HUMAN DEVELOPMENT

SIXTH EDITION

HUMAN DEVELOPMENT

DIANE E. PAPALIA

SALLY WENDKOS OLDS

McGRAW-HILL, INC.

New York St. Louis San Francisco Auckland Bogotá
Caracas Lisbon London Madrid Mexico City
Milan Montreal New Delhi San Juan
Singapore Sydney Tokyo Toronto

HUMAN DEVELOPMENT

Permissions Acknowledgments appear on pages 673–676
and on this page by reference.

This book is printed on acid-free paper.

    4 5 6 7 8 9 0   VNH   VNH   9 0 9 8 7 6

ISBN 0-07-048760-X

Library of Congress Cataloging-in-Publication Data

Papalia, Diane E.
    Human development / Diane E. Papalia, Sally Wendkos
Olds.—6th ed.
        p.   cm.
    Includes bibliographical references and indexes.
    ISBN 0-07-048760-X
    1. Developmental psychology.   2. Developmental
psychobiology.   I. Olds, Sally Wendkos.   II. Title.
BF713.P35   1995   94-7636
155—dc20

This book was set in Palatino by York Graphic Services, Inc.
The editors were Jane Vaicunas and James R. Belser;
the designer was Joan E. O'Connor;
the production supervisor was Leroy A. Young.
The photo editor was Inge King.
The permissions editor was Barbara Hale.
Von Hoffmann Press, Inc., was printer and binder.

Photo of Diane E. Papalia, © 1994, Erika Stone.
Photo of Sally Wendkos Olds, © 1994, Mark Olds.

Chapter-Opening Photo Credits

Chapter 1 Scott Thode/International Stock;   *Chapter 2*
Taeke Henstra/Photo Researchers;   *Chapter 3* Laura
Dwight;   *Chapter 4* Sally Cassidy/The Picture Cube;
Chapter 5 Jean-Claude Lejeune;   *Chapter 6* Erika Stone;
Chapter 7 Jeffrey W. Myers/The Stock Market;   *Chapter 8*
Richard Hutchings/Photo Researchers;   *Chapter 9* Mark
Bolster/International Stock Photo;   *Chapter 10* Will and
Deni McIntyre/Photo Researchers;   *Chapter 11* Bob
Daemmrich/Stock, Boston;   *Chapter 12* Frank Niemeir/
The Atlanta Constitution;   *Chapter 13* Spencer Grant/
Stock, Boston;   *Chapter 14* Joseph Nettis/Photo
Researchers;   *Chapter 15* Erika Stone;   *Chapter 16* Doug
Plummer/Photo Researchers;   *Chapter 17* Junebug Clark/
Photo Researchers;   *Chapter 18* Dennis Stock/Magnum.

ABOUT
THE AUTHORS

As a professor, **Diane E. Papalia** has taught thousands of undergraduates at the University of Wisconsin. She received her bachelor's degree, majoring in psychology, from Vassar College, and both her master's degree in child development and family relations and her Ph.D. in lifespan developmental psychology from West Virginia University. She has published numerous articles in such professional journals as *Human Development, The International Journal of Aging and Human Development, Sex Roles, The Journal of Experimental Child Psychology,* and *The Journal of Gerontology.* Most of these papers have dealt with her major research focus, cognitive development from childhood through old age. She is especially interested in intelligence in old age and in factors that contribute to the maintenance of intellectual functioning in late adulthood. She is a Fellow in the Gerontological Society of America.

Sally Wendkos Olds is an award-winning professional writer who has written more than 200 articles in leading magazines and is the author or coauthor of six books addressed to general readers, in addition to the three textbooks she has coauthored with Dr. Papalia. Her book *The Complete Book of Breastfeeding,* a classic since its publication in 1972, has been issued in a completely updated and expanded edition. She is also the author of *The Working Parents' Survival Guide* and *The Eternal Garden: Seasons of Our Sexuality,* and the coauthor of *Raising a Hyperactive Child* (winner of The Family Service Association of America National Media Award) and *Helping Your Child Find Values to Live By.* She received her bachelor's degree from the University of Pennsylvania, where she majored in English literature and minored in psychology. She was elected to Phi Beta Kappa and was graduated summa cum laude.

To our husbands,
Jonathan L. Finlay
and
David Mark Olds

—our loved and loving partners
in growth and development

CONTENTS
IN BRIEF

List of Boxes   xix
Preface   xxiii
Resources   xxix

1   ABOUT HUMAN DEVELOPMENT   1

■ **PART ONE**   BEGINNINGS   43

2   CONCEPTION THROUGH BIRTH   45

3   PHYSICAL DEVELOPMENT IN INFANCY
        AND TODDLERHOOD   91

4   INTELLECTUAL DEVELOPMENT
        IN INFANCY AND TODDLERHOOD   127

5   PERSONALITY AND SOCIAL
        DEVELOPMENT IN INFANCY
        AND TODDLERHOOD   161

■ **PART TWO**   EARLY CHILDHOOD   197

6   PHYSICAL AND INTELLECTUAL
        DEVELOPMENT IN EARLY CHILDHOOD   199

7   PERSONALITY AND SOCIAL
        DEVELOPMENT IN EARLY CHILDHOOD 239

■ **PART THREE** MIDDLE CHILDHOOD   269

8   PHYSICAL AND INTELLECTUAL
        DEVELOPMENT IN MIDDLE
        CHILDHOOD   271

9   PERSONALITY AND SOCIAL
        DEVELOPMENT IN MIDDLE
        CHILDHOOD   307

■ **PART FOUR**   ADOLESCENCE   339

10 PHYSICAL AND INTELLECTUAL
        DEVELOPMENT IN ADOLESCENCE   341

11 PERSONALITY AND SOCIAL
        DEVELOPMENT IN ADOLESCENCE   379

■ **PART FIVE**   YOUNG ADULTHOOD   407

12 PHYSICAL AND INTELLECTUAL
        DEVELOPMENT IN YOUNG
        ADULTHOOD   409

13 PERSONALITY AND SOCIAL
        DEVELOPMENT IN YOUNG
        ADULTHOOD   435

■ **PART SIX**   MIDDLE ADULTHOOD   469

14   PHYSICAL AND INTELLECTUAL
DEVELOPMENT IN MIDDLE
ADULTHOOD   471

15   PERSONALITY AND SOCIAL
DEVELOPMENT IN MIDDLE
ADULTHOOD   499

■ **PART SEVEN**   LATE ADULTHOOD   523

16   PHYSICAL AND INTELLECTUAL
DEVELOPMENT IN LATE
ADULTHOOD   525

17   PERSONALITY AND SOCIAL
DEVELOPMENT IN LATE
ADULTHOOD   557

■ **PART EIGHT**   THE END OF LIFE   585

18   DEATH AND BEREAVEMENT   587

Glossary   615
Bibliography   627
Permissions Acknowledgments   673
Indexes   677

CONTENTS

List of Boxes   xix
Preface   xxiii
Resources   xxix

■ CHAPTER ONE
ABOUT HUMAN DEVELOPMENT   1

HUMAN DEVELOPMENT:
THE SUBJECT AND THE TEXT   3
    What Is Human Development?   3
    How This Book Approaches Human
        Development   4

HUMAN DEVELOPMENT:
THE STUDY AND ITS HISTORY   5
    Aspects of Development   6
    Periods of the Life Span   6
    Individual Differences in Development   6
    Influences on Development   8
    How the Study of Human Development
        Has Evolved   11

HUMAN DEVELOPMENT:
RESEARCH METHODS   12
    Correlation   14
    Nonexperimental Methods   14

Experimental Methods   17
Data Collection Methods   21
Ethics of Research   22

HUMAN DEVELOPMENT:
THEORETICAL PERSPECTIVES   23
    Theories and Hypotheses   23
    Psychoanalytic Perspective   24
    Learning Perspective   30
    Cognitive Perspective   34
    Humanistic Perspective   37

A WORD TO STUDENTS   38

■ PART ONE
BEGINNINGS   43

■ CHAPTER TWO
CONCEPTION THROUGH BIRTH   45

FERTILIZATION   46
    How Does Fertilization Take Place?   46
    What Causes Multiple Births?   47
    What Determines Sex?   48

HEREDITY AND ENVIRONMENT 49
What Is the Role of Heredity? 49
How Do Heredity and Environment
Interact? 60

PRENATAL DEVELOPMENT 70
Stages of Prenatal Development 70
The Prenatal Environment 73

BIRTH 81
Stages of Childbirth 81
Methods of Childbirth 82
Settings for Childbirth 85

■ CHAPTER THREE
PHYSICAL DEVELOPMENT IN
INFANCY AND TODDLERHOOD 91

THE NEONATE 92
Physical Characteristics 92
Body Systems 93
The Brain and Reflex Behavior 94
The Newborn's Health 96
Immunization for Better Health 105

DEVELOPMENT DURING THE FIRST
3 YEARS OF LIFE 107
Principles of Development 107
States of Arousal: The Body's Cycles 108
Growth and Nourishment 110
The Senses 113
Motor Development 117
How Different Are Boys and Girls? 124

■ CHAPTER FOUR
INTELLECTUAL DEVELOPMENT IN
INFANCY AND TODDLERHOOD 127

HOW INFANTS LEARN 128
Learning and Maturation 128
Types of Learning 129
Infant Memory 131

STUDYING INTELLECTUAL DEVELOPMENT:
THREE APPROACHES 132
Psychometric Approach: Intelligence Tests 133
Piagetian Approach: Cognitive Stages 135
Information-Processing Approach:
Perceptions and Symbols 142

DEVELOPMENT OF LANGUAGE 144
Stages in Development of Language 146
Theories of Language Acquisition 150
Influences on Language Development 151
Delayed Language Development 153

DEVELOPMENT OF COMPETENCE 154
What Influences Competence? 155
HOME: The Home Observation for
Measurement of the Environment 155

■ CHAPTER FIVE
PERSONALITY AND SOCIAL
DEVELOPMENT IN INFANCY
AND TODDLERHOOD 161

EARLY PERSONALITY DEVELOPMENT 162
Trust versus Mistrust 162
Autonomy versus Shame and Doubt 163

EMOTIONS: THE FOUNDATION OF
PERSONALITY 165
How Infants' Emotions Are Studied 165
How Emotions Develop: The Emerging
Sense of Self 166
How Infants Show Their Emotions 167
How Emotions Are Communicated
between Infants and Adults 168

DIFFERENCES IN PERSONALITY
DEVELOPMENT 171
Temperamental Differences 171
Gender Differences 173

THE FAMILY AND PERSONALITY
DEVELOPMENT 174
The Mother's Role 174
The Father's Role 180
Stranger Anxiety and Separation
Anxiety 183
Disturbances in Family Relationships 183

RELATIONSHIPS WITH OTHER
CHILDREN 187
Siblings 187
Sociability 189

THE IMPACT OF EARLY DAY CARE 189
Cognitive Development 190
Emotional Development 192

■ PART TWO
EARLY CHILDHOOD 197

■ CHAPTER SIX
PHYSICAL AND INTELLECTUAL
DEVELOPMENT IN EARLY CHILDHOOD 199

PHYSICAL DEVELOPMENT 200

PHYSICAL GROWTH AND CHANGE 200
Height, Weight, and Appearance 200
Structural and Systemic Changes 201
Nutrition 201

HEALTH 201
Health Problems in Early Childhood 201
Influences on Health 204

SLEEP: PATTERNS AND PROBLEMS 207
Normal Sleep Patterns 207
Sleep Disturbances 208
Bed-Wetting 208

MOTOR SKILLS 209
Large-Muscle Coordination 210
Small-Muscle and Eye-Hand
Coordination 210

INTELLECTUAL DEVELOPMENT 210

ASPECTS OF INTELLECTUAL
DEVELOPMENT 212
Development of Memory:
Information Processing 212
Cognitive Development:
Piaget's Preoperational Stage 213
Development of Language 221
Development of Intelligence 224

THE WIDENING ENVIRONMENT 227
Preschool and Day Care 227
Kindergarten 234

■ CHAPTER SEVEN
PERSONALITY AND SOCIAL
DEVELOPMENT IN EARLY
CHILDHOOD 239

IMPORTANT PERSONALITY
DEVELOPMENTS IN EARLY CHILDHOOD 240
Initiative versus Guilt 240
Identification 241
Gender Identity 241

ASPECTS AND ISSUES OF PERSONALITY
DEVELOPMENT 245
Gender 245
Fears 249
Aggression 250
Altruism: Prosocial Behavior 254
Child-Rearing Practices 255
Relating to Other Children 259
Play 263

■ PART THREE
MIDDLE CHILDHOOD 269

■ CHAPTER EIGHT
PHYSICAL AND INTELLECTUAL
DEVELOPMENT IN MIDDLE
CHILDHOOD 271

PHYSICAL DEVELOPMENT 272

GROWTH DURING MIDDLE CHILDHOOD 272
Growth Rates 272
Nutrition and Growth 273

HEALTH, FITNESS, AND SAFETY 274
Children's Health 274
Children's Safety 277

MOTOR DEVELOPMENT IN MIDDLE
CHILDHOOD 278

INTELLECTUAL DEVELOPMENT 278

ASPECTS OF INTELLECTUAL
DEVELOPMENT IN MIDDLE
CHILDHOOD 279
Cognitive Development: Piaget's Stage
of Concrete Operations 279
Moral Reasoning: Two Theories 280
Development of Memory:
Information Processing 284
Development of Intelligence:
Psychometrics 286
Development of Language:
Communication 289

CHILDREN IN SCHOOL 293
Educational Trends 293
Teachers' Characteristics and Expectations 293
Parents' Influence 295
Education for Special Needs 296
Bilingualism and Bilingual Education 301

■ CHAPTER NINE
PERSONALITY AND SOCIAL
DEVELOPMENT IN MIDDLE
CHILDHOOD 307

THE SELF-CONCEPT 308
Developing a Self-Concept 308
Self-Esteem 309

ASPECTS OF PERSONALITY DEVELOPMENT
IN MIDDLE CHILDHOOD   311
  Everyday Life   311
  The Child in the Peer Group   313
  The Child in the Family   318

CHILDHOOD EMOTIONAL
DISTURBANCES   330
  Types of Emotional Problems   331
  Treatment for Emotional Problems 332

STRESS AND RESILIENCE   334
  Sources of Stress: Life Events, Fears,
    and the "Hurried Child"   334
  Coping with Stress: The Resilient Child 334

■ PART FOUR
ADOLESCENCE   339

■ CHAPTER TEN
PHYSICAL AND INTELLECTUAL
DEVELOPMENT IN ADOLESCENCE   341

ADOLESCENCE: A DEVELOPMENTAL
TRANSITION   342

PHYSICAL DEVELOPMENT   344

MATURATION IN ADOLESCENCE   344
  Physical Changes   344
  Psychological Issues Related to
    Physical Changes   348

HEALTH CONCERNS OF
ADOLESCENCE   351
  Nutrition and Eating Disorders 352
  Use and Abuse of Drugs   354
  Sexually Transmitted Diseases (STDs) 357

INTELLECTUAL DEVELOPMENT   360

ASPECTS OF INTELLECTUAL
DEVELOPMENT IN ADOLESCENCE   360
  Cognitive Development: Piaget's Stage of
    Formal Operations   360
  Adolescent Egocentrism   362
  Moral Development: Kohlberg's Levels
    of Morality   364

SECONDARY SCHOOL   367

The Transition to Junior High or
  High School   367
High School Today   368
Home Influences on Achievement in
  High School   369
Dropping Out of High School   371

DEVELOPING A CAREER   372
  Stages in Vocational Planning 373
  Influences on Vocational Planning 373

■ CHAPTER ELEVEN
PERSONALITY AND SOCIAL
DEVELOPMENT IN ADOLESCENCE   379

THE SEARCH FOR IDENTITY   380
  Identity versus Identity Confusion 380
  Research on Identity   381
  Achieving Sexual Identity   385

SOCIAL ASPECTS OF PERSONALITY
DEVELOPMENT IN ADOLESCENCE   389
  Relationships with Parents   390
  Sibling Relationships   394
  Relationships with Peers   395

TWO PROBLEMS OF ADOLESCENCE   398
  Teenage Pregnancy   398
  Juvenile Delinquency   402

A POSITIVE VIEW OF ADOLESCENCE:
THREE COHORT STUDIES   404

■ PART FIVE
YOUNG ADULTHOOD   407

■ CHAPTER TWELVE
PHYSICAL AND INTELLECTUAL
DEVELOPMENT IN YOUNG
ADULTHOOD   409

PHYSICAL DEVELOPMENT   410

SENSORY AND PSYCHOMOTOR
FUNCTIONING   410
HEALTH AND FITNESS IN YOUNG
ADULTHOOD   411

Health Status   411
Influences on Health and Fitness   412

INTELLECTUAL DEVELOPMENT   420

ADULT THOUGHT:
THEORETICAL APPROACHES   420
   K. Warner Schaie: Stages of Cognitive
      Development   420
   Robert Sternberg: Three Aspects
      of Intelligence   421
   Beyond Jean Piaget: Postformal Thought   422

ADULT MORAL DEVELOPMENT   423
   How Does Experience Affect Moral
      Judgments?   423
   Are There Gender Differences in Moral
      Development?   424

COLLEGE   426
   Who Goes to College?   426
   Intellectual Growth in College   426
   Gender Differences in Achievement
      in College   427
   Leaving College   428

STARTING A CAREER   428
   Work and Age   428
   Work and Gender   430

**■ CHAPTER THIRTEEN
PERSONALITY AND SOCIAL
DEVELOPMENT IN YOUNG
ADULTHOOD**   435

PERSONALITY DEVELOPMENT
IN YOUNG ADULTHOOD:
TWO MODELS   436
   Normative-Crisis Model   436
   Timing-of-Events Model   442

INTIMATE RELATIONSHIPS AND
PERSONAL LIFESTYLES   443
   Love   443
   Marriage   446
   Divorce   449
   Single Life   452
   Cohabitation   453
   Sexuality   453
   Parenthood   455
   Remaining Childless   464
   Friendship   464

**■ PART SIX
MIDDLE ADULTHOOD**   469

**■ CHAPTER FOURTEEN
PHYSICAL AND INTELLECTUAL
DEVELOPMENT IN MIDDLE
ADULTHOOD**   471

PHYSICAL DEVELOPMENT   473

PHYSICAL CHANGES OF MIDDLE AGE   473
   Sensory and Psychomotor Functioning   473
   Sexuality   474
   Appearance: The Double Standard
      of Aging   478

HEALTH IN MIDDLE AGE   479
   Health Status   479
   Health Problems   479
   The Impact of Race and Socioeconomics
      on Health   482

INTELLECTUAL DEVELOPMENT   484

ASPECTS OF INTELLECTUAL
DEVELOPMENT IN MIDDLE
ADULTHOOD   484
   Intelligence and Cognition   484
   The Adult Learner   489

WORK IN MIDDLE ADULTHOOD   489
   Occupational Patterns   490
   Occupational Stress   491
   Unemployment   492
   Work and Intellectual Growth   493

**■ CHAPTER FIFTEEN
PERSONALITY AND SOCIAL
DEVELOPMENT IN MIDDLE
ADULTHOOD**   499

MIDLIFE: THE NORMATIVE-CRISIS
APPROACH   500
   The "Midlife Crisis"   500
   Theories and Research   501
   Evaluating the Normative-Crisis Model   508

PERSONAL RELATIONSHIPS AND TIMING
OF EVENTS IN MIDLIFE   511
   Marriage and Divorce   511
   Relationships with Siblings   513

Friendships 514
Relationships with Maturing Children 514
Relationships with Aging Parents 517

■ PART SEVEN
LATE ADULTHOOD 523

■ CHAPTER SIXTEEN
PHYSICAL AND INTELLECTUAL
DEVELOPMENT IN LATE ADULTHOOD 525

OLD AGE TODAY 526
What Is Our Attitude toward Old Age? 526
Who Are the Elderly? 526
How Can We Make the Most of the
Later Years? 529

PHYSICAL DEVELOPMENT 530

LONGEVITY AND THE AGING PROCESS 530
Life Expectancy 531
Why People Age: Two Theories 533

PHYSICAL CHANGES OF OLD AGE 534
Sensory and Psychomotor Functioning 534
The Brain in Late Adulthood 536
Other Physical Changes 537
Reserve Capacity 537

HEALTH IN OLD AGE 537
Health Care and Health Problems 538
Influences on Health and Fitness 539
Mental and Behavioral Disorders 540

INTELLECTUAL DEVELOPMENT 543

ASPECTS OF INTELLECTUAL
DEVELOPMENT 543
Does Intelligence Decline in Late
Adulthood? 543
How Does Memory Change in Late
Adulthood? 547

LIFELONG LEARNING:
ADULT EDUCATION IN LATE LIFE 550

WORK AND RETIREMENT 551
Why People Retire 551
How People Feel about Retirement 552
Making the Most of Retirement 552

■ CHAPTER SEVENTEEN
PERSONALITY AND SOCIAL
DEVELOPMENT IN LATE ADULTHOOD 557

THEORY AND RESEARCH ON PERSONALITY
DEVELOPMENT 558
Erik Erikson: Crisis 8—Integrity versus
Despair 558
Robert Peck: Three Adjustments of Late
Adulthood 559
George Vaillant: Factors in Emotional
Health 560
Research on Stability and Change in
Personality 561
Approaches to "Successful Aging" 562
Personality and Patterns of Aging 563

SOCIAL ISSUES RELATED TO AGING 566
Income 566
Living Arrangements 566
Abuse of the Elderly 570

PERSONAL RELATIONSHIPS IN LATE LIFE 572
Marriage 572
Being Single Again: Divorce and
Widowhood 574
Remarriage 574
Single Life: The "Never Marrieds" 574
Sexual Relationships 575
Relationships with Siblings 576
Friendships 576
Relationships with Adult Children 577
Childlessness 578
Grandparenthood and
Great-Grandparenthood 580

■ PART EIGHT
THE END OF LIFE 585

■ CHAPTER EIGHTEEN
DEATH AND BEREAVEMENT 587

THREE ASPECTS OF DEATH 589

FACING DEATH 589
Attitudes toward Death and Dying across
the Life Span 589
Confronting One's Own Death 592
Bereavement, Mourning, and Grief 593
Widowhood: Surviving a Spouse 601

CONTROVERSIAL ISSUES OF DEATH
AND DYING 603

Euthanasia and the Right to Die   603
Suicide   605

FINDING A PURPOSE IN LIFE AND DEATH   610
The Meaning of Death   610
Reviewing a Life   611

Glossary   615
Bibliography   627
Permissions Acknowledgments   673
Indexes
    Name Index   677
    Subject Index   684

LIST
OF BOXES

■ CHAPTER ONE

1-1 Window on the World: The Purpose
of Cross-Cultural Research   10
1-2 Food for Thought: What Longitudinal
Studies Can Tell Us   13

■ CHAPTER TWO

2-1 Practically Speaking: Prenatal Assessment   61
2-2 Take a Stand: Genetic Testing   64
2-3 Food for Thought: Shyness   68
2-4 Practically Speaking: Reducing Risks
during Pregnancy   74
2-5 Window on the World: Maternity Care
in Western Europe and the United States   86

■ CHAPTER THREE

3-1 Window on the World: How Universal Is
"Normal" Development?   99
3-2 Food for Thought: When Does Obesity
Begin, and What Should Be Done about It?   114
3-3 Take a Stand: Should Baby Boys Be
Circumcised?   118
3-4 Practically Speaking: Are "Walkers"
Worth the Risk?   122

3-5 Practically Speaking: Putting Research
Findings to Work   123

■ CHAPTER FOUR

4-1 Window on the World: Eastern and
Western Learning Styles   144
4-2 Food for Thought: What the Babbling
of Hearing-Impaired Babies Tells Us
about the Development of Language   147
4-3 Practically Speaking: Talking with Babies
and Toddlers   154
4-4 Practically Speaking: How Parents Can
Help Their Children to Be More
Competent   156

■ CHAPTER FIVE

5-1 Practically Speaking: Reducing
Negativism and Encouraging
Self-Regulation   165
5-2 Food for Thought: How a Mother's
Depression Affects Her Baby   170
5-3 Practically Speaking: How to Choose
a Good Day Care Center   191

5-4 Window on the World: How Sweden Cares
for Parents and Children — 193
5-5 Practically Speaking: Putting Research
to Work — 194

■ **CHAPTER SIX**

6-1 Practically Speaking: Encouraging Healthy
Eating Habits — 203
6-2 Food for Thought: How Homelessness
Affects Children — 207
6-3 Practically Speaking: Helping Children
to Sleep Well — 209
6-4 Food for Thought: Theories of Mind — 219
6-5 Take a Stand: Should Preschool Be about
the Three Rs? — 231
6-6 Window on the World: Preschools in Three
Cultures — 232

■ **CHAPTER SEVEN**

7-1 Practically Speaking: Guiding Children's
Television Viewing — 253
7-2 Window on the World: A Nation of Only
Children — 260
7-3 Practically Speaking: Helping Young
Children to Make Friends — 263
7-4 Food for Thought: Imaginary Playmates — 266

■ **CHAPTER EIGHT**

8-1 Food for Thought: Children's Understanding
of Health and Illness — 275
8-2 Take a Stand: Should IQ Tests Be Used? — 287
8-3 Window on the World: How Can Asian
Children Achieve So Much? — 290
8-4 Practically Speaking: Teaching Children
to Think — 294

■ **CHAPTER NINE**

9-1 Window on the World: Family Ecologies
of Children from Ethnic Minority Groups — 319
9-2 Food for Thought: After-School Care:
Which Kind Is Best? — 323
9-3 Practically Speaking: Helping Children
Adjust to Divorce — 326
9-4 Food for Thought: Children Who Live
in Chronic Danger — 335

■ **CHAPTER TEN**

10-1 Window on the World: An Apache Girl
Comes of Age — 343
10-2 Window on the World: Female Genital
Mutilation — 344
10-3 Practically Speaking: Protecting against
Sexually Transmitted Diseases — 358
10-4 Food for Thought: Gender Differences
in Moral Development — 366
10-5 Take a Stand: Should Teenagers Hold
Part-Time Jobs? — 374

■ **CHAPTER ELEVEN**

11-1 Food for Thought: Gender Differences
in Personality Development — 383
11-2 Practically Speaking: Communicating
about Sex — 389
11-3 Window on the World: Preventing
Teenage Pregnancy — 401

■ **CHAPTER TWELVE**

12-1 Practically Speaking: What You Can Do
to Improve Your Health — 413
12-2 Window on the World: A Chinese
Perspective on Moral Development — 424
12-3 Food for Thought: How Dual-Earner
Couples Cope — 429

■ **CHAPTER THIRTEEN**

13-1 Food for Thought: Establishing Mature
Relationships with Parents — 440
13-2 Window on the World: Marriage and
Divorce Patterns — 447
13-3 Take a Stand: Advantages to Having
Children Early or Late — 457
13-4 Practically Speaking: The Hassles
of Raising Young Children — 461
13-5 Food for Thought: Both Job and Family
Roles Affect Men's Psychological
Well-Being — 463

■ **CHAPTER FOURTEEN**

14-1 Practically Speaking: Preventing
Osteoporosis — 476
14-2 Window on the World: Japanese Women's
Experience of Menopause — 478
14-3 Food for Thought: Moral Leadership
in Middle and Late Adulthood — 487
14-4 Food for Thought: Creativity Takes Hard
Work — 494

■ **CHAPTER FIFTEEN**

15-1 Take a Stand: Does Personality Change
in Middle Age? — 505
15-2 Window on the World: A Society
without Middle Age? — 509
15-3 Practically Speaking: Enhancing Marriage
at Midlife — 512
15-4 Food for Thought: Reacting to a Parent's
Death — 520

■ **CHAPTER SIXTEEN**

16-1 Window on the World: Aging in Asia — 527
16-2 Practically Speaking: You and the Older
People in Your Life — 530
16-3 Food for Thought: Wisdom in Late
Adulthood — 548

the physical, intellectual, social, and personality influences on development. There are, however, a number of differences. The changes in this revision continue to represent growth and development in our own thinking, as we present human development from the moment of conception until that moment at the other end of the life span when death ends the continuing process.

OUR AIMS FOR THIS EDITION

The goal of this sixth edition is the same as that of the first five—to emphasize the continuity of development throughout the life span, to show how experiences at one time of life affect future development, and to understand the influences upon people from their genes, their families, and the world they live in. We are still looking at the findings of scientific research and the theories of social scientists. We are still applying these to our understanding of humankind. And we are still asking the same basic questions: What influences have made people living in the final decades of the twentieth century the way they are? What factors are likely to affect all of us in the future? How much control do people have over their lives? How are people like each other? How is each person unique? What is normal? What is cause for concern?

We are also asking some new questions and coming up with some new answers. This revision continues to update the literature, as we discuss new research and new theories, a number of which have been published in the decade of the 1990s. We continue to synthesize research findings and to help students interpret them and think critically about controversial issues. Our continuing work on two other college textbooks, *A Child's World* (for courses in child development) and *Psychology* (for introductory courses), has helped us refine and sharpen our thinking about life-span development. The changes in this revision, then, represent growth and development in our own ideas.

THE SIXTH EDITION

ORGANIZATION

There are two major approaches to writing about and teaching human development—the *chronolog-*

ical approach (looking at the functioning of all aspects of development at different stages of life, such as infancy or late adulthood) and the *topical approach* (tracing one aspect of development at a time). We have chosen the *chronological* approach, which provides a sense of the multifaceted sweep of human development, as we get to know first the infant and toddler, then the young child, the schoolchild, the adolescent, the young adult, the adult at midlife, and the person in late adulthood. As we discuss the ages and stages of human beings, we provide evenhanded treatment of *all* periods of the life span; we have taken special pains not to overemphasize some and slight others.

In line with our chronological approach, we have divided this book into eight parts. After the Introduction (Part One), we discuss the physical, the intellectual, and the social and personality development for the life-span stages presented above. Readers who prefer a *topical* approach may read the book in this order: Chapters 1, 2, and 3 (general theories and issues and prenatal and early physical development); the first sections of Chapters 6, 8, 10, 12, 14, and 16 (physical development); the second sections of these chapters, plus Chapter 4 (intellectual functioning); then Chapters 5, 7, 9, 11, 13, 15, and 17 (social and personality development); and end the book with Chapter 18 (death and bereavement).

CONTENT

This new edition continues to provide comprehensive coverage of development from the crucial prenatal period through late adulthood. Full descriptions of each age period draw on the most up-to-date information available about physical, intellectual, and social and personality development. The text integrates theoretical, research-related, and practical concerns pertaining to every stage of the life span, reflecting our belief that all stages of life are important, challenging, and full of opportunities for growth and change.

As in the previous edition, we communicate a major personal involvement with the issues we have discussed. The book presents many personal examples from the authors' own lives, which relate to the material and personalize it. The most dramatic example is the story of how Anna (Diane Papalia's daughter) develops a proficiency with language, which serves as a springboard for the discussion of many developmental issues.

PREFACE

I n the preface to the previous five editions of *Human Development*, we spoke of change as a principle that governs all our lives. As we said then, people change, grow, and develop throughout life. We, the authors, have known many changes in our own lives since we began writing together back in 1973. Our life experiences, as much as our professional backgrounds (which are detailed in the section "About the Authors" on page v), have enabled us to become more sensitive to a number of the issues covered in this book.

When we first launched our collaboration—and our eventual friendship—with the first edition of *A Child's World*, our textbook about child development, Diane Papalia was a single, childless assistant professor at the University of Wisconsin in Madison. Sally Olds, a professional writer, was a married mother of three children—one in high school, one in junior high, and one in elementary school. Both parents of both authors were living, and we dedicated our first textbook to them.

Since then, as both of us have moved from young adulthood into midlife, our lives have changed in many ways. Diane took on more academic responsibilities as she became first an associate professor, then a dean, then a full professor. Her personal life changed dramatically when she married, moved to California, and came back to Wisconsin where she and her husband adopted a baby girl. Since then other career changes took her and her family to New York City, where they now live. Meanwhile, Sally's children grew up, went to college, chose careers, and left the nest; her husband retired; she knew the grief of mourning first her father and then her mother; and then she knew the joy of celebrating the marriages of two daughters and the births of three grandchildren.

As we and our lives have changed, this book has reflected some of what we have learned along the way. This sixth edition still retains much of the flavor of earlier editions, especially in its emphasis on the interrelationships among the different stages of the life span and among

■ **CHAPTER SEVENTEEN**

17-1 Food for Thought: Religion and Emotional
Well-Being in Late Life 565
17-2 Window on the World: Aging among
African Americans, Hispanic Americans,
and Other American Minority Groups 567
17-3 Practically Speaking: Visiting Someone
in a Nursing Home 571
17-4 Window on the World: Extended Family
Living in Latin America 579

■ **CHAPTER EIGHTEEN**

18-1 Food for Thought: Postponing Death 594
18-2 Window on the World: Mourning Customs
among Traditional Jews 596
18-3 Take a Stand: Should Anencephalic Babies
Be Used as Organ Donors? 604
18-4 Practically Speaking: The Living Will and
Medical Durable Power of Attorney 609
18-5 Practically Speaking: Evoking Memories
for a "Life Review" 612

While we have retained the scope, emphasis, and level of previous editions of *Human Development*, we have made a number of significant changes in this sixth edition.

■ Our *photo program* has evolved with an even greater commitment than ever before to diversity—in ethnicity, race, age, gender, and ability (or disability). We have carefully chosen our illustrations to be teaching tools—of points in the text and of the demographic diversity in the population, in the United States and in other countries around the world.

■ We have added a *Resource Guide*, so that interested readers can seek information and help with regard to various conditions discussed in the book.

■ As in previous editions, we have *updated the text* whenever new findings or interpretations have been available, reorganized some material to make it more effective, and added completely new sections. We have added tables and figures and updated statistics.

Among the important changes are the following:

■ *New sections:* Jean Baker Miller's self-in-relation theory, genetic testing, advantages and drawbacks of circumcision, theories of mind, encouraging healthy eating and sleeping habits, bilingualism and bilingual education, imaginary playmates, female genital mutilation, ethnic factors in identity formation, menopause in Japanese women, and the importance of free radicals in the physiology of aging.

■ *Important revisions:* Discussions of prenatal hazards and their effects on fetal development; the effects of day care on children's development; Freudian theory (all now contained in Chapter 1); prenatal diagnosis of various conditions; the impact of AIDS on children, adolescents, and adults; the development of the self-concept; women's development in adulthood; children's reactions to death; and cross-cultural attitudes toward death.

SPECIAL FEATURES IN THIS EDITION

This edition of *Human Development* includes four kinds of boxed material:

■ *"Window on the World"* boxes appear in every chapter of the book. These give readers glimpses

of human development in societies other than our own, showing that people grow up, live, and thrive in many different kinds of cultures, under many different influences. These discussions treat such issues as cross-cultural differences in acquiring physical, intellectual, and social skills; education and learning styles; child care for working parents; family ecologies of children from ethnic minority groups; and marriage and divorce patterns.

■ *"Practically Speaking"* boxes build bridges between academic study and everyday life by showing ways to apply research findings on various aspects of human development. They cover such topics as talking with babies; helping children make friends, do well in school, and cope with being on their own without adult supervision; enhancing marriage in midlife; visiting people in nursing homes; helping potential suicides; easing the lives of older adults; and evoking life review memories.

■ *"Food for Thought"* boxes explore important research issues. Some of these include discussions of what the babbling of hearing-impaired babies tells us about language development; the transition to junior high or high school; gender differences in moral and personality development; how job and family roles affect men's psychological well-being; and moral leadership in middle and late adulthood.

■ *"Take a Stand"* boxes have been added to each part, to encourage critical thinking about controversial issues. These boxes include discussions about genetic testing, circumcision, part-time work for teenagers, whether personality changes in middle age, and the use of anencephalic babies as organ donors.

LEARNING AIDS

We also continue to provide a number of basic teaching aids, including:

■ *Part overviews:* At the beginning of each part, an overview provides the rationale for the chapters that follow.

■ *Chapter-opening outlines:* At the beginning of each chapter, an outline clearly previews the major topics included in the chapter.

■ *"Ask Yourself" questions:* At the beginning of each chapter, a few key questions highlight the most important issues addressed in the chapter.

- *Key terms:* Whenever an important new term is introduced in the text, it is highlighted in **bold-face italic** and defined, both in the text and in the end-of-book Glossary.
- *End-of-chapter lists of key terms:* At the end of every chapter, key terms are listed in the order in which they first appear and cross-referenced to pages where they are defined.
- *End-of-book glossary:* The extensive glossary at the back of the book repeats the definitions of key terms and indicates the pages on which they first appear.
- *Chapter summaries:* At the end of every chapter, a series of brief statements, organized by the major topics in the chapter, clearly restate the most important points.
- *Bibliography:* A complete listing of references enables students to evaluate the sources of major statements of fact or theory.
- *Recommended readings:* Annotated lists of readings (classic works or lively contemporary treatments) are provided for students who want to explore issues in greater depth than is possible within these covers.
- *Index:* Separate indexes, by subject and by author, appear at the end of the book.
- *Illustrations:* Many points in the text are underscored pictorially through carefully selected drawings, graphs, and photographs. The illustration program includes new figures and many full-color photographs.

SUPPLEMENTARY MATERIALS

Human Development, Sixth Edition, is accompanied by a complete learning and teaching package. Each component of this package has been thoroughly revised and expanded to include important new course material. The package consists of a *Student Study Guide with Readings* by Thomas Crandell of Broome Community College and George Bieger of Indiana University of Pennsylvania; an *Instructor's Manual* by Thomas Crandell; and a *Test Bank* by Thomas Moye of Coe College. Computerized versions of the Study Guide and Test Bank are available for IBM and Macintosh computers. The *Human Development* supplements package also includes a newly revised set of full-color overhead transparencies.

In addition, the text will be supplemented regularly by a newsletter for adopters. The *Human Development* newsletter will highlight recent re-search and current issues related to the themes of the text—including cultural diversity issues within the United States and around the world.

ACKNOWLEDGMENTS

We would like to express our gratitude to the many friends and colleagues who, through their work and their interest, helped us clarify our thinking about human development. We are especially grateful for the valuable help given by those who reviewed the fifth edition of *Human Development* and the manuscript drafts of this sixth edition, whose evaluations and suggestions helped greatly in the preparation of this new edition. These reviewers, who are affiliated with both two- and four-year institutions, are as follows: David Bailey, Community College of Allegheny County; James A. Blackburn, University of Wisconsin–Milwaukee; Doris A. Blazer, Furman University; Martha B. Boston, Neumann College; Kyle Ann Campos, Des Moines Area Community College; Richard C. Carney, Community College of Allegheny County; Andrea Chen, State University of New York–Binghamton; David B. Conner, Northeast Missouri State University; Cynthia A. Edwards, Meredith College; Juanita L. Garcia, University of South Florida; Eulalio G. Gonzalez, Lorain County Community College; Vernon Haynes, Youngstown State University; Janice H. Kennedy, Georgia Southern University; Wendy Kliewer, Virginia Commonwealth University; Anita R. McLeod, Anderson College; Karen Macrae, University of South Carolina–Spartanburg; John M. Nash, Worcester State College; Leslee K. Pollina, Southeast Missouri State University; D. Kim Sawrey, University of North Carolina at Wilmington; Cynthia Scheibe, Ithaca College; Joe M. Tinnin, Richland College; Alvin Y. Wang, University of Central Florida; and Martha S. Zlokovich, Southeast Missouri State University.

We appreciate the strong support we have had from our publisher and would like to express our special thanks to Jane Vaicunas, editorial sponsor of this book; to our conscientious production editor, James R. Belser; and to Beth Kaufman, who helped in innumerable ways. Inge King, photo editor of all six editions of *Human Development,* again used her sensitivity, her interest, and her good eye to find outstanding photographs. Joan O'Connor and the artists working with her produced a creative, unique cover and book design noteworthy for esthetics, as well as the rendering of concepts. Kim Gelé provided valuable help with the glossary, bibliography, suggested readings, and resource sections; and Dorri Olds conceived graphic representation of some information.

Diane E. Papalia
Sally Wendkos Olds

Diane E. Papalia and Sally Wendkos Olds are the coauthors of *A Child's World* (in press for its seventh edition) and *Psychology* (in its second edition).

RESOURCES

Throughout this book we discuss many medical and psychological issues and disorders that affect health and well-being. You may want more detailed information on specific conditions, for either academic or personal reasons. To help in the search for further details, we have included the following listing. It provides the names of organizations that offer information, counseling, or other help for some of the specific conditions mentioned in this book. It is, of course, not all-inclusive. Many organizations exist in addition to the ones listed here.

Some of these agencies are public, some private. Some distribute literature or offer counseling directly. Others, including those listed here for which only a telephone number is given, provide referrals to local resources.

If a topic in which you are interested is not included, look in your local telephone directory (in the yellow pages, under "Associations," "Social Service Organizations," or "Human Services Organizations") or in the *Encyclopedia of Associations* in the reference room of your local library. Or ask the library's reference librarian.

Telephone numbers and addresses listed here are subject to change or disconnection without notice. To obtain information about toll-free numbers, dial 1-800-555-1212.

ALCOHOL AND DRUG INFORMATION AND TREATMENT

Al-Anon Family Group Headquarters
200 Park Avenue, Room 814
New York, NY 10003
800-356-9996

Local phone numbers can be obtained from local AA chapter or telephone directory.

Offers information and help to family and friends of people with drinking and drug problems.

Alcoholics Anonymous World Services
475 Riverside Drive
New York, NY 10115
212-870-3400

Local phone numbers are given in the white pages of telephone directories of communities around the world.

The largest and most successful organization in the world for recovery from alcoholism, through meetings and peer support. All services are free.

Center for Substance Abuse and Treatment
1-800-662-HELP

A 24-hour hotline sponsored by the federal government and affiliated with the National Institute of Drug Abuse.

Hazelden Educational Materials
Pleasant Valley Road
Box 176
Center City, MN 55012-0176
1-800-328-9000

Nonprofit organization which publishes and sells a wide range of books, pamphlets, and video and audio cassettes about chemical dependency, both for users and those close to them. Free catalog.

National Clearinghouse for Alcohol and Drug Information
P.O. Box 2345
Rockville, MD 20847
301-468-2600

Government-sponsored source of literature.

BIRTH DEFECTS AND DISEASES

National Down Syndrome Society
666 Broadway, Room 810
New York, NY 10012
212-460-9330

Gives information about parent support groups, publications, and special programs.

National Muscular Dystrophy Association
3300 East Sunrise Drive
Tucson, AZ 85718
602-529-2000

Supplies general information about the disease and services offered.

National Multiple Sclerosis Society
733 Third Avenue
New York, NY 10017
212-986-3240

Gives information about research and treatment.

Spina Bifida Information and Referral
4590 MacArthur Boulevard NW, Suite 250
Washington, DC 20007
800-621-3141

Provides general information and referrals.

DEATH AND DYING

Choice in Dying
200 Varick Street
New York, NY 10014
212-366-5540

A national nonprofit organization that advocates the rights of dying patients through professional and public education. Choice in Dying distributes, free of charge, state-specific forms for medical power of attorney or executing a living will.

CANCER

American Cancer Society
1599 Clifton Road NE
Atlanta, GA 30329
800-ACS-2345

For free information on almost any concern about cancer, this number will aid you in finding local resources.

National Cancer Institute
Building 31, Room 10-A-24
9000 Rockville Pike
Bethesda, MD 20892
800-4-CANCER

Persons at this number will answer cancer-related questions in addition to providing free information on cancer prevention.

CHILD ABUSE AND ADVOCACY

Child Help USA
P.O. Box 630
Hollywood, CA 90028
800-422-4453

A 24-hour hotline providing crisis intervention, information, and referral for anyone concerned about child abuse.

Children's Defense Fund
25 E Street NW
Washington, DC 20001
800-CDF-1200

Provides information and resources on a wide range of issues concerning children.

EDUCATION AND CHILD CARE

ChildCare Action Campaign
330 Seventh Avenue, 17th floor
New York, NY 10001
212-239-0138

This national coalition of leaders from various institutions and organizations serves as an advocacy group offering information on many aspects of child care through individual information sheets, a bimonthly newsletter, and audio training tapes for family day care providers.

National Association for Bilingual Education
1220 L Street NW, Suite 605
Washington, DC 20005-4018
202-898-1829

A nationwide advocacy organization that promotes equal opportunity for language-minority students and academic excellence for all students.

National Association for the Education of Young Children
1509 16th Street NW
Washington, DC 20036-1426
800-424-2460

This professional association accredits child-care centers and preschools around the country, holds regional and national meetings, and distributes publications for both professionals and parents.

National Black Child Development Institute
1023 15th Street NW, Suite 600
Washington, DC 20005
202-387-1281

This national nonprofit organization focuses on child care, health, education, and welfare. It holds conferences, conducts tutorial programs, and helps homeless children find adoptive families.

FAMILY SUPPORT

Family Resource Coalition
200 South Michigan Avenue, Suite 1520
Chicago, IL 60604
312-341-0900

Provides information on support groups nationwide, offering a broad array of services.

National Coalition of Grandparents
137 Larkin Street
Madison, WI 53705
608-238-8751

A nationwide consortium of groups and individuals concerned with grandparents and children. A source of information, support, and attorney referrals.

Well Spouse Foundation
P.O. Box 801
New York, NY 10023
212-724-5209

Provides information and support for husbands and wives who are caring for a terminally ill spouse.

GENERAL HEALTH

Melpomene Institute for Women's Health Research
1010 University Avenue
St. Paul, MN 55104
612-642-1951

Researches and publishes information on issues affecting physically active girls and women.

National Health Information Clearinghouse
U.S. Office of Disease Prevention and Health Promotion
P.O. Box 1133
Washington, DC 20013-1133
800-336-4797

Government service answering almost any health-related concern.

National Women's Health Network
1325 G Street NW
Washington, DC 20005
202-347-1140

A source of extensive information about women's health topics and related legislation.

INFANT MORTALITY

Compassionate Friends, Inc.
P.O. Box 3696
Oak Brook, IL 60522-3696
708-990-0010

Offers support to bereaved parents and siblings of infants and older children through 660 chapters in the United States.

National Sudden Infant Death Syndrome Clearinghouse
8201 Greensboro Drive, Suite 600
McLean, VA 22102
703-821-8955

Provides resources and information.

MEDICAL HELP

American Trauma Society
8903 Presidential Parkway, Suite 512
Upper Marlboro, MD 20772-2656
1-800-556-7890
Offers literature on accident prevention.

Orton Dyslexia Society
P.O. Box 9888
Baltimore, MD 21284
800-222-3123
Provides information about reading and writing
disorders.

MENTAL HEALTH

National Institute of Mental Health
Public Inquiries Branch
5600 Fishers Lane, Room 7C02
Rockville, MD 20857
310-443-4513
Federally sponsored agency which answers questions
about depression and other psychological disorders.

MISSING AND RUNAWAY CHILDREN

Child Find
P.O. Box 277
New Paltz, NY 12561
800-I AM LOST
Hotline to report disappearances or sightings.

National Center for Missing and Exploited Children
2101 Wilson Boulevard, Suite 550
Arlington, VA 22201
Hotline to report disappearances or sightings.

National Runaway Switchboard
3080 North Lincoln Avenue
Chicago, IL 60657
800-621-4000
Confidential crisis intervention and referral for
runaway homeless youth and their families, and
youth in crisis throughout the country.

PREGNANCY AND CHILDBIRTH

American Society for Psychoprophylaxis in Obstetrics/Lamaze
1101 Connecticut Avenue NW, Suite 700
Washington, DC 20036
800-368-4404
Makes referrals to local Lamaze instructors, which
help prospective parents prepare for childbirth and
infant care.

International Childbirth Education Association
P.O. Box 20048
Minneapolis, MN 55420
800-624-4934
Offers a free catalog of materials on pregnancy,
childbirth, and child care.

SELF-HELP

American Self-Help Clearinghouse
St. Clares-Riverside Medical Center
Denville, NJ 07834
201-625-7101
Provides information and contacts for self-help groups
nationwide. Will also assist you in starting a self-help
group in your area.

SEXUALLY TRANSMITTED DISEASES AND AIDS

American Foundation for the Prevention of Venereal Disease
799 Broadway, Suite 638
New York, NY 10003
212-759-2069
Publishes a booklet and other educational materials on
sexually transmitted diseases.

AIDS Hotline
800-342-AIDS
Run by the Centers for Disease Control, this 24-hour
hotline provides basic information on AIDS, HIV
testing, prevention, and referral to treatment centers.

National AIDS Clearinghouse
Box 60003
Rockville, MD 20849-6003
800-458-5231
Resources and free publications; a service of the
Centers for Disease Control.

VD/STD National Hotline
800-227-8922
Provides basic information on sexually transmitted
diseases, as well as referrals to free or low-cost clinics
in your area.

SPEECH AND HEARING

National Center for Stuttering
200 East 33rd Street
New York, NY 10016
800-221-2483
212-532-1460 (in New York)
Provides information and literature on treatment
programs.

HUMAN DEVELOPMENT

CHAPTER ONE

ABOUT HUMAN DEVELOPMENT

There is nothing permanent except change.

Heraclitus,
Fragment, (sixth century B.C.)

■ **HUMAN DEVELOPMENT:**
THE SUBJECT AND THE TEXT

What Is Human Development?
How This Book Approaches Human
   Development

■ **HUMAN DEVELOPMENT:**
THE STUDY AND ITS HISTORY

Aspects of Development
Periods of the Life Span
Individual Differences in Development
Influences on Development
How the Study of Human Development
   Has Evolved

■ **HUMAN DEVELOPMENT:**
RESEARCH METHODS

Correlation
Nonexperimental Methods

Experimental Methods
Data Collection Methods
Ethics of Research

■ **HUMAN DEVELOPMENT:**
THEORETICAL PERSPECTIVES

Theories and Hypotheses
Psychoanalytic Perspective
Learning Perspective
Cognitive Perspective
Humanistic Perspective

■ **A WORD TO STUDENTS**

■ **BOXES**

1-1 Window on the World: The Purpose
of Cross-Cultural Research
1-2 Food for Thought: What Longitudinal
Studies Can Tell Us

■ What can you gain from the study of human development, and how does this book approach the subject?

■ How has the study of human development evolved?

■ What are the major changes in the course of human life, and what common and individual influences affect people?

■ How do social scientists study people, and what are some ethical considerations about their methods?

■ What major theoretical perspectives try to explain human development, and what are their strengths and weaknesses?

The study of human development is endlessly fascinating because it is the study of real lives: yours, the reader's; ours, the authors'; and those of millions of people around the world. To introduce the subject matter of this book, we'd like to introduce Anna Victoria Finlay. By focusing on one aspect of her life, her early language development, we can better understand some of the reasons for studying human development and some of the ways it is studied.

At the time of this writing Anna—who was born in Santiago, Chile—is a bright-eyed, cheerful, lively 7-year-old. When she was 8 weeks old, Jonathan Finlay, her adoptive father, flew to Santiago and brought her home, to the waiting arms of her adoptive mother, a developmental psychologist and a professor at the University of Wisconsin-Madison named Diane E. Papalia.*

Anna was already cooing—making happy squeals, gurgles, and vowel sounds—when she came to Diane and Jonathan, and in the manner of parents around the world they began to coo back and to talk to their baby in dozens of daily "conversations." At about 6 months Anna added consonants to her "speech" and began to babble. And at 11 months, she toddled over to a next-door neighbor and said her first word—"Hi." Basking in the excited response she received from both her mother and her neighbor, Anna immediately repeated her first word six more times. She added three more words to her vocabulary over the next month and a few more soon after her first birthday. A favorite word was "glee," which originally meant Gregory, the family cat, and then came to mean all furry animals. Anna seemed to be right on schedule in becoming a speaker.

*Diane Papalia is, of course, one of the two authors of this textbook; the other is Sally Olds. Throughout, we will use a first name—Diane or Sally—whenever we are referring to only one of us.

But then Anna's progress slowed down, and by the time she was 2½, her parents began to worry. Anna seemed to understand what was said to her, but she spoke only a few words and was not putting them together in two-word sentences— though the average child does this considerably earlier, at about 18 months of age. They mentioned their anxieties to their pediatrician, who suggested a language assessment at a speech clinic. There, the speech pathologist told Diane and Jonathan that their daughter understood what a child her age was expected to, but that at the age of 30 months, she had the expressive language of a 15-month-old child.

"Was it something I did?" Diane asked, guilt-ridden and struck by the possible irony that she, a psychologist who writes about child development, might have contributed to Anna's language delay. The speech pathologist assured both parents that they did not seem to be to blame. Speech, she told them, may be late in developing for a number of reasons, unrelated to the child's intelligence or the environment provided by the parents. She then recommended a two-part program of speech therapy to bring Anna's speech up to normal for her age.

One aspect of the program, which began just before Anna's third birthday, was language stimulation. A trained speech therapist "played" with Anna, using toys to teach such concepts as *up-down*, *soft-hard*, and *big-little*. The therapist helped Anna to articulate her words more clearly and communicate more effectively—to use speech the way most people use it (or try to use it) much of the time—to get what she wanted.

The other part of Anna's speech therapy rested with her parents. Since her infancy, Diane and Jonathan had taken great joy in talking and reading to Anna, and they had generally spoken to her in "motherese," a simplified type of speech that most adults use almost automatically with babies. Now they were encouraged to simplify their speech even further. Instead of asking Anna, "Want to get up on Mommy's lap?" for example, they were to ask, "Want up?" Diane and Jonathan carried out this suggestion, gradually moving to more advanced levels of language as Anna's own speech improved. They also expanded on whatever Anna said and talked about whatever she showed interest in; and they used some effective new reading routines, which are described on page 17.

After 4 months of speech therapy, Diane and Jonathan received good news: at 3 years, 4 months, Anna had the usual vocabulary for her age. By 3 years, 9 months of age, her vocabulary was at an *advanced* level—4 years, 4 months. In addition, she was speaking sentences that averaged 5 to 7 words each and included some of up to 10 words.

By age 4, Anna was chattering away constantly, making requests, giving orders, asking questions, issuing comments. She would tell her mother, "Do your happy face, Mommy. Do your crying face. Do your mean face." She could name her favorite books and videotapes, sing "Eensy Weensy Spider," and use pronouns and past and future tenses correctly. At this writing, Anna is 7 years old and has just finished first grade. She has learned about time and money, she adds and subtracts "in her head," and she uses a computer. In light of her linguistic history, however, her progress in language thrills her parents the most. She loves to read and to be read to, and is also an imaginative storyteller. As her final first-grade class project, she wrote and illustrated a 16-page book, "Kara and the Magic Fish."

In many ways, language is a good illustration of the study of human development: it involves both the changes and the consistency that are typical of development, and it lends itself to study by all the basic methods of developmentalists. In this chapter, then, we focus on the study of language ability to show how learning about human development can enable us to understand and help children and adults.

As we describe our own approach to the study of human development, we will chart some major changes in the course of human life, and some influences on development. We will also touch on the history of the field, methods of social science, and ethical considerations in research. Finally, we will outline the major theoretical perspectives that try to explain human development.

Besides being an enjoyable shared activity, reading with a child—as Anna's father is doing with her—is an important way to help language skills develop. *(Erika Stone)*

HUMAN DEVELOPMENT: THE SUBJECT AND THE TEXT

WHAT IS HUMAN DEVELOPMENT?

Human development is the scientific study of how people change, as well as how they stay the same over time.

Change is most obvious in childhood but occurs throughout life. It takes two forms, quantitative and qualitative. *Quantitative change* is a change in the number or amount of something, such as height and weight—or the increase in the number of words, phrases, and sentences that Anna uses. *Qualitative change* is a change in kind, structure, or organization, such as the nature of a person's intelligence, the way the mind works—or Anna's development from a nonverbal infant to a child who understands and speaks a language. Like the emergence of a butterfly from a cocoon, qualitative change is marked by the appearance of new phenomena that could not have been predicted from earlier functioning. Speech is one such phenomenon.

In some ways, people show an underlying continuity, or consistency, from one time of life to another. In other ways, they change. One area with aspects of both continuity and change is personality development. According to recent research, for example, about 10 to 15 percent of children are consistently shy, while another 10 to 15 percent are, by and large, very sociable. (Most children fall between these extremes.) Although various factors in a child's life can modify these traits to some degree, the psychologist Jerome Kagan (1989) has found that they persist moderately through at least the first 7½ years, especially in children at one extreme or the other. Some characteristics—like outgoingness, neuroticism, and openness to new experiences—seem to persist through adulthood. But some others change in adulthood: at midlife, for instance, women typically become more assertive, men become more intimate and nurturing, and both sexes tend to become more introspective (that is, to think more about their lives).

Students of development are interested in factors that affect everyone. But since each member of the human species is unique, developmentalists also want to know why one person turns out different from another. Because human development is so complex, scientists cannot always answer that question. But by examining how people develop throughout life, they have learned much about what people need to develop normally, how they react to the many influences upon and within them, and how they can best fulfill their potential as individuals and as a species.

HOW THIS BOOK APPROACHES HUMAN DEVELOPMENT

Before introducing the study of human development, we will introduce some of our own ideas on the subject—the assumptions and beliefs that underlie this book—so that you may keep them in mind as you read.

We Celebrate the Human Being

We are interested in what theory and research have to tell us, specifically, about human beings. Whenever possible, we cite research that was done with people rather than animals. Sometimes, of course, we have to refer to studies of animals—in cases where ethical standards preclude research on humans. When we present conclusions based on animal research, we do so with caution, since we cannot assume that they apply equally to humans.

More important, our interest is in uniquely human qualities. So that you can explore this rich diversity, every chapter in this book has at least one "Window on the World" box, focusing on some aspect of a culture other than the dominant one in the United States. We will also examine cross-cultural differences at appropriate points in the main body of the text.

We Respect All Periods of the Life Span

We are convinced that people have the potential to change as long as they live. As we have pointed out, the changes of early life are especially dramatic, as almost helpless newborns transform themselves into competent, exploring children. Change in childhood normally involves increased size and improved abilities, but change in adulthood occurs in more than one direction.

Some abilities, like vocabulary, continue to grow; others, like strength and reaction time, diminish. Still other capacities may emerge for the first time in adulthood, like the synthesis of knowledge and experience into wisdom. Very old people can show growth, and even the experience of dying can be a final attempt to come to terms with one's life—in short, to develop.

We Believe in Human Resilience

We believe that people can often bounce back from difficult early circumstances or stressful experiences to make a good adaptation to life. A traumatic incident or a severely deprived childhood may well have grave emotional consequences; but the stories of countless people, some of whom researchers have followed into late adulthood, show that a single experience—even one as painful as the death of a parent in childhood—is not likely to cause irreversible damage (Vaillant & Vaillant, 1990). A nurturing environment can help a child overcome effects of early deprivation or trauma.

We Recognize That People Help Shape Their Own Development

People are not passive sponges, soaking up influences. They actively shape their own environment,

Oprah Winfrey is an example of human resilience. Sexually molested as a child and rebellious as a teenager, she blossomed when she went to live with her father, who encouraged her to learn. Today, as a host of a nationwide television talk show—and also an actor and producer—she is one of the most successful entertainers in the country. *(AP/Wide World Photo)*

and then they respond to the environmental forces that they have helped bring about. You can see this bidirectional influence over and over. When infants babble and coo, they encourage adults to talk to them, and this talk in turn stimulates the babies' language development. Teenagers' burgeoning sexuality may evoke their parents' fears of growing older and regrets for lost youth; the parents' reactions, in turn, may affect the teenagers' attitudes toward the changes they are undergoing. Older adults shape their own development by deciding when to retire from paid work, by taking up new activities, and by forming new relationships.

We Believe That Knowledge Is Useful

As people who live in the real world, we are concerned with how research findings can be used to solve practical problems. There are two kinds of research, which complement each other. *Basic* research is launched in the spirit of intellectual curiosity with no direct practical goal in mind; and *applied* research addresses immediate problems. Whenever possible, we extract from both kinds of research findings and theories with practical implications for everyday life.

Each chapter contains many examples and guidelines for action, some of them highlighted in the "Practically Speaking" boxes. The "Take a Stand" boxes use a pro-and-con format to focus on controversial issues, encouraging the reader to analyze and draw conclusions about the information presented. The "Food for Thought" boxes report on important issues, many based on cutting-edge research. And, as we pointed out, the "Window on the World" boxes explore topics involving various aspects of development in different cultures.

Now that you know something about how we approach human development, we introduce the study itself, sketching its outline and summarizing its history. Then we describe various ways of studying human development, their advantages, and their pitfalls. And finally, we present the perspectives of the field's most influential thinkers.

HUMAN DEVELOPMENT: THE STUDY AND ITS HISTORY

The study of human development originally focused on *describing* behavior in order to derive age norms. Today, developmentalists also want to *explain* why behaviors occur by looking at factors that influence development; the next step is to *predict* behavior and, in some cases, to try to *modify* or *optimize* development through training or therapy.

We can see the interrelationship of these four steps by looking at language development. *Description* leads to establishing norms for language at various ages. *Explanation* involves trying to uncover how children acquire language and get better at using it. *Prediction* entails determining what "language status" at a given age can tell us about later behavior: Does Anna's language delay at age 2½, for example, predict reading problems for her in second grade? *Modification* involves finding ways to change behavior, such as speech therapy to stimulate language growth. Of course, these four activities work together. Before starting language therapy, for instance, you need to know what is normal; to design a program, a therapist has to know how people acquire language skills.

The study of human development has many practical implications. After noting Anna's delayed speech development, her parents could, with the proper knowledge, be reassured that she was basically normal and could also learn how to help her overcome this specific problem. Similarly, understanding adult development helps professionals and laypersons alike to prepare for life transitions: a woman returning to work after maternity leave; a 50-year-old man who realizes that he will never be a company president; a person about to retire; a widow or widower; a dying patient.

Students of development draw on many disciplines, including psychology, sociology, anthropology, biology, education, and medicine. These disciplines are all reflected in this book.

ASPECTS OF DEVELOPMENT

One reason for the complexity of human development is that growth and change occur in different aspects of the self. In this book we talk separately about *physical, intellectual or cognitive,* and *personality and social* development at each period of life, but actually these strands are intertwined. Each aspect of development affects the others.

Physical Development

Changes in the body, the brain, sensory capacities, and motor skills are all part of physical development. They exert a major influence on both intellect and personality. For example, much of an infant's knowledge of the world comes from the senses and from motor activity. Thus, a child who has a hearing loss may be at risk of delayed language development. And in late adulthood, physical changes in the brain, as in Alzheimer's disease (which has been estimated to affect about 10 percent of people over the age of 65: Evans et al., 1989) can cause intellectual and personality deterioration.

Intellectual (Cognitive) Development

Changes in mental abilities—such as learning, memory, reasoning, thinking, and language—are aspects of intellectual, or cognitive, development. These changes are closely related to both physical

and emotional development. A baby's growing memory, for example, is related to the emotional experience of *separation anxiety,* the fear that the mother will not return once she has gone away. If children could not remember the past and anticipate the future, they would not be as likely to worry about the mother's absence. Memory also affects babies' physical actions. A 1-year-old boy who remembers being scolded for hitting the baby *may* refrain from doing it again.

Personality and Social Development

Personality is the unique way in which each person deals with the world and expresses emotions. Social development refers to changes in relationships with others. Both of these affect the cognitive and physical aspects of functioning. Anxiety about taking a test, for example, can impair performance. And social support from friends helps people cope with the potentially negative effects of stress on their physical and mental health. Similarly, physical and intellectual characteristics also affect social and personality development. Children who do not speak well may hit people to try to get what they want or have temper tantrums because of frustration over their inability to express their needs. This behavior affects their relationships with others in a negative way.

PERIODS OF THE LIFE SPAN

In this book we divide the human life span into eight periods: (1) prenatal, (2) infancy and toddlerhood, (3) early childhood, (4) middle childhood, (5) adolescence, (6) young adulthood, (7) middle age, and (8) late adulthood. These age divisions are approximate and somewhat arbitrary, especially in adulthood, when there are no clear-cut social or physical criteria like those in childhood (such as starting school and entering puberty) to signal a shift from one period to another.

Each period has its own characteristic events and issues; the major ones are described in Table 1-1.

INDIVIDUAL DIFFERENCES IN DEVELOPMENT

Although people typically proceed through the same general sequence of development, there is a wide range of individual differences in the timing

TABLE 1-1

Major Developments in Eight Periods of the Life Span	
Age Period	**Major Developments**
Prenatal stage (conception to birth)	Basic body structure and organs form. Physical growth is most rapid in life span. Vulnerability to environmental influences is great.
Infancy and toddlerhood (birth to age 3)	Newborn is dependent but competent. All senses operate at birth. Physical growth and development of motor skills are rapid. Ability to learn and remember is present, even in early weeks of life. Attachments to parents and others form toward end of first year. Self-awareness develops in second year. Comprehension and speech develop rapidly. Interest in other children increases.
Early childhood (3 to 6 years)	Family is still focus of life, although other children become more important. Fine and gross motor skills and strength improve. Independence, self-control, and self-care increase. Play, creativity, and imagination become more elaborate. Cognitive immaturity leads to many "illogical" ideas about the world. Behavior is largely egocentric, but understanding of other people's perspective grows.
Middle childhood (6 to 12 years)	Peers assume central importance. Children begin to think logically, although largely concretely. Egocentrism diminishes. Memory and language skills increase. Cognitive gains improve ability to benefit from formal schooling. Self-concept develops, affecting self-esteem. Physical growth slows. Strength and athletic skills improve.
Adolescence (12 to about 20 years)	Physical changes are rapid and profound. Reproductive maturity arrives. Search for identity becomes central. Peer groups help to develop and test self-concept. Ability to think abstractly and use scientific reasoning develops. Adolescent egocentrism persists in some behaviors. Relationships with parents are generally good.
Young adulthood (20 to 40 years)	Decisions are made about intimate relationships. Most people marry; most become parents. Physical health peaks, then declines slightly. Career choices are made. Sense of identity continues to develop. Intellectual abilities assume new complexity.
Middle age (40 to 65 years)	Search for meaning in life assumes central importance. Some deterioration of physical health, stamina, and prowess takes place. Women experience menopause. Wisdom and practical problem-solving skills are high; ability to solve novel problems declines. Double responsibilities of caring for children and elderly parents may cause stress. Time orientation changes to "time left to live." Launching of children typically leaves empty nest. Typically, women become more assertive, men more nurturant and expressive. For some, career success and earning powers peak; for others, "burnout" occurs. For a minority, there is a midlife "crisis."

(continued)

TABLE 1-1 *(Continued)*	
Age Period	**Major Developments**
Late adulthood (65 years and over)	Most people are healthy and active, although health and physical abilities decline somewhat.
	Most people are mentally alert. Although intelligence and memory deteriorate somewhat, most people find ways to compensate.
	Slowing of reaction time affects many aspects of functioning.
	Need to cope with losses in many areas (loss of one's own faculties, loss of loved ones).
	Retirement from work force creates more leisure time but may reduce economic circumstances.
	Need arises to find purpose in life to face impending death.

and expression of developmental changes. Throughout this book, we talk about average ages for the occurrence of certain phenomena: the first word, the first menstruation, the development of abstract thought. In all cases, these ages are *merely* averages. Only when deviation from these norms is extreme is there cause to consider a person's development exceptionally advanced or delayed. (Was Anna's language delay, for example, serious deviation from the norm or a normal individual difference? Would she eventually have reached her age level without therapy?)

The range of individual differences increases as people grow older. Normal children pass the same milestones in development at nearly the same ages because many changes of childhood are tied to maturation of the body and brain. Later in life, experiences and environment exert more influence, and since we undergo different experiences and live in different kinds of worlds, it is natural that we should reflect these differences.

Not only rates but also results of development vary. People differ in height, weight, and body build; in constitutional factors like health and energy level; in comprehension of complex ideas; and in emotional reactions. Their lifestyles differ too: the work they do, how well they do it, and how much they like it; the homes and communities they live in and how they feel about them; the people they see and the relationships they have; and how they spend their leisure time.

INFLUENCES ON DEVELOPMENT

Development is subject to many influences: the characteristics people are born with plus the effects of the experiences they have. Some experiences are purely individual, while others are common to certain groups—age groups, generations, or people who live in or were raised in particular societies and cultures. People's own behavior and lifestyle also influence their development.

Types of Influences: Sources and Effects

Internal and External Influences
Internal influences on development originate with *heredity*—the inborn genetic endowment that people receive from their parents. External influences, or *environmental influences*, come from people's experiences with the world outside the self.

But this distinction soon blurs: we change our world even as it changes us. A baby girl born with a cheerful disposition, for example, brings out positive reactions from other people, which in turn strengthen her trust that her efforts will be rewarded. With this self-confidence, she is motivated to try to do more—and is likelier to succeed than a child who lacks such trust.

Normative and Nonnormative Influences
The effects of certain major events have led some researchers to distinguish between normative and nonnormative influences on development (Baltes, Reese, & Lipsitt, 1980).

Something is "normative" when it occurs in a similar way for most people in a given group. *Normative age-graded influences* are biological and environmental influences on development that are highly similar for people in a particular age group, no matter when and where they live. These influences include biological events like puberty and menopause, as well as cultural events like entry into formal education (at about age 6 in most societies) and retirement from paid employment (usually between ages 55 and 70).

DRIVERS
LICENSE

⌐ WW II

Normative history-graded influences are biological and environmental influences common to a particular generation, or *cohort* (people growing up at the same time in the same place). These influences include the political turmoil in the United States during the 1960s and 1970s in reaction to the war in Vietnam, the massive famines in Africa during the 1980s and 1990s, and the violent conflicts in Eastern Europe in the early 1990s. They also encompass such cultural factors as the changing roles of women, the use of anesthesia during childbirth, and the impact of television and computers.

Nonnormative life events are unusual events that have a major impact on individual lives—typical events that happen to a person at an atypical time of life or events that do not happen at all to most other people. Nonnormative events include the death of a parent when a child is young, life-threatening illnesses, and birth defects. They can also, of course, be happy events, like Anna's adoption or being offered an exciting job. Whether such an event is positive or negative, it is likely to cause stress when a person does not expect it; if the person is not prepared for the event, she or he may need special help in adapting to it.

Birth of child

People often help create their own nonnormative life events by, say, applying for a new job or taking up a risky hobby like skydiving. Thus they are active participants in their own development.

Normative history-graded influences, like the impact of computers on education, can affect an entire cohort. Children like these kindergartners learning to use computers at such an early age will probably grow up thinking differently from the way their parents did. *(Bob Daemmrich/The Image Works)*

Contexts of Influences: An Ecological Approach

Both normative and nonnormative influences occur at particular "levels" of the environment. In his *ecological approach* to development, Urie Bronfenbrenner (1979) identifies four different levels of environmental influence, extending from the most intimate to the most global. To understand individual development, we must understand each person in the context of multiple environments.

■ The *microsystem* is the everyday immediate environment of home or school or work, including relationships with parents, siblings, caregivers, classmates, and teachers. These relationships are *bidirectional*, with each one affecting others. Not only did the personalities and value systems of Sally and her husband, Mark, influence the development of their children, but each child affected her parents as well as her sisters. The birth of Sally's first child, Nancy, for example, affected the lives of both her parents—of Sally, who left her full-time job as an advertising copy-

writer, and of Mark, who now felt an increased sense of responsibility for supporting his family. Then, the births of Sally's other two children affected the lives of their sisters as well as their parents. The attitudes of the three girls' teachers affected each girl's performance in school, positively when the teacher was encouraging and supportive, negatively when she or he was sarcastic or impersonal.

■ The *mesosystem* is the interlocking of various microsystems a person is involved with—the linkages between home and school, home and work, work and community, and so on. When Anna's grandfather fell ill, he required many hours of Diane's time and Anna did less well in school for a while.

■ The *exosystem* refers to the larger environment of institutions, like school, church, media, and government agencies. These larger environments also affect a person's experience. For example, being on welfare can affect a person's ambitions, and television can affect a person's

BOX 1-1 WINDOW ON THE WORLD

THE PURPOSE OF CROSS-CULTURAL RESEARCH

When Kpelle adults (people from central Liberia in Africa) were asked to sort 20 objects, they consistently did so on the basis of "functional" categories (that is, knife with orange or potato with hoe). Western psychologists associate functional sorting with a low level of thought; but since the subjects kept saying that this was the way a "wise man" would do it, the experimenter finally asked, "How would a fool do it?" He then received the "higher-order" categories he had originally expected—four neat piles with food in one, tools in another, and so on (Glick, 1975, p. 636).

This story illustrates one important reason why psychologists conduct research among different cultural groups—to recognize biases in traditional western theories and perspectives that often go unquestioned until they are shown to be a product of cultural influences. "Working with people from a quite different background can make one aware of aspects of human activity that are not noticeable until they are missing or differently arranged, as with the fish who reputedly is unaware of water until removed from it" (Rogoff & Morelli, 1989, p. 343).

By looking at people from different cultural and ethnic groups, researchers can learn which aspects of development are universal (and thus seem an intrinsic part of the human condition), and which are culturally determined. For example, no matter where children live, they learn to speak in the same sequence, going from cooing and babbling to single words and then to simple combinations of words. The words vary from culture to culture, but the sentences of toddlers around the world are structured similarly. Findings like this suggest that there is an inborn capacity for learning language. On the other hand, culture can exert a surprisingly large influence on such seemingly basic aspects of functioning as babies' early motor development. African babies tend to sit and walk earlier than American babies, apparently because of cultural practices. For example, Africans often prop infants in a sitting position and bounce them on their feet (Rogoff & Morelli, 1989).

In this book we present several examples of influential theories developed from research on western subjects which do not hold up when tested on people from other cultures—theories about gender roles, abstract thinking, moral reasoning, and a number of other concepts. We also look at people in cultures other than the dominant one in the United States, to show how closely human development is tied to culture and society and to understand normal development in a variety of settings.

---

gender attitudes. At age 5, Anna believed that only boys could be doctors, saying, "I'd have to get a penis for that," even though her own pediatrician was a woman.

■ The widest-ranging environment is the *macrosystem:* overarching cultural patterns of government, religion, education, and the economy. Sally's husband Mark, who experienced poverty as a child during the depression of the 1930s, is more concerned with economic security than Sally, since she never had to wonder where her next meal was coming from. Because of the current economic climate, both Nancy* and her husband need to work outside the home, which means that their daughter, Annie, receives a good part of her care from nonrelatives. People are affected by their country's values, too. If the United States offered subsidies to new parents,

*Sally and Mark's eldest daughter

as many other industrialized countries do, one of Annie's parents would have been able to stay home with her full time for at least her first year.

By emphasizing systems in and beyond the family, the ecological approach helps us to see the variety of influences upon human development. The relationship between culture and development is particularly apparent in this approach. Thus today, many developmentalists do cross-cultural research, studying people who live in different societies or in different cultural groups within the same society. Looking at development in context helps us to gain insight into the relative impact of environmental and biological influences on behavior (see Box 1-1).

Timing of Influences: Critical Periods

A *critical period* is a specific time during development when a given event has its greatest impact. For example, if a woman receives x-rays, takes certain drugs, or contracts certain diseases at specific times during pregnancy, the fetus may show specific ill effects; the amount and kind of damage to the fetus will vary, depending on the nature of the "shock" and on its timing.

The concept of critical periods has been applied to psychological as well as physical development. For example, Lenneberg (1969) proposed a critical period for language development, before puberty. This might explain why, when Sally's daughter Jennifer moved with her husband and son from the United States to her husband's native Germany, 5-year-old Stefan quickly learned to speak German with no accent at all; although Jennifer also became quite fluent, she was immediately recognizable as a foreigner.

Some of the evidence for critical periods of *physical* development, particularly fetal development, is undeniable. For other aspects of development, however, the concept of critical periods and irreversible effects is very controversial and seems too limiting. In these areas, although the human organism may be particularly *sensitive* to certain experiences at certain times of life, later events can often reverse the effects of early ones.

HOW THE STUDY OF HUMAN DEVELOPMENT HAS EVOLVED

Human development has, of course, been going on as long as human beings have existed; but ideas about it have changed drastically. This is an exciting time to study it, since formal *scientific study* of human development is relatively new, and changes in the way adults look at children are particularly dramatic.

Studies of Childhood

People have long held different ideas about what children are like and how they should be raised. According to the French historian Philippe Ariès (1962), not until the seventeenth century were children seen as qualitatively different from adults; before that, children were considered simply smaller, weaker, and less intelligent. Ariès based his opinion on such historical sources as old paintings, documents showing that children worked long hours and left their parents at early ages for apprenticeships, and statistics showing high infant mortality rates. He also concluded that parents, afraid that their children would die young, were reluctant to love them wholeheartedly.

This seventeenth-century painting by Georges de La Tour captures a tender moment between mother and baby, suggesting that, contrary to one widely held view, the recognition and appreciation of children's special nature is not a recent phenomenon. *(Musée des Beaux Arts de Rennes)*

Ariès's view has been widely accepted, but more recent analyses suggest a different picture. The psychologist David Elkind (1987a) finds recognition of children's special nature in the Bible and in the works of the ancient Greeks and Romans. And after examining autobiographies, diaries, and literature going back to the sixteenth century, Linda A. Pollock (1983) makes a strong argument that children have always been seen and treated differently from adults.

Books of advice for parents appeared in the sixteenth century. In most, physicians expressed their pet theories, telling mothers not to nurse their babies after feeling anger, lest their milk prove fatal; to begin toilet training at the age of 3 weeks; and to bind babies' arms for several months after birth to prevent thumb-sucking (Ryerson, 1961).

By the nineteenth century, several important trends had prepared the way for the study of child development. Scientists had unlocked the mystery of conception and were beginning to argue about the relative importance of heredity and environment (discussed in Chapter 2). The discovery of germs and immunization allowed parents to protect their children from the plagues and fevers that had made survival so uncertain. Adults also came to feel more responsible for the way children turned out, instead of simply accepting misfortune or misbehavior as fated. Moreover, new laws protecting children from long hours of labor meant that they could spend more time in school. The spirit of democracy filtered into home and classroom, as parents and teachers rejected the old, autocratic methods and focused on identifying and meeting children's needs. And the new science of psychology held that people could understand themselves by learning what influences had affected them during childhood.

Studies of Adolescence, Adulthood, and Aging

Adolescence was not considered a separate stage of development until the twentieth century, when G. Stanley Hall, a pioneer in child study, formulated a theory of adolescence. His two-volume work *Adolescence,* published in 1904, was popular and provoked much thought and discussion; but it had very little scientific basis, serving mainly as a platform for his own ideas.

Hall was also one of the first psychologists to become interested in aging. In 1922, at age 78, he published *Senescence: The Last Half of Life.* Six years later, Stanford University opened the first major scientific research unit devoted to aging. Not until a generation later, though, did this area of study blossom. By 1946, the National Institutes of Health (NIH) had set up a large-scale research unit, and specialized organizations and journals were reporting the newest findings—at first mainly on such topics as intellectual ability and reaction time, and later on emotional aspects of aging.

Since the late 1930s, a number of long-term studies have focused on adults. A major one is the Grant Study of Adult Development, which followed its subjects from the time when they were 18-year-old Harvard University students into late adulthood. In the mid-1950s Bernice Neugarten and her associates at the University of Chicago began their studies of middle-aged people, and K. Warner Schaie launched his ongoing study of adult intelligence. These studies and others, discussed in this book, add to our understanding. We still, however, know much more about children and the elderly than we do about young and middle-aged adults, although a growing emphasis on studies about these age groups should yield fruit.

Life-Span Studies

Today most psychologists recognize that human development is a lifelong process. Each period of a person's life span is influenced by the past and will affect the future.

Life-span studies in the United States grew out of programs designed to follow children over a period of years, through adulthood. The Stanford Studies of Gifted Children (begun in 1921 under the direction of Lewis Terman) focus on the development of people who were identified as unusually intelligent children. Other major studies that began around 1930—the Fels Research Institute Study, the Berkeley Growth and Guidance Studies, and the Adolescent (Oakland) Growth Study—have also yielded information on long-term development (see Box 1-2).

These and other studies have drawn on a wide variety of research tools; often, several different methods are used in the same study. Let's see what some of these methods are.

HUMAN DEVELOPMENT: RESEARCH METHODS

How do we know what people are like at various stages of development? Researchers in different

BOX 1-2   FOOD FOR THOUGHT

WHAT LONGITUDINAL STUDIES CAN TELL US

Stuart Campbell, orphaned at age 6 by his mother's death and his alcoholic father's abandonment, was raised in near-poverty by his stern but loving grandmother. At age 11 he entered a longitudinal study, and in junior high school and high school, he was judged to be unusually mature, intelligent, and mentally healthy, with a good sense of humor. By age 17 he knew he wanted to be a doctor. He became a pediatrician, married and divorced early in life, married again happily, had five children with his second wife, and established a home and a reputation in an upper-middle-class community.

Stuart was one of more than 500 children recruited for three studies known collectively as the Berkeley Longitudinal Studies. For the Berkeley Guidance Study and the Berkeley Growth Study, which were both launched in 1928, infants were enrolled right after birth. The Guidance Study gave parents help in coping with their children's problems, and the Growth Study examined mental development and physical growth. The Adolescent (Oakland) Growth Study was designed to assess how early or late puberty affected social and emotional development. This one enrolled children aged 10 to 12; Stuart was 11 when he joined it. More than 300 of the subjects in the three studies were followed into old age.

MEASURES

All subjects were given medical exams and periodic intelligence and psychological tests, including personality inventories. Family histories and descriptions of current family situations were recorded.

Life histories (case studies) were developed for 60 subjects, based on recorded data and interviews.

FINDINGS

These studies showed how people help to shape their own development. Sociologist John A. Clausen (1993) concluded that "adolescent planful competence," a combination of self-confidence, dependability, and intellectual involvement, helped people to mobilize resources and cope with difficulties. Other aspects of personality, appearance, and social background also had long-term consequences. Planful competence did not *guarantee* success in life, nor did its absence ensure failure. But adolescent planful competence was the most powerful influence on the course of a person's life. Competent teenagers like Stuart Campbell made good choices early in life, which often led to promising opportunities (like scholarships, competent spouses, and good jobs). Less competent adolescents made poorer early decisions and then tended to lead crisis-ridden lives.

A key goal of human development research is the ability to predict development and behavior. In these studies the personalities of people who as adolescents had shown planful competence changed less, and were less turmoil ridden, than did those of less competent teenagers. For example, at age 61, Stuart Campbell was found to be self-confident, intellectually involved, dependable, warm and agreeable, outgoing, and modestly assertive—all qualities that he had had in early adolescence.

How do people develop planful competence? In these studies, par-

enting that combined high standards, loving support, and firm control emerged as a major influence.

METHODOLOGY ISSUES

Planful competence in senior high school was a dependent variable and factors like parenting practices, intelligence test scores, and social class were independent variables. Then planful competence became an independent variable, with life success (as defined by the researchers) becoming the dependent variable.

Although the report of these studies is titled *American Lives*, it is actually a report of only *some* American lives. The lives studied are those of a cohort of people born in the 1920s and in one part of the country (the Bay area of San Francisco). The sample reflected the people living there at that time. It was almost entirely white, mostly native-born, Christian, and middle-class, with a few working-class subjects. Therefore, its findings might well not apply to people who, say, have to deal with poverty or racial or religious discrimination.

Of the approximately 200 subjects who dropped out, a disproportionate number were from families that had problems involving money, conflict, and divorce. So the skewing of the sample toward those with fewer family problems may have affected the findings. Still, with these caveats, the findings from these studies can be very helpful to developmentalists, parents, and teachers—and individuals looking for a better life.

SOURCE: Clausen, 1993.

branches of the physical and social sciences use different methods. But the term *scientific method* refers to certain underlying principles that characterize scientific inquiry in any field: careful observation and recording of data; testing of alternative hypotheses, or different explanations for data; and widespread public dissemination of findings and conclusions so that other observers can learn from, analyze, repeat, and build on the results. Only when developmentalists stick to these principles can they produce sound conclusions that explain and predict human behavior.

CORRELATION

In almost all research methods, some attempt will be made to find a *correlation,* or statistical relationship, between two or more factors.

Suppose you want to measure the relationship between two separate factors, like the amount of violence children see on television and the amount of aggressive behavior children show during free play. Each of these factors is called a *variable,* because it varies among members of a group or can be varied for purposes of an experiment.

The relationships between variables are expressed in terms of a *correlation.* Correlations show the *direction* and *magnitude* of a relationship between variables. Two variables may be related *positively:* they increase or decrease together. A *positive correlation* between televised violence and aggressiveness in children would exist if we found that the more they watch, the more they hit, bite, or kick other children; and conversely, the less violent television a child watches, the less aggressive his or her behavior is. Or two variables may have a *negative correlation:* as one increases, the other decreases. A *negative correlation* would exist if we found that the more violent television children watch, the less they fight.

Correlations are reported as numbers ranging from -1.0 (a perfect negative, or inverse, relationship) to $+1.0$ (a perfect positive, or direct, relationship). The higher the number (whether + or $-$), the stronger the relationship (either positive or negative). A correlation of zero indicates that there is no relationship between the two variables. Correlations practically never reach either -1.0 or $+1.0$, but range somewhere between 0 and 1.

Correlations allow us to *predict* one variable on the basis of another. If, for example, there is a positive correlation between watching televised violence and fighting, we would predict that children who watch violent shows are more likely to get into fights. Obviously, the greater the correlation between two variables, the greater the ability to predict one from the other.

Although correlations suggest *possible* causes for outcomes, they do *not* allow us to draw conclusions about cause and effect. We cannot conclude, for example, that watching violence on television *causes* aggressive play or makes it less likely; we can conclude *only* that the two variables are related. It is possible that being aggressive makes children want to watch violence on television. It is also possible that a third factor—perhaps an inborn predisposition toward aggressiveness—causes a child both to watch violent programs and to act aggressively. A correlation does not let us conclude that one factor causes the other. To do this, we need to design a controlled experiment.

In the next section we describe the research methods used to study human development, illustrating a number of them with real studies. Many of these studies are on development of language in young children, but the methods can be applied to other aspects of development and to people of any age. Table 1-2 compares methods.

NONEXPERIMENTAL METHODS

Nonexperimental techniques fall into three categories: case studies, observations, and interviews.

Case Studies

Case studies are studies of a single case or individual. Much of the data for psychoanalytic theories, which we discuss later in this chapter, comes from case studies—careful notes and interpretations of what patients have said under psychoanalysis. Our earliest sources of information about infants' development are case studies called *baby biographies,* journals in which parents recorded children's day-by-day development.

An important recent case study is the poignant story of "Genie" (Curtiss, 1977; Fromkin, Krashen, Curtiss, Rigler, & Rigler, 1974; Rymer, 1993). From the age of 20 months until she was discovered at age 13½, Genie had been confined in a small room where no one spoke to her. When found, she weighed only 59 pounds, could not straighten her arms or legs, and did not speak. She recognized

TABLE 1-2

Characteristics of Major Research Methods

Type	Main Characteristics	Advantages	Disadvantages
Nonexperimental Methods			
Case study	Study of single individual in depth.	Provides detailed picture of one person's behavior and development. Provides good description of behavior.	May not generalize to others; may reflect observer bias.
Naturalistic observation	Observation of people in their normal setting with no attempt to manipulate behavior.	Provides good description of behavior. Does not subject people to unnatural settings (such as the laboratory) that may distort behavior. Is a source of research hypotheses.	Lack of control; inability to explain cause-and-effect relationships. Observer bias possible.
Laboratory observation	Observation of people in the laboratory with no attempt to manipulate behavior.	Provides good descriptions. Greater control than naturalistic observation. Is a source of research hypotheses.	Inability to explain cause-and-effect relationships. Observer bias. Controlled situation can be artificial.
Interview	Participants asked about some aspect of their lives; ranges from highly structured to more flexible questioning.	Goes beyond observation in getting information about a person's life, attitudes, or opinions.	Interviewee may not remember information accurately or may distort responses in a socially desirable way. How question is asked may affect answer.
Experimental Methods			
Experiment	Controlled procedure in which an experimenter manipulates the independent variable to determine its effect on the dependent variable; may be conducted in the laboratory or field or make use of naturally occurring events.	Establishes cause-and-effect relationships; highly controlled procedure that can be repeated by another investigator. Degree of control is greatest in the laboratory experiment and least in the natural experiment.	Findings, especially when derived from laboratory experiments, may not generalize to situations outside the laboratory.

only her own name and the word *sorry*. Over the next 9 years Genie received intensive therapy that helped her learn many words and string them together in primitive sentences. Yet at last report, her language was still not normal.

Case studies offer useful, in-depth information, giving a rich description of an individual. But these studies have shortcomings. From studying Genie, for instance, we learn much about the development of a single child. However, like any case study, this one does not yield information about causes and effects. Even though it seems reasonable that Genie's severely deprived environment caused her deficiency in language, we cannot make this connection with certainty. It is impossible to know if Genie would have developed language normally if she had been raised by adequate parents. Furthermore, case studies do not explain behavior, and if they try to, there is no way to test the validity of their explanations. Also, case studies may be affected by *observer bias;* that is, the recorder may emphasize some aspects of a person's development and minimize others. While case studies may tell a great deal about individuals, then, it is questionable how well the information applies to people in general.

Observation

Observation takes two forms: naturalistic and laboratory. Both types can provide good descriptions of behavior, and both also have shortcomings.

Naturalistic Observation

In *naturalistic observation,* researchers observe and record people's behavior in real-life settings (like preschools or nursing homes). They do not manipulate the environment or alter behavior.

One type of naturalistic observation is *time sampling,* a technique used to determine how often a particular behavior (like aggression, babbling, or crying) occurs during a given period of time. One researcher used this method to study how infants and their parents act with each other. He went into the homes of forty 15-month-old babies and looked around during two typical 2-hour periods on separate days, without giving the parents any guidance or instructions. He recorded the presence or absence of 15 parental behaviors and 8 infant behaviors during alternating 15-second observe-record periods. He found that the mothers and fathers were more alike than different in the ways they treated their babies, that a parent paid slightly more attention to a child of his or her own sex, that a parent did more with a baby when he or she was alone with the baby than when the other parent was also present, and that the babies were more sociable when alone with one parent (Belsky, 1979).

Laboratory Observation

In *laboratory observation,* researchers observe and record behavior in settings that have been designed to place all the subjects in the same basic situation and to yield information on the subjects' behaviors in this experimental situation.

One research team looked at how mothers and fathers spoke to their babies of two different ages, either 2½ to 3½ months or 8½ to 9½ months (Kruper & Uzgiris, 1987). There were 40 mother-baby pairs and 32 father-baby pairs, equally divided between older and younger infants. Each parent-child pair was videotaped for about 10 minutes as the parent sat on a stool facing the baby. The parent had been asked to remain seated unless the baby needed attention and to play with the baby without toys as she or he would at home. Even though there were some differences between mothers' and fathers' speech, by and large fathers and mothers spoke similarly to their babies, asking many questions and repeating often. These parents treated their children as "communicating partners" from a very early age, as they asked questions, interpreted the babies' actions as answers, sometimes responded for the babies, and commented on the babies' thoughts and feelings.

Evaluation of Observational Studies

Observational studies cannot explain behavior or

Playing with babies is work for the psychologist Tiffany Field, who studies children by laboratory observation. At a child development center affiliated with a university medical school and hospital, Field follows up high-risk infants to assess the effects of early social interactions. *(Roe DiBona)*

determine its causes and effects. In naturalistic observation, investigators cannot control the conditions under which observation occurs. And in laboratory studies, the conditions may not be typical of real life. The laboratory study described above does not tell us *why* mothers and fathers talk to babies the way they do—why they seem to explain more to boy babies or try harder to get the attention of older babies. Furthermore, the very presence of an observer can alter the behavior being observed. Observers station themselves behind one-way mirrors (so they can observe subjects but cannot be seen themselves) or try to "blend in" with the background. Still, older children and adults often know that they are being observed and, realizing this, may act differently.

Interviews

In an *interview,* researchers ask questions about people's attitudes or opinions or some other aspect of their lives. By interviewing a large number of people, investigators get a picture of what people *say* they believe or do or have done.

An exploratory study of symbolic gestures—movements often used by toddlers to communicate before they can say words—was based largely on interviews with 38 mothers of 16- to 18-month-olds (Acredolo & Goodwyn, 1988). The researchers first sent the mothers a letter outlining the kind of gestures they were interested in (like those in Anna's repertoire, such as waving her hands up and down with small, quick motions to ask Jonathan to turn on the light or waving a piece of paper sideways to tell Diane that the wind was blowing). Interviewers then asked each woman about her child and about any gestures the child used.

From the interviews, the researchers learned that many children use such gestures as a transitional kind of communication. This shows that even before they can talk, they understand that objects and concepts have names and that they can use symbols to refer to a variety of things and happenings in their lives.

A problem with interviews is that the memory and accuracy of interviewees may be faulty. Some subjects forget when and how events actually took place. Others distort their replies to make them more acceptable to questioners or to themselves. Finally, the wording of a question can influence how people answer it. Thus, to corroborate the mothers' reports, these researchers followed up by looking at 11-month-old babies for 9 months.

This interview study had been inspired by a case study of a toddler who used 13 different gestures. It is a good example of the importance of understanding and knowing how to use all the research methods. It also shows the potential for using more than one method in a way that allows each one to contribute to our understanding in a different way.

EXPERIMENTAL METHODS

An *experiment* is a rigorously controlled procedure in which the investigator, called the *experimenter,* manipulates variables to learn how one affects another. Scientific experiments must be conducted and reported in such a way that another investigator can replicate (repeat) them to verify the results and conclusions.

Before recommending a program of speech therapy for a child like Anna, for example, a speech pathologist would want evidence that the program would be effective in helping children with expressive language delay. Such evidence could come from an experiment specifically designed to assess such therapy. Table 1-3 shows how such an experiment might be designed.

One actual team of researchers designed an experiment to examine the influence on children's language and vocabulary skills of a certain kind of reading by parents. The parents read picture books to the children, encourage the children's active participation, and give frequent, age-based feedback (Whitehurst, Falco, et al., 1988). The researchers compared two groups of middle-class children aged 21 to 35 months. In the *experimental group,* the parents adopted the new reading routines; in the *control group,* the parents continued their usual routines.

The parents of the children in the experimental group asked the children challenging open-ended questions rather than questions calling for simple yes-no answers. (Instead of asking, "Is the cat asleep?", they would ask, "What is the cat doing?") They expanded on the children's answers to their questions, corrected wrong answers, gave alternative possibilities, and bestowed praise. After 1 month of the program, the children in the experimental group were 8.5 months ahead of the control group in level of speech and 6 months ahead in vocabulary; 9 months later, the experimental group was still 6 months ahead of the controls. It is fair to conclude, then, that the new reading routines improve children's language and vocabulary

TABLE 1-3

Design for an Experiment	
Procedures	**Rationale**
1 Frame your research question: "Does speech therapy improve the rate of expressive language acquisition?"	You have chosen a problem that interests you and is relevant for either basic or applied research.
2 Review the literature on the topic.	You want to know what other work has been done, and you want a basis for formulating your hypothesis.
3 State your hypothesis: "Speech therapy improves the rate of expressive language acquisition."	This is the statement you will seek to support or not support.
4 Specify your operational definition of language acquisition: score on a standardized vocabulary test.	You need an objective way to measure your findings.
5 Specify your independent and dependent variables: the independent variable is the speech therapy; the dependent variable is the score on the vocabulary test.	You have developed a systematic framework for arriving at your data.
6 Identify the population you're concerned with: 3-year-olds with a delay of 1 year in expressive language. (There are 1000 children with this diagnosis at a certain speech clinic.)	This is the group that might ultimately be affected by your findings, but it is so large that you could not include everyone in your experiment.
7 Choose a sample, a subgroup of the population. You could do this by picking 50 children at random, say every twentieth child with this diagnosis at this clinic.	If the sample is chosen randomly so that each member of the population has an equal chance of being selected, you can generalize your results from the sample to the population.
8 Assign the subjects randomly to either the experimental or the control group, so that each group has 25 3-year-olds with a 1-year language delay.	Use random assignment of subjects to control for differences such as IQ, sex, geographic background, and learning ability.
9 Expose only the experimental group to the independent variable, the treatment (6 months of speech therapy given two times a week in 30-minute sessions). The control group does not receive the treatment.	All other conditions are the same for the two groups.
10 After 6 months give members of both groups a test of expressive language (the dependent variable).	All subjects receive the same evaluation.
11 Determine your results: calculate test scores for both groups and perform a statistical analysis. Is there a significant difference in scores between the experimental and control groups?	Statistical techniques are used to determine whether the two groups differ significantly in average test scores.
12 Analyze your findings: "Children in the experimental group scored significantly better on average on the expressive language test than those in the control group."	Because of the various objective, systematic controls, we can conclude that exposure to the treatment caused the statistical difference (higher scores on the test of expressive language), which probably represents greater linguistic progress.
13 Draw your conclusion: "The findings support the hypothesis that speech therapy is effective in improving expressive language acquisition."	Because of this evidence, you may decide to apply your findings by offering speech therapy to all 3-year-olds with a 1-year expressive language delay.

skills. (And this is why Diane and Jonathan adopted these new routines in reading to Anna.)

Variables and Groups

In the experiment just described, the type of reading approach was the *independent variable* and the children's language skills were the *dependent variable*. An **independent variable** is something over which the experimenter has direct control. A **dependent variable** is something that may or may not change as a result of changes in the independent variable; in other words, it *depends* on the independent variable. In an experiment, a researcher manipulates the independent variable to see how changes in it will affect the dependent variable.

To conduct an experiment, we need two groups of subjects: experimental and control groups. An **experimental group** is composed of people who will be exposed to the experimental manipulation or *treatment* (such as being read to in a new way). Following exposure, the effect of the treatment on the dependent variable is measured one or more times. A **control group** is composed of people who are similar to the experimental group but do not receive the treatment whose effects we want to measure. An experiment must include one or more of each type of group.

Sampling and Assignment

If experimental results show a cause-and-effect relationship between two variables, how do we know that this relationship is true *generally,* and not just for the subjects of the experiment? And how can we be sure that the relationship is not due to some third factor? The answers hinge on how subjects are selected and on how they are assigned to experimental and control groups.

First of all, we must make sure that our **sample** (the group of subjects chosen for the experiment) is representative of the entire population under study (that is, all the members of the larger group we want to generalize about). We generally cannot study an entire population (this would be too costly and time-consuming); but only if the sample is representative of the larger group can we generalize the results of the experiment to the population as a whole.

Experimenters ensure representativeness by random sampling. In a **random sample,** each member of the population has an equal and independent chance of being selected. For example, if we

want a random sample of the students in a human development class, we might put all their names into a hat, shake it, and then draw out the number of names we want.

Next, we should randomly *assign* these subjects to experimental and control groups. If the sample is large enough, differences in such factors as age, sex, race, IQ, and socioeconomic status will be evenly distributed so that the groups are as alike as possible in every respect except for the independent variable, the one to be tested. Random assignment *controls* for all other variables; that is, it prevents them from affecting the results. Thus the results of our experiment will reflect only the impact of the independent variable and not some other factor.

We could, of course, try to control for any and all factors we could think of that might have an effect by deliberately matching the experimental and control groups. But no matter how carefully we match groups for certain characteristics, we will probably miss others that may be just as important. The best way to control for unforeseen factors is to assign subjects randomly to the experimental and control groups so that each subject has an equal chance of being assigned to either group.

Note that in the reading experiment described above, although the researchers did not select a sample from a larger population, they did divide their subjects randomly into experimental and control groups.

Types of Experiments

There are three types of experiments: those conducted in the laboratory; those conducted in the "field," a setting that is part of the subject's everyday life; and those that make use of naturally occurring events.

Laboratory Experiments

In a *laboratory experiment* the subject is brought to a specific place and experiences conditions under the experimenter's control. The researcher records the subject's reaction to these conditions, possibly contrasting it with the same person's behavior under different conditions or with the behavior of people who experience a different set of conditions. In the first type of laboratory experiment, parents and children might be brought into a room so that researchers can measure the strength of parent-child attachment by seeing what happens when the mother leaves the child, when the father

Experiments use strictly controlled procedures that manipulate variables to determine how one affects another. To study emotional resiliency, this research project at the University of California at San Francisco monitors the heart rate and blood pressure of young children as they explain their feelings in response to a hand puppet's happy or angry face. *(James Wilson/Woodfin Camp & Assoc.)*

leaves the child, or when a stranger leaves the child. In the second type of laboratory experiment, some children might see a person acting aggressively while other children do not; then both groups of children would be measured on the degree to which they act aggressively themselves.

Laboratory experiments permit the greatest control over the situation and are the easiest studies to replicate (that is, the easiest for other researchers to carry out in exactly the same way). But because of the artificiality of the situation, subjects may not always act as they would in real life.

Field Experiments

In a *field experiment,* experimenters make a change in a familiar setting, like school or home. The experiment in which parents adopted new reading routines was a field experiment.

Natural Experiments

A *natural experiment* compares people who have been accidentally divided into separate groups by circumstances of life—one group who were exposed to some naturally occurring event and another group who were not. Natural experiments are not true experiments, because they do not try to manipulate behavior; but they provide a way of studying events that cannot be created artificially. For example, it would be unethical to separate identical twins at birth just to do an interesting experiment, but if we discover identical twins who *did* happen to be separated at birth and were raised in different circumstances, we can compare the ef-

fects of different environments on people with the same heredity. A number of the studies described in Chapter 2 did just this.

Comparing Experimentation with Other Methods

Experiments have several advantages over nonexperimental methods. Only experiments can tell us about cause-and-effect relationships. Also, the experimental method allows studies to be replicated by other researchers with different groups of subjects, to check the consistency of results.

Experiments also have drawbacks. For one thing, they may be designed so narrowly that they focus on one or two aspects of development and miss the overall picture. A second concern arises from the differences in the three types of experiments. Laboratory experiments, which allow the greatest control and thus tend to be the most reliable, are typically the *least* generalizable. That is, we cannot be sure that conclusions drawn from the laboratory apply to real life. Experimental manipulation shows what *can* happen if certain conditions are present: for example, that children who watch violent television shows in the laboratory *can* become more aggressive in that setting. It does not tell us what actually *does* happen in the real world. *Do* children who watch a lot of shoot-'em-ups hit their little brothers or sisters more than children who watch a different kind of show?

Greater understanding of human development

may well result from combining nonexperimental and experimental approaches. First, researchers can observe people as they go about their everyday lives and determine what correlations exist. Then they can design experimental studies of apparent relationships to assess cause and effect.

As we have seen in our examples of studies of language development, there is no one "right" way to examine an issue. Many questions can be approached from several different angles, each one yielding different kinds of information. Very often one type of study leads into another. For example, the case study of Genie suggests that language stimulation is important. To look at this further, we could design an experiment to test how different kinds of stimulation promote language development. And observations of the way parents talk to their children, as well as information gleaned from interviews, can generate hypotheses and inspire experiments to test them.

DATA COLLECTION METHODS

Information about development is most commonly gathered by *cross-sectional* or *longitudinal* studies (see Figure 1-1). In some cases *sequential* designs are used. These data collection techniques provide information about how people change or stay the same over time.

Cross-Sectional and Longitudinal Studies

In a ***cross-sectional study,*** people of different ages are assessed on one occasion. This kind of study provides information about *differences* in development among different age groups, rather than *changes* with age in the same person or people (which longitudinal studies show).

In one cross-sectional study, people in six different age groups from age 6 to old age took a battery of cognitive tests. Age differences in performance appeared: middle-aged subjects scored highest, and young children and older people scored lowest (Papalia, 1972). You could not conclude from these findings, however, that when the younger subjects in this study became older themselves, their scores would drop to the lower levels of the older people in the original sample. The older subjects may, as a cohort, have had poorer education or other experiences that affected their performance so that they would *never* have scored as well as the middle-aged subjects. The only way

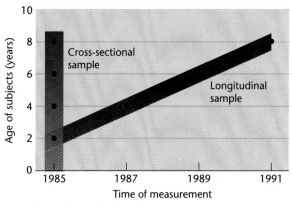

FIGURE 1-1
The two most important ways to obtain data about development. In a *cross-sectional* study, people of different ages are measured at one time. Here, groups of 2-, 4-, 6-, and 8-year-olds were tested in 1985 to obtain data about age differences in performance. In a *longitudinal* study, the same people are measured more than once. Here, a sample of children were first measured in 1985 when they were 2 years old; follow-up testing was done in 1987, 1989, and 1991, when the children were 4, 6, and 8, respectively. This technique shows age changes in performance.

to see whether change occurs over time in the same person is to conduct a longitudinal study.

In a ***longitudinal study,*** researchers measure the same people more than once to see changes in development over time. The researchers may measure one characteristic, such as vocabulary size, IQ, height, or aggressiveness. Or they may look at several aspects of development, to find interrelationships among factors. Since the same people are measured more than once, this design gives a picture of the *process* of development.

One important longitudinal study, started by Terman, followed young schoolchildren with high IQs into old age; it found that their intellectual, scholastic, and vocational superiority held up over time. Also, looking at differences within the group itself, researchers identified factors besides intelligence (like parental encouragement) that seem to foster success in life (P. Sears & Barbee, 1978; Terman & Oden, 1959).

Cross-sectional studies, then, look at *differences* among groups of people; longitudinal studies assess *changes* undergone by one or more persons. Each design has strengths and weaknesses.

The advantages of the cross-sectional method include speed and economy: it is faster and cheaper than the longitudinal method. In addition, since subjects are assessed only once, it does not lose subjects who drop out. Among its drawbacks is its masking of differences among individuals, since it looks at group averages. Its *major* disadvantage is that it cannot eliminate cohort, or generational, influences on subjects born at different times. Cross-sectional studies are sometimes misinterpreted as yielding information about developmental *changes* in groups or individuals; but such information is often misleading and may contradict longitudinal research. For example, it would be incorrect to conclude from the cross-sectional study described above (Papalia, 1972) that intellectual functioning declines in later years. This may be so, but longitudinal data would be needed to determine whether there were actual age changes. All that the cross-sectional method can show is that there were age *differences* in performance.

The great strength of *longitudinal* studies is their sensitivity to individual patterns of change, since data about individuals can be tracked. Also, they avoid cohort effects *within* a study—although longitudinal studies done on one particular cohort may not apply to a different cohort. (In other words, a study done with people born in 1930 may not apply to subjects born in 1990.) Longitudinal studies, however, are time-consuming and expensive. Another shortcoming is probable bias in the sample: people who volunteer tend to be of higher-than-average socioeconomic status and intelligence, and those who stay with the project over time may differ from those who drop out. Also, results can be affected by repeated testing: people tend to do better in later tests because of a "practice effect," that is, a familiarity with test materials and procedures. (Refer to Box 1-2 for a discussion of the Berkeley Longitudinal Studies.)

Sequential Studies

The *cross-sequential study* is one of several sequential strategies designed to overcome the drawbacks of longitudinal and cross-sectional studies. This method combines the other two: people in a cross-sectional sample are tested more than once, and the results are analyzed to determine the differences that show up over time for the different groups of subjects.

Some important research on intellectual functioning in adulthood employs sequential techniques. As we will see in Chapter 16, these techniques seem to provide a more realistic assessment than either the cross-sectional method (which tends to overestimate the drop in intellectual functioning in later years) or the longitudinal method (which tends to underestimate it).

ETHICS OF RESEARCH

Ethical Issues

Some years ago, a doctor recommended giving psychological tests to young underprivileged children in the hope of predicting which ones might someday become delinquent. These children could then be watched and given social support to forestall their criminal tendencies. Many people—justifiably, we believe—attacked the proposal, pointing out that the test results might be a "self-fulfilling prophecy": the children who were labeled as potential delinquents and were therefore treated differently might actually *become* delinquent as a result.

Should research like this—research that might harm its subjects—ever be undertaken? Might it be undertaken if the risk of harm is small and the likelihood of gaining valuable knowledge is great? How can we balance the possible benefits to humanity against the risk of intellectual, emotional, or physical injury to individuals? Researchers confront many such questions about consent, deception, self-esteem, and privacy.

Informed Consent

When parents consent to a child's participation in research, can we assume that they are acting in the child's best interests? According to one panel on ethics, children aged 7 or over should be asked for their own consent and should be overruled only if the research promises some direct benefit to the child, as in the use of a new drug (National Commission for the Protection of Human Subjects of Biomedical and Behavioral Research, 1978).

Informed consent can also be an issue with adults; for example, we need to make sure that institutionalized older subjects are competent to give consent and are not being exploited.

Deception

An issue that is often linked with consent is deception. How much do subjects need to know about an experiment before their consent can be considered informed? Suppose that children are told they are trying out a new game when they are actually being tested on their reactions to success or failure? Suppose that adults are told they are participating in a study on learning when they are really being tested on their willingness to inflict pain? Experiments like these, which cannot be carried out without deception, have been done—and they have added significantly to our knowledge, but at the cost of the subjects' right to know what they are getting involved in.

Self-esteem

Subjects may also be affected by their own behavior in an experiment. For instance, research on the limits of children's capabilities has a built-in "failure factor": the investigator keeps presenting questions or problems until the child is unable to answer. How seriously might such failure affect subjects' self-confidence? Also, when researchers publish findings that middle-class children are academically superior to poor children, unintentional harm may be done to the latter's self-esteem. Furthermore, such studies may become self-fulfilling prophecies, affecting teachers' expectations and students' performance.

Privacy

Is it ethical to use one-way mirrors and hidden cameras to observe people without their knowledge? How can we protect the confidentiality of personal information (for example, about income or family relationships or even about illegal activities, like smoking marijuana or shoplifting) that subjects may reveal?

Ethical Standards

Since the 1970s, federally mandated committees have been set up at colleges, universities, and other institutions to review proposed research from an ethical standpoint. In 1982 the American Psychological Association adopted guidelines covering such points as protection of subjects from harm and loss of dignity, guarantees of privacy and confidentiality, informed consent, avoidance of deception wherever possible, subjects' right to decline or withdraw from an experiment at any time, and the responsibility of investigators to correct any undesirable short-term or long-term effects of participation. Still, specific situations often call for hard judgments. Everyone in the field of human development must accept the responsibility to try to do good and, at the very least, to do no harm.

HUMAN DEVELOPMENT: THEORETICAL PERSPECTIVES

THEORIES AND HYPOTHESES

How people explain development depends on how they view the fundamental nature of human beings. Different thinkers, looking through different lenses, have come up with different explanations, or theories, about why people behave as they do.

A *theory* is a set of related statements about *data,* the information obtained through research. Scientists use theories to help them organize, or make sense of, their data and then to predict what data might be obtained under certain conditions. Theories, then, are important in helping scientists to *describe, explain, interpret,* and *predict* behavior.

Both research and theory are essential. Painstaking research adds, bit by bit, to the body of knowledge. Theories help researchers to find a coherent structure in the data—to go beyond isolated observations and make generalizations.

Theories guide future research by suggesting hypotheses to be tested. A *hypothesis* is a possible explanation for a phenomenon and is used to predict the outcome of an experiment. Sometimes research confirms a hypothesis, providing support for a theory. At other times, scientists must modify theories to account for unexpected facts that emerge from research.

The perspectives from which theorists look at development are important because they shape the questions researchers ask, the methods they use, and the way they interpret their results. Today human development is studied from at least four perspectives: psychoanalytic, learning, cognitive, and humanistic. Each has its dedicated supporters and its equally impassioned critics, and each has made important contributions to our understanding of human development.

In this book we examine and evaluate some of the more influential theories, and we emphasize the interplay between theory and research. The following brief overview summarizes the four perspectives (including their strengths and weaknesses), and Table 1-4 compares them. We present and analyze age-related aspects of the theories more fully throughout the book.

TABLE 1-4

Four Perspectives on Human Development			
Perspective	Important Theories	Basic Belief	Technique Used
Psychoanalytic	Freud's psychosexual theory	Sigmund Freud: Behavior is controlled by powerful unconscious urges.	Clinical observation
	Erikson's psychosocial theory	Erik Erikson: Personality is influenced by society and develops through a series of crises.	
	Self-in-relation theory	Jean Baker Miller: Personality develops in the context of emotional relationships, not separate from them.	
Learning	Behaviorism, or traditional learning theory (Pavlov, Skinner, Watson)	Behaviorism: People are responders; the environment controls behavior.	Rigorous and scientific (experimental) procedures
	Social-learning theory (Bandura)	Social-learning theory: Children learn in a social context, by observing and imitating models; person is an active contributor to learning.	
Cognitive	Piaget's cognitive-stage theory	There are qualitative changes in the way children think that develop in a series of four stages between infancy and adolescence. Person is an active initiator of development.	Flexible interviews; meticulous observation
	Information-processing theory	Human beings are processors of information.	Laboratory research; technological monitoring of physiologic responses
Humanistic	Maslow's self-actualization theory	People have the ability to take charge of their lives and foster their own development.	Discussion of feelings

PSYCHOANALYTIC PERSPECTIVE

Do you ever try to analyze your dreams? Do you believe that people often act in response to unconscious feelings—that is, feelings they are not aware of? If so, you are taking the *psychoanalytic perspective,* which is concerned with the unconscious forces motivating human behavior. This view originated at the beginning of the twentieth century, when a Viennese physician named Sigmund Freud first developed psychoanalysis, a therapeutic approach based on giving people in-

sights into unconscious conflicts, stemming from childhood, that affect their behavior and emotions.

The psychoanalytic perspective delves below the surface of our feelings to explore unconscious forces, which people are not even aware of but which motivate behavior. Originated by Sigmund Freud, it has been expanded and modified by other theorists; the most influential is Erik H. Erikson. Even though contemporary psychologists do not subscribe to many Freudian concepts—partly because so few have held up to efforts to test them scientifically, we present his theory here because of its historic importance, and because Freud did influence and inspire developmentalists who followed him.

Sigmund Freud: Psychosexual Theory

Sigmund Freud (1856–1939), the oldest of eight children, believed that he was his mother's favorite, and he expected to accomplish great things (E. Jones, 1961). His initial goal was medical research, but limited funds and barriers to academic advancement for Jews in Austria forced him into the private practice of medicine.

One of his main interests was neurology, the study of the brain and treatment of disorders of the nervous system—a branch of medicine then in its infancy. To relieve symptoms with no apparent physical cause, Freud began to ask questions designed to summon up his patients' long-buried memories. He then concluded that the source of emotional disturbances lay in traumatic experiences of early childhood which people repressed.

Freud believed that personality is decisively formed in the first few years of life, as children deal with conflicts between their inborn biological, sexually related urges and the requirements of society. He proposed that these conflicts occur in an unvarying sequence of stages of *psychosexual development,* in which pleasure shifts from one body zone to another—from the mouth to the anus and then to the genitals. At each stage, the behavior that is the chief source of gratification changes—from feeding to elimination and eventually to sexual activity.

Id, Ego, and Superego

Freud believed that newborns are initially governed by the *id,* a source of motives and desires that is present at birth. The id seeks immediate satisfaction under the *pleasure principle.* Infants do not see themselves as separate from the outside world; all they are concerned about is what they want. But when gratification is delayed (as when they have to wait for food), they begin to see themselves as other than their surroundings. At this point, sometime during the first year of life, they begin to develop an ego. The *ego,* which represents reason or common sense, operates under the *reality principle.* The ego's aim is to find realistic ways to gratify the id. The *superego,* which develops by about age 5 or 6, includes the conscience. As the child identifies with the parent of the same

The Viennese physician Sigmund Freud developed an orginal, influential, and controversial theory of emotional development in childhood, based on his adult patients' recollections. His daughter, Anna, shown here with her father, followed in his professional footsteps and constructed her own theories of development. *(Mary Evans/Sigmund Freud Copyrights)*

sex, the superego incorporates socially approved "shoulds" and "should nots" into the child's own value system.

Defense Mechanisms

Freud also described a number of *defense mechanisms,* ways in which people unconsciously distort reality to protect their egos against anxiety. Everyone uses defense mechanisms at times; only when they are so overused that they interfere with healthy emotional development are they pathological. (See Table 1-5.)

Stages of Psychosexual Development

Freud described five stages of personality development (see Table 1-6). He considered the first three the most crucial, and believed that children are at risk of fixation, an arrest in development, if they receive too little or too much gratification in

TABLE 1-5

Some Freudian Defense Mechanisms

Mechanism	Description and Examples
Regression	Return to behavior characteristic of an earlier age, during trying times, to try to recapture remembered security. A girl who has just entered school may go back to sucking her thumb or wetting the bed. Or a young man in college may react to his parents' recent separation by asking them to make decisions for him as they did when he was a child. When the crisis becomes less acute or the person is better able to deal with it, the inappropriate behavior usually disappears.
Repression	Blocking from consciousness those feelings and experiences that arouse anxiety. Freud believed that people's inability to remember much about their early years is due to their having repressed disturbing sexual feelings toward their parents. (See the discussion of the Oedipus and Electra complexes in Chapter 7.)
Sublimation	Channeling uncomfortable sexual or aggressive impulses into such socially acceptable activities as study, work, sports, and hobbies.
Projection	Attribution of unacceptable thoughts and feelings to another person. For example, a little girl talks about how jealous of her the new baby is, when she herself is jealous of the baby; or a husband who entertains fantasies of having an affair accuses his wife of being unfaithful.
Reaction formation	Saying the opposite of what one really feels. Buddy says, "I don't want to play with Tony, because I don't like him," when the truth is that Buddy likes Tony a lot but is afraid that Tony doesn't want to play with *him*.

any of these stages. A child may become emotionally "stuck" and may need help in order to move beyond that stage. Such evidence of childhood fixation shows up in adult personality.

Oral Stage (Birth to 12–18 Months)* During infancy, feeding is the main source of sensual pleasure. Babies whose oral needs are not met may grow up to become nail-biters or develop "bitingly" critical personalities. Babies who received so *much* oral pleasure that they do not want to abandon this stage may become compulsive eaters or smokers.

Anal Stage (12–18 Months to 3 Years) During toddlerhood, the chief source of pleasure shifts from the mouth to the anus. Moving the bowels produces great relief and pleasure. Too-strict toilet training may lead a child to hold back feces or release them at inappropriate times. An anally fixated adult may have a "constipated" personality, becoming obsessively clean and neat or rigidly tied to schedules and routines. Or the person may become defiantly messy.

Phallic (Early Genital) Stage (3 to 6 Years) During

*All ages are approximate

early childhood, the site of pleasure shifts from the anus to the genital area. During this stage, boys are influenced by sexual attachments to their mothers and girls to their fathers, and by rivalry with the same-sex parent. The boy, now aware that little girls do not have penises, assumes that they were cut off and worries that his father will castrate him too. The girl feels what Freud called *penis envy* and blames her mother for not having given her a penis. Children resolve the anxiety from both situations by identifying with the parent of the same sex, either through the Oedipus complex (for boys) or the Electra complex (for girls).

Both boys and girls deal with guilt and fear by identifying with the same-sex parent and developing a superego. The early superego is rigid. The daughter of parents who value cleanliness may want to change her clothes six times a day. Or a little boy may be tormented by guilt because he wrestled harmlessly with a friend. With maturity, the superego becomes more realistic and flexible, as it is better controlled by the ego.

Latency (6 to 12 Years) According to Freud, middle childhood is relatively calm sexually. Youngsters have resolved their Oedipal and Electra conflicts, adopted gender roles, and developed superegos. Because of this sexual calm, they can

TABLE 1-6

Developmental Stages According to Various Theories

Psychosexual Stages (Freud)	Psychosocial Stages (Erikson)	Cognitive Stages (Piaget)	Relational Stages (Miller)
Oral (birth to 12–18 months). Baby's chief source of pleasure is mouth-oriented activities like sucking and eating.	*Basic trust versus mistrust (birth to 12–18 months)*. Baby develops sense of whether world can be trusted. Virtue: hope.	*Sensorimotor (birth to 2 years)*. Infant changes from a being who responds primarily through reflexes to one who can organize activities in relation to the environment. Learns through sensory and motor activity.	*Infancy.* Baby identifies with caretaking activity; responds to caregiver's emotions; develops sense of comfort when other person is also comfortable; acts to move the relationship forward toward greater mutual well-being.
Anal (12–18 months to 3 years). Child derives sensual gratification from withholding and expelling feces. Zone of gratification is anal region.	*Autonomy versus shame and doubt (12–18 months to 3 years)*. Child develops a balance of independence over doubt and shame. Virtue: will.	*Preoperational (2 to 7 years)*. Child develops a representational system and uses symbols such as words to represent people, places, and events.	*Toddlerhood.* Child has more abilities, more physical and mental resources, new understandings of relationships, more complex sense of self and more complex relationships. Maintaining relationships with main people in the child's life is the most important thing.
Phallic (3 to 6 years). Time of the "family romance": Oedipus complex in boys and Electra complex in girls. Zone of gratification shifts to genital region.	*Initiative versus guilt (3 to 6 years)*. Child develops initiative when trying out new things and is not overwhelmed by failure. Virtue: purpose.		*Early childhood.* No Oedipus or Electra complex. Relationship to early caregivers continues. If these exalt the father's role as more valuable and more important than the mother's, the child will absorb that belief.
Latency (6 years to puberty). Time of relative calm between more turbulent stages.	*Industry versus inferiority (6 years to puberty)*. Child must learn skills of the culture or face feelings of inferiority. Virtue: skill.	*Concrete operations (7 to 12 years)*. Child can solve problems logically if they are focused on the here and now.	*School years.* Girls show deep interest in relationships, family, and emotional issues. Because of socialization, boys do not show this interest; instead they do a lot of competitive games and strategies.
Genital (puberty through adulthood). Time of mature adult sexuality.	*Identity versus identity confusion (puberty to young adulthood)*. Adolescent must determine own sense of self. Virtue: fidelity	*Formal operations (12 years through adulthood)*. Person can think in abstract terms, deal with hypothetical situations, and think about possibilities.	*Adolescence.* Girls "shut down" in response to societal directives to serve boys and men and to prepare to serve future children. They experience physical and sexual stirrings as bad and wrong. They receive societal message to be less active, both in relationships and with regard to self.

(continued)

TABLE 1-6   *(Continued)*

Psychosexual Stages (Freud)	Psychosocial Stages (Erikson)	Cognitive Stages (Piaget)	Relational Stages (Miller)
			Boys continue to shut down emotional responses, place autonomy above emotional connections.
	Intimacy versus isolation (young adulthood). Person seeks to make commitments to others; if unsuccessful, may suffer from sense of isolation and self-absorption. Virtue: love.		*Young adulthood.* Young women continue to seek mutual relationships in personal and work life; they also plan for continuing work life or career. Young men still feel the primacy of establishing themselves in work life or career; they seek intimate relationships but often do not give them primacy.
	Generativity versus stagnation (middle adulthood). Mature adult is concerned with establishing and guiding the next generation or else feels personal impoverishment. Virtue: care.		*Midlife.* Women continue to seek mutuality in growth-fostering relationships. Many men become able to pursue generative activities; other men continue the quest for self-enhancement.
	Integrity versus despair (old age). Elderly person achieves a sense of acceptance of own life, allowing the acceptance of death, or else falls into despair. Virtue: wisdom.		*Old age.* Reworking of relationships with family and enlargement of the relational world is essential for integrity in aging.

become socialized, develop skills, and learn about themselves and society.

Genital Stage (Adolescence and Adulthood) The physiological changes of puberty reawaken the libido, the basic energy that fuels the sex drive. The sexual urges of the phallic stage, repressed during latency, now resurface to flow in socially approved channels—heterosexual relations with people outside the family. The genital stage is the final psychosexual stage, lasting through adulthood.

Erik Erikson: Psychosocial Theory

Erik Erikson (b. 1902–1994), a German-born psychoanalyst, trained in Vienna under Sigmund

Freud's daughter, Anna Freud, who also became a psychoanalyst. Erikson fled from the threat of Nazism (which eventually forced the breakup of Sigmund Freud's entire circle) and came to the United States in 1933. His personal and professional experience—far broader than Freud's—led him to modify and extend Freudian theory.

Erikson's Approach

Erikson was of mixed Danish and Jewish parentage. After his parents' divorce, he had no contact with his father; as a youth he floundered before settling on a vocation, and when he came to the United States, he needed to redefine his identity as an immigrant. All these issues found echoes in the "identity crises" he observed among disturbed adolescents, soldiers in combat during World War II, and members of minority groups (Erikson, 1968, 1973; R. I. Evans, 1967). He concluded that the quest for identity is the major theme throughout life.

Erikson was influenced by his work with children. Before becoming a psychoanalyst, he taught art in a school in Vienna. He was also trained in the Montessori method of educating young children which stresses learning through play. His later studies ranged from child-rearing practices of Native Americans to social customs in India.

Erikson believed that Freudian theory undervalued the influence of society on the developing personality. For example, a girl growing up on a Sioux Indian reservation will develop different personality patterns and different skills from a girl who grew up in a wealthy family in turn-of-the-century Vienna, as most of Freud's patients did. Erikson also felt that Freud's view of society was too negative. Freud saw civilization as a source of discontent, an impediment to biological drives; Erikson, on the other hand, sees society as a potentially positive force that shapes the development of the ego, or self.

Erikson's Eight Crises

Erikson's theory of *psychosocial development* traces personality development across the life span. It emphasizes societal and cultural influences on the ego at each of eight age periods (1950). Each stage involves a "crisis" in personality involving a different major conflict. Each crisis is a turning point for dealing with an issue that is particularly important at the time, even though it will remain an issue to some degree throughout life. The crises emerge according to a timetable based on a person's level of maturation. If the person adjusts to the demands of each crisis, the ego will develop toward the next crisis; if any crisis is not satisfactorily resolved, continued struggle with it will interfere with healthy ego development.

Successful resolution of each of the eight crises (listed in Table 1-6 and discussed in detail in appropriate chapters) requires balancing a positive trait and a corresponding negative one. Although the positive quality should predominate, some degree of the negative is needed too. The crisis of infancy, for example, is *trust versus mistrust*. People need to trust the world and the people in it—but they also need to learn some mistrust so that they can protect themselves from danger. The successful outcome of each crisis involves the develop-

The psychoanalyst Erik H. Erikson departed from Freudian thought in emphasizing societal, rather than chiefly biological, influences on personality. Erikson sees development as proceeding through eight significant turning points at different times throughout life. *(UPI/Bettmann Newsphotos)*

ment of a particular "virtue" or strength—in this first case, the virtue of hope.

Jean Baker Miller: Relational Theory

Miller (b. 1927), a psychiatrist who founded the Stone Center for Developmental Services and Studies at Wellesley College, originally reacted against the male orientation in prevalent theories of personality development on the grounds that these theories did not explain women's development. She and other researchers at the Stone Center also came to believe that such theories do not describe well what occurs in men, either.

According to this *relational theory* (Miller, 1991), all personality growth occurs within emotional connections, not separate from them, beginning in infancy (see Table 1-6). The beginnings of the concept of self are not those of a static and lone person being ministered to by another, but of a person in a dynamic interaction with another.

The infant identifies with the first caregiver not because of who that person is but because of what the person does. The baby responds to other people's emotions, becomes comfortable when others are also comfortable, and acts to move relationships forward toward closer connections.

In the next stage of childhood, instead of striving only for autonomy and individuation, children, according to Miller, still consider the most important things in their life their emotional connections with people. Not unless they receive messages from their caregivers about the greater importance of men will young children—male or female—exalt the male role over the female.

A major split between male and female development occurs during the school years, when girls are encouraged to continue showing a deep interest in relationships, family, and emotional issues, but boys are discouraged from expressing such interests. Instead, they are steered toward personal achievements and competition. Both sexes are shortchanged. This dichotomy widens during adolescence and adulthood, to the detriment of both men and women. Women's growth within relationships is devalued, and men's deficiencies in participating in growth-fostering relationships are not addressed early enough.

Evaluation of Psychoanalytic Perspective

Freud's original and creative thinking made immense contributions to our understanding of children and has had a major impact on child rearing. He communicated the importance of unconscious thoughts and emotions, the importance and the ambivalence of early parent-child relationships, and many other aspects of emotional functioning. He also made us aware that people are sexual creatures from birth. And he originated psychoanalysis, an important influence on modern-day psychotherapy.

Yet Freud's theory grew out of his own place in history and in society. Much of it seems to patronize or demean women, no doubt because of its roots in the social system of a Victorian-era European culture convinced of male superiority. Also, Freud based his theories about normal development not on a population of average children but on a clientele of upper-middle-class neurotic adults in therapy. His concentration on body-centered conflicts seems too narrow, and his emphasis on the importance of early experience does not take into account such other influences on personality as genes and later experiences. His theories are hard to test, but what research there has been has questioned or invalidated many of his concepts. For example, research does not support Freud's contention that the superego or gender identity are outcomes of the Oedipus or Electra complexes (Emde, 1992).

Erikson's theory has held up somewhat better. One strength is its emphasis on social and cultural influences on development, which takes it beyond Freud's narrow focus on biological and maturational factors. Also, it covers the entire life span, whereas Freud's stops at adolescence. This life-span approach is important because it sees the possibility for growth, change, and development throughout life. For Erikson, development does not stop at adolescence. But Erikson, like Freud, has been criticized for an antifemale bias, since he uses the male as the norm for healthy development. His description of development in childhood as leading toward increased autonomy and independence seems to be particularly inappropriate in describing female development, and may be limited in its applicability to healthy male development, as well. Furthermore, some of his concepts are also hard to assess objectively or to use as the basis for research.

Miller's relational theory highlights the importance of relationships rather than separation for healthy development, and does not consider female development as a deviation from the norm. This theory, largely based on clinical observation, is quite new, and many aspects of it need to be confirmed by research.

LEARNING PERSPECTIVE

Unlike psychoanalytic theorists, theorists of the *learning perspective* are concerned with behavior that can be observed rather than with unconscious forces. They try to study behavior objectively and scientifically.

Learning theorists see development as quantitative (changes in amount rather than kind) and continuous (rather than occurring in stages). Thus, they predict later behaviors from earlier ones. Research spurred by this view focuses on how experiences affect behavior. Learning theorists develop laws of behavior that apply to people of all ages. Two important learning theories are behaviorism and social-learning theory.

Behaviorism

Behaviorism focuses on behaviors that can be seen, measured, and recorded. Behaviorists look for immediate, observable factors that determine whether a particular behavior will continue. They recognize that biology sets limits on what people

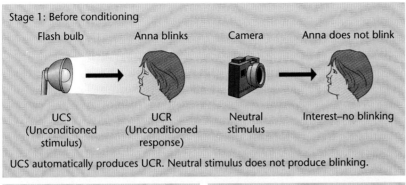

Stage 1: Before conditioning

Flash bulb → Anna blinks   Camera → Anna does not blink

UCS
(Unconditioned
stimulus)

UCR
(Unconditioned
response)

Neutral
stimulus

Interest–no blinking

UCS automatically produces UCR. Neutral stimulus does not produce blinking.

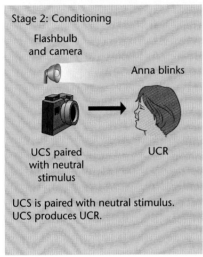

Stage 2: Conditioning

Flashbulb
and camera → Anna blinks

UCS paired
with neutral
stimulus

UCR

UCS is paired with neutral stimulus.
UCS produces UCR.

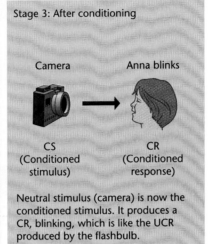

Stage 3: After conditioning

Camera → Anna blinks

CS
(Conditioned
stimulus)

CR
(Conditioned
response)

Neutral stimulus (camera) is now the
conditioned stimulus. It produces a
CR, blinking, which is like the UCR
produced by the flashbulb.

FIGURE 1-2
Classical conditioning occurs in three
stages. The neutral stimulus eventually
produces a conditioned response.

do, but they view the environment as much more influential in directing behavior. Behaviorists believe that *learning* changes behavior and advances development. They hold that human beings learn about the world like other animals: by reacting to aspects of their environments that they find pleasing, painful, or threatening.

Behaviorists have focused on two basic kinds of learning: classical and operant conditioning.

Classical Conditioning

Eager to capture Anna's memorable moments on film, Jonathan took pictures of her smiling, crawling, and showing off her other achievements. Whenever the flashbulb went off, Anna blinked. One evening when Anna was 11 months old, she saw Jonathan hold the camera up to his eye—and she blinked *before* the flash. She had learned to associate the camera with the bright light, and her blinking reflex operated without the flash.

Anna's blinking is an example of classical conditioning. While doing research on the salivating reflex of dogs, the Russian physiologist Ivan

Pavlov (1849–1936) accidentally discovered that his dogs had learned to associate sound with food. The dogs would salivate when they heard the food being brought to them. Pavlov then devised experiments in which dogs learned to salivate at the sound of a bell, which had been paired with food. This confirmed the power of *classical conditioning*, a kind of learning in which an animal or person learns a response to a stimulus that did not originally bring it, after the stimulus is repeatedly associated with a stimulus that *does* bring the response. Figure 1-2 shows the steps in classical conditioning.

1 *Before conditioning:* Anna blinks when the flashbulb goes off. The light is an unconditioned stimulus; it automatically elicits an unlearned, or unconditioned, response. Blinking is an automatic, unlearned response to bright light. The camera is a neutral stimulus; it does not ordinarily cause blinking.

2 *During conditioning:* Since Jonathan often takes photos indoors, he repeatedly pairs the camera

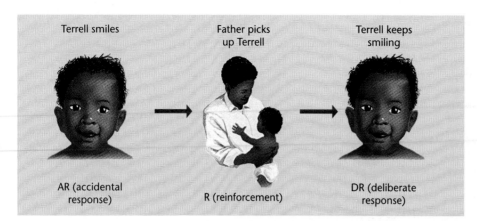

Terrell smiles

Father picks
up Terrell

Terrell keeps
smiling

AR (accidental
response)

R (reinforcement)

DR (deliberate
response)

FIGURE 1-3
Operant, or instrumental,
conditioning.

with the light. Every time he holds up the camera, the light flashes. Anna reflexively blinks at the light.

3   *After conditioning:* Anna blinks at the sight of the camera alone. She has learned to associate the camera with the light and to respond in the same way to both. The camera has become a conditioned stimulus; it was originally neutral, but after repeatedly being paired with the light, it now evokes blinking. The blinking has become a conditioned response; it is now elicited by the camera.

John B. Watson (1878–1958) was an American behaviorist who applied stimulus-response theories of learning to the study of child development. He expressed his philosophy in these words:

> Give me a dozen healthy infants, well formed, and my own special world to bring them up in, and I'll guarantee to take any one at random and train him to become any type of specialist I might select—doctor, lawyer, artist, merchant, chief, and yes, even beggar and thief, regardless of his talents, penchants, tendencies, abilities, vocations and race of his ancestors. (1958, p. 104)

Watson never got his dozen infants, but he did manage to teach one baby, known as "Little Albert," to fear furry white objects by classical conditioning techniques. We describe this famous experiment in Chapter 6.

Operant Conditioning

Terrell, a baby lying peacefully in his crib, smiles. His mother sees him smile, goes over to the crib, picks him up, and plays with him. Another time his father does the same thing. If this sequence continues to be repeated, Terrell will learn that some-

thing that he does (smiles) can produce something that he likes (loving attention from a parent).

This kind of learning is called *operant conditioning* because the person or animal involved is "operating" on the environment. Terrell learns that if he smiles at his parents, they will play with him. Thus, smiling, which began as an "accidental response," has become conditioned as the result of reinforcement.

The American psychologist B. F. Skinner (1904–1990) first formulated the basic principles of operant conditioning. He believed that an organism will tend to repeat a response that has been reinforced and will suppress a response that has been punished. Skinner worked primarily with rats and pigeons—and maintained that the same principles applied to human beings (Skinner, 1938).

Figure 1-3 shows the sequence in operant conditioning: Terrell happens to smile. This random, or accidental, response is reinforced by his parents' playing with him. He keeps smiling to attract their attention. The originally accidental response is now a deliberate response.

Reinforcement and Punishment   In operant conditioning, the consequences of a behavior determine its fate. In technical terms, a consequence that follows a behavior and *increases* the likelihood that the behavior will be repeated is called a *reinforcement.* Reinforcement can be either positive or negative. *Positive reinforcement* consists of giving a reward like food, gold stars, money, or praise. *Negative reinforcement* consists of taking away something that the person does not like (known as an *aversive* event), like a loud noise.

Negative reinforcement is sometimes confused with punishment. However, they are different. *Punishment* is a consequence that follows a behavior and *decreases* the likelihood that a behavior will be repeated. Punishment suppresses a behavior by *bringing on* an aversive event (like spanking a child or giving an electric shock to an animal), or by *withdrawing* a positive event (like watching television). Negative reinforcement encourages repetition of a behavior by *taking away* an aversive event. Whether or not something is reinforcing or punishing depends on the particular person involved. What is reinforcing for one person may be punishing for another.

Reinforcement is most effective when it immediately follows a behavior. If a response is no longer reinforced, it will eventually return to its original (baseline) level in a process called *extinction.* If no one picks Terrell up when he smiles, he may not stop smiling; but he will do so far less than if his smiles bring reinforcement. Thus, behaviors are strengthened when they are reinforced and weakened when they are punished.

Intermittent reinforcement—reinforcing a response at some times and not at others—produces more durable behaviors than reinforcing it every time. Because it takes longer for a person to realize that reinforcement has ended, the behavior tends to persist. This is why parents who only occasionally give in to a child's temper tantrum strengthen that kind of behavior even more than if they gave in every time—and then stopped. If they had been reinforcing every tantrum, once they stopped doing so, the child would realize almost at once that the tantrum was not producing the desired result.

Shaping New Responses   What can be done if a person or animal does not show any of the desired behavior? *Shaping* is a way to bring about a new response by reinforcing responses that are progressively like the desired one. For example, 3-year-old Joey stopped talking when his father left home. Joey's mother first gave him a little toy after he made any sound at all. Then she gave Joey the toy only after he said a word, and then only after he spoke a sentence.

Shaping is often part of *behavioral modification,* a form of operant conditioning that is often used to eliminate undesirable behavior. This type of learning is used to teach a variety of behaviors, including toilet training and obeying classroom rules. It is used most often for children with special needs, like mentally handicapped or emotionally disturbed youngsters, but its techniques are also effective with normal children.

Social-Learning Theory

An outgrowth of behaviorism, *social-learning theory* maintains that children, in particular, learn social behaviors by observing and imitating models (usually their parents). Albert Bandura (b. 1925), a professor at Stanford University, developed many of the principles of modern social-learning theory, also known as social-cognitive theory, which today is more influential than behaviorism.

Social-learning theory differs from behaviorism in several ways. First, it regards the learner as an active contributor to his or her learning. Second, although social-learning theorists also emphasize rigorous laboratory experimentation, they believe that theories based on animal research cannot explain human behavior. People learn in a social context, and human learning is more complex than simple conditioning allows for. And third, it acknowledges cognitive influence on behavior. It maintains that observational learning, rather than direct reinforcement or punishment, is central.

According to social-learning theory, children's identification with their parents is the most important element in how they learn a language, deal with aggression, develop a moral sense, and learn the behaviors their society holds as appropriate for their gender.

These little girls having a tea party demonstrate the social-learning theory that children tend to imitate dress, speech, and other behavior of the models they see both in real life and on television, thus resulting in gender-typed behavior. *(Erika Stone)*

Children actively advance their own social learning. For one thing, they choose the models they want to imitate. The choice is influenced by characteristics of the model, the child, and the environment. A child may choose one parent over the other and other adults (like a teacher, a television personality, a sports figure, or a drug dealer) in addition to—or instead of—either parent. Children tend to imitate people of high status and people who reflect their own personalities. So Benji, who already has aggressive tendencies, imitates Rambo rather than Mr. Rogers.

Behaviorists see the environment as molding the child, but social-learning theorists believe that the child also acts upon the environment—in fact, *creates* the environment to some extent. For example, Alicia, who spends hours at a time watching television rather than playing with other children, takes her models from people on the screen.

The specific behavior that children imitate depends on the behavior that is present and valued in their culture. If all the teachers in Carlos's school are women, he will not model their behavior, thinking that he would not be "manly." But if he meets a male teacher he likes, he may change his mind. He learns by observation and modifies his behavior.

Cognitive processes are at work as people observe models, learn "chunks" of behavior, and mentally put the chunks together into complex new behavior patterns. Thus, a woman may try to model her tennis serve on Steffi Graf's and her backhand on Monica Seles's. Cognitive factors, like the ability to pay attention and to mentally organize sensory information, affect the way a person will incorporate observed behavior. Children's developing ability to use mental symbols to stand for a model's behavior enables them to form standards for judging their own behavior.

Evaluation of Learning Perspective

Both behaviorism and social-learning theory have helped to make the study of psychology more scientific. This comes from two major emphases: defining terms precisely and conducting rigorous laboratory experiments. By stressing environmental influences, learning theories explain cultural differences in behavior very well (Horowitz, 1992). But they underplay the importance of heredity and biology. Further, they are not really developmental, since they apply the same basic laws of learning to explain behavior at all ages—from infancy

through adulthood—and are not concerned with differences in various stages of development.

Behaviorism has been especially useful in designing programs and therapies designed to effect rapid changes in behavior (like giving up smoking) or to teach new behaviors (like using the toilet). But because behaviorists are not interested in the causes of symptoms, they may eliminate one undesirable behavior (like stealing) by punishing it, only to see the substitution of another negative behavior (like bed-wetting), leaving the basic problem unresolved. Also, some people object to behaviorism on ethical grounds; they say that behaviorists "play God" by controlling other people's behavior.

Social-learning theory serves as a bridge between behaviorism and the cognitive perspective; it acknowledges the active role people play in their own learning and the cognitive influences on behavior.

COGNITIVE PERSPECTIVE

The third major theoretical perspective views people as living, growing beings with their own internal impulses and patterns for development. The *cognitive perspective* is concerned with the development of thought processes. It has two major characteristics. First, it views people as active, not reactive. Second, it emphasizes qualitative change—changes in the way people of different ages think—rather than quantitative change.

Cognitive theorists do not try to determine how reinforcements shape a person's responses. Nor do they focus on underlying motivational forces of which a person is unaware. They are concerned with how changes in behavior reflect changes in thinking. From childhood, everyone, they say, is a doer who actively constructs his or her world.

The Cognitive-Stage Theory of Jean Piaget

Much of what we know about how children think is due to the creative inquiry of the Swiss theoretician Jean Piaget (1896–1980), who applied his broad knowledge of biology, philosophy, and psychology to meticulous observations of children. He built complex theories about *cognitive development:* changes in children's thought processes that result in a growing ability to acquire and use knowledge about their world.

Born in Switzerland, Jean Piaget was a serious little boy who was interested in mechanics, birds, fossils, and seashells. He published his first scientific paper at the age of 10, on an albino sparrow he had seen in a park. At about this time, he began to assist the director of a museum of natural history and thus learned about mollusks, a kind of shellfish. He wrote about them—and had to turn down the offer of a curatorship of mollusks at another museum because he was still in school!

Piaget continued his scientific studies and also took up the study of psychoanalysis, psychology, and philosophy. While studying in Paris, he set out to standardize the tests that Alfred Binet had developed to assess the intelligence of French schoolchildren. Piaget became intrigued by the children's wrong answers, finding in them clues to their thought processes.

Continuing his interest in how children's minds develop, Piaget became director of a Swiss institute for studying children and training teachers. The institute student whom he married eventually helped him study the day-by-day intellectual development of their three children. From his meticulous observations of his own and other children, Piaget built a comprehensive theory of cognitive development.

Up to the time of his death at age 84, Piaget continued to study and write. He wrote more than 40 books and more than 100 articles on child psychology, as well as works on biology, philosophy, and education. Much of his work was done with his longtime collaborator, Barbel Inhelder, an experimental child psychologist who did her own research on how children and adolescents come to understand the laws of natural science.

Piaget described cognitive development as occurring in a series of stages. At each stage a new way of thinking about and responding to the world develops. Thus, each stage constitutes a qualitative change from one type of thought or behavior to another. Each stage builds on the stage before it and constructs the foundation for the one that comes next. And each stage has many facets. All people go through the same stages in the same order, even though the actual timing varies from one person to another, making any age cutoff only approximate. (Table 1-6 summarizes Piaget's stages; they are described and discussed fully in appropriate chapters throughout this book.)

Piaget reached many of his conclusions by combining observation with flexible questioning in what he called the *clinical method*. To find out how

The influential Swiss psychologist Jean Piaget studied children's cognitive development by observing and talking with his own youngsters and others. *(Yves DeBraine/Black Star)*

children think, Piaget followed up their answers to his questions by asking more questions. In this way, he discovered, for example, that a typical 4-year-old believed that pennies or flowers were more numerous when arranged in a line than when heaped or piled up. He individualized each interview, probing further into interesting responses, using language that he thought the child would understand, and even changing to the language that a child was using spontaneously.

Let us look at some of the principal features of Piaget's theory.

Cognitive Structures

EXPLORING + EXPERIMENTING

Piaget believed that the core of intelligent behavior is an inborn ability to adapt to the environment. Children build on their sensory, motor, and reflex capacities to learn about and act upon their world—from feeling a pebble, say, or exploring the boundaries of a living room. As they learn from their experiences, they develop more complex cognitive structures.

At each stage of development, a person has his or her individual representation of the world. Within this representation lie a number of basic cognitive structures known as *schemes*. A *scheme* is an organized pattern of behavior that a person uses to think about and act in a situation. In infancy, schemes are known by the behavior they involve: sucking, biting, shaking, grasping, and so forth. From the first days of life, infants have many schemes. As babies vary the schemes, they differentiate them. For example, babies develop different ways to suck at the breast, a bottle, or a thumb.

The earliest schemes are motor actions. As children develop intellectually, their schemes become patterns of thought related to particular behaviors. They also become more complex, going from concrete thinking about things that they can see, hear, smell, taste, or feel to abstract thought.

Principles of Cognitive Development

How does this cognitive growth occur? According to Piaget, a two-step process of taking in new information about the world (assimilation) and changing one's ideas to include the new knowledge (accommodation) is accomplished by three interrelated principles: organization, adaptation, and equilibration. These principles are inherited, they operate at all stages of development, and they affect all interactions with the environment.

Cognitive *organization* is a tendency to create systems that bring together all of a person's knowledge of the environment. From infancy on, people try to make sense of their world by organizing their knowledge. Development progresses from simple organizational structures to more complex ones. At first, for example, an infant's schemes of looking and grasping operate independently. Later, she integrates, or organizes, these separate schemes into a single more complex scheme that allows her to look at an object while holding it— to coordinate eye and hand—and thus to better understand that particular part of her environment. More complex organization comes about as she acquires more information.

Adaptation is Piaget's term for how a person deals with new information. It includes the two-step complementary processes of *assimilation* and *accommodation*. For example, when a baby begins to suck on a rubber nipple, he is showing assimilation; that is, he is using an old scheme to deal with a new object or situation. When he discovers that sucking on a bottle requires somewhat different tongue and mouth movements from those used to suck on a breast, he accommodates by modifying the old scheme. He has adapted his original sucking scheme to deal with a new experience—

the bottle. Thus, assimilation and accommodation work together to produce cognitive growth.

Equilibration is a constant striving for equilibrium, a state of balance between a child and the outside world and among the child's own cognitive structures. The need for equilibrium leads a child to shift from assimilation to accommodation. When children cannot handle new experiences with their existing structures, they organize new mental patterns, restoring a state of mental balance.

Evaluation of Piaget's Theory

Piaget was the forerunner of today's "cognitive revolution" in psychology, with its emphasis on internal cognitive processes, as opposed to learning theory's emphasis on outside influences and overt behaviors. Although American psychologists were slow to accept his ideas, Piaget has inspired more research on children's cognitive development than any other theorist. Among the important offshoots of Piaget's theory are Lawrence Kohlberg's cognitive-developmental approaches to gender identity and moral reasoning (discussed in Chapters 8, 10, and 12) and information-processing theory, which is concerned with how people manipulate incoming sensory information.

Piaget's careful observations have yielded a wealth of information, including some surprising insights. Who, for example, would have thought that not until age 6 or 7 do even very bright children realize that a ball of clay that has been rolled into a "worm" before their eyes still contains the same amount of clay? Or that an infant might think that a person no longer in sight may no longer exist? Piaget has shown us that children think differently from adults. Understanding how children think makes it easier for parents to teach them about money, about illness, about family crises. And it helps teachers to know how and when to introduce topics in school.

Yet Piaget can be criticized. He spoke primarily of the "average" child's abilities and took little notice of individual differences or of the ways in which culture, education, and individual motivation affect performance. He says little about emotional and personality development, except as they relate to cognitive growth. Many of his ideas emerged not from scientific research but from his highly personal observations of his own three children and from his idiosyncratic way of interviewing other children. Finally, he seems to have underestimated the abilities of young children.

On a more basic level, many developmentalists question the idea of clearly demarcated stages of cognitive growth. Today, many psychologists view such growth as gradual and continuous rather than as changing abruptly from one stage to the next. It also seems that many people do not reach Piaget's highest level of thought, formal logic, even in adulthood. In fact, formal logic (or abstract thinking) may not even be the best model of mature thought, since it fails to acknowledge such critical aspects of adult intellectual functioning as practical problem-solving ability and the development of wisdom.

Information-Processing Approach

The *information-processing approach* to understanding cognitive development depends on analysis of the mental processes underlying intelligent behavior. To learn how people manipulate incoming sensory information, scientists using this approach examine processes like perception, attention, memory, and problem solving. They see people as active manipulators of symbols and look at the processes by which they use these symbols and transform information.

To find out, for example, how infants process information, researchers use sensitive equipment to monitor such physiologic responses as eye movements, heart rate, and brain activity. They gauge the efficiency of infants' information processing by measuring variations in attention: how quickly different babies stop paying attention to familiar stimuli, how fast their attention recovers when they are exposed to new stimuli, and how much time they spend looking at the new versus the old. Through such studies we now know that even very young infants can remember and recognize something they have seen.

The information-processing approach, like Piaget's, sees people as active. Unlike Piaget's theory, it does not propose stages of development. And it ignores many important aspects of development like creativity, motivation, and social relations. Still, information-processing techniques provide a way to assess intelligence and to gather information about the development of memory. This is a burgeoning area of research.

HUMANISTIC PERSPECTIVE

In 1962, a group of psychologists founded the Association of Humanistic Psychology. Protesting against what they considered the essentially negative beliefs underlying behaviorist and psychoanalytic theory, they maintained that human nature is either neutral or good and that any bad characteristics are the result of damage that has been inflicted on the developing self.

Like the cognitive approach, the *humanistic perspective* views people as able to take charge of their lives and foster their own development. Humanistic theorists emphasize the potential for positive, healthy development and the distinctively human capacities of choice, creativity, and self-realization.

The humanistic approach is not truly developmental, since its proponents generally do not distinguish stages of the life span but make a broad distinction only between the periods before and after adolescence. We mention it here because it offers an influential view of personality development.

Abraham Maslow: Self-Actualization and the Hierarchy of Needs

One important humanistic psychologist, Abraham Maslow (1908–1970), identified a hierarchy of needs that motivate human behavior (see Figure 1-4). According to Maslow (1954), only when people have satisfied the most basic needs can they strive to meet higher needs.

The first need is physiological survival. Starving persons will take great risks to get food; only when they have obtained it can they worry about the next level of needs, those concerning personal safety and security. These needs, in turn, must be met (at least in part) before people can seek love and acceptance, esteem and achievement, and finally self-actualization, or the full realization of potential.

Maslow's ideal, a self-actualized person, shows high levels of all the following characteristics (Maslow, 1968): perception of reality; acceptance of self, of others, and of nature; spontaneity; problem-solving ability, self-direction; detachment and the desire for privacy; freshness of appreciation and richness of emotional reaction; frequency of peak experiences; identification with other human beings; satisfying and changing relationships with other people; democratic character structure, creativity, and a sense of values. Only about 1 person in 100 is said to attain this lofty ideal (R. Thomas, 1979). But no one is ever completely self-actualized; the healthy person is always moving up to levels that are even more fulfilling.

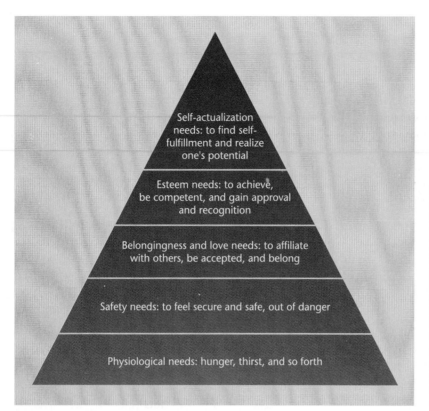

FIGURE 1-4
Maslow's hierarchy of needs. According to Maslow, human needs have different priorities. First comes survival (base of pyramid). Starving people will take great risks to obtain food; once they know they will not die of starvation, they start to worry about safety. Then the need for security must be met, at least in part, before people think about the need for love. As each level of needs is met, a person looks to the needs at the next higher level. This progression is not invariant, however; for example, self-sacrifice would be an exception. *(Maslow, 1954.)*

On first impression, Maslow's hierarchy of needs seems to be grounded in human experience. But the priorities he outlined do not invariably hold true. For example, history is full of accounts of self-sacrifice, in which people give up what they need for survival so that someone else (a loved one or even a stranger) can live.

Evaluation of Humanistic Theory

The humanistic outlook offers a positive, optimistic model of humankind and its potential for development, as opposed to the negative Freudian viewpoint; and it goes deeper than learning theory by considering internal factors, like feelings, values, and hopes. Humanistic theories have made a valuable contribution by promoting child-rearing approaches that respect the child's uniqueness.

Its limitations as a scientific theory have to do largely with its subjectiveness: since its concepts are not clearly defined, they are hard to communicate and to use as the basis for research designs. Furthermore, since humanistic theories do not fo-

cus on issues at different times of life, they do not provide insights into the process of development. However, since humanists are more interested in bettering the human condition than in increasing scientific knowledge about it, they make no apologies for the approach.

A WORD TO STUDENTS

Our final word in this introductory chapter is that this entire book is far from the final word. While we have tried to incorporate the most important and the most up-to-date information about how people develop, developmentalists are constantly learning more. As you read this book, you are certain to come up with your own questions. By thinking about them, and perhaps eventually conducting research to find answers, it is possible that you yourself, now just embarking on the study of human development, will someday add to our knowledge about the interesting species to which we all belong.

SUMMARY

HUMAN DEVELOPMENT: THE SUBJECT AND THE TEXT

■ Human development is the scientific study of the quantitative and qualitative ways people change over time. Quantitative change is change in number or amount, such as height, weight, and vocabulary. Qualitative change is change in kind, structure, or organization, such as in the nature of intelligence. Qualitative change is marked by the appearance of new phenomena that cannot be predicted from earlier functioning.

■ This book emphasizes human research, appreciates the lifelong capacity for change, acknowledges human resilience, recognizes that people help shape their own development, and is practically oriented.

HUMAN DEVELOPMENT: THE STUDY AND ITS HISTORY

■ The study of human development focuses on describing, explaining, predicting, and modifying development.

■ Although we can look separately at various aspects of development (such as physical, intellectual, and personality and social development), we must remember that these do not occur in isolation. Each affects the other.

■ Although we have divided the human life span into eight periods, the age ranges are often subjective. Individual differences must be taken into account.

■ Influences on development are both internal (hereditary) and external (environmental). Influences that affect large groups of people are called either *normative age-graded* or *normative history-graded*. *Nonnormative* life events are those that are unusual in themselves or in their timing; they often have a major impact.

■ According to the ecological approach, environmental influences on development occur at four levels: microsystem, mesosystem, exosystem, and macrosystem. The microsystem is the everyday environment. The mesosystem is the interlocking of various microsystems. The exosystem refers to the larger environment of institutions, while the macrosystem is the overarching cultural patterns of government, religion, education, and the economy.

■ The concept of a critical period, or time when an event has its greatest impact, seems more applicable to physical (and especially prenatal) development than to psychological development.

■ Attitudes about children were different in the past and affected how children were studied. As researchers became interested in following development into adulthood, life-span development expanded as a subject for study.

HUMAN DEVELOPMENT: RESEARCH METHODS

■ Correlational studies show the direction and magnitude of a relationship between variables.

■ There are three major nonexperimental techniques for studying people: case studies, observation, and interviews. Each one has strengths and weaknesses.

1 Case studies are studies of individuals.
2 Observation is of two types, naturalistic and laboratory. Each provides a good description of behaviors.
3 In an interview, researchers ask questions about peoples' attitudes, their opinions, or some other aspect of their lives.

■ Controlled experiments are the only method of discovering cause-and-effect relationships. The three principal types are laboratory, field, and natural experiments.

■ The two major methods of collecting data about development are the cross-sectional and the longitudinal. Cross-sectional studies describe age differences; longitudinal studies describe age changes. Each method has strengths and weaknesses. Sequential strategies have been developed to overcome the weaknesses of the other two designs.

■ Studies of people must reflect certain ethical considerations. In a carefully designed study, researchers consider its effect on the participants, as well as its potential benefit to the field.

HUMAN DEVELOPMENT: THEORETICAL PERSPECTIVES

■ A theory is a set of related statements about data, the information obtained from research. Theories are important in explaining, interpreting, and predicting behavior and in guiding future research. We consider four theoretical perspectives: psychoanalytic, learning, cognitive, and humanistic.

■ Theories from the psychoanalytic perspective focus on the underlying forces that motivate behavior. Although they differ markedly in some of the specifics of their theories, Sigmund Freud and Erik Erikson take this perspective. Freud described a series of psychosexual stages in which gratification shifts from one body zone to another (from mouth, to anus, to genitals); the child's maturational level determines when the shift will occur. Erikson described eight stages of psychosocial development between infancy and old age. Each stage involves the resolution of a particular crisis, achieving a balance between extremes; the crises emerge according to a maturationally based timetable. Jean Baker Miller's relational theory holds that personality growth occurs within emotional connections, not separate from them.

■ The learning perspective views human development primarily as a response to events and change as quantitative. Its focus is on observable behaviors. Behaviorism and social-learning theory reflect the learning perspective. Behaviorists are interested in shaping behavior through conditioning. Social-learning theory, which stresses imitation of models, incorporates some elements of this perspective as well as cognitive aspects. The person is considered to be an active contributor to learning.

■ The cognitive perspective sees people as active contributors to their own development and views development as occurring in a series of qualitatively different stages. The cognitive developmental theory of Jean Piaget is the most important example. Piaget described children's cognitive development as occurring through a series of four qualitatively different stages: sensorimotor (birth to 2 years), preoperational (2 to 7 years), concrete operations (7 to 12 years), and formal operations (12 years through adulthood). The information-processing approach analyzes the processes underlying intelligent behavior. It focuses on perception, attention, memory, and problem solving.

■ The humanistic perspective, represented by Abraham Maslow, views people as fostering their own development through choice, creativity, and self-realization.

KEY TERMS

human development (page 3)
quantitative change (3)
qualitative change (3)
heredity (8)
environmental influences (8)
cohort (9)
ecological approach (9)
critical period (10)
scientific method (14)
correlation (14)
case studies (14)
naturalistic observation (16)
laboratory observation (16)
interview (17)
experiment (17)
independent variable (19)
dependent variable (19)
experimental group (19)

control group (19)
sample (19)
random sample (19)
cross-sectional study (21)
longitudinal study (21)
cross-sequential study (22)
theory (23)
data (23)
hypothesis (23)
psychoanalytic perspective (24)
psychosexual development (25)
id (25)
ego (25)
superego (25)
defense mechanisms (25)
psychosocial development (29)
relational theory (29)
learning perspective (30)

behaviorism (30)
classical conditioning (31)
operant conditioning (32)
reinforcement (32)
punishment (32)
extinction (33)
shaping (33)
social-learning theory (33)
cognitive perspective (34)
cognitive development (34)
scheme (35)
organization (36)
adaptation (36)
assimilation (36)
accommodation (36)
equilibration (36)
humanistic perspective (37)

SUGGESTED READINGS

Calvert, K. (1992). *Children in the house: The material culture of early childhood, 1600–1900.* Boston: Northeastern University Press. An intriguing history of society's perceptions of early childhood, based on the objects used for child rearing. The author analyzes cultural assumptions about the innocence of children, their need to be protected, and gender roles, based on the clothing and equipment used by parents.

Clausen, J. A. (1993). *American lives: Looking back at the children of the great depression.* New York: Free Press. An engrossing account of three major longitudinal studies and their findings of the characteristics that lead to success in life. Richly detailed case histories of happy and successful adults and of those whose lives were unhappy and trouble-ridden dramatically illustrate the studies' findings.

Chudacoff, H. P. (1990). *How old are you? Age consciousness in American culture.* Princeton, NJ: Princeton University Press. The historian author of this lively book traces the development of age consciousness in urban middle-class culture from its beginnings in the late 1800s and discusses both advantages (policymakers can better identify groups that need special help) and disadvantages (ageism, or discrimination against certain age groups, most often the elderly).

Erikson, E. H. (1963). *Childhood and society.* New York: Norton. A collection of Erikson's writings that includes the classic "Eight Ages of Man," in which he outlines his theory of psychosocial development from infancy through old age.

Kagan, J. (1984). *The nature of the child.* New York: Basic Books. A beautifully written and compelling argument against the idea of the irreversibility of early experience. Kagan believes that people have the ability to change throughout life and that later events transform early childhood experiences.

Katz, D. (1992). *Home fires: An intimate portrait of one middle-class family in postwar America.* New York: HarperCollins. A true story that spans over 40 years (from 1946 through 1992), reads like an epic novel, and dramatically illustrates the ecological theory of development in context. The author integrates the events in the lives of the parents and four children in the Gordon family into an account of American social history, from World War II, through the tumultuous 1960s, up to the last decade of this century.

Miller, J. B. et al. (1991). *Women's growth in connection.* Cambridge, MA: Harvard University Press. A diverse collection of scholarly articles from the Stone Center for Developmental Services and Studies, focusing on the self-in-relation theory. The theory is applied to such issues as depression and eating disorders in women.

Rymer, R. (1993). *An abused child: Flight from silence.* New York: HarperCollins. This absorbing and controversial in-depth exploration of Genie's case follows her from the time of her discovery by the outside world into adulthood. It discusses the roles that psychologists, linguists, and social workers played in her life and traces the failure, despite many people's efforts, to enable her to live anything like a normal life.

Shapiro, J. P. (1993). *No pity: People with disabilities forging a new civil rights movement.* New York: Times Books. A fascinating account of the birth and development of the disability rights movement, which led to the enactment of the Americans with Disabilities Act of 1992. The book deals with many of the issues involved in this struggle and includes many personal stories of people with physical, mental, or emotional disabilities who were instrumental in changing the way such people were looked at and treated.

PART ONE

BEGINNINGS

L ife is change. From the moment of conception to the moment of death, human beings undergo many complex processes of development. Throughout life, people have the potential to grow, to change, to develop.

The study of human development will help you to understand yourself and the people you know. You will become aware of influences and choices that have made you the person you are, and of forces that can affect the person you will become. In Part One you will read about the dramatic changes that occur during the earliest stages of human development, changes broader in scope and faster in pace than any that you have experienced since or will ever experience again.

■ **Chapter 2** begins our discussion of the exciting human journey. We examine how conception occurs and which of the forces that guide development are already present through the mechanisms of heredity. We then trace the growth of the new life in the womb and see what factors influence it, for both good and ill, during gestation. We touch on the revolutionary techniques now being used to intervene in the natural process of prenatal development. And finally, we focus on the complex process of birth itself.

You will then learn some fascinating things about the impressive capabilities of newborn babies and their even more impressive potential for future growth. In the rest of Part One, you will follow human development through the first 3 years of life, the stages known as *infancy* and *toddlerhood*.

■ **In Chapter 3,** we see how newborns make the transition from the womb to the outside world, how their body systems function, and how their brains develop. We explore low birthweight and some other issues. Then, we go on to look at typical, normal sensory and motor development and at important health concerns during the first 3 years of life.

■ **In Chapter 4,** we cover intellectual growth. We see how babies learn and how social scientists study and measure their learning and their cognitive functioning. We pay particular attention to language skills, which are specifically human capabilities. And we explore competence—what it is and how it develops early in life.

■ **In Chapter 5,** we see how babies begin to show their unique personalities right from birth. We examine prominent theories about personality and social development, as we seek to explain why each child develops in his or her own way. Helping to explain this are such influences as inborn temperament and the family, which affect the development of sociability and of babies' ability to regulate their own behavior.

As in the rest of this book we see, right from the beginning, how the various kinds of development—physical, intellectual, and personality—overlap and affect each other.

CHAPTER TWO

CONCEPTION THROUGH BIRTH

*If I could have watched you grow as a magical mother
might, if I could have seen through my magical transparent
belly, there would have been such ripening within. . . .*

Anne Sexton, 1966

■ **FERTILIZATION**

How Does Fertilization Take Place?
What Causes Multiple Births?
What Determines Sex?

■ **HEREDITY AND ENVIRONMENT**

What Is the Role of Heredity?
How Do Heredity and Environment Interact?

■ **PRENATAL DEVELOPMENT**

Stages of Prenatal Development
The Prenatal Environment

■ **BIRTH**

Stages of Childbirth
Methods of Childbirth
Settings for Childbirth

■ **BOXES**

2-1 Practically Speaking: Prenatal Assessment
2-2 Take a Stand: Genetic Testing
2-3 Food for Thought: Shyness
2-4 Practically Speaking: Reducing Risks
during Pregnancy
2-5 Window on the World: Maternity Care
in Western Europe and the United States

■ How does human life begin?
■ How do heredity and environment affect a new human being's sex, appearance, health, intelligence, and personality?
■ How does a baby develop inside the mother's body?

■ How does the prenatal environment influence development?
■ What happens during birth, and how can medical intervention affect the natural birth process?

The beginning of human life has always inspired wonder and curiosity, and over the years both scientists and laypersons have held some surprising notions about it. Even today, when we know much more about the origin of life, an element of awe remains. The beginning for you, as for everyone, came long before you gave your first yell after leaving your mother's womb. In this chapter we will explain that beginning. We will then talk about the influences of what you inherited from your parents and of what you have experienced, both before and after birth. We also discuss the birth process itself, choices about childbirth, and the role of medical intervention.

Your true biological beginning was a split-second event when a single spermatozoon, one of millions of sperm cells from your father, joined an ovum (egg cell), one of the several hundred thousand ova produced and stored in your mother's body during her lifetime.

Which sperm meets which ovum has tremendous implications for the new person: for sex, appearance, susceptibility to disease, and even personality. The sperm and the ovum are partial microcosms of the two human beings, man and woman, who bring the new life into existence. There are also environmental influences. Who the mother and father are, what talents they have, where and how they live, how they feel about each other and their child—these and many other factors profoundly affect the child's development. Let us see how this important union takes place and what occurs during the 9 months when the new life grows inside the womb.

FERTILIZATION

Fertilization, or conception, the process by which sperm and ovum fuse to form a single new cell, is most likely to occur about 14 days after the beginning of a woman's menstrual period. The new single cell formed by the two *gametes,* or sex cells—the ovum and the sperm—is called a *zygote.* Once conceived, this zygote duplicates itself again and again by cell division.

HOW DOES FERTILIZATION TAKE PLACE?

At birth, a human female has about 400,000 immature ova in her two ovaries; each ovum is in its own small sac, or follicle. The ovum—though only about one-fourth the size of the period that ends this sentence—is the largest cell in the human body. From the time a female matures sexually until menopause, *ovulation* occurs about once each menstrual cycle (for most women, about every 28 days): a mature follicle in one ovary ruptures and expels its ovum. The ovum is swept along through the fallopian tube by tiny hair cells, called *cilia,* toward the uterus, or womb. It is in the fallopian tube that, if the ovum meets a sperm cell, fertilization normally occurs. (Figure 2-1 shows the female and male reproductive systems.)

The sperm—shaped like a tadpole but only $\frac{1}{600}$ inch from head to tail—is one of the smallest cells in the body. Sperm are produced in the testicles (testes), or reproductive glands, of a mature male at a rate of several hundred million a day and are ejaculated in the semen at sexual climax.

The sperm enter the vagina and begin to swim up through the opening of the cervix, the neck of the uterus. From the uterus they head into the fallopian tube, but only a few sperm actually get that far. The recent discovery that sperm cells have odor receptors, like those in the nose, suggests that they may locate a fertile egg by its scent (Parmentier et al., 1992). The protective layer around the ovum needs to be worn down so that one, and only one, sperm will actually penetrate the membrane. About 20 million sperm must enter a woman's body at one time to make fertilization likely, but only one of them can fertilize an ovum to conceive a new human being.

From the time of ejaculation, sperm maintain their ability to fertilize an ovum for up to 48 hours; and ova can be fertilized for about 24 hours after release from the ovary. Thus there is a "window" of about 48 hours during each menstrual cycle when sexual intercourse can result in fertilization. Sperm that reach a woman's reproductive tract up to 24 hours before or after an ovum is released are capable of fertilizing that ovum. If fertilization does not occur, the ovum and any sperm cells in the woman's body die. The sperm are absorbed by the woman's white blood cells, and the ovum passes into the uterus and exits through the vagina (see Figure 2-2). If sperm and ovum do meet, they conceive a new life and endow it with a rich genetic legacy.

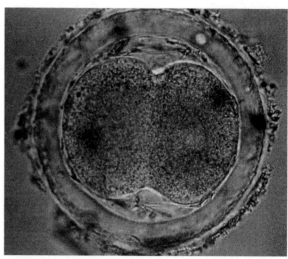

Fertilization takes place when a sperm cell unites with an ovum to form a single new cell. The fertilized ovum shown here has begun to grow by cell division. It will eventually differentiate into 800 billion or more cells with specialized functions. *(Petit Format/Science Source/Photo Researchers)*

WHAT CAUSES MULTIPLE BIRTHS?

Unlike most animals, the human baby usually comes into the world alone. Exceptions—multiple births—occur in two different ways.

One mechanism occurs when the woman's body releases two ova within a short time of each other, and both are fertilized. The two babies that are conceived are called *fraternal, two-egg,* or **dizygotic** *twins.* Since they are created by different ova and different sperm cells, they are no more alike in genetic makeup than any other siblings. They may be of the same sex or different sexes.

The other mechanism is the division of a single ovum after fertilization. *Identical, one-egg,* or *monozygotic twins,* who result from this cell division, have the same genetic heritage. Any differences they will later show must be due to the influences of environment. They are always of the same sex. Triplets, quadruplets, and other multi-

FIGURE 2-1
Human reproductive systems.

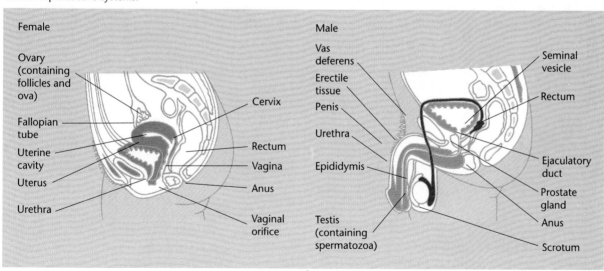

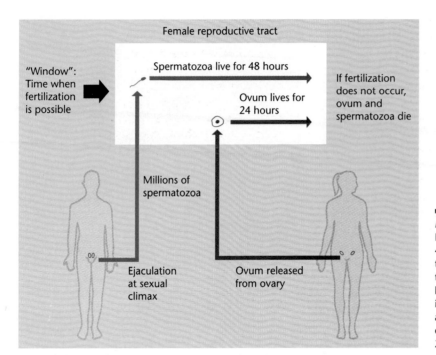

Female reproductive tract

"Window": Time when fertilization is possible

Spermatozoa live for 48 hours

Ovum lives for 24 hours

If fertilization does not occur, ovum and spermatozoa die

Millions of spermatozoa

Ejaculation at sexual climax

Ovum released from ovary

FIGURE 2-2
Fertilization. Spermatozoa can live for 48 hours in a woman's reproductive tract. If a live sperm is present during the 24-hour period after an ovum has been released, fertilization may occur. If it does not, both ovum and sperm die, and fertilization cannot occur until another ovum is released, usually about 28 days later.

Monozygotic twins seem to be born through an accident of prenatal life and their incidence is about the same in all ethnic groups. They are always of the same sex and have exactly the same genetic heritage: these 2-year-olds look so much alike that at first, this photo looks like one child sitting by a mirror. *(John Coletti/The Picture Cube)*

ple births result from either one of these processes or a combination of both.

Identical twins seem to be the result of an "accident" in prenatal development, unrelated to either genetic or environmental influences. They account for one-fourth to one-third of all twins.

Fraternal twins are more common under some circumstances. More are being born these days because of fertility drugs that stimulate ovulation and often cause the release of more than one ovum. These twins are more likely to be born to women who have had two or more pregnancies, to older women, in families with a history of fraternal twins, and in various ethnic groups. Fraternal twin births are most common among African Americans (1 in 70 births), East Indians, and northern Europeans, and least common among Asians other than East Indians (1 in 150 births among the Japanese and 1 in 300 among the Chinese). These differences are probably due to hormonal differences in women (Vaughan, McKay, & Behrman, 1979).

WHAT DETERMINES SEX?

Henry VIII of England divorced Catherine of Aragon because (among other reasons) she had borne him a daughter rather than the son he desperately wanted. It is ironic that this basis for divorce has been recognized in many societies, since we now know that the sperm cell—that is, the father—determines the sex of a child.

At conception, the zygote receives 23 chromosomes (segments of hereditary materials, described below) from the sperm and 23 from the ovum. They align themselves in pairs: 22 pairs are *autosomes,* or nonsex chromosomes; the twenty-third pair are *sex chromosomes,* which determine if the new human being will be male or female.

In a female, the two sex chromosomes—called X chromosomes—are the same. In a male, an X chromosome is paired with a smaller Y chromosome. An ovum can carry only an X chromosome, but sperm can carry either an X or a Y. When an ovum is fertilized by an X-carrying sperm, the resulting zygote has the pair XX, which makes it female. When an ovum is fertilized by a Y-carrying sperm, the zygote has the pair XY and so is male (see Figure 2-3). Thus, the sex of the child depends entirely on whether the sex chromosome carried by the sperm cell that fertilized the ovum was X or Y.

Differences between the sexes begin to appear at conception. About 120 to 170 males are conceived for every 100 females, but since males are more likely to be spontaneously aborted or stillborn, only 106 are born for every 100 females (U.S. Department of Health and Human Services [USDHHS], 1982). Boys' births average 1 hour longer than girls' births, which is one reason why more boys have birth defects (Jacklin, 1989). More males die early in life, and at every age males are more susceptible to many disorders, and so there are only 95 males for every 100 females in the United States (USDHHS, 1982). Furthermore, the male develops more slowly than the female from early fetal life into adulthood. At 20 weeks after conception, males are, on average, 2 weeks behind females; at 40 weeks they are 4 weeks behind; and they continue to lag behind till maturity.

Why are males more vulnerable? A number of theories have been proposed. The X chromosome may contain genes that protect females, the Y chromosome may contain harmful genes, or there may be different mechanisms in the sexes for providing immunity to various infections and diseases. One controversial hypothesis suggests that the mother's body produces damaging antibodies that act against a male fetus (Gualtieri & Hicks, 1985).

FIGURE 2-3

Determination of sex. All babies receive an X chromosome from the mother; therefore, sex is determined by whether an X or a Y chromosome is received from the father.

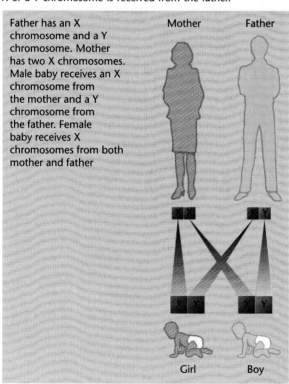

Father has an X chromosome and a Y chromosome. Mother has two X chromosomes. Male baby receives an X chromosome from the mother and a Y chromosome from the father. Female baby receives X chromosomes from both mother and father

Mother   Father

Girl   Boy

HEREDITY AND ENVIRONMENT

WHAT IS THE ROLE OF HEREDITY?

Do you ever read horoscopes? These popular but unreliable predictions are based on an ancient pseudoscience, astrology. Astrologers claim that a new life is influenced or controlled by the positions of heavenly bodies at the moment of birth. But if we want to understand the true sources of our physical, intellectual, and emotional makeup, the best place to look is, as Shakespeare put it, "not in our stars, but in ourselves."

The science of *genetics* is the study of *heredity*—the inborn factors, inherited from our parents, that affect our development. Genetics tells us that it is the meeting of ovum and sperm, not the crossing of heavenly orbits, which determines much of our future course. When two gametes unite to form a zygote, they give the new life a unique genetic makeup.

Body cells of women and men contain 23 pairs of chromosomes.

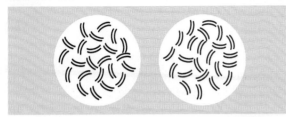

At maturity, each sex cell has only 23 single chromosomes. Through meiosis, a member is taken randomly from each original pair of chromosomes.

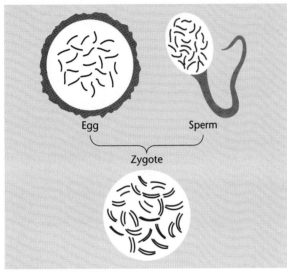

Egg   Sperm

Zygote

FIGURE 2-4
Hereditary composition of the zygote.

Mechanisms of Heredity: Genes and Chromosomes

The basic unit of heredity is the *gene*, a bit of *deoxyribonucleic acid (DNA)*. Genes determine inherited characteristics. DNA carries the instructions that tell each cell in the body what specific functions it will perform and how it will perform them. Human beings have an estimated 100,000 genes distributed among 46 *chromosomes*, which are larger segments of DNA that carry the genes. Each gene seems to be located by function in a definite position on a particular chromosome. As we said, half the chromosomes come from each parent: 23 from the ovum and 23 from the sperm. At conception, the single-cell zygote has all the biological information needed to guide its development into a complete human being.

This single cell develops into a complex organism, with billions of cells specializing in different functions. Through a process of cell division called *mitosis*, each cell except the sex cells will have 46 chromosomes identical to those in the original zygote. Thus each has the same genetic information. Mature gametes (human reproductive cells: ova in females, sperm in males) contain only 23 chromosomes each. This is the result of *meiosis*, a form of cell division in which the number of chromosomes is reduced by half (see Figure 2-4). This special type of division, which implies an almost unlimited variety of combinations of chromosomes and genes in ova and sperm, accounts for the differences in genetic makeup of children of the same parents.

Patterns of Genetic Transmission

Why does one person have blue eyes and another brown? Why is one person tall and another short? What causes such defects as color blindness? To answer questions like these, we need to see how the genes transmit hereditary characteristics.

Mendel's Laws

Gregor Mendel, an Austrian monk, experimented with plants during the 1860s and laid the foundation for our understanding of inheritance in all living things. He cross-pollinated purebred pea plants that produced only yellow seeds with pea plants that produced only green seeds. All the resulting plants—hybrids—produced yellow seeds. But when he bred those hybrids, 75 percent of their offspring had yellow seeds, and the other 25 percent had green seeds.

Mendel explained his findings by what he called the law of *dominant inheritance:* when an organism inherits competing traits (like green and yellow coloring), only one of the traits will be expressed. The expressed trait is called the *dominant* one, and the trait that is not revealed is called *recessive.*

Mendel also tried breeding for two traits at once. Mating pea plants that produced round yellow seeds with plants that produced wrinkled green seeds, he found that color and shape were transmitted independently of each other. In the first generation of hybrids, all the seeds were yellow and round—dominant traits. When the hybrid plants self-fertilized, most of the offspring still produced seeds that were yellow and round; but some (less than half) were either yellow and wrinkled, or green and round; and the smallest number were green and wrinkled. Thus Mendel proved that hereditary traits are transmitted as separate units.

He called this principle the law of *independent segregation.*

Dominant and Recessive Inheritance

How do dominant inheritance and recessive inheritance work? Genes that govern alternative expressions of a characteristic (like the color of seeds) are called *alleles.* A plant or animal receives a pair of alleles for a given characteristic, one from each parent. When both alleles are the same, the organism is *homozygous* for the characteristic; when they are different, the organism is *heterozygous.* In a heterozygous situation, the dominant allele is expressed. *Recessive inheritance* occurs only when a homozygous organism has received the same recessive allele from each parent; it is then that the recessive trait shows up.

Mendel's original purebred plants were homozygous—each had two alleles for either yellow or green seeds. The crossbred plants were heterozygous, having inherited alleles for both colors. Since yellow is dominant and green recessive, the crossbred plants all had yellow seeds. When those hybrids reproduced, one-fourth of the offspring had two yellow alleles, half had yellow and green, and one-fourth had two green alleles. Because of the law of dominance, three out of four plants in

the third generation bore yellow seeds and one bore green seeds (see Figure 2-5).

An observable trait (like the color of seeds) is called a *phenotype;* the underlying, invisible genetic pattern that causes certain traits to be expressed is a *genotype.* Organisms with identical phenotypes may have different genotypes, since (because of the principle of dominant inheritance) the same observable trait (like yellow seeds) can result from different genetic patterns, such as two yellow alleles or one yellow and one green allele.

The difference in genotypes explains why Mendel's first generation of homozygous yellow-seeded plants could have only yellow-seeded offspring, while the heterozygous second generation—just as consistently bearing yellow seeds—could produce some green-seeded offspring when mated with other hybrids of that generation. This difference also explains why recessive traits, like albino skin in humans, may "skip" several generations and then suddenly show up when two people carrying the recessive gene happen to mate. Also, phenotypes may be modified by environmental factors. For example, illness or malnutrition can make a person whose genetic "blueprint" calls for tallness shorter than his genes would dictate.

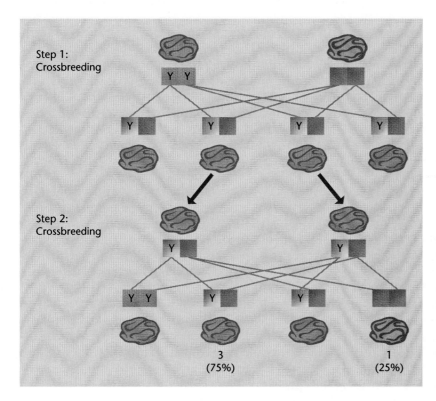

FIGURE 2-5
Mendel's experiments with colors of pea seeds. Mendel's experiments with peas established the pattern of dominant inheritance. When the plants are crossbred, the dominant characteristic (yellow seeds) is expressed. When the offspring breed, dominant and recessive characteristics show up in a 3:1 ratio. Because of dominant inheritance, the same observable phenotype (in this case, yellow seeds) can result from two different genotypes (yellow-yellow and yellow-green). However, a phenotype expressing a recessive characteristic (like green seeds) can have only one genotype (green-green).

Sex-Linked Inheritance and Other Forms

Dominance and recessiveness are not always absolute. *Incomplete dominance* is seen when red and white snapdragons are crossbred and pink flowers result; and in people with blood type AB, who have alleles for types A and B.

In *sex-linked inheritance,* certain recessive genes carried on a sex chromosome—usually the X chromosome—are not counteracted by a gene on the male's Y chromosome. Thus they are expressed more often in males. Red-green color blindness is a recessive trait that usually shows up only in males.

The genetic picture in humans is enormously complex. It is hard to find a normal trait that people inherit through simple dominant transmission—other than the ability to curl the tongue lengthwise! Some genes, like those for blood types A, B, and O, exist in three or more alternative forms known as *multiple alleles.* Most characteristics—like height, weight, and intelligence—are probably affected by many genes as well as environmental factors, through a pattern called *multifactorial inheritance.*

Scientists have recently discovered *genetic imprinting,* a process that contradicts one aspect of Mendel's theory—that genes from each parent behave the same way. Instead, some genes are imprinted, or chemically altered, by either the mother or the father. An imprinted gene will dominate one that has not been imprinted. For example, about 90 percent of children who develop Huntington's disease (a progressive degeneration of the nervous system that usually appears in middle age) seem to have inherited the gene from their fathers. This suggests that the source of the gene affects the outcome (Sapienza, 1990).

It is in genetic defects and diseases that we see most clearly the operation of dominant, recessive, and sex-linked transmission in humans.

Genetic and Chromosomal Abnormalities

With the birth of each of Sally's three children, her first concern, like that of virtually every new parent, was "Is my baby normal?" Fortunately, like almost all babies born in the United States, hers were healthy and normal. Still, each year more than 250,000 babies are born with physical or mental handicaps (March of Dimes Birth Defects Foundation, 1987). These babies account for about 6 percent of total births (4.1 million in 1991) but for about 21 percent of deaths in infancy (Wegman,

1992). Nearly half the serious malformations involve the central nervous system (see Table 2-1).

Some defects are transmitted by genes, some by chromosomes. Some are due to mutations—alterations in genes or chromosomes. Some arise when an inherited predisposition interacts with an environmental factor, either before or after birth. Spina bifida (a defect in the closure of the vertebral canal) and cleft palate (incomplete fusion of the roof of the mouth or upper lip) are probably passed on through an interaction of factors. Schizophrenia (an emotional disorder) and hyperactivity (a behavioral disorder) are also thought to be transmitted multifactorially.

Not all genetic or chromosomal abnormalities are seen at birth. Symptoms of Tay-Sachs disease and sickle-cell anemia may not appear until 6 months of age or later; those of cystic fibrosis not until age 4; and those of glaucoma and Huntington's disease usually not until the late thirties or later.

Defects Transmitted by Dominant Inheritance

Usually, normal genes are dominant over those carrying abnormal traits, but sometimes this situation is reversed and an abnormal trait is carried by a dominant gene. When one parent—say, the mother—has one normal gene that is recessive and one abnormal gene that is dominant, and the other parent (the father) has two normal genes, each of their children will have a 50-50 chance of inheriting the abnormal gene from the mother and of having the same defect she has (see Figure 2-6). Every offspring who has this abnormal gene will have the defect. The defect cannot be one that kills a person before the age of reproduction: if it did, the defect could not be passed to the next generation. Two disorders passed on this way are achondroplasia (a type of dwarfism) and Huntington's disease (a nervous system disorder).

Defects Transmitted by Recessive Inheritance

Diseases transmitted by recessive genes are often fatal in infancy. An example is Tay-Sachs disease, a degenerative disease of the central nervous system that occurs mainly among Jews of eastern European ancestry.

Some apparently healthy people act as carriers of such diseases and defects. Recessive traits show up only if a child has received the same recessive gene from each parent. When only one parent—for instance, the father—has the faulty recessive gene, none of the children will show the defect.

TABLE 2-1

Birth Defects

Problem	Characteristics of the Condition	Who Is at Risk	Tests and Their Accuracy	What Can Be Done
Alpha₁ antitrypsin deficiency	Enzyme deficiency that can lead to cirrhosis of the liver in early infancy and pulmonary emphysema and degenerative lung disease in middle age.	1 in 1000 Caucasians	Amniocentesis, CVS (chorionic villus sampling). Accuracy varies, but can sometimes predict severity.	No treatment
Alpha thalassemia	Severe anemia that reduces ability of the blood to carry oxygen. Nearly all affected infants are still-born or die soon after birth.	Primarily families of Malaysian, African, and southeast Asian descent	Amniocentesis, CVS. Accuracy varies; more accurate if other family members tested for gene.	Frequent blood transfusions
Beta thalessemia (Cooley's anemia)	Severe anemia resulting in weakness, fatigue, and frequent illness. Usually fatal in adolescence or young adulthood.	Primarily families of Mediterranean descent	Amniocentesis, CVS; 95% accurate.	Frequent blood transfusions
Cystic fibrosis	Body makes too much mucus, which collects in the lungs and digestive tract. Children do not grow normally and usually do not live beyond age 30, although some live longer. The most common inherited *lethal* defect among white people.	1 in 2000 Caucasians	Amniocentesis, CVS. Accuracy varies; more accurate if other family members tested for gene.	Daily physical therapy to loosen mucus; antibiotics for lung infections; enzymes to improve digestion; gene therapy (in experimental stage); lung transplants (in experimental stage)
Down syndrome	Minor to severe mental retardation caused by an extra 21st chromosome. The most common chromosomal defect.	1 in 350 women over age 35; 1 in 800, all women	Amniocentesis, CVS; nearly 100% accurate.	Programs of intellectual stimulation are effective

(continued)

TABLE 2-1   (Continued)

Problem	Characteristics of the Condition	Who Is at Risk	Tests and Their Accuracy	What Can Be Done
Duchenne's muscular dystrophy	Fatal disease found only in males, marked by muscle weakness. Minor mental retardation is common. Respiratory failure and death usually occur in young adulthood.	1 in 7000 male births	Amniocentesis, CVS; 95% accurate.	No treatment
Fragile X syndrome	Minor to severe mental retardation. Symptoms, which are more severe in males, include delayed speech and motor development, speech impairments, and hyperactivity. Considered one of the main causes of autism. The most common inherited form of mental retardation.	1 in 1200 male births; 1 in 2000 female births	Amniocentesis, CVS; 95% accurate.	Educational and behavioral therapy when appropriate
Hemophilia	Excessive bleeding, usually affecting males rather than females. In its most severe form, can lead to crippling arthritis in adulthood.	1 in 10,000 families with a history of hemophilia	Amniocentesis, CVS; 95% accurate.	Frequent transfusions of blood with clotting factors
Neural tube defects: Anencephaly	Absence of brain tissue. Infants are stillborn or die soon after birth.	1 in 1000	Ultrasound, amniocentesis; 100% accurate.	No treatment
Spina bifida	Incompletely closed spinal canal, resulting in muscle weakness or paralysis and loss of bladder and bowel control. Often accompanied by hydrocephalus, an accumulation of spinal fluid in the brain, which can	1 in 1000	Ultrasound, amniocentesis. Test works only if the spinal cord is leaking fluid into the uterus or is exposed and visible during ultrasound.	Surgery to close spinal canal prevents further injury; shunt placed in brain drains excess fluid and prevents mental retardation

(continued)

TABLE 2-1   (Continued)

Problem	Characteristics of the Condition	Who Is at Risk	Tests and Their Accuracy	What Can Be Done
	lead to mental retardation. The two types of neural tube defects together constitute the most common serious type of birth defect in the United States.			
Polycystic kidney disease	*Infantile form:* enlarged kidneys, leading to respiratory problems and congestive heart failure. *Adult form:* kidney pain, kidney stones, and hypertension resulting in chronic kidney failure. Symptoms usually begin around age 30.	1 in 1000	*Infantile form:* ultrasound; 100% accurate. *Adult form:* amniocentesis; 95% accurate.	Kidney transplants
Sex chromosome abnormality	Minor to severe developmental and learning disabilities, caused by missing X or extra X or Y chromosome.	1 in 500	Amniocentesis, CVS; nearly 100% accurate.	Hormonal treatments to trigger puberty when needed; special education for some
Sickle-cell anemia	Deformed, fragile red blood cells that can clog the blood vessels, depriving the body of oxygen. Symptoms include severe pain, stunted growth, frequent infections, leg ulcers, gallstones, susceptibility to pneumonia, and stroke.	1 in 500 blacks	Amniocentesis, CVS; 95% accurate.	Painkillers, transfusions for anemia, antibiotics for infections
Tay-Sachs disease	Degenerative disease of the brain and nerve cells, resulting in death before age 5.	1 in 3000 eastern European Jews	Amniocentesis, CVS; 100% accurate.	No treatment

SOURCE: Adapted from Tisdale, 1988, pp. 68–69.

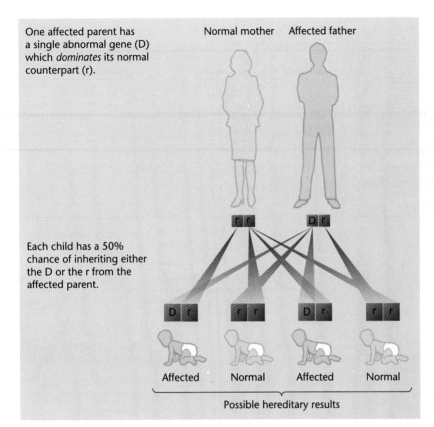

One affected parent has a single abnormal gene (D) which *dominates* its normal counterpart (r).

Normal mother   Affected father

Each child has a 50% chance of inheriting either the D or the r from the affected parent.

Affected   Normal   Affected   Normal

Possible hereditary results

FIGURE 2-6
Dominant inheritance of a birth defect.

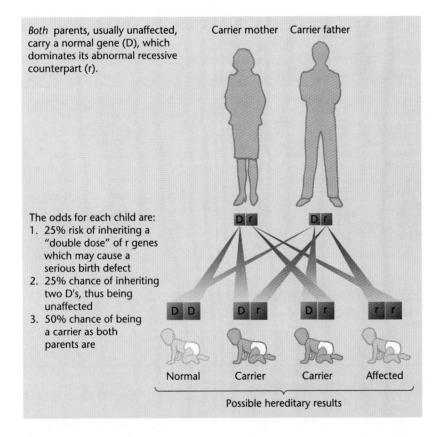

Both parents, usually unaffected, carry a normal gene (D), which dominates its abnormal recessive counterpart (r).

Carrier mother   Carrier father

The odds for each child are:
1. 25% risk of inheriting a "double dose" of r genes which may cause a serious birth defect
2. 25% chance of inheriting two D's, thus being unaffected
3. 50% chance of being a carrier as both parents are

Normal   Carrier   Carrier   Affected

Possible hereditary results

FIGURE 2-7
Recessive inheritance of a birth defect.

Each child, though, will have a 50-50 chance of being a carrier like the father and of passing the recessive gene on to his or her own children. Sometimes both parents carry the faulty gene, and though both are unaffected, they are capable of passing it on to their children. In such cases, a child has a 25 percent chance of a birth defect and a 50 percent chance of being a carrier (see Figure 2-7).

Inbreeding—marriage of close relatives—used to be common among the European upper classes. Today, such marriages are usually prohibited by law to lower the risk of children's inheriting a disease passed on through recessive genes that both parents may have inherited from a common ancestor. (See Table 2-2.)

Defects Transmitted by Sex-Linked Inheritance

Hemophilia, a blood-clotting disorder, used to be called the "royal disease" because it was prevalent among the highly inbred ruling families of Europe. Hemophilia is a sex-linked condition transmitted by a recessive gene. Because they are carried on one of the X chromosomes of an unaffected mother, sex-linked recessive traits almost always show up only in male children, who do not have an opposite dominant trait on the Y chromosome.

The sons of a normal man and a woman with one abnormal gene will have a 50 percent chance of inheriting the abnormal X chromosome and thus inheriting the disorder, and a 50 percent chance of inheriting the mother's normal X chromosome and being unaffected. Daughters will have a 50 percent chance of being carriers (see Figure 2-8). An affected father can never pass on such a gene to his sons, since he contributes a Y chromosome to them; but he can pass the gene on to his daughters. The daughters can become carriers or, if the mother is a carrier and passes on the recessive gene, they may inherit the disease themselves.

Chromosomal Abnormalities

Usually, chromosomal development proceeds normally, but when something does go wrong, serious abnormalities may develop. Some chromosomal defects are inherited; others result from accidents that occur during development. Accidental abnormalities are not likely to recur in the same family. About 1 in every 156 children born

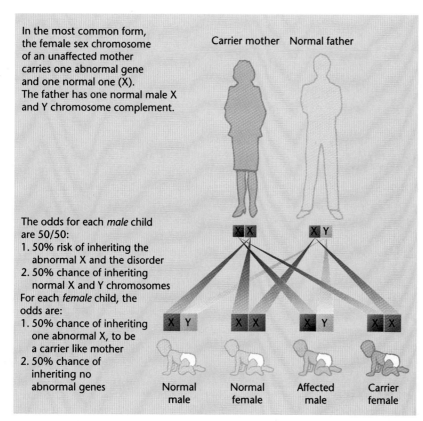

In the most common form, the female sex chromosome of an unaffected mother carries one abnormal gene and one normal one (X). The father has one normal male X and Y chromosome complement.

Carrier mother   Normal father

The odds for each *male* child are 50/50:
1. 50% risk of inheriting the abnormal X and the disorder
2. 50% chance of inheriting normal X and Y chromosomes

For each *female* child, the odds are:
1. 50% chance of inheriting one abnormal X, to be a carrier like mother
2. 50% chance of inheriting no abnormal genes

Normal male   Normal female   Affected male   Carrier female

FIGURE 2-8
Sex-linked inheritance of a birth defect.

TABLE 2-2

Chances of Genetic Disorders for Various Ethnic Groups

If You Are	The Chance Is About	That
African American	1 in 12	You are ... cell anem...
	7 in 10	You will ... ance as ... ple, deve...
African American and male	1 in 10	You have ... dispositi...
African American and female	1 in 50	molytic a... sulfa or c...
white	1 in 25	You are a ... fibrosis
	1 in 80	You are a ... phenylke...
Jewish (Ashkenazic)	1 in 30	You are a ... Sachs dis...
	1 in 100	You are a ... dysauton...
Italian American or Greek American	1 in 10	You are a carrier of beta thalassemia
Armenian or Jewish (Sephardic)	1 in 45	You are a carrier of familial Mediterranean fever
Afrikaner (white South African)	1 in 330	You have porphyria
Asian	100%	You will have milk intolerance as an adult

SOURCE: Adapted from Milunsky, 1992, p. 122.

Handwritten note overlaying table:

> Dowd's
> MI — MO RETARDATION
> HEARING IMP.
> POOR VISUAL ACUITY
> HEART DEFECTS
> SUSCEPTIBLE TO
> RESP. PROBLEMS
> OVERWEIGHT

in western countries has some chromosomal abnormality (Milunsky, 1992).

Some relatively rare chromosomal disorders are caused by either a missing (O) or an extra sex chromosome (either X or Y). Examples are Klinefelter's syndrome (with the pattern XXY), Turner's syndrome (with the pattern XO, and thus missing a second sex chromosome), and the XYY and XXX syndromes. The most obvious effects are sexually related characteristics (underdevelopment, sterility, or secondary sex characteristics of the other sex). These children, while not usually seriously retarded, often have reading problems and general learning disabilities ("Long-term outlook," 1982).

Down syndrome is the most common chromosomal disorder. Its most obvious symptom is a downward-sloping skin fold at the inner corners of the eyes. Other signs are a small head, a flat nose, a protruding tongue, mild to severe mental and motor retardation, and defective heart, eyes, and ears. Down syndrome is caused by an extra twenty-first chromosome or the translocation of part of the twenty-first chromosome onto another chromosome. Today, more than 70 percent of people with the syndrome live at least until age 30 (Baird & Sadovnick, 1987).

About 1 in every 800 babies born alive has Down syndrome. The risk is greatest with older parents: the chances rise from 1 such birth in 2000 among 25-year-old mothers to 1 in 40 for women over 45. The risk also rises with the father's age, especially among men over 50 (Abroms & Bennett, 1981). For years, the father's influence was ignored as researchers concentrated on the mother's age, fail-

Handwritten notes at bottom: TRISOMY 21   OVER 70% LIVE TO OVER AGE 30

ing to consider the fact that the older a woman is, the older her husband is likely to be. Although new DNA analysis has shown that the extra chromosome seems to come from the mother's ovum in 95 percent of cases (Antonarakis & Down Syndrome Collaborative Group, 1991), the other 5 percent of cases may be related to the father's age.

More than 90 percent of cases of Down syndrome are caused by an accident, a mistake in chromosome distribution during development of the ovum, sperm, or zygote (D. W. Smith & Wilson, 1973). But among mothers under age 35, the disorder is more likely to be hereditary. A clue to its genetic basis is the discovery of a gene on chromosome 21; this gene expresses a brain protein that seems to lead to Down syndrome (Allore et al., 1988).

Many children with Down syndrome can be taught skills with which they can support themselves as adults; the progress of these children has caused educators to revise their expectations upward (Hayden & Haring, 1976). Support groups help parents learn about and deal with the condition.

Genetic Counseling

Genetic counseling helps couples who believe that they may be at high risk of bearing a child with a birth defect. People who have already borne one handicapped child, who have a family history of hereditary illness, or who suffer from conditions known or suspected to be inherited can get information about their likelihood of producing affected children.

After they have given a thorough family history, both parents and any children in the family are examined physically. They may also take tests that identify carriers of genetic defects. One test involves laboratory investigations of blood, skin, urine, or fingerprints. Chromosomes prepared from body tissue are analyzed and photographed. Enlarged photographs of the chromosomes are then cut out and arranged according to size and structure on a chart called a *karyotype* to demonstrate any chromosomal abnormalities (see Figure 2-9).

On the basis of such tests, the genetic counselor calculates the mathematical odds for having an affected child but does not advise a couple on whether to take the risk. Rather, the counselor helps couples understand the implications of particular diseases and defects and makes them aware of what they can do. Sometimes counseling can show that a risk is either very slight or nonexistent. If a risk is high, one partner may choose to be sterilized or the couple may consider adoption or artificial insemination by donor (see Chapter 13). If a disorder is not extremely disabling or is treatable, a couple may take a chance. (An analogous type of help for prospective parents is assessment of fetal development and well-being before birth; see Box 2-1).

Geneticists hope that in the future they will be able to do much more to help parents. One source of help may be a national registry to track birth de-

This 2½-year-old has Down syndrome. Although her intellectual potential is limited, loving care and patient teaching are likely to help her achieve much more than was once thought possible for such children. *(Laura Dwight)*

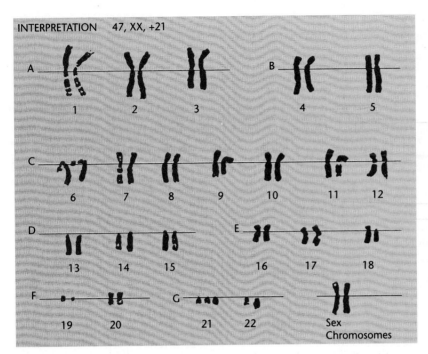

INTERPRETATION   47, XX, +21

FIGURE 2-9
Karyotype. Chromosomes of a child with Down syndrome, showing three chromosomes on number 21. (In the normal pattern, there are two chromosomes on number 21.) Since pair 23 consists of two X's, we know that this is the karyotype of a girl. *(Vanderbilt University and March of Dimes.)*

fects. A registry listing the occurrence of specific birth defects can help to identify people who may be at risk, provide preventive services, and help agencies meet the needs of affected people and their families.

Many advances may also come from current progress in locating defective genes on chromosomes. Investigators use complex instruments to identify and locate specific genes; so far they have mapped several thousand human genes. They determine what proteins are made by these genes and detect the presence or absence of proteins associated with particular disorders. Such knowledge can lead to new predictive tests, both before and after birth; to drugs to prevent or treat disease; and to "gene therapy"—technology for repairing abnormal genes (see Box 2-2 on page 64).

HOW DO HEREDITY AND ENVIRONMENT INTERACT?

From what you have read so far, you might have the impression that almost everything about human beings—how we look, how our minds work, and how we feel—is determined at conception. Heredity, of course, is only part of the story. The environment (both before and after birth) also plays a critical role in making us what we are and what we will become.

"Nature versus Nurture": Hereditary and Environmental Factors

Which has more effect—nature or nurture, heredity or environment? People have asked this question for years, and the answer differs for different traits. Some physical characteristics, like eye color and blood type, are clearly inherited. But more complex traits having to do with health, intelligence, and personality are subject to an interplay of both hereditary and environmental forces. (The different-shaded bands in Figure 2-10 show how these two forces, in varying degrees, can cause or contribute to mental retardation.)

How much is inherited? How much is environmentally influenced? These questions matter. Among other reasons, they affect the way people act toward children. For example, if it is possible to enhance a baby's intelligence through environmental factors, we can try to make the environment as favorable as possible. On the other hand, if a child's activity level is set mainly by heredity, parents and teachers need to have realistic expectations. And knowing which birth defects are hereditary makes genetic counseling possible.

The answer to the question "Nature or nurture?" is rarely either–or. Which of the two has the greater influence may depend on many factors.

Hereditary and Environmental Influences on Traits
Some traits governed by genes (like eye color) do

BOX 2-1 *PRACTICALLY SPEAKING*

PRENATAL ASSESSMENT

Not long ago, almost the only decision parents had to make about their babies before birth was the decision to conceive; most of what happened in the intervening 9 months was beyond their control. But we now have an array of new tools to assess fetal development and well-being.

AMNIOCENTESIS

In *amniocentesis,* a sample of the fluid in the amniotic sac is withdrawn and analyzed to detect the presence of about 200 (out of 4000) genetic defects, all recognizable chromosomal disorders, and other problems, including neural-tube defects (Milunsky, 1992). This fluid, in which the fetus floats in the uterus, contains fetal cells. The procedure is usually done between the fourteenth to sixteenth weeks of pregnancy; it takes about 2 weeks to get the results. Amniocentesis can also reveal the sex of the fetus, which may be crucial in the case of a sex-linked disorder like hemophilia.

Amniocentesis is generally recommended for pregnant women if they are at least 35 years old, if they and their partners are both known carriers of diseases such as Tay-Sachs or sickle-cell anemia, or if they or their partners have a family history of such conditions as Down syndrome, spina bifida, Rh disease, or muscular dystrophy. One analysis of 3000 women who had the procedure indicated that it was "safe, highly reliable and extremely accurate" (Golbus et al., 1979, p. 157). But another study of 4600 women found a slightly higher risk of miscarriage in women who had the procedure (Tabor et al., 1986). According to a Canadian study of 100 babies whose mothers had undergone amniocentesis and 56 untested infants, tested babies are no more

likely than untested ones to suffer problems relating to intelligence, language, or behavior. They seem to be at slightly greater risk of ear infections and middle-ear abnormalities, although their hearing is not affected (Finegan et al., 1990). Attempts are now being made to do amniocentesis before 15 weeks of pregnancy, although its safety remains unknown (D'Alton & De-Cherney, 1993).

CHORIONIC VILLUS SAMPLING

Chorionic villus sampling (CVS) consists of taking tissue from the end of one or more villi—hairlike projections of the membrane around the embryo, which are made up of fetal cells. These cells are then tested for the presence of various conditions. This procedure can be performed earlier than amniocentesis (between 8 and 13 weeks of pregnancy), and it yields results sooner (within about a week). Unfortunately, however, research has revealed a number of problems with CVS, compared with amniocentesis. Some women who used CVS experienced almost 5 percent more deaths of their fetuses or newborns than did those who chose amniocentesis. In addition, CVS diagnoses are at times ambiguous, so women may have to undergo amniocentesis anyway (D'Alton & DeCherney, 1993).

MATERNAL BLOOD TESTS

Blood taken from the mother between the sixteenth and eighteenth weeks of pregnancy can be tested for the amount of alpha fetoprotein (AFP) it contains. This *maternal blood test* is appropriate for women at risk of bearing children with defects in the formation of the brain or spinal cord (like anencephaly or spina bifida), which may be detected by high

AFP levels. To confirm or refute the presence of suspected conditions, ultrasound or amniocentesis, or both, may be performed.

One study found that using three blood tests from samples taken from the fifteenth to twentieth weeks of gestation—for AFP and two hormones (unconjugated estriol and chorionic gonadotropin)—predicted about 60 percent of cases of Down syndrome. These could then be confirmed by amniocentesis. This test is particularly important for women under 35 (who bear 80 percent of all Down syndrome babies), because they are not usually targeted to receive amniocentesis (Haddow et al., 1992).

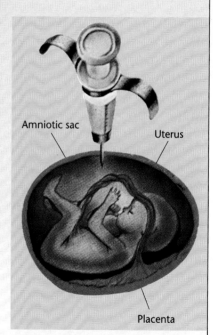

Amniocentesis. A sample of amniotic fluid can be withdrawn (by inserting a needle through the mother's abdominal wall) and analyzed for the presence of several birth defects. Analysis of the sampled fluid generally takes about 2 weeks *(F. Fuchs, 1980.)*

(continued)

BOX 2-1 (Continued)

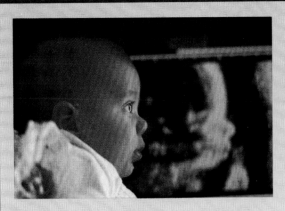

This 6-month-old baby is shown next to an ultrasound picture taken during his fourth month of gestation. Ultrasound is a popular diagnostic tool that presents an immediate image of the fetus in the womb. *(J. Pavlovsky/Sygma)*

Blood tests can also identify carriers of such diseases as sickle-cell anemia (a blood disorder seen mostly in black people), Tay-Sachs disease, and thalassemia (a blood disorder that affects people of Mediterranean origin). And they can reveal the sex of a fetus, which can be of help with sex-linked disorders (Lo et al., 1989).

ULTRASOUND

Some parents see their baby for the first time in a *sonogram,* a picture of the uterus, fetus, and placenta that is created by high-frequency sound waves directed into the woman's abdomen. The technique of **ultrasound** provides the clearest images yet obtained of a fetus in the womb, with little or no discomfort to the woman. Ultrasound is used to measure a baby's growth, to judge gestational age, to detect multiple pregnancies, to evaluate uterine abnormalities, to detect major structural abnormalities in the fetus, and to determine whether a fetus has died, as well as to guide other procedures like amniocentesis. Results from ultrasound can then be followed up with other procedures (D'Alton & DeCherney, 1993).

A new use for ultrasound involves guiding physicians to do a fetal biopsy (a test on a sample of fetal skin) to diagnose certain disorders. Fetal biopsy is still experimental, with its safety and accuracy in question (D'Alton & DeCherney, 1993). However, a recent report indicates that screening ultrasound does not improve perinatal outcome (such as fetal and neonatal death). Thus, routine ultrasound in low-risk pregnancies appears to be unnecessary (Ewigman et al., 1993).

UMBILICAL CORD BLOOD SAMPLING

By threading a needle into tiny blood vessels of the umbilical cord under the guidance of ultrasound, doctors can take samples of a fetus's blood. They can then get a blood count, examine liver function, and assess various other body functions.

This procedure can test for infection, anemia, certain metabolic disorders and immunodeficiencies, and heart failure, and it seems to offer promise for identifying still other conditions. The technique is associated with such problems as pregnancy loss, bleeding from the umbilical cord, early labor, and infection (Chervenak, Isaacson, & Mahoney, 1986; Kolata, 1988). It should be used only when diagnostic information cannot be obtained by other, safer means (D'Alton & DeCherney, 1993).

PREIMPLANTATION GENETIC DIAGNOSIS

The newest prenatal technique identified genetic defects in embryos of from 4 to 8 cells, which were conceived by in vitro fertilization (see Chapter 13). By extracting and examining a single cell for cystic fibrosis, researchers were able to determine whether this disease was present (Handyside, Lesko, Tarín, Winston, & Hughes, 1992). Defective embryos would not be implanted.

These techniques for prenatal diagnosis of birth defects, coupled with the legalization of induced abortion, have encouraged many couples with troubling medical histories to take a chance on conception. For example, a couple who know that they both carry a recessive gene for a disorder may conceive and then take tests to learn whether the fetus has the condition. They may be reassured that their baby will be normal, or, if the fetus is affected, they may terminate the pregnancy or plan for the special needs of a handicapped child.

NATURE
Hereditary defect causes mental retardation. Superior environment has no salutary effect.
Hereditary defect or disease (deafness, long-term illness) interferes with normal life and may contribute to retarded development.
Inherited factors that have social implications (color, sex, body build) may affect environment and limit opportunities for personal development.
Lower social class, poor education, or emotional deprivation may stunt intellectual development.
Birth injury or prenatal insult causes physical problem that interferes with regular schooling and retards development.
Birth injury or prenatal insult is so massive that it causes mental retardation despite normal, healthy genetic endowment.
NURTURE

FIGURE 2-10
How nature and nurture can contribute to intellectual retardation. As colors can be mixed to different shades and intensities, so heredity and environment interact to varying degrees to shape a trait like intellectual retardation. *(Adapted from Anastasi, 1958.)*

not seem to be affected by the environment or by a person's own behavior. But many traits are subject to variation, within the limits set by the genes. Genetic influences are not necessarily all-powerful, then; they may set up a range of possible reactions among people living in a particular range of environmental conditions. Also, genes are not expressed directly as behavior; thus they may be expressed differently in different environments. How our genetic inheritance shows itself depends to a considerable extent on our specific environment.

For example, genes have a strong effect on weight and height, but actual body size can depend on what a person does. A genetic tendency for fatness does not make a person eat a lot, but someone who does take in more calories than his or her body needs will be fatter than another person with a similar genetic tendency who eats less. In societies where nutrition improves, an entire generation of people may tower over their parents. The children have inherited their parents' genes for height, but within the range those genes allow, the second generation has responded to its healthier world. And as we saw in discussing phenotypes, illness or malnutrition may stunt growth.

Maturation

One reason it is so hard to untangle the relative effects of heredity and environment is that human beings keep changing throughout life, and some of these changes seem to be caused by the environment whereas others are clearly programmed by the genes. *Maturation* is the unfolding of a biologically determined, age-related sequence of behavior patterns. For example, crawling, walking, and running develop in that order at certain approximate ages. Behaviors that depend largely on maturation generally appear when the organism is ready—not before, and rarely afterward.

Yet environmental forces can affect this hereditary timetable, particularly in extreme cases like long-term deprivation. This was seen in infants in Iranian orphanages who received little attention and had no exercise. These babies did not sit up or walk until quite late, compared with well-cared-for Iranian children (Dennis, 1960). But even under these extreme conditions, maturation did occur, at a slowed pace.

The balance between nature and nurture seems most complex in the development of intellect and personality. Consider language. The genetic timetable dictates that before children can talk, they have to reach a certain level of neurological and muscular maturation. No 6-month-old could speak this sentence, no matter how enriched his or her home life might be. Yet environment seems to play a large part in language development. If parents encourage babies' first sounds by talking back to them, children will start to speak earlier than they would if their early vocalizing had been ignored. Heredity, then, draws the blueprint for development, but environment affects the pace at which "construction" proceeds and even the specific form of the structure.

Ways to Study the Relative Effects of Heredity and Environment

Researchers use a variety of methods to find out how heredity and environment interact to create differences between people. Some focus more on inherited factors, others on those in the environment. The most powerful way to study genetic influences on behavior involves breeding animals for certain traits, like aggressiveness or activity level. Because, for ethical reasons, similar studies cannot be done on human beings, scientists have relied on three other types of research: family, adoption, and twin studies.

BOX 2-2   *TAKE A STAND*

GENETIC TESTING

The Human Genome Project, a 15-year, $3 billion research effort under the joint leadership of the National Institutes of Health and the U.S. Department of Energy, is designed to map all the human genes and identify those that seem to cause particular disorders. The genetic information gained from such research could save many lives and improve the quality of many others by increasing our ability to control, treat, and cure disease.

However, to implement the findings from the project would almost certainly involve genetic testing of individuals to find out whether people carry harmful genes. What are the implications of such testing, and what do people say about its controversial aspects?

THE BENEFITS OF GENETIC TESTING

1   Knowing one's genetic profile can lead to early detection and more effective treatment of hereditary disorders. For example, a woman who learns that she has a genetic tendency for breast cancer might be advised to undergo mammograms (x-ray photographs of the breast, which are taken to reveal the presence of malignant tumors) at an earlier age and at more frequent intervals than would otherwise be recommended. If a cancer is caught in its early stage, her life may be saved.
2   Early detection may lead to prevention. A person who learns of a genetic predisposition to lung cancer may be motivated to stop smoking.
3   Such information can be helpful in making major life deci-

sions, such as whether to have children, what type of occupation to pursue, what climate to live in, and other such lifestyle choices.
4   Society may be able to protect the general welfare by testing people in jobs that bear on the public's safety. For example, if a test were developed to screen for a gene that controls Alzheimer's disease, airlines might screen pilots to see whether they were at risk; similarly, a railroad might screen engineers for a gene that might cause alcoholism. Of course, just because people have a gene that might predispose them toward certain diseases does not mean that they would in fact develop those diseases (Orentlicher, 1990).

THE DANGERS OF GENETIC TESTING

1   The presence of genetic information may be disseminated in a way that violates the individual's privacy. Although medical data are supposed to be kept confidential, it is almost impossible to keep such information private. A study at the University of Minnesota found that at least 50 people had access to each patient's medical charts (Gruson, 1992).
2   Discrimination on the basis of genetic information is possible. In 1983, 17 of the Fortune 500 companies had used genetic tests, and another 59 were considering using them to help them make decisions about employment, training, and promotion (Henig, 1989). An

informal survey found 50 cases in which people had been denied jobs, insurance claims, or other benefits because of their genes (Gruson, 1992). One man, who had been driving well, with no accidents and no traffic tickets for 20 years, had his auto insurance policy canceled when the insurance company learned that he carried a gene for a rare neurological condition (Henig, 1989). Because of such abuses, as of April 1992, four states have passed laws prohibiting job discrimination on the basis of genetic information, and at least 17 others are considering such legislation (Gruson, 1992).
3   The tests in current use are too often imprecise and thus are unreliable in predicting when, or even whether, a particular person may develop a particular disease. People deemed at risk of a disease may never develop it. Therefore, unless someone is currently disabled, his or her genetic profile should not be used to deny a job or insurance benefits. In fact, such a person should be covered under the Americans with Disabilities Act.
4   It would be extremely anxiety-producing for a person to learn that she or he has the gene for a disease for which there is no cure. What is the point of knowing you have a potentially debilitating condition when you cannot do anything about it?

Are we, then, premature in using genetic testing before it has been further perfected? Or do the benefits outweigh the risks?

In *family (consanguinity) studies*, researchers look at resemblances among people who are related to each other. Through this method, they discover the degree to which relatives share certain traits and whether the closeness of the genetic relationship affects the degree of similarity. If the closeness of the relationship is associated with degree of similarity in a trait, we can see the influence of heredity. One problem with family studies, however, is their inability to assess possible environmental sources of similarity (Plomin, 1990). With only a family study, for example, we cannot know whether obese children of obese parents inherited the tendency or whether they are fat because their diet is similar to that of their parents.

Adoption studies try to determine this by looking at the levels of similarity between adopted children and their adoptive parents and siblings, and between the children and their biological families. When adopted children are more like their biological parents and siblings on a particular trait (like obesity), we see the influence of heredity. When they resemble their adoptive families more, we see the influence of environment.

In the *study of twins* we compare identical twins (who have the same genetic makeup) with fraternal twins (who are no more similar genetically than are any other siblings). When identical twins are more alike on a trait than fraternal twins, we see the effects of heredity.

A number of studies have examined identical twins who had been separated in infancy and then reared apart from each other. These studies, which combine twin and adoption strategies, have shown strong resemblances between the twins. Such findings support a strong hereditary basis for a wide variety of physical and psychological characteristics. One problem with this approach, however, is that the home environments of both twins are often quite similar, even though their adoptive families are different. For example, both children are likely to grow up in homes that are at similar socioeconomic levels. Thus, the similarity between identical twins reared apart may reflect environmental similarities, as well as genes.

Some Characteristics Influenced by Heredity and Environment

Physical and Physiological Traits

When Robert Shafran went away to college, students he had never met greeted him like an old

Identical twins separated at birth are sought after by researchers who want to determine the impact of genes on personality. These twins, adopted by different families and not reunited till age 31, both became firefighters. Was this coincidence or heredity? *(Bob Sacha)*

friend and called him "Eddy." After seeing a snapshot of Eddy Galland, who had attended the same school the year before, Robert said, "What I saw was a photograph of myself." When a third lookalike turned up, the youths learned that they were identical triplets who had been separated at birth (Battelle, 1981).

The carbon-copy physical appearance of identical twins is well known. They are also more concordant (alike) than fraternal twins in traits such as blood pressure; rates of breathing, perspiration, and pulse; height and weight (Jost & Sontag, 1944), and age of first menstruation (Petri, 1934).

Obesity is strongly influenced by heredity. It is twice as likely that both identical twins will be overweight as that both fraternal twins will be (Stunkard, Harris, Pedersen, & McClearn, 1990). This does not mean that environment has no effect; it means that people genetically at risk of obesity must work harder not to get fat.

Even our days on earth may be numbered by our genes. Identical twin men are more concordant for strokes (17.7 percent, compared to 3.6 percent for male fraternal twins; Brass, Isaacsohn, Merikangas, & Robinette, 1992). And senescence (the process of growing old) and death occur at more similar ages for identical twins than for fraternal twins (Jarvik, Kallmann, & Klaber, 1957). In one study, adopted children (born in the 1920s) whose biological parents died before age 50 were twice as likely to have died young as adopted children whose biological parents were alive at 50 (T. Sorensen, Nielsen, Andersen, & Teasdale, 1988).

Intelligence

Behavioral geneticists have focused more on intelligence than on all other characteristics combined, generally using IQ scores as its measure. They have found that heredity exerts a major influence on intelligence, more clearly so with age (McGue, Bouchard, Iacono, & Lykken, 1993).

Since genes do not direct specific behaviors, how do they affect intellectual performance? Apparently, many genes—each with its own small effect—combine to influence intelligence. Genes establish a range of possible reactions to a range of possible experiences (Weinberg, 1989).

There is *no* evidence that differences in IQ scores between cultural, ethnic, or racial groups are due to hereditary factors. But many studies point to a strong genetic influence on differences between individuals *within a group*. About 50 percent of the difference in intelligence between persons in a group is believed to be genetically determined, with the remaining variation due to each person's experiences (Weinberg, 1989). This has implications for social policy, since the half of the variance that is environmentally determined is responsive to strategies that help children with low IQ scores do better both academically and socially. Changes in environment seem to be able to affect IQ by a range of 20 to 25 points (Weinberg, 1989).

Evidence for the role of heredity in intelligence has emerged from adoption and twin studies. Adopted children's IQs have been compared with those of their adoptive siblings and parents, and with the IQs or the educational levels of their biological mothers (from whom they had been separated since the first week of life). Resemblances have been consistently higher to the biological mothers than to the family members children have lived with (J. Horn, 1983; Scarr & Weinberg, 1983).

Also, heredity seems to become more important as people grow older. In the adoption studies, young siblings scored similarly, whether related by blood or adoption; but adolescents' scores had zero correlation with those of their adoptive siblings. Furthermore, the adolescents' IQs correlated more highly with their biological mothers' levels of schooling than with their adoptive parents' IQs. Scarr and Weinberg (1983) concluded that family environment is more important for younger children, but that older adolescents find their niches in life on the basis of inborn abilities and interests.

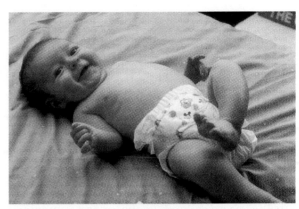

According to findings of longitudinal research, the basically cheerful mood of a baby like 14-month-old Annie seems to be the result of inborn temperament. However, life experiences can influence, for good or ill, the way a person approaches life. *(Nancy Olds)*

In other words, they actively select environments that are compatible with their heredity.

Longitudinal twin studies have also found the influence of heredity on intelligence increasing with age. Among 500 pairs of twins, identical twins grew more alike in IQ from infancy to adolescence, while fraternal twins became less alike. And individual children followed their own distinct patterns of "spurts and lags" in mental development. The home environment had an impact, but genetic factors had more (Plomin, Pedersen, McClearn, Nesselroade, & Bergeman, 1988).

We have to remember, however, that genetics accounts only in part for variations in intelligence; changing the environment can have considerable impact. The fact that much of intelligence seems to be inherited does not mean that it cannot be changed, given a better (or worse) environment.

Personality

Personality is a person's overall pattern of character, behavioral, temperamental, emotional, and mental traits. Something so complicated cannot be ascribed to any one major influence, either hereditary or environmental. But specific aspects of personality appear to be inherited, at least in part.

In 1956, two psychiatrists and a pediatrician (A. Thomas & Chess, 1984; A. Thomas, Chess, & Birch, 1968) launched the New York Longitudinal Study (NYLS), following 133 children from infancy into adulthood. These researchers concluded that *temperament*, or a person's basic style of approaching and reacting to situations, seems to be inborn. They looked at how active children were;

how regular they were in hunger, sleep, and bowel habits; how readily they accepted new people and situations; how they adapted to changes in routine; how sensitive ~~they were~~ ~~bright~~ lights, and ~~either~~ ~~they~~ tended to be ~~low intensely~~ they responded; a~~nd~~ ~~ks or~~ were easily ~~enor-~~ mously in a ~~from~~ birth, and th~~But~~ many childre~~, ap-~~ parently reac~~ental~~ handling (se~~~~

[handwritten note obscuring text: AUTISM NEED PREDICTABILITY REHEARSAL OF EVENTS]

There is ev~~~~vide range of per~~Ba-~~ con, & Lykke~~sig-~~ nificant gene~~vel,~~ sociability an~~ions~~ considered ne~~Ka-~~ gan, Reznick, ~~bies~~ from differen~~that~~ some tempera~~are inborn (see Box 2-3).~~

Some Disorders Influenced by Heredity and Environment

Alcoholism

Alcoholics may be largely born, not made. There is considerable evidence that alcoholism runs in families and that a heightened risk results from the interaction of genetic and environmental factors (McGue, 1993). Identical twins are significantly more concordant for alcoholism than fraternal twins. Sons of alcoholic men are 4 times as likely as sons of nonalcoholic men to develop alcoholism themselves, even when they are adopted at birth, and regardless of whether their adoptive parents are alcoholic. Children do not seem to be at unusual risk if their adoptive parents are alcoholic but their biological parents are not (Schuckit, 1985, 1987). Some recent research suggests the same magnitude of heritability for women, who at one time had been thought to become alcoholic largely as a result of social and psychological forces (Kendler, Heath, Neale, Kessler, & Eaves, 1992).

No one is predestined to develop alcoholism. But since genetic factors seem to make some people more vulnerable, children of alcoholic parents should be warned that they may not be able to handle liquor the way their peers do.

Schizophrenia

Schizophrenia is a group of mental disorders

RIGID PATTERNS

marked by a loss of contact with reality and by such symptoms as hallucinations, delusions, and other thought disorders. Many studies suggest that it has a strong genetic element. The biological children of women with schizophrenia are more likely than people in the general population to suffer from the disorder themselves; identical twins are more likely than fraternal twins to be concordant for it; and the closer a person's biological relation to someone with schizophrenia, the more likely the person is to develop it (Gottesman, 1993).

Although there is, then, strong evidence of biological transmission of schizophrenia, we have to ask why not all identical twins are concordant for this disorder. One answer may be that it is not the illness itself that is transmitted, but a predisposition toward it. If certain environmental stresses occur in the life of someone who is genetically predisposed, that person may develop schizophrenia.

The reputation that city life has for being stressful, as well as exciting, may be only too well deserved. After controlling for use of marijuana, parental divorce, and family history of psychiatric disorders, a Swedish study found that males who had grown up in a city were more likely to develop schizophrenia than were those from rural areas (Lewis, David, Andreasson, & Allebeck, 1992).

Infantile Autism

PERSEVERATION

Infantile autism is a rare developmental disorder involving an inability to communicate with or respond to other people. It develops within the first 2½ years of life, sometimes as early as the fourth month, when a baby may lie in the crib, oblivious to other people. The child does not cuddle; does not make eye contact with caregivers; either treats adults as interchangeable or clings mechanically to one person; and may never learn to speak but may be able to sing a wide repertory of songs. Boys are 3 times more likely than girls to be afflicted.

NO PHYS. DEFORMity

Many autistic children are retarded; only 30 percent have an IQ of 70 or more. They often, however, do well on tasks of manipulative or visual-spatial skill and may perform unusual mental feats (like memorizing entire train schedules). They may scream when their place at the table is changed, insist on always carrying a particular object (like a rubber band), clap their hands constantly, or be fascinated by moving objects—staring for hours at an electric fan.

Although "cold and unresponsive" parents have been blamed for causing autism, it is now recognized as a biological disorder of the nervous sys-

LIMITED LANG. UNDERSTANDING HIGH PAIN THRESHOLD

BOX 2-3 FOOD FOR THOUGHT

SHYNESS

At age 4, Jason went with his parents to an office Christmas party. For the first hour he didn't say a word; for the next hour he clung to his mother's side as he stared wide-eyed at the other children, the strange adults, and the array of toys. By the time he felt comfortable enough to venture away from her, the party was over.

Vicky, also 4, was at the same party. She had barely burst into the room when she ran up to the Christmas tree, grabbed the nearest brightly wrapped package, asked a strange man standing nearby if he could help her open it, and hardly gave her parents a backward glance.

Which of these two children do you think will have an easier time in our society?

Classical psychoanalytic thought has held for years that such differences between children are created by early experience: perhaps Jason is wary of the world because he has not learned to trust, while Vicky's experiences have been more positive. A major body of research, however, strongly suggests that shyness and boldness are inborn characteristics, which are related to various physiological functions and which tend to stay with people throughout life. These traits do not seem related to sex or socioeconomic class (Plomin, 1989).

Jerome Kagan, a professor of psychology at Harvard University, has conducted a series of longitudinal studies of some 400 children who were followed for over 5 years, starting at just under 2 years of age (Garcia-Coll, Kagan, & Reznick, 1984; Kagan, 1989; Kagan, Reznick, Clarke, Snidman, & Garcia-Coll, 1984; Reznick et al., 1986; Robinson, Kagan, Reznick, & Corley, 1992). Shyness, or what these researchers call "inhibition to the unfamiliar," was marked in about

Shyness seems to be inborn, to be related to various physiological functions, and to persist into adulthood. Should parents try to help a shy child, like this boy, become more outgoing; or should they try to help the child accept his or her personality as it is? Or should they try to do both? *(Rick Friedman/Black Star)*

10 to 15 percent of the children, first showing up at 21 months of age and persisting in most cases at 7½ years. The opposite trait, "boldness," or comfort in strange situations, was also especially strong in about 10 to 15 percent. Most of the children fell between the two extremes.

Both the genetic influence and the stability of the trait were strongest for the children at either extreme, whose personality characteristics were associated with various physiological signs that may give clues to the heritability of the traits. When asked to solve problems or learn new information, the very shy children had higher and less variable heart rates than the middle-range and bolder children, and the pupils of the shy children's eyes dilated more. The

shy children seemed to feel more anxious in situations that the other youngsters did not find particularly stressful.

A genetic factor in shyness also showed up in another study. Two-year-olds who had been adopted soon after birth closely resembled their biological mothers in terms of shyness. However, these babies also resembled their adoptive mothers, showing an environmental influence as well (Daniels & Plomin, 1985). The parents of shy babies tended to have less active social lives, exposing neither themselves nor their babies to new social situations. This was true for the adoptive parents, and even more so for biological parents raising their own children.

Thus, there is an intertwining of factors. While a *tendency* toward shyness may be inherited, the environment can either accentuate or modify this tendency. Some shy children become more outgoing and spontaneous, apparently in response to parents' efforts to help them become more comfortable with new people and situations.

In some societies children are encouraged to stay close to their parents, not to speak, and to hold back in the presence of strangers. Our society, however, values boldness. Therefore, parents are often advised to help shy children become more outgoing, by protecting them from as much stress as possible, by teaching them coping skills for stressful situations, and by bringing other children into the home. "Parents need to push their children—gently and not too much—into doing the things they fear" (Kagan, in J. Asher, 1987). In the long run, though, would it perhaps be better if society itself changed to place more value on all types of personalities? If so, how could this be done?

O/D AGE

tem, sometimes associated with epilepsy (*Diagnostic and Statistical Manual of Mental Disorders*, 3d ed., rev. [DSM III-R], 1987). New research has revealed that the brain of an autistic person is not fully developed and that the interference with development seems to occur either during early prenatal life or during the first or second year after birth (Courchesne, Yeung-Courchesne, Press, Hesselink, & Jernigan, 1988). Since concordance between identical twins is much higher than for fraternal twins (96 percent versus 23 percent, according to Ritvo, Freeman, Mason-Brothers, Mo, & Ritvo, 1985), autism is probably inherited, perhaps through a recessive gene, and the impact of the environment is minimal. Fortunately, the disorder is very rare (about 3 cases per 10,000 people).

Depression

The serious clinical syndrome called *depression* is different from normal temporary sadness. It is an affective disorder (a disorder of mood) in which a person feels unhappy and often has trouble eating, sleeping, or concentrating. It seems to involve a variety of causes, mechanisms, and symptoms. Some 6 percent of American adults are depressed in any 6-month period (J. K. Myers et al., 1984). Children—even infants—may also become depressed (see Chapter 9).

Since 1950, studies in countries including the United States, Canada, Sweden, Germany, Italy, Lebanon, Taiwan, and New Zealand have shown increasing rates of depression (Cross-National Collaborative Group, 1992; Klerman & Weissman, 1989). Depression affects more people and strikes earlier, in adolescence and young adulthood. Women are 2 to 3 times as likely as men to be depressed, but this imbalance is narrowing as more young men are affected. These trends have not shown up in studies of Koreans, Puerto Ricans, or Mexican Americans (Cross-National Collaborative Group, 1992; Klerman & Weissman, 1989).

Clearly, depression has a strong genetic basis. It is 2 to 3 times higher in close relatives of depressed people than in the general population (Klerman & Weissman, 1989). Identical twins have a 70 percent concordance rate, while fraternal twins, other siblings, and parents and children have only a 15 percent concordance rate (USDHHS, 1981b).

However, heredity cannot be the entire story, or we would not have seen significantly higher rates of depression over the past 40 years: genes are not likely to change in such a short time. Apparently, many forms of depression result from interaction between an inherited biochemical sensitivity and life stresses. Some stresses are physical, like bodily illness, changes in the chemistry of the central nervous system, and effects of various drugs. Others, however, are psychological, including changes in family stucture, shifts in male and female roles, increasing urbanization, and greater geographic mobility that disrupts networks of relationships (Cross-National Collaborative Group, 1992; Klerman & Weissman, 1989). Because of hereditary factors, different people respond to the same environment in different ways.

The Importance of the Environment

The power of heredity is great—but so is the power of environment. Recent efforts to acknowledge the role of genetics may have gone too far, attributing too much human outcome to our genes. According to one team of behavioral geneticists, research indicates that environmental factors are at least as important as genetic factors (Plomin & Rende, 1991). Since the heritability of a trait generally does not exceed 50 percent, there is a great deal of room for environmental influences.

One particularly important force is a person's *individual* environment, within the family as well as outside it. Even within the same family, every child grows up in a different environment. For example, Sally's daughter Nancy was a first baby, born to a 23-year-old mother who had worked in an advertising agency until 3 weeks before the birth, had been married just over 1 year, and lived 500 miles from any relatives. Her second child, Jennifer, had an older sibling and a family that was better established in the community and living in a suburban house rather than an apartment. Dorri, the third daughter, had two older sisters, a mother who was restless and wanted to go back to work, a father who had recently taken a new job in New York, and loving grandparents who lived nearby.

These are just a few of the obvious differences within one family. In addition, there were, of course, differences in the way the same parents reacted to each child's personality. Moreover, other events in these children's lives—illnesses, injuries, the schools they went to, the friends they made, and other individual experiences—also became environmental influences. It is easy to see, then, why even children growing up in the same family are not very similar. Usually, in fact, siblings are more different than alike. Correlations among sib-

GENETIC PRE-DISPOSITION

lings are only about .40 for cognitive abilities, and about .20 for personality (Plomin, 1989).

PRENATAL DEVELOPMENT

Many overlapping influences, then—both hereditary traits and environmental factors—affect everyone from the moment of conception onward. Some of the most far-reaching of these numerous influences come to bear during the prenatal period, long before an infant leaves the womb.

STAGES OF PRENATAL DEVELOPMENT

Prenatal development proceeds according to genetic instructions, from a single cell to an extremely complex being. This development before birth, called *gestation*, takes place in three stages: germinal, embryonic, and fetal. A month-by-month description is given in Table 2-3. Let's look at some of the highlights of each stage.

Germinal Stage (Fertilization to about 2 Weeks)

During the *germinal stage*, the organism divides, becomes more complex, and is implanted in the wall of the uterus.

Within 36 hours after fertilization, the single-cell zygote enters a period of rapid cell division. Seventy-two hours after fertilization, it has divided into 32 cells; a day later it has divided into 64 cells. Cell division continues until the original cell has become the 800 billion or more cells that make up the adult human body.

While the fertilized egg is dividing, it is also making its way down the fallopian tube to the uterus, a journey of 3 or 4 days. Meanwhile, its form has changed into a fluid-filled sphere, a *blastocyst,* which then floats freely in the uterus for a day or two. Some cells around the edge of the blastocyst cluster on one side to form the *embryonic disk*, a thickened cell mass from which the baby will develop. This mass is already differentiating into two layers. The upper layer, the *ectoderm,* will become the nails, hair, teeth, sensory organs, the outer layer of skin, and the nervous system, including the brain and spinal cord. The lower layer, the *endoderm,* will develop into the digestive system, liver, pancreas, salivary glands, and respiratory system. Later, a middle layer, the *mesoderm,* will develop and differentiate into the inner layer

of skin, muscles, skeleton, and excretory and circulatory systems.

During the germinal stage, other parts of the blastocyst develop into the nurturing and protective organs: the *placenta*, the *umbilical cord,* and the *amniotic sac.* The placenta, which has several important functions, is connected to the embryo by the umbilical cord, through which it delivers oxygen and nourishment to the embryo and removes its body wastes. The placenta also helps to combat internal infection and protects the unborn child from various diseases. It produces the hormones that support pregnancy and prepare the mother's breasts for lactation. The amniotic sac, a fluid-filled membrane, encases the baby, protecting it and giving it room to move.

The *trophoblast,* the outer cell layer of the blastocyst, produces tiny threadlike structures that penetrate the lining of the uterine wall. In this way, the blastocyst burrows into the wall of the uterus until it is implanted in a nesting place where it will receive nourishment from the mother's body. Upon implantation, the blastocyst has about 150 cells; when it is fully implanted in the uterus, it is an embryo (see Figure 2-11 on page 73).

Embryonic Stage (2 to 8–12 Weeks)

During the *embryonic stage*—the second stage of gestation—the major body systems (respiratory, alimentary, nervous) and organs develop.

Because of its rapid growth and development, the embryo is very vulnerable to environmental influences. Almost all developmental birth defects (like cleft palate, incomplete or missing limbs, blindness, and deafness) occur during the critical first 3 months of pregnancy. The most severely defective embryos usually do not survive beyond this time and are aborted spontaneously.

A *spontaneous abortion*, commonly called a *miscarriage*, is the expulsion from the uterus of a conceptus (prenatal organism) that cannot survive outside the womb. Three out of four spontaneous abortions occur within the first 3 months, affecting an estimated 31 percent of all pregnancies (Wilcox et al., 1988). A woman's risk of dying from a spontaneous abortion, while quite small, is greater after the first 3 months (S. M. Berman, MacKay, Grimes, & Binkin, 1985).

In ancient times, people believed that miscarriage could be brought on by the pregnant woman's fear of a sudden loud thunderclap, for example, or by jostling when her chariot hit a rut in the

TABLE 2-3

Development of Embryo and Fetus

Approximate Date	Description
1 month 	During the first month, the new life grows more quickly than at any other time during its life, achieving a size 10,000 times greater than the zygote. It now measures from ¼ to ½ inch in length. Blood is flowing through its tiny veins and arteries. Its minuscule heart beats 65 times a minute. It already has the beginnings of a brain, kidneys, a liver, and a digestive tract. The umbilical cord, its lifeline to its mother, is working. By looking very closely through a microscope, it is possible to see the swellings on the head that will eventually become its eyes, ears, mouth, and nose. Its sex cannot yet be distinguished.
2 months 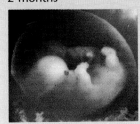	The embryo is less than 1 inch long and weighs only ¹⁄₁₃ ounce. Its head is one-half its total body length. Facial parts are clearly developed, with tongue and teeth buds. Arms have hands, fingers, and thumbs, and legs have knees, ankles, and toes. It has a thin covering of skin and can make hand and foot prints. The embryo's brain impulses coordinate the function of its organ systems. Sex organs are developing; the heartbeat is steady. The stomach produces digestive juices; the liver, blood cells. The kidneys remove uric acid from the body. The skin is now sensitive enough to react to tactile stimulation. If an aborted 8-week-old embryo is stroked, it reacts by flexing its trunk, extending its head, and moving back its arms.
3 months 	The developing person, now a fetus, weighs 1 ounce and measures about 3 inches in length. It has fingernails, toenails, eyelids (still closed), vocal cords, lips, and a prominent nose. Its head is still large—about one-third its total length—and its forehead is high. Its sex can be easily determined. The organ systems are functioning, so that the fetus may now breathe, swallow amniotic fluid in and out of the lungs, and occasionally urinate. Its ribs and vertebrae have turned to cartilage, and its internal reproductive organs have primitive egg or sperm cells. The fetus can now make a variety of specialized responses: it can move its legs, feet, thumbs, and head; open and close its mouth; and swallow. If its eyelids are touched, it squints; if its palm is touched, it makes a partial fist; if its lip is touched, it will suck; and if the sole of the foot is stroked, the toes will fan out. These reflex behaviors will be present at birth but will disappear during the first months of life.
4 months 	The body is catching up to the head, which is now only one-fourth the total body length, the same proportion it will be at birth. The fetus now measures 6 to 10 inches and weighs about 7 ounces. The umbilical cord is as long as the fetus and will continue to grow with it. The placenta is now fully developed, and all organs are formed. The mother may be able to feel the fetus kicking, a movement known as *quickening,* which some societies and religious groups consider the beginning of human life. The reflex activities that appeared in the third month are now brisker, because of increased muscular development.
5 months 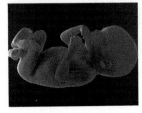	The fetus, now weighing about 12 ounces to 1 pound and measuring about 1 foot, begins to show signs of an individual personality. It has definite sleep-wake patterns, has a favorite position in the uterus (called its *lie*), and becomes more active—kicking, stretching, squirming, and even hiccuping. By putting an ear to the mother's abdomen, it is possible to hear the fetal heartbeat. The sweat and sebaceous glands are functioning. The respiratory system is not yet adequate to sustain life outside the womb; a baby born at this time typically does not survive. Coarse hair has begun to grow on the eyebrows and eyelashes, fine hair is on the head, and a woolly hair called *lanugo* covers the body.

(continued)

TABLE 2-3   (Continued)

Approximate Date	Description
6 months 	The rate of fetal growth has slowed down a little—the fetus is now about 14 inches long and weighs 1¼ pounds. It is getting fat pads under the skin; the eyes are complete, opening and closing and looking in all directions. It can maintain regular breathing for 24 hours; it cries; and it can make a fist with a strong grip. If the fetus were to be born now, it would have a slim chance of survival because its breathing apparatus is still very immature. There have been instances, however, when a fetus of this age has survived outside the womb, and these are becoming more common.
7 months 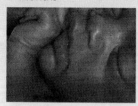	The fetus, about 16 inches long and weighing 3 to 5 pounds, has fully developed reflex patterns. It cries, breathes, swallows, and may suck its thumb. The lanugo may disappear at about this time, or it may remain until shortly after birth. Head hair may continue to grow. Survival chances for a fetus weighing at least 3½ pounds are fairly good, provided it receives intensive medical attention. It will probably have to live in an isolette until a weight of 5 pounds is attained.
8 months 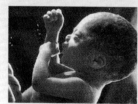	The fetus is now about 18 to 20 inches long and weighs between 5 and 7½ pounds. Its movements are curtailed because it is fast outgrowing its living quarters. During this month and the next, a layer of fat is developing over the fetus's entire body to enable it to adjust to varying temperatures outside the womb.
9 months 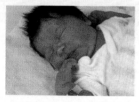	About a week before birth, the baby stops growing, having reached an average weight of about 7½ pounds and a length of about 20 inches, with boys tending to be a little longer and heavier than girls. Fat pads continue to form, the organ system is operating more efficiently, the heart rate increases, and more wastes are expelled. The reddish color of the skin is fading. On its birth day, the fetus will have been in the womb for approximately 266 days, although gestation age is usually estimated at 280 days, since doctors date the pregnancy from the mother's last menstrual period.

Note: Even in these early stages, individuals differ. The figures and descriptions given here represent averages.

street. Today we realize that the *normal* conceptus is well protected from almost all such jolts. About half of all spontaneous abortions are associated with chromosomal abnormalities (Ash, Vennart, & Carter, 1977). Most other miscarriages result from a defective ovum or sperm, an unfavorable location for implantation, a breakdown in the supply of oxygen or nourishment caused by abnormal de-velopment of the umbilical cord, or some physiologic abnormality of the mother.

Fetal Stage (8–12 Weeks to Birth)

With the appearance of the first bone cells at about 8 weeks, the embryo begins to become a fetus, and by 12 weeks it is fully in the *fetal stage*, the final

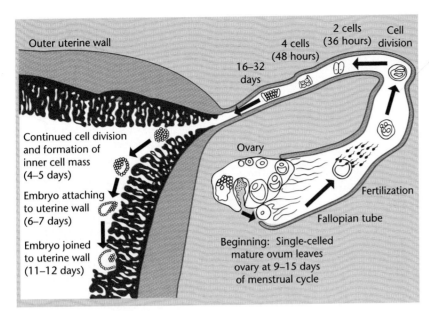

FIGURE 2-11
How an ovum becomes an embryo.

stage of gestation. From now until birth, the finishing touches are put on the various body parts, and the body changes in form and eventually grows about 20 times in length. Babies born as early as 22 weeks sometimes survive.

The fetus is far from being a passive passenger in its mother's womb. It kicks, turns, flexes its body, somersaults, squints, swallows, makes a fist, hiccups, and sucks its thumb. It responds to both sound and vibrations, showing that it can hear and feel. Its brain continues to develop.

Even within the womb, each of us is unique. Fetuses' activities vary in amount and kind, and their heart rates vary in regularity and speed. Some of these patterns seem to persist into adulthood, supporting the notion of inborn temperament.

THE PRENATAL ENVIRONMENT

Only recently have we become aware of some of the myriad environmental influences that can affect the developing fetus. The role of the father, for example, used to be almost ignored. Today we know that various environmental factors can affect a man's sperm—and the children he conceives. While the mother's role has been recognized far longer, we are still discovering many elements that can affect her fetus. (Box 2-4 suggests what prospective mothers can do to have a healthy pregnancy.)

Maternal Factors

Most of our knowledge about prenatal hazards comes from animal research or from studies in which mothers reported on such factors as what they had eaten while pregnant, what drugs they had taken, how much radiation they had been exposed to, and what illnesses they had contracted. Both these methods have limitations: it is not always accurate to apply findings from animals to human beings, and people do not always remember what they did in the past.

Various influences in the prenatal environment affect different fetuses differently. Some environmental factors that are *teratogenic,* or birth defect–producing, in some cases have little or no effect in others. Research suggests that the timing of an environmental event, its intensity, and its interaction with other factors are all relevant.

Prenatal Nourishment

Why Is Prenatal Nutrition Important? Babies develop best when their mothers eat well. A woman's diet *before* as well as during pregnancy is crucial to her child's future health. Diet during pregnancy may be even more vital. Pregnant women who gain between 22 and 46 pounds are less likely to miscarry or to bear stillborn or low-birthweight babies (Abrams & Parker, 1990).

Well-nourished mothers bear healthier babies, while mothers with inadequate diets are more

BOX 2-4   PRACTICALLY SPEAKING

REDUCING RISKS DURING PREGNANCY

Women can help ensure the best prenatal environment for their children by following these guidelines:

■ *Begin good medical care early:* Even a low-risk pregnancy can become high-risk if prenatal care is absent or poor. See a qualified practitioner regularly, beginning as soon as you suspect you are pregnant. If you are in a high-risk category, use an obstetrician who has experience with your condition. Participate actively in your medical care by asking questions and reporting symptoms.

■ *Eat well:* Eat a balanced diet to increase your odds of having a successful pregnancy and a healthy baby, and to prevent various disorders of pregnancy.

■ *Be fit:* If you didn't begin pregnancy with a well-toned, exercised body, start to get fit now. Regular moderate exercise pre-

vents constipation and improves respiration, circulation, muscle tone, and skin elasticity, all of which contribute to a more comfortable pregnancy and an easier, safer delivery.

■ *Gain weight sensibly:* Gain weight gradually, steadily, and moderately to help prevent a variety of complications, including diabetes, hypertension, varicose veins, hemorrhoids, and a difficult delivery owing to an overly large fetus.

■ *Don't smoke:* Stop smoking as early in pregnancy as possible to reduce risks to yourself and the baby.

■ *Don't drink alcohol:* Stop drinking to reduce the risk of birth defects, particularly of fetal alcohol syndrome.

■ *Don't take drugs:* Avoid taking any drugs that are not essential and prescribed by your doctor when you are pregnant or breastfeeding.

■ *Prevent infections or treat them promptly:* Try to prevent all infections—from common colds and flu to urinary tract and vaginal infections to the increasingly common sexually transmitted diseases—whenever possible. If you do contract an infection, have it treated promptly by a physician who knows you are pregnant.

■ *Don't try to be Superwoman:* Resist the temptation to overachieve and overdo. Getting enough rest during pregnancy is far more important then getting everything done, especially in high-risk pregnancies. If your doctor recommends that you begin your maternity leave earlier than you've planned, take the advice.

SOURCE: Adapted from A. Eisenberg, Murkoff, & Hathaway, 1986, p. 52.

---

likely to bear premature or low-birthweight infants, babies who are stillborn (born dead) or die soon after birth, or babies whose brains do not develop normally (J. L. Brown, 1987; Read, Habicht, Lechtig, & Klein, 1973; Winick, Brasel, & Rosso, 1972). In low-income families, other kinds of deprivation may aggravate the effects of poor nutrition.

Malnourished pregnant women who take dietary supplements have bigger, healthier, more active, and more visually alert infants (J. L. Brown, 1987; Vuori et al., 1979). In addition, better-nourished mothers tend to breastfeed longer, thus benefiting their babies (Read et al., 1973). Furthermore, recent findings point to a reduced risk of neural-tube defects in the babies of women who received supplements of folic acid (a vitamin in the B group) even before pregnancy, leading to the recommendation that all women of childbearing age receive

this vitamin (MRC Vitamin Study Research Group, 1991; Werler, Shapiro, & Mitchell, 1993).

The great importance of a pregnant woman's diet has emerged in recent findings about the devastating results of a lack of folic acid. In the 1980s, scientists connected the fact that China has the highest incidence in the world of babies born with neural tube defects (like anencephaly or spina bifida) with the timing of the babies' conception. Traditionally, Chinese couples marry at the time of the New Year, in January or February, and try to conceive as soon as possible after marriage.

Conception often occurs in the barren winter when rural women have few fresh fruits and vegetables. As a result, their diet is lacking in folic acid. After medical detective work established the lack of folic acid as a potent cause of these defects,

China embarked on a mass program to give folic acid supplements to prospective mothers (Tyler, 1994).

What Should Pregnant Women Eat? A well-balanced daily diet for pregnant women includes foods from each of the following categories: protein (meat and meat alternatives), dairy products, bread and cereals, fruits and vegetables rich in vitamin C, dark-green vegetables, other fruits and vegetables (including yellow ones rich in vitamin A), and fats and oils. Women need to eat more than usual when pregnant: typically, 300 to 500 more calories a day, including extra protein (Winick, 1981). Teenagers, women who are ill or undernourished or under stress, and those who took birth control pills until shortly before pregnancy need extra nutrients (J. E. Brown, 1983).

Maternal Drug Intake

Practically everything the mother takes in makes its way to the new life in her uterus. Drugs may cross the placenta, just as oxygen, carbon dioxide, and water do. Each year as many as 375,000 infants may be affected by their mothers' drug abuse during pregnancy (Silverman, 1989). The organism is especially vulnerable in its first few months, when development is most rapid. Thus drugs taken early in pregnancy have the strongest effects.

A number of extremely serious problems have shown up in a mother's—or father's—use of drugs. Some of these problems can be treated if the presence of a drug in a newborn baby's body can be detected early. But it is often difficult to determine exactly which drugs a person has taken, since doctors usually have to rely on the parents' own, often inaccurate, testimony.

A new test for the presence of drugs in a newborn's system analyzes the baby's meconium, the fetal waste matter that is excreted during the first few days after birth. By doing this with 3010 newborns from a high-risk urban population, researchers found that 44 percent tested positive for cocaine, morphine, or cannabinoid, the active ingredient in marijuana, even though only 11 percent of the mothers had admitted to using drugs (Ostrea, Brady, Gause, Raymundo, & Stevens, 1992). It is clear that the technique used to assess the extent of drug abuse influences the result. Since identifying these babies early can make a major

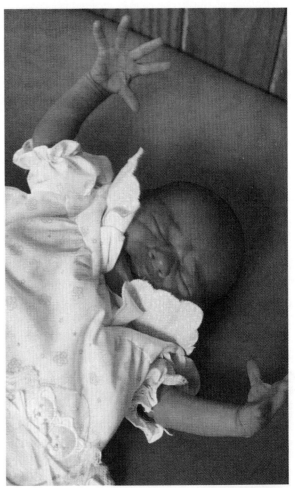

Babies whose mothers used cocaine during pregnancy begin life with massive problems. Many are preterm and small, many have neurological problems, and many, like this 1-month-old baby girl, cry for long periods of time and cannot be comforted. *(Steve Leonard/Black Star)*

difference in their lives, it is important to be as accurate as possible. Let's look now at the effects on children of their mothers' use of various drugs.

Medical Drugs Drugs known to be harmful include the antibiotics streptomycin and tetracycline; the sulfanomides; excessive amounts of vitamins A, B_6, C, D, and K; certain barbiturates, opiates, and other central nervous system depressants; several hormones, including birth control pills (Bracken, Holford, White, & Kelsey, 1978), progestin, diethylstilbestrol (DES), androgen, and synthetic estrogen; Accutane, a drug often prescribed for severe acne (Lott, Bocian, Pribram, & Leitner, 1984); and even aspirin (Stuart, Gross,

Elrad, & Graeber, 1982). The American Academy of Pediatrics (AAP) Committee on Drugs (1982) recommends that *no* medication be prescribed for a pregnant or breastfeeding woman unless it is essential for her own or her child's health.

The effects of taking a drug during pregnancy do not always show up immediately. In the late 1940s and early 1950s, the synthetic hormone diethylstilbestrol (DES) was widely prescribed (ineffectually, as it turned out) to prevent miscarriage. Years later, when the daughters of women who had taken DES during pregnancy reached puberty, about 1 in 1000 developed a rare form of vaginal or cervical cancer (Melnick, Cole, Anderson, & Herbst, 1987). "DES daughters" also have had more trouble bearing their own children, with higher risks of miscarriage or premature delivery (A. Barnes et al., 1980), and "DES sons" seem to show a higher rate of infertility and reproductive abnormalities (Stenchever et al., 1981). Therefore, all children of women who took DES during pregnancy should get regular medical checkups.

Alcohol   Each year in the United States, more than 40,000 babies are born with alcohol-related birth defects. About 1 infant in 750, according to American and European studies, suffers from *fetal alcohol syndrome (FAS),* a combination of slowed prenatal and postnatal growth, facial and bodily malformations, and disorders of the central nervous system. Central nervous system problems can involve poor sucking response, brain-wave abnormalities, and sleep disturbances in infancy; and, throughout childhood, a short attention span, restlessness, irritability, hyperactivity, learning disabilities, and motor impairments.

Some of the problems of FAS recede after birth; but problems like retardation, learning disabilities and hyperactivity persist into adulthood, and some malformations require surgery (Charness, Simon, & Greenberg, 1989; Streissguth et al., 1991).

For every child with fetal alcohol syndrome (about 6 percent of the offspring of alcoholic mothers), as many as 10 others may be born with *fetal alcohol effects,* a less severe condition that can include mental retardation, retardation of intrauterine growth, and minor congenital abnormalities.

Even moderate drinking may harm the fetus. A study of nearly 32,000 pregnancies found that the risk of fetal growth retardation increases if the mother has even one or two drinks a day. The effect increased sharply with heavier alcohol intake; taking less than one drink a day had a minimal ef-

fect (Mills, Graubard, Harley, Rhoads, & Berendes, 1984). Another study found that 4-year-old children of mothers who had 3 or more drinks a day in the first month of pregnancy scored an average of 5 points less on IQ tests than the average for the other children in the study (Streissguth, Barr, Sampson, Darby, & Martin, 1989). But not all the children were affected.

Because *no* level of drinking has been clearly established as "safe," women should avoid alcohol completely during pregnancy—better yet, from the time they begin *thinking* about becoming pregnant until they stop breastfeeding (AAP Committee on Substance Abuse and Committee on Children with Disabilities, 1993). One study showed that breastfed babies of mothers who have one or two drinks a day are slightly slower learning to crawl and walk (Little, Anderson, Ervin, Worthington-Roberts, & Clarren, 1989).

Marijuana   Evidence is mounting that heavy marijuana use by pregnant women can lead to birth defects. Researchers analyzed the cries of newborns in Jamaica (where marijuana use is common) and concluded that a mother's heavy use affects her infant's nervous system (Lester & Dreher, 1989). A Canadian study found transient neurological disturbances, like tremors and startles, and higher rates of premature and small-for-date infants (Fried, Watkinson, & Willan, 1984). Another study found a link between marijuana use just before and during pregnancy and a childhood cancer—acute lymphoblastic leukemia—possibly because of pesticide contamination of the cannabis leaves (Robison et al., 1989). In sum, women of childbearing age should not use marijuana.

Nicotine   Pregnant smokers are at higher risk than nonsmokers of bearing preterm and small-for-date babies, and of complications ranging from bleeding during pregnancy to death of the fetus or newborn. (Armstrong, McDonald, & Sloan, 1992; Landesman-Dwyer & Emanuel, 1979; McDonald, Armstrong, & Sloan, 1992b; Sexton & Hebel, 1984). However, women who cut down on smoking during pregnancy tend to have bigger babies than those who continue to smoke at previous levels (Li, Windsor, Perkins, Goldenberg, & Lowe, 1993).

Smoking in pregnancy seems to have some of the same effects on school-age children as drinking in pregnancy: poor attention span, hyperactivity, learning problems, perceptual-motor and linguistic losses, social maladjustment, poor IQ scores, low grade placement, and minimal brain dysfunction (Landesman-Dwyer & Emanuel, 1979; Naeye & Peters, 1984; Streissguth et al., 1984; Wright et al., 1983). A Swedish study found that children whose mothers smoke 10 or more cigarettes a day during pregnancy run a 50 percent greater risk than other children of contracting a childhood cancer (Stjernfeldt, Berglund, Lindsten, & Ludvigsson, 1986). Of course, since women who smoke during pregnancy also tend to smoke after the birth, it is hard to separate the effects of prenatal and postnatal exposure.

In one study of 2256 children aged 4 to 11, those whose mothers smoked at least a pack a day after pregnancy were twice as likely to be anxious, disobedient, or hyperactive or to exhibit some other behavior problem than were children of non-smokers. The effect was dose-related; that is, it was more pronounced in children whose mothers smoked more than a pack a day. And the risk was not lessened if the mother had stopped smoking during pregnancy but resumed afterward (Weitzman, Gortmaker, & Sobol, 1992). It is possible that smoking during pregnancy may alter the child's brain structure or function, with resulting long-term effects on behavior; that passive exposure to cigarette smoke after birth may affect a child's central nervous system; that smoking may alter the mother's behavior, thus affecting her child's; or that mothers who smoke may be less tolerant of their children's behavior.

Opiates   Women addicted to such drugs as morphine, heroin, and codeine are likely to bear premature, addicted babies who show effects until at least age 6. Addicted newborns are restless and irritable and often have tremors, convulsions, fever, vomiting, and breathing difficulties; they are twice as likely to die soon after birth as nonaddicted babies (Cobrinick, Hood, & Chused, 1959; Henly & Fitch, 1966; Ostrea & Chavez, 1979). As older babies, they cry often and are less alert and less responsive (Strauss, Lessen-Firestone, Starr, & Ostrea, 1975). And in early childhood—from approximately ages 3 to 6—they weigh less, are shorter, are less well adjusted, and score lower on tests of perceptual and learning abilities (G. Wilson, McCreary, Kean, & Baxter, 1979). Long-term follow-up studies on these children have found that they tend not to do well in school, are unusually anxious in social situations, and have trouble making friends (Householder, Hatcher, Burns, & Chasnoff, 1982).

Cocaine   Since cocaine (including crack, its smokable form) is now reported to be the number one illicit drug used by pregnant women in the United States (Schutter & Brinker, 1992), its effects are of grave importance. Although the immediate medical results of a pregnant woman's use of cocaine (such as prematurity, low birthweight, and smaller head circumference) are well known, little is known about later developmental consequences. It seems, though, that organizational and language skills and secure emotional attachment may be affected for the worse (Hawley & Disney, 1992). Pregnant cocaine users have a higher rate of spontaneous abortion, and their babies are at greater risk of neurological problems. Cocaine use seems to interfere with the flow of blood through the placenta, and it may act on fetal brain chemicals to cause behavioral change. These babies are not as alert as other babies, do not respond as well to various stimuli, and are more likely to be preterm, to weigh less, to be shorter and have smaller head circumferences at birth, and to have urinary tract defects (Chasnoff et al., 1989; Chasnoff, Griffith, Freier, & Murray, 1992; Chavez et al., 1989; Eisen et al., 1991; Hadeed & Siegel, 1989; Zuckerman et al., 1989).

Although babies whose mothers stopped using cocaine early in pregnancy grew as normally as babies of drug-free mothers, many were less alert and responsive. Cocaine-exposed newborns also showed more stress behaviors, such as tremors, restlessness, irritability, abnormal reflex behaviors, and excessive high-pitched crying (Eisen et al., 1991). Between ages 1 and 2 years, they scored lower on tests of infant mental development (Chasnoff et al., 1992).

Analysis of the cries of 160 infants, half of whom had been exposed to cocaine prenatally, found that the cocaine-exposed babies responded differently, depending partly on their health and birthweight (Lester et al., 1991). Low-birthweight babies exposed to cocaine tended to be sluggish and depressed, but, once provoked, they often screamed and were almost impossible to calm.

The baby's initial reaction to the effects of the drug was then influenced by the child's early environment. Drug-abusing parents are impaired themselves and often depressed, frequently leading to abuse or neglect of their children. Furthermore, the lethargic or irritable behavior of a cocaine-affected infant does not inspire loving feelings. So the fact that in early childhood, many of these children have trouble loving their parents,

NATURE
VS.
NURTURE

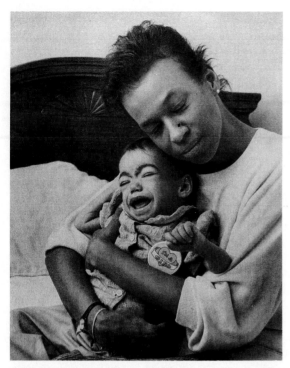

This 26-year-old mother contracted AIDS from her husband, who had gotten it from a former girlfriend, an intravenous drug user. The father died first of this modern plague, then the 21-month-old baby, and lastly the mother. *(Fred R. Conrad/The New York Times)*

making friends, and playing normally may stem from a self-perpetuating cycle of poor parenting. Furthermore, children of addicted mothers often face other environmental risks, such as poverty and unstable homes. But some studies have shown that cocaine-exposed infants can catch up in weight, length, and head circumference by 1 year of age (Weathers, Crane, Sauvain, & Blackhurst, 1993). They may also be able to catch up in other ways. So it is important for policymakers and people who care for such children not to give up on them—and to recognize that they can be helped after birth.

Caffeine Can the caffeine that a pregnant woman swallows in coffee, tea, cola, or chocolate cause trouble for her fetus? A recent study suggests that the amount of caffeine in 1½ to 3 cups of coffee a day may nearly double the risk of miscarriage, and drinking more than 3 cups nearly triples the risk (Infant-Rivard, Fernández, Gauthier, David, & Rivard, 1993). This conflicts with an earlier study that suggested that drinking up to 3 cups of cof-

fee a day during pregnancy does not increase the risk of miscarriage or affect fetal development (Mills, Holmes, Aarons, & Simpson, 1993). Because such serious questions remain, the U.S. Food and Drug Administration recommends that pregnant women avoid or use sparingly any food, beverages, or drugs that contain caffeine.

Other Maternal Factors

Illness A number of illnesses can have serious effects on the developing fetus, depending partly on *when* a pregnant woman gets sick.

Rubella (German measles) before the eleventh week of pregnancy is almost certain to cause deafness and heart defects in the baby; but the chance of these consequences drops to about 1 in 3 between 13 and 16 weeks of pregnancy and is almost nil after 16 weeks (E. Miller, Cradock-Watson, & Pollock, 1982). The syndrome can be prevented by immunizing women before pregnancy—ideally, by immunizing girls before puberty.

Diabetes, tuberculosis, and syphilis have also led to problems in fetal development, and both gonorrhea and genital herpes can have harmful effects on the baby at the time of delivery.

Acquired Immune Deficiency Syndrome Acquired immune deficiency syndrome (AIDS) may be contracted by a fetus if the mother has the disease or even has the human immunodeficiency virus (HIV) in her blood. The contents of the mother's blood are shared with the fetus through the placenta, and blood is a carrier of the virus that causes AIDS. HIV disproportionately affects disadvantaged women and children and is most often contracted by intravenous drug use or by sexual intercourse with a drug user.

An analysis of 721 children born to AIDS-infected mothers in 19 European locations found that premature babies are more susceptible, perhaps because they miss the protection of antibodies that may not appear until the last 3 months of gestation. Other associations were found with such birth complications as use of forceps and episiotomy. Babies delivered by cesarean surgery were less likely to be affected, but the researchers believe that it is premature to recommend surgical deliveries routinely. Breastfed infants of these mothers are more likely to develop the infection, but, still, in most populations breastfeeding is still to be preferred, unless the prevalence of HIV infection is very high or the difference in death rates between breastfed and bottle-fed babies is very low (European Collaborative Study, 1992; Lederman, 1992).

Although between 14 and 30 percent of HIV-positive mothers transmit the virus to their newborns, the Working Group on HIV Testing of Pregnant Women and Newborns (1990) does not believe that mandatory screening is called for. Instead, it favors informing all pregnant women and new mothers about AIDS and the tests for it and providing medical care to those who need it. One test can often detect the infection soon after birth, allowing the infant to be treated immediately with a drug approved for this condition. Early diagnosis and treatment are important, since children who acquire AIDS at about the time of birth often show symptoms before 1 year of age (Scott et al., 1989).

Incompatibility of Blood Types A problem resulting from the interaction of heredity with the prenatal environment is incompatibility of blood type between mother and baby. When a fetus's blood contains the *Rh factor*—a protein substance—but the mother's blood does not, antibodies in the mother's blood may attack the fetus and possibly bring about spontaneous abortion, stillbirth, jaundice, anemia, heart defects, mental retardation, or death. Usually the first Rh-positive baby is not affected, but with each succeeding pregnancy the risk becomes greater. A vaccine can now be given to an Rh-negative mother; when it is administered within 3 days after childbirth or abortion, it will prevent her body from making antibodies. Babies affected with Rh disease can be treated by repeated blood transfusions, sometimes before birth.

Medical X-rays We have known for more than 60 years that radiation can cause gene mutations, minor changes that alter a gene to produce a new, often harmful characteristic (D. P. Murphy, 1929). Although we don't know what exact dosage of x-rays will harm a fetus, the greatest potential for harm seems to occur early in pregnancy. Radiation exposure should be avoided, especially during the first 3 months (Kleinman, Cooke, Machlin, & Kessel, 1983). With the availability of ultrasound (see Box 2-3) medical x-rays are less necessary and less prevalent today than they were in the past.

Maternal Age What is the best age to have a baby?

In Chapter 11, we discuss the ramifications for teenage mothers and their babies, most of which are social rather than medical. The concerns for mothers past 30, however, have historically been for the physical well-being of mother and child. In recent years, as more women have delayed childbearing until the mid-thirties or even the forties, researchers have focused on the risks involved, and have come up with largely encouraging findings. In one group of almost 4000 pregnancies of mostly white, well-educated nonsmokers who received prenatal care, women over 35 had only a slightly higher risk of bearing unusually small babies and were no more likely to deliver prematurely or to have stillbirths than were younger first-time mothers (Berkowitz, Skovron, Lapinski, & Berkowitz, 1990). However, older mothers were twice as likely to have such complications of pregnancy as diabetes and high blood pressure. Furthermore, as women age, they become less fertile, are more likely to have miscarriages, and are more at risk of having children with birth defects.

Environmental Hazards Anything that affects a pregnant woman can affect her fetus: chemicals, radiation, extremes of heat and humidity, and other hazards of modern life. For example, babies whose mothers ate fish contaminated with PCBs (chemicals widely used in industry before they were banned in 1976) weighed less at birth, had smaller heads, and showed weaker reflexes and more jerky movements than infants whose mothers did not eat the fish; and they showed poor visual-recognition memory at 7 months and poor memory for words and numbers at 4 years (J. L. Jacobson, Jacobson, Fein, Schwartz, & Dowler, 1984; J. L. Jacobson, Jacobson, & Humphrey, 1990; S. W. Jacobson et al., 1985). At age 4, such children also tended to be less able to discriminate between visual stimuli and to have more problems with short-term memory (Jacobson, Jacobson, Padgett, Brumitt, & Billings, 1992).

Women who took saunas or soaked in hot tubs early in their pregnancies seem to run a higher risk of bearing babies with neural-tube defects (Milunsky et al., 1992).

Infants exposed to high levels of lead prenatally scored lower on intelligence tests than those exposed to low or moderate levels (Bellinger, Leviton, Watermaux, Needleman, & Rabinowitz, 1987; Needleman & Gatsonis, 1990). Children exposed prenatally to heavy metals showed higher rates of childhood illness and lower levels of performance on the McCarthy Scale of Children's Abilities (Lewis, Worobey, Ramsay, & McCormack, 1992). And a study conducted by researchers at Johns Hopkins University found that women who worked with chemicals widely used in manufacturing semiconductor chips had about double the rate of miscarriages as did women workers who did not handle the chemicals, suggesting a potential health risk (Markoff, 1992).

Radiation is especially dangerous. It affected Japanese infants after the atomic bomb explosions in Hiroshima and Nagasaki (Yamazaki & Schull, 1990) and German infants after the spill-out at the nuclear power plant at Chernobyl in the Soviet Union (West Berlin Human Genetics Institute, 1987). In utero exposure to radiation has been linked to greater risk of mental retardation, small head size, chromosomal malformations, Down syndrome, seizure, and poor performance on IQ tests and in school. The critical period seems to be 8 through 15 weeks after fertilization (Yamazaki & Schull, 1990).

Physical Activity   Fortunately, not all things an expectant mother does or is exposed to are harmful to a fetus. She can continue to jog, cycle, swim, play tennis, and so forth, since moderate exercise does not seem to endanger the fetuses of healthy women (Carpenter et al., 1988). A study of 45 women in mid-pregnancy who pedaled exercise bicycles found that only when the women were at the point of exhaustion did their fetuses show any decline in heart rate. Even in these cases, this decline was short-lived and occurred only just after the exercise was stopped; all the fetuses showed normal heart response within half an hour after the exercise session. Moreover, all the babies, except two who had unrelated complications, were fine at birth. The researchers recommend that pregnant women continue to exercise moderately—not pushing themselves to the limit and not raising their heart rate above 150—and that they taper off their workouts rather than stop abruptly.

Physically demanding, highly stressful work during pregnancy does not harm the mother or the baby either, at least in an otherwise healthy, financially secure population. Earlier research associated a woman's working long hours, working nights, or standing for long periods with high risks of preterm delivery. But in those studies, researchers were unable to separate factors related to poverty and poor medical care from the work

situation itself. To address this issue, one study compared the pregnancy outcomes of 4412 female resident physicians, who worked long hours in a stressful occupation, with those of 4236 wives of male classmates. The doctors were no more likely to deliver early than were the women in the control group (Klebanoff, Shiono, & Rhoads, 1990).

Paternal Factors: Environmental Influences Transmitted by the Father

The father, too, can transmit environmentally caused defects. Exposure to lead, marijuana and tobacco smoke, large amounts of alcohol and radiation, DES, and certain pesticides may result in the production of abnormal sperm (R. Lester & Van Theil, 1977). Associations have appeared between nervous system tumors in children and such occupations of their fathers as electrical or electronic worker, auto mechanic, miner, printer, paper or pulp mill worker, and aircraft industry worker (M. R. Spitz & Johnson, 1985). And one study showed a relationship between a paternal diet low in vitamin C and birth defects and certain types of cancers in the children (Fraga et al., 1991).

A harmful influence on both mother and baby is nicotine from a father's smoking. In one study, babies of fathers who smoked were lighter at birth by about 4 ounces per pack of cigarettes smoked per day by the father (or the cigar or pipe equivalent) (D. H. Rubin et al., 1986). Another study found that children of male smokers were twice as likely as other children to contract cancer as adults (Sandler, Everson, Wilcox, & Browder, 1985). In both studies, however, it was hard to distinguish between prebirth and childhood exposure to smoke.

A man's use of cocaine can also cause birth defects in his children, since cocaine seems to attach itself to his sperm. This cocaine-bearing sperm then enters the ovum at the time of conception. This research contradicts another earlier belief: that the significant drug exposure occurs when the baby's organs are developing, from 3 to 12 weeks into the pregnancy. It now appears that fathers must share the responsibility for such birth defects—not only those caused by cocaine, but also those caused by other toxins, such as lead and mercury, which might also "hitchhike" onto sperm in the same way (Yazigi, Odem, & Polakoski, 1991).

And it now seems that some drug-induced abnormalities may occur much earlier than previously thought, even before the fertilized ovum is implanted in the uterus. One route for the transmission of cocaine from the sperm to the baby may still lie with the mother, however. It is possible that when a cocaine-using woman has sexual intercourse, the man's sperm in her reproductive tract can pick up the drug and carry it to the ovum, where it will do its damage.

A later paternal age (average in the late thirties) is associated with increases in several rare conditions, including one type of dwarfism; Marfan's syndrome (deformities of the head and limbs); and a kind of bone malformation (G. Evans, 1976). The father's age may also be a factor in about 5 percent of cases of Down syndrome (Antonarakis & Down Syndrome Collaborative Group, 1991).

BIRTH

Birth is both a beginning and an end: the climax of all that has happened from the moment of fertilization through 9 months (or an average pregnancy of 266 days) of growth in the womb.

The uterine contractions that expel the fetus begin as mild tightenings of the uterus, each lasting 15 to 25 seconds. A woman may have felt similar contractions from time to time during the final months of pregnancy, but she can often recognize birth contractions as the "real thing" because of their greater regularity and intensity.

STAGES OF CHILDBIRTH

Childbirth, or labor, takes place in three stages (see Figure 2-12). The *first stage,* which is the longest, lasts an average of 12 to 24 hours for a woman having her first child. During this stage, uterine contractions cause the cervix to widen until it becomes large enough for the baby's head to pass through, a process called *dilation.* At the beginning of this stage, the contractions occur about every 8 to 10 minutes and last 30 seconds. Toward the end of labor they may come every 2 minutes and last 60 to 90 seconds. Women who have prepared for childbirth through special classes learn certain breathing techniques to make labor more comfortable.

The *second stage,* which typically lasts about 1½ hours, begins when the baby's head begins to move through the cervix into the vaginal canal, and it ends when the baby emerges completely from the mother's body. During the second stage,

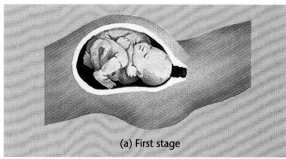

(a) First stage

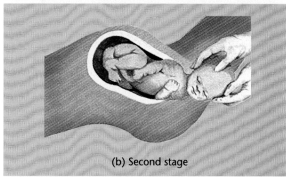

(b) Second stage

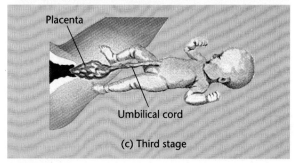

Placenta

Umbilical cord

(c) Third stage

FIGURE 2-12
Birth of a baby. (a) During the first stage of labor, a series of stronger and stronger contractions dilates the cervix, the opening to the mother's womb. (b) During the second stage, the baby's head moves down the birth canal and emerges from the vagina. (c) During the brief third stage, the placenta and umbilical cord are expelled from the womb. Then, the cord is cut. *(Adapted from Lagercrantz & Slotkin, 1986.)*

the "prepared" mother bears down hard with her abdominal muscles during each contraction, helping the baby in its efforts to leave her body. At the end of this stage, the baby is born. The umbilical cord, which is still attached to the placenta, is cut and clamped.

During the *third stage,* which lasts only a few minutes, what is left of the umbilical cord and the placenta are expelled.

In classes for expectant parents, mothers learn breathing and muscular exercises to make labor easier, and fathers learn how to assist through labor and delivery. *(Lawrence Migdale/Photo Researchers)*

METHODS OF CHILDBIRTH

Babies are delivered in a variety of ways. Historically, two concerns have been primary during delivery: the baby's safety and the mother's comfort. Another concern, growing sensitivity to the emotional needs of family members, has more recently resulted in efforts to bring the father and sometimes the other children into the experience.

Medicated Delivery

Most societies have evolved techniques to hasten delivery, make the mother's work easier, and lessen her discomfort. Most western women expect some pain relief during labor and delivery, usually a *medicated delivery*—that is, a delivery involving anesthesia. Anesthesia can be general, rendering the woman completely unconscious; or regional (local), blocking the nerve pathways that would carry the sensation of pain to the brain. Or the mother can receive a relaxing analgesic. All these drugs pass through the placenta to enter the fetal blood supply and tissues.

A number of studies have emphasized that obstetric medication involves dangers for the baby. Children have shown the effects of such medication as early as the first day of life, in poorer motor and physiologic responses (A. D. Murray, Dolby, Nation, & Thomas, 1981); and through the first year, in slower development in sitting, standing, and moving around (Brackbill & Broman, 1979).

In one study, the babies had caught up by 1 month of age, but their mothers felt differently about them (A. D. Murray et al., 1981). This could

be for one of two reasons. Many professionals believe that there is no such thing in human beings as a "maternal instinct." According to this theory, much of a woman's motherly feeling comes about because of her baby's behavior. An infant who nurses eagerly and acts alert sets up positive feelings in the mother. On the other hand, if the first encounters between mother and baby do not draw a strong reaction from the baby, the effects of this early impression may remain. It is also possible that mothers who choose unmedicated deliveries may feel more positive about parenting and that this attitude affects how they act with their babies.

However, in contradiction to these findings, one team of researchers compared babies born to medicated and nonmedicated mothers on several characteristics: strength and tactile sensitivity, activity and irritability, and sleep. They found *no* evidence of *any* drug effect (Kraemer, Korner, Anders, Jacklin, & Dimiceli, 1985). These investigators charge that research in this area has been poorly designed and misleading; that it may keep appropriate drugs from some mothers, making them suffer unnecessary pain and discomfort; and that it may cause others, who did receive drugs, to feel guilty.

Because the woman is the only person who can gauge her pain and is the most concerned about her child, she should have a strong voice in decisions about obstetric medication. The AAP Committee on Drugs (1978) recommends the minimum dose for relief of the mother's pain.

Alternative methods of childbirth, which we'll consider next, seek to minimize the use of harmful drugs while maximizing the parents' satisfaction as participants.

Natural and Prepared Childbirth

In 1914 a British physician, Dr. Grantly Dick-Read, claiming that fear causes most of the pain in childbirth, put forth the theory of *natural childbirth.* This method aims to eliminate fear by educating women in the physiology of reproduction and delivery and training them in breathing, relaxation, and physical fitness. By mid-century, Dr. Fernand Lamaze was using the psychoprophylactic method—*prepared childbirth*—substituting new breathing and muscular responses to the sensations of uterine contractions for the old responses of fear and pain.

The Lamaze method of prepared childbirth instructs women in anatomy to remove fear of the unknown and trains them to vary their patterns of breathing to match the strength of contractions and to concentrate on sensations other than the contractions. The mother learns to relax her muscles as a conditioned response to the voice of her "coach" (usually the father or a friend). Social support is also a factor. The coach attends classes with the expectant mother, takes part in the delivery, and helps with the exercises—enhancing her sense of self-worth and reducing her fear of being alone at the time of birth (Wideman & Singer, 1984).

Cesarean Delivery

Cesarean delivery is a surgical procedure to remove the baby from the uterus. Almost 1 in 4 babies are delivered in this way in the United States (nearly 1 million a year), an increase from 5.5 percent in 1970 to 23.5 percent in 1991 (Centers for Disease Control, 1993). The operation is commonly performed when labor is not progressing as quickly as it should, the baby seems to be in trouble, or the mother is bleeding vaginally. Often a cesarean is needed when the baby is in the breech position (head last) or in the transverse position (lying crosswise in the uterus), or when the head is too big to pass through the mother's pelvis.

Cesarean deliveries have a superior safety record in delivering breech babies (Sachs et al., 1983). But there is little evidence that they improve the overall survival of very low birthweight infants (Malloy, Rhoads, Schramm, & Land, 1989). And in a comparison of 21 countries, Notzon (1990) found no association between national cesarean rates and birth outcomes. Disadvantages of cesarean deliveries include a higher risk of maternal infection than in vaginal deliveries, a longer hospital stay and recovery from childbirth, greater expense, and the psychological and physical impact of any surgery (Sachs et al., 1983).

Also, the benefits need to be weighed against the risks, one of which is depriving the infant of the experience of labor. It now seems that the birth struggle may help the baby adjust to life outside the uterus (Lagercrantz & Slotkin, 1986). The stress of being born apparently stimulates the production in the infant's body of huge amounts of hormones called *catecholamines* (see Figure 2-13). This burst of catecholamines clears the lungs for breathing, mobilizes stored fuel for cell nourishment, and sends blood to the heart and brain. By sharpening

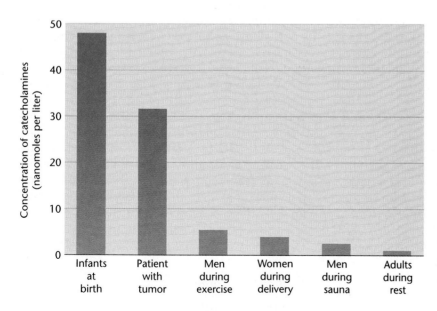

FIGURE 2-13
Stress hormones in newborn babies and adults. Umbilical samples from newborns show a level of stress hormones 20 times higher than that in resting adults. The surge of hormones during birth is also greater than that found in adults who are exercising or under great physical stress. *(Adapted from Lagercrantz & Slotkin, 1986.)*

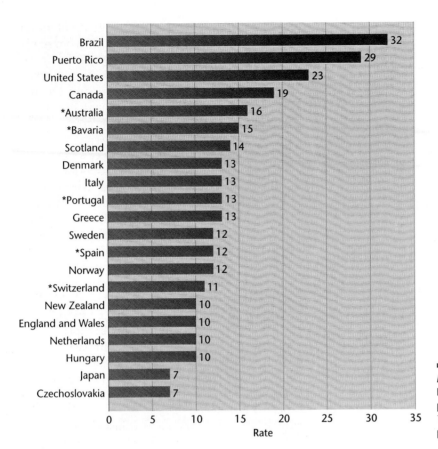

FIGURE 2-14
Rates of cesarean delivery per 100 hospital deliveries in selected countries, 1985. (Note: Asterisks indicate incomplete information.) *(Notzon, 1990.)*

the newborn's alertness, it may even foster early bonding between mother and child. Infants born by emergency cesarean surgery, after the onset of labor, show levels of catecholamines that are almost as high as vaginally born infants. But babies born through elective cesarean deliveries *before labor has begun* do not experience this surge of hormones, which seems to be triggered by contractions of the mother's uterus. The breathing problems that cesarean-delivered babies often suffer may be traceable to this lack of catecholamines, which help absorb liquid in the lungs.

Critics of current childbirth practices claim that too many unnecessary cesareans are performed, especially in the United States, where rates are among the highest in the world (see Figure 2-14). Perhaps in response to such criticism, the rate of increase has slackened since 1980 (Notzon, 1990).

Studies have linked cesarean rates with a number of nonmedical factors. For example, women with median family incomes of over $30,000 a year have cesarean deliveries at nearly twice the rate as women with median incomes under $11,000 (Gould, Davey, & Stafford, 1989). In a study of four Brooklyn hospitals, private physicians performed more cesareans than hospital residents did, possi-

bly because of concerns about being sued if a baby is born with problems, scheduling pressures, and less familiarity with new techniques to judge fetal distress (deRegt, Minkoff, Feldman, & Schwartz, 1986). More recent research also supports the association between cesarean delivery and the physician's opinion that she or he may be sued for malpractice (Localio et al., 1993).

A California study of more than 45,000 births to women who had had a previous cesarean delivery found that future babies were more likely to be delivered vaginally if the women had private medical insurance and if they went to a nonprofit teaching hospital with a high volume of births rather than a proprietary, nonteaching hospital with fewer births (Stafford, 1990). Two reports warn against the increasingly common practice of vaginal delivery in subsequent births after an initial cesarean delivery. Although most such births go well, there is some risk (1 in 100, according to one study) of rupturing the uterus, with potential injury to the baby (R. O. Jones et al., 1991).

Medical Monitoring

In *electronic fetal monitoring,* machines monitor

the fetal heartbeat throughout labor and delivery. This procedure provides valuable information (especially in detecting a lack of oxygen) for high-risk deliveries, including those of premature and low-birthweight babies and fetuses who seem to be in distress.

Routine monitoring in low-risk pregnancies, on the other hand, is costly and uncomfortable for the mother; it also results in twice as many deliveries by the riskier cesarean method, without corresponding improvements in outcome (Leveno et al., 1986; Lewin, 1988). Therefore it seems best *not* to perform continuous, routine monitoring when a pregnancy seems to be uncomplicated.

SETTINGS FOR CHILDBIRTH

Although 99 percent of babies born in the United States are born in hospitals and attended by physicians, a small but growing number of women with good medical histories and normal pregnancies are opting for more intimate, less impersonal settings. Some mothers elect to be attended by midwives, and to have their babies in the comfort of their homes or in small, homelike birth centers.

If a pregnancy is of low risk and the birth is uncomplicated, almost any of these arrangements can work well. It is often impossible to predict a sudden emergency during childbirth, however, and so it is vital to have backup plans in case of trouble. A good birth center has a contract with an ambu-

lance service, an agreement with a nearby hospital, and on-premises equipment for resuscitation and for administering oxygen. Provisions for a home birth should include arrangements for emergency transportation to a nearby hospital.

Many hospitals *are* big and impersonal, with rules that seem designed for the smooth functioning of the institution rather than for the benefit of the patients. But in recent years, as hospitals have competed for maternity cases, they have become more responsive to the desires of patients. Many now have birthing centers, where fathers or other birth coaches may remain with the mother during labor and delivery, and rooming-in policies that allow babies to stay in the mother's room for much or all of the day.

Freestanding maternity centers are usually staffed principally by nurse-midwives, with one or more physicians and nurse-assistants; they are designed for low-risk, uncomplicated births; and they offer prenatal care and birth in a homelike setting, with discharge the same day.

In many cultures, childbearing women are attended by a *doula*, a woman who has had a baby herself and can give emotional support to the mother. New research indicates that this practice can be very beneficial. In a study of 412 women having their first babies, 212 had a doula with them, while 200 did not (Kennell, Klaus, McGrath, Robertson, & Hinkley, 1991). The doula-present group had fewer cesarean deliveries, less use of anesthesia, shorter labors, and fewer forceps de-

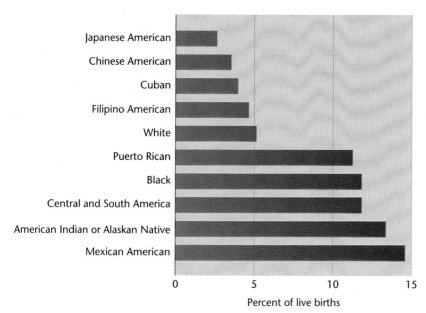

FIGURE 2-15
Proportion of mothers with late or no prenatal care, according to race and ethnicity of mother: United States, 1989. Early prenatal care is defined as care beginning in the first 3 months of pregnancy. Late prenatal care begins in the last 3 months. *(USDHHS, 1992, p. 37.)*

BOX 2-5   WINDOW ON THE WORLD

MATERNITY CARE IN WESTERN EUROPE AND THE UNITED STATES

Why do proportionately more babies die at or soon after birth in the United States compared with a number of western European countries? Why has this nation's rate of infant mortality risen over the past several decades in the world rankings? An answer may lie in differences in health care (Behrman, 1985; C. A. Miller, 1987).

Suppose you are a woman in one of 10 western European countries that have high standards of maternity care and entitlements to health services and social support (Belgium, Denmark, Germany, France, Ireland, Netherlands, Norway, Spain, Switzerland, and Great Britain). In all these countries you would receive either free or very low cost prenatal and postnatal care, including a paid maternity leave from work. Research has demonstrated that early prenatal care reduces rates of infant death, low birthweight, and other birth complications.

You would want to seek prenatal care early because only after your pregnancy was confirmed and officially registered would you begin to get benefits like transportation privileges and preferential hospital booking for delivery. You would probably go first to a general practitioner, who would coordinate your care with a midwife and an obstetrician. The midwife would give you most of your prenatal care and attend the birth—unless your pregnancy was considered high-risk, in which case a doctor would assist you.

If you had a complicated pregnancy, your midwife would visit you at home; in some countries you would receive such visits routinely.

After the baby was born, you would probably receive at least one home visit to get counseling about infant care, family planning, and your own health. If you were a single mother, you would get extra help; if you were an employed mother or the mother of a large family, you would get priority for day care and public housing. You would receive a monthly family allowance for each child, usually until adulthood or completion of education. And in most countries you would get a financial bonus at time of delivery to help pay for baby supplies and equipment. This bonus might hinge on the number of prenatal visits you made, and it might be larger if you breastfed.

In the Netherlands you could pay a token fee for a trained helper to stay with you for up to 8 hours a day for 10 days, helping you shop, cook, and take care of the baby and your other children. In Germany either you *or* your husband could take paid child-care leave, and unpaid leave might last for 3 years.

The bottom line is that as a pregnant woman in Europe, you would never need to ask how or where you would receive care or who would pay for it. As a pregnant woman in the United States, you would face a very different situation. You would not get the benefits of uniform national standards

for maternity care, and thus you would not be ensured of consistent, high-quality care. Furthermore, you could not count on financial coverage.

In the United States, about 24 percent of pregnant women do not receive care in the first 3 months, and those most at risk of bearing low-birthweight babies—teenage, minority, and unmarried women, and women with little education—get the least (S. S. Brown, 1985; Ingram, Makuc, & Kleinman, 1986; Singh, Forrest, & Torres, 1989; USDHHS, 1992). In 1989, about 5 percent of white mothers and 12 percent of African-American mothers had none at all or none until the last 3 months of pregnancy (see Figure 2-15). Latina women are 3 times as likely as other groups to receive no prenatal care at all (Council on Scientific Affairs of the American Medical Association, 1991).

This bleak picture might change if local and federal governments linked prenatal care to comprehensive social and financial benefits. There is need for a wide range of educational, social, and medical services (including outreach workers to identify women in need and help with transportation, baby-sitting, and housing problems). The state of New Jersey has launched a program offering a full range of prenatal health services to all women in the state (J. F. Sullivan, 1989). As more states follow suit, the future should be brighter for many American babies.

liveries (in which a tonglike instrument is used to bring the baby out of the mother's body). Such positive benefits of the emotional support gained from a female companion argue for the provision of such a person as part of the childbirth support team.

Still, in the United States, childbirth is seen mostly as a medical event that occurs in a hospital under the supervision of a physician. In the Netherlands, pregnancy and labor are thought of as normal events that require medical intervention only when there is a specific reason. About 35 percent of Dutch babies are born at home, and about 43 percent of deliveries are attended by midwives (Treffers, Eskes, Kleiverda, & van Alten, 1990). Most of these births are to women deemed to be at low risk, and their outcomes compare very favorably with hospital births attended by obstetricians.

What are the psychological implications of the new ways of giving birth? First, techniques that mini-mize drugs provide a better start in life for the baby. Second, the active participation of both parents reinforces close family attachments between mother, father, and infant. Last, women's insistence on assuming a strong role in the birth of their children has helped spur a general movement in which people take active responsibility for their own health rather than sitting back passively and relying on doctors. Of course, there are many ways to have a healthy baby, and many healthy, well-adjusted adults have been born in traditional hospital settings. One of the best guarantees of a healthy pregnancy and delivery is good prenatal care—something that, unfortunately, many American women do not receive (see Box 2-5).

In view of the importance of feeling in control of one's life, the availability of alternative means and sites of childbirth is a healthy trend. Choice is the crucial element. Children born in a variety of ways and places can grow up physically and psychologically healthy.

SUMMARY

FERTILIZATION

■ Fertilization is the process by which sperm and ovum unite to form a one-celled zygote. The zygote duplicates by cell division.

■ Although conception usually results in single births, multiple births can occur. When two ova are fertilized, fraternal (dizygotic) twins will be born; these have different genetic makeups and may be of different sexes. When a single fertilized ovum divides in two, identical (monozygotic) twins will be born; they have the same genetic makeup and are of the same sex. Larger multiple births result from either one of these processes or a combination of the two.

■ At conception, each normal human being receives 23 chromosomes from the mother and 23 from the father. These align into 23 pairs of chromosomes—22 pairs of autosomes and 1 pair of sex chromosomes. Chromosomes carry the genes that determine inherited characteristics.

■ A child who receives an X chromosome from each parent will be a female. But if the child receives a Y chromosome from the father, a male will be conceived.

HEREDITY AND ENVIRONMENT

■ The science of genetics is the study of heredity. The basic unit of heredity is the gene, which is made up of DNA.

■ The chief patterns of genetic transmission are dominant, recessive, sex-linked, and multifactorial inheritance. Various birth defects and diseases can be transmitted through each of these patterns.

■ An observable trait is called a phenotype; the underlying genetic pattern is the genotype.

■ Chromosomal abnormalities can also result in birth defects. Down syndrome is the most common.

■ Through genetic counseling, prospective parents can receive information about the mathematical odds of having children with certain birth defects.

■ Amniocentesis, chorionic villus sampling, maternal blood testing, ultrasound, umbilical cord blood sampling, and preimplantation genetic diagnosis are used to determine if a fetus is developing normally or is affected by certain abnormal conditions.

■ It is hard to disentangle the relative contributions of heredity and environment to development. Today, developmentalists look at the interaction of heredity and environment rather than attributing development exclusively to one factor or the other. Family studies, adoption studies, and studies of twins are important research techniques.

■ Physical and physiologic traits, intelligence, personality and temperament, and certain emotional and behavioral disorders are influenced by heredity, although certain aspects of development are influenced more by heredity and others more by environment.

PRENATAL DEVELOPMENT

■ Prenatal development occurs in three stages. The germinal stage is characterized by rapid cell division, increased complexity of the organism, and implantation of the organism in the wall of the uterus. The embryonic stage is characterized by rapid growth and differentiation of major body systems and organs. The fetal stage is characterized by the appearance of bone cells, rapid growth, and changes in body form.

■ Nearly all birth defects and three-quarters of all spontaneous abortions occur during the critical first 3 months of pregnancy.

■ The conceptus is affected by its prenatal environment. Important dangers include maternal nutrition, maternal drug intake, maternal illness, incompatibility of blood type with the mother's blood type, medical x-rays, maternal age and physical activity, and external environmental hazards. Paternal factors are also important. Environmental factors that can produce birth defects are called teratogenic.

BIRTH

■ Birth normally begins 266 days after conception and occurs in three stages: (1) dilation of the cervix; (2) descent and emergence of the baby; (3) expulsion of the umbilical cord and the placenta.

■ Excessive anesthesia in medicated deliveries may have a harmful effect on the newborn.

■ Natural and prepared childbirth can offer both physical and psychological benefits.

■ In recent years the rate of cesarean deliveries has risen to almost 24 percent in the United States.

■ Electronic fetal monitoring is widely used during labor and delivery, especially in high-risk births, to detect signs of fetal distress.

■ Delivery at home or in birth centers is an alternative to hospital delivery for some women with normal, low-risk pregnancies.

KEY TERMS

fertilization (page 46)
gametes (46)
zygote (46)
ovulation (46)
dizygotic twins (47)
monozygotic twins (47)
autosomes (49)
sex chromosomes (49)
genetics (49)
heredity (49)
gene (50)
deoxyribonucleic acid (DNA) (50)
chromosomes (50)
dominant inheritance (50)
independent segregation (51)
alleles (51)

homozygous (51)
heterozygous (51)
recessive inheritance (51)
phenotype (51)
genotype (51)
sex-linked inheritance (52)
multiple alleles (52)
multifactorial inheritance (52)
Down syndrome (58)
genetic counseling (59)
karyotype (59)
amniocentesis (61)
chorionic villus sampling (CVS) (61)
maternal blood test (61)
ultrasound (62)
maturation (63)

personality (66)
temperament (66)
schizophrenia (67)
infantile autism (67)
depression (69)
germinal stage (70)
embryonic stage (70)
spontaneous abortion (70)
fetal stage (72)
teratogenic (73)
fetal alcohol syndrome (FAS) (76)
medicated delivery (82)
natural childbirth (83)
prepared childbirth (83)
cesarean delivery (83)
electronic fetal monitoring (84)

SUGGESTED READINGS

DeFrain, J., Montens, L., Stork, J., & Stork, W. (1986). *Stillborn: An invisible death.* Lexington, MA: Heath. A sensitive study of the effects of stillbirth on families, based on data from 300 questionnaires and 25 in-depth interviews. The book provides concrete information about the reactions of parents, family, and friends to this experience and gives suggestions for coping.

Dorris, M. (1990). *The broken cord.* New York: Harper-Collins. A moving account of the struggles of a child with fetal alcohol syndrome, written by his adoptive father.

Eisenberg, A., Murkoff, H. E., & Hathaway, S. E. (1991). *What to expect when you're expecting* (rev. 2d ed.). New York: Workman. An excellent, comprehensive description of pregnancy, month to month, that incorporates research on care for both mother and baby.

Friedman, R., & Gradstein, B. (1992). *Surviving pregnancy loss.* Boston: Little, Brown. This book provides guidance on dealing with a pregnancy loss, be it a miscarriage, stillbirth, ectopic pregnancy, or a loss associated with a technology-assisted pregnancy. The personal accounts by women who have experienced pregnancy loss firsthand are especially moving.

Nilsson, L., Ingelman-Sundberg, A., & Wirsen, C. (1990). *A child is born* (2d ed.). New York: Delacorte. A new edition of this classic depiction of fetal development. The material about the parents' experience of pregnancy has been updated but the beautiful photographs of the developing fetus are unchanged.

Reuben, C. (1992). *The healthy baby book.* New York: Tarcher-Perigee. This guide to preventing birth defects includes specific "what to do" guidelines for before, during, and after pregnancy. Examines the effects of diet, medications, infectious diseases, environmental hazards, among others.

Stoppard, M. (1993). *Conception, pregnancy, and birth.* New York: Dorling Kindersley. A comprehensive source for information, unusual in focusing on the experiences of both the mother and the newborn. Clear and easy to read, with case studies and in-depth coverage of obstetrical tests used in the '90s.

CHAPTER THREE

PHYSICAL DEVELOPMENT IN INFANCY AND TODDLERHOOD

The experiences of the first three years of life are almost entirely lost to us, and when we attempt to enter into a small child's world, we come as foreigners who have forgotten the landscape and no longer speak the native tongue.

Selma Fraiberg,
The Magic Years, *1959*

■ **THE NEONATE**

Physical Characteristics
Body Systems
The Brain and Reflex Behavior
The Newborn's Health
Immunization for Better Health

■ **DEVELOPMENT DURING THE FIRST 3 YEARS OF LIFE**

Principles of Development
States of Arousal: The Body's Cycles
Growth and Nourishment
The Senses

Motor Development
How Different Are Boys and Girls?

■ **BOXES**

3-1 Window on the World: How Universal Is "Normal" Development?
3-2 Food for Thought: When Does Obesity Begin, and What Should Be Done about It?
3-3 Take a Stand: Should Baby Boys Be Circumcised?
3-4 Practically Speaking: Are "Walkers" Worth the Risk?
3-5 Practically Speaking: Putting Research Findings to Work

ASK YOURSELF

- How do newborn infants adjust to life outside the womb, and how can we tell whether they are healthy and are developing normally?
- What conditions can complicate newborn babies' adjustment and even endanger their lives?

- What can infants do at birth, and how do they acquire more sophisticated sensory and motor capabilities over the first 3 years?
- What can and should be done to foster infants' and toddlers' physical growth and development?

Suppose that after a rough voyage, you are cast ashore in an unknown land alone and without possessions. You are cared for by giants, who act strangely and speak gibberish. What's more, you are physically helpless and unable to tell anyone what you need or want.

You have been through just such an experience—at birth. A newborn baby is, in an extreme sense, an immigrant. After struggling through a difficult passage, the infant is faced with much more than learning a language and customs. A baby must start to breathe, eat, adapt to the climate, and respond to confusing surroundings—a mighty challenge for someone who weighs but a few pounds and whose organ systems are not fully mature. But as we'll see, infants normally come into the world with body systems and senses all working and ready to meet that challenge.

In this chapter we see what newborn babies look like, how their body systems work, and how the brain develops, permitting reflex behaviors to operate. We describe some ways to evaluate newborns, and we discuss how birth trauma and low birthweight affect development. Then we go on to chart some aspects of development during the first 3 years of life—basic principles, states of arousal, the importance of nutrition, early sensory and motor development, and similarities and differences between boys and girls.

As you read this chapter, keep in mind that because human beings live and behave as whole persons, all aspects of their development are intimately connected. When we try to separate these aspects, as we do here, we make arbitrary divisions, as if we were cutting the person into jigsaw pieces. For example, although we usually think of learning as a mental function, infants learn a great deal by physical action. Babies cannot tell themselves apart from their surroundings until they be-

gin to explore their environment and learn from their own movements where their bodies end and the rest of the world begins. As they drop toys, splash water, and hurl sand, they learn how their bodies can affect their world. Physical gestures often accompany a baby's first attempts to speak. As Maika says "Bye-bye," she opens and closes her hand. When Darryl says "Up," he raises his arms, showing Grandpa where he wants to go. Even more to the point, if Maika and Darryl had not developed the motor coordination needed to form certain sounds, they would not be able to speak at all. Because the brain itself—the center of intellectual as well as much of emotional functioning—is a physical organ, links exist between the physical aspects of growth and development and intelligence, learning, and personality.

Thus as we look at early physical growth and sensory and motor development of infants and toddlers in this chapter, at their intellectual development in Chapter 4, and at their personality and social development in Chapter 5, we should remember that these categories overlap, with each affecting the others.

THE NEONATE

The first 4 weeks of life are the *neonatal period*—a time of transition from intrauterine life, when a fetus is supported entirely by a mother's body, to an independent existence. Who are these newcomers to the world? What do they look like? What can they do?

PHYSICAL CHARACTERISTICS

An average *neonate*, or newborn, is about 20 inches long and weighs about 7½ pounds. At birth,

95 percent of full-term babies weigh between 5½ and 10 pounds and are between 18 and 22 inches long (Behrman & Vaughan, 1983). Size at birth is related to such factors as race, sex, parents' size, maternal nutrition, and maternal health. Boys tend to be slightly longer and heavier than girls, and a firstborn child is likely to weigh less at birth than later-borns. Size at birth is related to size during childhood (Behrman & Vaughan, 1983).

In their first few days, neonates lose as much as 10 percent of their body weight, primarily because of a loss of fluids. They begin to gain weight again at about the fifth day and are generally back to birthweight by the tenth to the fourteenth day. Light full-term infants lose less weight than heavy ones, and firstborns lose less than later-borns (Behrman & Vaughan, 1983).

The neonate's head may be long and misshapen because of the "molding" that eased its passage through the mother's pelvis. This temporary molding was possible because the baby's skull bones are not yet fused; they will not be completely joined for 18 months. The places on the head where the bones have not yet grown together—the soft spots, or *fontanels*—are covered by a tough membrane. Since the cartilage in the baby's nose is also malleable, the trip through the birth canal may leave the nose looking squashed for a few days.

Newborns are quite pale; even black babies who will later be very dark have a light complexion at birth. But newborns have a pinkish cast because of the thinness of their skin, which barely covers the blood flowing through their capillaries. The *vernix caseosa* ("cheesy varnish"), an oily covering that protects new babies against infection, dries in a few days' time. Some neonates are very hairy, covered with *lanugo,* a fuzzy prenatal hair that drops off within a few days.

"Witch's milk," a secretion that sometimes issues from the swollen breasts of both female and male newborns, was believed during the Middle Ages to have special healing powers. Like the blood-tinged vaginal discharge of some baby girls, this fluid emission results from high levels of the hormone estrogen, which is secreted by the placenta just before birth.

BODY SYSTEMS

Before birth, the fetus's blood circulation, respiration, nourishment, elimination, and temperature

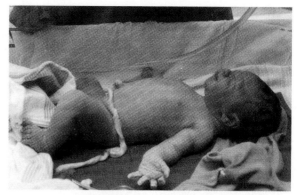

Annie, shown here only moments after her birth, is still attached to her umbilical cord. According to her weight and measurement, she was exactly average—but according to her parents, she is well above average in every other way! *(Phil Hollembeak)*

regulation are all accomplished through its connection with the mother's body. After birth, infants must perform these functions on their own. The transition from intrauterine life to life on the outside makes major demands on all body systems (see Table 3-1). This transition takes longer for low-birthweight babies, who are born with less fully developed body systems.

Circulatory System

Before birth, mother and baby have independent circulatory systems and separate heartbeats; but the fetus's blood is cleansed through the umbilical cord, which carries blood to and from the placenta. At birth, the baby's own system must take over. The heartbeat is fast and irregular; blood pressure does not stabilize until about the tenth day.

Respiratory System

The fetus gets oxygen through the umbilical cord, which also carries away carbon dioxide. The newborn, who needs much more oxygen, must now get it independently. Most infants start to breathe as soon as they emerge into the air. A baby who is not breathing within 2 minutes after birth is in trouble; if breathing has not begun in 5 minutes or so, some degree of brain injury from *anoxia*—lack of oxygen—may result. Infants' lungs have only one-tenth as many air sacs as adults'; thus infants are susceptible to respiratory problems, especially when born prematurely.

TABLE 3-1

A Comparison of Prenatal and Postnatal Life

Characteristic	Prenatal Life	Postnatal Life
Environment	Amniotic fluid	Air
Temperature	Relatively constant	Fluctuates with atmosphere
Stimulation	Minimal	All senses stimulated by various stimuli
Nutrition	Dependent on mother's blood	Dependent on external food and functioning of digestive system
Oxygen supply	Passed from maternal bloodstream via placenta	Passed from neonate's lungs to pulmonary blood vessels
Metabolic elimination	Passed into maternal bloodstream via placenta	Discharged by skin, kidneys, lungs, and gastrointestinal tract

SOURCE: Timiras, 1972, p. 174.

Gastrointestinal System

The fetus relies on the umbilical cord to bring food and carry body wastes away. The newborn has a strong sucking reflex to take in milk and has gastrointestinal secretions to digest it. *Meconium* (stringy, greenish-black waste matter formed in the fetal intestinal tract) is excreted during the first 2 days or so after birth. When the neonate's bowels and bladder are full, the sphincter muscles open automatically. Many months will pass before the baby can control these muscles.

Three or four days after birth, about half of all babies—and a larger proportion of babies born prematurely—develop *physiologic jaundice:* their skin and eyeballs look yellow. This kind of jaundice is caused by the immaturity of the liver; usually it is not serious and has no long-term effects. In some cases, it is treated by putting the baby under fluorescent lights.

Temperature Regulation

The layers of fat that develop during the last months of fetal life enable healthy full-term infants to keep their body temperature constant despite changes in air temperature. Newborn babies also maintain body temperature by increasing their activity in response to a drop in air temperature.

THE BRAIN AND REFLEX BEHAVIOR

What makes newborns respond to a nipple? What tells them to start the sucking movements that allow them to control their intake of milk?

These are functions of the nervous system, which consists of the brain, the spinal cord (a bundle of nerves running through the backbone), and a network of nerves that eventually reaches every part of the body. Through this network, sensory messages travel to the brain and motor commands travel back. This complex communication system governs what a person can do both physically and mentally. Normal growth of the brain, before and after birth, is fundamental to future development.

Growth and Development of the Brain

We can think of brain development by using an analogy: sculpture. A sculptor starts with a block of stone and chisels away the unwanted pieces. This is roughly what happens in the brain (Kolb, 1989). Starting in the womb, the brain produces more cells than it needs, and those that do not function well die out after birth. This removal of excess cells helps to create an efficient nervous system; in fact, some neurobiologists believe that certain disorders are caused by the persistence of extra cells (I. Feinberg, 1982).

The human brain grows fastest prenatally and soon after birth. In the uterus an estimated 250,000 brain cells form every minute through cell division (mitosis), and by birth most of the 100 billion cells in a mature brain are already formed (Cowan, 1979; see Figure 3-1).

A spurt in the formation of brain cells comes just before birth and shortly afterward. Within 2 months after birth, practically no new cells are forming (Lipsitt, 1986), though existing cells continue to grow in size. The cells sort themselves out

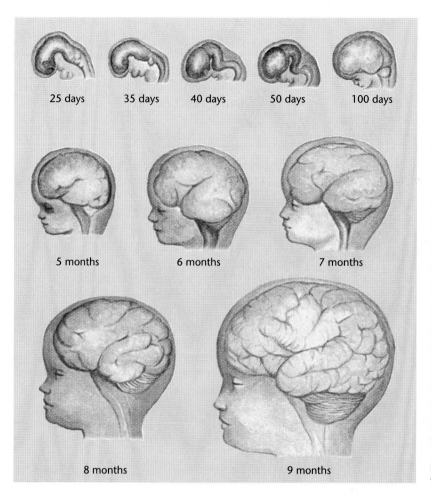

25 days   35 days   40 days   50 days   100 days

5 months   6 months   7 months

8 months   9 months

FIGURE 3-1
Fetal brain development from 25 days of gestation through birth. As the brain develops, the front part expands greatly to form the cerebrum (the large, convoluted upper mass). Specific areas of the cerebral cortex (the gray outer covering of the brain) have specific functions, such as sensory and motor activity; but large areas are "uncommitted" and thus are free for higher intellectual activity, such as thinking, remembering, and problem solving. The subcortex (the brain stem and other structures below the cortical layer) handles reflex behavior and other lower-level functions. The newborn's brain contains most of the cells it will eventually have, but it is only about 25 percent of its adult weight. A rapid increase in cortical connections during the first 2 years of life results in a dramatic weight gain (to four-fifths of adult brain weight) and in the capacity for thought. *(Restak, 1984.)*

by function, migrating to their proper positions either in the *cerebral cortex* (the upper level of the brain) or in the subcortical levels (below the cortex). In a newborn infant, the subcortical structures (which regulate such basic biological functions as breathing and digestion) are the most fully developed; cells in the cortex (which is responsible for thinking and problem solving) are not yet well connected. Connections between cortical cells increase astronomically as the child matures, allowing more flexible, higher-level motor and intellectual functioning.

The development of the cortex occurs in several stages. The innermost layers develop first; then the outer layers develop. This is why the timing of prenatal "insults" (from drugs or other causes) makes such a difference in the kind of defect that may result. An "insult" may block the formation of an entire cell group. On the other hand, if an "insult" damages the brain after new cells have stopped forming, the remaining cells often change to compensate for the injured ones (Kolb, 1989).

The brain, which is only 25 percent of its adult weight at birth, reaches about two-thirds of its

eventual weight during the first year and four-fifths by the end of the second year. It continues to grow more slowly until, by age 12, it is nearly of adult size. An infant's neurological growth permits development in motor and intellectual activities. Although programmed by genes, this development is also affected by the environment.

The brain is, figuratively speaking, plastic, especially while it is developing rapidly: it can be easily molded. Experiences of early life may have lasting effects, for better or worse, on the capacity of the central nervous system to learn and store information (Wittrock, 1980). For example, chronic malnutrition during either the prenatal period or the critical period shortly after birth can cause brain damage.

Furthermore, when rats and other animals were raised in "enriched" cages with stimulating apparatus, they developed heavier brains with thicker cortical layers, more connective cells, and higher levels of neurochemical activity (which helps to form connections between brain cells) than littermates raised in "standard" cages or in isolation (Rosenzweig, 1984; Rosenzweig & Bennett, 1976). And the brain's plasticity seems to continue to a

CAN'T MAKE CONSCIOUS CHOICES

lesser degree throughout most of the life span; similar neural differences appeared when older animals were exposed to different environments.

Such findings have sparked successful efforts to maximize the functioning of children with Down syndrome, to keep aging people mentally fit, and to help victims of brain damage recover. Brain plasticity can also help some infants with birth complications to develop normally.

REFLEX'S - SURVIVAL + PROTECTION

A Newborn's Reflexes

When babies (or adults) blink at a bright light, they are acting involuntarily. Such automatic responses to external stimulation are called ***reflex behaviors.***

Human beings have an array of reflexes, many of which are present before birth, at birth, or very soon after birth (see Table 3-2). Some of them seem to promote survival or offer protection. These "primitive" reflexes—or their absence—are early signs of brain development. Normally, the primitive reflexes disappear during the first year or so; for example, the Moro, or "startle," reflex drops out at 2 to 3 months, and rooting for the nipple at about 9 months. Such protective reflexes as blinking, yawning, coughing, gagging, sneezing, and the pupillary reflex (dilation of the pupils in the dark) remain. (Reflexes vary somewhat, however, according to culture; see Box 3-1).

Because the subcortex controls the primitive reflexes, their disappearance indicates development of the cortex and a shift to voluntary behavior. Since there is a timetable for shedding these reflexes, their presence or absence in the first few months of life is a guide to evaluating neurological development. Testing for normal reflexes immediately after birth is one of many ways to assess a baby's health and functioning.

THE NEWBORN'S HEALTH

How can we tell whether a neonate's systems are functioning normally? What can be done to help infants who suffer from complications of birth, who are born prematurely, or whose birthweight is dangerously low? How can we ensure that babies will live, grow, and develop as they should?

Effects of Birth Trauma

For a small minority of babies, the passage through the birth canal is a particularly harrowing journey.

Among more than 15,000 births over a period of 6 years at an outstanding medical school (A. Rubin, 1977), fewer than 1 percent of the infants suffered ***birth trauma***—injury sustained at the time of birth. Birth trauma may be caused by anoxia (oxygen deprivation at birth), neonatal diseases or infections, or mechanical injury. Some traumas leave permanent brain damage, causing mental retardation or behavior problems.

Often, however, the effects of birth injuries can be counteracted by a favorable environment. In a longitudinal study of almost 900 children born on the island of Kauai, Hawaii, those whose births had been difficult, whose birthweight had been low, or who had been sick when born were examined at age 10, at age 18, and in their early thirties. The findings were clear: complications at the time of birth were consistently related to later impaired physical and psychological development *only* when the children grew up in inadequate environments (E. E. Werner, 1985). Unless damage was so severe as to require institutionalization, these children—when in stable and enriching homes—did better in school and had fewer language, perceptual, and emotional problems than children who had not experienced unusual stress at birth but who had suffered "environmental trauma" in homes where they got little intellectual stimulation or emotional support (E. E. Werner, 1989; E. E. Werner et al., 1968).

We see, then, that children are remarkably resilient. Even very alarming one-time events can often be less important than day-to-day experience.

Medical and Behavioral Screening

Because the first few weeks, days, and even minutes after birth are crucial for development, it is important to know as soon as possible whether a baby has any problem that needs special care. To find out, doctors and psychologists use such tools as the Apgar and Brazelton scales and screen for certain medical conditions.

Immediate Medical Assessment: The Apgar Scale
One minute after delivery, and then again 5 minutes after delivery, infants are evaluated using the ***Apgar scale*** (see Table 3-3). The name of this scale commemorates its developer, Dr. Virginia Apgar (1953), and also helps us remember its five subtests: *a*ppearance (color), *p*ulse (heart rate), *g*rimace (reflex irritability), *a*ctivity (muscle tone), and *r*espiration (breathing).

TABLE 3-2

Human Primitive Reflexes

Reflex	Stimulation	Behavior
Rooting	Baby's cheek is stroked with finger or nipple.	Baby's head turns; mouth opens; sucking movements begin.
Darwinian (grasping)	Palm of baby's hand is stroked.	Baby makes strong fist; can be raised to standing position if both fists are closed around a stick.
Swimming	Baby is put into water face down.	Baby makes well-coordinated swimming movements.
Tonic neck	Baby is laid down on back.	Baby turns head to one side, assumes "fencer" position, extends arms and legs on preferred side, flexes opposite limbs.
Moro (startle)	Baby is dropped or hears loud noise.	Baby extends legs, arms, and fingers; arches back; draws back head.
Babinski	Sole of baby's foot is stroked.	Baby's toes fan out; foot twists in.
Walking	Baby is held under arms, with bare feet touching flat surface.	Baby makes steplike motions that look like well-coordinated walking.
Placing	Backs of baby's feet are drawn against edge of flat surface.	Baby withdraws foot.

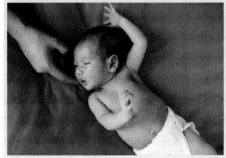

Rooting reflex *(Kathryn Abbe)*

Darwinian reflex *(Lew Merrim/Monkmeyer)*

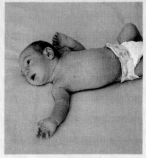

Tonic neck reflex *(Laura Dwight/Black Star)*

Moro reflex *(Elizabeth Crews)*

Babinski reflex *(Elizabeth Crews)*

Walking reflex *(Elizabeth Crews)*

TABLE 3-3

Apgar Scale			
Sign*	**0**	**1**	**2**
Appearance (color)	Blue, pale	Body pink, extremities blue	Entirely pink
Pulse (heart rate)	Absent	Slow (below 100)	Rapid (over 100)
Grimace (reflex irritability)	No response	Grimace	Coughing, sneezing, crying
Activity (muscle tone)	Limp	Weak, inactive	Strong, active
Respiration (breathing)	Absent	Irregular, slow	Good, crying

*Each sign is rated in terms of absence or presence from 0 to 2; highest overall score is 10.
SOURCE: Adapted from Apgar, 1953.

The newborn receives a rating of 0, 1, or 2 on each measure, for a possible maximum of 10. Ninety percent of normal infants score 7 or better. A score below 7 generally means that the baby needs help to establish breathing. A score below 4 means that the baby is in danger and needs immediate life-saving treatment. In that case, the test is repeated at 5-minute intervals to check on the effectiveness of resuscitation. If the effort succeeds and the score rises to at least 4, there are usually no serious long-term consequences. A score of 0 to 3 at 10, 15, and 20 minutes suggests a greater risk of neurological damage (AAP Committee on Fetus and Newborn, 1986).

A low Apgar score does not always indicate that a baby is suffocating. An infant's tone and responsiveness may be affected by the amount of sedation or pain-killing medication the mother received. Neurological and cardiorespiratory conditions may interfere with one or more vital signs. Premature infants may score low simply because of their physiological immaturity.

Recently, there has been some criticism of the Apgar test, partly because it is not as sensitive as newer measures (one new test, for instance, measures the oxygen in the newborn's blood). Another important charge is that the Apgar has little predictive value, mostly because of sloppy administration. However, since the Apgar test is quick, inexpensive, and easy to administer, it should probably not be abandoned; rather, hospital workers should be taught to perform it better and to act quickly on the basis of its results.

Neonatal Screening for Medical Conditions

Children who inherit the enzyme disorder phenylketonuria (PKU) will become mentally retarded unless they are fed a special diet beginning in the first 3 to 6 weeks of life. Screening tests that can be administered immediately after birth can often discover such correctable defects. Routine screening of all newborn babies for such rare conditions as PKU (1 case in 14,000 births), hypothyroidism (1 in 4250), and galactosemia (1 in 62,000)—or for other, even rarer disorders—is, of course, expensive. Yet the cost of detecting one case of a rare disease is often less than the cost of caring for a mentally retarded child for a lifetime. For this reason, all states now require routine screening for PKU and congenital hypothyroidism; states vary on requirements for other screening tests (AAP Committee on Genetics, 1992; Williams & Miller, 1991).

Assessing Responses: The Brazelton Scale

The *Brazelton Neonatal Behavioral Assessment Scale* is a neurological and behavioral test used to measure neonates' responses to their environment (Brazelton, 1973). The Brazelton scale assesses four dimensions of infants' behavior:

1 *Interactive behaviors,* like alertness and cuddling
2 *Motor behaviors* (reflexes, muscle tone, and hand-mouth coordination)
3 *Physiological control,* like the ability to quiet down after being upset
4 *Response to stress* (the startle reaction)

The Brazelton test takes about 30 minutes, and

BOX 3-1 WINDOW ON THE WORLD

HOW UNIVERSAL IS "NORMAL" DEVELOPMENT?

What happens if you briefly press a baby's nose with a cloth? Western babies will normally turn their heads away or swipe at the cloth. But Chinese babies will probably open their mouths promptly to restore breathing, without a fight. What happens if you lift a baby's body, supporting its head, and then release the head support, allowing the head to drop? Typical white newborns show the Moro reflex: they extend both arms and legs, cry persistently, and move about in an agitated way. Navajo infants, however, typically respond with a reduced reflex extension of the limbs. They rarely cry and almost immediately stop any agitated behavior. These differences suggest that some reflex behaviors are not universal, as we might expect (D. G. Freedman, 1979).

Are motor skills universal? When the Denver Developmental Screening Test was given to southeast Asian children (V. Miller, Onotera, & Deinard, 1984), the youngsters "failed" on three standard measures of normal development: they did not play pat-a-cake, they did not pick up raisins, and they did not dress themselves at the usual ages. But we cannot jump to the conclusion that these youngsters were backward in development. In their culture, children do not play pat-a-cake; raisins look like a medicine they are taught to avoid; and Asian parents do not expect children to dress themselves as early as American parents do. Because this test was devised for American children, sections of it may be inappropriate for children in cultures with different customs.

Even for universal behaviors like sitting and walking, what is "normal" or "typical" in one culture

may not be in another. African babies seem to be more precocious in gross motor skills, and Asian infants less so, than infants of European origin. These differences may be related to cultural differences in temperament. Asian infants, for example, are typically more docile and thus may tend to stay closer to their parents (Kaplan & Dove, 1987).

Although short-term experiments suggest that it is difficult (and not necessarily desirable) to speed up or modify a child's motor development, certain child-rearing practices that are widespread in a culture may advance or retard it. The anthropologist Margaret Mead saw that Arapesh infants in New Guinea could stand while holding on to something before they could sit alone. The reason, Mead reported, was that these infants were often held in a standing position, "so that they can push with their feet against the arms or legs of the person who holds them" (1935, p. 57).

At 3 months of age, babies from the Yucatan peninsula in Mexico are ahead of American babies in manipulative motor skills; yet by 11 months the Yucatecan babies are far behind in locomotive skills— so much so that the same pattern in an American child might be taken as an indication of neurologic disease (Solomons, 1978). The Yucatecan babies' manipulative precocity may result from their having no toys and thus discovering and playing with their fingers sooner. Their delayed skills in moving about may have to do with their being swaddled as infants and restrained in various ways as they get older. However, Navajo babies—who are also swaddled for most of the day—begin to walk at

Some observers have suggested that babies from the Yucatan develop motor skills later than American babies because they are swaddled. But Native American babies, like this one in a traditional cradle board, are also swaddled for most of the day, and they begin to walk at about the same time as other American babies. Another explanation for such developmental variations might be hereditary differences. *(Greenlar/The Image Works)*

about the same time as other American babies (Chisholm, 1983).

Some cultural differences in motor development may reflect genetic differences among peoples that have arisen through the process of natural selection. This evolutionary process occurs as individuals who adapt successfully to their environment survive and reproduce, passing on their hereditary traits to their offspring. This may explain why Ache children in eastern Paraguay show delays in gross motor skills, walking about 9 months later than American babies (Kaplan & Dove, 1987). Until the mid-1970s, the Ache economy relied on hunting and foraging. Natural selection may have favored more cautious, less exploratory individuals. Another explanation

(continued)

BOX 3-1   *(Continued)*

may lie in the tendency of Ache mothers to pull their babies back when they begin to crawl away, to protect them from danger. Perhaps when mothers spend less time in direct child care, children become independent sooner because their caretakers are less vigilant—an observation that may be relevant to-

day, when day care is prevalent and some aspects of development seem to be occurring at earlier ages than they did previously.

Children in other cultures who show early developmental lags often catch up to American children later. Ache 8- to 10-year-olds climb tall trees, chop branches, and play

in ways that enhance their motor skills. Development, then, may be viewed "as a series of immediate adjustments to current conditions as well as a cumulative process in which succeeding stages build upon earlier ones" (Kaplan & Dove, 1987, p. 197).

---

scores are based on a baby's best performance rather than an average. Testers try to get babies to do their best, sometimes repeating an item and sometimes asking the mother to alert her baby. The Brazelton scale may be a better predictor of future development than the Apgar scale or standard neurological testing (Behrman & Vaughan, 1983).

Low Birthweight

Seven percent of all babies born in the United States are of *low birthweight,* that is, they weigh less than 2500 grams (5½ pounds) at birth. Very low birthweight babies weigh 1500 grams (3⅓ pounds) or less; they account for 1.28 percent of births in the United States.

Low birthweight is associated with more than 60 percent of deaths in the first year of life (Morbidity and Mortality Weekly Report [MMWR], 1993). These infants are at least 5 times more likely to die during the first 4 weeks of life than are those weighing 6½ pounds or more; and for very low birthweight babies, the risk jumps to 90 times. These figures are better than they used to be because of improved ways to keep these tiny babies alive, but public health authorities are concerned because the rate of low birthweight itself is rising.

Some low-birthweight babies are born early. They are called *preterm* (premature) infants, and they may or may not be the appropriate size for their gestational age. Others are *small-for-date* babies. They weigh less than 90 percent of all babies of the same gestational age because they experienced delayed fetal growth, probably because of inadequate prenatal nutrition. They may or may not be preterm.

The risks to both types of babies are similar, but premature babies are more likely to die in infancy than small-for-date babies (Behrman, 1985). The

shorter the gestation period (if less than 36 weeks), the more problems the baby is likely to have. The neonatal transition takes longer for preterm babies because they enter the world with less fully developed body systems.

Who Is Likely to Have a Low-Birthweight Baby?

A number of factors are associated with the tendency to give birth to underweight infants (see Table 3-4). These include the following correlates of low birthweight (S. S. Brown, 1985):

- *Demographic factors,* like race, age, education, and marital status
- *Medical factors predating the pregnancy,* like previous abortions, stillbirths, or medical conditions
- *Medical factors associated with the current pregnancy,* like vaginal bleeding or too little weight gain
- *Prenatal behavioral and environmental factors,* like poor nutrition, inadequate prenatal care, smoking, use of alcohol and drugs, and exposure to toxic substances.

Many of these factors are interrelated. Teenagers' higher risk probably stems more from poor nutrition and inadequate prenatal care than from age. And socioeconomic status cuts across almost all risk factors. Poor women who smoke are more likely to have low-birthweight babies than affluent women who smoke, probably because such factors as poor nutrition and poor prenatal care compound the effects of smoking.

Even before pregnancy, women can cut down their chances of having a low-birthweight baby by eating well, not smoking or using drugs, drinking little or no alcohol, and getting good medical

TABLE 3-4

Principal Maternal Risk Factors for Delivering Underweight Infants

Category	Risks
Demographic and socio-economic factors	Age (under 17 or over 40) Race (black) Poverty Unmarried Low level of education
Medical risks predating current pregnancy	No children or more than four Low weight for height Genital or urinary abnormalities or past surgery Diseases such as diabetes or chronic hypertension Lack of immunity to certain infections, such as rubella Poor obstetric history, including previous low-birthweight infant and multiple miscarriages Genetic factors in the mother (such as low weight at her own birth)
Conditions of current pregnancy	Multiple pregnancy (twins or more) Poor weight gain (less than 14 pounds) Less than 6 months since previous pregnancy Low blood pressure Hypertension or toxemia Certain infections, such as rubella and urinary infections Vaginal bleeding in the first or second trimester Placental problems Anemia or abnormal blood count Fetal abnormalities Incompetent cervix Spontaneous premature rupture of membranes
Lifestyle factors	Smoking Poor nutritional status Abuse of alcohol and other substances Exposure to DES and other toxins, including those in the workplace High altitude
Risks involving health care	Absent or inadequate prenatal care Premature delivery by cesarean section or induced labor

SOURCE: Adapted from S. S. Brown, 1985; Wegman, 1992.

care. The most effective way to reduce the number of low-birthweight babies is widespread prenatal care. Because it is a social problem as well as a medical one, low birthweight can often be prevented with enough effort. This effort can pay off for society: more than $1.5 billion is spent every year on neonatal intensive care, most for low-birthweight babies. For every dollar spent on prenatal care, more than $3 is saved on care for low-birthweight infants (S. S. Brown, 1985).

Cross-cultural Aspects of Low Birthweight

Although the United States is more successful than any other country in the world in *saving* low-birthweight babies, the rate of such births in the United States is higher than those in 30 other European, Asian, and Middle East nations. And the low-birthweight rates among African American babies are higher than those in 73 other countries, including a number of African, Asian, and South American nations (UNICEF, 1992).

The high rates for African American women (see Table 3-5) reflect greater poverty and a greater ten-

TABLE 3-5

Comparison of Black and White Infants, 1990

	Black Infants	White Infants
Percent low birthweight (<5 lb or 2500 g)	13.3%	5.7%
Percent very low birthweight (<3.3 lb or 1500 g)	2.95%	.95%
Infant mortality rate per 1000 births	18.0	7.6
Percent decline in infant mortality rate, 1989–1990	3%	6%

Note: Black infants are more likely than white ones to die in the first year from SIDS, respiratory distress syndrome, infections, injuries, disorders related to short gestation and low birthweight, pneumonia and influenza, and as a result of maternal complications of pregnancy. Rates for deaths due to congenital abnormalities are virtually the same for black and white infants.
SOURCE: Based on information in USDHHS, 1992; MMWR, 1993.

dency to become a teenage mother. But even when these factors are controlled for, black women—even college-educated women—are more likely than white women to bear low-birthweight babies (S. S. Brown, 1985; Schoendorf, Hogue, Kleinman, & Rowley, 1992). This may be due to poorer medical care. Or it may stem from health problems that span generations, since there is some evidence that a mother's birthweight and her early childhood environment may predict her children's birthweights. In any case, the high ratio of low-birthweight babies is the major factor in the high mortality rates of black babies.

Consequences of Low Birthweight

The most pressing fear for very small babies is that they will die in infancy. Because their immune systems are not fully developed, they are more vulnerable to infection (Jason, 1989). Their reflexes may not be mature enough to perform functions basic to survival, like sucking, and they may need to be fed intravenously (through the veins). Because they have less fat to insulate them and to generate heat, it is harder for them to stay warm enough. Respiratory distress syndrome, also called *hyaline membrane disease,* is common. Because many low-birthweight babies lack an essential lung-coating substance, they may breathe irregularly or stop breathing altogether and die. Medical progress has caused such deaths to decline by almost one-third between 1988 and 1990 (Wegman, 1991).

Even with these potential problems, more *extremely* low birthweight babies are surviving today. One study found that among 128 infants weighing less than 1.76 pounds (800 grams) born from 1983 to 1985, 36 percent survived, compared with only 20 percent of such babies born from 1977 to 1980 at the same hospital (E. L. Hoffman & Bennett, 1990). The more the babies weighed, the better their chances were.

In the past, even when low-birthweight babies survived the dangerous early days, they were left with disabling conditions. Now many survivors do fairly well. In one analysis of 80 studies published since 1979, only about a 6-point difference in IQ showed up between low-birthweight infants and normal controls: 97.7 versus 103.78—both in the average range (Aylward, Pfeiffer, Wright, & Verhulst, 1989). This difference, although statistically significant, may not have made an actual difference in the children's lives. However, *very* low birthweight babies have a less promising prognosis. A study comparing eighty-eight 7-year-olds who had weighed less than 3.3 pounds at birth with children who had been full-term found that those who had been premature were more likely to need special education (48 percent versus 15 percent for the controls). They also did more poorly on tests of intelligence, verbal ability, and auditory memory (Ross, Lipper, & Auld, 1991).

Even babies who seem normal as toddlers may have problems later on. Among 36 children who had weighed less than 2.2 pounds at birth, 67 percent tested normal on neurodevelopmental measures at 19 months, but only 31 percent were still in the normal range at ages 3 to 4½ years (Collin, Halsey, & Anderson, 1991).

Furthermore, learning disabilities, which are more common in these children, may not be picked up by IQ measures. Among 90 Canadian 5½-year-olds who had weighed less than 3.3 pounds at birth, about half seemed to be at mild to moderate risk of future learning disabilities (Saigal, Szatmari, Rosenbaum, Campbell, & King, 1990). Whether they actually would have such problems might depend partly on the homes they grew up in. Children in higher socioeconomic circumstances are better able to overcome the early disadvantage of low birthweight (Aylward et al., 1989; McGauhey, Starfield, Alexander, & Ensminget, 1991; Ross, Lipper, & Auld, 1991).

Treatment of Low-Birthweight Babies

Much of the increase in neonatal survival is due to improved care. The low-birthweight baby is placed in an *isolette* (an antiseptic, temperature-controlled crib) and fed through tubes. Jaundiced babies are put under special lights, anemic babies get iron supplements, and those with low blood sugar are fed glucose intravenously.

Parents tend to view a low-birthweight baby negatively and are likely to be anxious about the baby's health. Afraid that the baby may die, they may also be afraid of becoming too attached. This often makes them treat the child differently, perhaps touching the baby less, offering more immature toys, and feeling less comfortable around the infant (Stern & Hildebrandt, 1986).

Frequent visits can give parents a more realistic idea of how the baby is doing and help them become more attached. And regularly visited babies seem to recover more quickly and leave the hospital sooner (Levy-Shiff, Hoffman, Mogilner, Levinger, & Mogilner, 1990; Zeskind & Iacino, 1984).

Promising results emerged from one study of 985 low-birthweight babies, most from poor inner-city families (Infant Health & Development Program, 1990). The parents of about half the babies received counseling and information about children's health and development and learned games and activities to play with their children. At 1 year, these babies entered an educational day care program. By age 3, these children were functioning better than a control group of low-birthweight children who had not received the intervention. The 3-year-olds in the experimental group were doing better on both cognitive and social measures, were much less likely to show mental retardation, and showed fewer behavior problems.

Other research has shown the value of stimulating infants through massage. Hospitals used to maintain a hands-off policy in the belief that low-birthweight babies were best left undisturbed once their basic needs were met. But life in the womb, where sounds and motion reach the fetus, is more interesting than life in an isolette. Isolation and its resulting sensory impoverishment may cause problems for these infants. Gentle massage of such infants seems to foster growth, behavioral organization, weight gain, motor activity, and alertness (T. M. Field, 1986; Schanberg & Field, 1987).

Both preventing low birthweight and intervening when it occurs may help to increase the number of babies who survive the neonatal period and the first year of life.

Postmaturity

Instead of coming too early, some babies do not show any signs of readiness for birth for weeks after they are expected. As many as 7 percent of women have not gone into labor 2 weeks after the due date. At this point, 42 weeks after the mother's last menstrual period, a baby is considered *postmature.* Sometimes as many as 5 weeks go by.

Postmature babies tend to be long and thin, because they have kept growing in the womb but have had an insufficient blood supply at the end. This may be because the placenta has aged and become less efficient; if so, its delivery of oxygen may also be reduced. The babies' greater size also complicates labor: the mother has to deliver a baby the size of a normal 1-month-old.

Since postmature fetuses are at higher risk of brain damage or even death, doctors faced with a gestation of more than 42 weeks sometimes induce labor with drugs and sometimes perform cesarean deliveries. These courses carry their own risks; for example, if the due date has been miscalculated, a

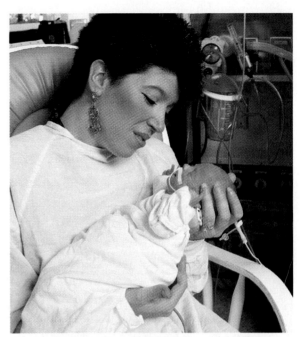

The tiniest babies thrive on human touch. This mother's holding and stroking of her low-birthweight baby girl will help establish a bond between mother and child, and will also help the baby grow and be more alert. *(Hank Morgan/ Science Source/Photo Researchers)*

baby who is actually premature may be delivered. To help in this difficult decision, doctors monitor the baby's status with ultrasound. This lets them see whether the heart rate speeds up when the fetus moves; if not, the baby may be short of oxygen. Another test involves examining the volume of amniotic fluid; a low level may mean insufficient food. To help provide answers, the National Institute of Child Health and Human Development has launched a study of 2800 women whose babies are late.

Infant Mortality

We have made great strides in protecting the lives of new babies. Today in the United States the *infant mortality rate*—the proportion of babies who die within the first year of life—is the lowest in our history. In 1990, for every 1000 live births there were 9.1 deaths in the first year—a decline of about 80 percent since 1940 (Wegman, 1992).* Still, American babies have poorer chances for survival than

*This is the latest year for which we have complete figures. Provisional statistics for 1991 indicate a further decline in the United States, to 8.9 infant deaths per 1000 live births (Wegman, 1992).

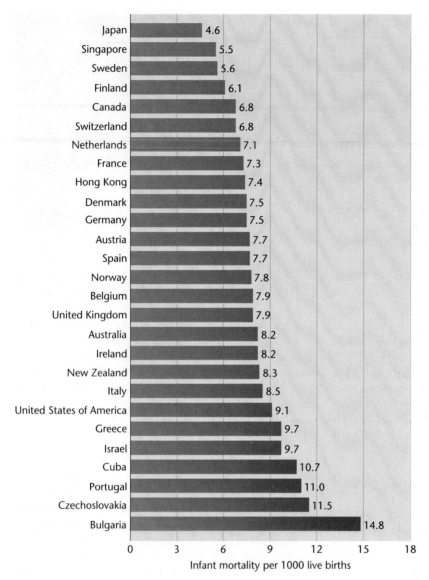

FIGURE 3-2
Infant mortality rates in industrialized countries as of 1990. A nation's infant mortality rate is one indicator of its health status. The United States is only twenty-first among 28 industrialized nations with populations of 2.5 million or more, largely because of its very high mortality rate for minority babies. The overall infant mortality rate in the United States was 9.1 per 1000 births, but the rate for white babies was only 7.6 while the rate for black babies was 18. In recent years almost all nations surveyed have shown improvements. *(Wegman, 1992.)*

babies in 20 other countries with populations greater than 2.5 million (Wegman, 1992) (see Figure 3-2). The nearly 37,000 infants who died before their first birthday represented the largest number of deaths in any age group up to the early forties. Almost two-thirds of those babies died in their first 4 weeks (USDHHS, 1992; Wegman, 1992).

The infant mortality rate for African American babies is more than twice as high as for white ones, as shown in Table 3-5. This difference is largely due to the greater number of low-birthweight babies born to black mothers, even those at middle-income levels. Newborn black and white babies born to college educated mothers who were not underweight at birth have an equal chance of survival (Schoen-

dorf, Hogue, Kleinman, & Rowley, 1992).

Birth defects are the leading cause of infant mortality. Second is sudden infant death syndrome (SIDS), which is followed by disorders relating to short gestation and unspecified low birthweight, respiratory distress syndrome, and the effects of maternal complications of pregnancy (USDHHS, 1992). Given the amount of research devoted to SIDS, we still know little about it.

Sudden Infant Death Syndrome

One kind of death in infancy follows a typical, sad scenario: a baby falls asleep peacefully, but a parent comes in later and finds the baby dead. *Sud-*

den infant death syndrome (SIDS) is the sudden death of an apparently healthy infant under 1 year of age, which remains unexplained after a complete postmortem examination. More than 5000 babies a year, or about 1.5 out of every 1000 babies born, die of SIDS. It is the leading cause of deaths in infants from 1 to 12 months old in the United States and in a number of other industrial countries (Kleinman & Kiely, 1990; USDHHS, 1992). SIDS occurs most often between 2 and 4 months of age, very rarely before 3 weeks or after 9 months (Zylke, 1989).

The little we know about SIDS includes the following: the death is not caused by suffocation, vomiting, or choking. It is most common in winter. It is not contagious, and so far doctors know of no way to predict or prevent it.

Several risk factors are related to SIDS. Babies who succumb are more likely to be of low birthweight, black, and male. Their mothers are more likely to be young, unmarried, and poor; to have received little or no prenatal care; to have been ill during pregnancy; to smoke or abuse drugs or both; and to have had another baby less than a year before the one who died. The fathers are also more likely to be young (Babson & Clark, 1983; Hunt & Brouillette, 1987; Kleinberg, 1984; Mitchell et al., 1993; D. C. Shannon & Kelly, 1982a, 1982b; USDHHS, 1990; Valdes-Dapena, 1980). SIDS occurs more frequently in families of low socioeconomic status, but it also strikes infants in advantaged families.

Current theories about the cause of SIDS include the possibility of neurological dysfunction, with perhaps an abnormality in brain chemistry. Difficulties in the regulation of respiratory control (Hunt & Brouillette, 1987), or in making the transition from sleep to wakefulness have both been suggested by research (Schechtman, Harper, Wilson, & Southall, 1992). And further confirmation of parental smoking has come from two studies. In one, infants whose mothers smoked after the babies' birth were twice as likely to have died from SIDS as were babies of nonsmokers. The risk rose to three times higher for babies whose mothers smoked both during and after pregnancy (Schoendorf & Kiely, 1992). The other found that if the mother smoked, the father's smoking increased the risk of SIDS (Mitchell et al., 1993). Another study suggested that some SIDS-labeled deaths were really accidents (Bass, Kravath, & Glass, 1986).

A major change in recommendations for the care of newborns has come from studies in Australia, the Netherlands, New Zealand, and the United Kingdom. They suggest that SIDS may be related to a baby's sleeping in the prone position (lying on the stomach). Although there is controversy within medical circles about the generalizability of this research, the American Academy of Pediatrics now recommends putting healthy babies to sleep on their back or side. The only babies who should still be put to bed stomach-down are premature infants with respiratory distress, infants with swallowing or upper-airway difficulties, or babies with other special problems (AAP Task Force on Infant Positioning and SIDS, 1992; Dwyer, Ponsonby, Newman, & Gibbons, 1991.)

Whatever the cause of SIDS deaths, the bereaved families suffer greatly. In studies of these families, all the parents contacted rated SIDS as the most severe family crisis they had ever experienced (DeFrain & Ernst, 1978; DeFrain, Taylor, & Ernst, 1982). One woman described it this way:

> This is the most painful time I have ever had to accept. It is hard to be a mother one day and not the next. The first months my arms actually ached to hold her again. I kept thinking I could hear her in bed playing, but it was just the furnace kicking on. (DeFrain et al., 1982, p. 19)

Parents also feel guilty and under criticism, and siblings react with emotional troubles, which may show up as nightmares or school problems. It usually takes about 18 months for a family to regain happiness. A mother recalled:

> So many people tell you when your child dies that things will someday be okay. At that time you seriously doubt that you can ever feel happy and normal again. But it does happen; and it is a blessing and a relief that it does. (DeFrain et al., 1982, p. 69)

IMMUNIZATION FOR BETTER HEALTH

Until recently, immunization seemed to have banished the specter of such contagious diseases as measles, rubella (German measles), mumps, pertussis (whooping cough), diphtheria, and poliomyelitis, at least in the United States. Until the middle of the twentieth century, these illnesses were widespread and often fatal. But between 1980 and 1985, the proportion of American children aged 1 to 4 who were immunized against the major childhood illnesses dropped. Since the mid-

1980s, whooping cough, mumps, measles, rubella, and pertussis cases have risen (USDHHS, 1992). Now about 1 in 4 2-year-olds and 1 in 3 poor children are not protected against measles, rubella, polio, mumps, diptheria, pertussis, and tetanus (National Association of Children's Hospitals and Related Institutions [NACHRI] & American Academy of Pediatrics, 1990; USDHHS, 1992). Table 3-6 shows current recommendations for childhood immunization.

Apparently, we have developed a new disease cycle: "alarm-action" and "relaxation-inaction." The rising disease rate in 1977 provoked renewed alarm and action, leading to a new federal program to promote education and provide money for vaccinations. Again, the disease rate among children declined, until 1981, when the budget of the Childhood Immunization Initiative program was

cut by one-third and the rate began to climb again (Bumpers, 1984), as shown in Table 3-7.

Immunizations also dropped because some parents feared that the vaccines themselves might cause brain damage to their children. Some cases of neurologic illness in children were attributed to the children's having been injected with diphtheria-pertussis-tetanus (DPT) vaccine. However, the association between DPT vaccine and serious acute neurologic illness is very small (1 case for every 100,000 to 1 million immunizations) and actual brain damage is rarer yet (Wentz & Marcuse, 1991). The danger from the diseases that this vaccine prevents still seems greater than the danger from the vaccine itself.

The contagious diseases of childhood are largely the same the world over. Rates of immunization in third world countries have been rising—from

TABLE 3-6

Recommended Childhood Immunizations

	DPT	Polio	MMR*	Hepatitis B†	Haemophilus‡	Tetanus-Diphtheria
Birth				✔		
1–2 months				✔		
2 months	✔	✔			✔	
4 months	✔	✔			✔	
6 months	✔				‡	
6–18 months				✔		
12–15 months					‡	
15 months			✔		‡	
15–18 months	✔	✔				
4–6 years	✔	✔				
11–12 years*			(✔)			
14–16 years						✔

*Measles, mumps, rubella
(✔)Except where public health authorities require otherwise.
†The AAP Committee on Infectious Disease (1992) has just recommended both universal infant immunization and adolescent immunization against hepatitis B (HBV), since selective immunization to high-risk populations failed to control the infection.
‡As of March 1991, two vaccines for *Haemophilus influenzae* infections have been approved for use in children younger than 15 months of age. The schedule varies for doses after 4 months of age depending on which vaccine for *Haemophilus influenzae* infections was previously given.
SOURCE: American Academy of Pediatrics, 1992.

TABLE 3-7

Trends in Preventable Childhood Diseases			
	Lowest Number of Cases (Year)	Number of Cases in 1991*	Increase from Best Year to 1991
Measles	1,497 (1983)	9,488	533.8%
Mumps	2,982 (1985)	4,031	35.2
Pertussis	1,248 (1981)	2,575	106.3
Rubella	225 (1988)	1,372	509.8

*Provisional data reported through December 28, 1991.
SOURCE: Centers for Disease Control,

5 percent of children in 1974 to 50 percent in 1987, with special progress noted in China, India, Nigeria, and Tanzania (Brooke, 1988; Warren, 1988). At the UN World Summit for Children in September 1990, more than 70 world leaders agreed to work for public health goals for children. Among these goals was the eradication of more than 35 percent of children's deaths worldwide by immunizing them (United Nations, 1990).

There is an irony in the fact that this summit meeting was held in the United States, where rates of routine immunization among preschool children fell steadily during the 1980s. A comparison of immunization rates in 1985, 1986, and 1987 in the United States and in several European countries (Denmark, France, West Germany, Netherlands, Norway, and England and Wales) found that American preschoolers are less likely to be protected against such diseases as polio, tetanus, diphtheria, and measles than are their European counterparts (B. C. Williams, 1990). Immunization rates are especially low among American children from minority groups.

Why are immunization rates so much higher in these other countries? The major difference seems to be the way health care is provided. All the European countries examined have systems of publicly subsidized health surveillance, which offer easy access with little or no cost. In the United States, on the other hand, many children are not covered by any health insurance and those who are often have no coverage for preventive care.

As of this writing, there is no national child health policy in the United States. This lack is not only a detriment to children's health; it is also an inefficient way to administer public funds, since every dollar spent on immunization against measles, mumps, and rubella saves $13.40 over treating children with these illnesses, and every dollar spent on pertussis immunization saves $11.10 (Harvey, 1990).

DEVELOPMENT DURING THE FIRST 3 YEARS OF LIFE

Fortunately, as we'll now see, most infants develop normally and grow up healthy.

PRINCIPLES OF DEVELOPMENT

Development is not haphazard or idiosyncratic. Rather, it progresses along logical lines that are similar for all human beings. Three guiding principles are at work in growth and development both before and after birth.

Top-to-Bottom Development

Babies develop head first. The *cephalocaudal principle* ("head to tail," from Greek and Latin roots) dictates that development proceeds from the head to the lower parts of the body. As we saw in Table 2-2, an embryo's head, brain, and eyes develop earliest; the head of a 2-month-old embryo is half the length of the entire body. By the time of birth, the head is only one-fourth the length of the body but is still disproportionately large; it becomes less so as the child grows (see Figure 3-3).

And infants learn to *use* the upper parts of the body before the lower parts. Babies can see objects before they can control the trunk, and they can use their hands to grasp long before they can walk.

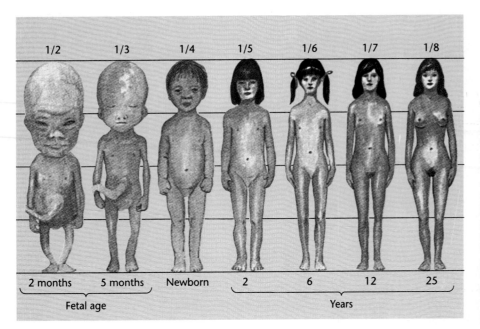

| 1/2 | 1/3 | 1/4 | 1/5 | 1/6 | 1/7 | 1/8 |

| 2 months | 5 months | Newborn | 2 | 6 | 12 | 25 |

Fetal age   Years

FIGURE 3-3
Changes in proportions of the human body during growth. The most striking change is that the head becomes smaller relative to the rest of the body: the fractions indicate head size as a proportion of total body length at several ages. More subtle is the stability of the trunk proportion (from neck to crotch). The increasing leg proportion is almost exactly the reverse of the decreasing head proportion.

Inner-to-Outer Development

Before infants can use their hands purposefully, they are quite adept at moving their arms. This is evidence of a second principle of development that is at work beginning in the womb. According to the *proximodistal principle* ("near to far," from Latin roots), development proceeds from the central part of the body to the outer parts. The embryonic head and trunk develop before the limbs, and the arms and legs before the fingers and toes. Babies first develop the ability to use their upper arms and upper legs (which are closest to the central axis), then their forearms and forelegs, then hands and feet, and finally fingers and toes.

Simple-to-Complex Development

Although Kim was able to sit up at 6 months and Modan not until 11 months, both could sit with support before they could sit alone. The third rule of development is obvious yet profound: in acquiring practically all skills, physical or other, we progress from the simple to the complex.

Maturation follows an apparently predetermined course. The times when individual babies reach specific milestones vary widely: there is no "right" age for being able to stand or speak. But almost all children progress in a definite order from simpler movements and activities to more complicated ones. (Only with specific kinds of stimulation, like those found in mother-child in-

teractions in some nonwestern cultures, is the sequence altered noticeably; see Box 3-1).

We now look at specific aspects of physical development during the first 3 years of life. Let's first see how babies spend their time, noting the increasing wakefulness that allows them to develop in response to the world around them. We'll then consider their dramatic physical growth; after that, we'll examine their growing sensory and motor capabilities.

STATES OF AROUSAL: THE BODY'S CYCLES

The human body has an inner "clock" that regulates cycles of eating, sleeping, elimination, and perhaps even mood. These patterns of timing, which are apparently inborn, govern infants' various *states of arousal*—the periodic variations in their daily cycles of wakefulness, sleep, and activity (see Table 3-8).

Neonates sleep more than they do anything else, but each baby's sleep pattern is different. The average is about 16 hours of sleep a day, yet one healthy baby may sleep only 11 hours while another sleeps 21 (Parmelee, Wenner, & Schulz, 1964). This sleep, of course, is not continuous. The next time you say "I slept like a baby," remember that new babies usually wake up every 2 to 3 hours around the clock.

To the heartfelt relief of parents, this pattern

soon changes. At about 3 months, babies grow more wakeful in the late afternoon and early evening and start to sleep through the night. By that age, most babies "sleep through" without eating or crying; by 6 months, babies do more than half their sleeping at night. Their increasing daytime wakefulness, alertness, and activity are accompanied by rapid physical, intellectual, and emotional development.

Sleep patterns change, too. Newborns have about six to eight sleep periods, which alternate between quiet and active sleep. Babies cannot tell us if they dream, but active sleep (probably the equivalent of rapid eye movement, or REM, sleep, which in adults is associated with dreaming) appears rhythmically in cycles of about 1 hour and accounts for 50 to 80 percent of a newborn's total sleep time. During the first 6 months, active sleep diminishes until it is only 30 percent of sleep time, and the lengths of the cycles become more consistent (Coons & Guilleminault, 1982).

Babies' states give us clues to how their bodies work and how they are responding to what goes on around them. A baby in a state of deep sleep responds to stimulation very differently from an alert baby or a drowsy one. And parents' reactions to a baby who is almost always sleepy or who spends a great deal of time in a state of interested, quiet wakefulness are different from their reactions to a baby who is often awake and crying. Thus infants' states influence how their parents treat them, which in turn influences what kinds of people they will turn out to be.

Parents try to change a baby's state when they pick up or feed a crying infant or soothe a fussy one to sleep. In most cases, crying is more distressing than serious. But for low-birthweight babies, crying interferes with maintenance of weight. The age-old way to soothe crying babies involves steady stimulation: rocking or walking them, wrapping them snugly, or letting them hear rhythmic sounds or suck on pacifiers. A baby who is

TABLE 3-8

States of Arousal in Infancy

State	Eyes	Breathing	Movements	Responsiveness
Regular sleep	Closed; no eye movement	Regular and slow	None, except for sudden, generalized startles	Cannot be aroused by mild stimuli
Irregular sleep	Closed; occasional rapid eye movements	Irregular	Muscles twitch, but no major movements	Sounds or light bring smiles or grimaces in sleep
Drowsiness	Open or closed	Irregular	Somewhat active	May smile, startle, suck, or have erections in response to stimuli
Alert inactivity	Open	Even	Quiet; may move head, limbs, and trunk while looking around	An interesting environment (with people or things to watch) may initiate or maintain this state
Waking activity and crying	Open	Irregular	Much activity	External stimuli (such as hunger, cold, pain, being restrained, or being put down) bring about more activity, perhaps starting with soft whimpering and gentle movements and turning into a rhythmic crescendo of crying or kicking, or perhaps beginning and enduring as uncoordinated thrashing and spasmodic screeching

SOURCES: Adapted from information in Prechtl & Beintema, 1964; Wolff, 1966.

easy to soothe enhances a caregiver's sense of competence and self-worth, thereby helping to set up a mutually reinforcing cycle.

Some research confirms what parents have long suspected: what an infant eats or drinks affects how much the baby sleeps and cries. Fifty-three healthy bottle-fed and breastfed newborns received an extra feeding of either water, carbohydrate (lactose), or formula. The babies who got water were more likely to need soothing, and those who had gotten the most nutritious feeding, the formula, slept more. The infants were most likely to be emotionally and cognitively "available" in the first 10 minutes after feeding (Oberlander, Barr, Young, & Brian, 1992).

Beginning at birth, babies show unique behaviors during wakeful periods. Annie sticks her tongue in and out; Davey makes rhythmic sucking movements. Some infants smile often; others do not. Some boys have erections frequently, others rarely.

The level and kind of activity a newborn shows can also provide a glimpse into the child's future. One study, which followed up children at ages 4 and 8 whose movements had been electronically monitored during the first 3 days of life, shows the continuity in development we noted in Chapter 1. The most vigorous newborns tended to become highly active children; the least vigorous newborns tended to be the least active when they got older (Korner et al., 1985).

increases by about 10 to 12 inches during the first year, making the typical 1-year-old about 30 inches tall. The average 2-year-old has grown about 6 inches and is 3 feet tall; another 3 to 4 inches will be added in the third year.

This growth, however, is not smooth and continuous. Rather, research has found that it occurs in spurts, often after long periods of no growth. In studying growth patterns of 31 babies who were 3 days to 21 months old when first measured, researchers found that the babies would stay the same size for 2 to 63 days, and then they would spring up as much as a full inch in less than 24 hours (Lampl, Veldhuis, & Johnson, 1992). This finding has important implications. Instead of worrying when a child's growth seems to have halted for weeks at a time, parents and physicians should give the child several months to catch up.

As young children grow in size, their shape also changes. The rest of the body catches up with the head, which becomes proportionately smaller until full adult height is reached (as was shown in Figure 3-4). Most children become leaner; the 3-year old is slender, compared with the chubby, potbellied 1-year-old.

Teething usually begins around 3 or 4 months (when infants begin grabbing almost everything in sight to put into their mouths), but the first tooth may not arrive until sometime between 5 and 9 months of age or even later. By the first birthday, babies generally have 6 to 8 teeth; by age 2½, they have a mouthful—20 (Behrman & Vaughan, 1983).

GROWTH AND NOURISHMENT

Growth is faster during the first 3 years—and especially during the first few months—than it ever will be again (see Figure 3-4). Early physical growth and muscular development make possible the rapid motor advancements of this period.

At 5 months, the typical baby's birthweight has doubled. This brings a baby who weighed 7½ pounds (the average birthweight) to about 15 pounds. By 1 year, babies weigh 3 times their birthweight—on average, about 22 pounds. During the second year, this rapid growth tapers off; the child gains 5 or 6 pounds and by the second birthday weighs about 4 times his or her birthweight. During the third year, the gain is even less—about 4 to 5 pounds, for an average weight of 31 or 32 pounds.

A similar pattern holds true for height, which

FIGURE 3-4
Growth in height and weight during infancy and toddlerhood. Babies grow most rapidly in both height and weight during the first few months of life, then taper off somewhat by age 3.

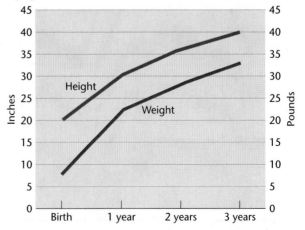

Breastfeeding brings many benefits beyond the milk itself, to both mothers and babies. Besides its nutritional advantages to the infant, there are other physical and emotional pluses to both members of the nursing couple. *(Nancy Durrell McKenna/Photo Researchers)*

Influences on Growth

The genes that babies inherit have the biggest say in shaping the body: whether it will be tall and thin, short and stocky, or somewhere in between (Stunkard, Foch, & Hrubec, 1986; Stunkard, Harris, Pedersen, & McClearn, 1990). However, height and weight are also affected by such environmental influences as nutrition, living conditions, and general health, again showing how hereditary and environmental factors interact.

Some differences show up between racial groups. The bones of black children harden earlier than those of white children, and the permanent teeth appear sooner. Also, black children mature earlier and tend to be larger than white children (American Academy of Pediatrics, 1973).

Well-fed, well-cared-for children grow taller and heavier than those who are less well nourished and nurtured. They also mature sexually and attain maximum height earlier, and their teeth erupt sooner. The differences usually begin to show up by the first year and remain consistent throughout life (American Academy of Pediatrics, 1973). Today, children are growing taller and achieving maturity sooner than they did a century ago, probably because of better nutrition, improved sanitation, and the decrease in child labor. Better medical care, especially the use of immunization and antibiotic drugs, also plays a part, since heart disease, kidney disease, and some infectious illnesses can have grave effects on growth. Children who are ill for a long time may never achieve their genetically programmed stature because they may never be able to make up for the growth time lost while they were sick.

We see, then, how heredity and environment interact in the process of physical growth. Now let's look at how different kinds of nourishment can influence babies' growth and development.

Breastfeeding

After a 50-year decline in popularity, breastfeeding has made a strong comeback, especially among better-educated, high-income women. In 1971, only 25 percent of new mothers breastfed their babies. When Sally was growing up, she never saw a child being nursed, but when she first became a mother, she decided to breastfeed her baby—and found the experience so gratifying that she went on to nurse her other two children (and was inspired to write both her first published article and her first book about breastfeeding). Today, more than half of new mothers breastfeed, and at least 5 times as many mothers now (as compared with 1971) continue to nurse their babies until at least the fifth or sixth month, even though breastfeeding rates declined again between 1984 and 1989 (Eiger & Olds, 1987; Ryan, Rush, Krieger, & Lewandowski, 1991).

The Benefits of Breastfeeding

Even though modern infant formulas approximate human milk and many babies thrive beautifully on them, breast milk is still almost always the best food for newborns. It has been called the "ultimate health food" because it offers so many benefits (Eiger & Olds, 1987, p. 26). Breast milk is a complete source of nutrients for young infants, more digestible than cow's milk, and less likely to produce allergic reactions. Because the way babies suck at the breast is different from the way they suck on a bottle, their teeth and jaws tend to develop better when they are breastfed (Labbok & Hendershot, 1987). Babies who are fed exclusively by breast for their first 4 months are less likely to suffer from otitis media, a disorder of the inner ear (Duncan et al., 1993).

Low-birthweight infants digest and absorb the fat in breast milk better than that in cow's milk formula. The milk of mothers of premature babies has a different composition from that of mothers of full-term infants. This may be nature's way of meeting premature babies' needs (Alemi, Hamosh, Scanlon, Salzman-Mann, & Hamosh, 1981).

Breastfed children get varying degrees of protection against diarrhea and respiratory infections like pneumonia and bronchitis (Fallot, Boyd, & Oski, 1980; Forman et al., 1984; Howie et al., 1990; Wright, Holberg, Martinez, Morgan, & Taussig, 1989). However, a Danish study of infectious illness during the first year found that breastfeeding did not protect children in a middle-class urban population in a developed country (D. H. Rubin et al., 1990). But these findings may not apply either to children in a developing nation or to rural or poor urban babies in a developed country, where breastfeeding *is* protective. Again, we must consider the context in which development occurs before drawing firm conclusions. (Here we see a good example of how the ecological approach, described in Chapter 1, helps us to evaluate and interpret findings about child development.)

Breastfeeding is an emotional as well as a physical act. The warm contact with the mother's body fosters bonding, or emotional linkage, between mother and baby, although such bonding also, of course, takes place with bottle-feeding. A mother's health, her emotional state, her lifestyle, and her attitude toward breastfeeding affect her ability to nurse her child. A very small proportion of women are physically unable to nurse; other women have strong feelings against it or are prevented by work or travel. Women are more likely to breastfeed if they begin within the first 10 hours after birth, have had a vaginal rather than a cesarean delivery (because a surgical delivery demands a longer re-

covery time), and do not return to work soon after the baby's birth (Romero-Gwynn & Carias, 1989). A mother's ethnic, cultural, and socioeconomic status also affect her decision on how she feeds her baby.

The Cultural Context of Breastfeeding

Although increases in breastfeeding rates have occurred across socioeconomic and educational levels (Martinez & Krieger, 1985), breastfeeding is still less popular than bottle-feeding among younger, poorer, and minority women (Fetterly & Graubard, 1984; Jacobson, Jacobson, & Frye, 1991; Rassin et al., 1984). Some of these women may not choose to nurse because they do not have information about the benefits of breastfeeding; others because they do not want to go against the norms of their community. Black inner-city mothers who do nurse their babies tend to show a higher level of ego maturity than do their counterparts who use the bottle (Jacobson, Jacobson, & Frye, 1991). Another source of difficulty involves unrealistic expectations; expecting nursing to be easy and natural, women who encounter problems at the beginning often become discouraged and switch to the bottle. Yet, most mothers need to learn to nurse and many babies have to learn to suckle, a process that may take some weeks. Support from family, friends, and professionals during these early weeks is often crucial to breastfeeding success.

Many hospital practices still discourage breastfeeding, and many doctors do not know enough about it to help and encourage new mothers, especially women in populations that are least likely to breastfeed. For example, women who receive free samples of infant formula from the hospital stop breastfeeding sooner than do women who receive discharge gifts of a breast pump (Dungy, Christensen-Szalanski, Losch, & Russell, 1992). Another category of women who tend to bottle-feed are those who must return to work full-time soon after their babies' births.

To encourage new mothers to consider breastfeeding, doctors, nurses, expectant parents, and schoolchildren need information about nutrition and lactation. Hospitals should make it possible for mothers to nurse on demand rather than restrict babies' feedings to rigid 3- or 4-hour schedules. And employers should help parents by offering help in finding child care near the workplace and by giving mothers "breastfeeding breaks" from work.

Bottle Feeding

Babies who are fed with properly prepared formula and raised with love also grow up healthy and well adjusted. Most bottle-fed babies receive a formula based on either cow's milk or soy protein. These formulas are manufactured to resemble mother's milk as closely as possible, but they contain supplemental vitamins and minerals that breast milk does not have. Breast milk or formula is the only food most babies need until they are about 4 to 6 months of age. After 4 months, breast-fed infants may need to receive supplemental iron; one group of Argentinian babies who received no food other than breast milk showed a higher incidence of anemia than did babies fed with formula (Calvo, Galindo, & Aspres, 1992).

Long-term studies that have compared breast-fed and bottle-fed children have found no significant differences either in terms of physical health or psychological adjustment (McClelland, Constantian, Regalado, & Stone, 1978; M. H. Schmitt, 1970). The quality of the relationship between mother and child seems to be more important than the feeding method.

Cow's Milk and Solid Foods

Because infants who were fed plain cow's milk in the early months of life were found to suffer from iron deficiency (Sadowitz & Oski, 1983), the American Academy of Pediatrics (AAP, 1989b; AAP Committeee on Nutrition, 1992b) recommends that babies receive breast milk or iron-fortified formula for the first year of life. Infants who were fed cow's milk in the second half of the first year showed a 30 percent increase in intestinal blood loss and a significant loss of iron in their stools. At 1 year, babies can switch to cow's milk if they are getting a balanced diet of supplementary solid foods providing one-third of their caloric intake. They should get homogenized whole milk fortified with vitamin D, not skim milk or reduced-fat (2 percent) milk, since babies need the calories in whole milk for proper growth. They do not need specially blended follow-up, or "weaning," formulas (AAP, 1989b).

The AAP strongly recommends waiting to start solid foods and fruit juices until 4 to 6 months of age. But because of aggressive marketing of baby food, parents' competitiveness, and the false belief that solid food helps babies sleep through the night, many infants begin getting solids—usually cereal or strained fruits—by the age of 2 months.

Some nutritionists condemn early feeding of solids as a form of forced feeding (Fomon, Filer, Anderson & Ziegler, 1979, p. 54), because babies who cannot sit without support or control their heads and necks cannot effectively communicate when they have had enough. (See Box 3-2 for a discussion of obesity in infants.)

The diet of children over age 2 should contain no more than 30 percent of total calories from fat (10 percent from saturated fats, those fats that are solid at room temperature) and less than 300 milligrams of cholesterol daily (AAP Committee on Nutrition, 1992a). However, children do need adequate amounts of dietary fat for normal growth and development. Cholesterol screening in small children is controversial, but the AAP does endorse it for children over 2 with a family history of heart disease, high cholesterol, or several other risk factors. If a high level is found, these children's diets should be modified accordingly. Drugs, however, should be used only with great caution because of the risk of side effects, including the potential of interfering with growth.

THE SENSES

"The baby, assailed by eyes, ears, nose, skin, and entrails at once, feels that all is one great blooming, buzzing confusion," wrote the psychologist William James in 1890. We now know that this is far from true. Infants are able to make some sense of their perceptions, and they can discriminate in the areas of sight, hearing, taste, smell, and touch.

Sight

Vision is the least well developed sense at birth. The eyes of newborns are smaller than those of adults, the retinal structures are incomplete, and the optic nerve is underdeveloped. At birth, normal babies blink at bright lights. The ability to shift their gaze to follow a moving target develops rapidly in the first months.

Peripheral vision is very narrow at birth. It more than doubles between 2 and 10 weeks of age (Tronick, 1972). A baby's eyesight is poor at first, but an infant's eyes focus best from about 1 foot away—just about the typical distance from the face of a person holding a newborn.

Vision becomes much more acute during the first year, reaching 20/20 levels by about the sixth month (Aslin, 1987). (This measure of vision means

BOX 3-2 FOOD FOR THOUGHT

WHEN DOES OBESITY BEGIN, AND WHAT SHOULD BE DONE ABOUT IT?

Obesity is a major problem among American children today. The latest studies suggest that the tendency to get fat is mainly genetic, and it is possible that some people inherit more subcutaneous fat or a more sluggish metabolism.

The belief that people may become obese later in life from being overfed in infancy rests on research in rats (Jelliffe & Jelliffe, 1974; Mayer, 1973). Feeding rat pups too many calories makes them develop too many fat cells, which persist through life (Hirsch, 1972). More recent research has cast doubt, however, on the long-term effects of how much food human babies eat.

Roche (1981) found almost no correlation between obesity before age 6 and at age 16. But after age 6 there was an increasingly strong correlation: children who were fat at age 6 or later were more likely to be fat as adults. A 40-year follow-up of Swedish children found that whether obese babies became obese adults depended very much on obesity in the family, especially in the mother. If she was fat, her child was likely to remain fat, even on a recommended diet (Mossberg, 1989). This seems to confirm a genetic basis for obesity.

Because we have no evidence that fatness hurts babies, and because children have critical growth needs, the AAP Committee on Nutrition (1981) warns against putting young children on any kind of weight-loss diet. As usual, moderation seems to be the safest course. Babies should be fed as much as they reasonably seem to need—neither more nor less.

Should efforts be made early to control children's weight? If so, why? For one thing, obese people are subject to more physical illness and tend to die sooner than people of normal weight. For another, starting in childhood they begin to suffer from our society's negative and judgmental reactions to fatness. Or should our society spend more efforts on changing our image of the more abundantly endowed among us?

---

that a person can read letters on a specified line on a standard eye chart from 20 feet away.) The first 3 years of life seem to represent a critical period for the development of binocular vision (using both eyes to focus on objects, allowing the perception of depth and distance). If children whose two eyes are not aligned properly do not have corrective surgery by age 3, their binocular sight does not develop as well as those whose visual problem is repaired early (Bertenthal & Campos, 1987).

The ability to perceive color also improves in the first few months. By about 2 months, babies can tell red and green; by about 3 months, they can see blue (Haith, 1986). Four-month-old babies can distinguish among red, green, blue, and yellow; and, like adults, they prefer red and blue (Bornstein, Kessen, & Weiskopf, 1976; Teller & Bornstein, 1987).

Depth Perception

A classic contribution to the study of infants' perceptions, and to the nature-nurture controversy (see Chapter 2), made use of a *visual cliff* (Walk & Gibson, 1961). Some observers of children believe that children are born with no knowledge of space and come to know about height, depth, and distance only through experience. To test this thesis, researchers put babies on a glass tabletop, over a checkerboard pattern. The glass formed a continuous surface, but to an adult's eye, it appeared that one side of the checkerboard pattern was a flat ledge and the other a vertical drop—that is, there was an illusion of depth (a "visual cliff"). Would infants see the same illusion and feel themselves in danger?

Young infants do see a *difference* between the "ledge" and the "drop." Six-month-old babies crawl freely on the ledge, but they avoid the drop, even when they see their mothers on the "far side." When even younger infants, aged 2 and 3 months, are placed face down over the visual cliff, their hearts slow down, probably in response to the illusion of depth (Campos, Langer, & Krowitz, 1970).

These findings suggest that depth perception is either innate or learned very early. However, the ability to *perceive* depth (as shown by a slowed heart rate, which indicates interest) does not indicate a *fear* of heights (a *faster* heart rate would indicate fear). The sense of danger does not develop until later and is related to children's ability to get around by themselves. Apparently, some mix of innate abilities and learned responses is reflected in the visual cliff experience. As usual, when researchers attempt to sort out nature and nurture, they end up seeing how closely the two interact.

Visual Preferences

The amounts of time that babies spend looking at different sights tell us about their *visual preferences,* which depend on the ability to tell one sight from another. This ability to view things selectively is present from birth.

Using an apparatus that lets an observer watch an infant's eyes and time how long she or he looks at a visual stimulus, researchers have found that babies less than 2 days old show definite preferences. Babies prefer curved lines to straight, complex patterns to simple, three-dimensional objects to two-dimensional objects, pictures of faces to pictures of other things, and new sights to familiar ones (Fantz, 1963, 1964, 1965; Fantz, Fagen, & Miranda, 1975; Fantz & Nevis, 1967).

Neonatal "pattern vision," which is related to visual preferences, can predict future development. Thirty-three newborns thought to be at high risk for developing neurologic and intellectual handicaps were tested on their ability to tell one pattern from another. On the basis of their performance, they were designated "normal," "suspect," or "abnormal." Then, their reflexes and neuromuscular maturation were examined. At age 3 or 4 years, 19 of them took the Stanford-Binet Intelligence Scale. The ratings on the neonatal visual pattern test predicted the children's IQ scores better than the ratings on the neurological tests (Miranda, Hack, Fantz, Fanaroff, & Klaus, 1977).

Hearing

Hearing is apparently good in the womb just before birth. Fetuses respond to sounds, and they may even learn some sounds while still in the womb. But immediately after birth, hearing may be impaired because of fluid that fills the inner ears as a result of the birth process. A day or two after birth, when the fluid disappears, hearing becomes efficient again.

Not only can newborns hear; they can also discriminate some sounds from others. At less than 3 days old, a baby can tell her mother's voice from a stranger's, and the mother's voice seems to have a special importance. In one study of young infants, a baby was able—by sucking on a nipple that was connected to a special apparatus—to turn on a recording of his or her mother reading a story. At certain times, though, the baby's sucking turned on a recording of another woman reading a story. As young as they were, these babies sucked about 24 percent more when it was their mother's

No matter how enticing a mother's arms are, this baby is staying away from them. As young as she is, she can perceive depth and wants to avoid falling off what looks like a cliff. *(Innervisions)*

voice on the recording (DeCasper & Fifer, 1980). Apparently, since they knew this voice, they were more interested in hearing it. Other research suggests that babies may also be born knowing their fathers' voices (Richards, 1993). Early recognition of these voices may be an important mechanism for bonding between parents and child and may be based on recognition of voices heard while the fetus is still in the womb.

Other experiments show that 3-day-old infants can distinguish between new speech sounds and those they have heard before (L. R. Brody, Zelazo, & Chaika, 1984), and that 1-month-old babies can discriminate between sounds as close as "ba" and "pa" (Eimas, Siqueland, Jusczyk, & Vigorito, 1971). Such findings suggest that newborns are biologically prepared for acquiring language.

This early sensitivity to sounds may provide a way to estimate infants' intelligence. Most attempts to predict later IQ scores have proved disappointing, but one study found significant correlations between ability to discriminate between sounds at 4 months of age and IQ score at 5 years. Thus, auditory sensitivity to changes in the environment may be one of the earliest indicators of cognitive functioning (O'Connor, Cohen, & Parmelee, 1984). In Chapter 4, we will look further at the relationship between childhood IQ and early

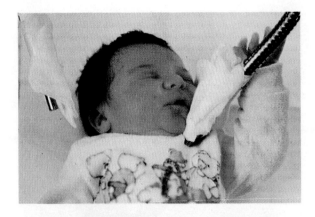

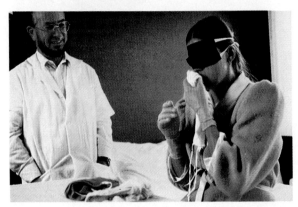

The nose knows. Three-day-old infants, like this one, act more peaceful when they smell pieces of gauze that their mothers have worn than when they smell cloth worn by other women. And blindfolded mothers can distinguish by smell between shirts their own babies have worn and shirts worn by other babies. *(J. Guichard/Sygma)*

sensory abilities (specifically, the ability to process sensory information efficiently).

Smell

Newborns can tell distinctive odors apart, and they seem to show by their expression that they like the way vanilla and strawberries smell but they do not like the smell of rotten eggs or fish (Steiner, 1979). They can also tell where odors are coming from. When an ammonium compound is dabbed on one side of the nose, babies in the first day of life will turn their noses to the other side (Rieser, Yonas, & Wilkner, 1976).

Smell is a powerful means of communication among human beings, beginning soon after birth. Six-day-old breastfed infants prefer their own mother's breast pad over that of another nursing mother, but 2-day-old infants do not, suggesting

that babies need a few days' experience to learn how their mothers smell (Macfarlane, 1975). This preference helps infants find food.

Taste

Most people's preference for lemonade over lemons seems to suggest an inborn sweet tooth. Newborns can tell different tastes apart, and they seem to prefer sweet tastes to sour or bitter ones. The sweeter the fluid, the harder they suck and the more they drink (Haith, 1986). This preference for sweet tastes is adaptive, since human breast milk is quite sweet. Newborns reject bad-tasting food, an ability that probably also serves as a survival mechanism.

Touch and Pain

Touch seems to be the earliest sense to develop, and for the first several months of life, it is the most mature sensory system. When you stroke a hungry newborn's cheek near the mouth, the baby responds by trying to find and connect with a nipple. Early signs of this rooting reflex show up in 2-month-old fetuses. By 32 weeks of gestation, all body parts are sensitive to touch (Haith, 1986), and infants' sensitivity to touch—and particularly, to pain—increases during the first 5 days of life.

Historically, when an 8-day-old Jewish boy was circumcised by a ritual practitioner, the baby was given a piece of wine-soaked cloth to suck on to dull the pain. In recent years, however, physicians have shied away from giving newborn babies anesthesia during surgery because of the belief that neonates cannot feel pain and because of the known side effects of many pain relievers. Parents have suffered as their infants have cried out in apparent pain from various procedures, wondering whether there might be long-term psychological effects of early painful experiences.

Even on the first day of life, babies can and do feel pain. Preterm and full-term newborns undergoing circumcision and such procedures as heel lancing (to obtain blood samples) cry more, have higher heart rates and blood pressure, and sweat more during and after the procedures. They also react to pain through body movements, like pulling a leg away from a pinprick, grimacing, and crying (Anand & Hickey, 1987). It seems, then, that the nervous system of a newborn is more highly developed than we used to think.

These findings have had important practical

MATURATION

consequences, like the following:

■ *Changes in some neonatal surgical procedures:* A newer mechanical method of heel lancing seems less painful than the manual method.
■ *Reconsideration of some procedures:* Nonritual circumcision is no longer performed as widely as it once was in the United States. (See Box 3-3.)
■ *Administration of safe levels of pain medication to infants:* The American Academy of Pediatrics now recommends the use of pain relievers in most surgery on infants. In one study of 415 newborns undergoing heart operations, those who received deep anesthesia that protected them from pain during the surgery and kept them unconscious for a day afterward recovered much better than babies given light anesthesia. This second group produced high levels of stress hormones, which may have made them more susceptible to various problems (Anand & Hickey, 1992).

MOTOR DEVELOPMENT

Newborn babies are busy. They turn their heads, kick their legs, flail their arms, and display an array of reflex behaviors. Even fetuses move around in the womb; they turn somersaults, kick, and suck their thumbs. But neither fetuses nor neonates have much conscious control over their movements.

By about the fourth month, voluntary, cortex-directed movements largely take over. Motor control, the ability to move deliberately and accurately, develops rapidly and continuously during the first 3 years as babies begin to use specific body parts consciously. The order in which they acquire this control follows the three principles of development outlined earlier: head to toe, inner to outer, and simple to complex.

Two of the most distinctively human motor capacities are the precision grip, in which thumb and index finger meet at their tips to form a circle, and the ability to walk on two legs. Neither of these capacities is present at birth, and both develop gradually. First, for example, Sofia picked things up with her whole hand, with her fingers closing against her palm; then she began to use neat little pincer motions with her thumb and forefinger to pick up tiny objects. First she gained control of separate movements of her arms, legs, and feet; then she was ready to put these movements together to manage walking.

Milestones of Motor Development

Babies do not have to be taught the basic motor skills; they just need freedom from interference. As soon as the central nervous system, muscles, and bones are mature enough, they need only room and freedom to move in order to keep showing new abilities. They are persistent, too; as soon as they acquire a new skill, they usually keep practicing and improving it. Parents soon grow tired of picking up a small object that a baby keeps dropping over the side of a high chair, only to cry for it and drop it again once it is retrieved; but this repetition is an important part of mastery and social interaction. Each newly mastered skill prepares a child to tackle the next one in the preordained sequence. And the proliferation of motor skills gives a child more of a chance to explore and manipulate the environment, and thus to obtain sensory and mental stimulation.

Motor development is marked by a series of milestones: achievements that signal how far development has come. The *Denver Developmental Screening Test* was designed to identify children who are not developing normally (Frankenburg, Dodds, Fandal, Kazuk, & Cohrs, 1975), but it may also be used as a benchmark for normal development between the ages of 1 month and 6 years. The test covers such gross motor skills as rolling over and catching a ball and such fine motor skills as grasping a rattle and copying a circle. It also assesses language development (for example, knowing the definition of words) and personal and social development (like smiling spontaneously and dressing). The newest edition of the test, now known as the Denver II (Frankenburg, Dodds, Archer, Shapiro, & Bresnick, 1992), has revised norms and a number of new items, including an 86 percent increase in language items.

The Denver Developmental Screening Test provides norms for the ages at which 25 percent, 50 percent, 75 percent, and 90 percent of children show each skill (see Table 3-9 for selected milestones). A child who fails to show a skill at an age when 90 percent of children ordinarily show it is considered developmentally delayed. A child with two or more delays in two or more sectors is thought to need special attention.

In the following discussion, when we talk about what the "average" baby can do, for convenience we will be referring to the 50 percent Denver norms. There is, however, no "average" baby. Normality covers a wide range; about half of all ba-

BOX 3-3   TAKE A STAND

SHOULD BABY BOYS BE CIRCUMCISED?

At one time routine nonritual circumcision was performed on almost 90 percent of newborn boys in the United States. This procedure surgically removes the foreskin, a retractable hood that covers the head, or glans, of the penis. The surgery itself takes about 15 minutes; healing takes from a week to 10 days.

The current rate, for about 60 percent of baby boys (Schoen, 1990), may rise again in response to the 1989 report by the AAP Task Force on Circumcision. Although the Task Force did not take a position on the advisability of the procedure, it did report that circumcision prevents several penile conditions, lowers the rate of cancer of the penis in adult men, and may protect against urinary tract infection in the male and cervical cancer in female sexual partners (AAP Task Force on Circumcision, 1989).

Jewish and Muslim boys are circumcised for cultural reasons. What, though, are the medical indications for or against circumcision? Both the professional and the lay community are divided—and often hotly emotional about the issue. Recently, two physicians summarized the arguments for and against routine nonritual circumcision.

IN FAVOR OF ROUTINE CIRCUMCISION

According to the chairman of the AAP Task Force on Circumcision, "The benefits of routine circumcision of newborns as a preventive health measure far exceed the risks of the procedure" (Schoen, 1990, p. 1311). This physician points to evidence favoring circumcision:

■ Lifelong genital hygiene is accomplished more easily, thus preventing the growth of bacteria that can cause several penile disorders.

■ Urinary tract infections in baby boys are much more common in uncircumcised infants.

■ Cancer of the penis is hardly ever found in a circumcised male.

■ Cervical cancer seems to be more common among the wives of men with penile cancer.

■ Uncircumcised men seem to be more susceptible to some sexually transmitted diseases, including genital ulcers, which may be a risk factor in transmitting the human immunodeficiency virus that causes AIDS.

■ Although infants do feel the pain of circumcision, there is no evidence of long-term effects, and a new local anesthetic, *dorsal penile-nerve block with lidocaine,* reduces babies' discomfort.

■ The disadvantages of circumcision are short-term, while its benefits are long-term.

AGAINST ROUTINE CIRCUMCISION

"Although the risks of routine neonatal circumcision are small, the benefits appear to be uncertain. It therefore seems prudent to consider neonatal circumcision a procedure to be performed at the discretion of the parents, not as a part of routine medical care" (Poland, 1990, p. 1315). This physician emphasizes other points:

■ Although the immediate risks are small, infection or excessive bleeding may occur in circumcision, as in any operation.

■ Babies definitely show signs of pain and stress when the procedure is performed without anesthesia.

■ There is no reliable information about the short- or long-term effects of dorsal penile-nerve block.

■ The benefits cited for the procedure are not proven. Penile hygiene can be achieved in uncircumcised males; penile disorders can occur in circumcised males. Studies showing the protective effects of circumcision may actually be reflecting sexual and other practices that are common in the cultural and economic groups that favor circumcision.

■ The procedure is costly, especially on a society-wide basis if third parties (like insurance companies and the government) pay for it.

In sum, then, there are valid arguments on both sides of the issue. Although the procedure is fast and usually safe when done by an experienced practitioner, and serious complications are rare and relatively minor (Wiswell & Geschke, 1989), the AAP Task Force on Circumcision (1989) recommends that the surgery should be performed only on stable, healthy babies and urges that parents should understand both benefits and risks before deciding to have their sons circumcised.

TABLE 3-9

Milestones of Motor Development

Skill	25 percent	50 percent	90 percent
Rolling over	2 months	3 months	5 months
Grasping rattle	2½ months	3½ months	4½ months
Sitting without support	5 months	5½ months	8 months
Standing while holding on	5 months	6 months	10 months
Grasping with thumb and finger	7½ months	8½ months	10½ months
Standing alone well	10 months	11½ months	14 months
Walking well	11 months	12 months	14½ months
Building tower of two cubes	12 months	14 months	20 months
Walking up steps	14 months	17 months	22 months
Jumping in place	20½ months	22 months	36 months
Copying circle	26 months	33 months	39 months

Note: This table shows the approximate ages when 25 percent, 50 percent, and 90 percent of children can perform each skill, according to the Denver Developmental Screening Test II.
SOURCE: Adapted from Frankenburg, Dodds, Archer, Shapiro, & Bresnick, 1992.

bies master these skills before the ages given, and about half afterward.

Head Control

At birth, most newborns can turn their heads from side to side while lying on their backs. While lying chest down, many can lift their heads enough to turn them. Within the first 2 to 3 months, they lift their heads higher and higher. By 4 months of age, almost all infants can keep their heads erect while being held or supported in a sitting position.

Hand Control

Newborns are born with a grasping reflex. If the palm of an infant's hand is stroked, the baby automatically closes the hand tightly. At about 3½ months, most infants can grasp an object of moderate size, like a rattle, but have trouble holding a small object. Next they begin to grasp objects with one hand and transfer them to the other, and then to hold (but not pick up) small objects. Sometime between 7 and 11 months, their hands become coordinated enough to pick up a tiny object like a pea with pincer-like motion. After that, hand control becomes increasingly precise. At 14 months, the average baby can build a tower of two cubes. About 3 months before the third birthday, the average toddler can copy a circle fairly well.

Locomotion

After 3 months, the average infant begins to roll over purposefully, first from front to back and then from back to front. (Before this time, however, babies sometimes roll over accidentally, and so even the youngest ones should never be left alone on a surface they might roll off.)

Babies sit either by raising themselves from a prone position or by plopping down from a standing position. The average baby can sit without support by 5 to 6 months and can assume a sitting position without help 2 months later.

At about 6 months, most babies begin to get around under their own power, in several primitive ways. They wriggle on their bellies and pull their bodies along with their arms, dragging their feet behind. They hitch or scoot by moving along in a sitting position, pushing forward with their arms and legs. They bear-walk, with hands and feet touching the ground. And they crawl on hands and knees with their trunks raised, parallel to the floor. By 9 or 10 months, babies get around quite well by such means, and so parents have to keep a close eye on them.

This kind of locomotion has important psychological implications. Did you ever drive for the first time to a place where you had gone only as a passenger? When you first had to find your own way, you probably saw landmarks you had never noticed, were aware of turns you had never felt, and—after getting there on your own—felt much more familiar with the entire route. The same kind of thing happens when babies begin to get around on their own, after having been carried or wheeled everywhere. "Self-produced locomotion" seems to

Lifting and holding up the head from a prone position, having enough hand control to use an aunt's nose as a handhold, and crawling along the floor to reach something enticing are all important early milestones of motor development. (a: *Phil Hollembeak;* b: *Mark Olds;* c: *Laura Dwight*)

be a turning point in the second half of the first year of life, influencing many aspects of physical, intellectual, and emotional development.

Between 7 and 9 months of age, babies show vast changes. They show a new understanding of concepts like "near" and "far"; they imitate more complex behaviors; they show new fears; and, on the other hand, they show a new sense of security around their parents or other caregivers. All these changes may result from a major reorganization of brain function, initiated by the new ability to crawl (Bertenthal & Campos, 1987; Bertenthal, Campos, & Barrett, 1984).

Crawling gives children a new view of the

world. They become very sensitive to where and what size objects are, whether objects are rooted or movable, and how objects are positioned relative to each other (Campos, Bertenthal, & Benson, 1980). In one study, babies were more successful at finding a toy hidden in a box when they had crawled around the box than when they had been carried around it (Benson & Uzgiris, 1985).

The ability to move from one place to another also has social implications. Crawling babies seem to be better able to tell themselves apart from the rest of the world: they see that people and objects around them can look different, depending on distance and closeness. Also, being able to get around means that a child is no longer a "prisoner" of a particular location. If Milly wants to be close to her mother and far away from a strange dog, for example, she can move toward the one and away from the other. This is an important step in developing a sense of mastery over the world, which enhances self-confidence and self-esteem.

Crawling babies get into new situations, and they learn to look for clues as to whether an ambiguous situation is secure or frightening, showing growth in a skill known as *social referencing.* Crawling babies look at ("socially reference") their mothers more than babies who have not yet begun to crawl, apparently to try to pick up emotional signals from their mothers' faces or gestures, which in turn influence the babies' behavior (Garland, 1982). The physical milestone of crawling seems to have far-reaching effects in helping babies see their world and themselves in a new way.

The next milestone is standing. By holding onto a helping hand or a piece of furniture, the average baby can stand at a little less than 6 months of age, but will only occasionally stand erect. About 4 months later, after dogged practice in pulling themselves to an upright posture, babies can at last let go and stand alone. The average baby can stand well about 2 weeks or so before the first birthday.

All these developments are milestones along the way to the major motor achievement of infancy: walking. For some months before they can stand without support, babies practice walking while holding onto furniture—sitting down abruptly when they reach table's end and crawling or lurching from chair to sofa. Soon after they can stand alone well, most infants take their first unaided steps, tumble, go back to crawling, and then try again. The average baby is walking regularly, if shakily, within a few days after that, and within a few weeks—soon after the first birthday—is walking well and thus achieves the status of toddler.

During the second year, children begin to climb stairs one at a time. (Since they can crawl upstairs before that—and tumble down long before, vigilance and baby gates are needed.) At first they put one foot and then the other on the same step before going on to the next higher one; later they will alternate feet. Going down the stairs comes later. In their second year, toddlers are running and jumping; their parents, trying to keep up with them, are running out of energy. At age 3, most children can balance briefly on one foot, and some begin to hop.

Environmental Influences on Motor Development

Human beings seem to be genetically programmed to sit, stand, and walk. Motor skills like these unfold in a regular, largely preordained pattern. Children must reach a certain level of physiologic maturation before they are ready to exercise each ability.

The role of the environment in this timetable is usually quite limited, although early experience can affect maturation rates in some areas, like vision (Lipsitt, 1986). In general, when children are well fed and well cared for and have physical free-

The major motor achievement of infancy, walking, occurs at different ages. Some babies find it easier to take their first steps when they have something to push. At this age, the pushability of the toy is more important than its service as a doll carriage. *(Margaret Miller/ Photo Researchers)*

BOX 3-4   PRACTICALLY SPEAKING

ARE "WALKERS" WORTH THE RISK?

The infant walker—a seat in a collapsible frame on wheels—is a very popular piece of equipment. More than half of American babies are placed in them at some time before they begin to walk.

Many parents buy a walker partly to amuse their babies but also because they believe it will help the babies learn to walk sooner. Unfortunately, some of these babies hurt themselves very badly. Thousands of walker-related injuries have been reported in the United States and Canada.

In 1984, in a single hospital in Toronto, 139 children who had used infant walkers were treated for such injuries as skull fractures (75 percent of the injuries in this group) and fractures of exposed body parts. One 6-month-old baby died after falling down 14 steps and hitting its head on a concrete floor (Rieder, Schwartz, & Newman, 1986). Most injuries came from the baby's tipping over the walker or falling down steps while in it. In one-third of the cases in this study, stair gates had been in place but were improperly attached or left unlatched. In 10 cases, the baby fell from the walker itself. In 21 cases, no one was in the room with the baby.

Surprisingly, 2 months after the accidents, nearly one-third of the babies were still being placed in their walkers; another one-third had stopped being placed in walkers only after learning to walk. The parents' most frequently stated reasons for using the walkers were that they made the babies happier by helping them get around, that they served as "baby-sitters," and that they encouraged early walking.

Ironically, a study of twins found that infant walkers do not speed up independent walking (Ridenour, 1982). One twin in each pair was placed in a walker for 1 hour a day from 4 months of age until walking began; the other twin was not. Twins in the two groups walked at about the same average age.

These findings reinforce others, cited in this chapter, that motor control and coordination generally develop at a natural pace (Gesell, 1929; McGraw, 1940). Efforts to hurry the process are likely to be useless or even harmful. At the very least, walkers should be used only when a parent or caretaker is within arm's reach—and never near open stairs.

---

dom and the chance to practice motor skills, their motor development will be normal. When the environment is grossly deficient in any of these areas, development can suffer—as in a classic study of three orphanages in Iran.

In this study, the overworked attendants in two of the orphanages hardly ever handled the children. Babies spent almost all their time on their backs in cribs. They sucked from propped-up bottles. They were never put in a sitting position or placed on their stomachs. They had no toys and were not taken out of bed until they could sit without help (often not till 2 years of age, as compared with 5½ months for the average American child). Once a child who could sit did reach the floor, there was no child-sized furniture or play equipment. These children were delayed in their motor development, apparently because of the deficient environment, which kept them from moving around and provided little stimulation. By contrast, the children in a third orphanage were fed in the arms of trained attendants, were placed on their stomachs and propped up to sit, and had many toys. These children showed normal levels of motor development.

When the children in the first two orphanages did start to get about, they scooted (moved around in a sitting position, pushing the body forward with their arms and feet), rather than crawling on hands and knees. Since they had never been placed on their stomachs, they had no opportunity to practice raising their heads or pulling their arms and legs beneath their bodies—the movements needed for crawling. Also, since they had never been propped in a sitting position, they had not practiced raising their heads or shoulders to learn how to sit at the usual age. Surprisingly, however, these delays seemed temporary. Older children in one of these two institutions, who presumably had also been delayed as toddlers, worked and played normally (Dennis, 1960).

Fortunately, such severe environmental deprivation is rare. But it is clear that the environment can play a part in motor development, and that the more restricted a child's environment is, the greater its effect will be.

Can Motor Development Be Speeded Up?

A number of researchers have tried to train children to walk, climb stairs, and control their bladder and bowels earlier than usual.

In a classic experiment, Gesell (1929) studied a pair of identical twins. He trained twin T, but not twin C, in climbing stairs, building with blocks, and hand coordination. With age, however, twin C became just as expert as twin T. Gesell therefore demonstrated the powerful influence of maturation on infants' behavior. Even though this study was conducted almost 70 years ago, and on only two infants, Gesell's conclusion about the importance of maturation still stands.

Toilet training also depends on maturation. It is often begun long before babies can control their sphincter muscles. When a child seems to be suc-

cessfully trained at a very early age, it is usually because the *parent* has been trained to recognize the child's readiness and can get the child to a potty or toilet in time. Before children can really control elimination, they have a lot to learn. Initially, elimination is involuntary: when an infant's bladder or bowels are full, the sphincter muscles open automatically. To control these muscles, children have to know that there is a proper time and place to allow them to open. They have to become familiar with the feelings that indicate the need to eliminate, and they have to learn to tighten the sphincter muscles until seated on the potty, and only then to loosen them.

In a study of another pair of twins, McGraw

BOX 3-5 PRACTICALLY SPEAKING

PUTTING RESEARCH FINDINGS TO WORK

If you are, or are about to become, a parent—or if you have occasion to care for infants or toddlers—you can put into practice important findings that have emerged from research in child development. The following recommendations are based on theories and findings discussed in Chapters 3, 4, and 5.

1 *Respond to babies' signals:* This is probably the single most important thing that caregivers can do. Meeting the needs of an infant, whether for food, cuddling, or comforting, establishes a sense of trust and gives the child a sense that the world is a friendly place. Answering cries or requests for help gives a baby a sense of having some control over his or her life, an important awareness for emotional and intellectual development. Adults often worry about spoiling children by reacting too quickly, but the children who have the most problems are those whose needs go unmet.

2 *Provide interesting things for babies to look at and do:* By first

watching a mobile hanging over a crib and then handling brightly colored toys and simple household objects, babies learn about shapes, sizes, and textures. Playing helps them develop their senses and motor skills. And handling objects helps them realize the difference between themselves and things that are separate from them.

3 *Be patient:* When a baby keeps throwing toys or other objects out of the crib or high chair, the purpose is not to annoy but to learn. By throwing things, babies learn such concepts as space and distance, what hands can do, and the fact that objects remain the same even when they are moved to a different place. It may be easier on your back and disposition if you tie one or two items to a string that can be pulled up each time. Of course, you should not leave the string near an unattended baby—or leave a baby alone in a high chair.

4 *Give babies the power to make changes:* If you hang a mobile

over the crib, make it possible for the baby to make the mobile move rather than depend on currents of air. Give toys that the baby can shake to make a noise, or can change in shape, or can make move. Babies need to learn that they have some control over their world and that they can have an effect on the things in it.

5 *Give babies freedom to explore:* It is better to baby-proof a room than to confine the baby in a playpen. Take away breakables, small things that can be swallowed, and sharp objects that can injure. Jam books so tightly into a bookcase that a baby cannot pull them out. But leave plenty of unbreakable objects around. Babies need opportunities to crawl and eventually to walk, to exercise their large muscles. They need to learn about their environment, to feel a sense of mastery over it. They also need freedom to go off on their own (under a caregiver's watchful eye) and develop a sense of independence.

(1940) measured the effects of very early toilet training. She put one twin on the toilet every hour of every day starting at 2 months of age; the other twin was not put on the toilet until 23 months of age. The first twin did not begin to show some control until about 20 months and did not achieve consistent success until about 23 months; and the other twin quickly caught up. Maturation has to occur before training can be effective.

While it is usually not advisable to attempt to speed up motor development for an individual child (see Box 3-4 on page 122), developmental ages for certain skills do, as we've seen, appear to vary somewhat from one culture to another.

HOW DIFFERENT ARE BOYS AND GIRLS?

Males are physically more vulnerable than females from conception throughout life. Boys are slightly longer and heavier than girls at birth and remain larger throughout adulthood, except for a brief time during puberty, when girls' earlier growth spurt causes them to overtake boys. Aside from these two differences, however, infant boys and girls are, for the most part, similar.

Although some research has found baby boys to be more active than baby girls (Maccoby & Jacklin, 1974), other studies have found the two sexes equally active during the first 2 years of life (Maccoby, 1980). Gender differences do not show up in sensitivity to touch, and very little difference appears in strength (although boys may be a little bit stronger). Further, girls and boys are more alike than different in reaching such maturational milestones as sitting up, walking, and teething. Gender differences are somewhat more pronounced in personality and social development, as we will see in Chapter 5.

By the time small children of either sex can run, jump, and play with toys requiring fairly sophisticated coordination, they are very different from the neonates that we described at the beginning of this chapter. The changes that have taken place in their intellectual capacity and activity while this physical development has gone on are equally dramatic, as we'll see in Chapter 4. Research has told us much about the way infants and toddlers develop physically, intellectually, emotionally, and socially (see Box 3-5 for ways to apply some of the findings discussed in Chapters 3, 4, and 5).

SUMMARY

THE NEONATE

- The neonatal period, the first 4 weeks of life, is a time of transition from intrauterine to extrauterine life. At birth, the neonate's circulatory, respiratory, gastrointestinal, and temperature regulation systems become independent of the mother's.
- A newborn baby's brain is one-fourth the weight of an adult's brain and grows to 80 percent of adult weight by the end of the second year. Primitive reflexes drop out as involuntary (subcortical) control of behavior gives way to voluntary (cortical) control. The brain can be molded by experience.
- At 1 minute and 5 minutes after birth, the neonate is assessed medically by the Apgar scale, which measures five factors (appearance, pulse, grimace, activity, and respiration) that indicate how well the newborn is adjusting to extrauterine life. The neonate may also be screened for one or more medical conditions. A small minority of infants suffer from birth trauma, injury sustained at the time of birth.
- The Brazelton Neonatal Behavioral Assessment Scale may be given to assess a newborn's responses to the environment and to predict future development.

- Low birthweight can influence early adjustment to life outside the womb and may even exert an influence on later development. A supportive postnatal environment can often improve the outcome. However, very low birthweight babies (those weighing 3½ pounds or less) have a less promising prognosis than those who weigh more.
- Low birthweight is a major factor in infant mortality. Although the infant mortality rate in the United States has improved, it is still disturbingly high, especially for African American babies. Birth defects are the leading cause of death in the first year.
- Sudden infant death syndrome (SIDS) is the leading cause of death in infants between 1 month and 1 year of age, affecting more than 5000 infants each year in the United States. There are many theories about the cause of SIDS, and none is universally accepted, although the most important one relates it to a brain abnormality.
- Rates of immunization are particularly poor in the United States, especially among minority-group children.

DEVELOPMENT DURING THE FIRST 3 YEARS OF LIFE

■ Normal physical growth and motor development proceed in a largely preordained sequence, according to three principles:

1 According to the cephalocaudal principle, development proceeds from the head to lower body parts.
2 According to the proximodistal principle, development proceeds from the center of the body to the outer parts.
3 Development usually proceeds from simple to complex behavior.

■ Newborn babies alternate between states of sleep, wakefulness, and activity, with sleep taking up the major (but diminishing) amount of their time. State patterns are indicators of how an infant is responding to the environment.
■ A child's body grows most dramatically during the first year of life; growth proceeds at a rapid but diminishing rate throughout the child's first 3 years.
■ Breastfeeding seems to offer physiologic benefits to the infant and facilitates formation of the mother-infant bond. However, the quality of the relationship between parents and the infant is more important than the feeding method in promoting healthy development.
■ Sensory capacities—present from birth—develop rapidly in the first months of life. Very young infants show pronounced abilities to discriminate between stimuli. Some sensory abilities appear to be related to later functioning.
■ During the first 3 months of life, infants gain control over their body movements. Motor skills normally develop when an infant is maturationally ready.
■ The Denver Developmental Screening Test is widely used to assess motor, linguistic, and personal and social development.
■ Environmental factors may retard motor development if deprivation is extreme. Environmental factors that are pervasive in a culture may affect the timetable of motor development, but short-term experiments aimed at accelerating specific types of motor development—such as stair climbing and toilet training—have generally had little effect.
■ Although infant boys are somewhat larger and more vulnerable than girls, researchers have found few other significant physical or maturational differences between the sexes in infancy.

KEY TERMS

neonatal period (page 92)
neonate (92)
fontanels (93)
vernix caseosa (93)
lanugo (93)
anoxia (93)
meconium (94)
cerebral cortex (95)
reflex behaviors (96)

birth trauma (96)
Apgar scale (96)
Brazelton Neonatal Behavioral Assessment Scale (98)
low birthweight (100)
preterm (100)
small-for-date (100)
infant mortality rate (103)
sudden infant death syndrome (SIDS) (105)

cephalocaudal principle (107)
proximodistal principle (108)
states of arousal (108)
visual cliff (114)
visual preferences (115)
Denver Developmental Screening Test (117)

SUGGESTED READINGS

DeFrain, J., Taylor, J., & Ernst, L. (1982). *Coping with sudden infant death.* Lexington, MA: Heath. An investigation of the experiences and special problems of families who have lost a child to sudden infant death syndrome.

Eiger, M. S., & Olds, S. W. (1987). *The complete book of breastfeeding.* New York: Workman, Bantam. A classic guidebook for nursing mothers that draws on research findings and incorporates many suggestions appropriate for the lifestyles of today's families.

Kopp, C. (1994). *Baby's steps: The "whys" of your child's behavior in the first two years.* New York: W. H. Freeman. An authority in the field focuses on how development leads children to act the way they do. Special "Snapshot" sections give entertaining, real-life examples, and there are suggestions for how you can help your own baby or toddler.

Leach, P. (1990). *Babyhood* (rev. ed.). New York: Knopf. A comprehensive look at the period of infancy, covering everything about a newborn baby. Although written for the layperson, the text covers the whole field of study about babies.

Manginello, F. P., & DiGeronimo, T. F. (1991). *Your premature baby.* New York: Wiley. This book helps parents with the challenge of parenting a premature infant. Medical issues such as diagnosis, treatment, and prognosis are discussed in depth. It also includes advice on caring for the baby at home, how to handle medical bills, and a discussion on ethical issues about premature babies.

Worth, C. (1988). *The birth of a father.* New York: McGraw-Hill. A supportive book that answers new fathers' questions about their new world, using interviews with fathers taken during the first year of parenthood.

CHAPTER FOUR

INTELLECTUAL DEVELOPMENT IN INFANCY AND TODDLERHOOD

So runs my dream; but what am I?
An infant crying in the night;
An infant crying for the light,
And with no language but a cry.

Alfred, Lord Tennyson,
In Memoriam, *Canto 54*

■ **HOW INFANTS LEARN**

Learning and Maturation
Types of Learning
Infant Memory

■ **STUDYING INTELLECTUAL DEVELOPMENT: THREE APPROACHES**

Psychometric Approach: Intelligence Tests
Piagetian Approach: Cognitive Stages
Information-Processing Approach: Perceptions and Symbols

■ **DEVELOPMENT OF LANGUAGE**

Stages in Development of Language
Theories of Language Acquisition
Influences on Language Development
Delayed Language Development

■ **DEVELOPMENT OF COMPETENCE**

What Influences Competence?
HOME: The Home Observation for Measurement of the Environment

■ **BOXES**

4-1 Window on the World: Eastern and Western Learning Styles
4-2 Food for Thought: What the Babbling of Hearing-Impaired Babies Tells Us about the Development of Language
4-3 Practically Speaking: Talking with Babies and Toddlers
4-4 Practically Speaking: How Parents Can Help Their Children to Be More Competent

- What can infants learn, and how can they learn it?
- What can the psychometric, Piagetian, and information-processing approaches tell us about infants' and toddlers' intellectual development?
- Can we measure or predict an infant's or toddler's intelligence?

- How does language ability develop in the early years?
- How do babies begin to develop a sense of competence?

If newborn infants could speak, they would protest that their intelligence has been underestimated for centuries. This underestimation persisted almost to the present through a coincidence of two major social movements toward the end of the nineteenth century. On one hand, psychologists were beginning to propose theories of human development. Meanwhile, on the other, doctors were establishing a routine under which babies were born in hospitals and were exposed to sedative drugs and isolated from their mothers. Thus, observations of newborns were strongly biased. Furthermore, the first tests to study infants' intelligence were based on the tests they were using for adults or animals, none of which was suited to human infants. Fortunately, all this has changed over the past few decades, which have seen more research on infants' abilities than took place during all previous history.

We now know that the normal, healthy human baby is remarkably competent. Infants enter the world with all their senses working, with the ability to learn, and with a capacity for using language. Beginning at birth, humans take an active part in affecting their environment as well as reacting to it.

In this chapter we draw on some of this research to explain the different ways babies learn. We describe the three major approaches to studying intellectual development. We follow the development of language in infancy and toddlerhood. And we discuss competence—what it is and how adults can help children to become competent.

HOW INFANTS LEARN

Do babies learn to suck on a nipple? They probably do not; sucking is a reflex they are born with. But sucking quickly becomes a learned behavior when it leads to a comfortably full stomach. Similarly, a baby's first cry is not learned behavior; but babies soon learn to *use* crying to get what they need or want.

Learning is a relatively permanent change in behavior that results from experience. Human beings are born with the *ability* to learn, but learning itself takes place only with experience. Babies learn from what they see, hear, smell, taste, and touch. Newborns begin sizing up what their senses tell them. They use their intellect to distinguish between sensory experiences (like the sounds of different voices) and to build on their small inborn repertoire of behaviors (like sucking).

Learning, then, is a form of adaptation to the environment. Before we examine some of the ways in which learning takes place and consider learning and memory, we need to clarify the relationship between learning and maturation.

LEARNING AND MATURATION

People often say things like "Sean has learned to walk" and "Vanessa is learning to talk." Learning based on experience undoubtedly played a part in Sean's walking, but that ability could not develop until he was ready, no matter how much his parents danced him on the floor. And even if Vanessa was born with the soul of a poet, she will not be able to speak like one until her mouth and vocal cords have developed enough to form verbal sounds and her brain and nervous system are mature enough to assign meanings to sounds and remember them. Certain neurological, sensory, and motor capacities must be present before related learning can take place.

We see, therefore, the importance of *maturation*, the unfolding of patterns of behavior in a biologically determined age-related sequence. These changes are programmed by the genes. In other words, before children can master new abilities, they have to be biologically ready. As we saw in Chapter 3, maturation is important for such motor skills as crawling, walking, and toilet training, and for many other physical and cognitive abilities. Maturation, then, is a necessary condition for learning to take place.

The connection between maturation and learning can be seen in the development of crawling. Very young babies placed on a "visual cliff" (see Chapter 3) show that they perceive depth, but they do not become afraid of the "deep" side until they have begun to get around on their own, as by crawling (Bertenthal & Campos, 1987). Perhaps they have fallen off something—or perhaps when they crawled on a high place they heard a caretaker cry out in fear. In any case, experience has allowed them to learn that the edge of a "cliff" is something to be afraid of. Thus, a skill that has come about through maturation (crawling) apparently contributes to a baby's ability to learn about and interpret the environment.

TYPES OF LEARNING

Babies learn in a number of ways—through the more or less simple processes of habituation, classical conditioning, and operant conditioning; and also through more complex learning that combines more than one mode.

Habituation

Habituation is a process by which repeated exposure to a particular stimulus (like a sound or a sight) results in a reduced response to the stimulus. Since habituation involves a change in behavior based on experience, it is a simple form of learning. Habituation allows us to conserve energy by remaining alert to things and events in the environment only as long as they seem to merit attention, because they seem either desirable or threatening.

Researchers study habituation in newborns by repeatedly presenting a stimulus (usually a sound or visual pattern). Typically, a baby stops sucking when the stimulus is first presented and does not start again until after the stimulation has ended. After the same sound or sight has been presented again and again, it loses its novelty and no longer influences the baby's sucking. At this point, the infant has habituated to it. A new sight or sound, however, will capture the baby's attention and

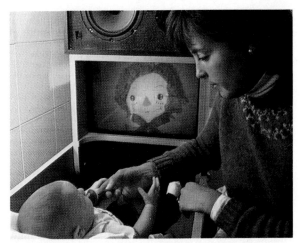

Can this baby tell the difference between Raggedy Ann and Raggedy Andy? This researcher may find out by seeing whether the baby has habituated—gotten used to one face—and then stops sucking on the nipple when a new face appears, showing recognition of the difference. *(James Kilkelly/DOT)*

again interrupt sucking. This increase in responding to a new stimulus is called *dishabituation*.

Studies based on habituation have found that newborns can tell sounds they have already heard from those they have not. In the first week of life, neonates can also distinguish between visual patterns (J. S. Werner & Siqueland, 1978). Their discriminatory ability becomes more refined by 5 months of age (Fantz, Fagan, & Miranda, 1975). The greater the difference between patterns, the less time a baby needs to tell them apart (J. F. Fagan, 1982; see Figure 4-1).

FIGURE 4-1
Visual recognition in infancy. The more two pictures differ, the less time a baby needs to distinguish them. A 5-month-old may need only 4 seconds to distinguish two very different patterns, but need 17 seconds for less varied patterns, and 20 to 30 seconds for faces. (*Source:* Fagan, 1982.)

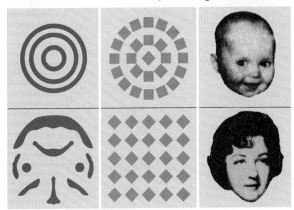

Because habituation is associated with normal development, its presence or absence, as well as the speed with which it occurs, can tell us a great deal about a baby's development. Since the capacity for habituation increases during the first 10 weeks of life, it is regarded as a sign of maturation (Rovee-Collier, 1987). Habituation studies show us how well babies can see and hear, how much they can remember, and what their neurological status is. Babies with low Apgar scores and those with brain damage, distress at the time of birth, or Down syndrome show impaired habituation (Lipsitt, 1986), as do neonates whose mothers were heavily medicated during childbirth (Bowes, Brackbill, Conway, & Steinschneider, 1970) or who took cocaine while pregnant (Eisen et al., 1991). Full-term neonates can habituate to stimuli in all sensory modalities (sight, hearing, touch, taste, and smell), while preterm newborns can generally habituate only to some stimuli in some circumstances (Rovee-Collier, 1987).

Speed of habituation shows promise as a predictor of intelligence, especially of verbal abilities. Poor habituation during the neonatal period often foreshadows slow development; a child who does not habituate at all is likely to have future learning problems (Lipsitt, 1986).

Conditioning

In Chapter 1, we saw how Anna, after her father had taken many pictures of her, eventually blinked *before* the flashbulb on his camera went off. This is an example of *classical conditioning,* in which a person or an animal learns to respond automatically to a stimulus that originally did not provoke the response. In Anna's case, this stimulus was Jonathan's camera. Classical conditioning lets the learner anticipate an event before it happens.

One of the earliest demonstrations of classical conditioning in human beings showed that emotions, such as fear, can be conditioned (Watson & Rayner, 1920). An 11-month-old baby known as "Little Albert," who loved furry animals, was brought into a laboratory. Just as he was about to grasp a furry white rat, a loud noise frightened him, and he began to cry. After repeated pairings of the rat with the loud noise, the child whimpered with fear when he saw the rat. The fear also generalized to rabbits, dogs, a Santa Claus mask, and other furry white objects. Under today's ethical standards, this experiment would never be permitted because it would be unethical to arouse fear in the name of science. However, the experiment did show that a baby could be conditioned to fear things that he had not been afraid of before.

Little Albert was almost a year old when his experiment began, but research has shown that infants can be conditioned within hours after birth (Rovee-Collier, 1987). Babies only 2 hours old have been classically conditioned to turn their heads and suck if their foreheads are stroked at the same time that they are given a bottle of sweetened water (Blass et al., 1984, in Rovee-Collier, 1987). Furthermore, newborn infants have learned to suck when they hear a buzzer or a tone; to show the Babkin reflex (turning their heads and opening their mouths) when their arms are moved (in-

An Indian snake charmer's baby eagerly plays with a snake the father has trained, showing that fear of snakes is a learned response. Children can be conditioned to fear animals that are associated with unpleasant or frightening experiences, as "Little Albert" was in a classic study by John B. Watson and Rosalie Rayner. *(Mary Ellen Mark)*

stead of the usual stimulus, pressure on the palm of the hand); to dilate and constrict the pupils of their eyes; to blink; and to show a change in heart rate (Rovee-Collier & Lipsitt, 1982).

Terrell's smiling to get loving attention from his parents (also described in Chapter 1) is an example of *operant (instrumental) conditioning,* in which a baby learns to make a certain response in order to produce a particular effect. Operant conditioning, in which the learner influences the environment, can be used to learn voluntary behaviors (as opposed to involuntary behaviors like blinking).

In one study, 2-day-old infants were rewarded with music as long as they sucked on a dry nipple. The babies would keep sucking as long as the music played, but would stop sucking when their sucking turned the music off (Butterfield & Siperstein, 1972). Studies like this, which change what babies do by reinforcing certain kinds of behavior, show that neonates can learn by operant conditioning, *if* the conditioning encourages them to perform some kind of behavior that they already know (like sucking or turning the head), rather than something they would not ordinarily do.

Classical and operant conditioning can occur separately or in combination to produce increasingly complex behavior. In one series of studies involving 1- to 20-week-old infants, babies received milk if they turned their heads left at the sound of a bell. The babies who did not learn to turn their heads through this operant conditioning were then classically conditioned. When the bell sounded, the left corner of the baby's mouth was touched, and the baby turned its head and received the milk. (The touch was the unconditioned stimulus and turning the head the unconditioned response. The bell was the conditioned stimulus; turning the head to the bell became the conditioned response.)

By the age of 4 to 6 weeks, all the babies had learned to turn their heads when hearing the bell. Then the babies learned to differentiate the bell from a buzzer (Papousek, 1959, 1960a, 1960b, 1961). When the bell rang, they were fed on the left; when the buzzer rasped, they were fed on the right. At about 3 months of age, the babies had learned to turn to the side that had brought food. By 4 months, they even learned to reverse their responses to bell and buzzer—an impressively complex response.

Babies learn in other ways besides habituation and conditioning. For example, they learn from observing and imitating models (social learning, described in Chapter 1, is also discussed later in this book). Children learn many complicated abilities through a mix of different kinds of learning and natural growth, or maturation.

INFANT MEMORY

Can you remember anything that happened when you were less than 1 year old? Chances are that you can't. We're not sure why this is so. Perhaps, as Freud believed, we repress our early memories; or perhaps we simply replace them with later, more complex ones.

But it is clear that infants do have memory. If they did not possess at least a short-term ability to remember, they would not be able to learn (Lipsitt, 1986). Moreover, even very young infants have shown a surprising ability to remember. For example, newborns who heard a certain speech sound one day after birth remembered that sound 24 hours later (Swain, Zelazo, & Clifton, 1993).

Babies less than 2 months old can remember past events, especially if the events gave them pleasure. Researchers studying 6-week-old babies tied a ribbon to each baby's left leg and also attached the ribbon to a bright mobile hung above the crib. The babies quickly learned that kicking would activate the mobile. Then the mobile was removed. When the mobiles were hung again 2 to 4 weeks later, ribbons were *not* attached to the babies' legs. But the babies still kicked when they saw the mobiles, especially with their left legs; they remembered that kicking activated the mobile (Rovee-Collier & Fagan, 1976, 1981; M. W. Sullivan, 1982).

In another study, babies who were trained with different mobiles on different days learned to expect a different one each time (Fagan, Morrongiello, Rovee-Collier, & Gekoski, 1984). Their ability to mentally incorporate the idea of change was shown by their responding more to a new mobile than to the old one. Findings like these "suggest that infants are 'built' to organize and find structure in what must otherwise appear to be a random and chaotic world" (p. 942).

Part of this structure involves the context (setting) in which a baby learns something. Infants as young as 3 to 6 months of age can recognize differences in settings, and they seem to encode information about the context, along with whatever else they are learning.

This finding emerged from a series of studies in which babies learned to activate a mobile by kicking. The babies were trained in a playpen with two sides covered by cloth in one of four patterns: stripes, squares, dots, or triangles. Upon retesting,

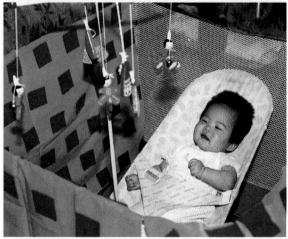

Babies less than 2 months old can remember, after a hiatus of 2 to 4 weeks, that they were able to activate a mobile by kicking their foot; they show this by kicking as soon as they see the mobile. The series of experiments in this research varied the contexts in which the babies learned, and contextual cues helped to establish memory. *(Carolyn Rovee-Collier)*

either 24 hours, 3 weeks, or 6 months later, the babies remembered how to activate the mobile if they were retested in a playpen with the same pattern. But if they were retested in a differently patterned playpen, they did not retrieve the original memory. This inability to recognize the original training cue in a different context may be adaptive by ensuring that old memories, no longer appropriate, will not be recovered (Rovee-Collier, Schechter, Shyi, & Shields, 1992; Shields & Rovee-Collier, 1992; Amabile & Rovee-Collier, 1991).

Early memories can last a long time. One recent study found that 2½-year-olds remembered an experience with a rattle that occurred at the age of 6½ months (Perris, Myers, & Clifton, 1990). The

ability that memory provides to organize the world is closely tied in with the development of intelligence. The research just described shows that from a very early age, infants can remember past events and can use mental symbols to do so. We can also see a connection between infants' cognitive and emotional development. If long-term memory exists for a distinctive but unemotional event like an experiment with a rattle, we need to ask: What important emotional consequences might follow an early traumatic experience?

This ability to organize the world is closely tied to the development of intelligence. Later in this chapter, we'll see how Piaget's concept of deferred imitation helps researchers assess infants' ability to recall events.

STUDYING INTELLECTUAL DEVELOPMENT: THREE APPROACHES

Rebecca, at 1 year, loved Cheerios—and she loved to play games with her father, Dan. One day Dan put some Cheerios into his hand, closed it, and put his fist on the tray of her high chair. Rebecca immediately pulled his fingers open and reached for the Cheerios. But as soon as she released Dan's fingers, they snapped closed. After two tries, she discovered that she could hold his fingers open with one hand while she picked up Cheerios with the other. One day, when one hand held a toy that she did not want to drop, Rebecca came up with another solution. She opened Dan's fingers with her free hand and held them open with her chin, so that she could use the free hand to get the Cheerios.

Rebecca's problem solving demonstrates the intelligent behavior that many babies of her age are capable of—behavior involving self-initiated learning far more complex than conditioning or habituation. How did her intelligence develop? Why do some children appear to be more intelligent than others of the same age? Can we measure a baby's intelligence, and can we predict how smart that baby will be as an older child or as an adult? Such questions have implications for how children are raised and schooled and what opportunities are made available to them. The questions are hard to answer because intelligence is a complicated subject: difficult to analyze, difficult to describe, and difficult to account for fully.

First, what do we mean by intelligence? Although there are many definitions, ***intelligent be-***

havior is generally considered to have two key aspects: it is *goal-oriented*, meaning that it is conscious and deliberate rather than accidental; and it is *adaptive*, meaning that human beings use their intelligence to identify and solve problems. Intelligence is affected by both inherited ability and environmental experience, as we saw in Chapter 1. Intelligence results in a person's being able to acquire, remember, and use knowledge; to understand concepts and relationships among objects, ideas, and events; and to apply knowledge and understanding to everyday problems.

Most investigators of intelligence have taken one of three approaches:

■ *Psychometric approach:* This approach tries to measure intelligence in terms of quantity, or *how much* intelligence a person has. It uses *intelligence tests;* the higher the test score, the more intelligent a person is assumed to be.
■ *Piagetian approach:* This approach looks at the quality of intellectual functioning, or *what* people can do. It is concerned with the evolution of mental structures and how children adapt to their environment, and it maintains that cognition develops in stages.
■ *Information-processing approach:* This approach analyzes the processes underlying intelligent behavior, or *how* people use their intelligence.

All three approaches help us to understand intelligence. No single approach gives us a full picture, but a combination of approaches opens several windows to let us examine intelligent, effective behavior. Let us see what each of the three approaches can tell us—particularly about the intellectual development of infants and toddlers.

PSYCHOMETRIC APPROACH: INTELLIGENCE TESTS

At the beginning of the twentieth century, school administrators in Paris asked the psychologist Alfred Binet to devise a test to identify children who were unable to handle academic work. These children could then be removed from regular classes and given more suitable programs. The test that Binet and his colleague Theodore Simon developed was the forerunner of psychometric tests that try to score intelligence by numbers. Since these tests have traditionally been given to older children (and are still being given to them), we will discuss this approach in detail in Chapter 6.

The *psychometric approach* tries to determine and measure quantitatively the factors that make up intelligence. This approach is used much less today, especially in assessing the development of very young children. But since it is historically important, we will briefly describe its use and its limitations in assessing infants and toddlers.

Why Is It Difficult to Measure Infants' and Toddlers' Intelligence?

Though we now know that infants are intelligent, measuring their intelligence is another matter. For one thing, babies cannot talk. You can't ask them questions and get answers. They can't tell you what they know and how they think. The most obvious way to gauge their intelligence is by what they can do, but very young infants do not do very much. An experimenter may try to catch their attention and coax them into some behavior; but if they do not grasp a rattle, say, it is hard to tell whether they do not know how, do not feel like doing it, or do not realize what is expected of them.

Not surprisingly, an infant's test scores tend to vary widely from one time to another. Their value in assessing a baby's *current* abilities is questionable; and they are almost useless for predicting *future* functioning. It is next to impossible to predict adult or even childhood IQ from psychometric scores of normal children before age 2. A more useful predictor of childhood IQ is the parents' IQ or educational level (Kopp & Kaler, 1989; Kopp & McCall, 1982). Not until the third year of life do the child's own scores, along with these factors, increase the reliability of prediction.

Even for toddlers, predictions based on psychometric tests are highly unreliable. In one longitudinal study, individual IQs changed by an average of 28½ points between ages 2½ and 17, and the IQs of 1 in 7 children shifted by more than 40 points (McCall, Appelbaum, & Hogarty, 1973). As youngsters are tested closer to their fifth birthday, the relationship between their intelligence scores and those in later childhood becomes stronger (Bornstein & Sigman, 1986).

Why do early intelligence scores fail to predict later scores? One answer probably has to do with the fact that the tests traditionally used for babies (see the discussion of developmental testing below) are primarily sensory and motor whereas the tests used for older children are heavily verbal. This implies that the tests measure different and largely unrelated kinds of intelligence (Bornstein & Sigman, 1986). Even when we look at motor skills alone, children who are good at the large-muscle activities tested at an early age may not be as adept at fine motor, or manipulative, skills considered to be a sign of intelligence a little later on. For example, a child who at 1 year could build towers with blocks may not by the age of 7 be able to copy a design made from colored blocks.

It is somewhat easier to predict the future IQ of a handicapped infant. Yet some children born with mental and motor disabilities make impressive strides in tested intelligence as they grow older. A supportive environment can help such a child learn special ways to cope (Kopp & Kaler, 1989; Kopp & McCall, 1982). In addition, human beings seem to have what some observers call a "strong self-righting tendency" (Kopp & McCall, 1982). That is, given a favorable environment, infants will generally follow normal developmental patterns unless they have suffered severe damage. Sometime between the ages of 18 and 24 months, however, this self-righting tendency seems to diminish as children begin to acquire skills (like verbal abilities) in which there will eventually be great variations in proficiency. As these sophisticated skills develop, individual differences become more pronounced and more lasting.

What Is Developmental Testing?

Despite the difficulties in measuring the intelligence of very young children, sometimes there are reasons for testing them. If parents are worried that a baby is not doing the same things as other babies of the same age, early testing may reassure them that their child's development is normal, though different. Or it may alert them to abnormal development and to the need to make special arrangements for the child.

Developmental tests are tests specially designed to chart the progress of infants and toddlers. These tests are primarily nonverbal, because they are designed for children who do not yet have a command of language (Anastasi, 1988). Many of these tests measure sensory and motor development.

Developmental tests are based on careful observations of large numbers of children. After determining what most infants or toddlers can do at particular ages, researchers develop standardized norms, assigning a developmental age to each specific activity. An individual child's performance is then evaluated in comparison to these norms.

One important test for this purpose is the *Bayley Scales of Infant Development* (Bayley, 1969; revised Bayley II, 1993). The Bayley II, which is used

to assess the developmental status of children from 1 to 42 months of age (3½ years), is now used primarily with children who are at risk or suspected of being at risk for abnormal development. The items in the Bayley II (see Table 4-1) fall into three categories:

1 *Mental scale:* measures such abilities as perception, memory, learning, and verbal communication.
2 *Motor scale:* measures gross and fine motor skills.
3 *Behavior rating scale:* a thirty-item rating completed by the examiner of the child's test-taking behaviors.

The separate scores calculated for each scale are useful for assessing a child's current abilities, but not for predicting later intelligence. They are most helpful for early detection of emotional disturbances and sensory, neurological, and environmental deficits (Anastasi, 1988).

Can Children's Scores on Intelligence Tests Be Improved?

Improved parenting skills and an enriched day care environment can apparently increase very young children's intelligence test scores. In Project CARE, one group of babies from disadvantaged backgrounds in North Carolina received two kinds of intervention, starting before they were 5 months old (Wasik, Ramey, Bryant, & Sparling, 1990). Home visitors met with the babies' parents, helping them to solve various problems of child rearing and daily life, and encouraging them to play educational games with their children. Meanwhile, activities at the day care center were designed to stimulate language and to foster social and cognitive development. A second group of babies received only the home visit program, and a third, control group got no systematic education.

At nine different times, from ages 6 months to 4½ years, the 65 children in the study were given cognitive tests. On each test after the 6-month assessment, those who received *both* home and day care intervention did better than the other two groups. The children who received only the home visits did no better than the control group. However, some other studies that found no effects during the preschool years did find them later on, after the children started school. So it is possible that such effects might show up for these children, too. In any case, these results show that the kind of care

TABLE 4-1

Sample Tasks in the Bayley Scales of Infant Development	
Age (in months)	**Tasks Most Children This Age Can Do**
5.8	Grasp edge of piece of paper held out by examiner
5.9	Vocalize pleasure and displeasure
6.0	Reach persistently for cube placed just out of reach
6.1	Turn head to watch spoon dropped to floor by child's side
6.3	Say several syllables
11.5	Stop doing something (like putting an object into the mouth) when adult says "no, no"
11.7	Try to imitate words like *mama, dada,* and *baby*
12.1	Imitate rattling of spoon in cup with stirring motion to make noise
12.6	Put round block into round hole of form board

SOURCE: Kessen, Haith, & Salapatek, 1970.

EXPLORATION OF ENVIRONMENT

babies get, both at home and in day care, can affect their intellectual development.

PIAGETIAN APPROACH: COGNITIVE STAGES

The Swiss psychologist Jean Piaget took a different approach from that of the psychometricians to the question of children's *cognitive development,* the growth in their thought processes that enables them to acquire and use knowledge about the world. To examine how children's thought evolves, Piaget closely watched the development of his own three children. His observations provided the basis for his theory of the first stage of cognitive development—the sensorimotor stage—and inspired much research on infant cognition and intelligence. Now, however, it seems that Piaget underestimated infants' and children's abilities. We will discuss research evidence for this belief in our evaluation of the *Piagetian approach.* First, we describe the highlights of the sensorimotor stage and the Piagetian concepts of object permanence and causality.

Piaget's Sensorimotor Stage (Birth to About 2 Years)

Piaget's first cognitive stage is called the *sensorimotor stage.* In this stage, during the first 2 years

of life, infants learn about themselves and their world through their own developing sensory and motor activity. Babies change from creatures who respond primarily through reflexes and random behavior into goal-oriented toddlers. They now organize their activities in relation to their environment, coordinate information they receive from their senses, and progress from trial-and-error learning to using rudimentary insights in solving simple problems.

This change is very obvious in any bookshop with a good section of children's books. Many books for babies are made of cloth or heavy board or vinyl, reflecting the fact that a baby first reacts to books by banging them, chewing on them, and taking them into the bathtub—in short, using them as objects. Not until babies are well into the sensorimotor stage do they realize that pictures in books stand for objects in the real world, and not until still later do they understand that black marks in books represent ideas as well as things.

Substages of the Sensorimotor Stage

Let's see how development proceeds in the sensorimotor stage. Table 4-2 shows in detail the great cognitive growth of the first two years.

Much of this growth in the sensorimotor period occurs through what Piaget called *circular reactions,* in which the child learns how to reproduce pleasurable or interesting events originally discovered by chance. The process has elements of

TABLE 4-2

Six Substages of Piaget's Sensorimotor Stage of Cognitive Development

Substage	Description
Substage 1 (birth to 1 month): Use of reflexes	Infants exercise their inborn reflexes and gain some control over them. They do not coordinate information from their senses. They do not grasp an object they are looking at. They have not developed object permanence.
Substage 2 (1 to 4 months): Primary circular reactions	Infants repeat pleasurable behaviors that first occur by chance (such as sucking). Activities focus on infant's body rather than the effects of the behavior on the environment. Infants make first acquired adaptations; that is, they suck different objects differently. They begin to coordinate sensory information. They have still not developed object permanence.
Substage 3 (4 to 8 months): Secondary circular reactions	Infants become more interested in the environment and repeat actions that bring interesting results and prolong interesting experiences. Actions are intentional but not initially goal-directed. Infants show partial object permanence. They will search for a partially hidden object.
Substage 4 (8 to 12 months): Coordination of secondary schemes	Behavior is more deliberate and purposeful as infants coordinate previously learned schemes (such as looking at and grasping a rattle) and use previously learned behaviors to attain their goals (such as crawling across the room to get a desired toy). They can anticipate events. Object permanence is developing, although infants will search for an object in its first hiding place, even if they saw it being moved.
Substage 5 (12 to 18 months): Tertiary circular reactions	Infants show curiosity as they purposefully vary their actions to see results. They actively explore their world to determine how an object, event, or situation is novel. They try out new activities and use trial and error in solving problems. Concerning object permanence, infants will follow a series of object displacements, but since they cannot imagine movement they do not see, they will not search for an object where they have not observed it being hidden.
Substage 6 (18 to 24 months): Mental combinations	Since toddlers have developed a primitive symbol system (such as language) to represent events, they are no longer confined to trial and error to solve problems. Their symbol system allows toddlers to begin to think about events and anticipate their consequences without always resorting to action. Toddlers begin to demonstrate insight. Object permanence is fully developed.

Note: Infants show enormous cognitive growth during Piaget's sensorimotor stage, as they learn about the world through their senses and their motor activities. Note their progress in problem solving, object permanence, and the coordination of sensory information.

operant conditioning. At first, an activity produces a sensation so welcome that the child wants to repeat it. The repetition then feeds on itself in a continuous cycle in which cause and effect become almost indistinguishable (see Figure 4-2).

The sensorimotor stage consists of six substages, which flow from one to another as a baby's *schemes*, or organized patterns of behavior, become more elaborate.

At first (birth to 1 month), neonates gain some control over their inborn reflexes. They engage in certain behaviors even when the reflex itself is not operating. For example, newborns suck reflexively when their lips are touched. They soon learn to find the nipple even when they are not touched, and they begin to suck when they are not hungry. Thus infants initiate activity.

The second stage (1 to 4 months) involves re-peating a pleasant sensation first achieved by chance (like sucking their thumbs). They learn to adjust by, say, sucking their thumbs differently from the way they suck on a nipple. They also start to coordinate and organize different kinds of sensory information, like vision and hearing. They turn toward sounds.

The third substage (4 to 8 months) coincides with a new interest in reaching out for objects. The baby begins to engage in intentional actions repeated not merely for their own sake, but to get results beyond the infant's own body, like shaking a rattle to hear the sound.

By the time they reach the fourth substage (8 to 12 months), infants have built on the few schemes they were born with. They generalize from past experience, calling on previously mastered responses in order to solve new problems. They will crawl to get something they want, grab it, or push away a barrier to it (like someone else's hand). They try out, modify, and coordinate previous schemes, to find one that works.

In the fifth substage (12 to 18 months), babies begin to experiment with new behavior. Once they begin to walk, they are curious and they explore. They now vary their original actions to see what will happen rather than merely repeating pleasing behavior they have accidentally discovered.

For the first time, children show originality in problem solving. By trial and error, they try out new behaviors until they find the best way to attain a goal. When Rebecca, for example, wanted to get the Cheerios from her father's hand, she tried prying and holding his fingers open first with one hand, then with both hands, and finally by using her chin as an additional tool.

At about 18 months, said Piaget, children, now in the sixth stage, become capable of symbolic thought. They can use language to think about actions before taking them. Since they now have some understanding of cause and effect, they no longer have to go through laborious trial and error to solve new problems. Piaget's daughter Lucienne demonstrated this breakthrough—the development of insight—when she figured out how to pry open a partially closed matchbox to remove a watch chain from it, opening and closing her mouth to signify her idea of widening the slit in the box (Piaget, 1952).

The ability to manipulate symbols frees children from immediate experience. They can now imitate actions even after whatever or whomever they are copying is no longer in front of them. They are now able to pretend, as Anna does at 20 months when she is given a tea set and immediately "serves tea" to Diane and Jonathan. This simple "pretend" play is the forerunner of more elaborate dramatic play that occurs at age 3 and later, as symbolic abilities and behaviors flourish during the preoperational stage (see Chapter 6).

Cognitive Concepts of the Sensorimotor Stage

During the sensorimotor stage, children develop several important cognitive concepts. One is *object permanence:* the realization that an object or person continues to exist even when out of sight. At first, infants have no concept that people and objects continue to exist when they cannot be seen. By the third substage, they will look for something they have dropped, but if they cannot see any part of it, they act as if it no longer exists. By the sixth substage, toddlers can follow a series of displace-

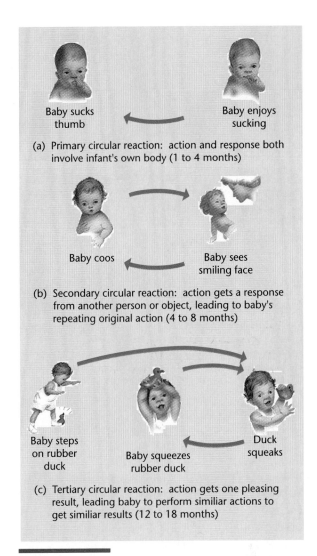

(a) Primary circular reaction: action and response both involve infant's own body (1 to 4 months)

(b) Secondary circular reaction: action gets a response from another person or object, leading to baby's repeating original action (4 to 8 months)

(c) Tertiary circular reaction: action gets one pleasing result, leading baby to perform similiar actions to get similiar results (12 to 18 months)

FIGURE 4-2

Primary, secondary, and tertiary circular reactions. According to Piaget, infants learn to reproduce pleasing events they have discovered accidentally.

(a) Primary circular reaction: A baby happens to suck a thumb, enjoys sucking, and puts the thumb back into the mouth or keeps it there. The stimulus (thumb) elicits the sucking reflex; pleasure then stimulates the baby to keep on sucking.

(b) Secondary circular reaction: This involves something outside the baby's body. The baby coos; the mother smiles; and because the baby likes to see the mother smile, the baby coos again.

(c) Tertiary circular reaction: The baby tries different ways to reproduce an accidentally discovered response. When the baby steps on a rubber duck, the duck squeaks. The baby then tries to produce the squeak in other ways, as by squeezing it or sitting on it.

This baby seems to be showing at least the beginning of the concept of object permanence by searching for an object that is partially hidden. She will have the complete concept by 18 months of age, when she will look for objects or people even when she has not seen where they were hidden. *(Doug Goodman/Monkmeyer)*

ments, looking for an object in the last place where it was hidden, even if they cannot see it.

Object permanence is the basis for children's awareness that they exist apart from objects and other people. It allows a child whose parent has left the room to feel secure in the knowledge that the parent continues to exist and will return. It is essential to understanding time, space, and a world full of objects and events.

Another important concept that emerges during this stage is *causality,* the Piagetian term for the recognition that certain events cause other events. In one study, babies saw films that showed physically impossible events, like a ball moving toward a second ball which then moved before the first ball touched it. Infants under 10 months of age showed no surprise, but older babies did. Evidently the older infants realized that a cause—such as something necessary for the movement of the second ball—was missing (Michotte, 1962, in Siegler & Richards, 1982).

It is not surprising that awareness of causality develops at about 10 months, since that is when many babies begin making their own experiments. They play with light switches and delight in making the light go on and off. Their favorite toys are those they can do something with—roll, drop, or make noise. By their actions, infants of this age show an understanding that *they* can cause things to happen.

While the roots of such important concepts as causality are taking hold now, infants cannot fully grasp them. The reason, according to Piaget, is that children of this age have limited *representational ability*—that is, a limited capacity to mentally represent objects and actions in memory. But this ability to remember and imagine things and events—largely through the use of symbols like words, numbers, and mental pictures—blossoms as children enter the next cognitive stage, the preoperational stage (discussed in Chapter 6).

Evaluation of Piaget's Sensorimotor Stage

Piaget's theories are still highly regarded for their innovative contribution to our understanding of cognitive development. But while research has supported some of his claims, it has refuted others.

Support for Piaget's Theory

According to some research, object permanence progresses in the sequence Piaget described (Kramer, Hill, & Cohen, 1975). Also, a positive relationship has been found between infants' scores on the subtests of a scale of sensorimotor development (the Infant Psychological Development Scales) and their childhood intelligence test scores.

Researchers have developed tests based on Piaget's theories to measure intellectual development in infants. Standardized tests of sensorimotor development, like the Infant Psychological Development Scales (IPDS) (Uzgiris & Hunt, 1975) combine the psychometric and Piagetian approaches. In one study, 23 babies were tested on the IPDS every 3 months between 1 and 2 years of age, and at 31 months, they were given the Stanford-Binet Intelligence Scale. A positive relationship was found between scores on the Stanford-Binet and scores on each of the eight subscales of the IPDS. The age of attaining object permanence was the strongest predictor of later scores on intelligence tests (Wachs, 1975). This seems to be a useful way to predict childhood intelligence from infants' abilities, a goal that has been hard to achieve.

Limitations of the Sensorimotor Stage Concept

Research that began to appear in the late 1970s challenges Piaget's view that infants go through a period of about 18 months when they cannot think about objects that are not physically present or about past events. In fact, infants seem able to con-

Habituation Events

Short carrot event

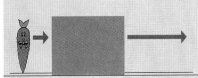

Tall carrot event

Test Events

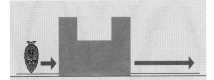

Possible event

Impossible event

FIGURE 4-3

Object permanence in infants. In this experiment, 3½-month-old infants watched a short or a tall carrot slide along a track. The track's center was hidden by a screen with a large window. The short carrot did not appear in the window when passing behind the screen; the tall carrot should have appeared in the window but did not. The babies looked longer at the tall than the short carrot event, suggesting that they were surprised that the tall carrot did not appear. (*Source:* Baillargeon & DeVos, 1991.)

ceptualize much earlier. One powerful demonstration of this is the research on very early memory abilities, described earlier. This shows that very young infants have symbolic capabilities and can remember past events. Other studies contradict Piaget's timing of several achievements.

Piaget may have underestimated infants' grasp of *object permanence* because of his testing methods. Young babies may fail to search for hidden objects because they are not able to perform a sequence of actions—like moving a cushion to look for something hidden behind it. Infants as young as 3½ months of age, tested by a more age-appropriate procedure, behaved as if they remembered an object they could not see (Baillargeon & DeVos, 1991; see Figure 4-3).

One Piagetian notion that research also seems to refute is the belief that the *senses are unconnected at birth* and are only gradually integrated through experience. We now know that right after birth, newborn infants will look at a source of sound, showing a connection between hearing and sight. And 1-month-olds will look longer at either a bumpy or smooth pacifier, depending on which kind they had sucked, suggesting an integration between vision and touch (Meltzoff & Borton, 1979; see Figure 4-4).

Another ability that seems to develop earlier than Piaget described is *invisible imitation,* imitation using parts of the body that babies cannot see, like the mouth. Piaget maintained that this followed a period of *visible imitation*—using the hands or feet, for example, which babies can see. In fact, babies less than 72 hours old (including one

who was tested only 42 minutes after birth) imitated an adult's opening the mouth and sticking out the tongue (Meltzoff & Moore, 1983). Newborns under 72 hours copied head movements of

FIGURE 4-4

Research refutation of Piaget's belief that the senses are unconnected at birth and are only gradually integrated through experience. One-month-old infants sucked on either a bumpy or smooth pacifier, which they could not see. After the pacifier was removed, the babies looked longer at the kind they had sucked, suggesting an integration between vision and touch. (*Source:* Mandler, 1990, p. 238.)

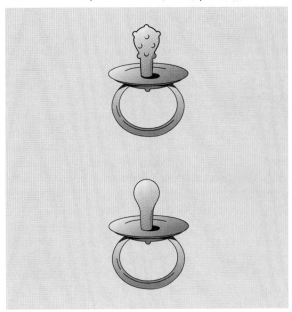

These photos show a 14-month-old in a series of experiments by A. N. Meltzoff. First, the boy sees an adult pulling apart a two-piece toy. The child is then shown receiving the toy, and then imitating the adult's action in pulling it apart. Babies of 9 months showed such deferred imitation 24 hours later, and 14-month-olds showed it as much as a week later. *(Courtesy of A. N. Meltzoff.)*

adults (Meltzoff & Moore, 1989). And babies at an average age of 36 hours imitated three different emotional expressions—a smile, a pout, and the wide-opened mouth and eyes that usually denote surprise (T. M. Field, Woodson, Greenberg, & Cohen, 1982). This shows a link between cognitive and emotional development. Such early imitation is not limited to babies from western countries. A study in Nepal, for example, found that 1-hour-old newborns in that Asian land imitated widened and pursed lips of adults (Reissland, 1988).

Neonatal invisible imitation suggests that human beings are born with a primitive ability to match the acts of other human beings. This may be one aspect of an underlying representational system that lets babies both perceive and produce human acts (Meltzoff & Moore, 1989). Early imitation may be the means by which infants identify people they see (Meltzoff & Moore, 1992). Through early imitation, infants distinguish "those like me" (that is, people) from things. Early mutual-imitation games, so common between parents and young infants, may be an important type of early communication. Such games reinforce this aspect of development (Meltzoff & Gopnik, 1993).

Another area of study is *deferred imitation,* the ability to imitate an action a baby saw some time before. This ability shows that a baby has a long-term memory for an event, and thus, that the baby has a mental representation for it, a "picture" in the mind. Piaget said that children cannot do this

until age 18 months, but recent research has found deferred imitation in infants aged 14 months (Meltzoff, 1985, 1988b) and even 9 months (Meltzoff, 1988a).

In one series of studies, adults pulled apart a two-piece wooden toy or shook a plastic rattle in front of the babies, who could not touch the toys at the time. The babies returned to the lab 24 hours later (for the 9-month-olds), or 1 week later (for the 14-months-olds). Upon seeing the toys again, more of the babies who had seen the adults' action did the same things than did the control babies, who had also been in the lab the same day and had seen the toys but not the actions. Older babies were more likely to reproduce the actions, perhaps showing a superior ability to receive and encode the information in memory. These findings suggest that deferred imitation occurs before other substage-6 representational abilities.

And finally, research suggests that an *understanding of number* begins long before age 2, when Piaget claimed children first begin to use symbols like words and numbers. There is some evidence that babies as young as 5 months may be able to add and subtract small numbers of objects (Wynn, 1992). This seems to provide some support for the idea that the ability to grasp the rudiments of arithmetic may be inborn (as language may be), and that when parents teach their babies numbers, they are only teaching them the names ("one, two, three") for concepts that babies already know.

Babies as young as this 5-month-old have the ability to add and subtract small numbers of objects, as shown in this experiment using different numbers of dolls. It is possible that the ability to grasp the rudiments of arithmetic may be inborn and that when parents teach their babies numbers, they are only teaching them the names ("one, two, three") for concepts that babies already know. *(David Sanders/Arizona Daily Star)*

Karen Wynn used 4-inch-high rubber Mickey Mouse dolls in a series of rigorously designed experiments (see Figure 4-5). For the problem "1 plus 1," she showed the baby one doll, then hid the doll behind a screen. The baby saw a hand place an-other doll behind the screen, and then the screen was pulled away to show two dolls. The length of time that the baby looked at the dolls was timed.

Sometimes the screen was pulled away to show a false answer; in the "1 plus 1" situation, the ba-

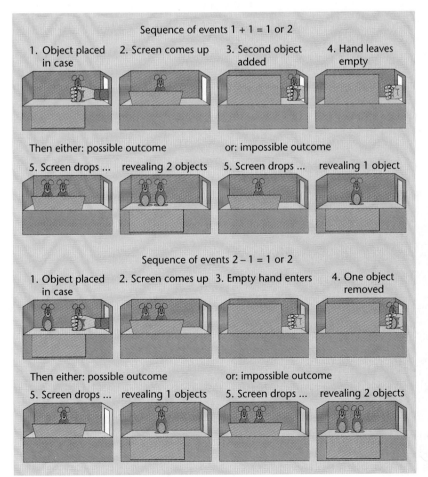

Sequence of events 1 + 1 = 1 or 2

1. Object placed in case
2. Screen comes up
3. Second object added
4. Hand leaves empty

Then either: possible outcome   or: impossible outcome

5. Screen drops ... revealing 2 objects   5. Screen drops ... revealing 1 object

Sequence of events 2 − 1 = 1 or 2

1. Object placed in case
2. Screen comes up
3. Empty hand enters
4. One object removed

Then either: possible outcome   or: impossible outcome

5. Screen drops ... revealing 1 objects   5. Screen drops ... revealing 2 objects

FIGURE 4-5
Can 5-month-old infants count? For the problem "1 plus 1," the researcher showed a baby 1 doll, then hid it behind a screen. The baby saw a hand place another doll behind the screen; then the screen was pulled away. Sometimes there was a false answer; the babies sometimes saw only 1 doll or 3 dolls. In the "2 minus 1" trials the researcher showed 2 dolls, then took 1 away, and the babies saw either 1 or 2 dolls. The babies consistently looked longer at the surprising "wrong" answers than the expected right ones, which suggests that they had "computed" the right answers in their minds.

bies sometimes saw only one doll or three dolls. In other experiments the researcher started by showing two dolls, then took one away, and the babies saw either one or two dolls. In all the experiments, the babies looked longer at the surprising "wrong" answers than the expected right ones, which suggests that they had "computed" the right answers in their minds.

The conclusion from studies like these is that babies seem to be able to think earlier than Piaget thought they could. Either they are born with the capacity to form concepts, or they acquire it very early in life, without having to go through a long sensorimotor stage.

INFORMATION-PROCESSING APPROACH: PERCEPTIONS AND SYMBOLS

At 6 weeks, Annie begins to make sucking noises and wave her arms excitedly as Nancy approaches. It is clear that the baby recognizes her mother and that the sight and sound of her fill the infant with a joy she is bursting to express. But just how does recognition take place? What is going on in Annie's head? Neither Piaget nor the psychometricians have a good answer.

The *information-processing approach* is the newest scientific explanation of how intelligence works. This approach sees people as manipulators of perceptions and symbols. Its goal is to discover what infants, children, and adults do with information from the time they perceive it until they use it. Like the psychometric approach, information-processing theory focuses on individual differences in intelligence. But it concentrates on describing the processes that people go through in acquiring information or solving problems, rather than merely assuming differences in mental functioning from answers given or problems solved.

Information Processing during Infancy as a Predictor of Intelligence

The popularity of the psychometric approach, along with the difficulty of measuring infant intelligence this way, has led to serious misconceptions about infant intelligence. Because of discrepancies between scores on developmental tests for infants and later IQ tests, many people believed that the intellectual functioning of an infant had little in common with that of older children and adults—in other words, that there was a discontinuity in intellectual development. Today, discoveries about the ability of very young babies to process visual and auditory stimuli counter this view. In fact, when we look at how infants process information rather than at how they perform on psychometric tests, we find that mental development is fairly continuous from birth into childhood (McCall & Carriger, 1993; Bornstein & Sigman, 1986; Thompson, Fagan, & Fulker, 1991).

How *do* infants process information? The answers come from studies that use sensitive equipment to monitor such responses as eye movements, heart rate, and brain activity. For example, even very young infants show *visual-recognition*

This 2-year-old is taking part in a new kind of intelligence test, especially effective with developmentally disabled babies. Electrodes attached to the child's chest measure changes in heart rate, which speeds up when events violate expectations. Here, light bulbs glow and darken in response to a wand. Testers estimate children's intelligence on the basis of how long it takes them to learn what to expect. This child was previously thought to be a slow learner, but the test indicated normal intelligence. *(Richard Howard)*

memory, the ability to remember and recognize something they have seen. If infants pay more attention to new patterns than to familiar ones, they can tell the new from the old; therefore, they must be able to remember the old. To compare new information with information they already have, they must be able to form mental images or representations of stimuli. Infants apparently acquire information by forming such images, and the efficiency of their information processing depends on the speed with which they form and refer to them.

Researchers gauge the efficiency of infants' information processing by measuring variations in attention: how quickly babies habituate to familiar stimuli, how fast their attention recovers when they are exposed to new stimuli, and how much time they spend looking at the new and the old (McCall & Carriger, 1993; Bornstein, 1985; Bornstein & Sigman, 1986). Mental development is the process of transforming the novel into the familiar, the unknown into the known (Rheingold, 1985). Efficient habituation correlates with other signs of advanced mental development—like a preference for complexity, rapid exploration of the environment, relatively sophisticated play, fast problem solving, and the ability to match pictures.

Infants who are efficient at taking in and interpreting what they see, or at remembering what they see or hear, score well later on childhood intelligence tests. In several longitudinal studies, habituation and attention-recovery abilities during the first 6 months of life were moderately useful in predicting scores on psychometric tests taken between ages 2 and 8 (Bornstein & Sigman, 1986). Infants' attention is particularly related to later language ability: infants' visual recognition correlates positively with their scores 4 and 7 years later on vocabulary tests (Fagan & McGrath, 1981).

A recent study assessed the relationship between visual *novelty preference* at 5 and 7 months to general IQ and specific cognitive measures at 1, 2, and 3 years. At 5 and 7 months, 113 infants were shown sets of abstract patterns and photographs of faces. The babies who seemed to prefer looking at new pictures more than those they had seen before tended to score higher on the Bayley Scales at 2 years and the Stanford-Binet at 3 years. Thus, novelty preference seems to predict general intelligence at 2 and 3 years. Also, infant novelty preference predicted several specific abilities at later ages, including language skills and memory ability at 3 years (Thompson et al., 1991).

Other research has looked at infants' information processing skills in terms of how well they are able to identify items by sight that they had felt with their hands earlier but did not see. This ability, known as *cross-modal transference*, shows a fairly high level of abstraction; it implies central processing of tactile and visual information. One study compared high-risk very low birthweight babies with normal full-term infants from the same low-income population. The combination of two scores—on the infants' visual recognition memory at 7 months and cross-modal transfer at 1 year—was significantly associated with the children's IQ scores at 3, 4, and 5 years of age (S. A. Rose, Feldman, Wallace, & McCarton, 1991).

Early sensitivity to sounds, too, may predict aspects of infants' later cognitive functioning. A highly significant positive correlation showed up between 4-month-old infants' ability to discriminate sounds and their IQ scores at age 5 (O'Connor, Cohen, & Parmelee, 1984).

Influences on Information Processing and Cognitive Development

A major influence on cognitive development is the way parents and other caregivers act toward children. In several studies, researchers looked at how responsive American and Japanese mothers were to their babies, seen first when the babies were 2 to 5 months old, and then again at 1, 1½, 2½, or 4 years of age, when the children were assessed on various cognitive abilities (Bornstein & Tamis-LeMonda, 1989). Responsiveness was defined as behavior that promptly and appropriately followed some behavior of the baby. In other words, when the baby babbled or looked at the mother (nondistress activities) or cried (a sign of distress), what did the mother do? Did she smile at, talk to, pick up, pat, feed, or pay attention to the baby in some other way?

While almost all the mothers responded quickly when their babies were distressed, their rate of nondistress responsiveness varied greatly, showing no links to the mothers' education or socioeconomic status. Although the responses mothers made to 2-month-old babies were not associated with the children's later development, the way the women acted when the babies were 4 or 5 months old was. As toddlers, the children of the most responsive mothers had more advanced representational abilities, and as 4-year-olds, scored higher on the Wechsler Preschool and Primary Scale of Intelligence (WPPSI) and other learning tasks. In other research, mothers' responsiveness to 4-month-old babies was associated with later cogni-

BOX 4-1 WINDOW ON THE WORLD

EASTERN AND WESTERN LEARNING STYLES

Benjamin, aged 1½ years, loved to play with the key to his family's hotel room in Nanjing, China. He liked to shake it vigorously, enjoying the sounds it made. He also liked to hold the plastic block attached to the key and to try to insert the key into the narrow slot at the front desk where guests dropped their keys. It didn't seem to bother him at all that he usually failed to get the key in the slot, and his parents were happy to let him continue banging the key around.

But then his parents noticed something related to their mission, to investigate early childhood education and creativity in China. Benjamin's father, Howard Gardner, a professor of education at Harvard University, describes a typical scene:

Any Chinese attendant nearby would come over to watch Benjamin and, noting his lack of initial success, attempt to intervene. He or she would hold

onto Benjamin's hand and, gently but firmly, guide it directly toward the slot, reorient it as necessary, and help him to insert it. The "teacher" would then smile somewhat expectantly at Ellen or me, as if awaiting a thank you (1989, p. 54).

What did this experience tell this educational psychologist? It illuminated a major difference in cultural attitudes toward helping children learn. Benjamin's American parents encourage his exploratory behavior, wanting him to become self-reliant, to learn that he could solve problems on his own, and to come up with creative solutions to new problems. Chinese educators and parents, however, believe that molding a child's behavior by guiding him gently into tasks that are beyond him will diminish a child's frustration, make him happy, and help him learn how to do one task so that he can then go on to a harder one.

Dr. Gardner calls the Chinese view of creativity "evolutionary": helping children become competent through approved means will enable them to deviate from the traditional approved forms. In contrast, the American view is "revolutionary": the young westerner makes bold departures first and gradually moves into the tradition. Americans value originality and independence, and worry that creativity will never emerge unless children acquire it early. The Chinese fear that children may never acquire skills if they do not learn them early.

Concluding that both cultures produce competent, creative people, Gardner asks, "Can we glean, from the Chinese and American extremes, a superior way to approach education, perhaps striking an optimal balance between the poles of creativity and basic skills?" (p. 56).

SOURCE: Gardner, 1989.

---

tive achievements (in conjunction with the babies' abilities in processing information); but the way they acted with their 1-year-olds was not (Bornstein, 1985). These different findings may point to a sensitive period, when babies are about 4 months old, for caregivers' impact on intellectual growth.

How does adult responsiveness help children develop intellectually? It might raise their self-esteem and make them feel that they have some control over their lives. It might make them feel secure enough to explore, and motivate them to persist. And it might also help them regulate themselves to pay attention and thus learn.

Other research focused on mothers' responsiveness to preterm infants. The ones whose mothers were most sensitive, responsive, and positively involved with them became adolescents who scored higher on IQ tests and considered themselves more competent than the children of less responsive mothers (Beckwith & Cohen, 1989). Findings like these confirm other data showing that the environ-

ment a child grows up in can do a great deal to offset the negative effects of complications at the time of birth. Although most of these studies have been done with mothers, their findings are probably just as relevant for fathers and other primary caregivers. Parents' involvement—or noninvolvement—in their children's learning is strongly affected by the culture they live in, as shown in Box 4-1.

DEVELOPMENT OF LANGUAGE

At 4½ months, Stefan chuckles out loud. He also says "Ngoo-ooo" and "Ngaaah." At 7 months he makes more sounds, mostly sounding like "Da" or "Ga." At 11 months he says "Dada," and at 14 months he points to everything, asking "What zis?" or saying "Da" for "I want that." At 17 months he points to the right places when asked "Where is your nose? Tongue? Belly button?"

By 21 months he says, or tries to say, at least 50 words, and understands many more. He can now tell you, in his own language, exactly what he does or does not want. When asked "Do you want to go to bed?" his answer is "Eh-eh-eh," accompanied by vigorous arm waving. In other words, "No!" He has also said his first three-word sentence: "Choo-choo bye-bye da-da." (Translation: "The train went away, and now it's all gone.")

Aside from being a source of amusement, delight, and pride to his parents (and a source of information for Sally, his grandmother), Stefan's language ability is a crucial element in his cognitive growth. Once he knows the words for things, he can use a system of symbols to stand for the objects around him; he can reflect on people, places, and things in his world; and he can communicate his needs, feelings, and ideas in order to exert control over his life. (See Table 4-3 for a list of early language milestones.)

Studying the way early language develops, psychologists constantly come up with new findings—some expected, some surprising—about this universal human phenomenon. While the essential process still remains a mystery, we do know some facts about it. For example, children's level of maturation and their living environment are both important in learning language. And as we shall see, human beings seem to be born with a predisposition for learning language.

Findings like these have come about through a variety of methods for studying language development in infancy. Studies of habituation, based on heart rate or sucking behavior, tell us when babies can distinguish one sound from another. A procedure in which electrodes fastened to a baby's scalp measure the brain responses elicited by sounds, and any difference in these responses, also measures a baby's ability to differentiate between sounds. Researchers audiotape and videotape children, and they rely on records kept by trained observers during set intervals. We have been able to learn a great deal about babies' ability to communicate even before they can say a single word.

TABLE 4-3

Language Milestones from Birth to 3 Years

Age in Months	Development
Birth:	Baby can perceive speech, cry, make some response to sound.
1½ to 3 months	Coos and laughs.
3 months	Plays with speech sounds.
5 to 6 months	Makes consonant sounds, trying to match what she or he hears.
6 to 10 months	Babbles in strings of consonants and vowels.
9 months	Uses gestures to communicate and plays gesture games.
9 to 10 months	Begins to understand words (usually "no" and baby's own name); imitates sounds.
10 months	Loses ability to discriminate sounds not in own language.
10 to 14 months	Says first word (usually a label for something); imitates sounds.
13 months	Understands symbolic function of naming.
14 months	Uses symbolic gesturing.
16 to 24 months	Learns many new words, expanding vocabulary rapidly, going from about 50 words to up to 400; uses verbs and adjectives. Speaks two-word sentences.
18 to 24 months	Says first sentence.
20 months	Uses fewer gestures; names more things.
20 to 22 months	Comprehension spurt.
24 months	Uses many two-word phrases; no longer babbles; wants to talk.
30 months	Learns new words almost every day; speaks in combinations of three or more words; understands very well; makes many grammatical mistakes.
36 months	Says up to 1000 words, 80 percent intelligible; makes few mistakes in syntax; grammar is close to informal adult speech.

SOURCES: Reznick & Goldfield, 1992; Bates, O'Connell, & Shore, 1987; Capute, Shapiro, & Palmer, 1987; Lenneberg, 1969.

STAGES IN DEVELOPMENT OF LANGUAGE

Prespeech

The word *infant* is based on the Latin for "without speech." Before babies say their first "real" words, they make a variety of sounds that progress in a fairly set sequence from crying to cooing and babbling, accidental imitation, and then deliberate imitation. These sounds are known as *prelinguistic speech.*

Crying

Crying is the newborn's first and only means of communication. To a stranger, a baby's cries may sound alike, but the baby's parents can often tell the cry for food from the cry of pain. Different pitches, patterns, and intensities signal hunger, sleepiness, or anger.

Cooing

Anywhere from 6 weeks to 3 months, babies start to laugh and coo when they are happy, making squeals, gurgles, and vowel sounds like "ahhh." A kind of "vocal tennis" begins at about 3 months when they begin to play with speech sounds, producing a variety that seem to match the ones they hear from the people around them (Bates et al., 1987). Cross-cultural studies—like one that looked at babies growing up in families that spoke French, Chinese, and Arabic—found that babies do not, as was once believed, "try out" all speech sounds in all human languages, but instead move in the direction of their own language (Boysson-Bardies, Sagart, & Durand, 1984).

Babbling

Babbling—repeating consonant-vowel strings like "ma-ma-ma-ma"—occurs rather suddenly between 6 and 10 months of age, and these strings are often mistaken for a baby's first word. Early babbling is not real language, since it does not hold meaning for the baby, but it becomes more word-like, leading into early speech. In this stage, one kind of difference shows up between babies. "Word babies" seem to understand words earlier and produce word sounds in their babbling, while "intonation babies" babble in sentencelike patterns and tend not to break their babbling strings down into individual words (Dore, 1975). The importance of babbling is underscored by its appearance, in a different form, among deaf babies (Petitto & Marentette, 1991; see Box 4-2). Although these babies may also babble vocally, they do so about 5 months later than hearing babies do (Oller & Eilers, 1988).

Imitating Language Sounds

In the usual course of language development, among babies with normal hearing and speech, babies begin by accidentally imitating sounds they hear. Then they imitate themselves making these sounds. At about 9 to 10 months, they deliberately imitate other sounds, without understanding them. Once they have this basic repertoire of sounds, they string them together in patterns that sound like language but seem to have no meaning (Eisenson, Auer, & Irwin, 1963; Lenneberg, 1967).

This prelinguistic speech can be rich in emotional expression. Starting at about 2 months, when infants' cooing begins to express contentment, the range of emotional tone increases steadily. Long before children can express ideas in words, parents become attuned to their babies' feelings through the sounds they make (Tonkova-Yompol'skaya, 1973).

Recognizing Language Sounds

Long before babies can utter anything but a cry, they can distinguish between speech sounds. In the first months of life, they can tell apart such similar sounds as "ba" and "pa" (Eimas, Siqueland, Jusczyk, & Vigorito, 1971). This ability seems to be inborn.

But children lose the ability to differentiate sounds that are not relevant to the language they hear spoken around them. Japanese infants can easily tell "ra" from "la," but Japanese adults, who speak a language that does not have the "L" sound, have trouble with the same discrimination (Bates, O'Connell, & Shore, 1987). Before 6 months of age, babies have learned the basic sounds of their native language, thus taking the first step in understanding speech. In one recent study, 6-month-old Swedish and American babies routinely ignored variations in sounds common to their own language, but could distinguish variations in an unfamiliar language (Kuhl, Williams, Lacerda, Stevens, & Lindblom, 1992).

By 9 or 10 months of age, when babies begin to understand meaningful speech, but before they are physically mature enough to produce their own, they have lost the ability to differentiate sounds not common in their own language. Language perception is, then, shaped by experience earlier than had been thought.

Babies understand many words before they can

BOX 4-2 *FOOD FOR THOUGHT*

WHAT THE BABBLING OF HEARING-IMPAIRED BABIES TELLS US ABOUT THE DEVELOPMENT OF LANGUAGE

A profoundly deaf baby, whose parents are also deaf, makes a series of rhythmic, repetitive motions in front of her torso. Another baby, also the nonhearing child of nonhearing parents, makes similar hand motions around his head and face. What these children are doing is babbling. But instead of repeating syllables with their voices ("ma-ma-ma") as hearing babies do, they are using gestures. The gestures, like the syllables uttered by hearing babblers, do not have any meaning by themselves. But the babies repeat and string together a few motions over and over again (see Figure 4-6). The hand-babbling begins before 10 months of age, the same time when hearing infants begin voice-babbling.

Apparently, these babies are copying the sign language they see their parents using, just as hearing babies copy voice utterances. The researchers who described and analyzed the hand motions of two nonhearing babies and two hear-

ing babies found that the nonhearing babies' motions were much more systematic and deliberate than the random clenching fists and fluttering fingers of the hearing babies (Petitto & Marentette, 1991). They then concluded that babies learn sign language (which is structured very much like spoken languages) in the same basic way that other babies learn speech. First, they string together meaningless units; then, as parents reinforce the gestures, the babies attach meaning to them. This suggests that there is an inborn language capacity in the brain that underlies the acquisition of both spoken and signed language. In other words, babbling—whether vocal or man-

FIGURE 4-6
Example of manual babbling used by a nonhearing baby who had been exposed to sign language. These four hand shapes represent a sequence, as the baby repeated the series of hand movements over and over again. Each motion is comparable to a syllable in a sequence of vocal babbling. (*Source:* Petitto & Marentette, 1991.)

ual—is tied to brain maturation rather than to maturation of the vocal cords. This suggests that both nativist and learning-theory explanations for how children learn language are valid.

---

say them. The first words most babies understand are either their own names or the word "no." This is not surprising, considering the fact that these are the two words an active baby is likely to hear most often. They also pick up other words with special meaning for them; Emma's parents sometimes have to start spelling words in front of her if it is not time yet to give the 14-month-old her b-a-n-a-n-a.

Throughout the prespeech period, parents and other caregivers have been actively communicating with babies in many ways. By the end of the first year, the baby has some sense of intentional communication, a primitive idea of reference, and a set of signals to communicate with familiar caregivers (Bates et al., 1987). The linguistic stage is now set for speech.

Gestures

But before babies say their first words, they have

developed a rich repertoire of nonverbal gestures (Anna did this, as we saw in Chapter 1). At 9 months of age, for example, Antonio *pointed* to things, sometimes making a noise ("eh-eh-eh") to show that he wanted an object. Between 9 and 12 months, he learned a few *conventional social gestures:* saying bye-bye, nodding his head to mean *yes*, and shaking his head to signify *no.* Then by about 13 months, he was using more elaborate *representational gestures* that carried a more complex meaning: for example, he would hold up his arms to show that he wanted to be picked up or hold an empty cup to his mouth.

These *symbolic gestures* go beyond pointing and games like pat-a-cake, to represent specific objects, events, desires, and conditions. They emerge just before or at about the same time that babies say their first words.

At first, typically at about 14 months, children

This toddler is clearly communicating something—maybe saying a word meaning "block" as she points to the structure. The most common first words are names of things, either general ("baby") or specific (the doll's name). *(Laura Dwight)*

use symbolic gestures to make requests; at about 15 months to describe attributes (like blowing to mean "hot"); and about 2 weeks later to "name" objects. These gestures usually appear before children have a vocabulary of 25 words. They tend to drop out when children learn the word for the idea they were expressing in gestures, and can use speech as their main mode of communication (Lock, Young, Service, & Chandler, 1990). Among thirty-eight 17-month-olds, 87 percent used at least one such gesture, and the average child used four (Acredolo & Goodwyn, 1988).

More than half the children developed symbolic gestures as a result of routines with their parents. Mitsuko, for example, bounces her torso to mean "horse," stemming from bouncing on her father's knee. While children make up most of these gestures themselves, their parents' role is important. It takes two to communicate, and if parents do not interpret and respond to the gestures, children are likely to drop them and try to get adults' attention in other ways—like grabbing or making sounds.

Symbolic gestures show that even before children can talk, they understand that objects and concepts have names and that they can use symbols to refer to the things and happenings in their everyday lives.

First Words

When Stefan said "Dada" and Anna said "Hi"—their first words—both were right on time. The average baby says his or her first word sometime between 10 and 14 months, initiating *linguistic speech*—the use of spoken language to convey meaning. Before long, the baby will use many words, and will show some understanding of grammar, pronunciation, intonation, and rhythm as well. At this point, though, the sum total of an infant's repertoire is likely to be "mama" or "dada." Or it may be a simple syllable that has more than one meaning, depending on what is on the baby's mind at the moment. As with Stefan, "Da" may mean "I want that," "I want to go out," "Where's Daddy?" and so forth. A word like this is called a *holophrase*, because it expresses a complete thought in a single word. Its meaning depends upon the context in which the child utters it.

How Vocabulary Grows

Typically, by 15 months of age, a child has spoken 10 different words or names (Nelson, 1973). Vocabulary continues to grow throughout the single-word stage, which tends to last until the age of about 18 months. Children rely more and more on words, as more and more occasions inspire them to speak a word or a name. The sounds and rhythms of speech grow more elaborate, and even if a great deal of speech is still babbling—even over the age of 1 year—it does seem quite expressive.

In studying the first 50 words spoken by a group of 1- and 2-year-olds, K. Nelson (1973, 1981) found that the most common were *names* of things, either in the general sense ("bow-wow" for dog) or the specific ("Unga" for one particular dog). Others were *action* words ("bye-bye"), modifiers ("hot"), words that express *feelings or relationships* ("no"), and a few *grammatical* words ("for").

Some children use their first words primarily to *refer* to objects and events (using nouns and verbs to name and describe things); while others use them to *express* social routines (using pronouns and repeating formulas, like "stop it") (Nelson, 1981). "Referential" children tend to learn new words faster than "expressive" children do (E. V. Clark, 1983). The differences between these two kinds of speakers seem to be related to environmental factors, including parental speaking styles (Lieven, 1978; Olsen-Fulero, 1982). Referential children are more often firstborns from better-educated families, whose parents seem to encourage labeling by asking their children many questions (Nelson, 1973). In contrast, parents of expressive children speak to them more often to tell them what to do.

By 13 months, most children seem to understand the symbolic function of naming; that is, that a word stands for a specific thing or event. They add words slowly to their vocabulary until a "naming explosion" occurs sometime between 16 and 24 months. Within a few weeks, the toddler goes from saying about 50 words to saying about 400 (Bates, Bretherton, & Snyder, 1988).

Language development often proceeds in spurts, with some children showing a surge in understanding at about 20 to 22 months of age. However, such a spurt can occur at almost any point in the second year, and some children never seem to show one. For those who do, a spurt in the number of words the child says often occurs within two months (Reznick & Goldfield, 1992).

Creating Sentences

At 18 months, Sally's daughter Nancy first spoke two words to express one idea. "Shoe fall," she said to her father, who was pushing her in her stroller. Her father paused, saw the shoe on the sidewalk, and picked it up. In this first sentence, Nancy put two words together to express a single thought.

First Sentences

The age at which children begin combining words varies, and the ranges are similar for children learning spoken language and for children of deaf parents who learn sign language. Generally, children put words together between 18 and 24 months, about 8 to 12 months after they say their first word. But this is very variable. Although prelinguistic speech is fairly closely tied to chronological age, linguistic speech is not. Knowing a child's age tells us very little about his or her language development (Brown, 1973a, 1973b).

Furthermore, there does not seem to be a direct relationship between different aspects of language development. In one study, children who at 20 months of age were early talkers continued to be verbally precocious at age 4½, but were not likely to be early readers (Crain-Thoreson & Dale, 1992.)

Nancy's first sentence was typical in that it dealt with everyday events, things, people, or activities (Braine, 1976; Rice, 1989; Slobin, 1973). This early speech is called "telegraphic" because it includes only essential words, like early telegrams. When Stefan says, "Deda fweep," he seems to mean "I want to sweep." Telegraphic speech was once thought to be universal, but we now know that children vary in the extent to which they use it (Braine, 1976) and the form itself varies depending on the language being learned (Slobin, 1983). It still conforms to some degree to the grammar a child hears; Stefan does not say "Fweep Deda" when he wants to push a toy broom around. Again, interpretation of these early sentences often depends on their context.

Learning Grammar

Children's speech becomes increasingly complex. First, tense and case endings, articles, and prepositions are missing ("shoe fall"); and frequently, so are subjects or verbs ("That ball" and "Mommy sock"). Next, the child may string two basic relationships together ("Adam hit" and "Hit ball") to get a more complicated relationship ("Adam hit ball"). Generally, the first sentences consist of nouns, verbs, and adjectives.

Sometime between ages 20 and 30 months, children acquire the fundamentals of syntax. They begin to use articles (*a, the*), prepositions (*in, on*), conjunctions (*and, but*), plurals, verb endings, past tense, and forms of the verb *to be* (*am, are, is*). By 3 years of age, their speech becomes longer and more complex. Although they often omit parts of speech, they get their meaning across, and they are fluent speakers (R. Brown, 1973a, 1973b). At 2 years, 10 months, for example, Maika, who wanted to help her mother wash dishes, said clearly and grammatically (despite her frustration), "I can't get this glove on my hand." It was a simple sentence, but since she had never heard it before, her saying something completely novel like this illustrates the complex achievement that language is.

Language continues to develop, of course, and by late childhood, children are fully competent in grammar, although they continue to enlarge their vocabulary and improve their style.

Characteristics of Early Speech

Children's speech is not just an immature version of adult speech. It has a character all its own. By and large, this is true whether the child is speaking German, Russian, Finnish, Samoan, or English (Slobin, 1971). There are a number of characteristics of early speech.

Jason's Uncle Tyrone gave him a toy car, which Jason, at 13 months, called his "koo-ka." Then Jason's father came home with a gift and said, "Look, Jason, here's a little car for you." But Jason said "koo-ka," and ran and got the one from his uncle. To him, *that* was a little car, and it took some time before he called any other toy cars by the same word. Jason was *underextending* a concept by restricting "little car" to one object.

When Diane's nephew, Eddie, was 14 months old, he jumped in excitement at the sight of a gray-haired man on the television screen and shouted, "Gampa!" When Stefan was 15 months old, he saw a cow and squealed, "Oof-woof!" Both these toddlers were overgeneralizing, or *overextending* concepts. Eddie thought that because his grandfather had gray hair, all gray-haired men could be called "Grandpa." Stefan may have thought that because a dog has four legs and a tail, all animals with these characteristics are "oof-woofs"; or, not knowing the word for cow, he simply may have used the closest one he knew.

As children develop a larger vocabulary, they overextend less and less. Feedback from adults on the appropriateness of what they say is a major way to move beyond this tendency. ("No, honey, that man looks like Grandpa, but he's somebody else's grandpa, not yours." "Sweetie, that is a *cow*.")

Children *simplify*. They use telegraphic speech to say just enough to get their meaning across ("No drink milk!").

Children *overregularize rules*, applying them rigidly, without knowing that some rules have exceptions. But when John says "mouses" instead of "mice" or Anna says "I thinked" rather than "I thought," this represents progress. Both children initially used the correct forms of these irregular words, in simple imitation of what they heard. Once they learn grammatical rules for plurals and past tense (a crucial step in learning language), they apply them universally. The next step in their development involves learning the exceptions to the rules, which they will do by early school age.

Children *understand grammatical relationships that they cannot yet express*. At first, Erica may under-stand that a dog is chasing a cat, but cannot string together enough words to express the complete action. Her sentence comes out as "Puppy chase" rather than "Puppy chase kitty."

THEORIES OF LANGUAGE ACQUISITION

Although both maturation and environment are important in the development of language, different linguists assign major importance to one or the other of these influences. B. F. Skinner (1957) was the foremost proponent of *learning theory*, which says that language learning is based on experience—specifically, on aspects of the child's environment. Noam Chomsky (1957), on the other hand, upholds a view called *nativism*, which maintains that there is an inborn capacity for learning language.

Learning Theory

According to learning theory, children learn language in the same way they learn other kinds of behavior—through conditioning and reinforcement. Parents reinforce children (usually by smiling, paying attention, and talking) for making sounds that resemble adult speech. So children make more of these sounds, generalizing and abstracting as they go along. At first, children utter sounds at random, and those that sound like adult speech are then reinforced. The children repeat the reinforced sounds. Then children imitate the sound they hear adults making and are again reinforced for doing so. Thus, children in English-speaking countries learn English rather than another language. Imitation may explain why children generally outgrow incorrect usages even though parents, who generally correct the *truth* of children's statements, usually do not correct their grammar (R. Brown, Cazden, & Bellugi, 1969).

As support for their position, learning theorists point to the fact that children reared at home, who presumably hear more adult speech and get more attention and more reinforcement than those who grow up in institutions, do babble more (Brodbeck & Irwin, 1946). However, learning theory does not account for children's marvelously imaginative ways of saying things they have never heard. Anna, for example, described the brown smudge left on a napkin she used to wipe chocolate from her lips as her "lip shadow," a sprained ankle as a "sprangle," and told Diane she didn't want to go to sleep yet because she wasn't "yawny."

Nativism

In the nativist view, human beings have an inborn capacity in the brain for acquiring language and learn to talk as naturally as they learn to walk. Evidence for this viewpoint comes from several facts:

■ Almost all children learn their native language, no matter how complex, mastering it in the same age-related sequence without formal teaching.
■ Human beings, the only animals to master a spoken language, are the only species whose brain is larger on one side than the other, and who seem to have an inborn mechanism for language localized in the larger hemisphere (the left for most people).
■ Newborns respond to language in sophisticated ways. They move their bodies in the rhythm of the adult speech they hear (Condon & Sander, 1974); they can tell their mother's voice from those of strangers (DeCasper & Fifer, 1980); and, in the first months of life, they can tell apart very similar sounds (Eimas et al., 1971).

One researcher suggests that neonates can put sounds into categories because all human beings are "born with perceptual mechanisms that are tuned to the properties of speech" (Eimas, 1985, p. 49). Contact with the sounds of a particular language leads children to "tune in" the corresponding preset "channels" and "tune out" unused ones. These perceptual mechanisms, along with the vocal cords and the specialized speech centers of the brain, let a child "join the community of language" quickly (p. 52).

How, starting with simple sound recognition, do babies go on to create complex utterances that follow the specific rules of language in their society? Noam Chomsky (1972) proposes that an inborn *language acquisition device (LAD)* programs children's brains to analyze the language they hear and to extract from it the rules of grammar. Using these rules, they can make up new sentences.

Deaf children make up their own sign language when they do not have models to follow—more evidence that internal mechanisms play a large role in a young child's growing capacity for linguistic expression (H. Feldman, Goldin-Meadow, & Gleitman, 1979; Hoff-Ginsberg & Shatz, 1982). The case of 9-year-old Simon, a deaf child of deaf parents, is also cited as support for this theory. Simon used correct grammar in American Sign Language (ASL), even though he learned incorrect grammar from his parents and a different sign language, with different rules of grammar, at his school (Newport, 1992).

Still, the nativist approach does not explain why children differ so much in grammatical skill and fluency, how they come to understand the meanings of words, or why speech development depends on having someone to talk with.

Most developmentalists today draw on both nativism and learning theory. They believe that children have an inborn capacity to acquire a language, which is then activated and enhanced by learning through experience.

INFLUENCES ON LANGUAGE DEVELOPMENT

What determines how quickly and how well a baby learns to speak? Again, we see both nature and nurture.

A genetic influence is apparent in the moderate relationship that exists between parents' intelligence and the rate at which their biological children develop communication skills during the first year of life. Such a relationship has been found for adopted children and their biological mothers, but not their adoptive parents. It also seems likely that environmental factors, like parents' imitation of the sounds infants make, affect the pace of linguistic learning (Hardy-Brown & Plomin, 1985; Hardy-Brown, Plomin, & DeFries, 1981).

Other research attributes many of the marked differences in language abilities that surface by the end of a child's second year to differences in children's surroundings (Nelson, 1981). One important environmental influence, of course, is how much and what kind of speech babies hear (M. K. Rosenthal, 1982).

Child-Directed Speech ("Motherese")

You do not have to be a mother to speak "motherese." If you pitch your voice high, simplify your speech by using short words and sentences, speak slowly, ask questions, and repeat your words often when you speak to a baby or toddler, you are speaking motherese, or—as it is also called—*child-directed speech* (CDS). Most adults—and even

"Motherese"—a simplified form of language used for speaking to babies and toddlers—seems to come naturally, not only to parents and grandparents, but even to slightly older children. *(Larry Lawfer/The Picture Cube)*

young children—do it intuitively. Until recently, the idea that CDS enables children to learn their native language, or at least to pick it up faster, was generally accepted. Recently, however, some have questioned its value. Let us look at the debate.

Those who consider CDS important believe that it serves several functions (C. E. Snow, 1972). Emotionally, it helps adults to develop a relationship with children. Socially, it teaches children how to carry on a conversation—how to introduce a topic, comment and expand on an idea, and take turns talking. Linguistically, it teaches children how to use new words, structure phrases, and put ideas into language. Because CDS is confined to simple, down-to-earth topics, children can use their own knowledge of familiar things to help them work out the meanings of the words they hear (C. E. Snow, 1977). Of course, parents may not consciously have such purposes in mind when they say, "Where is your nose? I see your nose! Here's your nose!" That kind of talk just seems to come naturally.

Infants' preference for this kind of simplified speech is already present before 1 month of age; it does not seem to depend on any specific experience (R. P. Cooper & Aslin, 1990). However, parents usually do not start speaking CDS until babies show by their expressions, actions, and

sounds that they have some understanding of what is being said to them. Since women use CDS less when asked to make tapes addressed to unseen children (C. E. Snow, 1972), it seems that interaction with an infant encourages its use.

Some researchers have found positive correlations between use of CDS and the rate of 2-year-olds' language growth (Hoff-Ginsberg, 1985, 1986). Social class differences have also shown up. Upper-middle-class mothers are more likely to follow their children's conversational cues, as by answering questions or pursuing a topic that the child has brought up, whereas working-class mothers more often speak to their children to tell them what to do (Hoff-Ginsberg, 1991). Activity—what parent and child are doing together—is also important. Reading to a child is especially conducive to a supportive style of parent-child conversation, while toy play leads to the highest rates of mothers' directives (Hoff-Ginsberg, 1991).

The value of CDS seems to be supported by research on twins. It has been known for more than 50 years that twins usually speak later than single-born children; one study sheds some light on the reasons. After observing 6 pairs of twins and 12 firstborn singleton children at ages 15 and 21 months, researchers found substantial differences in mother-child interactions, mostly due to the practical pressures on harried mothers of twin infants (Tomasello, Mannle, & Kruger, 1986).

Mothers of twins speak to and interact with their babies about as much as mothers of singletons, but since they have to divide their attention between two babies, each one often gets less. Compared with mothers of singletons, mothers of twins do not speak to each child as often, pay less attention to each one, and have shorter conversations. When they do speak to their babies, more of what they say involves directing a child to do something rather than chattier comments and questions. They imitate more, and elaborate less on topics the children bring up. Directive speech is not as effective as questioning in encouraging children's fluency (Nelson, 1981). Thus, while twins have each other to talk to—and often develop a private language between them—their interaction is not as influential as the kind that they would have with an adult.

Another researcher found modest support for the value of CDS in a study of language functioning in 2½-year-olds, but still concluded that "the differences among mothers that predicted rate of language growth in their children were not differences in the use of motherese per se" (Hoff-Gins-

LANG- STIMULATION

berg, 1985, p. 384). What are these differences? One seems to be an adult's goals in talking to a child—whether, for example, she or he prods a child to speak in ways just beyond the range of the child's current competence, which may motivate the child to move up to the next level of language skill (Hoff-Ginsberg, 1986).

Investigators who question the value of CDS contend that children speak sooner and better if they hear and can respond to more complex speech from adults. The children, then, can select from this speech the parts that they are interested in and are able to deal with. In fact, these researchers say, children discover the rules of language faster when they hear complex sentences that use these rules more often and in more ways (Gleitman, Newport, & Gleitman, 1984).

What are we to conclude about this controversy? It seems that however parents speak, the important element is their interest in and close interaction with their babies. The more they talk with their children, the sooner the babies can pick up the nuances of speech and correct wrong assumptions. Ultimately, as one review of the research literature concluded, "No child has been observed to speak a human language without having had a communicative partner from whom to learn" (Hoff-Ginsberg & Shatz, 1982, p. 22).

The Impact of Different Aspects of Adult Speech

In one study, the vocabularies of children aged 14 to 26 months were directly related to the amount of speech directed to them by their caregivers—in this case, their mothers (Huttenlocher, Haight, Bryk, Seltzer, & Lyons, 1991). Furthermore, there was a strong relationship between the frequency of various words in the mothers' speech and the order in which the children learned these words. Another study looked at 2-year-olds in day care centers in Bermuda. The children whose caregivers spoke to them often (especially to give or ask for information rather than to control their behavior) were more advanced in language development than children who did not have such conversations with adults (McCartney, 1984). On the other hand, when children with normal hearing grow up in homes with deaf parents who communicate only through sign language, the children's speech development is slowed (Moskowitz, 1978).

In order to speak and communicate, children need practice and interaction. Hearing speech on television is not enough; Dutch children who

watch German television every day do not learn German (C. E. Snow et al., 1976). Language is a social act.

Unquestionably, conversation with babies is important. The question is, What sort of conversation? Too much direction—commands, requests, and instructions—is not helpful (K. Nelson, 1973). Among the most helpful things adults can do are to paraphrase what a child says, expand on it, talk about what interests the child, remain quiet long enough to give the child a chance to respond, and use read-aloud sessions to ask specific questions (Rice, 1989). See Box 4-3.

DELAYED LANGUAGE DEVELOPMENT

Albert Einstein did not start to speak until he was 3 years old, a fact that heartens the parents of other children whose speech develops later than usual. About 40 percent of late talkers have other problems, like hearing impairment or mental retardation (Rice, 1989). Some have a history of otitis media (an inflammation of the middle ear) between 12 and 18 months of age, and these children improve when the infection and the related hearing loss are cleared up (Lonigan, Fischel, Whitehurst, Arnold, & Valdez-Menchaca, 1992). About 3 percent of preschool-age children are significantly behind their age-mates in language skills; their intelligence is normal, however (Rice, 1989).

It is unclear why these children speak later than others. They are not necessarily from homes where they do not get enough linguistic input. Even though some of their parents talk to them more in terms of what the children can say rather than what they can understand (Whitehurst, et al., 1989), this may be more the result than the cause of their delay. Current investigations focus on problems in information processing, or "fast-mapping" new words; that is, absorbing the meaning of a new word based on having heard it in conversation (Rice, 1989). It is also possible that these children have a specific cognitive limitation that makes it hard for them to learn the rules of language (Scarborough, 1990).

In any case, children whose language is delayed can often benefit from special teaching programs at home, at preschool, and from a qualified professional. It is important to address the problem early: research has found that schoolchildren with reading disabilities often had early language defects, such as mispronunciation at age 2, poor vo-

BOX 4-3   PRACTICALLY SPEAKING

TALKING WITH BABIES AND TODDLERS

"Yes, you like this, don't you? . . . Yes, you do. . . . You love your bath. . . . And your mommy loves your little noises. . . . Now let's wash your little tummy. . . . Now. . . ." Although this typical commentary from a parent to a child may not sound as if it is on the highest intellectual plane, it is a vital influence on the baby's cognitive and emotional development.

Talking, reading, and singing to babies are not only among the joys of child rearing; they also help children's cognitive and emotional development. This is how babies learn a language; learn that they are valued, special people; and learn how to get along with other people.

Here are some suggestions for talking with a baby at different stages of language development:

▪ *Babbling stage:* When a baby babbles, repeat the syllables. Make a game of it, and soon the baby will repeat your sound. Aside from being fun, this kind of game gives a baby the idea that a conversation consists of taking turns, an idea babies seem to grasp at about 7½ or 8 months of age. A round of stimulating chitchat like "dee, dee, dee; dah, dah, dah" helps babies to experience the social aspect of speech.

▪ *First words:* By the time babies speak their first words, at about 1 year, parents can help them learn even more by repeating these first words and pronouncing them correctly. If you can't understand what the baby is saying, smile in approval and say something yourself. Babies can understand many more words than they can utter, and they can learn the names for the objects in their world. For example, point to Sean's doll and say, "Please give me Kermit." If Sean doesn't respond, reach over, pick up the doll, and say, "Kermit." Sean's ability to understand grows as he learns to discover through language what another person is thinking.

▪ *Multiword speech:* You can help a toddler who has begun to string words together to make sentences by expanding on what the child says. If Tessa says "Mommy sock," you can reply, "Yes, that is Mommy's sock." Even though expansion may not speed up the acquisition of grammar, it has a strong social use.

▪ *Reading to young children:* A child will participate more in reading-aloud sessions if you ask challenging open-ended questions rather than those calling for a yes or a no. Thus,

ask "What is the cat doing?" instead of "Is the cat asleep?" Start with simple questions ("Where is the ball?") and then pose more challenging ones ("What color is the ball?" "Who is playing with the ball?" "What is happening to the boy in the corner?"). Then expand on the child's answers, correct wrong ones, give alternative possibilities, and bestow praise.

A study comparing methods like these with standard reading-aloud practices found that 21- to 35-month-old children participating in this kind of reading session scored 6 months higher in vocabulary and expressive language skills than did a group of control children (Whitehurst et al., 1988). Another study found that children who were read to often, especially in this way, when they were 2 years old had better language skills at ages 2½ and 4½ (Crain-Thoreson & Dale, 1992).

Above all, talking and reading with a child should be fun. Not every conversation should be a lesson or a test. And the baby should be able to decline to play occasionally, because sometimes a small child just doesn't feel like talking. Most children who begin talking fairly late catch up eventually—and many make up for lost time by talking nonstop to anyone who will listen!

cabularies at age 3, or weaknesses in naming objects at age 5 (Scarborough, 1990).

DEVELOPMENT OF COMPETENCE

Why do some children persevere in finding a way around an obstacle (as Rebecca did when she went after the Cheerios) while others burst into tears

and give up? A child's competence is rarely such a life-and-death issue as it was for one 17-month-old girl who survived untended for 2 to 3 weeks after her parents had been shot dead, apparently by eating potato chips and drinking water from a toilet (Associated Press, 1987). But since the ability to function well from day to day has many other implications, Burton L. White and his colleagues wanted to find out why some children get along in life much better than others. In 1965, they began the Harvard Preschool Project to test and observe some 400 preschoolers and rate them on their competence in cognitive and social skills (B. L. White, 1971; B. L. White, Kaban, & Attanucci, 1979).

The most competent children—the researchers called them A's—showed such *social skills* as getting and holding the attention of adults in acceptable ways, using adults as resources, and showing both affection and hostility. They got along well with other children, were proud of their accomplishments, and wanted to act in grown-up ways. Among their *cognitive skills* were using language well, showing a range of intellectual abilities, planning and carrying out complicated activities, and "dual focusing" (paying attention to a task while being aware of what else was going on). Children classified as B's were less accomplished in these skills; and children classified as C's were very deficient. Follow-up studies 2 years later showed a notable stability in the classifications.

WHAT INFLUENCES COMPETENCE?

To find out how the A and C children became the way they were, the researchers identified A's and C's who had younger siblings, and they looked at the ways the A and C mothers acted with their younger children. (The researchers focused on mothers, feeling that few fathers spent enough time with children of this age to be influential, a conclusion they might not draw today, as will be seen in Chapter 7.) As it turned out, there were sizable differences in mothering after children were about 8 months old. At this age, children start to understand language, and so the way parents talk to them is important. They also begin to crawl; some parents react with pleasure, and some with annoyance. And since they become attached to the person they spend the most time with, this person's personality becomes more important.

The major differences revolved around three aspects of child rearing—the ability to "design" a child's world, to serve as a "consultant" for a child, and to provide a good balance between freedom and restraint. Mothers from all socioeconomic levels fell into both groups.

The A mothers designed a safe physical environment full of interesting things to see and touch (common household objects as often as expensive toys). They tended to be "on call" with their babies, without devoting their entire lives to them. A number had part-time jobs, and those who did stay home generally spent less than 10 percent of their

time interacting with their infants. They went about their daily routine but made themselves available for a few seconds or minutes when needed to answer a question, label an object, help a toddler climb stairs, or share in an exciting discovery. These women generally had positive attitudes toward life, enjoyed being with young children, and gave generously of themselves. They were energetic, patient, tolerant of messiness, and fairly casual about minor risks. They were firm and consistent, setting reasonable limits while showing love and respect. When they wanted to change their babies' behavior, they distracted infants under 1 year of age, and used a combination of distraction, physical removal, and firm words with older children.

The C mothers were a diverse group. Some were overwhelmed by life, ran chaotic homes, and were too absorbed by daily struggles to spend much time with their children. Others spent *too much* time with them: hovering, being overprotective, pushing their babies to learn, and making them dependent. Some were physically present but rarely made real contact, apparently because they did not really enjoy the company of small children. They provided for their children materially but confined them in cribs or playpens.

The researchers identified several guidelines for successful parenting (see Box 4-4). But they did not investigate the children's own contributions to their mothers' child-rearing styles. Children are actors, reactors, and interactors. It is quite possible that the children of the A mothers showed the kind of personalities that made their mothers *want* to respond as they did. Perhaps they showed more curiosity, more independence, and more interest in what their mothers did than did the C children.

HOME: THE HOME OBSERVATION FOR MEASUREMENT OF THE ENVIRONMENT

To look at the impact of a child's home surroundings in infancy and early childhood on later intellectual growth, researchers often use a measure called the *Home Observation for Measurement of the Environment (HOME)* (R. H. Bradley, 1989). HOME includes scales of parental responsiveness, which, as we saw earlier, influences children's cognitive development. It gives credit to the parent of a toddler for caressing or kissing the child once during the examiner's visit; to the parent of a preschooler for spontaneously praising the child twice during

BOX 4-4   PRACTICALLY SPEAKING

HOW PARENTS CAN HELP THEIR CHILDREN TO BE MORE COMPETENT

The findings from the Harvard Preschool Project and from studies using the HOME scales can be useful to any parents of young children and can be translated into the following guidelines:

1   The best time for enhancing your child's competence is from the age of 6 to 8 months up until about 2 years, but it is never too late.

2   Encourage your children to have close social relationships with important people in their lives, especially from the first few months after their first birthday.

3   Do not worry if you are not with your child full-time. Instead, make the most of the time you do spend with your child, and provide the best parent substitutes you can find.

4   Give your children help when they need it rather than pressing it on them too soon, ignoring them, or seeing them as a burden to be dealt with quickly.

5   Stay fairly close to your young children, but do not hover so much that you discourage them from developing attention-seeking skills.

6   Talk to them about whatever they are interested in at the moment and play with them on their level instead of trying to redirect their attention to something else.

7   Speak to them. They will not pick up language from listening to the radio or television, or overhearing conversations. They need interaction with adults.

8   Create an environment that fosters learning. It should include books, challenging toys, and an interesting place to play.

9   Give them physical freedom to explore. Do not confine them regularly in a playpen, crib, jump seat, or small room.

10 Use punishment sparingly; instead, find opportunities for positive feedback.

SOURCES: Bradley & Caldwell, 1982; Bradley, Caldwell, & Rock, 1988; Bradley et al., 1989; Stevens & Bakeman, 1985; B. L. White, 1971; B. L. White, Kaban, & Attanucci, 1979.

---

the visit; and to the parent of an older child for answering the child's questions. Examiners evaluate how parent and child talk to each other, and they give high marks for a parent's friendly, nonpunitive attitude.

This measure also evaluates the number of books in the home, the presence of challenging toys that encourage the development of concepts, and parents' involvement in children's play. High scores on all these factors are fairly reliable in predicting children's IQ; when combined with the parent's level of education, they are even more accurate.

In one study, researchers compared HOME scores for low-income 2-year-olds with the children's Stanford-Binet intelligence test scores two years later. The single most important factor in predicting high intelligence was the mother's ability to create and structure an environment that fostered learning (Stevens & Bakeman, 1985). This result supports the findings of the Harvard Preschool Project. And a longitudinal study in Little Rock, Arkansas, found positive correlations between how responsive parents were to their 6-month-old babies and how well the children did at age 10 on IQ and achievement test scores and teachers' ratings of behavior (R. Bradley & Caldwell, 1982; R. Bradley, Caldwell, & Rock, 1988).

Other people besides mothers can also offer children the same kinds of benefits. Fathers and other caregivers can provide books and toys that encourage conceptual thinking and language development, can talk with and read regularly to children, can pay attention to and get involved in their play, and can use punishment sparingly.

The importance of what parents do can be seen in the findings of one study of children from three different ethnic groups. It found that day-to-day aspects of a child's home environment (like parental responsiveness and the availability of stimulating play materials) are more closely related to the child's development than are such aspects of the child's wider environment as socioeconomic status (R. H. Bradley et al., 1989). This conclusion emerged from a study in which researchers looked at 931 white, African American, and Mexican American children up to age 3. Across all the ethnic groups, a favorable home environment could offset problems in infancy, but when a child's early developmental status was low *and* his or her early home environment was poor, the chances for a good outcome for the child were much less than when only one of these measures was low.

Interaction is a key to much of childhood development—intellectual, social, and emotional.

Children call forth responses from the people around them and they, in turn, react to those responses. In the next chapter—Chapter 5—we'll look more closely at these bidirectional influences as we explore early personality and social development.

SUMMARY

HOW INFANTS LEARN

■ Learning is a relatively permanent change in behavior that occurs as a result of experience. Maturation refers to the unfolding of patterns of behavior in a biologically determined age-related sequence. Learning and maturation interact to produce changes in cognitive abilities.

■ Very young infants are capable of several types of learning, including habituation and classical and operant conditioning, as well as combinations of several types.

■ Habituation is a process by which repeated exposure to a stimulus results in a reduced response to the stimulus. Dishabituation is the increase in responding when a new stimulus is presented. Speed of habituation shows promise as a predictor of intelligence.

■ In classical conditioning a person or animal learns to respond automatically to a stimulus that did not originally provoke the response. In operant conditioning a certain response is produced to bring about a particular effect. Both types of conditioning occur early in infancy.

■ Infants exhibit some memory ability virtually from birth, and memory ability develops rapidly.

STUDYING INTELLECTUAL DEVELOPMENT: THREE APPROACHES

■ Intelligence involves both adaptive and goal-oriented behavior. Three major approaches for studying intelligence are the psychometric, Piagetian, and information-processing approaches.

■ The psychometric approach seeks to determine and measure quantitatively the factors that make up intelligence. Psychometric testing for infants emphasizes motor skills, which may not measure the same thing as verbal tests do. Psychometric tests of infant intelligence are generally poor predictors of intelligence in later childhood and adulthood.

■ Developmental tests are especially designed to assess infants and toddlers. An important one is the Bayley Scales of Infant Development.

■ The Piagetian approach is concerned with qualitative stages of cognitive development, or the way people develop the ability to acquire and use knowledge about the world.

■ During the sensorimotor stage, infants develop from primarily reflexive creatures to goal-oriented toddlers capable of some symbolic thought. A major development during this stage is object permanence, the realization that a person or object continues to exist even when out of sight. Considerable recent research suggests that a number of aspects of Piaget's sensorimotor stage occur earlier than Piaget described. These include object permanence, the coordination of the senses, invisible and deferred imitation, and the concept of number.

■ The information processing approach is concerned with the process underlying intelligent behavior; that is, how people manipulate symbols and what they do with the information they perceive. Important ways to assess infant information processing include measurement of visual-recognition memory, novelty preference, and cross-modal transfer. Such assessment show promise of predicting later intelligence.

■ Information processing ability is influenced by the responsiveness of significant adults toward infants.

DEVELOPMENT OF LANGUAGE

■ Prelinguistic speech, which precedes the first word, includes crying, cooing, babbling, and imitating language sounds. Neonates can distinguish speech sounds; by 6 months, babies have learned the basic sounds of their language. By 9 or 10 months they begin to understand meaningful speech. Before they say their first word, babies use many gestures, including pointing, conventional social gestures, and, for many babies, symbolic gestures.

■ During the second year of life, the typical toddler begins to speak the language of the culture. That year seems to be particularly important for understanding language. Sometime between 10 and 14 months the typical baby utters a first word, thus initiating linguistic speech. These single words are called holophrases because they express a complete thought in a single word. Linguistic speech, unlike prelinguistic speech, is not closely tied to chronological age.

■ Early speech is characterized by underextending and overextending concepts, simplicity, and overregularizing rules. The child can understand grammatical relationships before being able to express them in speech.

■ The major theories of language acquisition are learning theory (which emphasizes the role of conditioning, reinforcement, and imitation) and nativism (which maintains that people have an inborn capacity to acquire language). Today, most developmentalists hold that children have an inborn capacity to learn language that is activated and enhanced by certain environmental experiences.

■ Communication between caregivers and children is important for language development. It is not clear whether hearing simple, direct language (child-directed speech or motherese) is crucial. The causes of delayed language development are also unclear.

DEVELOPMENT OF COMPETENCE

■ Parents' child-rearing styles (especially during the first 2 years) affect children's intellectual, social, and emotional competence.

■ Parents of the most competent children are those who are skilled at "designing" a child's environment, are available as "consultants" to a child, and use appropriate controls. Parental responsiveness is associated with optimal cognitive development.

KEY TERMS

learning (page 128)
maturation (128)
habituation (129)
classical conditioning (130)
operant (instrumental) conditioning (131)
intelligent behavior (132)
psychometric approach (133)
Bayley Scales of Infant Development (134)
cognitive development (135)
Piagetian approach (135)

sensorimotor stage (135)
circular reactions (135)
schemes (136)
object permanence (137)
causality (138)
representational ability (138)
invisible imitation (139)
visible imitation (139)
deferred imitation (140)
information-processing approach (142)
visual-recognition memory (142)

novelty preference (143)
cross-modal transference (143)
prelinguistic speech (146)
linguistic speech (148)
holophrase (148)
learning theory (150)
nativism (150)
language acquisition device (LAD) (151)
child-directed speech (151)

SUGGESTED READINGS

Baron, N. S. (1992).   *Growing up with language: How children learn to talk.* Reading, MA: Addison-Wesley. The author, a mother and linguistics professor, unravels the mystery of how children, in just a few short years, crack the code and master language. She explains the processes by which they become coherent readers and speakers, and how parents play a vital role. This work is both highly informative and eminently readable.

Brown, R. (1973).   *A first language: The early stages.* Cambridge, MA: Harvard University Press. A classic book that describes the language development of three young children: Adam, Eve, and Sarah.

Ginsburg, H., & Opper, S. (1979).   *Piaget's theory of intellectual development* (2d ed.). Englewood Cliffs, NJ: Prentice-Hall. A clear, readable discussion of Piaget's concepts. It includes outlines of Piaget's basic ideas, his early research and theory, his use of logic as a model for adolescents' thinking, and a discussion of the implications of his work.

Piaget, J. (1952).   *The origins of intelligence in children.* New York: International Universities Press. Piaget's now classic presentation of the six substages of sensorimotor development. Based on abundant observations of his three children.

Pinker, S. (1994).   *The language instinct: How the mind creates language.* New York: Morrow. This in-depth work on language development proposes that language is an instinct, wired into our brains from birth. The author, a well-known linguist, answers questions such as how language evolves, how the brain computes it, and how children learn it. He discusses modern linguistic theory in a way that is easily understandable to the average reader.

White, B. L. (1985).   *The first three years of life* (rev. ed.). Englewood Cliffs, NJ: Prentice-Hall. A presentation for lay readers of White's findings on children's competence. It is a thorough treatment of cognitive changes during infancy and toddlerhood.

Wilde, J. A. (1993).   *The child's discovery of the mind.* Cambridge, MA: Harvard University Press. According to Piaget, children have little understanding of the mind before the age of six. But in the last 20 years, Piaget's methods have been challenged and his conclusions revised. Here is a fascinating survey of the research in this area, studying the implications for children's intellectual and social development.

CHAPTER FIVE

PERSONALITY AND SOCIAL DEVELOPMENT IN INFANCY AND TODDLERHOOD

I'm like a child
trying to do everything
say everything
and be everything
all at once

John Hartford,
"Life Prayer," 1971

■ **EARLY PERSONALITY DEVELOPMENT**

Trust versus Mistrust
Autonomy versus Shame and Doubt

■ **EMOTIONS: THE FOUNDATION OF PERSONALITY**

How Infants' Emotions Are Studied
How Emotions Develop: The Emerging Sense of Self
How Infants Show Their Emotions
How Emotions Are Communicated between Infants and Adults

■ **DIFFERENCES IN PERSONALITY DEVELOPMENT**

Temperamental Differences
Gender Differences

■ **THE FAMILY AND PERSONALITY DEVELOPMENT**

The Mother's Role
The Father's Role
Stranger Anxiety and Separation Anxiety
Disturbances in Family Relationships

■ **RELATIONSHIPS WITH OTHER CHILDREN**

Siblings
Sociability

■ **THE IMPACT OF EARLY DAY CARE**

Cognitive Development
Social Development
Emotional Development

■ **BOXES**

5-1 Practically Speaking: Reducing Negativism and Encouraging Self-Regulation
5-2 Food for Thought: How a Mother's Depression Affects Her Baby
5-3 Practically Speaking: How to Choose a Good Day Care Center
5-4 Window on the World: How Sweden Cares for Parents and Children
5-5 Practically Speaking: Putting Research to Work

- What are some common influences on personality and social development, and how do infants and toddlers develop distinct personalities?
- What does Erikson say about personality and social development in the first 3 years of life?
- What emotions do infants and toddlers have, and how do they show their emotions?

- What are the effects of differences in temperament and gender?
- How do family relationships contribute to personality and social development?
- What causes child abuse and neglect, and what can be done to combat these problems?
- What impact does day care have upon infants and toddlers?

At 2 years, 10 months, Anna shouted, "No! Won't go!" running away from Jonathan as soon as she saw him walking over to the sandbox. Getting Anna to do anything her parents suggested had become harder and harder. Even though Diane and Jonathan knew that their daughter's constant "no's" were a normal and healthy aspect of this stage of life, it was sometimes hard for them to keep smiling through the "terrible twos."

This period—in which many children express their urge for independence by resisting almost everything they are told to do—is an important stage. Dependent, docile infants who trustingly accept what their parents want them to do are often transformed into strong-willed, sometimes ill-tempered little creatures with minds of their own. This time in a child's life—often ushered in before the second birthday and lasting well beyond it—dramatizes one of the most important aspects of early psychosocial development. When we look beyond the tears and the tantrums, the "no's" and the noise, we can appreciate that toddlers' emphatic expressions of what *they* want to do, as opposed to what *we* want them to do, signal the important shift from the dependency of infancy to the independence of childhood. Tracing the course of this shift is one major theme of this chapter.

The parent-child relationship is another theme. This chapter explores the ways in which parents influence their children in infancy and toddlerhood—and how children influence their parents. It also examines the development and measurement of emotions in infancy, when these emotions and their expression are highly organized and quite varied. We look at the ways in which babies are like each other, and the many ways they differ because of temperament, sex, and early experiences.

These issues underlie the psychosocial theory of early personality development, developed by Erik Erikson. They have also inspired research into the relationships between babies and their parents, as well as their other caretakers, their siblings, and other babies. And they have spurred study of situations when parent-child relationships are disrupted by separation or when they go tragically wrong, resulting in abuse and neglect. All these issues raise basic questions about the roots of personality.

EARLY PERSONALITY DEVELOPMENT

Personality is a person's unique and relatively consistent way of feeling, thinking, and behaving. (Table 5-1 shows some highlights of early personality and social development.) As we have noted, some aspects of personality seem to be inherited, while others seem to come about through early experience. First, we will discuss the vital awareness, which begins in infancy, that some aspects of the world and some of the people in it can be trusted, while others cannot. Then, we will talk about the autonomy that develops in toddlerhood, an essential step toward independence.

TRUST VERSUS MISTRUST

Infants come into this world needing a huge amount of care and sustenance. They are totally dependent on other people for food, protection, their very lives. How do they come to trust that their needs will be met? Infants' early experiences are the key element in developing this trust, according to Erik H. Erikson (1950).

The first of Erikson's eight crises, or critical developmental stages, *basic trust versus basic mistrust*, begins in infancy and continues till about 18 months of age. In these early months, babies develop a sense of how reliable the people and objects in their world are (refer to Table 1-1). They need to develop the right balance between trust (which allows them to form intimate relationships) and mistrust (which enables them to protect themselves). If trust predominates, as it should, children develop the virtue of *hope:* the belief that they can fulfill their needs and obtain their desires. If mistrust predominates, children will view the world as unfriendly and unpredictable and will have trouble forming close relationships.

According to Erikson, the feeding situation is the setting for establishing the right mix of trust and mistrust, and the mother plays an all-important role. Does she respond quickly enough? Can the baby count on being fed when hungry, and can the baby therefore trust the mother as a representative of the world? Trust enables an infant to let the mother out of sight "because she has become an inner certainty as well as an outer predictability" (Erikson, 1950, p. 247). It also is a critical element in forming attachments to important people, as we shall see when we discuss attachment later in this chapter.

The critical element in developing trust seems to be sensitive, responsive, consistent caregiving. This can be provided by a person or persons other than the mother—despite Erikson's emphasis on the mother's prime responsibility for how children turn out. Mothers are influential in their children's development, but they are not the only important influences. Furthermore, a child's own contribution to his or her life's journey—either as a result of inborn temperament or of responses to other people or life circumstances (as, for example, prenatal or birth complications)—can be substantial.

AUTONOMY VERSUS SHAME AND DOUBT

Starting at about 18 months, another major development occurs. As children mature—physically, cognitively, and emotionally—they are driven toward achieving independence from the very people they were so dependent on. The first sign of this drive toward autonomy, or self-determination,

---

TABLE 5-1

Highlights of Infants' and Toddlers' Personality and Social Development, Birth to 36 Months

Approximate Age, Months	Characteristics
0–3	Infants become open to stimulation. They begin to show interest and curiosity, and they smile readily at people.
3–6	Infants can anticipate what is about to happen and experience disappointment when it does not. They show this by becoming angry or acting wary. They smile, coo, and laugh often. This is a time of social awakening and early reciprocal exchanges between the baby and the caregiver.
7–9	Infants play "social games" and try to get responses from people. They "talk" to, touch, and cajole other babies to get them to respond. They express more differentiated emotions, showing joy, fear, anger, and surprise.
9–12	Infants are intensely preoccupied with their principal caregiver, may become afraid of strangers, and act subdued in new situations. By 1 year, they communicate emotions more clearly, showing moods, ambivalence, and gradations of feeling.
12–18	Babies explore their environment, using the people they are most attached to as a secure base. As they master the environment, they become more confident and more eager to assert themselves.
18–36	Toddlers sometimes become anxious because they now realize how much they are separating from their caregiver. They work out their awareness of their limitations in fantasy, in play, and by identifying with adults.

SOURCE: Adapted from Sroufe, 1979.

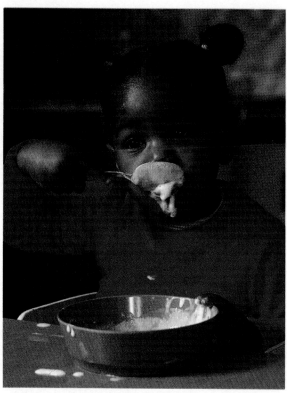

According to Erikson, toddlers need to develop autonomy. During this stage, parents need to ignore messy faces, bibs, tables, and floors, and let children learn how to master such basic tasks as feeding themselves. *(Gary Gladstone/The Image Bank)*

comes as the result of physical maturation. "Me do!" is the byword as toddlers use their developing muscles to try to do everything themselves—to walk, to feed and dress themselves, and to expand the boundaries of their world.

Erikson referred to this stage as the second crisis: *autonomy versus shame and doubt.* From about 18 months to 3 years, children begin to make their own decisions and to use some self-restraint. Thus a key issue during toddlerhood is the development of self-regulation and self-control versus outside regulation and control. Ideally, having come through the first stage with a sense of basic trust in the world and an awakening sense of self, toddlers begin to trust their own judgment and to substitute it for their parents'. Erikson referred to the emergence now of the virtue of *will.* This often looks like *negativism,* the tendency to say "no" just for the sake of resisting authority. But will is an essential characteristic of this stage.

Shame and doubt also have a place in toddlers'

learning how to regulate themselves, says Erikson, since unlimited liberty is neither safe nor healthy. Some self-doubt helps them recognize what they are not yet ready to do, and a sense of shame helps them learn to live by reasonable rules. Toddlers need adults to set appropriate limits. Too few or too many may make children compulsive about controlling themselves; and fear of losing self-control may fill a child with inhibitions and loss of self-esteem.

Self-control is children's ability to adjust what they do to fit what they know is socially acceptable. However, when they want *very* badly to do something, they easily forget the rules; thus, Renée runs into the street after a ball and Jacques takes a forbidden cookie. Not until they are about 3 do they develop *self-regulation,* or control of their own behavior to conform with social expectations. This involves greater flexibility, conscious thought, and the ability to wait for gratification.

The growth of self-regulation parallels that of cognitive awareness. Children continually absorb information about the kinds of behavior that their parents approve of. Parents are the most important people in a toddler's life and the ones whose approval matters more than anything else in the world. As children process, store, and act upon this information, a gradual shift from external to internal control takes place.

Toilet training, which Freud saw as the imposition of social control on a child's natural function, is for Erikson an important step toward self-control and autonomy. So is language; as children are better able to make their wishes understood, they become more powerful and independent. Meanwhile, parents and other caregivers provide a safe harbor from which the child can set out and discover the world, and to which the child can keep coming back for support.

The "terrible twos" are a normal manifestation of this need for autonomy. The emergence of a strong and often stubborn will in a 2-year-old is normal. Toddlers *have to* test the new notion that they are individuals, that they have some control over their world, and that they have new, exciting powers. No longer content to let someone else decide what they should do, they are now driven to try out their own ideas and find their own preferences. Because one of their favorite ways of testing is to shout "No!" this behavior is called *negativism.* This negative behavior is both healthy and normal (see Box 5-1).

BOX 5-1   PRACTICALLY SPEAKING

REDUCING NEGATIVISM AND ENCOURAGING SELF-REGULATION

Parents and other caregivers who view children's expressions of self-will as a normal, healthy striving for independence, not as stubbornness, can help them learn to regulate themselves, contribute to their sense of competence, and avoid excessive conflict. Almost all children show negativism to some degree; it usually begins before 2 years of age, tends to peak at about 3½ to 4, and declines by age 6. Many children playfully tease their parents to show their control—but do not really mean what they say and will eventually comply with requests. Suggestions like the following can help parents help both themselves and their children (Haswell, Hock, & Wenar, 1981; Kopp, 1982; Power & Chapieski, 1986):

Be flexible. Learn the child's natural rhythms and special likes and dislikes. The most flexible parents tend to have the least resistant children.

Think of yourself as a safe harbor, with safe limits, from which a child can set out and discover the world—and keep coming back for support.

Make your home "child-friendly." Fill it with unbreakable objects that are safe to explore.

Avoid physical punishment. It does not work and may even lead a toddler to do more damage.

Offer a choice—even a limited one—to give the child some control. For example, "Would you like to have your bath now, or after we read a book?"

Be consistent in enforcing necessary requests.

Don't interrupt an activity unless absolutely necessary. Try to wait until the child's attention has shifted to something else.

If you must interrupt, give warning: "We have to leave the playground soon." This gives the child time to prepare and either finish an activity or think about resuming it another time.

Suggest alternative activities. When Ashley is throwing sand in Keiko's face, say, "Oh, look! Nobody's on the swings now. Let's go over and I'll give you a good push!"

Suggest; don't command. Accompany requests with smiles or hugs, not criticism, threats, or physical restraint.

Link requests with pleasurable activities: "It's time to stop playing, so that you can go to the store with me."

Remind the child of what you expect: "When we go to this playground, we *never* go outside the gate."

Wait a few moments before repeating a request when a child doesn't comply immediately.

Use "time out" to end conflicts. In a nonpunitive way, remove either yourself or the child from a situation. Very often this results in the resistance diminishing or even disappearing.

Expect less self-control during times of stress (like illness, divorce, the birth of a sibling, or a move to a new home).

EMOTIONS: THE FOUNDATION OF PERSONALITY

All normal human beings seem to have the same basic *emotions*—such subjective feelings as sadness, joy, and fear—which motivate human behavior. These emotions are expressed in characteristic ways, are accompanied by certain neurochemical processes in the body, and arise in response to various situations and experiences. Each one has a unique function in adapting to life (Izard & Malatesta, 1987). But people differ in how often they feel a particular emotion, what kinds of events call it forth, and how they act as a result. Emotional reactions to events and people, which are intimately tied in with cognitive perceptions, form a fundamental element of personality.

HOW INFANTS' EMOTIONS ARE STUDIED

It is hard to tell what babies are feeling; and it is hard to learn how their feelings first develop. However, a series of innovative studies suggest that in the first few months of life babies express a fairly wide range of emotions (Izard, Huebner, Resser, McGinness, & Dougherty, 1980). Researchers videotaped the facial expressions of 5-, 7-, and 9-month-olds as the babies played games with their mothers, were surprised by a jack-in-the-box, were given shots by a doctor, and were approached by a stranger. When college students and health professionals were asked to identify the babies' emotional expressions just from the tapes, they believed that they were able to recognize joy, sadness, interest, and fear, and to a lesser degree anger, surprise, and disgust. When observers were trained with Izard's Facial Expression Scoring Manual, which is based on patterns of facial movements, they felt even more confident about their identifications (Izard, 1971, 1977).

Although we do not know that these babies actually had the feelings they were credited with, they did show a range of expressions that were very similar to adults' expressions of these emotions. So it is at least possible that these expressions reflected similar feelings.

HOW EMOTIONS DEVELOP: THE EMERGING SENSE OF SELF

Babies' emotions, like everything else about them, are products of a dynamic process of development. As with motor development, the emergence of various emotions (see Table 5-2) seems to be governed by the biological "clock" of the brain's maturation. But this timetable can be altered by environmental influences. Abused infants typically show fear several months earlier than other babies do, very

TABLE 5-2

Timetable of Emotional Development

Emotion	Approximate Age of Emergence
Interest Distress (in response to pain) Disgust (in response to unpleasant taste or smell)	Present at birth
Anger, surprise, joy, fear, sadness	First 6 months
Empathy, jealousy, shyness, embarrassment, surprise	18–24 months
Shame, guilt, pride	30–36 months

SOURCES: Adapted from information in Izard & Malatesta, 1987; and M. Lewis, 1987; 1992.

likely having learned fear through their unhappy experiences (Gaensbauer & Hiatt, 1984).

Very soon after birth, babies show signs of interest, distress, and disgust. Within the next few months these primary emotions differentiate into joy, anger, surprise, sadness, and fear. Not until the second year do babies typically develop *self-awareness*, the understanding that they are separate from other people and things. Once they have this understanding, they can feel such "self-conscious" emotions as pride or embarrassment, which imply that the children are evaluating themselves, a necessary step for regulating themselves.

They can now begin to reflect on their actions and measure them against social standards (Stipek, Gralinski, & Kopp, 1990; Izard & Malatesta, 1987; Kopp, 1982; M. Lewis, 1987). It seems likely that until children misbehave and feel bad about it that they won't hold back from doing what they know they are not supposed to do, in the absence of authority figures (Stipek et al., 1990).

When does self-awareness emerge? After interviewing the mothers of 123 toddlers, aged 14 to 40 months, one team of researchers (Stipek et al., 1990) found this sequence of self-concept development:

1 *Physical self-recognition:* Most recognized themselves in mirrors or pictures by 18 months, about the time when Piaget said object permanence is fully developed (see Chapter 4). This confirms previous findings; in an earlier study researchers counted the number of times children aged 6 to 24 months touched their noses. Then the researchers dabbed rouge on the babies' noses, sat them in front of a mirror, and noted whether they touched their noses more often. The 18-month-olds touched their red noses much more often than younger children did. The researchers concluded that the 18-month-olds did this because they knew that they didn't normally have red noses, and that this is, then, the age when babies recognize themselves (M. Lewis & Brooks, 1974).

2 *Self-description:* Sometime between 19 and 30 months, children use either neutral descriptions (like "little" or "curly hair") or evaluative ones (like "good" or "dirty") about themselves. Children will not apply descriptive and evaluative terms to themselves unless they have a concept of themselves as *distinct* physical beings.

3 *Emotional response to wrongdoing:* Sometime after the previous developments, children show that they are upset by a parent's disap-

Although it looks as if 9-month-old Annie recognizes the photo of herself on her grandmother's tee shirt, such self-recognition does not normally occur until about 18 months of age. Annie may be interested in the picture because she can see that it is a human face. Babies as young as 1 month can recognize their mothers' faces (see Chapter 3). *(Phil Hollembeak)*

proval and will stop doing something they're not supposed to do, at least while they're being watched. This signals the beginning of moral understanding and an early sense of conscience. Even the youngest children in the study, however, showed autonomy, asserting their will apparently just to be contrary and resisting attempts to restrain them physically.

HOW INFANTS SHOW THEIR EMOTIONS

Newborns plainly show when they are unhappy. They let out piercing yells, flail their arms and legs, and stiffen their bodies. It is harder to tell when they are happy. During the first month, they become quiet at the sound of a human voice or when they are picked up, and they smile when their hands are moved together to play pat-a-cake. With every passing day, infants respond more to people—smiling, cooing, reaching out, and eventually moving toward them. These signals, if we become adept at reading them, are fairly reliable clues to a baby's emotional state.

By expressing their feelings, babies gain a grow-

ing amount of control. When they want or need something, they cry; when they feel sociable, they smile or laugh. When these early messages get a response, babies' sense of connection with other people is strengthened. Their sense of power grows as they see that their cries bring help and comfort and that their smiles and laughter elicit smiles and laughter in return.

The meaning of this emotional language changes as babies develop. At first, crying signals physical discomfort (at 2 months, to an injection; at 4 months, to arm restraint); later it more often expresses psychological distress. The early smile is a spontaneous expression of internal well-being; later smiles show pleasure in other people—as early as 3 to 4 weeks of age in response to a high-pitched human voice, and at 4 to 6 weeks in response to a nodding face (Izard & Malatesta, 1987).

Crying

Crying is the most powerful way—sometimes the only way—by which infants can communicate their vital needs. Babies have four patterns of crying (Wolff, 1969): the basic *hunger cry* (a rhythmic cry, not always associated with hunger), the *angry cry* (a variation in which excess air is forced through the vocal cords), the *pain cry* (a sudden onset of loud crying without preliminary moaning, sometimes followed by breath-holding), and the *frustration cry* (two or three drawn-out cries, with no prolonged breath-holding). Babies in distress cry louder, longer, and more irregularly than hungry babies and are more apt to gag and to interrupt their crying (Oswald & Peltzman, 1974).

Parents often worry that they will spoil a child by responding to crying, but research puts this fear to rest. Babies whose cries bring relief apparently gain confidence that their actions will bring results. By the end of the first year, babies whose mothers have regularly responded to their crying with tender, soothing care cry less (Ainsworth & Bell, 1977; S. Bell & Ainsworth, 1972). By now they are communicating more in other ways—with babbling, gestures, and facial expressions—than the babies of more punitive or ignoring mothers, who cry more. So although parents do not need to leap to a baby's side at every whimper, it seems safer to respond more rather than less.

Smiling

A baby's smile is irresistible. Parents usually greet a baby's first smile with great excitement, and adults who see a smiling baby will almost always smile back.

The early faint smile that appears soon after birth occurs spontaneously as a result of central nervous system activity. It generally appears without outside stimulation, often when the infant is falling asleep (Sroufe & Waters, 1976). In their second week, babies often smile after a feeding, when they are drowsy and may be responding to the caregiver's sounds. After this, smiles come more often when babies are alert but inactive. At about 1 month, smiles become more frequent and more social, directed toward people. Babies smile now when their hands are clapped together or when they hear a familiar voice (Kreutzer & Charlesworth, 1973; Wolff, 1963). During the second month, as visual recognition develops, babies respond more selectively, smiling more at people they know than at those they do not know.

Some infants smile much more than others. Babies who generously reward caretaking with smiles and gurgles are likely to form more positive relationships with their caregivers than babies who smile less readily.

Laughing

At about the fourth month of life, infants start to laugh out loud. They chortle at being kissed on the stomach, hearing various sounds, and seeing their parents do unusual things. Some of their laughter

may be related to fear. Babies sometimes react to the same stimulus (like an object looming toward them) with both fear and laughter (Sroufe & Wunsch, 1972).

As babies grow older, they laugh more often and at more things. A 4- to 6-month-old may respond to sounds and touch; a 7- to 9-month-old may delight in a game of peekaboo or howl with glee when a parent puts on a funny mask. This shift reflects cognitive development: the older baby has learned to recognize what is expected and to perceive an incongruity. Laughter, then, is a response to the environment; it helps babies discharge tension in situations that otherwise might be upsetting, and is "an important tie between cognitive development and emotional growth and expression" (Sroufe & Wunsch, 1972, p. 1341).

HOW EMOTIONS ARE COMMUNICATED BETWEEN INFANTS AND ADULTS

Mutual-Regulation Model

Max smiles at his mother, a signal she takes as an invitation to play; as she kisses his stomach, he goes into gales of giggles. But the next day, when she begins to kiss his stomach again, the baby looks at her glassy-eyed and turns his head away. His mother interprets this as a message saying, "I want to stay quiet now." Following this cue, she tucks him into a baby carrier and lets him rest quietly against her body.

This process, called the *mutual-regulation model* (E. Z. Tronick & Gianino, 1986), shows how infants as young as 3 months of age take an active part in regulating their emotional states. Babies differ in the amount of stimulation they need or want: too little leaves them uninterested; too much overwhelms them. Overstimulation is a special danger for low-birthweight infants, but it can also affect other babies.

Babies and adults send a variety of signals to each other, and a healthy interaction occurs when a caregiver "reads" a baby's behaviors accurately and responds appropriately. Adults do not, of course, always receive or understand babies' messages. When babies do not get the results they want, they may be upset at first, but they usually keep on sending signals so that they can "repair" the interaction. Normally, interaction moves back and forth between poorly regulated and well-regulated states, and babies learn from these shifts

This baby won't be "spoiled" by being picked up; instead, father and child will improve their communication with each other. When a caregiver "reads" a baby's behaviors accurately and responds appropriately, the baby learns how to send signals. This is known as the *mutual regulation* model. *(Lawrence Migdale)*

how to send signals and what to do when the first signal does not bring what they want.

When a baby's goals for connecting with people and objects and for retaining a comfortable emotional balance are met, the baby feels joyful or at least interested. But if someone taking care of a baby like Max either ignores his invitation to play or insists on playing after he has signaled that he does not feel like it just then, the baby would feel angry or sad. Both partners are important and each stimulates the other (E. Z. Tronick (1989). (See Box 5-2 for an example of what can happen when this mutual-regulation model breaks down.)

"Reading" the Emotions of Another Person

The ability to decipher other people's feelings seems to be an inborn ability that helps human beings form attachments to others, live in society, and protect themselves. Even very young normal infants can perceive emotions expressed by other people, and they adjust their own behavior accordingly. At 10 weeks of age, they meet anger with anger (Lelwica & Haviland, 1983). At 3 months, infants faced with a stony-faced, unresponsive mother will make faces, sounds, and gestures to get a reaction (J. F. Cohn & Tronick, 1983; E. Z. Tronick, 1980). And 9-month-olds show more joy, play more, and look longer when their mothers seem happy; and look sad and turn away when their mothers seem sad (Termine & Izard, 1988). This is one more example of the competence very young babies show. They do not passively receive other people's actions; they do a great deal to act on and change the way people act toward them.

When this ability to "read" other people is not present, it severely handicaps a person right from infancy. One recent study examined the responses of three groups of children—normal, mentally retarded, and autistic—to adults' negative emotions. The adults expressed fear (using facial expressions and gestures upon seeing a toy robot), distress (pretending to hurt themselves), and discomfort (pretending to feel sick). The normal children (average age 20 months) and the retarded ones (average, 42 months) were very attentive to the adults in all three situations. But the autistic children (average age about 42 months) seemed to ignore or not notice these adults. This failure to notice the emotional signals of the people around them is a typical symptom of autism, and is a crucial one, since it limits children's social and emotional development and thus contributes to their deficiencies (Sigman, Kasari, Kwon, & Yirmiya, 1992).

The ability to "read" other people's unspoken signals helps children learn how to act in specific situations, through the system known as social referencing.

Social Referencing

If, at a formal dinner table, you have ever cast a sidelong glance to see which fork the person next to you was using, you have read another person's nonverbal signals to get information on how to act. Babies learn how to do this at a very early age.

Through *social referencing,* one person forms an understanding of an ambiguous situation by seeking out another person's perception of it. Babies are confronted by many situations that they neither understand nor know how to respond to. They learn to interpret other people's emotional and cognitive reactions some time after 6 months of age, when they begin to judge the possible consequences of events, imitate complex behaviors, and distinguish among and react to various emotional expressions. They show referencing by the way they look at their caregivers when they encounter a new person or toy.

A study using the visual cliff (described in Chapters 3 and 4) found that when the drop looked very shallow or very deep, 1-year-olds did not look to their mothers; they were able to judge for themselves whether to cross over or not. But when they were uncertain about the depth of the "cliff," they paused at the "edge," looked down, and then looked up to their mothers' faces. Meanwhile, the mother posed one of several expressions—fear, anger, interest, happiness, or sadness. The particular emotion shown influenced the babies' actions. Most of those whose mothers showed joy or interest crossed the "drop"; very few whose mothers looked angry or afraid crossed it; and an intermediate number of those whose mothers looked sad did (Sorce, Emde, Campos, & Klinnert, 1985). Apparently, babies turn to social referencing of facial expressions most often in puzzling situations.

The link between the physical, the cognitive, and the emotional aspects of development shows clearly in a study of social referencing in forty 12- to 18-month-old babies, half of whom suffered some level of hearing loss. The hearing-impaired babies achieved the ability to socially reference their mothers later than the babies with normal hearing. This may be due to a delay in the hearing-loss babies' achievement of self-awareness (MacTurk & Koester, 1991).

BOX 5-2   FOOD FOR THOUGHT

HOW A MOTHER'S DEPRESSION AFFECTS HER BABY

What happens when a baby's emotional signals to a caregiver are ignored or overridden? When this keeps happening, as it often does between depressed women and their babies, the system of mutual regulation breaks down, often with severe consequences.

THE DEPRESSED MOTHER: HOW SHE FEELS AND ACTS

Some 12 to 20 percent of American mothers with children under age 5 suffer from *depression*, an emotional state characterized by sadness and such other symptoms as difficulties in eating, sleeping, and concentrating (Garrison & Earls, 1986). The risk is higher for mothers who are poor, poorly educated, single, immigrants, and dissatisfied with their marriage or living conditions; and for those who have a temperamentally difficult or handicapped child and no family and friends to turn to (W. T. Garrison & Earls, 1986; B. S. Zuckerman & Beardslee, 1987). About 20 percent of new mothers suffer from postpartum depression, which lasts 6 to 8 weeks after birth (B. S. Zuckerman & Beardslee, 1987). Depressed mothers tend to be punitive, to consider their children bothersome and hard to care for, and to feel as if their lives are out of control (T. M. Field et al., 1985; Whiffen & Gotlib, 1989; B. S. Zuckerman & Beardslee, 1987).

BABIES OF DEPRESSED MOTHERS: HOW THEY ACT

Babies of depressed mothers often stop sending emotional signals and try to comfort themselves by such behaviors as sucking or rocking. The babies will try for a while to repair the interaction; but with repeated failures, they will fall back on their own resources. If this defensive reaction becomes habitual, it can create major problems for babies who feel that they have no power to draw responses from other people, that their mothers are unreliable, and that the world is untrustworthy. The babies themselves then become sad, not as a reflection of the mother's depression but as the result of impaired interaction.

This cycle may explain why children of depressed mothers are at risk of various emotional and cognitive disturbances. As infants, they are more likely to be drowsy, to show tension by squirming and arching their backs, and to cry often. As toddlers they tend to engage in a low level of symbolic play. Later they are likely to grow poorly and perform poorly on cognitive measures, to have accidents, and to have behavior problems that often last into adolescence (T. M. Field et al., 1985; B. S. Zuckerman & Beardslee, 1987).

Babies of depressed mothers seem less upset when separated from their mothers than do babies of nondepressed mothers (Dawson et al., 1992). Such infants are also less motivated than other babies to explore the environment and more apt to prefer less challenging tasks (Redding, Harmon, & Morgan, 1990). Among forty-five 2-year-olds whose reactions to such mishaps as a doll breaking and juice spilling were studied, the children of depressed mothers tended to suppress their frustration and tension (Cole, Barrett, & Zahn-Waxler, 1992). Clearly, these children react differently from other children from an early age, apparently in direct response to the changes that depression causes in a mother's behavior.

Furthermore, babies of depressed mothers may be at risk of becoming depressed themselves. The left frontal region of the human brain seems to be specialized for "approach" emotions like joy, whereas the right frontal region is specialized for "withdrawal" emotions like distress. In one study of the brain activity of 11- to 17-month-old infants, babies of depressed mothers showed less activity in the left frontal region than did other babies. This may suggest that they are predisposed to depression later on (Dawson et al., 1992).

HELPING DEPRESSED MOTHERS AND THEIR CHILDREN

Most depressed mothers know that their feelings affect their children, and they often feel guilty about feeling depressed. Such women and their babies can benefit by a program in which professional or paraprofessional home visitors help families get access to community resources, model and reinforce positive interaction with the babies, and offer the mothers the chance to take part in parenting groups or a drop-in social hour (Lyons-Ruth, Connell, & Grunebaum, 1990). After an average of about 47 home visits over a 13-month period, 18-month-olds whose families had been visited scored higher on the Bayley mental scale than did a control group of nonvisited infants. Furthermore, the visited infants were twice as likely to be rated as securely attached to their mothers (showing better emotional health, as we will see in our discussion of attachment later in this chapter).

DIFFERENCES IN PERSONALITY DEVELOPMENT

Even in the womb each person begins to show a unique personality. Differences already exist prenatally in fetal activity levels and favorite positions in utero. After birth, personality differences become even more apparent. Very young infants' normal emotional responses seem to reflect patterns or traits that persist as they get older, suggesting that some aspects of personality are inborn.

A considerable body of research has shown that some characteristic emotional reactions may stem from differences in temperament, which seems to be largely genetic in origin, though it is also influenced by the environment. Other research has looked at personality differences between the sexes, which seem to be mostly socially influenced, although there may also be a biological component.

TEMPERAMENTAL DIFFERENCES

A 2-month-old who screams in outrage when given a shot is likely to become just as infuriated at 19 months when a playmate takes away a toy, whereas a 2-month-old who takes the shot more calmly will probably put up with later indignities without much fuss. In other words, infants not more than 8 weeks old already show signs of temperamental differences that form an important part of their personalities (Izard, in Trotter, 1987).

We can see how this works by looking at three sisters. Aretha, the eldest, was a cheerful, calm baby who ate, slept, and eliminated at regular times. She greeted each day and most people with a smile, and the only sign that she was awake during the night was the tinkle of the musical toy in her crib. When Belinda, the second sister, woke up, she would open her mouth to cry before she even opened her eyes. She slept and ate little and irregularly; she laughed and cried loudly, often bursting into tantrums; and she had to be convinced that new people and new experiences were not threatening before she would have anything to do with them. The youngest sister, Clarissa, was mild in her responses, both positive and negative. She did not like most new situations, but if allowed to proceed at her own slow pace, she would eventually become interested and involved.

Each of these children was showing her own *temperament*—her characteristic style of approaching and reacting to people and situations. Temperament has been defined as the *how* of behavior:

not *what* people do, or *why*, but how they go about doing it. Two toddlers, for example, may be equally able to dress themselves and equally motivated to do it, but the ways they approach the task may be different (A. Thomas & Chess, 1984).

Components of Temperament

The New York Longitudinal Study (NYLS—introduced in Chapter 2) followed 133 people from early infancy into adulthood. Researchers collected data by interviewing, testing, and observing the subjects, and interviewing their parents and teachers. Based on the findings, they identified nine aspects or components of temperament that showed up soon after birth (A. Thomas, Chess, & Birch, 1968). These are:

1 *Activity level*—how and how much a person moves
2 *Rhythmicity, or regularity*—predictability of biological cycles like hunger, sleep, and elimination
3 *Approach or withdrawal*—how a person initially responds to a new stimulus, like a new toy, food, or person
4 *Adaptability*—how easily an initial response is modified in a desired direction to a new or altered situation
5 *Threshold of responsiveness*—how much stimulation is needed to evoke a response
6 *Intensity of reaction*—how energetically a person responds
7 *Quality of mood*—whether a person's behavior is predominantly pleasant, joyful, and friendly; or unpleasant, unhappy, and unfriendly
8 *Distractibility*—how easily an irrelevant stimulus can alter or interfere with a person's behavior
9 *Attention span and persistence*—how long a person pursues an activity and continues in the face of obstacles.

Three Patterns of Temperament

Almost two-thirds of the children studied fitted into one of three categories identified by these researchers (see Table 5-3). Aretha, in our example, is an *easy* child (like 40 percent in the NYLS sample): generally happy, rhythmic in biological functioning, and accepting of new experiences. Belinda is a *difficult* child (like 10 percent in the sample): more irritable, irregular in biological rhythms, and more intense in expressing emotion. And Clarissa

TABLE 5-3

Three Temperamental Patterns		
Easy Child	**Difficult Child**	**Slow-to-Warm-Up Child**
Responds well to novelty and change	Responds poorly to novelty and change	Responds slowly to novelty and change
Quickly develops regular sleep and feeding schedules	Has irregular sleep and feeding schedules	Sleeps and feeds more regularly than difficult child; less regularly than easy child
Takes to new foods easily	Accepts new foods slowly	Shows mildly negative initial response to new stimuli (e.g., a first encounter with a bath; a new food, person, or place; entering school)
Smiles at strangers	Is suspicious of strangers	
Adapts easily to new situations	Adapts slowly to new situations	
Accepts most frustrations with minimal fuss	Reacts to frustration with tantrums	
Adapts quickly to new routines and rules of new games	Adjusts slowly to new routines	Gradually develops liking for new stimuli after repeated, unpressured exposures
Has moods of mild to moderate intensity, usually positive	Has frequent periods of loud crying; also laughs loudly	Has mildly intense reactions, both positive and negative
	Displays intense and frequently negative moods	

SOURCE: Adapted from A. Thomas & Chess, 1984.

is a *slow-to-warm-up* child (like 15 percent in the sample): generally mild and slow to adapt to new experiences (A. Thomas & Chess, 1977, 1984).

Many children (like 35 percent of the NYLS sample) do not fit neatly into any of these three groups. A baby may have regular eating and sleeping schedules, yet be fearful of strangers. A child may be extremely easy or relatively easy most of the time but not always. Another child may warm up slowly to new foods but adapt quickly to new baby-sitters. All of these variations are normal (A. Thomas & Chess, 1984).

Influences on Temperament

Temperament seems to be largely determined by heredity (A. Thomas & Chess, 1977, 1984; Braungart, Plomin, DeFries, & Fulker, 1992; Emde et al., 1992). Individual differences in basic temperament do not seem to be determined by parents' attitudes (A. Thomas & Chess, 1984) or by gender, birth order, or social class (Persson-Blennow & McNeil, 1981). However, temperamental style can change over time. What accounts for such change?

The NYLS found that although the nine primary aspects of temperament remained relatively stable, some people did show considerable change (A. Thomas & Chess, 1984). Sometimes this seemed due to unusual events or parents' handling of a child. One "difficult" girl in the NYLS who was having a hard time in childhood suddenly showed musical and dramatic talent at about age 10, leading her parents to see her in a new way and to respond differently to her; by age 22 she was well-adjusted. Another "difficult" child was doing well with quiet and firm limit-setting by her parents—until she was 13, when her father died and her overwhelmed mother could not cope with the child's needs; this girl developed a severe behavior disorder. An "easy" child got into trouble at age 14 after experimenting with drugs; he gave up drugs a year later when he began following an Indian guru; several years later he broke with the guru; in his early twenties he was doing well (A. Thomas & Chess, 1984).

Changes in temperament also appeared in a study of preterm infants, observed at 3 months and again at 7 months (Garcia-Coll, Halpern, Vohr, Seifer, & Oh, 1992). Changes in sociability, irritability, and approachability might be due to the infants' recovery from difficulties experienced around the time of birth. This, then, shows the possible influence of the environment, as well as the self-righting tendency children so often have, which may enable a genetic predisposition to a certain temperamental style to reassert itself.

Other evidence of the influence of environmental factors comes from a study of babies from three African cultures. The researchers attributed the temperamental differences that they found across cultures to different child-rearing customs (like unconcern with "clock time" in a tribe whose babies have irregular biological rhythms), mothers' attitudes (expecting different behaviors from boys and girls), and ecological settings (DeVries & Sameroff, 1984).

While cross-cultural variations may result to some extent from genetic differences among the three groups, they also seem to reflect early life experiences. The NYLS researchers found the same thing—that children respond to the way their parents treat them. One analysis of NYLS data found that the way mothers feel about their roles— whether they are happy or unhappy about either being employed or being at home full time—seems to affect their children's adjustment. Mothers who were dissatisfied either with their jobs or with being homemakers were more likely to be intolerant of, to disapprove of, or to reject their 3-year-olds' behavior, and the rejected children were apt to become "difficult" (J. V. Lerner & Galambos, 1985).

Effects of Temperament on Adjustment: "Goodness of Fit"

About one-third of the NYLS subjects developed behavior problems at some time. Most were mild disturbances that showed up between ages 3 and 5 and cleared up by adolescence, but some remained or grew worse by adulthood.

No temperamental type was immune to problems. Even easy children had them when their lives held too much stress. One kind of stress is being expected to act in ways contrary to basic temperament. If a highly active child is confined to a small apartment and expected to sit still for long periods, if a slow-to-warm-up child is pushed to adjust to many new people and situations, or if a persistent child is constantly taken away from absorbing projects, trouble may result. The key to healthy adjustment is "goodness of fit" between children and the demands made upon them.

"Goodness of fit" between parent and child— the degree to which parents feel comfortable with the child they have—is extremely important, because it affects parents' feelings toward their children. Thus, energetic, active parents may become impatient with a slow-moving, docile child, while more easygoing parents might welcome such a personality. An Australian study found that children who as infants were seen by their mothers as having "difficult" temperaments were more likely to have behavior problems as preschoolers. In fact, the mothers' perceptions were the most powerful predictors of the later behavior problems (Oberklaid, Sanson, Pedlow, & Prior, 1993).

One of the most important things that parents can do is ride with a child's basic temperament instead of trying to cast him or her into a mold of the parents' design. For example, the parents of a rhythmic child can use a "demand" feeding schedule, letting the child set the pace; the parents of an irregular child can help by setting a flexible schedule. The parents of a slow-to-warm-up child need to give the child time to adjust to new situations and need to ask other people, like relatives and nursery school teachers, to do the same.

Recognition of inborn temperament relieves parents of some heavy emotional baggage. When they understand that a child acts a certain way not out of willfulness, laziness, or stupidity, but because of inborn temperament, they are less likely to feel guilty, anxious, or hostile, or to act rigid or impatient. They can focus on helping the child use his or her temperament as a strength, rather than seeing it as an impediment. They can change "poorness of fit" to "goodness of fit" and make positive contributions to the child's development.

GENDER DIFFERENCES

As we saw in Chapter 3, there are few physiological differences between baby boys and baby girls. Are there differences in personality?

Researchers have studied infants' activity levels, temperaments, responses to what they see as opposed to what they hear, how irritable they are, and their interest in exploring their surroundings versus staying close to a parent. Some studies have found differences between the sexes, but these findings have not always held up when the studies were repeated by the same or other investigators. After reviewing the literature, Birns (1976) concluded that gender differences cannot be described clearly until after age 2.

Other studies have focused on the ways adults act toward infants. The findings of these studies are much clearer. A baby, even a newborn, who is identified as a female will be treated differently from one identified as a male. When strangers think that a crying baby is a male, they are likely to assume that "he" is crying from anger; when they believe that the baby is female, they think that "she" is afraid (Condry & Condry, 1974).

In one study, twenty-four 14-month-old children, 12 boys and 12 girls, were introduced to adults who did not know them. Sometimes the babies were identified according to their real sex, and sometimes they were said to belong to the other sex. In playing with the children, the adults were more likely to encourage the "boys" in active play and more likely to choose a ball rather than a doll for them to play with. The adults tended to talk more to the "girls" and to choose a doll or a bottle for them to play with. Interestingly, though, the children themselves did not show gender differences; the boys and girls played in very similar ways, even though they were treated differently by the adults (Frisch, 1977).

Parents' behavior toward babies is affected by the parent's own sex and by the age and personality of the infant, but there are some consistent findings. Baby boys get more attention in infancy, but the attention baby girls get is designed to make them smile more and be more social (Birns, 1976). Mothers' facial expressions show a wider range of emotion with baby daughters than with sons—which may explain why girls are better than boys at interpreting emotional expression (Malatesta, in Trotter, 1983).

Thus, although differences may not be present at birth, environmental shaping of boys' and girls' personalities begins very early in life. As we look at the crucial influence of children's families, we will see other differences among children.

THE FAMILY AND PERSONALITY DEVELOPMENT

Was your birth planned and welcomed? How old were your parents? Were they physically and emotionally healthy? Were they wealthy, comfortable, or poor? How did your personality mesh with theirs? How many people lived in your home?

Such early social factors had a major influence on the child you were and the person you are now. Furthermore, you yourself influenced your family. Your parents' feelings and actions toward you were influenced by your sex, your temperament, your health, and your birth order.

The kind of family you grew up in was probably very different from what it would have been a century earlier, and family life will probably change even more in the future. A baby born today is likely to have only one sibling, a mother who works outside the home, and a father who is more involved in his children's lives than his own father was. An infant has a 40 to 50 percent chance of spending part of his or her childhood with only one parent, probably the mother, and probably because of divorce (P. C. Glick & Lin, 1986a).

These changes in family life are revolutionizing

research on *socialization*—how children learn the behaviors their culture deems appropriate. The relationships formed in infancy set the pattern for much of a child's early socialization. In the past, most research focused on the relationship between mothers and babies, but now we also recognize the importance of the relationships infants have with their fathers, their brothers and sisters, their grandparents, and other caregivers.

Another trend is a focus on how the entire family system operates. How does the marital relationship affect the relationship each spouse has with the baby? Do Joey's parents act differently with him when either one is alone with him and when they are all together? Questions like these have produced provocative answers. When both parents are present and talking to each other, for example, they pay less attention to their child. Some spouses' closeness to each other may detract from their ability to be close to their children; in other cases parenting itself either strengthens a marriage or strains it (Belsky, 1979). By looking at the family as a unit, we get a fuller picture of the web of relationships among all its members.

The ability to form intimate relationships throughout life may well be affected by relationships formed in infancy. Let us see how babies influence and are influenced by those close to them.

THE MOTHER'S ROLE

Until recently most developmentalists seemed to agree with Napoleon that "the future good or bad conduct of a child depends entirely on the mother." Although we now recognize that mothers are not the only important people in babies' lives, they are still central characters in the drama of development.

The Mother-Infant Bond

To find out how and when the special intimacy between mothers and their babies forms, some researchers have followed the *ethological approach.* This approach considers behavior to be biologically determined and is concerned with the evolutionary basis of behaviors. It relies on naturalistic observation, focuses on animals and birds, and emphasizes critical, or sensitive, periods for the development of behavior. In connection with his studies of animal behavior, the ethologist Konrad Lorenz (1957) waddled, honked, and flapped his arms—and got newborn ducklings to follow him

The family may well be the largest single influence on children's development, and children also influence other family members in many important ways. Research now focuses on relationships between children and their fathers and siblings, as well as their mothers. *(Michal Heron/Woodfin Camp & Assoc.)*

as they would the mother duck, and to "love him like a mother."

Newly hatched chicks will follow the first moving object they see, whether or not it is a member of their own species, and they become increasingly attached to it. Usually, this first attachment is to the mother; but if the natural course of events is disturbed, other (often bizarre) attachments (like the one to Lorenz) can occur. This behavior, termed *imprinting*, is an instinctual form of learning in which an organism's nervous system seems primed to acquire certain information during a brief critical period in the animal's early life. Imprinting is said to take place automatically and irreversibly. Lorenz found that if the chicks had no object to follow during the critical period, imprinting would not occur. Similarly, among goats and cows, certain rituals occur right after birth. If they are prevented or interrupted, mother and offspring will not recognize each other. The results for the baby animal are devastating—physical withering and death, or abnormal development (Blauvelt, 1955; A. U. Moore, 1960; J. P. Scott, 1958). These findings raise questions for human beings.

Is There a Critical Period for Mother-Infant Bonding?

In 1976, two researchers concluded that if mother and baby are separated during the first hours after birth, the ***mother-infant bond***—the mother's feeling of close, caring connection with her newborn—may not develop normally (Klaus & Kennell, 1976). Their studies inspired many hospitals to establish rooming-in policies, allowing mothers and babies to remain together. Such humane changes are welcome, even though follow-up research has not confirmed the notion of a critical time for bonding (Chess & Thomas, 1982; M. E. Lamb, 1982a, 1982b; Rutter, 1979b). No long-term effects showed up from early extended contact between mother and baby.

In 1982, Klaus and Kennell modified their original position; and in 1983, the researcher and psychiatrist Stella Chess wrote, "By now the whole 'critical period concept' has been generally discredited in human development theory" (p. 975). This finding relieved adoptive parents, and parents who had to be separated from their infants after birth, of much unnecessary worry and guilt. Concern with bonding is still a vital issue, however, and some developmentalists urge research on groups at risk of weak bonding (like poor, young, or single mothers and fathers) to find out what factors other than early contact affect parent-child bonds (Lamb et al., 1983).

What Do Babies Need from Their Mothers?

In a famous study, rhesus monkeys were separated from their mothers 6 to 12 hours after birth and raised in a laboratory. The infant monkeys were put into cages with one of two kinds of surrogate "mothers"—a plain cylindrical wire-mesh form or

In a series of classic experiments, Harry Harlow and Margaret Harlow showed that food is not the most important way to a baby's heart. When infant rhesus monkeys could choose whether to go to a wire surrogate "mother" or a warm, soft terry-cloth "mother," they spent more time clinging to the cloth mother, even if they were being fed by bottles connected to the wire mother. *(Harry Harlow Primate Laboratory/ University of Wisconsin)*

a form covered with terry cloth. Some monkeys were fed from bottles connected to the wire "mothers"; others were "nursed" by the warm, cuddly cloth ones.

When the monkeys were allowed to spend time with either kind of "mother," they all spent more time clinging to the cloth surrogates—even if they were being fed only by the wire ones. In an unfamiliar room, the babies "raised" by cloth surrogates showed more natural interest in exploring than those "raised" by wire surrogates—even when the appropriate "mothers" were there. Apparently, the monkeys also remembered the cloth surrogates better. After a year's separation, the "cloth-raised" monkeys eagerly ran to embrace the terry-cloth forms, whereas the "wire-raised" monkeys showed no interest in the wire forms (Harlow & Zimmerman, 1959). None of the monkeys in either group grew up normally, however (Harlow & Harlow, 1962), and none were able to mother their own offspring (Suomi & Harlow, 1972).

It is hardly surprising that a dummy mother would not provide the same kind of stimulation and opportunities for development as a live mother. These experiments show that (contrary to the psychoanalytic emphasis on satisfaction of biological needs) feeding is *not* the most important thing mothers do for their babies. "Mothering" includes the comfort of close bodily contact and, in monkeys, the satisfaction of an innate need to cling. Surely, human infants also have needs that

must be satisfied, or at least acted upon, if they are to grow up normally. A major task of psychology is to find out what those needs are.

Going beyond such one-way concepts as imprinting and the mother-infant bond, research over the past few decades has shifted its focus to the two-way process of *attachment* between babies and the important people in their lives.

Attachment: A Reciprocal Connection

When Ahmed's mother is near, he looks at her, smiles at her, talks to her, and crawls after her. When she leaves, he cries; when she comes back, he squeals with joy. When he is frightened or unhappy, he clings to her. Ahmed has formed his first attachment to another person.

Attachment is an active, affectionate reciprocal, enduring relationship between two people. In unscientific circles, we call it *love*. The interaction between the two people continues to strengthen their bond. It may be, as Mary Ainsworth (1979), a pioneering researcher on attachment, has said, "an essential part of the ground plan of the human species for an infant to become attached to a mother figure" (p. 932)—who does not have to be the infant's biological mother but may be any primary caregiver.

Studying Attachment
Attachment research dramatically illustrates how

TRUST MOTHER TO BE COUNTED ON

scientists build on the work of those who have gone before. Ainsworth first studied attachment in the early 1950s as a junior colleague of John Bowlby (1951). Bowlby was convinced of the importance of the mother-baby bond, partly from examining ethological studies of bonding in animals and partly from seeing disturbed children in a psychoanalytic clinic in London. He recognized the baby's role in fostering attachment and warned against separating mother and baby.

Ainsworth was also influenced by studies of attachment in monkeys and research on the behavior of babies in a strange room. After studying attachment in Ugandan babies (1967), she tried to replicate her studies in Baltimore. But because of cultural differences between Africa and the United States, she changed her approach, which had relied on naturalistic observation in babies' homes, and devised the now famous **Strange Situation.** This laboratory technique, designed to elicit behaviors of closeness between an adult and an infant, is now the most common way to study attachment. Typically, the adult is the mother (although other adults have also taken part in studies) and the infant is 10 to 24 months of age.

In the eight-episode *Strange Situation,* (1) the mother and baby enter an unfamiliar room; (2) the mother sits down and the baby is free to explore; (3) an unfamiliar adult enters; (4) the mother goes out, leaving the baby alone with the stranger; (5) the mother comes back and the stranger leaves the room; (6) the mother leaves the baby alone in the room; (7) the stranger comes back instead of the mother; and finally, (8) the stranger goes out as the mother returns. The mother encourages the baby to explore and play again, and gives comfort if the baby seems to need it (Ainsworth, Blehar, Waters, & Wall, 1978). Of particular concern is the response of the baby when the mother returns (episodes 5 and 8).

Patterns of Attachment

When Ainsworth and her colleagues observed 1-year-olds in the Strange Situation and also at home, they found three main patterns of attachment: *secure attachment* (the most common category, into which 66 percent of American babies fell) and two forms of anxious, or insecure, attachment—*avoidant attachment* (20 percent of the babies) and *ambivalent (or resistant) attachment* (12 percent).

Securely attached babies (like Ahmed) cry or protest when the mother leaves and greet her happily when she returns. They use her as a base: they leave her to go off and explore, returning from time to time for reassurance. They are usually cooperative and relatively free of anger. At 18 months they get around better on their own than anxiously attached toddlers (J. Cassidy, 1986). They are better at crossing open spaces and at reaching for, playing with, and holding on to toys; and they stumble and fall less. Perhaps, knowing that their mothers are available, they can pay more attention to their surroundings than babies who anxiously eye their mothers.

Avoidant babies rarely cry when the mother leaves, and they avoid her on her return. These babies do not reach out in time of need and tend to be very angry. They dislike being held, but dislike being put down even more.

Ambivalent (resistant) babies become anxious even before the mother leaves. They are very upset when she does go out. When she comes back, they show their ambivalence by seeking contact with her while at the same time resisting it by kicking or squirming. Resistant babies do little exploration and are hard to comfort (Egeland & Farber, 1984).

Babies with a fourth pattern, *disorganized-disoriented attachment,* often show inconsistent, contradictory behaviors (Main & Solomon, 1986). They greet the mother brightly when she returns but then turn away, or approach without looking at her. They seem confused and afraid and may represent the least secure pattern. This pattern is most often regarded as a version of one of the other patterns, typically the resistant one (O'Connor, Sigman, & Brill, 1987).

Secure attachment thrives when a mother is affectionate, attentive, and responsive to a baby's signals. The amount of positive parent-child interaction is more important than the amount of time Nancy, a working mother, is able to spend with Annie. *(Phil Hollembeak)*

Both Anna and Diane contribute to the attachment between them by the way they act toward each other. The way the baby molds herself to her mother's body shows her trust and reinforces Diane's feelings for her child, which she then displays through sensitivity to Anna's needs. Again we see how babies actively influence their world. *(Jonathan Finlay)*

How Attachment Is Established

A baby builds a "working model" of what can be expected from the mother, says Ainsworth. As long as the mother continues to act in basically the same ways, the model holds up. But if she changes her behavior—not just once or twice but consistently—the baby can revise the model, and the nature of attachment may change.

A baby's personality—the tendency to cuddle, cry, or adapt to new situations—also exerts an influence. Attachment is affected by what mother and baby do and how they respond to each other.

What the Mother Does Secure attachment thrives when the mother is affectionate, attentive, and responsive to her baby's signals. The amount of positive interaction between the two is more important than the mother's caretaking skills and the amount of time she spends with her baby (A. Clarke-Stewart, 1977).

Ainsworth and her colleagues (1978) found several important differences in the quality of mothering, which were related to babies' patterns of attachment. Mothers of securely attached babies were the most sensitive to their infants throughout the first year of life. They took their cues from their babies about when to feed them and responded to the babies' signals to stop, slow down, or speed up feeding (Ainsworth, 1979). More recent research also found that mothers of babies considered secure at 1 year of age had been more responsive to their infants at 1, 3, and 9 months—more likely to soothe the babies when they cried, to "answer" the babies' sounds, and to talk to the babies when they looked into the mothers' faces (Isabella, Belsky, & von Eye, 1989).

Furthermore, mothers of securely attached babies tended to hold them closer to the body than mothers in the other two groups (Cunningham, Anisfeld, Casper, & Nozyce, 1987). Babies whose mothers had carried them on their bodies in soft baby carriers rather than in infant seats in the first months of life were more securely attached at 13 months of age.

Mothers of avoidant babies were the angriest of all three groups. They had trouble expressing their feelings and shied away from close physical contact with their babies. Babies subjected to physical distancing and rebuffs became angry in turn.

In a group of low-income, mostly single mothers (Egeland & Farber, 1984), mothers of securely attached infants were responsive and skilled in caretaking and had positive feelings about themselves. Mothers of avoidant babies were tense, irritable, and lacking in confidence, and seemed uninterested in their babies. Mothers of resistant babies were well-meaning but less capable; they tended to score lower on IQ tests and understand less how to meet their babies' needs.

"Mother love" is not automatic, nor is love necessarily enough. Many factors affect the way a woman acts toward her baby. One is the mother's emotional state. For example, mothers who are mentally ill or who, for whatever reason, mistreat their children are more likely to have children who are insecurely attached (vanIJzendoorn, Goldberg, Kroonenberg, & Frenkel, 1992). Other factors include the mother's reasons for having the baby, her experience and competence in child care, her view of her life, her relationship with the baby's father, her interest in a job or other outside activities, her life circumstances, and the presence of other relatives in the home, like a supportive or intrusive grandmother (Egeland & Farber, 1984).

What the Baby Does   Infants actively influence the people who take care of them. Virtually any activity on a baby's part that leads to a response from an adult can be an attachment behavior: sucking, crying, smiling, clinging, and looking into the caregiver's eyes (Bowlby, 1958; Richards, 1971; Robson, 1967). As early as the eighth week of life, babies direct some of these behaviors more to their mothers than to anyone else. Their overtures are successful when the mothers respond warmly, express delight, and give the babies frequent physical contact along with freedom to explore (Ainsworth, 1969). The babies gain a sense of the consequence of their own actions—a feeling of power and confidence in their ability to bring about results.

An infant's early characteristics may be a predictor of whether the baby is likely to become securely or anxiously attached. Many resistant babies, for example, have had problems as neonates—about half of such babies in one study (Ainsworth et al., 1978). Many showed developmental lags that may have made them harder to care for (Egeland & Farber, 1984). A study of 17- to 21-month-old babies and their mothers in Chile found that underweight babies were more likely to be insecurely attached (Valenzuela, 1990). Infant irritability may also be related to resistant attachment. Babies who showed distress at 2 days of age when a pacifier was taken out of their mouths (a measure of distress reactivity) showed insecure attachments at 14 months (Calkins & Fox, 1992).

However, anxious attachment is not inevitable even for infants who have other problems. In many cases, the mother can do much to shape the quality of their attachment. Normal mothers can often compensate for the problems of physical or mental impairment in their children, so that the children develop a secure attachment (vanIJzendoorn et al., 1992). Also, very low birthweight does not seem to be associated with impaired attachment (Easterbrooks, 1989; Macey, Harmon, & Easter-

brooks, 1987). And a comparison of hearing-impaired toddlers and children with normal hearing found no differences in security of attachment and mother-toddler play between the two groups, suggesting that a good mother-child relationship does not depend on the early development of normal language (Lederberg & Mobley, 1990). "As in any relationship, the partner's responses are critical" (Egeland & Farber, 1984, p. 769). It is the interaction between adult and infant that determines the quality of attachment.

Changes in Attachment

Although attachment patterns normally persist, they can—and often do—change. In one study, almost half of a group of 43 middle-class babies changed attachment pattern between ages 12 and 19 months (R. A. Thompson, Lamb, & Estes, 1982). The changes were associated with changes in the babies' daily lives, including mothers' taking jobs outside the home and providing other kinds of child care. The changes were not all in one direction: some babies became less securely attached, but most became more securely attached.

What accounts for this? Although a mother's caretaking skills are important in forming the initial attachment, her emotional signals—the joy she shows in feeding or bathing her baby—may help the attachment pattern evolve, especially during the second year of life. Some initially resistant infants of young, immature mothers become more secure as their mothers gain experience, skill, and more positive attitudes (Egeland & Farber, 1984). Also, other people can make a difference in a child's life, allowing attachment to, say, a father, a grandmother, or a baby-sitter.

Long-term Effects of Attachment

Do infants who are securely attached to their mothers grow into children who are very dependent on adults? Research says no. In fact, the more secure a child's attachment is to a nurturing adult, the easier it is for the child to leave that adult. Children who have a secure base do not need to cling to their mothers. Their freedom to explore lets them try new things, attack problems in new ways, and be more comfortable with the unfamiliar.

These effects may persist for years after birth. At age 2, securely attached children are more enthusiastic, persistent, cooperative, and generally effective than insecurely attached children (Matas, Arend, & Sroufe, 1978). At ages 2 and 3, they know themselves and their mothers better; they are more likely to know their own names, identify their mother's shoe as hers, and know both their own and their mothers' sex (Pipp, Easterbrooks, & Harmon, 1992).

From ages 3 to 5, they are more curious, more competent, and get along better with other children and are more likely to form close friendships (J. L. Jacobson & Wille, 1986; Waters, Wippman, & Sroufe, 1979; Youngblade & Belsky, 1992; Arend, Gove, & Sroufe, 1979). Having had good relationships with their parents, they probably expect to have—and do have—good relationships with others. They are also more likely to be independent in preschool, seeking help from teachers only when they need it (Sroufe, Fox, & Pancake, 1983).

On the other hand, children with attachment problems often have other problems. Two-year-olds who had been resistant at 14 months are more inhibited than those who had been avoidant (Calkins & Fox, 1992). Also disorganized-disoriented attachment in infancy may predict hostile behavior toward other children at age 5 (Lyons-Ruth, Alpern, & Repacholi, 1993).

The controversial issue about the possible effects that child care by people besides the mother might have on babies' attachment to their mothers is discussed in the last section of this chapter. For now, let's evaluate the research on attachment.

Critique of Attachment Research

Almost all the research on attachment is based on the Strange Situation. This research has yielded many findings that help us understand attachment, but a number of critics question its conclusions.

The Strange Situation *is* strange, and also artificial. It sets up a series of eight 3-minute staged episodes, asks mothers not to initiate interaction, exposes children to repeated comings and goings of adults, and expects the children to pay attention to them. Attachment cuts across a wide range of behaviors; thus a more complex method may be needed to measure it more sensitively, especially to see how mother and infant interact during natural, *non*stressful situations (T. M. Field, 1987).

Furthermore, the Strange Situation may be an especially poor way to study attachment in certain situations. Children of employed mothers, for example, are used to routine separations from their mothers and to the presence of other caregivers, and may, therefore, not react "by the book" (K. A. Clarke-Stewart, 1989; L. W. Hoffman, 1989). And research on Japanese infants, who are less commonly separated from their mothers than are American babies, show high rates of resistant classifications, which may reflect the extreme stress-

fulness of the Strange Situation for these babies (Miyake, Chen, & Campos, 1985).

And finally, we do not know the long-term effects of early attachment. After reviewing the literature, M. E. Lamb (1987a) concluded that the association between attachment in infancy and development in childhood is weak and inconclusive. Differences among older children may stem from parent-child interaction after infancy. Because interaction patterns are often set early and remain consistent over the years, it is hard to tell when they are most influential. We will learn more about attachment as researchers use measures besides the Strange Situation and as they integrate new attachment patterns into research designs.

While the mother-child attachment is important, it is not the only meaningful tie that babies form. The mother may be the only one who can suckle her infants, but other people—fathers, grandparents, siblings, friends, and caregivers—can also comfort and play with them, and give them a sense of security. Fathers are especially important.

THE FATHER'S ROLE

Fortunately, the days of ignoring or minimizing a father's contribution to his children's development seem to be over. In television commercials fathers diaper and bathe their infants. Stores offer strollers with man-sized handles and baby carriers that fit men over 6 feet. And psychologists are devoting more research to the father's role in a child's life.

The findings from such research underscore the importance of sensitive, responsive fathering. Close ties form between fathers and babies during the first year of life, and fathers go on to exert a strong influence on their children's social, emotional, and cognitive development.

Bonds and Attachments between Fathers and Infants

Many fathers form close bonds with their babies soon after birth. Proud new fathers admire their babies and feel drawn to pick them up. The babies contribute to the bond by doing the things all normal babies do: opening their eyes, grasping their fathers' fingers, or moving in their fathers' arms.

As early as 3 months after birth, it may be possible to predict the security of attachment between father and child. Fathers who show delight in their 3-month-olds, who see themselves as important in

Fathers and children often form close bonds during the first year of life. This father, engrossed with his infant daughter, is likely to go on to exert a strong influence on her social, emotional, and cognitive development. *(Joel Gordon)*

their babies' development, are sensitive to their needs, and hold time with them as a high priority are likely to be securely attached at 1 year (Cox, Owen, Henderson, & Margand, 1992).

Babies develop attachments to both their parents at about the same time. In one classic study, babies 1 year old or older protested about equally against separation from both mother and father, while babies 9 months or younger did not protest against either parent's departure. When both parents were present, just over half of the babies were more likely to go to their mothers, but almost half showed as much or more attachment to their fathers (Kotelchuck, 1973).

Another study found that although babies prefer either the mother or the father to a stranger, they usually prefer their mothers to their fathers, especially when upset (M. E. Lamb, 1981). This is probably because mothers typically care for them more often than fathers do. It will be interesting to see if father-infant attachment changes in families in which the father is the primary caregiver.

How Do Fathers Act with Their Infants?

Despite a common belief that women are biologically predisposed to care for babies, research suggests that men can be just as sensitive and responsive to infants (M. E. Lamb, 1981). Fathers talk "motherese" (see Chapter 4); they adjust the pace of feeding to a baby's cues; and when they see crying or smiling infants on a television monitor, their physiological responses (changes in heart rate, blood pressure, and skin conductance) are similar

to those of mothers. Still, fathers are typically not as responsive as mothers. They usually take a less active role in child rearing, and the crucial factor in determining how sensitive an adult is to a baby's cues is the amount of care that the adult gives the baby (Zelazo, Kotelchuck, Barber, & David, 1977).

The amount of child care by men in industrialized countries seems, however, to be increasing (Lamb, 1987). One study of 48 working-class Irish fathers found a high level of child care and a strong relationship between father care and the babies' scores at age 1 on measures of cognitive development (Nugent, 1991). These fathers talked to their babies, played with them, fed, diapered, soothed, and sang to them. The men most likely to care for their infants were younger, happily married men who had been at the birth, and who subsequently modified their work schedules and shared domestic duties with their wives.

In the United States, fathers *care for* their babies less than they *play with* them (Easterbrooks & Goldberg, 1984). And they tend to do many things differently from the way mothers do them. Fathers videotaped face to face with 2- to 25-week-old infants typically provide a series of short, intense bursts of stimulation, whereas mothers tend to be gentler and more rhythmic. Fathers pat the babies; mothers talk softly to them (Yogman, Dixon, Tronick, Als, & Brazelton, 1977). Fathers toss infants up in the air and wrestle with toddlers; mothers typically play gentler games and sing and read to them (M. E. Lamb, 1977; Parke & Tinsley, 1981).

This very physical style of play is not, however,

typical of all cultures. Swedish and German fathers, for example, usually do not play with their babies this way (Lamb, Frodi, Frodi, & Hwang, 1982; Parke, Grossman, & Tinsley, 1981). And the fact that Swedish infants show more attachment behaviors to mothers than to fathers, unlike American babies who show attachment fairly equally to both parents, suggests that the distinctive father-infant play style in the United States may play an important role in fostering attachment between fathers and their babies (Lamb, Frodi, Hwang, & Frodi, 1983). Similarly, vigorous father-infant play is also absent among African Aka pygmies (Hewlett, 1987). Again, we see cross-cultural differences in the ways parents act with their children.

The father's involvement is influenced by many factors. One is the mother's attitude. She often serves as the "gatekeeper" of the father's involvement with the baby, both in her direct actions and in the way she talks about him (Yogman, 1984). Another factor is the mother's employment. Women who work full time stimulate their babies more than women who stay at home full time, and they play with their babies more than the fathers do. They still spend more time taking care of their babies, however, than do the babies' fathers (Pedersen, Cain, & Zaslow, 1982). A study of fathers who were their babies' primary caretakers found that these men behaved more like mothers than like "typical" fathers (T. M. Field, 1978).

Different roles and different societal expectations about what fathers and mothers are supposed to do clearly influence their styles of interacting with their babies.

What Is the Significance of the Father-Infant Relationship?

The differences between men and women, both biological and social, make each parent's role in the family unique—and each one's contribution special. For example, the physical way in which fathers typically play with babies offers excitement and a challenge to conquer fears. During the first 2 years, babies often smile and "talk" more to the father, probably because he is more of a novelty (M. E. Lamb, 1981).

In one study, a group of toddlers—two-thirds of whose mothers were employed outside the home—showed the benefits of the father's involvement in caring for and playing with them, especially when his attitude was sensitive and positive. The father's behavior had a particularly strong influence on competence in problem solv-

ing, and although the mother's behavior had more impact on attachment, the father's involvement helped to make boys' attachment to their mothers more secure (Easterbrooks & Goldberg, 1984). Furthermore, secure attachments to fathers seem to help children form close friendships at age 5 (Youngblade & Belsky, 1992).

Fathers also seem to play an important part in helping toddlers become independent. One study focused on the interaction between forty-four 2-year-old boys and girls, their fathers, and their mothers (who were the primary caregivers). The parents were instructed to get the toddlers to put away toys and not touch a tape recorder. Both parents dealt very similarly with their children. It seems, then, that fathers do *not* play the part of family disciplinarian but act in far less stereotyped ways (Yogman, Cooley, & Kindlon, 1988).

As we noted earlier, adults act differently toward babies depending on whether they think the baby is a boy or a girl. Fathers act *more* differently toward boys and girls than mothers do, even during a baby's first year (M. E. Snow, Jacklin, & Maccoby, 1983). By the second year, this difference intensifies: fathers talk more and spend more time with sons than with daughters (M. E. Lamb, 1981). For these reasons, fathers, more than mothers, seem to affect the development of gender identity and *gender-typing*—the process by which children learn behavior that their culture considers appropriate for each sex (Bronstein, 1988).

Fathers may also influence their sons' cognitive development more than mothers do. The more attention a father pays to his baby son, the brighter, more alert, more inquisitive, and happier that baby is likely to be at 5 or 6 months (Pedersen, Rubenstein, & Yarrow, 1973). Baby boys raised without fathers tend to lag cognitively behind boys in two-parent families, even when the mother does not act differently (Pedersen, Rubenstein, & Yarrow, 1979). This finding may be further evidence of the father's importance in cognitive development (Radin, 1988)—or it may reveal the economic or social disadvantages of growing up in a single-parent family.

The very fact that a child's two parents have two different personalities—no matter what those personalities are—influences development in unknown ways. We don't know, for example, what effects stem from babies' learning that the same action will bring different reactions from mother and father. It seems clear, though, that anyone who plays a large part in a baby's day-to-day life will exert an important influence.

STRANGER ANXIETY AND SEPARATION ANXIETY

Sophie used to be a friendly baby, smiling at strangers and going to them, continuing to coo happily as long as someone—anyone—was around. Now, at 8 months, she howls when a new person approaches her or when her parents try to leave her with a sitter. Sophie is experiencing both *stranger anxiety,* wariness of a person she does not know, and *separation anxiety,* distress when a familiar caregiver leaves her.

Separation anxiety and stranger anxiety used to be considered emotional and cognitive milestones of infancy, reflecting attachment to and recognition of the mother. It now seems, however, as if these phenomena are very variable and depend largely on a baby's temperament and life circumstances.

Although Sophie's reaction is typical, it is not universal. For one thing, there are cross-cultural differences in stranger anxiety. Navajo infants, for example, show less fear of strangers during the first year of life than Anglo infants do (Chisholm, 1983). Then, there are differences within a culture. The Navajo babies who had many opportunities to interact with other people—who belonged to an extended family or lived close to the trading post—were less wary of new people than were other Navajo infants.

In the dominant American culture, babies rarely react negatively to strangers before 6 months of age, commonly do so by 8 or 9 months, and do so more and more throughout the first year (Sroufe, 1977). However, subtle signs of stranger wariness often appear as early as 3 or 4 months of age, showing that the baby knows his or her usual caregiver and isn't quite sure about the newcomer. Even at the later ages, however, a baby may react positively to a new person—especially if the person doesn't swoop down on the infant, but waits for a little while and then approaches the baby gradually, gently, and playfully. With this kind of approach, the infant's natural curiosity and inborn tendency to relate to other people can take over.

In reacting to a stranger, a baby picks up cues from his or her caregiver. In one study, mothers of 10-month-old babies who were approached by an unfamiliar woman spoke to their babies either positively or neutrally about the woman, or spoke to the woman herself positively or neutrally, or remained silent (Feinman & Lewis, 1983). When the mothers spoke positively about the stranger, the babies were friendlier to her than in any of the other situations, and were more likely to lean toward her and offer her a toy. Apparently, the babies socially referenced their mothers in this ambiguous situation and acted accordingly. Sally experienced this phenomenon when she visited her 9-month-old granddaughter, Maika, in Germany, after not having seen her for 7 months. Since Sally's daughter, Jenny, greeted Sally eagerly, the baby apparently decided that this was a person she could trust, and she soon went willingly into her grandmother's arms.

Today, neither early and intense fear of strangers nor intense protest when the mother leaves is considered to be a sign of secure attachment. Researchers now measure attachment more by how easily the parent can comfort the baby upon their reunion than on how many tears the baby shed at departure time. And whether a baby cries when a parent leaves or someone new approaches may tell us more about a baby's temperament than about the security of his or her attachment (R. J. Davidson & Fox, 1989).

DISTURBANCES IN FAMILY RELATIONSHIPS

When the attachments between infants and their parents are disrupted or impaired because children are separated from their parents or have painful relationships with them, the consequences can be grave. What happens to children who are deprived of their parents very early in life? The answer may depend on a number of factors, including the reason for the separation, the kind of care the child receives, and the quality of relationships before and after the separation.

Institutionalization

When orphanages were the most common way to care for children whose parents were dead or unable to care for them, many babies in them died in the first year (R. A. Spitz, 1945). Children institutionalized for a long time often declined intellectually and developed psychological problems.

A classic study by R. A. Spitz (1945, 1946) compared 134 children reared in two institutions ("Nursery" and "Foundling Home") with 34 children reared in their own homes. At the end of a year, the children in "Nursery" and the children reared at home were healthy and normal. But those in "Foundling Home" were below average in height and weight, and their developmental scores had plummeted (from 124 to 75, and then to 45).

Early research in child development brought out the need for sensitive, individualized care when children, like these Romanian orphans, need to be in an institution. One of the most important factors is stability of caregivers, letting children become attached to particular people. *(James Nachtwey/Magnum)*

Also, they were highly susceptible to disease, often fatally. Paradoxically, many of the "Foundling Home" babies had favorable backgrounds, whereas those in "Nursery" had been born to delinquent girls, many of whom were emotionally disturbed or retarded. The most important difference between the institutions turned out to be how much personal attention the babies got. In "Nursery," all babies received full-time care from their own mothers or from full-time substitutes; but in "Foundling Home," eight children shared one nurse—a typical situation in institutions.

By showing the need for care approximating good mothering, Spitz's work hastened a trend toward placement in foster homes and much earlier adoption. True, his study and others showed that children in well-run institutions—which provide plenty of conversation and active, meaningful ex-

periences—suffer no impairment of intelligence. But even in these conditions, children remain at risk of social deprivation. The damage seems to come not from being separated from parents or having more than one caregiver, but from frequent changes in caregivers, a situation that prevents the formation of "early emotional bonds to particular individuals" (p. 151). This kind of damage can usually be avoided by abundant attention and stimulation from a person to whom a baby becomes attached as a "substitute mother" (A. Clarke-Stewart, 1977; Rheingold, 1956).

Research that measured physiological and behavioral responses of 9-month-olds to brief separations from their mothers suggests that infants' stress may be due less to the separation itself than to the quality of the substitute care. When caregivers were warm and responsive and played with the infants *before* they cried, the babies cried much less than when they were with less responsive caregivers (Gunnar, Larson, Hertsgaard, Harris, & Brodersen, 1992). This effect was most marked with babies whose temperaments disposed them to be quick to anger in situations where they seemed to feel a loss of control.

Hospitalization

Even a short stay in a hospital can be disturbing to infants and toddlers. Unless they get a great deal of attention, their intellectual responsiveness tends to decline until they return home. Hospitalized babies 15 to 30 months old go through three stages of separation anxiety (Bowlby, 1960).

First, they *protest:* they try to get their mothers back by shaking the crib and throwing themselves about. Then they *despair:* they become withdrawn and inactive, crying monotonously or intermittently. Because they are so quiet, it is often assumed that they have accepted the situation. And finally, they *detach:* they accept care from a succession of nurses and eat, play with toys, smile, and are sociable; but when their mothers visit, the babies remain apathetic and may turn away.

What can be done to reduce stress and fear when a young child must be hospitalized? One parent can stay, even sleeping overnight; and daily visits from other family members, familiar routines, and limits on the number of caregivers can relieve the strangeness of the situation (Rutter, 1979b). Providing occasional happy separations ahead of time can make an impending hospital visit less stressful. Children who are used to being left with grandparents or sitters or who have stayed overnight at friends' houses are less likely to be upset by hospitalization (Rutter, 1971; Stacey, Dearden, Pill, & Robinson, 1970).

Child Abuse and Neglect

Most parents try to do the best they can for their children, but some cannot or will not meet a child's most basic needs. Mistreatment can take several different forms. *Child abuse* involves physical injury. The typical pattern has been identified as the *battered child syndrome* (Kempe et al., 1962). *Sexual abuse* refers to any kind of sexual contact between a child and an older person. *Neglect* is withholding of adequate care, usually physical care like food, clothing, and supervision. Emotional neglect also occurs, sometimes resulting in *nonorganic failure to thrive,* in which a baby fails to grow and gain weight at home despite adequate nutrition, but improves rapidly when moved out of the home and given emotional attention.

In the late 1980s and early- to mid-1990s, more than 2 million children a year in the United States were reported to be victims of abuse and neglect. Many were victims of sexual abuse. This represented a rise in reported cases, which may reflect an increase in mistreatment, better reporting of mistreatment, or both.

Causes of Abuse and Neglect

Why do adults hurt or neglect children? Taking Bronfenbrenner's (1979) ecological approach to this problem, we can look at it in the social context of several levels of environmental influence—within the home, the community, and the wider culture (Belsky, 1980).

Abusers and Neglecters   More than 90 percent of all child abuse occurs at home (Child Welfare League of America, 1986; Bergman, Larsen, & Mueller, 1986; Browne & Finkelhor, 1986). Over 90 percent of abusers are not psychotic and do not have criminal personalities; but many are lonely, unhappy, depressed, angry, dissatisfied, isolated, and under great stress, or they have health problems that impair their ability to raise their children. They were often mistreated in their own childhood and felt rejected by their parents (Trickett & Susman, 1988). The power they exert over their children through abuse may be a misplaced effort to gain control over their own lives (B. D. Schmitt & Kempe, 1983; Wolfe, 1985).

Abusers often hate themselves for what they do and yet feel powerless to stop. Often they do not

know how to be good parents. They do not know how to make a baby stop crying, for example, and sometimes lose all control when they cannot get children to do what they want them to do. They tend to be ignorant of normal child development, expecting children to be toilet-trained or to stay clean and neat at unrealistically early ages. Furthermore, they often expect their children to take care of them, and they become abusive when this does not happen. They have more confrontations with their children than do nonabusive parents and are less effective in resolving problems (J. R. Reid, Patterson, & Loeber, 1982; Wolfe, 1985). Abusive parents have trouble reading babies' emotional signals and often misinterpret babies' needs. A parent may try to feed a child who is actually crying in pain, and then be frustrated when the baby spits out the food (Kropp & Haynes, 1987).

Neglectful parents, on the other hand, are likely to be irresponsible and apathetic, and to ignore their children (Wolfe, 1985). Mothers of infants who fail to thrive tend to have been poorly nurtured themselves and to have had stressful relationships with the babies' fathers. These mothers tend to have more complications of pregnancy and childbirth than other mothers. They gain less weight, deliver earlier, and bear smaller babies; they also have more trouble feeding their infants (Altemeir, O'Connor, Sherrod, & Vietze, 1985). They do not hug or talk to their babies, and they seem unable to organize a safe, warm home environment for these babies, whose presence they seem to resent (P. H. Casey, Bradley, & Wortham, 1984).

Victims   Abused children tend to need or demand more from their parents than other children. They are more likely to have been low-birthweight infants, or to be hyperactive, mentally retarded, or physically handicapped (J. R. Reid et al., 1982). They cry more and show more negative behavior (Tsai & Wagner, 1979). Babies who fail to thrive because of emotional neglect have often had medical problems at or soon after birth (Altemeir et al., 1985).

Families   Abusive parents are more likely than other couples to have marital problems and to fight physically with each other. They have more children and have them closer together, and their households are more disorganized. They experience more stressful events than other families (J. R. Reid et al., 1982). The arrival of a new man in the home—a stepfather or the mother's boyfriend—may trigger abuse from the man.

Abusive parents tend to cut themselves off from

neighbors, family, and friends. Consequently, there is no one to turn to in times of stress and no one to see what is happening in the family. Neglectful parents are isolated within the family, tending to be emotionally withdrawn from spouse and children (Wolfe, 1985).

Communities   The outside world can create a climate for family violence. Unemployment, job dissatisfaction, and chronic financial hardship are all closely correlated with child and spouse abuse (Wolfe, 1985). Men who are unhappy in their jobs or unemployed are more likely than other men to mistreat their wives and children (Gil, 1971; McKinley, 1964).

Cultures   A culture can set the stage for violence by fostering certain attitudes. Two factors that seem to lead to child abuse are violent crime and physical punishment. Child abuse is rare in countries where violent crime is infrequent and children are seldom spanked. In the United States, 30 states still permit corporal punishment in schools, and minority and handicapped children are paddled more often than their classmates (Celis, 1990).

Effects of Abuse and Neglect

Both childhood abuse and neglect can produce grave consequences, showing the link between physical, emotional, and cognitive development (Kendall-Tackett, Williams, & Finkelhor, 1993; Emery, 1989). Abused children often show speech delays (Coster, Gersten, Beeghly, & Cicchetti, 1989). They are more likely to repeat a grade, to do worse on cognitive tests, and to be discipline problems in school (Eckenrode, Laird, & Doris, 1993). They tend to be aggressive and uncooperative with other children and, consequently, less well liked (Salzinger, Feldman, Hammer, & Rosario, 1993; Haskett & Kistner, 1991). As adults they are more likely to become delinquent or criminal (Dodge, Bates, & Pettit, 1990; Widom, 1989). Abuse is most traumatic if a nonabusive parent is unsupportive on hearing of it and if more than one type of abuse has occurred (Browne & Finkelhor, 1986; Bryer, Nelson, Miller, & Krol, 1987; Burgess, Hartman, & McCormack, 1987).

Sexually abused children are likely to be fearful, have low self-esteem, become preoccupied with sex, and have problems with behavior and school achievement (Kendall-Tackett, Williams, & Finkelhor, 1993; Einbender & Friedrich, 1989). As adults, they tend to be fearful, anxious, depressed, angry, or hostile. They suffer from low self-esteem, do not

trust people, feel isolated and stigmatized, and are sexually maladjusted (Browne & Finkelhor, 1986).

Fortunately, many maltreated children are amazingly resilient, especially if there is a supportive family member to whom the child can become attached (Egeland & Sroufe, 1981). Two-thirds of all abused children go on to take good care of their own children. Those who become good parents are likely to have had people who cared for them and to whom they could turn for help, to be in a good marital or love relationship in adulthood, and to be openly angry about and able to describe their experiences. They were more likely to have been abused by only one parent and more apt to have had a loving, supportive relationship with one parent or a foster parent.

The link between being abused as a child and growing up to become an abuser is by no means inevitable. The expectation that the one always causes the other seems to be a self-fulfilling prophecy in some cases, and many parents who were abused feel like "walking time bombs," ready to explode into violence against their own children (Kaufman & Zigler, 1987).

Combating Abuse and Neglect

To *prevent* abuse and neglect, overwhelmed parents need help, especially in caring for children with special needs. They can get such help from community educational and support programs, subsidized day care, volunteer homemakers, and temporary "respite homes" or "relief parents" who take over the children when the parents feel too burdened (Wolfe, 1985). Such programs now exist in many communities.

One effective program trains parents thought to be at risk, giving them pointers in managing children's behavior (including the use of smiles and praise for good behavior and time-out procedures for misbehavior). Parents also learn how to help children develop language and social skills (Wolfe, Edwards, Manion, & Koverola, 1988).

One of the most effective ways to *stop* abuse is to treat abusers as criminal offenders: people who are arrested for family violence are less likely to continue the maltreatment (Sherman & Berk, 1984). Other valuable services for abused children and adults include shelters, education, and therapy. One effective program teaches parents child-management skills and gives therapy to help deal with stress (Patterson, Chamberlain, & Reid, 1982).

One "peer-helper" program helped abused or neglected 3- to 5-year-olds who were severely withdrawn. A teacher's aide and other children

This adult volunteer uses dolls to help young children realize that they have control over their bodies and need not let anyone—even friends or family members—touch them. Such programs for preventing sexual abuse need to walk a fine line between alerting children to danger and frightening them or discouraging appropriate affection. *(Janet Fries/TIME Magazine)*

(average age 4 years) were trained to suggest or direct play activities and to give or receive objects during play, to encourage the maltreated children to play with them. The actions of the 4-year-old initiators did more to help the withdrawn children become more sociable than did the adult's efforts (Fantuzzo et al., 1988). This kind of program shows the practical, real-world impact that child development research can have on the lives of children. It also underscores once more the close relationship among physical, intellectual, and social development in early childhood.

Preventing Sexual Abuse

Parents can help prevent the sexual abuse of their children by other people—their spouses, other relatives or friends, or such community workers as teachers or group leaders. First, they need to recognize the signs. These include any extreme changes in behavior, like loss of appetite, sleep disturbance, and nightmares; regression to bed-wetting, thumb-sucking, or frequent crying; torn or stained underclothes; vaginal or rectal bleeding or discharge; vaginal or throat infection; painful, itching, or swollen genitals; unusual interest in or knowledge of sexual matters; and fear or dislike of being left in a certain place or with a certain person (U.S. Department of Health and Human Services, USDHHS, 1984).

Parents also need to tell their children that their bodies belong to them and that they can say "no" to anyone who might try to touch them or kiss them when they do not want to, even if it is some-one they love and trust. Children need to know that they are never to blame for what an adult does, that they can talk to their parents about anything without fear of punishment, and that most adults do not hurt children.

RELATIONSHIPS WITH OTHER CHILDREN

Although parents exert a major influence over children's lives, other children are important, too.

SIBLINGS

If you have brothers or sisters, your relationships with them are likely to be the longest-lasting you'll ever have. You may have fought continually as children, or you may have been each other's best friends. In either case, these are the people who share your roots, who "knew you when," who accepted or rejected the same parental values, and who probably deal with you more candidly than almost anyone else you know. Lack of siblings, too, affects a person's life. An only child has a very different childhood from a child with brothers and sisters, as we'll see in Chapter 7.

How Children React to the Arrival of a New Baby

Chris, aged 3, came into the bedroom where his mother was feeding his new sister. He stared for a

Babies and toddlers become closely attached to their older brothers and sisters, especially when, as with these Chinese children, the older siblings assume a large measure of care for the younger ones. *(Eastcott/The Image Works)*

few minutes and then pleaded, "Mommy, why don't you throw that baby in the garbage?"

Children react in a variety of ways to the arrival of a sibling. Some regress to earlier behaviors: they suck their thumbs, wet their pants, ask to suck from breast or bottle, or use baby talk. Others withdraw, refusing to talk or play. Some suggest taking the baby back to the hospital, giving it away, or flushing it down the toilet. And some take pride in being the "big ones," who can dress themselves, use the potty, eat with the grown-ups, and help care for the baby. Most behavioral problems of older siblings disappear by the time the younger one reaches 8 months of age (Dunn, 1985).

The birth of a younger sibling seems to change the way a mother acts toward her first child. Chris's mother is likely to play less with him, to be less sensitive to his interests, to give more orders, to have more confrontations, and to initiate fewer conversations and games (Dunn, 1985; Dunn & Kendrick, 1982). Children who take the initiative by coming up to the mother to start a conversation or to play a game seem to have less of a problem with sibling rivalry than those who with-

draw, because they have found a way to salvage their close relationships with their mothers.

There is little research on helping children adjust to a new sibling. Popular wisdom advises parents to prepare the older child for the birth of a new baby and to make any changes in the child's life (like moving to another bedroom or from a crib to a bed, or changing school) well beforehand to minimize feelings of being displaced (Spock & Rothenberg, 1985). Parents should accept a child's anxiety and jealousy as normal, while at the same time protecting the new baby from any harmful expression of those feelings. They can encourage the older child to play and help with the baby, and emphasize how much they value *each* child.

Finally, older siblings adjust better if their fathers give extra time and attention to them to make up for the mother's sudden involvement with the infant (M. E. Lamb, 1978).

How Siblings Interact

Siblings have more to do with each other after the first 6 months of a baby's life. In many societies around the world, including our own, older siblings have some responsibility for caring for babies (Dunn, 1985). Children also teach younger siblings and influence the younger ones' cognitive development (Stewart, 1983).

How do siblings get along? In one study of 34 pairs of same-sex middle-class siblings at home, the younger ones averaged 20 months of age. Their brothers and sisters, 1 to 4 years older, more often initiated both positive and negative behaviors, while the younger ones imitated more. Older boys were more aggressive; older girls were more likely to share, cooperate, and hug. The sibling interaction was "rich and varied, clearly not based predominantly on rivalry" (Abramovitch, Corter, & Lando, 1979, p. 1003). Although rivalry is often present, so is genuine affection.

Young children usually become quite attached to their older brothers and sisters. (At 1 year, Sally's daughter Dorri referred to her older sisters as "my choo-jun"—"my children.") Babies become upset when their siblings go away, greet them when they come back, prefer them as playmates, and go to them for security when a stranger enters the room (Dunn, 1983; R. B. Stewart, 1983).

When little girls imitate their big brothers, they may take on some characteristics commonly thought of as masculine. The environment that siblings create for each other affects not only their future relationship but each one's personality development as well (Dunn, 1983). It may also affect how they react to other children.

SOCIABILITY

Although the family is the center of a baby's social world, infants and—even more so—toddlers show interest in people outside the home, particularly people their own size. More babies now spend time in day care settings with other babies, and more researchers are studying how they react to each other.

Babies' interest in other children rises and falls. From the first days of life in a hospital nursery, infants who have been lying quietly in their cribs will start to cry when they hear another baby's cries (G. B. Martin & Clark, 1982; Sagi & Hoffman, 1976; Simner, 1971). During the first few months of life, they respond to other babies in about the same way they respond to their mothers: they look, they smile, they coo (T. M. Field, 1978). From age 6 months till about 1 year, they increasingly smile at, touch, and babble to another baby, especially when they are not distracted by the presence of adults or toys (Hay, Pedersen, & Nash, 1982). At about 1 year, however, when the biggest items on their agenda are learning to walk and to manipulate objects, they pay more attention to toys and less to other people (T. M. Field & Roopnarine, 1982).

In their second year, babies become more sociable again, and now they understand relationships better. A 10-month-old who holds out a toy to another baby pays no attention to whether the other's back is turned, but a child in the second year of life knows when the offer has the best chance of being accepted and how to respond to another child's overtures (Eckerman, Davis, & Didow, 1989; Eckerman & Stein, 1982). This insight into other people seems to go along with children's understanding of themselves as separate individuals. A study of German 19-month-olds found that those who recognized themselves in a mirror were more likely to imitate how an unknown child played with a toy than toddlers who did not recognize themselves (Asendorpf & Baudonnière, 1993).

Some people, of course, are more sociable than others. Readiness to accept new people, ability to adapt to change, and a person's usual mood seem to be inherited traits (A. Thomas et al., 1968) that remain fairly stable over time. But babies are also influenced by the attitudes of those around them. Sociable infants tend to have sociable mothers (M. Stevenson & Lamb, 1979). And children who

spend time with other babies from infancy on seem to become sociable at earlier ages than those who spend all their time at home.

From just under 1½ years of age to almost 3, children show a growing interest in what their playmates do. They imitate each other—more in what they do than in what they say—like hiding, throwing something, knocking on a playhouse, or jumping off a box. They play more games like hide-and-seek and follow-the-leader. These strategies help them connect with other children and pave the way for the more complex games involving talking and symbolic play that take over during the preschool years (Eckerman et al., 1989). As children grow older and enter more and more into the world beyond their own home, their social skills become increasingly important. The first step into the wider world for many children is their entrance into out-of-home child care.

THE IMPACT OF EARLY DAY CARE

Only a short time ago, most babies of working mothers were cared for in their own homes (Hofferth, 1979). (All mothers are, of course, "working mothers," since rearing children and caring for a family are valuable—though unpaid—forms of work. Here, however, we define *working mother* as one who works for pay, usually outside the home.) Today, about 61 percent of children 4 or under (including 53 percent of infants under 1 year) receive care outside the home, from someone other than their mother (U.S. Bureau of the Census, 1990).

What happens to children who, from the age of a few weeks or a few months, are cared for by outside people, either baby-sitters or day care workers? Does day care—and, especially, infant day care—help or harm children? And what kinds of care are best, or worst? Few issues in child development arouse as much controversy and are so hard to answer.

The answer is important, since more than half of all American mothers of children under 1 year of age are going out to work, a higher proportion than at any time in the nation's history. The questions we ask are important, too. What kind of day care are we talking about, care in a center or the more common care in the home of a nonrelative who "takes in" children? What constitutes "high-quality" care? By what criteria do we judge harm and benefit? How can we isolate the day care experience itself from the parenting the child gets at

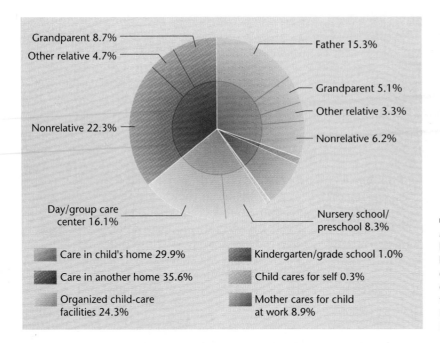

Grandparent 8.7%

Other relative 4.7%

Father 15.3%

Grandparent 5.1%

Other relative 3.3%

Nonrelative 22.3%

Nonrelative 6.2%

Day/group care center 16.1%

Nursery school/ preschool 8.3%

Care in child's home 29.9%

Kindergarten/grade school 1.0%

Care in another home 35.6%

Child cares for self 0.3%

Organized child-care facilities 24.3%

Mother cares for child at work 8.9%

FIGURE 5-1
Primary child-care arrangements used by employed mothers for children under 5. About 60 percent of these mothers use some form of day care outside the home, either in someone else's home or at group centers. (*Source*: U.S. Bureau of the Census, 1990.)

home? Do more competent, caring parents select better child care? What happens when parents *want* good care, but cannot find any that is available and affordable?

An increasing amount of research is being devoted to finding answers to these questions. But the studies are open to criticism, and the findings from them are often ambiguous, inconsistent, or contradictory. And since researchers are human beings, generally with strong opinions on the issue, there may be a tendency to explain data according to their own positions.

Furthermore, although most children are cared for either in their own homes or in someone else's home (see Figure 5-1), much of what we know about the effects of day care comes from studies of high-quality, well-funded, university-based centers. Unfortunately, this is hardly typical of the care most children receive. Therefore, we really have little idea of the effect of the most common kinds of child care. With these two caveats, let's look at what research has yielded so far about the impact of day care on children's cognitive, emotional, and social development.

Good day care is like good parenting. Children can thrive physically, intellectually, and emotionally in day care that has small groups, a high adult-to-child ratio, and a stable, competent, highly involved staff. Caregivers should be trained in child development, sensitive to children's needs, authoritative but not too restrictive, stimulating, and affectionate (Belsky, 1984). Children develop best when they have access to educational toys and ma-

terials, when they are cared for by adults who teach them and accept them (are neither too controlling nor merely custodial), and when they have a balance between structured activities and freedom to explore on their own (Clarke-Stewart, 1987).

By and large, children in good day care programs do at least as well, physically, cognitively, and socially as those raised at home. High-quality day care seems to enhance emotional development, too, and may even improve relationships with parents. Parents may feel less stress because their child is well cared for while they earn the income they need and because they get some relief from the demands of parenting. For suggestions on choosing good child care, see Box 5-3.

COGNITIVE DEVELOPMENT

The most straightforward data emerge in the cognitive realm for children aged 2 to 4 who attend day care centers. An analysis of the research literature, which seems to reflect the majority of day care programs (not confined to the best, but excluding the worst) suggests that "day care is not harmful to children, and may even help their development" (Clarke-Stewart, 1992, p. 64).

Children in adequate or superior group day care seem to do as well as, or better than, children raised at home by parents or baby-sitters or in day care homes, on a number of intellectual measures. Where differences appear, the day care children

BOX 5-3 PRACTICALLY SPEAKING

HOW TO CHOOSE A GOOD DAY CARE CENTER

What makes a day care center good? A number of factors are important. For one, children get the best care when small numbers of children interact with a few adults. When groups are too large, adding more adults to the staff does not help. It does not seem to matter how many years of formal education the caregivers have had. What does matter is how much they have specialized in a child-related field, like developmental psychology, early childhood education, or special education. Adults with such special training tend to give better care, and children in their care do better on tests of school readiness skills (Abt Associates, 1978).

A licensed center meets minimum state standards for health, fire, and safety (if it is inspected regularly), but many centers and home care facilities are not licensed or regulated. Furthermore, licensing does not tell anything about the program's quality (American Academy of Pediatrics, AAP, 1986c).

Here are some things to look for in deciding whether to use a particular day care facility (AAP, 1986c; Olds, 1989).

DOES THE CENTER . . .

Provide a safe, clean setting?

Have trained personnel who are warm and responsive to all the children?

Promote good health habits?

Offer a stimulating environment to help children master cognitive and communicative skills?

Encourage children to develop at their own rate?

Nurture self-confidence, curiosity, creativity, and self-discipline?

Stimulate children to ask questions, solve problems, make decisions, and engage in a variety of activities?

Foster social skills, self-esteem, and respect for others?

Help parents improve their child-rearing skills?

Promote cooperation between parents, personnel, public schools and private schools, and the community?

BE WARY IF THE PROGRAM . . .

Is not licensed or registered with the state

Refuses to let parents visit unannounced

Employs staff members who are not educated, trained, or experienced in child-related subjects

Is overcrowded, unclean, or poorly supervised

Does not have enough heat, light, or ventilation

Has no written plans for meals or emergencies

Has no smoke alarms, fire extinguishers, or first aid kits

Does not set aside separate areas for playing, feeding, resting, and diapering

Has no policy on managing injuries or infections, or managing sick children

Does not have a medical consultant

---

score higher on IQ tests, show more advanced eye-hand coordination, play more creatively, know more about the physical world, can count and measure better, show better language skills, and are more advanced in remembering and reciting back such information as their names and addresses.

This cognitive gain is often temporary—a speeding up in acquiring these skills rather than a permanent advantage over other children. Some studies show that the advantages do not hold up once the children leave the center, and by the end of first grade, home-reared children have caught up. The gains do not seem to be related to the length of time children are in day care nor to the age at which they entered (Clarke-Stewart, 1992).

Children from low-income families or stressful home environments benefit the most from good day care. Although the average child in a good program is not much affected for better or for worse, disadvantaged children in good programs tend not to show the declines in IQ often seen when such children reach school age. Children in day care may be more motivated to learn (AAP, 1986c; Belsky, 1984; Bronfenbrenner, Belsky, & Steinberg, 1977).

The findings about infant day care (under 1 year, or under 3 years, depending on who is defining it) are more complex. Some studies have shown that children aged 18 months to 5 years score higher on intelligence tests if they attended infant day care (Clarke-Stewart & Fein, 1983—in Clarke-Stewart, 1989, p. 269). This advantage also seems to be temporary. However, at least one study found that children who had been in high-quality infant care were more likely to be assigned to gifted programs in elementary school and, as sixth graders, to get higher math grades (T. Field, 1991).

But another study, of 1181 3- to 4-year-olds, suggests that while children from low-income families and girls from any families do as well or better than home-reared children, boys from high-income families in full-time infant care may be at risk for lower intellectual development. At 3 and 4 years of age, these children were tested on behavioral and cognitive measures, including a picture vocabulary test (Baydar & Brooks-Gunn, 1991).

Children whose mothers had gone to work in the second quarter of the first year did more poorly on these tests than those whose mothers had gone either earlier or later. Those whose mothers did not return to work until the second or third year of the children's lives (an economic impossibility for many parents) scored about the same as mother-reared children.

One study comparing care at different levels of quality suggests some reasons for cognitive gains. This research involved 166 children from nine day care centers in Bermuda, where 84 percent of 2-year-olds spend most of the workweek in day care. When caregivers spoke often to children—especially to give or ask for information rather than to control behavior—and encouraged children to start conversations with them, the children did better on tests of language development than children who did not have such conversations with adults (McCartney, 1984).

A follow-up study (D. Phillips, McCartney, & Scarr, 1987) found that the children who talked often with their caregivers were also more sociable and considerate. In fact, the quality and amount of verbal stimulation seemed even more important for social development than the children's family background. Here, then, we see the intertwining of different aspects of development and the connection between cognitive influences and personality.

SOCIAL DEVELOPMENT

Children who spent much of their first year in day care tend to be as, or more, sociable, self-confident, persistent, achieving, and better at solving problems than children who had been at home. Day care preschoolers also tend to be more comfortable in new situations, more outgoing, less timid and fearful, more helpful and cooperative, and more verbally expressive (Clarke-Stewart, 1989; 1992). One study of children who started day care at an average age of just under 7 months found that between 5 and 8 years of age, these children had more friends and were more physically affectionate with them, took part in more extracurricular

activities, and were more assertive than children who had been at home (T. Field, 1991).

Day care children also, however, tend to be more disobedient and less polite to adults, bossier and more aggressive with other children, louder, more boisterous, and more demanding in general (Clarke-Stewart, 1989; 1992). But are these "negative" characteristics bad for the children? Or is their negative aspect the inconvenience these traits pose for adults? Are children who have been in infant day care more advanced in thinking for themselves, and therefore less inclined to go along with what other people want?

Alison Clarke-Stewart suggests that these children may seem more "bratty than children who stay at home because they want their own way and do not have the skills to achieve it smoothly, rather than because they are maladjusted" (1989, p. 269).

EMOTIONAL DEVELOPMENT

The major emotional issue regarding infant child care that researchers have looked at is its effect on children's attachments to their mothers. Does being cared for by other people for much of a baby's time affect this bond? The effects may depend upon many factors, including the mother's satisfaction with her marriage; whether and why she works full time or part time; the child's age, sex, and temperament; and the kind and quality of care the baby gets. Early child care in itself does not seem to pose a risk; the risk lies in poor-quality care and poor family environments (Scarr, Phillips, & McCartney, 1989). The quality of child care tends to be higher outside the United States (see Box 5-4).

The first year of life seems the most critical. When babies from stable families receive high-quality care, most studies report positive findings (L. W. Hoffman, 1989). On the other hand, when infants get unstable or poor-quality day care, they are more likely to avoid their mothers and to have emotional and social problems later on. These effects are worse when there is a poor fit between the mother's and baby's personalities, when the family is under great stress, and when the mother is not responsive to the baby (Gamble & Zigler, 1986; Young & Zigler, 1986).

Some controversial research suggests that extensive substitute care in the first year may affect some children negatively, especially boys (Belsky & Rovine, 1988). In one study, most (57 percent) of a group of children who had been cared for by someone else for 20 or more hours a week, begin-

BOX 5-4 *WINDOW ON THE WORLD*

HOW SWEDEN CARES FOR PARENTS AND CHILDREN

Other people besides mothers have cared for children in most societies throughout history. Today the issue of nonparental child care in the United States has taken on a new urgency for several reasons: the great numbers of mothers now working outside the home, the rise of group day care as a business venture, and the belief that day care should enhance children's development rather than just offer baby-sitting.

Sweden, with its extensive policy of parental leaves and subsidized child care, often serves as a model (Lamb & Sternberg, 1992; Hwang & Broberg, 1992). But how good a model is it? Sweden is an affluent, homogeneous society of about 8 million people, all of whom speak the same language and are part of the same culture. Many specific practices may not apply to countries like ours, which are much larger and much more diverse racially and ethnically. However, should we adopt the Swedish philosophy that society as a whole shares responsibility for the care and welfare of its children?

Swedish family policy came about because of rapid industrialization, which caused a labor shortage. To enable women both to work and to bear and rear future workers, Sweden developed a sys-tem that included good pay for women, generous parental leaves for women and men, and high-quality early child care that would not require professional or financial sacrifices. Let's see what this system includes.

Every Swedish family receives an allowance from the state for each child, from birth through age 16. Both mothers and fathers can take parental leave, ranging from two weeks at 90 percent of regular salary through 18 months, part paid, part unpaid, for one parent at a time. Thus almost all Swedish babies have one parent home for the first year, and up to 18 months of age are cared for at home by their parents.

In 1989, more than 80 percent were cared for by parents, and 8 percent were cared for by relatives or private baby-sitters. Only 8 percent were in day care operated by local municipalities before 18 months, but about half of all children over this age receive such care. Since the national government sets guidelines for quality, municipal child care is of a very high caliber. Standards are set for the physical facility, staffing and staff training, size of groups, and so forth. Family day care, however, which is common, is almost unregulated; efforts are being made to develop guidelines for "daymothers."

Child care, seen as every family's right, is financed mostly from public funds. Parents pay an average of only 10 to 15 percent of the real cost of child care; the state and the municipality each contribute just under half, from revenues received from employers and both business and personal taxes.

Research has shown positive effects of high-quality infant day care in Sweden (Andersson, 1992). Children aged 8 and 13 who had entered out-of-home care before age 1 (usually during the second half of the first year) were compared with children who had been cared for at home. The day care youngsters generally did better in school and were rated more highly by their teachers on such social and emotional variables as school adjustment and social competence. The *type* of care given has not been found to affect children's social, emotional, or intellectual development. The most important factor seems to be how well children are cared for in their own homes and what the emotional climate is like at home. Parents are still the most important caregivers in children's lives, even if others care for them a good part of the time.

ning before age 9 months and through the first year, formed secure attachments to their mothers. But baby boys who received more than 35 hours a week of substitute care tended to be insecurely attached to both parents. The most vulnerable had been "difficult babies" at 3 months of age and had mothers who were dissatisfied with their marriages, insensitive to other people, and strongly career-motivated. Other research, however, has found that working mothers who are warm, accepting, and available when they are home do have securely attached 18-month-old sons (Benn, 1986). We cannot, then, make a blanket statement about day care without considering specific characteristics of the people, the care, and the situation.

The timing of the mother's first going out to work is related to quality of attachment. In one study, 18-month-old boys whose mothers started work in the second half of their first year of life were more likely to be insecurely attached than those whose mothers went to work when the babies were younger (Benn, 1986). This suggests that the second half of a child's (particularly a boy's) first year may not be the best time for a mother to return to work and that women who must, or choose to, go back to work by that time should try

BOX 5-5 PRACTICALLY SPEAKING

PUTTING RESEARCH TO WORK

If you are a parent, or are about to become a parent, or if you care for infants or toddlers, you can put into practice some of the most important findings to emerge from recent research into child development, as in the following recommendations.*

■ *Respond to babies' signals:* This is probably the single most important thing that caregivers can do. Meeting an infant's needs—whether for food, cuddling, or comforting—establishes a sense of trust that the world is a friendly place. Answering cries or requests for help gives babies a sense of having a measure of control over their lives, an important awareness for emotional and intellectual development. Adults often worry about spoiling children by meeting their needs quickly, but the children who have the most problems in life are those whose needs go unmet. As one saying goes,

"Baby a baby when he's a baby, and you won't have to baby him the rest of his life" (Chapters 4 and 5).

■ *Provide interesting things for babies to look at and do:* By watching a mobile hanging over a crib and handling brightly colored toys and simple household objects, babies learn about shapes, sizes, and textures. Playing helps them develop their senses and motor skills. And handling objects helps them distinguish between themselves and things that are not themselves (Chapters 3 and 4).

■ *Talk to babies and read to them:* By hearing and responding to speech directed especially to them, babies learn how to express themselves. You'll be most effective if you pitch your voice high and speak slowly, use short words and simple sentences, leave off word endings (saying "go" instead of "going," for example), ask questions, repeat words and phrases, and

talk about things in the baby's world. You'll probably do most of these things intuitively as you talk in "baby talk," or "motherese" (Chapter 4).

■ *Give babies freedom to explore:* It's better to baby-proof an environment (by taking away breakables, small things that can be swallowed, and sharp objects that can injure; and by jamming books into a bookcase so tightly that a baby can't pull them out) than it is to confine a baby in a playpen. Babies need opportunities to crawl and eventually walk and to exercise their large muscles. They also need to learn about their environment to feel in control of it. And they need the freedom to go off on their own to develop a sense of independence (Chapters 4 and 5).

*For research findings, see the chapter or chapters given in parentheses at the end of each entry.

to do so before the baby is 6 months old (Benn, 1986).

However, after reviewing studies of parent-infant attachment, Lois W. Hoffman (1989) concluded that if there is a relationship between a mother's employment during her baby's first year of life and the baby's attachment security, it is weak. Most studies find that most babies of full-time employed mothers are securely attached. It is possible that a mother's working outside the home during the first few months of a baby's life may be a form of stress that, when combined with other stresses, can interfere with attachment, but that in itself it does not make a difference.

Also, as suggested on page 180, the "Strange Situation" may not be the most appropriate measure of quality of attachment for children of working mothers. At least some babies who seem insecurely attached in the strange situation may really be showing independence. Because they are so

used to their mothers' comings and goings, they are not anxious about them, pay little attention to them, and simply do what works for them on a day-to-day basis—that is, they show an appropriate "avoidant" pattern (K. A. Clarke-Stewart, 1989). Clearly, day care is a complex issue. The importance of its quality has been shown by research findings that the most positive outcomes for children are associated with stable, high-quality care. The age at which a child enters day care also seems to matter, although different studies come up with diverse findings. However, knowing all of this will not help most children and their parents, unless societies adopt family-friendly policies.

Government, community and religious institutions, and employers can all cooperate in such policies. They might include subsidies that enable parents to stay home with their children for the first few months or years of their lives, or opportunities to work part time during these early years. In addition, high-quality child care, accessible to all families, can richly repay the investment in children, who are, after all, the future of any society.

In Part Three, we will see how young children build on the foundation laid during their first 3 years.

SUMMARY

EARLY PERSONALITY DEVELOPMENT

■ Personality is a person's unique and relatively consistent way of feeling, thinking, and behaving.

■ According to Erik Erikson, infants and toddlers experience the first two crises in a series of eight that influence personality development throughout life.

1 The first critical task, which infants face in the first 12 to 18 months, is to find a balance between basic trust and mistrust of the world. Successful resolution of this crisis results in the "virtue" of hope. Resolution is affected greatly by events surrounding feeding and by the quality of the mother-infant bond.

2 The second crisis, which a toddler faces from between 12 and 18 months to about 3 years, concerns autonomy versus shame and doubt. Successful resolution results in the "virtue" of will. Toilet training is a key event in resolving this crisis, which is greatly affected by help the child gets from parents. Negativism is a normal developmental manifestation during this time.

■ At about age 3 children develop self-regulation, or control of their behavior to conform to external expectations.

EMOTIONS: THE FOUNDATION OF PERSONALITY

■ Recent research suggests that the development and expression of different emotions are tied to brain maturation, although experiences and the development of self-awareness also affect the timing of their arrival.

■ Self-awareness appears to emerge in the following sequence: Physical self-recognition, self-description, and emotional response to wrongdoing.

■ Babies communicate their emotions through crying, smiling, and laughing.

■ According to the mutual regulation model, babies play an active part in regulating their emotional states. They "read" the emotions of others and, after about 6 months of age, display social referencing.

DIFFERENCES IN PERSONALITY DEVELOPMENT

■ Early differences in emotional expression, which may stem from temperament, are indicative of future personality development.

■ The New York Longitudinal Study identified nine fairly stable components of temperament, or a person's individual style of approaching people and situations. These traits appear to be largely genetic in origin but may be affected by significant environmental changes. On the basis of these temperamental patterns, most children can be classified as easy, difficult, or slow to warm up. "Goodness of fit" between the parent's and the child's temperament has an important effect on adjustment.

■ Significant physiological and behavioral differences between the sexes typically do not appear until after infancy. However, parents treat their sons and daughters differently from birth, and so some personality differences develop.

THE FAMILY AND PERSONALITY DEVELOPMENT

■ Some research has suggested that the first few hours or days of life constitute a critical period for forming the mother-infant bond, but follow-up research has failed to support this conclusion. However, infants do have strong needs for closeness and warmth as well as physical care from one caregiver or a few caregivers.

■ Mother-infant attachment, a reciprocal connection that forms and consolidates during infancy, is receiving considerable attention in research. Using the Strange Situation test, three main patterns of attachment have been found: secure attachment and two types of insecure attachment—avoidant attachment and ambivalent (resistant) attachment. A fourth pattern, disorganized-disoriented, may be a subtype of the resistant pattern. Patterns of attachment seem to have long-term implications for development.

■ Fathers and babies become attached early in a baby's life. Infants' and toddlers' experiences with mothers and fathers seem to differ, and the variety is valuable.

■ Separation anxiety and stranger anxiety are normal phenomena that arise during the second half of the first year and appear to be related to a baby's temperament and life circumstances. Separation anxiety is a child's distress upon the departure of the caregiver. Stranger anxiety is wariness of strangers. There is considerable individual difference in the expression of both separation anxiety and stranger anxiety.

■ Studies of parental deprivation—generally conducted among orphans in institutions in which considerable sensory deprivation is common—point to the need for consistent parenting or caregiving in a stimulating environment. Attempts at enriching institutional environments have dramatically benefited children's emotional and intellectual development.

▪ Effects of short-term separations, such as for hospitalization, depend on particular circumstances.

▪ Child abuse, including sexual abuse and neglect, has received widespread attention and medical documentation. Characteristics of the victim, abusers or neglecters, families, the community, and the larger culture are associated with or contribute to child abuse and neglect.

RELATIONSHIPS WITH OTHER CHILDREN

▪ Siblings influence each other both positively and negatively from an early age. Parents' actions and attitudes can help reduce sibling rivalry.

▪ Although infants' interest in other children fluctuates with their developmental priorities, individual differences in sociability tend to remain stable over time.

THE IMPACT OF EARLY DAY CARE

▪ Good-quality day care appears to have generally positive impact on cognitive, social, and emotional development. A major controversy concerns the effect of early and extensive day care on attachment behavior. Some research suggests that such a condition may affect attachment negatively. Unfortunately, much day care in the United States is not of high quality.

KEY TERMS

personality (page 162)
basic trust versus basic mistrust (163)
autonomy versus shame and doubt (164)
self-regulation (164)
negativism (164)
emotions (165)
self-awareness (166)
mutual-regulation model (168)
social referencing (169)

depression (170)
temperament (171)
socialization (174)
ethological approach (174)
mother-infant bond (175)
attachment (176)
Strange Situation (177)
secure attachment (177)
avoidant attachment (177)
ambivalent (resistant) attachment (177)

disorganized-disoriented attachment (177)
stranger anxiety (183)
separation anxiety (183)
child abuse (185)
battered child syndrome (185)
sexual abuse (185)
neglect (185)
nonorganic failure to thrive (185)

SUGGESTED READINGS

Brazelton, T. B., & Cramer, B. G. (1990). *The earliest relationship.* New York: Addison-Wesley. This book examines the parent-child relationship from its beginning in pregnancy to its further development after the child is born. It coordinates current research on infant behavior and parent-infant interaction with psychoanalytic theories about becoming a parent. The second half of the book consists of case studies that illustrate different types of parent-infant relationships.

Eyer, D. D. (1992). *Mother-infant bonding: A scientific fiction.* New Haven, CT: Yale University Press. An engrossing historical account of the bonding "myth," showing how the idea that mothers and infants must be physically close immediately after birth gained scientific currency despite its lack of validity, how it fell from favor, and what its effect has been on women, infants, and hospital practices.

Konner, M. (1991). *Childhood: A multicultural view.* Boston: Little Brown. This book shows how children around the globe develop, how parents and society shape them, and how science is beginning to understand them. It examines the nature-nurture question and reviews evidence showing the importance of biology in explaining experience and development. Theories of Piaget and Freud are also discussed. Originally a companion to the public television series *Childhood,* the book is full of photos of children around the world.

Shapiro, J. L. (1993). *The measure of a man: Becoming the father you wish your father had been.* New York: Delacorte Press. This insightful and moving book offers reflections on the changing role of men in the modern family. You'll also find practical tips for how to be an effective parent with a partner, as a single parent, and as a stepfather.

Stern, D. N. (1990). *Diary of a baby.* New York: Basic Books. A noted developmental psychologist describes what a baby sees, feels, and experiences in the first 22 months of life.

PART TWO

EARLY CHILDHOOD

The years from 3 to 6 used to be called the *preschool years*. Now, when so many children attend some kind of school starting at age 3, and many go to day care centers even earlier, a more accurate term for this stage is *early childhood*.

■ In **Chapter 6**, we discuss physical and intellectual development during these years. Children now look different, as they lose their babyish roundness. They act differently, too. They become better at fine motor tasks like tying shoelaces (in bows instead of knots), drawing with crayons (on paper rather than on walls), and pouring cereal (into the bowl, not onto the floor). They improve in gross motor abilities like running, hopping, skipping, jumping, and throwing balls. They also think differently, as they move forward in their ability to handle a wide range of intellectual concepts and to express their thoughts and feelings in the language of their culture.

■ In **Chapter 7**, we see how critical these years are for personality development. Children's conceptions of themselves grow stronger. They know what sex they are—and they want everyone else to affirm their sense of maleness or femaleness. Their behavior becomes more socially directed, sometimes helping other people, sometimes hurting them. The number of important people in their lives expands, as friends and playmates become more important.

All aspects of development—physical, intellectual, emotional, and social—continue to intertwine to make each person unique.

CHAPTER SIX

PHYSICAL AND INTELLECTUAL DEVELOPMENT IN EARLY CHILDHOOD

Children live in a world of imagination and feeling. . . .
They invest the most insignificant object with any form
they please, and see in it whatever they wish to see.

Adam G. Oehlenschlager

PHYSICAL DEVELOPMENT

■ PHYSICAL GROWTH AND CHANGE

Height, Weight, and Appearance
Structural and Systemic Changes
Nutrition

■ HEALTH

Health Problems in Early Childhood
Influences on Health

■ SLEEP: PATTERNS AND PROBLEMS

Normal Sleep Patterns
Sleep Disturbances
Bed-Wetting

■ MOTOR SKILLS

Large-Muscle Coordination
Small-Muscle and Eye-Hand Coordination

INTELLECTUAL DEVELOPMENT

■ ASPECTS OF INTELLECTUAL DEVELOPMENT

Development of Memory: Information
  Processing
Cognitive Development: Piaget's
  Preoperational Stage
Development of Language
Development of Intelligence

■ THE WIDENING ENVIRONMENT

Preschool and Day Care
Kindergarten

■ BOXES

6-1 Practically Speaking: Encouraging
Healthy Eating Habits
6-2 Food for Thought: How Homelessness
Affects Children
6-3 Practically Speaking: Helping Children
to Sleep Well
6-4 Food for Thought: Theories of Mind
6-5 Take a Stand: Should Preschool Be
about the Three R's?
6-6 Window on the World: Preschools
in Three Cultures

ASK YOURSELF

- How do children's bodies and motor skills grow and develop during early childhood?
- How can young children be kept healthy?
- What sleep patterns and problems develop during early childhood, and how can they be handled?
- How do young children think and remember, and what does research tell us about their cognitive competence?

- How does language ability flower in early childhood?
- How can we assess intelligence in early childhood, and how do parents influence intellectual performance?
- What options are available for young children's care and schooling, and how important is the quality of care and education?

I t is the day before Keisha's third birthday. "Pretty soon," she tells her mother, "I'll be big enough to sleep without sucking my thumb. And maybe tomorrow I'll be big enough to wear pajamas like Daddy's."

The big day dawns. Keisha leaps out of bed at her usual early hour and runs to the mirror. As she stands there, first on one foot and then on the other, she examines her mirror image closely; then she runs to her parents' room. "Mommy, Daddy!" she squeals into sleepy ears. "I'm 3!" But then a note of disappointment creeps into her voice as she acknowledges sadly, "But I don't look different."

Keisha's change from the day before may be infinitesimal, but in terms of what she was a year earlier, she is very different indeed. Her next 3 years of life will show greater changes.

Children who have celebrated their third birthday are no longer babies. They are capable of bigger and better things, both physically and intellectually. The 3-year-old is a sturdy adventurer, very much at home in the world and eager to explore its possibilities, as well as the developing capabilities of his or her own body. A child of this age has come through the most dangerous time of life—the years of infancy and toddlerhood—to enter a healthier, less threatening phase.

Youngsters grow more slowly between the ages of 3 and 6 than during the preceding 3 years, but they make so much progress in coordination and muscle development that they can do much more. Intellectual development, too, continues at a staggering pace. Children in this age group have taken huge leaps forward in their ability to remember, reason, speak, and think.

In this chapter, we'll trace all these developing capabilities and consider several important concerns. We'll also describe the profound effects of young children's expanding environment: at day care centers, preschool, and kindergarten.

■ PHYSICAL DEVELOPMENT

PHYSICAL GROWTH AND CHANGE

Physical changes may be less obvious during early childhood than during the first 3 years of life; but they are still important, making possible dramatic gains in motor skills and intellectual development.

HEIGHT, WEIGHT, AND APPEARANCE

At about age 3, children begin to lose their chubbiness and begin to take on the slender, athletic appearance of childhood. As abdominal muscles develop, potbellies slim down. The trunk, arms, and legs all grow longer. The head is still relatively large, but (in keeping with the cephalocaudal principle, described in Chapter 3) the other parts of the body continue to catch up as body proportions steadily become more adult. Within that overall pattern, children show a wide range of individual and sex-related differences. Boys tend to have more muscle per pound of body weight than girls, while girls have more fatty tissue.

Although Keisha's growth has slowed now that she is 3, she is 4 inches taller than she was a year ago; she now measures almost 38 inches and weighs almost 32 pounds. Her friend Felipe, whose birthday is within a week of hers, is slightly taller and heavier. Each year for the next 3 years, both grow about 2 to 3 inches and gain 4 to 6 pounds.

Boys' slight edge in height and weight normally continues until puberty when girls suddenly surpass boys. A year or two later boys again become taller and heavier than girls of the same age

STRUCTURAL AND SYSTEMIC CHANGES

The changes in children's appearance reflect important internal developments. Muscular and skeletal growth progresses, making children stronger. Cartilage turns to bone at a faster rate than before, and bones become harder, giving the child a firmer shape and protecting the internal organs. These changes, coordinated by the maturing brain and nervous system, allow an expansion of both large-muscle and small-muscle motor skills. In addition, the increased capacities of the respiratory and circulatory systems improve physical stamina and, along with the developing immune system, keep children healthier.

By the age of 3, all the primary, or deciduous, teeth are in place, and children can chew anything they want to. The permanent teeth, which will begin to appear at about age 6, are developing; therefore, if thumb-sucking persists past the age of 5, it can affect how evenly the teeth come in.

NUTRITION

Proper growth and health depend on good nutrition. As children's growth rate slows down, so does their appetite, and parents often worry that their children are not eating enough. Because caloric requirements per pound of body weight decline, children between ages 3 and 6 normally eat less in proportion to their size than infants do.

The nutritional demands of early childhood are easily satisfied. A small child's daily protein requirement, for example, can be met with two glasses of milk and one serving of meat or an alternative like fish, cheese, or eggs. Vitamin A needs can be met with modest amounts of carrots, spinach, egg yolk, or whole milk (among other foods). And vitamin C can be obtained from citrus fruits, tomatoes, and leafy dark-green vegetables (E. R. Williams & Caliendo, 1984). Lactose-intolerant children who cannot drink milk can get enough protein and minerals from other foods. No one food is essential to a child's diet.

Concerns about the cholesterol levels in chil-

dren's diets have led to recommendations that children over age 2 should receive about 30 percent of their total calories from fat, less than 10 percent of the total from saturated fat. They can now drink skim or low-fat milk and get protein, iron, and calcium from other low-fat dairy products, beans, and lean meats (AAP Committee on Nutrition, 1992a).

How much do young children eat? Over a 6-day period, 15 children aged 2 to 5 years took in roughly the same number of calories every day, even though they often ate very little at one meal and a great deal at another (Birch, Johnson, Andresen, Peters, & Schulte, 1991). Since small children are able to control their food intake in an orderly way, parents should not urge them to eat more than they want, as this might interfere with a child's normal mechanism for balancing energy intake.

What parents do need to do is to see that the foods they offer are nutritious (see Box 6-1). In a study comparing the 2- to 5-year-old children of mothers who work outside the home with children of nonemployed mothers, both ate equally well. But both groups of children had some dietary problems—too little calcium, iron, zinc, and Vitamin E, and too much fat (Johnson, Smiciklas-Wright, Crouter, & Willits, 1992).

One cause of children's dietary deficiencies is the impact of television commercials for foods heavy in sugar and fat. If children's diets include a lot of sugared cereals, chocolate cake, other snacks low in nutrients, and fast foods, their small appetites will not allow them room to eat the foods they need. Snacks should have nutritional value.

HEALTH

The early childhood years are basically healthy; yet some health problems do exist.

HEALTH PROBLEMS IN EARLY CHILDHOOD

EAR INFECTIONS

Minor Illnesses

Coughs, sniffles, stomachaches, and runny noses are part of early childhood. These minor illnesses typically last from 2 to 14 days but are seldom serious enough to need a doctor's attention. In fact, they may even have some cognitive and emotional as well as physical benefits, since illness helps children learn how to cope with physical distress, and

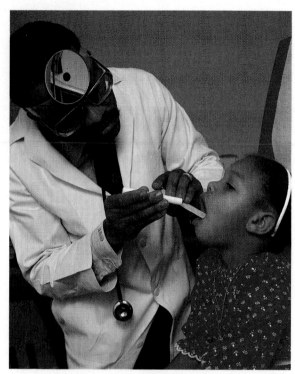

Although sore throats and other minor illnesses are common among 3- to 6-year-olds, they are usually not serious enough to require visits to the doctor. This 5-year-old will probably have fewer colds and sore throats in the next few years, as her respiratory and immune systems mature. *(Elliott Varner Smith/International Stock)*

the coping enhances their sense of competence. It also can make them more empathic, better able to understand someone else's physical problems.

Because the lungs are not fully developed, respiratory problems are common during these years, though less common than in infancy. Three- to five-year-olds average seven to eight colds and other respiratory illnesses a year; but later, during middle childhood, children average fewer than six such illnesses (Denny & Clyde, 1983), because of the gradual development of the respiratory system and natural immunity (resistance to disease).

Major Illnesses

What used to be a very vulnerable time of life is much safer now. Deaths in childhood are relatively rare compared with deaths in adulthood; most such deaths are caused by injury rather than illness (Starfield, 1991). Children's death rates from all kinds of illness have come down in recent years. Since 1950, deaths from influenza and pneumonia have dropped by 84 percent, although respiratory diseases are still the major cause of death among

infants and children worldwide. The 5-year survival rate for cancer (which in medical terms is considered a cure) has risen dramatically for children under 15 diagnosed between 1977 and 1988, compared with those diagnosed between 1967 and 1973 (American Cancer Society, 1993).

AIDS in Children

Aside from the devastating physical effects of acquired immune deficiency syndrome (AIDS), this fatal disease has severe psychological implications (AAP Task Force on Pediatric AIDS, 1991). For parents of a child with AIDS, who are themselves often limited in functioning because of drug use or lifestyle, caregiving is an even heavier burden. Most children with AIDS show developmental delays and often behave like younger, less competent children. Futhermore, the entire family may be stigmatized by the community, and the child may be shunned in the neighborhood or kept out of school, even though there is virtually no risk of infecting classmates. Infected preschoolers do not transmit the human immunodeficiency virus (HIV) to other people in the household, even when they share toys, toothbrushes, eating utensils, toilets, and bathtubs (M. F. Rogers et al., 1990).

Children who carry the HIV virus but do not show any disease symptoms should be treated like well children, both at home and in school. They do not need to be isolated, either for their own health or for that of other children. But children who show symptoms of HIV infection do need special care and special education. These children may develop central nervous system dysfunction that can interfere with their ability to learn and can also cause behavior problems. These children should, under the provisions of the Education for All Handicapped Children Act, be educated in the least restrictive environment—first at school, and then, as the disease progresses, at home (AAP Task Force on Pediatric AIDS, 1991).

The AIDS epidemic claims many more victims than those who die of related illnesses. Among those most grievously affected are children of stricken mothers. According to current estimates 24,600 children and 21,000 adolescents will have lost their mothers by the end of 1995 (Michaels & Levine, 1992). The great majority of these orphans will come from low-income black and Latino families.

Who will care for these children? Some will be taken in by relatives, often already overburdened by their own families or by age, as in the case of grandparents called upon to raise second families. Some will go into foster care or adoptive homes.

BOX 6-1 PRACTICALLY SPEAKING

ENCOURAGING HEALTHY EATING HABITS

Jennifer refuses to eat almost anything but peanut butter and jelly sandwiches. Tobias seems to live on bananas. Mealtimes sometimes seem more like art class, as they make snowmen out of mashed potatoes or lakes out of applesauce—and the food remains uneaten on the plate.

What is a parent to do? First, don't worry, since a diminished appetite in early childhood is normal. Don't urge children to eat more than they want, since young children, if offered a choice of nourishing food, tend to take in what they need. Then look at the child. A child who is energetic, with good muscle tone, bright eyes, glossy hair, and the ability to spring back quickly from fatigue is unlikely to be suffering from inadequate nutrition (E. R. Williams & Caliendo, 1984). The following suggestions can make mealtimes pleasanter, children healthier, and home atmospheres happier.

■ Keep a record of what your child actually eats. The child may be eating enough.
■ Serve simple, easily identifiable foods. Children like to know

what they are eating and often balk at mixed dishes.
■ Serve finger foods as often as possible.
■ Introduce only one new food at a time, along with a familiar, well-liked one.
■ Offer small servings, especially of new or previously disliked foods. It is better to give seconds than to set out what to a small child may look overwhelming.
■ After a reasonable time, remove the food and do not serve any more until the next meal. A healthy child will not suffer from missing a meal, and some children need to learn that certain times are appropriate for eating and others are not.
■ Give the child a choice—whether to have rye bread or whole wheat, whether to have a peach or an apple, whether to have yogurt or milk. No one food is essential; there is always a substitute that can provide the same nutrients.
■ Encourage your child to help prepare food by making sandwiches or mixing and spooning out cookie dough.

■ Allow for a quiet period before a meal to prevent fatigue or overexcitement.
■ Have nutritious snack foods handy, and allow the child to select favorites from among them.
■ Turn typically childish behavior to advantage. Serve food in appealing dishes; dress it up with garnishes or little toys; make a "party" out of an ordinary meal.
■ Don't fight "rituals," in which a child eats foods one at a time, in a certain order.
■ Make mealtimes pleasant with conversation on interesting topics, keeping any talk about eating itself to a minimum.
■ Provide a good example yourself by eating healthy, well-balanced meals.
■ To prevent choking, do not give children under 5 hard candies, nuts, grapes, and hot dogs; cut their food into small pieces; encourage them to chew vigorously; do not allow them to eat while talking, running, jumping, or lying down, or to toss or pour foods directly into their mouths.

Most will face periods of uncertainty and instability in which their grief at losing their mothers will be aggravated by their fears about the future. This social catastrophe poses great challenges to society.

Accidental Injuries

Accidents are the leading cause of death in childhood, most often because of automobiles. Children in the United States are far more likely to die as the result of injury than are European children (Williams & Miller, 1991, 1992).

All 50 states and the District of Columbia have laws requiring young children to be restrained in cars, either in specially designed seats or by standard seat belts. The *restraints* are effective: children who are *not* restrained are 11 times more likely to

die in an automobile accident than children who are restrained (Decker, Dewey, Hutcheson, & Schaffner, 1984). However, the *laws* are not always effective. Active young children often rebel against the discomfort of wearing seat belts, and parents—to avoid argument—frequently give in. An Australian study found that educating preschoolers about the importance of wearing restraints was more effective than threatening parents with police checks and fines (Bowman, Sanson-Fisher, & Webb, 1987). However, young children are more likely to be hit *by* cars than to be injured *in* them (Williams & Miller, 1992).

Most fatal nonvehicular accidents occur in and around the home: children drown in bathtubs, pools, and buckets containing liquids (as well as in lakes, rivers, and oceans); are burned in fires and explosions; fall from heights; drink or eat poisonous substances; get caught in mechanical contrivances; and suffocate in traps like abandoned refrigerators. One dangerous place is the ordinary supermarket shopping cart; the number of children injured through their use doubled during the 1980s, with more than 12,000 serious head injuries to children under 5 reported in 1989 (U.S. Consumer Product Safety Commission, 1991).

Considering how many child-hours are spent at day care centers, it is not surprising that injury sometimes occurs there, although children in day care actually suffer fewer injuries than do children cared for at home (Thacker, Addiss, Goodman, Holloway, & Spencer, 1992). Almost half of all injuries at day care centers occur on playgrounds; 1 in 3 are from falls, often resulting in skull injury and brain damage (Sacks et al., 1989). Children would be protected somewhat by covering ground surfaces with impact-absorbing materials like wood chips, loose sand, or mats.

Children are naturally venturesome and unaware of danger. It is hard for parents and other caretakers to tread the line between smothering children and exposing them to risk. Society needs to help, as in laws like those requiring car restraints and "child-proof" caps on medicine bottles.

INFLUENCES ON HEALTH

Why do some children have more illnesses or injuries than others? Heredity contributes to some illness: some children seem to be predisposed toward some medical conditions. Such environmental factors as nutrition and physical care also make a difference. So does frequency of contact with other children, who may be harboring bacteria or viruses. In addition, family situations involving stress and economic hardship may make some children more prone to illness or injury than others.

Exposure to Illness

Children in large families are sick more often than children in small families (Loda, 1980). And children in day care centers are 2 to 4 times more likely to pick up mild infectious diseases (like colds, flu, and diarrhea) than are children raised at home. They also have a higher risk of contracting more serious gastrointestinal diseases and hepatitis A (Thacker et al., 1992). Caregivers can cut the rate of illness by more than half by teaching children how to wash their hands after using the toilet;

washing their own hands frequently, especially after changing diapers; separating children in diapers from those who are toilet-trained; preparing food away from toilet areas; regularly disinfecting toys and equipment; and discouraging children from sharing food. Safe playground equipment and supervision can help prevent falls and other injuries. In fact, children in *high-quality* day care, where nutrition is well-planned and illnesses may be detected and treated early, tend to be healthier than those not in day care programs (AAP, 1986c).

Stress

Stressful events in the family—like moves, job changes, divorce, and death—seem to increase the frequency of minor illnesses and home accidents. In one study, children whose families had experienced 12 or more such events were more than twice as likely to have to go into the hospital as children from families who had experienced fewer than 4 events (Beautrais, Fergusson, & Shannon, 1982). Since entry into day care is stressful for many preschoolers (Craft, Montgomery, & Peters, 1992), parents and day care workers can try to alleviate this by giving children tours of the center before they enter and providing extra nurturance during the first days away from home.

Of course, stress also affects adults. Anything that reduces a caregiver's ability to cope may result in neglect of basic safety and sanitary precautions. A distraught adult is more likely than one who is not under stress to forget to put away a kitchen knife or a poisonous cleaning fluid, fasten a gate, or make sure that a child washes before eating.

Poverty

Poverty is unhealthy—and dangerous. Low income is the *chief* factor associated with ill health (J. L. Brown, 1987), and young children are the largest poverty group in the United States (NACHRI & AAP, 1990). Poor children often do not eat properly, do not grow properly, and do not get the immunizations or medical care they need. Poor families often live in crowded, unsanitary housing, where parents are too busy trying to feed and clothe their children to supervise them adequately. The children are at a disproportionately high risk of injury, partly because their parents do not know how to keep them safe or what to do if they swallow poison or hurt themselves, and partly because they do not have back-up caregivers (Santer & Stocking, 1991).

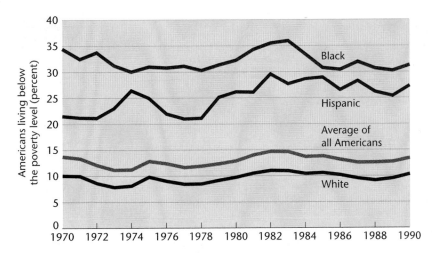

FIGURE 6-1
Although in actual numbers more white people are poor than those from minority groups, poverty rates in proportion to the numbers of people are highest for African American and Latino families. As a result, children from these backgrounds have higher rates of poverty-related problems. *(Bassuk, 1991, p. 69.)*

In the relatively affluent United States, about 1 in 4 children are poor, in terms of the official "poverty level" (about $12,500 a year for a family of four). The exact proportion varies somewhat by age, and minorities are at greatest risk. About 43 percent of black children and 40 percent of Latino children are poor, compared with fewer than 16 percent of white children (see Figure 6-1).

A nationwide survey of 2182 children 17 years old or younger found that about 10 percent had no medical insurance, 10 percent had no regular source of health care, and 18 percent got their medical care in emergency rooms, community clinics, or hospital outpatient departments (D. L. Wood, Hayward, Corey, Freeman, & Shapiro, 1990). Children who were uninsured, poor, or nonwhite were less likely to have seen a doctor in the past year, and uninsured children were less likely to have up-to-date immunizations.

The problems of poor children begin before birth. Poor mothers often do not eat well or receive adequate prenatal care, and their babies are likely to be of low birthweight, to be stillborn, or to die soon after birth. Poor children are often malnourished, and malnourished children tend to be weak and susceptible to disease. They are likely to suffer from such diverse maladies as lead poisoning, hearing and vision loss, and iron-deficiency anemia, as well as possibly stress-related conditions like asthma, headaches, insomnia, and irritable bowels. They also tend to have behavior problems, psychological disturbances, and learning disabilities (J. L. Brown, 1987; Egbuono & Starfield, 1982; Starfield, 1991). Poor children who do not have homes have the greatest problems of all (see Box 6-2).

In the United States, death rates for African American children and teenagers are considerably

higher than for whites for every cause except suicide, car injuries, and accidental poisoning and falls (Williams & Miller, 1992). Worldwide, the United States compares unfavorably with 10 European countries on low birthweight, infant survival rates, immunization rates, and children's death rates, especially those due to violence (National Center for Health Statistics, 1985–1988; World Health Organization, 1989). It also compares unfavorably on childhood deaths from injury (see Table 6-1).

The reason for this difference is plain. In these European countries, no child has to go without either preventive health services or medical care because the family cannot afford it. The government

TABLE 6-1

Injury Deaths per 100,000 among Children Age 0–19 (1984–1986) from All Causes	
United States	
Total	30.5
Black	34.4
White and Other	29.8
Belgium*	23.2
Denmark	18.7
France	21.5
West Germany**	23.3
Ireland	17.9
Netherlands	13.1
Norway	22.3
Spain†	16.9
Switzerland	24.9
England and Wales	15.6

*1983–84 and 1986
**The survey was taken before unification.
†1983–1985
SOURCE: National Center for Health Statistics, 1985–1988; World Health Organization, 1989.

BOX 6-2 FOOD FOR THOUGHT

HOW HOMELESSNESS AFFECTS CHILDREN

Young children and their single mothers constitute the fastest-growing segment of homeless people, more than one-third of this population. Although estimates of the homeless vary widely, this population includes somewhere between 250,000 and 3 million people (Bassuk, 1991). Every night, between 61,500 and 100,000 American children sleep in emergency shelters, welfare hotels, abandoned buildings, cars, or on the street. The effects of this kind of deprivation are devastating, both physically and psychologically (J. L. Bass, Brennan, Mehta, & Kodzis, 1990; Bassuk, 1991; Bassuk & Rosenberg, 1990; Rafferty & Shinn, 1991).

Most homeless children are under the age of 5. Since they are spending these crucial early years in an unstable, insecure, chaotic environment, it is not surprising that both as preschoolers and as schoolchildren, they tend to have high rates of developmental delays and learning difficulties, especially in language and motor skills, and severe depression and anxiety. A Massachusetts study found that about half the homeless children in 14 family shelters needed psychiatric referral (Bassuk & Rubin, 1987). Homeless youngsters show more developmental and behavioral problems than poor children with homes; both groups have higher rates than other children (Bassuk & Rosenberg, 1990).

Homeless children and their parents are deprived of much more than a physical home. They are cut off from a supportive community, from family ties, and from institutional resources. The children suffer more health problems than do poor children who have homes. They are three times more likely than other children to have missed immunizations, and they experience high rates of diarrhea, hunger and malnourishment, asthma, and elevated levels of lead. They are also

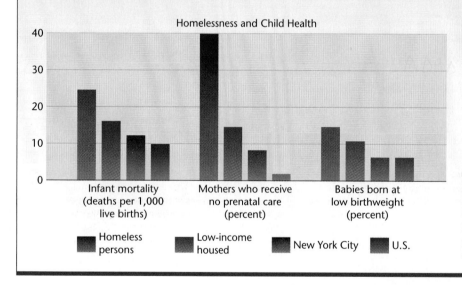

Homelessness and Child Health

FIGURE 6-2
Homelessness and child health. Homeless children suffer more health problems than do other poor children who have homes. *(Bassuk, 1991, p. 70.)*

provides free health care for everyone without asking whether they are "poor enough" to be eligible. More than 90 percent of European preschoolers receive recommended immunizations; in the United States we do not even have reliable data for either immunization or health care visits.

What can the United States do to raise the health standards for children? There are several approaches to this challenge. Reducing poverty, of course, needs to be the major goal. The government can also offer free or low-cost health care for pregnant and nursing women and for children; can institute systems to track health care so that children do not slip between the cracks of different agencies, especially between ages 1 and 4, the time when this is most likely to happen; can provide more health care workers in inner-city and rural areas; and can offer more birth control services to help prevent unwanted pregnancies.

In view of the far-reaching effects of poverty and hunger on the bodies and minds of growing children, it is essential to make sure that every child has an adequate diet and adequate health care. All of society suffers when hunger and disease flourish.

BOX 6-2   *(Continued)*

HOW HOMELESSNESS AFFECTS CHILDREN

at risk of anxiety, depression, and behavior problems like aggression and withdrawal (see Figure 6-2). These children have more problems in school, partly because they miss more of it; tend to do poorly on standardized reading and math tests; and are more likely to repeat a grade or be placed in special classes than are children with homes (Bassuk, 1991; Rafferty & Shinn, 1991). (See Figure 6-3.)

Homeless children can be

helped—*if* our society makes a major commitment. To prevent further homelessness, our elected representatives must allocate enough funds for housing, education, health care, child care, social services, and a higher minimum wage. Meanwhile, to take care of families that are already homeless, we need community programs to provide decent, permanent, and affordable housing. Families also

need safe, clean emergency shelters where they can get nutritious meals and have basic levels of privacy so that children can do their homework, get their sleep, and not be exposed to disease. Homeless families also need such services as prenatal, mental health, and pediatric care, along with help for substance abuse. Homelessness is a multifaceted problem that requires a multifaceted solution.

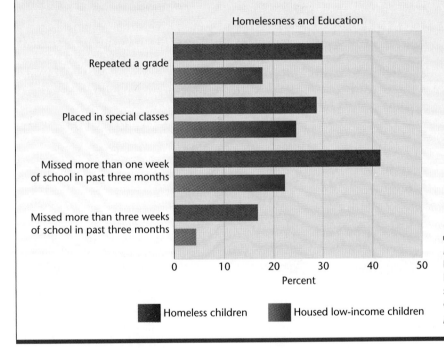

Homelessness and Education

FIGURE 6-3
Homelessness and education. Homeless children have more school-related problems than do other poor children. *(Bassuk, 1991, p. 70.)*

SLEEP: PATTERNS AND PROBLEMS

The baby who sleeps almost around the clock, waking up for feedings, grows into a toddler who sleeps 12 hours at night—plus 1 or 2 hours in the morning and afternoon; later, there is only one nap after lunch. By age 3, children often lie awake at nap time, but if they skip the nap altogether, they become fretful and cranky just before dinner. Food often perks them up for another couple of hours.

Sleep patterns change throughout life, and early

childhood has its own distinct rhythms. Young children generally sleep deeply through the night—more so than they will later in life (Webb & Bonnet, 1979)—and they need a daytime nap or quiet rest until about age 5.

NORMAL SLEEP PATTERNS

As children approach age 5, they try harder and harder to put off going to bed. They hate to part with a stimulating world full of people and be alone in their beds. Because of this, and because it now takes them longer to fall asleep, they often look for ways to postpone the inevitable. The elaborate bedtime routines that are common at this age also reflect children's increased mastery over the environment.

Children under age 2 will play quietly by themselves or with a sibling before falling asleep. Slightly older children are more likely to want a light left on in their rooms or to sleep with a favorite stuffed animal or blanket (Beltramini & Hertzig, 1983), and *everyone* loses sleep when a special "sleep pal" cannot go another day without being laundered—or is left behind when the family goes visiting. These *transitional objects* help a child make the transition from the dependence of infancy to the independence of later childhood.

Anna falls asleep clutching her stuffed "Grover," but Diane and Jonathan are not worried that she will become too dependent on a *thing*. A longitudinal study found that children who had insisted on taking cuddly objects to bed at age 4 were outgoing, self-confident, and self-sufficient at age 11. They enjoyed playing alone and were not likely to be worriers; at 16, they were just as well adjusted as boys and girls who had not used transitional objects (Newson, Newson, & Mahalski, 1982).

SLEEP DISTURBANCES

Sometimes more serious sleep problems develop during childhood. If they persist for a long time, they may be signs of emotional difficulties, but sometimes they just reflect habit patterns that interfere with sleep (see Box 6-3).

Many children—from 20 to 30 percent of those in their first 4 years of life—engage in long bedtime struggles (lasting more than an hour) and wake their parents frequently at night. The problem tends to be at its worst between ages 2 and 4. These children have often gone through such stresses as an accident or illness in the family, a depressed or ambivalent mother, or a mother's sudden absence during the day. They often sleep in the same bed with their parents—though this may be a reaction to, rather than a cause of, disturbed sleep (Lozoff, Wolf, & Davis, 1985).

At age 4, Anna went through a brief period of having nightmares about spiders, but they disappeared as suddenly as they had begun. About 1 in 4 children between ages 3 and 8 (most of them under age 6), have nightmares or night terrors (Hart-

mann, 1981). Nightmares are frightening dreams, often brought on by staying up too late, eating a heavy meal close to bedtime, or overexcitement. Upon awakening, a child can often recall the nightmare vividly. An occasional bad dream is no cause for alarm. Frequent nightmares, especially if they cause fear or anxiety during waking hours and if they persist past age 6, may signal excessive stress.

Night terrors are not connected with dreams; they seem to result from waking suddenly from deep sleep. Children wake in an unexplained state of panic. They may scream and sit up in bed, breathing rapidly and staring ahead unseeing; yet they are not aware of any frightening dreams or thoughts. They go back to sleep quickly, and in the morning they remember nothing. These episodes, which alarm parents more than children, are rarely serious and usually stop by themselves at about age 6.

Sleepwalking—literally, walking while asleep—is fairly common; usually, it is harmless and outgrown by age 6 (T. Anders, Caraskadon, & Dement, 1980). *Sleeptalking*—talking while asleep—is also rarely related to any problem and rarely requires any corrective action.

ADHD - Impulse control

BED-WETTING

Most children stay dry, day and night, by the age of 3 to 5 years; but *enuresis,* repeated urination during the day or night in clothing or in bed, is common, especially at night. It is not considered a problem unless it occurs at least twice a month after age 5. About 7 percent of 5-year-old boys and 3 percent of girls wet the bed; by age 10, the proportion is 3 percent of boys and 2 percent of girls (DSM III-R, 1987). Most outgrow the habit without any special help. Fewer than 1 percent of bedwetters have any physical disorder; the causes in the other 99 percent are thought to be heredity and developmental delay, not psychological dynamics.

Enuresis runs in families. About 75 percent of bed-wetters have a close relative who also wets the bed, and identical twins are more concordant for enuresis than fraternal twins (DSM III-R, 1987). Among more than 1000 children in New Zealand, family history was the strongest predictor of childhood bed-wetting (Fergusson, Horwood, & Shannon, 1986). Biological factors also seemed crucial. Children who were small at birth, slept more at ages 1 and 2, and developed slowly in the first 3 years attained bladder control later, with boys slightly slower than girls. The only significant en-

BOX 6-3   PRACTICALLY SPEAKING

HELPING CHILDREN TO SLEEP WELL

Aside from most parents' natural desires to help their children feel comfortable, helping a child get a good night's sleep helps the parents, too! When a young child has trouble going to sleep or wakes often during the night, the parents can neither relax nor sleep; they get cranky and become irritated with the child, and the entire family feels the strain. Fortunately, parents can take steps to make bedtime pleasant and nighttime refreshing for both generations. Here are some suggestions (AAP, 1992; L. A. Adams & Rickert, 1989; Graziano & Mooney, 1982):

HELPING CHILDREN GO TO SLEEP

- Establish a regular, unrushed bedtime routine—about 20 minutes of four to seven quiet activities, like reading a story, singing, or quiet conversation.
- Do not let the child watch scary or loud television shows.
- Avoid highly stimulating, active play just before bedtime.

- Keep a small night-light on if it makes the child feel more comfortable.
- Stay calm but don't yield to impulsive requests for "just one more story," "one more drink of water," or one more bathroom trip.
- If you're trying to break a habit, offer the child rewards for good bedtime behavior, like stickers on a chart or simple praise.
- Try putting your child to sleep a little later. Sending a child to bed too early is a common reason for sleep problems.
- If a child's fears about the dark or going to sleep have persisted for a long time, look for a program to help the child learn how to relax, substitute pleasant thoughts for frightening ones, and cope with stressful situations.

HELPING CHILDREN GO BACK TO SLEEP

- If a child gets up during the night, take him or her back to

bed. Speak calmly, pat the child gently on the back, but be pleasantly firm and consistent, even through the child's crying and fussing for a night or two.
- After a nightmare, reassure a frightened child and occasionally check in on the child. If frightening dreams persist for more than 6 weeks, consult your doctor.
- After night terrors, do not wake the child. If the child wakes, don't ask any questions. Just let the child go back to sleep. Help your child get enough sleep on a regular schedule; overtired or stressed children are more prone to night terrors.
- Walk or carry a sleepwalking child back to his or her own bed. Childproof your home with gates at the top of stairs and at windows, and bells on the child's bedroom door, so you'll know when she or he is out of bed.

---

vironmental influence was age of toilet training; when this began after 18 months, it took the child longer to attain bladder control. The only emotional factor in bed-wetting seems to be its tendency to recur in children who have already had the problem, especially at times of upset over such events as the birth of a sibling or entering school (DSM III-R, 1987).

A child who wets the bed should not be blamed or punished. Parents need not do anything about enuresis unless the child sees it as a problem. Treatments include rewarding children for staying dry; waking them when they begin to urinate by using devices that ring bells or buzzers; giving drugs (as a last resort, no more than 6 months after the last occurrence, and then tapered off; see McDaniel, 1986); and teaching children to practice controlling the sphincter muscles.

MOTOR SKILLS

When we see what 3-year-olds can do, it's hard to realize that they have been walking for only about 2 years. Tiffany puts on her older sister's tutu, stretches on tiptoe, and balances shakily on one foot; a few minutes later, she is back in overalls, riding her tricycle. With her stronger bones and muscles, greater lung power, and improved coordination between senses, limbs, and central nervous system, she can do more and more of the things she wants to do. Children aged 3 to 6 make great strides in motor skills—both *gross motor skills,* physical skills like jumping and running, which involve the large muscles, and *fine motor skills,* abilities like buttoning shirts and copying figures, which involve the small muscles.

NATURAL CONSEQUENCES

LARGE-MUSCLE COORDINATION

At 3, David could walk a straight line and stand on one foot—but only for about 1 second. At 4, he could hop on one foot; and he could catch a ball his father bounced to him, with hardly any misses. On his fifth birthday, he could jump nearly 3 feet and was learning to roller-skate.

Such motor skills—advanced far beyond the reflexes of infancy—are required for sports, dancing, and other activities that begin during middle childhood and may last a lifetime. (See Table 6-2 for a sampling of large-muscle skills that develop in early childhood.) However, children under the age of 6 are rarely ready to take part in any program preparing them for organized sports. Only 20 percent of 4-year-olds can throw a ball well, and only 30 percent are good at catching (AAP Committee on Sports Medicine and Fitness, 1992). The best way to help children develop physically is to encourage them to be active at an appropriate level for their state of maturity, in free-play situations, not structured ones.

SMALL-MUSCLE AND EYE-HAND COORDINATION

A few months ago, given a crayon and a large piece of paper, Winnie would cover the sheet with scribbles that only she could make sense of. Now, at age 3, she can draw a nearly straight line and a recognizable circle. At 4, Nelson can cut on a line with scissors, draw a person, make designs and crude letters, and fold paper into a double triangle. At 5, Juan can string beads and copy a square.

With their small muscles under control, children are able to tend to more of their own personal needs. This imparts a sense of competence and independence. By age 2 or 3, they use one hand more than the other (9 out of 10 are right-handed). At 3, Winnie can eat with a spoon and pour milk into her cereal bowl. She can button and unbutton her clothes well enough to dress herself without much help, although she still has trouble with zippers and shoelaces. She can use the toilet alone and can wash her hands afterward (with some reminding). By the time she starts kindergarten, she will be able to dress without supervision.

▪ INTELLECTUAL DEVELOPMENT

At the breakfast table, Terry, aged 3½, overhears his grandparents discussing the number of square feet of tile in their kitchen. In his small voice he pipes, "But then you'd need to have square shoes!" Later that morning he takes the P from his set of magnetic letters and puts it under his doll's mattress to find out whether the doll is a real princess. He defines spareribs as "sideways rectangle things with a bone in the middle."

Terry's growing facility with speech and ideas is helping him form his own unique view of the world—in ways that often surprise adults. From ages 3 to 6, Terry becomes more competent in cognition, intelligence, language, and learning. He is developing the ability to use symbols in thought and action, and to handle such concepts as age, time, and space more efficiently.

TABLE 6-2

Gross Motor Skills in Early Childhood		
3-Year-Olds	4-Year-Olds	5-Year-Olds
Cannot turn or stop suddenly or quickly	Have more effective control of stopping, starting, and turning	Start, turn, and stop effectively in games
Jump a distance of 15 to 24 inches	Jump a distance of 24 to 33 inches	Can make a running jump of 28 to 36 inches
Ascend a stairway unaided, alternating the feet	Descend a long stairway alternating the feet, if supported	Descend a long stairway unaided, alternating the feet
Can hop, using largely an irregular series of jumps with some variations added	Hop four to six steps on one foot	Easily hop a distance of 16 feet

SOURCE: Corbin, 1973.

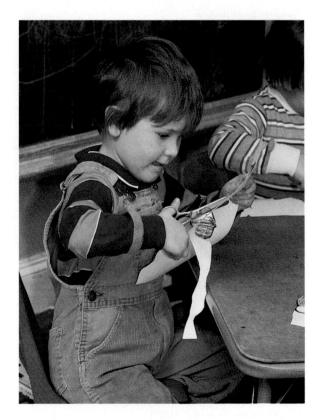

Children make significant advances in motor skills during the preschool years. As they develop physically, they are better able to make their bodies do what they want. Increasing eye-hand coordination helps them to use scissors or chopsticks, while normal large-muscle development lets them run, jump, hop, and ride a tricycle. Even children with disabilities can do many of these normal activities, with the help of special devices. *(a: Laura Dwight, b: Bob Daemmrich, c: Miro Vintoniv/Stock, Boston, d: Tom McCarthy/The Image Bank)*

"Remember when we went on the airplane to visit Grandma and Grandpa?" Young children remember better events that are unique and new, and they may recall many details from a special trip for a year or longer. *(Elizabeth Crews/The Image Works)*

ASPECTS OF INTELLECTUAL DEVELOPMENT

DEVELOPMENT OF MEMORY: INFORMATION PROCESSING

When Anna was 3 years old, she went on a trip with her preschool class to pick apples. Months later, she would still talk about riding on the bus, visiting the farm, picking the apples, bringing them home, and eating them. She clearly had vivid memories of the event.

Until recently, the kinds of things children ordinarily remember were rarely studied. Before the mid-1960s, there was very little research on memory in children younger than 5. And until about the 1980s, most of that research was done in the artificial setting of the psychological laboratory rather than in the real world. It focused mostly on tasks like recognition and recall.

Recognition is the ability to identify something that has been encountered before (like distinguishing pictures that you have seen before and those that are new). *Recall* is the ability to reproduce knowledge from memory (like describing pictures you have seen after they are no longer present). Preschool children, like all age groups, do better on recognition tasks than on recall, and ability improves with age (N. Myers & Perlmutter, 1978).

Today memory research uses more naturalistic tasks. When young children are tested by methods that identify their abilities, they turn out to have

better memories than was once thought. Their ability to remember continues to develop, becoming even more efficient in middle childhood. Let's see what memory is like in early childhood.

Influences on Children's Memory

General Knowledge
It stands to reason that the more familiar children are with items, the better they should be able to remember them. Early studies found that young children recalled material better when items bore an understandable relation to each other. When 3- and 4-year-olds in one study were shown pairs of pictures, they did much better recalling pairs that were related in some way than pairs that were unrelated (Staub, 1973). Also, children remembered pictures in which one member of the pair was a part of the other (like a tire and a car) better than those in which one item was the usual habitat of the other (like a fish and a lake). They remembered to a lesser degree those in which the two items belonged to the same category (like a hat and a sock). This suggests that the more children know about what is in the world, the better they can remember.

"Mastery Motivation" and Study Activities
Older children remember better than younger ones, and some children remember better than others, probably because of two other factors: a child's motivation to master skills in general and the child's way of approaching a specific task (Lange, MacKinnon, & Nida, 1989).

These conclusions emerged from studies of ninety-three 3- and 4-year-olds. During three sessions over 4 months, the children were tested on their knowledge of a variety of objects, were assessed on how reflective or impulsive they were, were videotaped to analyze how they did two tasks presented to them, and were rated by preschool teachers and parents on such characteristics as "takes initiative in carrying out activities," "uses problem-solving strategies," and "tries to pursue difficult tasks." One of the two tasks involved putting together a picture puzzle. In the other, the children were shown an array of toys, which they were permitted to handle before the toys were taken away and replaced by a set of new toys; the children were asked to label these new toys before they too were removed. Finally, the children were asked to recall what the toys were. The videotapes showed what the children did with the toys—how much they looked at them, picked them up, and moved them around; how they grouped and named them; and whether they repeated the names of the toys to themselves. Children varied considerably in these activities.

The best predictor of how well a child remembered the names of the toys was "mastery motivation," that is, a child's tendency to be independent, self-directed, and generally resourceful (as rated by the child's teacher). The only other factor related to recall was the child's activities while studying the toys. Children who named the toys, grouped the toys, or spent time thinking about the names of the toys or repeating those names to themselves (in other words, used strategies to help them remember) recalled better than children who did less of these specific activities. These two factors were not related to each other; that is, "mastery motivation" did not seem to encourage use of particular study activities (Lange et al., 1989).

Unusual Activities and New Experiences

Anna's memory of picking apples is an example of a finding that children as young as 3 years remember events better that are unique and new and may recall many details from, say, a trip to the zoo or to an unusual museum for a year or longer (Fivush, Hudson, & Nelson, 1983). They also remember events that recur regularly (having lunch or going to the park), but one such occasion tends to blur into another.

Naturalistic research confirms this. For example, one study found that preschoolers tend to remember activities they took part in better than objects they saw (D. C. Jones, Swift, & Johnson, 1988).

Sixty-five 3- and 4½-year-olds visited a child-size replica of a turn-of-the-century farmhouse, where they took part in five activities, including pretending to sew a blanket on a treadle sewing machine and chopping ice with a pick and hammer. Then they were interviewed—some later the same day, some 1 week later, and some 8 weeks later—to determine what they remembered. There were few age differences in the children's memories of what they had *done*. But the older children were better at recalling objects they had seen and objects they had handled (like the blanket). The best-remembered objects were those that the children had used to *do* something (like the sewing machine).

Social Interactions

The way people talk with a child about an event also influences how well the child will remember it. In one field experiment, ten 3-year-olds and their mothers visited a natural history museum (Tessler, in Nelson, 1989). Half the mothers talked naturally with their children as they walked through the museum. The other half, as requested, did not open discussions but only responded to their children's comments. All the conversations were tape-recorded. A week later the researchers interviewed the mothers and children separately and asked 30 questions about objects seen the week before. The results were dramatic. The children remembered *only* those objects that they had talked about with their mothers. Furthermore, the children in the "natural conversation" group remembered better.

In this study, the mothers' styles of talking to the children also had an effect. Four of the mothers had a narrative style, reminiscing about shared experiences ("Remember when we went to Vermont and saw Cousin Bill?"); six mothers had a more practical style, using memory for a specific purpose like solving a problem ("Where does this puzzle piece go? You remember we did that one yesterday."). The children of the "narrative" mothers averaged 13 correct answers, compared with fewer than 5 for the children of the "practical" mothers.

COGNITIVE DEVELOPMENT: PIAGET'S PREOPERATIONAL STAGE

Although Piaget made his observations of children's intellectual development long before the recent research on memory, the growth of recall is fundamental to his description of the way thought processes develop during early childhood. When children can recall events and objects, they can begin to form and use *concepts*—representations of things not in their present environment. Communication improves as they can share their representational systems with others.

Between ages 3 and 6, children are in Piaget's second major stage of cognitive development—the preoperational stage, in which, he said, children can think in symbols but cannot yet use logic. Piaget proposed that symbolic thought begins in the sixth and last substage of the sensorimotor period; toddlers begin to generate ideas and solve problems through mental representations, which are limited to things that are physically present. (As we noted in Chapter 4, however, babies can form some types of mental representations much earlier than Piaget's theory allows for.)

In the *preoperational stage,* children can think about objects, people, or events in their absence, by using mental representations of them. The preoperational stage is a significant step beyond the sensorimotor period because children can now learn not only by sensing and doing but by thinking symbolically as well; not only by acting but also by reflecting on their actions. They still cannot think logically, however, said Piaget, as they will be able to do in the stage of concrete operations, which they reach in middle childhood (see Chapter 8). Again, it seems that Piaget underestimated the capabilities of children. However, his theory is a critical starting point for studying cognitive development and the inspiration for much current research. Let us see what he had to say about preoperational thought.

The Symbolic Function

"I want an ice cream cone!" Sharon, aged 4, says, trudging indoors from the hot, dusty street. She has not seen anything that triggered this desire—no open freezer door or television commercial. She no longer needs this kind of sensory cue to think about something. She remembers ice cream (her mental representation includes coldness and taste), and she purposefully seeks it out. This absence of sensory or motor cues characterizes the major important development of this stage, the *symbolic function:* the ability to learn by using symbols.

A *symbol* is a mental representation to which a person has attached meaning. It is something that stands for something else. Symbols allow us to think about things without having to have the ac-

tual objects or events in front of us. An object can be a symbol, taking on in people's minds the qualities of whatever it stands for. This is why there is such controversy about how a piece of cloth with stripes and stars is treated. It would not be such an emotional issue if in people's minds the nation's flag did not symbolize the United States of America.

The most common symbol (and probably the most important one for thought) is the word, at first spoken, and then written. Knowing the symbols for things helps us to think about them and their qualities, remember them, and talk about them with other people. Preoperational children can now use language to stand for absent things and for events that are not taking place at the present time. Symbolic thought is, therefore, a great advance over the sensorimotor stage.

Indications of the Symbolic Function

Children show the symbolic function in three ways: deferred imitation, symbolic play, and language. *Deferred imitation* is the imitation of an observed action after time has passed. In *symbolic play,* children make an object stand for something else. One evening in the bathtub, Anna, at age 5, illustrates both of these, plus language. First Anna "swims" around, moving her mouth in fishlike motions. She then asks Diane to throw her some foam bathtub letters, which Anna catches in her mouth and "eats." Anna is showing *deferred imitation*: she saw pet fish, formed and stored a mental symbol of their swimming and eating (probably a visual image), and later—when she could no longer see the fish—reproduced the behavior by calling up the stored symbol. She shows *symbolic play* by making toys stand for fish food. And she uses *language* when she asks Diane to give her the toys. (We will talk more about language, perhaps the most impressive manifestation of the symbolic function, later in this chapter.)

Achievements of Preoperational Thought

By using symbols based on recall, preoperational children think in new and creative ways. Although their thinking is not yet fully logical, it does show partial logic. Let us see how a child at this preoperational level of cognitive development thinks.

Understanding of Identities and Functions

The world is more orderly and predictable now, because preoperational children have a basic knowledge of both identities and functions. Rico,

SOUP / SPOKEN WRITTEN

aged 5, now understands that certain things stay the same even though they may change in form, size, or appearance. For example, the day Pumpkin, his cat, was nowhere to be found, Rico suggested, "Maybe Pumpkin put on a bear suit and went to someone else's house to be their pet bear." When his baby-sitter questioned him about this possible turn of events, however, Rico showed that he still believed Pumpkin would, even underneath her disguise, continue to be his beloved cat.

Children in this stage also understand some basic functional relationships between things and events. Tanya, age 3, knows that when she pulls a cord, the curtain opens; and that when she flicks a switch, the ceiling light goes on. Although she does not yet understand fully how one action causes the other, she does perceive a connection between them.

Limitations of Preoperational Thought

Preoperational thinking is still rudimentary compared with what children will be able to do when they reach the stage of concrete operations in middle childhood. For example, preoperational children do not yet clearly differentiate reality from fantasy. What are some other ways in which, according to Piaget, children in this stage are intellectually different from older children?

Centration

Preoperational children show *centration:* they focus, or center, on one aspect of a situation and neglect others, often coming to illogical conclusions. They cannot *decenter,* or think simultaneously about several aspects of a situation.

A classic example is Piaget's most famous experiment. He designed it to test children's development of *conservation*—the awareness that two things that are equal remain so if their shape is altered so long as nothing is added or taken away. He found that children do not fully understand this principle until the stage of concrete operations, normally in middle childhood.

Let's consider a typical conservation experiment (see Figure 6-4). A child, Nils, is shown two identical clear glasses, both short and wide and holding the same amount of water. Then the water in one glass is poured into a third glass—a tall, thin one. Nils is now asked whether both glasses contain the same amount of water, or whether one contains more. In early childhood—even after watching an experimenter pour the water out of

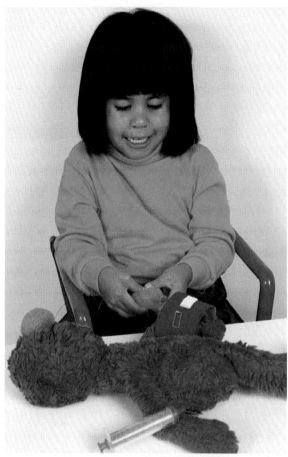

As Anna pretends to take Grover's blood pressure, she is showing a major cognitive achievement, deferred imitation—the ability to act out an action she observed some time before. *(Erika Stone)*

one of the short, fat glasses into a tall, thin glass or even after pouring it himself—Nils will say that the taller glass (or the wide glass) contains more water. When asked why, he says, "This one is bigger this way," stretching his arms to show height (or width). Preoperational children cannot consider height and width at the same time. They center on one aspect and so cannot understand what is happening. Their logic is flawed because their thinking is tied to what they "see"; if one glass *looks* bigger, they seem to think it must *be* bigger.

Irreversibility

Preoperational children's logic is also limited by *irreversibility:* failure to understand that an operation can go two ways. Once a child can conceptualize restoring the original state of the water by pouring it back into the other glass, she or he will realize that the amount of water in both glasses is

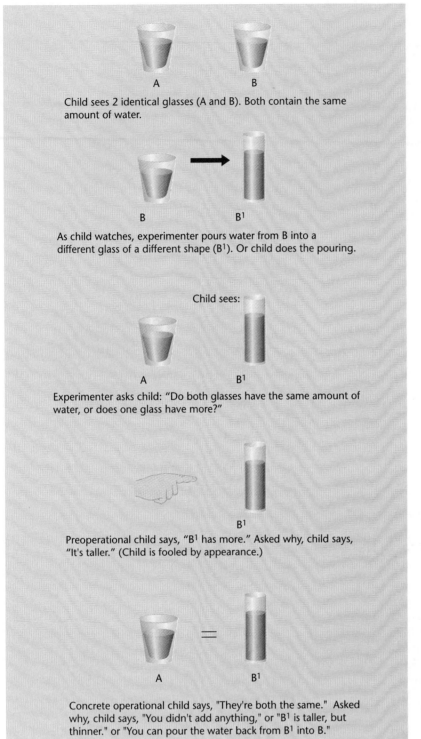

Child sees 2 identical glasses (A and B). Both contain the same amount of water.

As child watches, experimenter pours water from B into a different glass of a different shape (B¹). Or child does the pouring.

Child sees:

Experimenter asks child: "Do both glasses have the same amount of water, or does one glass have more?"

Preoperational child says, "B¹ has more." Asked why, child says, "It's taller." (Child is fooled by appearance.)

Concrete operational child says, "They're both the same." Asked why, child says, "You didn't add anything," or "B¹ is taller, but thinner." or "You can pour the water back from B¹ into B."

FIGURE 6-4
Piaget's most famous experiment: a test of conservation.

the same. The preoperational child does not understand this.

Focus on States Rather Than on Transformations

Preoperational children think as if they were watching a filmstrip with a series of static frames. They focus on successive states and are not able to understand the meaning of the transformation from one state to another. We saw this in the experiment with conservation (refer back to Figure 6-4). Preoperational children do not grasp the meaning of pouring the water from the original glass to the new one. They do not understand the implication of transforming B into B^1—even though the appearance changes, the amount does not.

Transductive Reasoning

Logical reasoning is of two basic types: deduction and induction. Deduction goes from the general to the particular: "Eating a lot of candy can make people sick. I ate a lot of candy today, and so I may get sick." Induction goes from the particular to the general: "Yesterday I ate a lot of candy and felt sick. Last week I ate a lot of candy and felt sick. The same thing happened to Emily and Bret. Therefore it looks as if eating a lot of candy can make people sick."

Preoperational children, said Piaget, do not think along either of these lines. Instead, they reason by *transduction:* they move from one particular to another particular without taking the general into account. This kind of reasoning leads Adam to see a causal relationship where none actually exists: "I had bad thoughts about my sister. My sister got sick. Therefore, I made my sister sick." Because the bad thoughts and the sister's sickness occurred around the same time, Adam assumes, illogically, that one caused the other.

Egocentrism

At age 4, Sally's daughter Jenny was at the beach. Awed by the constant thundering of the waves, she turned to her father and asked, "But when does it stop?" "It doesn't," he replied. "Not even when I'm *asleep?*" asked Jenny incredulously. Her thinking was so egocentric, so focused on herself as the center of her universe, that she could not consider anything—even the mighty ocean—as continuing its motion when she was not there to see it.

Egocentrism is an inability to see things from another's point of view. A classic Piagetian experiment known as the *mountain task* illustrates egocentric thinking (see Figure 6-5). A child would sit

FIGURE 6-5

Piaget's mountain task. A preoperational child is unable to describe the "mountain" from the doll's point of view—an indication of egocentrism.

on a chair facing a table on which were three large mounds. The experimenter would place a doll on another chair, on the opposite side of the table, and would ask the child to tell or show how the "mountains" looked to the doll. Young children could not answer the question; instead, they would describe the mountains from their own perspective. Piaget took this as proof that they could not imagine a different point of view (Piaget & Inhelder, 1967).

Egocentrism, to Piaget, is not selfishness but self-centered understanding, and it is fundamental to the limited thinking of young children. Egocentrism is a form of centration: these children are so centered on their own point of view that they cannot take in another's view at the same time. Three-year-olds are not as egocentric as newborn babies, who cannot distinguish between the universe and their own bodies; but young children still think that the universe centers on them. This inability to decenter helps explain why they have trouble separating reality from what goes on inside their own heads and why they show confusion about what causes what. When Adam believes that his "bad thoughts" have made his sister sick, he is thinking egocentrically. Egocentrism explains why young children often talk to themselves or seem to "talk past" other people. It also explains why young children so often feel guilty for "causing" such events as their parents' divorce.

Assessing Piaget's Theory

No thinker about cognitive development during early childhood has been more influential than Piaget. Yet recent research suggests that he underes-

Story A

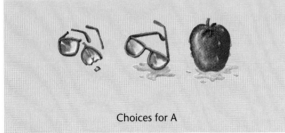

Choices for A

FIGURE 6-6
Examples of sequences to test understanding of causality. A child is asked to look at pictures like those in the top row, to pick the one in the bottom row that would show what happened, and to tell a story about what happened. *(Gelman, Bullock, & Meck, 1980.)*

timated the cognitive abilities of young children.

One problem seems to have been his tendency to *over*estimate young children's understanding of language. He assumed that wrong answers revealed faults in thinking, when some of the errors may actually have arisen from the way he phrased the questions. In many of his experiments, children apparently misinterpreted tasks they were asked to do and answered questions that may not have been the ones the experimenter was asking.

Do Young Children Understand Cause and Effect?

Young children apparently have more understanding of cause and effect than Piaget thought. One psychologist, who looked up some of the stories Piaget had asked children to retell, found that she had trouble remembering them herself. When she simplified the stories to clarify cause-and-effect connections, first-graders had no trouble retelling them correctly (Mandler, in Pines, 1983).

To eliminate the complicating factor of language, other researchers asked 3- and 4-year-olds to look at pictures like those on the top in Figure 6-6, and then to choose the picture on the bottom that would tell "what happened" (Gelman, Bullock, & Meck, 1980). These children showed an understanding of causality, telling stories like: "First you

have dry glasses, and then water gets on the glasses, and you end up with wet glasses."

When we listen to children talk, we hear them spontaneously using such words as *because* and *so*. "He's crying because he doesn't want to put his pajamas on—he wants to be naked," said Marie at 27 months, watching her twin brother's bedtime struggle. Even at this early age, children seem to understand some causal relationships, long before they can answer adults' "why" questions.

How Animistic Are Young Children?

Animism is a tendency to attribute life to objects that are not alive. When Piaget asked children about the sun, the wind, and clouds, answers then led him to think that young children are confused about what is alive and what is not. Piaget attributed this to egocentrism; one child, for example, said that the moon is alive "because we are."

However, when a later researcher questioned 3- and 4-year-olds about differences between a rock, a person, and a doll, the children showed that they understood that people are alive and rocks are not (Gelman, Spelke, & Meck, 1983). They did not attribute thoughts or emotions to rocks, and they talked about the fact that dolls cannot move on their own as evidence that dolls are not alive. The confusion Piaget observed may have arisen because the objects he asked about are all capable of movement and, in addition, are very far away. Since children know so little about sun, wind, and clouds, they are less certain about the nature of these phenomena than about the nature of more familiar objects like rocks and dolls.

Even 3-year-olds realize that animals can go uphill by themselves and that statues (even statues that look like animals), wheeled vehicles, and rigid objects cannot, showing an understanding of which things are capable of independent movement (Massey & Gelman, 1988). When faced with an array of photos of such objects, children of this age are not always accurate in *saying* which ones are alive and which are not, but many know which ones can do things that live creatures can do and which cannot.

How Egocentric Are Young Children?

Four-year-old Anna was sitting on her father's lap. She said to Jonathan, "I see Annas in your eyes." When he asked her, "And what do I see in your eyes?" she replied, "You see Daddys in my eyes." Anna's ability to take another person's point of view at an earlier age than Piaget had said this was

BOX 6-4   FOOD FOR THOUGHT

THEORIES OF MIND

How and when do children come to understand what another person is thinking and feeling? This question is currently a hot topic, as researchers delve into the area known as "theory of mind." A child's ability to make sense of what other people are doing is a major step in cognitive development. Babies begin to develop some sort of theory of mind as young as 9 months of age when they begin to communicate (Bretherton, 1991). By age 2 or 3, this understanding is crucial for a child's day-to-day interaction with other people. The lack of such a development in autistic children is undoubtedly tied to their inability to form relationships (Moore & Frye, 1991).

Social referencing (see Chapter 5) is one example of a child's "reading" another person's mind. This kind of understanding quickly becomes more sophisticated. Naturalistic studies done in the home have seen evidence of it as children help or argue with others, respond to other people's distress, cooper-ate, pretend, tell jokes, and talk about other people. As early as the second year of life, a child who wants to annoy an older sibling will often grab the sibling's favorite toy. By the third year, children regularly make excuses for themselves by saying "I didn't mean to" and protest another child's actions by saying "He did it on purpose!" (Dunn, 1991).

This kind of understanding is a cognitive concept; a 3-year-old's ability to understand another person's thinking is related to the child's performance at age 6 on a task that requires taking the perspective of someone else and imagining how that person feels (Dunn, Brown, & Beardsall, 1991). The close relationship between the cognitive and the emotional is underscored by the fact that children from families that talk a lot about feelings and causality generally achieve such understanding at an earlier age (Dunn, 1991; Dunn, Brown, Slomkowski, Tesla, & Youngblade, 1991).

Telling a lie is a sign of cognitive development! For a child to de-ceive someone, that child has to be able to imagine what another person might think. Studies have revealed that 3-year-olds will lie to a stranger to protect their mothers if they think that the mother did something wrong, but they will tell the truth when speaking to the mother (Ceci & Leichtman, 1992).

Research along these lines has a number of practical implications. One is in the realm of legal testimony. Research has found that children can be coached to tell a lie or to withhold information. This raises the possibility that some parents may urge their children to make false allegations of abuse, sometimes against the other parent (Tate, Warren, & Hess, 1992), and also that children may be pressured by a parent to deny that such abuse took place (Bussey, 1992). In view of other findings—that having to testify in court may impede the recovery of a sexually abused child—advocates for children need to exercise great sensitivity in handling these issues.

---

possible has been confirmed by research, in a variation on Piaget's mountain task.

A child is seated in front of a square board, with dividers that separate it into four equal sectors. A figure of a police officer is put at the edge of the board. Then a doll is put into one sector after another; each time, the child is asked whether the police officer can see the doll. Another toy police officer is then brought into the action, and the child is told to hide the doll from both officers. When 30 children between the ages of 3½ and 5 were given this task, they gave the correct answer or did the right thing 90 percent of the time (Hughes, 1975).

Why were these children able to take another person's point of view—in this case the police officer's—whereas children doing Piaget's classic mountain task were not? The difference may be that this task calls for thinking about more famil-iar, less abstract materials. Most children do not look at mountains and do not think about what other people might see when looking at a mountain, but even 3-year-olds know about dolls and police officers and hiding.

An example from real life shows a similar ability to take another viewpoint. When Anna, age 4, was going back to the United States with her parents after a family visit to England, she said, "Don't be sad, Grandma. We'll come see you again. And you can come see us in New York." Anna's grandmother had not cried or talked about feeling sad, but Anna imagined how she must have been feeling.

Anna's statement reflects the findings of much recent research on children's developing "theories of mind," which concerns when children understand the mental states of other people (see Box 6-4). Between the ages of 3 and 5, children begin

These children's building of a tower shows that they can classify by at least two different attributes—in this case, by color and size. *(Charles Gupton/Stock, Boston)*

to think about how other people are thinking and feeling, and their understanding of other people's actions grows significantly (Dunn, Brown, Slomkowski, Tesla, & Youngblade, 1991). In Anna's family, feelings are often discussed. Children in such families are better able to recognize emotions in others (Dunn, Brown, & Beardsall, 1991).

How Well Can Young Children Classify?

Researchers today also differ with Piaget on children's ability to classify. Piaget identified three stages of classification (Inhelder & Piaget, 1964):

Stage 1 (2½ to 5 years): Children group items to form a design or figure (like a house); or they group them according to criteria that keep changing (like adding a blue square to a red square because they are both squares and then adding a red triangle to the group because it is red, like the red square).

Stage 2 (5 to 7 or 8 years): Children group by similarity but may switch criteria in midtask, sorting some groups by color and others by shape or size. They often subclassify: they may put all the red items into one group and then group the red squares, triangles, and circles.

Stage 3 (7 to 8 years): At the stage of concrete operations, children are truly classifying. They *start out* with a plan to group items by two criteria (like color and shape), showing that they understand the relationships between classes and subclasses.

Researchers after Piaget, however, have found that many 4-year-olds can classify by two criteria (Denney, 1972) and that children can begin to classify early in the second year of life (Gopnik & Meltzoff, 1987). In one study, researchers brought 12 babies (whose average age was 15½ months at the beginning of the study) into the laboratory and set out three different sets of eight objects, four of one kind and four of another. The sets included (1) four flat yellow rectangles and four brightly colored plastic people figures, (2) four clear pillboxes and four balls of red modeling clay, and (3) four rag dolls and four red cars. The children were told to "play with these things" or "fix them all up." The problems, posed at 3-week intervals and continuing until every baby had passed a series of cognitive tests, elicited an unvarying sequence of classification ability:

Level 1—Single-category grouping (average age 16.04 months): The child moves four objects of one kind and groups them together.

Level 2—Serial touching (average age 16.39 months): The child touches four items from one group and then four from the other group.

Level 3—Two-category grouping (average age 17.24 months): The child moves all eight objects and either sorts them into two distinct groups or establishes one-to-one correspondence (like putting each of the four dolls on top of a car).

At about 18 months babies typically go through a "naming explosion" when they suddenly acquire many new words with which to label objects. This interest in naming things seems to show that babies now realize that objects belong to different categories. It is not surprising that they develop two-category classification at about the same time as they feverishly try to name all the objects in their world. (Gopnik & Meltzoff, 1987).

Can Cognitive Abilities Be Accelerated?

Programs to teach specific cognitive abilities seem to work when a child is already on the verge of acquiring the concept being taught. However, certain kinds of training are more effective than others.

In one experiment to teach conservation (D. Field, 1981), 3- and 4-year-olds were shown various arrangements of checkers, candies, jacks, sticks, and rods. The child was asked to pick the two rows that had the same number of items or to show which two objects were the same length. Then the objects were moved or changed in some way, and the child was asked whether they were the same as before (see Figure 6-7).

The child was then given one of three rules to explain why items that did not appear the same might *be* the same:

1 *Identity*, or sameness of the materials: "No matter where you put them, they're still the same candies."
2 *Reversibility*, or the possibility of returning the items to their original arrangement: "Look, we just have to put the sticks back together to see that they are the same length."
3 *Compensation*, showing that a change in one dimension was balanced by a change in the other: "Yes, this stick does go farther in this direction, but at the other end the stick is going farther, and so they balance each other."

The children who were given the identity rule made the most progress in learning the principle of conservation. Those who learned reversibility also advanced, but those who were taught compensation benefited little from the training.

The 4-year-olds (who presumably were closer to acquiring conservation on their own) were more apt than the 3-year-olds to learn the concept and to retain it up to 5 months later. The 3-year-olds were not able to conserve as many quantities and tended to lose whatever abilities they did gain. This kind of training seems, then, to benefit children only when their intellectual structures are well enough developed to handle the principle of conservation. The training then gives them a strategy for integrating it into their thought processes.

It seems, then, that young children are more competent than Piaget believed. "Preoperational" children do, of course, have more cognitive limitations

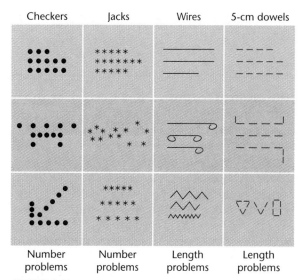

FIGURE 6-7

Examples of conservation training problems. In these experiments, a child was shown arrangements of items like those in the top row, and then was shown rearrangements of the same objects (as in the second or third row) and asked whether they were the same. The child was then told why they were the same on the basis of identity, reversibility, or compensation. Identity was the strongest concept for teaching conservation. *(D. Field, 1977.)*

than children in the next higher stage of development, concrete operations. However, when faced with tasks compatible with what they are familiar with and explained in language they understand, they show greater competence than they do on traditional Piagetian tasks. Our estimation of young children's intellectual abilities has changed for the better as a result of newer, more age-appropriate research techniques.

DEVELOPMENT OF LANGUAGE

During early childhood Anna is full of questions: "How many sleeps until tomorrow?" "Who filled the river with water?" "Do babies have muscles?" "Do smells come from inside my nose?"

Young children are interested in the whole wide world, and they ask questions about everything—partly because they are hungry for knowledge and partly because they quickly learn that asking "why" will almost always keep a conversation going. At the beginning of early childhood, children can give and follow commands that include more than one step, like "Pick up your toys and put them in the closet." And they can name familiar things like pets, body parts, and people. Their linguistic skills progress rapidly through early childhood.

Using Words, Sentences, and Grammar

Once children pass the age of 3, speech becomes more adultlike. At 3, they use plurals and past tense, and they know the difference between *I, you,* and *we.* Between ages 3 and 6, children typically learn from two to four new words a day, but they do not always use the words as adults use them. Anna uses the word *tomorrow* to refer to any time in the future and *yesterday* as an all-purpose word for the past (Pease & Gleason, 1985).

Between ages 4 and 5, children's sentences average four to five words. They can now deal with prepositions like *over, under, in, on,* and *behind;* can name colors; and can count to 10. Between ages 5 and 6, children use longer and more complex sentences. They can define simple words, and they know some opposites. They use more conjunctions, prepositions, and articles. Between 6 and 7 years of age, children's speech becomes quite sophisticated. They now speak in grammatically correct (for the most part!) compound and complex sentences, and they use all parts of speech. They can also do some simple reading and writing, sometimes "inventing" phonetic spelling, as when Anna wrote about "padung (petting) a cat."

Although young children speak fluently, understandably, and fairly grammatically, they often make errors by failing to note exceptions to rules. A mistake like saying "holded" instead of "held" or "eated" instead of "ate" is a normal sign of progress in learning a language. Younger children correctly say, "I held the baby" or "I ate the pizza," but at that point they are merely repeating expressions they have heard. When children begin to discover rules (like adding *-ed* for past tense), they tend to *overregularize*—that is, to use a rule on all occasions. This is appropriate most of the time, but not with irregular verbs like *to hold* and *to eat.* Eventually, as children hear people talking and take part in conversations themselves, they notice that *-ed* is not always used to form the past tense of a verb. Thus "mistakes" like "I holded the baby" and "I eated the pizza" involve taking one step backward in order to take two steps forward.

An aspect of immature language comprehension shows up in the frequency with which children misinterpret complex sentences. If Noah's mother tells the 4-year-old, "You may watch TV after you pick up your toys," Noah may process the words he hears in the order in which he hears them, and think that he may first watch television and then pick up his toys. At 5, Anna told her mother that she had kissed her dentist goodbye. When Diane asked, "Did Dr. Margot kiss you back?" Anna said no. Rephrasing the question, Diane asked, "Did Dr. Margot kiss you?" This time Anna said yes. She had thought her mother was asking whether the dentist had kissed Anna's back! Such misunderstandings have important implications for adults who talk to children, since children often receive a very different meaning from the one adults intend to communicate.

From a very early age, children communicate through social speech. They take into account other people's needs and use words to establish and maintain social contacts—and to tell jokes. Whatever these tots are talking about clearly strikes them as funny. *(Bob Daemmrich/The Image Works)*

Speaking to Others: Social Speech

The form and function of speech are linked. As children master words, sentences, and grammar, they communicate better. *Social speech* is intended to be understood by someone other than the speaker. It takes other people's needs into account and is used to establish and maintain communication with others. It must be adapted to the other person's speech patterns and behavior. It may take the form of questions and answers or other means of exchanging information, or it may involve criticism, commands, requests, or threats.

Piaget characterized most of young children's speech as egocentric (not adapted to the listener), but research suggests that children's speech is quite social from an early age (see Table 6-3). When 3- to 5-year-olds were asked to communicate their choice of a toy, they behaved very differently with a person who could see and with one who could not. They pointed to the toy for a sighted listener, but described it to a blindfolded listener (Maratsos, 1973). In addition, 4-year-olds use "motherese" (see Chapter 4) when speaking to 2-year-olds (Shatz & Gelman, 1973). And even 2-year-olds use social speech as they point out or show objects to others. Most of the time (almost 80 percent in one study), the feedback they get shows that they have captured their listeners' attention (Wellman & Lempers, 1977).

Children's general knowledge affects their ability to communicate. Asked to describe a variety of pictures, 4½-year-olds did very well with simple, familiar subjects like monkeys and people but not with abstract designs (Dickson, 1979). Even teenagers as old as 14 were unable to describe unusual designs clearly enough for others of their age to understand (Krauss & Glucksberg, 1977).

Children's ability to communicate is related to their popularity with their peers—one more example of the close tie between cognitive and emotional aspects of development. Well-liked preschoolers can start and keep up conversations better than less popular children, who are not as good at adapting the way they speak to the needs of a listener and the demands of a situation (Hazen & Black, 1989).

Research suggests, however, that when children do not communicate with others, it is often not because they are unable to but because they do not intend to. In one study, 3- to 5-year-old lower- and middle-class urban children had little trouble making themselves understood when they *tried* to communicate with others (Berk, 1986). But sometimes

TABLE 6-3

Development of Social Speech	
Age	**Characteristics of Speech**
2½	*Beginnings of conversation:* Speech is increasingly relevant to others' remarks. Need for clarity is being recognized.
3	*Breakthrough in attention to communication:* Child seeks ways to clarify and correct misunderstandings. Pronunciation and grammar improve markedly. Speech with children the same age expands dramatically. Use of language as instrument of control increases.
4	*Knowledge of fundamentals of conversation:* Child shifts speech according to listener's knowledge. Literal definitions are no longer a sure guide to meaning. Disputes can be resolved with words.
5	*Good control of elements of conversation.*

SOURCE: Adapted from E. B. Bolles, 1982, p. 93.

children engage in *private speech:* they are not trying to communicate with anyone else.

Speaking to Oneself: Private Speech

Anna, age 4, is alone in her room painting. When she finishes, she is overheard saying aloud, "Now I have to put the pictures somewhere to dry. I'll put them by the window. They need to get dry now. I'll paint some more dinosaurs."

Private speech—talking aloud to oneself with no intent to communicate with others—is normal and common in early and middle childhood. From 20 to 60 percent of what children say at these ages consists of private utterances, ranging from playful rhythmic repetition (something like babies' babbling) to the kind of "thinking out loud" Anna does or barely audible muttering.

What is the function of private speech? Piaget considered it an egocentric inability to recognize another person's viewpoint and therefore an inability to communicate. He believed that young children talk while they do things because they do not yet fully differentiate between words, or symbols, and what the words represent.

On the other hand, the Russian psychologist Lev Semenovich Vygotsky (1962) saw private speech as a special form of communication: communication with oneself. Like Piaget, he believed that private speech helps children integrate language with thought. But unlike Piaget, he believed that private speech *increases* through the early school years as children use it to guide and master their actions and then fades away as they establish internal control through silent thought.

A number of studies support Vygotsky's position. Among nearly 150 middle-class children 4 to 10 years old, private speech rose and then fell with age. And the most sociable children used the most private speech—apparently confirming Vygotsky's view that private speech is stimulated by social experience (Berk, 1986; Kohlberg, Yaeger, & Hjertholm, 1968). Private speech peaked earliest—around age 4—for the brightest children and between ages 5 and 7 for the average child; it was virtually nonexistent by age 9.

A similar but slower pattern appeared among low-income 5- to 10-year-olds in the Appalachian mountains of Kentucky. In this culture, where people tend to talk little, 25 percent of the children (especially boys) still used private speech at age 10. These youngsters talked to themselves most when they were trying to solve difficult problems and no adults were around (Berk & Garvin, 1984). This suggests that private speech guides children's behavior and helps them think. If so, talking out loud in school is not necessarily "naughty," and forbidding such behavior may slow learning (Berk, 1986).

DEVELOPMENT OF INTELLIGENCE

Assessing Intelligence by Traditional, Psychometric Measures

Traditionally, according to the psychometric approach, psychologists have tried to determine and measure quantitatively the factors that make up intelligence. They have used *intelligence quotient (IQ) tests* to assess how much a person has of certain abilities, like comprehension and reasoning abilities. These tests consist of certain questions or tasks (usually verbal and performance) that seem to be indicators of intellectual functioning in these areas. The test scores show how well someone can perform the tasks relative to other people. Children's performance in such tests can predict future school performance fairly accurately.

Because children normally get better at solving

tasks as they grow, a child's performance is evaluated on the basis of age. Each child's score is compared with *standardized norms,* standards obtained from the scores of a large, representative sample of children of the same age who took the test while it was in the process of preparation.

Besides providing standardized norms, test developers must devise techniques to try to ensure that the tests are *valid* (that they measure the abilities they claim to measure) and *reliable* (that the results are reasonably consistent from one time to another). These are rigorous criteria, but tests can be meaningful and useful only if they are both valid and reliable.

What Do Scores on Intelligence Tests Mean?

Unfortunately, many people have the misconception that the score on an intelligence test represents a fixed quantity of intelligence that people are born with, rather than simply an indicator of relative intellectual functioning. Intelligence tests are often presumed to measure innate ability, but they actually measure achievement and performance, which are affected by factors beyond "pure" intelligence. Although IQ scores of school-age children and adults tend to be fairly stable, some people show marked changes, perhaps reflecting environmental circumstances (Kopp & McCall, 1982).

Indeed, test-takers on the whole have been doing better on the Stanford-Binet in recent years (Anastasi, 1988), forcing test developers to raise previously established norms. This improvement probably reflects exposure to educational television programs, preschools, better-educated parents, and a wider variety of experiences—as well as exposure to the tests themselves—rather than genetic changes in the population.

Intelligence is difficult to define and even more difficult to measure. Undoubtedly there are real differences in intellectual ability among children, but there is serious disagreement over how accurately psychometric tests assess those differences. We will continue to explore issues concerning intelligence testing in Chapter 8, when we examine the intellectual development of school-age children. For now we'll discuss measurement of intelligence in preschool children.

Because the child of 3, 4, or 5 is quite proficient with language, intelligence tests can now include verbal items. As a result, from this age on tests produce more reliable results than the largely nonverbal tests used in infancy. As children approach age 5, there is a higher correlation between their scores on intelligence tests and the scores they will achieve later (Bornstein & Sigman, 1986).

Children are now easier to test than infants and toddlers, but they still need to be tested individually. Let's look at two important individual tests.

Stanford-Binet Intelligence Scale

The *Stanford-Binet Intelligence Scale,* the first individual childhood intelligence test to be developed, takes 30 to 40 minutes. The child is asked to define words, string beads, build with blocks, identify the missing parts of a picture, trace mazes, and show an understanding of numbers. The child's score is supposed to measure practical judgment in real-life situations, memory, and spatial orientation.

The fourth edition of the Stanford-Binet, revised in 1985, differs in several ways from previous editions. It is less verbal: there is an equal balance of verbal and nonverbal, quantitative, and memory items. It assesses patterns and levels of cognitive development instead of providing the IQ as a single overall measure of intelligence. The revamped standardization sample is well balanced geographically, over the United States; ethnically, in proportion to ethnic groups' representation in the population; and by gender, representing both sexes equally. Also, the corrected norms offer a socioeconomic balance and include handicapped children. (In Chapter 8 we will discuss this test in more detail and explore some of the controversy over intelligence testing of schoolchildren.)

Wechsler Preschool and Primary Scale of Intelligence

The *Wechsler Preschool and Primary Scale of Intelligence, Revised (WPPSI-R),* an hour-long individual test used with children aged 3 to 7, yields separate scores for verbal and performance items as well as a combined score. Its separate scales are similar to those in the Wechsler Intelligence Scale for Children (WISC-III), discussed in Chapter 8. The 1989 revision includes a number of new subtests and has new picture items. It too has been restandardized on a sample of children representing the population of preschool-age children in the United States. Because children of this age tire quickly and are easily distracted, the test may be given in two separate sessions.

The "Zone of Proximal Development"

A form of testing that has become popular in Russia and is now influencing testing in the United States is based on the theory of the psychologist Vygotsky (1978). He argues that all higher planning and organizing functions in cognitive development appear twice: first as the result of interaction with other people, usually adults, and then after the child has internalized what the adults have taught.

First, adults have to direct and organize a child's learning. They do this most effectively in what Vygotsky calls the *zone of proximal development (ZPD).* Children in this "zone" for a particular task can almost—but not completely—perform the task on their own. ("proximal" means "near"). With the right kind of teaching, they can accomplish it successfully. A good teacher seeks out a child's ZPD and helps the child learn within it. The adult then gradually gives less support until the child can perform the task unaided.

Vygotsky (1956) gives an example of two children, both with a mental age of 7 years (based on their ability to do various cognitive tasks). With the help of leading questions, examples, and demonstrations, Natasha can easily solve test items taken from 2 years above her level of actual development. But Ivan, with the same kind of help from an adult, can solve test items only half a year above his level of actual development. If you measure these children by what they can do on their own, their mental development is about the same. But if you measure them from their immediate potential development, they are quite different. In other words, Natasha and Ivan have different ZPDs.

To take stock, then, not only of completed stages of development but also of those in the process of developing, testers using the ZPD approach give children test items up to 2 years above their level of actual development. They help them to answer the items by asking leading questions and giving examples. The testers can then find the child's current ZPD, or level of potential development. This tells more about a child's potential than does a traditional test score.

Parents' Influence on Children's Intelligence

How well children do on intelligence tests is influenced by many factors, including their temperament, their genes, the match between their cognitive style and the tasks they are asked to do, their social and emotional maturity, their ease or unease in the testing situation, and their socioeconomic status and ethnic background. (We'll examine the last two factors in Chapter 8.) One of the most important influences of all is a child's parents.

A home full of books and toys is a key factor in this boy's intellectual growth. Parents who provide an enriched environment for learning are most likely to have children with high IQs. *(Gregory K. Scott/Photo Researchers)*

Providing an Environment for Learning

Do parents who raise bright children do something special? On the basis of many studies (A. Clarke-Stewart, 1977), we can draw a picture of the parents of young children who score high on intelligence tests and whose scores *increase* in early childhood. Parents can help their children grow intellectually in a number of ways.

Parents of children with higher scores are often sensitive, warm, and loving. They are very accepting of their children's behavior, letting them express themselves and explore. When they want to change a child's behavior, they often use reasoning or appeals to feelings rather than enforcing rigid rules. They use relatively sophisticated language and teaching strategies, and they encourage their children's independence, creativity, and growth by reading to them, teaching them to do things, and playing with them. The children respond by showing curiosity and creativity, exploring new situations, and doing well in school. The findings from studies using HOME (discussed in Chapter 4) showed that the children of parents who were responsive to them and who provided stimulating play materials tended to earn higher intelligence scores. Apparently, parents who pro-

vide challenging, pleasurable learning opportunities for the child can lay a foundation for optimum intellectual growth.

"Scaffolding"

The metaphor of scaffolds—temporary platforms where building workers stand—has been applied to a way of teaching children based on the concept of ZPD (Wood, 1980; Wood, Bruner, & Ross, 1976). *Scaffolding* is the temporary support that parents give a child to do a task. There is an inverse relationship between the child's current ability and the amount of support needed. In other words, the less ability a child has in doing a task, the more direction the parent should give; and the more ability the child has, the less direction the parent should give. As the child becomes able to do more and more, the parent helps less and less. Once the job is done, the parent takes away the temporary support—or scaffold—that is no longer needed.

In one study of scaffolding, parents worked with their 3-year-old children on three difficult tasks: copying a model made of blocks; classifying by size, color, and shape; and having the children retell a story they had heard. Both mothers and fathers tended to be guided by their child's level of competence. Parents gave more help when children had more trouble. Furthermore, the parents became more sensitive to their children's needs later in the experiment than they had been at first. This sensitivity was important, because the more finely tuned the parents' help was, the better a child did (Pratt, Kerig, Cowan, & Cowan, 1988).

The Father's Role

Most studies have concentrated on the mother's role in children's intellectual development, but research also shows the father's impact. The father influences his children through how he feels and acts toward them, the kind of relationship he has with their mother, and his position in the family. Probably because of sons' identification with their fathers (see Chapter 7), fathers influence their sons more than their daughters. As boys take on their fathers' attitudes, values, roles, gestures, and emotional reactions, they also pick up their fathers' styles of thinking, their problem-solving strategies—even the very words they use. Boys are especially likely to imitate fathers who are nurturant and approving and who are seen as strong but do not dominate or intimidate (Radin, 1981).

In one study, the preschool sons of alcoholic fathers did more poorly than a control group on a number of measures: fine motor tasks, language, and adaptive and personal and social abilities (Noll, Zucker, Fitzgerald, & Curtis, 1992). This may be because the quality of cognitive, social, and emotional stimulation in homes with an alcoholic father is deficient. Or other factors, possibly hereditary ones, may have caused both the sons' deficits on the tests and the fathers' alcoholism. In either case, these boys represent a population at risk.

A father's influence on his daughter seems to be more complex, but girls whose fathers show interest in their intellectual development and encourage independence seem to develop best. Neither boys nor girls develop as well intellectually when their fathers are strict, dogmatic, and authoritarian (Radin, 1981).

What happens when there is no father in the home? The father's absence seems to inhibit children's cognitive development. A mother's reaction to a father's absence is likely to affect her child's response. So will any changes in the family's financial situation. Economic hardship—often a direct result of loss of the father—can handicap children's development in many ways.

However, much of the research on the father's absence was done when single-parent families were rarer than they are today. Now that this lifestyle is more common, some of its disadvantages, like social stigma and the lack of male models and other support systems, may be diminishing. Sometimes a supportive stepfather, an older brother, a grandfather, or an uncle helps make up for the lack of a father.

The Mother's Role: When Mothers Are Employed

What happens when the mother works outside the home—as more than half of mothers of babies under 1 year of age now do in the United States? Overall, the cognitive, social, and emotional development of preschool children seems at least as good when mothers are employed as when they are not (L. W. Hoffman, 1989; Zimmerman & Bernstein, 1983).

Some research suggests that mothers' employment has a gender-related influence. Daughters of working mothers tend to be more independent and to have a more positive attitude toward being female than daughters of mothers who are at home (Bronfenbrenner, Alvarez, & Henderson, 1984). Other research has found that middle-class boys—but not girls, and not boys in lower-income families—do worse in school when the mother works, especially if she worked full time during their preschool years (D. Gold & Andres, 1978b; D. Gold, Andres, & Glorieux, 1979).

What accounts for these differences? Interviews with 152 parents of 3-year-olds suggest a possible explanation: children's intellectual development may be affected by the way their parents view them. Working parents—when the mother is well educated and works full-time—are likely to regard young girls more positively than young boys. Both mothers and fathers praised girls as competent and self-reliant but described boys as disobedient and aggressive. The parents' attitudes may reflect professional women's aspirations for their daughters as well as boys' tendency to be more active and to need more supervision and control, which may cause extra stress for the parents (Bronfenbrenner et al., 1984; L. W. Hoffman, 1989).

Parents' view of a child—and thus, arguably, the child's intellectual progress—may be influenced by the mother's attitude toward her role. Both husbands and wives described their 3-year-olds (of both sexes) less favorably when a mother worked out of necessity rather than choice and when she felt conflict between demands of work and home. This was particularly true for women with little education who worked full-time. The more positive attitudes of mothers who worked part-time toward both sons and daughters may reflect the fact that balancing work and child care was easier for them (Alvarez, 1985; L. W. Hoffman, 1989).

We have to be careful in interpreting such results, however. Although the attitudes the parents expressed toward their sons and daughters seem to mesh with the earlier findings about differences in boys' and girls' development when mothers work, the studies did not prove a link; further investigation is needed. (We will discuss gender-role differences more fully in Chapter 7 and the effects of both parents' work in Chapter 9.)

THE WIDENING ENVIRONMENT

As important as parents are in a young child's life, they are far from the only influence. Today more young children than ever spend part or most of the day in preschool, day care, or kindergarten.

PRESCHOOL AND DAY CARE

The difference between preschool and day care lies in their primary purpose. Preschool emphasizes educational experiences geared to children's developmental needs, typically in sessions of only 2 hours or so. Day care provides a safe place where children can be cared for, usually all day, while parents are at work or school. But the distinction has blurred: good day care centers seek to meet children's intellectual and emotional needs, and many preschools offer longer days in response to the growing number of families in which a single parent or both parents work outside the home.

One reason for the rapid growth of day care has been a scarcity of affordable preschools. Although preschools have flourished in the United States since 1919, when the first public nursery schools were established, many privately run preschools serve mainly well-educated, affluent families.

Today, however, more and more public schools are moving into preschool education. As a result, preschool enrollment has grown dramatically since 1970. Another sign of the acceptance of preschool as an important aid in children's development is the great expansion throughout the country of free preschool programs for disabled 3- to 5-year-olds, in recognition that early intervention can make a major difference in these children's lives (Hinds, 1991).

How Good Preschools Foster Development

When Sally's daughter Jenny was 4 years old, she broke her leg in a sledding accident. But 2 weeks later, still in her cast, she was back in school finger painting, building block towers, and making paper placemats. She went to a good preschool— and she did not want to miss anything.

A good preschool helps children learn and grow in many ways, and is fun as well. Autonomy flour-

ishes as children explore a world outside the home and choose from among many activities tailored to their interests and abilities. From their successes they build confidence and self-image. Preschool is particularly valuable in helping children from one- or two-child families (like most families today) learn how to get along with other children.

Some preschools stress social and emotional growth. Others, like those based on the theories of Piaget or the Italian educator Maria Montessori, have a stronger cognitive emphasis. To assess preschool programs for 4- and 5-year-olds, the National Association for the Education of Young Children (NAEYC) drew up a list of appropriate and inappropriate classroom practices (see Table 6-4).

Over the past decade, pressures have built to offer more formal education in preschool. The rising demand for day care, the recognition of the "head start" obtained by disadvantaged children in compensatory programs, the numbers of teachers put out of work by declining school enrollments, and the growing desire among parents to give their children a leg up on the educational ladder have all combined to bring the three R's into nursery school. Many educators and psychologists, however, maintain that the only children who benefit from early schooling are those from disadvantaged families—and that most middle-class children are better served by a relaxed preschool experience (see Box 6-5).

One study compared children who had been enrolled in a heavily academic preschool with children from more relaxed (traditional) preschools. In the early grades the children from the academic

Not every preschooler wants to do the same thing at the same time. Preschool provides a certain level of individual freedom, while it helps children grow in many ways—physically, intellectually, socially, and emotionally. *(K. B. Kaplan/ The Picture Cube)*

TABLE 6-4

Integrated Components of Appropriate and Inappropriate Practice for 4- and 5-Year-Old Children

Component	Appropriate Practice	Inappropriate Practice
Curriculum Goals	Experiences are provided that meet children's needs and stimulate learning in all developmental areas–physical, social, emotional, and intellectual.	Experiences are narrowly focused on the child's intellectual development without recognition that all areas of a child's development are interrelated.
	Each child is viewed as a unique person with an individual pattern and timing of growth and development. The curriculum and adults' interaction are responsive to individual differences in ability and interests. Different levels of ability, development, and learning styles are expected, accepted, and used to design appropriate activities.	Children are evaluated only against a predetermined measure, such as a standardized group norm or adult standard of behavior. All are expected to perform the same tasks and achieve the same narrowly defined, easily measured skills.
	Interactions and activities are designed to develop children's self-esteem and positive feelings toward learning.	Children's worth is measured by how well they conform to rigid expectations and perform on standardized tests.
Teaching Strategies	Teachers prepare the environment for children to learn through active exploration and interaction with adults, other children, and materials.	Teachers use highly structured, teacher-directed lessons almost exclusively.
	Children select many of their own activities from among a variety of learning areas the teacher prepares, including dramatic play, blocks, science, math, games, and puzzles, books, recordings, art, and music.	The teacher directs all the activity, deciding what children will do and when. The teacher does most of the activity for the children, such as cutting shapes, performing steps in an experiment.
	Children are expected to be physically and mentally active. Children choose from among activities the teacher has set up or the children spontaneously initiate.	Children are expected to sit down, watch, be quiet, and listen, or do paper-and-pencil tasks for inappropriately long periods of time. A major portion of time is spent passively sitting, listening, and waiting.
	Children work individually or in small, informal groups most of the time.	Large group, teacher-directed instruction is used most of the time.
	Children are provided concrete learning activities with materials and people relevant to their own life experiences.	Workbooks, ditto sheets, flashcards, and other similarly structured abstract materials dominate the curriculum.
	Teachers move among groups and individuals to facilitate children's involvement with materials and activities by asking questions, offering suggestions, or adding more complex materials or ideas to a situation.	Teachers dominate the environment by talking to the whole group most of the time and telling children what to do.
	Teachers accept that there is often more than one right answer. Teachers recognize that children learn from self-directed problem solving and experimentation.	Children are expected to respond correctly with one right answer. Rote memorization and drill are emphasized.

(continued)

TABLE 6-4   (Continued)

Integrated Components of Appropriate and Inappropriate Practice for 4- and 5-Year-Old Children

Component	Appropriate Practice	Inappropriate Practice
Guidance of socioemotional development	Teachers facilitate the development of self-control in children by using positive guidance techniques such as modeling and encouraging expected behavior, redirecting children to a more acceptable activity, and setting clear limits. Teachers' expectations match and respect children's developing capabilities.	Teachers spend a great deal of time enforcing rules, punishing unacceptable behavior, demeaning children who misbehave, making children sit and be quiet, or refereeing disagreements.
	Children are provided many opportunities to develop social skills such as cooperating, helping, negotiating, and talking with the person involved to solve interpersonal problems. Teachers facilitate the development of these positive social skills at all times.	Children work individually at desks or tables most of the time or listen to teacher directions in the total group. Teachers intervene to resolve disputes or enforce classroom rules and schedules.
Language development and literacy	Children are provided many opportunities to see how reading and writing are useful before they are instructed in letter names, sounds, and word identification. Basic skills develop when they are meaningful to children. An abundance of these types of activities is provided to develop language and literacy through meaningful experience: listening to and reading stories and poems; taking field trips; dictating stories; seeing classroom charts and other print in use; participating in dramatic play and other experiences requiring communication; talking informally with other children and adults; and experimenting with writing by drawing, copying, and inventing their own spelling.	Reading and writing instruction stresses isolated skill development such as recognizing single letters, reciting the alphabet, singing the alphabet song, coloring within predefined lines, or being instructed in correct formation of letters on a printed line.

SOURCE: National Association for the Education of Young Children,

preschool did better, but 10 years later the boys from the traditional preschools did better in reading and mathematics than boys from the academic preschool. The girls from the academic school did better in reading, but not in mathematics (L. B. Miller & Bizzel, 1983). Although children may learn more in the short term, an early academic emphasis may have a negative impact on their interest in learning or their ability to learn over the long run.

Another study found that children who had gone to a traditional preschool did as well in kindergarten as those who had attended more academic programs. Furthermore, children from academically accelerated preschools were more anxious when taking tests, less creative, and more negative about school than those who went to low-key preschools (Hirsh-Pasek, 1991; Hirsh-Pasek, Hyson, & Rescorla, 1989).

The most important contribution of preschool may well be the feeling children get there: that school is fun, that learning is satisfying, and that they are competent in a school setting. The answer to "What makes a good preschool?" depends on the values of particular cultures, which vary considerably, as Box 6-6 shows.

BOX 6-5   *TAKE A STAND*

SHOULD PRESCHOOL BE ABOUT THE THREE R'S?

Brandi has been writing in her diary for two years, sometimes in English, sometimes in Japanese. She began playing the violin at 13 months, and at the age of 5, jogs 2.5 miles a day (Slevin, 1986). Brandi is one of a number of children whose parents have taken part in a program that extends academic education down into the cradle (Doman, 1979, 1984). These parents teach babies as young as 1 year how to read, do math, and understand a foreign language; they continue to teach them skills usually considered much too difficult for preschoolers.

Efforts like these, which came into prominence in the early 1960s, coincided with a mounting body of research showing that infants and young children are much more competent than they had previously been thought to be. In an increasingly competitive world, some parents and educators believe that children should learn as much as they can, as soon as they can. This philosophy is most often carried out in preschools that emphasize teaching children the rudiments of reading, arithmetic, and other subjects usually taught in elementary school. But other child-care professionals express strong opinions about the folly, and even the danger, of teaching children academic skills before they enter first grade. Here are some of the arguments on both sides.

IN FAVOR OF EARLY ACADEMICS

1 The learning curve in the first few years of life is greater than

it will ever be again. We should take advantage of children's natural enthusiasm and curiosity and teach them what they're capable of learning, as soon as possible.

2 When we don't teach children material that they are capable of learning, we thwart children's natural tendencies, artificially retard their cognitive development, and prevent them from fulfilling their intellectual potential.

3 The ability to acquire language is particularly keen in early childhood, and this ability diminishes, certainly by puberty. We should capitalize on this "window of opportunity."

4 Teaching children to read at an early age enhances their natural ability and can produce intellectual superiority later in life. This has been especially impressive in compensatory preschool programs for disadvantaged children. If these children can benefit so much, why not offer the same kind of advantage to all children?

5 Children who read early do not have any more learning problems than children who learn later; in fact, they tend to have fewer, if the teaching is done in a sensitive, nonpressured way (Doman, 1979; 1984).

AGAINST EARLY ACADEMICS

1 Children who do not learn the knowledge and skills being taught right away may think of themselves as "stupid," be-

come more anxious about learning situations, and learn to hate school.

2 Giving children chances to engage in conversation does more to help them develop such basic language skills as communicating, expressing themselves, and reasoning than just exposing them to language (Katz, 1987).

3 It is more important for children to follow their own interests in these early years than to be pushed to learn things that they don't care about. If parents and teachers reward them too much for learning, they become more interested in the rewards and less interested in the tasks (Katz, 1987).

4 Following too academic a curriculum tends to stifle the creativity of young children (Hirsh-Pasek, 1991)

5 The most important skill that children need to learn is how to get along with other people. If they can do this, they will have a great asset that will serve them throughout life.

6 The business of childhood is play. Even though children are capable of learning many facts and skills at very early ages, the first few years of life are better spent in the kind of relaxed learning that comes through play.

What kind of preschool experience do *you* think is better for children?

BOX 6-6 WINDOW ON THE WORLD

PRESCHOOLS IN THREE CULTURES

It is morning in a Japanese preschool. After a half-hour workbook session—lively with talk, laughter, and playful fighting among the children—twenty-eight 4-year-olds sing in unison (in Japanese): "As I sit here with my lunch, I think of Mom. I bet it's delicious; I wonder what she's made?" The children speak freely, loudly, even vulgarly to each other for much of the day, but then have periods of formal, teacher-directed group recitations of polite expressions of greeting, thanks, and blessings.

In a Chinese preschool, twenty-six 4-year-olds sing a cheerful song about a train, acting out the words by hooking onto each other's backs and chugging around the room. They then sit down and for the next 20 minutes follow their teacher's direction to put together blocks, copying pictures she has handed out. They work in an orderly way, and their errors are corrected as the session proceeds. The teacher has taught the children to recite long pieces and sing complicated songs, emphasizing enunciation, diction, and self-confidence, but she discourages spontaneous talk as a possible distraction from work.

The eighteen 4-year-olds at an American preschool begin their day with a show-and-tell session in which they speak individually. Then they all sing a song about monkeys. For the next 45 minutes, they separate into groups for different activities, including painting, blocks, puzzles, a housekeeping corner, and listening to a story. The teacher moves around the room, talking with the children about their activities, mediating fights,

and keeping order. She encourages children to express their own feelings and opinions, helps them learn new words to express concepts, and corrects their speech.

What makes a good preschool? Your answer to this question depends on what you regard as the ideal child, the ideal adult, and the ideal society. How schools reflect such values shows up in a comparison between preschools in Japan, China, and the United States (Tobin, Wu, & Davidson, 1989). This wide-ranging study involved videotaping preschool activities in the three countries; showing the tapes and discussing them with parents and educators; and asking 750 preschool teachers, administrators, parents, and child development specialists to fill out questionnaires. The classroom activities were consistent with the opinions expressed in the questionnaires from each cultural group. (Excerpts from the questionnaire data are given in Table 6-5.)

At a time when many American educators worry about a trend for preschools to teach children about science, computers, and foreign languages, as well as reading and arithmetic, it is noteworthy that one of the biggest differences was the importance given to the teaching of actual subject matter. Over 50 percent of the Americans who answered the questionnaires listed "to give children a good start academically" as one of their top three reasons for a society to have preschools. But only 2 percent of the Japanese gave this reason, since the Japanese tend to see preschools as a haven, before the academic pressure and competition

that children will face in the years to come.

Japanese preschoolers are encouraged to develop more basic skills like concentration and the ability to function in a group, which will help them learn academic subjects later on. Teachers cultivate perseverance, for example, by refusing to help children dress and undress themselves.

The Chinese, however, emphasized academics even more than the Americans: 67 percent gave this reason. Their emphasis on early learning seems to have several sources: the Confucian tradition of early, strenuous study; the Cultural Revolution, which discouraged frivolous play and stressed such productive skills as reading, writing, working with numbers, and clear speaking; and the desire of parents to compensate through their children for their own disrupted educations. This early stress on academics is controversial, though, and a less academically oriented preschool curriculum is becoming more popular, especially among child development specialists.

By and large, then, although preschoolers in all three cultures do many of the same activities, China stresses academic instruction, Japan stresses play, and the United States presents a mixed picture. But in all three countries, parents often pressure preschools to give their children a strong educational start so that they will achieve prominent positions in the society. It would be interesting to follow today's children to find out whether those who work harder at ages 3 or 4 or 5 do in fact achieve more as adults.

TABLE 6-5

Cultural Attitudes Toward Preschools in China, Japan, and the United States

Question 1: What Are the Most Important Things for Children to Learn in Preschool?

Top 3 answers in each country
China:
1 Good health, hygiene, and grooming habits
2 Cooperation and how to be a member of a group
3 Creativity

Japan:
1 Sympathy, empathy, concern for others
2 Cooperation and how to be a member of a group
3 Good health, hygiene, and grooming habits

United States:
1 Self-reliance, self-confidence
2 Cooperation and how to be a member of a group
3 Sympathy, empathy, concern for others

Question 2: Why Should a Society Have Preschools?

Top 3 answers in each country
China:
1 To give children a good start academically*
2 To make young children more independent and self-reliant*
3 To free parents for work and other pursuits

Japan:
1 To give children experience being a member of a group
2 To make young children more independent and self-reliant
3 To give children a chance to play with other children

United States:
1 To make young children more independent and self-reliant
2 To give children experience being a member of a group
3 To give children a good start academically

Note: The two items marked with an asterisk were tied for first place.
SOURCE: Tobin, Wu, & Davidson, 1989.

Montessori Preschools

A remarkably successful system, designed originally by Dr. Maria Montessori to teach poor and retarded Italian children, spread rapidly in the United States during the 1960s, when Montessori schools became popular with affluent parents.

Recently, public school administrators have turned to this approach because so many of its tenets coincide with proposals for reforming schools to help disadvantaged children.

The Montessori curriculum is child-centered, based on respect for the child's natural abilities. It focuses on motor, sensory, and language education. Children enter a "prepared environment," a carefully planned arrangement of surroundings, equipment, and materials in which they advance at their own pace in a graduated sequence from the simple to the complex. Preschoolers learn from their own experiences, with the guidance, support, and help of skilled teachers. Students select their own materials, which are designed so that they can tell whether they are using them correctly. The method aims to foster moral development by emphasizing order, patience, self-control, responsibility, and cooperation.

Compensatory Preschool Programs

Children from deprived socioeconomic backgrounds often enter school with a considerable handicap. Since the 1960s, large-scale programs have been developed to help such disadvantaged children compensate for the experiences they have missed and to prepare them for school.

Project Head Start

The best-known compensatory preschool program in the United States is *Project Head Start.* It was developed in 1965 as a major weapon in the federal government's war against poverty. Its goal is to improve the lives of children of low-income families by providing health care, intellectual enrichment, and a supportive environment. Today, some 30 years later, Project Head Start has provided services to over 8 million children and their families. Still, it reaches a relatively small proportion of poor 3- and 4-year-olds.

Has Head Start lived up to its name? Head Start children have shown substantial intellectual and language gains, with the neediest children benefiting most. One reason why Head Start children do as well as they do in school is that they are absent less than other youngsters from impoverished homes. They are healthier, are more likely to be of average height and weight, and do better on tests of motor control and physical development. Still, Head Start children have not equaled the average middle-class child in performance in school or on standardized tests (R. C. Collins & Deloria, 1983).

The most successful Head Start programs have been those with the most participation by parents, the best teachers, the smallest groups, and the most extensive services. Benefits have often gone beyond the children themselves; families report educational and financial gains and an increased sense of satisfaction with and control over their lives.

Long-term Benefits of Compensatory Preschool Education

Children enrolled in good compensatory preschool programs show long-lasting gains that repay society's initial investment. While increases in IQ scores have been short-lived, some positive effects of Head Start have held up through high school. Head Start students are less likely than other needy children to be held back and more likely to stay in school and to be in regular rather than special classes (L. B. Miller & Bizzel, 1983).

A number of studies have found long-term benefits for children enrolled in high-quality compensatory preschool programs, which incorporated many special services like those in Head Start (Darlington, 1991; Haskins, 1989). Children who had preschool education were less likely than those who had no formal schooling until kindergarten or first grade to need special education for slow learners. They were also much more likely at age 19 to have finished high school, to have enrolled in college or vocational training, and to have jobs. They did better on tests of competence and were less likely to have been arrested, and the women were less likely to have become pregnant (Berrueta-Clement, Schweinhart, Barnett, Epstein, & Weikart, 1985; Haskins, 1989).

But a warning against too strong an academic emphasis in preschool came from one longitudinal study that compared low-income youngsters from three different types of preschool programs (Schweinhart, Weikart, & Larner, 1986). One program stressed social and emotional development and activities initiated by the child; the second was highly structured, emphasizing the teaching of numbers, letters, and words; and the third took a middle ground. Children from all three programs did better in elementary school than children with no preschool experience. The children from the academic program narrowly outperformed the others—but they had more behavior problems. And by 15 years of age, many had lost interest in school and developed serious social and emotional problems, such as vandalism and delinquency.

It seems, then, that early childhood education can help to compensate for deprivation and that well-planned programs produce long-term benefits that exceed their original cost (Haskins, 1989). However, we need to keep in mind the developmental needs of young children for play, exploration, and freedom from undue demands—and we need to look closely at particular programs. Today, similar questions are being raised about the benefits of different kinds of education for 5-year-olds.

KINDERGARTEN

The typical 5-year-old gets a preview of "real school" when she or he attends kindergarten, a traditional introduction to formal schooling, often situated in a neighborhood public school. Historically, kindergarten has been a year of transition between the relative freedom of home or preschool and the structure of the primary grades. Since the 1970s, it has become more like first grade.

In fact, the pressures that have made preschools more academically oriented filtered down from kindergarten, where today many children spend less time on freely chosen activities that stretch their muscles and imaginations, and more time on worksheets and learning to read (Egertson, 1987).

Many kindergartners now spend a full day in school rather than the traditional half day. Results of studies on the effects of all-day kindergarten are mixed (Robertson, 1984; Rust, in Connecticut Early Childhood Education Council, [CECEC], 1983). Advocates of full-day kindergarten stress its longer blocks of uninterrupted time for unhurried experiences and educational activities; its greater opportunities for pupil-teacher and parent-teacher contact, since a teacher is responsible for one rather than two classes; teachers' and childrens' higher energy levels, resulting from a structured morning start and a more relaxed afternoon. Opponents believe that some 5-year-olds cannot handle a 6-hour day and a long separation from their parents and point to a danger of overemphasizing academic skills and sedentary activities.

Some educators and psychologists express alarm over "treating kindergarten like a miniature elementary school with a heavy cognitive-academic orientation" (Zigler, 1987, p. 258). Furthermore, they caution against sending children to kindergarten too early, pointing to studies showing the "age effect"—that the youngest children in a class do more poorly than the oldest (Sweetland & DeSimone, 1987). One alternative is a half-day kindergarten program taught by licensed, qualified teachers, followed by a half-day of care given by certified caregivers to children who need day care (Zigler, 1987). This gives some academic preparation and also all-day supervision for those who need it.

We know that many 5-year-olds—and even some younger children—can be taught that 2 times 2 equals 4, just as we know that 9-month-old infants can be taught to recognize words printed on flash cards. But unless motivation comes from the children themselves, and unless learning arises naturally from their experiences, their time might be better spent on the business of early childhood. Young children need concrete sensory activities that help them make sense of their world. They also need a widening network of social interactions that, as we'll see in Chapter 7, help them define their emerging identity.

SUMMARY

PHYSICAL GROWTH AND CHANGE

- Physical growth increases during the years from 3 to 6, but more slowly than during infancy and toddlerhood. Boys are on average slightly taller and heavier than girls.
- The muscular, skeletal, nervous, respiratory, circulatory, and immune systems are maturing, and all primary teeth are present.
- Proper growth and health depend on nutrition. Children eat less than before and need a balanced diet.

HEALTH

- Minor illnesses help build immunity to disease and may also have cognitive and emotional benefits.
- Major contagious illnesses are rare when children receive vaccinations. Respiratory diseases are the major cause of death in infants and children worldwide.
- Accidents, the leading cause of death in childhood in the United States, are most common in cars, at home, or at day care.
- Factors such as exposure to other children, stress in the home, poverty, homelessness, and hunger increase children's risk of illness or injury.

SLEEP: PATTERNS AND PROBLEMS

- Sleep patterns change during early childhood. Young children tend to sleep through the night, take one daytime nap, and sleep more deeply than later in life.
- It is normal for children close to age 5 to develop bedtime rituals that delay going to sleep. However, prolonged bedtime struggles and nighttime fears may indicate emotional disturbances that need attention.
- Night terrors, nightmares, sleepwalking, and sleep-talking may appear in early childhood.
- Bed-wetting is common, especially at night. It is a cause for concern when it occurs at least twice a month after age 5.

MOTOR SKILLS

- Motor development advances rapidly during early childhood. Children progress in gross- and fine motor skills and eye-hand coordination.

- By the time they are 6 years old, children can tend to many of their own personal needs.

ASPECTS OF INTELLECTUAL DEVELOPMENT

- Studies of memory development indicate that recognition ability is better than recall ability in early childhood, but both increase during this period. Recall is required for the processing and use of information. Children's memory is influenced by mastery motivation, study strategies, general knowledge, unusual activities, and social interactions.
- According to Piaget, the child is in the preoperational stage of cognitive development from approximately 2 years to 7 years of age. Because of the development of recall, thought is not limited to events in the immediate evironment as in the sensorimotor stage. But the child cannot yet think logically as in the next stage, concrete operations.
- The symbolic function—as shown in deferred imitation, symbolic play, and language—enables children to mentally represent and reflect upon people, objects, and events.
- Preoperational children can understand basic functional relationships and the concept of identity. However, they confuse reality and fantasy, they are unable to decenter, they reason transductively, and they do not understand reversibility and the implications of transformations. They are unable to conserve.
- Research shows that in some ways, Piaget may have underestimated abilities of the children he described as "preoperational." They seem better able to understand causal relationships and classification than he thought, and they appear to be less animistic and egocentric. Researchers have been able to teach conservation when children are mature enough to grasp it.
- During early childhood, speech and grammar become fairly sophisticated. Speech is of two main types: social and private.

  1 Social speech is intended to communicate with others. Piaget characterized much of early speech as egocentric, but recent research indicates that young children engage in social speech more than was previously thought.

2   Private speech—children's talking aloud to themselves—is not intended to communicate but appears to help children gain control over their actions. It usually disappears by age 9 or 10.

▪ Since psychometric intelligence tests for young children (such as the Stanford-Binet Intelligence Scale and Wechsler Preschool and Primary Scale of Intelligence) include verbal items, they are better predictors of later IQ than infant tests.

▪ Test developers must provide standardized norms as well as insure that tests are valid and reliable.

▪ According to Vygotsky, the zone of proximal development (ZPD) for a task is the "zone" in which children *almost* perform the task successfully alone. With help, they can perform it successfully.

▪ Parents have a major influence on intelligence test performance. Scaffolding refers to the temporary support parents give to help children do a task.

THE WIDENING ENVIRONMENT

▪ Many children between 3 and 6 years of age attend day care centers, preschools, and kindergartens. Some of these programs are changing to meet the needs of working parents as well as children's intellectual and other developmental needs.

▪ Preschools and kindergartens prepare children for formal schooling. Some programs focus more on structured cognitive tasks, others on activities initiated by the children. Since the 1970's, the academic content of early childhood education programs has increased.

▪ Evaluations of compensatory preschool programs, such as Project Head Start, demonstrate that they can have long-term positive outcomes. However, it is important not to put too much academic pressure on young children.

KEY TERMS

transitional objects (page 208)
enuresis (208)
gross motor skills (209)
fine motor skills (209)
recognition (212)
recall (212)
preoperational stage (214)
symbolic function (214)
symbol (214)
deferred imitation (214)
symbolic play (214)

centration (215)
decenter (215)
conservation (215)
irreversibility (215)
transduction (217)
egocentrism (217)
animism (218)
social speech (223)
private speech (223)
intelligence quotient (IQ) tests (224)
standardized norms (224)

valid (224)
reliable (224)
Stanford-Binet Intelligence Scale (225)
Wechsler Preschool and Primary Scale of Intelligence (WPPSI-R) (225)
zone of proximal development (ZPD) (225)
scaffolding (226)
Project Head Start (233)

SUGGESTED READINGS

Beardsley, L. (1990). *Good day bad day: The child's experience of child care.* New York: Teachers College Press, Columbia University. The author introduces a group of fictional preschool-age children and contrasts their experiences through a hypothetical day in each of two very different child care situations. Although fictional, it is based on real observations on good and poor-quality day care settings.

Beckman, P. J., & Beckman Boyes, G. (1993). *Deciphering the system: A guide for families of young children with disabilities.* Cambridge, MA: Brookline. This comprehensive guide provides basic information about parents' rights under recent legislation affecting young children with disabilities, including the Individuals with Disabilities Education Act. It will take you through the service system, telling you what to expect from the educational assessment process, how to work with multiple service providers, and how to set up due process meetings. You'll also find a resource list and a glossary to help you understand professional jargon.

Ingersoll, B. D., & Goldstein, S. (1993). *Attention deficit disorder and learning disabilities.* New York: Doubleday. This book helps sort out the realities and myths of treatments for ADD and learning disabilities. The authors discuss established as well as "alternative" treatments, focusing on the latest evidence from scientific studies.

Leach, P. (1990). *Your baby and child from birth to age 5.* New York: Knopf. A *very* comprehensive book on child care, encompassing physical, cognitive, and emotional development in the first five years of a child's life.

Schorr, L., & Schorr, D. (1988). *Within our reach—Breaking the cycle of disadvantage.* New York: Doubleday. An optimistic book describing how the cycle of disadvantage can be turned around by large-scale social programs for children.

Tobin, J. J., Wu, D. W. H., & Davidson, D. H. (1991). *Preschool in three cultures: Japan, China, and the United States.* New Haven: Yale University Press. A thought-provoking study of preschools in three countries shows that the Japanese, Chinese, and Americans have very different ideas about how to train children for their future roles in society.

Treiber, P. M. (1993). *Keys to dealing with stuttering.* Hauppague, NY: Barron's. The latest research is summarized to help parents understand and manage a child's stuttering, helping the child at home and at school.

Webber, J. (1993). *Children's medications guide book.* Englewood Cliffs, NJ: Prentice-Hall. A mother and pharmacist is the author of this guide for parents who want to know more about the medications that are prescribed for their children and about nonprescription medications. Provides information on use, dosage, precautions, and side effects.

Wilson, M. H., Baker, S. P., Teret, S. P., Shock, S., and Garbarino, J. (1991). *Saving children: A guide to injury prevention.* New York: Oxford University Press. This comprehensive book, written by a team of safety experts affiliated with the Johns Hopkins Injury Prevention Center, takes a developmental approach to understanding the reasons why children of different ages become injured. It focuses on preventing injuries in three key environments: the street, the home, and the school and play areas.

CHAPTER SEVEN

PERSONALITY AND SOCIAL DEVELOPMENT IN EARLY CHILDHOOD

*Children's playings are not sports and should
be deemed as their most serious actions.*

Montaigne,
Essays

■ **IMPORTANT PERSONALITY
DEVELOPMENTS IN EARLY CHILDHOOD**

Initiative versus Guilt
Identification
Gender Identity

■ **ASPECTS AND ISSUES OF PERSONALITY
DEVELOPMENT**

Gender
Fears
Aggression
Altruism: Prosocial Behavior

Child-Rearing Practices
Relating to Other Children
Play

■ **BOXES**

7-1 Practically Speaking: Guiding Children's
Television Viewing
7-2 Window on the World: A Nation of Only
Children
7-3 Practically Speaking: Helping Young
Children to Make Friends
7-4 Food for Thought: Imaginary Playmates

- How do various theories explain important personality developments of early childhood?
- How do boys and girls identify their sex, and how does this identification affect their personalities and standards of behavior?
- What accounts for common fears in early childhood, and what can be done about them?
- What makes young children act aggressively or altruistically?

- How do parents' child-rearing practices influence young children's personality development?
- How do young children get along with their siblings, and how do they begin to form friendships?
- What kinds of play do children engage in?

At 5 years of age, Anna usually gets along very well with her friend Danielle as they build with wooden blocks or pretend to fix hot dogs for lunch. They do fight sometimes, though; one day Anna took Danielle's pail and shovel, and Danielle threw sand in Anna's face. On another day Danielle was crying; Anna said, "Danielle is upset," and kissed her "best friend." Danielle is an important presence in Anna's life. As they play and talk, and even as they fight, it is apparent how they have changed since infancy and toddlerhood. "They're becoming real people," Anna's father says.

What does it mean to become a real person? It means that Anna is developing a sense of herself as someone different from Danielle or anyone else, with her own traits, her own likes and dislikes, and her own ideas about what she wants to do and believes she ought to do. This uniqueness did not come to Anna overnight on her third, fourth, or fifth birthday; her basic temperament, for example, showed up quite early, soon after birth. Nor is the process anywhere near complete; Anna's self-concept will continue to develop throughout life; and she will not focus on some important issues about her identity until adolescence or later.

But now, in early childhood, she has left behind the days of infantile dependence, she is coming out of the stage of saying "no" for its own sake, and she shows definite signs of her singular personality. She is also becoming a more social being, defining herself through her relationships with others.

In this chapter, we discuss several aspects of personality development in early childhood. First we see how Erik Erikson analyzes the continuing evolution of personality in the years from 3 to 6. Then we discuss some building blocks of personality. One of the most important is identification, which influences children's recognition of their own gender and also affects the degree to which they will be altruistic, aggressive, or fearful. In these years, as always, personality affects and is affected by a child's social network, including relations with parents, brothers and sisters, and playmates. We close the chapter by exploring a crucial activity of these years, one that brings together social, physical, and cognitive abilities. This is the "business" of early childhood—*play*.

IMPORTANT PERSONALITY DEVELOPMENTS IN EARLY CHILDHOOD

As Stefan, aged 5, and Sally, his grandmother, walk to a new playground, Stefan confides, "I like to hold your hand. I'm a big boy now, so I don't have to hold it, but I like to—it feels good. I like you." Once there, Stefan holds his temper when a toddler tumbles onto the sand castle he has worked on for 20 minutes, but he loses it when a little girl grabs his pail. He is brave enough to run after her, but his courage leaves him when Sally suggests that he climb to the top of the tallest slide. In this incident, as in much of his life these days, Stefan is dealing with important issues—initiative, identification and gender identity, affection, altruism, aggression, fears, and fun. The most basic concern of early childhood is the ongoing process of developing a personal identity.

INITIATIVE VERSUS GUILT

As children leave toddlerhood behind and enter early childhood, they are faced with two contradictory pressures. They *can* do more and more—and they *want* to do more and more. At the same time, they are learning that some of the things they want to do (like, say, singing a cute little song) meet social approval, while others (like taking apart Mommy's alarm clock) do not. How do they resolve their desire to do with their desire to be approved of by their parents and other important people in their lives?

According to Erik Erikson, this struggle is the basis for the third crisis of personality development, *initiative versus guilt.* This entails a conflict between the sense of purpose, or initiative, which allows a child to plan and carry out activities, and the moral reservations the child may have about such plans.

This conflict marks a split between two parts of the personality—the part that remains a *child,* full of exuberance and a desire to try new things and test new powers, and the part that is becoming an *adult,* constantly examining the propriety of motives and actions. Children who learn how to regulate these opposing drives develop the *virtue of purpose,* the courage to envision and pursue goals, without being inhibited by guilt or fear of punishment (Erikson, 1964). If this crisis is not resolved adequately, says Erikson, a child may turn into an adult who suffers from psychosomatic illness, inhibition, or impotence; who overcompensates by showing off; or who becomes self-righteous and intolerant, concerned more with prohibiting impulses than with enjoying spontaneity.

How can parents help their children strike a healthy balance between a developing sense of initiative that may lead them to overdo new things and a tendency to become too repressed and guilty? They can give children opportunities to do things on their own while protecting them with guidance and firm limits, so that they can turn out to be people who are responsible—and who also enjoy life.

IDENTIFICATION

Anna, age 5, insists on dressing in a new way, begging to wear leggings with a skirt over them, and boots, indoors and out. When Diane asks her why she wants to make this new fashion statement, Anna replies, "Because Katie dresses like this—and Katie's the king of the girls!"

Anna's interest in changing her "look" illustrates an important personality development: *identification,* a child's adoption of the character-

According to Sandra Bem's gender-schema theory, boys and girls look at their culture's gender schema and adapt their own attitudes and behavior. These children have clearly picked up a societal message that cooking and serving fit the female role, while being waited on fits the male's. *(David Young-Wolff/PhotoEdit)*

istics, beliefs, attitudes, values, and behaviors of another person or of a group.

GENDER IDENTITY

The sex we are born with is a key element of our identity. It is one of the first things people want to know about us at birth and one of the first things others notice about us throughout our lives. It affects how we look, how we move our bodies, and how we work, play, and dress. It influences what we think about ourselves and what others think of us. All those characteristics—and more—are included when we use the word *gender:* what it means to be male or female.

How do young children achieve *gender identity,* the awareness and identification of themselves as male or female? How do they develop *gender roles,* the behaviors that their society expects of males and females, as well as general standards of socially and morally correct behavior? And how do

TABLE 7-1

Four Perspectives on Gender Identification

Theory	Major Theorist	Key Process	Basic Belief
Psychoanalytic	Sigmund Freud	Emotional	Gender identification occurs at the resolution of the Oedipus (for boys) and Electra (for girls) complexes when child identifies with same-sex parent.
Social-learning	Jerome Kagan	Learning	Identification is a result of observing and imitating models and being reinforced for gender-appropriate behavior.
Cognitive-developmental	Lawrence Kohlberg	Cognitive	Once child learns she is a girl or he is a boy, child actively sorts information by gender into what girls do and what boys do, and acts accordingly.
Gender-schema	Sandra Bem	Cognitive and learning	Child organizes information about what is considered appropriate for a boy or a girl on the basis of what a particular culture dictates, and behaves accordingly. Child sorts by gender because the culture dictates that gender is an important schema.

other important aspects of personality develop? Let us see what insights several theoretical perspectives can give us (see Table 7-1).

The earliest explanation for identification—and gender identity—was the psychoanalytic theory. But the most commonly accepted current explanations for the development of gender identity are the social-learning theories of Albert Bandura, Jerome Kagan, and others, and the cognitive theories of Lawrence Kohlberg and Sandra Bem. Since all these approaches contribute to our understanding of the development of personality, we will examine each of them.

Psychoanalytic Theory

Psychoanalytic theory explained identification as the result of resolving the Oedipus or Electra conflict, both of which were named after characters in classical Greek literature. Through a series of circumstances, Oedipus killed a stranger (actually, his father) and married the man's widow (his bi-

ological mother). Upon learning the awful truth, his guilt led him to blind himself. Freud gave the name of this tragic hero to his concept that every little boy falls in love with his mother, has murderous thoughts about his father, and feels guilty about both feelings. He named the similar process for girls after Electra, who killed her mother.

According to Freud, identification results when a child represses the wish to possess the parent of the other sex and identifies with the same-sex parent, whom the child sees as the "aggressor." This allows the superego to develop and to lead the child into the latency stage. This view, however, is no longer widely accepted by psychologists, who tend to favor one of the following theories.

Social-Learning Theory: Observing and Imitating Models

Social-learning theorists explain identification in general, and gender identification in particular, as the consequence of observing and imitating models. Typically, one model is a parent, but children also model themselves after other people, as Anna did with her classmate, Katie. An older brother or sister, a teacher, a peer, or a TV personality can also serve as models. Children may adopt characteristics from several different models.

How Identification Occurs

According to Jerome Kagan (1958, 1971), four interrelated processes establish and strengthen identification. First, children *want* to be like the model. For example, a boy may look to a famous baseball player, thinking that he will be able to do what the athlete can do. Second, children believe that they *are* like the model. Thus, a girl believes that she looks like her mother, tells jokes like her mother, walks like her mother. Other people affirm this identification with comments like "You have your mother's eyes." Third, children *experience emotions* like those the model is feeling. When Sally's 5-year-old daughter Dorri saw Sally cry after her own brother's death, Dorri felt sad and cried too, not for an uncle she barely knew but because her mother's grief made her feel sad. And finally, children *act* like the model. In play and in everyday conversation, they adopt the mannerisms of the model. Preschool teachers and parents are often startled to hear their own words and tone of voice come out of children's mouths.

Through identification, then, children come to believe that they have the same characteristics as a model. Thus, when they identify with a nurturant and competent model, children are pleased and proud. When the model is inadequate, they may feel unhappy and insecure.

Effects of Identification

According to social-learning theory, young children generally identify with the parent of the same sex; and when they imitate that parent, they are reinforced. A little boy sees that he is physically more like his father than like his mother. He imitates his father (especially when he sees him as nurturant, competent, and powerful) and is rewarded for acting "like a boy." The same kind of process occurs for a girl. According to this approach, children learn morally acceptable behavior in the same way as gender identity, by imitation and reinforcement. By the end of early childhood, these lessons are largely internalized; a child no longer needs frequent praise or punishment or the presence of a model to act in socially appropriate ways.

Music is a language all its own—and here it fosters an important aspect of growth. As this little girl plays and sings along with her father, she demonstrates identification, one of the most important personality developments of early childhood. *(Anthony Jalandoni/Monkmeyer)*

Evaluating Social-Learning Theory

Although social-learning theory seems to make sense, it has been hard to prove. Children do imitate adults, but not always those of the same sex. For example, a little girl may put on her father's hat or a little boy, his mother's shoes (Maccoby & Jacklin, 1974; Raskin & Israel, 1981). And often children do not imitate a parent at all. When children are tested for similarity to their parents, they are found to be no more like them than like other parents chosen at random. And those who do score as similar to their own parents are no more like the same-sex parent than like the other parent (Hetherington, 1965; Mussen & Rutherford, 1963).

An analysis of a large number of studies suggests that parents do encourage gender-typed activities in play and chores, and that fathers are more likely than mothers to differentiate between boys and girls. However, it is possible that parents may be simply reinforcing children's existing preferences rather than creating them (Lytton & Romney, 1991). (We will be describing a study that shows that girls with high levels of prenatal masculine hormones preferred to play with "boys'" toys, suggesting a possible biological influence.)

Social learning may underlie children's acquisition of gender identity and behavioral standards. But simple imitation and reinforcement do not seem to explain fully how this occurs.

Cognitive-Developmental Theory: Mental Processes

Cindy learns that she is something called a "girl" because people call her a girl. She figures out the kinds of things girls are "supposed" to do, and she does them. In other words, she learns her gender in the same way she learns everything else—by actively thinking about her experience. This is the heart of the cognitive-developmental theory proposed by Lawrence Kohlberg (1966).

Gender Identity and Gender Constancy

To learn their gender, Kohlberg says, children do not depend on adults as models or dispensers of reinforcements and punishments; instead, they actively classify themselves and others as male or female and then organize their behaviors around their gender.

Gender identity typically begins at about age 2. By age 3, according to Kohlberg, most children have a firm idea of which sex they belong to. When Dorri, at age 3, had a very short haircut, she indignantly corrected people who thought she was a boy. But gender constancy comes later, at about age 4 or 5. It is this that Kohlberg considers important in the behaviors that children adopt.

Gender constancy, or *gender conservation,* is a child's realization that his or her sex will *always* be the same. Three-year-old David, for example, told his mother, "When I grow up, I want to be a mommy just like you so I can play tennis and drive a car." But Anna, at 4, said that she would always be a girl and that her friend David would always be a boy—even if he played with dolls. David had not achieved gender constancy; Anna had.

According to Kohlberg, gender differences in behavior *follow* the establishment of gender constancy. Thus the reason Anna prefers dolls and dresses is not the approval she gets for those preferences (as in social-learning theory) but her cognitive awareness that such things are consistent with her idea of herself as a girl. Once children realize that they will *always* be male or female, they try to adopt "sex-appropriate" behaviors.

Gender-Schema Theory: A "Cognitive-Social" Approach

Going beyond cognitive-developmental theory, Sandra Bem developed *gender-schema theory,* a "cognitive-social" approach that contains elements of both cognitive-developmental theory and social-learning theory. It focuses on the concept of

gender schema (Bem, 1983, 1985). A schema is a mentally organized pattern of behavior that helps a child sort information. A gender schema, then, is a pattern of behavior organized around gender.

Bem maintains that children socialize themselves in their gender roles. First, they develop a concept of what it means to be male or female by organizing information around the schema of gender. They organize on the basis of gender because they see that society classifies people more by gender than by anything else: males and females wear different clothes, play with different toys, and use separate bathrooms. Thus Marie asks, "Is this a toy that girls play with?" and Eddie asks, "Do boys wear this kind of Halloween costume?"

Then, as children see what boys and girls are "supposed" to be and do—the culture's gender schema—they adapt their own attitudes and behavior. From the full range of human attributes, they display those that, according to their society's gender schema, fit them. In the United States, for example, girls learn that it is important to be nurturant, while boys learn that it is important to be strong and aggressive. Children then look at themselves. If they act "gender-appropriate," their self-esteem rises; if not, they feel inadequate.

This theory assumes that since the gender schema is learned, it can be modified. Bem (1983, 1985) says that adults can teach children to substitute other schemas for a prevailing cultural schema, thus freeing them from constraints of gender stereotypes. She suggests that adults model nonstereotyped behavior by sharing household tasks, that they give children nonstereotyped gifts (like dolls for boys and trucks for girls), that they expose children to men and women in nontraditional occupations, monitor young children's reading and television viewing, and emphasize anatomy and reproduction (rather than clothing and behavior) as the main distinctions between males and females.

Evaluating the Cognitive Theories

Research supports a link between gender concepts and cognitive development. Two-year-olds can classify pictures as "boys" or "girls" and "mommies" or "daddies." By age 2½, children can tell which pictures they themselves resemble, and they know whether they will be fathers or mothers when they grow up (S. K. Thompson, 1975).

However, cognitive-developmental theory has its weaknesses. Children often act in "gender-appropriate" ways *before* they achieve gender constancy, contradicting Kohlberg's predictions. In

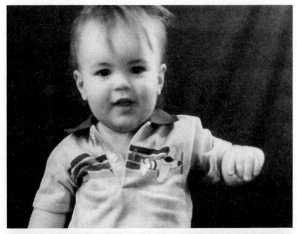

In one study, children saw three photos of this little boy—nude, dressed in boys' clothes, and dressed in girls' clothes. Preschoolers who identified the child's sex by genitals rather than by dress were more likely to show gender constancy—to know that they themselves would remain the sex they were. *(Sandra Lipsitz Bem)*

addition, the theory does not explain why—of all the differences among people—children pay so much attention to sex in setting up the classifications by which they make sense of their world.

Gender-schema theory is supported by the fact that very little evidence directly links children's acquisition of gender constancy to their gender-related behavior, as Kohlberg's theory predicts. Rather, research shows that children who do not yet have gender constancy still know a good deal about what is "appropriate" for males and females (G. D. Levy & Carter, 1989). So instead of saying, as Kohlberg does, that gender-role development depends on a single essential cognitive factor, like gender constancy, it seems reasonable to look at a number of different factors. These can include how

much children know about gender-role stereotypes and how likely they are to categorize various activities or objects by gender, two factors that have been found important in children's gender-typing (G. D. Levy & Carter, 1989).

Bem's idea that a culture's gender schema can be deliberately changed is a desirable goal if that means freeing people from the constraints of stereotypes. But change in ingrained attitudes about basic aspects of human behavior is slow. As far back as 1910, for instance, the founders of kibbutzim (communal settlements) in Israel tried to do away with special roles for men and women by changing family structure and assigning chores without regard to sex. But today, work on the kibbutz generally follows traditional gender lines, with men doing agricultural and mechanical work, and women cooking, laundering, and caring for children (Tiger & Shepher, 1975). Also, while the past several decades have brought major changes in the way American men and women—and boys and girls—think, feel, and act about gender, many of the old patterns persist. Women, even those with full-time jobs, still do most of the child care and housework; and men are still, by and large, more career-oriented.

ASPECTS AND ISSUES OF PERSONALITY DEVELOPMENT

GENDER

Two 4-year-olds, Kendra and Michael, are neighbors. They were wheeled together in the park as babies. They learned to ride tricycles at about the same time and pedaled up and down the sidewalk, often colliding with each other. They go to preschool together. Kendra and Michael have followed very similar paths. But there is a definite difference between them: their sex. How much difference does being a girl or a boy make?

How Different Are Girls and Boys?

Besides having different sex organs, Kendra and Michael are different in size, strength, appearance, physical and intellectual abilities, and personality. Which of their differences are due to the fact that Kendra is a girl and Michael is a boy, and which are simply differences between them as two individual human beings? As we discuss this question, we need to distinguish between *sex differences,* which are the biological differences between males and females, and *gender differences*, which are psychological or behavioral differences.

In their landmark review of more than 2000 studies, Maccoby and Jacklin (1974) found only a few characteristics on which boys and girls differed significantly. Three cognitive differences—girls' superior verbal ability and boys' better mathematical and spatial abilities—do not show up until after the age of 10 or 11. Moreover, more recent analyses have found these differences to be very small indeed. Gender differences in verbal abilities are so small as to be almost meaningless (Hyde & Linn, 1988). Those in math are complex, but also small, and have been getting smaller in recent years. In the general population, neither sex shows better understanding of mathematical concepts, girls excel in computation (adding, subtracting, and so on), and boys do not show superior problem-solving ability until high school (Hyde, Fennema, & Lamon, 1990).

Personality differences, too, are few. The clearest gender difference in personality, which shows up in early childhood, is that males tend to be more aggressive. Boys play more boisterously; they roughhouse more and are more apt to try to dominate other children and challenge their parents. Boys argue and fight more often and are more apt to use force or threats of force to get their way, while girls try to defuse conflicts by persuasion rather than confrontation (P. M. Miller, Danaher, & Forbes, 1986). Girls are more likely to cooperate with their parents and they tend to set up rules (like taking turns) to avoid clashes with playmates (Maccoby, 1980).

Girls are more likely to be *empathic*, that is, to identify with other people's feelings (N. Eisenberg, Fabes, Schaller, & Miller, 1989; M. Hoffman, 1977). Until about age 4 or 5, boys and girls show equal interest in babies. And even after this age, boys know just as much about babies and respond as enthusiastically to adult encouragement to take an interest in and help care for a baby (Berman, 1987; Berman & Goodman, 1984).

Thus, we need to be careful not to overemphasize differences between the sexes. Those that do exist are statistically small and are valid for large groups of boys and girls but not necessarily for individuals. Some girls love rough play and some boys hate it. But despite the rarity of behavioral sex differences, both males and females *believe* that they are more different than they actually are (Matlin, 1987). Where does that belief come from, and what are its effects?

Attitudes toward Gender Differences

When Kendra and Michael play house in the family corner at preschool, Kendra, as the "mommy," is likely to "cook" and "take care of the baby" while Michael puts on a hat and "goes to work." When he comes home, sits at the table, and says "I'm hungry," Kendra drops what she is doing to wait on him. This scenario would be less surprising if both children's mothers did not work outside the home and if both their fathers did not do a fair amount of the housework. These children have absorbed the gender roles of their culture rather than those of their own households.

Gender Roles and Gender-Typing

Gender roles are the behaviors, interests, attitudes, and skills that a culture considers appropriate for males and females and expects them to fulfill. By tradition, American women have been expected to devote most of their time to being wives and mothers, while men were supposed to devote most of their time to earning money. Those roles include personality expectations too: for example, that women are compliant and nurturant while men are active and competitive.

Gender-typing is a child's learning of his or her gender role. Children learn gender roles early, through socialization, and become increasingly gender-typed between ages 3 and 6. Moreover, the brighter children are, the faster they tend to learn them. Bright children are the first to notice the physical differences between the sexes and the expectations of their society for each sex—and to try to live up to those expectations (S. B. Greenberg & L. Peck, personal communication, 1974).

Strong gender-typing in early childhood may help children develop their gender identity. Ultimately, of course, people vary in the degree to which they take on gender roles. Perhaps children can become more flexible in their thinking about gender differences only after they know for sure that they are male or female and will always remain so.

Gender Stereotypes

Gender stereotypes are exaggerated generalizations about male or female behavior: for example, that a female is bound to be passive and dependent, while a male is aggressive and independent. Such stereotyped attitudes are found in children as young as age 3. The children in one study described babies differently, depending on whether the baby was identified as a girl or a boy. They tended to call a "boy" big, and a "girl" little; a "boy" mad, a "girl" scared; a "boy" strong, a "girl" weak (Haugh, Hoffman, & Cowan, 1980).

Gender stereotypes can restrict children's views of themselves and their future. They affect people in their simplest, most everyday endeavors as well as in far-reaching life decisions. Children who absorb these stereotypes may become men who will not give a baby a bottle or change a diaper, or women who "can't" nail boards together or bait a fish hook (Bem, 1976). By viewing certain activities as unmasculine or unfeminine, people may deny their natural inclinations and abilities and force themselves into ill-fitting academic, vocational, or social molds.

Androgyny: A Different View of Gender

The healthiest personality, says Bem (1974, 1976), includes a balance of positive characteristics normally thought of as more appropriate for one sex or the other. A person having such a balance—whom Bem describes as **androgynous**—might be assertive, dominant, and self-reliant (so-called masculine traits), as well as compassionate, sympathetic, and understanding ("feminine" traits). Androgynous men and women are free to judge a particular situation on its merits and to act on the basis of what seems most effective rather than on what is considered appropriate for their gender.

How Do Gender Differences Come About?

Some people insist that the root of gender differences is biological. But many psychologists besides Bem believe that the cultural environment, as interpreted to young children through such influences as parents and the media, is at least as important. Research does not yield an either-or answer.

Biological Influences

Hormones circulating before or about the time of birth seem to cause sex differences in animals. The male hormone testosterone has been linked to aggressive behavior in mice, guinea pigs, rats, and primates; and the female hormone prolactin can cause motherly behavior in virgin or male animals (Bronson & Desjardins, 1969; Levy, 1966; R. M. Rose, Gordon, & Bernstein, 1972). But human beings are influenced far more by learning than animals are.

Two classic studies suggest that both biology and environment play a role. In one (Ehrhardt & Money, 1967), girls whose mothers had taken the male hormone androgen during pregnancy were

Anna's enjoyment of her truck shows that she is not restricted in her play by gender stereotypes. Contemporary developmentalists discourage such stereotypes, usually favoring encouraging children to pursue their own interests, even when these interests are unconventional for their gender. *(Erika Stone)*

born with abnormal external sex organs, but after surgery, they looked normal and could eventually have babies. Still, they acted "boyish" by playing with trucks and guns and competing with boys in sports. Were these behaviors due to prenatal hormonal exposure, parental reinforcement of "tomboy" behavior, or some combination? It is unclear. The other study (Money, Ehrhardt, & Masica, 1968) more clearly highlights the role of environment. These subjects were chromosomally male and had testes instead of ovaries but looked like females and had been brought up as girls. All were "typically female" in behavior and outlook: all considered marriage and raising a family to be very important, and most had played primarily with dolls and other "girls'" toys. In this case, biology fails to account for gender-typing.

A study of men with a hormonal deficiency disorder (Hier & Crowley, 1982) suggests that androgens may be responsible for normal males' superior spatial abilities. But once again, environmental influences cannot be ruled out. This gender difference does not exist in all cultures. Where it does, women (or men who do not feel fully masculine) may give up on a task that they do not deem "sex-appropriate" (Kagan, 1982).

Hormones may, then, predispose people toward certain behaviors, but then the environment shapes these behaviors. In all the above studies, samples were very small, making the findings inconclusive. Furthermore, since variations among people of the same sex are larger than the average differences between the sexes, biology fails to explain fully the differences that do exist in males' and females' behavior.

Family Influences

Even in today's more "liberated" society, parents—and especially fathers—treat sons and daughters differently, beginning in infancy. The biggest area of difference is in encouraging gender-typed activities, according to an analysis of 172 studies between 1952 and 1987 (Lytton & Romney, 1991). Parents pressure boys more to act "like real boys" and avoid acting "like girls" than they pressure girls to avoid "boyish" behavior and act in "feminine" ways. Girls have much more freedom in the clothes they wear, the games they play, and the people they play with.

On such other measures as the amount of parent-child interaction, encouragement to achieve or to be independent, strictness, clear communication, and warmth and nurturance, most differences are small and nonsignificant. However, those that did appear were in the expected direction—as, for example, accepting aggression more in boys and being warmer with girls.

Fathers are more apt to be social with, more approving of, and more affectionate toward their preschool daughters, but more controlling and directive toward their sons, and more concerned with their sons' cognitive achievements than with their daughters' (Bronstein, 1988). But adult men and women who get along well at work and in relationships are most apt to have had warm ties to fathers who were competent, strong, secure in their own masculinity, and nurturant toward their children (Biller, 1981). Children from one-parent families (usually headed by the mother) tend to be less stereotyped than those from two-parent families (Katz, 1987). This seems partly due to the fact that a single parent serves as both mother and father,

doing everything herself, and thus provides a more androgynous model.

What parents do has long-range implications. Even if parents are merely reinforcing behavioral tendencies that are already there, by accentuating them and limited a child's behavior to what is "appropriate" for one sex or the other, we are limiting children's views of themselves, the chance to experience different activities, and to fulfill their own unique personalities.

Media Influences

The typical high school graduate has watched more than 25,000 hours of television (Action for Children's Television, n.d.) and has absorbed highly gender-stereotyped attitudes from the little screen. Television is more stereotyped than real life: there are about twice as many males as females on TV, and the males are usually more powerful, dominant, and authoritative than females (Calvert & Huston, 1987). TV men are typically more aggressive, more active, and more competent than women (Mamay & Simpson, 1981; D. M. Zuckerman & Zuckerman, 1985).

Some changes have been made in recent years. But while TV women are now more likely to be working out of the home and using their brains for activities other than housework or child care—and while men are sometimes shown caring for children or doing the marketing—a high level of gender-stereotyping still prevails. According to social-learning theory, children who watch a great deal of television will imitate the models they see and become more gender-typed themselves. Research has borne this out.

Can the media help abolish stereotypes? The answer seems to be "Yes, but . . . " By and large, children come to the TV set with preformed attitudes, and they watch and process information selectively. Boys turn on more cartoons and action adventure programs than girls do, and both sexes remember television sequences that confirm the stereotypes they already hold better than they remember nonstereotypical sequences (Calvert & Huston, 1987). However, if a serious effort were made, the media could probably shape children's views of themselves and other people in terms of possibilities rather than limitations.

Cultural Influences

In China, India, and a number of other developing countries, new statistics showing an unexpectedly high ratio of males in the population sound an alarming result of sex discrimination.

Because of parental preferences for sons, female fetuses are disproportionately aborted, newborn girls are sometimes drowned, and many little girls die because they get less food and medical attention than do little boys (Kristof, 1991). It is easy to see how, in such societies, personalities would be strongly influenced by gender. But even in the United States, males and females are treated and valued differently.

Do societal forces encourage and accentuate biological differences, or does the culture itself create gender differences? This question is hard to answer. We do know that all societies mandate gender roles. They vary from culture to culture, but in most societies men are more aggressive, competitive, and powerful than women, and the pattern is hard to change. Yet attitudes and roles *are* changing. Today women are moving into nontraditional occupations and are gaining power in business, government, and the family. Egalitarian attitudes are becoming more prevalent, especially among younger, better-educated, and higher-income people (Deaux, 1985). And both men and women are exploring aspects of their personalities that were suppressed by the old gender stereotypes.

FEARS

When Kelly was 3 years old, she was frightened by a neighbor's large, barking dog. The next day, she refused to go out to play. When her mother asked why, she said she had a stomachache; but when dinnertime came, she cleaned her plate. The next day, Kelly again refused to go outside. When her father insisted on taking her to the store, Kelly burst into tears and clung to his arm. Kelly had developed a fear of dogs, one of the most common fears of this fearful age. Yet by her sixth birthday, this fear had gone away; in fact, she had to be stopped from patting strange dogs in the park.

Why do girls express more fears than boys do? It may be because parents encourage girls to be more dependent, because girls' fears are accepted and boys' fears are discouraged, or because boys do not admit having fears (Bauer, 1976; Croake, 1973; Jersild & Holmes, 1935).

What Do Children Fear, and Why?

Temporary fears are common in 2- to 4-year-olds, many of whom are afraid of animals, especially dogs. By 6 years of age, children are more likely to

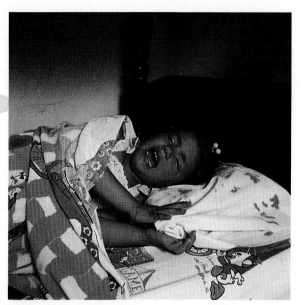

Many 6-year-olds develop fear of the dark. This and other characteristic fears of early childhood are usually short-lived. *(Bill Stanton/International Stock)*

be afraid of the dark. Other common fears are of thunderstorms and doctors (DuPont, 1983). Most of these fears evaporate as children grow older and lose their sense of powerlessness (see Table 7-2).

Why do children become so fearful at this age? The reasons may stem from their intense fantasy life—their inability to clearly distinguish "pretending" from reality. In one study, 75 percent of kindergartners and 50 percent of second-graders—as compared with only 5 percent of sixth-graders—expressed fear of ghosts and monsters. Older children are afraid of different things. Ten- to twelve-year-olds, who understand cause and effect, are more likely to fear bodily injury and physical danger, while 4- to 6-year-olds may fear a person who "looks ugly" (Bauer, 1976). Underlying anxieties (like the inner conflicts discussed at the beginning of this chapter) may cause some fears. Violent television shows and movies may then provide frightening images for these anxieties.

Sometimes young children's imaginations are carried away, making them worry about being attacked by a lion or being abandoned. But often their fears come from appraisal of real dangers—like being bitten by a dog—or from actual events, as when a child who has been hit by a car becomes afraid to cross the street. Children of this age know more and have experienced more than they did before, and one thing they know is that there are many things to be afraid of.

TABLE 7-2

Childhood Fears	
Age	**Fears**
0–6 months	Loss of support, loud noises
7–12 months	Strangers; heights; sudden, unexpected, and looming objects
1 year	Separation from parent; toilet, injury, strangers
2 years	A multitude of stimuli, including loud noises (vacuum cleaners, sirens and alarms, trucks, and thunder), animals, dark rooms, separation from parent, large objects or machines, changes in personal environment, strange peers
3 years	Masks, dark, animals, separation from parent
4 years	Separation from parent, animals, dark, noises (including noises at night)
5 years	Animals, "bad" people, dark, separation from parent, bodily harm
6 years	Supernatural beings (e.g., ghosts, witches), bodily injury, thunder and lightning, dark, sleeping or staying alone, separation from parent
7–8 years	Supernatural beings, dark, media events (e.g., news reports on the threat of nuclear war or child kidnapping), staying alone, bodily injury
9–12 years	Tests and examinations in school, school performances, bodily injury, physical appearance, thunder and lightning, death, dark
Teens	Social performance, sexuality

SOURCE: Adapted from Morris & Kratochwill, 1983.

Preventing and Dealing with Fears

We don't know why some fears vanish and others persist. It seems, though, that adults' reactions play a part. Parents should accept fears as normal, offer reassurance, and encourage children to express their feelings without being ridiculed or punished. But children should not be allowed to avoid what they fear; avoidance does not remove the cause of the fear.

Fears that linger can be treated before they become handicapping. Through conditioning, modeling, and gradual exposure to the feared object, the fear can be attacked directly, not treated as a symptom of a deeper problem (C. M. Murphy & Bootzin, 1973). Some children seem to mask fears in aggression, which surfaces in a new way in early childhood.

AGGRESSION

Babies do not show truly *aggressive behavior,* hostile actions intended to hurt somebody or to establish dominance. But anyone who is around children past the age of 2½ or 3 has seen enough punching, kicking, biting, and throwing to know that the age of *hostile aggression* has arrived. In the next 3 years or so, children normally shift from showing aggression with blows to showing it with words. Let's see how that happens—and why it sometimes doesn't happen.

A toddler who roughly snatches a toy away from another child is interested only in getting the toy, not in hurting or dominating the other child. This is *instrumental aggression,* or aggression used as an instrument to reach a goal.

In the early stages of aggression, children often focus single-mindedly on something they want and make threatening gestures against anyone who is keeping it from them. Between ages 2½ and 5, they commonly struggle over toys and the control of space. Aggression surfaces mostly during social play. Some aggression is normal, and the children who fight the most tend to be the most sociable and competent. The ability to show *some* aggression may be a necessary step in the social development of human beings.

As children move through early childhood from ages 2 to 5 and are better able to express themselves with words, aggression declines in frequency, initiation, and average length of episodes (Cummings, Iannotti, & Zahn-Waxler, 1989). However, individual differences that show up at age 2 tend to be fairly stable, especially among boys. Boys who hit or grab toys from other children at age 2 are still acting aggressively at age 5.

Most children become less aggressive after age 6 or 7, as empathy more commonly replaces egocentrism. Children are now better able to put themselves in someone else's place, can understand why someone is acting in a certain way, and can develop positive ways to deal with others.

But not all children learn to control aggression. Some become more and more destructive. Aggression may be a reaction to major problems in a child's life. It may also *cause* major problems, by making other children and adults dislike a child. Even in a normal child, aggression can get out of hand and become dangerous. Therefore, researchers have looked at what stimulates aggression.

Triggers of Aggression

Although the male hormone testosterone may well underlie the tendency toward aggressive behavior and explain why males are more likely to be aggressive than females, social-learning theorists point to other contributing factors, a number of which show up in homes where parenting is ineffective (Patterson, DeBaryshe, & Ramsey, 1989). Parents of children who later become antisocial often fail to reinforce good behavior and are harsh or inconsistent or both in punishing misbehavior. They are not closely involved in their children's lives in positive ways like making sure that the children do their homework. The children tend to do poorly in school and to be rejected by their peers. Depressed, they then seek out other troubled children, who spur them on to more antisocial behavior.

Triggers of aggression that often show up in the early lives of these children include reinforcement for aggressive behavior, frustration, and imitation of aggressive models in real life or on television.

Reinforcement

Children's clearest reward for aggression, of course, is getting what they want. But sometimes even scolding or spanking can reinforce aggressive behavior, since some children would rather get negative attention than none at all. Preschool teachers have decreased the amount of aggression shown by 3- and 4-year-old boys by ignoring aggressive behavior and reinforcing cooperative activities (P. Brown & Elliott, 1965). But it is not always safe to ignore aggression, and permitting it by not interfering with it can communicate approval.

Some parents actively encourage aggression toward other children while discouraging it toward themselves. Their children learn not to hit their parents, but they still hit others (Bandura, 1960).

Frustration and Imitation

Frustration—often resulting from punishment, insults, and fears—does not necessarily lead to aggression, but a frustrated child is more likely to act aggressively than a contented one.

Frustration and imitation can work together, as in a classic social-learning study in which children were exposed to one of two types of models or to no model (Bandura, Ross, & Ross, 1961). Seventy-two 3- to 6-year-olds were divided into three groups. One by one, each child in each group went

The kind of aggression involved in fighting over a toy, without intention to hurt the other child, is known as *instrumental aggression*. It surfaces mostly during social play and normally declines as children learn to ask for what they want. *(Elizabeth Crews/The Image Works)*

got DESENSITIZED TO AGGRESSION

into a playroom for 10 minutes. For those in the first group, an adult model (male for half of the children, female for the other half) would be playing quietly in a corner with toys. For the second group, the adult model would begin to assemble a construction toy, but after a minute would spend the rest of the session punching, throwing, and kicking a 5-foot-tall inflated doll. For the third group, there was no model.

After the sessions, all three groups of children were mildly frustrated, since they had seen toys that they were not allowed to play with. They then went into another playroom. The children who had seen the aggressive model were much more aggressive than those in the other groups, imitating many of the things they had seen the model say and do. Both boys and girls were more strongly influenced by an aggressive male model than by an aggressive female model, apparently because they considered aggression more appropriate for males (gender-schema theorists would say that this was in line with the gender schema the children had learned). The children who had been with the quiet model were less aggressive than those who had not seen any model. We see, then, how adult models can influence children's behavior in more than one direction.

Televised Violence

When Anna was 3, her teacher reported that she was butting heads with her classmates. Her parents were disturbed and puzzled about this new behavior, but then they remembered that Anna had just seen a videocassette of the movie *Bambi*, which shows animals fighting in just this way. Diane and Jonathan quickly moved in to teach Anna that this might be acceptable behavior for stags in the forest but not for children in preschool. They also put away the *Bambi* cassette.

Research suggests that children are influenced more by seeing filmed violence than by seeing real people acting aggressively (Bandura, Ross, & Ross, 1963). And children's programs are much more violent than adults' programs (Signorielli, Gross, & Morgan, 1982). One Canadian study found that from 28 to 40 percent of children aged 3 to 10 watched violent programs (Bernard-Bonnin, Gilbert, Rousseau, Masson, & Maheux, 1991).

A body of research since the 1950s shows that children who see televised violence behave more aggressively (National Institute of Mental Health [NIMH], 1982). This is true across geographic locations and socioeconomic levels, for both boys and girls, and for normal children as well as children with emotional problems. This does not necessarily mean that televised violence *causes* aggression. It is possible that children already prone to violence become more so after seeing it onscreen. Also, they may watch more violent television. Finally, it is possible that some third factor is involved: maybe children who watch and react aggressively to televised violence are spanked more than other children.

In any case, aggressive children do watch more television than nonaggressive children, identify more strongly with aggressive characters, and are more likely to believe that aggression on television reflects real life (Eron, 1982). Aggressive acts make a more vivid impression than any punishment the "bad guy" receives (Liebert & Poulos, 1976, in Lickona, 1976). Television encourages aggressive behavior in two ways: children imitate what they see on television, and they also absorb the value that aggression is acceptable (NIMH, 1982).

Children who see television characters—both heroes and villains—getting what they want through violence and lawbreaking may fail to intervene when another child is being victimized by a bully. They are also more likely to break rules and less likely to cooperate to resolve differences. And they seem to become more willing to hurt people.

In one study, one group of 5- to 9-year-olds watched 3½ minutes of a chase, two fistfights, two shootings, and a knifing. A control group watched 3½ minutes of sports. Then the children were asked to play a "game" that involved pushing either a "help" button (to help an unseen child win a game) or a "hurt" button (to make a handle touched by that child painfully hot). Of course, there was no such child; the only child in the experiment was the one pushing the buttons. The children who had watched the violence were more willing to hurt the unseen child and to inflict more severe pain than were the others (Liebert, 1972).

Some effects of televised violence endure for years. Among 427 young adults whose viewing habits had been studied at the age of 8, the best predictor of aggressiveness in 19-year-old men and women was the degree of violence in the programs they had seen as children (Eron, 1980, 1982).

Meanwhile, television becomes more and more violent. Broadcasts of war cartoons soared from 1½ hours a week in 1982 to 48 hours a week in 1987, and the average child in the United States saw 250 episodes of such cartoons in a year. Sales of war toys jumped 700 percent during that period. In one small Canadian community that had been without

BOX 7-1   PRACTICALLY SPEAKING

GUIDING CHILDREN'S TELEVISION VIEWING

Jason loves television and watches several hours every day. By his third birthday, Jason, like most American children, watches 2 to 3 hours a day; by age 5, he watches a little more; and then from ages 5 to 7, he views less. There are wide individual differences, however. Like many boys his age, Jason watches more cartoons and action-adventure shows than does Vicky, a "typical" girl (A. C. Huston, Wright, Rice, Kerkman, & St. Peters, 1990). By the time both graduate from high school, they will have spent more time in front of the television set than in the classroom (American Academy of Pediatrics, 1986a).

Television influences children's attitudes about hurting or helping other people, gender roles, alcohol and other drugs, and sexuality and relationships. It can send positive messages—or negative ones. Children are active viewers of television, at least most of the time: they choose the programs to watch. As they grow older, they watch more complex shows and more cartoons and comedies rather than information shows designed for children. Viewing patterns seem to be set quite early in life and are greatly influenced by parents' patterns (A. C. Huston et al., 1990).

To help children reap the benefits and avoid the dangers of this electronic teacher, parents, teachers, and other adults can follow these guidelines suggested by the American Academy of Pediatrics (1986a) and Action for Children's Television (n.d.):

■ *Plan your child's viewing in advance:* Approach television the way you would a movie by deciding with your child which show to watch, turning the set on for that program and turning it off when the program is over.

■ *Set limits:* Restrict your child's viewing to 1 or 2 hours a day at certain set times, taking into account the child's favorite programs. Many 3- to 10-year-old children watch television with no parental limits (Bernard-Bonnin et al., 1991).

■ *Do not use television as a reward or punishment:* You may, however, want to reserve viewing time until after the child has carried out responsibilities like homework and chores.

■ *Watch with your child:* This way, you will know what your child is seeing, and you will be able to use television to express your own values and feelings about complex issues and to explain confusing scenes.

■ *Talk to your child about such topics as love, work, war, family life, sex, drugs, and crime:* You can open up conversations about the difference between make-believe and real life, about ways characters could solve problems without violence, and about violence and how it hurts.

■ *Set a good example:* Examine your own viewing habits, and change them if necessary to help your children develop good habits.

■ *Provide alternatives:* Encourage and participate in both indoor and outdoor activities like games, sports, hobbies, reading, and household duties. Use television as a baby-sitter as little as possible.

■ *Resist commercials:* Help your child become a smart consumer by teaching how to recognize a sales pitch and how to tell when a product on a television show is presented as an advertisement. Talk about foods that can cause cavities and about toys that may break too soon.

■ *Use available technologies:* If you have a videocassette recorder, tape desirable shows or rent movies or special tapes made for children. If you have cable, ask about devices to lock out inappropriate channels.

■ *Recognize your power:* You can channel the power of television so that it will enhance your child's life.

television, both verbal and physical aggression increased after its introduction (T. M. Williams, 1978). And 40 studies assessing more than 4500 children in seven countries show the effects of cartoon violence and violent play: increases in fighting, kicking, choking, loss of temper, cruelty to animals, and disrespect for others, as well as decreases in sharing, imagination, and school performance (National Coalition on Television Violence, n.d.).

Reducing Aggression

Parents can often nip aggressive tendencies in the bud by changing what they do early in their children's lives. Help is available from parent-training programs that instruct parents in how to reinforce good behavior, discipline consistently and appropriately, and become positively involved in their children's lives (Patterson et al., 1989).

Reasoning with children, making them feel

guilty, and withdrawing approval and affection are all more likely to produce children with a strong conscience. On the other hand, children who are disciplined by spanking, threats, or withdrawal of privileges are more likely to be aggressive. (Of course, parents may also be more likely to spank aggressive children.)

Punishment—especially spanking—may backfire, because hitting children provides a double incentive for violence. The child not only suffers frustration, pain, and humiliation but sees aggressive behavior in an adult. Parents who spank provide a model of aggressive behavior, even as they are trying to teach children not to be aggressive. Parents need to think about what kind of behavior they want to encourage—and how to encourage it.

Parents can also monitor their children's television watching, limiting total time and selecting appropriate programs (see Box 7-1). Television—especially educational television—can also promote prosocial behavior.

ALTRUISM: PROSOCIAL BEHAVIOR

Anna, at 3½, responded to two fellow preschoolers' complaints that they did not have enough modeling clay—her favorite toy—by giving them half of hers. Anna was showing altruistic behavior, or *prosocial behavior,* acting out of concern for another person, with no expectation of reward. Prosocial acts often entail cost, self-sacrifice, or risk on the part of the person who makes them.

Origins of Prosocial Behavior

Why do some children reach out to comfort a crying friend or stop to help someone who has fallen while crossing a street? What makes these children generous, compassionate, and sensitive to other people's needs? From many studies dating from the 1970s, we have learned about caring behavior.

Socioeconomic status, for example, is *not* a factor: parents' income or social standing makes no difference in how a youngster will behave toward others. And in most studies, no sex differences turned up either.

Prosocial behavior emerges early. Even before their second birthday, children often help others, share belongings and food, and offer comfort. These altruistic behaviors emerge at about the same time that children are increasingly able to use symbols and to pretend. What we may be seeing,

then, is a child's ability to imagine how another person might feel and to develop a feeling of responsibility for others. This ability enables children to develop a moral sense at a very young age (Zahn-Waxler, Radke-Yarrow, Wagner, & Chapman, 1992).

Altruistic children tend to be advanced in mental reasoning and able to take the role of others (Carlo, Knight, Eisenberg, & Rotenberg, 1991). They are also relatively active and self-confident. Not surprisingly, other children respond to them and tend to prefer prosocial preschoolers as playmates (Hart, DeWolf, Wozniak, & Burts, 1992). How do they become this way? The findings of many studies point to the home. The family is important as a model, as a source of explicit standards, and as a guide to adopting models.

Encouraging Prosocial Behavior: What Parents Do

One important way that parents encourage altruism is to love and respect a child, since altruistic children generally feel secure in their parents' love and affection. Preschoolers who were securely attached as infants are more likely than insecurely attached children to respond to other children's distress. They have more friends, and their teachers consider them more socially competent. Children who received empathic, nurturant, responsive care as infants develop those qualities themselves (Kestenbaum, Farber, & Sroufe, 1989; Sroufe, 1983).

Parents of prosocial children typically set an example, encourage them to empathize with others and to reflect on the implications of their actions. When Sara took candy from a store, her father did not give her an abstract lecture on honesty or tell her what a bad girl she had been. Instead, he explained how the owner of the store would be harmed because she had not paid for the candy, and then he took her back to the store to return it. When incidents like this occur, Sara's parents ask, for example, "How do you think Mr. Jones feels?" or "How would you feel if you were Maria?"

Parents of prosocial children usually hold them to high standards. The children know that they are expected to be honest and helpful. They have responsibilities in the home and are expected to meet them. Parents also point out other models, and steer their children toward stories and television programs—like *Mister Rogers' Neighborhood*—that depict cooperation, sharing, and empathy. Such programs encourage children to be more sympathetic, generous, and helpful (Mussen & Eisenberg-Berg, 1977; NIMH, 1982; D. M. Zuckerman & Zuckerman, 1985).

One study identified 406 non-Jewish Europeans who, during the 1930s and 1940s, had risked their lives to rescue Jews in Nazi-occupied countries and then compared these rescuers with people who did not help. The researchers found that the rescuers' childhood homes were different from the others' (Oliner & Oliner, 1988). Rescuers' parents had emphasized strong ethical principles—compassion and caring for others and a sense of fairness extending to people one did not know. They put less emphasis on values like obedience, earning money, and the importance of self. The rescuers also reported closer early family relationships, especially with parents who disciplined them more by reasoning, explanations, persuasion, advice, and suggestions of how to right a wrong than by spanking. Furthermore, the parents often behaved altruistically themselves.

A more recent examination of the relationship between parents' behavior and children's prosocial behavior found similar results (Hart et al., 1992). Among 106 children aged 3 to 6, the most prosocial children had parents who disciplined them by inductive techniques—setting limits and logical consequences, explaining, and getting ideas from the children, rather than punishing, threatening, belittling, or making flat demands. The strongest relationships held for the older preschool daughters of inductive mothers. Mothers are still the primary caregivers of most young children, and their behavior seems to make more of an impact than fathers' behavior.

Obviously, parents can have an enormous impact on children's personalities. Let's look more closely at how they use that influence.

CHILD-REARING PRACTICES

"Just as the twig is bent, the tree's inclined," wrote the eighteenth-century English poet Alexander Pope. But raising children is not so simple. Children are not saplings to be bent to their parents' will. In early childhood, as children become their own persons, their upbringing can be a baffling, complex challenge. How are parents raising their children today? Some parents, of course, repeat the child-rearing patterns that their own parents followed. Others adopt practices that are very different from those their parents used.

What parents themselves do and say is a major influence on whether children will be likely to help other people, strangers or those in their own families. *(Peter Vandermark/Stock, Boston)*

Parents' Use of Reinforcement and Punishment

Almost all parents sometimes offer rewards to get children to do something they want them to do, and use punishment to get the children to stop doing what they do *not* want them to do. Many parents are less comfortable with rewards—seeing them as bribes—than punishment, but the weight of research shows that children learn more by being reinforced for good behavior than by being punished for bad behavior.

Reinforcement

Behavior modification, or behavior therapy (a form of operant, or instrumental, learning, described in Chapter 1), is a new name for the old practice of providing positive consequences when children do what parents want them to do and negative consequences when they do something the parents disapprove of. The most effective discipline involves "catching a child being good" and reinforcing the desirable behavior.

External reinforcers may be social ones like a smile, a hug, praise, or a special privilege. Or they may be more tangible—candy, money, toys, or gold stars. Whatever the reinforcer, the child must see it as rewarding and must get it fairly consistently after showing the desired behavior. Eventually, the behavior should provide its own *internal* reward to the child—such as a sense of pleasure and accomplishment.

Ineffective Punishment: "Rewarding" with Punishment

"What are we going to do with that child?" Noel's mother says. "The more we punish him, the more he misbehaves!" No wonder: Noel's parents usually ignore him when he behaves well but scold or spank him when he acts up. In effect, they reinforce his misbehavior by paying attention to it.

Most children, of course, prefer approval to disapproval. But children who get little positive attention may like disapproval more than no attention at all, and so they deliberately misbehave. Punishment thus "rewards" the very behavior it is intended to stop.

Effective Punishment: When Does Punishment Work?

Most researchers stress the negative effects of punishment. But although the carrot is usually a better motivator than the stick, there are times when punishment seems necessary. For example, children have to learn very quickly not to run out into traffic and not to bash each other over the head with wooden trucks. Sometimes, too, undesirable behavior may be so deep-seated that it is hard to find any good behavior to reinforce.

If punishment must be used, findings from laboratory and field research suggest the most effective ways to use it (Parke, 1977). The following criteria are important:

■ *Timing:* The shorter the time between misbehavior and punishment, the more effective the punishment. When children are punished as they *begin* to engage in a forbidden act such as approaching an object they have been told to stay away from, they will go to it less often than if they are not punished until *after* they have actually touched it. Parents and teachers need to move in quickly when a child is about to repeat misbehavior. And they should act immediately after the event rather than postponing punishment "until your father gets home" (a practice that has, fortunately, diminished over the years).

■ *Explanation:* Punishment is more effective when accompanied by a short explanation at a level the child can understand. For example, children are less likely to play with a fragile vase if, the last time they broke one, they were told "That vase belongs to Aunt Martha" than if they were punished with no explanation. When possible, rules should be explained in advance, along with a warning of the consequences of breaking them. (This can't always be done, since children often misbehave in ways that parents never dreamed of!)

■ *Consistency.* The more consistently a child is punished, the more effective the punishment will be. When the same behavior brings punishment only some of the time, it is likely to continue longer than if unpunished all the time.

■ *The person who punishes:* The better the relationship between the punishing adult and the child, the more effective the punishment. Punishment is two-edged: as it presents something negative, it withholds something positive. Therefore, the more positive the element that is being withheld (acceptance by an affectionate, nurturing adult), the more effective the punishment.

Used with care, then, punishment can be effective, at least in the short run. However, it can be harmful when it is inconsistent and is administered in a hostile way. Unwanted long-term effects may include a child's avoidance of a punitive parent, undermining the parent's ability to influence behavior. Physical punishment (aside from the risk of injury it carries) may encourage children to imitate the aggression modeled by the parent. And children who are punished often may become passive because they feel helpless to escape punishment.

Some children are punished more often than others, and not necessarily because of the seriousness of their offenses. Parents tend to spare the rod for a child who expresses remorse and tries to make up for misdeeds, whereas a child who is defiant or who ignores parents' rebukes is punished severely.

Child rearing, of course, involves far more than reinforcing and rewarding specific kinds of behaviors. Let's look at other aspects of parenting.

Parents' Styles and Children's Competence: Baumrind's Research

Why does Nicole hit and bite the nearest person when she cannot finish a jigsaw puzzle? Why does

Parenting styles influence children's personality development. Children of authoritative parents, who balance firmness with love and respect, are often the most self-reliant, self-controlled, and content. *(Bill Stanton/International Stock)*

David sit with the puzzle for an hour until he solves it? Why does Michele walk away from it after a minute's effort? In short, why are children so different in their responses to the same task? What makes them turn out the way they do?

One effort to answer these questions has related different styles of parenting to different levels of children's competence.

Three Parenting Styles

Diana Baumrind set out to discover relationships between children's social competence and parents' different styles of child rearing. Her research combined lengthy interviews, standardized testing, and home studies of 103 preschool children from 95 families. She identified children who were functioning at various levels and then sought to relate the children's adjustment to their parents' child-rearing styles. She then categorized three child-rearing styles and described typical behavior patterns of children raised according to each style (Baumrind, 1971; Baumrind & Black, 1967).

Authoritarian parents value control and unquestioning obedience. They try to make children conform to a set standard of conduct, and they punish them forcefully for acting contrary to that standard. They are more detached and less warm than other parents; their children tend to be more discontented, withdrawn, and distrustful.

Permissive parents value self-expression and self-regulation. They make few demands, allowing children to monitor their own activities as much as possible. They consider themselves

resources, not standard-bearers or models. They explain the reasons underlying the few family rules that do exist, consult with children about policy decisions, and rarely punish. They are noncontrolling, nondemanding, and relatively warm; their children tend to be immature—the least self-controlled and the least exploratory.

Authoritative parents respect a child's individuality, while at the same time stressing social values. They direct their children's activities rationally, paying attention to the issues rather than to a child's fear of punishment or loss of love. While they have confidence in their ability to guide children, they respect the children's interests, opinions, and unique personalities. They are loving, consistent, demanding, and respectful of children's independent decisions, but they are firm in maintaining standards and willing to impose limited punishment. They explain the reasoning behind their stands and encourage verbal give-and-take. They combine control with encouragement. Their children apparently feel secure in knowing that they are loved and in knowing what is expected of them. As preschoolers, children of authoritative parents tend to be most self-reliant, self-controlled, self-assertive, exploratory, and content.

Research based on Baumrind's work has also found a link between authoritative parenting and learning. The study by Pratt and his colleagues on "scaffolding," the temporary help that parents give children to do a task (described in Chapter 6), found that authoritative parents were more sensitive in knowing when to shift their level of help and that their children were more successful at various tasks.

Evaluation of Baumrind's Conclusions

The questions Diana Baumrind was interested in answering forced her to rely on correlational data, as do many developmental researchers. Using such data, she could not prove that these three styles of child rearing *caused* the children in her study to turn out as they did. Rather, she established that relationships did exist between each parenting style and a particular set of behaviors. Also, it is impossible to know from her data whether the children were actually raised in a particular style: it is possible, for example, that some of the well-adjusted children had been raised inconsistently, but by the time of the study, their parents had adopted the authoritative pattern. Furthermore, Baumrind did not consider a child's influence on parents: for example, "easy" children may stimulate parents to be authoritative while "difficult" children may drive their parents to authoritarianism. Therefore, we cannot draw firm conclusions about the effects of the different styles.

But if authoritative parenting does indeed further children's development, its success may be related to the parents' reasonable expectations and realistic standards. Children from authoritarian homes are so strictly controlled, by either punishment or guilt, that often they cannot make a conscious choice about a particular behavior because they are too concerned about what their parents will do. Children from permissive homes receive so little guidance that they often become uncertain and anxious about whether they are doing the right thing. But in authoritative homes, children know when they are meeting expectations, and they are able to decide when it is worth risking their parents' displeasure or other unpleasant consequences to pursue some goal. These children are expected to perform well, to fulfill their commitments, and to participate actively in family duties as well as in family fun. They know the satisfaction of meeting responsibilities and achieving success.

Determinants of Child-Rearing Styles

Of course, no parent is always authoritarian, permissive, or authoritative. Being human, parents have different moods and react differently to various situations (Carter & Welch, 1981). And although it is easy to *know* the "right" way to act with children, it is not always easy to put it into action.

But what makes a parent adopt a particular pattern of child rearing most of the time? Some clues to the answer to this question have emerged from a study of 42 low-income African American mothers and grandmothers who were caring for 3- to 6-year-old children (Kelley, Power, & Wimbush, 1992). In the past, African American mothers have been described as largely authoritarian parents, but this study found a wide range of approaches within this group, leading to a number of conclusions. The principal one is that it is misleading to characterize a cultural group with a single term. Other findings point to some of the influences upon the women that resulted in different child-rearing attitudes and practices.

Some of the important factors turned out to be how religious a woman was, how old she was, how much education she had, and whether she was a single parent. Furthermore, cultural background more than any of these factors seemed to indicate whether a woman spanked her child or not. More religious mothers tended to be more sensitive to their children's needs (in Baumrind's terminology, more "authoritative"), as did more mature, more educated, and married mothers. Younger, less educated single mothers, who were less involved in organized religion, tended to emphasize obedience and respect for elders. This latter approach may be more adaptive for children in a stressful inner-city community, in which respect for authority leads to success in a highly structured school and work situation. Finally, what this study teaches us is that "different" does not imply "worse," and that values developed by studying attitudes and behaviors in the majority culture may not apply to all families—especially those from minority groups.

Parents' Love and Maturity

In the long run, specific parenting practices during a child's first 5 years may be less important than how parents feel about their children and how they show their feelings. That is the conclusion of a major follow-up study (McClelland, Constantian, Regalado, & Stone, 1978) of young adults whose mothers had been interviewed about their child-rearing techniques 20 years earlier (R. R. Sears et al., 1957).

The way these adults turned out seemed to bear little or no relation to how long they had been breastfed, whether they had gone to bed early or late, or a number of other factors. The most important influence—overshadowing all others—

was how much their parents, especially their mothers, had loved them, enjoyed them, and shown affection for them.

The most beloved children grew up to be the most prosocially mature: most tolerant of other people, most understanding, and most likely to show active concern for others. The least mature adults had grown up in homes with adult-centered standards where they were considered a nuisance and an interference. Their parents had tolerated no noise, mess, or roughhousing at home and had reacted unkindly to aggressiveness, sex play, or expressions of normal dependency. Although the children of "easygoing, loving parents" had often behaved less acceptably when they were growing up than the children of stricter parents, this may be a necessary step toward independence from parental values (McClelland et al., 1978, p. 114).

RELATING TO OTHER CHILDREN

Although babies are aware of other babies almost from birth, the most important people in their world are the adults who take care of them. Relationships with peers become important in early childhood. Almost every characteristic activity and personality issue of this age—such as play, gender identity, or aggressive or prosocial behavior—involves relationships with other children, either siblings or friends. But before we look at these relationships, let's look at the children who grow up without any siblings—only children.

The Only Child

Better verbal ability

Since the 1970s, couples have had fewer babies; today, about 1 couple in 10 has an only child. Although people often think of only children as spoiled, selfish, lonely, or maladjusted, research does not bear out this negative view. In fact, according to a statistical analysis of 115 studies comparing only children of various ages and backgrounds and children with siblings (Falbo & Polit, 1986), only children do very well. In occupational and educational achievement, intelligence, and character (or personality), the "onlies" surpassed children with siblings, especially those with many siblings or older siblings. In these three categories, as well as in adjustment and sociability, only children were like firstborns and people with only one sibling. The authors of this statistical analysis point out that only children, like firstborns and children with one sibling, have parents who can spend

Sibling rivalry is *not* the main pattern for brothers and sisters early in life. While some rivalry exists, so do affection, interest, companionship—and influence. *(David Young-Wolff/ PhotoEdit)*

more time and focus more attention on them. Perhaps these children do better because their parents talk to them more, do more with them, and expect more of them.

Being an only child has implications for future development, and these implications may vary from one culture to another. Box 7-2 discusses China, which encourages one-child families.

Brothers and Sisters

When Sally brought her third baby, Dorri, home from the hospital, both Jenny (then 3) and Nancy (5) had colds. The older sisters were so eager to hold the baby that they willingly put on hospital-type face masks. Their interest in their baby sister continued; Jenny often fed Dorri bottles of juice, and Nancy would dry and dress her after her bath. Once Dorri could toddle around, Nancy and Jenny brought her into their fantasy play, making allowances for her inability to follow their instructions or the rules of their games.

Sibling rivalry is *not* the main pattern for brothers and sisters early in life. While some rivalry exists, so do affection, interest, companionship—and influence. Siblings separated by as little as 1 year or as much as 4 years interact closely with each other in many ways (Abramovitch, Corter, & Lando, 1979; Abramovitch, Corter, Pepler, & Stanhope, 1986; Abramovitch, Pepler, & Corter, 1982).

Spend time w/ adults — Lang - Stim.

BOX 7-2   WINDOW ON THE WORLD

A NATION OF ONLY CHILDREN

A group of Chinese kindergartners are learning a new skill: how to fold paper to make toys. When the toys do not come out right, some of the children try again on their own or watch their classmates and copy what they do. But other children become bored and impatient and ask someone else to do it for them, or else they give up, bursting into tears. In some research (Jiao, Ji, & Jing, 1986), the children in the second category tended to come from one-child families—a fact that has worried citizens of the People's Republic of China, which in 1979 established an official policy of limiting families to one child each.

The government is intensely serious about this policy, since China's exploding population means that there are not enough places in classrooms for all its children, not enough jobs for adults, not enough food for everyone. To lower the birthrate, family-planning workers oversee factory workshops and agricultural brigades, and special birth control departments exist in every inhabited area. The policy goes beyond using propaganda campaigns and rewards (housing, money, child care, and school priorities) to induce voluntary compliance. There have been millions of involuntary abortions, sterilizations, and vasectomies, and people who have children without permission are fined and denied job promotions and bonuses. As a result, more only children live in China than in any other country, even though most families formed since 1979 in rural areas (where the policy has not been rigidly enforced until a recent harsh crackdown) have two or three children.

The nursery schools, kindergartens, and early elementary grades of China are filled with children who have no brothers or sisters. This situation marks a great change in Chinese society, in which newlywed couples were traditionally congratulated with the wish, "May you have a hundred sons and a thousand grandsons." No culture in human history has ever been composed entirely of only children. And now that the Chinese are seeing a real possibility of achieving this goal, some critics have asked whether they are sowing the seeds of their own destruction.

Some research, for example, has suggested that only children are more egocentric, less persistent, less cooperative, and less well liked than children with siblings. They were more likely to refuse to help another child or to help grudgingly, less likely to share their toys or to enjoy playing or working with other children, less modest, less helpful in group activities, and more irresponsible (Jiao et al., 1986).

However, new research comparing Chinese schoolchildren with and without siblings contradicts previous findings that only children are spoiled, overindulged "little emperors" (Falbo & Poston, 1993). A sample of 4000 third- and sixth-graders from both urban and rural districts were assessed on academic achievement, physical growth, and personality. Personality traits looked at are those considered desirable in China, such as: "good manners, doesn't cry, keeps trying until finishes task, not selfish, modest, likes to do things better than others, has own ideas, confident, likes to help others, respects elders, doesn't start fights, and pays attention to teacher." These and other traits were rated by the children themselves and by other children, parents, and teachers.

Overall, this research did not point to a risk of abnormal development for only children. In fact, for academic achievement and physical growth, only children did about the same as or better than children with siblings. They did especially well in tests of verbal achievement, and in two of the four provinces studied, only children were either taller or heavier than the others.

Very few personality differences were found, and these varied by sex and by urban or rural residence. In general, only children living in urban areas, and especially boys, were seen to have less desirable personalities, whereas those from rural areas, especially girls, had more desirable personalities. The poorer showing of city children may have been due partly to the fact that the data for this project were collected immediately after the disastrous 1989 Tiananmen demonstrations, and the Beijing schools undoubtedly reflected the turmoil in the country. The better showing of girls may mean that girls are more easily socialized into Chinese personality norms than are boys. In sum, then, birth order and the presence or absence of siblings are not necessarily determining factors for children's development, but have to be weighed in context with the other influences on their lives.

China's population policy also has wider implications of considerable concern. If it succeeds, eventually most Chinese will lack not only siblings but also aunts and uncles, nephews and nieces, and cousins. How this would affect individuals, families, and the social fabric is at present incalculable.

By and large, older siblings initiate more behavior, both friendly (sharing a toy, smiling, hugging, or starting a game) and unfriendly (hitting, fighting over a toy, teasing, or tattling). The younger children tend to imitate the older ones—whether in using scissors or blowing cake crumbs out of their mouths. As children reach their fifth birthdays, siblings are less physical and more verbal in showing aggression (through commands, insults, threats, tattling, put-downs, bribes, and teasing) and care and affection (through compliments and comfort rather than hugs and kisses).

The age difference between siblings apparently has only one effect: in closely spaced pairs, older siblings initiate more prosocial behavior. Same-sex siblings tend to be a bit closer and to play together more peaceably than boy-girl pairs. Siblings tend to get along better when their mother is not with them, suggesting that squabbling is often a bid for parental attention.

Despite some sibling rivalry, then, prosocial and play-oriented behaviors usually constitute a majority of sibling interactions, and their relationships, at least during the preschool years, do not seem to be primarily competitive or negative (Abramovitch et al., 1986).

Relationships between siblings set the stage for other relationships. If relationships with brothers and sisters are marked by trust and companionship, children may carry this pattern over into their dealings with playmates, classmates, and eventually friends and lovers in adulthood. If early sibling relationships are aggressive, this too may influence later social relations.

First Friends

At 3, Sally's daughter Nancy already had a best friend. She and Janie wore a path between their backyards, they asked for each other as soon as they woke up in the morning, and neither was so happy as when she was with her best friend.

Friendship develops as people develop. Although younger children may play alongside or near each other, it is only at about age 3 or so that they begin to have friends. Through friendships and more casual interactions with other children, young children learn how to get along with others. They learn the importance of *being* a friend in order to *have* a friend. They learn how to solve problems in relationships, they learn how to put themselves in another person's place, and they see models of other kinds of behavior. They learn val-

ues (including moral judgments and gender-role norms), and they practice adult roles.

Young children define a friend as "someone you like." Because friendships are voluntary, they are more fragile than the more permanent ties with parents, siblings, and other relatives.

A study of the conceptions of friendship held by 4- to 7-year-olds confirms and adds to these findings (Furman & Bierman, 1983). The children were interviewed and were asked to recognize and rate pictured activities that would make children friends. The most important features of friendships were *common activities* (doing things together), *affection* (liking and caring for each other), *support* (sharing and helping), and, to a lesser degree, *propinquity* (living nearby or going to the same school). Older children rated affection and support higher and *physical characteristics* (appearance and size) lower than younger children did.

Behavior Patterns and Choice of Playmates and Friends

Although playing with someone and being friends are not the same, the traits that make young children desirable or undesirable seem quite similar for both purposes. Children who have friends talk more and take turns directing and following. Children who do not have friends tend to fight with those who do, or to stand on the sidelines and watch them (Roopnarine & Field, 1984). Children like to play with peers who smile and offer a toy or a hand; they reject overtures from disruptive or aggressive children and ignore those who are shy or withdrawn (Roopnarine & Honig, 1985).

One important task of early childhood is learning how to cope with anger-causing situations. Well-liked preschoolers and kindergartners tend to cope well with anger. They respond in relatively direct, active ways that tend to minimize further conflict and help them to keep relationships going. Boys are more likely to express their angry feelings or resist the actions of the child provoking them, whereas girls are more likely to express their disapproval of the other child. Unpopular children are more likely to hit back or tattle to the teacher (S. Asher, Renshaw, Geraci, & Dor, 1979; Fabes & Eisenberg, 1992).

However, popularity itself helps. Popular children are less likely to be involved in angry conflicts, because other children are less likely to attack them or try to take their toys. Then, popular children have a strong coping tool: they can

Young children learn the importance of *being* a friend in order to *have* a friend. One way of being a friend can involve a sighted child's helping a blind playmate to enjoy the feel of the sand and the sound of the surf. *(Nita Winter)*

threaten not to play with or not to like the other child (Fabes & Eisenberg, 1992). While there is something of a cycle going on here, it seems that children who can regulate their anger—either because of inner resources or what they have learned—can handle social situations better than children who cannot. And this translates into popularity.

Family Ties and Popularity

Although young children's relationships with their brothers and sisters often carry over to relationships with other children, patterns established with siblings are not always repeated with friends. A child who is dominated by an elder sibling can easily step into a dominant role with a playmate. And by and large, children are more prosocial and playful with playmates than with siblings (Abramovitch et al., 1986).

Young children's relationships with their parents may be more significant. The parents of popular children generally have warm, positive relationships with their children. They teach by reasoning more than punishment (Kochanska, 1992; Roopnarine & Honig, 1985). They are more likely to be authoritative, and their children have learned to be both assertive and cooperative. Parents of rejected or isolated children have a different profile. The mothers do not have confidence in their parenting, rarely praise their children, and do not encourage independence. The fathers pay little attention to their children, dislike being disturbed by them, and consider child rearing women's work (Peery, Jensen, & Adams, 1984, in Roopnarine & Honig, 1985).

The parents' relationship with each other is another factor. Children whose parents do not get along sometimes respond to this stress in their lives by playing with other children in ways that try to avoid conflict. As a result, they don't participate fully, they miss having fun, and they don't learn the skills of getting along with others (Gottman & Katz, 1989).

Furthermore, children seem to pick up social behaviors from their parents. An Australian study found a close link between the social skills of kindergartners and their mothers (A. Russell & Finnie, 1990). Mothers were asked to help their preschool children join the play of two other children whom the target child did not know. The mothers of popular children were most likely to offer effective, group-oriented suggestions that drew their own child's attention to what the other two were doing; they made positive comments about the playing children and gave ideas about joining the pair. On the other hand, the mothers of children who were either disliked or generally ignored by their classmates showed a lack of sensitivity toward the needs of the pair who were playing. They either disrupted the play by taking charge to make the other children let their own child play, or they gave little or no effective help to their child.

Parents can help their children to make friends by setting up play dates for them. When parents actively arrange their children's social lives, the children have more playmates and see them more often (Ladd & Colter, 1988). Parents who monitor preschoolers' play indirectly—by staying nearby

BOX 7-3 PRACTICALLY SPEAKING

HELPING YOUNG CHILDREN TO MAKE FRIENDS

Having friends helps children develop and contributes to their mental health.

Research suggests that parents and other adults can help children who have trouble finding playmates or making friends by following these recommendations and suggestions (Roopnarine & Honig, 1985):

■ Use positive disciplinary techniques. Give rewards, make rules and their reasons clear,

and encourage cooperation in nonpunitive ways.

■ Be models of warm, nurturing, attentive behavior, and work to build children's self-esteem.

■ Show prosocial behavior yourself, and praise signs of children's budding empathy and responsiveness.

■ Make a special effort to find a play group for children if they do not often have an opportunity to be with other children.

Social skills grow through experience.

■ Encourage "loners" to play with small groups of two or three children at first, and give them ample time to get acquainted before getting involved.

■ Teach "friendship skills" indirectly through puppetry, role-playing, and books about animals and children who learn to make friends.

---

but not getting involved—tend to have more socially competent children than do parents who participate in the play activity. It is not clear, though, which comes first. Parents' early monitoring styles may influence the way their children play with others, or parents of children who are aggressive or do not play well on their own may feel the need to maintain more of a presence. See Box 7-3 for suggestions for helping children make friends.

How children get along with their age-mates affects one of the most important activities of early childhood—play—which we'll look at now.

PLAY

The Importance of Play

Carmen, age 4, wakes up to see her clothes laid out for her. She tries putting her overalls on backward, her shoes on the wrong feet, her socks on her hands, and her shirt inside out. At breakfast, she pretends that the pieces of cereal in her bowl are "fishies" swimming in the milk, and, spoonful by spoonful, she goes fishing. Throughout the long, busy morning, she plays. She puts on an old hat of her mother's, picks up a briefcase, and is a "mommy" going to work. Next she is a doctor, giving her doll a "shot." She runs outside to splash in puddles with a friend and then comes in for an imaginary telephone conversation.

An adult might be tempted to smile indulgently (or enviously) at Carmen and to dismiss her activities as no more than a pleasant way to pass

time. This would be grievously in error. For play is the work of the young of virtually all species.

Through play, children grow. They learn how to use their muscles, they coordinate what they see with what they do, and they gain mastery over their bodies. They find out what the world is like and what *they* are like. They stimulate their senses by playing with water, sand, and mud. They acquire new skills and learn when to use them. And they cope with complex and conflicting emotions by reenacting real life.

Perspectives on Play

We can look at play from different perspectives. Children have different styles of playing, and they play at different things. One kindergartner spends most of her free time playing with other children, while another likes to build block towers by himself. What can we learn about individual children by seeing how they play? To answer such questions, researchers have approached play in two broadly different ways—as a social phenomenon and as an aspect of cognition. Considering play as a social activity, researchers evaluate children's social competence on the basis of how they play. *Social play* reflects the extent to which children interact with other children in play. *Cognitive play* reveals the level of a child's cognitive development, and also enhances that development.

Social and Nonsocial Play

In the 1920s, Mildred B. Parten (1932) observed forty-two 2- to 5-year-olds during free-play periods at nursery school. She identified six types of

TABLE 7-3

Types of Social and Nonsocial Play in Early Childhood

Category	Description
Unoccupied behavior	The child does not seem to be playing, but watches anything of momentary interest.
Onlooker behavior	The child spends most of the time watching other children play. The onlooker talks to them, asking questions or making suggestions, but does not enter into the play. The onlooker is definitely observing particular groups of children rather than anything in general that happens to be exciting.
Solitary independent play	The child plays alone with toys that are different from those used by nearby children and makes no effort to get close to the other children.
Parallel play	The child plays independently but among other children, playing with toys like those used by the other children, but not necessarily in the same way. Playing *beside* rather than *with* the others, the parallel player does not try to influence the other children's play.
Associative play	The child plays with other children. They talk about their play, borrow and lend toys, follow one another, and try to control who may play in the group. All the children play similarly if not identically; there is no division of labor and no organization around any goal. Each child acts as he or she wishes and is interested more in being with the other children than in the activity itself.
Cooperative or organized supplementary play	The child plays in a group organized for some goal—to make something, play a formal game, or dramatize a situation. One or two children control who belongs to the group and direct activities. By a division of labor, children take on different roles and supplement each other's efforts.

SOURCE: Adapted from Parten, 1932, pp. 249–251.

play, ranging from the most nonsocial to the most social (see Table 7-3), determined the time devoted to each type, and charted the children's activities. She found that as children get older, their play tends to become more social and cooperative.

More recent research, however, suggests different conclusions. In a similar study done 40 years later, forty-four 3- and 4-year-olds played much less sociably than the children in Parten's group (K. E. Barnes, 1971). Why was this so? The change might have reflected a changed environment: because these children watched television, they may have become more passive; because they had more elaborate toys and fewer siblings, they may have played alone more.

Is solitary play less mature than group play? Some observers have suggested that young children who play alone may be at risk of developing social, psychological, and educational problems. But research has found that much nonsocial play consists of constructive or educational activities and furthers a child's cognitive, physical, and social development.

In an analysis of children in six kindergartens, about one-third of solitary play consisted of such goal-directed activities as block building and artwork, about one-fourth was large-muscle play, about 15 percent was educational, and only about 10 percent involved just looking at the other children (N. Moore, Evertson, & Brophy, 1974). Solitary play can be a sign of independence and maturity rather than poor social adjustment.

Another study looked at nonsocial play in relation to the cognitive and social competence of 4-year-olds. It used roletaking and problem-solving tests, teachers' ratings of social competence, and popularity with other children. Some kinds of nonsocial play turned out to be associated with a high level of competence. For example, parallel constructive play (activities like playing with blocks or working on puzzles near another child) is most common among children who are good problem solvers, are popular, and are seen by teachers as socially skilled (K. Rubin, 1982).

Not all nonsocial play, then, is immature. Children need some time alone to concentrate on tasks and problems, and some simply enjoy nonsocial activities more than group activities. We need to pay attention to what children *do* when they play, not just at whether they play alone or with someone else.

Cognitive Play

According to Piaget (1951) and Smilansky (1968), children's cognitive development in early childhood lets them progress (as shown in Table 7-4) from simple functional (repetitive) play (like rolling a ball) to constructive play (like building a block tower), dramatic play (like playing doctor), and then formal games with rules (like hopscotch and marbles). These more complex forms of play, in turn, foster further cognitive development.

Imaginative (Dramatic) Play

Kaia, at 13 months, pushes an imaginary spoon holding imaginary food into the mouth of her very real father. Joseph, at 2 years, "talks" to a doll as if it were a real person. Lee, at 3 years, wears a kitchen towel as a cape and runs around as Batman.

These children are engaged in *imaginative play,* play involving invented situations. (Imaginative play is also called *fantasy play, dramatic play,* or *pretend play.*) At one time, professionals' main interest in such play was its supposed role in helping children express their emotional concerns, but interest now focuses more on its role in cognitive and general personality development.

Imaginative play emerges during the second year of life when sensorimotor play is on the wane. It increases during the next 3 to 4 years and then declines as children become more interested in playing games with formal rules, like checkers and other board games. Piaget (1962) maintained that children's ability to pretend rests on their ability to use and remember symbols—to retain in their minds pictures of things they have seen or heard—and that its emergence marks the beginning of the preoperational stage (see Chapter 6).

This preschooler playing with toy people and miniature everyday objects is showing an important cognitive development of early childhood: the ability to use symbols to stand for people or things in the real world. *(John Coletti/The Picture Cube)*

About 10 to 17 percent of preschoolers' play is imaginative play, and the proportion rises to about 33 percent among kindergartners (K. Rubin et al., 1976; K. Rubin, Watson, & Jambor, 1978). The kind of play, as well as its amount, changes during these years from solitary pretending to *sociodramatic play*

TABLE 7-4

Types of Cognitive Play

Category	Description
Functional play (sensorimotor play)	Any simple, repetitive muscle movement with or without objects, such as rolling a ball or pulling a pull toy
Constructive play	Manipulation of objects to construct or to "create" something
Dramatic play (imaginative play)	Substitution of an imaginary situation to satisfy the child's personal wishes and needs. Pretending to be someone or something (doctor, nurse, Batman), beginning with fairly simple activities but going on to develop more elaborate plots
Games with rules	Any activity with rules, structure, and a goal (such as winning), like tag, hopscotch, marbles
	Acceptance of prearranged rules and adjustment to them

SOURCE: Piaget, 1951; Smilansky, 1968.

BOX 7-4   FOOD FOR THOUGHT

IMAGINARY PLAYMATES

At age 3½, Anna had 23 sisters, with such names as Och, Elmo, Zeni, Aggie, and Ankie. She often talked to them on the telephone, since they lived about 100 miles away, in the town where her family used to live. Over the next year, most of the sisters disappeared, but Och has continued to visit, especially for birthday parties. Och has a cat and a dog (which Anna has begged for in vain), and whenever Anna is denied something that she wants advertised on television, she announces that she already has one at her sister's house.

All 23 sisters—and some "boys" and "girls" who have followed them—live only in Anna's imagination. Like about 15 to 30 percent of children between ages 3 and 10, she has created imaginary companions, with whom she talks and plays. This normal phenomenon of childhood is seen most often in bright, creative firstborn and only children (Manosevitz, Prentice, & Wilson, 1973). Girls are more likely to have them than are boys (or are at least more likely to acknowledge them), and girls' imaginary playmates are usually human, while boys' are more often animals (D. G. Singer & Singer, 1990).

Children who have such imaginary companions are able to distinguish fantasy from reality, but in free-play sessions they are more likely to engage in fantasy play than are children without imaginary companions (Taylor, Cartwright, & Carlson, 1993). They play more happily and more imaginatively than other children and are more cooperative with other children and adults (D. G. Singer & Singer, 1990; J. L. Singer & Singer, 1981). They are more fluent with language, watch less television, and show more curiosity, excitement, and persistence during play.

What role do these companions play in a child's life? They are good company for an only child (like Anna) and provide wish-fulfillment mechanisms ("There was a monster in my room, but Elmo scared it off with magic dust"), scapegoats ("I didn't eat those cookies—Och must have done it!"), supports in difficult situations (like the 6-year-old who "took" her imaginary companion with her to see a scary movie), and displacement agents for the child's own fears ("Aggie is afraid she's going to be washed down the drain"). In sum, children usually use such companions to help them get along better in the real world.

---

involving other children. Jessie, who at age 3 would climb inside a box by herself and pretend to be a train conductor, will by age 6 want to have passengers on her train with whom she can enact minidramas. Through pretending, children learn how to understand another person's viewpoint, develop skills in solving social problems, and become more creative (Doyle, Doehring, Tessier, deLorimier, & Shapiro, 1992; Singer & Singer, 1990). Many children's imaginative play extends to imaginary playmates (see Box 7-4).

Influences on Play: Parents, Day Care Centers, and Gender

Parents of children who play imaginatively tend to get along well with each other, expose their children to interesting experiences, talk with them, and not spank them. Children who watch a lot of television play less imaginatively, possibly because they passively absorb images rather than generating their own (Fein, 1981). Mothers who engage their children in a lot of imaginative play tend to have children who play more and for longer times with other children (Vandell & Ramanan, 1991).

Time in good group-based day care tends to be associated with sociable play. In one study of children from three centers, those in a large community center and those in a small university-based center played more sociably the longer they had been in day care (Schindler, Moely, & Frank, 1987). This was not true of children in a small private center. The other two centers had mixed-age groups and higher adult-child ratios and emphasized social skills more than academic ones. Another study found that children in high-quality day care played at more complex levels than children in barely adequate care (Howes & Matheson, 1992). The different effects of various care situations underscore the need to look at every day care situation individually, rather than making sweeping statements about "effects of day care."

At age 4, Anna much prefers to play with other girls than with boys (even her imaginary companions are all female now). She constantly classifies toys, games, and activities as "girls'" things or "boys'" things, and when she is not sure about a particular item, she asks Diane to tell her. Stefan, too, is more interested these days in playing with children of his own sex.

The tendency toward sex segregation in play is common among preschoolers; it becomes more so in middle childhood, and it is universal across cultures (Maccoby, 1988, 1990). One reason for the split seems to be the different styles of play that boys and girls typically adopt; and neither sex, by and large, seems to like the other's approach. Although there are, of course, many individual exceptions, boys tend to like rough-and-tumble play in fairly large groups, while girls are more inclined to quieter play with one other child. School-age boys more often play in the streets and other public places, whereas girls are more likely to meet in each other's home or yard.

Another factor seems to be girls' realization, at an age when children try to influence their playmates more and more frequently, that boys do not pay attention to girls' requests and suggestions, and that boys tend to make their own wishes known by direct demands. Even among 33-month-old children, boys tend not to withdraw from a place when a girl asks them to, but they are more likely to do so when a boy tells them to. Eleanor Maccoby (1990) suggests that girls withdraw from boys when they sense this lack of responsiveness. It is also possible that the realization by girls that boys do not respond to them as readily as to other boys may contribute to the lower self-esteem noted in girls nearing puberty (see Chapter 11).

We'll look at issues like self-esteem, as well as the other aspects of development in middle childhood (from about age 6 to 12) in Chapters 8 and 9.

SUMMARY

IMPORTANT PERSONALITY DEVELOPMENTS IN EARLY CHILDHOOD

■ Several types of theories attempt to explain how young children acquire gender identity—awareness that they are male or female—moral standards, and other aspects of personality. These perspectives are the psychoanalytic, social-learning, cognitive-developmental, and cognitive-social approaches.

■ Erikson maintains that the chief developmental crisis of early childhood is the development of a balance between initiative and guilt. The successful resolution of this conflict is the virtue of purpose; this enables the child to undertake, plan, and carry out activities in pursuit of goals. The outcome of this stage is strongly influenced by how parents deal with their children.

■ Identification is the adoption of the characteristics, beliefs, attitudes, values, and behaviors of another person or a group. It is an important personality development of early childhood.

■ Gender identification is the awareness and identification of oneself as male or female.

■ In Freudian terms, the child identifies with the same-sex parent at the resolution of the Oedipus or Electra complex.

■ According to social-learning theory, identification occurs when the child observes and imitates one or more models.

■ The cognitive-developmental theory maintains that the development of gender identity is related to cognitive development.

■ The gender-schema theory, a variation of cognitive-developmental theory that draws on aspects of social learning, holds that children fit their self-concept to the gender schema for their culture, a socially organized pattern of behavior for males and females. According to this theory, the gender schema of a culture or an individual can be changed.

ASPECTS AND ISSUES OF PERSONALITY DEVELOPMENT

■ Sex differences are physical differences between males and females; gender differences are psychological or behavioral differences between the sexes that may or may not be based on biology.

■ Gender roles are the behaviors and attitudes a culture deems appropriate for males and females. Gender-typing refers to the learning of culturally determined gender roles.

■ There are few actual behavioral differences between the sexes. After about age 10 or 11, girls do better in verbal abilities, and boys do better in math and spatial abilities. Boys are more aggressive than girls from early childhood, and girls are more empathic. However, these differences are quite small and usually meaningless. Boys and girls are more similar than different.

■ Despite these relatively minor gender differences, our society holds strong ideas about appropriate behaviors for the two sexes, and children learn these expectations at an early age.

■ Gender stereotypes—exaggerated generalizations that may not be true of individuals—have the potential to restrict the development of both sexes. Androgynous child rearing, which encourages the expression of both "male" and "female" characteristics, is being fostered by many individuals and social institutions.

■ Explanations for gender differences have focused on both biological and environmental factors. Both types of influences appear to have an impact.

■ Preschool children show many fears of both real and imaginary objects and events. Conditioning and modeling can help children overcome fears.

■ Whether children exhibit aggression or prosocial behavior is influenced by the way their parents treat them as well as by other factors, such as what they learn from the media and whether they observe aggressive or prosocial models.

▪ Parents influence children's behavior partly through rewards and punishments. Rewards are generally more effective than punishments.

▪ Punishments are most effective when they are immediate, consistent, accompanied by an explanation, and carried out by a person who has a good relationship with the child. Physical punishment can have damaging effects.

▪ Baumrind has identified three types of child-rearing styles: authoritarian, permissive, and authoritative. Each is related to certain personality traits in children. The authoritative style has the most positive outcomes.

▪ Parents' love is the most important influence on the social maturity that their children will exhibit as adults.

▪ Relationships with siblings and peers appear to be important in determining the pattern of relationships later in life.

▪ As siblings move through early childhood, most of their interactions are positive. Sibling rivalry is not the dominant pattern. As they mature, their interaction is less often physical and more often verbal. Older siblings tend to be dominant and are both more aggressive and more prosocial.

▪ Only children develop at least as well as children with siblings.

▪ Children who are aggressive or withdrawn tend to be less popular with playmates than children who act friendly. The type of attachment they have had in infancy—as well as their parents' attitudes, disciplinary techniques, and child-rearing styles—affects the ease with which young children find playmates and friends.

▪ Play is both a social and a cognitive activity. Changes in the type of play children engage in reflect their development. Through play, children exercise their physical abilities, grow cognitively, and learn to interact with other children. Play is influenced by parents, type of day care, and gender. Having imaginary companions in childhood is associated with healthy psychological development.

KEY TERMS

initiative versus guilt (page 241)
identification (241)
gender (241)
gender identity (241)
gender roles (241)
gender constancy (gender conservation) (244)
gender-schema theory (244)

gender schema (244)
sex differences (245)
gender differences (246)
gender-typing (246)
gender stereotypes (246)
androgynous (247)
aggressive behavior (250)
prosocial behavior (254)

behavior modification (255)
authoritarian parents (257)
permissive parents (257)
authoritative parents (257)
social play (263)
cognitive play (263)
imaginative play (265)

SUGGESTED READINGS

Anthony, E. J., & Cohler, B. J. (Eds.). (1987). *The invulnerable child.* New York: Guilford. An important sourcebook of scholarly papers on the development of competence, the interaction of personality and experience in early childhood, and the extraordinary resilience shown by many children subjected to a variety of calamities.

Axline, V. M. (1967). *Dibs in search of self.* New York: Ballantine. This immensely moving and readable classic is the story of the play therapy that enabled a silent, withdrawn child to become his true, intelligent, and emotionally expressive self.

Brazelton, T. B. (1992). *Touchpoints: Your child's emotional and behavioral development.* Reading, MA: Addison-Wesley. This comprehensive reference book by the pediatrician who developed the Brazelton Neonatal Behavioral Assessment Scale discusses and gives advice to parents relating to issues that come up during the first six years of children's lives. The author defines "touchpoints" as universal spurts of development and periods of regression during childhood.

Faber, A., & Mazlish, E. (1988). *Siblings without rivalry.* New York: Avon. This book offers dozens of practical guidelines and real-life examples for fostering healthy and cooperative sibling relationships.

Hopson, D., & Powell-Hopson, D. (1990). *Different and wonderful: Raising black children in a race-conscious society.* Englewood Cliffs, NJ: Prentice-Hall. On the basis of their research in this area and their experience as parents, two clinical psychologists advise on such issues as toys, choosing day care and schools, and enhancing self-esteem. This book is not just for African American parents; it is a great source for anyone working with children of different races.

Turecki, S., with Wernick, S. (1994). *The emotional problems of normal children.* New York: Bantam. A compassionate and practical guide with two basic points: Normal children can have problems, and parents can help them. Illustrated with vivid vignettes from the author's practice as a child and family psychiatrist, this work shows how parents can use their intimate knowledge of the child to intervene. You'll also find guidelines for deciding when to seek professional help and what to expect if you do.

PART THREE

MIDDLE CHILDHOOD

uring the middle years of childhood—the elementary school years, from about age 6 to about age 12—children continue to make great strides in development.

■ In **Chapter 8**, we note children's physical and intellectual progress as they continue to grow taller, heavier, and stronger and to learn new skills and cognitive concepts. And children become better at things they have already been doing. They can throw a ball farther and more accurately and can run faster and for a longer time. They apply their knowledge of numbers, words, and concepts more and more effectively.

■ The personality traits that children have already begun to display are etched more deeply, as we'll see in **Chapter 9.** While parents still exert an important influence, the peer group now becomes very important too. Children want to be with their friends, and they develop socially through their contacts with other youngsters.

Childhood is not, of course, a time of pure bliss. The stresses children deal with include family upheavals, difficulties in getting along with other children, demands of schoolwork, and events in the world beyond their own circle. Some children suffer emotional disturbances, partly in response to such stresses. Others seem to be energized to build healthy, fulfilling lives. To meet the challenge of these years, children develop more competence in all realms of development.

CHAPTER EIGHT

PHYSICAL AND INTELLECTUAL DEVELOPMENT IN MIDDLE CHILDHOOD

What we must remember above all in the education of our children is that their love of life should never weaken.

Natalia Ginzburg,
The Little Virtues, 1985

PHYSICAL DEVELOPMENT

■ **GROWTH DURING MIDDLE CHILDHOOD**

Growth Rates
Nutrition and Growth

■ **HEALTH, FITNESS, AND SAFETY**

Children's Health
Children's Safety

■ **MOTOR DEVELOPMENT IN MIDDLE CHILDHOOD**

INTELLECTUAL DEVELOPMENT

■ **ASPECTS OF INTELLECTUAL DEVELOPMENT IN MIDDLE CHILDHOOD**

Cognitive Development: Piaget's Stage
of Concrete Operations
Moral Reasoning: Two Theories

Development of Memory: Information
Processing
Development of Intelligence: Psychometrics
Development of Language: Communication

■ **CHILDREN IN SCHOOL**

Educational Trends
Teachers' Characteristics and Expectations
Parents' Influence
Education for Special Needs
Bilingualism and Bilingual Education

■ **BOXES**

8-1 Food for Thought: Children's
Understanding of Health and Illness
8-2 Take a Stand: Should IQ Tests Be Used?
8-3 Window on the World: How Can Asian
Children Achieve So Much?
8-4 Practically Speaking: Teaching Children
to Think

■ What gains in growth and motor development do children make in middle childhood, and what health hazards do they face?

■ How do schoolchildren think and remember, and what progress do they make in moral development and communicative abilities?

■ How can intelligence be measured, particularly in minority and disadvantaged children?

■ How can schools and parents enhance children's intellectual development?

■ What are the special needs of disabled and gifted children, and how can they be met?

■ What is creativity, and how can it be nurtured?

Compared with the pace of physical and intellectual development in early childhood, development between the ages of 6 and 12 may seem slow. Physical growth has slowed down considerably—except for the growth spurt toward the end of this period—and while motor abilities continue to improve, changes are less dramatic than they were earlier. But development is still highly significant. Intellectual growth is substantial, as the once-egocentric child becomes more logical. And with many day-by-day changes, there is a startling difference between 6-year-olds, who are still small children, and 12-year-olds, now almost adults.

Although these years are among the healthiest in the life span, many children are not as healthy or as physically fit as they should be. We'll consider why this is so. We'll also look at cognitive development, which proceeds largely within the framework of school. It is hardly coincidental that the usual age in the western world for beginning formal study coincides with important changes in children's mental abilities. These changes are recognized by each of three major approaches to intellectual development: Jean Piaget described entry into the stage of concrete operations; the information-processing approach focuses on improvements in memory and problem solving; and psychometric intelligence tests are more accurate now at predicting school performance. We'll examine these three approaches, along with children's moral development and their development of language. After looking at all these changes, we'll consider several aspects of schools, including how they try to meet the special needs of children with physical or mental disabilities or exceptional gifts.

■ PHYSICAL DEVELOPMENT

Walk by a typical elementary school just after the last bell, and you will see an eruption of children of all shapes and sizes. Tall ones, short ones, chubby ones, and thin ones dash helter-skelter through the school doors and into the freedom of the open air. Although it may not be obvious, many of these children are not as physically fit as they should be.

Follow these children on their way home from school, and you'll see some leaping up onto narrow ledges and then walking along, balancing themselves, until they jump off, trying to break distance records—but occasionally breaking bones instead. Some children will reach home (or, often, a baby-sitter's house) not to emerge for the rest of the day. They could be outdoors honing new skills in jumping, running, throwing, catching, balancing, cycling, or climbing—becoming stronger, faster, and better coordinated. Instead, many will stay indoors watching television or playing quietly.

GROWTH DURING MIDDLE CHILDHOOD

GROWTH RATES

Both boys and girls gain an average of 7 pounds and 2 to 3 inches a year until the adolescent growth spurt, which begins at about age 10 for girls. Then, girls are on average taller and heavier than boys until the boys begin *their* spurt at about age 12 or 13 and overtake the girls.

Children vary widely, however—so widely that "if a child who was of exactly average height at his seventh birthday grew not at all for two years, he would still be just within the normal limits of height attained at age nine" (Tanner, 1973, p. 35).

Growth rates vary with race, national origin, and socioeconomic level. A study of 8-year-old children in different parts of the world yielded a range of about 9 inches between the average height of the shortest children (mostly from southeast Asia, Oceania, and South America) and the tallest ones (mostly from northern and central Europe, eastern Australia, and the United States) (Meredith, 1969). Although genetic differences account for some of this diversity, environmental influences are important. The tallest children come from parts of the world where malnutrition and infectious disease are not major problems. For similar reasons, children from affluent homes tend to be larger and more mature than children from poorer homes.

Given the wide variance in size during middle childhood, we have to be careful about assessing children's health or identifying possible abnormalities in physical growth. Especially in the United States, which is racially and ethnically diverse, we may need to develop separate growth standards for different groups.

NUTRITION AND GROWTH

In the middle years, children usually have good appetites. They need to eat well: their play demands energy, and their body weight will double in these years. To support constant exertion and steady growth, children need a daily average of 2400 calories, 34 grams of protein, and high levels of complex carbohydrates, like those in potatoes and grains. Refined carbohydrates (sweeteners) should be kept to a minimum (E. R. Williams & Caliendo, 1984).

For some years, the idea that sugar makes children hyperactive, interferes with learning, or has other negative effects on behavior or mood has gained currency. However, although sweets are less desirable in anyone's diet because they generally provide nonnutritive calories, neither sugar nor the artificial sweetener aspartame affects children's behavior or mood adversely (Rosen et al., 1988; Saravis, Schachar, Zlotkin, Leiter, & Anderson, 1990). Sugar's "bad press" may have resulted from its reputation as an energy food and also from its presence in large amounts at such events as birthday parties, where the real cause of disruptive behavior is the situation, not the sweets.

What children need to stay alive, and then to grow normally, are rich sources of energy and protein. When meals cannot support survival and growth, growth is sacrificed to maintain the body.

Malnutrition

Nutrition also has social implications. Children cannot play and stay alert without enough food. The effects of poor nutrition can be long-lasting. A longitudinal study in Guatemala, where malnutrition is a serious problem, found that diet from birth to age 2 is a good predictor of social behavior in

In the middle years, children need to eat well: their play demands energy, and their body weight will double in these years. To support constant exertion and steady growth, children need high levels of complex carbohydrates, like those in potatoes and grains, and a minimum of refined carbohydrates (sweets). *(Tom McCarthy/PhotoEdit)*

middle childhood. Of 138 children, ages 6 to 8, who had received dietary supplements in infancy, all had received extra calories and vitamins but only some had received proteins. The children who had not had extra proteins as infants tended to be passive, anxious, and dependent on adults, while the better-nourished children were happier, feistier, and more sociable with their peers (D. E. Barrett, Radke-Yarrow, & Klein, 1982).

Furthermore, poor nutrition may cause problems in family relationships. Mothers may respond less frequently and less sensitively to malnourished babies, who lack the energy to engage a mother's attention. The infants, in turn, become unresponsive and develop poor interpersonal skills, further reducing their mothers' and other people's inclination or desire to interact with them (B. M. Lester, 1979). If the mother is malnourished too, the cycle worsens (Rosetti-Ferreira, 1978).

Links between nutrition and cognitive development are also clear. African children in Kenya who suffered mild to moderate undernutrition scored lower than well-nourished children on a test of verbal abilities and on a matrix test that asked the child to select a pattern to fit in with a set of other patterns (Sigman, Neumann, Jansen, & Bwibo, 1989). And low-income third- to sixth-graders who took part in a school breakfast program in Massachusetts improved their scores on achievement tests (A. F. Meyers, Sampson, Weitzman, Rogers, & Kayne, 1989). Here again, we see how closely the different domains of development—physical, personality, and cognitive—are related.

Obesity

Obesity—fatness—in children has become a major health issue in the United States since the 1970s, as it has become more common among 6- to 11-year-olds. In a 6-year study of nearly 2600 mostly white, middle-class children under age 12, about 5½ percent of 8- to 11-year-olds were obese (Gortmaker, Dietz, Sobol, & Wehler, 1987; Starfield et al., 1984).

What makes children fat? Research findings are most often correlational, meaning that we cannot draw cause-and-effect conclusions. However, there seems to be a strong basis for believing that overweight often results from an inherited predisposition, aggravated by behavior involving too little exercise and too much food.

Some people seem to be genetically predisposed toward obesity. As we pointed out in Chapter 2, it

is twice as likely that both identical twins will be overweight than that both fraternal twins will be (A. J. Stunkard, Harris, Pederson, & McClearn, 1990). Environment also has a strong influence: obesity is more common among lower socioeconomic groups, especially among women. Fat children are less active than other children and tend to watch more television (Dietz & Gortmaker, 1985; Kolata, 1986).

Fat children do not usually "outgrow" being fat; they tend to become fat adults (Kolata, 1986), and obesity in adulthood puts them at risk of health problems like high blood pressure, diabetes, and orthopedic problems.

Childhood obesity can be treated. Behavioral therapy, which helps children change their eating and exercise habits, is especially effective when it also involves parents (L. H. Epstein & Wing, 1987). Parents learn not to use foods as rewards for good behavior, to provide a smaller variety of foods, and to stop buying tempting high-calorie foods.

HEALTH, FITNESS, AND SAFETY

CHILDREN'S HEALTH

Richard, aged 10, is home in bed with a cold. He sneezes, snoozes, watches television, pulls out his old books and toys, and, in general, enjoys the rest from his usual routine. He is lucky. He has had no illnesses this year other than two colds, while some of his classmates have had six or seven respiratory infections. That number of respiratory infections is common during middle childhood, as germs pass freely among youngsters at school or at play (Behrman & Vaughan, 1983).

But even though children do get a lot of colds at this age, most of them are healthier than their counterparts early in this century. The development of vaccines for many childhood illnesses has made middle childhood a relatively safe time of life, physically. Vaccination rates are much better for children of this age than for younger ones, since immunization is required for school admission. This may be one reason the death rate in middle childhood is the lowest in the life span.

However, some recent research has found that about 1 in 4 children aged 4 to 8 show some kind of psychosocial or developmental problem. The children's problems include learning disabilities, speech delay, temper tantrums, and bed-wetting;

BOX 8-1 FOOD FOR THOUGHT

CHILDREN'S UNDERSTANDING OF HEALTH AND ILLNESS

Children's understanding of health and illness is closely tied to their cognitive development.

At the beginning of middle childhood, children do not always think logically. During this period, children tend to believe that illness is magically produced by human actions, often their own. Magical explanations can last well into childhood. One 12-year-old with leukemia said, "I know that my doctor told me that my illness is caused by too many white cells, but I still wonder if it was caused by something I did" (Brewster, 1982, p. 361). It would be hard for a parent or professional who overheard this remark to keep from saying, "There, there, of course it wasn't anything you did." But this reaction may not be as supportive as we might think. Egocentric explanations for illness can serve as a defense against feelings of helplessness. Children may feel that if something they did made them ill, perhaps they can do something else to get better. One researcher warns, "It is never wise to break down defenses until one is sure that more desirable concepts will take their place" (Brewster, 1982, p. 362).

With cognitive development, children's explanations for disease change. They enter a stage in which they explain all diseases—hardly less magically—by germs. "Watch out for germs" is the motto of children of this age, who believe that germs cause disease automatically. The only "prevention" is a variety of superstitious behaviors to ward off germs. Last, as children approach adolescence, they enter a third stage when they see that there can be multiple causes of disease, that contact with the dreaded germs does not automatically lead to illness, and that people can do much to keep healthy.

Over the past few years, as acquired immune deficiency syndrome (AIDS) has spread, many attempts have been made to educate the public, including children. To find out how much children understand about this disease, researchers interviewed preschoolers and first-, third-, and fifth-graders (Schvaneveldt, Lindauer, & Young, 1990). The children's knowledge was related to their general perceptions about illness, and accurate understanding was directly related to age. Preschoolers knew practically nothing about AIDS; some did not even remember conversations about it with their parents just the evening before their interviews. Third- and fifth-graders had a fair amount of accurate information about the causes, outcome, and prevention of AIDS, although in both age levels the children held such mistaken beliefs as that AIDS could be contracted from mosquito bites or that it could be prevented by good nutrition.

It is important to gear any teaching about illness to children's levels of understanding. The most informative curriculum in the world will fail if it goes over the heads of the pupils for whom it is meant.

family problems include divorce or a parent's illness or absence because of imprisonment (Horwitz, Leaf, Leventhal, Forsyth, & Speechley, 1992).

Because of their cognitive development, which we'll discuss in the next section of this chapter, children in this age group are beginning to understand the causes of health and illness and that people can do much to promote their own health (see Box 8-1). Let's look now at some aspects of health and fitness in middle childhood.

Minor Medical Conditions

What health problems crop up in these years? The study of mostly white middle-class children in a health maintenance plan found varied conditions, from allergies to warts. Almost all the youngsters got sick from time to time, but their ailments tended to be brief. During the 6 years of the study, almost all the children had acute (short-term) medical conditions—usually upper-respiratory infections, viruses, or eczema—but only 1 in 9 had chronic (persistent) conditions like migraine headaches or nearsightedness. Eighty percent were treated for injuries. Upper-respiratory illnesses, sore throats, strep throats, ear infections, and bed-wetting decreased with age; but acne, headaches, and transitory emotional disturbances increased as youngsters approached puberty (Starfield et al., 1984). There has been an increase in this age group in chronic conditions that limit children's activity (Starfield, 1991).

Vision

Most schoolchildren have much keener vision than they had earlier in life. Children under 6 years of age tend to be farsighted because their eyes have

These girls proudly show off a childhood milestone—the normal loss of baby teeth, which will be replaced by permanent ones. American children today have about one-third fewer dental cavities than did children of a decade earlier, probably owing to the widespread use of fluoride and to better dental care. *(Mary Kate Denny/PhotoEdit)*

not matured and are shaped differently from those of adults. After that age, the eyes can focus better.

In a minority of children, however, vision does not develop normally. Ten percent of 6-year-olds have defective near vision, and 7 percent have defective distant vision; by 11 years of age 17 percent have problems seeing things at a distance (U.S. Department of Health, Education, and Welfare, USDHEW, 1976).

Dental Health

Most of the teeth that must serve people for the rest of their lives appear near the onset of middle childhood. The primary teeth begin to fall out at about age 6, to be replaced by about four permanent teeth per year for the next 5 years. The first molars erupt at about age 6, followed by the second molars at about 13, and the third molars (the wisdom teeth) usually during the early twenties (Behrman & Vaughan, 1983).

About one-half of 5- to 17-year-olds in the United States have no tooth decay (U.S. Department of Health and Human Services, USDHHS, 1988). American children today have about one-third fewer dental cavities than were reported in similar surveys at the beginning of the 1980s, when they had an average of almost five decayed or missing teeth or filled surfaces (USDHHS, 1981a, 1988). This improvement seems to be due to the widespread use of fluoride in tablets, and also in drinking water, toothpaste, mouthwash, and foods prepared with fluoridated water—and to better dental care. Two-thirds of the decay in children's

teeth is on the rough chewing surfaces; much of this can be prevented with the use of adhesive *sealants*, plastic films that harden after being painted onto teeth.

General Fitness

Today's schoolchildren are less physically fit than children were during the mid-1960s. Their hearts and lungs are in worse shape than those of an average middle-aged jogger. In one typical midwestern working-class community, 98 percent of the 7- to 12-year-olds had at least one of the following major risk factors for developing heart disease later in life: their levels of body fat averaged 2 to 5 percent above the national average (which itself is unhealthily high), 41 percent had high levels of cholesterol, and 28 percent had higher than normal blood pressure (C. T. Kuntzleman, personal communication, 1984).

Why are these children in such poor physical shape? It may be because they are not active enough. Only half take physical education classes as often as twice a week, fewer than half stay active during cold weather, and most do not spend enough time learning such lifetime fitness skills as running, swimming, bicycling, and walking. Many watch too much television. Most physical activities, in and outside of school, are team and competitive sports and games, which do not promote fitness, are usually dropped once the young person is out of school, and are generally played by the most athletic youngsters, not by those who need more exercise.

POOR ATHLETES ARE DISCOURAGED

Improving Health and Fitness

Children's health and fitness *can* be improved. One important step is to bring down high blood pressure. If a child's blood pressure is above the 95th percentile for age and sex after three measurements, treatment should begin. Taking off excess weight, reducing salt intake, and increasing aerobic exercise usually help, but some children are also given drugs to avoid heart damage (American Academy of Pediatrics, AAP, Task Force on Blood Pressure Control in Children, 1987).

Sometimes, just changing everyday behavior brings about considerable improvement. Parents, for example, can make exercise a family activity, by regularly hiking or playing ball together, replacing driving with walking whenever possible, and limiting television viewing, which has been linked to high cholesterol levels in children (Wong et al., 1992). Excessive TV viewing also seems to lower children's metabolic rates, putting them at risk of obesity because their resting energy expenditures become lower than if they were doing nothing at all (Klesges, Shelton, & Klesges, 1993).

One education and behavior modification program taught about 24,000 Michigan children how to analyze foods; how to measure their blood pressure, heart rate, and body fat; and how to withstand advertising and peer pressures to smoke and to eat "junk" foods. The program also encouraged children to take part in vigorous games. Results for 360 second-, fifth-, and seventh-graders were heartening. They had become faster at running a mile; they had lowered levels of cholesterol, blood pressure, and body fat; and the number without any risk factors for developing coronary disease had risen by 55 percent (Fitness Finders, 1984).

Schools should provide sound physical education programs with a variety of sports, with an emphasis on enjoyment rather than winning, and on activities that can be part of a lifetime fitness regimen—like tennis, bowling, running, swimming, golf, and skating (AAP Committee on Sports Medicine and Committee on School Health, 1989).

CHILDREN'S SAFETY

Almost 22 million children are injured in the United States each year, making injury the leading cause of disability and death in children over 1 year of age (Sheps & Evans, 1987). Boys average more accidents than girls, probably because they take more physical risks (Ginsburg & Miller, 1982). Injuries increase from ages 5 to 14, as children become involved in more physical activities and are supervised less (Schor, 1987).

A child's family also affects safety. A longitudinal study of 693 families who sought medical care over a 6-year period found that a small number of families accounted for a large number of injuries. After adjustment for family size, 10 percent of the families accounted for almost 25 percent of the injuries (Schor, 1987). Children with siblings have more injuries than only children. Parents of more than one child may not be as vigilant as parents of one child, or younger children may imitate their older siblings and take more risks, or children in

These enthusiastic soccer players are proving that girls are often much better athletes than they were given credit for (or given the opportunity to be) in the past. Studies show that boys and girls who take part in similar activities show similar abilities. *(George Ancona/International Stock)*

larger families may be more active. Families with high injury rates may be undergoing stress that interferes with the ability to make the home safe or watch over children.

The most common cause of serious injury and death in young schoolchildren is being hit by a moving vehicle. Parents tend to overestimate the safety skills of young children. Many kindergartners and first-graders walk alone to school, often crossing busy streets without traffic lights, although they do not have the skills to do this safely. Parents have to know their children's limitations as pedestrians, and schools should offer transportation (Dunne, Asher, & Rivara, 1992; Rivara, Bergman, & Drake, 1989).

Most childhood accidents occur in (or are inflicted by) automobiles, or occur in the home; but between 10 and 20 percent take place in and around schools. Elementary school children are most likely to be injured from playground falls (Sheps & Evans, 1987). Secondary school students are most often injured in sports. Some of these injuries could be avoided if players were grouped by size, skill, and maturational level rather than by age (AAP Committee on Sports Medicine and Committee on School Health, 1989).

Each year about 300,000 visits to emergency rooms and 600 deaths to children under 15 are attributed to bicycle accidents. Head injury is the leading cause of disability and death in these accidents (Cushman, Down, MacMillan, & Waclawik, 1991). The dangers of riding a bike can be reduced dramatically by using safety-approved helmets, but only 5 percent of child bicyclists wear them (AAP Committee on Accident and Poison Prevention, 1990). Children should also wear protective headgear for football, roller skating, skateboarding, horseback riding, hockey, speed sledding, and tobogganing. School programs to encourage helmet use can be effective (Weiss, 1992).

MOTOR DEVELOPMENT IN MIDDLE CHILDHOOD

Studies of 7- to 12-year-olds done more than 30 years ago, when children seem to have been more active physically, suggested that motor abilities improve with age (see the examples in Table 8-1). These studies also found sex differences: boys tended to run faster, jump higher, throw farther, and show more strength than girls (Espenschade, 1960; Gavotos, 1959). After age 13, the gap between the sexes widened; boys improved, while girls stayed the same or declined (Espenschade, 1960).

Today, however, it seems clear that much of the difference between the sexes' motor abilities has been due to differences in expectations and participation. Prepubescent boys and girls who take part in similar activities show similar abilities. When third-, fourth-, and fifth-grade boys and girls who had been in excellent coeducational physical education classes for at least a year were compared on their scores on sit-ups, shuttle run, 50-yard dash, broad jump, and 600-yard walk-run, both sexes improved with age, and the girls performed about as well as the boys on most measures. Girls who were tested in the third year of the program performed even better than the boys on a number of measures (E. G. Hall & Lee, 1984).

There is no reason to separate prepubertal boys and girls for physical activities. After puberty, however, girls should not play in collision sports with boys, because their lighter, smaller frames make them too susceptible to being injured by the heavier boys (American Academy of Pediatrics Committee on Pediatric Aspects of Physical Fitness, Recreation, and Sports, 1981).

To help all children improve their motor skills, organized athletic programs should offer children the chance to try a variety of sports, should focus coaching on improving skills rather than on winning games, and should include as many youngsters as possible rather than concentrating on a few star athletes (AAP Committee on Sports Medicine and Committee on School Health, 1989).

▪ INTELLECTUAL DEVELOPMENT

Even today, when many children go to preschool and most go to kindergarten, starting first grade is a milestone, approached with a mixture of eagerness and anxiety. "What will the teacher be like?" Julia, aged 6, wonders as she walks up the steps to the big red-brick schoolhouse, wearing her new backpack. "What will we learn? Will I be able to do the work?" Julia's ability to learn and to do schoolwork will expand greatly during the next 6 years, because of her growing capacity to think conceptually, solve problems, remember, and use language—developments we'll examine in this section. But the first day of school will always be a special day, a day of promise and anticipation.

TABLE 8-1

Motor Development of Boys and Girls in Middle Childhood

Age	Selected Behaviors
6	Girls are superior in accuracy of movement; boys are superior in forceful, less complex acts. Skipping is possible. Children can throw with proper weight shift and step.
7	Balancing on one foot without looking becomes possible. Children can walk 2-inch-wide balance beams. Children can hop and jump accurately into small squares. Children can execute accurate jumping-jack exercise.
8	Grip strength permits steady 12-pound pressure. Number of games participated in by both sexes is greatest at this age. Children can engage in alternate rhythmic hopping in a 2-2, 2-3, or 3-3 pattern. Girls can throw a small ball 40 feet.
9	Girls can jump vertically to a height of 8½ inches, and boys, 10 inches. Boys can run 16½ feet per second. Boys can throw a small ball 70 feet.
10	Children can judge and intercept pathways of small balls thrown from a distance. Girls can run 17 feet per second.
11	Standing broad jump of 5 feet is possible for boys; 6 inches less for girls.
12	Standing high jump of 3 feet is possible.

SOURCE: Adapted from Cratty, 1979, p. 222.

ASPECTS OF INTELLECTUAL DEVELOPMENT IN MIDDLE CHILDHOOD

COGNITIVE DEVELOPMENT: PIAGET'S STAGE OF CONCRETE OPERATIONS

Sometime between 5 and 7 years of age, according to Piaget, children enter the stage of *concrete operations,* when they can think logically about the here and now.

Operational Thinking

Children in Piaget's third stage are capable of *operational thinking:* they can use symbols to carry out *operations*—that is, mental activities, as opposed to the physical activities that were the basis for most of their earlier thinking. For the first time, logic becomes possible. Even though preoperational children can make mental representations of objects and events that are not immediately present, their learning is still closely tied to physical experience. Concrete operational children are much better than preoperational children at classifying, working with numbers, dealing with

concepts of time and space, and distinguishing reality from fantasy.

Because they are much less egocentric by now, children in the stage of concrete operations can *decenter.* That is, they can take all aspects of a situation into account rather than focusing on only one aspect, as they did in the preoperational stage. They realize that most physical operations are reversible. Their increased ability to understand other people's viewpoints lets them communicate more effectively and be more flexible in their moral thinking.

But although school-age children think more logically than younger children, their thinking is still anchored in the here and now. According to Piaget, not until the stage of formal operations, which usually comes with adolescence (see Chapter 10), will young people be able to think abstractly, test hypotheses, and understand probabilities.

Conservation

What Is Conservation?
Conservation is the ability to recognize that two equal quantities of matter remain equal—in substance, weight, or volume—so long as nothing is added or taken away (as explained in Chapter 6).

In a typical conservation task, Stacy is shown two equal balls of clay. She agrees that they are equal. She is said to conserve *substance* if she recognizes that even after one of the balls has been rolled into the shape of a worm, the two lumps of clay still have an equal amount of matter. In *weight* conservation, she recognizes that the ball and the worm weigh the same. And in conservation of *volume,* she realizes that the ball and the worm displace equal amounts of liquid when they are placed in glasses of water.

Children develop different types of conservation at different times. At age 6 or 7, they typically are able to conserve substance; at 9 or 10, weight; and at 11 or 12, volume. The underlying principle is identical for all three kinds of conservation, but children are unable to transfer what they have learned about one type of conservation to a different type. **Horizontal décalage** is the term Piaget used for this inability.

Thus, we see how concrete a child's reasoning still is. It is tied so closely to particular situations that children cannot easily apply the same basic mental operation to a different situation.

How Is Conservation Developed?

Children typically go through three stages in mastering conservation. Let's see how this works for conservation of substance.

In the *first* stage, preoperational children fail to conserve. They center or focus on one aspect of the situation—for example, that the ball of clay becomes longer when it is rolled into a "worm"—and do not notice that the worm is also narrower than the ball. Evidently, they are fooled by appearances and decide that the worm contains more clay. Because they do not yet understand the concept of reversibility, they do not realize that they could restore the original shape by rolling the worm back into a ball.

The *second* stage is transitional. When Diane asks Anna, age 6, whether she'll have the same amount of cheese to eat if it's in one big piece or several smaller ones, Anna answers, "The same." Then she adds, "But please cut it into pieces because I'm *very* hungry!" Children in transition, as Anna now is, go back and forth, sometimes conserving and sometimes not. They may notice more than one aspect of a situation—such as height, width, length, and thickness—but may fail to recognize how these dimensions are related. These children may answer correctly when they see a short worm but fail to conserve if the worm is very long and thin.

In the *third* and final stage, children conserve and give logical reasons for their answers. These reasons may refer to *reversibility* ("If the clay worm were shaped into a ball, it would be the same as the other ball"); *identity* ("It's the same clay; you haven't added any or taken any away"); or *compensation* ("The ball is shorter than the worm, but the worm is thinner than the ball, so they both have the same amount of clay"). Thus concrete operational children show a qualitative cognitive advance over preoperational children. Their thinking is reversible, they decenter, and they are aware that transformations are only perceptual changes.

Piaget stressed that children develop the ability to conserve when they are neurologically mature enough. He believed that conservation is only minimally affected by experience. However, factors other than maturation do affect conservation. Children who learn conservation skills earliest have high grades, high IQs, and high verbal ability (Almy, Chittenden, & Miller, 1966; Goldschmid & Bentler, 1968). Black children from higher socioeconomic levels do better than black children of lower socioeconomic levels on conservation tasks, as well as on other Piagetian operations (Bardouille-Crema, Black, & Feldhusen, 1986). Also, children from different countries—Switzerland, the United States, Great Britain, and other nations—achieve conservation at different average ages. Therefore culture, and not maturation alone, plays a role.

MORAL REASONING: TWO THEORIES

An important explanation of moral development today is that moral values develop in a rational process coinciding with cognitive growth. Jean Piaget and Lawrence Kohlberg, two of the most influential theorists on the development of moral reasoning, maintained that children cannot make sound moral judgments until they shed egocentric thinking and achieve a certain level of cognitive maturity. Let's examine these theories.

Piaget and Two Moral Stages

According to Piaget, children's conception of morality develops in two major stages (summarized in Table 8-2), which coincide approximately with the preoperational and concrete operational stages. People go through these moral stages at varying times, but the sequence is always the same.

The first stage, **morality of constraint** (also called *heteronomous morality*), is characterized by rigid, simplistic judgments. Young children see

PRE-OPERATIONAL / CONCRETE OPERATIONAL

TABLE 8-2

Piaget's Two Stages of Moral Development		
Aspect of Morality	**Morality of Constraint**	**Morality of Cooperation**
Point of view	Child views an act as either totally right or totally wrong and thinks everyone sees it the same way. Children cannot put themselves in place of others.	Children can put themselves in place of others. They are not absolutist in judgments but see that more than one point of view is possible.
Intentionality	Child judges acts in terms of actual physical consequences, not the motivation behind them.	Child judges acts by intentions, not consequences.
Rules	Child obeys rules because they are sacred and unalterable.	Child recognizes that rules were made by people and can be changed by people. Children consider themselves just as capable of changing rules as anyone else.
Respect for authority	Unilateral respect leads to feeling of obligation to conform to adult standards and obey adult rules.	Mutual respect for authority and peers allows children to value their own opinions and abilities and to judge other people realistically.
Punishment	Child favors severe punishment. Child feels that punishment itself defines the wrongness of an act; an act is bad if it will elicit punishment.	Child favors milder punishment that compensates the victim and helps the culprit recognize why an act was wrong, thus leading to reform.
"Immanent justice"	Child confuses moral law with physical law and believes that any physical accident or misfortune that occurs after a misdeed is a punishment willed by God or some other supernatural force.	Child does not confuse natural misfortune with punishment.

SOURCE: Adapted partly from M. Hoffman, 1970; Kohlberg, in M. Hoffman & Hoffman, 1964.

everything in black and white, not gray. Because of their egocentrism, they cannot conceive of more than one way of looking at a moral question. They believe that rules are unalterable, that behavior is either right or wrong, and that any offense—no matter how minor—deserves severe punishment.

The second stage, *morality of cooperation* (or *autonomous morality*), is characterized by moral flexibility. As children mature and interact more with other children and with adults, they think less egocentrically. They have ever-increasing contact with a wide range of viewpoints, many of which contradict what they have learned at home. Children conclude that there is not one unchangeable, absolute moral standard, but that rules are made by people and can be changed by people, including themselves. They look for the intent behind the act, and they believe that punishment should fit

the "crime." They are on the way to formulating their own moral codes.

To illustrate one aspect of this change, Piaget (1932) told this story:

Once upon a time there were two little boys, Augustus and Julian. Augustus noticed one day that his father's inkpot was empty, and he decided to help his father by filling it. But in opening the bottle, he spilled the ink and made a large stain on the tablecloth. Julian played with his father's inkpot and made a small stain on the tablecloth. Piaget then asked, "Which boy is naughtier and why?"

A child in the stage of constraint is likely to consider Augustus the greater offender, because he made the larger stain. But a child in the stage of cooperation will recognize that Augustus meant well, whereas the smaller stain Julian made was the result of doing something he should not have been doing. Immature moral judgments, being egocentric, center on one dimension: the magnitude of the offense. Mature judgments take intention into account.

However, the issue of intention versus consequences is far from clear-cut even among adults, as we can see in our criminal codes. Penalties are more severe for murder than for *attempted* murder, even though both may involve wanting to kill. And a drunken driver who has injured someone is usually punished more harshly than one who has not, even though neither driver intended to hurt anyone. Consequences matter so much to most people that society has institutionalized its responses on the basis of what actually happens.

Kohlberg and Moral Reasoning

How would *you* respond to this moral dilemma? A woman is near death from cancer. A druggist has discovered a drug that doctors believe might save her. The druggist is charging $2000 for a small dose—10 times what it costs him to make the drug. The sick woman's husband, Heinz, borrows from everyone he knows but can scrape together only $1000. He begs the druggist to sell him the drug for less or let him pay later. The druggist refuses, saying, "I discovered this, and I'm going to make money from it." Heinz, desperate, breaks into the man's store and steals the drug. Should Heinz have done that? Why, or why not? (Kohlberg, 1969).

Kohlberg's Moral Dilemmas
"Heinz's" problem is the most famous example of Kohlberg's approach. For some 20 years, he studied a group of 75 boys who were from 10 to 16 years old when he began. Kohlberg told them stories posing hypothetical moral problems about unfamiliar people—dilemmas like Heinz's—and he asked how they would solve them. At the center of each dilemma was the concept of justice.

Then Kohlberg and his colleagues asked the boys questions to find out how they came to their decisions. He was less interested in answers than in the reasoning that led to them; thus two boys who gave opposite answers to a dilemma could both be at the same moral level if their reasoning was based on similar factors.

Kohlberg's Three Levels of Moral Reasoning
From the boys' responses, Kohlberg concluded that levels of moral reasoning are related to cognitive levels. The reasoning behind the boys' an-

swers convinced Kohlberg that many people arrive at moral judgments independently rather than merely "internalizing" the standards of others. On the basis of the different thought processes shown by the answers, Kohlberg described three levels of moral reasoning:

- *Level I—Preconventional morality* (ages 4 to 10). Children, under external controls, obey rules to get rewards or avoid punishment.
- *Level II—Conventional morality* (ages 10 to 13). Children have internalized the standards of authority figures. They obey rules to please others or to maintain order.
- *Level III—Postconventional morality* (age 13 or later, if ever). Morality is fully internal. People now recognize conflicts between moral standards and choose between them.

Each of the three levels is divided into two stages. Table 8-3 gives descriptions of the six stages with illustrative answers to Heinz's dilemma.

Kohlberg's lower stages are similar to Piaget's, but his advanced stages go farther, into adulthood. And the more advanced a person is in the ability to assume the role of another, the more complicated Heinz's dilemma becomes.

Evaluating Kohlberg's Theory
Kohlberg has had a major impact on our thinking about how moral judgment develops, has supported an association between cognitive maturity and moral maturity, and has stimulated both research and the elaboration of theories of moral development. However, his theory is limited in a number of ways.

First, the early empathy shown by very young children seems to signal the emergence of an early moral sense (see Chapter 6). The theory also falters when applied to the moral development of females and people in other cultures, as we will show in Chapters 10 and 12.

The American boys whom Kohlberg and his colleagues followed for 20 years progressed through Kohlberg's stages in sequence. None skipped a stage. Moral judgments correlated positively with the boys' age, education, IQ, and socioeconomic status (Colby, Kohlberg, Gibbs, & Lieberman, 1983). But since people from nonwestern cultures rarely score above stage 4, Kohlberg's definition of morality as a system of justice may miss higher levels of reasoning in some cultural groups (Nisan & Kohlberg, 1982; Snarey, 1985). Furthermore, as Carol Gilligan (1982) states, Kohlberg's theory stresses

TABLE 8-3

Kohlberg's Six Stages of Moral Reasoning

Levels	Stages of Reasoning	Typical Answers to Heinz's Dilemma
Level 1: Preconventional Morality (ages 4 to 10) Emphasis in this level is on external control. The standards are those of others, and they are observed either to avoid punishment or to reap rewards.	**Stage 1** *Orientation to punishment and obedience.* "What will happen to me?" Children obey the rules of others to avoid punishment. They ignore the motives of an act and focus on its physical form (such as the size of a lie) or its consequences (for example, the amount of physical damage).	*Pro:* "He should steal the drug. It isn't really bad to take it. It isn't as if he hadn't asked to pay for it first. The drug he'd take is worth only $200: he's not really taking a $2000 drug." *Con:* "He shouldn't steal the drug. It's a big crime. He didn't get permission; he used force and broke and entered. He did a lot of damage, stealing a very expensive drug and breaking up the store, too."
	Stage 2 *Instrumental purpose and exchange.* "You scratch my back, and I'll scratch yours." Children conform to rules out of self-interest and consideration for what others can do for them in return. They look at an act in terms of the human needs it meets and differentiate this value from the act's physical form and consequences.	*Pro:* "It's all right to steal the drug, because his wife needs it and he wants her to live. It isn't that he wants to steal, but that's what he has to do to get the drug to save her." *Con:* "He shouldn't steal it. The druggist isn't wrong or bad; he just wants to make a profit. That's what you're in business for—to make money."
Level II: Conventional Morality (ages 10 to 13) Children now want to please other people. They still observe the standards of others, but they have internalized these standards to some extent. Now they want to be considered "good" by those persons whose opinions are important to them. They are now able to take the roles of authority figures well enough to decide whether an action is good by their standards.	**Stage 3** *Maintaining mutual relations, approval of others, the golden rule.* "Am I a good boy or girl?" Children want to please and help others, can judge the intentions of others, and develop their own ideas of what a good person is. They evaluate an act according to the motive behind it or the person performing it, and they take circumstances into account.	*Pro:* "He should steal the drug. He is only doing something that is natural for a good husband to do. You can't blame him for doing something out of love for his wife. You'd blame him if he didn't love his wife enough to save her." *Con:* "He shouldn't steal. If his wife dies, he can't be blamed. It isn't because he's heartless or that he doesn't love her enough to do everything that he legally can. The druggist is the selfish or heartless one."
	Stage 4 *Social system and conscience.* "What if everybody did it?" People are concerned with doing their duty, showing respect for higher authority, and maintaining the social order. They consider an act always wrong, regardless of motive or circumstances, if it violates a rule and harms others.	*Pro:* "You should steal it. If you did nothing you'd be letting your wife die. It's your responsibility if she dies. You have to take it with the idea of paying the druggist." *Con:* "It is a natural thing for Heinz to want to save his wife, but it's still always wrong to steal. He still knows that he's stealing and taking a valuable drug from the man who made it."

(continued)

TABLE 8-3 *(Continued)*

Kohlberg's Six Stages of Moral Reasoning

Levels	Stages of Reasoning	Typical Answers to Heinz's Dilemma
Level III: Postconventional Morality (age 13, or not until young adulthood, or never) This level marks the attainment of true morality. For the first time, the person acknowledges the possibility of conflict between two socially accepted standards and tries to decide between them. The control of conduct is now internal, both in the standards observed and in the reasoning about right and wrong. Stages 5 and 6 may be alternative methods of the highest level of moral reasoning.	**Stage 5** *Morality of contract, of individual rights, and of democratically accepted law.* People think in rational terms, valuing the will of the majority and the welfare of society. They generally see these values best supported by adherence to the law. While they recognize that there are times when human need and the law conflict, they believe that it is better for society in the long run if they obey the law. **Stage 6** *Morality of universal ethical principles.* People do what they as individuals think right, regardless of legal restrictions or the opinions of others. They act in accordance with internalized standards, knowing that they would condemn themselves if they did not.	*Pro:* "The law wasn't set up for these circumstances. Taking the drug in this situation isn't really right, but it's justified." *Con:* "You can't completely blame someone for stealing, but extreme circumstances don't really justify taking the law into your own hands. You can't have people stealing whenever they are desperate. The end may be good, but the ends don't justify the means." *Pro:* "This is a situation that forces him to choose between stealing and letting his wife die. In a situation where the choice must be made, it is morally right to steal. He has to act in terms of the principle of preserving and respecting life." *Con:* "Heinz is faced with the decision of whether to consider the other people who need the drug just as badly as his wife. Heinz ought to act not according to his particular feelings toward his wife, but considering the value of all the lives involved."

SOURCE: Adapted from Kohlberg, 1969, 1976, in Goslin, 1969.

"masculine" values (justice and fairness) rather than "feminine" values (caring for others).

Also questionable is Kohlberg's belief that children are "moral philosophers" who work out their moral systems by independent discovery. On the contrary, studies show that moral judgments are strongly influenced by education—as by simply telling children the "right" answers to moral reasoning tasks (Carroll & Rest, 1982; Lickona, 1973).

Still another issue is the relationship between moral reasoning and action. Kohlberg's theory describes moral *judgments* (thinking about moral issues typically involving justice) rather than moral actions. (We will take up the issue of moral action in Chapter 14.) People at postconventional levels of thought do not necessarily act more morally than those at lower levels (Kupfersmid & Wonderly, 1980). This is not surprising in view of research findings on cheating: almost all children who cheat are just as likely as noncheaters to *say* that

cheating is wrong (Hartshorne & May, 1928–1930).

At one point Kohlberg himself questioned his sixth stage, citing the difficulty of finding people at such a high level of moral development (Muuss, 1988). Still later, however, he proposed a seventh stage that was more religious in orientation (Kohlberg, 1981). Kohlberg's rethinking of his concepts illustrates the dynamic nature of theories—that they change in response to new research findings or new insights.

DEVELOPMENT OF MEMORY: INFORMATION PROCESSING

The information-processing approach to cognitive development pays particular attention to memory. As cognitive development advances, so does memory. The ability to remember thus improves greatly by middle childhood. This happens in part because children's memory capacity—the amount of information they can remember—increases, and in part because they learn to use a variety of mnemonic devices, or deliberate strategies, to help them remember. An important development is metamemory, an understanding of how memory processes work.

How Memory Works: Encoding, Storing, and Retrieving

According to information-processing theory, memory is like a filing system. It operates through three basic steps: encoding, storage, and retrieval. After perceiving something, we need to file it. Thus the first step is to *encode,* or classify it—for example, under "people I know" or "places I've been." Second, we must *store* the material so that it stays in memory. And third, we need to be able to *retrieve* information, or get it out of storage. Forgetting can occur because of a problem in any of the three steps.

Immediate memory increases rapidly in middle childhood. We can see this by asking children to recall a series of digits in the reverse of the order in which they heard them (to recite "8-3-7-5-1-6" if they have heard "6-1-5-7-3-8"). At ages 5 to 6, children typically can remember only two digits; by adolescence they can remember six. Younger children's relatively poor immediate memory may help to explain why they have trouble solving certain kinds of problems (such as conservation). They may not be able to hold all the relevant pieces of information in memory (Siegler & Richards, 1982). They may, for example, forget that two differently shaped balls of clay were equal in the first place, and so by the time they are asked about the ball and the "worm," they can judge only on present appearance.

Mnemonic Devices: Strategies for Remembering

Older children can usually remember a list of numbers better than younger children can, partly because they have discovered that they can take deliberate actions to help them remember. Strategies to aid memory are called ***mnemonic devices.*** As children get older, they develop better strategies and tailor them to meet the need to remember specific things.

Mnemonic techniques need not be discovered haphazardly. Children can be taught to use them earlier than they would use them spontaneously. Some teachers make a special point of teaching the use of strategies, pointing out that they will help

Contestants in a spelling bee can make good use of mnemonic strategies—devices to aid memory. This boy may be trying to remember by putting a word into a mental category with other words that contain similar elements. *(Charles Gupton/Stock, Boston)*

children remember. Such teaching is especially helpful to children of low to average achievement levels (Moely et al., 1992). Some of the most common memory strategies are rehearsal, organization, elaboration, and use of external memory aids.

Rehearsal

Anna, at 6½, repeats to herself a telephone number that she wants to remember. *Rehearsal* (conscious repetition) is a common mnemonic device.

When do children begin using rehearsal? In one study (Flavell, Beach, & Chinsky, 1966), first-graders who had been told that they would be asked to recall a sequence of pictures sat and waited until they were asked for the information. Second- and fifth-graders, on the other hand, moved their lips and muttered, suggesting that they were rehearsing the material. Not surprisingly, the older children remembered the material better than the younger ones. When the experimenters asked first-graders to name the pictures out loud when they first saw them (a form of rehearsal), the children recalled the order better.

Young children who were taught to rehearse applied the technique to the immediate situation but did not apply it to new situations (Keeney, Canizzo, & Flavell, 1967).

More recent research shows that some children between 3 and 6 years old do use rehearsal. And although 6-year-olds are more likely than 3-year-olds to rehearse, those 3-year-olds who do rehearse can remember a grocery list just as well as 6-year-olds (Paris & Weissberg-Benchell, in Chance & Fischman, 1987). Children older than 6 learn and use more sophisticated mnemonic techniques: organization, elaboration, and external aids.

Organization

It is easier to remember material if we mentally organize it into categories. Adults generally do this automatically. Children younger than 10 or 11 do *not* normally use *organization* spontaneously; but they can be taught to do it, or they may pick it up by imitating others (Chance & Fischman, 1987). If they see randomly arranged pictures of, say, animals, furniture, and clothing, they do not mentally sort the items into categories. If shown how to organize, they recall the pictures as well as older children do; but they do not generalize the learning to other situations.

Elaboration

To help ourselves remember items, we can link them together in an imagined scene or story—a strategy called *elaboration.* To remember to buy lemons, ketchup, and napkins, for example, we might imagine a ketchup bottle balanced on a lemon, with napkins handy to wipe up spilled ketchup. Older children are more likely than younger ones to use elaboration spontaneously, and they remember better when they make up the elaborations themselves. Younger children remember better when someone else makes up the elaborations for them (Paris & Lindauer, 1976; Reese, 1977). Diane, wanting Anna, 6½, to help her remember to buy coffee and lettuce, told Anna to visualize her mother making coffee and tossing a salad, and Anna remembered the images and items several days later.

External Memory Aids

The mnemonic strategies used most commonly by both children and adults involve prompting by something outside the person. You write down a telephone number or the spelling of a new word, make a list, tie a string around your finger, set a timer, or ask someone to remind you. Even kindergartners recognize the value of such *external memory aids,* and as children mature, they use them more (Kreutzer, Leonard, & Flavell, 1975).

Metamemory: Understanding the Processes of Memory

At 6 years old, Anna has trouble remembering her dreams. Then she has an idea: "Maybe I can put a piece of paper in my brain to take a picture of my dream. This would help me remember." Anna is showing her new awareness of *metamemory*—knowledge of the processes of memory.

From kindergarten through fifth grade, children advance steadily in understanding memory (Kreutzer et al., 1975). Kindergartners and first-graders know that people remember better if they study longer, that people forget things with time, that relearning something is easier than learning it for the first time, and that external aids can help them remember. By third grade, children typically know that some people remember more than others and that some things are easier to remember than others.

DEVELOPMENT OF INTELLIGENCE: PSYCHOMETRICS

IQ Tests

Bart's third-grade teacher told the boy's parents, "Bart is underachieving—he's not working up to his ability." It is likely that what she meant by Bart's *ability* was his score on an IQ test. What she meant by *underachieving* could have been either his classwork or his scores on group achievement tests, which measure how much children know in various subject areas, like mathematics, history, and so forth. Achievement tests assess children's progress and let the school know how effectively it is teaching. They are different from the group intelligence tests that students in many schools receive every few years, which aim to measure children's basic *aptitude,* or general intelligence.

Because individual tests are more precise, youngsters are sometimes tested individually either for admission to a selective program or to uncover specific problems or strengths that the school should address.

The most widely used *individual* test for schoolchildren is the *Wechsler Intelligence Scale for Children (WISC-III).* This test measures verbal and performance abilities, yielding separate scores for

BOX 8-2   TAKE A STAND

SHOULD IQ TESTS BE USED?

Many schools give group intelligence tests every few years, partly to assess students' ability and partly to judge how well they are being prepared. Such tests help administrators decide whether to admit particular students, whether they would benefit from an enriched program, or whether they need special help.

Yet the use of intelligence tests is controversial, having both pros and cons.

IN FAVOR OF IQ TESTING

1 Since these tests have been standardized and thus are the same for all test-takers, extensive information exists about their norms, validity, and reliability. They are frequently updated, making them more accurate.

2 IQ scores are good predictors of achievement in school, especially for highly verbal children. Since school achievement is important for success in American society, this prediction is useful.

3 They help identify youngsters who are especially bright or who need special help in school.

4 They measure abilities that are highly valued in our verbal society.

AGAINST IQ TESTING

1 IQ tests do not assess skills directly, but instead, infer ability from how children score. This leads to problems of cultural bias.

2 IQ tests are not appropriate for a number of groups. Infant scores are not good predictors of later intelligence. People whose intelligence is probably underestimated include those belonging to minority groups, those with disabilities, and the elderly.

3 They define intelligence narrowly, missing many aspects of intelligent behavior, such as "street smarts" (common sense and shrewdness in everyday life), social skills (getting along with other people), creative insight as in music and art, and self-knowledge (Gardner, 1983; Sternberg, 1987).

4 Because IQ tests are timed, they wrongly equate intelligence with speed.

5 IQ scores, which purport to measure inborn aptitude rather than what a child has learned, are more closely related to the amount of schooling a child has had than to the child's age (Ceci, 1991; Cahan & Cohen, 1989). Schooling has the greatest impact on verbal abilities, but it also affects performance on number and figure tasks.

What, then, should we as a culture do about intelligence tests? Should we do away with their use altogether? Or, if we retain them for the information that they can give, are there ways in which we can make their use less biased against children who have not grown up in the majority culture of our society? In a heterogeneous nation like the United States, such questions are at the core of an eventual harmony among disparate racial, ethnic, and socioeconomic groups. How they are answered affects the future of our country.

each, as well as a total score. Separating the subtest scores makes the diagnosis of specific problems easier. For example, if a child does much better on the verbal tests (by, say, understanding a written passage and knowing vocabulary words) than on the performance tests (as in mastering mazes and copying a block design), this may signal problems with perceptual or motor development. If the child does much better on the performance tests, there may be a problem with language development.

A widely used *group* test is the **Otis-Lennon School Ability Test,** which assesses children from kindergarten to twelfth grade. Paper-and-pencil tests like this are usually given to children in small groups. They are asked to classify items, to show an understanding of verbal and numerical concepts, to display general information, and to follow directions.

Norms, Reliability, and Validity

There are pros and cons to using the familiar IQ tests (see Box 8-2). Some criteria for judging any test are the degree to which it has been standardized and the amount of information about norms (standards of performance), reliability (consistency of results), and validity (whether the tests measure what they claim to measure).

Norms are established by giving a test to a representative group of test-takers; their average performance becomes the standard against which later test-takers' performance is measured (see Chapter 6). *Reliability* can be determined by giving the same person the same test more than once, or (to eliminate variables like differences in testing conditions and the tendency to do better the second time) by comparing a person's score on half the answers with his or her score on the other half. *Validity* depends on how well the results correlate with other measures or predict outcomes, like performance in school.

Race, Culture, and IQ Tests

The failings of IQ tests become especially serious when the tests are misused to classify people and to limit expectations and opportunities on the basis of test scores. The importance and sensitivity of this issue are most evident when we consider racial and cultural differences in test results.

Intelligence Testing of African American Children
Black Americans tend to score about 15 points lower on IQ tests than white Americans (E. B. Brody & Brody, 1976). There is considerable overlap: some black people score higher than most white people. Still, an average difference exists, and what it means is highly controversial. There are two basic ways of interpreting it. Most modern educators maintain that it reflects typical differences in environments between the two groups—in education, living conditions, and other circumstances that affect self-esteem and motivation as well as academic performance itself (Kamin, 1974). The other view is that disparities in IQ reflect hereditary (genetic) differences and therefore that black people are innately inferior intellectually (Jensen, 1969). This latter view overlooks much evidence showing the importance of the environment. Let us see why the first position seems more solidly based.

For one thing, differences favoring white children do not appear until about age 2 or 3 (Golden, Birns, & Bridger, 1973). Some research suggests, in fact, that black babies are precocious on infant intelligence tests, especially in motor abilities (Bayley, 1965; Geber, 1962; Geber & Dean, 1957). The difference that shows up later may reflect the switch from predominantly motor tests to verbal tests. Verbal ability is highly influenced by environmental factors.

We also see the importance of the environment when we compare people from different socioeconomic levels. The same pattern that holds between white American and black American test-takers (an average difference of 15 points) also holds for American middle-class and deprived rural and mountain children, and for English middle-class and low-income canal-boat and Gypsy children (Pettigrew, 1964). Furthermore, black children who live in northern cities score higher than those in the rural south (Baughman, 1971), and middle-class black children score better than poor black children (Loehlin, Lindzey, & Spuhler, 1975). The relationship between schooling and test scores (Cahan & Cohen, 1989) may point to differences in the quantity and quality of typical school experiences between black American and white American children.

Another argument is that the apparent differences between black people's and white people's average intelligence reflect culture-related defects in the construction of the tests.

Cultural Bias
In 1986, a 15-year lawsuit ended with the upholding of a federal court order that because IQ tests are "culturally biased," California schools may not use them to place black students in special classes. The court had found that a disproportionate number of black youngsters were being wrongly consigned to classes for the mentally retarded.

This controversial decision was unprecedented; but as far back as 1920, researchers had recognized the difficulty of devising tests to measure intelligence in different cultural groups. Since then, test developers have tried in vain to devise tests that can measure innate intelligence without introducing *cultural bias*—the tendency to include test elements or procedures that are more familiar, significant, or comfortable for members of certain cultures. Language, of course, is one factor. Another is the nature of the test questions themselves, which—because they do not adequately separate what children have already learned from their ability to acquire new knowledge—favor children from advantaged backgrounds (Sternberg, 1985b).

Finally, according to Miller-Jones (1989), test developers' decisions about which answers to accept sometimes seem arbitrary. For example, a 4- to 6-year-old taking the 1973 edition of the Stanford-Binet Intelligence Scale is asked, "What is a house made of?" The answer "A house is made of walls" would be considered incorrect; a "correct" answer must give materials—like wood, bricks, or stone. Miller-Jones concludes, "The accepted responses do not incorporate all reasonably intelligent responses to the question" (p. 361).

"Culture-Free" and "Culture-Fair" Tests
Some tests do not require language. Testers use

gestures, pantomime, and demonstrations for tasks like tracing mazes, finding absurdities in pictures, putting the right shapes in the right holes, and completing pictures. But it has not been possible to eliminate all cultural content from these tests. For example, in a test asking for absurdities in a picture, a culture's artistic conventions may affect the way people view the picture. A group of Asian immigrant children in Israel, when asked to provide the missing detail for a picture of a face with no mouth, said that the *body* was missing. They were not used to considering a drawing of a head as a complete picture and "regarded the absence of a body as more important than the omission of a mere detail like the mouth" (Anastasi, 1988, p. 360).

Recognizing the impossibility of designing a *culture-free test*—one with no culture-linked content—test developers have tried to produce *culture-fair tests* that deal with experiences common to various cultures. But these tests are not really culture-fair. For one thing, they almost invariably call for skills that are more familiar to some groups than to others (Anastasi, 1988; Sternberg, 1985a).

Furthermore, it is almost impossible to screen for culturally determined values and attitudes. Different cultures define intelligent behavior differently. The ability to sort names of living things according to their biological classifications (for example, to put *bird* and *fish* under *animal*) is considered intelligent in western society. But among the Kpelle tribe of Liberia, it is considered more intelligent to sort things according to what they do (see Box 1-1 in Chapter 1); for example, a Kpelle might put *animal* with *eat*. In the United States, parents at lower socioeconomic levels tend to value rote memory, while middle- and upper-class parents are more apt to encourage their children to reason (Sternberg, 1985b; Sternberg, 1986; Sternberg, in Quinby, 1985). (See Box 8-3 for a discussion of cultural factors affecting academic performance and measurement of intelligence in Asian and American children.)

Nowhere are the effects of heredity and environment more closely interwoven than in the measurement of whatever it is that we mean by *intelligence*. To separate inborn potential from the impact of life experience is a goal that, for the most part, has eluded test designers.

The Test Situation

Cultural attitudes may bias the testing situation as well as the test itself. Such factors as rapport with the test-giver, knowing how to sit still and pay at-tention to adult questions or instructions, interest in the tasks, motivation to excel, knowing test strategies (like quickly giving answers a child is sure of, and then going back to more problematic questions), and modes of problem solving may be influenced by what children learn, either in or out of school (Ceci, 1991; Anastasi, 1988). A child in a society that stresses slow, deliberate work is handicapped in a timed test. A child from a culture that stresses sociability is handicapped in taking a test alone. And a child who is not accustomed to being asked questions by an adult who knows the answers is dealing with a new situation when being tested individually (Miller-Jones, 1989).

Black and Hispanic students, as well as students who are disabled and students from low socioeconomic backgrounds, often do better in familiar settings (like their own classrooms) with examiners they know (like their own teachers) than in strange rooms with unfamiliar examiners. These children also do better when they are tested more than once with standardized tests based on the curricula they have been studying (D. Fuchs & L. S. Fuchs, 1986; L. S. Fuchs & D. Fuchs, 1986).

The function of intelligence tests is not just to measure intelligence but to find out how to improve it. Since research has shown close ties between schooling and intelligence test scores, it makes sense to improve school for all children, and most especially for those from minority groups, who have traditionally scored lower on such tests than children in the majority culture. We will look at the impact of school in these middle years later in this chapter.

DEVELOPMENT OF LANGUAGE: COMMUNICATION

Language, too, develops quickly in middle childhood. Children can understand and interpret communications better, their vocabulary and ability to define words grow, and they are better able to make themselves understood.

Grammar: The Structure of Language

Suppose that you are looking at a snow-covered driveway and you ask someone how you are going to get the family car out of the garage. You might be told either (1) "Ken *promised* Barbie to shovel the driveway" or (2) "Ken *told* Barbie to

BOX 8-3   WINDOW ON THE WORLD

HOW CAN ASIAN CHILDREN ACHIEVE SO MUCH?

They seem to have three strikes against them—Southeast Asian boat children. They suffered disruption and trauma as they escaped from their native countries; they lost months, or even years, of formal schooling; and they knew no English when they arrived in the United States. Still, these Indochinese refugee children quickly began to excel in their new schools (Caplan, Choy, & Whitmore, 1992). The academic success of these children mirrors that of many children from Asian families. How are young Asian Americans able to make such a strong showing by almost every educational measure? Research has yielded a number of answers.

GENERAL COGNITIVE ABILITY

In a cross-cultural study of American, Japanese, and Chinese children, an international research team designed a test to assess children's cognitive abilities based on common experiences (H. W. Stevenson et al., 1985). Test items, given in all three languages, included verbal tasks (like answering questions about stories and everyday facts and defining words) and nonverbal tasks (like matching shapes and recalling rhythms). Urban first- and fifth-graders in all three countries also took specially designed reading and math tests.

Asian students do not start out with any overall cognitive superiority. In fact, in one study, American first-graders outperformed Asians on many tasks, possibly because they were more used to answering adults' questions (Chinese children are expected to "be seen but not heard") and had had more cultural experiences, like going to museums, zoos, and movies (which Asian children do not have until

Children from Asian families often do better in school than other American youngsters. The reasons seem to be cultural, not genetic. *(Peter Dublin/Stock, Boston)*

they go to school) (Song & Ginsburg, 1987).

The most recent comparisons of Asian and American students found two trends. Although the American students' mathematical abilities declined from first to eleventh grade when compared with those of Asian students, their general information scores became increasingly similar (H. W. Stevenson, Chen, & Lee, 1993). These authors concluded that these differences indict American schools. Since children learn math skills almost entirely in school, high-level teaching makes the difference. But because general information can be learned outside of school, American students, who seem to be just as capable as Asian students, manage to pick it up. The superior performance of Asian children seems to be related to cultural and educational differences.

FAMILY AND CULTURAL ATTITUDES

In Japan, a child's entrance into school is a greater occasion for celebration than graduation from high school; first-graders receive such expensive gifts as desks, chairs, and leather backpacks. Japanese and Korean parents spend a great deal of time helping children with schoolwork, and Japanese children who fall behind receive private tutoring or go to *jukus,* private remedial and enrichment schools (McKinney, 1987; Song & Ginsburg, 1987). Chinese and Japanese mothers—but not Americans—view academic achievement as their children's most important pursuit; and Asian mothers hold higher standards for their children's academic achievement (H. W. Stevenson et al., 1993; H. W. Stevenson & Lee, 1990; H. W. Stevenson et al.,

BOX 8-3   (Continued)

HOW CAN ASIAN CHILDREN ACHIEVE SO MUCH?

1990). Even in light of the poorer showings made by American students compared with Asians, American mothers express much higher degrees of satisfaction with their children's school performances and their children's schools than Asian mothers do (H. W. Stevenson et al., 1993).

Family attitudes and involvement are very important. In the southeast Asian families, children spend much more time on homework than American children do; parents help them by setting daily goals and relieving the children of household chores. Parents read aloud to the children, set examples of egalitarian role sharing, and expect equivalent achievements from boys and girls. And older brothers and sisters help the younger ones, learning as they are teaching. Asian students are expected to devote themselves almost entirely to study, whereas American students are more likely to hold after-school jobs, go out on dates, engage in sports, and do chores at home. Most important, perhaps, is an overwhelming feeling that learning is valuable, that mastery is satisfying in and of itself, and that effort is more important than ability (H. W. Stevenson et al., 1993; Caplan, Choy, & Whitmore, 1992).

In their (often valid) perception of limited chances for success in American life, partly because of language limitations, partly because of unfamiliarity with the culture, and partly because of prejudice from other Americans, many Asian Americans see education as the best route to upward mobility. They are, therefore, highly motivated to succeed academically (Sue & Okazaki, 1990).

EDUCATIONAL PRACTICES

Academic and classroom practices differ, too (Song & Ginsburg, 1987; Stigler, Lee, & Stevenson, 1987). Asian teachers spend more time teaching the class as a whole, whereas American teachers focus more on small groups. Japanese and Chinese teachers spend more than three-quarters of their time with the entire class, whereas American teachers spend less than half. American children spend more time working alone (often at problems they do not understand) or in small groups (with other children who do not understand the work), rather than listening to the teacher teach. Although the American approach offers more individual attention, each child ends up with less total instruction.

Classroom behavior plays a part. American children are out of their seats and engaged in irrelevant activities 5 times more often than Chinese and Japanese children are, and Asian children are more obedient. And Chinese and Japanese children spend more time on homework, get more help from parents, and like doing it more than American children do (Chen & Stevenson, 1989).

Finally, Asian children spend more time in school each year, more time in classes each day, and more time being taught mathematics—partly because the curriculum is centrally set rather than left up to individual teachers. Although Asian teachers generally do not have as much education as their American counterparts, they are more knowledgeable in their own subjects. To raise American students' proficiency in math and science, it would be necessary not

only to provide more hours of education, possibly by lengthening the school day and school year, but also to help American teachers improve their own proficiency and motivate them to teach these subjects.

PSYCHOLOGICAL ADJUSTMENT

The common belief is that high-achieving Asian students suffer psychologically. However, American students report more frequent feelings of stress, academic anxiety, and aggression—with school seen as the most common source of stress, over peers, family, sports, and jobs (H. W. Stevenson et al., 1993). So the poorer academic achievement of American students does not buy them peace of mind.

What happens to students when they leave school? Although 90 percent of Japanese students graduate from high school, compared with 76 percent of American students, only 29 percent go to college, compared with 58 percent in the United States (Simons, 1987). And what are these people like as adults? A growing number of Japanese parents, students, and lawyers argue that regimentation stifles individuality; and they are raising legal challenges to many long-established practices (Chira, 1988). Culture shapes attitudes and encourages some kinds of behaviors rather than others. It is apparently culture rather than inborn ability that has helped Asian students achieve so much in school. If cultural standards in either the East or the West change, the relative standing of students will probably change too. In any case, the citizens in a culture determine priorities, which are then reflected in their children's lives.

These girls sharing a secret demonstrate growing sophistication in the use of language to communicate. By the early school years, most children use complex grammar and have vocabularies of several thousand words. But because they still do not fully understand the processes of communication, they sometimes misinterpret what they hear. *(Erika Stone)*

shovel the driveway." Depending on which answer you received, you would know whether Ken or Barbie would be getting to work. But many children under 5 or 6 years of age do not understand the structural difference between these two sentences and think that *both* mean that Barbie is to do the shoveling (C. S. Chomsky, 1969). Their confusion is understandable, since almost all English verbs that might replace *told* in the second sentence (such as *ordered, wanted,* and *expected*) would put the shovel in Barbie's hand.

Most 6-year-olds have not yet learned how to deal with grammatical constructions in which a word is used as *promise* is used in the first sentence, even though they know what a promise is and are able to use and understand the word correctly in other sentences. But by age 8, most children can interpret the first sentence correctly.

Even though 6-year-olds speak on a rather sophisticated level, using complex grammar and several thousand words, they still have a way to go before they master syntax—the way in which

words are organized in phrases and sentences. During the early school years, they rarely use the passive voice, verbs that include the form *have,* or conditional ("if . . . then") sentences.

Children develop an increasingly complex understanding of syntax up to and possibly after age 9 (C. S. Chomsky, 1969). When testing forty 5- to 10-year-olds on their understanding of syntactic structures, Chomsky found considerable variation in the ages of children who understood them and those who did not (see Table 8-4).

Metacommunication: Understanding the Processes of Communication

When Leroy, age 6, received a fluoride treatment from his dentist, he was told by the hygienist not to swallow anything for half an hour. Soon after leaving the examining room, Leroy started to drool and to look very upset. He was greatly relieved when the dentist saw his concern and reassured him that he *could* swallow his saliva.

Despite Leroy's sophisticated linguistic ability, he was still having problems with communication, as do many children of his age. Of course, adults, too, often misinterpret what other people say. But children's failures in interpreting messages often stem from difficulties in **metacommunication,** their knowledge of the processes of communication. This knowledge grows during middle childhood.

To study children's ability to transmit and understand spoken information, kindergartners and second-graders were asked to construct block buildings exactly like those built by another child and to do this on the basis of the first child's audiotaped instructions—without seeing the buildings themselves. The instructions were often incomplete, ambiguous, or contradictory. The "builders" were then asked whether they thought that their buildings looked like the ones they were supposed to be copies of and whether they thought that the instructions were good or bad.

The older children monitored their understanding better. When instructions were inadequate, they noticed more and paused or looked puzzled. They were more likely to know when they did not understand something and to see the implications of unclear communication—that their buildings might not look exactly like the ones they were copying because the instructions were not good enough. Younger children sometimes knew that the instructions were unclear, but they did not realize that this meant that they could not do their job well. And even the older children (who, after

TABLE 8-4

Acquisition of Complex Syntactic Structures

Structure	Difficult Concept	Age of Acquisition
Ken is easy to see	Who is doing the seeing?	5.6 to 9 years.*
Ken promised Barbie to go	Who is going?	5.6 to 9 years.*
Ken asked Barbie what to do	Who is doing it?	Some 10-year-olds have still not learned this.
He knew that Ken was going to win the race.	Does the "he" refer to Ken?	5.6 years.

*All normal children aged 9 and over know this.
SOURCE: C. S. Chomsky, 1969.

all, were only 8 years old or so) lacked complete awareness of the communication process (Flavell, Speer, Green, & August, 1981).

Findings like these have important implications. Young children do not understand all of what they see, hear, or read, but often they do not know that they do not understand. They may be so used to not understanding things in the world around them that this does not seem unusual. Adults therefore must be aware that children's understanding cannot be taken for granted. For the sake of children's safety, well-being, and academic progress, we need to determine whether children do, in fact, know what we want them to know.

CHILDREN IN SCHOOL

Because school is central in children's lives, it affects and is affected by every aspect of their development. However, child-care professionals and educators often disagree on how school can best enhance children's development.

EDUCATIONAL TRENDS

Conflicting views, along with historical events, have brought great swings in educational theory and practice during this century. The traditional curriculum, centered on the "three R's" (reading, 'riting, and 'rithmetic), gave way first to "child-centered" methods that focused on children's interests and then, during the late 1950s, to an emphasis on science and mathematics in order to overcome a Soviet lead in the space race. Rigorous studies were then replaced during the turbulent 1960s by student-directed learning in "open classrooms," where children engaged in varied activi-

ties and teachers served as "facilitators." High school students took more electives and student-initiated courses. Then, in the mid-1970s, a decline in high school students' scores on the Scholastic Aptitude Test (SAT) sent schools back to the "basics" (Ravitch, 1983).

Today, in the 1990s, many educators oppose the "back-to-basics" approach. Instead, they favor a different approach to educating children in the early primary grades (Rescorla, 1991). They recommend teaching in a way that builds on children's natural interests and talents: teaching reading and writing, for example, in the context of a social studies project, or teaching math concepts in the study of music. They urge the use of cooperative projects, hands-on experience, using concrete materials to solve problems, and close parent-teacher cooperation. Contemporary educators also emphasize a "fourth R"—reasoning. Children who are taught thinking skills perform better on intelligence tests and in school (see Box 8-4).

What do all these changes mean for children? They illustrate, for one thing, the underlying faith that our future depends on the way our children turn out, and that an important way to affect children's development is through education.

TEACHERS' CHARACTERISTICS AND EXPECTATIONS

If you're lucky, you may have had a special teacher who had a major influence on you—who inspired a love of knowledge and spurred you to work and to learn. One study showed the power of a teacher's influence by linking the success of a number of people who had grown up in a poor city neighborhood with a very special first-grade teacher. Many more of "Miss A's" former pupils

BOX 8-4 PRACTICALLY SPEAKING

TEACHING CHILDREN TO THINK

Teachers complain that it is easier to teach children bald facts to give back on tests than it is to teach them how to think for themselves. *Can* children be taught to think? Research says "yes."

Thinking arises at least partly from experience. Therefore, for children to learn how to think—which includes how to evaluate a situation, how to focus on the most important aspects, how to decide what to do, and how to go about doing it—they need experiences. The following suggestions for ways by which parents and teachers can provide such experiences come from findings in cognitive studies (Marzano & Hutchins, 1987; Maxwell, 1987):

- Teach thinking skills in connection with everyday activities at home or at school. This can begin very early. Asking toddlers open-ended questions (beginning with *what, why,* and *how*) while reading to them encourages them to improve their verbal skills; it also helps them to learn to think. The same kind of approach helps older children.
- Ask children to "match" information, to compare new data with what they already know. This helps them to learn to identify links among words or concepts (what two items have in common or how they differ). Schoolchildren can categorize a country as European

or African, democratic or totalitarian. Categorization can help them to remember facts better, too, as we point out in our discussion of memory.
- Demonstrate "critical thinking," the ability to evaluate information. Teach children to ask four questions about anything they hear or read: (1) Is it unusual? (2) Is it common knowledge ("the sky is sometimes blue")? (3) If not, what is the evidence? (4) If there is evidence, is it reliable? If not, they should learn not to accept the statement.
- Show children how to approach a problem: (1) They need to identify what they know, what they do not know, and what has to be done. They can then (2) design a plan to solve it, (3) carry out the plan, and (4) evaluate the plan (decide whether it worked).
- Use "guided imagery" (imagining an event or experience). Sensory images help us store information in long-term memory, and the more senses are invoked, the better. Thus children studying the Sahara Desert might be asked to "see" it, "touch" the sand, "hear" the wind, and "feel" hot and thirsty. This approach uses elaboration, a memory strategy discussed in this chapter.
- Teach children to go beyond what they have learned. Children studying the American

Revolution might be asked, "How did the soldiers feel at Valley Forge? What were they wearing? Imagine that you were there, and write a letter to your family."
- Inspire invention. Ask children to create new information or products, like a household gadget to help in some regular chore.
- Suggest creative projects, like writing a poem or drawing a picture. Encourage children to produce a first version—and then to polish or revise it.
- Give children basic tools by teaching them how and when to use procedures, like reading a map, doing arithmetic, and using a microscope.
- Encourage children to set goals within a time frame and to write down the goals so that they can check their progress.
- Help children learn how to find the most important points in what they read, see, or hear.
- Encourage children to write, since the process of putting thoughts down on paper forces the writer to organize them. Projects that children can enjoy, as well as learn from, include keeping a journal, presenting an argument to one's parents (for an allowance increase or a special purchase or privilege), and writing a letter to a business or famous person.

than other disadvantaged youngsters showed increases in IQ over the years. Alumni of Miss A's classroom also scored higher on measures of work status, type of housing, and personal appearance than other graduates of the same school (Pederson, Faucher, & Eaton, 1978). What did Miss A do? She showed her confidence in children's ability,

gave extra time to those who needed it, was affectionate and generous, and remembered pupils by name, even 20 years later.

Miss A's belief in her pupils undoubtedly had much to do with how well they did. According to the principle of the *self-fulfilling prophecy,* students live up to (or down to) the expectations that

An exceptional teacher's influence can extend far into the future, and an interest she or he inspires may shape a child's entire life. *(George Ancona/International Stock)*

other people have for them. In the famous "Oak School" experiment, teachers were told at the beginning of the term that some students had shown unusual potential for intellectual growth. Actually, the children named as potential "bloomers" had been chosen at random. Yet several months later, many of them—especially first- and second-graders—showed unusual gains in IQ. The teachers did not spend more time with these children than with the others, nor did they treat them differently in any obvious ways. Subtler influences may have been at work—possibly the teachers' tone of voice, facial expressions, touch, and posture (R. Rosenthal & Jacobson, 1968).

Although this research has been criticized for methodological flaws, work by many other researchers using a variety of methods has confirmed the basic principle—that teachers' expectations "can and do function as self-fulfilling prophecies, although not always or automatically" (Brophy & Good, 1974, p. 32). This principle has important implications for minority-group and poor children. Since many middle-class teachers may be convinced (often subconsciously) that such students have intellectual limitations, they may somehow convey their limited expectations to the children, thus getting from them the little that they expect.

PARENTS' INFLUENCE

Teachers are not, of course, the only adults who influence how well children do in school. Parents'

involvement improves children's grades and their scores on IQ and achievement tests, as well as their behavior and attitude toward school. It also results in better schools (A. Henderson, 1987).

Parents of achieving children do a number of specific things (U.S. Department of Education, 1986b). They read, talk to, and listen to children. They tell their children stories, play games, share hobbies, and discuss news, television programs, and current events; they provide a place to study and to keep books and supplies; they set and insist on times for meals, sleep, and homework, making sure that children meet school deadlines; they monitor how much television their children watch and what their children do after school; and they show interest in their children's lives at school, partly by talking about school events and also about the children's problems and successes.

One study of about 1000 black, white, and Hispanic mothers and their elementary school children in the Chicago metropolitan area found that in general the mothers thought that parents should work closely with their children on schoolwork and that certain changes should be made in the schools to improve children's performance (Stevenson, Chen, & Uttal, 1990). Mothers in all three groups thought that the children should be in smaller classes, should get more individualized instruction, and should spend more time on studying mathematics. However, some ethnic differences showed up. The black and Hispanic mothers showed a greater emphasis on and concern about their children's education than the white mothers did. They believed that their children should be tested more on what they had learned, should have a longer school day, and should be doing more homework (although children in mostly minority schools were already doing more homework than children in mostly white schools).

The black and Hispanic children were enthusiastic about school and had high expectations about their future success; they showed initiative, self-discipline, self-direction, high self-esteem, and a high desire for achievement. Since a high proportion of these children expected to go to college, it is especially sad that the rates of school failure and dropping out of school are so high among minority students in junior and senior high schools. What happens after the elementary school years that destroys motivation for school achievement? (We'll discuss these issues in Chapter 10.)

EDUCATION FOR SPECIAL NEEDS

Children with Disabilities

Education for children with disabilities has come a long way since the beginning of this century, when the family of Helen Keller had to travel to distant cities to find help for their deaf and blind daughter, who later became a famous author and lecturer. Let us look at three of the most common educational disabilities—and then at how children with them are educated.

Mental Retardation

Most retarded children can benefit from schooling, at least up to sixth-grade level. *Mental retardation* is defined as below-average intellectual functioning, a deficiency in adaptive behavior appropriate to current age, and the appearance of such characteristics before age 18 (*Diagnostic and Statistical Manual of Mental Disorders*, 3d ed., rev., DSM-III-R, 1987). Low-level intellectual functioning (defined as a score of 75 or below on IQ tests) is important in determining retardation. But so is the person's behavior in everyday life—skills of communication, sociability, and daily living. A supportive and stimulating early environment and a continued level of guidance and help bring about a promising outcome for many of these children, including many born with Down syndrome (see Chapter 2).

The mentally retarded account for about 1 percent of the population; about 1.5 males are affected for every female. The retarded are generally classified by four categories, based on severity—mildly, moderately, severely, and profoundly retarded (see Table 8-5).

In 30 to 40 percent of cases, the cause of retardation is unknown. Known causes include problems in embryonic development (30 percent), environmental influences and mental disorders (15 to 20 percent), problems with pregnancy and childbirth (10 percent), hereditary factors (5 percent), and physical disorders acquired in childhood (5 percent) (DSM-III-R, 1987).

Learning Disabilities

Nelson Rockefeller, who was a governor of New York and a vice president of the United States, had so much trouble reading that he ad-libbed his speeches instead of using a script. Thomas Edison never learned how to spell or write grammatically. General George Patton read poorly and got through West Point by memorizing entire lectures (Schulman, 1986). All these people suffered from *dyslexia*—a developmental reading disorder in which reading achievement is at least 2 years below the expected level.

Dyslexic children—some 3 to 6 percent of the school population—often confuse up and down and left and right; they may read *saw* for *was* and have trouble with arithmetic as well as reading. Dyslexia affects males and females equally, is more common in children from large families and in lower socioeconomic levels, and seems to be partly hereditary (Council on Scientific Affairs of the American Medical Association, 1989; DeFries, Fulker, & LaBuda, 1987; S. E. Shaywitz, Shaywitz, Fletcher, & Escobar, 1990). It is usually not caused by vision problems, and there is no scientific evidence that it can be helped by any kind of "visual training" using exercises or special glasses (American Academy of Pediatrics Committee on Children with Disabilities, 1992). However, new studies suggest that dyslexia may sometimes be caused by a defect in the pathway between the eyes and the brain (S. Lehmkuhle, et al., 1993).

The reading problem is part of a generalized language impairment ("Dyslexia," 1989). Dyslexic children tend to be late in starting to talk, suffer subtle deficits in both spoken and written language, and have limited memory for verbal materials. If diagnosed before third grade, the child's prognosis is better.

Dyslexia is only one of a number of *learning disabilities (LDs)*—disorders that interfere with a specific aspect of school achievement. An estimated 5 to 10 percent of the population is affected (Interagency Committee on Learning Disabilities,

DELAYED LANG. DEVELOPMENT

TABLE 8-5

Levels of Mental Retardation	
Level	**Description**
Mildly retarded	About 85 percent of the retarded population. Mildly retarded people can acquire skills up to about the sixth-grade level, hold low-level paid jobs in adulthood, and live in the community. Although they can usually function on their own, they may need guidance and help at times of unusual stress.
Moderately retarded	About 10 percent of the retarded population. Moderately retarded people can learn academic subjects to the second-grade level, can learn occupational and social skills, and in adulthood may work in sheltered workshops or in regular jobs with close supervision. They can do a fair amount for themselves, but usually live in supervised group homes.
Severely retarded	About 3 to 4 percent of the retarded population. Severely retarded people may learn to talk during the school years, can be trained in personal hygiene, and can sometimes learn to recognize such "survival" words as *men, women,* and *stop.* They typically live in group homes or with their families.
Profoundly retarded	About 1 to 2 percent of the retarded population. Profoundly retarded people have minimal sensorimotor functioning, but may respond to some training in getting around, in self-care, and in communicating, especially if they have a one-to-one relationship with a caregiver. They live in group homes, in intermediate-care facilities, with their families, or in institutions.

1987). Since success in school is important for self-esteem, learning disabilities can have devastating effects on the psyche as well as on the report card.

Children with learning disabilities typically have average or higher general intelligence and normal vision and hearing. But they have trouble processing what comes through their senses. As one child said, "I know it in my head, but I can't get it into my hand."

Many different disorders affect one or more aspects of learning, including reading, processing spoken words, small-motor or large-motor coordination, and speech. The cause of most of these disabilities is unknown. They may be related to behavioral problems; "LD children" tend to be less task-oriented, more easily distracted, and less able to concentrate than other children. There may be a failure of cognitive processing; these children are less organized as learners and are less likely to use memory strategies (Feagans, 1983). Or the cause may be physiological; some differences have been found in the brains of people with learning disabilities (Hynd & Semrud-Clikeman, 1989). Learning disabilities often run in families, and research suggests that genetic transmission of chromosomal abnormalities may play a role (DeFries et al., 1987; M. D. Levine, 1987). But it is also possible that many children classified as learning-disabled are simply youngsters whom schools have failed to teach and control effectively (McGuinness, 1986).

Children at highest risk of learning disabilities are those who were very low birthweight infants, who suffered birth trauma or malnutrition, who have a "difficult" temperament, or who come from poor, chaotic families. Those whose problems were discovered and responded to early do the best (M. D. Levine, 1987). Among the most successful aids are behavioral modification techniques to help concentration, techniques for improving basic skills and using cognitive strategies, help in organizing life outside school as well as in it, and encouragement of progress in both academic and nonacademic areas.

Children do not outgrow learning disabilities; some 5 to 10 million adults suffer from them (Schulman, 1986). But if children take tests to establish their strengths and weaknesses, if they learn skills to help them use their strengths to compensate for their weaknesses, and if they get psychological help for such problems as poor self-esteem (often caused by school problems), they can often lead satisfying, productive lives. Some go on to college and professional careers and, while never cured of their disabilities, learn how to cope with them.

Hyperactivity

A behavior disorder that often accompanies learning disorders is hyperactivity. The story is all too familiar to many parents and teachers. Johnny cannot sit still, cannot finish even a simple task, cannot keep a friend, and is always in trouble. His teacher says, "I can't do a thing with him." His family doctor says, "Don't worry; he'll grow out of it." And his next-door neighbor says, "He's just a spoiled brat."

The syndrome Johnny is suffering from, formally known as *attention deficit hyperactivity disorder (ADHD)*, is marked by inattention, impulsivity, low tolerance of frustration, temper tantrums, and a great deal of activity at the wrong time and in the wrong place, like the classroom. These traits appear to some degree in all children; but in about 3 percent of school-age children (6 to 9 times more boys than girls), they are so pervasive that they interfere with the child's functioning in school and daily life. These children are considered hyperactive. Hyperactivity shows up before age 4 in about half the cases, but it is often not recognized until the child starts school (DSM-III-R, 1987).

Hyperactivity is probably caused by a combination of genetic, neurological, biochemical, and environmental factors (Weiss, 1990). One team of researchers found that the brains of adults who had been hyperactive as children metabolized glucose (a sugar) differently from the brains of other adults. These differences were especially notable in the areas associated with regulation of attention and motor activity (Zametkin et al., 1990). This suggests that the disorder has a specific neurological aspect. However, there are so many possible causes of hyperactivity that it is difficult to determine the origin of any one case. It often runs in families, and data suggest that it may be at least partly inherited (DSM-III-R, 1987).

Whatever the cause, parents and teachers can help these children do better at home and in school. First, they have to understand and accept the child's basic temperament. Then they can teach the child how to break up work into small, manageable segments; they can incorporate physical activity into the daily classroom schedule; and they can offer alternative ways for children to show what they have learned, such as individual conferences or tape-recorded reports, instead of written reports (M. A. Stewart & Olds, 1973).

ADHD is sometimes treated with drugs. Stimulants may be prescribed to help children focus on the task at hand and reduce problem behaviors. However, not all hyperactive children are helped by drugs, and we do not know the long-range effects of giving drugs to what many believe to be basically normal children. Although findings on brain abnormalities seem to support the use of stimulants, it still seems best to consider drugs

only after trying other approaches, and then to use them only in combination with behavior modification programs that teach social skills and control of impulsive behavior (AAP Committee on Children with Disabilities and Committee on Drugs, 1987; McDaniel, 1986; M. A. Stewart and Olds, 1973).

One treatment that has received much attention is a diet free of artificial food colorings and flavorings. However, an additive-free diet seems to help only a small number of hyperactive children, and the National Institutes of Health does not recommend it in all cases (Hadley, 1984). Other research suggests that these children may benefit from eating protein-rich breakfasts (Conners, 1988).

The long-range prognosis for children diagnosed as hyperactive is mixed. Some evidence suggests that about half grow up to function normally as adults (Mannuzza, Klein, Bonagura, Konig, & Shenker, 1988). Other research finds that by age 15 only one-quarter have "recovered"; most continue to show poorer cognitive skills and disruptive behaviors at home and school (McGee, Partridge, Williams, & Silva, 1991). As adults, many have higher rates of job changes, marital disruption, traffic accidents, and brushes with the law (B. Henker & Whalen, 1989). The long-range problems that occur are most likely to revolve around getting along with other people, drug abuse, and conduct disorders. On the bright side, although hyperactive people generally continue to be restless and impulsive, they also tend to have such positive traits as spontaneity, zest, and energy.

Educating Children with Disabilities

In 1975, Congress passed the Education for All Handicapped Children Act (Public Law 94.142), which ensures an appropriate public education for all disabled children. This law provides for an evaluation of each child's needs and the design of an appropriate program, for the involvement of parents in the decision about their children's education, and for the allocation of necessary funds. Eight out of ten children affected by this law are mentally retarded, learning-disabled, or speech-impaired.

This law requires that children be educated in the least restrictive environment. Generally, this involves *mainstreaming*, the integration of disabled and nondisabled students, as much as possible. Under mainstreaming, disabled children are in regular classes with nondisabled youngsters for all or part of the day, instead of being segregated in special classes. Thus, disabled people learn to get along in a society where most people do not share

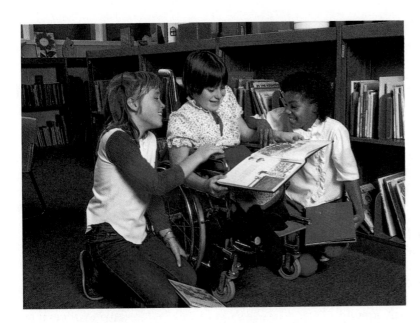

Mainstreaming in schools gives disabled and nondisabled children an opportunity to learn how to get along with and understand each other.
(Will McIntyre/Photo Researchers)

their impediments, and nondisabled people get to know and understand the disabled. However, critics of this policy maintain that disabled children can be taught better and more humanely by specially trained teachers in small classes.

Retarded children do about the same academically in mainstreamed classes as in special classes (Gruen, Korte, & Baum, 1974). But the other children in regular classes tend not to accept them socially; mainstreaming does not diminish the stigma of being retarded (A. R. Taylor, Asher, & Williams, 1987).

Mainstreaming requires innovative teaching techniques that meet the needs of all students. Not all teachers can rise to the challenge, but many have effectively taught classes of both disabled and nondisabled students, drawing on teachers' aides, individual tutors, and computers (D. Thomas, 1985). The best solution seems to be a combination of mainstreaming and special classes. A retarded child, for example, might be able to take physical education in a regular class, while receiving academic instruction in a class with slow learners. Or a child with cerebral palsy might be in a regular academic class but receive special physical training while classmates go to gym.

Gifted, Talented, and Creative Children

At age 12, Balamurati Krishna Ambati, who was born in India, was a third-year premedical student at New York University. He had mastered calculus at age 4, had scored 750 on the math SAT at age 10, and hoped to be a doctor before age 18

(Stanley, 1990). His path has not been easy: although his parents encouraged his achievements from the beginning, his teachers urged him to slow down and his peers have not always understood his drive to excel.

Giftedness can be a mixed blessing. Many promising children—more than half, by one report—achieve below their tested potential (National Commission on Excellence in Education, 1983). Why? One reason is that schools often do not meet their needs for intellectual stimulation.

About 2.5 million children—some 3 to 5 percent of the school population—are estimated to be gifted, but fewer than 1 million get special attention. The number of mentally retarded children in the population is about the same, but more funds are spent on their education (Horowitz & O'Brien, 1986).

Defining and Identifying Giftedness

Like intelligence, giftedness is hard to define. The traditional definition, the one most often used to select children for special programs, is narrow—an IQ score of 130 or higher (Horowitz & O'Brien, 1986). This definition does not identify creative children (whose unusual answers often lower their test scores), gifted children from minority groups (whose abilities may not be well developed, though the potential is there), or children with aptitudes in specific areas.

We favor a broader definition of *giftedness,* including—but not limited to—one or more of the following: superior general intellect, superiority in a single domain (like mathematics or science), talent in the arts (like painting, writing, or acting), leadership, or creative thinking (looking at problems in a new way).

Two new ways of looking at giftedness stem from new theories of intelligence. According to Sternberg (1985b; J. E. Davidson & Sternberg, 1984), gifted children process information efficiently, especially on novel tasks requiring insight. And according to Gardner's theory of multiple intelligences (Gardner, 1983), people can be gifted in one or more of at least seven separate and relatively independent intelligences. Some of these intelligences—musical, bodily kinesthetic (moving precisely as in dance), interpersonal (understanding others), and intrapersonal (knowing oneself)—are not tapped by traditional intelligence tests. The others are linguistic (reading and writing), logical-mathematical (using numbers and solving logical problems), and spatial (finding one's way around an environment).

The use of IQ tests to identify gifted children goes back to Lewis M. Terman, the professor who brought the Binet test to the United States. In the 1920s, Terman began a major longitudinal study of more than 1500 California children with IQs of 135 or more. The intellectual, scholastic, and vocational superiority of Terman's subjects has held up over 60 years. They were 10 times more likely than an unselected group to have graduated from college and 3 times more likely to have been elected to honorary societies like Phi Beta Kappa. By midlife, they were highly represented in listings like *Who's Who in America.* Almost 90 percent of the men were professional or semiprofessional or were in high echelons of business (Terman & Oden, 1959).

Thus IQ tests (even in their early days) correctly identified some children of unusual promise. Yet Terman's bright group never produced a great musician, an exceptional painter, or a Nobel prize winner—evidence that IQ does not predict creative achievement. Indeed, the most academically able children are not necessarily the most creative thinkers—innovators who solve problems in original ways or find problems that others overlook (Getzels, 1964, 1984; Getzels & Jackson, 1962). And the most creative children, whose minds take twists that teachers do not expect, may not do well in school (Renzulli & McGreevy, 1984).

One line of research has tried to identify creative children by analyzing how they think. Guilford (1959) distinguished between two kinds of thought: *convergent thinking,* which seeks a single "right" answer (usually the traditional one); and *divergent thinking,* which comes up with fresh, unusual possibilities.

Special tests have been devised to identify divergent thinkers. The Torrance Tests of Creative Thinking, for example, ask children to find ways of improving a toy, to list unusual uses for common objects, to draw pictures starting with a few given lines, and to write down what various sounds bring to mind. One problem with these tests is that the score depends partly on speed, which is not a hallmark of creativity. Furthermore, although the tests are fairly reliable (they yield consistent results), there is little evidence that they are valid—that children who do well on them are creative in real life (Anastasi, 1988; Mansfield & Busse, 1981). Much more research needs to be done before we can identify youngsters who will be creative adults (see Chapter 14).

Educating and Nurturing Gifted Children

When Terman's study began, the popular image of a bright child was a puny, pasty-faced bookworm. Terman debunked that stereotype. The children in his sample tended to be taller, healthier, and better coordinated than average, as well as better adjusted and more popular with other children (Wallach & Kogan, 1965). Other studies, however, have found that gifted underachievers and extremely gifted children—those with IQs of 180 or more—do tend to have social and emotional problems that may be caused in part by unchallenging school experiences (Janos & Robinson, 1985).

Three elements essential to the flowering of gifts and talents seem to be inborn ability, a drive to excel, and encouragement by adults (B. S. Bloom, 1985). Nurturing appears to be especially crucial (Horowitz & O'Brien, 1986). Children identified as gifted are likely to have well-educated, well-to-do, emotionally supportive, happily married parents who spend time with them, answer their questions, and encourage their curiosity (Janos & Robinson, 1985). Undoubtedly many talented and gifted children do not fulfill their potential because they don't grow up in this kind of family.

Parents of creative children tend to be special themselves, according to a review of 61 studies. They usually have occupations they consider meaningful or pursue intellectual or artistic hobbies. They are uninhibited and unconventional and do not worry about what "the Joneses" think. They expect their children to do well, and they give them both freedom and responsibility. These parents are not rigidly controlling; they let their children be themselves (B. Miller & Gerard, 1979).

However, another report of studies on the rearing of future scientists found a less clear-cut relationship between creativity and parental control (Mansfield & Busse, 1981).

Creativity often fades after children enter school, where they are rewarded for doing what adults want them to do. Those who remain creative tend to be the rebellious ones who annoy teachers with questions like "What would birds look like if they couldn't fly?" or get lost in imagination instead of doing homework. When teachers accept unconventional questions, praise original ideas, and refrain from grading everything children do, school-children are more creative and better behaved (Torrance, in Chance & Fischman, 1987).

What kind of education is best for gifted and talented students? One successful approach involves coaching by *mentors*—experts in the child's field of talent or interest (B. S. Bloom, 1985). Another approach involves special schools or classes for the artistically talented or intellectually gifted.

Most programs concentrate on enrichment (broadening and deepening studies through special activities like field trips and research projects) or acceleration (rapid movement through the curriculum), as exemplified by the "Talent Search" for mathematically and verbally precocious youth begun at Johns Hopkins University (Horowitz & O'Brien, 1986). A comprehensive national study concluded that a wide range of "able learners"—perhaps 25 percent of all students—should be served through a combination of enrichment and acceleration, geared to their individual needs (Cox, Daniel, & Boston, 1985).

There is no firm line between being gifted and not being gifted. What we learn about fostering intelligence, creativity, and talent for the small, special population of the gifted and talented can help all children make the most of their potential.

BILINGUALISM AND BILINGUAL EDUCATION

More than 2.5 million school-aged American children come from non-English-speaking homes (Hakuta & Garcia, 1989). To help these children, many school districts have implemented programs of *bilingual education,* a system of teaching children in two languages—their native language and English. To encourage *bilingualism,* or fluency in two languages, some schools teach children basic subjects in their native language first and then switch over to English (the *transitional* model).

Would Wolfgang Amadeus Mozart have composed some of the world's most beautiful music if his gifts had not been recognized, nurtured—and exploited—at an early age? His father, a fine musician and composer himself, taught Wolfgang, shown here with his sister, and encouraged him to perform. *(The National Gallery, London)*

Others immerse them in English from the very beginning, using a TESL (Teaching English as a Second Language) approach (the *immersion* model).

One controversy about bilingual education revolves around which of the above approaches is more effective. This question is hard to answer, since most research has focused only on how well children learn English—and not how well they do in school and life (Hakuta & Garcia, 1989). One plus for the transitional approach is that by emphasizing the value of reading and writing their native language, children become truly bilingual and can also feel proud of their cultural identity. This approach seems to be gaining ground in light of research that suggests that children who develop skills in their native language first make a smoother transition to all-English classrooms (Padilla et al., 1991; Celis, 1991).

But will a child with two languages fail to become really fluent in either one? This does not seem to be a problem. In fact, when the second language has been added with no sacrifice to the first and where bilingualism is admired, children who speak two languages tend to achieve more academically (Padilla et al., 1991; Diaz, 1983). In general, knowing one language does not interfere with learning a second; and learning the second does not rob a child of fluency in the first. As one observer commented, having two languages is more like having two children than like having two spouses (Fallows, 1986).

Bilingual children can usually switch easily from one language to the other, depending on the situation. This process of changing one's speech to match the situation, or *code-switching,* seems to come naturally to children. They learn very early, for example, to talk to their parents differently from the way they talk to their friends. One common example of code-switching occurs among some African Americans who speak standard English at school or work and in the wider world, and then switch to "black English" when talking with family or friends. Black English, which is spoken by some but not all black Americans, has a distinctive grammar that seems to derive from African

languages. Since it does not conform to standard English, its use in the wider society can be a drawback, whereas its informal use can be a means of emphasizing cultural bonds.

Still another concern is the expense of bilingual education. For a program to be effective, teachers need to know and be able to teach both languages, and classes need to be small. Many school districts consider bilingual programs a luxury they cannot afford. However, many children who are plunged into English-speaking classrooms without special instruction in English fall behind in their schoolwork and drop out, which may eventually cost society more (Cardenas, 1977; Cummins, 1986; McLaughlin, 1985).

The question is more than an educational one. Bilingualism is a major political issue. In Canada, Canadian-born children are expected to learn both English and French, but some districts are populated more by one cultural group than the other. In the United States, the issue is about how best to integrate newcomers. Either way, bilingualism has psychological ramifications, since identity is entwined with culture and language, and self-esteem is bound up with proficiency in the society in which a child lives. We'll explore issues of self-concept and other aspects of personality in Chapter 9.

SUMMARY

GROWTH DURING MIDDLE CHILDHOOD

▪ Physical development is less rapid in middle childhood than in the earlier years. Boys are slightly larger than girls at the beginning of this period, but girls undergo the growth spurt of adolescence at an earlier age and thus tend to be larger than boys at the end of the period. Wide differences in height and weight exist between individuals and between groups.

▪ Proper nutrition is essential for normal growth and health. Malnutrition can impair activity, sociability, and cognitive functioning.

HEALTH, FITNESS, AND SAFETY

▪ Obesity among children is increasingly common. It is influenced by genetic and environmental factors and can be treated.

▪ Respiratory infections and other common health problems of middle childhood tend to be of short duration and tend to run in clusters.

▪ Vision becomes keener in middle childhood, but up to 17 percent of children have defective distance vision by the age of 11.

▪ Although about one-half of American children aged 5 to 17 have no tooth decay, there are some dental problems in this group. Use of fluoride has resulted in improved dental health.

▪ Children today are less healthy and less fit than children in the mid-1960s. This disturbing trend seems to be occurring because children are less physically active today.

▪ Accidents are the leading cause of death in children over age 1. Most childhood accidents occur in or from automobiles, or in the home. A smaller amount occur in or around school.

MOTOR DEVELOPMENT IN MIDDLE CHILDHOOD

▪ Because of improved motor development, boys and girls in middle childhood can engage in a wider range of motor activities than preschoolers.

▪ Studies conducted several decades ago suggested that boys excel in motor skills, but more recent research indicates that boys and girls have similar motor abilities.

ASPECTS OF INTELLECTUAL DEVELOPMENT IN MIDDLE CHILDHOOD

■ The child from about age 7 to age 11 is in the Piagetian stage of concrete operations and can use symbols (mental representations) to carry out operations (mental activities).

■ Children at this stage are less egocentric than before and are more proficient at tasks requiring logical reasoning, such as conservation. However, their reasoning is largely limited to the here and now.

■ According to Piaget and Kohlberg, moral development coincides with cognitive development. Moral development is influenced by a child's maturational level, social role-taking skills, and interactions with adults and other children.

1 According to Piaget, moral development occurs in two stages. The first, morality of constraint, is characterized by moral rigidity. The second, morality of cooperation, is characterized by moral flexibility.

2 Kohlberg, who defines morality as a sense of justice, extended Piaget's view to include six stages of moral reasoning organized on three levels: preconventional morality, conventional morality, and postconventional morality.

■ Memory involves encoding, storage, and retrieval. It improves greatly during middle childhood because children's capacity increases rapidly and because they become more adept at using memory devices such as rehearsal, organization, elaboration, and external aids. Metamemory (the understanding of how memory works) also improves.

■ The intelligence of school-age children is assessed by group tests (such as the Otis-Lennon School Ability Test) and individual tests (such as the WISC-III).

■ Critics claim that psychometric intelligence tests overlook practical intelligence and creative insight and falsely equate mental efficiency with speed. New methods are being devised to test and train intelligence.

■ African Americans tend to score lower on intelligence tests than white Americans. Numerous findings indicate that the difference in scores is more likely to reflect environmental than innate racial differences.

■ Developers of intelligence tests have attempted to devise "culture-free" tests, tests with no culture-linked content and "culture-fair" tests, tests that focus on experiences common across cultures. None of the attempts has been completely successful.

■ Children's understanding of increasingly complex syntax develops up to and perhaps even after age 9. Although the ability to communicate improves, even older children may not have a complete awareness of the processes of communication.

CHILDREN IN SCHOOL

■ Teachers influence children's success in school and thus their self-esteem. Self-fulfilling prophecies often limit the achievement of poor and minority children.

■ Parents' involvement in children's education enhances children's learning.

■ Mental retardation is defined as below-average intellectual functioning, a deficiency in age-appropriate adaptive behavior, and the appearance of these characteristics before age 18. Most retarded people can benefit from schooling at least up to sixth grade.

■ Learning disabilities interfere with learning to read (dyslexia) and other school tasks. The causes of these disabilities are unclear. Many learning-disabled children can lead productive lives if they get individual attention early.

■ Under the law in the United States, every handicapped child is entitled to an appropriate education at public expense, and parents must be consulted in planning the child's program. Children must be educated in the least restrictive environment possible. They generally are mainstreamed, or placed in regular classes, as much as possible.

■ An IQ of 130 or higher is the most common standard for identifying gifted children for special programs, but this measure misses some children.

■ Creativity is sometimes identified as divergent (rather than convergent) thinking. The validity of tests for creativity is questionable.

■ Although Terman's study found that gifted children tend to be unusually successful adults, some gifted children do not live up to their apparent potential, possibly because schools do not meet their needs.

■ The development of gifts, talents, and creativity depends greatly on nurturance. The child's drive to excel is another crucial factor. Most special school programs for the gifted stress enrichment or acceleration. Each meets the needs of some students.

■ Bilingualism is fluency in two languages. Bilingual education is a system of teaching children in two languages. In general, knowing one language does not interfere with learning a second; and learning a second does not lessen fluency in the first. Bilingual children can usually switch easily from one language to the other.

KEY TERMS

concrete operations (page 279)
operational thinking (279)
decenter (279)
conservation (279)
horizontal décalage (280)
morality of constraint (280)
morality of cooperation (281)
preconventional morality (282)
conventional morality (282)
postconventional morality (282)
mnemonic devices (285)
rehearsal (285)

organization (286)
elaboration (286)
external memory aids (286)
metamemory (286)
Wechsler Intelligence Scale for
    Children (WISC-III) (286)
Otis-Lennon School Ability Test
    (286)
culture-free test (289)
culture-fair test (289)
metacommunication (292)
self-fulfilling prophecy (294)

mental retardation (296)
dyslexia (296)
learning disabilities (LDs) (296)
attention deficit hyperactivity dis-
    order (ADHD) (298)
mainstreaming (298)
giftedness (299)
convergent thinking (300)
divergent thinking (300)
bilingual education (301)
bilingualism (301)
code-switching (302)

SUGGESTED READINGS

Berger, L., Lithwick, D., and Seven Campers (1992). *I will sing life: Voices from the Hole in the Wall Gang Camp.* Boston: Little, Brown. This spirited and inspiring collection of writings by seven children, ages 7 to 17, who have all attended a camp for children with life-threatening diseases, and the counselors who lead the camp's creative-writing program, offers a window into the minds of children who live with cancer, sickle cell anemia, disability, or AIDS. In moving and witty poetry and prose, they talk about their families, their friends, their beliefs in God, and their feelings about their illnesses.

Coles, R. (1986). *The moral life of children.* Boston: Atlantic Monthly. Coles, a prominent child psychiatrist, offers his rebuttal to Kohlberg's theory that moral development rests on cognitive development and that schoolchildren are too young to live moral lives. The book contains many moving quotations from children discussing morality in their own experience.

Gardner, H. (1989). *To open minds: Chinese clues to the dilemma of contemporary education.* New York: Basic Books. This thoughtful and readable book by a leading cognitive psychologist draws on his extensive research on creativity at Harvard University and his observations of children in modern Chinese classrooms. He discusses both the progressive and the traditional approaches to education, using many lively anecdotes to make his points.

Healy, J. M. (1990). *Endangered minds: Why our children don't think.* New York: Simon & Schuster. In this thought-provoking book a noted educator examines the reasons children today are less able to concentrate and less able to absorb information than previous generations. Healy's theory is that forces in today's society (such as the electronic media, unstable family patterns, and environmental hazards) are changing the way children think and may even be changing the brain's physical structure.

Kennedy, P., Terdal, L., & Fusetti, L. (1993). *The hyperactive child book.* New York: St. Martin's Press. A practical and up-to-date guide on treating, educating, and living with an Attention Deficit–Hyperactivity Disorder child. The three authors are a unique team consisting of a clinical psychologist, a pediatrician, and a mother. They provide help in dealing with diagnosis, medications, schools, and the parents' needs.

Kidder, T. (1990). *Among schoolchildren.* New York: Avon. The author spent an entire school year observing a fifth-grade class in Holyoke, Massachusetts. This story of that teacher and her students is a remarkable depiction of the demands on a teacher; it portrays with compassion the triumphs and failures of her students.

Radford, J. (1990). *Child prodigies and exceptional early achievers.* New York: Free Press/Macmillan. This exploration of the lives of gifted children charts the impact of environmental and genetic influences in their lives. Telling the stories of dozens of early achieving children, the author, a psychology professor, discusses their problems and stresses the importance of stimulating environments and of inspiring mentors.

Shekerjian, D. (1990). *Uncommon genius: How great ideas are born.* New York: Viking. This fascinating exploration of creativity draws on interviews with 40 winners of the MacArthur Foundation fellowships (the so-called "genius awards"), as well as the findings of research and the lives of creative people. It tells some good stories—and offers suggestions for nurturing creativity in our own lives.

CHAPTER NINE

PERSONALITY AND SOCIAL DEVELOPMENT IN MIDDLE CHILDHOOD

The healthy human child will keep
Away from home, except to sleep.
Were it not for the common cold
Our young we never would behold.

Ogden Nash,
You Can't Get There from Here, 1956

■ **THE SELF-CONCEPT**

Developing a Self-Concept
Self-Esteem

■ **ASPECTS OF PERSONALITY DEVELOPMENT IN MIDDLE CHILDHOOD**

Everyday Life
The Child in the Peer Group
The Child in the Family

■ **CHILDHOOD EMOTIONAL DISTURBANCES**

Types of Emotional Problems
Treatment for Emotional Problems

■ **STRESS AND RESILIENCE**

Sources of Stress: Life Events, Fears, and the "Hurried Child"
Coping with Stress: The Resilient Child

■ **BOXES**

9-1 Window on the World: Family Ecologies of Children from Ethnic Minority Groups
9-2 Food for Thought: After-School Care: What Kind Is Best?
9-3 Practically Speaking: Helping Children Adjust to Divorce
9-4 Food for Thought: Children Who Live in Chronic Danger

- How does the self-concept develop, and how does it affect children's behavior?
- What do schoolchildren do with their time, and how does a schoolchild's daily life today differ from the daily life of children in previous generations?
- How does the peer group influence children, and why do some children make friends more easily than others?
- What changes occur in family relationships in middle childhood, and how are children affected by parents' employment, by parents' divorce, and by living in a single-parent family?
- What are some emotional disturbances of childhood, and how are they treated?
- How do school-age children handle stress?

A t age 6, Anna became a "published author" when she and her fellow first-graders wrote and illustrated their own books. Anna's self-esteem jumped when she saw her book, "Anna in Outer Space," exhibited for all to see. At age 10, Stefan's self-concept relies on other bases: his proficiency in math, his daredevil exploits on his new bike, his ability to speak two languages. Schoolchildren's new interests and abilities affect how they feel about themselves— and change them in far-reaching ways. In this chapter, we trace the social and personality growth that goes along with the cognitive changes of middle childhood.

The self-concept, of course, develops continuously from infancy onward. We examine it in depth at this point because it is particularly important for personality and social development during the years of middle childhood. From about age 6 to the onset of puberty at about age 12, youngsters develop more realistic concepts of themselves and of what they need to survive and succeed in their culture. They become more independent of their parents and more involved with other people, particularly other children. Through interaction with their peers, they make discoveries about their own attitudes, values, and skills. But the family remains a vital influence. Children have been profoundly affected by new patterns of family life, as well as by other societal changes.

Although most children are healthy, both physically and emotionally, some succumb to emotional disorders of one kind or another, sometimes in response to stress, sometimes because of biological malfunction. Other, more resilient children face childhood stresses and emerge from them healthier and stronger.

THE SELF-CONCEPT

DEVELOPING A SELF-CONCEPT

"'Who in the world am I?' Ah, *that's* the great puzzle," said Alice in Wonderland, after her size had abruptly changed—again. Solving Alice's "puzzle" entails a lifelong process of getting to know our developing selves.

The *self-concept* is our sense of self, including self-understanding and self-control or self-regulation. The self-concepts that are built during middle childhood are often strong and lasting. Positive ones (like "I am popular," "I am a good artist," "I am a fast runner") may take shape as children's physical, intellectual, and social abilities let them see themselves as valuable members of society. This is also the time when a negative self-image may arise, to stay with a person long after childhood has been left behind. Let us see how children develop self-knowledge, self-regulation, and then self-esteem.

Beginnings: Self-Recognition and Self-Definition

The sense of self grows slowly. It begins in infancy, with *self-awareness:* Vera gradually realizes that she is a being separate from other people and things, with the ability to reflect on herself and her actions. At about 18 months, she has her first moment of *self-recognition* when she recognizes herself in the mirror.

The next step is *self-definition.* This comes when Vera identifies the characteristics she considers important to describe herself. At age 3, Vera thinks of herself mostly in terms of externals—her ponytailed hair, her neat house, her activities in preschool. Not until about age 6 or 7 does Vera begin to define herself in psychological terms. She now develops a concept of who she is (the *real self*) and also of who she would like to be (the *ideal self*). By the time she achieves this self-understanding, Vera has made progress in a related area: her behavior is regulated less by her parents and more by herself. The ideal self incorporates many of the "shoulds" and "oughts" Vera has learned; it helps her control her impulses in order to be considered a "good" girl (Maccoby, 1980).

Coordination of Self-Regulation and Social Regulation

In middle childhood, Jimmy can do more things than he could as a preschooler. And, in fact, he does more things and is involved with more people. He is also handed more responsibilities: to do his homework, to wash dishes, to help clean the apartment, to obey rules at home and school. Jimmy begins to regulate his behavior not only to get what he needs and wants (as he did earlier), but also to meet other people's needs and wants. As Jimmy internalizes society's behavioral standards and values, he coordinates personal and social demands, and he now does things voluntarily (like cleaning his room) that he would have needed prodding to do at an earlier age.

The sense of self might seem like the most personal thing in the world. But many observers see self-concept as a *social* phenomenon, "the meeting ground of the individual and society" (Markus & Nurius, 1984, p. 147). School-age children look around themselves, see what society expects, and blends its expectations with the picture they already have of themselves—and the self-concept evolves.

As they strive to become functioning members of society, children must fulfill several important tasks toward the development of self-concept (Markus & Nurius, 1984). They must (among other things) do the following:

■ *Expand their self-understanding* to reflect other people's perceptions, needs, and expectations. They have to learn what it means to be a friend, a teammate, or a member of a dramatic cast.
■ *Learn more about how society works*—about complex relationships, roles, and rules. Jimmy comes to understand, for example, that his mother has a "boss" at work to whom she has to answer,

This newspaper deliverer is accomplishing several important tasks of middle childhood related to the self-concept. By taking on responsibilities to match her growing capabilites, she learns about how her society works, her role in it, and what doing a job well means. *(Elliott Varner Smith/Inernational Stock)*

and that his track coach can be "nice" at one moment and "mean" at another.
■ *Develop behavioral standards* that are both personally satisfying and accepted in society. This can be hard for children, since they belong to *two* societies—the peer group's and the adult one— which sometimes have conflicting standards.
■ *Manage their own behavior.* As children take responsibility for their own actions, they must *believe* that they can follow both personal and social standards, and they must develop the ability to *do* it.

SELF-ESTEEM

Middle childhood, then, is an important time for the development of *self-esteem,* a positive self-image or self-evaluation. As we pointed out earlier, children compare their *real selves* and their *ideal selves* and judge themselves by how well they measure up to the social standards and expectations

A child's sense of competence—which is enhanced by winning an athletic competition, as did this girl who won medals for her participation in New York State games for the physically challenged—contributes mightily to self-esteem. A positive self-image can strongly influence a child's future success and happiness. *(Hugh Rogers/Monkmeyer)*

they have taken into their self-concept and by how well they perform.

Children's opinions of themselves have a great impact on their personality development, and especially on their usual mood. Children who like themselves tend to be cheerful, whereas those with low self-esteem are more likely to be depressed (Harter, 1990). A depressed mood can lower a person's energy level, which in turn can affect competence, leading to lower self-esteem.

There are other differences, too, between children with high and low self-esteem (Harter, 1990). Keesha, for example, who has high self-esteem, is confident, curious, and independent. She trusts her own ideas, approaches challenges and initiates new activities with confidence, describes herself positively, and is proud of her work. She adjusts fairly easily to change, tolerates frustration, perseveres in pursuing a goal, and can handle criticism.

On the other hand, Kitty, who has low self-esteem, does not trust her own ideas, lacks confidence, hangs back and watches instead of exploring on her own, withdraws and sits apart from other children, and describes herself negatively, without pride in her work. She gives up easily when frustrated and reacts immaturely to stress and inappropriately to accidents.

Since self-esteem underlies so much in life, it is important to ask how children get a favorable self-image.

Industry and Self-Esteem

According to Erik Erikson, an important determinant of a good self-image is a child's view of his or her competence. The major crisis of middle childhood in Erikson's theory is that of *industry versus inferiority.* The issue to be resolved is a child's capacity for productive work. Children in all cultures have to learn the skills they need to survive; the specifics depend on what is important in a particular society. For example, Arapesh boys in New Guinea, no longer content merely to play, learn to make bows and arrows and to lay traps for rats; Arapesh girls learn to plant, weed, and harvest. Inuit children of Alaska learn to hunt and fish. Children in industrialized countries learn to do math, read, write, and use computers.

These efforts at mastery can help children form a positive self-concept. The "virtue" that develops with successful resolution of this crisis is *competence,* a view of the self as able to master skills and complete tasks. As children compare their own abilities with those of their peers, they construct a sense of who they are. If they feel inadequate by comparison, they may retreat to the familiar but less challenging nest of the family, where less may be expected of them. If, on the other hand, they become *too* industrious, says Erikson, they may neglect their relationships with other people and turn into "workaholic" adults.

Sources of Self-Esteem

Another view of how children form an overall favorable opinion of themselves, or a sense of *global self-worth,* comes from Susan Harter's (1990) research. This suggests that self-esteem comes from two major sources: how competent children think they are in various aspects of life and how much social support they receive from other people.

Children as young as 4 years old already seem to show by their behavior that they possess a sense of self-worth. But not until middle childhood (about age 8) are youngsters able to express self-judgments in words. This development parallels their growing ability to form cognitive concepts.

To measure self-worth, Harter (1985, 1987) asked children between the ages of 8 and 12 about five domains in life: how well they do in school, how good they are in sports, how accepted they feel by other children, how they behave, and what they look like. The children rated the importance of doing well in each domain in order to feel good about themselves, and then they rated themselves on their competence in each domain. They also answered questionnaire items tapping how much they liked themselves as persons and how happy they were with the way they were. And they assessed how they were treated by their parents, teachers, classmates, and close friends. Did these people care about and like the child, and treat him or her like a person who mattered and had valuable things to say?

According to this research, the most vital contributor to self-worth is the degree to which a child feels regard from the significant people in his or her life. The most important people were parents and classmates, followed by friends and teachers.

In the five separate domains, the major one was physical appearance; children rated this aspect as very important and judged themselves by how good-looking they thought they were. This domain was followed by social acceptance. Less critical at this age were competencies in school work, conduct, and athletics. These findings undermine to some extent the high value that Erikson put on competence in middle childhood. In these studies, the children's senses of their own adequacy mattered, but not as much as physical appearance and social acceptance.

In a child's global sense of self-worth, both large areas are important—competency in the five domains and a sense of support from significant people. One does not compensate for the lack of the other. Therefore, even if, say, Juanita thinks that it's important to be pretty and smart and considers herself both, she'll suffer some loss of self-worth if she doesn't feel valued by her family and other important people. On the other hand, even if Mike's family and friends shower him with praise and emotional support, if he thinks sports are important but that he is not athletic, he'll suffer a loss of self-esteem. A sense of self-worth affects virtually every area of life, and certainly other aspects of personality development.

ASPECTS OF PERSONALITY DEVELOPMENT IN MIDDLE CHILDHOOD

EVERYDAY LIFE

"You're it!" "No, *you're* it!" For thousands of years, impromptu games have served the time-honored mandate of childhood: to learn through play. Today, however, new social patterns in the larger society are replacing traditional ones. The impact of television, computer games, and more organized sports, all of which call for fewer social and physical skills, is just one example of these changes, which lead children of today's changing families to act, think, and live differently from children in previous cohorts.

How Do Children Spend Their Time?

American children spend about two-thirds of their time on essentials—sleeping, eating, school, personal care, housework, and religious observance—

Middle childhood is a time for learning the skills that one's culture considers important. In Tanzania, a Masai boy learns to herd cattle. In the United States, children learn to count, read, and use computers. *(Paul Conklin/Monkmeyer)*

TABLE 9-1

How School-Age Children Spend Their Time: Children's Top 10 Activities (Average Hours and Minutes Per Day)				
	Weekdays		Weekends	
Activity	Ages 6–8	Ages 9–11	Ages 6–8	Ages 9–11
Sleeping	9:55	9:09	10:41	9:56
School	4:52	5:15	—	—
Television	1:39	2:26	2:16	3:05
Playing	1:51	1:05	3:00	1:32
Eating	1:21	1:13	1:20	1:18
Personal care	0:49	0:40	0:45	0:44
Household work	0:15	0:18	0:27	0:51
Sports	0:24	0:21	0:30	0:42
Religious observance	0:09	0:09	0:56	0:53
Visiting	0:15	0:10	0:08	0:13

SOURCE: Adapted from Institute for Social Research, 1985.

leaving about 55 hours a week of leisure time (Institute for Social Research, 1985; see Table 9-1).

The two main things that children *choose* to do are playing (alone or with other children) and watching television. These two activities take up anywhere from 50 to 70 percent of their free time. Children aged 6 to 8 spend more time playing; by 9 years of age, the balance shifts in favor of television (Institute for Social Research, 1985).

Children watch television more in middle childhood than during any other period of childhood, and 11- and 12-year-old boys watch the most, particularly action and adventure shows. Disadvantaged children are 3 times as likely as other children to be heavy viewers (W. A. Collins, 1984; Institute for Social Research, 1985). Children who read for pleasure every day are, not surprisingly, likely to be less frequent viewers. But even children who read almost every day at age 9 are less likely to do so by age 13 (National Assessment of Educational Progress, 1982).

School-age youngsters spend many hours on sports, clubs, religious groups, scouting, camps, private lessons, and other organized activities (W. A. Collins, 1984). Participation in athletics and other activities is strongly influenced by the ethnic and social group. For example, black boys are more likely to be involved in team games; white boys, in individual sports like swimming and tennis (Medrich et al., 1982).

With Whom Do Children Spend Their Time?

When Sally's eldest daughter, Nancy, was 10 years old, her parents drove 300 miles to visit her at sum-

mer camp. She waved to them, called out "Hi," and then went back to playing softball. They had just received the first of many lessons about the powerful draw of the peer group.

School-age children spend relatively little time with their parents (Demo, 1992); the peer group becomes central. Just counting minutes and hours, however, can be deceptive. Relationships with parents continue to be the most important ones in children's lives.

Different relationships serve different purposes for children, as a questionnaire study of 199 mostly middle-class fifth- and sixth-graders showed (Furman & Buhrmester, 1985). In rating the important relationships in their lives, the children named their parents as most important. They looked to them for affection; guidance; lasting, dependable bonds; and affirmation of competence or value as a person. They rated mothers higher than fathers as companions, and they were generally more satisfied with their relationships with their mothers than those with their fathers. After parents, the most important people were grandparents, who were often warm and supportive, offering affection and enhancement of worth. Although the children looked for and got guidance from teachers, too, they were least satisfied with relationships with teachers.

Children turned most often to friends for companionship, and to friends and mothers for intimacy. Although they also looked to siblings (especially those of the same sex and close in age) for companionship and intimacy and to older siblings for guidance, sibling relationships generally involved the most conflict.

Some gender differences emerged. Girls were closer to their mothers than to their fathers; for boys, there was no difference. Also, girls relied on best friends more than boys did, and their friendships were more intimate, affectionate, and worth-enhancing. Since these three qualities seem to be more characteristic of older children's friendships, school-age girls' closest friendships may be more mature than those of boys.

Now let's look more closely at this diverse and nurturing social world to see the importance of the peer group and the family.

THE CHILD IN THE PEER GROUP

Babies are aware of one another, and preschoolers begin to make friends, but not until middle childhood does the peer group come into its own.

Functions and Influence of the Peer Group

In our highly mobile, age-segregated society, the peer group is a particularly strong influence, for both good and ill.

Positive Effects

To identify the peer group's role in children's lives, a team of Canadian researchers (Zarbatany, Hartmann, & Rankin, 1990) had 91 fifth- and sixth-graders keep week-long diaries of what they did with other children and what they liked and disliked about their friends' behavior. Then another group of 81 children the same age (average age 11½) rated the importance and prevalence of each activity and which behaviors they would most like or dislike in each activity (see Table 9-2). The researchers concluded that children develop psychologically in three major ways as the result of peer activities. First, they develop skills for sociability and intimacy, enhance relationships, and get a sense of belonging. Second, they are motivated to achieve and they attain "integrity of the self," or a sense of identity. And third, they learn.

Different peer activities contribute differently to these functions. Noncompetitive activities (like talking to each other) offer opportunities for enhancing relationships, while competitive ones (like sports) help children identify unique aspects of the self. Children need exposure to a variety of activities, and may need to be encouraged to take part in those they might not ordinarily seek out (like, say, team sports for girls and child care for boys).

In another time or place, these boys might have been out kicking a ball instead of playing video games. As technology changes the tools and habits of leisure, children's play is becoming less active and often calls for fewer social skills. *(Larry Kolvoord/The Image Works)*

It is among other children, as well as with their parents, that youngsters develop a self-concept and build self-esteem. They form opinions of themselves by seeing themselves as others see them. They have a basis of comparison—a realistic gauge of their own abilities and skills. Only within a large group of their peers can children get a sense of how smart, how athletic, and how personable they are. Then, the peer group helps children choose values to live by. Testing their opinions, feelings, and attitudes against those of other children helps them sift through the values they previously accepted unquestioningly from parents and decide which to keep, which to discard. The peer group also offers emotional security. Sometimes another child can provide comfort that an adult cannot. It is reassuring to find out that a friend also harbors "wicked" thoughts that would offend an adult.

Interacting with other children helps children in cognitive ways too. When children work on computer tasks with a partner, for example, they may seem to concentrate less on the task and more on the social interaction, but they enjoy the sessions more and learn more from them than children working alone do (Perlmutter, Behrend, Kuo, & Muller, 1989). Finally, the peer group helps children learn how to get along in society—how to adjust their needs and desires to those of others, when to yield, and when to stand firm.

On the positive side, the peer group counterbalances parents' influence, opens new perspectives, helps children form a self-concept and de-

TABLE 9-2

Important and Prevalent Peer Activities as Rated by Fifth- and Sixth-Graders

Most Common Activities*	Most Important Activities*
Conversation	Noncontact sports
Hanging out	Watching TV or listening
Walking around at school	to records
Talking on the telephone	Conversation
Traveling to and from school	Talking on the telephone
Watching TV or listening	Physical games
to records	Going to parties
Physical games	Hanging out

Most Liked Behaviors	
Invitations to participate	Sharing
Performing admirably	Facilitating achievements
Physically helping	Being nice or friendly
Complimenting or encouraging	Instructing
Loyalty	Helping
Humor	Absence of unpleasant
Giving permission	behavior

Most Disliked Behaviors	
Physical aggression	Annoying or bothersome
Interfering with achievements	behavior
Verbal aggression	Expressing anger
Dishonesty	Unfaithfulness
Teasing	Greed or bossiness
Ignoring	Violating rules
	Criticizing

*There were some gender differences. Boys liked sports more than girls did and spent more time in contact sports; girls spent more time shopping, talking on the telephone, and talking about hair styles and clothing than boys did.
SOURCE: Zarbatany, Hartmann, & Rankin, 1990.

velop social skills, helps them learn, and frees them to make independent judgments.

Negative Effects: Conformity

On the other hand, the peer group may hold out some undesirable values at this age of emerging self-regulation, and some children (especially those who have low status in the group) may not have the strength to resist. Children are most susceptible to pressure to conform during middle childhood. In some countries—such as Israel, the Soviet Union, and China—as well as in some behavior modification programs in the United States, the peer group is used deliberately to mold behavior. During middle childhood, children are especially susceptible to pressure to conform (Costanzo & Shaw, 1966).

Peer influence is strongest when issues are am-biguous. Since we live in a world with many ambiguous issues that require careful judgment, the consequences of peer-group influences can be severe. And although peer groups do many constructive things together—playing games, scouting, and the like—it is usually in the company of friends that children also begin to smoke and drink, sneak into the movies, and perform other antisocial acts. On the other hand, youngsters who are headed for more serious trouble with the law tend *not* to get along with their peers. These children are often immature, and they lack social skills (Hartup, 1989).

For children—as for adults—some degree of conformity to group standards is a healthy mechanism of adaptation. Conformity is unhealthy only when it becomes destructive or causes people to act against their better judgment.

Members of a neighborhood peer group are usually—but not always—of the same age, sex, race, and socioeconomic status, and they enjoy doing things together. While the peer group helps children build their self-concept and become independent from parents, it also exerts pressure to conform to group standards of dress, hair style, and behavior. *(Jeff Greenberg/Photo Researchers)*

Makeup of the Peer Group

Peer groups form naturally among children who live in the same neighborhood or go to school together (Hartup, 1984). Children who play together are usually within a year or two of the same age, though an occasional neighborhood play group will form that includes small children along with older ones. Too wide an age range brings problems with differences in size, interests, and levels of ability.

In the elementary school years, peer groups are usually all girls or boys, partly because children of the same sex have common interests, and girls are generally more mature than boys. These same-sex groupings offer "classrooms" for learning "gender-appropriate" behaviors.

Members of a peer group are usually of the same race and of the same or similar socioeconomic status, especially in segregated neighborhoods. Racial segregation in peer groups (as in adult society) often results from *prejudice*—negative attitudes toward certain groups, which can corrode the self-esteem of members of these groups. Studies conducted from the 1960s to the mid-1970s found bias against blacks among both white and black children in northern and southern American cities, from preschool through the early school years (Morland, 1966; J. Williams, Best, & Boswell, 1975).

Court-ordered school integration, which began in the mid-1950s, has brought more acceptance of racial differences, even though children still tend to choose friends of the same race. One study of midwestern third- and sixth-graders who had been in integrated classrooms since kindergarten found that although the youngsters (particularly the older African-American children) preferred members of their own race, they rated classmates of the other race quite positively (Singleton & Asher, 1979).

Some schools have worked to reduce prejudice by recruiting and training more minority-group teachers and by emphasizing the cultural contributions of minorities. The most effective programs, however, are those that get children from different racial groups to work together. Like sports teams, interracial learning groups provide a common goal—and result in positive feelings between children of different races (Gaertner, Mann, Murrell, & Dovidio, 1989).

Friendship

Jordan met his best friend at school; their favorite activity is playing ball together. Melissa and her best friend eat lunch together, play together at recess, walk home together, and then talk on the phone to each other.

Children may spend much of their free time in groups, but only as individuals do they form friendships. Children's ideas about friendship change enormously during the elementary school years. Now a friend is someone a child feels comfortable with, likes to do things with, and can share feelings and secrets with. Friendships make children more sensitive and loving, more able to give and receive respect. Children cannot be true friends or have true friends until they achieve the cogni-

TABLE 9-3

Stages of Friendship		
Stage	**Ages***	**Characteristics**
0 Momentary playmateship (undifferentiated)	3–7	Children are egocentric—they think only about what they want from a relationship. Children define friends by how close they live. ("She's my friend—she lives on my street.") Children value friends for material or physical attributes. ("He's my friend—he's got a giant Superman doll and a real swing set.")
1 One-way assistance (unilateral)	4–9	Children define a good friend as someone who does what they want the friend to do. ("He's my friend—he lets me borrow his eraser," or, "She's not my friend anymore—she wouldn't go skating with me.")
2 Two-way, fair-weather cooperation (reciprocal)	6–12	Friendship involves give-and-take but still serves separate self-interests rather than common interests. ("We're friends—we do things for each other," or, "A friend is someone who plays with you when you don't have anybody else to play with.")
3 Intimate, shared relationships (mutual)	9–15	Children view friendship as an ongoing, systematic, committed relationship involving more than doing things for each other. Children become possessive of their friends, demanding exclusivity. ("It takes a long time to make a close friend, and so you feel bad if she gets to be friends with someone else.") Girls develop one or two close friendships; boys have more, but less intimate, friends.
4 Autonomous interdependence (interdependent)	12 on	Children respect friends' needs for both dependency and autonomy. ("A good friendship is a real commitment, a risk you have to take. You have to be able to support and trust and give, but you have to be able to let go, too.")

*Ages of the various stages may overlap.
SOURCE: Selman & Selman, 1979.

tive maturity to consider other people's viewpoints and needs as well as their own.

Robert Selman has traced changing forms of friendship through five overlapping stages, on the basis of interviews with more than 250 people between the ages of 3 and 45 (Selman & Selman, 1979; see Table 9-3). Most school-age children are in either stage 2 (fair-weather relationships based on reciprocal self-interest) or stage 3 (intimate, mutual relationships). In general, girls value *depth* of relationships, while boys value *number* of relationships (Furman, 1982). Middle-childhood friends are typically of the same sex and have common interests (Hartup, 1989).

Having a true friend is a milestone in development. Mutual affection enables children to express intimacy, to bask in a sense of self-worth, and to learn what being human is all about (Furman, 1982; H. S. Sullivan, 1953).

Popularity

We all want other people to like us. What our peers think of us matters terribly, affecting our present happiness and often echoing through the years to affect later success and well-being.

Why are some children sought out while others are ignored or rebuffed? Why do some children have many friends while others have none? What are popular and unpopular children like? What can be done to help children who are neglected or rejected by their peers? Let's look at these issues.

The Popular Child

Popular children share a number of characteristics. Typically, they are sociable and have good cognitive abilities. They are good at solving social problems and they help other children, are assertive without being disruptive or aggressive. Their behavior enhances, rather than undermines, other children's goals. They are trustworthy, loyal, and self-disclosing enough to provide emotional support for other children. They are not goodie-goodies, but they have superior social skills that make other people enjoy being with them (Newcomb, Bukowski, & Pattee, 1993).

The Unpopular Child

One of childhood's saddest figures is the child who is chosen last for every team, is on the fringes of every group, walks home alone after school, is not invited to birthday parties, and sobs in despair, "Nobody wants to play with me."

Children can be unpopular for many reasons; some causes are within their power to change, but others are not. Some unpopular youngsters are aggressive, some are hyperactive and inattentive, and some are withdrawn (Newcomb et al., 1993; Pope, Bierman, & Mumma, 1991; Dodge, Coie, Pettit, & Price, 1990). Others act silly and infantile, showing off in immature ways; or are anxious and uncertain, so pathetic in their lack of confidence that they repel other children, who find them no fun to be with. Very fat or unattractive children, children who act strange in any way, and retarded or slow-learning youngsters also tend to be outcasts. Unpopular children do not have the social skills that popular ones do.

A major problem may be a child's expectation of not being liked. Two groups of unpopular children—third-grade boys and fourth- and fifth-grade girls—took part in an experiment. Some were told that other children whom they had met only once before really liked them and looked forward to seeing them again, and then they were brought back together with these other children. The children who got this positive "feedback" were liked better by their new acquaintances than children in a control group who had received no such message. Furthermore, when the children were rated on their behavior by independent observers, the girls who got positive messages behaved in more socially competent ways (Rabiner & Coie, 1989). Apparently, some unpopular children, expecting not to be liked, do not exert themselves with others.

Family Influences on Popularity

It is often in the family setting that children acquire the behaviors that affect popularity (as we pointed out in Chapter 7). Among 112 six- to eleven-year-olds and their parents, the children of authoritative parents (who guided their children by suggesting, explaining, supporting, and encouraging) were more popular than children of authoritarian parents (who criticized, commanded, and prohibited more, and explained less—Dekovic & Janssens, 1992). The parents of aggressive children are often either coercive or inept in dealing with them. Then, the children are so impulsive, mean, and disruptive that other children dislike them. As a result, they tend to seek out friends who are just as antisocial as they are (Hartup, 1989). (It is not clear, though, whether unpopularity during middle childhood *causes* later disturbances or *reflects* developmental problems that show up in more serious form later on.)

Children of mothers who punish and threaten are likely to try to threaten or act mean with other children. These children are less popular than children of mothers who reason and try to help a child understand how another person might feel (Hart, Ladd, & Burleson, 1990). Unpopular children also report the least supportive relationships with their fathers (C. J. Patterson, Kupersmidt, & Griesler, 1990).

How Can Unpopular Children Be Helped?

Popularity in childhood is not a frivolous issue. Aside from their sadness, sense of rejection, and poor self-esteem, unpopular children are also deprived of a basic developmental experience: the positive interaction with other youngsters that helps them grow. Unpopularity during the preschool years is not necessarily cause for concern, but by middle childhood peer relationships are strong predictors of later adjustment. Children whose elementary school peers like them are more likely to be well-adjusted as adolescents. But children who have trouble getting along with peers are more likely to have psychological problems, to drop out of school, and to become delinquent (Newcomb et al., 1993; Morison & Masten, 1991; Kupersmidt & Coie, 1990; Parker & Asher, 1987).

How can adults help? Children who are simply *neglected* or overlooked by their classmates or other peers may do better in a different class or a new school, or if they join a new club or go to a new camp. But children who are actively *rejected* by peers—the ones most at risk of developing emotional and behavioral difficulties in later life—need to learn how to make other children like them.

In one study, fifth- and sixth-graders were trained in social skills. They learned how to carry on a conversation: how to share information about themselves, how to show interest in others by asking questions, and how to give help, suggestions, invitations, and advice. When they had a chance to practice their new conversational skills in a group project with other children, they became better liked by the others and interacted more with them (Bierman & Furman, 1984).

The children who received the training showed more general and lasting improvement over a 6-week period (on measures of conversational skills, rates of interaction, peer acceptance, and self-perception) than those who received no training, those who received the training but then did not participate in the peer-group project, and those who took part in the group project but were not taught any skills.

We see, then, that children not only need social skills but also need to be in situations in which they can use these skills and in which other children can see the changes that have taken place in them. Otherwise, other children may hold on to their former opinions about these youngsters and may not give them a chance to show their new skills.

Furthermore, since it seems that children who expect to be liked actually are better liked (Rabiner & Coie, 1989), some kind of positive expectation should be built into programs that are developed to increase children's popularity. However, findings about the impact of family relations on popularity show that to be effective, intervention has to look at, and possibly try to change, the quality of parent-child relations rather than focus only on the individual child.

THE CHILD IN THE FAMILY

School-age children spend more time away from home than they used to. School, friends, games, and movies all draw them away from the house and keep them apart from the family. Yet home is still the most important part of their world, and the people who live there are the most important to them (Furman & Buhrmester, 1985).

Relationships with parents and siblings continue to develop during middle childhood and, as proposed in Bronfenbrenner's ecological theory, societal change affects family life, which in turn affects children's development. The major changes in recent years involve the rising rates of divorce, single-parent families, and mothers working outside the home. Although all these factors exert influence, a review of family research suggests that their negative effects have been greatly exagger-

Parents who enjoy being with their children, like this mother giving a lesson in making tortillas, are likely to raise children who feel good about themselves—and about their parents. *(Lawrence Migdale/Photo Researchers)*

ated—and that the most important social processes affecting children's development involve economic well-being or its lack, and the atmosphere within the home—whether it is warm and loving or conflict-ridden (Demo, 1991). Cross-cultural research shows how the family ecology differs among ethnic groups (see Box 9-1).

Parent-Child Relationships

Outside obligations and interests increase at a time when children are more self-sufficient and need less physical care and supervision than before. Parents spend less than half as much time caring for 5- to 12-year-olds—teaching them, reading and talking to them, and playing with them—as they spend caring for preschoolers (C. R. Hill & Stafford, 1980). Still, the job of parenting is far from over. And even though parents spend relatively little time directly interacting with their school-age children (about 30 minutes on an average work-

BOX 9-1 WINDOW ON THE WORLD

FAMILY ECOLOGIES OF CHILDREN FROM ETHNIC MINORITY GROUPS

A genuine multicultural viewpoint involves looking at far deeper issues than whether people wear saris or kunte cloth, or whether they eat sushi or empañadas. It means delving into the values passed on through the generations and expressed in behavior. The ecological perspective (proposed by Bronfenbrenner, discussed in Chapter 1) considers how people develop in their immediate social environments, and how aspects of the larger social context affect what goes on in the family. Taking this approach, one team of researchers identified distinctive socialization goals, adaptive strategies, and the resulting behavior of children in African American, Native American, Asian Pacific American, and Hispanic families (Harrison, Wilson, Pine, Chan, and Buriel, 1990).

The worldviews of all these ethnic groups emphasize a loyalty to the group and a collective philosophy that emphasizes group values rather than individual ones. Many of the specific adaptive strategies, those cultural patterns that promote the survival and well-being of people in these groups, stem from

these worldviews. Thus, in these ethnic minority families, ties are strong among extended family members, who are more likely than white families to share living quarters and to interact with each other in daily life. These family ties are important in solving problems and coping with stress, especially for recent immigrants and single-parent families.

By and large, ethnic minority children are encouraged to cooperate, share, and develop an interdependence with others—values that contrast sharply with western ideals of competition, autonomy, individualism, and self-reliance.

In socializing children, parents often set their goals in terms of their specific situations within the larger society. Thus social roles in minority families tend to be more flexible than in majority-culture families. Older siblings assume more responsibilities for younger ones, adults more often share breadwinning (often out of economic need), and alternative family arrangements are more common (often because of a perceived, or real, awareness of inadequate support systems in

the larger society). The parents of well-motivated, achieving African American children emphasize ethnic pride and self-development, while acknowledging the existence of racial barriers.

Another common adaptive strategy is to become comfortable in two cultures. Children learn two languages: the one spoken in the home, which helps to give children a sense of their ethnic identity, and the one spoken in the larger society, which is essential for getting along socially, academically, and eventually at work. These children learn to switch languages and behavior appropriately from one situation to the other.

Anyone planning public policy or working directly with children from ethnic minorities needs to be aware of the way their families differ from the overall majority culture, and also of the ways in which families in one minority culture differ from those in another. Only by acknowledging and respecting the differences among people can we overcome the barriers that prevent children from reaching their full potential.

day, according to some research), most parents are highly supportive, loving, and involved with their children (Demo, 1992).

Issues between Parents and Children

As children's lives change, the issues that arise between them and their parents change, too (Maccoby, 1984). One important new area of concern is school. Parents worry about how a child is doing with schoolwork and wonder how involved they should become. They may have to deal with a child who complains about his or her teacher, pretends to be sick to avoid going to school, or cuts school.

Parents usually want to know where their children are and whom they are with when they are not in school. Some parents even tell children with whom they may and may not play. Parents and

children often disagree over what household chores children should do, whether they should be paid for doing them, and how much allowance they should get. (Of course, many of these issues do not even come up in some societies, where children over the age of 6 must work to help the family survive.)

The profound changes of middle childhood in children's lives and in the kinds of issues that arise between them and their parents bring changes in the ways parents handle discipline and control. Yet, as we'll see, most parents do *not* change their basic approach to their job as their children mature.

Discipline

Every parent struggles with the constant decisions involved in bringing up human beings who will think well of themselves, fulfill their potential, and become happy, productive people. This struggle is what *discipline* is all about. Many people think of *discipline* as a synonym for *punishment,* but the word is from the Latin for "knowledge" or "instruction" and is principally defined this way in dictionaries. Parents differ in the way they try to teach their children character, self-control, and morality. And most parents go about it differently with school-age and younger children (Maccoby, 1984; G. C. Roberts, Block, & Block, 1984).

For example, the parents of 8-year-old Jared rely more on praise for what he does right than on punishment for what he does wrong. When they do feel that punishment is called for, they usually deprive him of some privilege, like watching a favorite television show. They employ an "inductive disciplinary strategy" in which they give reasons. For example, Jared's father tells him, "You shouldn't hit Craig because this will hurt him and make him feel bad." Jared sees from this how his actions can affect others.

His parents appeal to his self-esteem ("What happened to the helpful boy who was here yesterday?"), sense of humor ("If you go one more day without a bath, we'll know when you're coming without looking!"), moral values ("A big, strong boy like you shouldn't sit on the train and let an old person stand"), or appreciation ("Aren't you glad that we care enough to remind you to wear boots so that you won't catch a cold?"). Above all, Jared's parents let him know that he is responsible for what happens to him and has to bear the consequences of his behavior ("No wonder you missed the school bus today—you stayed up too late last night! Now you'll have to walk.").

This evolution is typical as children gain cognitive awareness. School-age children are less likely to knuckle under to sheer power. They are more likely to defer to parents' wishes because they recognize that their parents are fair, that they contribute to the whole family's well-being, and that they often "know better" because of their wider experience. On the other hand, parents often defer to children's growing judgment and take strong stands only on important issues. Thus, parents of schoolchildren are less likely to impose their own taste in clothing except for special occasions, recognizing that children use dress to express personality and assert independence (Schiro, 1988).

Yet a parent's underlying philosophy seems to remain fairly consistent over time, especially with regard to control, enjoyment, and emotional investment. In one longitudinal study, parents of 3-year-old boys and girls from a wide range of backgrounds filled out long questionnaires—and answered the same questions again when the children were 12 years old. The questions related to independence, control, handling aggression and sex, early training, emphasis on health and achievement, expression of feelings, protectiveness, supervision, and punishment. Over the 9-year period, the parents' basic values and approach to child rearing seemed to remain constant, emphasizing rational guidance and praise. Shifts that occurred were appropriate to the children's development (G. C. Roberts et al., 1984).

Control and Coregulation

Control of a child's behavior gradually shifts from the parents to the child. The process begins during the second year of life; then, a child's gradual acquisition of self-control and self-regulation steadily reduces the need for constant parental scrutiny. But not until adolescence or even later do most people make their own decisions about how late they should stay out, with whom they should associate, and how they should spend their money.

Middle childhood is a transitional stage of *coregulation,* in which parent and child share power; parents continue to supervise, while children begin to exercise self-regulation (Maccoby, 1984). Coregulation reflects the child's developing self-concept. As children of this age begin to coordinate their own wishes with societal demands, they are more likely to anticipate how their parents or other people will react to what they do, or to accept a reminder from adults that others will think better of them if they behave differently.

Coregulation is a cooperative process; it succeeds only when parents and children communicate clearly. If children do not tell their parents where they are, what they are doing, and what problems they are facing, or if parents are preoccupied with their own activities and do not take an interest in their children's, the parents will not be able to judge when to step in.

To make this transitional phase work, parents need to influence their children when they are with them and monitor them when they are not, by phone or baby-sitter. They also need to teach children to monitor their *own* behavior—to adopt acceptable standards, avoid undue risks, and recognize when they need their parents' support or guidance (Maccoby, 1984).

Parents' Work: How It Affects Their Children

Much of adults' time, effort, and ego involvement

goes into their occupations. How do these occupations affect the family—especially now, when adults' roles are in transition? Let's look at some of the ways parents' work affects children.*

Mothers' Work

Most of the research on the way women's work affects their children has focused not on the kind of work they do or its demands on them, but on whether they work at all for pay. And much of this research refers to a time when the working mother was the exception rather than the rule, as she is today, when almost 7 out of 10 married women with children under 18 and 8 out of 10 single mothers are in the work force. With more than half of all new mothers going to work soon after giving birth, many children have never known a time when their mothers were *not* working.

How does a mother's employment affect her children? That depends on many variables. Is she married or single? Does she work full time or part time? How does she feel about her work? Does the family need the money? How are the children cared for? Fifty years of research do not show any overall ill effect of working. Rather, many contemporary researchers emphasize the positive effects of a mother's employment on her entire family.

The Mother's Psychological State   Despite the guilt many working mothers feel over being away from their children, employed women often feel more competent, more economically secure, and more in charge of their lives. Their self-esteem tends to be higher than that of homemakers, whose work is generally undervalued in our society. By and large, the more satisfied a woman is with her life, the more effective she is as a parent. This effect cuts across socioeconomic levels, but may be especially significant at lower incomes, especially for single mothers who have had little education. One way the benefits of mothers' work shows up is in the lower rates of child abuse from mothers working full time, compared with unemployed or part-time workers (Gelles & Maynard, 1987).

Interactions in Working-Mother Families   The husband of a working mother can spend more time with his children, since he is less likely to hold a second job. In working-mother families, the divi-

This mother, taking her child to day care, is typical of the majority of today's mothers, who have jobs outside the home. How a mother's employment affects her children depends on many variables. *(Charles Gupton/Stock, Boston)*

sion of labor between the parents is somewhat less traditional. Even though the typical working mother still has more responsibility for housework and child care, her husband tends to be more involved than men in homemaker-mother families (Demo, 1991). He is most involved when the mother works full time, when they have more than one child, when the children are quite young, and when she earns close to what he does (L. Hoffman, 1986). The involved father shows his children a nurturing side—expresses love, tries to help them with their worries and problems, makes them feel better when they are upset, and gives them continuing care and attention (Carlson, 1984). Thus his children see a side of the personality that has traditionally been less visible in men.

Working Mothers and Children's Values   Daughters of working women and sons of involved fathers have fewer stereotypes about gender roles than children in "traditional" families (Carlson, 1984). This effect seems to depend more on the mother's attitude toward the father's participation in home duties than on how much he actually does (G. K. Baruch & Barnett, 1986).

Children's Reactions to Mothers' Work   School-age children of employed mothers seem to have two advantages over children of homemakers. They tend to live in more structured homes, with clear-

---

*This section about the impact of parents' work on their children is indebted to Lois Wladis Hoffman (1984, 1989), who conceptualized and researched many of these issues. Statements not otherwise referenced in this discussion rely on her analysis.

cut rules giving them more household responsibilities; and they are encouraged to be more independent. Encouragement of independence seems to be especially good for girls, helping them to become more competent, to achieve more in school, and to have higher self-esteem; but it may put pressure on some boys (Bronfenbrenner & Crouter, 1982).

Findings for boys are less clear-cut and more varied by social class. Boys in both single-parent and two-parent lower-income families seem to benefit when their mothers work; these boys achieve more in school. They are probably benefiting from the family's higher income. Sons of middle-class working mothers, however, have done less well in school than have the sons of homemakers (Heyns & Catsambis, 1986). However, the data for this study were collected in the 1960s and 1970s, when opportunities for women and options for child care were not as broad as they are today. As society adjusts to the fact that now the *typical* mother is a working mother, there should be fewer negative effects on boys.

Children do complain that they have too little time with their working mothers (General Mills, 1977). And many mothers worry about finding competent day care and after-school care for younger children and of supervising older ones, especially when the children care for themselves part of the day (see Box 9-2). Time-related problems are not, of course, as severe for women who work part-time or have flexible hours.

The dual-income family does not follow one single pattern. Probably the most influential factor is the parents' attitudes. "Where the pattern itself produces difficulties, they seem often to stem mainly from the slow pace with which society has adapted to this new family form" (L. W. Hoffman, 1989, p. 290). When good child care is more available and affordable, when men assume a larger role in the home, and when employers support workers' family roles, the benefits will be felt in millions of American families.

Fathers' Work

Most of the research on how men's work affects their families has focused on the nature of the work itself. Some of the findings regarding men can also apply to women.

When work does not fully satisfy a man's (or a woman's) psychological needs, children may benefit. A man whose work is not exciting may throw himself enthusiastically into family life and, through his children, gain a sense of accomplishment, fun, intellectual stimulation, moral values, and self-esteem. But children may also suffer if a man takes out his frustration at having little autonomy at work by being hostile and severe with his children (McKinley, 1964), or if a man's work is so fulfilling that he does not invest much of himself in his family (Veroff, Douvan, & Kulka, 1981). The dominant mood of a man's work may also go home with him—whether it is a feeling of satisfaction or the kind of tension that, for example, often follows police officers home (Nordlicht, 1979).

How does a father's work schedule affect his children? There seems to be little if any relationship between the number of hours a father works and how much interest he takes in his children (Clark & Gecas, 1977).

When a father loses his job and becomes irritable and pessimistic, he is likely to nurture his children less and punish them more. The children may react to this treatment with emotional or behavior problems and reduced aspirations (McLoyd, 1989; 1990). Not all unemployed fathers react this way, however; a man's reactions are tempered by his wife's relationship with him and his children—and by the children's personalities and temperaments. Some fathers find something positive in being out of work—the chance to spend more time with their children. In general, though, a father's not having a job is considered to have damaging effects on his children, while a mother's having one has been thought disruptive for her family (Bronfenbrenner & Crouter, 1982).

We see, then, that the work lives of both mothers and fathers affect their children in many different ways. But—as we note so often in this book—a single influence (like parents' employment) always has to be considered in context with other aspects of a child's world.

Children of Divorce

Children suffer when their parents split up. The children, as much as or more than the parents, may feel pain, confusion, anger, hate, bitter disappointment, a sense of failure, and self-doubt. For many, this family disruption is the central event of childhood, with ramifications that follow them into adult life.

More than 1 million children under the age of 18 are involved in divorces each year. About half of the children born in the late 1970s and early

BOX 9-2 FOOD FOR THOUGHT

AFTER-SCHOOL CARE: WHAT KIND IS BEST?

When Kim, 11, comes home from school, she unlocks the front door, throws down her books, and feeds her cat before sitting down for her own snack. Then she calls her mother to check in and tell her whether she will be staying home, going outside to play, or going to a friend's home. Depending on what needs to be done, she may fold clean laundry, set the table, or start dinner. If she wants to watch a special television show at night, she will do her homework in the afternoon.

Kim is among some 2 million *self-care children,* who regularly care for themselves at home without adult supervision because both parents or a single custodial parent works outside the home (Cole & Rodman, 1987). Although most self-care takes place after school, some children spend time alone in the morning or evening, too. Most are alone for no more than 2 hours a day (Cain & Hofferth, 1989). Other children go to a structured after-school program, where they do their homework under adult supervision, take music or art lessons, or engage in other activities. Others are cared for by a baby-sitter or a relative; and some are cared for by their own parents. Does it matter what kind of after-school care a child gets?

As in so many other aspects of human development, there is no simple answer. Among 150 suburban middle-class children, for example, no differences were found between mother-care and self-care children on a number of dimensions (Vandell & Corasaniti, 1988). Both groups did about the same in classroom work, standardized tests, popularity with other children, and parent and teacher ratings. However, children who went to after-school programs or stayed with baby-sitters tended to get lower school grades, do worse on tests, and be less popular. It's possible that parents who think their children are having problems are more likely to see that they're supervised.

It's also possible that in middle-class neighborhoods a stigma is attached to children who go to after-school care. This does not seem to hold true in low-income neighborhoods. In these areas, another study found, both black and white third-graders from single-parent and two-parent families thrived in formal after-school programs (Posner & Vandell, 1900). These children got higher grades in school, had better work habits, and were better adjusted than children who stayed alone or were cared for by their mothers or baby-sitters.

Still another examination of after-school care for 390 third-through fifth-graders found that when family income and parental emotional support were controlled, the type of after-school care was less important than the quality of children's experiences with their families (Vandell & Ramanan, 1991).

Studies like these are removing the stereotyped picture of the "latchkey child" as a lonely, neglected youngster. In addition, research has dispelled another misconception—that most self-care children are from poor, single-parent families in high-risk inner-city settings. Many are, in fact, from well-educated, middle- to upper-class suburban or rural families (Cain & Hofferth, 1989).

How can parents tell when a child is ready for self-care, and how can they make the situation as comfortable as possible for the child? The following guidelines can help answer these questions (Cole & Rodman, 1987; Olds, 1989).

Before children take care of themselves, they should be able to control their bodies well enough to keep from injuring themselves; keep track of keys and handle doors well enough to avoid locking themselves in or out; safely operate necessary household equipment; stay alone without being too afraid or lonely; be resourceful enough to handle the unexpected; be responsible enough to follow important rules; understand and remember spoken and written instructions; read and write well enough to take telephone messages and use a pay phone in an emergency; know what to say and do about visitors and callers (not tell people they do not know that they are alone, and not open the door to anyone but family and close friends); and know how to get help in an emergency (how to call police and firefighters, which friends and neighbors to call, and what other resources to call on).

Parents and guardians can help by staying in touch by phone (preferably by setting up a regular time for check-in calls); telling children what to do and how to reach a responsible adult in an emergency; setting up a structure for self-care time; and instituting safety procedures.

1980s will experience their parents' divorce and then spend an average of 5 years in a single-parent home before the custodial parent remarries (P. C. Glick & Lin, 1986b; Wegman, 1986).

No matter how unhappy a marriage has been, its breakup usually comes as a shock to the children. The children of divorcing parents often feel afraid of the future, guilty about their own (usually imaginary) role in causing the divorce, hurt at the rejection they feel from the parent who moves out, and angry at both parents. They may become depressed, hostile, disruptive, irritable, lonely, sad, accident-prone, or even suicidal; they may suffer from fatigue, insomnia, skin disorders, loss of appetite, or inability to concentrate; and they may lose interest in schoolwork and in social life. Children of different ages react to divorce differently.

Children's Adjustment to Divorce

"Tasks" of Adjustment The children of divorcing parents face special challenges and burdens in addition to the usual issues of emotional development. In a longitudinal study of 60 divorcing families whose children ranged in age from 3 to 18 at the time of the separation, six special "tasks" emerged as crucial to the children's adjustment (Wallerstein, 1983; Wallerstein & Kelly, 1980):

1 *Acknowledging the reality of the marital rupture:* Small children often do not understand what happened, and many older children initially deny the separation. Others either are overwhelmed by fears of total abandonment or retreat into fantasies of reconciliation. Most children face the facts by the end of the first year of separation.

2 *Disengaging from parental conflict and distress and resuming customary pursuits:* At first, children are often so worried that they cannot play, do schoolwork, or take part in other usual activities. They need to put some distance between themselves and their distraught parents and go on with living their own lives. Most children do this by the end of the first 1 to 1½ years after the separation.

3 *Resolving loss:* Absorbing all the losses caused by divorce may be the single most difficult task. Children need to adjust to many losses: of the parent they are not living with, the security of feeling loved and cared for by both parents, familiar daily routines and family traditions, and often a whole way of life. Some children take

years to deal with these losses, and some never do, carrying a sense of being rejected, unworthy, and unlovable into adulthood.

4 *Resolving anger and self-blame:* Children realize that divorce, unlike death, is voluntary, and they often stay angry for years at the parent (or parents) who could do such a terrible thing to them. They also look for the cause of divorce in something they did—or didn't do. When and if they do forgive their parents and themselves, they feel more powerful and more in control of their lives.

5 *Accepting the permanence of the divorce:* Many children hold on for years to the fantasy that their parents will be reunited, even after both have remarried. Many accept the permanence of the situation only after they achieve psychological separation from their parents in adolescence or early adulthood.

6 *Achieving realistic hope regarding relationships:* Many children who have adjusted well in other ways come through a divorce feeling afraid to take a chance on intimate relationships themselves, for fear that they will fail as their parents did. They may become cynical, depressed, or simply doubtful of the possibility of finding lasting love.

Many children do, of course, succeed at all these tasks and come through the painful experience of divorce with a basically intact ego. The ability to do this seems to be related partly to a child's own resilience (see the discussion later in the chapter). It also seems to be related partly to the way parents handle issues entailed by the separation (see Box 9-3) and the challenge of raising children alone.

Influences on Children's Adjustment to Divorce

Children—especially boys—who live with their divorced mothers have more social, academic, and behavioral problems than children in intact homes (J. B. Kelly, 1987). However, a number of factors influence how well children adjust to divorce.

Parenting Styles and Parents' Satisfaction Children of divorced authoritative parents usually show fewer behavior problems (Hetherington, 1987), do better in school, and have fewer problems getting along with other children (Guidubaldi & Perry, 1985) than children of authoritarian or permissive parents. These effects are especially significant for boys. Children whose parents are able to control their anger, cooperate in parenting, and not expose the children to quarreling have fewer emotional and social problems (Hetherington, Stanley-Hagen, & Anderson, 1989).

Children who do have these problems after divorce are often responding to the conflict between their parents rather than the separation itself. They may also be reacting to predivorce parental conflicts (Amato, et al., 1993). This may be an indirect result of their mothers' distress, which interferes with the ability to be warm and empathic with the children (Kline, Johnston, & Tschann, 1991).

In families in which the parents had divorced 6 years earlier, custodial mothers who did not remarry had more emotional problems and were less satisfied with their lives than remarried or nondivorced mothers. The unmarried mothers were still in intense, ambivalent, conflicted relationships with their sons, who tended to show behavior problems and spend less time at home with adults. However, the mothers had good relationships with their daughters, who tended to be fairly well adjusted (Hetherington, 1986).

Remarriage of the Mother   It generally takes 2 to 3 years for children to adjust to a single-parent household; when a mother remarries, they have to adjust again; and sometimes they have to adjust to the breakup of this new marriage (Hetherington et al., 1989). Remarried mothers tend to be happier, better adjusted, and more satisfied with life, and their sons do better with a stepfather. However, their daughters often have more problems than the daughters of divorced women who have not remarried or of nondivorced mothers. Typically, however, these girls do adjust eventually (Hetherington, 1986).

Relationship with the Father   The majority of fathers are not closely involved with their children after separation, but fortunately there are exceptions. Those who do see their children often and help to make child-rearing decisions also tend to pay child support. The closer the fathers live to their children, the higher their socioeconomic status, and the more recent the separation, the more involved they tend to be (Amato & Keith, 1991a). All these factors have implications for postdivorce counseling and legislation: perhaps encouraging fathers to take a larger role in their children's lives soon after the separation will set a pattern of child support and intimacy that will continue over the years.

This kind of encouragement is vital since fathers are important to their children. Among 16- to 18-year-old boys whose parents had divorced 10 years earlier, the boys' relationships with their fathers were important to the boys' adjustment. The sons of erratic and rejecting fathers felt hurt, trapped, and humiliated; and they often reacted with anger against their mothers (Wallerstein, 1987).

Accessibility of Both Parents   Predictable and frequent contact with the noncustodial parent is important for children, who are deprived by the typical practice of limited visitation for fathers. Children who have reliable, frequent contact with the noncustodial parent are usually better adjusted; this is especially true for boys (J. B. Kelly, 1987). However, joint custody—shared custody by both parents—does not seem to improve a child's situation in an amicable divorce and may worsen it in a bitter divorce (Kline, Tschann, Johnston, & Wallerstein, 1989). Although some observers hold that the best custody arrangement is with the parent of the same sex, a recent analysis finds no advantage to this arrangement (Downey & Powell, 1993).

Adolescents who do not get along with their mothers and are able to make their homes with their fathers often have adjustment problems at the time of the divorce, but they show psychological growth in the long run. When the parent a young person turns to is responsive, this parent can protect and help the child; but when this is not the case, "bitter, even tragic disappointment" can result (Wallerstein, 1987, p. 211).

Long-term Effects of Divorce on Children

Longitudinal studies that have followed up children of divorcing parents have found that many children adjust well, but that others are still troubled 10 or more years later. Among thirty-eight 16- to 18-year-olds whose parents had divorced 10 years earlier, three-quarters of the girls and about half of the boys were doing fairly well (Wallerstein, 1987). Most were in school full time, working part time, law-abiding, and living at home (3 out of 4 with their mothers; those living with their fathers had moved during adolescence). The girls were getting along well with their mothers and were likely to be dating and involved in sexual relationships, while the boys were far more likely to be lonely, to be emotionally constricted, and to hold back in relationships with girls. The divorce had left its mark on most of these young people. Burdened by sadness, neediness, and a sense of their own powerlessness, they missed their fathers (whom they tended to idealize), were anxious about their own love relationships and chances for

BOX 9-3   PRACTICALLY SPEAKING

HELPING CHILDREN ADJUST TO DIVORCE

Parents can help their children to make the difficult adjustment to divorce. The following guidelines are based on the advice of experts on family relations:

All the children should be told at the same time about the divorce, in language suited to their age: Some 80 percent of preschoolers are given no explanation because their parents think they are too young to understand (Wallerstein & Kelly, 1980). But even very young children know that a change is taking place, and they need to be told often, in various ways, what is happening. Both parents should tell them together, to let the children see that both are still involved in their lives and will continue to be available to them.

Children should be told only as much as they need to know: It may be tempting for parents to talk about what they see as causes for the divorce—an affair, alcoholism, gambling, sexual incompatibility. Yet this talk may confuse and wound children far more than it helps them. It puts a heavy burden on them to judge the parent "in the wrong." At a time when they need as much emotional support as possible, they may lose faith in at least one parent, and perhaps both.

Children need to know that they have not caused the divorce: Young children are egocentric. They tend to see the whole world as revolving around themselves, to assume that something they did or thought drove their parents to divorce, and to become tortured by guilt.

Parents must emphasize the fi-

nality of their decision: The fantasy of a reunion is almost universal. As long as children dream of reunion, they cannot accept reality. Once they give up this dream, they can pay attention to lessening the pain of the rupture.

Arrangements for the children's care should be carefully explained: Although children may not talk about their fear of abandonment, they need reassurance that they will continue to be cared for. Parents should explain custody arrangements and should emphasize (if it is true) that they will continue to consult each other on important issues concerning the children.

Children should be reassured of both parents' continuing love: They need to know that there is no such thing as divorce between parent and child and that the noncustodial parent will continue to love and care for them.

Children should be encouraged to express fear, sadness, and anger: When they can show these emotions openly, they can begin to understand and deal with them. Parents can admit their own sadness, anger, and confusion, and can seek out a discussion group for children of divorced parents.

Limits should be set on children's behavior: Parents should maintain firm, friendly discipline. Children need to know that someone stronger loves them enough to stop them from losing control.

Parents should enlist the help of other adults: A person outside the immediate family—like a teacher, scout leader, relative, or friend—can show a caring

concern that helps a child through the crisis.

Battling parents should declare a truce when they are with the children: Divorced parents do not have to be friends, but they help their children by cooperating on child-rearing issues.

Children should not be used as weapons: Children suffer when they are forced to transmit angry messages, when they are drawn into arguments, when they are asked to choose sides, or when family visits turn into battles. Parents who use children this way are sacrificing a child's welfare for their own immediate satisfaction.

Parents must recognize the conflict between their needs and their children's needs: Parents need to spend time with other adults, but children need their parents' company. Adults have to be sensitive to this problem and work out solutions that will meet the needs of both generations.

Children's lives should be changed as little as possible: Any change is stressful; the fewer minor adjustments children have to make, the more energy they have to cope with the major one. If possible, the parent who has custody should postpone taking a job for the first time or moving into a new house. If changes must be made, parents should realize that children need extra understanding.

Parents should use whatever resources they can find for themselves and their children: These include helpful books, discussion groups, and community programs.

successful marriage, and were afraid of being betrayed, hurt, and abandoned (Wallerstein, 1987).

What happens to children of divorce when they reach adulthood? One analysis of 37 studies involving more than 81,000 people found some differences between adult children of divorce and people who had grown up in intact families (Amato & Keith, 1991b). The divorce group tended to be slightly more depressed, to have more marital problems themselves, to be in poorer physical health, and to have a lower socioeconomic status. However, the differences were small, were stronger in earlier studies (perhaps showing that divorce is less traumatic now than it had been in the past), were weaker among black people (where one-parent families are more common), and were stronger among people who had sought counseling or therapy. In the general community, the link between parental divorce and negative long-term results for their children was weak.

While divorce is a wrenching experience for everyone in the family, the resilience of the human spirit allows many children to come through the painful times with an increased sensitivity and compassion that serve them well in adulthood.

The One-Parent Family

Current Trends   One consequence of a high divorce rate is the large number of children being raised by single parents. One-parent families may be created by the death of a parent, or by parents' never marrying, a situation that has become more common in recent years. Nearly a quarter of the nation's unmarried women (23.7 percent) now become mothers, an increase of almost 60 percent since 1982 (U.S. Bureau of the Census, 1993). The increase was especially marked among white women and women who attended college, but it was also there for African American and Hispanic women and women at all educational levels.

But single-parent families most often result from divorce, separation, or desertion. About 22 percent of American children (more than 10 million) live in homes with only one parent (U.S. Bureau of the Census, 1993). The number of single-parent families in the United States almost tripled between 1960 and 1986, but the rate of increase has slowed.

The rates for single-parenthood are different among different ethnic groups in the United States. The highest rates occur among African Americans (62.6 percent in 1991), followed by Hispanic families (33.1 percent), and totaling some 23.0 percent among white families (U.S. Bureau of the Census,

1991). Rates are also different in different countries (see Figure 9-1). An Australian report comparing rates in the mid-1980s for eight industrialized countries* found that the United States has the highest percentage of single-parent families (then, 28.9 percent), with the lowest rate by far in Japan (4.1 percent—Burns, 1992).

In 86 percent of single-parent households the mother is the custodial parent, but the number of unmarried father-only families more than doubled between 1980 and 1992. Fathers now head 14 percent of single-parent households (U.S. Bureau of Census, 1993).

Almost 60 percent of custodial fathers are not married; about 40 percent have remarried (Meyer & Garasky, 1993). (We discuss stepfamilies later in this chapter.) Custodial fathers typically are older, make more money, and are better educated than custodial mothers. Married fathers earn the most, followed by single fathers and then single mothers. Still, a substantial number of custodial fathers are poor or nearly poor; 18 percent of father-only families are poor, compared with 43 percent of single-mother families (U.S. Bureau of Census, 1993). More single fathers than married fathers are black, under 30 years old, and less highly educated (Meyer & Garasky, 1993).

Custodial fathers who do best were actively involved in child care and household tasks before the divorce, sought extra counseling after it, and purposefully worked toward a good relationship with their children. Most are happy with their decision and feel that they are the better choice for custodial parent (Hanson, 1988).

Effects on Children   Children growing up with one parent do not have two adults who can share child-rearing responsibilities, take children to activities, serve as gender role models, and model the interplay of personalities. What is more, divorce often brings a family's income down to or near the poverty level, and financial hardship has negative effects on children's health, well-being, and school achievement. Typically, mother-only families suffer from the mother's low earning capacity, the father's failure to pay child support, and meager public benefits (McLanahan & Booth, 1989).

The strains of divorce also affect parenting. For several years following a separation, the single parent may be preoccupied with personal concerns and be less attentive and responsive to the child

*Australia, France, Japan, Sweden, United Kingdom, United States, Soviet Republic, and West Germany.

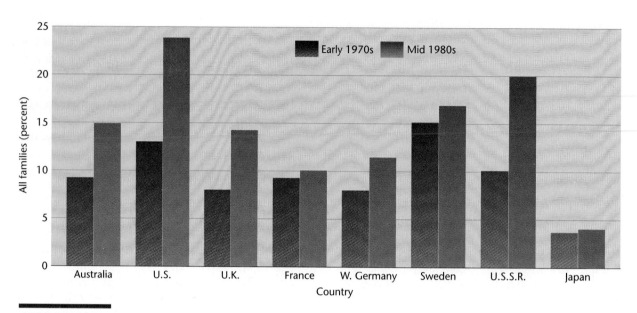

FIGURE 9-1
Single-parent families as a percentage of all families. (*Source:* Burns, 1992.)

(Kline, Johnston, & Tschann, 1991). Housekeeping and normal routines like bedtime and bath time may be neglected (Hetherington, Cox, & Cox, 1975). These effects wear off in time, especially if the custodial parent forms a new relationship. But school-age children may continue to feel torn between two hostile parents and to reject a stepparent.

In general, children in one-parent families report more autonomy and household responsibility; more conflict with siblings and less family cohesion; and less support, control, or punishment from fathers, compared with children in intact families (Amato, 1987).

Effects on Schooling   Among 18,000 elementary school and high school students in 14 states, students from one-parent homes achieved less in school, liked school less, had more problems with peers, and were more likely to need disciplinary action than those with two parents. However, a follow-up analysis and interviews with parents showed that the critical factor was family income. Lower income affected achievement more strongly than the number of parents at home (Zakariya, 1982). What looks like a "single-parent" effect is often a "low-income" effect. Other factors that influence achievement are parents' expectations and the number of books in the home (Milne, Myers, Rosenthal, & Ginsburg, 1986).

Teachers can help these children. When elementary school teachers make systematic efforts to get parents to help their children at home, single parents help as much and as effectively as married ones (J. L. Epstein, 1984). Schools have begun to look at other ways to cooperate with single parents, most of whom are working mothers. They offer evening, breakfast, or weekend meetings, conferences, and programs; baby-sitters for younger children during school events and late-afternoon transportation for students after sports or band practice; and send notices and report cards to the noncustodial parent.

Long-term Effects   Do youngsters with only one parent get into more trouble than those with two parents? Some studies say that they do, and that they may also be at greater risk, later in life, of marital and parenting problems themselves (Rutter, 1979a). As adults, children from mother-only families are more likely to be poor themselves and to become single parents than are children who live with both parents (McLanahan & Booth, 1989). Children benefit from rich family relationships—and as they grow older and more independent, parents need more help in guiding them.

Yet the one-parent home is not necessarily pathological, and the two-parent family is not always healthy (Demo, 1991). In general, children grow up better adjusted when they have a good relationship with one parent than when they grow up in a two-parent home filled with discord and discontent (Rutter, 1983); and an inaccessible, rejecting, or hostile parent is worse than an absent one (Hetherington, 1980).

This "blended" family consists of a couple and three sets of children: a teenager from the husband's first marriage, two children from the wife's first marriage, and a toddler from the present marriage. Life is more complex in such families, but studies show that most of the children in them adjust and thrive. *(Erika Stone)*

Stepfamilies   The word *stepparent* conjures up vivid storybook images of wicked and cruel interlopers. Such images often sabotage the efforts of the kindest stepparents to form close, warm relationships with their spouses' children. Yet many make the effort, and many succeed. With today's high rate of divorce and remarriage, families made up of "yours, mine, and ours" are common.

The stepfamily—also called the *blended* or *reconstituted* family—is different from the "natural" family. It has a larger cast, with all the relatives from four adults (the married pair, plus both former spouses). And it has many stresses to deal with. Because of losses resulting from death or divorce, both children and adults may be afraid to trust or to love. A child's loyalties to an absent or dead parent may interfere with forming ties to a stepparent, especially when the child goes back and forth between two households. Disparities in life cycles often arise, as when a father of adolescents marries a childless woman (E. Visher & Visher, 1983).

The most common stepfamily consists of a mother, her children, and a stepfather. One study (Santrock, Sitterle, & Warshak, 1988) found that these remarried mothers were just as involved, nurturant, and available to their children as mothers in intact marriages. These women's greater satisfaction with life seems to carry over to their relationships with their children.

Most of the children were doing well and had good feelings about their stepfathers, who had been in the role an average of 3 years. These men were somewhat involved with the children's care but were relatively distant from them. Their detachment seemed to be deliberate, prompted by what they saw as the children's needs. Nearly one-fourth of the men said that they had tried to assume a parental role too fast and that this had caused problems in their relationships with the children. Some research has found that a man has the best chance of being accepted by his stepson if he makes friends with the boy first, supports the mother's parenting, and later moves into an authoritative role (Hetherington, 1986). This does not work so well with a girl, who is less likely to accept a stepfather as a parent. Boys benefit from having a stepfather, while stepdaughters seem to have more behavioral problems than daughters of nondivorced women or of women who have not remarried (J. B. Kelly, 1987).

In a comparison group, the stepmothers were much more involved, taking their stepchildren to and from school and other activities, providing emotional support and comfort, and disciplining them (Santrock et al., 1988). Still, for most stepchildren their most enduring ties are with their biological custodial parents, and "the positive nature of the relationship between the remarried parent and the child [is] a key ingredient in helping the child through the disruption and disequilibrium, as the family [moves] from the status of intact to divorced to becoming a stepfamily" (Santrock et al., 1988, p. 161).

Sibling Relationships

"I fight more with my little brother than I do with my friends," reports Monique, 10. "But when I fight with Billy, we always make up." The tie between Monique and Billy is deeper and more lasting than ordinary friendships, which may founder on a quarrel or just fade away. It is also ambiva-

Relationships with siblings are important during middle childhood. Older sisters talk and explain more to their younger siblings than older brothers do. *(Cary Wolinsky/Stock, Boston)*

lent, marked by special affection as well as by intense competition and resentment.

Siblings influence each other *directly* through interaction, and *indirectly* through their impact on each other's relationship with the parents. A major direct influence is the way siblings help one another develop a self-concept. When Monique sees that she and her brother are different despite all their shared bonds, she forms a stronger sense of herself as an individual.

Sibling relations are also a laboratory for learning how to resolve conflicts. The ties of blood and physical closeness impel siblings to make up after quarrels, since they know they will see each other every day. They learn that expressing anger does not end a relationship. Younger siblings become quite skillful at sensing other people's needs, negotiating for what they want, and compromising. While firstborns like Monique tend to be bossy and more likely to attack, interfere with, ignore, or bribe their siblings, later-borns like Billy plead, reason, and cajole (Cicirelli, 1976a).

Monique and Billy's relationship is helped by the fact that she is a girl and he is a boy. Children are more apt to squabble with same-sex siblings; two brothers quarrel more than any other combination (Cicirelli, 1976a).

Siblings learn how to deal with dependence in relationships by depending on each other. Although children in America care for younger brothers and sisters less than do children in many other countries, a good deal of caretaking does take place. Older children often mind younger ones when parents are at work; they also help younger siblings with homework. This help is most likely to be effective (and accepted) when it comes from a sibling—especially a sister—who is at least 4 years older (Cicirelli, 1976a, 1976b).

A recent study looked at interaction among 64 threesomes: a kindergartner or first-grader; a same-sex older sibling in second- or third- grade; and a same-sex, same-age friend of the older sibling (Azmitia & Hesser, 1993). The older siblings proved to be better teachers of the younger children than were the older peers. The older siblings were more likely to give spontaneous guidance, and the younger ones often prompted explanations and pressured their older siblings into giving them more control of the task. It seems clear that both older and younger siblings influence the relationship, and make it a very special one.

Girls explain more to younger siblings than boys do, and when girls want younger siblings to do something, they are more apt to reason with them or to make them feel obligated; older brothers tend to attack (Cicirelli, 1976a, 1976b). Gender differences also affect the way parents divide their time among their children. Mothers tend to talk more, explain more, and give more feedback to children with older brothers than to children with older sisters, maybe because of girls' greater effectiveness with younger siblings (Cicirelli, 1976a).

CHILDHOOD EMOTIONAL DISTURBANCES

One child's fear of the dark keeps him from going to summer camp, another's anxiety requires large doses of reassurance before such routine events as exams and doctor's visits, and a third's constant temper tantrums antagonize the most important adults in her life.

These children are typical of as many as 20 to 25 percent of school-age children whose lives are impaired by psychiatric problems. Only about 1 in 5 of these troubled children receives help. This disturbing finding emerges from several surveys of children's mental health. A study in Pittsburgh found that 22 percent of 789 seven- to eleven-year-olds visiting their pediatricians had had a psychiatric problem during the previous year (Costello et al., 1988). Other studies have found a lower percentage of troubled children—from 5 to 15 percent—but this lower figure still represents some 3 to 9 million children (Knitzer, 1984; U.S. Department of Health and Human Services, USDHHS, 1980).

Boys, African American children, and children from poor families are at especially high risk, as are those who have recently experienced a stressful life event, who have repeated a grade in school, or whose parents are having difficulties or have a psychiatric problem (Costello et al., 1988). Some problems seem to be associated with a particular phase of a child's life and will go away on their own, but others need to be treated to prevent problems in the future.

TYPES OF EMOTIONAL PROBLEMS

We have discussed sleep problems (Chapter 6) and hyperactivity (Chapter 8); now we'll look at some other childhood problems—acting-out behavior, anxiety disorders, and depression.

Acting-Out Behavior

Children's emotional troubles often surface in their behavior: they show by what they do that they need help. They fight, they lie, they steal, they destroy property, and they break rules. These are common forms of *acting-out behavior:* misbehavior that is an outward expression of emotional turmoil.

Of course, almost all children make up fanciful stories as a form of make-believe or lie occasionally to avoid punishment. But when children past the age of 6 or 7 continue to tell tall tales, they are often signaling a sense of insecurity. They may need to make up glamorous stories to secure the attention and esteem of others; or obvious or habitual lying may be a way to show hostility toward their parents (Chapman, 1974).

Occasional minor stealing, too, is common. Although it needs to be dealt with, it is not necessarily a sign that anything is seriously wrong. But when children repeatedly steal from their parents or steal so openly from others that they are easily caught, they are—again—often showing hostility toward their parents and their parents' standards. In some cases, the stolen items seem to symbolize parents' love, power, or authority, of which the child feels deprived.

Any chronic antisocial behavior should be regarded as a possible symptom of deep-seated emotional upset. In Chapter 11, we'll discuss some extreme forms of misbehavior, those that get adolescents into trouble with the law.

Anxiety Disorders

Various anxiety disorders begin in childhood. Here, we'll consider separation anxiety disorder and school phobia.

Separation Anxiety Disorder
Jessica wakes up complaining of nausea. Yesterday morning it was a headache, the day before that it was a stomachache, and last week she vomited three mornings in a row. Yet as soon as her mother says she can stay home from day camp, her symptoms disappear, and she spends the rest of the day happily playing in her room. Jessica is suffering from *separation anxiety disorder,* a condition involving excessive anxiety for at least 2 weeks, concerning separation from people to whom the child is attached. This condition is very different from the normal separation anxiety children show in the first year or two of life (see Chapter 5).

A child like Jessica may refuse to visit or sleep at friends' homes, go on errands, or attend camp or school; may "cling" to and shadow a parent around the house; and may complain of stomachaches, headaches, nausea, and vomiting before or during a separation. The condition affects boys and girls equally and may begin in early childhood and persist through the college years. Affected children tend to come from close-knit, caring families and to develop the anxiety after a life stress like the death of a pet, an illness, or a move.

School Phobia
School phobia—unrealistic fear that keeps children away from school—may be a form of separation anxiety disorder. It seems to have more to do with a fear of leaving the mother than a fear of school itself. Virtually no research has been done on the school situation of school-phobic youngsters, and so we know very little about their perceptions of school or how they get along there. If there *is* a problem at school—a sarcastic teacher, a bully in the schoolyard, or overly difficult work—the child's fears may be realistic; the environment, not the child, may need changing.

What *do* we know about school-phobic children? First, they are not truants; their parents usually know when they are absent. They tend to have average or higher than average intelligence and to be average or good students. Their ages are evenly

Everyone feels "blue" at times, but a child's chronic depression can be a danger signal and should be taken seriously, especially when it represents a marked change from the child's usual behavior. *(Mimi Cotter/International Stock)*

distributed from 5 to 15, and they are equally likely to be boys or girls. Although they come from a variety of backgrounds, their parents tend to be professionals. Their parents are also more likely than a control group to be depressed, to suffer from anxiety disorders themselves, and to report disturbed family functioning (Bernstein & Garfinkel, 1988).

The most important element in the treatment of a school-phobic child is an early—but gradual—return to school. Usually children go back to school without too much difficulty once treatment is begun.

Childhood Depression

"Nobody likes me" is a common complaint in middle childhood, when children tend to be popularity-conscious. But when these words were addressed to a school principal by an 8-year-old boy whose classmates had accused him of stealing, it was a danger signal. The boy vowed that he would never return to school—and he never did. Two days later, he hanged himself by a belt from the top rail of his bunk bed ("Doctors rule out," 1984).

Fortunately, depressed children rarely go to such lengths, though suicide among young people is on the increase (see Chapter 18). How can we tell the difference between a harmless period of the "blues" (which we all go through at times) and a major *affective disorder*—that is, a disorder of mood? The basic symptoms of an affective disorder are similar from childhood through adulthood, but some features are age-specific *(Diagnostic and Statistical Manual of Mental Disorders*, 3d ed., rev., DSM III-R, 1987).

Friendlessness is one sign of *childhood depression.* The disorder also involves an inability to have fun, to concentrate, and to show normal emotional reactions. Depressed children are often tired, extremely active, or inactive. They talk very little, cry a great deal, have trouble concentrating, sleep too much or too little, lose their appetite, start doing poorly in school, look unhappy, complain of physical ailments, feel overwhelmingly guilty, suffer severe separation anxiety (as in school phobia), or think often about death or suicide (Malmquist, 1983; Poznanski 1982). Any four or five of these symptoms may support a diagnosis of depression, especially when they represent a marked change from the child's usual pattern. Parents do not always recognize "minor" problems like sleep disturbances, loss of appetite, and irritability as signs of depression, but children themselves can often describe how they feel.

No one is sure of the cause of depression in either children or adults. There is some evidence for a biochemical predisposition, which may be triggered by specific experiences. The parents of depressed children are more likely to be depressed themselves, suggesting a possible genetic factor, a reflection of general stress in these families, or a result of poor parenting practices by disturbed parents (Weissman et al., 1987).

Moderate to severe depression is fairly easy to spot, but milder forms are harder to diagnose. The presence of any of the above symptoms should, therefore, be followed closely; if they persist, the child should get psychological help.

TREATMENT FOR EMOTIONAL PROBLEMS

The choice of a specific kind of treatment for a particular disorder depends on many factors: the nature of the problem, the child's personality, the family's willingness to participate, the availability of treatment in the community, the family's financial resources, and, often, the orientation of the professional first consulted.

Therapies

Psychological treatment can take several forms. In *individual psychotherapy* a therapist sees a child one on one, to help the child gain insights into his or her personality and relationships, and interpret feelings and behavior. This may be helpful at a time of great stress in the child's life, like the death of a parent, even when a child has not shown any signs of disturbance. The therapist shows acceptance of the child's feelings—and the child's right to them. Child psychotherapy is usually more effective when combined with counseling for parents.

Sometimes the parents come with the child, as in *family therapy.* The family therapist sees the whole family together, observes the way members act with one another, and points out their patterns of functioning—both growth-producing patterns and inhibiting or destructive patterns. Sometimes the child whose problem brings the family into therapy is, ironically, the healthiest member, responding to a troubled family situation. Through therapy, parents are often able to confront their own differences and begin to resolve them—the first step toward solving the children's problems as well.

Behavior therapy, or *behavior modification,* uses principles of learning theory to alter behavior—to eliminate undesirable behaviors like temper tantrums or to develop desirable ones like doing homework. A behavior therapist does not look for underlying reasons for behavior and typically does not try to offer a child insight into his or her situation, but aims simply to change the behavior. The therapist may use operant conditioning to encourage a behavior like putting dirty clothes into the hamper. Every time the child does it, she or he gets a reward, like words of praise, some kind of treat, or a token that can be exchanged for toys.

During the 1980s, an increase occurred in the use of *drug therapy* to treat childhood emotional problems (Tuma, 1989). Now, antidepressants are commonly prescribed for bed-wetters, stimulants for hyperactive children, and antipsychotics for children with severe psychological problems.

Effectiveness of Therapy

Psychological therapy generally helps (R. J. Casey & Berman, 1985). In a review of 75 studies, children who received treatment scored better than children with similar problems who did not receive it, on a variety of measures (including self-concept, adjustment, personality, social skills, achievement in school, cognitive functioning, and resolution of fears and anxieties).

Treatment for specific problems (like impulsiveness or hyperactivity) brings more improvement than therapy aimed at better social adjustment. No one form of therapy (play or nonplay, individual or group, "child-only" or treatment of child and parents) seems superior to another overall, but some kinds of treatment are better for certain problems (Tuma, 1989). Behavior therapy is especially effective for phobias, bed-wetting, and problems with general self-control.

Drugs help in the treatment of some childhood emotional disturbances, but their use should not eliminate psychotherapy. Drugs are usually most effective when combined with other treatments. But giving pills in order to change children's behavior is a radical step. Many medicines have undesirable side effects; and in some cases the drugs relieve only behavioral symptoms and do not get at underlying causes. Thus many therapists use drugs only as a last resort.

Although parents, therapists, and researchers often see definite gains in children who receive therapy, teachers and peers tend not to notice much improvement. First impressions are hard to overcome. It often helps when parents point out a child's improvement to the teacher and help the child make new friends who do not know what she or he was like before treatment.

Therapists who work with troubled children often encourage them to express themselves through play, which helps bring out their emotions. *(Michal Heron/Monkmeyer)*

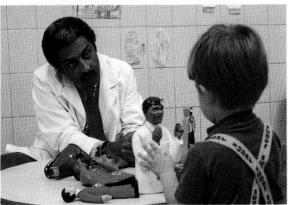

STRESS AND RESILIENCE

SOURCES OF STRESS: LIFE EVENTS, FEARS, AND THE "HURRIED CHILD"

Stressful events are part of every childhood. Illness, the birth of a sibling, sibling rivalry, frustration, and temporary absences of parents are common sources of stress. In addition, the divorce or death of parents, hospitalization, and the day-in, day-out grind of poverty affect the lives of many children. Other children live through homelessness, wars, and earthquakes. Violent events like kidnappings and attacks by playground snipers make children realize that their world is not as safe as they had thought and that their parents cannot always protect them. Such realizations affect children in the short and possibly the long run (Garmezy, 1983; Pynoos et al., 1987). (See Box 9-4.)

Sometimes, as in physical or psychological abuse, the parents themselves are a source of difficulty. Too many parents say to their children things like, "Why are you so stupid?" "I wish you had never been born!" "Some athlete you are!" "Can't you do anything right?" "Don't bother me!"

These parents are inflicting *psychological maltreatment*, which has been broadly defined as action (or a failure to act) that damages children's behavioral, cognitive, emotional, or physical functioning (Hart & Brassard, 1987). Abusing parents may reject, terrorize, isolate, exploit, degrade, ridicule, insult, and corrupt children and be emotionally unresponsive to them.

Psychological maltreatment is part of the more than 2 million cases of child abuse and neglect reported annually. It often occurs without physical abuse and is inflicted by adults who would be horrified to hear themselves called "abusers." It has been linked to children's lying, stealing, low self-esteem, emotional maladjustment, dependency, underachievement, depression, failure to thrive, aggression, homicide, and suicide, as well as to psychological distress in later life, and it may also play a part in learning disorders (Hart & Brassard, 1987).

In other cases, society imposes pressures, like forcing children to grow up too soon. Children today have a special set of pressures to cope with. Because families move around more than they used to, children are more likely to change schools and friends and less likely to know many adults well. They know more about technology, sex, and violence than children of previous generations, and because of single-parent homes and parents' work schedules, they are likely to shoulder adult responsibilities.

The child psychologist David Elkind has called today's child the "hurried child" (1981, 1987b). He believes that the pressures of life today are making children grow up too soon and are making their shortened childhood too stressful. Today's children are pressured to succeed in school, to compete in sports, and to meet their parents' emotional needs. On television and in real life, children are exposed to many adult problems before they have mastered the problems of childhood. Yet children are not small adults. They feel and think like children, and they need these years of childhood for healthy development.

COPING WITH STRESS: THE RESILIENT CHILD

Children's reactions to stressful events may depend on such factors as the event itself (children respond differently to a parent's death than to divorce), the child's age (preschoolers and adolescents react differently), and the child's sex (boys are often more vulnerable than girls) (Rutter, 1984). Yet if two children of the same age and sex are exposed to the same stressful experience, one may crumble while the other copes well. Why?

Resilient children are those who bounce back from circumstances that would blight the emotional development of most children. These are children of the ghetto who go on to distinguish themselves in the professions. These are neglected or abused children who go on to form intimate relationships, be good parents to their own children, and lead fulfilling lives. These are survivors of a trauma like the Holocaust of Nazi Germany who went on to lead normal, successful lives as adults (Helmreich, 1991). What is special about such children?

Several studies have identified "protective factors" that may operate to reduce the effects of such stressors as kidnapping, poor parenting, or psychological abuse (Anthony & Koupernik, 1974; Garmezy, 1983; Rutter, 1984; M. S. Rosenberg, 1987). Factors like the following seem to contribute to children's resilience:

■ *The child's personality:* Resilient children tend to be adaptable enough to cope with changing circumstances, and to be positive thinkers who are friendly, sensitive to other people, and inde-

BOX 9-4 FOOD FOR THOUGHT

CHILDREN WHO LIVE IN CHRONIC DANGER

A 6-year-old from Washington, D.C., asked whether there is anywhere she feels safe, said, "In my basement," because it had no windows for bullets to fly through. A 10-year-old told about running away in terror after he saw a man shot in the back on the street. A 6-year-old saw her mother punched in the face by a drug addict. These inner-city children are, unfortunately, typical of many who live surrounded by violence and, as a result, are fearful, anxious, distressed, and depressed.

Possibly because the subject is so painful or because children may not be reporting all that they see or experience, mothers, who are usually these children's primary caretakers, tend to underestimate the extent of their children's exposure to violence and how it affects them. This, then, may hinder parents' efforts to shield their children from seeing violent acts or becoming victims of it. The children themselves may take violent behavior so for granted that they become desensitized to it and may not take necessary precautions to protect themselves.

Children who experience an initial trauma before age 11 are 3 times more likely than those who undergo this as teenagers to develop psychiatric symptoms (David-son & Smith, 1990). (See Table 9-4 for typical reactions at different ages.) Furthermore, children in an environment with multiple risks are most likely to suffer permanent developmental damage (Rutter, 1987). Besides living in a violent community, some other common risks go along with living in poverty—such as poor housing, schools, and medical care. Also, parents overwhelmed by their own stresses are often unable to give their children the kind of home lives they would like to. Families often split up and parenting is often inadequate, sometimes even extending to neglect or abuse.

What happens to children who grow up surrounded by violence? They often have trouble concentrating and remembering because they don't get enough sleep and are troubled by their fears; they may become anxious and afraid that their mothers will abandon them; some become aggressive to hide their fears, to protect themselves, or to imitate actions they've seen; many do not allow themselves to care for other people, since they're afraid of more hurt and loss.

These children need islands of safety in their lives. They need to have caring relationships with adults, like teachers or community leaders, who can deal with their concerns in the day-to-day context of classroom or group meeting. Play and art activities can help a child express feelings about a traumatic event, reinstate a sense of inner control, develop a feeling of self-worth, and set the stage for a dialogue with an adult whom the child can trust (Garbarino, Dubrow, Kostelny, & Pardo, 1992).

Also, much can be done on the larger societal level. The American Psychological Association's Commission on Violence and Youth recommends community programs built around the interests and needs of young people, including health care, recreation, and vocational training (Youngstrom, 1992). Role models from the community, peer-group discussions, and family intervention should all be offered to deter youths from drugs and violence. The American Academy of Pediatrics urges regulating and restricting ownership of handguns and ammunition, not romanticizing gun use in television and movies, identifying high-risk adolescents (teenage boys and drug and alcohol abusers) to provide services to them, and developing more resources in the community (AAP, 1992).

TABLE 9-4

Typical Reactions to Violence at Different Ages

Early childhood	Passive reactions and regression (like bed-wetting, clinging, and speaking less), fear of leaving the mother or of sleeping alone, aggressive play, sleep problems
School-age	Aggressiveness, inhibition, somatic complaints (headaches, stomachaches, etc.), learning difficulties (forgetfulness, trouble concentrating), psychological difficulties (like anxiety, phobias, withdrawal, denial), grief and loss reactions (hopelessness, despair, depression, inability to play, suicidal thoughts, uncaring behavior, destructiveness), acting tough to hide fears, constricted activities
Adolescence	Some symptoms of school-age children, plus acting-out and self-destructive behavior (like drug abuse, delinquency, promiscuity, life-threatening reenactments of the trauma), identification with the aggressor (becoming violent, joining a gang)

SOURCE: Garbarino, Dubrow, Kostelny, & Pardo, 1992.

pendent. They feel competent and have high self-esteem. Intelligence, too, may be a factor; good students seem to cope better (Rutter, 1984).

▪ *The child's family:* Resilient children tend to have good relationships with parents who are emotionally supportive to them and to each other, or, failing that, to have a close relationship with at least one parent. If they lack even this, they are likely to be close to at least one other adult who expresses interest in them and obviously cares for them, and whom they trust.

▪ *Learning experiences:* Resilient children are likely to have had experience solving social problems. They have seen parents, older siblings, or others deal with frustration and make the best of a bad situation. They have faced challenges themselves, have worked out solutions, and have learned that they can exert some control over their lives.

▪ *Reduced risk:* Children who have been exposed to only one of a number of factors strongly related to psychiatric disorders (such as discord between the parents, low social status, overcrowding at home, a disturbed mother, a crim-

inal father, or experience in foster care or institutions) are often able to overcome the stress. But when two or more of these factors are present, the children's risk of developing an emotional disturbance goes up fourfold or more (Rutter, 1987). When children are not besieged on all sides, they can often cope with adverse circumstances.

▪ *Compensating experiences:* A supportive school environment and successful experiences—for example, in sports, in music, or with other children—can help make up for a dismal home life, and in adulthood a good marriage can compensate for poor relationships earlier in life.

All this research does not, of course, mean that what happens in a child's life does not matter. In general, children with unfavorable backgrounds have more problems in adjustment than those with favorable backgrounds. The heartening promise of these findings, however, lies in the recognition that what happens in childhood does not necessarily determine the outcome of a person's life.

SUMMARY

THE SELF-CONCEPT

▪ The self-concept is the sense of self-worth. It helps people understand themselves and regulate their behavior. The self-concept develops greatly during middle childhood; many aspects are strong and lasting.

▪ Self-esteem, or a positive self-image, is an important development of middle childhood. Self-esteem is associated with dominant mood, which, in turn, affects competence.

▪ Erikson's fourth crisis, which takes place during middle childhood, is industry versus inferiority. The issue to be resolved is the child's capacity for productive work according to the demands of one's culture. The virtue of this period is competence.

▪ According to Susan Harter's research, children's global self-worth arises from two major sources: how competent children think they are and how much social support they receive. Feelings about physical appearance as well as support from parents and classmates are particularly important.

ASPECTS OF PERSONALITY DEVELOPMENT IN MIDDLE CHILDHOOD

▪ Schoolchildren spend most of their leisure time watching television and playing alone or with others. As children move through elementary school,

they read less for pleasure. Many children are involved in sports and other organized activities.

▪ The society of childhood mirrors changes in adult society. Many children today are from more mobile families and thus have weaker social bonds than children in previous generations, and so the peer group sometimes tends to substitute for kinship bonds.

▪ The peer group is an important arena for the building of self-concept and self-esteem.

▪ School-age youngsters are most susceptible to pressure to conform, which may encourage antisocial behavior in children who are too weak to resist.

▪ Most children select peers who are like them in age, sex, race, and socioeconomic status. Racial prejudice among schoolchildren appears to be diminishing as a result of school integration.

▪ The basis of friendship changes in middle childhood. Children choose friends they feel comfortable with and see friendship as involving give-and-take. Friends typically are of the same sex and have common interests.

▪ Popularity influences self-esteem. Children who are not only ignored by their peers but rejected by them are at risk of emotional and behavioral problems. They need to learn social skills. Family influences on popularity are significant.

▪ Although school-age children spend less time with

their parents than with their peers, relationships with parents continue to be most important. Other important relationships are with grandparents, siblings, friends, and teachers. Different relationships serve different purposes for children.

■ New issues related to school and the use of leisure time arise during this period.

1 Although school-age children require less direct care and supervision than younger children, it is still important for parents to monitor their children's activities.
2 Although disciplinary methods evolve with children's cognitive development, there appears to be an underlying consistency in parents' child-rearing attitudes. There are some differences among social classes in parents' interactions with school-age children.
3 Coregulation is an intermediate stage in the transfer of control from parent to child, during which children make more of their own day-to-day decisions under their parents' general supervision.

■ Children today are growing up in a variety of family situations besides the traditional nuclear family. These include families in which mothers work outside the home (now a majority of families), families with divorced parents, one-parent families, and step families. In any of these, an atmosphere of love, support, and respect for family members will provide an excellent prognosis for healthy development.

1 Age affects children's reactions to both mothers' employment and divorce. Whether children make a successful adjustment to either situation depends largely on the way the parents handle it.
2 Children of employed mothers (particularly girls) may benefit from their mothers' enhanced self-esteem, from added family income, and from less stereotyped gender attitudes. However, sons may show some negative effects, and self-care children may be at greater risk if they are not mature enough to care for themselves.

3 Children living with only one parent are under special stress and are at risk of lower achievement in school and other problems. These children do better in school when their parents are involved with the children's schooling.

■ Siblings exert a powerful influence on each other either directly (through their interactions) or indirectly (through their impact on each other's relationship with their parents).

CHILDHOOD EMOTIONAL DISTURBANCES

■ Some 3 to 9 million or more children suffer from a variety of emotional disorders, including acting-out behavior, anxiety disorders, and childhood depression.
■ Studies show that psychological therapy is generally effective. Yet only 1 in 5 troubled children gets help.

STRESS AND RESILIENCE

■ Normal childhood stesses take many forms and can affect the healthy emotional development of children. Unusual stresses, such as natural disasters and wars, also affect many children.
■ Psychological maltreatment of children appears to be widespread among both families and institutions. It results in damage to children's behavioral, cognitive, emotional, or physical functioning and may prevent them from fulfilling their potential.
■ As a result of advanced technology, family responsibilities, and pressure to grow up too soon, many children today are experiencing a shortened and stressful childhood.
■ Psychologists have studied factors that enable some children to withstand stress better than others. Resilient children are those who are able to "bounce back" from unfortunate circumstances. Factors contributing to children's resilience include the child's personality, family, learning experiences, small number of risk factors, and compensating experiences.

KEY TERMS

self-concept (page 308)
self-definition (308)
real self (309)
ideal self (309)
self-esteem (309)
industry versus inferiority (310)
global self-worth (310)

prejudice (315)
discipline (320)
coregulation (320)
self-care children (323)
acting-out behavior (331)
separation anxiety disorder (331)
school phobia (331)

affective disorder (332)
childhood depression (332)
individual psychotherapy (333)
family therapy (333)
behavior therapy (333)
drug therapy (333)
psychological maltreatment (334)

SUGGESTED READINGS

Coles, R. (1990). *The spiritual life of children*. Boston: Houghton Mifflin. The author, a child psychiatrist, interviewed hundreds of children of many faiths about their religious beliefs. In this book he reports their opinions on heaven, hell, and God's wishes for humankind, and their doubts.

Comer, J. P., & Poussaint, A. F. (1992). *Raising black children*. New York: Plume. Two leading psychiatrists discuss the special pressures parents face in raising black children, dealing with such issues as drugs, AIDS, and educational pressures. They also offer guidance in helping children cope with the unconscious racism in society. The insights they provide are relevant for *all* parents and children.

Elkind, D. (1988). *The hurried child* (rev. ed.). New York: Addison-Wesley. This book, by a well-known psychologist, examines how parents can raise healthy children who enjoy childhood, despite a social trend toward pressure to grow up fast.

Helmreich, W. (1991). *Against all odds: Holocaust survivors and the successful lives they made in America*. New York: Simon & Schuster. This account of several hundred Jewish people who came to the United States after living through the Nazi years in Germany shows the resiliency of the human spirit as it describes and analyzes the surprisingly normal lives these survivors forged for themselves after major trauma.

Lansky, V. (1989). *Vicky Lansky's divorce book for parents: Helping your children cope with divorce and its aftermath*. New York: New American Library. Based on the author's own experiences as well as those of other families, this practical guide for divorcing parents deals with issues chronologically, from the decision to separation to long-term adjustment.

Marston, S. (1994). *The divorced parent*. New York: Morrow. This book offers success strategies for raising children after the parents' separation or divorce. With a sense of humor and insight into how families work, the author manages to keep in mind the complexity of divorce while offering sound practical suggestions.

Simon, S. B., & Olds, S. W. (1991). *Helping your child find values to live by*. Hadley, MA: Values Press. A self-help manual for parents for establishing moral values and emotional self-awareness in children. The authors explain why values themselves cannot be taught but how parents can teach children a process for arriving at their own values.

PART FOUR

ADOLESCENCE

I n adolescence, young people's appearance changes as a result of the hormonal events of puberty. Their thinking changes as they develop the ability to deal with abstractions. Their feelings change about almost everything. All areas of development converge as adolescents confront their major task, establishing an adult identity.

■ In **Chapter 10**, we examine the dramatic physical and intellectual development that occurs from about age 12 till about age 20. We see the impact of early and late maturation, we look at health problems that affect adolescents, and we see how their advances in intellectual competence help them consider abstract ideas, moral issues, and career choices. Finally, we look at the roles of school and work in teenagers' lives.

■ In **Chapter 11**, we see how adolescents incorporate their new appearance, their puzzling physical yearnings, and their new intellectual abilities into their sense of self. We examine the major task of adolescence—the quest for identity, including sexual identity. We look at the relationships adolescents have with their parents and their peers, and we see how the peer group serves as the testing ground for teenagers' ideas about life and about themselves. We look at some problems that arise during the teenage years, as well as some of the strengths of adolescents.

CHAPTER TEN

PHYSICAL AND INTELLECTUAL DEVELOPMENT IN ADOLESCENCE

I think what is happening to me is so wonderful, and not only what can be seen on my body, but all that is taking place inside.

Anne Frank, The Diary of a Young Girl, *1952*
(entry written January 5, 1944)

■ **ADOLESCENCE: A DEVELOPMENTAL TRANSITION**

PHYSICAL DEVELOPMENT

■ **MATURATION IN ADOLESCENCE**

Physical Changes
Psychological Issues Related to Physical Changes

■ **HEALTH CONCERNS OF ADOLESCENCE**

Nutrition and Eating Disorders
Use and Abuse of Drugs
Sexually Transmitted Diseases (STDs)

INTELLECTUAL DEVELOPMENT

■ **ASPECTS OF INTELLECTUAL DEVELOPMENT IN ADOLESCENCE**

Cognitive Development: Piaget's Stage of Formal Operations
Adolescent Egocentrism
Moral Reasoning: Kohlberg's Levels of Morality

■ **SECONDARY SCHOOL**

The Transition to Junior High or High School
High School Today
Home Influences on Achievement in High School
Dropping Out of High School

■ **DEVELOPING A CAREER**

Stages in Vocational Planning
Influences on Vocational Planning

■ **BOXES**

10-1 Window on the World: An Apache Girl Comes of Age
10-2 Window on the World: Female Genital Mutilation
10-3 Practically Speaking: Protecting against Sexually Transmitted Diseases
10-4 Food for Thought: Gender Differences in Moral Development
10-5 Take a Stand: Should Teenagers Hold Part-Time Jobs?

- What physical changes do adolescents experience, and how do these changes affect them psychologically?
- How prevalent are eating disorders, drug abuse, and sexually transmitted diseases in adolescence, and what can be done about them?
- How does cognitive development affect the way adolescents solve problems and make moral judgments and life decisions?

- What factors affect the value of secondary schooling, and why do some adolescents drop out of school?
- What factors influence young people's vocational choices?

Apache Indians in the southwestern United States denote a girl's sexual maturation with a traditional ritual: after she menstruates for the first time, her elders chant from sunrise to sunset for 4 days (see Box 10-1). Jewish people welcome 13-year-old boys and girls into the adult community with bar mitzvah and bat mitzvah celebrations. In Nepal a girl's transition to womanhood is marked by her exchanging the simple short skirt she wore as a child for the ankle-length wrapped skirt worn by adult women.

Such coming-of-age rites are common in many traditional societies in which the attainment of sexual maturity is considered the beginning of adulthood. Rites of passage may include religious blessings; separation from the family; severe tests of strength and endurance; bodily mutilation (see Box 10-2), piercing of ears, filing of teeth, or elaborate tattooing; and acts of magic.

In modern industrial societies, no single initiation rite marks the passage from childhood to adulthood, and the sexual aspects of coming-of-age are often only whispered about. Instead, we recognize a lengthy transitional stage known as *adolescence.*

Adolescence is a developmental transition between childhood and adulthood. It is generally considered to begin at about age 12 or 13 and to end in the late teens or early twenties. However, its physical basis has actually begun long before, and its psychological ramifications may continue long after. In this chapter we look at the dramatic physical changes of this stage and at how they affect and are affected by psychological changes. Then we see how adolescents develop intellectually as they become able to think abstractly, even though they retain elements of egocentric thought. Their thinking processes affect not only their moral

reasoning but also their education and career goals, as we'll see. We'll delve more deeply into the adolescent quest for identity in Chapter 11.

ADOLESCENCE: A DEVELOPMENTAL TRANSITION

Adolescence is generally considered to begin with *puberty,* the process that leads to sexual maturity, when a person is able to reproduce.* Although the physical changes of this time of life are dramatic, they do not burst full-blown at the end of childhood. Instead, puberty is part of a long and complex process that began even before birth. The biological changes that signal the end of childhood produce rapid growth in height and weight (a rate of growth second only to that of infancy), changes in body proportions and form, and the attainment of sexual maturity. But adolescence is also a social and emotional process. It has been said that "adolescence begins in biology and ends in culture" (Conger & Peterson, 1984, p. 92).

Before the twentieth century, children entered the adult world when their bodies were mature or when they began a vocational apprenticeship. Today, the entry into adulthood is not so clear-cut. Puberty occurs earlier than it used to (see our discussion of the *secular trend* in this chapter). And because of the longer period of education required by our complex society, adulthood arrives later.

Americans consider themselves adult at various ages, depending on which marker they use. They may draw on a variety of legal definitions. James

*Some people use the term *puberty* to mean the end point of sexual maturation and refer to the process as *pubescence,* but our usage conforms to that of most psychologists today.

BOX 10-1 *WINDOW ON THE WORLD*

AN APACHE GIRL COMES OF AGE

Among the Apache Indians of the American Southwest, a girl's entrance into puberty is celebrated by a 4-day ceremony of chanting from sunrise to sunset, which reenacts the tribe's version of how the world was created (Heard Museum of Anthropology and Primitive Art, 1987).

According to Apache lore, the first woman on earth was a deity called Changing Woman, the mother of twins who cleansed the world of evil so that human beings could live well. During the puberty rite (also called "gifts of Changing Woman"), the deity's spirit is believed to enter the girl to prepare her for her role as a mother and life-giver. Among the gifts that Changing Woman is believed to bestow upon her are strength, an even temperament, prosperity, and a long life.

As male members of the tribe gather around, chanting, the girl approaches a ceremonial blanket laid out on the ground, on which a buckskin has been placed. She wears an abalone shell on her forehead and carries a staff to represent longevity and a cane that she will need when she is old. The buckskin on which she stands symbolizes the hope that she will always have plenty of meat and not go hungry.

The girl kneels before the sun and is massaged to "mold" her

The Apache Indians of the American southwest celebrate a girl's entrance into puberty with a 4-day ritual that includes special clothing, a symbolic blanket, and singing from sunrise to sunset. In modern industrial societies, there is no single comparable initiation rite. *(Bill Gillette/Stock, Boston)*

body into adult form and to give her strength. In the past, the girl danced throughout the night, but more recently a surrogate—usually a godmother or best friend—has been allowed to take over for her. On the last day of the ceremony, the girl is blessed with pollen, sym-

bolizing her newfound reproductive powers.

In many traditional cultures, ceremonies like this one recognize the importance and value of the physical changes that prepare a young person for an adult role in the society.

---

may consider himself an adult at 17 when he can enlist in the army, Madeline at age 18 when she can marry without her parents' permission; others may go by the age when they can be held legally responsible for contracts (18 to 21, depending on the state). People may feel that they have achieved sociological adulthood when they are self-supporting or have chosen a career, or married, or founded a family. Intellectual maturity is generally

considered to coincide with the capacity for abstract thought. Emotional maturity depends on such achievements as discovery of identity, independence from parents, development of a system of values, and ability to form mature relationships of friendship and love (see Chapter 11). Some people, of course, never leave adolescence emotionally or socially, no matter what their chronological age.

BOX 10-2   *WINDOW ON THE WORLD*

FEMALE GENITAL MUTILATION

Many traditional societies have coming-of-age rituals that signal membership in the adult community. These ceremonies often include putting an enduring mark on the body—tattooing or scarring the face, removing the foreskin from the penis, sharpening the teeth, and so forth. One custom widely practiced in some parts of Africa, the Middle East, and southeast Asia is surgery on the female genitals, euphemistically called *female circumcision* but termed *female genital mutilation (FGM)* by the World Health Organization. The operation, performed on girls of varying ages from infancy to puberty, may entail *clitoridectomy,* the removal of part or all of the clitoris, or *infibulation,* which involves clitoridectomy plus removal of parts of the labia, the raw edges of which are then sewn together with catgut or held by thorns.

The purposes of these procedures include preserving virginity, reducing the sex drive, maintaining cleanliness, and enhancing beauty. The consequences are often dreadful, including—besides the complete loss of sexual fulfillment—psychological dysfunction and sometimes life-threatening infection from unsterilized instruments and serious loss of blood (Lightfoot-Klein, 1989).

The operations have been extremely controversial for years. In the countries where they are practiced, government officials, physicians, and women's groups have tried to end them, but because most women in the tribes that practice them believe in the procedures and are often the ones who carry them out, they still go on. Furthermore, they are now being carried out in Europe and North America, where many East African refugees have immigrated (Farnsworth, 1993; Zimmerman, 1993).

In some areas, attitudes do seem to be changing. A survey of 150 female third-year high school students in the Sudan found that even though about 96 percent of these girls had had some form of FGM performed on them, more than 70 percent were strongly opposed to the same operation for their sisters and other young girls (Pugh, 1983). These girls' attitudes may have been influenced by the campaign to do away with FGM being led by a growing number of women throughout Africa and the world.

■ PHYSICAL DEVELOPMENT

MATURATION IN ADOLESCENCE

Adolescents' maturation involves not only physical changes but also the psychological effects of these changes. Let's explore both aspects.

PHYSICAL CHANGES

The biological changes that signal the end of childhood include the adolescent growth spurt, the beginning of menstruation for girls, the presence of sperm in males, the maturation of reproductive organs, and the development of secondary sex characteristics. When do most young people in the United States experience these changes?

Puberty and the Secular Trend

Any eighth- or ninth-grade class picture presents startling contrasts. Flat-chested little girls stand next to full-bosomed, full-grown young women. Skinny little boys are seen next to broad-shouldered, mustached young men. This variance is normal. There is about a 6- to 7-year range for puberty in both boys and girls.

During puberty, the reproductive functions mature, the sex organs enlarge (see Table 10-1), and the secondary sex characteristics appear (see Table 10-2). The process takes about 4 years and begins about 2 years earlier for girls than for boys. Girls, on the average, begin to show pubertal change at 9 or 10 years of age, achieving sexual

TABLE 10-1

Primary Sex Characteristics: Sex Organs	
Female	**Male**
Ovaries	Testes
Fallopian tubes	Penis
Uterus	Scrotum
Vagina	Seminal vesicles
	Prostate gland

TABLE 10-2

Secondary Sex Characteristics	
Girls	**Boys**
Breasts	Pubic hair
Pubic hair	Axillary (underarm)
Axillary (underarm)	hair
hair	Facial hair
Increased width and	Changes in voice
depth of pelvis	Changes in skin
Changes in voice	Broadening of shoulders
Changes in skin	

maturation by 13 or 14. Normal girls, however, may show the first signs as early as age 7 or as late as 14 (becoming sexually mature at ages 9 to 16). The average age for boys' entry into puberty is 12, with sexual maturity coming at age 14. But normal boys may begin to show changes from ages 9 to 16 (achieving maturity from ages 11 to 18) (Chumlea, 1982). Maturing early or late often has social and psychological consequences.

The physical changes of adolescence unfold in a sequence that is much more consistent than their actual timing, though even this order varies somewhat from one person to another. The usual sequences are shown in Table 10-3. Some people move through puberty very quickly, while for others the process takes much longer. One girl, for example, may be developing breasts and body hair at about the same rate; but the body hair of another may grow so much faster than her breasts that her adult hair pattern appears a year or so before her breasts develop. The same kinds of variations occur among boys (Tobin-Richards, Boxer, Kavrell, & Petersen, 1984).

Puberty begins when, at some biologically determined time, the pituitary gland sends a message to a young person's sex glands, which then secrete hormones. This time is apparently regulated by the interaction of genes, health, and environment; it may be related to a critical weight level.

Puberty, then, occurs in response to changes in the body's hormone system, which are triggered by a physiologic signal. In girls the ovaries sharply step up their production of the female hormone estrogen; and in boys, the testes increase the manufacture of androgens, particularly testosterone. Both boys and girls have both types of hormones, but girls have higher levels of estrogen and boys have higher levels of androgens. As early as age 7, the levels of these sex hormones begin to increase, setting in motion the pubertal events. Estrogen stimulates growth of female genitals and development of breasts, while androgens stimulate growth of male genitals and body hair.

TABLE 10-3

Usual Sequence of Physiologic Changes in Adolescence	
Girls' Characteristics	**Age of First Appearance**
Growth of breasts	8–13
Growth of pubic hair	8–14
Body growth	9.5–14.5 (average peak, 12)
Menarche	10–16.5 (average, 12.5)
Underarm hair	About 2 years after pubic hair
Increased output of oil- and sweat-producing glands (which may lead to acne)	About the same time as underarm hair
Boys' Characteristics	**Age of First Appearance**
Growth of testes, scrotal sac	10–13.5
Growth of pubic hair	10–15
Body growth	10.5–16 (average peak, 14)
Growth of penis, prostate gland, seminal vesicles	11–14.5 (average, 12.5)
Change in voice	About the same time as growth of penis
First ejaculation of semen	About 1 year after beginning of growth of penis
Facial and underarm hair	About 2 years after appearance of pubic hair
Increased output of oil- and sweat-producing glands (which may lead to acne)	About the same time as underarm hair

Hormones are also closely associated with emotions, specifically with aggression in boys and with both aggression and depression in girls (Brooks-Gunn, 1988). Some researchers attribute the increased emotionality and moodiness of early adolescence to hormones, but we need to remember that in human beings social influences combine with hormonal ones and sometimes predominate. Thus, even though there is a well-established relationship between the production of the hormone testosterone and sexuality, adolescents begin sexual activity more in accord with what their friends do than with what their glands secrete (Brooks-Gunn & Reiter, 1990).

On the basis of historical sources, developmentalists have inferred the existence of a *secular trend,* a lowering of the age when puberty begins and young people reach adult height and sexual maturity. A secular trend is a trend that can be seen only by observing several generations. This trend, which also involves increases in adult height and weight, began about 100 years ago and has occurred in the United States, western Europe, and Japan, but apparently not in some other countries (Chumlea, 1982).

The most obvious explanation for this secular trend seems to be a higher standard of living. Children who are healthier, better nourished, and better cared for mature earlier and grow bigger. This explanation is supported by evidence: the age of sexual maturity is later in less developed countries than in more industrialized countries. In New Guinea, girls do not begin to menstruate until sometime between age 15.4 and age 18.4, compared with an average age of 12.5 years in the United States (Eveleth & Tanner, 1976).

The secular trend appears to have ended, at least in the United States, probably as a reflection of higher living standards in most segments of our population (Schmeck, 1976). The leveling of the trend suggests that the age of sexual maturity has now reached some genetically determined limit and that better nutrition is unlikely to lower the age any further.

The Adolescent Growth Spurt

An early sign of maturation is the *adolescent growth spurt,* a dramatic increase in height and weight. It generally begins to appear in girls between ages 9½ and 14½ (usually at about age 10) and in boys between ages 10½ and 16 (usually at about age 12 or 13). It typically lasts about 2 years. Soon after the spurt ends, the young person reaches

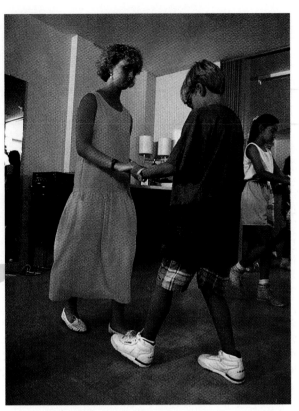

As these young dancers demonstrate, during the years from ages 11 to 13, girls are on the average taller, heavier, and stronger than boys, who achieve their adolescent growth spurt later than girls do. If our society did not have such a rigid idea that males must be taller than females, this temporary state would be less embarrassing for the boys. *(Dagmar Fabricius/Stock, Boston)*

sexual maturity. Growth in height is virtually complete by age 18 (Behrman & Vaughan, 1983).

Before the growth spurt, boys are typically only about 2 percent taller than girls. Since girls' growth spurt usually occurs earlier than that of boys, for a period of several years girls are taller, heavier, and stronger. After the growth spurt, boys are larger again, now by about 8 percent. The growth spurt in boys is more intense, and its later appearance allows for an extra period of growth, since growth goes on at a faster rate before puberty.

Boys and girls grow differently during adolescence. A boy becomes larger overall, his shoulders are wider, his legs are longer relative to his trunk, and his forearms are longer relative to both his upper arms and his height. A girl's pelvis widens during adolescence to make childbearing easier, and layers of fat are laid down just under the skin, giving her a more rounded appearance.

In both sexes, the adolescent growth spurt affects practically all skeletal and muscular dimensions. The changes, which are greater in boys than in girls, follow their own timetables, so parts of the body may be out of proportion for a while. The result is the familiar teenage gawkiness that accompanies unbalanced, accelerated growth.

Primary Sex Characteristics

The *primary sex characteristics* are the organs necessary for reproduction. In the female, the sex organs are the ovaries, uterus, and vagina; in the male, the testes, prostate gland, penis, and seminal vesicles (see Figure 2-1 in Chapter 2 and Table 10-1). The gradual enlargement of these body parts occurs during puberty, leading to sexual maturation.

The principal sign of sexual maturity in girls is menstruation. In boys, the principal sign is the presence of sperm in the urine (a boy is fertile as soon as sperm are present). Both the onset of menstruation and the first appearance of sperm in the urine are highly variable. One longitudinal study found that only 2 percent of 11- to 12-year-old boys showed sperm in the urine compared with 24 percent of 15-year-olds (Richardson & Short, 1978).

Another sign of puberty in a boy is the occurrence of an ejaculation of semen while he is asleep, known as a *nocturnal emission* (commonly referred to as a *wet dream*). Most adolescent boys, whether or not they are having sexual intercourse or masturbating on a fairly regular basis, have these emissions, which are perfectly normal and may or may not occur in connection with an erotic dream.

Secondary Sex Characteristics

The *secondary sex characteristics* are physiologic signs of sexual maturation that do not directly involve the sex organs. They include the breasts of females and the broad shoulders of males. Other secondary sex characteristics involve changes in the voice, skin texture, and body hair. The timing of these signs is variable, but the sequence is fairly consistent (see Table 10-2).

The first sign of puberty for girls is usually the budding of the breasts. The nipples enlarge and protrude; the areolae, the pigmented areas surrounding the nipples, enlarge; and the breasts assume first a conical and then a rounded shape. The breasts are usually fully developed before menstruation begins. Much to their distress, some adolescent boys experience temporary breast enlargement; this is normal and may last up to 18 months.

Various forms of hair growth, including pubic hair and axillary (armpit) hair, also signal maturation. Boys usually welcome the appearance of hair on the face and chest, but girls tend to be dismayed if any hair appears on their faces and around their nipples, though this is normal.

The skin of adolescent boys and girls becomes coarser and oilier, and the increased activity of the sebaceous glands causes outbreaks of pimples and blackheads. Acne is more common in boys than in girls and seems to be related to increased amounts of the male hormone testosterone. The voices of both boys and girls deepen, partly in response to growth of the larynx and partly—in boys—in response to the production of male hormones.

Menarche

The most dramatic sign of a girl's sexual maturity is *menarche*—the first menstruation, or monthly shedding of tissue from the lining of the womb.

These young ballerinas show the budding breasts that are usually the first sign of puberty for girls. Other secondary sex characteristics will soon follow. *(Andy Levin/Black Star)*

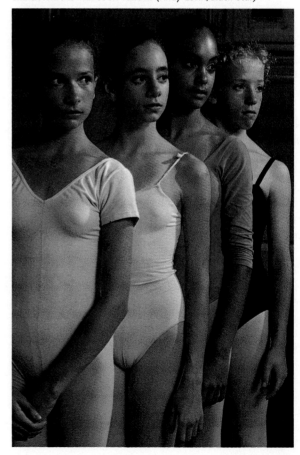

Adolescent boys usually welcome the need to shave, because facial hair is one of the secondary sex characteristics that signal sexual maturation. *(Mark Antman/The Image Works)*

Menarche occurs fairly late in the sequence of female development (see Table 10-3). On the average, a girl in the United States first menstruates at the age of 12½, about 2 years after her breasts have begun to develop and her uterus has begun to grow, and after her growth spurt has slowed down.

Although in many cultures menarche is taken as the sign that a girl has become a woman, the early menstrual periods usually do not include ovulation, and many girls are unable to conceive for 12 to 18 months after menarche. Since ovulation and conception do sometimes occur in these early months, girls who have begun to menstruate should assume that they can become pregnant.

What effect does strenuous exercise have on the menstrual cycle? Most female athletes do not experience menstrual irregularity; but those who do usually become regular when they stop training and can then go on to have normal childbearing experiences (Bullen et al., 1985; Shangold, 1978).

PSYCHOLOGICAL ISSUES RELATED TO PHYSICAL CHANGES

The physical changes of adolescence have many psychological ramifications. Let's look at some.

Effects of Early and Late Maturation

One of the great paradoxes of adolescence is the conflict between a young person's yearning to find an individual identity—to assert a unique self—and an overwhelming desire to be exactly like his or her friends. Anything that sets an adolescent apart from the crowd can be unsettling, and youngsters are often disturbed if they mature sexually either much earlier or much later than their friends. Though neither late maturing nor early maturing is necessarily an advantage or a drawback, the timing of maturation can have psychological effects.

Early and Late Maturation in Boys

Some research has found early-maturing boys to be more poised, relaxed, good-natured, popular with peers, and likely to be leaders—and less impulsive than late maturers. Other studies have found them to be more worried about being liked, more cautious, and more bound by rules.

Late maturers have been variously found to feel more inadequate, rejected, and dominated; to be more dependent, aggressive, and insecure; to rebel more against their parents; and to think less of themselves (Mussen & Jones, 1957; Peskin, 1967, 1973; Siegel, 1982). While some studies have shown that early maturers retain a head start in intellectual performance into late adolescence and adulthood (Gross & Duke, 1980; Tanner, 1978), many differences seem to disappear by adulthood (M. C. Jones, 1957).

There are pluses and minuses in both situations. Boys like to mature early, and those who do seem to have an advantage over late maturers, reaping a number of benefits to self-esteem (Alsaker, 1992). Being more muscular, they are stronger and better in sports, and they have a more favorable body image. They have an edge in dating, since they enjoy the benefit of being at the same maturity level as typical girls their own age (Blyth et al., 1981).

But an early maturer is likely to be given more responsibility by adults than a late maturer and sometimes has trouble living up to others' expectations that he should act as mature as he looks. Furthermore, he may have too little time to prepare for the changes of adolescence. Late maturers may feel and act more childish; but they may benefit from the longer period of childhood, when they do not have to deal with the new and different demands of adolescence, and they may become more flexible as they adapt to the problems of being smaller and more childish-looking than their peers (N. Livson & Peskin, 1980).

Early and Late Maturation in Girls

Advantages and disadvantages of early and late maturation are less clear-cut for girls. Girls tend not to like maturing early; they are generally happier when they mature neither earlier nor later than their peers. Early-maturing girls tend to be less sociable, expressive, and poised; more introverted and shy; and more negative about menarche (M. C. Jones, 1958; N. Livson & Peskin, 1980; Ruble & Brooks-Gunn, 1982). They are apt to have a poor body image and lower self-esteem than later-maturing girls (Alsaker, 1992; Simmons, Blyth, Van Cleave, & Bush, 1979).

One reason why an early-maturing girl may feel less attractive (Crockett & Petersen, 1987) is that her new curviness clashes with cultural standards equating beauty with thinness. She may also be reacting to other people's concerns about her sexuality. Parents and teachers sometimes assume that girls with mature bodies *are* sexually active because they look as if they *could* be. Therefore, adults may treat an early-maturing girl more strictly and more disapprovingly than they treat less-developed girls. Other adolescents may also stereotype and put pressures on her that she is ill-equipped to handle.

A girl who is bigger than many of the boys she knows and more bosomy than other girls will often feel uncomfortably conspicuous; but working through these problems may give her valuable experience in dealing with problems later in life. Some researchers have, in fact, found that early-maturing girls make better adjustments in adulthood (M. C. Jones & Mussen, 1958; N. Livson & Peskin, 1980).

In general, effects of early or late maturation are most likely to be negative when adolescents are very different from their peers—either by being much more or much less developed—and when they do not see the changes as advantageous (Simmons, Blyth, & McKinney, 1983). But it is hard to generalize about the psychological effects of timing of puberty, because they depend, at least in part, on how the adolescent and the people in his or her world interpret this event. Adults need to be sensitive to the potential impact of these changes so that they can help young people experience these years as positively as possible.

The Relationship between Stress and the Timing of Puberty

Some controversial research suggests that conflict between parents and young adolescents may be re-

lated more to puberty than to chronological age, and that stress may even cause early maturation (Steinberg, 1988). Girls who argue more with their mothers mature faster physically than girls who have calmer relationships. It's possible that a very close mother-daughter tie at a time when a girl is striving for independence might be stressful, and that stress might in turn affect the hormonal secretions that govern puberty. Following up these findings, researchers who had followed a group of girls since age 3 found that 16-year-olds who had grown up in a conflict-ridden family or whose fathers had not lived with the family in the girls' childhood tended to reach menarche earlier than girls with calmer family settings (Moffitt, Caspi, Belsky, & Silva, 1992).

What might account for this relationship? One possibility is an interaction between heredity and environment. Mothers and daughters resemble each other in age of first menstruation (Garn, 1980). Early maturers tend to marry earlier and have children earlier than their peers. Early marriages are more likely to end in divorce. It is possible that early-maturing mothers tend to have early-maturing daughters, whose fathers are more likely to be absent because of their mothers' higher probability of divorce (Surbey, 1990). These conclusions are still being debated, but they again point out the interrelationship among various aspects of development.

Reactions to Menarche and Menstruation

Menarche is more than a physical event; it is "a concrete symbol of a shift from girl to woman" (Ruble & Brooks-Gunn, 1982, p. 1557). Girls who have begun to menstruate seem more conscious of their femaleness than girls of the same age who have not yet reached menarche. They are more interested in boy-girl relations and in adorning their bodies, and when they draw female figures, they show more explicit breasts. They also seem more mature in certain personality characteristics (Grief & Ulman, 1982).

Unfortunately, in the past, the negative side of menarche—the sometimes unexpected discomfort and embarrassment that may accompany it—has been emphasized. Cultural taboos have reinforced negative attitudes and have prevented the development of rituals to welcome young girls to womanhood (Grief & Ulman, 1982). Western culture treats menarche not as a rite of passage (as in Box 10-1) but as a hygienic crisis, arousing girls' anxieties about staying clean and sweet-smelling

Most teenagers are more concerned about their physical appearance than about any other aspect of themselves. Unfortunately, anxiety about looks and image sometimes turns a happy mother-daughter shopping trip into a tense, unhappy experience, but parents who don't take their adolescent's unhappiness as a personal rebuke can help maintain or restore self-esteem. *(Rhoda Sidney/The Image Works)*

but not instilling pride in their womanliness (Whisnant & Zegans, 1975).

Today, although many girls have mixed feelings about menarche and menstruation, most take them in stride. The better prepared a girl is for menarche, the more positive her feelings and the less her distress (Koff, Rierdan, & Sheingold, 1982; Ruble & Brooks-Gunn, 1982). Unfortunately, though, some girls are uninformed or, worse yet, misinformed; as a result, they have unhappy memories of first menstruation (Rierdan, Koff, & Flaherty, 1986). Those whose menarche comes early are most likely to find it disruptive (Ruble & Brooks-Gunn, 1982), possibly because they are less prepared or because they simply feel out of step with their friends.

How can menstruation be a more positive experience? Young girls need good information, neither too technical nor too impersonal. They need to be told about the body parts and processes and what they can expect. They need to realize that menstruation is a special, universal female experience, different from injury or disease. Parents should bring up the subject as soon as a girl's breasts and pubic hair begin to develop. They should reassure her that menstruation is normal and that she will be able to continue with all her usual activities, like sports, swimming, and bathing. They should encourage her to ask questions, and all family members, including fathers and brothers, should maintain an open, matter-of-fact attitude. Celebrating menarche with a family ritual can underline the positive meaning of this event in a girl's life.

Feelings about Physical Appearance

Most young teenagers are more concerned about their looks than about any other aspect of themselves, and many do not like what they see in the mirror. Boys want to be tall, broad-shouldered, and athletic; girls want to be pretty, slim but shapely, with nice hair and skin (Tobin-Richards, Boxer, & Petersen, 1983). Anything that makes boys think that they look feminine or girls think that they look masculine makes them miserable. Teenagers of both sexes worry about their weight, their complexion, and their facial features.

Girls tend to be unhappier about their looks than boys of the same age, no doubt because our culture places greater emphasis on women's physical attributes. When adolescents are asked what they like least about their bodies, boys often say "nothing," while girls complain mostly about their legs and hips (Tobin-Richards et al., 1983). Adolescent girls are more prone to depression than boys, mainly because of worries about their appearance. They feel "ugly"; consider themselves too fat, too short, or too tall; or hate their hair or their complexion. Before puberty, rates for depression are the same in boys and girls; but at about age 12 girls start to have higher rates, and by age 14 girls' rates are twice as high as boys' (Lewinsohn, in Goleman, 1990b; Rierdan, Koff, & Stubbs, 1988, 1989).

Adults often dismiss adolescents' preoccupation with their looks. But in a society in which personality is often judged by appearance, self-image can have long-lasting effects on young people's feelings about themselves. Adults who thought they were attractive during their teenage years have higher self-esteem and are happier than those who did not. Not until the mid-forties do the differences in self-esteem and happiness disappear (Berscheid, Walster, & Bohrnstedt, 1973).

HEALTH CONCERNS OF ADOLESCENCE

Illness is rare among adolescents, who have low rates of disability and chronic disease. The health problems they do have are often preventable, stemming as they do from personality, poverty, and lifestyle factors. Across racial, ethnic, and class lines, young adolescents (aged 11 to 14), especially boys, tend to risk their health by smoking, drinking, using marijuana, and being sexually active. Adolescents whose families have been disrupted by parental separation or death are more likely to start these activities early and to engage in them even more over the next few years (Millstein et al., 1992). Adolescents' increasing tendency to take risks is reflected in the fact that the leading causes of death at this age are accidents, homicide, and suicide. For African American males aged 15 to 24, homicide is the number one killer—seven times greater than the rate for white males (McGinnis, Richmond, Brandt, Windom, & Mason, 1992).

Teenagers' concerns about their health tend to revolve around stress and nervousness (R. Blum, 1987). They consult physicians most often for skin and cosmetic problems, coughs and sore throats, and (for girls) prenatal care (Gans, 1990). Adults' concerns about teenagers' health focus on their high rates of sexually transmitted diseases, drug abuse, and pregnancy (Millstein, 1989).

These are relatively healthy years. Only 6 percent of adolescents suffer from chronic disabilities; in 32 percent of these cases, a mental disorder is responsible (Newacheck, 1989). Other disabilities are caused by chronic respiratory conditions, diseases of the muscle and skeletal system and connective tissue, nervous system disorders, and hearing impairment (Gans, 1990; Newacheck, 1989; see Figure 10-1). Dental health is often a problem: 96 percent of high school students have some tooth decay; about 50 percent wear—or should be wearing—braces to correct poor contact between upper and lower jaws; and 23 percent of 15-year-olds have untreated decay in at least one tooth (Gans, 1990).

The health status of adolescents is expected to get worse over the next few decades, largely because more will be living in poverty. Adolescents from poor families are 3 times as likely to be in fair or poor health and 47 percent more likely to suffer from disabling chronic illnesses than those from families above the poverty line. These teenagers need access to medical care; research shows that they will use it. In one study, teenagers with Medicaid coverage went to doctors at rates similar to teenagers from more affluent families; those without coverage sought less care (Newacheck, 1989). But in the early 1990s, 15 percent of Americans aged 10 to 18 did not have medical insurance; rates were particularly high among poor, near-poor, and minority adolescents (Newacheck, McManus, & Gephart, 1992).

An estimated 14 percent of young people under age 18 do not receive the medical care they need. This is a particular problem for adolescents, who are less likely to see a physician regularly than are younger children (Gans, 1990). Why don't teenagers get medical care? Some of the reasons include lack of money or insurance coverage, office hours that conflict with school hours, requirements for parental consent, and a lack of assurance of confidentiality on the part of the health care provider.

In Chapter 11 we examine teenage pregnancy,

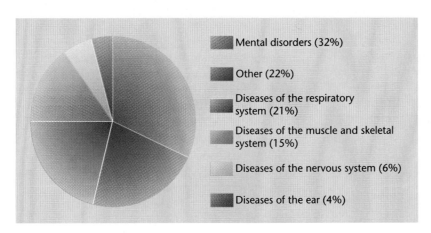

Mental disorders (32%)

Other (22%)

Diseases of the respiratory system (21%)

Diseases of the muscle and skeletal system (15%)

Diseases of the nervous system (6%)

Diseases of the ear (4%)

FIGURE 10-1
Causes of mental and physical disability among 10- to 18-year-olds. Six percent of adolescents in this age range have a serious chronic condition that limits their activity. In 32 percent of cases, a mental disorder is responsible. (Adapted from Gans, 1990.)

and in Chapter 18 we discuss the growing rates of suicide among adolescents. In this chapter we deal with such major health problems as eating disorders, drug abuse, and sexually transmitted diseases.

NUTRITION AND EATING DISORDERS

Nutritional Needs

The adolescent growth spurt is accompanied by an eating spurt, especially among boys. Since boys grow more during adolescence, they need more calories than girls. On the average, a girl needs about 2200 calories per day, and a boy needs about 2800. Protein is important to sustain growth, and teenagers should avoid eating large amounts of junk food like french fries, soft drinks, ice cream, fatty meats, and snack chips and dips.

The most common mineral deficiencies of adolescents are of calcium, iron, and zinc. The need for calcium, which supports bone growth, is best met by drinking enough milk. Girls are especially prone to calcium deficiency, a problem that may haunt them later in the form of osteoporosis (thinning of the bones), which afflicts 1 in 4 postmenopausal women (see Chapter 14). Teenagers need a steady source of iron-rich foods like iron-fortified breads, dried fruits, and leafy green vegetables. Iron-deficiency anemia is common among American adolescents because their diet tends to be iron-poor. Foods containing zinc—like meats, eggs, seafood, and whole-grain cereal products—are also important, since even a mild zinc deficiency can delay sexual maturity (E. R. Williams & Caliendo, 1984).

Many adolescents put on weight, and some—especially girls—react by embarking on a lifelong struggle to reduce for the sake of health and beauty. Some are fighting real obesity. But in recent years, two eating problems—*anorexia* and *bulimia*—have become increasingly common. Both reflect our society's stringent standards of female beauty, exalting slenderness above all else, and individual pathologies of people who try to meet those standards through bizarre eating patterns.

Obesity

Obesity, overweight involving a skinfold measurement in the 85th percentile, is the most common eating disorder in the United States, affecting some 15 percent of adolescents (see Figure 10-2). Obese

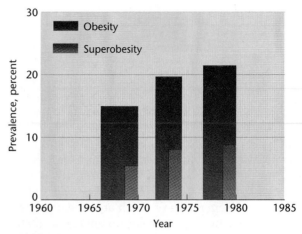

FIGURE 10-2
Estimated trends in obesity and superobesity in adolescents 12 to 17 years old in the United States. Even in these years, obesity is associated with a number of health problems. (Adapted from Gortmaker, Dietz, Sobol, & Wehler, 1987.)

teenagers tend to become obese adults, subject to a variety of health risks. A 60-year longitudinal study found that overweight in adolescence can lead to life-threatening chronic conditions in adulthood—even if the excess weight is lost. The effects are particularly strong for heavy boys, who as adults have death rates nearly double those of men who were slender as teenagers (Must et al., 1992). Further, overweight is associated with poor psychological adjustment (Alsaker, 1992).

Obesity results when people consume more calories than they expend. Obese adolescents—and adults—are widely regarded as having too little "willpower," but this is an oversimplification. Risk factors having nothing to do with willpower seem to make some people likely to become overweight. These factors include genetic regulation of metabolism (obesity often runs in families, as noted in Chapter 2); developmental history (inability to recognize body clues about hunger and when it should be satisfied, or the development of an abnormally large number of fat cells during childhood); rates of physical activity; emotional stress; and brain damage. No matter what the cause, however, obese people can lose weight. Programs using behavior modification to help adolescents make changes in diet and exercise have had some success in taking off pounds.

Anorexia Nervosa and Bulimia Nervosa

Sometimes a determination *not* to become obese can result in even graver problems than obesity itself, as in the disorders of anorexia nervosa and bulimia nervosa. Both tend to reflect problems in society as well as in families and individuals, since they stem in large part from today's idea of female beauty—with its unrealistic glorification of slenderness. This cultural influence interacts with family and personal factors to make many girls and young women obsessed with weight.

Preoccupations with dieting and weight have become widespread among teenage girls, especially white girls; black girls are less weight- and diet-conscious. Girls who gain weight or diet to lose it are dissatisfied with their self-image and often depressed. Among 497 urban and suburban high school seniors, two-thirds of the girls were preoccupied with weight and dieting, compared with only 15 percent of the boys (Casper & Offer, 1990). In a different group of 1400 high school students, 63 percent of the girls were trying to lose weight and 28.4 percent of the boys were trying to gain—although most of these adolescents were already of normal weight (Rosen & Gross, 1987). Another study found that more than half of female high school seniors have dieted "seriously." Some never stop (J. D. Brown, Childers, & Waszak, 1988); and some adopt bizarre eating habits.

Anorexia

Someone suggests to Susanna, 14, that she could stand to lose a few pounds. She loses them—and then continues to diet obsessively, refusing to eat, until she has lost at least 15 to 25 percent of her original body weight. Meanwhile, Susanna stops menstruating, thick soft hair spreads over her body, and she becomes intensely overactive.

This is a typical scenario for *anorexia nervosa,* or self-starvation, an eating disorder seen mostly in young white women (*DSM-III-R*, 1987). The disorder may affect people of both sexes from preadolescence to middle age; but it is most likely to occur during adolescence. It occurs across socioeconomic levels and is estimated to affect from 0.5 to 1 percent of 12- to 18-year-old girls. Only about 5 to 10 percent of patients are adolescent boys, although the number of males affected is increasing (*DSM-III-R*, 1987; Garner, 1993). From 2 to 8 percent of people with anorexia eventually die of starvation (D. B. Herzog, Keller, & Lavori, 1988).

Typically, Susanna is preoccupied with food—cooking it, talking about it, and urging others to eat—but she eats very little herself. She has a distorted view of herself: she cannot see how shockingly thin she is. She is a good student, described by her parents as a "model" child; but she is also

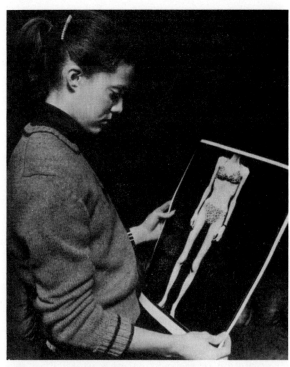

Before this girl received therapy for anorexia nervosa, she had a grossly distorted body image. When she looked like the girl in the picture she is holding, she could not see how shockingly thin she was. *(Patt Blue)*

withdrawn, depressed, and obsessed with repetitive, perfectionist behavior (Garner, 1993).

The cause of anorexia is unknown. Many observers consider it a reaction to extreme societal pressure to be slender—a response to a standard of attractiveness in the media that is thinner for women than for men and the thinnest it has been since the 1920s, the time of the last epidemic of similar eating disorders (Silverstein, et al., 1986; Silverstein, Peterson, & Perdue, 1986).

Others see it as a psychological disturbance related to a fear of growing up, a fear of sexuality, or an extremely malfunctioning family. Such families often seem harmonious on the surface, but they are actually overdependent and too involved in each other's lives and have difficulty dealing with conflict (Dove, n.d.). Some people with anorexia seem to feel that controlling their weight is the only way to control any part of their lives. Depression is often a part of the disorder. A Canadian study that followed anorexic patients (some of whom also had bulimia, which we discuss below) between 5 and 14 years after treatment found that they were likely to suffer from depression or anxiety disorders later in life (Toner, Garfinkel, & Garner, 1986).

Still others suggest that anorexia may be a physical disorder caused by a deficiency of a crucial chemical in the brain or by a disturbance of the hypothalamus. Others believe that it may develop because of inadequate coping skills to face new experiences or adverse life events (Garner, 1993). Anorexia is probably due to a combination of factors.

Early warning signs include a dieter's lowering weight goals after reaching an initial desired weight, determined dieting in isolation, excessive exercising, dissatisfaction even after losing weight, and interruption of menstruation. As soon as symptoms like these appear, treatment should be sought.

Bulimia

An eating disorder closely related to anorexia also affects mostly adolescent girls and young women. In *bulimia nervosa*, a person regularly (at least twice a week) goes on huge eating binges (consuming up to 5000 calories in a single sitting, nearly always in secret) and then tries to nullify the high caloric intake by self-induced vomiting, strict dieting or fasting, vigorous exercise, or use of laxatives or diuretics (*DSM-III-R*, 1987). People with bulimia are obsessed with their weight and body shape. They do not become abnormally thin, but they become overwhelmed with shame, self-contempt, and depression over their abnormal eating habits. They also suffer extensive tooth decay (caused by repeated vomiting of stomach acid), gastric irritation, skin problems, and loss of hair. There is some overlap between anorexia and bulimia; some victims of anorexia have bulimic episodes, and some people with bulimia lose weight. But the two are separate disorders.

Bulimia seems to be related to low levels of the brain chemical serotonin, providing a biological basis for the disorder. Another theory provides a psychoanalytic explanation: that these people use food to appease their hunger for love and attention. There is some basis for this explanation: some bulimic patients report that they felt abused, neglected, and deprived of nurturing from their parents (Humphrey, 1986).

Treatment for Anorexia and Bulimia

Both these eating disorders can be treated, but the relapse rate for anorexia is very high, with up to 25 percent of patients progressing to chronic invalidism and many dying prematurely (Beumont, Russell, & Touyz, 1993).

The immediate goal of treatment for anorexia is to get patients to eat, to gain weight—and to live. They are likely to be admitted to a hospital, where they may be given 24-hour nursing, drugs to encourage eating and inhibit vomiting, and behavior therapy, which rewards eating by granting such privileges as getting out of bed and leaving the room. People with anorexia or bulimia often need medical treatment too (Beumont, et al., 1993).

Both anorexia and bulimia are treated by therapies that help patients gain insight into their feelings. Since these patients are at risk of depression and suicide, the discovery that antidepressant drugs can help is heartening (Fluoxetine-Bulimia Collaborative Study Group, 1992; Hudson & Pope, 1990; Kaye, Weltzin, Hsu, & Bulik, 1991).

Patients with anorexia seem to need long-term support even after they have stopped starving themselves. Some 27 months after completion of treatment, most of the 63 females in one study had continued to gain weight, had resumed menstruating, and were functioning in school or at work. Still, they continued to have problems with body image. Even though they averaged 8 percent below ideal weight, most thought of themselves as being overweight and as having excessive appetites, and many felt depressed and lonely (Nussbaum, Shenker, Baird, & Saravay, 1985). Since the transition from hospital to home can be difficult, good supervision and counseling are important (Beumont et al., 1993).

USE AND ABUSE OF DRUGS

Current Trends

Throughout recorded history, people have used drugs to relieve physical ills as well as to alleviate unhappiness and to give their lives a lift. Why, then, is the use of drugs so troubling today? Major causes for concern include the early age at which many people begin to abuse drugs and the prevalence of drug abuse among adolescents, many of whom begin taking drugs mainly out of curiosity or because of peer pressure.

Use of drugs among adolescents is less prevalent than it was at its peak during the 1960s. Surveys of eighth-, tenth-, and twelfth-grade students around the United States show an almost continuous overall decline in use of most drugs from 1979 to 1992 (National Institute on Drug Abuse [NIDA], 1993). These surveys probably underestimate drug use since they do not reach high school dropouts, who are thought to have higher rates. But they do show a steady decline among students and recent graduates. One disturbing trend, however, is an overall increase in drug use by eighth-graders.*

Many young people are using such drugs as alcohol, nicotine, marijuana, LSD, amphetamines, barbiturates, heroin, and cocaine; and many begin to use them in elementary school. The Monitoring the Future Survey (NIDA, 1993) found that in 1992 69.3 percent of eighth-graders had tried alcohol, 45.2 percent had smoked tobacco, 17.4 percent had tried inhalants, and 11.2 percent had used marijuana. In the same survey, of almost 16,000 1992 high school seniors, 14.4 percent admitted using illicit drugs at least once in the previous month, and 40.7 percent said that they had tried an illicit drug at some time. (Both figures were lower than in 1991.)

Twelfth-graders' use of cocaine in the previous 30 days continued the decline begun in 1986; it was down to 1.3 percent in 1992, compared with 1.6 percent in 1988. Lifetime use of crack for seniors was 2.6 percent in 1992 (see Table 10-4).

The effects of drugs are harmful in adolescence and beyond. In one longitudinal study, more than 1000 high school sophomores and juniors were interviewed again at age 24 or 25. Those who had

begun using a certain drug in their teens tended to continue to use it (Kandel, Davies, Karus, & Yamaguchi, 1986). Users of illicit drugs, including marijuana, were in poorer health than nonusers, had more unstable job and marital histories, and were more likely to have been delinquent. Cigarette smokers tended to be depressed and to have lung problems and breathing problems.

Alcohol, marijuana, and tobacco are the three drugs most popular with adolescents.

Alcohol

Many of the same people who worry about the illegal use of marijuana by young people are brought up short when reminded that alcohol too is a potent, mind-altering drug, that it is illegal for most high school students and many college students (even though it is usually easy to get), and that it is a much more serious problem nationwide. High school students seem to be drinking less than they used to, but college students and young adults have shown much slighter decreases. Although nearly all high school seniors (87.5 percent) in the 1992 NIDA survey reported drinking alcoholic beverages in the previous year, the percentage who had had a drink during the previous month dropped to 51.3 percent from the peak rate of 72 percent in 1980. Fewer students reported

*At this writing, preliminary reports from a NIDA study of secondary school students, published in 1994, point to a troubling resurgence of drug use among adolescents.

TABLE 10-4

Lifetime Prevalence of Drug Use by Students, 1991 and 1992			
	Eighth-graders	**Tenth-graders**	**Twelfth-graders**
Marijuana	1991: 10.2% 1992: 11.2%	1991: 23.4% 1992: 21.4%	1991: 36.0% 1992: 32.6%
Cocaine	1991: 2.3% 1992: 2.9%	1991: 4.1% 1992: 3.3%	1991: 7.8% 1992: 6.1%
Crack cocaine	1991: 1.3% 1992: 1.6%	1991: 1.7% 1992: 1.5%	1991: 3.1% 1992: 2.6%
Inhalants	1991: 17.6% 1992: 17.4%	1991: 15.7% 1992: 16.6%	1991: 17.6% 1992: 16.6%
LSD	1991: 2.7% 1992: 3.2%	1991: 5.6% 1992: 5.8%	1991: 8.8% 1992: 8.6%
Alcohol	1991: 70.1% 1992: 69.3%	1991: 83.8% 1992: 82.3%	1991: 88.0% 1992: 87.5%
Cigarettes	1991: 44.0% 1992: 45.2%	1991: 55.1% 1992: 53.5%	1991: 63.1% 1992: 61.8%
All illicit drugs	Not available	Not available	1991: 44.1% 1992: 40.7%

Note: The overall rate of illicit drug use among twelfth-graders was 65.6% in 1981, considerably higher than in 1991 and 1992.
SOURCE: National Institute on Drug Abuse, 1993.

MEDIA PORTRAYAL OF ALCOHOL —

SHOULD TV COMMERCIALS BE BANNED like TOBACCO?

To prevent deaths among young Americans caused by alcohol-related motor vehicle accidents, educational campaigns now stress the importance of naming a "designated driver," one person in a group who will take the wheel and will agree not to drink on a specific night. *(Louis Fernandez/Black Star)*

drinking heavily, too: 29.9 percent said that they had been drunk during the previous 30 days, compared with 31.6 percent in 1991.

Most teenagers start to drink because it seems a grown-up thing to do, and they continue to do so for the same reasons adults do: to add a pleasant glow to social situations, to reduce anxiety, and to escape from problems. Although the average teenager drinks moderately and has no problems with alcohol, some young people, like some adults, cannot handle this drug. In a survey sponsored by the National Institute on Alcohol Abuse and Alcoholism (NIAAA), more than 3 out of 10 young people were classified as "problem drinkers." These youngsters had been drunk at least four times in the previous year or had gotten into trouble through drinking at least twice in the previous year (Rachal et al., 1980). The dangers of driving after drinking are well known: the leading cause of death among 15- to 24-year-olds is alcohol-related vehicle accidents (AAP Committee on Adolescence, 1987).

Marijuana

Marijuana has been used all over the world for centuries, but only since the 1960s has it become popular among the American middle class. Despite a decline in use since 1979 (from 37 percent to 11.9 percent of high school seniors in 1992 who smoked it during the past 30 days, according to the NIDA survey), it is still by far the most widely used illicit drug in this country.

Adolescents start to smoke marijuana for many of the same reasons they begin to drink alcohol. They are curious, they want to do what their friends do, and they want to hurtle into adulthood. Another appeal of marijuana was its value as a symbol of rebellion against parents' values, but this attraction may be slipping, since today's teenagers are much more likely to have parents who smoked (or smoke) marijuana themselves.

Heavy use of marijuana can lead to heart and lung trouble, contribute to traffic accidents, and impede memory and learning. It may also lessen motivation, interfere with schoolwork, and cause family problems. Among 49 boys in one study (average age about 16), those who drank alcoholic beverages and also smoked marijuana more than twice a week were more likely than those who did not smoke marijuana to have poor eating habits and such health problems as respiratory infections and general fatigue (Farrow, Rees, & Worthington-Roberts, 1987).

Tobacco

Sneaking a cigarette behind the barn was once a humorous staple of adolescent lore. But adults' amused indulgence toward young people's use of tobacco has turned to distress, with new awareness of health hazards. The publication in 1964 of the U.S. Surgeon General's report clearly linked smoking to lung cancer, heart disease, emphysema, and several other illnesses.

Many adolescents got the message. Teenagers express concern about the effects of smoking on health, and smokers feel the disapproval of their peers. Still, in 1992, 27.8 percent of high school seniors smoke regularly, a rate that has not dropped substantially in the past decade (NIDA, 1993).

Today, more teenage girls than boys smoke, reversing the former male-female ratio. As a result, one type of equality women have achieved is a death rate from lung cancer almost equal to that of men, although about 2.5 times as many men develop the disease (American Cancer Society, 1985).

Smokers usually take their first puff between 10 and 12 years of age; they continue to smoke even though they do not enjoy it at first, and they become physically dependent on nicotine at about age 15. Young people are more likely to smoke if their friends and family do (McAlister, Perry, & Maccoby, 1979; National Institute of Child Health and Human Development, 1978). Since peer pressure has been effective in inducing people to smoke, its influence in the other direction may be the best preventive mechanism (L. D. Johnston, Bachman, & O'Malley, 1982; McAlister et al., 1979).

SEXUALLY TRANSMITTED DISEASES (STDs)

What Are STDs?

Sexually transmitted diseases (STDs), also referred to as *venereal diseases,* are diseases spread by sexual contact. Rates of STDs have soared for all ages since the 1960s, with severe effects on adolescents. Of the 12 million cases of STDs each year in the United States, 2 out of 3 occur among young people under 25 years old (Donovan, 1993).

The most prevalent STD is chlamydia, which causes infections of the urinary tract, rectum, and cervix and can lead, in women, to pelvic inflammatory disease (PID), a serious abdominal infection. Other STDs, in order of incidence, are trichomoniasis, gonorrhea, genital (venereal) warts, herpes simplex, hepatitis B, syphilis, and acquired immune deficiency syndrome (AIDS).

Genital herpes simplex is a chronic, recurring, often painful disease caused by a virus (a different strain of which also causes cold sores on the face). Although no hard figures on its incidence are available, it is highly contagious, with about 500,000 new cases reported every year (Goldsmith, 1989). The condition can be fatal to the newborn infant of a mother who has an outbreak of genital herpes at the time of delivery and to a person with a deficiency of the immune system. It has been associated with increased incidence of cervical cancer. There is no cure, but the antiviral drug acyclovir can prevent active outbreaks.

AIDS is a failure of the body's immune system that leaves affected persons vulnerable to a variety of fatal diseases. The virus that causes it is transmitted through bodily fluids (mainly blood and semen) and stays in the body for life, even though the person carrying it may not show any signs of illness. Symptoms may not appear until from 6 months to 7 or more years after initial infection. Most victims in the United States are drug abusers who share contaminated hypodermic needles, homosexual and bisexual men, people who have received transfusions of infected blood or blood products, and infants who have been infected in the womb or during birth. Worldwide, most HIV-infected adults are heterosexual.

A 1993 report by the United Nations identifies sexually active teenage girls as the "next leading edge" of the AIDS epidemic. In an analysis of information from 31 European, Asian, and African countries, the rate of human immunodeficiency virus (HIV) peaked for women at ages 15 to 25, compared to the male peak at ages 25 to 35. Young girls' greater susceptibility to this virus may stem from both physical and cultural causes. Physically, they are less well protected, partly because the membranes in their vaginas are thinner than those of older women, the mucous these membranes produce is thinner, and it contains fewer immunity-producing cells (Futterman et al., 1993).

Many teenagers put themselves at risk for AIDS. Among 1091 tenth-graders from urban working-class, welfare, and middle-class suburban families, more than two-thirds of sexually active students reported inconsistent or no use of condoms; at least one-third had had two or more partners; and more than 5 percent had had intercourse with a presumably high-risk partner (Walter, Vaughan, & Cohall, 1991). Fortunately, educating teenagers about AIDS does have an effect. Among 15- to 19-year-old males, those who received AIDS education and sex education had fewer sexual partners, used condoms more consistently, and had less frequent intercourse (Ku, Sonenstein, & Pleck, 1992). This study, then, counters the widely held notion that educating teenagers about sex makes them *more* sexually active.

AIDS has continued to spread since the early 1980s, when it first exploded as a public health concern. Education has reduced its spread in the homosexual community, blood screening has reduced the risk of contraction by transfusion, and current efforts focus on halting it among drug users. As of now, it is incurable.

Box 10-3 lists steps that sexually active people can take to protect themselves from STDs. Table 10-5 summarizes the most common STDs and their incidence, causes, most frequent symptoms, treatment, and consequences.

STDs and Adolescents

The reasons for the high rates of sexually transmitted diseases among adolescents are many: increased sexual activity, especially among girls; use of oral contraceptives, which do not protect against STDs, instead of condoms, which often do; the assumption that STDs can be cured easily; adolescents' belief that they and their sexual partners are immune to the diseases that affect other people; and teenagers' willingness to take risks because they want sex more than they fear disease.

BOX 10-3 PRACTICALLY SPEAKING

PROTECTING AGAINST SEXUALLY TRANSMITTED DISEASES

How can people who are sexually active protect themselves against sexually transmitted diseases (STDs)? The following guidelines (adapted from American Foundation for the Prevention of Venereal Disease [AFPVD], 1986; and Upjohn Company, 1984) minimize the possibility of acquiring an STD and maximize the chances of getting good treatment if one is acquired.

■ Have regular medical checkups. All sexually active persons should request tests specifically aimed at diagnosing STDs.
■ Know your partner. The more discriminating you are, the less likely you are to be exposed to STDs. Partners with whom you develop a relationship are more likely than partners you do not know well to inform you of any medical problems they have.
■ Avoid having sexual intercourse with many partners, promiscuous persons, and drug abusers.
■ Practice "safe sex." Avoid sexual activity involving exchange of bodily fluids. Use a latex condom during intercourse and oral sex.
■ Avoid anal intercourse.
■ Use a contraceptive foam, cream, or jelly; it will kill many germs and help to prevent certain STDs.
■ Learn the symptoms of STDs: vaginal or penile discharge; inflammation, itching, or pain in the genital or anal area; burning during urination; pain during intercourse; genital, body, or mouth sores, blisters, bumps, or rashes; pain in the lower abdomen or in the testicles; discharge from or itching of eyes; and fever or swollen glands.
■ Inspect your partner for any visible symptoms.
■ If you develop any symptoms yourself, get immediate medical attention.
■ Just before and just after sexual contact, wash genital and rectal areas with soap and water; males should urinate after washing.
■ Do not have any sexual contact if you suspect that you or your partner may be infected. Abstinence is the most reliable preventive measure.
■ Avoid exposing any cut or break in the skin to anyone else's blood (including menstrual blood), body fluids, or secretions.
■ Practice good hygiene routinely: frequent, thorough hand washing and daily fingernail brushing.
■ Make sure needles used for ear piercing, tattooing, acupuncture, or any kind of injection are either sterile or disposable. Never share a needle.
■ If you contract any STD, notify all recent sexual partners immediately so that they can obtain treatment and avoid passing the infection back to you or on to someone else. Inform your doctor or dentist of your condition so that precautions can be taken to prevent transmission. Do not donate blood, plasma, sperm, body organs, or other body tissue.

For more information, contact American Foundation for the Prevention of Venereal Disease, 799 Broadway, Suite 638, New York, NY 10003.

TABLE 10-5

The Most Common Sexually Transmitted Diseases

Disease	New Cases Annually	Cause	Symptoms: Male	Symptoms: Female	Treatment	Consequences If Untreated
Chlamydia	4 million	Bacterial infection	Pain during urination, discharge from penis.	Vaginal discharge, abdominal discomfort.†	Tetracycline or erythromycin.	Can cause pelvic inflammatory disease or eventual sterility.
Tricho-moniasis	3 million	Parasitic infection, sometimes passed on in moist objects like towels and bathing suits	Often absent.	May be absent, or may include vaginal discharge, discomfort during intercourse, odor, painful urination.	Oral antibiotic.	May lead to abnormal growth of cervical cells.

Disease	New Cases Annually	Cause	Symptoms: Male	Symptoms: Female	Treatment	Consequences If Untreated
Gonorrhea	1–2 million	Bacterial infection	Discharge from penis, pain during urination.*	Discomfort when urinating, vaginal discharge, abnormal menses.†	Penicillin or other antibiotics.	Can cause pelvic inflammatory disease or eventual sterility; can also cause arthritis, dermatitis, and meningitis.
Genital warts	750,000	Viral infection	Painless growths that usually appear on penis, but may also appear on urethra or in rectal area.*	Small, painless growths on genitalia and anus; may also occur inside the vagina without external symptoms.*	Removal of warts.	May be associated with cervical cancer; in pregnancy, warts enlarge and may obstruct birth canal.
Herpes	500,000	Viral infection	Painful blisters anywhere on the genitalia, usually on the penis.*	Painful blisters on the genitalia, sometimes with fever and aching muscles; women with sores on cervix may be unaware of outbreaks.*	No known cure, but controlled with antiviral drug acyclovir.	Possible increased risk of cervical cancer.
Hepatitis B	100,000–200,000	Viral infection	Skin and eyes become yellow.	Skin and eyes become yellow.	No specific treatment; no alcohol.	Can cause liver damage, development of chronic hepatitis.
Syphilis	100,000	Bacterial infection	In first stage, reddish-brown sores on the mouth or genitalia or both, which may disappear, though the bacteria remain; in the second, more infectious stage, a widespread skin rash.*	Same as in men.	Penicillin or other antibiotics.	Paralysis, convulsions, brain damage, and sometimes death.
AIDS (acquired immune deficiency syndrome)	80,000 (projected in 1992)	Viral infection	Extreme fatigue, fever, swollen lymph nodes, weight loss, diarrhea, night sweats, susceptibility to other diseases.*	Same as in men.	No known cure, but experimental drug AZT may extend life.	Death, usually due to other diseases, such as cancer.

*May be asymptomatic.
†Often asymptomatic.
SOURCES: Adapted from Centers for Disease Control, 1986, 1992; Goldsmith, 1989; Morbidity and Mortality Weekly Report, 1987.

Young girls may be even more susceptible than mature women to STD-caused infections of the upper genital tract, which can lead to serious, even dangerous, complications. Teenagers are more likely than adults to put off getting medical care (often out of worry that their parents will find out), they are less likely to follow through with treatment, they are often embarrassed to alert their sexual partners when they contract an STD, and STDs are more likely to be misdiagnosed in young people (Centers for Disease Control, 1983). Most campaigns aimed at eradicating STDs focus on early diagnosis and treatment. Not until at least equal prominence is given to prevention and to the moral obligation to avoid passing them on will headway be made in stopping this epidemic.

■ INTELLECTUAL DEVELOPMENT

The major element that puts adolescent thinking on a higher level than the thought processes of childhood is the concept "What if . . . ?" Adolescents can think in terms of what *might* be true, rather than just in terms of what they see. Since they can imagine an infinite variety of possibilities, they are capable of hypothetical reasoning. They are able to think in broader terms about moral issues and about plans for their own future.

ASPECTS OF INTELLECTUAL DEVELOPMENT IN ADOLESCENCE

COGNITIVE DEVELOPMENT: PIAGET'S STAGE OF FORMAL OPERATIONS

The dominant explanation for the changes in the way teenagers think has been that of Jean Piaget, who saw them entering the highest level of cognitive development people are capable of. Piaget called this level, which is marked by the capacity for abstract thought, *formal operations.*

Cognitive Maturity: The Nature of Formal Operations

The attainment of formal operations gives adolescents a new way to manipulate—or operate on—information. They are no longer limited to thinking about the here and now, as they were in the previous cognitive stage, concrete operations. Now, they can deal with abstractions, test hypotheses, and see infinite possibilities.

This advance opens many new doors. It lets teenagers analyze political and philosophical doctrines, and sometimes construct their own elaborate theories, with an eye to reforming society. It even allows them to recognize the fact that in some situations there are no definite answers. Much of childhood appears to be a struggle to come to grips with the world as it is. Now young people become aware of the world as it could be.

The ability to think abstractly has emotional ramifications too. "Whereas earlier the adolescent could love his mother or hate a peer, now he can love freedom or hate exploitation. The adolescent has developed a new mode of life: the possible and the ideal captivate both mind and feeling" (Ginsburg & Opper, 1979, p. 201).

We can glimpse the nature of formal operations in different reactions to a story told by Peel (1967):

Only brave pilots are allowed to fly over high mountains. A fighter pilot flying over the Alps collided with an aerial cable-way and cut a main cable, causing some cars to fall to the glacier below. Several people were killed.

A child still at the concrete operations level said, "I think that the pilot was not very good at flying. He would have been better off if he went on fighting." Only one answer springs to the child's mind— that the pilot was inept and not doing his real job, fighting.

By contrast, an adolescent who had reached the level of *formal operations* found a variety of possible explanations for what happened: "He was either not informed of the mountain railway on his route, or he was flying too low; also, his flying compass may have been affected by something before or after takeoff, thus setting him off course and causing the collision with the cable" (Peel, 1967). We see in the adolescent a new flexibility and complexity of thinking.

Tracing Cognitive Development: The Pendulum Problem

Cognitive development can be traced from stage to stage by following the progress of a typical child in dealing with a classical Piagetian problem in formal reasoning: the pendulum problem. The child, Adam, is shown the pendulum—an object hanging from a string. He is then shown how he can change the length of the string, the weight of the object, the height from which the object is released, and the amount of force he can use to push the object. Then he is asked to figure out which factor or combination of factors determines how fast the pendulum swings.

When Adam first sees the pendulum, he is not yet 7 years old and is in the preoperational stage. Unable to formulate a plan for attacking the problem, he tries one thing after another in a hit-or-miss manner. First he puts a light weight on a long pendulum and pushes it, then he tries swinging a heavy weight on a short pendulum; then he removes the weight entirely. His method is random, and he cannot understand or report what has actually happened. He is convinced that his pushes make the pendulum go faster; even though this is not so, he reports it as observed fact.

Adam next encounters the pendulum at age 11, when he is in the stage of concrete operations. This time, he looks at some possible solutions, and he even hits upon a partially correct answer. But he fails to try out every possible solution systematically. He varies the length of the string and the weight of the object, and he thinks that both length and weight affect the speed of the swing. But because he varied both factors at the same time, he cannot tell which one is critical or whether both are.

Not until Adam is confronted with the pendulum again when he is 15 years old does he go at the problem systematically. He now realizes that any one of the four factors, or some combination of them, might affect the speed of the swing. He carefully designs an experiment to test all the possible hypotheses by varying one factor at a time while holding the others constant. By doing this, he is able to determine that only one factor—the length of the string—determines how fast the pendulum swings.*

Adam's last solution to the pendulum problem shows that he has arrived at the stage of formal operations, a cognitive level usually attained at about age 12. Adam can now think in terms of what might be true and not just in terms of what he sees. Since he can imagine a variety of possibilities, he is, for the first time, capable of *hypothetical-deductive* reasoning. Once he develops a hypothesis, he can construct a scientific experiment to test it. He considers all the possible relationships that might exist and goes through them

What determines how fast the pendulum swings: The length of the string? The weight of the object suspended from it? The height from which the object is released? The amount of force used to push the object? According to Piaget, an adolescent who has achieved the stage of formal operations can form a hypothesis and figure out a logical way to test it. Research suggests, however, that as many as half of all teenagers and more than one-third of all adults cannot solve this problem. *(Mimi Forsyth/Monkmeyer)*

one by one, to eliminate the false and arrive at the true.

This systematic reasoning process operates for all kinds of problems, from the simple mechanics of day-to-day living to the construction of elaborate political and philosophical theories. Adam can bring to bear what he has learned in the past to fix the family car or to plan for his future career. However, people who are capable of systematic formal thought do not always use it.

What Brings about Cognitive Maturity?

Inner and outer changes in adolescents' lives combine to bring about cognitive maturity, according to Piaget. The brain has matured and the social environment is widening, offering more opportunities for experimentation. Interaction between the two kinds of changes is essential. Even if young

*This description of age-related differences in the approach to the pendulum problem has been adapted from Ginsburg and Opper (1979).

people's neurological development has advanced enough to allow them to reach the stage of formal reasoning, they may never attain it if they are not encouraged culturally and educationally.

Peer interaction can help advance cognitive maturity. In one study college students (average age 18.5 years) were faced with a chemistry problem, asked a series of questions, and told to set up their own experiments (Dimant & Bearison, 1991). Students were randomly assigned to work alone or with a partner. Those working in a twosome were told to discuss their answers to the questions; and their responses (after being videotaped) were categorized as (1) disagreement, (2) explanation, (3) question, (4) agreement, or (5) extraneous. One dialogue was coded as follows (Dimant & Bearison, 1991, p. 280):

SUBJECT A: "What you said can't be. It's no sense." *(disagreement)*

SUBJECT B: "I'm right. I know it." *(disagreement)*

SUBJECT A: "Look here, see *B* [a container in the experiment] didn't work with *D* and *E*, so it can't be *B*. *(explanation)*

SUBJECT B: "Oh, you're right." *(agreement)*

The students who worked in pairs solved more problems than did those who worked alone. However, the nature of the interaction within a pair was important. The more answers a student received from the first three response categories, all of which challenged the subject's reasoning, the greater advances in reasoning occurred. The quality and frequency of the interactions brought about cognitive gains.

A 4-year longitudinal study of 165 undergraduates found that students majoring in the natural sciences, humanities, or social sciences showed improvements in reasoning from their first year of college to their fourth (Lehman & Nisbett, 1990). Although the different courses of study taught different kinds of reasoning abilities, students in all three fields improved the quality of their everyday reasoning. This shows that reasoning skills can be taught and suggests that such teaching can help people change the way they think about uncertainty in everyday life.

Assessing Piaget's Theory

What do *knowing* and *thinking* mean? How do we establish the "highest reaches" of cognitive development? Measuring these things by a person's

ability to solve problems (like the pendulum problem) or to conserve volume defines cognition in terms of mathematical and scientific thinking. This is a narrow perspective, which "conveys a view of the individual as living in a timeless world of abstract rules" (Gilligan, 1987, p. 67).

Furthermore, one-third to one-half of American adults never seem to attain the stage of formal operations as measured by the pendulum problem and volume conservation (Kohlberg & Gilligan, 1971; Papalia, 1972). Even by late adolescence or adulthood not everyone is capable of abstract thought.

Also, the Piagetian view does not consider the importance of other aspects of intelligence. It does not allow for practical intelligence—the ability to handle real-world problems or the wisdom that helps people cope with an often chaotic world. Nor would it tend to foster such "nonscientific" subjects as history, languages, writing, and the arts. In fact, as more psychologists have defined cognition in Piaget's terms, more educators have emphasized scientific subjects and taken less interest in the humanities. Piaget's definition of cognitive maturity is important; but formal reasoning is not the only—or even the most prominent—aspect of mature thinking.

ADOLESCENT EGOCENTRISM

Those totally egocentric beings whose interest extended not much farther than the nipple have developed, by adolescence, into people who can solve complex problems, analyze moral dilemmas, and envision ideal societies. Yet in some ways, adolescents' thought often remains immature. They tend to be extremely critical (especially of authority figures), argumentative, self-conscious, self-centered, indecisive, and apparently hypocritical—characteristics that still reflect some egocentrism.

The psychologist David Elkind (1984) has described several typical adolescent behaviors that indicate egocentric thinking. Let's consider them.

Finding Fault with Authority Figures

Adolescents have a new ability to imagine an ideal world. They realize that the people they once nearly worshiped fall far short of their ideal, and they feel compelled to say so—often. Parents who do not take this criticism personally but rather look at it as a necessary stage in teenagers' cognitive and social development will be able to answer

Even when a parent's viewpoint is valid, an adolescent's egocentrism often leads to argumentativeness. Those people who once seemed so perfect—the teenager's parents—are now handy targets for criticism. *(Erika Stone)*

such comments matter-of-factly (and with a touch of humor), indicating that nothing—and nobody (not even a teenager!)—is perfect.

Argumentativeness

Adolescents want to practice their new ability to see the many nuances in an issue. If adults encourage and take part in arguments about principles while carefully avoiding discussion of personality, they can help young people stretch their reasoning ability without getting embroiled in family feuding.

Self-Consciousness

Hearing his parents whispering, Dale "knows" that they are talking about him; and when Mesha passes some boys laughing raucously, she "knows" that they are ridiculing her. The extreme self-consciousness of adolescents can be explained by the concept of the *imaginary audience:* an observer who exists only in their own minds and who is as concerned with their thoughts and behaviors as they are themselves.

Adolescents can put themselves into the mind of someone else—they can think about someone else's thinking. Since they have trouble distinguishing what is interesting to them from what is interesting to someone else, however, they assume that everyone else is thinking about the same thing they are thinking about—themselves.

The imaginary audience stays with us to a certain degree in adulthood. Who among us, for ex-

ample, has not agonized over what to wear to an event—thinking that others present will actually care what clothes we have on—and then realized that most people were so busy thinking about the impression *they* were making that they hardly noticed our carefully chosen outfit at all! Because this kind of self-consciousness is especially agonizing in adolescence, Elkind emphasizes the importance of adults' avoiding any public criticism or ridicule of young teenagers.

Self-Centeredness

Elkind uses the term *personal fable* for the conviction that we are special, that our experience is unique, and that we are not subject to the natural rules that govern the rest of the world. This egocentric belief accounts for much self-destructive behavior by young teenagers who think that they are magically protected from harm. Amanda thinks that *she* cannot get pregnant; Tony thinks that *he* cannot get killed on the highway; teenagers who experiment with drugs think that *they* cannot get hooked. "These things happen only to other people, not to me" is the unconscious assumption that helps explain much adolescent risk taking. Young people have to maintain a sense of being special while realizing that they are not exempt from the natural order of things.

Indecisiveness

Teenagers have trouble making up their minds about even the simplest things because they are suddenly aware of the multiplicity of choices in virtually every aspect of life.

Apparent Hypocrisy

Adolescents often do not recognize the difference between expressing an ideal and working toward it. Thus Will marches against pollution while littering along the way, and Beth becomes aggressive while protesting for peace. Part of growing up involves the realization that "thinking does *not* make it so," that values have to be acted upon to bring about change.

The more adolescents talk about their personal theories and listen to those of other people, the sooner they arrive at a mature level of thinking (Looft, 1971). As their thought processes mature, they are better able to think about their own identities, to form adult relationships, and to determine how and where they fit into society.

MORAL REASONING: KOHLBERG'S LEVELS OF MORALITY

Obviously, a person cannot have a moral code based on ideals before developing a mind that is capable of imagining ideals. In Kohlberg's theory (introduced in Chapter 8), moral reasoning is a function of cognitive development. Moral development generally continues in adolescence, as the ability to think abstractly lets young people understand universal moral principles. Of course, advanced cognition does not *guarantee* advanced morality (intelligence and evil are too often linked), but, according to Kohlberg, it must *exist* for moral development to take place.

Adolescents apply moral reasoning to many kinds of problems, from lofty social issues to personal choices. Just as not all adolescents are at Piaget's stage of formal operations, not all of them are on the same rung of Kohlberg's moral ladder (see Table 8-3 in Chapter 8). In Kohlberg's view, it is the reasoning underlying the conclusion someone reaches in response to a moral problem, not the conclusion itself, that indicates the person's stage of moral development. Adolescents may be found at each of Kohlberg's three levels.

Most adolescents—like most adults—seem to be at Kohlberg's conventional level of moral development, level II, which contains stages 3 and 4. They have internalized the standards of others, and they conform to social conventions, support

the status quo, and think in terms of doing the right thing to please others or to obey the law. As we listen to law-and-order political speeches, we realize how many adults are at stage 4.

Only a small number of people seem to attain level III, postconventional morality. At level III, which may be attained in adolescence or adulthood, people can look at two socially accepted standards and choose the one that seems right to them. But even people who have achieved a high level of cognitive development do not always reach a comparably high level of moral development. This is because other factors besides cognition affect moral reasoning. Thus, a certain level of cognitive development is *necessary* but not *sufficient* for a comparable level of moral development.

How Adolescents at Different Levels React to Kohlberg's Dilemmas

In Kohlberg's theory, it is the reasoning underlying a person's response to a moral dilemma, not the answer itself, which indicates a person's stage of development. Let us see how young people at all three levels respond to questions about the value of human life (Kohlberg, 1968).

Preconventional Level. Stage 1: When Tommy, aged 10, is asked, "Is it better to save the life of one important person or a lot of unimportant people?" he says, "All the people that aren't important because one man just has one house, maybe a lot of furniture, but a whole bunch of people have an awful lot of furniture."

He seems to be confusing the value of people with the value of their property, and since *many* people have more property than just *one* person, he believes it is better to save their lives.

Stage 2: At age 13, Tommy is asked about "mercy killing": Should a doctor kill a fatally ill woman who requests death because of pain? He answers, "Maybe it would be good to put her out of her pain; she'd be better off that way. But the husband wouldn't want it; it's not like an animal. If a pet dies, you can get along without it—it isn't something you really need. Well, you can get a new wife, but it's not really the same."

He thinks of the woman's value in terms of what she can do for her husband.

Conventional Level. Stage 3: At 16, Tommy answers the question about mercy killing by saying, "It might be best for her, but her husband—it's a human life—not like an animal; it just doesn't have the same relationship that a human being does to a family."

He identifies with the husband's distinctively human empathy and love, but he still does not seem to realize that the woman's life would have value even if her husband did not love her or even if she had no husband.

Stage 4: Richard, aged 16, answers by saying, "I don't know. In one way, it's murder; it's not a right or privilege of humans to decide who shall live and who should die. God put life into everybody on earth, and you're taking away something from that person that came directly from God, and you're destroying something that is very sacred; it's in a way part of God, and it's almost destroying a part of God when you kill a person."

He sees life as sacred because it was created by God, an authority.

Postconventional Level. Stage 5: At 20, Richard says: "There are more and more people in the medical profession who think it is a hardship on everyone, the person, the family, when you know they are going to die. When a person is kept alive by an artificial lung or kidney, it's more like being a vegetable than being a human. If it's her own choice, I think there are certain rights and privileges that go along with being a human being."

He now defines the value of life relative to other values: equal and universal human rights, concern for the quality of life, and concern for practical consequences.

Stage 6: At age 24, Richard answers, "A human life takes precedence over any other moral or legal value, whoever it is. A human life has inherent value whether or not it is valued by a particular individual."

Richard now sees the value of human life as absolute, not as derived from or dependent on social or divine authority.

Kohlberg maintains that moral thinking is universal, transcending cultural boundaries. Other research, however, suggests that culture exerts a major influence on moral reasoning (see Box 12-2 in Chapter 12 for an example of the Chinese perspective). And although both Piaget and Kohlberg considered parents minimally important in helping their children's moral development, recent research has found that, on the contrary, parents can make a major contribution in this area.

The most effective way to help children and adolescents move to higher levels of moral reasoning seems to be to give them ample opportunities to talk about, interpret, and enact moral dilemmas and to expose them to people at a level of moral thinking slightly higher than their own present level. In a study of 63 family triads (mother, father, and child from grades 1, 4, 7, and 10), Walker and Taylor (1991) found that parents could help their children reason at higher levels. These parents were asked to talk with their children about two dilemmas—a hypothetical one and an actual one from the child's own life, which the child described—most commonly, one about friendships, fighting, or honesty.

The young people who developed the most over a 2-year period had parents who used humor and praise, who listened to the children, asked for their opinions, and in other ways encouraged them to participate. These parents asked clarifying questions, reworded answers, and checked to be sure the children understood the issues (as in the Socratic style of questioning). They tended to reason at a slightly higher level than their children were currently at, in a style reminiscent of scaffolding, or of Vygotsky's notion of "zone of proximal development" (see Chapter 6).

On the other hand, the children who progressed the least had parents who either lectured about their own opinions or challenged their children's opinions by questioning and contradicting them, making the children feel defensive or under attack. Moral development arises from both cognitive and emotional bases, and parents can help their children in both domains.

Carol Gilligan (1982) maintains that Kohlberg's approach to moral development is oriented toward values that are generally more important to males than to females, and that it fails to take into account girls' and women's major concerns and perspectives. Recent research confirms Gilligan's (1982) findings of gender differences in moral reasoning (discussed in Chapter 12) and suggests that such differences may show up in early adolescence (see Box 10-4).

Progress to the highest levels of moral thinking seems to depend on appreciating the relative nature of moral standards. Adolescents need to understand that every society evolves its own definition of right and wrong and that the values of one culture may seem shocking to another. Many young people discover arguments about morality when they enter the wider world of high school or college and meet people whose values, culture, and ethnic background differ from their own.

BOX 10-4   FOOD FOR THOUGHT

GENDER DIFFERENCES IN MORAL DEVELOPMENT

Morality has at least two major dimensions: justice with regard to individual rights, and care elicited by a sense of responsibility in relationships. Kohlberg's theory of moral reasoning focuses on the first dimension, which seems to be a more male-oriented point of view, whereas Gilligan has developed a different way of looking at morality, one that seems to fit in more with a female viewpoint.

Some recent research seems to bear out this dichotomy and to suggest that it shows up in early adolescence (Skoe & Gooden, 1993). Forty-six girls and boys aged 11 and 12 years old were interviewed using a new technique, the ethic-of-care interview. These interviews incorporate one real-life conflict introduced by the adolescent, along with three hypothetical dilemmas involving family and friends. One, for example, asked what a hypothetical young person should do if "Nicole" or "Jason" has accepted a friend's dinner invitation—and then receives an invitation from another friend to see a favorite rock band (from good seats!) on the same evening.

When the students were scored according to five ethic-of-care levels (see Table 10-6), girls scored higher than boys. The girls generated more personal real-life dilemmas (those involving a specific person or group of people whom the subject knows well), whereas boys were more likely to talk about moral conflicts involving people they did not know well, institutions, or issues intrinsic to the self. Girls also tended to be more concerned than boys about maintaining friendships and not hurting other people. The boys were more likely to be concerned about themselves, emphasizing, for example, staying out of trouble.

There seems to be a developmental progression in the ethic of care, with older subjects scoring higher than younger ones (Skoe & Gooden, 1993). Since research on the ethic-of-care dimension is fairly new, further study is needed to determine whether people do, in fact, become more responsible as they mature and whether their statements about care are reflected in their actions.

TABLE 10-6

Ethics-of-Care Levels

Levels	Description	Example
1: Survival	Caring for self, with the aim of ensuring one's happiness and avoiding suffering or being hurt.	"Maybe Nicole should tell Janice that she wants to go to a rock band and maybe she could go to Janice's place some other time."
1.5: Transition from survival to responsibility	A new understanding of the connection between self and others, along with concept of selfishness. Although aware of needs of others, care of self is still uppermost.	"Jason should go to his friend who asked him first, because they might not want to ask you ever again if you go with your other friend."
2: Goodness	Caring for others, elaborating the concept of responsibility. "Right" is defined by church, parents, society, etc. Conflict arises over issue of hurting.	"Nicole might be able to go to Janice's house for dinner and to the concert with Pam, or she should invite Janice over for the next night. She wouldn't want to hurt either one's feelings."
2.5: Transition from goodness to truth in relationships	Reconsideration of relationship between self and other: is it "good" to protect others at one's own expense? More flexibility, thoughtfulness, and struggle with dilemmas.	No children scored at this level.
3: Caring for both self and others	Focus on dynamics of relationships through a new understanding of the interconnection between others and self. Condemns hurt and exploitation, takes responsibility for choices.	No children scored at this level.

SOURCE: Adapted from Skoe & Gooden, 1993.

SECONDARY SCHOOL

THE TRANSITION TO JUNIOR HIGH OR HIGH SCHOOL

Urie Bronfenbrenner's *ecological approach* (see Chapter 1) emphasizes the interaction between the various environments in a child's life. This approach to development in context helps us to understand some of the issues that arise in early adolescence, like the move out of elementary school.

Patterns of Transition

At the end of sixth grade, most American children leave the familiar surroundings of a small elementary school to enter a junior high school with many more students and a more impersonal setting in which teachers, classrooms, and classmates change constantly throughout the day. In 3 more years they move again, to an even larger high school. This typical sequence is known as the *6-3-3 pattern*. A few children follow the *8-4 pattern*—staying in elementary school through eighth grade and then going directly to high school.

The second pattern may well be better, since a number of stresses are associated with the more typical sequence. One 5-year longitudinal study followed 594 white students in the Milwaukee public schools from sixth through tenth grades, comparing students in the 6-3-3 pattern with those in the 8-4 pattern (Blyth, Simmons, & Carlton-Ford, 1983). Researchers looked at students' self-esteem, social adjustment (based on extracurricular activity), academic progress (by grade-point average and performance on achievement tests), and perception of the "anonymity" of their schools (how much they felt other people knew them).

Students who went to junior high school in seventh grade had more problems than those who did not leave elementary school until ninth grade. Girls were especially vulnerable.

Effects of the Transition

Both boys and girls in the 6-3-3 pattern had a decrease in grade-point averages (GPA), took less part in extracurricular activities, and saw their schools as more anonymous. Furthermore, the girls' self-esteem dropped, an effect that persisted into tenth grade (Blyth et al., 1983).

Gender-related Causes

Why do girls have more problems? One clue emerges from a study that found that the more life changes are taking place in a student's life, the more likely both GPA and extracurricular participation are to decrease for both sexes and the more likely girls' self-esteem is to drop (Simmons, Burgeson, Carlton-Ford, & Blyth, 1987).

Girls usually enter puberty sooner than boys and begin to date earlier, making it more likely that they will experience "life-change overload." Furthermore, there is more emphasis on girls' looks and popularity, and they may miss the security of being with old friends. Other research, too, has shown that girls react more negatively than boys to stress in adolescence, unlike childhood, when males are more vulnerable.

School-related Causes

Some of the negative changes associated with this transition may result from a mismatch between the needs of adolescents and the characteristics of the new school. Typically, junior high school students have fewer opportunities to make decisions than do elementary school students; they have less personal, less positive relationships with their teachers; they are more likely to be grouped by ability, a practice that increases competitiveness and concerns about evaluation; and their classwork often requires lower-level cognitive skills than did their work in earlier grades. Furthermore, since junior high teachers tend to judge students by a higher standard, this often results in lowered grades; and since grades are a powerful predictor of self-confidence, a drop in grades can lead to a drop in self-esteem (Eccles et al., 1993).

Home-related Causes

Another factor that can affect adjustment to the new school status is a change in parents' work status. One study found that when parents had either been demoted or laid off at about the same time that their children were moving into junior high school, these young adolescents had a hard time adjusting to their new school status. They had more trouble getting along with other students and were more disruptive in school than were youngsters from stable families or families in which a parent had just been rehired or promoted. They had even more problems than did children whose parents had been laid off permanently during the two years of this study (Flanagan & Eccles, 1993).

These high school graduates are taking an important step toward their future careers. Dropping out of school does not guarantee poverty, but dropouts do have to scramble harder to start a career. Today, more Americans than ever graduate from high school, an increase over previous generations that results from many causes—a general widening of educational opportunities, encouragement of minority-group students, and financial aid programs for students from low-income families. *(Spencer Grant/Photo Researchers)*

Total comfort and complete stability, of course, are not only impossible to achieve at any age but also undesirable. Throughout life, we grow and develop as we learn to cope with challenges. We do this best, however, if we can deal with one change at a time. Although this is not always possible to provide, educators and families can focus on designing environments for early adolescents that will help them meet the needs and desires special to this developmental stage. This may involve opportunities for decision making, participation in rule making, continued close relationships with adults both within and outside the family, and a level of independence appropriate for their age and level of development.

HIGH SCHOOL TODAY

High school is the central organizing experience in most adolescents' lives. It offers the chance to learn new information, master new skills, and sharpen old ones; to preview career choices; to take part in sports; and to get together with friends. It widens young people's intellectual and social horizons as it combines encounters with peers and a variety of adults. It also provides an important life transition as young people move from the security of the simpler world of childhood to a large-scale organizational environment.

The social, vocational, and athletic functions of high school are important, but its primary focus continues to be on basic academic subjects. During the past two decades standardized test scores

fell, most dramatically in vocabulary and reading. One analysis attributed this decline to a decreased emphasis on academics (Rock, Ekstrom, Goertz, Hilton, & Pollack, 1985). However, another reason seems to be the broader base of students who now go to high school. The National Commission on Excellence in Education (1983) found that the average high school or college *graduate* today is not as well educated as the average graduate of previous generations, when fewer people finished high school or college. However, the average *citizen* today is better educated than the average citizen of the past.

In response to concern over falling academic performance, the 1980s and 1990s have seen a greater emphasis on basic academic subjects. More students are studying foreign languages (Maeroff, 1984), but some observers still believe that American high school students do not study as much science and mathematics as they should (National Center for Education Statistics [NCES], 1984).

What makes a high school good? Research points to such factors as an active, energetic principal; an orderly, unoppressive atmosphere; teachers who take part in making decisions; a principal and teachers with high expectations for students; an emphasis on academics (as opposed to athletics and other extracurricular activities); and frequent monitoring of students' performance (Linney & Seidman, 1989).

Today, more than three-fourths of Americans who are 25 years old and older (76.5 percent) have graduated from high school; some finished at the usual age, and others earned their diplomas later

(U.S. Bureau of the Census, 1988). This increase stems from many causes: a general widening of educational opportunities, encouragement of minority-group students, and financial aid programs for students from low-income families. Still, the United States lags behind several other countries in graduation rates of younger adults (see Figure 10-3).

HOME INFLUENCES ON ACHIEVEMENT IN HIGH SCHOOL

Even though adolescents are more independent than elementary school children and are less likely to look to their parents for direct help with schoolwork, more subtle home influences still affect how well they do in school.

Parents' Interest

A survey of more than 30,000 high school seniors in more than 1000 schools showed that the students with the best grades tend to be those whose parents are most involved in their children's lives (NCES, 1985; see Table 10-7). This is particularly true of fathers, whose involvement is more variable than that of mothers: in general, the more involved a father is, the better his children fare. In this survey, 85 percent of the A students but only 64 percent of the D students had fathers who kept close track of their progress in school.

These correlational findings do not prove that parents' involvement improves students' grades. A cause-and-effect relationship may, in fact, work the other way: that is, children who do well in school may spur their parents' interest. But it seems more likely that parents' involvement and concern stimulate their children to do better in school.

The parents of students who do the best are interested in more than homework and grades. They make time to talk to their children, to know what they are doing, and to be available. They go to PTA meetings. They take the children seriously both in and out of school, and the children reward that interest. Three-fourths of the youngsters with top grades in the NCES (1985) study had parents who talked with them almost every day, compared with only 45 percent of the D students.

Parenting Styles

Several studies of about 6400 California high school students compared their achievement based

on their parents' fitting into one of the following child-rearing styles:

Authoritative parents tell adolescents to look at both sides of issues, admit that children sometimes know more than parents, talk about politics, and welcome teenagers' participation in family decisions. Students receive praise and freedom if they get good grades; poor grades bring encouragement to try harder, offers of help, and loss of freedom. *Authoritarian parents* tell adolescents not to argue with or question adults and tell them they will "know better when they are grown up." Good grades bring admonitions to do even better, and poor grades upset parents, who then punish by reducing allowances or "grounding." *Permissive par-*

FIGURE 10-3

High school graduation rates. Although the United States boasts a higher rate of high school graduation for adults aged 25 to 64 than seven other industrialized countries, American rates have lagged behind for younger adults. The high rates among American minority groups explain the drop in part, and some observers recommend more minority-group and more male teachers in the nation's schools. (*Source:* U.S. Department of Education, 1992.)

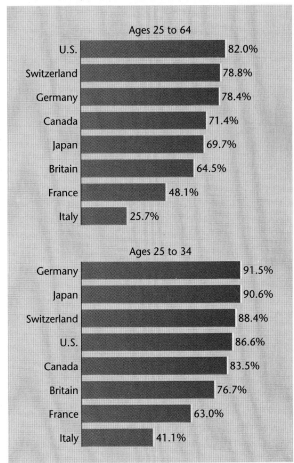

Ages 25 to 64

U.S.	82.0%
Switzerland	78.8%
Germany	78.4%
Canada	71.4%
Japan	69.7%
Britain	64.5%
France	48.1%
Italy	25.7%

Ages 25 to 34

Germany	91.5%
Japan	90.6%
Switzerland	88.4%
U.S.	86.6%
Canada	83.5%
Britain	76.7%
France	63.0%
Italy	41.1%

TABLE 10-7

Parents' Involvement and High School Students' Grades				
	Self-Reported Grades			
Survey Item	Mostly A's	Mostly B's	Mostly C's	Mostly D's
Mother keeps close track of how well child does in school.	92%	89%	84%	80%
Father keeps close track of how well child does in school.	85%	79%	69%	64%
Parents almost always know child's whereabouts.	88%	81%	72%	61%
Child talks with mother or father almost every day.	75%	67%	59%	45%
Parents attend PTA meetings at least once in a while.	25%	22%	20%	15%
Child lives in household with both parents.	80%	71%	64%	60%

Note: This table, based on a survey of more than 30,000 high school seniors, shows the percentage of students with various grade averages who gave positive answers to each survey item. In each instance, the higher the grades were, the more likely the parents were to be involved with the child.
SOURCE: National Center for Education Statistics, 1985.

ents do not care about grades, make no rules about watching television, do not attend school programs, and neither help with nor check their children's homework. (Permissive parents may be neglectful and uncaring, or caring and concerned but convinced that children should be responsible for their own lives.)

Children of authoritative parents tend to do better in school than do those of parents in the other two groups (Dornbusch, Ritter, Leiderman, Roberts, & Fraleigh, 1987; Steinberg, Lamborn, Dornbusch, & Darling, 1992; Steinberg & Darling, in press). Students who get low grades are more likely to have authoritarian or permissive parents or parents who waffle between styles. Inconsistency is associated with the lowest grades, possibly because children who do not know what to expect from their parents become anxious and less able to concentrate on their work. A particularly strong influence is parents' involvement with their children's education as shown by going to school programs, helping to select courses, and monitoring progress.

Ethnic differences showed up among the students, confirming the basis of the ecological approach to development in context (Steinberg, Dornbusch, & Brown, 1992). The above relationships hold up for white teenagers. But Asian American students, whose parents tend to be authoritarian, still do well, largely, it seems, because of the influence of peers, who also value academic achievement. However, Latino and African American students—even those of authoritative parents—do not do as well in school, apparently because there is little support from their peers for academic achievement. Parents cannot always overcome influences in the larger environment. If young people feel that shining in school will make them less popular with their peers or will not result in life success, they will not be motivated to succeed in school.

This work suggests another influence of context. The lower school achievement of children of single parents, who tend to be more permissive, may well be due to the style of parenting, not the single-parent status itself.

Socioeconomic Status

So many educators consider socioeconomic status so important to school achievement that the association between the two is often taken for granted. However, a statistical analysis of 101 studies (K. R. White, 1982) found that socioeconomic status (traditionally defined by income, occupation, and education) is only weakly correlated with academic achievement. The correlation decreases as students get older, partly because schools provide enriching experiences and partly because many students have dropped out—and dropping out is more common among both low achievers and students from low-income homes.

The major influence on achievement is a student's home atmosphere: how much reading matter is available, how the parents feel about education, what they want for their children, what they do for and with their children, how and how much they talk to their children, and how stable the family is. Both rich and poor families can create a climate that fosters learning. "Even though family background does have a strong relationship to achievement, it may be *how* parents rear their children . . . and not the parents' occupation, income, or education that really makes the difference" (K. R. White, 1982, p. 471).

DROPPING OUT OF HIGH SCHOOL

Students who leave school before receiving a diploma make a crucial decision that reduces their opportunities in the future. Dropping out of high school does not guarantee poverty, but dropouts do have to scramble harder to start a career—if they ever have one. Many employers require a high school diploma, and many jobs require skills that are based on a solid education.

Who Drops Out?

In 1991, 8.9 percent of white people aged 16 to 24 in the United States were not in school and had never received a high school degree. For African Americans, the percentage was 13.6 percent. Both these percentages represented an increase in school graduation rates over the previous 19 years. However, the dropout rates for Latinos—35.3 percent in 1991—was roughly the same as it had been in 1972 (see Figure 10-4). Among the possible reasons for the high Latino dropout rates are language difficulties, financial pressures, and a culture that puts family first. Almost one-half of dropouts leave in the eleventh grade, almost one-third in the senior year, and about one-fourth in the tenth grade. Boys are more likely to drop out than girls ("Students' Learning," 1990).

Asian American students have the lowest dropout rate, followed by (in increasing order) white, African American, Latino, and Native American students. When socioeconomic status is held constant, however, the large difference among white, African American, and Latino young people narrows or even vanishes. In fact, at equal socioeconomic levels, black students' attainment is higher than white students' (NCES, 1987). Thus although socioeconomic status does not seem to af-

fect performance while students are actually in school, it does make a difference in whether they stay there long enough to graduate.

Why Do They Drop Out?

The reasons dropouts give for their decision are not surprising, although they do not tell the whole story. When asked 2 years later why they had dropped out, one group of young men mentioned poor grades (36 percent), not liking school (25 percent), being expelled or suspended (13 percent), or having to support a family (26 percent). Women attributed dropping out to marriage or plans to marry (31 percent), feeling that "school is not for me" (31 percent), poor grades (30 percent), pregnancy (23 percent), and a job (11 percent) (NCES, 1983).*

It is hard to pin down the reasons for dropping

*The figures total more than 100 percent because some respondents gave more than one reason for dropping out.

FIGURE 10-4
High school dropout rates. Although rates have declined for white and African American students, they have remained high for Latino students, who often leave school to help support their families. (*Source:* U.S. Department of Education, 1992.)

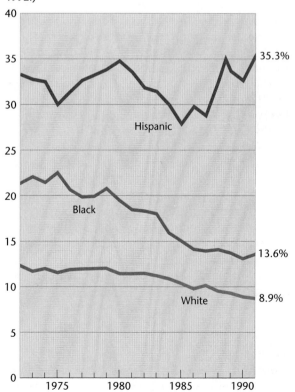

out. More than half the women said that they left because of pregnancy or marriage—but they may have become pregnant or gotten married because they were not doing well or were not interested in school. The men's explanations tell us just as little. Some researchers have attributed dropping out to lack of motivation and low self-esteem, minimal parental encouragement of education, teachers' low expectations, and disciplinary problems at home and at school (Rule, 1981).

Which students are most likely to drop out of school? Those whose parents are poorly educated and in low-level jobs and who are in large single-parent families are 3 to 5 times more likely to drop out than children in more privileged circumstances (NCES, 1987). Even in more affluent families, teenagers from single-parent and remarried families are more likely to drop out than are those living with both parents, according to a study of more than 13,000 high school sophomores (Zimiles & Lee, 1991). A gender effect showed up in this study: an adolescent living with a parent of the same sex is less likely to drop out when the custodial parent has not remarried and is more likely to do so in a stepfamily. This may be related to the strong attachment that often develops between a child and a same-sex single parent, a relationship that may be disrupted when the parent remarries.

Dropping out in high school can sometimes be predicted as early as the seventh grade. In a longitudinal study, 475 seventh-graders were followed for 5 years. The dropout rates were higher for those students who, when first seen, showed aggressive behavior *and* did poorly in school (Cairns, Cairns, & Neckerman, 1989). More than 80 percent of the boys and 47 percent of the girls who showed this behavioral combination in seventh grade dropped out before finishing eleventh grade. Being unpopular with peers in seventh grade did *not* predict dropping out, probably because young people tend to have friends who are like themselves (that is, at similar risk for dropping out or graduating).

Other factors associated with dropping out include having repeated a grade in elementary school, working more than 15 hours a week while in high school, being married, having a child, and such signs of antisocial behavior as suspension, probation, or trouble with the law (NCES, 1987).

What Happens to Dropouts?

Dropouts have trouble getting jobs; the work they do get is in low-level, poor-paying occupations;

and they are more likely to lose their jobs. In one national study of high school dropouts, 27 percent of males and 31 percent of females were looking for work; 32 percent of the women were not looking for work because they were full-time homemakers. Of those who were working, only about 14 percent of the men and 3 percent of the women had jobs that required technical skills. Typical jobs were waiting on tables, manual labor, factory work, clerking in stores, baby-sitting, clerical work, and farm work. More than half regretted leaving school very soon after they had done so, and only a small percentage were taking part in educational programs (NCES, 1987).

How Can Dropping Out Be Prevented?

Society suffers when many young people do not finish school. Dropouts are more likely to end up on welfare, to be unemployed, and to become involved with drugs, crime, and delinquency. In addition, the loss of taxable income burdens the public treasury (NCES, 1987). Both public and private organizations have developed a variety of programs to encourage young people to stay in school.

One successful federally funded program, Upward Bound, was established in 1964 and by 1988 had seen 80 percent of its graduates go on to 4-year colleges. Students from low-income families whose parents and siblings did not go to college are selected on the basis of school records, teachers' recommendations, a personal interview, and an assessment of applicants' and parents' commitment to the program. The program stresses high expectations; has a rigorous curriculum; and offers tutoring, peer counseling, and counseling on drug abuse, self-esteem, study skills, preparing for the Scholastic Aptitude Tests (SATs), applying to colleges, and planning careers (Wells, 1988).

It is possible to prevent dropping out. With commitment by government, educators, and parents, millions of young people can be helped to have a brighter future.

DEVELOPING A CAREER

"Is there life after high school? Where will this education lead to? What kind of work will I do? Do I need still more education?" These are the questions that adolescents ask themselves with more urgency as their high school years come to an end.

Volunteer work is one way to preview the rewards and frustrations of a particular career. If this teenage tutor finds teaching rewarding, she may pursue a career in education. *(David M. Grossman/Photo Researchers)*

STAGES IN VOCATIONAL PLANNING

At age 6, Sally's daughter Nancy wanted to be a ballerina. Then a ninth-grade honors biology class awakened her interest in science. In high school, she considered studying anthropology or sociology (not knowing exactly what either field was); later, in college, she ended up majoring in environmental studies. An internship at a natural history museum (as part of her college requirements) inspired her to study for a doctorate in biology; and after earning her Ph.D., she became the curator of natural sciences at a different museum.

Nancy's progression of goals was typical, following three classic stages in career planning: (1) the fantasy period, (2) the tentative period, and (3) the realistic period (Ginzberg et al., 1951). During the *fantasy* period, in the early school years, children's career choices are active and exciting rather than realistic, and their decisions are emotional rather than practical. The *tentative* period, which comes at puberty, ushers in a somewhat more realistic effort by youngsters to match interests with abilities and values. By the end of high school, students enter the *realistic* period and can plan for the appropriate education to meet their career requirements.

Many young people, however, are still not realistic in late adolescence. In one study, more than 6000 high school seniors in Texas were asked to name their top three career choices and to report on their interests and their educational plans. At a time when they had to make crucial choices about education and work, these students showed very limited knowledge about occupations. Not surprisingly, they tended to know more about their first career choice and increasingly less about the next two choices. But even of those who felt that they had a good understanding of their first career choice, only about half were planning to get the right amount of education. Some seemed bent on schooling that would leave them overeducated for their chosen careers, and others were not planning for enough training. Furthermore, most of the students did not seem to be making a good match between their career choices and their own interests (Grotevant & Durrett, 1980).

INFLUENCES ON VOCATIONAL PLANNING

How do adolescents make career choices? Many factors enter in, including individual ability and personality; education; socioeconomic, racial, or ethnic background; societal values; and the accidents of particular life experiences. (See Box 10-5 for a discussion of part-time work for high school students.) Two important influences are parents and gender. Let's consider each of these.

Parents

Parents' encouragement and financial support influence their children's aspirations and achievement. If parents do not encourage children to pursue higher education and do not help them financially, it is much harder for the children.

BOX 10-5   TAKE A STAND

SHOULD TEENAGERS HOLD PART-TIME JOBS?

The traditional American ethic gives a quick, unqualified "yes" to the question, "Does work help adolescents develop?" But some recent research makes us wonder whether "common sense" is really so sensible, whether part-time work has real value for high school students. Some students, of course, have to work to help support their families, and until society moves to help these families, for these students the question is academic. But for those who work to earn pocket money, research has shown that the issue is more complex than it appears at first blush.

AGAINST PART-TIME WORK
FOR ADOLESCENTS

1 Teenagers who work are no more independent in making financial decisions than their classmates who do not hold jobs (Greenberger & Steinberg, 1986).
2 Most students who work part time during high school are in low-level, repetitive jobs and do not learn skills that will be useful later in life (Hamilton & Crouter, 1980).
3 Working teenagers are not likely to earn any more money as adults than those who did not hold jobs during high school (Greenberger & Steinberg, 1986).
4 Work seems to undermine performance in school, especially

for teenagers who work more han 15 or 20 hours per week. Grades, involvement in school, and attendance decline. Working more than 15 hours a week is related to dropping out of school (NCES, 1987). Since education is so important as preparation for careers and for life, working at an early age may interfere with it. It may make more sense to take on a volunteer assignment.
5 Working has hidden costs. Some teenagers spend their earnings on alcohol or drugs, develop cynical attitudes toward work, and cheat or steal from their employers. Teenagers who work tend to spend less time with their families and to feel less close to them. Furthermore, they have little contact with adults on the job, and they are usually placed in gender-stereotyped jobs (Greenberger & Steinberg, 1986; Steinberg, Fegley, & Dornbusch, 1993). When teenagers work long hours, they are less likely to eat breakfast, exercise, get enough sleep, or have enough leisure time (Bachman & Schulenberg, 1993).

IN FAVOR OF PART-TIME WORK
FOR ADOLESCENTS

1 Paid work teaches young people to handle money responsibly.
2 It helps them develop good work habits, like promptness,

reliability, and efficient management of time (National Commission on Youth, 1980).
3 A good part-time job (one that helps a teenager to master new skills, assume responsibility, and work with people of different ages and backgrounds) helps students learn about a particular field, thus guiding them in choosing a career (National Commission on Youth, 1980).
4 It helps them learn workplace skills, like how to find a job, and how to get along with a variety of people—employers, coworkers, and sometimes the public.
5 By showing adolescents how demanding and difficult the world of work is and how unprepared they are for it, part-time jobs—especially menial ones—sometimes help to motivate young people to continue their education.
6 Some undesirable tendencies of working adolescents may be caused not by working itself but by the factors that motivate some teenagers to take jobs. Some teenagers may want to work because they are uninterested in school, are alienated from their families, and want money to buy drugs and liquor. Their jobs may actually keep them out of trouble by providing legal ways for them to earn money.

Parental encouragement is a better predictor of high ambition than social class. When 2622 sixth-, eighth-, tenth-, and twelfth-grade students—black and white, from all social strata—were asked to describe their own expectations for their education and their fathers' and mothers' expectations for them, more than half the students agreed with the perceived goals of each parent. A greater level of agreement existed between students and their

mothers than between students and their fathers, probably because women have traditionally spent more time with children (T. E. Smith, 1981).

Gender

A woman who entered engineering school at Ohio State University in 1945 was one of only six females in her class. Some 35 years later, women made up about 30 percent of the entering class (R. D. Feldman, 1982). Similar increases have been seen in medicine, law, and other former bastions of male prominence.

But although gender-typing in occupational choice has broken down to a great extent, it is still a factor. Some counselors still steer young people into gender-typed careers on the basis of females' supposed superiority in verbal abilities and males' supposed superiority in mathematics (Matlin, 1987).

However, there is little or no difference between boys and girls in either mathematical or verbal ability (J. S. Hyde, Fennema, & Lamon, 1990; J. Hyde & Linn, 1988). Gender differences in verbal abilities are so small as to be almost meaningless (J. Hyde & Linn, 1988). And overall, males do not have more mathematical ability than females. Females actually excel at computation, neither sex shows better understanding of mathematical concepts, and males' advantage in problem solving does not show up until high school (see Chapter 7). Furthermore, gender differences have decreased in recent years (J. S. Hyde et al., 1990).

Among mathematically gifted seventh- and eighth-grade students some gender differences favoring boys have shown up (Benbow & Stanley, 1980, 1983). But some researchers believe that the findings may reflect differences in socialization, attitudes, and experience with mathematics (Matlin, 1987). Another explanation for gender differences in high school is that more boys than girls drop out of school, thereby removing many low-scoring boys from high school samples. Furthermore, more girls than boys take the SAT, and the girls tend to be drawn from a wider socioeconomic background.

The fact that high school girls begin to perform more poorly than boys at mathematical problem-solving tasks is troublesome, however. Such problem solving is critical for success in many occupations, and people with less developed mathematical skills are not likely to choose careers in such fields as engineering, chemistry, or physics.

Furthermore, girls' lower scores on the mathematics portions of the SAT are a serious disadvantage in applying to college. The tests themselves need to be examined, not only for evidence of gender bias but also to determine whether they require skills that are not being taught well enough in high school (J. S. Hyde et al., 1990). However, the gender disparity in mathematics is not likely to diminish until educators consider remedial math teaching (which would probably help more girls) just as important as remedial reading programs (which reach higher proportions of boys).

Finally, studies published before 1973 showed larger gender differences than more recent research. The differences may have declined as a result of increased flexibility in gender roles. Or perhaps researchers are more likely now than they used to be to publish when they have found *no* significant gender differences. In any case, the small differences that still do show up have no real psychological or educational implications. There is no basis for steering boys and girls toward different careers. It does not matter whether *most* boys are better at mathematics or *most* girls are better at writing; it is how well a particular person solves mathematical problems or writes that will affect the individual's chances of career success.

The choice of a career is closely tied in with a central personality issue during adolescence: the continuing effort to define the self, to discover and mold an identity. The question "Who shall I be?" is very close to "What shall I do?" If we choose a career that we feel is worth doing and one we can do well, we feel good about ourselves. On the contrary, if we feel that it wouldn't matter to anyone whether we did our work or not, or if we feel that we're not very good at it, the core of our emotional well-being can be threatened.

How adolescents' sense of identity develops will be discussed in Chapter 11, along with other personality issues.

SUMMARY

ADOLESCENCE: A DEVELOPMENTAL TRANSITION

▪ Adolescence is a developmental transition between childhood and adulthood. It begins with puberty, a process that leads to sexual maturity, when a person is able to reproduce.

▪ The end of adolescence is not clear-cut in western societies; no single sign indicates that adulthood has been reached. In some nonwestern cultures, adulthood is regarded as beginning at puberty and is signified by puberty rites, which take a variety of forms.

MATURATION IN ADOLESCENCE

▪ A secular trend is a trend that can be observed over several generations. A secular trend toward earlier attainment of adult height and sexual maturity began about 100 years ago, probably because of improvements in living standards; it seems to have ended in the United States.

▪ Dramatic physiologic changes mark adolescence.

1 Both sexes undergo an adolescent growth spurt: sharp growth in height, weight, and muscular and skeletal development.

2 Primary sex characteristics are the characteristics directly related to reproduction, namely, the female and male reproductive organs. These enlarge and mature during puberty.

3 The secondary sex characteristics include the breasts in females, the broadened shoulders in males, and the adult voices, skin, and growth of body hair characteristic of men and women.

4 Menarche in females occurs at an average age of 12½ in the United States. Males experience sperm in their urine and nocturnal emissions.

▪ An adolescent's rapid body changes and physical appearance affect self-concept and personality. The effect of early or late maturing is particularly pronounced during adolescence but generally disappears in adulthood.

▪ Girls adjust better to menarche if they are prepared for it with accurate information.

HEALTH CONCERNS IN ADOLESCENCE

▪ Adolescents have low rates of disability and chronic disease. Their tendency to take risks is reflected in their high death rates from accidents, homicide, and suicide. Health problems such as obesity, anorexia nervosa, bulimia nervosa, drug abuse, and sexually transmitted diseases affect a sizable number of adolescents.

ASPECTS OF INTELLECTUAL DEVELOPMENT IN ADOLESCENCE

▪ Many adolescents attain Piaget's stage of formal operations, which is characterized by the ability to think abstractly.

1 People in the stage of formal operations can engage in hypothetical-deductive reasoning. They can think in terms of possibilities, deal flexibly with problems, and test hypotheses.

2 Since experience plays a more important part in the attainment of this cognitive stage than in that of previous Piagetian stages, not all people become capable of formal operations.

▪ Although the adolescent is not egocentric in the sense that a younger child is, adolescents show egocentric tendencies. These include finding fault with authority figures, argumentativeness, self-consciousness, self-centeredness, indecisiveness, and apparent hypocrisy.

▪ Most adolescents are at Kohlberg's conventional level (stages 3 and 4) of moral development. However, some young people in adolescence are at the preconventional stage and some are at the postconventional stage. Gender differences show up in early adolescence.

SECONDARY SCHOOL

▪ Stress is associated with the transition to secondary school, especially in the 6-3-3 pattern and especially for girls.

▪ With the achievement of virtually universal secondary education in the United States, high school is the central organizing experience, intellectually and otherwise, in the lives of most adolescents.

▪ Home atmosphere, parents' involvement, and family relationships appear to make a greater difference than socioeconomic status in how well adolescents do in school.

▪ Although most adolescents graduate from high school, differences exist in who drops out before graduating. It is hard to pin down the precise reason for dropping out. Programs are being developed to prevent it.

DEVELOPING A CAREER

▪ The search for identity is closely linked to vocational choice. Vocational choice is linked to a number of factors including whether or not the adolescent works part time. Part-time work appears to have little educational, social, or occupational benefit.

▪ Parental attitudes and gender also influence educational and vocational aspirations and choices.

KEY TERMS

adolescence (page 342)
puberty (342)
secular trend (346)
adolescent growth spurt (346)
primary sex characteristics (347)
secondary sex characteristics (347)

menarche (347)
obesity (352)
anorexia nervosa (353)
bulimia nervosa (354)
sexually transmitted diseases
(STDs) (357)

formal operations (360)
imaginary audience (363)
personal fable (363)
ecological approach(367)

SUGGESTED READINGS

Byrne, K. (1987).   *A parent's guide to anorexia and bulimia.* New York: Holt. In this sensible and reassuring book, the author, herself the mother of a recovering anorexic, discusses how to identify eating disorders, when to seek professional help, and what to expect from these professionals. She also offers suggestions on how to communicate with the eating-disordered member of the family.

Elkind, D. (1984).   *All grown up and no place to go.* Reading, MA: Addison-Wesley. A thought-provoking book about the difficulties today of being a teenager and raising teenagers. Elkind argues that teenagers are unprepared for the adult challenges they are asked to face, so they exhibit many problem behaviors. The chapter relating formal operational thinking abilities to behaviors such as self-centeredness, self-consciousness, and argumentativeness is outstanding.

Freedman, S. G. (1990).   *Small victories: The real world of a teacher, her students, and their high school.* New York: Harper & Row. This account of a year in the life of a New York City teacher shows what an imaginative, dedicated person can bring to the lives of immigrant students and others who live and go to high school in a rundown inner-city neighborhood. The book also includes portraits of other faculty members as well as students. It leaves the reader with the sense that good teaching is a vocation, not a job.

Greenberger, E., & Steinberg, L. (1986).   *When teenagers work.* New York: Basic Books. An absorbing and controversial analysis of research on the impact that working has on teenagers. The authors conclude that working during the teens entails a number of hidden costs that affect development negatively.

Walker, A., & Parmar, P. (1993).   *Warrior marks: Female genital mutilation and the sexual blinding of women.* New York: Harcourt Brace. An account by a novelist and a filmmaker of their research for, and making of, a documentary film about female genital mutilation. The book includes transcripts of interviews with people either involved with or concerned about the practice, and photographs of people and places.

CHAPTER ELEVEN

PERSONALITY AND SOCIAL DEVELOPMENT IN ADOLESCENCE

This face in the mirror
stares at me
demanding Who are you? What will you become?
And taunting, You don't even know.
Chastened, I cringe and agree
and then
because I'm still young,
I stick out my tongue.

Eve Merriam,
"Conversation with Myself," 1964

■ **THE SEARCH FOR IDENTITY**

Identity versus Identity Confusion
Research on Identity
Achieving Sexual Identity

■ **SOCIAL ASPECTS OF PERSONALITY DEVELOPMENT IN ADOLESCENCE**

Relationships with Parents
Sibling Relationships
Relationships with Peers

■ **TWO PROBLEMS OF ADOLESCENCE**

Teenage Pregnancy
Juvenile Delinquency

■ **A POSITIVE VIEW OF ADOLESCENCE: THREE COHORT STUDIES**

■ **BOXES**

11-1 Food for Thought: Gender Differences in Personality Development
11-2 Practically Speaking: Communicating about Sex
11-3 Window on the World: Preventing Teenage Pregnancy

ASK YOURSELF

■ How do adolescents search for their identity?
■ What sexual practices and attitudes are current among adolescents?
■ How inevitable is "adolescent rebellion," and how are adolescents' attitudes and behavior influenced by parents and peers?

■ What are the causes and consequences of teenage pregnancy and juvenile delinquency?
■ What are these years like for most adolescents?

A central question in the drama of adolescence is "Who am I?" The theme of these years—and a major theme for years to come—is the search for identity: what makes each person an individual unlike any other who has ever lived or will ever live. The question "Who am I?" begins to form in infancy, when babies first discover that they are separate from their mothers. Children begin to find answers as they learn the boundaries of self, shed much of their egocentric thinking, and size up their skills and values in the mirror of the peer group.

The question of selfhood crests in adolescence and is related to physical, cognitive, and social and emotional development. At the age of 15, for example, Meredith has the body of a woman. Now capable of adult sexual behavior and of advanced problem solving, she knows that she will soon be responsible for her own life. How will she choose to live it? What kind of work will she do? What decisions will she make about sexual relationships and other ties? What beliefs and values will she live by?

These choices are not easy, and they are often accompanied by emotional turmoil. Underlying teenagers' alternating high and low spirits are two major preoccupations—identity and intimacy. These years are not easy for parents, either. Adolescents trying their wings are often as erratic and unpredictable as birds taking their first flights from the nest. Chafing at the ties that bind them to an older generation, they often see mothers and fathers as inhibiting more than helpful. Yet while teenagers look to their peers as companions in the struggle for independence, they still turn to their parents for important guidance and emotional support.

In this chapter, we examine some fundamental issues of personality development in adolescence from the perspectives of theory and research. We discuss relationships with peers and parents and how adolescents come to terms with their sexual-

ity. Then we turn to two serious problems, teenage pregnancy and juvenile delinquency. Finally, we look at positive aspects of adolescence—what it is like for most normal young people.

THE SEARCH FOR IDENTITY

The search for identity is a lifelong voyage, launched in childhood and propelled further in adolescence. As Erik Erikson (1950) emphasizes, this effort to make sense of the self and the world is not "a kind of maturational malaise." It is, instead, a healthy, vital process that contributes to the ego strength of the adult. We have already looked at some of the issues that contribute to an adolescent's sense of self, like moral reasoning, achievement in and out of school, and thinking about future careers. Now we explore some of the other conflicts in this struggle which spur personal growth and development.

IDENTITY VERSUS IDENTITY CONFUSION

The chief task of this stage of life, says Erikson (1968), is to resolve the conflict of *identity versus identity confusion*—to become a unique adult with an important role in life. To form an identity, the ego organizes a person's abilities, needs, and desires and helps to adapt them to the demands of society.

Based on his own life (see Chapter 1) and on his research with adolescents in various societies, Erikson concluded that a crucial aspect in the search for identity is deciding on a career. In the previous stage, that of *industry versus inferiority*, a child acquires the skills needed for success in the culture. Now, adolescents need to find ways to use these skills. Rapid physical growth and new genital maturity alert young people to their impending adulthood, and they begin to wonder about their roles in adult society.

Erikson sees the prime danger of this stage as identity (or role) confusion, which can express itself in a young person's taking an excessively long time to reach adulthood (after age 30). (He himself did not resolve his own identity crisis until his mid-twenties.) A certain amount of identity confusion is normal. It accounts for both the chaotic nature of much adolescent behavior and teenagers' painful self-consciousness about their looks.

Cliquishness and intolerance of differences—both hallmarks of adolescence—are defenses against identity confusion, says Erikson. Adolescents may also show confusion by regressing into childishness to avoid resolving conflicts or by committing themselves impulsively to poorly thought-out courses of action. During the *psychosocial moratorium*—the "time out" period that adolescence and youth provide—many people search for commitments to which they can be faithful. Naomi commits herself to working for racial harmony in her community, Raul becomes a vegetarian, Michelle diligently studies the violin. Very often these youthful commitments, which are both ideological and personal, will shape a person's life for many years to come. The extent to which young people can be true to them determines their ability to resolve this crisis.

The fundamental "virtue" that arises from this identity crisis is the *virtue of fidelity*—sustained loyalty, faith, or a sense of belonging to a loved one or to friends and companions. Fidelity also involves identifying with a set of values, an ideology, a religion, a political movement, a creative pursuit, or an ethnic group. Self-identification emerges when young people choose values and people to be loyal to, rather than having accepted them whole-cloth from parents.

Fidelity represents an extensively developed sense of trust. In infancy, it was important to trust in others, especially parents; now it is important to be trustworthy oneself. In addition, adolescents now transfer their trust from their parents to other people, like mentors or loved ones, who can help guide them through life. Love is part of the avenue toward identity, says Erikson. By becoming intimate with another person and sharing thoughts and feelings, the adolescent offers up his or her own tentative identity, sees it reflected in the loved one, and is better able to clarify the self.

Adolescent intimacies differ from mature intimacy, which will involve commitment, sacrifice,

"Who am I?" is the major question of adolescence, as young people search for identity and ponder their life choices. *(Dario Perla/International Stock Photo)*

and compromise. Mature intimacy cannot take place until after a person has achieved a stable identity, says Erikson. But this sequence describes males' development. Erikson's theory considers women's development as a deviation from a male norm. He said that women achieve identity and intimacy at the same time: an adolescent girl puts her identity aside as she prepares to define herself through the man she will marry. This male orientation has brought important criticisms of Erikson's theory. We will now look at one line of research that has explored differences between males' and females' identity development.

RESEARCH ON IDENTITY

Kate, Mark, Nick, and Andrea are all about to graduate from high school. Kate has weighed her interests and talents and has settled on a career in music therapy. After carefully researching colleges, she has applied to three that offer good programs. Mark also knows exactly what he is going to do: his parents have always assumed that he will go into the family business, and he has never given

TABLE 11-1

Criteria for Identity Statuses		
	Position on Occupation and Ideology	
Identity Status	Crisis (Period of Considering Alternatives)	Commitment (Adherence to a Path of Action)
Identity achievement	Present	Present
Foreclosure	Absent	Present
Identity diffusion	Present or absent	Absent
Moratorium	In crisis	Present but vague

SOURCE: Adapted from Marcia, 1980.

much thought to doing anything else. Nick has no idea of what he wants to do, but he is not worried. He figures that he will go to college, have a good time, and see what happens. Andrea has not yet made a decision about her life goals and is agonizing over them. She thinks that she may be interested in something having to do with science, but she is torn between a premedical program and engineering school.

All four of these high school seniors are wrestling with issues of identity formation. What accounts for the differences in the way they are going about it—and in the eventual results?

Identity Statuses: Crisis and Commitment

The psychologist James E. Marcia has expanded and clarified Erikson's theory by identifying several identity statuses and correlating these statuses with other aspects of personality. Marcia defines identity as "an internal, self-constructed, dynamic organization of drives, abilities, beliefs, and individual history" (1980, p. 159). He identified four different statuses according to the presence or absence of crisis and commitment, the two elements that Erikson maintained were crucial to forming identity (see Table 11-1). He then related these identity statuses to various personality characteristics, including anxiety, self-esteem, moral reasoning, and patterns of behavior. The categories are not permanent; they change as people continue to develop (Marcia, 1979).

Marcia defines *crisis* as a period of conscious decision making, and *commitment* as a personal investment in an occupation or a system of beliefs (ideology). To evaluate identity status, Marcia (1966) developed a 30-minute semistructured interview (see Table 11-2).

TABLE 11-2

Identity-Status Interview	
Sample Questions	Typical Answers for the Four Statuses
About occupational commitment: "How willing do you think you'd be to give up going into _____ if something better came along?"	*Identity achievement.* "Well, I might, but I doubt it. I can't see what 'something better' would be for me." *Foreclosure.* "Not very willing. It's what I've always wanted to do. The folks are happy with it and so am I." *Identity diffusion.* "Oh sure. If something better came along, I'd change just like that." *Moratorium.* "I guess that if I knew for sure, I could answer that better. It would have to be something in the general area—something related. . . ."
About ideological commitment: "Have you ever had any doubts about your religious beliefs?"	*Identity achievement.* "Yes, I even started wondering whether there is a god. I've pretty much resolved that now, though. The way it seems to me is . . ." *Foreclosure.* "No, not really; our family is pretty much in agreement on these things." *Identity diffusion.* "Oh, I don't know. I guess so. Everyone goes through some sort of stage like that. But it really doesn't bother me much. I figure that one religion is about as good as another!" *Moratorium.* "Yes, I guess I'm going through that now. I just don't see how there can be a god and still so much evil in the world or . . ."

SOURCE: Adapted from Marcia, 1966.

On the basis of their answers, people are classified into one of the following four categories:

1 *Identity achievement (crisis leading to commitment):* Kate is in this category. She has devoted much thought to important issues in her life (the crisis period), she has made choices, and she now expresses strong commitment to those choices.
2 *Foreclosure (commitment with no crisis):* Mark is in foreclosure. He has made commitments, but instead of questioning them and exploring other possible choices (going through the crisis period), he has accepted other people's plans for his life.
3 *Identity diffusion (no commitment, crisis uncertain):* In a carefree way, Nick has considered various options but so far has actively avoided commitment.
4 *Moratorium (crisis, no commitment):* Andrea, still in crisis, is struggling with a decision, seems to be heading for a commitment, and will probably achieve identity.

Gender Differences in Identity Formation

Sigmund Freud's infamous statement "Biology is destiny" implies that the different patterns of development seen in males and females in almost all cultures are an inevitable result of their anatomical differences. Today, however, psychologists are more likely to believe that "socialization is destiny." The prevailing modern belief is that most differences between males and females arise from societal attitudes and practices, although some research suggests differing rates of maturation between the sexes (see Box 11-1). Whatever the reasons, the sexes differ in the struggle to define identity. Only in recent years have researchers explored the female quest for identity.

Research on Female Identity Formation

Carol Gilligan (1982, 1987; L. M. Brown & Gilligan, 1990) has studied girls and women in several contexts. She has concluded that the female definition of self is less concerned with achieving a separate identity than with relationships with other people. Girls and women judge themselves on their re-

BOX 11-1 FOOD FOR THOUGHT

GENDER DIFFERENCES IN PERSONALITY DEVELOPMENT

Popular wisdom holds that boys and girls develop differently, that girls mature earlier and are more empathic, and that boys are more aggressive. But in 80 years of research about development, this belief has rarely been investigated scientifically. A statistical analysis of 65 studies of personality growth, involving about 9000 subjects, *has* found gender differences (Cohn, 1991). Adolescent girls apparently do mature earlier in some ways. This difference is small in general, most notable in junior high and high school; it declines markedly among college-age adults and disappears entirely among older men and women. This lessening of gender differences may be the result of maturation.

The analysis used research conducted on the Washington University Sentence Completion Test, which consists of 36 sentence stems that respondents have to complete. Examples are: "At times she (he) worried about . . . ," "A woman (man) should always . . ."

Overall, gender differences in personality development favored females. Such differences arose by late childhood, increased at about age 13, and were fairly large throughout adolescence. When boys were still egocentric, girls moved toward social conformity; when boys began to be conformists, girls were becoming more self-aware. It's ironic, then, that boys are often granted earlier dating privileges, independence, and freedom from adult supervision, when it's the girls who are more mature.

Gender differences in personality development seem to stem from differences in boys' and girls' social experiences. The sexes play quite differently, for example. The looser structure of girls' games, which are less rule-bound than those played by boys, may foster the development of moral reasoning. The small groups in which girls play provide more opportunities for conversation and for mimicking adult relationships than do the large groups common in boys' play. Furthermore, children may attach their own meanings to social roles: the competitiveness encouraged in boys may reinforce a tendency toward impulsiveness that all children have, but that is discouraged in girls.

Later in life, both men and women base their moral reasoning on issues related to both justice (as in Kohlberg's theory) and care (as in Gilligan's), supporting this author's belief that "a single path toward maturity exists for both sexes" (Cohn, 1991, p. 263).

The psychologist Carol Gilligan has studied females' identity formation in adolescence and adulthood and concluded that girls and women achieve identity differently from boys and men. The female route is less through competition and more through cooperation. *(Harvard University News Office)*

sponsibilities and on their ability to care for others as well as themselves. Even highly achieving women attain identity more through cooperation than through competition.

James E. Marcia (1979) modified his original interviews to explore issues of female identity. He added questions about attitudes toward premarital intercourse, views on women's role, and concerns related to lifestyle. His findings were surprising: the men in moratorium (those who were in crisis but had not yet made commitments) most closely resembled men who had achieved identity. But the women who most closely resembled the men in the identity achievement category were in foreclosure: they had made a commitment but had not undergone a personal crisis.

Why should this be? Marcia's explanation is that society pressures women to carry on social values from one generation to the next, and therefore stability of identity is extremely important for them. He has suggested that for women, foreclosure of identity is just as adaptive as a struggle to achieve identity. However, with the many changes that

have taken place over the past couple of decades in terms of women's roles, identity foreclosure may no longer be adaptive for them.

Marcia's belief that identity and intimacy develop together for women supports other research indicating that intimacy is more important for girls than for boys, even in grade school friendships (Blyth & Foster-Clarke, 1987).

Research on Female Self-Esteem

In studying girls from kindergarten through twelfth grade, Gilligan and her colleagues have come up with other important findings (L. M. Brown & Gilligan, 1990). An analysis of interviews with 99 girls in several age groups showed that girls' confidence in themselves and in their perceptions of the world stays fairly high until age 11 or 12. Until then they tend to be quite perceptive about relationship issues and assertive about their feelings. But when they hit adolescence, they accept stereotyped notions of how they should be, and they repress their true feelings for the sake of being "nice."

As they recognize that they are burying parts of themselves, which means they can no longer have authentic relationships, their confidence falters. Only those who continue to be honest with themselves and with others by acknowledging their true feelings and by expressing them appropriately, are able to stay in healthy relationship with themselves, with others, and with the society they are entering, says Gilligan. These girls' self-esteem stays high, they see themselves as competent, and they are more apt to choose nontraditional careers.

A broad-based survey sponsored by the American Association of University Women (AAUW) of 3000 children in grades 4 through 10 (2400 girls and 600 boys) yielded similar results (Daley, 1991). Although boys' self-worth dropped, too, by high school age they were still ahead of the girls, and the drop was less steep.

The AAUW survey also found culture a factor in self-esteem. Many more black girls were still confident in high school compared to white and Hispanic girls, and white girls lost their self-assurance earliest of all three groups. African American girls may feel more self-confident because they often see strong women around them. They seem less dependent on school achievement for their self-esteem, drawing their sense of themselves more from family and community. Ethnicity is an important issue in the development of self-esteem.

Ethnic Factors in Identity Formation

Identity development is especially complicated for young people from minority-group backgrounds. How do skin color, language differences, physical features, and stereotyped social standing affect a person's self-concept? One review of the literature on these issues concludes that they are extremely important and that, for young people's optimal development, adults can and should take various actions (Spencer & Markstrom-Adams, 1990).

Some research using Marcia's (1966) identity-status measures has shown a larger proportion of minority-group adolescents than white adolescents scoring in "foreclosure" (Spencer & Markstrom-Adams, 1990). This may be adaptive. For example, Latino adolescents living in predominantly Latino communities may pick up messages that they will find social recognition, strength, and a robust sense of ethnic identity by following the norms of their culture.

What happens when a young person confronts conflicting values between the larger society and the ethnic community, as, say, when a Native American is expected to participate in a ceremony being held on a day when she or he is supposed to be in school? Or when someone internalizes popular prejudice against his or her racial or ethnic group? Or when parents do not discuss such issues with their children? All these situations can cause identity confusion.

Some positive steps that can be taken to foster healthy identity formation among minority-group children include encouraging them to stay in school so that they can get a good education; caring for health, both physical and mental; encouraging social support systems like kin networks and religious centers; stressing cultural heritage; and supporting parents and teachers who work in minority communities (Spencer & Markstrom-Adams, 1990).

ACHIEVING SEXUAL IDENTITY

How do adolescents achieve sexual identity? And how do they deal with their parents concerning this exciting yet stressful new aspect of their lives?

A profound change in an adolescent's life is the movement from close friendships only with people of the same sex to friendships and romantic attachments with members of the other sex (or same-sex romantic feelings). Seeing oneself as a sexual being, coming to terms with one's sexual stirrings, and developing an intimate romantic relationship are important aspects of achieving sexual identity.

Adolescents' self-images and relationships with peers and parents are bound up with sexuality. Sexual activity—casual kissing, necking and petting, and genital contact—fulfills a number of adolescents' important needs, only one of which is physical pleasure. Teenagers become sexually active to enhance intimacy, to seek new experience, to prove their maturity, to keep up with their peers, to find relief from pressures, and to investigate the mysteries of love.

Studying Adolescents' Sexuality

It is extremely difficult to do research on sexuality. Virtually every study about sex, from Kinsey's surveys in the 1940s to those being done now, has been criticized for inaccuracy, on the basis that people who answer questions about sex tend to be sexually active and liberal in their attitude toward sex and are therefore not a representative sample of the population. Also, there is no way to corroborate what people say: some may lie to conceal their sexual activities while others may exaggerate. The problems multiply when young people are involved. For one thing, parental consent is often needed for the participation of minors, and parents who grant permission may not be typical.

Still, surveys have merit: even if we cannot generalize findings to the population as a whole, within the groups that take part we can see trends over time, that reveal changes in sexual mores. We need to remember, however, that attitudes may be changing more than behavior. Although teenagers today *seem* to be more sexually active than teenagers of a generation or two ago, it is possible that they are not acting much differently but are more willing to talk about their sexual activities.

Sexual Attitudes and Behavior

Masturbation

Masturbation, or sexual self-stimulation, is the first sexual experience for most people and is almost universal. Yet because most adults in our society are more anxious about discussing masturbation than any other aspect of sexuality (E. J. Roberts, Kline, & Gagnon, 1978), there has been very little research on it.

The research we do have shows an increase since the early 1960s in the number of adolescents who say that they masturbate (Dreyer, 1982). In the early 1970s, 50 percent of boys and 30 percent of girls under 15 years of age said that they masturbated; by the late 1970s, 70 percent of boys and 45 percent of girls under the age of 15 admitted to it. Apparently, a significant change did take place, even though we do not know whether boys and girls actually did masturbate more or whether they were simply more willing to say they did.

Still, teenagers continue to regard masturbation as shameful; fewer than one-third questioned by Coles and Stokes (1985) said that they felt no guilt about it. This suggests that attitudes toward masturbation have changed more radically among sex educators than among teenagers. Educators today stress that masturbation is normal and healthy, that it cannot cause physical harm, that it helps people learn how to give and receive sexual pleasure, and that it provides a way to gratify sexual desire without entering into a relationship for which a person is not emotionally ready.

Sexual Orientation

It is in adolescence that a person's *sexual orientation* is usually expressed: whether that person will consistently be sexually and affectionally interested in members of the other sex *(heterosexual)* or in persons of the same sex *(homosexual).*

In one study of 38,000 students in grades 7 through 12, 88.2 percent described themselves as predominantly heterosexual, 1.1 percent as predominantly homosexual or bisexual (being interested in members of both sexes), and 10.7 percent were unsure of their sexual orientation (Remafedi, Resnick, Blum, & Harris, 1992). The older students were more certain about their sexual orientation than the younger ones: 25.9 percent of 12-year-olds were unsure of their sexual orientation, compared with only 5 percent of 18-year-olds. Those who were "unsure" were more likely to report having homosexual fantasies and attractions, and less likely to have had heterosexual experiences (Remafedi et al., 1992).

What Determines Sexual Orientation?

Why do people become heterosexual or homosexual? Much of the research on this question has been spurred by efforts to explain the less common pattern, homosexuality; and a number of hypotheses have been advanced to account for it.

The oldest theory is that homosexuality represents a kind of mental illness. But in a classic study, Hooker (1957) could find no evidence to support this contention. Her conclusions and those of other

researchers (along with political lobbying and changes in public attitudes) eventually led the American Psychiatric Association to stop classifying homosexuality as a "mental disorder." The *Diagnostic and Statistical Manual of Mental Disorders* now classifies as a disorder only "persistent and marked distress about one's sexual orientation" (*DSM-III-R*, 1987, p. 296).

Other theories consider biological factors, a family with a dominating mother and a weak father (thought by some to cause male homosexuality), and chance learning (developing a preference for one's own sex after having been seduced by a homosexual). So far, no scientific support has been found for family constellation or chance learning as a cause, but there is some evidence for a biological origin. One recent report has linked male homosexuality to a small region of one chromosome (Hamer, Hu, Magnuson, Hu, & Pattatucci, 1993), and the researchers are now looking at the chromosomes of female homosexuals.

According to one theory, sexual orientation is determined by a complex prenatal process involving both hormonal and neurological factors (Ellis & Ames, 1987). If the levels of sex hormones in a fetus of either sex are in the typical female range between the second and fifth months of gestation, the person will be attracted to males after puberty. If the hormone levels are in the male range, the person will be attracted to females. Another finding—of differences in an area of the brain that governs sexual behavior—also points to a possible biological origin for homosexuality (LeVay, 1991). If there is such a predisposition toward either heterosexuality or homosexuality, it appears that social and environmental influences would have to be very strong to overcome the original biological programming.

The prevailing view today is that there are a number of different reasons why a person becomes heterosexual or homosexual, and that interaction among various biological and environmental events is crucial.

Homosexuality

Many young people have one or more homosexual experiences as they are growing up, usually before age 15. But isolated experiences, or even homosexual attractions or fantasies, do not determine eventual sexual orientation; few go on to make this a regular pattern. Only about 3 percent of adolescent boys and 2 percent of girls have ongoing homosexual relationships, even though about 15 percent of boys and 10 percent of girls have had a homosexual contact during adolescence (Chilman, 1980). Boys who say they are religious are less likely than nonreligious boys to consider themselves homosexual (Remafedi et al., 1992).

Despite the fact that homosexuality is more visible today than it used to be, with more people openly declaring their preference for people of the same sex, research suggests that homosexual behavior has been stable or has declined during the past 30 years (Chilman, 1980). Its incidence seems to be similar in a number of cultures (J. S. Hyde, 1986).

Attitudes, Behavior, and the "Sexual Evolution"

The early 1920s through the late 1970s witnessed a sexual *evolution* (rather than a *revolution*), both in what people do sexually and in how they feel about their sexual behavior. There has been a steady trend toward acceptance of more sexual activity in more situations. One major change has been the approval of premarital sex in a loving relationship. Another is a decline in the *double standard*—the code that gives males more sexual freedom than females. The sexual evolution may now have reached a plateau or may even be reversing itself; but meanwhile, like the rest of the population, today's teenagers are more sexually active and liberal than the generation before them. This is especially true of girls.

In 1965, among students at a large southern university, 33 percent of the males and 70 percent of the females believed that premarital sexual intercourse was immoral. By 1985, there was a much closer correspondence between the sexes, with only 15.9 percent of the males and 17.1 percent of the females thinking this (Robinson, Ziss, Ganza, Katz, & Robinson, 1991). Rates for premarital sexual activity also rose, especially for women (see Table 11-3). The double standard is not dead, though. Both men and women consider it more immoral for a woman to have many sexual partners than for a man to do so, and college men still espouse more liberal attitudes than college women.

Although more teenage boys report being sexually experienced today than was the case in 1979, some evidence suggests that today's typical youth has intercourse less frequently and with fewer partners. A study of 1880 male 15- to 19-year-olds drew a profile of the average sexually active boy. During the previous year he had relationships with two girls at different times, each one lasting a few months, and for long periods of time—as much as six months—he had no sexual partner

Over the past fifty years attitudes toward sexuality have changed, to include the approval of premarital sex in a loving relationship and a decline in the double standard by which males are freer sexually than females. Most teenagers are not promiscuous; sexual activity usually occurs within a monogamous relationship. *(Bob Daemmrich/The Image Works)*

(Sonenstein, Pleck, & Ku, 1991). A girl is likely to have her first sexual relations with a steady boyfriend; a boy is likely to have his with someone he knows casually (Dreyer, 1982; Zelnik, Kantner, & Ford, 1981; Zelnik & Shah, 1983).

There is often a discrepancy between what people of any age *say* about sex and what they *do*. Most teenagers apparently become sexually active earlier than they say they should. In one poll (Louis Harris & Associates, 1986), teenagers gave a median age of 18 as the "right age" to start having intercourse, even though most of the 17-year-olds and nearly half of the 16-year-olds were no longer virgins (see Table 11-4). In another study, of 3500 junior high and high school students, 83 percent of nonvirgins gave a "best age for first intercourse" higher than the age at which they had experienced it themselves, and 88 percent of young mothers

TABLE 11-3

Premarital Sexual Intercourse among College Students		
	Males (%)	**Females (%)**
1965	65.1	28.7
1970	65.0	37.3
1975	73.9	57.1
1980	77.4	63.5
1985	79.3	63.0

SOURCE: Robinson, Ziss, Ganza, Katz, & Robinson, 1991.

TABLE 11-4

Incidence of Sexual Intercourse, 1988	Males (%)	Females (%)
By age 15	33	25
By age 19	86	80

SOURCES: London, Masher, Pratt, & Williams, 1989; Pratt, 1990; Sonenstein, Pleck, & Ku, 1989; as reported in Miller & Moore, 1990.

gave a higher "best age for first birth" (Zabin, Hirsch, Smith, & Hardy, 1984).

Many adolescents, then, hold "values and attitudes consistent with responsible sexual conduct, but not all of them are able to translate these attitudes into personal behavior" (Zabin et al., 1984, p. 185). Helping such teenagers act according to the values they already hold may be more productive than trying to persuade adolescents with different attitudes to change their behavior.

Why do so many adolescents begin having sexual relations so early? Teenage girls (and, to a lesser extent, boys) often feel under pressure to engage in activities that they do not feel ready for. Social

pressure was the chief reason given by 73 percent of the girls and 50 percent of the boys in the Harris poll when asked why many teenagers do not wait for sex until they are older. One-fourth of the teenagers reported that they had felt pressured to go further sexually than they wanted to. Both boys and girls also mentioned curiosity as a reason for early sex; more boys than girls cited sexual feelings and desires. Only 6 percent of the boys and 11 percent of the girls gave love as a reason. Various social and psychological factors also exert influence (see Table 11-5).

Furthermore, the media present a distorted view of sex. On television, as opposed to real life, unmarried couples have sex from 4 to 8 times more often than married couples; contraceptives are almost never used, but women seldom get pregnant; and only prostitutes or homosexuals contract sexually transmitted diseases (STDs). Not surprisingly, then, adolescents who get their information about sex from television tend to accept the idea of premarital and extramarital intercourse with multiple partners and without protection against pregnancy or disease. This may change, since some television producers, responding to the AIDS epidemic and to pressure from public interest groups, are incorporating birth control and other evidence

TABLE 11-5

Factors Associated with Timing of First Intercourse	Factors Associated with Early Age	Factors Associated with Later Age
Timing of puberty	Early	Late
Personality style	Risk-taking, impulsive	Traditional values, religious orientation
Substance use	Use of drugs, alcohol, tobacco	Nonuse
Education	Fewer years of schooling	More years of schooling; valuing academic achievement
Family structure	Single-parent family	Two-parent family
Socioeconomic status	Disadvantaged	Advantaged
Race	Black	White, Latino

SOURCES: Miller and Moore, 1990; Sonenstein, Pleck, and Ku, 1991.

BOX 11-2 *PRACTICALLY SPEAKING*

COMMUNICATING ABOUT SEX

Parental attitudes toward teenagers' sexuality are more liberal than they used to be, and many parents do talk to their children about sex in helpful ways. An extensive survey of contemporary teenagers' views on, and experiences with, sex found that when parents give guidance, it is overwhelmingly positive. Only 3 percent of the teenagers recalled hearing from parents that sex was not normal and healthy (Coles & Stokes, 1985).

Yet communication about sex remains a problem. Most parents are still not giving their children enough information, and youngsters still get most of their information (including much misinformation) from friends (Conger, 1988). Parents often think that they have said more than their children have actually heard. One girl, already a mother at age 15, reported, "[My mother] told me that she'd told me to come to her when it was time for me to have sex and she'd get me some birth control, but she must have said it *very* softly" (Coles & Stokes, 1985, p. 37).

According to one survey (Louis Harris & Associates, 1986), 31 percent of American teenagers—28 percent of those who are sexually active—have never talked with their parents about sex, and 42 percent are nervous or afraid to

bring it up. Furthermore, 64 percent have never discussed birth control at home. This is important, because sexually active teenagers who *have* had discussions with parents about sexual matters are more likely to use birth control consistently than those who have not. Teenagers' confusion and ignorance increase the risk of pregnancy. Boys, Latino teenagers, and teenagers whose parents are not college graduates are least likely to have talked about sex with their parents (Louis Harris & Associates, 1986).

Adolescents' ambivalence, however, makes it hard for parents to discuss sex with them. Although teenagers say that they would like to be open and frank with their parents about sexual behavior, they often resent being questioned, and they tend to consider their sexual activities nobody else's business. But when parents ignore obvious signs of sexual activity, young people sometimes become puzzled and angry. As one 16-year-old girl said, looking ahead to the time when *she* would be a parent:

I'm not going to pretend that I don't know what's happening. If my daughter comes in at five in the morning, her skirt backwards and wearing some guy's sweater, I'm not going to ask her, "Did

you have a nice time at the movies?" . . . I don't plan to fail! (R. C. Sorensen, 1973, p. 61)

How, then, can parents help their children? Experts on adolescent behavior recommend the following:

■ Be sensitive to your teenager's desire to talk to you, and give your undivided attention.
■ Keep the door open on any subject. Be an "askable" parent.
■ Reassure a teenager of your support and help in any kind of trouble.
■ Be well informed yourself so that you can impart knowledge, or help your child find it.
■ Listen calmly, and concentrate on hearing and understanding your teenager's point of view.
■ Speak to your teenager as courteously as you would speak to a stranger.
■ Try to understand feelings even if you don't always approve of behavior. Do not judge.
■ Avoid belittling and humiliating your teenager and laughing at what may seem to you to be naive or foolish questions and statements.
■ Listen—and then offer your own views as plainly and honestly as possible.

---

of responsible sexual behavior into both daytime and prime-time shows (J. D. Brown, Childers, & Waszak, 1988).

A major reason for concern about early sexual activity is the risk of pregnancy (discussed later in this chapter) and of STDs (see Chapter 10). Teenagers who can go to their parents or other adults with questions about sex have a better chance of avoiding some of the common problems associated with burgeoning sexual activity and a better chance of achieving a mature sexual identity (see Box 11-2).

SOCIAL ASPECTS OF PERSONALITY DEVELOPMENT IN ADOLESCENCE

An essential aspect of the search for identity is the need to become independent of parents. An important path for this part of the search leads to the peer group. In this section we'll examine adolescents' relationships with parents and peers.

The storm and stress often associated with the teenage years in the United States and other western cultures have been called *adolescent rebellion.* Such rebellion may encompass not only conflict within the family but a general alienation from adult society and hostility toward its values. Yet studies of adolescents typically find that fewer than 1 out of 5 fit this "classical" pattern of tumult (Offer, Ostrov, & Howard, 1989).

Age does become a powerful bonding agent in adolescence—more powerful than race, religion, community, or sex. American teenagers spend much of their free time with people of their own age, with whom they feel comfortable and can identify. They have their best times with their friends, with whom they feel free, open, involved, excited, and motivated. These are the people they most want to be with. Young people are caught up in "generational chauvinism": they tend to believe that most other adolescents share their personal values and that most older people do not (Csikszentmihalyi & Larson, 1984; R. C. Sorensen, 1973).

Nevertheless, adolescents' rejection of parental values is often partial, temporary, or superficial. Teenagers' values tend to remain closer to those of their parents than many people realize, and "adolescent rebellion" often amounts to little more than a series of minor skirmishes.

RELATIONSHIPS WITH PARENTS

The myth is that parents and teenagers do not like each other and do not get along with each other. This belief may have been born in the first formal theory of adolescence, that of the psychologist G. Stanley Hall. Hall (1916/1904) believed that young people's efforts to adjust to their changing bodies and to the imminent demands of adulthood usher in a period of "storm and stress," which inevitably leads to conflict between the generations. Sigmund Freud (1953/1935) and his daughter, Anna Freud (1946), also thought that parent-child friction was inevitable, growing out of adolescents' need to free themselves from dependency on their parents. But the anthropologist Margaret Mead (1928, 1935), who studied adolescence in other cultures, concluded that when a culture provides a serene and gradual transition from childhood to adulthood, adolescent rebellion is not typical. Such peaceful transitions are most likely to occur in cultures where social change is minimal.

But even in more dynamic societies, more recent research has borne out the fact that rebellion does not have to be a hallmark of adolescence. Teenagers who are very rebellious may well need spe-

cial help. Despite some conflicts, most American adolescents feel close to and positive about their parents, have similar values on major issues, and value their parents' approval (Demo, 1992; J. P. Hill, 1987; Offer, Ostrov, & Howard, 1989). One possible reason for the lack of conflict between the generations may be the fact that teenagers typically spend no more than an hour a day with their parents (Demo, 1992). It's easier to get along with people you're not with!

This does not, of course, mean that teenagers and their parents live in a calm, stress-free relationship. Let's look at some aspects of the conflicts between them.

An Ambivalent Relationship

Young people feel a constant tension between needing to break away from their parents and realizing how dependent they really are on them. They have to give up the identity of "the Smiths' little boy" or "the Millers' little girl" and establish their own private identity, while at the same time keeping parental and family ties.

Adolescents' mixed feelings are often matched by their parents' own ambivalence. Torn between wanting their children to be independent and wanting to keep them dependent, parents often find it hard to let go. As a result, parents may give teenagers "double messages"; that is, the parents will say one thing but will actually communicate just the opposite by their actions.

Conflict is more likely to surface between adolescents and their mothers than with their fathers (Steinberg, 1981, 1987a). This may be partly because mothers have been more closely involved with their children and may find it harder to let go. It may also be because fathers sometimes tend to withdraw from their teenage children—from their developing daughters, out of discomfort with the sexual stirrings they may feel toward them; and from their sons, who may now be bigger than both parents and more aggressive.

Still, the emotions attending this transitional time do not necessarily lead to a break with either parental or societal values. In fact, a number of studies of American teenagers have found little turmoil (Brooks-Gunn, 1988; Offer et al., 1989). For one thing, although teenagers report slightly more negative moods than younger children, they do not report the wide swings in emotional states that are often considered inevitable in adolescence (Larson & Lampman-Petraitis, 1989). Research is fairly consistent in reporting significant conflict only in 15 to 25 percent of all families, and these are often families that had problems *before* the children approached adolescence (W. A. Collins, 1990; J. P. Hill, 1987; Offer et al., 1989).

In his classic studies of midwestern boys, Daniel Offer (1969) found a high level of bickering over relatively unimportant issues by 12- and 14-year-olds and their parents, but he found little "turmoil" or "chaos." A follow-up study of the same boys 8 years later (Offer & Offer, 1974) found most of them happy, reasonably well-adjusted, with a realistic self-image. Less than one-fifth had experienced a tumultuous adolescence. Similar results held true for wider groups of adolescents (Offer et al., 1989).

Conflict with Parents

By and large, parents and teenagers do not clash over economic, religious, social, or political values. Most arguments are about mundane matters like schoolwork, chores, friends, dating, curfews, and personal appearance (Montemayor, 1983; Smetana, Yau, Restrepo, & Braeges, 1991). Later in adolescence, conflict is more likely to revolve around dating and alcohol (Carlton-Ford & Collins, 1988). The nature of the conflict is quite similar in married and divorced families (Smetana et al., 1991).

Most disagreements are resolved with less trouble than popular mythology suggests. Quarrels may reflect some deep quest for independence (as is often speculated), or they may be just a continuation of parents' efforts to teach children to conform to social rules. "This [socializing] task inescapably produces a certain amount of tension. . . . At this point it is simply not clear whether parent-adolescent conflict has a 'deeper meaning' than this" (Montemayor, 1983, p. 91).

Discord generally increases during early adolescence, stabilizes during middle adolescence, and then decreases after the young person is about 18 years of age. But for most teenagers, the "storm and stress" concept is exaggerated. Conflict is part of every relationship, and since the transitions of adolescence challenge the established interaction between parent and child, it is not surprising that some contention arises. Usually, however, parents and children resolve their disagreements to their mutual satisfaction, and parents continue to exercise considerable influence on teenagers' basic values. When family conflicts are severe and cannot be resolved easily, however, adolescents are at risk of serious problems. Intervention and counseling can often help such families (Offer et al., 1989).

What Adolescents Need from Their Parents

Many of the arguments between teenagers and their parents are about "how much" and "how soon": how much freedom teenagers should have to schedule their own activities, or how soon they can take the family car. Parents of adolescents have to be more flexible in their thinking and more egalitarian with their children than they were when the children were younger. They need to walk a fine line between granting their children a gradually

Most adolescents feel close to and positive about their parents, have similar values on major issues, and appreciate their parents' approval. Also, they often enjoy being in each other's company. *(Erika Stone)*

Communication between parents and adolescents may flow more naturally when they are engaged in a shared pursuit. Grinding corn in the traditional manner strengthens the bond between this Navajo mother and daughter. *(Ruth Duskin Feldman)*

increasing level of independence and protecting them from immature lapses in judgment.

If separation or emotional independence from the family or other important adults comes too early, it can spell trouble for a teenager. This trouble can take the form of alienation, susceptibility to negative peer influences, and unhealthy behavior like drug abuse or premature sexual activity (Steinberg, 1987b; Steinberg & Silverberg, 1986). Still, parents should not try to keep their children from taking *any* risks. Positive exploration that involves trying a new activity, making new friends, learning a difficult skill, taking on a new challenge, or resisting peer pressure (thus taking the risk of alienating old friends) poses challenges that help people grow (Damon, 1984).

The kind of parenting that seems to provide the right balance is, still, authoritative parenting. This offers warmth and acceptance; assertiveness with regard to rules, norms, and values; willingness to listen, explain, and negotiate; and granting of psychological autonomy, encouraging children to form their own opinions (Lamborn, Mounts, Steinberg, & Dornbusch, 1991).

"Authoritative parents exert control over the child's behavior, but not over the child's sense of self" (Steinberg & Darling, in press, p. 7). Warmth seems to foster the development of self-esteem and social skills, behavioral control helps young peo-

ple to control their impulses, and granting psychological autonomy helps the development of responsibility and competence (Steinberg, 1990).

One reason this approach works so well with teenagers is that it takes their cognitive growth into account. By explaining their reasons, parents acknowledge that adolescents can often evaluate situations on a very sophisticated level. This kind of approach has also been shown to lead to higher school performance (Steinberg & Darling, in press), showing one way in which parents affect their children's performance in school. The stronger the parents' interest in teenagers' lives, the more likely the teenagers are to get high marks.

How Adolescents Are Affected by Their Parents' Life Situation

Parents' Employment

Most of the research about the impact of parents' work patterns on adolescents has involved mothers' employment, and the findings have been somewhat inconsistent.

In one study, 7 out of 10 teenagers said that their mothers' working had either a positive effect or no effect on them (General Mills, Inc., 1981). This is understandable. Teenagers want to be independent—to make their own decisions. Mothers who are at home are more likely to continue to direct their adolescents' activities, and a mother will often feel personally rebuffed if her well-meaning advice or questions are rejected. In another study, adolescent children of working mothers tended to be better adjusted socially, feel better about themselves, have more of a sense of belonging, and get along better with families and with school friends than other teenagers (D. Gold & Andres, 1978a).

On the negative side, teenage children of working mothers tend to spend less time on homework and reading and more time watching television (Milne, Myers, Rosenthal, & Ginsburg, 1986). With less supervision, they may also be more subject to peer pressure leading to behavior problems.

In the 1950s, 1960s, and 1970s, when most mothers who could afford to stay home did so, some research found certain differences between children of employed mothers and children of at-home mothers. For example, adolescent sons of working women held less stereotyped views of the female role; their daughters had higher and less gender-stereotyped career aspirations, were more outgoing, scored higher on academic measures, and seemed better adjusted on social and personality measures (L. Hoffman, 1979). More recent analysis, however, suggests that a mother's work status is just one of many factors that shape children's attitudes toward women's roles (Galambos, Petersen, & Lenerz, 1988). Since we seem to have come to the end of a historical period in which mothers' work outside the home was not the norm, maternal employment may be considered a history-graded influence on gender typing (see Chapter 1).

Today, maternal employment in itself does not seem to affect teenagers much for either good or ill. Rather, whatever effect it has is filtered through other factors, like the warmth of a relationship or a mother's satisfaction with her role. Teenage sons of working mothers are likely to have more flexible attitudes toward gender roles when they have warm relationships with their mothers, and teenage daughters have egalitarian attitudes toward gender roles when their mothers are happy with their own roles (Galambos et al., 1988).

"Self-Care" Adolescents

At 13, Karim is too old for day care or a babysitter, and like many other young people, he is responsible for himself for at least part of the day. Lack of supervision does not in itself make preteens and young teenagers especially vulnerable to peer pressure. But differences do show up, depending on the kind of self-care, parents' involvement with self-care, and parenting styles.

Steinberg (1986) gave questionnaires to 865 young people aged 10 to 15 years old in Madison, Wisconsin, asking them what they would do about hypothetical antisocial situations (like stealing, vandalism, and cheating on a test) if a best friend suggested one course while they themselves really thought they should do something else. Some of Steinberg's respondents, like Karim, stayed home alone after school; they were in telephone contact with their parents, followed an agreed-upon schedule of homework and chores, and were in a familiar environment that reminded them of family values. These young people were no more influenced by their friends than were youngsters who were at home with adults or older siblings. But the further removed his respondents were from even the possibility of adult supervision, the more they were affected by peers. Thus, those who spent time unsupervised at a friend's house were more influenced by peers than those who stayed home alone, and those who just "hung out" with a group were the most easily swayed. Yet even in this last category, youngsters whose parents knew where they were turned out to be only slightly more susceptible to peer influence than those who were actually with adults. Furthermore, young people whose parents were authoritative found it easier to resist peer pressure, apparently because they had taken their parents' standards as their own.

This study emphasizes the importance of considering differences among self-care adolescents. However, we need more research before we can draw general conclusions. For one thing, since most of Steinberg's subjects were suburban, his findings might not apply to rural or urban teenagers. For another, it is not clear whether being supervised by adults helps adolescents resist peer pressure or whether being more peer-oriented leads adolescents to resist adult supervision. Finally, these subjects were responding to hypothetical situations; their responses may have been very different from their behavior in real life. But another study of young people from the same schools did find that their responses to hypothetical situations were related to reports of actual misconduct (B. B. Brown, Clasen, & Eicher, 1986). So this approach may hold the promise of predicting behavior.

Adolescents with Single Parents

By and large, adolescents who do not live with their fathers run a greater risk of giving in to peer pressure and getting into trouble, and this risk is not alleviated by the mother's remarriage.

A nationwide study of 6710 adolescents aged 12

to 17 found that, across socioeconomic levels, teen-agers living with only their mothers were more likely than those living with both parents to be truant, to run away from home, to smoke, to have discipline problems in school, or to get into trouble with the police (Dornbusch et al., 1985). But the presence of another adult in the home—like a grandparent or a friend of the mother, but *not* a stepfather—lowers the risk almost to the level found in two-parent families, especially for boys. This suggests that some of the problems in single-parent homes may be due to the many pressures on the mother and that nontraditional family groupings can help relieve this pressure and thus help keep adolescents out of trouble.

Steinberg (1987b) analyzed the answers of the 865 Wisconsin adolescents whom he had studied and came to a similar conclusion. Adolescents living with both parents were less likely to be influenced to commit antisocial acts by their friends than were those in either single-parent homes or stepfamilies. Only among the oldest children was the presence of a stepfather even slightly helpful in lowering susceptibility to peer pressure.

Since single and remarried mothers are less likely to be authoritative parents (Dornbusch, Ritter, Leiderman, Roberts, & Fraleigh, 1987), their children's problems may stem from parenting style rather than the father's absence. In any case, their children are more likely to have trouble getting through adolescence.

SIBLING RELATIONSHIPS

Sherilynn, who used to enjoy playing and looking after her younger brother, is spending much less time with Kyle these days. In this, she is typical of most adolescents, whose relationships with their siblings change during these years, along with their relationships with their parents. Although there has been very little research about sibling ties in adolescence, what there is underscores the adolescent's need to find an identity beyond the family.*

In a study of 363 students in grades 3, 6, 9, and 12, Buhrmester and Furman (1990) found that as children grow older, their relationships with their siblings become progressively more egalitarian and also more distant. Adolescent siblings still show intimacy, affection, and admiration for their

brothers and sisters, but they spend less time with them (Raffaelli & Larson, 1987), and their relationships are less intense. Older siblings exercise less power over the younger ones, fight with them less, are not as likely to look to them for companionship, and are not as close to them. As teenagers work at separating from their families, they spend more time with close friends and with people they are romantically involved with. Simply, they have less time and less need for the emotional gratification they used to get from the sibling bond.

These changes in relationships seem to be fairly complete by the time the younger sibling is about 12 years old. By this time, children no longer need the same amount of supervision—supervision that has often been given by older brothers and sisters. At the same time that the younger siblings are becoming more competent and independent, the relative difference between older and younger siblings is shrinking. (A 6-year-old is vastly more competent than a 3-year-old, but an 18-year-old and a 15-year-old are more equal.) The change in the relationship between younger and older siblings parallels—and may well come before—the same kind of change between adolescents and their parents, with regard to greater equality, more independence, and less authority exerted by the older person over the younger.

The changes that occur in sibling relationships differ, depending on a child's place in the family. The older sister or brother has inherited a position of authority and responsibility that she or he never had in relation to either parents or peers. Then, as the younger sibling grows up, the older one has to give up some of the power and status that has been held for years. Maybe this is why so many older siblings look on their younger brothers and sisters as pesky annoyances. On the other hand, the younger ones still look up to their older siblings and try to be more "grown up" by identifying with them.

Spacing has an effect, too. Siblings who are further apart in years tend to be more affectionate toward each other and to get along better than do those who are close in age. The more frequent quarrels and greater antagonism between closely spaced brothers and sisters probably arise from a greater rivalry between siblings whose capabilities are close enough so that they compare themselves with each other—or are constantly compared by other people. Gender is another factor: same-sex siblings are usually closer than a brother and sister.

However, although these effects of birth order, spacing, and gender have held up across several

---

*For this discussion we are indebted to the work of Buhrmester and Furman, 1990.

studies, they are less important in the quality of sibling relationships than are such factors as the temperament of each child, how the parents act toward them, and how old the children are (Stocker, Dunn, & Plomin, 1989). Between ages 9 and 15, the amount of time that young people spend with both their parents and siblings declines dramatically (Larson & Richards, 1991). Although adolescents are alone for many of the hours that they used to be with their families, they also spend more time with friends.

RELATIONSHIPS WITH PEERS

An important source of support during the complex transition of adolescence, and a source of pressure for behavior that their parents may deplore, is young people's growing involvement with their peers.

Adolescents going through rapid physical changes take comfort from being with others who are going through similar changes. Young people questioning adult standards and the need for parental guidance find it reassuring to turn for advice to friends who can understand and symphathize because they are in the same position. Teenagers "trying on" new values can test their ideas with their peers with less fear of being ridiculed or "shot down" than they might have with adults. The peer group is a source of affection, sympathy, and understanding; a place for experimentation; and a supportive setting for achieving autonomy and independence from parents. It is also a place to form intimate relationships with others, providing the basis for adult intimacy (Coleman, 1980; Gecas & Seff, 1990; Newman, 1982). It is no wonder, then, that adolescents like to spend time with their peers.

How Adolescents Spend Their Time—and with Whom

What do teenagers do on a typical day? With whom do they do it? Where do they do it? And how do they feel about what they are doing? For 1 week, 75 high school students in a suburb of Chicago carried beepers that rang at random times once every 2 hours during the day. The students were asked to report what they were doing when the beeper sounded—and where, and with whom. The average student received and responded to 69 percent of the beeper signals, yielding a total of 4489 self-reports, from which researchers described

Adolescents, like these congregating at a mall, spend more than half their waking hours with other teenagers and only about 5 percent of their time with a parent. Before young people become truly independent, they go from being dependent on parents to being dependent on peers. *(Lawrence Migdale)*

what it is like to be a teenager today (Csikszentmihalyi & Larson, 1984).

The results (see Figures 11-1 and 11-2) showed the importance of peers. These adolescents spent more than half their waking hours with friends and classmates and only 5 percent of their time with one or both parents. They were happiest when with friends. Being with the family ranked second, next came being alone, and last, being with classmates. Teenagers have more fun with friends—joking, gossiping, and goofing around—than at home, where activities tend to be more serious and humdrum.

Friendships in Adolescence

"What *do* you talk about for so long?" Sally's mother used to ask her when she had been on the phone for an hour with the best friend she had seen no more than 2 hours before. Sally was not surprised, then, to see the same pattern emerge when her own daughters entered their teens. The

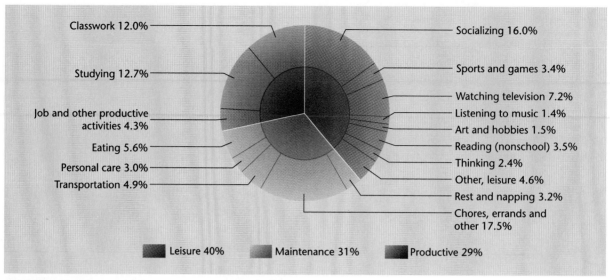

Classwork 12.0%
Studying 12.7%
Job and other productive activities 4.3%
Eating 5.6%
Personal care 3.0%
Transportation 4.9%

Socializing 16.0%
Sports and games 3.4%
Watching television 7.2%
Listening to music 1.4%
Art and hobbies 1.5%
Reading (nonschool) 3.5%
Thinking 2.4%
Other, leisure 4.6%
Rest and napping 3.2%
Chores, errands and other 17.5%

Leisure 40%   Maintenance 31%   Productive 29%

FIGURE 11-1

What adolescents spend their time doing: percentage of self-reports in each location by 2734 high school students. Here and in Figure 11-2, 1 percentage point is equivalent to about 1 hour per week spent in the given activity. (*Source:* Csikszentmihalyi & Larson, 1984, p. 63.)

intensity of friendships is greater in adolescence than at any other time in the life span (Berndt & Perry, 1990).

There is some continuity from middle childhood into adolescence: both age groups see mutual help, mutual interaction, and mutual liking as the core

of friendship. And for both, friendships seem to last about as long and to involve about the same level of conflict.

But there are also differences. In early adolescence, friends are more intimate and supportive than they are at earlier ages, adolescents regard

FIGURE 11-2

The people that adolescents spend their time with. (*Source:* Csikszentmihalyi & Larson, 1984, p. 71.)

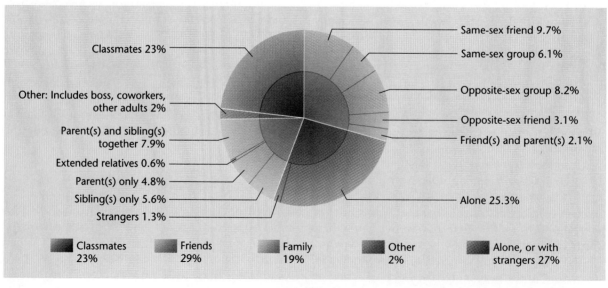

Classmates 23%
Other: Includes boss, coworkers, other adults 2%
Parent(s) and sibling(s) together 7.9%
Extended relatives 0.6%
Parent(s) only 4.8%
Sibling(s) only 5.6%
Strangers 1.3%

Same-sex friend 9.7%
Same-sex group 6.1%
Opposite-sex group 8.2%
Opposite-sex friend 3.1%
Friend(s) and parent(s) 2.1%
Alone 25.3%

Classmates 23%   Friends 29%   Family 19%   Other 2%   Alone, or with strangers 27%

Friendships are likely to be closer and more intense in adolescence than at any other time in the life span. Adolescents have the most fun when they are doing something with their friends, with whom they feel free, open, involved, excited, and motivated. *(Jeff Isaac Greenberg/Photo Researchers)*

loyalty as more critical to a friendship, and adolescents compete less and share more with their friends than do younger children (Berndt & Perry, 1990). These features of friendship continue into adulthood. Their appearance marks a transition to adultlike relationships.

Such changes are due partly to cognitive development. Adolescents are better able than younger children to express their thoughts and feelings and share them with friends; they are also better able to consider another person's point of view, so they can better understand their friends' thoughts and feelings.

Gender affects friendships, too. Emotional support and sharing of confidences are particularly vital to female friendships throughout life (Blyth & Foster-Clark, 1987; Bukowski & Kramer, 1986). Boys and men tend to count more people as friends than girls and women do, but male friendships are rarely as close as female friendships.

However, girls who seek from a best friend the intimacy they lack at home are likely to be disappointed. In a survey of 134 girls aged 16 to 18, those who had the closest friendships also had affectionate ties with their mothers, saw their mothers as nonauthoritarian, and wanted to be like them (M. Gold & Yanof, 1985). Their close relationships with their mothers may well have helped these girls to develop enough trust and autonomy to be ready for intimacy with other people.

Such differences illustrate some of the other factors that influence people's ability to make and keep friends. Adolescents who have close friends are high in self-esteem, consider themselves competent, and do well in school; those whose friendships involve a high degree of conflict score lower on all these measures (Berndt & Perry, 1990).

Adolescents tend to choose friends who are already like them; then, friends influence each other to become even more alike (Berndt, 1982; Berndt & Perry, 1990). Friends tend to have similar status within the larger peer group (Berndt & Perry, 1990). Similarity is more important to friendship in adolescence than later in life, probably because teenagers are struggling to differentiate themselves from their parents and, as a result, need support from people who are like them (Weiss & Lowenthal, 1975).

This need for support also shows in the way adolescents often imitate each other's behavior and are influenced by peer pressure. As a result, adolescents sometimes find themselves in a tug-of-war between parents and peers.

Peer Pressure versus Parents' Influence

If the other girls in her group wear ripped jeans and unlaced running shoes, Heather will not come to school in a plaid skirt and penny loafers. If her crowd gathers at a fast-food restaurant at night, Heather will not—at least by choice—spend her evenings in the library. Her friends influence not only her clothes and hairdos but also her social activities, sexual behavior, and use or nonuse of drugs. Members of the adolescent peer group are constantly influencing and being influenced by each other. Even the most outspoken "noncon-formists" usually follow the customs of their chosen group.

Still, "peer power" is not everything. Most teenagers have positive ties with their parents (J. P. Hill, 1987) and maintain two reference groups: parents and peers. Peers tend to have more to say about everyday social issues; parents have more influence about deeper concerns: what to do about a moral dilemma, what job to take, and what education to pursue (Brittain, 1963; Emmerick, 1978). Also, as adolescents become surer of themselves, they become more autonomous; they are more likely to make up their own minds and to stick with their decisions in the face of disagreement from either parents or peers (Newman, 1982).

Parents' Influence over Adolescents' Choice of Friends

Although adolescents' parents often feel they have lost any leverage they ever had over their children's choice of friends, they still seem to exert considerable indirect influence. One study of 3781 high school students found significant relationships between parents' behaviors and students' peer groups (Brown, Mounts, Lamborn, & Steinberg, 1993).

The researchers found that such parental practices as monitoring students' behavior and school work, encouraging achievement, and joint decision making were associated with such adolescent behaviors as academic achievement, drug use, and

self-reliance. In turn, these behaviors were related to membership in such common adolescent peer groups as "populars, jocks, brains, normals, druggies, and outcasts" (Brown et al., 1993, p. 471).

It seems that parents help to shape prosocial or antisocial behavior, which then predisposes their children to gravitate toward particular crowds. Thus, teenagers whose parents emphasize achievement do better in school. Then, the ones whose parents try to monitor their behavior tend to join the "brains" crowd, whereas the ones who are not monitored and do not take part in joint decision making are more likely to join the "popular" crowd, which is more likely to become involved in drug use.

TWO PROBLEMS OF ADOLESCENCE

Although most young people weather adolescence well, some have serious problems. Two that can affect the rest of a young person's life are unplanned pregnancy and juvenile delinquency. Neither of these problems is normal or typical. Both are signals that a young person is in trouble and needs help.

TEENAGE PREGNANCY

The teenage pregnancy rate in the United States is one of the highest in the world. In 1990, 1.1 mil-

One of the worst consequences of teenage pregnancy is the tendency for girls to drop out of school and to drift into lifelong financial dependency. These girls go to a school in Fort Worth, Texas, especially oriented toward pregnant students aged 12 to 21. Some of the girls keep their babies; others release them for adoption. Either way, the mothers can continue their education. *(D. Fineman/Sygma)*

lion teenage girls became pregnant (Children's Defense Fund [CDF], 1993). About half had their babies, 13 percent miscarried, and 40 percent had abortions (CDF, 1993; National Research Council, 1987). Almost 68 percent of births to 15- to 19-year-old girls occurred outside of marriage, compared to 15 percent in 1960 (CDF, 1993). A high number of both pregnancies and births were to girls from minority and disadvantaged groups (G. Adams, Adams-Taylor, & Pittman, 1989).

More than 9 out of 10 teenage mothers choose, at least at first, to keep their babies rather than give them up for adoption or place them in foster care. But caring for a baby is demanding, and these young mothers, barely more than children themselves, often cannot manage it. As a result, children of teenagers often enter the state's foster care system, and years may pass before a foster child's final status is settled (Alan Guttmacher Institute, 1981).

Consequences of Teenage Pregnancy

The consequences of pregnancy are enormous for adolescent girls and boys, their babies, and society.

Teenage girls are more prone to such complications of pregnancy as anemia, prolonged labor, and toxemia (McKenry, Walters, & Johnson, 1979). They are twice as likely as older mothers to bear low-birthweight babies and children with neurological defects and three times more likely to have babies who die in the first year (McKenry et al., 1979).

The health problems of teenage mothers and their children often result from social causes rather than medical ones. Many of the mothers are poor, do not eat properly, and get inadequate prenatal care or none at all (S. S. Brown, 1985). In two large-scale studies, one in the United States and one in Denmark, teenagers' pregnancies turned out better than those of women in any other age group, leading to the conclusion that "if early, regular, and high-quality medical care is made available to pregnant teenagers, the likelihood is that pregnancies and deliveries in this age group will not entail any higher medical risk than those of women in their twenties" (Mednick, Baker, & Sutton-Smith, 1979, p. 17).

Even with the best care, however, and the best of physical outcomes, teenage mothers still have problems. They are less likely to finish high school than their age-mates who do not have babies, and many who do finish do so at a later age. In one study, 5 years after giving birth, only half of urban black adolescent mothers had graduated from high school; however, 10 years later, two-thirds had graduated (Furstenberg, Brooks-Gunn, & Morgan, 1987).

Teenage mothers are also likely to have money troubles; many receive public assistance, at least for a while. Furthermore, they are at high risk of repeat pregnancies. The risk is highest for those who drop out of school, remain sexually active, and do not use reliable means of birth control. These girls "may have resigned themselves to few options other than repeated childbearing" (McAnarney & Hendee, 1989, p. 76).

Children of teenage parents are more likely than other children to have low IQ scores and to do poorly in school (Baldwin & Cain, 1980), and this likelihood increases over the years. As preschoolers, these children are often overactive, willful, and aggressive. In elementary school, they tend to be inattentive and easily distracted, and they give up easily. In high school, they are often low achievers (Brooks-Gunn & Furstenberg, 1986). However, a 20-year study that followed more than 400 teenage mothers in Baltimore found that two-thirds of their daughters did not become teenage mothers themselves, and most graduated from high school (Furstenberg, Levine, & Brooks-Gunn, 1990).

Why Teenagers Get Pregnant

Why, in an age of improved methods of contraception, do so many young girls become pregnant? Usually this is because they do not use any contraception. Two-thirds of sexually active teenagers do not always use birth control, and 27 percent never use it. Even after going to a health department clinic, only 13 percent used birth control pills correctly all the time, and only 4 in 10 took a pill every day (Oakley, Sereika, & Bogue, 1991).

Why don't teenagers use birth control? Most commonly, they say that they did not expect to have intercourse and therefore did not prepare for it. But when asked why their *peers* do not use contraceptives, many tell a different story. Nearly 40 percent say that young people either prefer not to use birth control, do not think about it, do not care, enjoy sex more without it, or want to get pregnant. Other often-mentioned reasons are lack of knowledge about or access to birth control, embarrassment about seeking contraception or fear that parents will find out that they are having sex, and the "personal fable" belief that pregnancy "won't happen to me" (Louis Harris & Associates, 1986).

Guilt feelings often underlie the explanation that sexual activity was unexpected. The saying "I'm not that kind of girl" sums up the attitude of some girls (Cassell, 1984). Believing that sexual intercourse is wrong, these girls preserve their self-respect by considering themselves swept away by love and unable to help themselves. Unpremeditated sex is acceptable; carefully planned sex is only for "bad" girls. The guiltier a girl feels about having premarital sex, the less likely she is to use effective contraception (Herold & Goodwin, 1981). A girl who feels guilty is embarrassed to go to a birth control clinic and have an internal physical examination. She is less likely than one who does not feel guilty to read about birth control, and she is more likely to think that oral contraceptives are hard to get.

Who Is Likely to Get Pregnant?

Social factors affect both premarital sexual activity and the use of birth control. African American and Latina girls, girls who live with a single parent, disadvantaged girls, and girls whose parents are relatively uneducated tend to use no birth control, or to use less effective methods than "the pill" or the diaphragm. On the other hand, girls who make high grades, have career aspirations, or are involved in sports or other activities *are* likely to use birth control effectively (Ford, Zelnick, & Kantner, 1979; Louis Harris & Associates, 1986; Miller & Moore, 1990).

Age, sexual knowledge, and experience are all major factors. The younger a girl is at first intercourse, the longer she is likely to wait before seeking help with contraception—and the more likely she is to become pregnant (Tanfer & Horn, 1985). The less she knows about sex, the less likely she is to protect herself (Louis Harris & Associates, 1986). And the newer she is to sexual activity, the more vulnerable she is. Half of first premarital pregnancies occur in the first 6 months of sexual activity, and 1 out of 5 occur in the first month (Zabin, Kantner, & Zelnik, 1979).

Historically, teenagers seldom sought advice about birth control until they had been sexually active for a year or more. But in recent years the proportion of American women using contraceptives at first intercourse has risen, from 47 percent in the years 1975 to 1979 to 65 percent in 1983 to 1988. This change may be partly owing to AIDS education, since the increase was largely due to an increased use of condoms. Ethnic differences appeared in one study of 8450 women aged 15 to 44: 68 percent of Jewish women, 54 percent of other white women, 45 percent of black women, and 32 percent of Latina women used contraception at first intercourse (Mosher & McNally, 1991).

What is the boy's role? Although boys are less likely to use contraceptives than girls, 2 out of 5 girls who used birth control during recent intercourse relied on their partners' male methods: condoms or withdrawal (G. Adams et al., 1989). This too may be changing, with the increased use of condoms. And the image of the irresponsible young man who abandons his pregnant sweetheart belies the amount of support supplied by many young fathers, especially in minority communities. Some of this support is mandated by law, since many states require fathers to pay child support for the first 18 years of a child's life. Enforcement often involves deducting set amounts from a man's pay. However, despite these laws (which are spottily enforced) and even though paternity can be clearly established through biological testing, many men do not assume responsibility for their children, leaving the mother with all the financial and emotional burdens of child rearing.

Preventing Teenage Pregnancy

Since teenagers who are knowledgeable about sex are more likely to use birth control, parents and schools can help to lower the high level of teenage pregnancy by offering education about sex and parenthood—both the facts and the feelings (Conger, 1988). Many people fear that if teenagers know about sex, they will want to put this knowledge into practice, but community- and school-based sex education does not result in more sexual activity by adolescents (Eisen & Zellman, 1987). Since the media are a powerful influence on adolescents' behavior, radio and television executives can mount campaigns to present sexual situations responsibly and to permit advertising of contraceptives. Since adolescents who have high aspirations for the future are also less likely to become pregnant, it is important to motivate young people in other areas of their lives and to raise their self-esteem. Programs that have focused on this approach rather than on the mechanics of contraception have achieved some success (Carrera, 1986). See Box 11-3 for other suggestions about how to prevent teenage pregnancy.

Helping Pregnant Teenagers
and Teenage Parents

Any pregnant woman needs to be reassured about her ability to bear and care for a child and about

BOX 11-3 *WINDOW ON THE WORLD*

PREVENTING TEENAGE PREGNANCY

Why do so many American teenagers get pregnant? Several factors commonly offered as causes—the prevalence of sexual activity among teenagers, an unusually large population of poor African American teenagers, high unemployment among teenagers, and federal welfare programs that ease the financial pressure of teenage parenthood—fail to explain the trend (E. F. Jones et al., 1985). Let's see why:

■ Rates of early intercourse are similar in the United States and the Netherlands, yet pregnancy and abortion rates for girls aged 15 to 19 are about 7 times higher in the United States. In Sweden, where girls become sexually active even earlier, rates of pregnancy and abortion are less than half the American rates.

■ Rates of pregnancy and abortion are far higher among both white and black American teenagers than they are for teenagers elsewhere.

■ Unemployment among teenagers is a serious problem in other industrial countries, too.

■ Industrial nations with more generous support programs for poor mothers have much lower rates of teenage pregnancy than the United States.

How, then, do other countries succeed in preventing teenage pregnancy?

■ *Easy availability of free or inexpensive contraceptives on a confidential basis:* In Britain,

France, the Netherlands, and Sweden, adolescents can get contraceptives free or at low cost from doctors or clinics. In Sweden, parents cannot be told that their children have sought contraceptives; in the Netherlands, teenagers can request confidentiality (E. F. Jones et al., 1985). American teenagers say that making contraceptives free, keeping their distribution confidential, and making them easy to get would be the three most effective ways to encourage use of birth control. Teenagers suggest establishing clinics close to (but not in) schools to make access easier (Louis Harris & Associates, 1986).

■ *Sex education and information about sex:* In Sweden, sex education is compulsory at all grade levels. Dutch schools have no special sex education programs, but mass media and private groups in the Netherlands provide extensive information about birth control, and Dutch teenagers are well informed (E. F. Jones et al., 1985). Realistic, comprehensive educational programs that include information on various means of contraception and how to obtain them are related to getting teenagers to use birth control consistently and effectively (Alan Guttmacher Institute, 1981).

■ *Delaying sexual activity is the most effective means of birth control:* When parents talk with children about sex from an early age, communicate healthy at-

titudes, and are available to answer questions, the children are likely to wait longer for sex (Conger, 1988; Jaslow, 1982). Community programs can also help young people stand up against peer pressure to be more sexually active than they want to be (Howard, 1983). Peers can also influence teenagers to delay sex. In the United States, teenage girls tend to respond especially well to counseling by other girls close to their own age (Jay, DuRant, Shoffitt, Linder, & Litt, 1984). Girls and boys often heed peers who say that having sex without birth control is foolish rather than romantic, when they might not pay attention to the same advice coming from an older person. The two arguments for delaying sex that teenagers find most convincing are the danger of getting STDs and the danger that a pregnancy will ruin a person's life (Louis Harris & Associates, 1986).

It seems clear that parents need support from communities to help prevent young people from becoming pregnant while they are still children themselves. Some school districts around the country have begun to provide such support, through programs of information and, increasingly, through distribution of condoms and other contraceptives (Barbanel, 1990). Perhaps steps like this, which other countries seem to use successfully, can also be effective in the United States.

her continued attractiveness. She needs to express her anxieties and to receive sympathy and reassurance. The unmarried girl is especially vulnerable. Whatever she decides to do about her pregnancy, she has conflicting feelings. And just when she needs the most emotional support, she often gets the least. Her boyfriend may be frightened by the responsibility and turn away from her, her family may be angry with her, and she may be isolated from her school friends. Pregnant teenagers often benefit from talking to an interested, sympathetic, and knowledgeable counselor.

Programs that help pregnant girls stay in school can teach both job and parenting skills (Buie, 1987). Some high schools operate day care centers for the children of unmarried students, to help the mothers continue their schooling. They also offer courses in parenting (Purnick, 1984).

The value of training young people to be parents showed up in one program in which 80 low-income teenage mothers learned either from a biweekly visit to their homes (by a graduate student and a teenage aide) or through paid job training as teachers' aides in the nursery of a medical school. The infants of both parent-training groups did better than babies in a control group. They weighed more, had more advanced motor skills, and interacted better with their mothers. The mothers who worked as teachers' aides and their children showed the most gains. These mothers had fewer additional pregnancies, more returned to work or school, and their babies made the most progress (T. M. Field, Widmayer, Greenberg, & Stoller, 1982).

The mother bears the major impact of teenage parenthood, but the young father's life is often affected as well. A boy who feels emotionally committed to the girl he has impregnated also has decisions to make. He may pay for an abortion. Or he may marry the girl, a move that will affect his educational and career plans. The father also needs someone to talk to, to help him sort out his own feelings so that he and the mother can make the best decision for themselves and their child.

JUVENILE DELINQUENCY

There are two kinds of young people who get into trouble with the law. One is the *status offender*. This is a young person who has been truant, has run away from home, has been sexually active, has not abided by parents' rules, or has done something else that is ordinarily not considered crimi-

nal—except when done by a minor. If Huckleberry Finn were alive and active today, he would fit perfectly into this category.

The second kind is one who has done something that is considered a crime no matter who commits it—like robbery, rape, or murder. People under the age of 16 or 18 (depending on the state) are usually treated differently from adult criminals. Court proceedings are likely to be secret, the offender is more likely to be tried and sentenced by a judge rather than a jury, and punishment is usually more lenient. However, for some particularly violent crimes, minors may be tried as adults.

Teenagers, especially boys, are responsible for more than their share of crimes. The rate among girls has increased a little recently, but still girls' crime rates are similar to those of boys only for status offenses like running away from home, incorrigibility, and engaging in sexual intercourse.

Personal Characteristics of Delinquents

What makes one child get into trouble when another who lives on the same street or even in the same household remains law-abiding? Not surprisingly, children who get into trouble early in life are more likely to get into deeper trouble later on. Stealing, lying, truancy, and poor achievement in school are all important predictors of delinquency (Loeber & Dishion, 1983).

Socioeconomic status is the poorest predictor of delinquency (Loeber & Dishion, 1983). A study of 55 delinquents who had been patients at a psychiatric institute led to the conclusion that delinquency is not a class phenomenon but a result of emotional turmoil that affects young people from all levels of society. Delinquents from affluent families are frequently taken to psychiatrists; those from poor families are more likely to be booked by the police (Offer, Ostrov, & Marohn, 1972).

In some cases, deliquency is related to a history of physical and sexual abuse and to neurological and psychiatric problems (D. O. Lewis et al., 1988). Relating problems like these to delinquency may make it possible to treat some youthful offenders with such medications as anticonvulsants and antidepressants.

The Delinquent's Family

Several family characteristics are associated with juvenile delinquency. In a 1987 study of 18,226 boys and girls under 18 in long-term state-operated

The increase among girls of drug use and running away from home seems to lead to some other illegal activities, like shoplifting. The strongest predictor of delinquency is a family's failure to supervise and discipline children; the poorest predictor is socioeconomic status. *(Mike Kagan/Monkmeyer)*

correction institutes, more than half reported that a family member had also been imprisoned at least once, and nearly 3 out of 4 had not grown up with both parents (U.S. Department of Justice, 1988). Of course, these figures apply only to young people who were arrested and convicted, and thus may reflect who gets caught up in the criminal justice system rather than who actually commits delinquent acts. Some young offenders' families have the resources to keep them out of jail.

The strongest predictor of delinquency is the family's supervision and discipline of the children. Antisocial behavior in adolescents is closely related to parents' inability to keep track of what their children do and with whom they do it. And parents of delinquent children are less likely to punish rule-breaking with anything more severe than a lecture or a threat (Patterson & Stouthamer-Loeber, 1984). The impact of ineffective parenting begins early in childhood. As we pointed out in Chapter 7, parents of delinquents often failed to reinforce their children's good behavior and were harsh or inconsistent or both in punishing misbehavior. And through the years they have not been closely involved in their children's lives in positive ways (Patterson, DeBaryshe, & Ramsey, 1989).

These findings support the discussion earlier in this chapter about adolescent rebellion. Much of the tension often considered a sign of such rebellion may arise over the conflict between adolescents' desire for instant gratification and parents' desire to socialize their children. When parents cannot or will not fill their role as socializers, their children may become problems for society.

The Influence of the Peer Group

Parents worry, with good reason, about a child's "falling in with the wrong crowd." Peers do exert a strong influence; young people who take drugs, drop out of school, and commit delinquent acts usually do all of these in the company of their friends. But children don't "fall in" with a group; they seek out their friends, or, when rejected by some young people, accept the overtures of others. Of all the groups in a school or neighborhood, what makes one youngster go with the "wrong" one?

Recent research suggests that the process starts out in childhood and has its roots in troubled parent-child interactions (Patterson, Reid, & Dishion, in press). Children get certain payoffs for antisocial behavior, possibly getting attention or their own way by acting up, or avoiding punishment by lying or cheating on school tests. The children's antisocial behavior then interferes with school work and with their ability to get along with their well-behaved classmates. As a result, these children—unpopular and nonachieving—seek out other antisocial children. These children keep influencing each other and often learn new forms of problem behavior from one another.

Since school failure is often related to antisocial behavior, and since contact with antisocial peers at age 10 is related to antisocial behavior at age 12, a common educational practice may be aggravating the problem. "Tracking" children, or grouping them together in the same classroom because of similar academic skills, keeps the nonachieving children together. Since these are often the antisocial children, the long-term friendships that grow up in the classroom may solidify the problem behaviors and discourage the children from improving either their school work or their behavior (Dishion, Patterson, Stoolmiller, & Skinner, 1991).

Dealing with Delinquency

How can we help young people lead productive, law-abiding lives? And how can we protect society? So far, the answers to both questions are unclear. Can we turn young offenders away from a life of crime by sentences that consider their youth, bolstered by social solutions like probation and counseling? Or would we have less crime if we treated young offenders as we treat adults, basing sentences on the seriousness of the crime rather than the age of the offender?

One study suggests that how young offenders are treated is less important in most cases than just letting them grow up. Except for a small group of "hard-core" offenders, it is almost impossible to predict which young people will commit crimes as adults (L. W. Shannon, 1982). In a longitudinal analysis of police and court records, plus interviews with more than 6000 adults in Racine, Wisconsin, more than 90 percent of the men and 65 to 70 percent of the women had engaged in some adolescent misbehavior, although many had not been caught. But only 5 to 8 percent had been booked for felonies as adults. Why did most of these people become law-abiding? Fewer than 8 percent said that they were afraid of getting caught. Most said that they had realized that what seemed like fun in their early years was no longer appropriate.

Most adolescents, then, outgrow their "wild oats" as maturity brings valuable reappraisals of attitudes and behavior. But society must continue to explore ways to help those who cannot climb out of the morass of delinquency and alienation on their own.

A POSITIVE VIEW OF ADOLESCENCE: THREE COHORT STUDIES

Fortunately, the great majority of adolescents neither become pregnant nor get into trouble with the law. With all its turbulence, normal adolescence is an exciting time, when all things seem possible. Teenagers are on the threshold of love, of their life's work, and of participation in adult society. They are getting to know the most interesting people in the world: themselves. And, according to an analysis of findings from three cohorts of adolescents, most of them manage very well during these years (Offer et al., 1989).

The data for this analysis came from three separate studies of adolescents: in the 1960s, the 1970s, and the 1980s. Although both similarities and differences showed up among the three cohorts, they were more alike than different. By and large, the findings were that most adolescents enjoy life, are happy with themselves most of the time, do not feel inferior to others, and do not have major problems with body image, physical development, or sexuality. They are usually relaxed and confident in new or challenging situations, and they take pleasure in doing good work.

Above all, most of the adolescents in the three groups did not show any evidence of either a "generation gap" or a "natural rebellion" against their parents. Instead, most got along well with their parents and did not see any major problems with them. Life may not always run smoothly at home, but apparently most teenagers like their families and are proud of them. As these investigators point out, "the family serves as a first line of psychological defense" for typical teenagers (Offer et al., 1989, p. 735).

The differences that emerged for the three cohorts showed that teenagers in the 1960s were best off, and those in the 1970s worst off. What accounts for this? One theory involves "baby booms" and "baby busts" (Easterlin, 1980). It suggests that the higher the ratio of adolescents in a population, the more problems they have. Adolescents who were part of a baby boom have to compete more fiercely for jobs and college admission. Such pressures may help to explain differences in self-image between generations. The adolescents studied in the 1960s were at the end of a baby bust generation, those studied in the 1970s were in the middle of a baby boom, and those in the 1980s were again in a baby bust period, offering some support for this theory.

Although high-risk groups like high school dropouts were not studied, this theory might help to explain the greater problems of disadvantaged populations, which tend to have higher proportions of young people than the population at large. In these studies, however, the data do not show systematic social class and racial differences (Offer et al., 1989).

The findings from a careful analysis like this one point to the importance of having an open mind

With all its turbulence, normal adolescence is an exciting time of life. Teenagers are on the threshold of love, of life's work, and of participation in adult society. They are getting to know the most interesting people in the world: themselves. And most of them manage very well during these years. *(Myrleen Ferguson/PhotoEdit)*

about development. Instead of looking through the filter of a preconceived theory, it is essential to look at the facts. If people believe that adolescence is normally a time of stress and disturbance, the 20 percent of the teenage population with real problems may not get the help they need, as the adults around them stand back, waiting for them to "grow out" of adolescence and out of their problems. Adolescents who show by their behavior that they are disturbed can, and should, be helped at once. With support, more of them can recognize and build on their strengths as they enter adult life.

SUMMARY

THE SEARCH FOR IDENTITY

▪ Erik Erikson's psychosocial crisis of adolescence is the conflict of identity versus identity confusion. The virtue that should arise from this crisis is fidelity.

▪ The most important task during adolescence is the search for identity. Research by James Marcia, based on Erikson's theory, examined the presence or absence of crisis and commitment in identity formation. He identified four categories of identity formation: achievement, foreclosure, diffusion, and moratorium.

▪ Marcia, Gilligan, and other researchers have found differences in how males and females achieve identity. Intimate relationships seem more important for females, and achievement seems more important for males. Ethnic differences also exist.

▪ Adolescents' sexuality strongly influences their developing identity. Masturbation and occasional early homosexual experiences are common. Sexual orientation appears to be influenced by an interaction of biological and environmental factors.

▪ Sexual attitudes and behaviors are more liberal today than in the past. There is more acceptance of premarital sexual activity, and there has been a decline in the double standard.

▪ Because of social pressure, many adolescents become sexually active sooner than they feel that they should. A majority have had intercourse by age 17.

▪ Although many parents are more accepting of teenage sexuality than in the past, many adolescents have difficulty discussing sexual matters with their parents.

SOCIAL ASPECTS OF PERSONALITY DEVELOPMENT IN ADOLESCENCE

▪ Although the relationship between adolescents and their parents is not always smooth, there is little evidence that a full-blown rebellion usually characterizes it. Parents and teenagers often hold similar values on major issues. "Authoritative" parenting appears to be associated with the most positive outcomes.

▪ The effect of maternal employment on adolescents' development is filtered through other factors, such as mothers' warmth and role satisfaction.

▪ As children grow older, their relationships with siblings become more egalitarian and more distant.

▪ Adolescents spend most of their time with their peers, who play an important role in their development. Friendships become more intimate, and relationships develop with peers of the other sex.

▪ Peer pressure influences some adolescents toward antisocial behavior, especially adolescents whose parents offer little supervision.

TWO PROBLEMS OF ADOLESCENCE

▪ Pregnancy is a major problem among adolescents today. The teenage pregnancy rate in the United States is one of the highest in the world.

▪ Although many pregnant teenagers have abortions, 90 percent of those who have their babies keep them. Teenage pregnancy often has negative consequences for mother, father, child, and society.

▪ Juvenile delinquents fall into two categories:

1   Status offenders, who commit acts (such as truancy and incorrigibility) that are not criminal for adults.

2   Young people (under age 16 or 18) who have been found guilty of an offense punishable by law.

▪ People under age 18 account for more than their share of crimes, particularly crimes against property. However, the vast majority of youngsters who have juvenile police records grow up to be law-abiding. Ineffective parenting is most strongly associated with delinquency.

A POSITIVE VIEW OF ADOLESCENCE: THREE COHORT STUDIES

▪ Even with all the difficulties of establishing a personal, sexual, social, and vocational identity, adolescence is typically an interesting, exciting, and positive threshold to adulthood.

KEY TERMS

identity versus identity confusion (page 380)
crisis (382)
commitment (382)
identity achievement (383)

foreclosure (383)
identity diffusion (383)
moratorium (383)
masturbation (385)
sexual orientation (386)

heterosexual (386)
homosexual (386)
adolescent rebellion (390)
status offender (402)

SUGGESTED READINGS

Apter, T. (1990).   *Altered loves: Mothers and daughters during adolescence.* New York: St. Martin's. This is an insightful study of changes in the mother-daughter relationship during adolescence. It is based on the author's interviews with mothers and daughters in England and the United States and on recent psychological studies of family interaction.

Brown, L. M. and Gilligan, C. (1992).   *Meeting at the crossroads: Women's psychology and girls' development.* Cambridge, MA: Harvard University Press. The result of a study of about 100 girls of various ages and ethnic backgrounds, this book examines the changes that commonly occur during adolescence, replacing girls' courage, honesty, and willingness to face conflict with fear of risk and reluctance to express strong opinions. It also offers suggestions, such as the need to talk honestly with other girls and women.

Edelman, M. W. (1992).   *The measure of our success: A letter to my children and yours.* Boston: Beacon. The founder and president of the Children's Defense Fund and the first black woman admitted to the Mississippi bar directs this book to her own three sons, born of an interracial, interfaith marriage, but its message and moral implications apply to any reader. The book's "lessons for life" emphasize service to society and a recognition of the bonds across race, class, and gender.

Hardy, J. B., & Zabin, L. S. (1991).   *Adolescent pregnancy in an urban environment: Issues, programs, and evaluations.* Washington, DC: Urban Institute Press; and Baltimore, MD: Urban & Schwarzenberg. The authors, with ten contributors, analyze the urban context for teenage pregnancy, discuss services available to young parents and their babies, and describe programs designed to prevent early pregnancies, including birth control and health education.

Hyde, J. (1994).   *Understanding human sexuality* (5th ed.). New York: McGraw-Hill. An exceptionally readable textbook covering a wide range of topics in the area of sexuality: physical and hormonal factors, contraception, research on sex, variations in sexual behavior, sexual dysfunction, and the treatment of sex in religion, the law, and education.

Steinberg, L., & Levine, A. (1990).   *You and your adolescent: A parent's guide for ages 10–20.* New York: Harper & Row. This informative book by a psychologist-writer team draws on current research (including the senior author's extensive investigations) to explain the physical and psychological changes of adolescence and to offer advice on communicating with teenagers and helping them through these years.

PART FIVE

YOUNG ADULTHOOD

People change and grow in many ways during the years from ages 20 to 40, the approximate boundaries by which we define *young adulthood*. During these two decades, they make many of the decisions that will affect the rest of their lives—their health, their happiness, and their success. It is in this stage of life that most people leave their parents' home, take their first job, get married, and have and raise children—all major transitions. No wonder many social scientists consider these years the most stressful in the life span!

■ How adults eat, how much they drink, whether they smoke, how much exercise they get, how they handle stress—all these choices involving lifestyle can have a major impact on both present and future physical functioning, as we see in **Chapter 12.** We also discuss here the ramifications of decisions about college and career, which are related to developments in intellectual functioning in early adulthood. And we see some ways in which adults' thought processes differ from those of younger people.

■ In **Chapter 13,** we discuss two different approaches to explaining social and emotional development in adulthood: Erik Erikson's age-related theory, which has inspired several intensive studies of adults; and the timing-of-events theory, which emphasizes life experiences more than chronological age in explaining why people feel and act as they do. With both theories as a background, it is easier to understand the events of young adulthood that relate to some core choices: to adopt a sexual lifestyle, to marry or remain single, to have children or not, and to make friends.

CHAPTER TWELVE

PHYSICAL AND INTELLECTUAL DEVELOPMENT IN YOUNG ADULTHOOD

If . . . happiness is the absence of fever then I will never know happiness. For I am possessed by a fever for knowledge, experience, and creation.

Diary of Anaïs Nin *(1931–1934),* written when she was between 28 and 31

PHYSICAL DEVELOPMENT

■ **SENSORY AND PSYCHOMOTOR FUNCTIONING**

■ **HEALTH AND FITNESS IN YOUNG ADULTHOOD**

Health Status
Influences on Health and Fitness

INTELLECTUAL DEVELOPMENT

■ **ADULT THOUGHT: THEORETICAL APPROACHES**

K. Warner Schaie: Stages of Cognitive Development
Robert Sternberg: Three Aspects of Intelligence
Beyond Jean Piaget: Postformal Thought

■ **ADULT MORAL DEVELOPMENT**

How Does Experience Affect Moral Judgments?
Are There Gender Differences in Moral Development?

■ **COLLEGE**

Who Goes to College?
Intellectual Growth in College
Gender Differences in Achievement in College
Leaving College

■ **STARTING A CAREER**

Work and Age
Work and Gender

■ **BOXES**

12-1 Practically Speaking: What You Can Do to Improve Your Health
12-2 Window on the World: A Chinese Perspective on Moral Development
12-3 Food for Thought: How Dual-Earner Couples Cope

■ How do the lifestyles and behavior of young adults affect their physical health?

■ How do intellectual functioning and moral reasoning develop in young adulthood?

■ How does the college experience influence development?

■ What impact do age, gender, and family have on career development and satisfaction with work?

For many people, the essence of young adulthood is captured in these words: "Time—there's never enough to do everything I want to do and everything I should do." A college senior is trying to fit in all the courses needed to prepare for medical school. A newly hired attorney works 80 hours a week while trying to find time to see her fiancé and her friends, run 5 miles a day, and occasionally relax. A middle-level management executive feels defensive when his boss questions his career commitment because he leaves work early enough to have dinner with his children. And a single mother, overwhelmed by the stresses of raising a baby alone and making ends meet, relieves her tensions by smoking too much and eating too little.

People set priorities every day of their lives. The important decisions made by young adults affect health, careers, and personal relationships. And the people making them are still maturing in many important ways. At one time, developmentalists considered the years from the end of adolescence to the onset of old age as a relatively uneventful plateau, but research now confirms our own personal experiences that this is not so.

The adult years hold great potential for intellectual, emotional, and even physical development. Important advances occur during young adulthood (which we define here as the span between ages 20 and 40), throughout middle age (from age 40 to age 65), and through late adulthood (age 65 and over).

Some of these advances come about as the result of new and significant roles that many people assume in adulthood: worker, spouse, parent. These roles affect how people think and how they act. And how they think and act affects how they fill those roles—or whether they take them on at all.

During young adulthood, as throughout life, the interactions among the various aspects of development—physical, intellectual, and social and emotional—are notable. We see how personality affects health when we look at factors that incline some people to smoke, drink, overeat, or exercise, or that increase the risk of heart attack. We examine such intellectual issues as the measurement of adult intelligence, whether there are adult stages of cognitive development, and whether men and women follow different routes to moral maturity. We also look at the college experience and the intellectual and personality development that occurs in college. We end this chapter with a discussion of one of the most important issues during this period of life, the choice of career, which will come up again in Chapter 13, when we explore personality development in adulthood and the choice of a personal lifestyle.

■ PHYSICAL DEVELOPMENT

SENSORY AND PSYCHOMOTOR FUNCTIONING

The typical young adult is likely to be at the height of his or her physical ability. Strength, energy, and endurance are now at their peak. From the middle twenties, when most body functions are fully developed, until about age 50, declines in physical capabilities are usually so gradual that they are hardly noticed—at least not until toward the end of this period.

Today's 20-year-olds tend to be taller than their parents because of a secular trend in growth (see Chapter 10). Between ages 30 and 45, height is stable; then it begins to decline (Tanner, 1978).

The peak of muscular strength occurs sometime around 25 to 30 years of age; it is followed by a gradual 10 percent loss of strength between ages 30 and 60. Most of the weakening occurs in the back and leg muscles, and slightly less in the arm muscles (Bromley, 1974). Manual dexterity is most efficient in young adulthood; agility of finger and hand movements begins to lessen after the mid-thirties (Troll, 1985).

The senses are also at their sharpest during young adulthood. Visual acuity is keenest at about age 20 and does not begin to decline until about age 40, when a tendency toward farsightedness makes many people put on reading glasses. A gradual hearing loss typically begins before age 25; after age 25, the loss becomes more apparent, especially for higher-pitched sounds. Taste, smell, and sensitivity to pain and temperature generally do not diminish until about age 45 or later.

HEALTH AND FITNESS IN YOUNG ADULTHOOD

HEALTH STATUS

Your favorite spectator sport may be tennis, basketball, figure skating, or football. Whatever it is, most of the athletes you root for are young adults, people in prime physical condition. Besides being at the peak of sensory and motor functioning, young adults are the healthiest age group in the United States. According to a recent U.S. government report, almost 95 percent of people aged 15 to 44 consider their health excellent, very good, or good (U.S. Department of Health and Human Services, USDHHS, 1992). Young adults get far fewer colds and respiratory infections than children do; and when they do get a cold, they usually shake it off easily. They tend to have outgrown childhood allergies, and they have fewer accidents than children do. Many young adults are never seriously sick or incapacitated; fewer than 1 percent are limited in the ability to get around and do things because of chronic (long-lasting) conditions or impairment. The most frequent chronic conditions, especially in low-income families, are back and spine problems, hearing impairment, arthritis, and hypertension (high blood pressure). Young black adults are more likely than young white adults to suffer from hypertension (USDHHS, 1992).

About half of all acute conditions that young adults experience are colds, coughs, and other respiratory illness; about 20 percent are injuries. When they are hospitalized, it is most often because of childbirth, accidents, and diseases of the digestive and genitourinary systems (USDHHS, 1985).

Given the healthy state of most young adults, it is not surprising that in the United States, accidents (primarily automobile accidents) are the leading cause of death for people aged 25 to 34.

The typical young adult is a good physical specimen—although few exhibit the kind of coordination, stamina, and endurance shown by Uta Pippig, fastest woman in the 1993 New York City Marathon. This 28-year-old runner completed the 26.2-mile distance in 2 hours, 26 minutes, and 24 seconds. *(Focus on Sports)*

Next comes cancer, followed by heart disease and suicide. With the growing incidence of AIDS among young adults, this may soon figure among these other major killers. Between the ages of 35 and 44, cancer and heart disease are the major threats to life. Age 35 represents a turning point—the first time since infancy when the chief cause of death is physical illness.

Gender, race, and ethnicity make a significant difference in both the rates and the causes of death. Men aged 25 to 44 are twice as likely to die as women in the same age range; men are most likely to die in automobile crashes and women of cancer (USDHHS, 1992). Young African American adults are more than twice as likely to die as white people of the same age (the impact of race on health is discussed in Chapter 14). And Hispanic Americans have a variety of health problems, sometimes fatal, partly because they are less likely than any

Killings per 100,000 men 15 through 24 years old for   1987

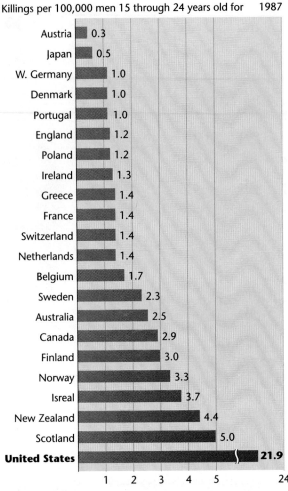

Austria	0.3
Japan	0.5
W. Germany	1.0
Denmark	1.0
Portugal	1.0
England	1.2
Poland	1.2
Ireland	1.3
Greece	1.4
France	1.4
Switzerland	1.4
Netherlands	1.4
Belgium	1.7
Sweden	2.3
Australia	2.5
Canada	2.9
Finland	3.0
Norway	3.3
Isreal	3.7
New Zealand	4.4
Scotland	5.0
United States	**21.9**

1   2   3   4   5   24

FIGURE 12-1
Young men at risk. Young American men are murdered at a rate 4 to 73 times that of other industrial nations. Are Americans more violent? Or is their greater accessibility to guns the reason for this high rate? (*Sources:* Fingerhut & Kleinman, 1990; *New York Times.*)

other ethnic group in the United States to have health insurance (Council on Scientific Affairs of the American Medical Association, 1991).

In the United States, murder is the fifth leading cause of death in young adulthood—and it is the *top* cause for young African American men and a major cause for Hispanic men. Young American men are slain at rates 4 to 73 times higher than the rates in other industrial nations (see Figure 12-1). Three-fourths of the killings in this country involve guns, compared with only one-fourth of those in other industrialized nations (Fingerhut & Kleinman, 1990). The high rate of murder might be a legacy of American frontier justice—a greater readiness to use violence. Or it may reflect the fact

that the United States has no effective gun control legislation, as many other countries do. Of course, the first reason may explain the second.

INFLUENCES ON HEALTH AND FITNESS

Good health is not just a matter of luck; it often reflects a way of life, a series of choices. Human beings are not passive victims or beneficiaries of their genes; they are to a remarkable degree the masters of their own destiny. The Centers for Disease Control (1980) estimates that 50 percent of deaths from the 10 leading causes in the United States are linked to factors over which people have some control. Apart from such obviously risky or self-destructive behaviors as reckless driving, failing to use seat belts, associating with dangerous people, and suicide, many other things that people do from day to day can either expand or sap their vigor and extend or shorten their lives.

Health, as defined by the World Health Organization, is "a state of complete physical, mental, and social well-being and is not merely the absence of disease and infirmity" (Danish, 1983). People can seek health by pursuing some activities and refraining from others.

One study of 7000 adults, aged 20 to 70, found that observing seven common habits (see Table 12-1) was directly related to health. People who followed all seven habits were the healthiest; the next-healthiest were those who followed six of the habits, then those who followed five, and so on (Belloc & Breslow, 1972). A follow-up study found that 10 or more years later, people who had six or seven poor health habits were twice as likely to be

▪ *TABLE 12-1*

Seven Health Habits
Common Practices Directly Related to Health
1 Eating breakfast
2 Eating regular meals and not snacking
3 Eating moderately to maintain normal weight
4 Exercising moderately
5 Sleeping regularly 7 to 8 hours a night
6 Not smoking
7 Drinking alcohol moderately or not at all

SOURCE: Belloc & Breslow, 1972.

BOX 12-1 *PRACTICALLY SPEAKING*

WHAT YOU CAN DO TO IMPROVE YOUR HEALTH

As research shows, people have a great deal of control over their health and longevity. How you feel and how long you live often depend on what you do. If you follow these recommendations, you will be doing your part to maximize good health and long life.

■ *Eat for health:* Eat breakfast, eat regular meals, and eat moderately to maintain normal weight. Eat a diet low in fat and cholesterol to help prevent heart disease: fish and poultry (without skin) rather than red meats; almost no high-fat and smoked meats such as bacon and sausage; low-fat or skim milk and yogurt made from it; no more than two to four egg yolks a week; less butter and other fats; and low-fat cheeses like low-fat cottage cheese, ricotta, goat cheese, and mozzarella instead of hard and creamy cheeses. Eat foods associated with low rates of cancer: high-fiber fruits and vegetables and whole-grain cereals; citrus fruits and dark-green and yellow vegetables that are high in vitamin A, vitamin C, or both; and vegetables in the cabbage family (like cauliflower, broccoli, and brussels sprouts).

■ *Exercise regularly:* Find an exercise program that you will enjoy enough to stick with it. Try to find someone to exercise with you. It doesn't matter whether you run, bicycle, swim, walk, or do aerobic dancing; what matters is working out for at least 20 minutes at a time three times a week. If you're under 16 or over 35, see your doctor first. Build up gradually; continue to warm up gradually at the beginning of each session and cool down afterward.

■ *Use your seat belt:* It's very likely that at some time in your life you will be in an automobile accident. Your chance of being killed in a crash is 25 times higher if you are thrown out of your car. Your belt doubles your chance of surviving a crash (Engelberg, 1984).

■ *Don't smoke:* If you have never smoked, don't start. If you smoke now, stop. The sooner you stop, the better it will be for your health, the health of people around you, and the health of any children you may bear and raise in the future. You can go to one of a number of groups or professionals who offer support, or you can chew a gum specially designed for the purpose.

■ *Don't drink alcohol to excess:* If you don't drink, there's no reason to start. If you consume no more than one or two drinks a day (of whiskey, beer, or wine), and if your drinking has not caused any problems for you, there is probably no need to stop. But if you are drinking more than this—or if your drinking has gotten you into trouble on the job, at home, or with the law—your life and those of others may depend on your giving up alcohol altogether. Many people with drinking problems have found help from Alcoholics Anonymous, an organization that has chapters in communities around the world.

■ *Avoid drugs:* Drugs can harm your health, affect your mind, weaken your motivation to work, and sour your relationships, as well as get you into trouble with the law. Pregnant women who use drugs endanger their unborn children.

■ *Lead a healthy sexual life:* Practice safe sex. Promiscuity has been linked to cervical cancer and to acquired immune deficiency syndrome (AIDS). Protect yourself from sexually transmitted diseases (see Box 10-2).

---

disabled than people with no more than two poor habits (Breslow & Breslow, 1993). Also, people who abuse drugs or alcohol and people who do not practice safe sex expose themselves to a heightened risk of disease.

The link between behavior and health points up the interrelationship among the physical, intellectual, and emotional aspects of development. What people do affects how they feel. But *knowing* the facts about good health habits is not enough. People's personalities, social settings, and emotional states often outweigh what they know they should do and lead them into unhealthy behavior.

Let's look at some of the behaviors that are strongly and directly linked with health (see also Box 12-1) and then at some factors that influence health indirectly: socioeconomic level, education, gender, and marital status.

Diet

The saying "You are what you eat" sums up the importance of diet for physical and mental health. The first three of the seven health habits in Table 12-1 relate to diet. What people eat affects how they look, how they feel, and how likely they

What people eat affects how they look, how they feel, and how likely they are to suffer from various diseases. This couple's spaghetti supper may taste even better to them in their knowledge that pasta and bread, both low-fat complex carbohydrates, are nutritionally sound. *(Steve Goldberg/ Monkmeyer)*

are to suffer from various diseases. Conditions like diabetes and gout, for example, are more common among people who eat rich foods.

Diet and Weight

In a society that values slenderness and judges people by their physical attractiveness, being overweight can lead to major emotional problems. It also carries physical risks—of high blood pressure, heart disease, and certain cancers.

The risk of becoming overweight is highest from ages 25 to 34, making young adults a prime target group for prevention (Williamson, Kahn, Remington, & Anda, 1990). At all ages, obesity is a serious health hazard; the National Institutes of Health (NIH, 1985) urges that the 34 million Americans who have medically significant obesity receive the same kind of attention given to patients with other life-threatening disorders. Lower levels of overweight can also impair health.

Research confirms the dangers of being fat. Among 8006 Japanese men aged 45 to 68, death rates were highest for the fattest and the thinnest. The thinnest men, however, had lost weight since their twenties, probably because of the illnesses they eventually died from. People who are normally thin or who deliberately lose weight have a better prognosis than heavy people and people who

lose weight as the result of ill health (Rhoads & Kagan, 1983).

The effort to lose weight is such a constant preoccupation for so many people that every year some new diet book becomes a best-seller. But although many overweight people do lose weight on fad diets, most gain it back almost immediately after resuming their usual eating patterns. This "yo-yo" pattern of weight fluctuation, or "cycling," may be the most dangerous pattern of all. Recent research has found that *both* weight loss and weight gain are associated with higher death rates from coronary heart disease—and from all causes except cancer (I.-M. Lee & Paffenbarger, 1992). The healthiest course for overweight people—which is, of course, usually difficult—is to lose weight slowly and then maintain that loss. The most effective way to lose weight is to eat less, and especially to decrease the amount of fat in the diet, to use behavior modification techniques to change eating patterns, and to exercise more.

Diet and Cholesterol

High levels in the bloodstream of a fatty substance called *cholesterol* pose a risk of heart disease. Cholesterol creates fat deposits in blood vessels throughout the body, sometimes narrowing those vessels so much that the blood supply to the heart can be cut off, leading to a heart attack. There are two kinds of cholesterol: HDL ("good" cholesterol) and LDL ("bad" cholesterol), and a favorable ratio between these two, with HDL higher than LDL, is even more important than a person's total cholesterol level. (A mnemonic for remembering the healthy ratio is: "HDL should be high, LDL should be low.")

The link between cholesterol and heart disease has been definitively established. In one large-scale study, almost 4000 middle-aged men with high cholesterol levels were observed for 7 years. All the men followed low-cholesterol diets, and some received a cholesterol-lowering drug. This study found that reducing cholesterol levels can lower the risk of heart disease and death (Lipid Research Clinics Program, 1984a, 1984b).

Since the most important determinant of cholesterol levels seems to be the kinds and amounts of food people eat, nine major voluntary and government health agencies have proposed a healthy American diet for everyone from age 2 up (American Heart Association, 1990). It emphasizes a variety of nutritionally sound foods, with less fat and salt, and more fiber and complex carbohydrates— cereals, grains, etc. (See Box 12-1).

Diet and Cancer

Extensive worldwide research points strongly to a link between diet and certain cancers. One of the most clear-cut relationships is between a high-fat diet and colon cancer (Willett, Stampfer, Colditz, Rosner, & Speizer, 1990). Another link has been found between diet and stomach and esophageal cancers, which are more common among people in Japan than among Americans of Japanese descent. These cancers are associated with eating pickled, smoked, and salted fish, which is more common in Japan than in the United States (Gorbach, Zimmerman, & Woods, 1984). Although a correlation between a high-fat diet and breast cancer has been found, some recent research has failed to confirm that link (Willett et al., 1992). The new "healthy American diet" takes the risk of cancer into account (American Heart Association, 1990).

Exercise

After a distinctly nonathletic adolescence, each of the authors of this book joined one of the biggest trends of the past decade—regular exercise. Now Diane makes a point of taking a long brisk walk every day, and Sally jogs every morning. To our surprise, like many who have become more active in adulthood, we've found that exercise can be fun—even though it is good for us!

Today's "exercise boom" is highly visible; while a recent survey indicates that only 40 percent of American adults exercise strenuously three or more times a week, 78 percent of American adults currently engage in some kind of regular physical activity (Prevention Index '93, 1993). Those who do—who jog or jump, dance or swim, bike or bounce—reap many benefits. Physical activity helps to maintain desirable body weight; build muscles; strengthen heart and lungs; lower blood pressure; protect against heart attacks, cancer, and osteoporosis (a thinning of the bones that tends to affect older women, causing fractures; see Chapter 14); relieve anxiety and depression; and possibly lengthen life (P. R. Lee, Franks, Thomas, & Paffenberger, 1981; McCann & Holmes, 1984; Notelovitz & Ware, 1983).

According to one study of more than 13,000 healthy men and women, the benefits of exercise are not reserved only for marathoners and aerobics fanatics (Blair et al., 1989). These subjects fell into five categories of heart and respiratory fitness, on the basis of how well they did on a treadmill. The least fit led the most sedentary lives; the fittest exercised strenuously, sometimes running as much as 40 miles per week. Eight years later, the death rates of the least fit group were more than three times higher than the death rates of the most fit, as Figure 12-2 shows. This held for both men and women and for death rates from heart disease, cancer, and several other causes. But the greatest benefit to health showed up at levels of fitness just above the lowest level. People who did as little as walking ½ hour to 1 hour every day at a fast but comfortable pace cut their health risks by half or more, as compared with those who did less. The

A moderate program of regular physical activity brings many benefits. It helps people feel and look good, builds muscles, strengthens heart and lungs, keeps weight down, and protects against various disorders. *(Jim Wilson/Woodfin Camp & Associates)*

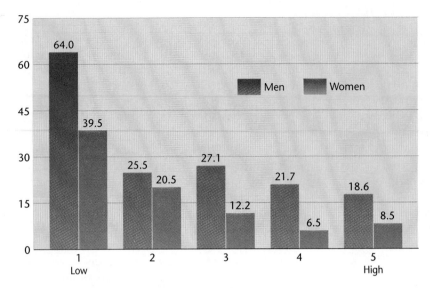

FIGURE 12-2
Death rates and fitness levels. In a study of adults at different levels of fitness, those at higher levels tended to live longer. The biggest difference showed up between the most sedentary group and the next higher level of fitness. (Note: Death rates are expressed as deaths per 10,000 person-years of follow-up.) (*Source:* Blair et al., 1989.)

message seems to be that instead of lying down when the urge to exercise hits, you can live longer if you take a brisk walk.

Smoking

Smoking is one of the worst of all health risks. Smokers expose themselves to an increased risk of cancer, heart disease, and a number of other disorders that can shorten their lives. The association between smoking and lung cancer is well established. Smoking is also related to cancer of the larynx, mouth, esophagus, bladder, kidney, pancreas, and cervix; and it is linked to gastrointestinal problems like ulcers, to heart attacks, and to respiratory illnesses like bronchitis and emphysema (USDHHS, 1987).

Nonsmokers are at risk of health problems because of *passive smoking;* that is, inhaling smoke when smoking by others is taking place around them. We noted in Chapter 2 how a pregnant woman's smoking can affect her unborn child. Nonsmokers in households in which more than two packs of cigarettes are smoked daily inhale smoke that is the equivalent of one or two cigarettes a day (Matsukura et al., 1984). Children of smoking mothers show diminished lung function (Tager, Weiss, Munoz, Rosner, & Speizer, 1983); and children of smokers and nonsmokers married to heavy smokers are at increased risk of lung cancer and heart disease. Passive smoking is a leading preventable cause of death in the United States today (Trichopoulos et al., 1992; Correa, Pickle, Fontham, Lin, & Haenszel, 1983; Fielding & Phenow, 1988).

The effects of smoking on smokers themselves have been well known for many years, and many people have gotten the message. But according to a national survey, 30 percent of U.S. adults smoke; this represents an increase of 5 percent since 1991 (Prevention Index '93, 1993). And the number of women who smoke has risen, to the point where women now smoke almost as much as men (Prevention Index '93, 1993).

At least 90 percent of the people who stop smoking do so on their own (Fiore, Novotny, Pierce,

Many people have gotten the message about the harmful effects of smoking. However, smoking rates have risen since 1991, especially among girls and women. (*Drawing by W. B. Park; © 1988 The New Yorker Magazine, Inc.*)

The American People Finally Speak Up

et al., 1990); others turn to specific programs for help. The most promising programs use a combination of cognitive, behavioral, and aversive techniques. Use of nicotine chewing gum, along with information on the drawbacks of smoking, has been successful (USDHHS, 1987). Quitting is usually not a one-time event, however, but rather a dynamic process that often occurs over a long cycle of stopping and relapsing (S. Cohen et al., 1989). As Sally's brother said, "It's easy to stop smoking—I've done it plenty of times."

However and whenever people stop smoking, their health is likely to improve. Over a 6-year follow-up in one study, middle-aged smokers who had heart disease were more likely to suffer a heart attack and to die than nonsmokers with heart disease or people with heart disease who had stopped smoking the year before the study began (Hermanson, Omenn, Kronmal, & Gersh, 1988). And in another study, women who had given up smoking and had not smoked for 3 or more years had a risk of heart attack no higher than that of women who had never smoked (L. Rosenberg, Palmer, & Shapiro, 1990).

Alcohol

The United States is a drinking society. Advertising equates hard liquor with the good life, and beer and wine with a good time. Drinking is the norm; according to a national survey, 59 percent of adults say that they sometimes drink (Prevention Index '93, 1993). Many adults extend hospitality by offering a glass of wine, a beer, or a cocktail; and a nondrinker is often pressed for explanations. However, drinking is less common than it used to be: alcohol consumption is now at a 3-decade low (Morbidity and Mortality Weekly Report, MMWR, 1989). According to their own reports, 46 percent of adults who drink alcohol consume three drinks or fewer in a given day, a 7 percent decline since 1983 (Prevention Index '93, 1993). The percentage of drinkers who consume four or more drinks a day is unchanged, however, since the early 1980s, remaining at 12 percent (Prevention Index '93, 1993).

For millions of drinkers and the people around them, alcohol can do great harm. For some 1 out of 10 adults, it can pose significant problems (USDHHS, 1992). Long-term heavy use may lead to such physical problems as cirrhosis of the liver, certain cancers, and heart failure. Besides liver damage, drinkers are likely to suffer from other gastrointestinal disorders (including ulcers), heart disease, nervous system damage, psychoses, and other medical problems. One controversial study (of a small sample of hospitalized people with alcoholism) suggested that women's bodies may metabolize alcohol less efficiently than men's, putting them at higher risk of liver disease (Frezza et al., 1990). As we pointed out earlier, drinking by a pregnant woman can damage her fetus.

Alcohol abuse is a major cause of fatal automobile accidents, and although 81 percent of drivers in one survey say that they never drive after drinking, 18 percent admit that they do drink and drive at least sometimes (these numbers do not add up to 100, because 1 percent say that they drive after drinking "all the time"—Prevention Index '93, 1993). Alcohol is also implicated in deaths from drowning, suicide, fire, and falls; and it is often a factor in family violence (National Institute on Alcohol Abuse and Alcoholism, NIAAA, 1981).

Despite the damage that alcohol can do to both physical and psychological health, many drinkers deny—or do not realize—that alcohol prevents them from functioning well on the job, at home, and in society.

Many experts consider alcoholism a chronic disease, with periods of remission and relapse, rather than a failure of willpower. Depending on the severity of the condition, treatment may include detoxification (removing all alcohol from the body), hospitalization, medicine and vitamins, individual and group psychotherapy, avoidance of all mood-altering drugs, involvement of the family, and referral to Alcoholics Anonymous. Treatment helps to give alcoholics new tools for coping with their addiction and leading a productive life, but it is not a cure. Treatment can be life-saving: in a study of 199 alcoholic men, those who stopped drinking lived as long as casual drinkers or teetotalers (Bullock, Reed, & Grant, 1992).

Indirect Influences on Health

Clearly, what people do or refrain from doing, or how they respond to life's changes and challenges, affects their health directly. There are also indirect influences on health and health-related behavior: these include economic status, education, gender, and marital status.

Socioeconomic Factors

Income is a major influence on health. More affluent people benefit both from access to better health care and from a healthier lifestyle. People without

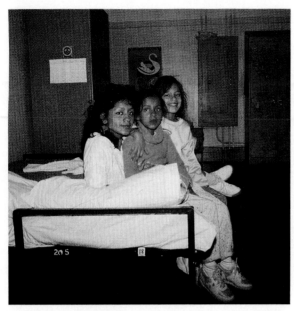

Income is a major influence on health. This family, living in a shelter for the homeless, may not be getting the nutrition and medical care needed for good health. *(Yvonne Hemsey/ Gamma-Liaison)*

health insurance have tended to receive substandard medical care, putting them at risk for a variety of medical problems (Burstin, Lipsitz, & Brennan, 1992). The association between poor living conditions and poor health helps to explain why the African American community, as well as other minority populations, has higher rates of sickness and death. But poverty is not the only reason.

Education

Adults who have not gone to college are at increased risk of developing chronic ailments like hypertension and heart disease. The less schooling people have had, the greater the chance that they will contract such a disease, that they will be seriously affected by it, and even that they will die of it. These findings—which hold true even when age, sex, race, and smoking or nonsmoking are controlled—come from a survey of a representative national sample of 5652 working people aged 18 to 64 (Pincus, Callahan, & Burkhauser, 1987).

Furthermore, while death rates have declined overall in the United States since 1960, death rates for poor and poorly educated people continue to be higher than those for more affluent, better educated people. In fact, this disparity increased between 1960 and 1986 (Pappas, Queen, Hadden, & Fisher, 1993).

This does not mean, of course, that formal edu-

cation *causes* good health. However, education is related to other factors that may be causative. The first, of course, is income. Other such factors may include health habits (like diet) and the ability to solve problems (including problems about personal health). People with more education tend to come from families with more money, and so they can afford a healthier diet and better preventive health care and medical treatment. In addition, better-educated people tend to have learned and to practice sensible personal habits. They tend to exercise more, to eat better, and to smoke less. Finally, education may help people to develop self-confidence and therefore to handle stress better.

Gender

Who are healthier—women or men? One problem in answering this question is that until recently women have been excluded from many, if not most, major studies (Healy, 1991). Thus much of what we know applies only to men. We do know that women have lower death rates throughout life. Yet women report being ill more often than men, and they use health services more often. What accounts for these differences? To remedy the lack of information about women's health, the National Institutes of Health recently launched a multidisciplinary study at a number of institutions across the United States, designed to gather data about major causes of death and disability among women. A major debate in medicine today revolves around the best way to treat women—by developing a new medical specialty devoted to women's health or by incorporating more attention to the health problems of women in standard medical school curriculums (Lewin, 1992).

Biological Differences   Female hardiness at every stage of life has been attributed to the genetic protection given by the presence of two X chromosomes, and, in mature women, to the beneficial effects of female hormones. Also, menstruation and pregnancy tend to make women aware of the body and its functioning, and cultural standards encourage medical management of those processes. Women see doctors during pregnancy, while trying to become pregnant, and for routine tests like the Pap smear, which detects cervical cancer; and they are more likely to be hospitalized than men, most often for surgery in connection with the reproductive system (Nathanson & Lorenz, 1982).

After women reach menopause, they are at about the same risk of heart disease as men of the same age (Healy, 1991). But in earlier years they are at lower risk, possibly because of the hormonal protection women enjoy during the years their bodies are producing estrogen (USDHHS, 1992). This may be a major benefit of the menstrual cycle, a powerful regulator of hormones that fluctuate in a woman's body for some 40 years of her life—from about age 12 until about age 50. To varying degrees, these hormones affect women's physiological, intellectual, and emotional states. For example, sight, hearing, smell, and touch operate differently at different phases of the menstrual cycle. Sight is keenest at the time of ovulation (usually midcycle), hearing peaks at the beginning of a menstrual period and again at ovulation, smell is most sensitive at midcycle and is reduced during menstruation, and sensitivity to pain is lowest just before a period (Parlee, 1983). Women's cognitive abilities are influenced so slightly that their daily lives are not affected in any meaningful way (Kimura, 1989).

Premenstrual syndrome (PMS) is a disorder involving physical discomfort and emotional tension; symptoms may appear up to 2 weeks before a menstrual period and then decline during and after it. Up to one-third of women have PMS, and about 10 percent have symptoms severe enough to interfere with their normal activities (Wurtman & Wurtman, 1989).

Symptoms may include headaches, swelling and tenderness of the breasts, abdominal bloating, weight gain, anxiety, fatigue, depression, irritability, acne, constipation, and other discomforts (American Council on Science and Health, 1985; M. Harrison, 1982; R. L. Reid & Yen, 1981). These symptoms are not distinctive in themselves; it is their timing that identifies PMS. Women who think that they may have PMS should keep a diary to keep track of when their symptoms occur.

The cause of PMS is not known: it may be related to cyclical hormonal and biochemical changes; there may also be psychological causes.

Little information is available on the effectiveness of various treatments for PMS, and the Food and Drug Administration has not approved any particular drug. Some doctors prescribe progesterone; others recommend vitamins, minerals, a healthy diet, elimination of caffeine and sugar, and exercise. Treatment may also target specific symptoms: for example, antidepressants for a woman who feels "blue" or diuretics for a woman who retains fluids. Since some women report relief after binge eating of carbohydrates, one research team suggests a high-carbohydrate diet (Wurtman & Wurtman, 1989). Treatment with a drug used to treat obesity has reduced some symptoms, apparently by affecting a transmitter chemical in the brain.

PMS is sometimes confused with *dysmenorrhea,* menstrual cramps. Cramps tend to afflict adolescents and young women; PMS is more typical in women in their thirties or older. Dysmenorrhea is caused by contractions of the uterus, which are set in motion by prostaglandin, a hormone-like substance; it can be treated with prostaglandin inhibitors.

Behavioral and Attitudinal Differences   Women's more frequent visits to physicians reflect greater sensitivity to their bodies. Women generally know more than men about health, think more and do more about preventing illness, are more aware of symptoms and susceptibility, and are more likely to talk about their medical fears and worries (Nathanson & Lorenz, 1982). Gender-role stereotyping may also enter in: men may feel that illness is not "masculine" and thus may be less likely to admit that they do not feel well.

Thus the fact that women say more often than men that they are sick does not necessarily mean that women are in worse health, nor does it mean that they are imagining ailments or that they have an unhealthy preoccupation with illness. It may well be that the better care women take of themselves helps them to live longer than men.

As women's lifestyles have become more like men's, their vulnerability to illness has also become more like men's. Today more women than ever before are dying from lung cancer (USDHHS, 1992), probably because they are smoking more. Since employment may be a factor in men's lower rates of reported illness, this may change too as more women join the work force. Employed women report less illness than homemakers, possibly because workers need to protect their jobs, their salaries, and their image as healthy producers (Nathanson & Lorenz, 1982).

The impact of gender-related behaviors and attitudes on physical health illustrates, once again, the relationship between the various domains of development. By and large, women are health-conscious not only for themselves but for their families—their husbands, their children, and (eventually) their aging parents. Now that women are under increasing pressures in the workplace, some observers are concerned that they will have less time and energy to monitor health, for themselves or for their families.

Marital Status

Marriage also enters the picture as a factor in health. Marriage seems to be healthful for both women and men, as we'll see in Chapter 13. But it is also possible that married people merely *seem* healthier, since family responsibilities discourage them from taking time off from work.

■ INTELLECTUAL DEVELOPMENT

Common sense tells us that when we become adults, we think differently from the way we did as children, or as adolescents. We can hold different kinds of conversations, understand more complicated material, and solve harder problems. Common sense, of course, is not always correct. But in this case, research confirms these beliefs.

We'll look at what is now made possible by the leaps beyond earlier levels of thinking, and at what intellectual strengths we generally see in young adulthood. (We'll talk about intellectual functioning in later adulthood in Chapters 14 and 16.)

ADULT THOUGHT: THEORETICAL APPROACHES

Piaget held that cognitive progress from infancy through adolescence results from a combination of maturation and experience. What happens, then, in an adult? Experience plays an especially important role in intellectual functioning. But the experiences of an adult are different from and usually far broader than those of a child, whose world is defined largely by home and school. Because adults have such diverse experiences, it is very hard to generalize about the effects of experience on cognition in adults. Still, some developmentalists have devised innovative ways to study and measure development in adulthood.

K. WARNER SCHAIE: STAGES OF COGNITIVE DEVELOPMENT

As a teenager, Spencer liked to match wits with participants on television quiz shows. By his mid-twenties, he had become impatient with such "games" and concentrated on using his extensive knowledge to develop computer software for museums. By his late thirties, he was focusing on ways to expand the small company he had started, in order to provide for his family and his two employees who had been with him from the beginning.

Spencer illustrates a progression identified by K. Warner Schaie (1977–1978), who believes that intellectual development proceeds in relation to people's recognition of what is meaningful and important in their own lives. The five stages in Schaie's theory chart a series of transitions from *"what* I need to know" (acquisition of skills in childhood and adolescence), through *"how* I should use what I know" (integration of these skills into a practical framework), to *"why* I should know" (a search for meaning and purpose that culminates in the "wisdom of old age"). Real-life experiences are important influences on this progression.

The sequence of stages in Schaie's model of cognitive development is as follows (see Figure 12-3):

1 *Acquisitive stage (childhood and adolescence):* In the **acquisitive stage,** information and skills are learned mainly for their own sake, without regard for the context, as a preparation for participation in society. Children and adolescents perform best on tests that give them a chance to show what they can do, even if the specific tasks have no meaning in their own lives.

2 *Achieving stage (late teens or early twenties to early thirties):* In the **achieving stage,** people no longer acquire knowledge merely for its own sake but use what they know to become competent and independent. Now, they do best on tasks that are relevant to the life goals they have set for themselves.

3 *Responsible stage (late thirties to early sixties):* People in the **responsible stage** are concerned with long-range goals and practical real-life problems that are likely to be associated with their responsibilities to others (like family members or employees).

4 *Executive stage (thirties or forties through middle age):* People in the **executive stage** are responsible for societal systems (like governmental or business concerns) rather than just family units; they need to integrate complex relationships on several levels.

5 *Reintegrative stage (late adulthood):* Older adults—who have let go of some social involvement and responsibility, and whose cognitive functioning may be limited by biological changes—are more selective about what tasks they will expend effort on. In this **reintegrative stage,** they think about the purpose of what they do and bother less with tasks that have no meaning for them.

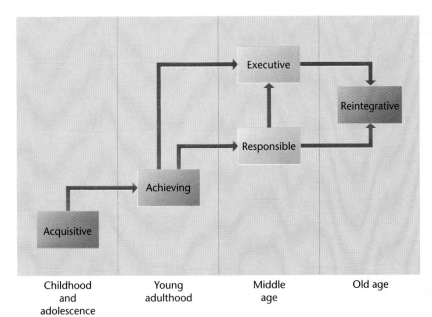

FIGURE 12-3
Stages of cognitive development in adults. (*Source:* Based on Schaie, 1977–1978.)

Childhood and adolescence | Young adulthood | Middle age | Old age

If adults do go through qualitative changes in intellectual functioning, traditional intelligence tests may be inappropriate for them (as we'll discuss further in Chapter 14). The challenge of developing new strategies to measure intellectual competence in adults is, Schaie says, "no less than that faced by Binet in initially measuring the intelligence of school children" (1977–1978, p. 135).

ROBERT STERNBERG: THREE ASPECTS OF INTELLIGENCE

Another way to think about thinking is in terms of the kinds of thought that become more important and more sophisticated in adult life. Let's look at an example involving three young women.

Alix, Barbara, and Courtney applied to graduate programs at Yale University. Alix had earned almost straight A's in college, scored very high on the Graduate Record Examination (GRE), and had excellent recommendations. Barbara's grades were only fair, and her GRE scores were low by Yale's high standards, but her letters of recommendation praised her exceptional research and creative ideas. Courtney's grades, GRE scores, and recommendations were good but not among the best.

Alix and Courtney were admitted to the graduate program. Barbara was not admitted to the program, but psychology professor Robert Sternberg hired her as a research associate, and she took graduate classes on the side. Alix did very well for the first year or so, but less well after that. Barbara

confounded the admissions committee by doing outstanding work. Courtney's performance in graduate school was only fair, but she had the easiest time getting a good job afterward (Trotter, 1986).

What explains these three stories? According to Sternberg (1985b, 1987), the women represent three different aspects of intelligence. Everyone has each element to a greater or lesser extent, and each is particularly useful in specific kinds of situations:

1 *Componential element—how efficiently people process and analyze information:* The **componential element** is the *critical* aspect of intelligence. It tells people how to approach problems, how to go about solving them, and how to monitor and evaluate the results. Alix was strong in this area; thus she was good at taking intelligence tests and finding holes in arguments.

2 *Experiential element—how people approach novel and familiar tasks:* The **experiential element** is the *insightful* aspect of intelligence. It allows people to compare new information with what they already know and to come up with new ways of putting facts together—in other words, to think in original ways (as Einstein did when he developed his theory of relativity). Automatic performance of familiar operations (like recognizing words) facilitates insight, because it leaves the mind free to tackle unfamiliar tasks (like decoding new words). Barbara was strong in this area.

3 *Contextual element—how people deal with their environment:* The **contextual element** is the *prac-*

These lawyers conferring about a case will be helped to achieve professional success by their tacit knowledge—the practical, "inside" information about how things are done, which is not formally taught but must be gained from experience. *(Mike Kagan/Monkmeyer)*

tical "real-world" aspect of intelligence. It becomes increasingly valuable in adult life—as in selecting a place to live or a field of work. It involves the ability to size up a situation and decide what to do: adapt to it, change it, or find a new, more comfortable setting. Courtney was strong in this area.

Alix's componential ability helped her to sail through tests in undergraduate school. But in graduate school, where more original thinking is expected, it was Barbara's superior experiential intelligence—her fresh insights and innovative ideas—that began to shine. Courtney was strongest in practical, contextual intelligence—"street smarts." She knew her way around. She chose "hot" research topics, submitted papers to the "right" journals, and knew where and how to apply for jobs.

Psychometric tests measure componential (critical) intelligence rather than experiential (insightful) or contextual (practical) intelligence. Since experiential and contextual intelligence are very important in adult life, psychometric tests are much less appropriate and useful in gauging adults' intelligence than in measuring children's.

An important component of contextual, or practical, intelligence is ***tacit knowledge***—"inside information" or "savvy" that is not formally taught or openly expressed, like knowing how to win a promotion or cut through red tape. (In the example above, Courtney was strong in tacit knowledge.) Getting ahead in a career, for instance, often depends on tacit knowledge. This includes

self-management (understanding motivation and knowing how to organize time and energy), *management of tasks* (knowing how to write a grant proposal), and *management of others* (knowing when to reward subordinates). Job performance typically shows only a weak correlation with IQ and employment tests; but one study in which hypothetical work-related scenarios were presented to experts and novices in psychology and business management found a significant relationship between job performance and these three kinds of tacit knowledge (Wagner & Sternberg, 1986).

BEYOND JEAN PIAGET: POSTFORMAL THOUGHT

Piaget considered formal operations to be the highest level of thought. Yet thought in adulthood is flexible, open, and adaptive in new ways that go beyond abstract logic. It is sometimes referred to as *postformal* thought.

Mature thinkers are able to combine both the *objective* (rational, or logical, elements) and the *subjective* (concrete elements, or elements based on personal experience). This helps people take their own feelings and experiences into account (Labouvie-Vief & Hakim-Larson, 1989). Wisdom can now flower, as more flexible thought enables people to accept inconsistency, contradiction, imperfection, and compromise so that they can solve real-life problems.

Thus mature thinking, or ***postformal thought***, relies on subjectivity and intuition, as well as on the pure logic that is characteristic of formal operational thought (Labouvie-Vief, 1985, 1986; Labouvie-Vief & Hakim-Larson, 1989). Mature thinkers personalize their reasoning, using the fruits of their experience when they are called on to deal with ambiguous situations. In one study, for example, novice nurses stuck to the clearly defined rules they had learned for taking care of babies, but experienced nurses drew on their intuition to guide them in deciding when it was better *not* to be bound by rules (Benner, 1984). Experience, then, contributes to adults' superior ability to solve practical problems.

We can see how postformal thinking develops in a study that asked people from preadolescence through middle age to interpret a story (Labouvie-Vief, Adams, Hakim-Larson, Hayden, & DeVoe, 1987). The subjects in this study were asked to consider the following problem:

> John is a heavy drinker, especially at parties. His wife, Mary, warns him that if he gets drunk once more, she will take the children and leave him. John does come home drunk after an office party. Does Mary leave John?

Children and most young adolescents said "yes"—Mary would leave John because she had said she would. Older adolescents saw that the problem was not so simple, but most of them still tried to approach it logically. However, the more mature adolescents and adults took into account the problem's "human dimensions." They realized that Mary might not go through with her threat, for a number of reasons. The *most* mature thinkers realized that there are a number of different ways to interpret the same problem, and that the way people look at such questions often depends on their individual life experiences.

In this study, that realization was partially age-related: it did not appear until late adolescence or early adulthood. Once in adulthood, however, age did not matter: people in their forties did not necessarily think more maturely than those in their twenties. Some adults seemed better able to understand issues having to do with certainty and logical conclusions, and to integrate these issues with emotion.

Postformal thought is also characterized by a shift from polarization (right versus wrong, logic versus emotion, mind versus body) to an integration of concepts. This shift often occurs in college, as we'll see in the work of Perry (1970), whose studies of college students we discuss later in this

chapter. One of its major effects is a new way of thinking about moral issues.

ADULT MORAL DEVELOPMENT

According to both Piaget and Kohlberg, moral development depends on cognitive development—a shedding of egocentric thought and a growing ability to think abstractly. But at Kohlberg's fifth and sixth stages of moral reasoning—fully principled, postconventional morality—moral development is chiefly a function of experience. Not until their twenties, if ever, do people reach this level.

HOW DOES EXPERIENCE AFFECT MORAL JUDGMENTS?

"Live and learn" sums up adult moral development. Experience leads people to reevaluate their criteria for judging what is right and fair. Experiences that promote such change are usually strongly colored by emotion, which triggers rethinking in a way that hypothetical, impersonal discussions cannot. People who undergo such experiences are more likely to see other people's points of view in social and moral conflicts.

For example, Bielby and Papalia (1975) noted that some adults spontaneously offer personal experiences as reasons for their answers to Kohlberg's moral dilemmas like Heinz's quandary (described in Chapter 8). People who have had cancer themselves, or whose family members or friends have had cancer, are more likely to condone a man's stealing an expensive drug to save his dying wife (as Heinz did), and to explain this view in terms of their own experience.

Two experiences that advance moral development, Kohlberg believed, are encountering conflicting values away from home (as happens in college or the military) and being responsible for the welfare of other people (as in parenthood—one reason parenthood is such a major transition). According to Kohlberg (1973), cognitive awareness of higher moral principles develops in adolescence, but most people do not commit themselves to acting upon these principles until adulthood, when the crises and turning points of identity often revolve around moral issues.

With regard to moral judgments, then, a person's cognitive stage is not the entire story. Of course, someone whose thinking is still at the level of concrete operations is unlikely to make moral

BOX 12-2   WINDOW ON THE WORLD

A CHINESE PERSPECTIVE ON MORAL DEVELOPMENT

Kohlberg's dilemma of "Heinz," who could not afford a drug for his sick wife (see Chapter 8), was revised for use in Taiwan: in the revision, a shopkeeper will not give a man food for his sick wife.

This version would seem unbelievable to Chinese villagers, who in real life are more accustomed to hearing a shopkeeper in such a dispute say, "You have to let people have things whether they have money or not" (Wolf, 1968, p. 21). In Kohlberg's format, subjects make an either-or decision based on their individual value systems. In Chinese society, people faced with such a dilemma discuss it openly, are guided by community standards, and try to find a way of resolving the problem to please as many parties as possible (Dien, 1982).

Other cultural differences are also involved here. In the west, even good people may be harshly punished if, under the force of circumstances, they break a law. The Chinese are unaccustomed to uni-versally applied laws; they prefer to abide by the sound decisions of a wise judge. The Chinese outlook is that human beings are born with moral tendencies, and their moral development rests on intuitive and spontaneous feelings supported by society, rather than on the kind of analytical thinking, individual choice, and personal responsibility envisioned by Kohlberg. Kohlberg's philosophy is based on abstract principles of justice; the Chinese ethos leans toward conciliation and harmony.

How, then, can Kohlberg's theory, rooted in western values and reflecting western ideals, be applied to moral development in an eastern society that works along very different lines? Some say that it cannot be applied and that an alternative view is required—a view that measures morality by the ability to make judgments based on norms of reciprocity, rules of exchange, available resources, and complex relationships (Dien, 1982).

This viewpoint echoes the forceful protests of Carol Gilligan (1982, 1987), who has studied moral development in American women. Gilligan argues that Kohlberg's stages esteem only male-oriented values, such as justice and fairness, and ignore such female-oriented moral values as compassion and responsibility for the welfare of others.

These issues are important to American society as a whole, not only to women and to people from other cultures. If our leaders stress justice and rights (Kohlberg's values) rather than alternative values like care and responsibility, we may be encouraging our citizens to see morality as a rigid, either-or issue and to dismiss attempts to resolve conflicts in a care-focused way as "utopian, outdated, impractical," or even "the outworn philosophy of hippies" (Gilligan, 1987, p. 75). In the interest of national and global harmony, we need to rethink our concepts of morality.

decisions at a postconventional level. But even someone who is at the stage of formal operations may not reach the highest level of moral thinking—unless experience catches up with cognition. Furthermore, experience is interpreted within a cultural context, affecting people differently in different countries or in different subcultures within the same country (see Box 12-2.)

ARE THERE GENDER DIFFERENCES IN MORAL DEVELOPMENT?

The issue of gender differences in moral development is a major controversy in developmental psychology. Many critics have assailed Freud's idea that women, because of their biological nature, are morally inferior to men. Kohlberg's theory of moral reasoning has also been attacked as being based on male values and excluding female values.

Some studies of moral reasoning in adulthood have shown differences in the levels achieved by men and women; these differences have consistently favored men. A review of the literature on moral development, however, found no significant gender differences in levels of moral reasoning across the life span (L. J. Walker, 1984). Only a few, inconsistent differences showed up in childhood and adolescence. Small differences in a few studies of adults did favor men, but the findings were not clearly gender-related, since the men were generally better educated and had better jobs than the women. The review therefore concluded that "the moral reasoning of males and females is more similar than different" (Walker, 1984, p. 687).

Still, men and women do seem to look at moral issues in different ways, to define morality differently, and to base their moral decisions on different values. One researcher who has focused on these differences is Carol Gilligan. Gilligan (1982) maintains that Kohlberg's approach to moral development is oriented toward values that are generally more important to males than to females, and that it fails to take into account women's major concerns and perspectives. While our society expects from men assertiveness and independent judgment, it expects from women concern for the well-being of others and self-sacrifice to ensure that well-being. A woman's central moral dilemma is the conflict between herself and others, a conflict that is not reflected in Kohlberg's theory and testing methods.

Gilligan examined women's reasoning about an area of their lives in which they have choices: the control of fertility. She interviewed and gave moral dilemmas to 29 women referred by abortion and pregnancy counseling services. These women talked about whether they would terminate or continue their pregnancies, and how they were arriving at their decisions. The women spoke "in distinct moral language whose evolution traces a sequence of development" (Gilligan, 1982, p. 73). They saw morality in terms of selfishness versus responsibility and as an obligation to exercise care and avoid hurting others. They viewed people who care for each other as the most responsible, and people who hurt someone else as selfish and immoral. Gilligan concluded that while men tend to think more in terms of abstract justice and fairness, women tend to think more about their responsibilities to specific people. (See Table 12-2 for Gilligan's description.)

We see here a dramatic illustration of two contrasting concepts: Kohlberg's morality of rights and Gilligan's morality of responsibility. An example of the abstract morality of Kohlberg's stage 6 is the biblical story of Abraham and Isaac: Abraham was ready to sacrifice his son's life when God demanded it as a proof of faith. An example of Gilligan's person-centered morality can also be found in the Bible, in the story of the woman who proved to King Solomon that she was a baby's mother when she agreed to give the infant to another woman rather than see it harmed. Acknowledging the female perspective on moral development lets us appreciate the importance for both sexes of connections with other people and of the universal need for compassion and care.

TABLE 12-2

Gilligan's Levels of Moral Development in Women	
Stage	**Description**
Level 1: Orientation of individual survival	The woman concentrates on herself—on what is practical and what is best for her.
Transition 1: From selfishness to responsibility	The woman realizes her connection to others and thinks about what the responsible choice would be in terms of other people (like the unborn baby), as well as herself.
Level 2: Goodness as self-sacrifice	This conventional feminine wisdom dictates sacrificing the woman's own wishes to what other people want—and will think of her. She considers herself responsible for the actions of others, while holding others responsible for her own choices. She is in a dependent position, one in which her indirect efforts to exert control often turn into manipulation, sometimes through the use of guilt.
Transition 2: From goodness to truth	She assesses her decisions not on the basis of how others will react to them but on her intentions and the consequences of her actions. She develops a new judgment that takes into account her own needs, along with those of others. She wants to be "good" by being responsible to others, but also wants to be "honest" by being responsible to herself. Survival returns as a major concern.
Level 3: Morality of nonviolence	By elevating the injunction against hurting anyone (including herself) to a principle that governs all moral judgment and action, the woman establishes a "moral equality" between herself and others and is then able to assume the responsibility for choice in moral dilemmas.

SOURCE: Adapted from Gilligan, 1982.

COLLEGE

College can mean anything from a 2-year community college stressing vocational training or a small 4-year liberal arts school to a large university with graduate divisions. Most colleges today are coeducational, but a few are still all-male or all-female. With such diversity, it is hard to generalize about the college experience.

WHO GOES TO COLLEGE?

Today's college classrooms include many different kinds of students. Juanita, for example, entered college directly from high school, having already decided on a premedical program. Vince worked for 2 years after high school and is now taking courses in music and journalism, unsure which to follow as a career. Otis wants a master's degree in business administration as the first step on his route to a six-figure salary. Marilyn came to college looking for a husband. Consuela interrupted her education to marry and to raise three children; now that they are in college, she herself came back to earn her degree. Toshio, retired from business after a lifetime of supporting a family, now has time to expand his intellectual horizons.

Nearly 14.2 million students are enrolled in American colleges and universities. Fifty-five percent are women, and an increasing percentage are ages 35 and older (National Center for Education Statistics, NCES, 1989a, 1991; see Chapter 14 for a discussion of learning in midlife).

INTELLECTUAL GROWTH IN COLLEGE

College can be a time of intellectual discovery and personal growth. For traditional students—those in transition from adolescence to adulthood—college offers a chance to question assumptions held over from childhood and thus to mold a new adult identity. Sometimes this questioning may lead to an identity crisis and to serious problems: abuse of alcohol or drugs, eating disorders, risk taking, and even suicide. Fortunately, however, it more often fosters healthy development.

Students change in response to other students who challenge long-held views and values; to the student culture itself, which is different from the culture of society at large; to the curriculum, which offers new insights and new ways of thinking; and

to faculty members, who often take a personal interest in students and provide new role models (Madison, 1969).

A 4-year longitudinal study of 165 undergraduates in three disciplines found that students majoring in the *natural sciences* (biology, chemistry, microbiology, physics), *humanities* (communications, English, history, journalism, linguistics, philosophy), or *social sciences* (psychology, anthropology, economics, political science, sociology) showed improvements in reasoning from their first year of college to their fourth (Lehman & Nisbett, 1990).

Students in all three fields improved the quality of their everyday reasoning. This shows that reasoning skills can be taught and suggests that such teaching can help people change the way they think about uncertainty in everyday life. The different major courses of study taught different kinds of reasoning abilities. For example, undergraduate training in the social sciences produced gains in statistical and methodological reasoning, or the ability to generalize patterns. Students majoring in the other two categories had better conditional reasoning, or the ability to use formal deductive logic, like that used in computer programming and mathematics. And all the students except the social science majors improved their verbal reasoning, the ability to recognize arguments, evaluate evidence, and detect analogies in reading passages. (These findings suggest that a narrow education in a single major field is not enough to realize one's intellectual potential.)

One avenue of self-discovery in college is the exploration of new, more realistic career choices. For example, Lucas was first attracted to a career in astronomy; but after exploring other fields, he decided that he really wanted to work with people.

The academic and social challenges of college can lead to intellectual and moral growth. In a study that has inspired much of the research on postformal thought, William Perry (1970) interviewed 67 Harvard and Radcliffe students throughout their undergraduate years and found that their thinking progressed from rigidity to flexibility and ultimately to freely chosen commitments:

■ As students encounter a wide variety of ideas, they accept the coexistence of several different points of view, and they also accept their own uncertainty. They consider this stage temporary, however, and expect to learn the "one right answer eventually."
■ Next they see the relativism of all knowledge

In the 1970s, high school girls were less likely than boys to go to college and less likely to finish. Today girls are *more* likely than boys to go to college and about as likely to aim for advanced degrees. Female college students may develop more interest and confidence in studying anatomy when taught by a female instructor who serves as a role model. *(Charles Gupton/ Stock, Boston)*

and values: they recognize that different societies, different cultures, and different individuals work out their own value systems. They now realize that their opinions on many issues are as valid as anyone else's, even if the other person is an authority figure.

■ Finally they affirm their identity through the values and commitments they choose for themselves.

GENDER DIFFERENCES IN ACHIEVEMENT IN COLLEGE

Looking around you at your classmates, you can probably see many signs of the rapid change in women's roles—in college enrollment, in the courses women choose, and in their personal, educational, and occupational goals. In the 1970s, high school girls were less likely than boys to go to college and less likely to finish. Today, girls are *more* likely than boys to go to college and about as likely to pursue advanced degrees (National Center for Education Statistics, NCES, 1989a, 1991).

And women are earning more degrees today than in the past. More than half of the bachelor's and master's degrees awarded in 1990–1991, and about 40 percent of doctoral and professional degrees, were awarded to women (NCES, 1991). And in recent years the percentage of women among students of dentistry, medicine, veterinary medicine, and law took large leaps (Congressional Caucus for Women's Issues, 1987).

Yet as recently as the late 1970s, some of the same girls who had outshone boys throughout high school slipped behind in college. Even the ablest female students had lower self-esteem and more limited aspirations than males. Women were avoiding academic risks and steering away from mathematics (Sells, 1980). Many overprepared for class and took careful notes, but panicked over assignments and examinations and felt less confident than their male classmates about their preparation for graduate study (Leland et al., 1979). Even highly gifted women tended to go to less selective colleges than men and were less likely to go on to prestigious graduate schools and high-status occupations (Kerr, 1985).

These patterns may well have resulted from gender socialization, since during adolescence girls tend to become more focused on relationships and boys tend to become more focused on careers (Kerr, 1985). Society gives girls messages that emphasize the roles of wife and mother and stress the difficulty or even the impossibility of combining personal achievement with love and family. Young men are given no reason to believe that their roles as future husbands and fathers might interfere with developing their career potential.

These gender-based messages to young people may help to explain why differences still persist today between adult men and women. The great majority of engineering, architecture, and science students are male, while most of the students of teaching, foreign languages, and home economics are female (Newhouse News Service, 1987).

LEAVING COLLEGE

The *college dropout* is variously defined as a student who leaves a college and takes some time off before resuming studies at the same school ("stopping out") or transfers to another school, or ends college studies altogether. About half of entering college students never earn a degree at all (National Institute of Education, NIE, 1984).

There is no "typical" college dropout. Students leave school for many reasons—marriage, the desire to be close to a loved one, a change in occupational status, or dissatisfaction with their school. Ability may be a factor; able students are more likely than they were in the early 1970s to remain in college (U.S. Department of Education, 1987). But although most dropouts have lower average aptitude scores than those who stay in school, they are usually doing satisfactory work.

Leaving college temporarily can be a positive step. Many students gain more by working for a while, enrolling at a more compatible institution, or just allowing themselves time to mature. After 2 years of academic work and 1 year of art school, for example, Sally's daughter Dorri took 2 years out to pursue a long-held dream of a career in rock music. She worked as a waitress and took music lessons while she was out of school—but then decided against following this route. Having learned more about herself, her goals, and the music business, she decided to go back to the school of design in which she had been enrolled, which had allowed her to "stop out" for up to 2 years without having to reapply. Dorri majored in illustration, received her Bachelor of Fine Arts degree, and is now working as a graphic artist.

Many colleges make it easy for students to take leaves of absence, to study part time, and to earn credit for independent study, life experiences, and work done at other institutions. "Stopping out," then, is generally not a major problem; but students who drop out and never earn degrees at all may limit their opportunities.

Formal education need not—and often does not—end in the early twenties. It can continue throughout adulthood. The trend toward lifelong learning can be seen in growing college enrollments over the past decade by people over 30, and especially by those over 35 (National Center for Education Statistics, NCES, 1989b). We'll discuss the place of educational programs in the lives of mature adults in later chapters.

STARTING A CAREER

On her way to becoming a professor of child development, Diane majored in psychology as an undergraduate and then went on to pursue a master's degree in child development and family relations, and a doctorate in life-span developmental psychology. Like many people, Diane embarked upon her first full-time job as a young adult. With her first faculty appointment, she carved out a major aspect of her identity, earned financial independence, and showed the ability to assume adult responsibilities.

Long before that time, however, and long after it, work had and will continue to have a major role in her development, as it does for most people. Many a career is born in a child's dream (as a young girl, Diane pored over her parents' book on child development); adolescents struggle with thoughts of future vocations; people in midlife often change careers (sometimes voluntarily, sometimes not); and older adults face issues concerning retirement.

Work is entwined with all aspects of development. Intellectual factors, physical factors, social factors, and emotional factors affect the kind of work people do; and people's work can affect every other area of their lives. Let's look now at some important aspects of work: how age and gender affect attitudes and performance, and how working life and family life intersect (see Box 12-3). (Other work-related issues are discussed in Chapter 14 and Chapter 16.)

WORK AND AGE

How does a person's stage of life affect the way she or he thinks about work and performs on the job? Age-related effects have been reported in an analysis of more than 185 studies (Rhodes, 1983).

How Young Adults Feel about Their Jobs

By and large, workers under age 40, who are in the process of forming their careers, are less satisfied with their jobs overall than they will be later on, at least until age 60. They are less involved with their jobs, less committed to their employers, and more likely to change jobs than they will be in later life (Rhodes, 1983).

The reason for the increase in "job satisfaction" with age is uncertain. There are no clear age dif-

BOX 12-3 *FOOD FOR THOUGHT*

HOW DUAL-EARNER COUPLES COPE

Both authors of this book have been personally involved in a significant trend in American life: marriages in which husband and wife both hold jobs outside the home. This represents a major change from traditional family patterns and—as both research and our own personal experiences testify—it offers both pluses and minuses. The way families deal with the issues in this lifestyle differs by ethnic group and economic level, but some generalities seem to apply to most such families.

A major advantage, of course, is financial. Most first-time home buyers are two-earner families, for example; and a second income raises some families from poverty to middle-income status and makes others affluent. Many women who work in mills and factories contribute almost half of the family income (L. Thompson & Walker, 1989). Other benefits over the one-income household often include:

■ More equal relationship between husband and wife
■ Greater sense of integrity for the woman
■ Closer relationship between a father and his children
■ Greater capacity for each partner to function and develop in both work and family roles

But this way of life also creates many stresses. Working couples face extra demands on their time and energy, conflicts between work and family roles, possible rivalry between spouses, and anxiety and guilt over meeting children's needs.

One source of strain is the fact that husband and wife are part of three role systems—the wife's work system, the husband's work system, and the joint family system. Each role makes demands at different times, and partners have to decide which should take priority at each time. The family is most demanding when there are young children; careers are especially demanding, and especially stressful, when a worker is getting established or being promoted. And both kinds of demands frequently occur around the same time, often in young adulthood.

Because these sweeping changes in family patterns and career aspirations are so new, today's hard-working, family-oriented men and women have few role models— and few institutional supports from society. Couples must therefore work out their own solutions.

There have been some changes in how these couples divide work within the home. However, women who work outside the home continue to hold the primary responsibility for homemaking and child care—doing almost 80 percent of all housework (Berardo, Sheehan, & Leslie, 1987). Lower-income and minority-group husbands are most likely to do more at home, and men are most likely to "help out" with cooking or child care (L. Thompson & Walker, 1989). Still, mothers spend from 3 to 5 hours of active involvement with their children for every hour fathers spend, and mothers carry 90 percent of the burden of responsibility for child care (M. Lamb, 1987b).

The issue of who does what is not related to how much the wife earns, how many hours she works, or whether she is the dominant partner in the marriage. In fact, husbands who have more say about running the household do more of the chores (Kamo, 1988). So far, then, it is not clear what distinguishes marriages in which wage earning and family work are shared equitably from marriages in which they are not.

What kinds of changes could society institute to alleviate the strains on dual-earner families as more couples adopt this lifestyle? One possibility involves redesigning living and working environments so that people could pool domestic services and thus split their time more easily between home and workplace. Also, employers could structure more jobs on a part-time basis; communities and employers could provide more child-care services; and the federal government could take a larger role in financing and offering tax incentives for child care, in subsidizing new parents to let them postpone their return to work, and in providing a higher wage base for child-care workers. Such measures would help parents, children, and society.

One encouraging sign of changing societal attitudes recognizing the value of family life was the passage of the Family Leave Act in 1993, providing 12 weeks of unpaid leave for such family events as the birth or adoption of a child or the care of an older person. Such leave would be available to employees in businesses with 50 or more workers.

Age differences in performance on the job seem to depend largely on how performance is measured and on the demands of a specific kind of work. Erik Weihenmayer's physical prowess helps him perform as a wrestling coach; the fact that he is blind does not interfere with either this job or his other work as an English teacher. *(James Salzano/American Foundation for the Blind)*

ferences for some specific aspects of job satisfaction (like promotion, supervision, and coworkers), and findings about satisfaction with pay are mixed. The relationship between age and overall job satisfaction may reflect the nature of the work itself. The longer people work at an occupation, the more rewarding the work may be (Rhodes, 1983). Or it may be that younger people, who are still seeking the best path in life, know that they can change career directions more easily now than later. They may look at their jobs more critically than they will when they have made a stronger commitment.

Again, we have to be careful about differences that show up in cross-sectional studies. For example, older people have shown a greater belief in the idea that people should work hard to develop character (the "work ethic"). This is probably a difference in values between cohorts rather than an effect of how long people have lived. There may be more of a developmental difference, however, in personality needs associated with work. Younger workers, for example, are more concerned with

how interesting their work is, with the opportunities it gives them to develop their abilities, and with their chances for advancement. Older workers care more about having friendly supervisors and coworkers and receiving help with their work.

How Young Adults Perform on the Job

Findings about the relationship between age and performance at work are mixed. Studies on absenteeism, for example, give conflicting results. But if we break the findings down into *avoidable* absences (those which seem voluntary on the worker's part) and *unavoidable* absences (like those caused by sickness), we do see effects of age. Younger workers have more avoidable absences than older workers, possibly because of a lower level of commitment. Older workers have more unavoidable absences, probably because of poorer health and slower recovery from accidents.

When we look at how well people do their work, the picture again is not clear-cut. The key factor may be experience rather than age: when older people perform better, it may be because they have been on the job longer, not because they are older.

Many workers continue to be productive very late in life. In general, age differences in performance seem to depend largely on how performance is measured and on the demands of a specific kind of work. A job requiring quick reflexes is likely to be done better by a young person; a job that depends on mature judgment may be better handled by an older person.

WORK AND GENDER

Today 46 percent of economists, 33 percent of computer analysts, and 28 percent of mail carriers are women (U.S. Department of Labor, 1992). Gender has less to do with vocational choice than it did 25 years ago, when most women—whatever their interests and talents—planned to devote most of their working lives to homemaking and child care. (This has rarely even been recognized as a vocational choice but has been seen as just something women are "supposed to do.")

Even in the past, many women worked for pay outside of the home. Today, there are more women in the labor force than ever before: 57 percent of women in 1992 (see Figure 12-4). Sixty-six percent of mothers of children under age 18 and 58.4 percent of mothers with children under 6 are em-

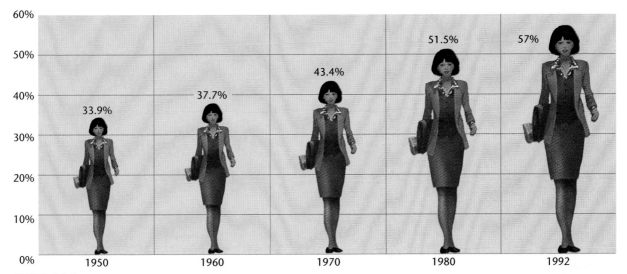

FIGURE 12-4
Percentage of American women in the labor force, 1950–1992. (*Sources:* Hayghe, personal communication, 1992; Matthews & Rodin, 1989.)

ployed outside the home (H. Hayghe of the U.S. Department of Labor, personal communication, March 1992).

Like men, women work to earn money, to achieve recognition, and to fulfill personal needs. Many women need to work because they are single, divorced, widowed, separated, or married to men who do not earn enough to support the family. Trends toward later marriage, later childbearing, and smaller families have made it easier for many women to pursue ambitious career goals. And both men and women take advantage of alternative work patterns like part-time and flexible schedules and job sharing.

Laws mandating equal opportunity in employment are designed to give both sexes equal rights in hiring, pay, and promotion. But reality still falls far short of this ideal. For every dollar that men earn, women earn only about 70 cents. This wage gap has narrowed slightly in the past few years—but that is not so much because women are paid more because men's earnings have dropped with the disappearance of many highly paid

manufacturing jobs (U.S. Bureau of Labor, 1989).

Although more women are getting better jobs these days (especially in business and the professions), a large proportion are still doing "pink-collar" work, low-paid work that has traditionally been done by women (and that tends to remain low-paid largely *because* it is done by women). Almost half of all employed women are clerks, salespersons, and the like; very few have skilled craft or construction jobs. Many enter the labor force in low-paying entry-level jobs, and often they do not advance as rapidly as men. This is due partly to discrimination, and partly to the problems of juggling work and family roles in a society that gives little support to families (Kessler-Harris, 1987).

New work patterns change day-to-day life for the whole family and bring new stresses and satisfactions. Once again, we see the interrelationship between different aspects of people's lives. In Chapter 13, we'll explore further the effects of both work and relationships on young men's and women's personality development.

SUMMARY

SENSORY AND PSYCHOMOTOR FUNCTIONING

■ The typical young adult is in good condition; physical and sensory abilities are usually excellent.

HEALTH AND FITNESS IN YOUNG ADULTHOOD

■ Almost 95 percent of 15- to 44-year-olds rate their health as good, very good, or excellent.

■ Specific behavior patterns such as diet, exercise, smoking, and drinking alcohol can affect health.

■ Good health is related to higher income, greater education, gender, and being married.

■ Women are usually more likely than men to report being ill, to use health services, and to be hospitalized. Women are more health-conscious than men and tend to arrange for health services for the family.

■ Hormones of the menstrual cycle seem to affect at least some women physically and emotionally. The effect on cognitive abilities does not seem to influence daily functioning.

ADULT THOUGHT: THEORETICAL APPROACHES

■ K. Warner Schaie has proposed five stages of cognitive development from childhood through late adulthood: acquisitive, achieving, responsible, executive, and reintegrative.

■ Robert Sternberg has proposed three aspects of intelligence: componential (critical), experiential (insightful), and contextual (practical). The experiential and contextual aspects develop and become particularly important during adulthood.

■ *Postformal thought* refers to thought in adulthood that is flexible, open, and adaptive, and goes beyond formal logic. It is characteristic of mature thinkers.

ADULT MORAL DEVELOPMENT

■ According to Lawrence Kohlberg, moral development in adulthood depends primarily on experience; but, as before, moral thinking cannot exceed the limits set by cognitive development.

■ Women's moral development has been explored by Carol Gilligan, who proposes that women have concerns and perspectives that are not tapped in Kohlberg's theory and research. Whereas men tend to think more about justice and fairness, women are more concerned with reponsibilities to specific people.

COLLEGE

■ The college experience affects intellect and personality, as college students question long-held assumptions and values.

■ In the past, girls often did better than boys in elementary school and high school, but that picture tended to change at the college level. Today, more women are going to college and are earning advanced degrees. The fields that men and women choose to study still differ markedly, however.

■ About 50 percent of college students never earn degrees.

STARTING A CAREER

■ Career development is important during young adulthood. Younger workers are less committed to their present jobs than older workers.

■ Dual-earner families, in which both spouses work outside the home, are becoming more prevalent. Both society and the working couples have to make changes to alleviate the stresses associated with the potentially conflicting demands of work and family.

■ Women, like men, work for a variety of reasons—to earn money, to achieve recognition, and to fulfill personal needs. Women tend to earn less than men, and although more women are getting better jobs than in previous decades, most are still doing low-paid work. Today an increasing number of women are pursuing careers in business, law, medicine, and other traditionally male-dominated areas.

KEY TERMS

premenstrual syndrome (PMS)
   (page 419)
acquisitive stage (420)
achieving stage (420)

responsible stage (420)
executive stage (420)
reintegrative stage (420)
componential element (421)

experiential element (421)
contextual element (421)
tacit knowledge (422)
postformal thought (422)

SUGGESTED READINGS

Belenky, M. F., Clinchy, B. McV., Goldberger, N. R., & Tarule, J. M. (1986). *Women's ways of knowing: The development of self, voice, and mind.* New York: Basic Books. A lively and thought-provoking report of an in-depth survey of 135 women. The authors maintain that women think differently from men and that women's mode of thought, which combines objectivity with intuition and personal knowledge, is just as or more legitimate than traditional male models of dispassionate thinking. The book describes five common modes of women's thought, illustrates the findings with quotations and anecdotes, and explores implications for education.

Gilligan, C., Ward, J. V., & Taylor, J. McL. (Eds.). (1988). *Mapping the moral domain: A contribution of women's thinking to psychological theory and education.* Cambridge, MA: Harvard University Press. In 14 articles, researchers and theoreticians examine the different ways that males and females, from childhood through adolescence into adulthood, think about relationships, loyalty, responsibility, violence, and other moral issues.

Griswold, R. L. (1993). *Fatherhood in america: A history.* New York: Basic Books. A fascinating account of the changing roles of fathers over the years, focusing on the connections between masculinity, feminism, and American culture. Drawing on personal letters and diaries, as well as analysis of movies, magazines, and other cultural aspects, the author shows how the role of father as breadwinner has expanded and changed.

Melpomene Institute for Women's Health Research. (1993). *The bodywise woman.* Champaign, IL: Human Kinetics Publishers. A research-based report on the relationship between women's health and physical activity, this reference book uses case histories, graphs, and charts in its discussion of body image, menstruation, pregnancy and fitness, and exercise for children and older women.

Pittman, F. (1993). *Man enough: Fathers, sons, and the search for masculinity.* New York: Putnam. In this partly autobiographical work, the author traces the development of masculine roles. He proposes an ideal of masculinity as based on teamwork and emulation with other men, rather than competition; and equality with women, rather than fear or domination.

Sternberg, R. (1985). *Beyond IQ.* Cambridge, MA: Cambridge University Press. Sternberg's statement of his triarchic theory of intelligence. The book describes and explains this new way of looking at intelligence.

Taylor, S. E. (1989). *Positive illusions: Creative self-deception and the healthy mind.* New York: Basic Books. This provocative book by a social psychologist draws on a large body of research demonstrating that the best adjusted people are not, as has traditionally been believed, firmly in touch with reality. Instead, the healthy human mind seems to cope with life by replacing negative information with positive, often unrealistically optimistic, beliefs.

CHAPTER THIRTEEN

PERSONALITY AND SOCIAL DEVELOPMENT IN YOUNG ADULTHOOD

*Human beings are not born once and for all on the day
their mothers give birth to them. . . . Life obliges them over
and over again to give birth to themselves.*

Gabríel Gárcia Marquez,
Love in the Time of Cholera, *1988*

■ **PERSONALITY DEVELOPMENT
IN YOUNG ADULTHOOD: TWO MODELS**

Normative-Crisis Model
Timing-of-Events Model

■ **INTIMATE RELATIONSHIPS
AND PERSONAL LIFESTYLES**

Love
Marriage
Divorce
Single Life
Cohabitation
Sexuality
Parenthood
Remaining Childless
Friendship

■ **BOXES**

13-1 Food for Thought: Establishing Mature
Relationships with Parents
13-2 Window on the World: Marriage
and Divorce Patterns
13-3 Take a Stand: Advantages to Having
Children Early or Late
13-4 Practically Speaking: The Hassles
of Raising Young Children
13-5 Food for Thought: Both Job and Family
Roles Affect Men's Psychological Well-being

- Do adults' personalities develop in definite, predictable patterns, or does the course of development depend on what happens in people's lives?
- How is personality development alike and different for young men and women?
- How do young adults get along with their parents?

- What are the effects of such lifestyle choices as marriage, divorce, single life, cohabitation, parenthood, stepparenthood, and remaining childless?
- What do love, sexuality, and friendship mean to young adults?

Looking back, both authors of this book—Diane now in her mid-forties, and Sally in her late fifties—would say, like most people at midlife, that they are very different from the people they were at age 20, when they entered young adulthood. And by age 60 or age 70, they are likely to have changed even more. It is difficult to realize, then, that until recently, students of human development paid very little attention to the social and emotional changes that take place during the 50 or more years of adult life.

Today, few people believe that the personality stops growing when the body does. Most developmentalists are now convinced that human beings can change and grow as long as they live. In this chapter, as well as in the other chapters from 12 through 17, we look at theories and research on adult development that have arisen over the past few decades.

Two main approaches to adult development are the normative-crisis model and the timing-of-events model. In this chapter, we look at research supporting both approaches. We also examine how young adults reach important decisions that frame their lives—decisions that revolve around love, sex, parenting, friendship, and work and career.

PERSONALITY DEVELOPMENT IN YOUNG ADULTHOOD: TWO MODELS

NORMATIVE-CRISIS MODEL

The *normative-crisis model* describes human development in terms of a definite sequence of age-related social and emotional changes. Those who follow this approach, like Erik Erikson and

researchers he inspired, believe that everyone follows the same basic built-in "ground plan" for human development (see Table 13-1). In this chapter we describe how these theories explain the changes of young adulthood; in Chapters 15 and 17 we discuss changes later in life.

Erik Erikson: Crisis 6—Intimacy versus Isolation

The sixth of Erikson's eight crises—and what he considers the major issue of young adulthood—is *intimacy versus isolation.* Young adults, says Erikson, need and want intimacy; they need to make deep personal commitments to others. If they are unable or afraid to do this, they may become isolated and self-absorbed. The ability to achieve an intimate relationship, which demands sacrifice and compromise, depends on the sense of identity, the critical issue in adolescence. A young adult who has a strong identity is ready to fuse it with that of another person.

Not until a person is ready for intimacy can what Erikson calls "true genitality" occur. Until this point, says Erikson, people's sex lives have been dominated by the search for identity or by "phallic or vaginal strivings which make of sex-life a kind of genital combat" (1950, p. 264). Now, however, psychologically healthy people are willing to risk temporary loss of self in coitus and orgasm, very close friendships, and other situations requiring self-abandon.

The young adult, then, can aspire to a "utopia of genitality"—mutual orgasm in a loving heterosexual relationship, in which trust is shared and cycles of work, procreation, and recreation are regulated. The ultimate aim is to help the children of this union achieve all the stages of their own development. Erikson sees this not as a purely sexual utopia but as an all-encompassing achievement. He distinguishes sexual *intimacies*, which

TABLE 13-1

Three Normative-Crisis Views of Phases in Adults' Development

Erikson	Vaillant	Levinson
Intimacy versus isolation (age 20 to age 40): Sense of identity, developed during adolescence, enables young adults to fuse their identity with that of others. Young adults resolve conflicting demands of intimacy, competitiveness, and distance, and develop an ethical sense. They are ready to enter into a loving heterosexual relationship with the ultimate aim of providing a nurturing environment for children.	*Age of establishment (age 20 to age 30):* Moving from under the parents' dominance to autonomy; finding a spouse; raising children; developing and deepening friendships.	*Novice phase of early adulthood (age 17 to age 33):* Building a provisional life structure; learning its limitations. 1 *Early adult transition (age 17 to age 22):* Moving out of the parents' home; becoming more independent. 2 *Entry life structure for early adulthood (age 22 to age 28):* Building a first life structure; choosing an occupation; marrying; establishing a home and a family; joining civic and social groups; following a dream of the future and finding an older mentor to help find ways to achieve that dream.
	Age of consolidation (age 25 to age 35): Doing what has to be done; consolidating career; strengthening marriage; not questioning goals.	3 *Age-30 transition (age 28 to age 33):* Reassessing work and family patterns; creating the basis for the next life structure. *Culminating phase of early adulthood (age 33 to age 45):* Bringing to fruition the efforts of early adulthood. 1 *Culminating life structure for early adulthood (age 33 to age 40):* a "Settling Down": Building a second adult life structure; making deeper commitments to work and family; setting timetables for specific life goals; establishing a niche in society; realizing youthful aspirations. b "Becoming One's Own Man": Getting out from under other people's power and authority; seeking independence and respect; discarding the mentor.
	Age of transition (around age 40): Leaving the compulsive busywork of occupational apprenticeships to examine the "world within."	2 *Midlife transition (age 40 to age 45):* Ending early adulthood; beginning middle adulthood.

SOURCES: Erikson, 1950; Levinson, 1978, 1986; Vaillant, 1977.

Intimacy, a major achievement of young adulthood, comes about through commitment to a relationship that may demand sacrifice and compromise. Erikson says that intimacy is possible only after each partner has achieved his or her own identity. But Gilligan and other researchers propose a different sequence for women, who, they say, often achieve intimacy first and then go on to find identity later, sometimes years later. *(Jeffrey Dunn/Stock, Boston)*

may take place in casual encounters, from *intimacy with a capital "I,"* characterized by mature mutuality that goes beyond sexuality (E. Hall, 1983).

The "virtue" that develops in young adulthood is the *virtue of love,* or *mutuality of devotion* between partners who have chosen to share their lives. People also need a certain amount of temporary isolation during this period in order to think about their lives on their own. As young adults work to resolve conflicting demands of intimacy, competitiveness, and distance, they develop an ethical sense, which Erikson considers the mark of the adult.

A decision not to fulfill the natural procreative urge has serious consequences for development, says Erikson. A major criticism of Erikson's theory is the fact that he limits "healthy" development to loving heterosexual relationships that produce children. In addition to his exclusion of single, celibate, homosexual, and childless lifestyles, his focus on a male pattern of development also limits the validity of his theory. Furthermore, his assertion that people establish their identity in adolescence is too narrow. The search for identity continues throughout adulthood.

Research projects inspired by Erikson's theories include those described by George Vaillant and Daniel Levinson. These pioneering studies of adult development have serious limitations, but they are historically important, mostly in the role they played in emphasizing how much development actually takes place after adolescence.

George Vaillant: Adaptation to Life

In adapting to life, people can change themselves, their surroundings, or both. What kinds of adaptations are healthiest, and how do various adaptations affect the quality of life?

In 1938, a select sample of 268 eighteen-year-old Harvard undergraduates—self-reliant and emotionally and physically healthy—were selected for longitudinal research called the *Grant Study.* Reporting on the findings when the men were in their fifties and again in their sixties, Vaillant (1977; Vaillant & Vaillant, 1990) came to several important conclusions: (1) that we change and develop throughout life, (2) that our lives are shaped not by isolated traumatic events but by the quality of sustained relationships with important people, and (3) that the mechanisms we use to adapt to circumstances are related to our level of mental health.

Vaillant's Adaptive Mechanisms

Vaillant identified four characteristic ways in which people adapt: (1) *mature* (such as using humor or helping others), (2) *immature* (such as developing aches and pains with no physical basis), (3) *psychotic* (distorting reality), and (4) *neurotic* (repressing anxiety, intellectualizing, or developing irrational fears). Men who used mature **adaptive mechanisms** were more successful in many ways. They were happier, were mentally and physically healthier, got more satisfaction from work, enjoyed richer friendships, made more money, and seemed better adjusted all around.

Career Consolidation and Stages of Development

The life histories of the men in the Grant Study support Erikson's progression, with the addition of a stage that Vaillant calls "career consolidation." In this stage, somewhere between their twenties and their forties, people become preoccupied with strengthening a career. This stage would come after Erikson's sixth crisis (development of intimacy) and before the seventh (generativity, or guiding the next generation).

The timing of career consolidation—after intimacy but before generativity—may suggest why many marriages run into trouble by the seventh year. For one thing, either partner may turn away from the relationship to focus on a career. Also, problems loom largest for partners who are at different points: if, say, a wife is focused on intimacy and a husband on career; or if a wife is wrapped up in a career while the husband is ready to move on to generativity.

The ages when changes take place vary, but Vaillant (1977) saw a typical pattern. At age 20, many of the men he studied were still under parental dominance. (This finding has also surfaced in recent research; see Box 13-1.) During their twenties— and sometimes thirties—they won autonomy from parents, married, raised children, and deepened friendships. Of the men who at age 47 were considered best adjusted, 93 percent had stable marriages before age 30 and were still married at 50.

Between ages 25 and 35, these men worked hard at consolidating their careers and devoted themselves to their families. They followed the rules, strove for promotions, accepted "the system," rarely questioning whether they had chosen the right woman or the right career. The excitement, charm, and promise they had radiated as students disappeared, so that they were now described as "colorless, hardworking, bland young men in gray flannel suits" (Vaillant, 1977, p. 217).

The stage of career consolidation ends in middle age when "men leave the compulsive, unreflective busywork of their occupational apprenticeships, and once more become explorers of the world within" (Vaillant, 1977, p. 220).

Daniel Levinson: Life Structure

In a much smaller study of only 40 men, Daniel Levinson (1978) and his colleagues at Yale University interviewed in depth and gave personality tests to 35- to 45-year-old men, 10 each from four occupations: hourly workers in industry, business executives, academic biologists, and novelists. He then constructed a theory of development in adulthood.

At the heart of Levinson's theory is the *life structure*—"the underlying pattern or design of a person's life at a given time" (Levinson, 1986, p. 6). It includes the people, places, things, institutions, and causes that a person finds most important, as well as the values, dreams, and emotions that make them so. Most people's life structures are built around work and family. Other elements may include race, religion, ethnic heritage, wars, economic depressions, and even influential books.

Levinson's Life Eras

According to Levinson, people shape their life structures during overlapping eras of about 20 to 25 years each, connected by brief transitional periods, when they appraise their structures and think about restructuring their lives (refer to Table 13-1). The accomplishment of each era's tasks provides a foundation for the next era's life structure.

Levinson divides early adulthood into two main phases* (see Table 13-1 for the tasks of each phase).

*All ages are approximate.

According to George Vaillant, who studied men from age 18 through adulthood, somewhere between their twenties and their forties, people typically become preoccupied with strengthening their careers. *(Henley & Savage/The Stock Market)*

BOX 13-1 FOOD FOR THOUGHT

ESTABLISHING MATURE RELATIONSHIPS WITH PARENTS

When does a person leave adolescence to become a mature adult? Research suggests that this transition usually occurs not in the teens but in the late twenties—at least for white middle-class high school graduates. A dramatic shift in psychological maturity typically occurs between ages 24 and 28; it can be tracked by measuring a young adult's relationship with his or her parents. Men and women mature differently, but whether a person is married or unmarried does not affect maturation.

These conclusions emerged from interviews with 78 women and 72 men between 22 and 32 years of age (Frank, Avery, & Laman, 1988). These 150 high school graduates from a midwestern suburb were assessed on their relationships with their parents, according to 10 different aspects of maturity. Five of the measures evaluated autonomy, including how well the young adults could make decisions and take responsibility for their own lives. Another five measures evaluated the relationships between the generations—how close they were, how they communicated, and how the young people felt about their parents. The researchers then described six major relationship patterns:

1 *Individuated:* Young adult (YA) feels respected by parents, freely seeks their advice and help, acknowledges their strengths, enjoys being with them, and has few conflicts with them. Yet YA feels separate from parents and is aware of and untroubled by a lack of intensity and depth in the relationship.
2 *Competent-connected:* YA is very strongly independent, with life views that differ radically from parents' beliefs, but feels more empathic toward parents than

individuated YA and often helps parents resolve their own problems of health, drinking, or relationships. The mother may be seen as demanding and critical, but YA understands her limitations, keeps conflicts within limits, and stays close to her.
3 *Pseudoautonomous:* YA pretends not to care about conflicts with parents and disengages rather than confronting parents openly. Fathers are often seen as uninterested and mothers as intrusive; both are seen as unable to accept YA for himself or herself.
4 *Identified:* In this unusually open and intimate relationship, YA accepts parents' values and outlook on life, seeks advice on most major decisions, and feels secure in the parents' availability. There are few tensions, and parents are seen as nonjudgmental and supportive.
5 *Dependent:* YA cannot cope with ordinary life situations without parents' help, feels troubled by this but unable to change, and sees parents as overbearing and judgmental or emotionally detached and preoccupied with themselves. YA either goes along with parents' wishes or gets into childish power struggles. This pattern is equivalent to insecure or avoidant attachment.
6 *Conflicted:* This profile emerged only with fathers. YA sees the father as hot-tempered and incapable of a close relationship, feels constantly under attack, is ashamed of the father's inadequacies, and longs to be closer to him.

The profiles of young women's relationships with their parents—and thus of their psychological maturity, according to this model—differed from those of young men. Women were most likely to be

"competent-connected" with their mothers and "identified" or "conflicted" with their fathers. Men were most often "individuated" with both parents or "pseudoautonomous" with their fathers. And women were somewhat more likely than men to be "dependent" on their mothers.

For both sexes, age was important. About half of those over 28 years old felt that they could cope with most aspects of life without asking their parents for help, and only 1 in 5 had serious doubts that they could manage on their own. For people under 24, however, these proportions were reversed: only 1 in 5 felt that they could cope with most aspects of life independently, and half had serious doubts that they could manage on their own.

If findings like these are borne out by more broad-based research, developmentalists will need to take a new look at the timetable for the end of adolescence and the beginning of adulthood, and what this means for education, career planning, and relationships between the generations.

However, we need to look closely at the population groups involved. This new schedule for achieving adulthood probably reflects the fact that middle-class young people remain dependent on their parents for support longer today than they did in the past. Adulthood may come sooner for less affluent young people, who become economically independent at earlier ages. Adulthood may also come sooner for children who leave the nest earlier. Children who grow up in stepfamilies and single-parent families, especially when they have many siblings, are likely to leave home at younger ages (Mitchell, Wister, & Burch, 1989). Once again, we have to guard against drawing sweeping conclusions from relatively small, limited samples.

In the "novice" phase (ages 17 to 33), a man needs to leave his parents' home and become financially and emotionally independent. Between age 22 and age 28, the emphasis is on relationships with friends and family, and with the other sex, usually leading to marriage and children; and on work, leading to choice of occupation.

Two important tasks of Levinson's "novice" phase involve the "dream" and the "mentor." A man's dream of the future is usually expressed in terms of his career: the vision of, say, winning a Nobel Prize. The realization, generally in midlife, that a cherished dream will not come true may trigger an emotional crisis. The way men substitute more attainable goals determines how well they will cope with life. Success during these years is influenced by a slightly older *mentor*—someone who offers guidance and inspiration, and passes on wisdom, moral support, and practical help in both career and personal matters. At about age 30, men reevaluate earlier commitments or make strong commitments for the first time. Some slide through this transition easily; others experience crises.

In Levinson's "culminating" phase of young adulthood, beginning at about age 33, men begin to settle down. They make deeper commitments and set career goals, with a time for achieving them. They anchor their lives in family, occupation, and community. A man now chafes under the authority of those with power and influence over him and wants to break away and speak with his own voice. He may discard his mentor and be at odds with his wife, children, lover, boss, friends, or coworkers. How he deals with the issues of this phase will affect the midlife transition (discussed in Chapter 15).

Women and Levinson's Theory

Levinson (1986) believes that women go through the same kinds of age-linked changes as men, but research on women's development has been even sparser and narrower than that for men. A review of four unpublished dissertations based on interviews with very small, select samples of women supports his view in general but suggests some differences. The women handled tasks differently from men, and their lives were more conflicted and less stable (P. Roberts & Newton, 1987).

The four investigators interviewed a total of 39 women, from 28 to 53 years old. In one study (D. Adams, 1983), the eight respondents were all black attorneys. In the other three studies (Droege, 1982; Furst, 1983; W. Stewart, 1977), all were white, and

from one-third to almost all were employed. At least half the women in each sample had been married at some time, and at least one-fourth were parents. How did these women deal with Levinson's "novice" tasks?

The Dream   The women's dreams were vaguer, more complex, and less motivating than men's, and their life structures were more tentative and temporary. Most dreams were split between achievement and relationships; women defined themselves in relation to others—husbands, children, or colleagues.

Erikson, Vaillant, and Levinson all contend that men "find themselves" by separating from their families of origin, becoming autonomous, and pursuing their own interests, a thesis now being questioned by proponents of relational theory (J. B. Miller, 1991). Other research on women suggests that they develop identity not by breaking away from others but through the responsibility and attachment in relationships (G. Baruch, Barnett, & Rivers, 1983; Chodorow, 1978; Gilligan, 1982).

The Love Relationship   All 39 women sought a "special man." Levinson's "special woman" helps a man pursue his dream; but these women mostly saw themselves as supporting a *man's* goals (rather than finding a "special man" to support their own). In fact, their husbands were the major obstacle to the individualistic part of their dreams. (The husband of one woman who considered applying for a Fulbright scholarship threatened to find another woman who would be more interested in marriage.)

The Mentor   Many of the women identified role models during their twenties, but only four achieved a true mentor relationship. If a mentor is as important as Levinson believes, and if these women's pattern was typical, we would expect many women to be hampered in their occupations by lack of a mentor.

Forming an Occupation   The task of forming an occupation stretched well into middle age for these women—both those who had raised children and then sought an occupation and those who had formed career goals in their twenties but had postponed them.

At about age 30, many of the women reversed career and family priorities, or at least paid more attention to the previously neglected aspect of their dream: either career or marriage and motherhood. They began making greater demands on their husbands to accommodate their interests and goals. Women who were unsatisfied with both their relationships and their occupational achievements during their twenties found the age-30 transition most stressful.

A longitudinal study of 132 college seniors found that women who committed themselves during their twenties to career, family, or both developed more fully than women who had no children and who chose work beneath their capabilities. Between age 27 and the early forties, women who had faced the challenges of career or parenthood became more disciplined, independent, hard-working, and confident and improved their "people skills." Compared with women who had made neither kind of commitment, they were more dominant, more motivated to achieve, more emotionally stable, more goal-oriented, and more interested in what was going on in the world (Helson & Moane, 1987). This research suggests that a range of satisfactory life structures is possible for young women who form dreams and set about making them come true.

Evaluating the Normative-Crisis Approach*

The theory of a predictable sequence of age-related changes throughout life has been influential. But a universal pattern of development for adults is questionable. Children's ages are fairly indicative of their level or sequence of development, but for adults, individual personality and life history reveal more about development than age does. Personality traits, which show some stability over the years, affect the course of people's lives. And people's unique experiences do much to shape their development. Furthermore, it is misleading to look at adult development as a series of stages, since many issues keep recurring.

It is also risky to generalize from studies with such limited samples. Both the Grant Study and Levinson's studies were based on small groups of mostly white middle-class to upper-middle-class men, all born in the 1920s or 1930s. Their development was most likely influenced by societal events that did not affect earlier or later cohorts, by their socioeconomic status, by their race, and by their sex. Adult female development has been studied even less extensively than adult male development. Although very limited, then, these

*We will offer a full critique of the normative-crisis approach in Chapter 15.

studies do help to identify developmental threads that run through the lives of many people.

TIMING-OF-EVENTS MODEL

Instead of looking at adults' development as a function of age, the *timing-of-events model* views *life events* as markers of development. According to this model, which allows for more individual variation, people develop in response to specific events in their lives and to the times when these events occur. If life events occur as expected, development proceeds smoothly. If not, stress can result, affecting development. Stress may occur in response to an unexpected event (like losing a job), in response to an event that happens earlier or later than expected (like being widowed at age 35), or in response to the failure of an expected event to occur at all (like the failure of grown children to leave home when anticipated). This model, which the gerontologist Bernice Neugarten supports, is concerned with age only as it relates to cultural norms regarding expected events.

Types and Timing of Life Events

In childhood and adolescence, internal maturational events signal the transition from one developmental stage to another. For example, a baby says the first word, takes the first step, loses the first tooth; and the body changes at the onset of puberty.

In adulthood, however, people move from "a biological to a social clocking of adult development" (Danish & D'Augelli, 1980, p. 111). Physiological and intellectual maturation are now less important to growth than the effects of events like marriage, parenthood, divorce, widowhood, and retirement. For example, menopause is generally less important in a woman's life than a job change.

Normative versus Nonnormative Events

Life events are of two types: those people expect (*normative life events*) and those they do not expect (*nonnormative life events*). Normative events include marriage and parenthood in early adulthood, and widowhood and retirement late in life. However, people's lives are also typically punctuated by such nonnormative events as a disabling accident, an unexpected promotion, the loss of a job, a lottery prize, or a notable achievement.

Whether or not an event is normative often depends on its timing. Most adults have strong feelings about the time in life when certain activities are acceptable (Neugarten, Moore, & Lowe, 1965). People are usually keenly aware of their own timing and describe themselves as "early," "late," or "on time" in marrying, having children, settling on a career, or retiring. Events that are normative when they are "on time" become nonnormative when they are "off time"; for example, marrying at 14 or, for the first time, at 41 or retiring at 41 or 91 would be a nonnormative event.

In contrast to the normative-crisis school, the timing-of-events model holds that normative events that come at expected times are generally taken in stride; "it is the events that upset the expected sequence and rhythm of the life cycle that cause problems" (Neugarten & Neugarten, 1987, p. 33).

Individual versus Cultural Events

An *individual event* happens to one person or one family (like pregnancy or a promotion). A *cultural event* shapes the context in which individuals develop; examples are an economic depression, an earthquake, a war, a famine, and an accident at a nuclear reactor or a chemical plant. Cultural attitudes affect people's "social clocks." A timetable that seems right and proper to people in one age cohort may feel jarring to the next generation. The typical timing of such events as marriage, for example, varies from culture to culture (see Box 13-2).

The Decline of Age-Consciousness

Over the past half-century, our society has become less age-conscious (Neugarten & Hagestad, 1976; Neugarten & Neugarten, 1987). The feeling that there is a "right time" to do certain things has become less widespread. In the 1950s, middle-aged middle-class people, when asked the "best age" for finishing school, marrying, and retiring, agreed far more than their counterparts two decades later (see Table 13-2). Today people are more accepting of 40-year-old first-time parents and 40-year-old grandparents, 50-year-old retirees and 75-year-old workers, 60-year-olds in blue jeans, and 30-year-old college presidents—as well as a President of the United States in his mid-forties.

Yet despite this blurring of traditional life periods, there are still societal expectations about appropriate ages for events to occur, and people often try to time major life events (marriage, parenthood, job changes) by this social clock. For example, a young woman who puts off marrying to get a foothold on the career ladder may then hurry to become a mother.

Responding to Life Events

No matter which kind of event we are talking about, the key issue is how someone responds to it. An event that energizes one person may depress, or lead to illness in, another (see Chapter 14).

How a person reacts to events depends on both internal and external factors (Brim & Ryff, 1980; Danish & D'Augelli, 1980; Danish, Smyer, & Nowak, 1980). These include anticipation and preparation (as through classes for prospective parents or seminars to plan retirement), cognitive understanding (interpreting the event), physical health (including resources for handling stress), personality factors (flexibility and resilience), life history (past success in coping with stressful events), and social support (emotional support from others).

In the next section, we look at important life events of young adulthood that revolve around intimate relationships like marriage and parenthood. We also examine some personal lifestyles in which some traditional events do not take place.

INTIMATE RELATIONSHIPS AND PERSONAL LIFESTYLES

During young adulthood, most people decide whether to marry, cohabit, or live alone, and whether or not to have children. Important relationships may include heterosexual or homosexual unions and kinship ties to members of an extended family—within and across generations.

From the late 1950s to the present—especially during the 1960s and 1970s—major changes occurred in American society. Current norms no longer dictate that people must get married, stay married, have children, or maintain separate roles for men and women (Thornton, 1989). Today's rules for acceptable family behavior are more elastic than they were during the first half of this century. Still, for most young adults a loving relationship is a pivotal factor in their lives; thus, we begin our consideration of relationships and lifestyles with love.

LOVE

Love has always been a favorite topic for poets, novelists, and songwriters. It has also become increasingly popular with social scientists, who have

TABLE 13-2

The "Right Time" for Life Events and Activities

Activity or Event	Appropriate Age Range	Late 1950s Study, % Who Agree		Late 1970s Study, % Who Agree	
		Men	Women	Men	Women
Best age for a man to marry	20–25	80	90	42	42
Best age for a woman to marry	19–25	85	90	44	36
When most people should become grandparents	45–50	84	79	64	57
Best age for most people to finish school and go to work	20–22	86	82	36	38
When most people should be ready to retire	60–65	83	86	66	41
When a man has the most responsibilities	35–50	79	75	49	50
When a man accomplishes most	40–50	82	71	46	41
When a woman has the most responsibilities	25–40	93	91	59	53
When a woman accomplishes most	30–45	94	92	57	48

Note: Table shows the percentage of middle-aged middle-class people who agreed on a "right time" for major life events and achievements in two surveys, one taken in the late 1950s and the other in the late 1970s.
SOURCES: Adapted from Rosenfeld & Stark, 1987; adapted, in turn, from Passuth, Maines, & Neugarten, 1984.

come up with some illuminating findings about "this thing called love."

Do opposites attract? Or do most people fall in love with someone like themselves? Some element of self-love must be involved in selecting a loved one, since lovers and spouses tend to resemble each other in many traits: physical appearance and attractiveness, mental and physical health, intelligence, popularity, warmth, parents' marital and individual happiness, and such other factors as socioeconomic status, race, religion, education, and income (Murstein, 1980). Sally and her husband, for example, have the same religious background, are both college graduates, and are enough alike physically that strangers have taken them for brother and sister.

On the other hand, many people choose partners whose qualities complement their own. Diane and her husband have different religious backgrounds and different countries of origin. Also, they feel differently about new situations and people: she prefers the comfort of the familiar; he is energized by the new. Still, they have much in common: both have graduate degrees, and they have similar values on many issues.

An intriguing conceptualization is Robert J. Sternberg's *triangular theory of love* (1985a; Sternberg & Barnes, 1985; Sternberg & Grajek, 1984). In this view, love has three faces, or elements—intimacy, passion, and commitment. *Intimacy*, the emotional element, involves self-disclosure, which leads to connection, warmth, and trust. *Passion*, the motivational element, is based on inner drives that translate physiological arousal into sexual desire. And *commitment*, the cognitive element, is the decision to love and to stay with the beloved. In this theory, the degree to which these three elements are present affects the kind of love people feel, and mismatches of the elements lead to problems. The eight types of love relationships that result from different combinations of the elements are shown in Table 13-3.

Research on love has dispelled some of the myths about it. A cross-sectional study of a small sample, of 24 couples, ranging in age from the teens to the seventies and described by acquaintances as "very much in love" (Neiswender, Birren, & Schaie, 1975), found that:

■ Married love is not different in kind from unmarried love. It is neither more realistic and mature nor less idealistic.
■ Love is not only for the young. Although people of different ages experience love somewhat differently, older people love just as much as younger people.

Lovers often resemble each other in appearance or personality, suggesting that a form of self-love plays a part in the choice of a partner. These two military cadets, for instance, have common career goals. *(Robert Kristofik/The Image Bank)*

TABLE 13-3

Patterns of Loving	
Type	**Description**
Nonlove	All three components of love—intimacy, passion, and commitment—are absent. This describes most of our personal relationships, which are simply casual interactions.
Liking	Intimacy is the only component present. This is what we feel in true friendship and in many loving relationships. There is closeness, understanding, emotional support, affection, bondedness, and warmth. Neither passion nor commitment is present.
Infatuation	Passion is the only component present. This is "love at first sight," a strong physical attraction and sexual arousal, without intimacy or commitment. This can flare up suddenly and die just as fast—or, given certain circumstances, can sometimes last for a long time.
Empty love	Commitment is the only component present. This is often found in long-term relationships that have lost both intimacy and passion, or in arranged marriages.
Romantic love	Intimacy and passion are both present. Romantic lovers are drawn to each other physically and bonded emotionally. They are not, however, committed to each other.
Companionate love	Intimacy and commitment are both present. This is a long-term, committed friendship, often occurring in marriages in which physical attraction has died down but in which the partners feel close to each other and have made the decision to stay together.
Fatuous love	Passion and commitment are present, without intimacy. This is the kind of love that leads to a whirlwind courtship, in which a couple make a commitment on the basis of passion without allowing themselves the time to develop intimacy. This kind of love usually does not last, despite the initial intent to commit.
Consummate love	All three components are present in this "complete" love, which many of us strive for, especially in romantic relationships. It is easier to reach it than to hold onto it. Either partner may change what he or she wants from the relationship. If the other partner changes, too, the relationship may endure in a different form. If the other partner does not change, the relationship may dissolve.

SOURCE: R. J. Sternberg, 1985a.

■ Physical intimacy becomes steadily more important from adolescence to middle age and then abruptly less so.

■ Young and middle-aged adults are the most realistic about their lovers' strengths and weaknesses; both adolescents and older adults tend to idealize their loved ones.

The more evenly balanced the partners' contributions to a relationship are, the happier a couple tends to be. When two people think that one or the other is favored, they usually try to make things fairer (by demanding more or giving more), or talk themselves into believing that things are fairer than they seem, or end the relationship (Walster & Walster, 1978).

MARRIAGE

Most adults marry, usually for the first time in young adulthood. But people have been marrying at later and later ages. In 1991, the median age of first-time bridegrooms was 26.3 and of first-time brides, 24.1 years, compared with 24.7 and 22 years, respectively, in 1980 (U.S. Bureau of the Census, 1992b).

Benefits of Marriage

The universality of marriage throughout history and around the world shows that it meets a variety of fundamental needs. Marriage is usually considered the best way to ensure orderly raising of children. Its economic benefits include providing for a division of labor and a consuming and working unit. Ideally, marriage also offers a source of intimacy, friendship, affection, sexual fulfillment, and companionship. It presents an opportunity for emotional growth through a bond that is more reciprocal than the bond with parents and more committed than bonds with siblings, friends, or lovers. (The high divorce rate shows how hard it is to attain these ideals, but the high remarriage rate shows the degree to which people keep trying.)

Marriage and Happiness

Studies done from the 1950s to the 1970s found that married people were happier than single people. Either marriage brought happiness, or happy people tended to marry.

In one study of 2000 adults around the country, married men and women of all ages reported more satisfaction than single, divorced, or widowed people. The happiest of all were married people in their twenties with no children—especially women. Young wives reported feeling much less stress after marriage, while young husbands, although happy, said that they felt more stress (A. Campbell, Converse, & Rodgers, 1975). Apparently marriage was still seen as an accomplishment and a source of security for a woman but as a responsibility for a man.

Women and men feel differently about marriage in other respects, too. Women see marriage as a place to express and talk about emotions; they consider the sharing of confidences a measure of intimacy. Men, however, define intimacy differently; they tend to express love through sex, practical help (like washing a wife's car), doing things together, or just being together (L. Thompson & Walker, 1989). As a result, men often get more of what is important to them, since women do the things that matter to men. Many men do not feel comfortable talking about feelings—or even listening to their wives talk about theirs—and this leaves their wives feeling dissatisfied. It is noteworthy that the association between marriage and psychological well-being is more pronounced for men (Ross, Mirowsky, & Goldsteen, 1990).

The ability of marriage to bring happiness seems to be changing (Glenn, 1987). Although more married people than people who have never married call themselves "very happy," the gap has narrowed dramatically—among 25- to 39-year-olds, from 31 percentage points in the early 1970s to 8 points in 1986. Apparently, never-married people (especially men) are happier today, while married people (especially women) are less happy. One possible reason is that some benefits of marriage are no longer confined to wedlock. Single people can get both sex and companionship outside of marriage, and marriage is no longer the sole (or even the most reliable) source of security for women. Also, since most women now continue to work, marriage is likely to *increase* rather than decrease their stress.

Marriage and Health

Married people tend to be healthier physically and psychologically than those who are separated, divorced, widowed, or never-married. The effect is stronger for men than for women (Ross et al., 1990). Married people have fewer disabilities or chronic conditions that limit their activities; and when they go to the hospital, their stays are gen-

BOX 13-2 *WINDOW ON THE WORLD*

MARRIAGE AND DIVORCE PATTERNS

Although marriage exists in every culture, and some means of ending a marriage is almost as universal, the patterns of becoming wed and unwed vary from society to society (Burns, 1992; Bianchi & Spain, 1986). One area of difference involves typical ages for marriage. In eastern Europe people tend to marry early; Scandinavians are likely to marry late. Variations in the typical "marrying age" in different cultures tell us something about those cultures.

The statistical differences are striking. In Hungary, for example, 70 percent of women and 33 percent of men aged 20 to 24 have already married, whereas in Nordic countries, 85 percent of the women and 95 percent of the men in this age group have not. Like other eastern European nations, Hungary encourages births. In Scandinavia, cohabitation is popular among young adults. Although most Scandinavians eventually marry, they do not marry in their early twenties. Japan, too, has a high proportion of unmarried young adults. But young men and women in Japan do not cohabit, like those in Scandinavia; they tend to live at home with their parents longer than young adults in other cultures.

Industrialized nations, in which a growing number of women go to college and then to work, are seeing a trend toward later marriage. In the United States, for example, well over half of the women and more than three-fourths of the men between ages 20 and 24 have not yet been married (see Table 13-6 later in this chapter).

In cultures with high divorce rates, even royalty is not exempt. This photograph of Prince Charles and Lady Diana of Great Britain was taken near the end of their relationship together and graphically foretells the different directions the Prince of Wales and his wife would soon be taking. *(Tim Graham/Sygma)*

Divorce rates too reflect differences among cultures. For example, the high rates in such countries as Sweden, the United States, and the former Soviet Union reflect unique national characteristics of these countries, while different cultural arrangements have delayed the trends in such countries as Italy and Ireland (Burns, 1992). Japan, a more traditional society, has the lowest, most stable divorce rate of eight countries studied from 1948 to 1988 (see Figure 13-1).

Higher divorce rates reflect the advent of more liberal laws passed in most western nations in the 1960s and 1970s. These laws have emphasized consent of both parties, or no-fault, as the basis for obtaining a divorce, as opposed to the need to find one partner at fault. In Sweden, however, liberal divorce laws have been in effect since 1920, although they were revised in 1974. Countries like Italy and Ireland, where religious opposition to divorce is strong, have not experienced higher rates. In fact, the Irish constitution continues to prohibit divorce, even though surveys show that most citizens are in favor of legal divorce. The laws did not cause the divorces; they merely followed public opinion and enabled people who wanted to end a marriage to do so.

erally short. Married people live longer, too, according to a study going back to 1940 in 16 industrial countries (Hu & Goldman, 1990). Those who have never married are the next-healthiest group, followed by widowed people and then by people who are divorced or separated.

Why should this be? Healthy people may attract mates more easily, may be more interested in getting married, and may be better marriage partners. Or married people may lead healthier, safer lives than single people. Because spouses can take care of each other, they may be less likely to need care in hospitals or institutions. Married people tend to be better off financially, a factor that seems to enhance physical and mental health (Ross et al., 1990). Then, even in less-than-ideal marriages, partners provide company for each other, offer emotional support, and do many things that ease day-to-day life. The loss of these supports through death or separation may make the widowed and divorced more vulnerable to mental and physical disorders (Doherty & Jacobson, 1982). This view is supported by a study of more than 25,000 women aged 18 to 55, which found that women who lived with another adult—whether married or not— were healthier than those who did not (Anson, 1989).

Predicting Success in Marriage

What *is* success in marriage? To answer this question, researchers rely on people's ratings of their own marriages, on the absence of marital counseling, or on the number of years partners stay together. All these criteria are flawed: people are sometimes less than honest, even with themselves; some people acknowledge problems and seek help more easily than others; and some put up longer with unhappiness. Even so, these criteria are the best ones we have.

Age at marriage is a major predictor of success. Teenagers have high divorce rates: early marriage may affect career or educational ambitions, restrict both partners' potential, and lock a couple into a relationship neither one is mature enough to handle. People who wait until their late twenties or later to marry have the best chances for success. A number of other factors are also associated with a greater probability of divorce (see Table 13-4).

Success in marriage is closely associated with the ways partners communicate, make decisions, and deal with conflict. One study found patterns that could predict the course of a marriage (Gottman & Krokoff, 1989). Whining, acting defensive, being stubborn, and withdrawing by walking away or not talking to the spouse are all

---

TABLE 13-4

Personal Factors Associated with Increased Probability of Divorce

Factor	Remarks
Premarital cohabitation	This factor has been explained as the result of the fact that people who live together are less conventional. As this lifestyle becomes more common, it should exert less influence. And in fact, for recent cohorts the effect is weaker.
Young age at marriage	This is the strongest predictor of divorce in the first 5 years of marriage.
Bearing a child before marriage	Premarital pregnancy of itself does not seem to increase the risk of divorce.
Having no children	Having at least one child reduces the risk of divorce, especially if that child is a boy. Fathers tend to be more involved with sons than with daughters, and greater father involvement in child care reduces divorce probability.
Stepchildren in the home	The presence of children from a previous marriage brings additional stresses and divided loyalties.
Divorce of own parents	This factor is still an important risk factor, even now when it is more common to have divorced parents.
Being African American	This difference still exists when socioeconomic status, fertility, sex ratios, and age at marriage are controlled.

SOURCES: L. K. White, 1990; Schoen, 1992.

signs of trouble. But arguing and showing anger (as a form of communication) seemed to be good for marriage. These authors suggest that wives who force confrontations of disagreement and anger will help their marriages—assuming that their husbands react without withdrawing, whining, or being stubborn, and that neither becomes defensive. The patterns set during young adulthood affect the quality of the marriage at midlife.

Domestic Violence

Spousal abuse typically begins with a man's shoving or slapping a woman, and then escalates into a beating. Some women become critically injured, some die, and others live in constant terror.

Violence is more common among young, poor, and unemployed couples, whether married or cohabiting (Lystad, 1975; Yllo & Straus, 1981). Lower levels of violence are surprisingly common early in relationships: 44 percent of women and 31 percent of men report pushing, shoving, or slapping their partners before marriage; and 36 percent of women and 27 percent of men in the first 18 months of marriage (O'Leary et al., 1989). Some people—men and women equally—restrict their aggression toward each other to words. This behavior is more common among younger couples and diminishes as they have more children. It often follows alcohol and drug use but is not associated with race or socioeconomic status (Straus & Sweet, 1992).

Violence committed by men against women causes the most harm. Men who abuse women tend to be social isolates, to have low self-esteem, to be sexually inadequate, to be inordinately jealous, and to deny and minimize the frequency and intensity of their violence, usually blaming the woman (J. L. Bernard & Bernard, 1984; Bouza, 1990; R. Harris & Bologh, 1985).

Why do women stay with men who abuse them? As many as one-fourth of women and one-third of men wed to aggressive spouses do not consider themselves unhappily married. Victims of aggression often minimize its importance; attribute it to alcohol, frustration, and stress; interpret it as a sign of love or of masculinity; and deny that their mates really mean to hurt them (O'Leary et al., 1989). Others have low self-esteem and feel that they deserve to be beaten. Financially dependent wives are especially vulnerable; battered wives who return to their husbands are usually not employed and feel they have nowhere else to go (Kalmuss &

Straus, 1982; Strube & Barbour, 1984). Some women are afraid to leave—a realistic fear, since some abusive husbands do track down and beat or even kill their estranged wives.

Abused women often feel that they have nowhere to turn. In many states, a wife cannot sue her husband for assault, and police officers called to break up a fight between husband and wife rarely arrest the husband. Yet men who are arrested for family violence are less likely to continue to abuse their families, and a growing number of communities are now adopting this approach (Bouza, 1990; Sherman & Berk, 1984; Sherman & Cohn, 1989).

Today, more attention is being paid to the plight of abused wives. In many places battered wives can go with their children to shelters for refuge and counseling, and they can get help from the legal system, including court orders to keep their husbands away. Programs are springing up to help abusive men stop their violent behavior, usually through group counseling (Bernard & Bernard, 1984; Feazell, Mayers, & Deschner, 1984). And family therapy, which treats the entire family together, can sometimes stop mild to moderate abuse before it becomes dangerous (Gelles & Maynard, 1987).

DIVORCE

"I'm still trying to figure out what happened," said Gary, a man in his thirties who had been married for 8 years and was now in a support group for people going through separation and divorce. "In October my wife tells me she's unhappy and doesn't love me anymore. In November she hands me a letter saying she wants a divorce" (Ketcham, 1990).

The dissolution of marriage is largely a phenomenon of young adulthood. The "seven-year itch" is more than folklore; this is a peak time for divorce. The United States has one of the highest divorce rates in the world, with more than 1 million divorces a year (U.S. Bureau of the Census, 1992b; Burns, 1992—see Figure 13-1 and Box 13-2). Although the divorce rate, after a two-decade rise, seems to have leveled off since 1980, about 2 out of 3 first marriages are estimated to end this way (T. C. Martin & Bumpass, 1989).

Why Divorce Has Increased

Divorce is more common now largely because society has changed in several ways. Women are less

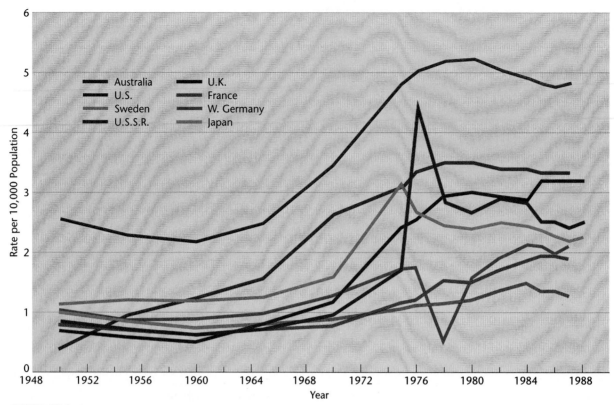

FIGURE 13-1

Divorce rates in selected countries before and after the passage of more lenient divorce laws. Similar patterns show low rates until mid-century, a postwar jump, a plateau through the 1950s and 1960s, sharp rises in the late 1960s and 1970s, a more gradual increase peaking at the end of the 1970s, and a slight decline and leveling off in the 1980s. (*Source:* Burns, 1992.)

financially dependent on their husbands and may be less likely to stay in bad marriages. There are fewer legal obstacles to divorce, there is less religious opposition to it, and it carries less social stigma. Couples used to stay together "for the sake of the children"; today, that is not always considered the wisest course. And since more couples today either postpone or decide against having children at all, it is easier to return to a single state (Berscheid & Campbell, 1981).

Perhaps a more fundamental change is even more important. While most people *hope* that their marriages will last, fewer strongly *expect* them to endure until the death of one partner. As one sociologist comments, "more honest vows would often be 'as long as we both shall love' or 'as long as no one better comes along'" (Glenn, 1991, p. 268). Furthermore, people now expect more from marriage—and with greater expectations, they are more likely to be disappointed. More people live far away from their extended families and want their spouses to be like parents and friends,

as well as lovers—to enrich their lives, help them develop their potential, and be loving companions and passionate sexual partners. When partners cannot fulfill this tall order, few people consider it shameful or immoral to seek a divorce. Then, various personal factors in people's lives make some more prone to divorce than others (see Table 13-4).

People today are also more likely to recognize that staying in an unhappy marriage may well damage the personalities of both spouses and their children. Marriage counseling helps some couples to work out their problems and save the marriage; it helps other couples to separate in the most positive way for everyone.

Reactions to Divorce

"You lose all your self-esteem," said one divorced wife. Said another," I never want to live through anything like that again. At the same time, I have grown so much; I feel so free and so optimistic that I can't say I'm sorry I'm where I am."

Ending even an unhappy marriage is always painful, especially when there are children. A divorce brings feelings of failure, blame, hostility, and self-recrimination. Divorce has many facets: emotional, legal, economic, parental (children's needs must be met), communal (relationships outside the family will also change), and psychic (both partners need to regain personal autonomy). In any one situation, some of these aspects will be more intense than others, but all cause stress.

Reactions to such stress may show up in poor health. Separated and divorced people have higher rates of illness and death (Kitson & Morgan, 1990). Another common reaction is difficulty in performing the social activities of everyday life, which, says some research, affects divorced women more than widows (Kitson & Roach, 1989).

Adjustment depends partly on how people feel toward themselves and their partners, and on how the divorce was handled. It also depends on other factors. Among 290 divorced parents—most of them white and well educated—some predictors of successful adjustment showed up 2 years after divorce (Tschann, Johnston, & Wallerstein, 1989). Those who made the best adjustments had more personal resources before the separation—like higher socioeconomic status for men and better psychological functioning for women. Even in this advantaged group, money was important: people whose income dropped less adjusted better. (Those in less advantaged groups suffer even more—in a lower standard of living, increased work hours, and continued hassles with an ex-spouse who defaults on child support—Kitson & Morgan, 1990.)

Another important factor in adjustment is the degree to which a person has detached from the former spouse. People who still argue with their former mates or have not found a new lover or spouse have more trouble. For both sexes, an active social life helps people cut the emotional ties to former spouses.

The person who takes the first step to end the marriage often feels a mixture of relief, sadness, guilt, apprehension, and anger. Nonetheless, she or he (more often she—women initiate divorce more often than men) is usually in better emotional shape in the early months of separation than the other partner, who feels the pain of rejection, loss of control, and powerlessness (J. B. Kelly, 1982; Pettit & Bloom, 1984). Anger, depression, and disorganized thinking and functioning are common after divorce, but they are balanced by relief, a continuing attachment to the former spouse, and the hope for a fresh chance in life (J. B. Kelly, 1982).

Remarriage after Divorce

Most divorced people do not remain single. Until the late 1960s, the remarriage rate kept pace with the rising divorce rate; it declined sharply in the 1970s and more moderately in the 1980s, as more divorced adults cohabited outside of marriage or continued to live alone. Still, an estimated three-quarters of divorced women remarry, and men are even likelier to remarry than women. An American woman is more likely to remarry if her first marriage was brief, if she was young when it ended, has no children, is non-Hispanic white, has a high school education, and lives in the west (Bumpass, Sweet, & Martin, 1990—see Table 13-5).

TABLE 13-5

Factors Influencing the Probability of Remarriage*

Variable	Estimated Percentage Expected to Remarry
Age at separation	
Under 25 years old	89
25–29	79
30–39	59
40+	31
Duration of first marriage	
0–1 years	89
2–4	82
5–9	76
10+	52
Age at first marriage	
14–17 years old	84
18–19	79
20–22	67
23+	51
Children at separation	
0	81
1–2	73
3+	57
Race	
White non-Hispanic	76
Black	46
Education	
0–11 years	67
12 years	75
13+	72
Region of U.S.	
Northeast	60
North Central	70
South	77
West	78
Total	72

*Based on 1982 experiences.
SOURCE: Bumpass, Sweet, & Martin, 1990, p. 754.

Redivorce, too, seems to have peaked in the late 1960s, when second marriages were more likely to dissolve than first marriages; now the incidence of redivorce is approaching that of first divorce (P. C. Glick, 1988, 1989; P. C. Glick & Lin, 1986b; A. J. Norton & Moorman, 1987).

The high divorce rate is not a sign that people do not want to be married. Instead, it often reflects a desire to be *happily* married and a belief that divorce is like surgery—painful and traumatic, but needed to make a better life.

SINGLE LIFE

The percentage of young men and women who have not yet married has increased dramatically during the past few decades in every age bracket from 20 to 39 (see Table 13-6). Some of these people will marry eventually, but it is possible that a growing number will never marry at all.

Some young adults stay single so that they can be freer to take social, economic, and physical risks. They can decide more easily to move across the country or across the world, to take chances on new kinds of work, to further their education, or

Single life is increasingly common among young adults, for a variety of reasons. This 30-year-old man with a master's degree in business administration returned to his Illinois farming community to manage land that has been in his family for a century. As a rural bachelor, he meets few eligible women; he spends his evenings reading by a wood-burning stove; when he gets lonely, he takes his dog for a walk. *(Paul L. Merideth/Tony Stone Worldwide)*

TABLE 13-6

Percentage of Women and Men Never Married at Various Ages, 1970–1991			
Women	**1970**	**1980**	**1991**
20–24 years	35.8	50.2	64.1
25–29 years	10.5	20.9	32.3
30–34 years	6.2	9.5	18.7
35–39 years	5.4	6.2	11.7
Men	**1970**	**1980**	**1991**
20–24 years	54.7	68.8	79.7
25–29 years	19.1	33.1	46.7
30–34 years	9.4	15.9	27.3
35–39 years	7.2	7.8	17.6

SOURCE: U.S. Bureau of the Census, March 1992.

to do creative work, without having to worry about how their quest for self-fulfillment affects another person. Others just like being alone. And others postpone or avoid marriage because of fear that it will end in divorce (P. C. Glick & Lin, 1986b). Postponement makes sense, since the younger people are when they first marry, the worse the chances for success. By and large, single young adults like their status (Cargan, 1981).

More than 60 single men and women, aged 22 to 62, told interviewers about the "pulls" (advantages of being single) and the "pushes" (disadvantages of being married) that made them opt for single life. Among the "pulls" were career opportunities, mobility, self-sufficiency, sexual freedom, exciting lifestyles, freedom to change, and opportunities for sustained friendships, a variety of experiences, a plurality of roles, and psychological and social autonomy. Among the "pushes" were the restrictions of monogamy (such as feeling trapped or bored, obstacles to self-development, unhappiness, anger, role-playing, and the need to conform to expectations), poor communication, sexual frustration, lack of friends, limited mobility, and limited availability of new experiences (Stein, 1976).

Single people's problems range from practical ones like finding a job, getting a place to live, and being totally responsible for themselves to the intangibles of wondering how they fit into the social world, how well friends and family accept them, and how being single affects their self-esteem.

Two common stereotypes—that single people are lonely and that they have many different sexual partners—are not supported by research.

When 400 never-married, divorced, and remarried Ohioans were interviewed, most of the never-married subjects did not express loneliness and fewer than 20 percent had multiple sexual partners (this was *before* the AIDS epidemic). In this study divorced people came closer to the stereotype than those who had never married (Cargan, 1981).

COHABITATION

An increasingly common arrangement is *cohabitation*, in which a couple in a romantic and sexual relationship live together without being married. By their early thirties, almost half the population in the United States has cohabited. Currently, about 4 percent of the population is cohabiting (Bumpass & Sweet, 1988).

Why do couples move in together without marrying? For one thing, the secular trend toward earlier maturation, along with the societal trend toward more education, creates a longer span between physiological maturity and social maturity. Many young people want close sexual relationships and yet are not ready for marriage. Living with someone can help people know themselves better, help them understand what an intimate relationship involves, and help them clarify what they want in marriage and in a mate. Often the experience is a maturing one.

Some of the problems of cohabiting couples are like those of newlyweds: overinvolvement with the partner, working out a sexual relationship, perceived loss of personal identity, overdependency on the partner, and becoming distant from other friends. Other problems are specific to cohabitation: discomfort about the ambiguity of the situation, jealousy, and a yearning for a commitment.

But living together is neither a trial marriage nor practice for marriage. It is like a modern equivalent of "going steady," and it usually does not last long: within a few years most cohabiting couples have either married or separated. People who lived together first do not have better marriages than those who did not. In fact, some research shows that couples who lived together before getting married report lower-quality marriages and a lower commitment to the institution of marriage—and a greater likelihood of divorce than noncohabiting couples (Thomson & Colella, 1992; Bumpass & Sweet, 1988).

The differences between live-together and wait-for-marriage couples probably reflect the kind of people who choose living together rather than the effect of the cohabitation itself. This conclusion is bolstered by the fact that the differential has become smaller in more recent cohorts as cohabitation has become more the norm and less a flouting of convention (Schoen, 1992).

SEXUALITY

Underlying all these lifestyle decisions is the need to express sexuality. People entering their twenties face the tasks of achieving independence, competence, responsibility, and equality, all in relation to their sexuality. During the next few years, most people make major decisions about sexual lifestyles: whether they will engage in casual, recreational sex or be monogamous—and whether they will express their sexuality in heterosexual, homosexual, or bisexual activity. Only 3 percent of adults over age 18 have not had sexual intercourse; estimates are that 91 to 93 percent are heterosexual, and 5 to 6 percent either homosexual or bisexual (T. W. Smith, 1991). Many of the issues young adults face have a sexual aspect: the decision to marry, the decision to have a child, the foray into extramarital sex that often comes with the "seven-year itch," and changes in sexual patterns following divorce.

Sexual Activity among Unmarried People

The relaxation of strictures against premarital sex reflects a major change in attitudes. Among women aged 30 and older, the proportion who said that premarital sex was always or almost always wrong dropped from 62 percent in 1972 to 45 percent in 1986; a similar decline was seen among men (Thornton, 1989). Furthermore, actions are speaking as loud as—or louder than—words. Most Americans engage in premarital intercourse; the later they marry, the less likely they are to be virgins on the wedding day.

In one study, 82 percent of women in their twenties who had never been married had had intercourse, and 53 percent were currently sexually active (Tanfer & Horn, 1985). However, some changes have occurred because of the risk of AIDS. In a nationally representative sample of 15- to 44-year-old unmarried sexually experienced women, one-third changed their behavior, most often by limiting the number of partners (McNally & Mosher, 1991). And among women who visited a health service at a large university in the northeast between 1975 and 1989, later cohorts were more likely to use condoms (25 percent in 1989, 6 percent in 1975). However, other research suggests that, along with overall levels of sexual activity, the frequency of specific practices like fellatio, cunnilingus, and anal intercourse remained stable (De-Buono, Zinner, Daamen, & McCormack, 1990).

Among younger people, sexual activity is generally part of an affectionate relationship, and there is little promiscuity. There is more casual sex among older single people and separated and divorced people. Young adults who do *not* engage in premarital sex hold back for a number of reasons: moral or religious scruples, concern about how it will affect a future marriage, or fear of pregnancy, sexually transmitted diseases (STDs), or public opinion. Women express such reservations more than men.

Sexual Activity in Marriage

It is surprising how little research exists about sex in marriage. We do know that most couples have sexual relations more frequently during the first year of marriage than they ever will again. And the more sexually active they are during that first year, the more active they are likely to be in the future. One survey found that, on average, spouses have intercourse about 67 times a year, ranging from a high of 105 times a year for those under 30, to 16 times a year for people older than 70 (T. W. Smith, 1991). Husbands and wives now seem to derive more pleasure from the sexual side of marriage (M. M. Hunt, 1974).

This has come about because of a societal evo-lution from Victorian attitudes about the "wickedness" of sex to an acceptance of sexual activity—especially in marriage—as normal, healthy, and pleasurable. More information about sex is available in the press, in professional journals, and from sex therapists. The greater reliability of contraceptives and the availability of legal and safe abortion have also contributed to this change, freeing husbands and wives from fears of unwanted pregnancy. And the feminist movement has helped many women to acknowledge their sexuality.

Extramarital Sex

Some married people seek sex outside of marriage—especially after the first few years, when the excitement and novelty of sex with the spouse wear off or problems in the relationship surface. Either or both spouses may turn to other sex partners out of boredom or anger at the husband or wife, to recapture a remembered joy or to seek a more vital relationship, or from a desire for sexual emancipation.

It is hard to know just how common extramarital affairs are, because there is no way to tell how truthful people are about their sexual practices. It does seem that more people, especially women, are having extramarital sex today than in the past, and that they are having it at younger ages.

In Kinsey's surveys done in the 1940s and 1950s, 51 percent of the men and 26 percent of the women reported extramarital intercourse (Kinsey, Pomeroy, & Martin, 1948; Kinsey, Pomeroy, Martin, & Gebhard, 1953). A more permissive attitude

Married people today seem to derive more pleasure from the sexual side of marriage than couples did in the past, as attitudes about sexual activity have become more open and more information is available. Sexual intimacy is not limited to genital contact; it is also involved in relaxed times of physical closeness. *(Mike Kagan/Monkmeyer)*

arose between 1965 and 1973, but after 1973 attitudes became more restrictive again, especially among people under age 30 (Lewis & Ventura, 1990; Thornton, 1989). According to one recent survey of married adults, 65 percent of women and 30 percent of men reported having had no more sexual partners than spouses since age 18, indicating that they had not had extramarital sex (T. W. Smith, 1991). This may mean that up to 35 percent of women and 70 percent of men *may* have had extramarital sex (some of these had sex with people other than their spouses either before or between marriages). Younger people were more likely to report more sexual partners, probably showing a cohort effect.

PARENTHOOD

The birth of a baby marks a major transition in the parents' lives. Moving from an intimate relationship between two people to one involving a totally dependent third person changes individuals and changes marriages. Parenthood is a developmental experience, whether the children are biological offspring, are adopted, or are the children of only one spouse.

Why People Have Children

At one time, the blessing offered newlyweds in the Asian country of Nepal was, "May you have enough sons to cover the hillsides!" (B. P. Arjyal, personal communication, Feb. 12, 1993). Having children has traditionally been regarded as not only the primary reason for marriage, but its ultimate fulfillment. In preindustrial societies, large families were a necessity: children helped with the family's work and eventually cared for their aging parents. And because the death rate in childhood was high, fewer children reached maturity. Because economic and social reasons for having children were so powerful, parenthood—especially motherhood—had a unique aura.

Today, Nepali couples are wished, "May you have a very bright son." Although sons are still preferred over daughters there, even boys are not wished for in such numbers as in the past, in the face of the lessening or even reversal of previous reasons for having children. Because of technological progress, fewer workers are needed; because of modern medical care, most children survive; and because of government programs, some care of the aged is being provided. Overpopulation is a major problem in many parts of the world, and children are an expense rather than an economic asset. Furthermore, children can have negative, as well as positive, effects on a marriage.

Still, the desire for children is almost universal. Why? Psychoanalytic theorists like Freud maintain that women have a deep instinctual wish to bear and nurture infants, that they thus replace their own mothers, and that their babies are a substitute for the penis they will never have. Ego psychologists like Erikson see generativity—a concern with establishing and guiding the next generation—as a basic developmental need. Functionalist sociologists attribute reproduction to people's need for immortality, achieved by replacing themselves with their children. Other theorists consider parenthood a part of nature, universal in the animal world. There is also continuing cultural pressure to have children, on the assumption that all normal people want them. For the subjects in one study of 199 married couples—nonparents to parents of four—the chief motivations for parenthood were the wish for a close relationship with another human being and the desire to educate and train a child (F. L. Campbell, Townes, & Beach, 1982).

When People Have Children

The authors of this book exemplify changing trends in parenthood over the past 30 years. Sally was 23 years old in 1957, when she had her first child; not until after her third child was born, 5 years later, did she actively pursue her writing career. Diane, who is younger, established her academic career first and was 39 when she and Jonathan adopted Anna in 1986 (see Box 13-3).

By and large, today's couples have fewer children and have them later in life than the previous generation did (see Figure 13-2); now many people spend the early years of marriage finishing an education and starting a career. More contemporary women—16 percent in 1987 versus 4 percent in 1970—have a first child after age 30 (National Center for Health Statistics, 1990).

This pattern is not an accident: today's women see a later "ideal age" for first birth. The most recently married women, the best educated, and the most strongly feminist choose the latest ideal ages (Pebley, 1981). And more educated women actually do have their children later; educational level is the most important predictor of the age when a woman will first give birth (Rindfuss, Morgan, & Swicegood, 1988; Rindfuss & St. John, 1983).

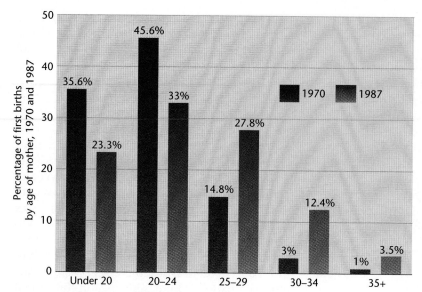

FIGURE 13-2
Today, women tend to have fewer children and have them later in life than their mothers' generation did. More women now have a first child after age 30. (*Source:* National Center for Health Statistics, 1990.)

The trend toward later motherhood seems to be a blessing for babies. Although mothers over 35 have a higher risk of birth-related complications, the risk to the baby's health is only slightly higher than for infants of younger women (Berkowitz, Skovron, Lapinski, & Berkowitz, 1990). On the positive side, babies of older mothers seem to benefit from their mothers' greater ease with parenthood. When 105 new mothers aged 16 to 38 were interviewed and observed with their infants, the older mothers reported more satisfaction with parenting and spent more time at it. They were more affectionate and sensitive to their babies and more effective in encouraging desired behavior (Ragozin, Basham, Crnic, Greenberg, & Robinson, 1982).

Finding Alternative Ways to Parenthood

Infertility

Mira and Lum planned to have a baby right after marriage. It never occurred to them that they might have trouble conceiving; but as more than a year went by without conception, they had to face the possibility that they might be among the 11 percent of married American couples who experience *infertility*—inability to conceive after 12 or more months of trying (Mosher & Pratt, 1990).

Psychological Effects of Infertility Infertility burdens a marriage emotionally. People—especially women—usually have trouble accepting the fact that they cannot do what comes so naturally and easily to others. Spouses may become angry with themselves and each other, and may feel empty,

worthless, and depressed (Abbey, Andrews, & Halman, 1992). Their sexual relationship suffers as sex becomes a matter of "making babies, not love" (Sabatelli, Meth, & Gavazzi, 1988). Such couples may benefit from professional counseling or support from other infertile couples; RESOLVE, a national nonprofit organization, offers such services.

Causes of Infertility Infertility becomes more of a problem with age. Only about 5 percent of couples are infertile when the woman is in her early twenties, but about 15 percent are infertile a decade later (Menken, Trussell, & Larsen, 1986). The ability to become pregnant seems to peak at about age 31, and then decline (van Noord-Zaadstra et al., 1991). Although most research is based on the woman's age, the man's age is also a factor; in early adulthood both partners are equally likely to be infertile (Glass, 1986).

The most common cause of infertility in men is the production of too few sperm. Only one sperm is needed to fertilize the ovum, but a sperm count lower than 60 to 200 million per ejaculation makes conception unlikely. Another cause is a blocked passageway, making sperm unable to exit; a third cause is sperm that are unable to swim well enough to reach the cervix. If the problem is in the woman's body, she may not be producing ova; the ova may be abnormal; the fallopian tubes may be blocked, preventing ova from reaching the uterus; mucus in the cervix may prevent sperm from penetrating it; or a disease of the uterine lining may prevent implantation of the fertilized ovum.

Sometimes surgery can correct the problem. And sometimes hormones can raise a man's sperm

BOX 13-3   TAKE A STAND

ADVANTAGES TO HAVING CHILDREN EARLY OR LATE

With advances in contraception, women and men have a choice in deciding when to have the children they want. Do they want to get an early start—or wait for a few years? Early or late childbearing—which is better for parents and for children? Both patterns have their own sets of pluses and minuses.

ADVANTAGES TO HAVING CHILDREN EARLY

- You are likely to have more physical energy. You can cope better with getting up in the middle of the night, staying up all night with a sick baby, keeping up with the heavy demands of both job and family.
- You are likely to have fewer medical problems with pregnancy and childbirth. Women who conceive after age 35 to 40 are statistically more likely to suffer from toxemia, high blood pressure, and kidney disorders, and they run a higher risk of bearing a child with a birth defect.
- You will be younger as your children grow—more energetic and psychologically in tune with them later as they become teenagers and then young adults.
- If your financial circumstances permit, you can use the children's early years to continue your education, work at a less demanding entry-level job, or work on a part-time schedule, then when your children demand less time and attention you will be free to concentrate more on your other work.
- You will be giving yourself a cushion of time if you have trouble conceiving. Couples who do not conceive right away often become anxious. The more trouble they have, the more anxious they get, and the anxiety may lead to further difficulty.

- You will have had fewer years to engage in activities that are risk factors in childbearing—such as smoking, drinking, and overeating. Hypertension and related circulatory problems, glucose intolerance, and diabetes are also more likely to develop in middle age.
- You will not be as apt to have built up an unrealistically high set of expectations for your children, as do some couples who have waited many years to have a family.

ADVANTAGES TO HAVING CHILDREN LATE

- You have had a chance to think more about your goals—what you want in life, both from family and career.
- You are more mature and can bring the benefits of your life experience to your role as parent.
- You will not have had to interrupt the course of your career between your schooling and starting to work.
- You will be better established in your career, so you won't have to press so hard on the job in the early years, when your children's needs are likely to be greatest.
- You've already proved to yourself that you can make it on the job, so you won't feel as if your children are keeping you from attaining career success, and you can relax and enjoy them.
- You are likely to have more money, which will make it easier to handle the expenses of children, buy time- and labor-saving services, and get more child care.
- You will be in a stronger position to negotiate a favorable maternity/paternity leave, a part-time work schedule, an arrangement whereby you can do some work at home, or

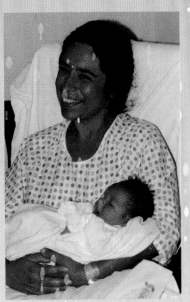

According to the timing-of-events model, the age at which people experience such major life events as a first baby can have an important influence on development. A normative event like parenthood, which most people expect during young adulthood, may become nonnormative and thus more difficult to deal with if it occurs earlier or later. (Phil Hollenbeak)

some other benefit. Knowing your value to the organization, your employer may be more likely to make concessions to keep you.
- Since you waited longer to have your children, you may have a keener appreciation of them and of the rewards of parenthood.

Ultimately, of course, deciding when to have children, like deciding whether to have them, is an intensely personal choice for people to determine in terms of their own lifestyles and life goals.

SOURCE: Olds, S. W. (1989). The working parents' survival guide. Rocklin, CA: Prima Publishing.

Anna, Diane Papalia's adopted daughter, seems to be a living embodiment of a recent study that found that adopted children viewed the world more positively than a control group of nonadopted children, felt better able to control their lives, and saw their adoptive parents as more nurturing. *(Erika Stone)*

count or increase a woman's ovulation; some fertility drugs cause superovulation, producing two, three, or more babies at a time. In more than 1 out of 10 cases, however, both man and woman seem perfectly normal but still are not able to conceive. Some infertile couples choose to remain childless; others adopt a child or turn to new technology.

Adoption

Adults adopt children for many reasons, only one of which is infertility. Since 1970, more Americans—including single and older people, working-class families, and homosexual couples—have become adoptive parents. Among African Americans, adoption is not so closely tied to infertility, but instead to the wish to provide a family for a known child, often a relative, who needs parents (Bachrach, London, & Maza, 1991). Because advances in contraception and legalization of abortion have reduced the number of adoptable

healthy white American babies, many adoptable children are disabled, beyond infancy, or of foreign birth (like Anna, Diane's daughter, who was born in Chile). Adoptions are more likely to be arranged independently—through private attorneys and doctors—than through agencies.

Adoption is well accepted in the United States, but there are still prejudices and mistaken ideas about it, like the belief that all adopted children have problems because they are not raised by their biological parents. Some negative views of adoption were reinforced by past studies that found elevated numbers of adoptees among people seeking mental health services. However, some more recent research has found that a difference between attitudes and characteristics of adopted and nonadopted children favored the adoptees. Adopted children were more confident, viewed the world more positively, felt better able to control their lives, and saw their adoptive parents as more nurturing than the nonadopted children in a control group (Marquis & Detweiler, 1985).

That is not to say that adopting a child is easier than bearing one. To the contrary, besides the usual issues of parenthood, adoptive parents have extra challenges—acceptance of their infertility (if this is why they adopted), awareness that they are not repeating their own parents' experience, the need to explain the adoption to their children, and discomfort about their children's interest in the biological parents.

New Methods of Becoming a Parent

Many couples yearn to have children who carry on their own hereditary legacy—to see in future generations the almond-shaped eyes of one ancestor or the artistic talent of another. Those who can afford the expense and the effort often realize their dreams through new technology that enables them to have children who are genetically at least half their own. The four following methods are all controversial.

Artificial Insemination Artificial insemination involves injection of sperm—often the husband's sperm—directly into the woman's cervix. If a husband seems infertile, a couple may choose artificial insemination by a donor (AID). The donor may be matched with the husband for physical characteristics, and the husband's sperm may be mixed with the donor's so that the possibility exists that the husband is the biological father. Many couples who conceive in this way never tell the children or anyone else about the children's origins. In the

United States, some 170,000 women are artificially inseminated each year, resulting in 65,000 births (Office of Technology Assessment, 1988).

In Vitro Fertilization   In 1978, headlines announced the birth of Louise Brown, the first "test-tube baby."* After 12 years of trying to conceive, Louise's parents had authorized a gynecologist to extract an ovum from Mrs. Brown's ovary, allow it to mature in an incubator, and then fertilize it with Mr. Brown's sperm. The doctor then implanted the embryo in Mrs. Brown's uterus, where it grew in the normal way.

In vitro fertilization (IVF), fertilization that takes place outside the mother's body, is becoming increasingly common for women whose fallopian tubes are blocked or damaged. Usually several ova are fertilized and implanted, to increase the chances of success. Conception and livebirth rates by IVF compare favorably with those for spontaneous conception, but decline with the mother's age (Tan et al., 1992). Although these children tend to be smaller than average, their head circumference is normal and their mental development is in the normal range (Brandes et al., 1992).

Ovum Transfer   Women who cannot produce normal ova may use donor eggs, ova donated by fertile women—the female counterpart of AID. There are two methods of *ovum transfer.* An ovum can be taken from a donor's body and fertilized in the laboratory, and the resulting embryo implanted in another woman's uterus (Lutjen et al., 1984). Or a donor egg can be fertilized by artificial insemination. The donor's uterus is flushed out a few days later, and the embryo is retrieved and inserted into the recipient's uterus (Bustillo et al., 1984). This procedure seems to be as effective with women 40 to 44 years old as with those under 35 (Sauer, Paulson, & Lobo, 1990).

Surrogate Motherhood   In *surrogate motherhood* a woman is impregnated by the prospective father (usually by artificial insemination). She carries the baby to term and gives the child to the father and his wife. The surrogate undergoes the entire pregnancy, with its risks and emotions. Surrogate motherhood is in legal limbo, partly as a result of the famous "Baby M" case, in which a surrogate mother changed her mind and wanted to keep the

baby (Hanley, 1988a, 1988b; Shipp, 1988). She was not granted custody of the child, but she does have visiting rights. The American Academy of Pediatrics Committee on Bioethics (1992) recommends that surrogate parenting be considered a tentative, preconception adoption agreement in which, before birth, the surrogate mother is the sole decision maker. The AAP also recommends a prebirth agreement on the period of time in which the surrogate may assert her parental rights.

Technology and Conception: Ethical Issues   To many people, the most objectionable aspect of surrogacy, aside from the possibility of forcing the surrogate to relinquish the baby, is the payment of money. Payment for adoption is forbidden in about 25 states, but surrogate motherhood is not adoption, since the biological father is also the social father. The creation of a "breeder class" of poor and disadvantaged women who carry the babies of the well-to-do strikes many people as wrong.

New means of conception raise other questions: must people who use them be infertile, or should they be free to make such arrangements simply for convenience? Should single people and homosexual couples have access to these methods? Should the children know about their parentage? Should chromosome tests be performed on all prospective donors and surrogates? What is the risk that children fathered or mothered by the same donor or surrogate (genetic half siblings) might someday meet and marry, putting their children at risk of birth defects? Can handling an embryo outside the body injure it? If a test-tube baby is born with a major defect, is the physician liable? What happens if a couple who have contracted with a surrogate divorce before the birth?

One thing seems certain: as long as there are people who want children but are unable to conceive or bear them, human ingenuity and technology will come up with new ways to satisfy their need.

The Transition to Parenthood

Both women and men often feel ambivalent about becoming parents. Along with excitement, they usually feel some anxiety about the responsibility of caring for a child and about the permanence that a pregnancy seems to impose on a marriage. Pregnancy also affects a couple's sexual relationship, sometimes making it even more intimate, but sometimes creating barriers.

What happens in a marriage from the time of the first pregnancy until the child's third birthday?

*This popular term is a misnomer: the fertilization is seldom performed in a test tube. Even the term *in vitro* is wrong; it is Latin for "in glass," but most labs use plastic dishes.

That varies considerably. One research team followed 128 middle- and working-class couples during this time; at the beginning of the study the husbands' ages averaged 29 years and the wives' 27 years. Although some marriages improved, many suffered overall, especially for the wives. Many spouses loved each other less, became more ambivalent about their relationship, argued more, and communicated less. This was true no matter what the sex of the child was and whether or not the couple had a second child by the time the first was 3 years old. But when the researchers looked, not at the *overall* quality of the marriage, but at such *individual* measures as love, conflict, ambivalence, and effort put into the relationship, at least half of the sample showed either no change on a particular measure or a small positive change (Belsky & Rovine, 1990).

What distinguishes marriages that deteriorate after parenthood from those that improve? This study found no single determining factor. Rather, a number of different factors related to both parents and child seemed influential. In deteriorating marriages, the partners were more likely to be younger and less well educated, to earn less money, and to have been married for fewer years. One or both partners tended to have low self-esteem, and husbands were likely to be less sensitive (Belsky & Rovine, 1990). The mothers who had the hardest time were those with babies who had irregular temperaments and were therefore harder to take care of. (Again, we see how babies influence their own environment.)

Two surprising findings emerged from Belsky and Rovine's study. First, couples who were most romantic "pre-baby" had more problems "post-baby," perhaps because they had unrealistic expectations. Second, women who had planned their pregnancies were unhappier, possibly because they had expected life with a baby to be better than it turned out to be. Another finding of unmet expectations emerged from a study of married, middle-class white women. These mothers too expected things to be better 1 year after their first babies were born—in terms of their relationships with their husbands, their own physical well-being, and their maternal competence and satisfaction—than they turned out to be, and had trouble adjusting (Kalmuss, Davidson, & Cushman, 1992).

One often violated expectation involves the division of chores. When a couple has shared them fairly equally before the baby is born, and then, post-baby, the burden shifts to the wife, marital happiness tends to decline, especially for nontraditional wives (Belsky, Lang, & Huston, 1986).

Parenthood as a Developmental Experience

As hard as it may be to take on the role of parent, keeping it up is even more demanding. Parenting has rich rewards, but anyone with children will testify that those rewards are earned. Caring for small children can be unsettling, irritating, frustrating, and overwhelming, as well as fulfilling and amusing (see Box 13-4).

About one-third of mothers find mothering both

These Nepalese parents enjoy the fun and stimulation of having a child— although by now Kusum's parents have realized that parenthood also has other aspects, especially when their 2½-year-old is unenthusiastic about being bathed. The physical, psychological, and financial stresses of rearing children contribute to the parents' own development. One of the best things about parenthood is that it is never predictable: parents must constantly meet the challenges of their children's changing needs. *(Sally Wendkos Olds)*

BOX 13-4   *PRACTICALLY SPEAKING*

THE HASSLES OF RAISING YOUNG CHILDREN

Parenthood has many rewards, many joyful moments. But it also carries a large measure of day-in, day-out stress. Being the parent of a young child means cleaning up messes, trying to accomplish some task while stepping over or around your child, running time-consuming errands when you would rather be going to the movies, planning your schedule around your child's needs—and then being ready to change your plans at the last minute. It also means listening to crying, whining, and nagging when you are tired and cranky yourself, reading to or playing with your child when you would really like to sink into a hot bath, having your conversation with another adult interrupted, and—occasionally—being embarrassed in public.

Researchers are now paying attention to these daily hassles. One team identified these and other normal, typical everyday stressors in a study to see how they determine families' levels of functioning, and what factors can relieve the stress they cause. Hassles, say Crnic and Greenberg (1990), are "the irritating, frustrating, annoying, and distressing demands that to some degree characterize everyday transactions with the environment" (p. 1629). The kind that come with parenting fall into two types—what parents have to do and what the children do that upsets the parents.

These researchers followed 74 mother-child pairs from the time the children were 1 month old until past their fifth birthdays. The pairs were mostly from white, two-parent families, and only 20 percent received any form of public assistance or welfare income. Not surprisingly, the more hassles these mothers experienced, the less sat-isfying parenting was for them. However, they did not seem to change their behavior toward their children as a result—at least not in the study's controlled laboratory observations. (Their behavior at home might present a different picture.)

According to the mothers, the best source of emotional support, which lessened the stress of parenting young children, came from friends, rather than the children's fathers. This may be because other mothers experience the same kinds of hassles, can sympathize with each other, and can also offer helpful suggestions from their own experience. On the other hand, the mothers need more than emotional support from their children's fathers; they need practical help in caring for the children.

---

enjoyable and meaningful, a third find it neither, and another third have mixed feelings (L. Thompson & Walker, 1989). Among couples who do not have children, husbands consider having children more important and are more apt to want them than their wives do (Seccombe, 1991). However, once the children come, although fathers treasure and are emotionally committed to them, they enjoy looking after them less than mothers do. Although fathers generally believe they should be involved in their children's lives, most are not nearly as involved as mothers are (Backett, 1987; Boulton, 1983; LaRossa, 1988). Still, men's families are very important to them (see Box 13-5).

In resolving conflicts among their personal roles (parent versus spouse versus worker), most successful parents define their situation positively. They believe that in any conflict, parental responsibilities clearly come first. They concentrate on one set of responsibilities at a time. And they compromise some standards when necessary, letting the furniture go undusted or becoming less active in community affairs to spend more time with their children (B. C. Miller & Myers-Walls, 1983; Myers-Walls, 1984; Paloma, 1972). As children develop, parents do too (see Table 13-7).

Unfortunately, some people cannot meet the physical, psychological, and financial demands and challenges of parenthood. They may abuse, neglect, maltreat, or abandon their children (see Chapters 5 and 9); or they may become physically or emotionally ill themselves. Most parents, however, do cope, sometimes with the help of their family, friends, and neighbors; books and articles about child rearing; and professional advice.

Blended Families

At a wedding that Sally recently attended, the bride's 9-year-old daughter from a previous marriage played a significant role in the creation of her new family. Jessica helped to make wedding favors, she read a short passage during the ceremony, and she received her own ring, as a symbol of her deep involvement in the new relationship.

With today's high rate of divorce and remarriage, families made up of "yours, mine, and ours" are becoming more common. In 1987 there were

TABLE 13-7

Stages of Parenting

What Children of Different Ages Need from Their Parents

INFANT AND TODDLER	PRESCHOOLER	SCHOOLCHILD	ADOLESCENT	YOUNG ADULT
Total care: feeding, clothing, bathing, protecting from harm, etc.	Continuing care balanced with encouragement of independence and autonomy	Help in balancing information from the outside world with what is learned at home	Help in balancing sexual drive in positive way	Encouragement of independence
Emotional attachment	Help in channeling aggression	Help in forming goals to strive for	Help in achieving independence from parents and other adult authorities	Awareness that parents can be consulted as older friends who will share their wisdom and experience without directing their children's lives from their own needs for vicarious success
A sense of security arising from trust that they are being cared for	Help in developing a good sense of gender identity	Help in developing moral reasoning	Encouragement to form own code of values	Role models for achieving intimacy, fulfillment, and integrating work and family roles
The beginnings of a feeling of control over life, achieved from parents' responsiveness	Help in forming a healthy acceptance of their bodies	Encouragement of achievement (academic, athletic, social)	Encouragement and help with educational and career goals	
	Encouragement of intellectual abilities, especially language	Encouragement of special talents and skills		
		Help in achieving high self-esteem		

How Adults Develop at Different Stages of Parenting

BEFORE BIRTH OF FIRST CHILD	PRESCHOOLER	SCHOOLCHILD	ADOLESCENT	YOUNG ADULT
Thinking about why they want children	Learning to change parenting behavior as the child's needs change (permitting more independence, for example)	Developing a realistic view of the child's abilities, separating their own achievement needs from the child's	Reexamining values in response to the child's questioning and testing of limits	Enjoying relationship with young adults who happen to be their children
Planning their lives as parents	Keeping the marital bond strong despite children's demands on time and energy	Appreciating the child for who he or she is, not for living out their own fantasies of being a genius or an athlete	Learning how to be flexible	Accepting children as independent people who need to make their own decisions and learn from their mistakes
INFANT AND TODDLER	Pursuing vocational goals more vigorously as the child begins to move out of the house	Learning how to be sensitive to the emotional needs of other people	Learning how to be strong in setting necessary limits	Learning how to offer help without being intrusive or controlling
Resolving conflicts between individual goals (career, comfort, and convenience) and baby's needs	Learning how to consult books, media, child-rearing experts without being too dependent on them	Participating in the child's school and extracurricular life to contribute in a public setting	Seeing the adolescent as an emerging adult with his or her own interests and not as a mirror of the parents	Rebuilding their marriage (or single social life) on a new basis without children at home
Change in image of themselves from parents' children to children's parents	Forgiving themselves for not being perfect parents	Recapturing the freshness of childhood by seeing things through the eyes of their child	Attending to own career goals, while not ignoring children's needs	Rethinking individual life goals after work of parenting is complete
Giving of self physically and emotionally		Rewriting their own childhood history by offering the child opportunities they never had		Embracing grandparenthood without interfering with the child's parenting of own children
Working through their relationship with their own parents—encouraging their role as grandparents, while not leaning on them for parenting decisions				

BOX 13-5 *FOOD FOR THOUGHT*

BOTH JOB AND FAMILY ROLES AFFECT MEN'S PSYCHOLOGICAL WELL-BEING

Traditionally, women's mental health has been assessed in terms of family relationships, and men's in terms of their work experiences. In recent years, however, researchers have paid more attention to the neglected aspects of both sexes' lives. A number of studies—notably those about women's multiple roles (see Chapter 15)—have emphasized the importance of work in women's lives, and recent research has shown the importance of family connections to men's well-being.

In one study, researchers interviewed 300 employed husbands, aged 25 to 40, in two-earner couples, asking them to evaluate work, marital, and parental roles for both rewards and concerns (Barnett, Marshall, & Pleck, 1992). For ex-

ample, in terms of work, they were asked how rewarding it was "to have a variety of tasks" and how much of a concern was "a lack of job security." For the marital role they rated rewards like "enjoying the same activities" and concerns like "your partner being critical of you." And for the parent role, rewards included "seeing your children mature and change" and concerns, "having too many arguments and conflicts with them." Each man received a role-quality score for each role: his reward score minus his concern score. The men were also assessed for anxiety and depression.

The study's main finding invalidated the widely held view that work is the main determinant of male mental health. Instead, men's

family roles are just as important, and their various roles are related. A man's good relationships with his wife and children often make up for a poor experience on the job, but when both job and family roles are unsatisfactory, psychological distress often results. One difference between men and women is that for working women merely being a parent often offsets job concerns, whereas for men it is not parenthood of itself, but how rewarding the parental role is that is important. Being a father may be less central to a man's sense of self than motherhood is to a woman, but getting rewards from parenthood is just as important to fathers as to mothers.

4.3 million such families and about 6 million stepchildren in the United States (P. C. Glick, 1989).

The stepfamily—also called the *blended,* or *reconstituted,* family—is different from a "natural" family. First, it has a larger supporting cast, including former spouses, former in-laws, and absent parents, as well as aunts, uncles, and cousins on both sides. Furthermore, it may be "contaminated with anger, guilt, jealousy, value conflicts, misperceptions, and fear" (Einstein, 1979, p. 64). It is, in short, burdened by much baggage not carried by an "original" family—and it cannot be expected to function in the same way.

Stepfamilies have to deal with the stress from losses (due to death or divorce) undergone by both children and adults, which can make them afraid to trust and to love. A welter of family histories can complicate present relationships. Previous bonds between children and their biological parents or loyalty to an absent or dead parent may interfere with forming ties to the stepparent—especially when children go back and forth between two households. Disparities in life experiences are also common, as when a father of adolescents marries a woman who has never had a child (E. Visher & Visher, 1983).

Stepfamilies cope in a number of ways. Some of the most successful strategies include the following (E. B. Visher & Visher, 1981; 1989):

■ *Having realistic expectations:* Members of a stepfamily have to remember that it is different from a biological family. They have to allow time for loving relationships to develop. They need to see what is positive about their differences: instead of resisting the diversity in two households, for example, they can welcome it as a doubling of resources and experiences.

■ *Developing new relationships within the family:* Stepfamilies need to build new traditions and develop new ways of doing things that will be right for them. They can plan activities to give the children time alone with the biological parent, time alone with the stepparent, and time with both parents—and activities that provide time alone for the couple. They can move to a new house or apartment, one that does not hold memories of a past life.

Stepparents need to understand children's emotions, to be sensitive and responsive to children's fears, hurts, and resentments at a time when the

Couples choose not to have children for many reasons, including commitment to social causes or careers, a feeling that they would not make good parents, a wish to retain the intimacy of the marital duo, a fear of financial burdens, and a desire to preserve their freedom to travel and make spur-of-the-moment decisions. *(Palmer Brilliant/The Picture Cube)*

adults may be euphoric about building a new life together. They need to maintain a courteous relationship with the former spouse. Children adjust best after divorce when they maintain close ties with both parents, when they are not used as weapons for angry parents to hurt each other, and when they are not subjected to the pain of hearing a parent or stepparent insult the absent parent. Divorced parents can form "coparenting teams" to meet their children's needs. And they can gain much by seeking social support. Sharing feelings, frustrations, and triumphs with other stepparents and children often helps people to view their own situation more realistically and to benefit from the experiences of others.

For people who have been bruised by loss, the blended family has the potential for providing the same benefits as any family that cares about all its members. Achieving complete caring within the family is not easy (even for biological families), but it can be done.

REMAINING CHILDLESS

"When are you going to have a baby?" This question is heard less often these days, as societal attitudes have moved away from the belief that all married couples who *can* have children *should* have them. Today, most people still want children, but those who do not no longer feel so pressured to have them (Thornton, 1989).

About 5 to 7 percent of American couples are childless by choice (D. E. Bloom & Pebley, 1982). Some decided before marriage never to have children. Most, however, kept postponing conception, waiting for "the right time" until they decided that that time would never come.

What makes people come to this decision? Some feel committed to social causes or careers to which they want to devote their time and energy. Some would rather have contact with other people's children than bring up their own, because they feel more comfortable with adults or think that they would not make good parents. Some want to retain the intimacy of their marriage, free from the emotional demands of parenting. Some do not want the financial burdens of parenthood. Some enjoy the freedom to travel or to make spur-of-the-moment decisions (F. L. Campbell et al., 1982).

In a study of 42 couples who had chosen either parenthood or childlessness, the two groups turned out to be very similar in family background and marital satisfaction, but different in their interaction with their spouses (H. Feldman, 1981). The childless couples had less traditional attitudes toward women and did more enjoyable activities together. (Parents may not need to do as much together, or even talk to each other as much, because being with their children meets some of their relational needs.)

Both groups in this study were happy in their marriages—a fact that may reflect their free choice of lifestyle. But some people who want children are discouraged by the costs and the difficulty of combining parenthood with employment. Better child care and other support services might help more couples make truly voluntary decisions (D. E. Bloom & Pebley, 1982).

FRIENDSHIP

Young adults often feel as if they have too little time to be with friends. Friends, however, do play an important role in these years. In fact, one study of friendships across the life span found that new-lyweds have more friends than adolescents, the middle-aged, or the elderly (Weiss & Lowenthal, 1975).

Characteristics of Adult Friendship

How does a close friendship differ from a romantic tie? According to 150 people—two-thirds of them college students and one-third adults who were no longer in school—friendships involve trust, respect, enjoyment of each other's company, understanding and acceptance of each other, willingness to help and to confide in one another, and spontaneity, or feeling free to be oneself (K. E. Davis, 1985). Romantic bonds also have these aspects, plus sexual passion and extreme caring. However, these subjects saw "best friendships" as more stable than ties to a spouse or lover. Most people's close and best friends were of the same sex.

Benefits of Friendship

Friendships not only nourish the soul; they are also balm for the body. People who are isolated from friends and family are twice as likely to fall ill and to die as people who maintain social ties (House, Landis, & Umberson, 1988). The 10 to 20 percent of people who have close contact with others less than once a week and have no one with whom to share feelings are most at risk. The effect is greater for men, probably because women's relationships are generally more intimate—even if a woman has few ties with others, the ties she has may be very nurturing, making up in quality what they lack in quantity. These findings are supported by Anson's (1989) finding, cited earlier, that living with another person seems to enhance health.

What is it about social relationships that fosters good health—or about their absence that undermines health? Early theories suggested that emotional support from other people helps minimize the effect of stress. But more recent observers propose other possible reasons (House et al., 1988). Social ties may foster a sense of meaning or coherence in life. It is also possible that people who keep in touch with others are more likely to behave in healthy ways—sleeping and eating sensibly, getting enough exercise, avoiding substance abuse, and getting medical care when it is needed.

Broad social forces underlie both social ties and health. However, American adults today, compared with those of 30 years ago, are less likely to be married, more likely to be living alone, less likely to belong to voluntary organizations, and less likely to visit with others. It is ironic that just as we are discovering how important social interactions are for health, people seem to be engaging in them less often.

The bonds forged in young adulthood with friends and family often endure throughout life. These relationships continue to influence people through middle age and into old age; and the changes people experience in their more mature years affect their relationships, as we'll see in Parts Six and Seven.

SUMMARY

PERSONALITY DEVELOPMENT IN YOUNG ADULTHOOD: TWO MODELS

■ Studies of adults show that development continues throughout life. In young adulthood, people develop as they confront the issues of leaving their parents' home, deciding on careers, establishing relationships and families, and setting life goals.

■ Two important perspectives on adulthood are the normative-crisis model and the timing-of-events model.

■ The normative-crisis model—exemplified by Erikson, Vaillant, and Levinson—proposes that there is a built-in plan for human development and that during each part of the life span, people face a particular crisis or task.

1 Erikson's sixth psychosocial crisis is intimacy versus isolation. To develop successfully, according to Erikson, young adults must fuse their identities in a close, intimate heterosexual relationship that leads to procreation. Negative outcomes that may result during this period are self-absorption and isolation.

2 In the Grant Study of Harvard men, Vaillant found that men who used "mature" defenses were more successful in many ways than those who used less mature adaptive techniques. This study also revealed a period of career consolidation that characterized men in their thirties.

3 According to Levinson, the goal of adults' development is building the life structure. In his studies of men, Levinson found periods of transition

and periods of stability alternating throughout adulthood. Two important influences during young adulthood are the mentor and the dream.

■ Studies of women suggest gender differences in paths to identity. Males traditionally define themselves in terms of separation and autonomy; females seem to achieve identity through relationships and attachment.

■ The timing-of-events model proposes that adult development is influenced by the specific important events that occur in a person's life, and that the timing of an event affects the person's reaction to it.

■ Life events may be expected (normative) or unexpected (nonnormative). Timing can affect "normativeness." Events perceived as "off time" are generally more stressful than those that occur "on time."

■ Although our society has become less age-conscious, many people still try to time major life events such as marriage, occupational progression, and parenthood by "social clocks."

INTIMATE RELATIONSHIPS AND PERSONAL LIFESTYLES

■ According to Robert Sternberg's triangular theory of love, love has three aspects: intimacy, passion, and commitment. These combine into eight types of love relationships.

■ During young adulthood, many people decide whether and whom to marry. Americans have been marrying later than in past generations. Marriage is related to happiness and health. Success in marriage is related to age at marriage and the way partners communicate.

■ The United States has one of the highest divorce rates in the world, with more than 1 million divorces each year. Although divorce usually entails a painful period of adjustment (even for the spouse who has initiated it), most divorced people remarry.

■ Today more people feel free to remain single until a late age or never marry. Advantages of being single include career opportunities, travel, and self-sufficiency. Possible negative aspects include being totally responsible for oneself and finding social acceptance.

■ Cohabiting is in many ways a maturing experience, though there may be problems associated with it, such as dealing with the ambiguity of the situation, jealousy, and the desire for a commitment.

■ Most young adults make basic decisions about their sexual lifestyles. Most Americans today are having sexual experiences before marriage. The more sexually active husbands and wives are during the first year of marriage, the more active they are likely to remain. More married people, especially young married people, appear to be having sexual relationships outside of marriage.

■ Infertile couples may suffer adverse psychological effects. Adoption is becoming more difficult because of a decreased number of adoptable American babies, and more couples are trying artificial insemination, in vitro fertilization, ovum transfer, and surrogate motherhood.

■ Having a child marks a major transition in a couple's life, from sharing reciprocal responsibilities to having total responsibility for a new life. Parenthood has a mixed impact on marriages.

■ Many couples today opt for fewer children or remain childless, and an increasing number of women, especially educated women, have children later in life.

■ Friendships are important during young adulthood. Social ties are valuable for health and well-being.

KEY TERMS

normative-crisis model (page 436)
intimacy versus isolation (436)
adaptive mechanisms (438)
life structure (439)
timing-of-events model (442)

normative life events (442)
nonnormative life events (442)
triangular theory of love (444)
cohabitation (453)
infertility (456)

artificial insemination (458)
in vitro fertilization (459)
ovum transfer (459)
surrogate motherhood (459)

SUGGESTED READINGS

Bartholet, E. (1993). *Family bonds: Adoption and the politics of parenting.* A tough, hard-hitting, intensely personal book that raises deep questions about the meaning of family and challenges the adoption policies in the United States and many other countries. The author, a law professor who made many efforts to conceive through new techniques and then adopted two Peruvian children, illumines her analysis of the issues with her own moving personal story.

Block, J. (1990). *Motherhood as metamorphosis: Change and continuity in the life of a new mother.* New York: Dutton. This examination of the psychological ramifications of becoming a mother explores how a woman's life is transformed in her baby's first year of life.

Bolles, E. B. (1993). *The Penguin adoption handbook.* New York: Penguin Books. This revised edition of a classic guide provides a comprehensive description of the adoption process. It covers agency, international, and independent adoptions, and notes the different tactics that work best for couples, single people, and minority families.

Cowan, C. P., & Cowan, P. A. (1992). *When partners become parents: The big life change for couples.* New York: Basic Books. Based on a ten-year study of 100 couples, this book charts the changes in their lives upon the arrival of a first child. The authors offer anecdotes and quotations from the couples, and come up with a number of interesting conclusions, set against an impressive body of other recent research.

Greer, J., with Myers, E. (1992). *Adult sibling rivalry: Understanding the legacy of childhood.* New York: Crown. The author, a psychotherapist specializing in sibling counseling, explores how conflicts that begin in childhood affect adult life and relationships, both within and outside the family, and offers suggestions for healing old wounds.

Hart, D. A. (1992). *Becoming men: The development of aspirations, values, and adaptational styles.* New York: Plenum. The fascinating results of a longitudinal study of men's lives. The men entered the study as adolescents and were interviewed extensively at four-year intervals for the next twenty years. The results shed light on how men and woman face the challenges of adolescence and adulthood.

Schnur, S. (1990). *Daddy's home! Reflections of a family man.* New York: Crown. A book of sensitive and sometimes humorous essays that touch on many of the emotional issues of young adulthood.

Tannen, D. (1990). *You just don't understand: Women and men in conversation.* New York: Morrow. A fascinating and fun-to-read analysis of the differences in the ways men and women communicate. The author is an expert in linguistics.

PART SIX

MIDDLE ADULTHOOD

When does middle age begin? Is it at the birthday party when you see your cake ablaze with 40 candles? Is it the day your "baby" leaves home and you now have time to pursue all those activities you've put on hold for so long? Is it the day when you notice that police officers are getting younger all the time? *Middle adulthood,* which we define in this book roughly as the years between ages 40 and 65, has many markers. In Chapters 14 and 15, we will see what sets these years apart from the years that come before and afterward.

■ In **Chapter 14,** we examine health in middle adulthood, looking at menopause, the male climacteric, the physical changes that appear in both sexes, and the impact of stress on health. We also consider the way thought processes continue to mature and how they

contribute to moral leadership. Finally, we examine the satisfactions that middle-aged people get from their work, as well as the effects of burnout, unemployment, and the challenge of changing careers at midlife.

■ The famous—or infamous—"midlife crisis" is discussed in **Chapter 15.** Should all middle-aged people get ready for it, or is it a figment of researchers' and journalists' imagination? Another controversial issue related to social and emotional development is whether personality is fixed early in adulthood or whether it changes over the years. Finally, we look at the relationships middle-aged adults have with important people in their lives: their spouses, their friends, and the generations on either side of them—their children and their parents. These are richly textured years.

CHAPTER FOURTEEN

PHYSICAL AND INTELLECTUAL DEVELOPMENT IN MIDDLE ADULTHOOD

The primitive, physical, functional pattern of the morning of life, the active years before forty or fifty, is outlived. But there is still the afternoon opening up, which one can spend not in the feverish pace of the morning but in having time at last for those intellectual, cultural, and spiritual activities that were pushed aside in the heat of the race.

Anne Morrow Lindbergh,
Gift from the Sea, *1955*

PHYSICAL DEVELOPMENT

■ **PHYSICAL CHANGES OF MIDDLE AGE**

Sensory and Psychomotor Functioning
Sexuality
Appearance: The Double Standard of Aging

■ **HEALTH IN MIDDLE AGE**

Health Status
Health Problems
The Impact of Race and Socioeconomics
  on Health

INTELLECTUAL DEVELOPMENT

■ **ASPECTS OF INTELLECTUAL
DEVELOPMENT IN MIDDLE ADULTHOOD**

Intelligence and Cognition
The Adult Learner

■ **WORK IN MIDDLE ADULTHOOD**

Occupational Patterns
Occupational Stress
Unemployment
Work and Intellectual Growth

■ **BOXES**

14-1 Practically Speaking: Preventing
Osteoporosis
14-2 Window on the World: Japanese
Women's Experience of Menopause
14-3 Food for Thought: Moral Leadership
in Middle and Late Adulthood
14-4 Food for Thought: Creativity Takes
Hard Work

ASK YOURSELF

■ What physical changes do men and women experience during the middle years, and how do they cope with them?

■ How do the physical changes of midlife affect sexuality?

■ Does intellectual functioning in middle adulthood have a distinctive character?

■ Why do some people continue their education or change careers at midlife?

■ What benefits do middle-aged people get from work?

The Spanish toast *Salud, amor, y pesetas—y el tiempo para gustarlos* ("Health, love, and money—and time to enjoy them") inspired the authors of a book about middle age to use it as a chapter title; they found it the "ideal summary of what middle age can offer" (B. Hunt & Hunt, 1974, p. 23).

What, though, *is* middle age? Since in this book we divide the life span chronologically, we define *middle age* as the years between ages 40 and 65. But it can also be defined contextually. One context is the family situation: a middle-aged person can be defined as one who has grown children or elderly parents (Troll, 1989).

A contextual definition may contradict a chronological one. In terms of chronology, both authors of this book are middle-aged. Contextually, Diane is a young adult in some ways, in midlife in others. Although she is in her mid-forties, her child is only 7—hardly ready to leave the nest. And until the past couple of years she did not need to assume the role of caregiver for her parents, who had, well into their seventies, been active, fit, and intellectually alert. A major life transition for Diane was her father's final illness and his death in 1992; since then she has been more of a supportive presence in her mother's life. Sally in her early forties was the mother of three teenagers, one of whom was already away at college; she had also been helping her own widowed mother, in poor health at age 75; and by Sally's late forties, she had become a grandmother.

Many people begin to feel middle-aged when they reach their fifties, a turning point that is often just as dramatic as adolescence. Younger colleagues call them "ma'am" or "sir," they suffer from arthritis or prostate trouble or some other physical condition associated with old age, sons go bald or daughters make them grandparents, they realize that they are the oldest people in the office, and they recognize more names in the obituaries.

Still, many people consider their middle years the best time of their lives. In general, middle-aged people are in good physical, financial, and psychological shape. They are likely to be in their peak earning years, and since their children are usually independent or nearly so, many are in the most secure financial position of their lives. Medical advances, awareness of preventive care, and fitness are keeping them, by and large, in good physical health. One of the greatest strengths of midlife stems from having lived long enough to acquire valuable social and professional experience and having opportunities to use that experience.

This "prime time" of life has its stresses too, of course. The middle-aged adult realizes that his or her body is not what it once was. In a youth- and fitness-oriented society like ours, wrinkles, sags, and stiff muscles are unwelcome signs of aging. Furthermore, signs of aging can hurt job seekers.

This last point is important because work strongly influences how people feel about midlife. This is a time of taking stock, a time of reevaluating earlier career aspirations and how well they have been fulfilled. Sometimes people respond by modifying their goals; sometimes they strike out in totally new directions.

Reevaluation—which extends to intimate relationships and other aspects of life—comes about because of a shift in people's orientation in time. Instead of thinking of their life span in terms of the years they have lived, people begin to think in terms of the time they have left to live (Neugarten, 1967). They realize that they cannot possibly do everything they want to do, and they are eager—sometimes desperately so—to make the most of their remaining years. This realization prompts some people to switch careers, some to leave their spouses, and some to retire.

In this chapter, we discuss physical and intellectual issues of middle age. We focus on sensory and psychomotor functioning, on sexual expression, on health, and on the distinctive ways in which people think and learn at midlife. We look at moral development and at adult education. And we consider the satisfactions and stresses of work and the challenge of career change. In Chapter 15, we will explore the social and emotional issues of midlife.

PHYSICAL DEVELOPMENT

From young adulthood through the middle years, biological changes generally take place gradually. They may not be noticed—until one day a 40-year-old man realizes that he cannot read the telephone directory without eyeglasses, or a 55-year-old woman has to admit that she is not as quick on her feet as she was.

Physical functioning and health are usually still good, though not at the peak level of young adulthood. Most people take changes in reproductive and sexual capacities—menopause and the male climacteric—in stride, and some experience a kind of sexual renaissance. Some, however—especially women—feel keenly a perceived decline in physical attractiveness.

PHYSICAL CHANGES OF MIDDLE AGE

SENSORY AND PSYCHOMOTOR FUNCTIONING

The changes in sensory and motor capabilities during midlife are usually fairly small, and most middle-aged people compensate well for them. These changes are real, however, and they affect people's self-concept and their interaction with others.

Vision, Hearing, Taste, and Smell

Throughout life, the lens of the eye becomes progressively less flexible, so its ability to focus diminishes; this common occurrence is usually noticed for the first time in early middle age. Many people now need reading glasses for *presbyopia,* the farsightedness associated with aging. This sometimes has a salutary effect. At age 50, for example, Sally, who has worn glasses for nearsightedness since she was 11, passed the vision test

for her driving license without glasses for the first time in her life. Bifocals—eyeglasses in which lenses for reading are combined with lenses for distant vision—help people make the adjustment between near and far objects. Middle-aged people also experience a slight loss in sharpness of vision; and because of changes in the pupil of the eye, they need about one-third more brightness to compensate for the loss of light reaching the retina (Belbin, 1967; Troll, 1985). Nearsightedness, though, tends to level off in these years.

There is also a gradual hearing loss during middle age, especially with regard to more high-pitched sounds; this condition is known as *presbycusis.* After about age 55, hearing loss is greater for men than for women (Troll, 1985). However, most hearing loss during these years is not even noticed, since it is limited to levels of sound that are unimportant to behavior. Hearing loss occurs at much later ages among some African tribespeople than it does in Europe and the United States, most likely because people in western countries suffer the effects of an environment full of blaring auto horns, loud radios, jet airplanes, and other harsh noises (Timiras, 1972).

Recent evidence indicates that sensitivity to taste and smell declines in midlife (Cain, Reid, & Stevens, 1990; Stevens, Cain, Demarque, & Ruthruff, 1991). Since the taste buds become less sensitive, foods that may be quite flavorful to a younger person may seem bland to a middle-aged person (Troll, 1985).

Strength, Coordination, and Reaction Time

"Use it or lose it" is the motto of many middle-aged people, who have taken up jogging, racquetball, tennis, aerobic dancing, and other forms of physical exercise that often make them fitter, stronger, and more energetic than they were in their youth.

Although strength and coordination decline gradually during the middle years (Spirduso & MacRae, 1990), a 10 percent reduction in physical strength from its peak during the twenties often means little to people who rarely if ever exert their full strength in daily life.

The more people do, the more they *can* do, and vice versa. People who become active early in life reap the benefits of more stamina and more resilience after age 60 (Spirduso & MacRae, 1990). But people who lead sedentary lives lose muscle tone and energy, and so they become even less inclined to exert themselves physically. A sedentary

Many middle-aged people find that their improved ability to use strategies in a sport, as a result of experience and better judgment, often outweigh the changes in strength, coordination, and reaction time that are common in midlife. Although such changes affect the status of top-flight athletes, they rarely interfere with typical recreational competitors, like these tennis players. *(David Lawrence/The Stock Market)*

lifestyle has recently emerged as the major correlate to deaths from heart attacks (J. Brody, 1990).

Simple reaction time (like the speed of lifting an index finger from a key) slows by about 20 percent, on the average, between ages 20 and 60 (Birren, Woods, & Williams, 1980). Complex motor skills (like those involved in driving), which increase during childhood and youth, gradually decline after people have achieved full growth. But the decline does not necessarily result in poorer performance.

Driving, for instance, requires such skills as coordination, quick reaction time, and ability to tolerate glare. After the age of about 30 to 35, each of these abilities declines (DeSilva, 1938, in Soddy & Kidson, 1967). Yet middle-aged drivers are typically better than younger ones (McFarland, Tune, & Welford, 1964). Also, 60-year-old typists are as efficient as 20-year-olds (Spirduso & MacRae, 1990). In these and other activities, the improvement that comes with experience more than makes up for the decrements that come with age. "Overpracticed" skills seem more resistant to the effects of age than skills that are used less.

Skilled industrial workers in their forties and fifties are often more productive than ever, partly because they are generally more conscientious and careful (Belbin, 1967). Furthermore, middle-aged workers are less likely than younger workers to suffer disabling injuries on the job—a likely result of experience and good judgment, which more than compensate for any lessening of coordination and motor skills (B. Hunt & Hunt, 1974).

Physiological Changes

Some of the physiological changes of midlife are a direct result of aging. Still, behavioral factors and lifestyle, dating from youth, often affect their timing and extent. People age at different rates, and the decline of the body systems is gradual. The most common of these changes include a diminished ability to pump blood; reduced kidney functioning; less enzyme secretion in the gastrointestinal tract, leading to indigestion and constipation; weakening of the diaphragm; and, in the male, enlargement of the prostate gland (the organ surrounding the neck of the urinary bladder), which may cause urinary and sexual problems.

SEXUALITY

Sexual Activity

Myths about sexuality in midlife (many of which were believed by middle-aged people themselves) have often interfered with happiness. But recent advances in health and medical care, more liberal attitudes toward sex throughout society, and new studies are now making people more aware that sex can be a vital part of life during these—and even later—years. Middle-aged people are engaging in sexual activity more often and in more varied ways than ever before (Brecher & the Editors of Consumer Reports Books, 1984; B. D. Starr & Weiner, 1981).

In fact, freed from worries about pregnancy and blessed with more time to spend with their partners, many people find that their sexual relationship is better than it has been in years. This is usually so for those who consider a sexual relationship part of an overall sensual attachment. Lovers who hold and caress each other, both in and out of bed, without confining such touching to "foreplay" for genital sex, can experience a global kind of arousal that permeates a relationship. For such couples, midlife can be a time of heightened sexuality as part of a caring, close relationship. This holds true for homosexual as well as heterosexual couples (Weg, 1989).

Sexual functioning is different in middle adulthood. Most men do not experience sexual tension as often as they did when they were younger: those who wanted intercourse every other day may now be content to go 3 to 5 days between orgasms. Erections arrive less often of their own accord and more often only with direct stimulation. Orgasms come more slowly and sometimes not at all. And men need a longer recovery time after one orgasm before they can ejaculate again. Also, after menopause, some women do not become aroused as readily as before, and some find intercourse painful because of thinning vaginal tissues and inadequate lubrication.

Very often, lessening of sexual activity is due to nonphysiological causes: monotony in a relationship, preoccupation with business or financial worries, mental or physical fatigue, depression, failure to make sex a high priority in the face of conflicting demands on one's time, fear of failure to attain an erection, and the lack of an available partner. Physical causes include chronic disease, surgery, some medications, and too much food or alcohol (Masters & Johnson, 1966; Weg, 1989).

Couples who recognize the normal changes of middle age, and who can redesign their sex life around them, can find great satisfaction. In fact, the slower reactions of men can prove a boon: couples may enjoy longer, more leisurely periods of sexual activity; and women may find the longer period of arousal helpful in reaching orgasm—often by means other than intercourse. In one study of 160 middle-aged women, most reported having a better sex life than they had earlier (L. B. Rubin, 1982). They knew their own sexual needs and desires better, felt freer to take the initiative, and had a higher level of interest in sex.

Reproductive and Sexual Capacity

One fundamental change of middle age—the decline of reproductive capacity—affects men and women differently. Women's ability to bear children comes to an end. Although men can continue to father children, they begin to experience reduced fertility and, in some cases, a decrease in potency, the ability to obtain and maintain an erection.

Menopause

The biological event of *menopause* occurs when a woman stops ovulating and menstruating and can no longer bear children. Menopause is generally considered to have occurred 1 year after the last menstrual period. For American women, this typically happens between ages 45 and 55, at an average age of 51. A small proportion of women, however, begin to experience menstrual changes in their thirties, a few others not until their sixties.

Physical Effects of Menopause   The time span of some 2 to 5 years during which a woman's body undergoes the various physiological changes that bring on the menopause is known as the *climacteric*. During the climacteric, a woman's body reduces its production of the female hormone estrogen. As a result, the woman usually menstruates irregularly, with either more or less bleeding than before and a shorter or longer time between cycles.

Some women—but not all—experience other physical effects. These may include hot flashes (sudden sensations of heat that flash through the body), thinning of the vaginal lining, or urinary dysfunction caused by tissue shrinkage. In a minority of postmenopausal women (1 in 4), the decrease in estrogen leads to *osteoporosis,* a condition in which the bones become thinner and more susceptible to fractures (see Box 14-1). Other discomforts sometimes reported by menopausal women, which do not seem to be directly related to the hormonal changes in their bodies, include joint pain, insomnia, dizziness, constipation, forgetfulness, irritability, and anxiety (Matthews, 1992).

The most troublesome physical effects of menopause, and other health problems like osteoporosis and a higher risk of heart disease, are linked to the lower levels of estrogen in a woman's body after menopause. Today, artificial estrogen is often prescribed, either in a pill or in a slow-release skin patch, but not every woman needs estrogen-replacement therapy (ERT), and not every woman should get it.

There is a great deal of contradictory research about the benefits and risks of ERT. Replacement of estrogen alone has been related to a higher risk of cancer of the lining of the uterus, but when artificial progesterone is given along with the

BOX 14-1   PRACTICALLY SPEAKING

PREVENTING OSTEOPOROSIS

Three-quarters of older women do *not* suffer from *osteoporosis,* or thinning of the bones. But those who do often suffer broken bones in old age (Figure 14-1). This decrease in bone mass is largely a disorder of women. It is most prevalent in white women, especially those of northern European background, and women who are thin, who smoke, whose menopause occurs before age 45, and who get too little calcium or too little exercise. It seems more common today than it used to be, with increasing incidence of hip fractures in the United States, Britain, and Canada. Recent analysis of old human bones, from 87 British women buried from 1729 to 1852 found that these older bones were stronger than contemporary ones (Lees et al., 1993).

Fortunately, osteoporosis seems to be preventable if women take steps in youth and middle age. Three major preventive measures are exercising, avoiding smoking, and (for some women) taking hormone supplements (Hopper & Seeman, 1994; Dawson-Hughes et al., 1990; National Institutes of Health [NIH], 1984). Perhaps the most important safeguard is calcium intake. Women who drink two cups of coffee a day tend to

have lower bone density—unless they also drink milk every day (Barrett-Connor, Chang, & Edelstein, 1994).

Most American women drink little milk and eat few foods rich in calcium; those who have osteoporosis tend to consume even less of this important mineral. Women should get between 1000 and 1500 milligrams of calcium a day or even more, starting early in life. They can easily do so by consuming such calcium-rich foods as the following:

■ *Dairy foods:* Skim milk and low-fat or fat-free yogurt provide the benefits of calcium without the fat, cholesterol, or high calories of cream.
■ *Certain kinds of seafood:* Canned sardines and salmon (if eaten with the bones) and oysters, canned or fresh.
■ *Certain vegetables:* broccoli; kale; collard, dandelion, turnip, and mustard greens.

Exercise seems to stimulate bone growth: it should become part of the daily routine early in life and should continue to some degree as long as possible throughout life. The best exercises for increasing bone

density are weight-bearing activities like walking, running, jumping rope, aerobic dancing, and bicycling.

The National Institutes of Health (1984a) also recommends administration of estrogen to women at particularly high risk of developing osteoporosis, such as those who have had their ovaries removed. One study of 75 postmenopausal women who already had osteoporosis found that estrogen skin patches reduced bone loss and numbers of vertebral fractures (Lufkin et al., 1992). Estrogen, however, which is associated with higher rates of breast cancer, is more controversial than the recommendations for diet and exercise, which can be safely followed by all women.

Efforts to find a safe, effective treatment for osteoporosis continue. One New Zealand study found that calcium supplements slowed bone loss in postmenopausal women (Heaney, 1993; Reid, 1993). Other therapies now being tested include the hormone calcitonin (as a nasal spray), a combined hormone therapy, and non-hormonal drugs that inhibit bone resorption (National Osteoporosis Foundation, 1992; Dawson Hughes et al., 1990; Skolnick, 1990).

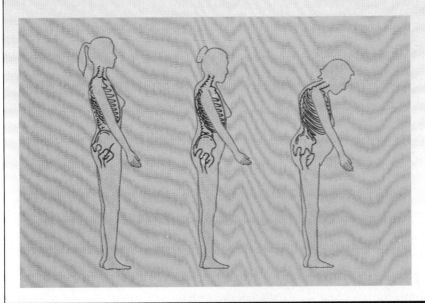

FIGURE 14-1
Osteoporosis. As osteoporosis weakens bones, fractures of vertebrae may cause women to become stooped from the waist up, and to lose 4 inches or more of height. (*Source:* Notelovitz & Ware, 1983.)

estrogen, some studies suggest that the risk of developing this kind of cancer falls below the level for women who receive no hormone at all (Bush et al., 1983; Hammond, Jelovsek, Lee, Creasman, & Parker, 1979). This estrogen-progesterone combination has been linked to an increase in breast cancer; but one recent analysis found that women who used postmenopausal estrogen were *not* at increased risk of breast cancer (Henrich, 1992).

Some physicians advise women with a history of breast cancer or blood clots not to use ERT. The safety of long-term combined estrogen-progesterone treatment is still hotly debated and under study. Meanwhile, women need to examine their own situation and their family health history and, if they do get ERT, to stay in close touch with their physicians.

Psychological Effects of Menopause For most women, menopause is a psychological *non*event. At one time, such problems as depression were blamed on menopause, but recent research shows no reason to attribute psychiatric illness to this normal event. In a classic study of several hundred women from 21 to 65 years old, women who had been through menopause felt much more positive than women who had not (Neugarten, Wood, Kraines, & Loomis, 1963). A typical comment was, "I've been healthier and in much better spirits since the change of life. I've been relieved of a lot of aches and pains" (Neugarten, 1968, p. 200).

In newer research, of 541 42- to 50-year-old healthy women who were premenopausal at the beginning of the study, many women reported some uncomfortable physical symptoms as they entered the climacteric, but tended to report *lower*

levels of stress in their daily lives after menopause than they had experienced before it (Matthews, 1992). Although about 10 percent of the women experienced slight depression as menopausal symptoms first appeared, the vast majority of the women did not become depressed either at this time or after menopause.

Psychological problems in midlife are more likely to be caused by attitude than by anatomy—especially by negative societal views of aging. Women's own expectations are important: women who expect discomfort tend to be more depressed and angry than women who expect benefits, who tend to have a better experience (Matthews, 1992). Menopause occurs at a time of life when many women are undergoing changes in roles, relationships, and responsibilities. These changes may be either stressful or exciting, and the way a woman perceives them affects her experience of menopause.

Societal attitudes toward aging seem to influence a menopausal woman's well-being far more than the hormones in her body do. In cultures that value older women, few problems are associated with menopause (see Box 14-2). Women who have problems or questions about menopause can often benefit from talking with postmenopausal women, who can reassure them and also pass on practical suggestions.

The Male Climacteric

Although men can continue to father children till quite late in life, some middle-aged men experience a decrease in fertility and frequency of orgasm and an increase in erectile failure. Furthermore,

These members of a support group meet regularly to talk about such menopause-related issues as the use of vaginal lubricants, bone scans to detect osteoporosis, whether or not to choose hormone replacement therapy, and how they can use this time of life to take stock of themselves and where they want to go with their lives.
(Darcy Padilla/NYT Pictures)

BOX 14-2   WINDOW ON THE WORLD

JAPANESE WOMEN'S EXPERIENCE OF MENOPAUSE

The value of doing cross-cultural research in making social scientists question long-held and widely accepted beliefs has shown up in the results of a cross-sectional survey of Japanese women between the ages of 45 and 55 (Lock, 1991). A total of 1316 factory workers, farm workers, and homemakers answered questionnaires, and 105 were interviewed in their homes. In addition, physicians and counselors were also interviewed.

Japanese women's experience of menopause turned out to be quite different from the experience of western women. For example, only 12.6 percent of Japanese women who were beginning to experience irregular menstruation reported experiencing hot flashes in the previous 2 weeks, compared to 47.4 percent of Canadian women. Fewer than 20 percent of Japanese women had ever had a hot flash, compared to almost 65 percent of Canadian women. In fact, there is

no specific Japanese word for a hot flash, and since the Japanese language makes many subtle distinctions about all kinds of body states, this lack of vocabulary supports the low incidence and perceived lack of problem of what most western women report as the most troubling symptom of menopause. Japanese women in this age group are more likely to report headaches, shoulder stiffness, ringing in the ears, dizziness, and other complaints that do not appear directly related to the hormonal changes of menopause.

What does this research tell us? For one thing, it emphasizes the importance of doing cross-cultural research and of developing appropriate tools in each culture. It would not be useful, for example, to use a list of menopausal symptoms drawn up in Canada to assess women in Japan, or vice versa. Then, it points to the possibility of biological interpopulation variations

in physical symptoms, like hot flashes. And finally, researchers have to consider that different cultures view events differently. For example, in Japan the end of menstruation seems to have far less significance than it does for western women.

"Menopause is not a disease, but a life-cycle transition to which powerful symbolic meanings, individual and social, are attached" (Lock, 1991, p. 1272). In Japan, "menopausal syndrome" is seen as a disease of modernity, which affects women with too much time on their hands. If, says the government, these women would busy themselves taking care of their elderly parents, they would not have physical complaints. This point of view may well arise from the fact that the greatest health problem in Japan is the aging of the population, and one of the greatest social problems is an erosion of traditional patterns of the extended family.

middle-aged men seem to have cyclic fluctuations in the production of hormones.

The **male climacteric** (sometimes inaccurately called the *male menopause*) is a period of physiological, emotional, and psychological change involving a man's reproductive system and other body systems. It generally begins about 10 years later than a woman's climacteric, and its physical effects vary (Weg, 1989). A small minority (about 5 percent) of middle-aged men experience depression, fatigue, lower libido, occasional erectile failure, and vaguely defined physical complaints (F. O. Henker, 1981; Weg, 1989). Since researchers have found no relationship between hormone levels and changes in mood (Doering, Kraemer, Brodie, & Hamburg, 1975), it is probable that most men's complaints are just as subject to nonphysiological pressures as women's are. Some problems may be related to such life events as illness, worries about work, children's leaving home, or the death of parents.

APPEARANCE: THE DOUBLE STANDARD OF AGING

Although both sexes suffer from our society's premium on youth, women are especially oppressed because of a traditional double standard of aging. Gray hair, coarsened skin, and "crow's feet" are considered attractive in men, as indicators of experience, mastery, and power; but in women they are regarded as telltale signs of being "over the hill." The ideal feminine look is "smooth, rounded, hairless, unlined, soft, unmuscled—the look of the very young; characteristics of the weak, of the vulnerable" (Sontag, 1972, p. 9). Once youth has faded, so (in some men's eyes) has a woman's value as a sexual and romantic partner, a prospective employee, or as a business associate.

Of course, the existence of a double standard does not mean that men are completely unaffected when they begin to look old. Homosexual men may lose their physical appeal as they age (Berger,

1982). And even heterosexual men, who historically have escaped societal penalties for showing the natural effects of aging, are sometimes at a disadvantage in the job market as they reach midlife.

The pressures created by a society that believes in looking young, acting young, and being young—added to the real physical losses that people may suffer as they get older—may contribute to what has been called the *midlife crisis*. (This crisis is not inevitable, however, as discussed in Chapter 15.) Men and women who can withstand these pressures while staying as fit as possible, and who can appreciate maturity as a positive achievement for both sexes, will be able to make the most of middle age—a time when both physical and intellectual functioning are likely to be at an impressively high level.

HEALTH IN MIDDLE AGE

HEALTH STATUS

The typical middle-aged American is quite healthy. In a recent government survey, about 84 percent of people 45 to 65 years old reported their health to be good, very good, or excellent (U.S. Department of Health and Human Services, 1992). Only 8.6 percent of people in this age range are unable to carry out important activities because of poor health (USDHHS, 1992). College-educated people, wealthier people (those with an income of $35,000 or more), and white people rate their health better than less-educated, lower-income, and minority-group people; the differences probably reflect the benefits of good health care and health habits set earlier in life (USDHHS, 1982, 1985, 1990, 1992).

HEALTH PROBLEMS

Diseases and Disorders

The most common chronic ailments of middle age are asthma, bronchitis, diabetes, nervous and men-

Wrinkles and graying hair often imply that a man is "in the prime of life" but that a woman is "over the hill." This double standard of aging, which downgrades the attractiveness of middle-aged women but not of their husbands, can affect a couple's sexual adjustment. *(Gabe Palmer/The Stock Market)*

The typical middle-aged American is quite healthy: about 84 percent of people 45 to 65 years old report their health as good, very good, or excellent. The healthiest are white and college-educated, with incomes over $35,000. Shown here is Sally Olds, who began to jog in her forties and, 14 years later, completed the 26.2 miles of the New York City Marathon. *(Mark Olds)*

tal disorders, arthritis and rheumatism, impaired sight and hearing, and malfunctions of the circulatory, digestive, and genito-urinary systems. These ills do not necessarily appear in middle age, however; and while three-fifths of 45- to 64-year-olds have one or more of them, so do two-fifths of people between ages 15 and 44 (Metropolitan Life Insurance Company, in B. Hunt & Hunt, 1974; USDHHS, 1992). One in 6 men aged 45 to 64 has some form of heart or blood vessel disease, while 1 in 9 women in this age bracket has some form of heart disease or stroke (American Heart Association, 1993).

One major health problem of midlife is **hypertension** (high blood pressure). This disorder often predisposes people to heart attack or strokes ("cerebrovascular accidents" in which a blood clot causes a loss of blood flow to the brain, often with disabling consequences). It affects about 40 percent of 20- to 74-year-old Americans and is particularly prevalent among African Americans and poor people (USDHHS, 1992). Blood pressure screening, a low-salt diet, and medication have prevented many deaths from heart disease and stroke. One recent study also found that middle-aged women who stopped smoking quickly lowered their risk of stroke, no matter how old they were or how much they had smoked (Kawachi et al., 1993).

As women enter middle age, their risks for coronary heart disease rise, especially after menopause. In the past, most of the research on heart disease risks, as on many other health conditions, was done on men. But the Healthy Women Study—a three-year study of 500 women who were from 42 to 50 years old when the study began—found that one way to lower women's risk of heart disease is to build more exercise into daily life. Even a moderate increase in exercise—such as taking three 20-minute brisk walks every week—seems to lower the risk (Owens, Matthews, Wing, & Kuller, 1992).

A controversial treatment to prevent heart disease in postmenopausal women involves administering estrogen. According to a 10-year study of 48,470 postmenopausal women (98 percent of whom were white) in the Nurses' Health Study, estrogen therapy can cut the risk of heart disease almost in half (Stampfer et al., 1991). The controversial aspect has to do with the fact that estrogen therapy has been linked to higher rates of breast cancer and cancer of the lining of the uterus. Some physicians maintain that the effects of estrogen in preventing heart disease, a major cause of death in women—especially postmenopausal women—

overwhelms any small increase in cancer deaths (Goldman & Tosteson, 1991).

However, the nurses' study was not a randomized study; it is possible, therefore, that healthier women may have chosen to take estrogen. Before a definitive statement on this topic can be made, a randomized study must be conducted; one is planned, but results would not be available for another 10 years.

Another health problem in this age group is AIDS, which now occurs more often in people over age 50 than in children under age 13. People over 50 now account for 10 percent of recorded cases. Although most cases occur in homosexual or bisexual men who contracted AIDS through sexual intercourse, or in drug abusers, about 17 percent of patients in this age group contracted it through contaminated blood transfusions before routine screening began in 1985. The disease seems to be more severe and to progress more rapidly in older people (Brozan, 1990; USDHHS, 1992).

Health problems in midlife are especially severe among Latinos because of poverty, low levels of education, and cultural and language barriers (Council on Scientific Affairs of the American Medical Association, 1991). Because their ailments tend to be diagnosed at a more advanced stage (since they often lack health insurance), they are less likely to benefit from treatment. This is a serious problem, since Latinos suffer disproportionately from high blood pressure, diabetes, kidney disease, certain cancers, AIDS, and lead poisoning.

The Impact of Stress on Health

Your department has been downsized, and your workload has just been doubled. Or you have to make an important speech to hundreds of colleagues. Or you've just had an argument with your spouse, your child, your parent, or your closest friend. You can be under stress for these or an infinite number of other reasons. *Stress* is the organism's physiological and psychological reaction to demands made on it.

Stress is, of course, an inevitable part of everyone's life, at every age. Stress—or rather, how people cope with stress—is coming under increasing scrutiny as a factor in causing or aggravating such diseases as hypertension, heart ailments, stroke, and ulcers. According to one recent survey, 62 percent of Americans feel great stress at least once or twice a week, compared with only 55 percent saying this in 1983 (Prevention Index, 1993).

The most commonly reported physical symptoms of stress are headaches, stomachaches, muscle aches or muscle tension, and fatigue. The most common psychological symptoms are nervousness, anxiety, tenseness, anger, irritability, and depression.

We'll first examine evidence for a connection between stressful life events and illness, and then we'll focus on personality factors that may link stress and heart disease.

Can Stressful Life Events Lead to Illness?

When two psychiatrists, Holmes and Rahe, looked at the life events that had preceded illness among 5000 hospital patients, they found that the more changes had taken place in a person's life—even positive changes—the greater the likelihood of illness within the next year or two (T. H. Holmes & Rahe, 1976). Change can bring stress, and some people react to stress by getting sick.

Going by people's assessments of how much adjustment various life events required, Holmes and Rahe gave numerical values to the events (see Table 14-1). About half the people with between 150 and 300 "life change units" (LCUs) in a single year—and about 70 percent of those with 300 or more LCUs—became ill.

Holmes and Rahe's research broke new ground in linking illness to stressful life events. But it has significant shortcomings. First, it presents human beings as *react*ors rather than *act*ors and does not consider the significance of how a person *interprets* a particular event. For example, divorce affects a person who initiates it differently from one on whom it is imposed. Then too, stress can also result from *lack* of change—boredom, inability to advance at work, or unrewarding personal relationships. Finally, their findings do not tell us *how* stress produces illness, or why some people get sick from stress while others thrive on it.

Why Does Stress Affect Some People More Than Others?

"Control" and Stress   One reason why the same event may be stressful for one person and not for another may have to do with control. When people feel that they can control stressful events, they are less likely to get sick. Research on human beings and animals has found links between stressful events perceived as uncontrollable and various illnesses, including cancer (Laudenslager, Ryan, Drugan, Hyson, & Maier, 1983; Matheny & Cupp, 1983; Sklar & Anisman, 1981).

Lack of control may also explain a finding based

TABLE 14-1

Some Typical Life Events and Weighted Values

Life Event	Value
Death of spouse	100
Divorce	73
Marital separation	65
Jail term	63
Death of close family member	63
Injury or illness	53
Marriage	50
Being fired at work	47
Marital reconciliation	45
Retirement	45
Change in health of family member	44
Pregnancy	40
Sex difficulties	39
Gain of new family member	39
Change in financial state	38

SOURCE: Adapted from T. H. Holmes & Rahe, 1976.

on a survey of 100 middle-class middle-aged Californians—that physical and psychological problems are more closely related to the irritations of everyday life than to major events (Lazarus, 1981). This might be because most people feel that they *should* be able to control the small things—such as avoiding traffic jams, keeping possessions from being lost or stolen, and getting along with others. When these things are uncontrollable, people feel at fault.

How can people minimize the impact of stress? Some research suggests that regular exercise, at least 6 hours of sleep a night, and socializing with family and friends at least once a week are all associated with reduced levels of stress (Prevention Index, 1993). Some people also benefit from attending stress management workshops, where they can learn how to control their reactions and to turn stress into an opportunity for constructive change. Such workshops frequently incorporate techniques like relaxation, meditation, and biofeedback.

Personality and Stress: Behavior Patterns and Heart Disease   How people experience stress or cope with it may reflect personality traits that have been implicated in heart disease. In one study of 227 middle-aged men, the 26 who had had heart attacks were more likely than the others to have worried and to have felt sad, anxious, tired, and lacking in sexual energy in the year before the attack (Crisp, Queenan, & D'Souza, 1984). And a study of 2320 men who survived heart attacks found that men who were socially isolated and under stress were more likely to die within 3 years after an attack than more sociable men who were under less stress (Ruberman, Weinblatt, Goldberg, & Chaudhary, 1984). It is possible that the state of mind of the high-risk men in both studies caused them to smoke more and to have unhealthy eating patterns and also affected their hormonal systems in ways that brought about heart disease.

Is a particular type of personality prone to heart attack? This is a highly controversial question. In the 1970s two doctors said that people who are impatient, competitive, aggressive, and hostile show *"Type A" behavior pattern*. Those who are more relaxed, easygoing, and unhurried, they said, show *"Type B" behavior pattern*. These doctors maintained that Type A people (mostly men) are more likely to suffer heart attacks in their thirties or forties, whereas Type B people almost never have heart attacks before age 70—even if they smoke, eat fatty foods, and do not exercise (Friedman & Rosenman, 1974). However, research has found little evidence for a relationship between overall Type A behavior and heart disease.

Death Rates and Causes of Death

Today, when people tend to live longer, death in middle age seems premature. It is not as unexpected as in earlier life stages, however. Beginning at age 35, the death rate at least doubles for each of the next two decades. Death is now more likely to come from natural causes than from accidents or violence. The five leading causes of death between ages 45 and 64 are cancer, heart disease, stroke, accidental injuries, and chronic obstructive pulmonary diseases and allied conditions (USDHHS, 1992).

Since 1977, mortality has declined by 30 percent for people aged 25 to 64, largely because of changes in personal lifestyle (USDHHS, 1992). Because many people have lowered their cholesterol—by changing their diets, or taking medicine, or both— and have sought medical care for high blood pressure, middle-aged people are less likely than they used to be to die of heart disease or stroke. Deaths from car crashes have also declined, largely because fewer people drink and drive, more drivers and passengers use seat belts, and highways have lower speed limits. But there are more fatal cancers. A 250 percent jump in lung cancer deaths has offset a decline in deaths from other kinds of cancer. Smoking is responsible for over 80

percent of these deaths (USDHHS, 1990).

As in young adulthood, death rates are higher for men than for women and higher for African Americans than for Latino, Asian American, Native American, and white people (USDHHS, 1992). Men aged 45 to 64 are almost twice as likely to die as women in this age bracket. Men are 3 times more likely to die from heart disease and 25 to 30 percent more likely to die from cancer or stroke. The leading cause of death for black and white women aged 45 to 54 continues to be cancer, mainly of the breast, genital organs, or lungs; the last, of course, is related to increased smoking by women (USDHHS, 1982, 1986, 1990, 1992). For 55- to 64-year-old women, cancer is the leading cause of death for white women, heart disease for black women (USDHHS, 1992).

THE IMPACT OF RACE AND SOCIOECONOMICS ON HEALTH

In the United States as a whole, adults are healthier and can look forward to a longer life span than ever before. But one segment of our population African-Americans who live in inner-city slums— is in as deplorable a state of health as people in some of the poorest and most backward nations in the world. Black men in New York's Harlem, for example, have a lower life expectancy than men in Bangladesh.

The death rate for middle-aged black people is about 1.8 times that for white people. This is a smaller difference than that between black and white young adults, but about 2 times as many black people as white people die of strokes, because more black people suffer from high blood pressure. In 1989 death rates of black people were about 45 percent higher than those of white people from heart disease and 40 percent higher from cancer (USDHHS, 1992). Overall death rates are considerably higher in inner-city African American communities than in some places that the government has designated "natural disaster areas" (McCord & Freeman, 1990). In Harlem, almost all the excess mortality involves people under age 65, possibly because those black people who have survived despite poorer medical care and other social and economic problems may be more vigorous than the larger numbers of white people the same age (see Figure 14-2). What accounts for this catastrophe in the midst of a prosperous, highly developed country?

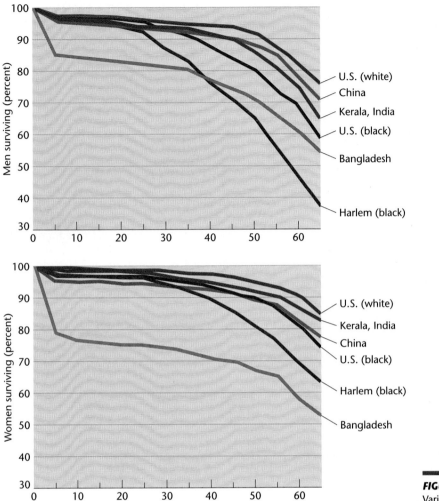

FIGURE 14-2
Variations in survival rates by sex, race, and region. (*Source:* Sen, 1993, p. 45.)

The largest single factor is poverty, which results in poor nutrition, substandard housing, inadequate prenatal care, and poor access to health care throughout life (Otten, Teutsch, Williamson, & Marks, 1990). Even when black people do have access to health care, they are less likely than white people to receive coronary bypass surgery, kidney transplants, and certain other treatments (Council on Ethical & Judicial Affairs, 1990).

Almost one-third (31 percent) of the excessive mortality of black people aged 35 to 54 can be accounted for by six risk factors: (1) high blood pressure, (2) high cholesterol, (3) excess weight, (4) diabetes, (5) smoking, and (6) alcohol intake (Otten et al., 1990). The first four of these factors may be partly attributable to heredity, which also predisposes black people to sickle cell disease. But lifestyle also plays a part in these four factors, as well as in factors 5 and 6.

Ill health, as we have seen, is often directly linked to how people live from day to day—how much they smoke and drink, whether they abuse drugs, what and how much they eat. By practically every measure, lifestyle factors that contribute to ill health are epidemic in poor African American communities. Poor black people have high rates of cancer (especially lung cancer), high blood pressure, heart disease, and cirrhosis (liver disease) (Chissell, 1989; McCord & Freeman, 1990). Young black women are at risk of obesity; young black men are at risk of being murdered; black babies are at risk of being born too early and too small (McCord & Freeman, 1990; Wegman, 1989; Williamson, Kahn, Remington, & Anda, 1990).

African Americans also have another enemy to grapple with: racism. Some observers attribute the widening health gap between black and white Americans in part to the stress created by prejudice (Chissell, 1989; Lawler, 1990, in Goleman, 1990a). Research has shown, for example, that people who suppress their anger have abnormally high blood pressure. It is possible that constant racial discrimination and consistent suppression of anger combine, fatally, with a physiological predisposition of many black people to retain sodium in the kidneys while under emotional stress, a reaction that raises blood pressure (Goleman, 1990a). Some observers also point to the effects of low self-esteem, which leads some African Americans to early childbearing, violence, poor eating habits, overreaction to stress, and use of smoking, drinking, and drugs to handle depression and frustration (Chissell, 1989).

Another danger for African Americans who suffer heart attacks is delaying too long before going to the hospital. Among 83 men and women who had heart attacks, black patients waited, on average, 23 hours before seeking medical treatment, while whites waited only an average of 8 hours (Simpson et al., 1991). This delay can be life-threatening. Treatment for heart attack (caused by a blood clot that blocks an artery feeding the heart muscle) involves giving drugs that break up the clot, but this treatment must be begun within 6 to 8 hours after the beginning of chest pain to insure that the heart muscle cells do not die.

African American heart attack sufferers tend to describe their symptoms as "suffocation" or "a sharp, stabbing chest pain," and often do not relate these symptoms to a heart problem. The African Americans in this study had less education than their white counterparts, so their delay in seeking help may be due more to social and economic factors than to race (Simpson et al., 1991).

African American men and women are nearly twice as likely to suffer strokes as are whites or Latinos (Sacco, Hauser, & Mohr, 1991). And physical impairment from strokes is worse among African Americans than among whites, according to a study of 145 hospitalized patients in North Carolina (Horner, Matchar, Divine, & Feussner, 1991). The black patients were impaired more severely at admission; they needed more help in eating, walking, and bathing; and they improved more slowly than whites. But within 3 to 6 months after the stroke, both groups were doing about the same. It is possible that black stroke victims also delay seeking medical help, and that this delay is responsible for the greater early impairment.

Although it is of course African Americans themselves who suffer most from these patterns, poor health and early death in the black popula-

tion affect the entire society—as in pressures on tax-supported institutions and demands on medical care. Government and communities must offer health education, access to basic health care, and employment that provides adequate income and decent housing—while eradicating racism from the body politic—if these trends are to be halted or reversed.

▪ INTELLECTUAL DEVELOPMENT

Happily, the adage "You can't teach an old dog new tricks" does not apply to people. Middle-aged and older people can and do continue to learn new "tricks," new facts, and new skills, and they can remember those they already know well. There is no evidence of decline in many types of intellectual functioning before age 60, and there are even increases in such areas as vocabulary and general information. Middle-aged people can learn new skills—unless they think they cannot. Furthermore, they show a distinct advantage in solving the problems of everyday life, which is attributable to their ability to synthesize their knowledge and experience.

ASPECTS OF INTELLECTUAL DEVELOPMENT IN MIDDLE ADULTHOOD

INTELLIGENCE AND COGNITION

As we discuss intellectual functioning in maturity, we need to raise questions about the nature of intelligence and the way it is tested in adults: what standardized psychometric tests can and cannot tell us about adults' intelligence, how appropriate these tests are for evaluating adults, and what kinds of intellectual abilities may improve through the years.

Psychometrics: Does Intelligence Change in Adulthood?

For years, psychologists have tried to find out whether intelligence increases or declines during adulthood by giving adults psychometric tests like those used with children. On such tests, young adults have done better than older adults in *cross-sectional* studies—studies in which people of different ages were tested at the same time (Doppelt & Wallace, 1955; H. Jones & Conrad, 1933; Miles & Miles, 1932). But young people's superior performance in these studies may be due more to cohort differences than to youth. That is, people in more recently born cohorts may know more because they have had better or longer schooling, because they have learned more from television, because they are healthier, or for some other reason unrelated to aging.

By contrast, *longitudinal studies*—studies in which the same people are tested periodically over the years—show an increase in intelligence at least until the fifties (Bayley & Oden, 1955; W. A. Owens, 1966). But these studies, too, present problems. Participants' higher scores on later tests may reflect "practice effects" like feeling more comfortable in the testing situation or remembering how similar problems were solved in earlier tests. Thus improvement may reflect better performance rather than better abilities. Also, subjects who stay with a study may differ from those who drop out. (The sequential approach of K. Warner Schaie is an attempt to overcome the drawbacks of both these methods of collecting data; we discuss Schaie's approach in Chapter 16 because the implications of an assumed decline in intelligence are especially relevant in late adulthood.)

Looking at adult intelligence is further complicated by the existence of different kinds of intellectual abilities. R. B. Cattell (1965) and J. L. Horn (1967, 1968, 1970; Horn & Hofer, 1992) proposed one such distinction: between "fluid" and "crystallized" intelligence.

Fluid intelligence is the capacity to apply intellectual ability in new situations. It involves the processes of perceiving relations, forming concepts, reasoning, and abstracting. Fluid intelligence is believed to depend on neurological development and to be relatively free from the influence of previous learning, education, or culture. It is assessed by tasks in which a problem is novel for everyone or else is an extremely common cultural element. Test-takers may be asked, for example, to group letters and numbers, to pair related words, or to remember a series of digits. Fluid intelligence is measured by tests like the Raven Progressive Matrices, in which a person is asked to select a pattern that best completes a series of patterns (see Figure 14-3).

Crystallized intelligence, on the other hand, is the ability to remember and use learned information. It depends on education and cultural background and is measured by tests of vocabulary,

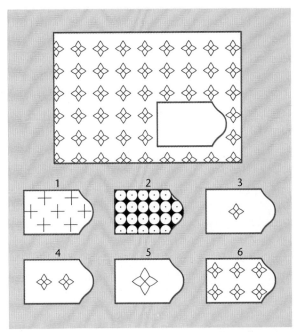

FIGURE 14-3

Item from the Raven Progressive Matrices Test. This test is a measure of fluid intelligence, since it represents a novel task that does not ostensibly depend on knowledge. Even without instructions, a test-taker can understand what to do. However, people from a culture in which fill-in or matching exercises are common may do better on tests like these than people from other cultures. (*Source:* Raven, 1983.)

general information, and responses to social situations and dilemmas. Crystallized intelligence represents knowledge acquired over a lifetime.

Fluid intelligence requires the ability to process *new* information. Crystallized intelligence depends on the use of *stored* information and on how *automatic* a person's information processing has become, especially in complex tasks like reading, which call on a large number of mental operations.

Traditional tests suggest that patterns of intelligence persist into midlife: adults with relatively high IQ scores generally had high scores as children; they also tend to be healthier, better educated, and at higher socioeconomic levels than adults whose scores are lower. Standardized tests also show that performance on some tasks improves during adulthood, with different abilities peaking at different times. Performance on fluid intelligence seems to be highest in young adulthood and to decline earlier than performance on crystallized intelligence (see Figure 14-4). But people may continue to improve on tests of crystallized intelligence through middle age, often until near the end of life (J. L. Horn & Donaldson, 1980). For example, verbal abilities rise, especially among

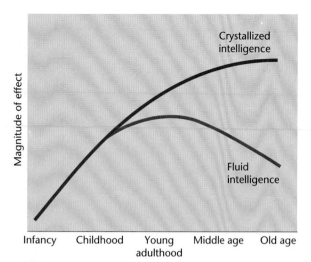

FIGURE 14-4
Changes in "fluid intelligence" and "crystallized intelligence"
over the life span. While there is a decline in fluid intelligence, there is a gradual increase in crystallized intelligence.
(*Source:* J. L. Horn & Donaldson, 1980.)

people who use their intellectual powers regularly,
either on the job or through reading or other mental stimulation.

So far, much of the research on fluid and crystallized intelligence has been cross-sectional; thus
the results may reflect differences between cohorts
rather than changes with age. Furthermore, we
have to ask how valid traditional IQ tests are for
adults. Many of these tests were originally designed for children, and adults often find the questions and tasks silly. In addition, adults may not
be motivated to do their best. Young people usually have a strong stake in performing well, partly
to prove themselves and partly because they hope
for some payoff, like admission to college. Adults,
especially older ones, rarely have so strong a goal.
Finally, we should ask whether these tests tap the
abilities that are most central to what intelligence
means in adulthood, like practicality and the ability to function well in various situations. Although
middle-aged people may take somewhat longer
than younger people to do certain tasks and may
not be as adept at solving novel problems, they
often compensate with judgment developed from
a wider range of experience.

K. Warner Schaie (whose stages of adult development are discussed in Chapter 12) has criticized
the use of conventional psychometric tests for
adults. As he points out, adults are usually more
interested in using knowledge for practical purposes than in acquiring knowledge and skills for
their own sake. In middle age, according to

Schaie's model (see Figure 12-2), adults who are in
either the "responsible" stage or the "executive"
stage use their intellectual abilities to solve real-
life problems associated with family, business, or
societal responsibilities. This ties in with Erikson's
belief (discussed in Chapter 15) that middle-aged
people are concerned with the task of generativity—
responsibility for establishing and guiding the next
generation.

When adults do not perform well on psychometric tests, then, it may not be a question of fal-
tering memory or reasoning ability, but rather that
this kind of test is simply not appropriate for their
age group.

Mature Thinkers: Does Cognition Change in Adulthood?

Integrative Thinking

Adults tend to think in an integrative way (see
Chapter 12). Middle-aged people, in particular,
tend to interpret what they read, see, or hear in
terms of its personal and psychological meaning
for them. Instead of accepting what they read at
face value, they filter it through their own life experience and learning and interpret it accordingly.
This has implications for every aspect of their lives.

In one series of studies, college students and
older adults were asked to summarize stories
(Labouvie-Vief & Hakim-Larson, 1989). One was a
fable about a wolf who promises to reward a crane
for removing a bone stuck in the wolf's throat
(Labouvie-Vief, Schell, & Weaverdyck, 1982). The
crane dislodges the bone with its beak—a maneu-
ver that involves putting its head into the wolf's
jaws—and then asks for the promised reward; the
wolf replies that the crane's reward is to get away
alive!

Both age groups recalled the story in detail, but
they gave very different summaries. The students
confined themselves to inferences from the text itself, while the older adults (their average age was
74) went beyond the text to draw out moral and
social meanings based on their own experiences
and real-world learning. The thinking of the older
people was, in fact, more flexible than that of the
younger ones, who rigidly stuck to the story as
given.

A similar study, built around a Sufi teaching tale,
also included a middle-aged group (R. G. Adams,
1986). In this study, it was clear that the middle-
aged adults were thinking on two levels at the
same time: they integrated what was in the text

BOX 14-3   FOOD FOR THOUGHT

MORAL LEADERSHIP IN MIDDLE AND LATE ADULTHOOD

What makes a single mother of four young children with no money and only a tenth-grade education dedicate her life to religious missionary work on behalf of her equally poor neighbors? What leads a pediatrician to devote much of his practice to the care of poor children instead of to patients whose parents could provide him with a lucrative income?

In the mid-1980s, two psychologists, Anne Colby and William Damon, sought answers to questions like these. They embarked on a two-year search for people who showed unusual moral excellence in their day-to-day lives. They eventually identified 23 "moral exemplars," interviewed them in depth, and studied the routes by which they had become the people they were (Colby & Damon, 1992).

In our previous discussions of moral development, we have emphasized the interaction of intellectual and emotional factors in contributing to the way people think about morality and to how they act about it. In the report of this research, these aspects of human development are closely intertwined.

MORAL EXEMPLARS:
WHO THEY ARE

To find their subjects, Colby and Damon worked with a panel of 22 "expert nominators," people who in their professional lives regularly think about moral ideas—philosophers, historians, religious thinkers, and so forth. Then the researchers drew up a final set of five criteria: a sustained commitment to principles that show respect for humanity; acting consistently with one's ideals; willingness to risk self-interest; inspiring others to moral action; and a sense of humility and lack of concern for one's own ego.

The final group ranged widely in age, education, occupation, and ethnicity. There were 10 men and 13 women, aged 35 to 86, of white, African American, and Latino backgrounds. Education levels went from eighth grade up through M.D.s, Ph.D.s, and law degrees; and occupations included religious callings, business, teaching, and social leadership. Areas of concern involved poverty, civil rights, education, ethics, the environment, peace, and religious freedom.

The research yielded a number of surprises, not least of which was this group's showing on Kohlberg's measure of moral judgment. Each exemplar was posed the Heinz dilemma (described in Chapter 8) and a follow-up dilemma asking how the man should be punished if he does steal the drug. Of the 22 exemplars (one response was not scorable), only half scored at the postconventional level; the other half scored at the conventional level. The major difference between the two groups was level of education: those with college and advanced degrees were much more likely to score at the higher level, and no one who had not gone to college scored above the conventional level. Clearly, it is not necessary to score at Kohlberg's highest stages to live an exemplary moral life.

LIFE INFLUENCES AND
PERSONAL CHARACTERISTICS

How does a person become morally committed? For the 23 moral exemplars, it became clear that they did not develop in isolation, but responded to social influences. Some of these influences, like those from parents and other inspiring models, were important from childhood on. Especially interesting, however, in discussing adult development, are the many influences significant in later years, which helped these people evaluate their own capacities, form moral goals, and develop strategies to achieve their goals.

Overall, the processes responsible for reliability and stability in moral commitments were *gradual*, taking many years to build up. They were also *collaborative*: leaders took advice from their supporters and people noted for independent judgment drew heavily upon feedback from those close to them. They thrived and grew in close action and communication both with people who shared their goals and with those who had different perspectives.

Furthermore, these people kept growing throughout life, remained open to new ideas, and continued to learn from others. This is where personality issues figure strongly. In Chapter 15 we will explore a question about personality in midlife: does it remain stable or does it change? These moral exemplars showed a combination of change and continuity. They held a lifelong commitment to change: they focused their energy on changing society and people's lives for the better. Meanwhile, they remained stable in their moral commitments, in what they felt was important in determining their actions.

Along with their enduring moral commitments, certain personality characteristics also seemed to remain with them throughout middle and late adulthood: an enjoyment of life, the ability to make the best of a bad situation, solidarity with others, a sense of absorption in work, a sense of humor, not taking themselves too seriously, and humility. They also tended to be optimistic in their belief that change was indeed possible, a trait

(continued)

BOX 14-3 (Continued)

MORAL LEADERSHIP IN MIDDLE AND LATE ADULTHOOD

that helped them battle what often seemed like overwhelming odds and to persist in the face of defeat.

While their decisions in the service of moral action often meant risk and hardship, these people did not see themselves as courageous. Nor did they agonize over the decisions they made. They just saw what had to be done, and since their personal and moral goals coincided, they went ahead and did it. Colby and Damon liken this attitude to the one felt by most people who see nothing extraordinary

about a simple moral action like not stealing even when you have an opportunity to do so—as, say, from a blind newsdealer. These moral exemplars took the same basic attitude toward moral actions that would be daunting for most people, not calculating personal consequences to themselves or their families, not feeling they were sacrificing or martyring themselves—just going ahead and doing what they believed needed to be done.

In the end, of course, there is no

clear blueprint for creating a "moral exemplar." Just as it does not seem possible to write directions to produce a genius in any other field, there does not seem to be a well-marked route for producing a moral giant. What studying the lives of such people can bring to our lives, however, is the knowledge that seemingly ordinary people can rise to greatness, that an openness to change and new ideas can persist throughout adulthood, and that their examples can inspire the rest of us.

---

with the psychological and metaphorical meaning the story held for them individually.

Integrative thinking has emotional and social implications. The ability to interpret events in a mature way enables many adults to come to terms with childhood events that once disturbed them, partly because of their earlier narrow interpretations (Schafer, 1980). Research has shown that women's adjustment in adulthood is related not to what actually happened between them and their mothers but to how they view their mothers' behavior toward them (Main, 1987).

Society benefits from this shift in adult thought. It is often middle-aged people who create inspirational myths and legends, who put truths about the human condition into symbols that younger generations can turn to for guidelines in leading their lives (Gutmann, 1977). People may need to be capable of integrative thought before they can become moral and spiritual leaders. Box 14-3 deals with some of the factors that contribute to moral leadership in middle and late adulthood.

Practical Problem Solving

Which do you think you would handle better—playing a game of Twenty Questions or figuring out what to do about a flooded basement?

In one study (Denney & Palmer, 1981), 84 adults between age 20 and age 79 were given two kinds of problems. One kind was like Twenty Questions (and like tasks on traditional intelligence tests): the subjects were shown 42 pictures of common ob-

jects and were told to figure out which one the examiner was thinking of, by asking questions that could be answered yes or no. Scoring was based on how many questions it took to get the answer and what percentage of the questions eliminated more than one item at a time ("Is it an animal?") rather than only one item ("Is it the cow?").

In the second kind of problem, the subjects were asked what they would do in real-life situations like the following: your basement is flooding; you are stranded in a car during a blizzard; your 8-year-old child is 1½ hours late coming home from school.

The results confirmed our central point about intelligence in adulthood. The older the subjects were, the worse they did on Twenty Questions; but the best *practical* problem solvers were people in their forties and fifties, who based their answers on the experiences of everyday living. A follow-up study, which tried to give the elderly an advantage by posing problems with which they would be most familiar (concerning issues of retirement, widowhood, and ill health), found that people in their forties were better problem solvers than younger and older adults (Denney & Pearce, 1989).

After all, what is the *purpose* of intelligence? Is it to play games or to solve the real problems that face people every day? If the purpose of intelligence is to deal with real-life problems, then it is clear why middle-aged people are known as the *command generation,* and why this age group wields the most authority in virtually all institutions in society. Even though middle-aged and older adults may not be as capable as younger people at solving novel problems, the many complex strengths of mature thought seem to compensate for—and can often outweigh—any deficiencies.

THE ADULT LEARNER

A woman marries at age 17, raises six children, and goes to college at 41 and to law school at 48; at 51 she is on the legal staff of the government of a major American city. A 56-year-old automotive mechanic takes a night course in philosophy. A 49-year-old physician signs up for a seminar on recent advances in endocrinology. These three people exemplify the boom in continuing education, the fastest-growing aspect of American education today.

Why do adults go to school? Almost two-thirds who take part-time classes do so for job-related reasons (U.S. Department of Education, 1986a). Some seek training to keep up with new developments in their fields. Many study in order to move up the career ladder or to prepare for different kinds of work. Some women who have devoted their young adult years to homemaking and parenting go back to school to embark on new careers. People close to retirement often want to expand their minds and skills to make more productive and interesting use of leisure. Some adults simply enjoy learning and want to keep on doing it throughout life.

Mature learners tend to be more motivated than those of traditional age. They have come to see that learning is not limited to the classroom but also occurs informally at home, on the job, and elsewhere. What they may lack in specific academic skills they make up for in the richness and variety of their life experiences, which they apply to the material they confront in school (Datan, Rodeheaver, & Hughes, 1987).

But adult learners are often more anxious and less self-confident than their younger classmates, who "know the ropes" because they have been going to school, usually without interruption, for the past 12 years or more. And older students often have special practical problems. They may have trouble fitting classes into busy schedules and juggling course work, parenting, and jobs. They may also have trouble just getting to class, and their friends and family are not always supportive.

To help meet their needs, a growing number of colleges are granting credits for practical life experience. They are also becoming more flexible in scheduling, letting more students matriculate part-time and do much of their work independently.

In today's complex society, education is never finished. And although not all learning takes place in school, more and more people are finding that some sort of formal learning is important for developing their full intellectual potential, as well as for keeping up with the challenges and opportunities of the world of work.

WORK IN MIDDLE ADULTHOOD

How do mature workers do on the job? Is age a good predictor of job performance? Congress now

This Spanish-speaking man and woman studying English are among the 14 percent of adults in the United States enrolled in part-time educational programs. Mature learners, who most often take classes for job-related reasons, tend to be more motivated than younger students. *(Blair Seitz/ Photo Researchers)*

permits mandatory retirement for police officers, fire fighters, and corrections officers. To determine how important age is in a public safety officer's job performance, an interdisciplinary task force commissioned by Congress conducted a 16-month study (Landy, 1992).

The team examined the effects of age on critical abilities, as well as the probability of a disabling medical emergency like a heart attack or stroke occurring on the job. They found that physical fitness and mental abilities, both of which vary regardless of age, predict job performance better than a person's years. Furthermore, they found that the likelihood of a major medical emergency occurring during a critical public safety task is very small. In a 500-member police department, such an event might occur only once every 25 years.

Furthermore, 60- to 65-year-old public safety officers turned out to be more fit than those aged 45 to 55, probably because those who are not fit and capable leave such jobs early. Also, older officers often move into desk jobs where their knowledge and wisdom can be passed on to younger workers. The task force recommends replacing mandatory retirement ages with tests to measure psychological, physical, and perceptual-motor abilities. Although such tests already exist, they are far from perfect and need further development.

OCCUPATIONAL PATTERNS

The typical middle-aged worker is likely to fit one of two descriptions. She or he may be at the peak of a career chosen in young adulthood—earning more money, exerting more influence, and commanding more respect than at any other period in life. Or a worker may be on the threshold of a new vocation, possibly spurred by the reevaluation that takes place during midlife—or by the need to seek a new line of work after being forced out of a job by cutbacks or for some other reason. A variation on the second pattern is that of some women, who enter or reenter the work force at this time of life, or move into more demanding work, because of the emptying of the nest or the need for money to send children to college.

Pattern 1: Stable Careers

People who follow the pattern of a stable career are reaping personal benefits and also letting society benefit from their years of experience in a chosen field. Most of them continue to enjoy the

work they have settled into. And because of their accumulated experience and wisdom, many reach positions of power and responsibility. Most business, academic, and political leaders, and many other prominent people in our society, tend to be in their middle years.

The top ranks of business, government, and the professions are still male-dominated, though women have made significant headway in these and other fields. In general, women still earn less than men and face barriers in both hiring and advancement.

Middle-aged men with stable careers tend to fall into two major categories, *workaholics* and the *mellowed*, says Tamir (1989). "Workaholics" may work at a frenzied pace either because of a last-ditch effort to reach financial security before they retire or because they find it hard to relinquish any of their authority.

The "mellowed" have come to terms with their level of achievement, even if they did not go as far in their careers as they had hoped. The best-adjusted among the "mellowed" have a sense of relaxation rather than failure. They are often happier, less cynical, and steadier in temperament than their more successful counterparts (Bray & Howard, 1983). Although these middle-aged men want to do challenging work, they do not pin their emotional well-being on their jobs as much as they used to. These findings contradict Levinson's belief (see Chapter 13) that failure to achieve youthful goals will send a man into a midlife crisis.

Pattern 2: Changing Careers

At age 40, the president of a multimillion-dollar corporation left his prestigious position to study architecture; eventually he opened his own architectural firm. At age 50, a homemaker who had held a variety of part-time jobs while her children were growing up earned a master's degree in social work; her job as a community organizer enabled her to draw on many of her past experiences.

Stories of midlife occupational changes abound these days, as people seek new careers for a variety of reasons. With longer life expectancies, many middle-aged people realize that they do not want to keep doing the same thing for the next 20 years and therefore strike out in totally new directions. Some are forced by unemployment to seek second careers. Some would rather change jobs than deal with competition from younger people moving up the career ladder. Some think, "I'm in a rut" or "I've gone as far as I can go with this company," and seek the challenge of a job that offers more opportunity for advancement or growth.

Common events of midlife can cause people to change careers. The emptying of the nest when the last child leaves home may change a woman's orientation from family to career and may also affect a man's outlook. People who have paid off the mortgage or put the last child through college may look for an easier work load, a job that pays less but is more satisfying, or a business venture that is risky but exciting. Others realize that they are ill-prepared for retirement and focus on accumulating a nest egg. And divorce or widowhood may create a need for more income.

How do career changers fare? The answer depends in part on whether the change is free or forced. People who freely choose to make a change often enjoy their lives more because they are contributing their valuable experience to new organizations or ventures; and they are often considered particularly valuable employees, since they are highly motivated and ambitious (Schultz & Schultz, 1986). But people who are forced to change careers may also do well, taking a layoff or forced retirement as an opportunity for growth.

Education and counseling can help people considering midlife career changes to see what possibilities are open to them and how they can make the most of those possibilities. The decision whether or not to stay in a job may hinge on the amount of intellectual and personal growth that the work provides.

People who follow this second pattern—changing careers—are getting considerable attention these days as part of a trend toward a lifetime of multiple careers. Many career changers are women. Although about half of middle-aged women now do paid work, compared with only about 20 percent in the 1920s (R. R. Bell, 1983), many have just entered the work force for the first time in their adult lives or have reentered it after "dropping out" to raise children. Such women not only face age and gender discrimination but are also handicapped by lack of experience, competing with people who may have a 20-year head start. Middle-aged men who change careers are more likely to have been in the work force throughout their adult life and thus are less often at such a disadvantage. This gender difference is likely to narrow, however, as the current generation of women, most of whom have been working straight through their child-rearing years, reach middle age.

We'll look at some of the motivations that lead peo-

ple to change jobs or careers, and then we'll see what kinds of work are most conducive to personal and intellectual growth.

OCCUPATIONAL STRESS

When workers are dissatisfied with their jobs, it is often because of occupational stress. The nature and structure of the work force is changing in profound ways. By the year 2000, most new workers will be female, minority-group, or both (A. Kaplan of the Stone Center, personal communication, 1993). This suggests that the existing workplace structure will have to change to keep up with the needs of these workers.

Many companies are moving to develop programs that speak more directly to the needs of women and minority-group members. This is especially important in the corporate sector, where higher positions are generally held by white men. Such programs should help to reduce a number of major stressors, like those listed in Table 14-2,

TABLE 14-2

Sources of Stress on the Job	
Rank	**Stressor**
1	Lack of promotions or raises
2	Low pay
3	Monotonous, repetitive work
4	No input into decision making
5	Heavy work load or overtime
6	Supervision problems
7	Unclear job descriptions
8	Unsupportive boss
9	Inability or reluctance to express frustration or anger
10	Production quotas
11	Difficulty juggling home and family responsibilities
12	Inadequate breaks
13	Sexual harassment

Note: Working conditions are listed in the order in which they were reported by 915 female office workers. In most cases the stressors are similar to those reported by workers in general, but there are some differences. Whereas these women rank low pay as the second greatest source of stress, this item is generally eighth or ninth in importance to men. Sexual harassment is almost always a woman's problem. One surprise is the low stress value given to "juggling work schedule with home and family responsibilities," which rates below elements of work life itself.
SOURCE: Adapted from Working Women Education Fund, 1981, p. 9.

which are related to various physical and emotional complaints.

One high-technology company established training opportunities geared specifically for women, and the firm also organized support groups for women, held on company time. Under these conditions of safety and trust, women workers feel supported by management, and able to work more productively both for the company and for their own needs (A. Kaplan, personal communication, 1993).

Certain patterns of stress are connected with certain occupations. Workers in low-status health care jobs (like technicians and aides) and personal service jobs (like waiters and telephone operators) have particularly high rates of admission to community mental health centers (Colligan, Smith, & Hurrell, 1977). These may be related to the strains of being in a subordinate position, in which workers experience pressure and authoritarian treatment but cannot respond to it (Holt, 1982).

Studies of 30- to 60-year-old men in a range of occupations also found that high psychological demands at work combined with little control resulted in "job strain" (Schnall et al., 1990). The men experiencing this kind of job strain were 3 times more likely to have high blood pressure and to show the changes in heart muscles that often precede heart attacks. This relationship held when the study controlled for smoking, alcohol, Type A behavior, and several other factors.

A major cause of daily stress on the job is conflict with supervisors, subordinates, and coworkers (Bolger, DeLongis, Kessler, & Schilling, 1989). Among 166 married couples who kept daily diaries for 6 weeks, the most upsetting stressors were arguments with other people. Dissension at work may be especially trying because people tend to suppress their anger instead of expressing it. Most reported incidents of stress had to do with work overloads: men felt more overloaded at work, and women who worked outside the home felt overloaded both at home and at work.

One approach to diminish stress for women workers often includes training in assertiveness, becoming more task-oriented, behaving more impersonally, and thinking more analytically. Such emphases, while improving some aspects of performance, tend to negate strengths that women often have, such as their abilities to work closely with other people. Some critics, in fact, suggest that employers would get better results by offering "relational training workshops" for both men and women, focusing on how people can work

together (I. Stiver of the Stone Center, personal communication, 1993).

Burnout is a reaction to work-related stress; it involves emotional exhaustion, a feeling of being unable to accomplish anything on the job, and a sense of helplessness and loss of control. It is especially common among people in the helping professions (like teaching, medicine, therapy, social work, and police work) who feel frustrated by their inability to help people as much as they would like to. Burnout is usually a response to long-term stress rather than an immediate crisis. Its symptoms include fatigue, insomnia, headaches, persistent colds, stomach troubles, alcohol or drug abuse, and trouble getting along with people. A burned-out worker may quit a job suddenly, pull away from family and friends, and sink into depression (Briley, 1980; Maslach & Jackson, 1985).

Measures that seem to help burned-out workers include cutting down on working hours and taking breaks, including long weekends and vacations. Other standard stress-reducing techniques—exercise, music, and meditation—also help.

UNEMPLOYMENT

The greatest work-related stressor is sudden, unexpected loss of a job. Research on unemployment since the 1930s (concentrating primarily on men) has linked it to physical illness, to mental illnesses such as depression and anxiety, and to problems in marital and family functioning for both the un-

Unemployment can be devastating, bringing not only loss of a paycheck but loss of identity and self-esteem. Both men and women cope with unemployment better when they can draw on financial, psychological, and social resources. Some, in fact, develop both emotionally and professionally by seeing this forced change as an opportunity to do something new or as a challenge for growth. *(Gilles Peress/Magnum)*

employed person and the spouse, as well as health, psychological, and behavior problems in their children (Voydanoff, 1990).

When people are unemployed, two major sources of stress are the loss of income (with its financial hardships) and the effect of this loss on their feelings about themselves. Workers who derive their identity from their work, men who define manhood as supporting a family, and people who define their worth in terms of their work's dollar value lose more than their paychecks when they lose their jobs. They lose a piece of themselves and their self-esteem (Voydanoff, 1983; 1990).

The ability to cope with unemployment depends on various factors. Those who cope best have some financial resources to draw on—savings, the earnings of other family members, and so on. They do not blame themselves for losing their jobs or see themselves as failures but assess their situation in more objective terms. They have the support of understanding, adaptable families and can draw on outside resources, like friends (Voydanoff, 1990).

Women are as likely as men to feel distressed over loss of a job, as was shown by a study of former employees of a plant in Indiana that closed in 1982 (Perrucci & Targ, 1988). Job-losers of both sexes reported headaches, stomach trouble, and high blood pressure and felt less in control of their lives. The women's responses support another study, which found that a woman's sense of pride and power is more strongly related to her paid work than to her personal life (G. Baruch, Barnett, & Rivers, 1983).

A crucial factor in adjustment to losing a job is the context in which a person sees the situation. People who can look at such a forced change as an opportunity to do something else or as a challenge for growth can develop emotionally and professionally. They may change not only jobs but the entire direction of their careers.

WORK AND INTELLECTUAL GROWTH

Do people develop as a result of the kind of work they do? Research says yes: people seem to grow in jobs that challenge their capabilities.

What specific aspects of work affect psychological functioning? In an examination of 50 different aspects of the work experience, from the pace of the work to relationships with coworkers and supervisors, the aspect that had the strongest impact was the *substantive complexity* of the work itself: "the degree to which the work, in its very substance, requires thought and independent judgment" (Kohn, 1980, p. 197). A sculptor's work, for example, is more complex than a ditchdigger's, a lawyer's work is more complex than a clerk's, and a computer programmer's work is more complex than a data processor's. (This "substantive complexity" may have something to do with creativity, discussed in Box 14-4.)

A combination of cross-sectional and longitudinal studies revealed a reinforcing interplay between the complexity of work and the worker's intellectual flexibility in coping with demanding situations. People with more complex work tend to become more flexible thinkers, not only on the job but in other areas of their lives. "They become more open to new experience. They come to value self-direction more highly. They even come to engage in more intellectually demanding leisure-time activities. In short, the lessons of work are directly carried over to nonoccupational realms" (Kohn, 1980, p. 204). At the same time, a person's intellectual flexibility influences the complexity of the work she or he will be doing 10 years down the road.

This circular relationship "may begin very early in life when children from culturally advantaged families develop skills and other qualities that result in their being placed in classroom situations and tracks that are relatively complex and demanding, which in turn contribute to further development of intellectual flexibility" (Smelser, 1980, p. 16). The circle continues in adulthood, as people begin their careers—and the gap widens between flexible thinkers in complex jobs and less flexible thinkers in less complex jobs. The flexible thinkers tend to go into increasingly complex work, which in turn enables their thinking to become more and more flexible, qualifying them for even more complex work. People who show less flexibility at the outset and do less complex work grow more slowly or not at all (Kohn, 1980).

Why is the complexity of work tied so closely to intellectual growth? One reason may be that, in a society like ours, in which work plays a central role in people's lives, mastery of complex tasks affects people's sense of self; it gives them a feeling of competence and teaches them that they can manage the problems they encounter (Kohn, 1980).

What is most important, then, about work is not income or status but what people actually do. Research about work—as well as about study, problem solving, and moral choices—also confirms that people's minds do not stop developing at the

BOX 14-4 FOOD FOR THOUGHT

CREATIVITY TAKES HARD WORK

At about age 40, Frank Lloyd Wright designed Robie House in Chicago, Agnes deMille choreographed the Broadway musical *Carousel,* and Louis Pasteur developed the germ theory of disease. At 48 the jazz singer Ella Fitzgerald began to record a 19-album series of nearly 250 popular classics; at 59 she finished it. Charles Darwin was 50 when he presented his theory of evolution, Leonardo da Vinci was 52 when he painted the *Mona Lisa,* and Leonard Bernstein was 53 when he composed his *Mass* in honor of John F. Kennedy. The novelist Toni Morrison, 1993 winner of the Nobel Prize in Literature, won the Pulitzer Prize for *Beloved,* a novel she wrote when she was about 55. These achievements are examples of the creative productivity possible in midlife.

Just what goes into the cognitive processes of highly creative minds is a puzzle that many researchers have tried to solve. The psychologist Howard Gruber (Gardner, 1981) has approached this question through intensive case studies of the intellectual lives of great scientists like Charles Darwin.

To find out how Darwin's mind worked, Gruber pored over Darwin's notebooks, trying to map the changes in his thinking during the 18 months after his 5-year voyage of exploration in which he had meticulously recorded his observations of fossils, plants, animals, and rocks along the coast of South America and in the Pacific islands.

There is a commonly held idea that the creative act involves sudden insight. But Gruber was struck by how long it took Darwin to think through a new idea. Darwin had gone down at least one blind alley before he came upon an essay by the English economist Thomas Malthus, which described how natural disasters and wars keep population increases under control. After reading Malthus's description of the struggle for survival, it occurred to Darwin that some species—those whose characteristics were best adapted to the environment—would survive and others would not. But even then, it took Darwin several months after reading Malthus's essay to develop his principle of natural selection, which explains how adaptive traits are passed on through reproduction. And it was not until 2 decades later that he finally published his theory and the supporting evidence.

Although each mind works somewhat differently, Gruber found some common characteristics of highly creative people:

■ They work *painstakingly and slowly* to master the knowledge and skills they need to solve a problem. Darwin studied barnacles for 8 years—until he probably knew more about them than anyone else in the world.

■ They constantly *visualize* ideas. Darwin drew one particular image—a branching tree—over and over, as he refined his theory of how more complex, highly developed species evolve on the "tree" of nature.

■ They are *goal-directed;* they have a strong "sense of purpose, a feeling of where they are and where they want to go" (Gardner, 1981, p. 69).

■ They have *networks* of *enterprises,* often juggling several seemingly unrelated projects or activities.

■ They are *able to set aside problems* they have too little information to solve and go on to something else, or to adopt temporary working assumptions. Darwin did this when he got stuck on questions about heredity for which he had no reliable answers.

■ They are *daring.* It took courage for Darwin to publish a theory that broke away from the entrenched ideas of his day.

■ Rather than work in isolation (as they are often thought to do), they *collaborate* or discuss their ideas with others, by choosing peers and designing

A popular myth attributes creation to sudden flashes of inspiration, but the author Toni Morrison, 1993 winner of the Nobel Prize in Literature, worked long, hard hours throughout her prolific career. Her achievements are examples of the creative productivity possible in midlife. *(Ulf Andersen/ Gamma-Liaison)*

environments that nurture their work.

■ They *enjoy turning over ideas* in their minds "and would not dream of doing anything else" (Gardner, 1981, p. 70). Darwin was reading Malthus's essay for amusement.

■ Through hard work, they *transform themselves,* until what would be difficult for someone else seems easy for them. This last point, in particular, is reminiscent of Kohn's belief (1980) that substantively complex work, requiring deep thought and independent judgment, can contribute to intellectual growth—not only in a Darwin but in anyone.

The challenge, then, for a society that depends on the creativity of its citizens is how to encourage these characteristics. Are there, for example, ways to train people to visualize their ideas, to learn when to persist in pursuing a train of thought—and when to set aside a problem for the time being? In sum, how much of creativity can be expanded by what goes on in the home, the school, and the workplace?

end of adolescence or young adulthood. Such research also continues to confirm the links between intellectual development and the social and emotional aspects of personality, to which we turn in Chapter 15.

SUMMARY

■ Middle adulthood is a time of reevaluation. There is no single biological marker or behavioral sign denoting the beginning of middle age. In this book, *middle age* is defined as the period from 40 to 65 years of age.

PHYSICAL CHANGES OF MIDDLE AGE

■ Middle-aged adults experience some declines in sensory abilities: strength, coordination, reaction time, and complex motor skills. They can often compensate for these declines with such aids as eyeglasses and with the application of experience and judgment.
■ Middle-aged couples today are engaging in sexual relations more often and in more varied ways than their counterparts in the past. Sexual compatibility is not the most important factor in a happy marriage, but sexual activity and sexual satisfaction can and often do continue throughout middle age and the older adult years.
■ Menopause, the cessation of menstruation and reproductive ability in women, typically occurs around age 50, when a decrease in the production of estrogen brings about the end of ovulation. It is associated with hot flashes, thinning of the vaginal lining, and urinary dysfunction. Osteoporosis, a condition in which bones become thinner and more susceptible to fractures, affects 1 out of 4 postmenopausal women. There is no reason to attribute psychological problems to menopause.
■ Although men can continue to father children until late in life, in some men the male climacteric brings a decline in fertility and in frequency of orgasm, an increase in impotence, and other symptoms.
■ The "double standard of aging" in American society causes women more than men to seem less desirable as they lose their youthful looks. For both sexes, the problems of getting older are often amplified by living in a society that places a premium on youth.

HEALTH IN MIDDLE AGE

■ Most middle-aged people rate their health as good or better. Three-fifths of middle-aged people suffer from chronic health conditions of varying degrees of severity; however, two-fifths of young adults already have these conditions. Stress, particularly when associated with lack of control, is related to a variety of physical and psychological problems.

■ Although death rates have declined in recent generations (especially death from heart disease and stroke), death rates increase throughout midlife. Death is more likely to occur in this period from natural causes than from accidents or violence. The leading causes of death are cancer, heart disease, accidents, and stroke. As in younger age groups, death rates are higher for males than for females and higher for black people than for white people.

ASPECTS OF INTELLECTUAL DEVELOPMENT IN MIDDLE ADULTHOOD

■ Performance on many standardized intelligence measures increases during adulthood, especially for verbal abilities and tasks involving stored knowledge. However, the appropriateness of conventional IQ tests for adults is questionable.
■ Although middle-aged people may perform more slowly and may not be as adept at solving novel problems, some research suggests that the ability to solve practical problems based on experience peaks at midlife. Many middle-aged adults think in an integrative way.
■ Continuing education for adults is the fastest-growing area of education in the United States.
■ Adults go to school for many reasons, but chiefly to improve their work-related skills and knowledge or to prepare for a change of career. Adult learners tend to be more motivated but less self-confident than young students.

WORK IN MIDDLE ADULTHOOD

■ Many middle-aged people are at the peak of their careers, but others are involved in career changes that may be triggered by the self-evaluation process of midlife. For some, occupational stresses such as burnout, unemployment, and specific working conditions affect physical and emotional well-being.
■ The kind of work adults do affects the degree to which they grow intellectually. There seems to be a direct relationship between the complexity of the work a person does and intellectual flexibility.
■ Some people do extremely creative work in middle age. Studies of scientists show that creativity appears to have more to do with slow, painstaking work than with sudden inspiration.

KEY TERMS

presbyopia (page 473)

presbycusis (473)

menopause (475)

climacteric (475)

osteoporosis (475)

male climacteric (478)

hypertension (480)

stress (480)

fluid intelligence (485)

crystallized intelligence (485)

burnout (492)

substantive complexity (493)

SUGGESTED READINGS

Banner, L. W. (1992). *In full flower: Aging women, power, and sexuality. A history.* New York: Knopf. A richly researched trip through history and literature finding models in which gender roles blur.

Bird, C. (1992). *Second careers: New ways of working after 50.* Boston: Little, Brown. A report on the second careers of 6347 readers of *Modern Maturity* magazine, arranged by first careers so that readers can learn what other mature workers have done. The book includes a vocational aptitude test that has been validated on older people.

Colby, A., and Damon, W. (1992). *Some do care: Contemporary lives of moral commitment.* An absorbing and inspiring report of the authors' research on the lives of 23 outstanding moral leaders in communities across the United States. Drawing on in-depth interviews, the authors discuss how these people acquired their moral goals, how these goals changed and grew over the years, and what their lives can teach readers about moral courage.

Cooper, K. H. (1990). *Preventing osteoporosis.* New York: Bantam. Showing that osteoporosis is not just a disease of the elderly and is not limited to women,

Dr. Cooper explains how to develop bone density, investigates probable causes, and explains how to determine if you have osteoporosis or are at risk. The book includes complete diet and exercise plans that reduce the risk of developing this disease.

Greenwood, S. (1989). *Menopause, naturally: Preparing for the second half of life.* Volcano, CA: Volcano Press. This optimistic book by a woman doctor explains menopause in physical and psychological terms.

Marks, J. (1993). *The hidden children: The secret survivors of the Holocaust.* New York: Fawcett Columbine. Many children survived the Holocaust by remaining in hiding for months or years. In this powerful work, twenty-three of these children, now adults, share their stressful experiences and the profound impact that they have had on their lives.

Steinberg, W. (1993). *Masculinity: Identity, conflict, and transformation.* Boston: Shambala. A Jungian analyst uses dreams, myths, and experiences of real men to illustrate how an inner balance can be reached, and how this balance can be the key to establishing a free and strong masculinity.

PERSONALITY AND SOCIAL DEVELOPMENT IN MIDDLE ADULTHOOD

PERSONALITY AND SOCIAL DEVELOPMENT IN MIDDLE ADULTHOOD

What happens to a dream deferred?
Does it dry up
Like a raisin in the sun?
Maybe it just sags
Like a heavy load.
Or does it explode?

Langston Hughes,
"Montage of a Dream Deferred," 1951

■ **MIDLIFE: THE NORMATIVE-CRISIS APPROACH**

The "Midlife Crisis"
Theories and Research
Evaluating the Normative-Crisis Model

■ **PERSONAL RELATIONSHIPS AND TIMING OF EVENTS IN MIDLIFE**

Marriage and Divorce
Relationships with Siblings
Friendships

Relationships with Maturing Children
Relationships with Aging Parents

■ **BOXES**

15-1 Take a Stand: Does Personality Change in Middle Age?
15-2 Window on the World: A Society without Middle Age?
15-3 Practically Speaking: Enhancing Marriage at Midlife
15-4 Food for Thought: Reacting to a Parent's Death

When asked, "How are you?" a vivacious speech therapist replied, "I'm going to have my fortieth birthday in 2 weeks, and I can't talk to anyone without mentioning it. So I guess I'm having my midlife crisis. Isn't everybody?"

MIDLIFE: THE NORMATIVE-CRISIS APPROACH

THE "MIDLIFE CRISIS"

Changes in personality and lifestyle during middle adulthood are often attributed to the *midlife crisis,* a supposedly stressful period during the early to middle forties, which is triggered by a review and reevaluation of one's past life and which heralds the onset of middle age. This idea burst into public consciousness in the late 1970s, with the popularization of data from studies building on Erik Erikson's conceptualization of the normative-crisis approach to human development. This is the view that the human personality goes through a universal sequence of critical changes at certain ages.

Many psychologists talk about a *midlife transition,* which may or may not involve upset. The term *midlife crisis,* however, implies a disturbing transition. It has become a trendy catchphrase, popping up as an explanation for depression, extramarital affairs, or career changes. Such events are taken as signs of a shift from an outward orientation, a concern with finding a place in society, to an inward orientation, a search for meaning within the self (Jung, 1966). This inward turn may be unsettling; as people question their life goals, they may temporarily lose their moorings.

What brings on the "midlife crisis," says Jacques (1967), is awareness of mortality. The first part of

adulthood is over, its tasks largely done. Most people have formed their families and are now tasting freedom from the daily responsibilities of child care. They have established their occupations and have, by and large, accepted their level of success. They have become independent of their parents, who may now be turning to *them* for advice and help. They are in the prime of life—but they now realize that their time has become shorter and they will not be able to fulfill all the dreams of their youth; or, if they have fulfilled their dreams, they may realize that they have not found the satisfaction they had hoped for.

This realization is not necessarily traumatic, however. For many people, it is just one more of life's many transitions, and they adjust easily. People can emerge from this time of questioning with more awareness and understanding of themselves and of others; with more wisdom, strength, and courage; and with a greater capacity for love and enjoyment.

In one way, talking about a "midlife crisis" is helpful, because it calls attention to the dynamic nature of personality in middle age. In another way, it is not helpful, since it can lead to a rigid notion that everyone must undergo a crisis in order to develop emotionally during midlife.

Today, attention is shifting from the "midlife crisis" and the normative-crisis model from which it springs, to the timing-of-events model (introduced in Chapter 13). According to this model, personality development is influenced less by age than by the events in people's lives and when they occur. Twenty or thirty years ago, the occurrence and timing of such major events as marriage, first job, and the birth of children and grandchildren were fairly predictable, so age may have been a generally adequate indicator of development. But today, lifestyles are more diverse, people's "social clocks" tick at different rates, and a "fluid life cycle" has washed out the old boundaries between youth and adulthood, and between middle age and old age (Neugarten & Neugarten, 1987). As a result, it may be more useful to consider adult development in terms of life events.

The timing-of-events model also recognizes that societal changes affect the significance of events and their impact on personality. For example, when women's lives tended to revolve around bearing and rearing children, the end of the reproductive years meant something different from what it means now, when most women are only in their mid-thirties by the time their youngest child has started school. When people died earlier, survivors felt old earlier, since the death of friends, relatives, and public figures close to their own age reminded them that someday they too would die.

Whether or not an actual crisis takes place, however, a sharper awareness of life's limits often leads middle-aged people to recognize that if they want to change direction, they have to act quickly. Midlife is a time of stock taking, not only in regard to careers but also in intimate relationships.

In this chapter we look at midlife first through the prism of the normative-crisis model of development; we also present a critique of that model. Then, we look at important events in relationships, which are pertinent to the timing-of-events model. As we examine changes in marriage, sexuality, sibling bonds, and friendship, as well as relationships with maturing children and with aging parents, we see variations in the shape and timing of these events.

THEORIES AND RESEARCH

Much of the major theoretical and research work on adult development of the past few decades has taken a normative-crisis viewpoint. This is the perspective of Carl Jung's analysis of a necessary midlife transition, Erikson's stage of generativity versus stagnation, Robert Peck's expansion of Erikson's work, and Vaillant's and Levinson's research (introduced in Chapter 13). These views are summarized in Table 15-1; they are discussed in the following sections, along with several studies of women's development, which, until recently, have not received the same attention as men's. Then the various perspectives are evaluated according to current psychological thought.

Carl Jung: Balancing the Personality

Carl Jung, a disciple of Freud, later broke with Freud over a number of issues. One of these was

THE TERRIBLE FORTY-TWOS

The concept of a "midlife crisis" can lead to a rigid notion that everyone must have one. For many people, however, the transition to middle age is not particularly stressful. The timing and acuteness of the transition and the way people cope with it may reflect their circumstances and personalities more than their age. This disgruntled executive may be using the "midlife crisis" to excuse his temper tantrum. *(Drawing by M. Twohy: © 1990 The New Yorker Magazine, Inc.)*

Jung's conviction that people grow and change throughout life—that their personalities are not unalterably set in childhood.

Jung (1953) emphasized the quest for meaning in life and the process of developing an individual personality. He considered the midlife transition very important in psychological development. Up until about age 40, according to Jung, women and men concentrate on their obligations to their families and to society, and they develop those aspects of personality that further these goals. Women emphasize expressiveness and nurturance; men emphasize an orientation toward achievement.

But when people's careers are established and their children are grown, both men and women are free to balance their personalities. They achieve a "union of opposites" by expressing those aspects of themselves that had been suppressed earlier. To do this, they need to pay more attention to their inner selves, often becoming preoccupied with the tasks of this stage. Two necessary tasks are giving up the image of youth and youthful lifestyles and acknowledging eventual mortality. Since these tasks and the inner dialogue they call for involve threatening concepts, midlife is often stressful. But people who avoid the transition and do not reorient their lives appropriately will not make a good psychological adjustment at this stage or in the future.

TABLE 15-1

Six Views of Development in Middle Adulthood

Jung	Erikson	Peck	Vaillant	Levinson	Helson
Midlife transition (about age 40): After child-rearing obligations have diminished, women and men can balance their personalities by expressing characteristics that had previously been suppressed. Women become more assertive and men become more emotionally expressive. People become more inner-oriented and pre-occupied with their inner world. They now need to give up the image of youth, adopt a more appropriate lifestyle, and acknowledge that their lives are finite. This inner work creates stress but is necessary for healthy adjustment.	*Crisis 7—Generativity versus stagnation* The impulse to foster the development of the next generation leads middle-aged persons to become mentors to young adults. The wish to have children is instinctual, and so childless people must acknowledge their sense of loss and express their generative impulses in other ways, helping to care for other people's children directly or as protégés in the workplace. Some stagnation could provide a rest that leads to greater future creativity. Too much stagnation could lead to physical or psychological invalidism.	1 *Valuing wisdom versus valuing physical powers:* People realize that the wisdom they have gained through the years makes up for declining physical powers and youthful attractiveness. 2 *Socializing versus sexualizing in human relationships:* People appreciate the personalities of others as they value them as friends rather than sex objects. 3 *Emotional flexibility versus emotional impoverishment:* Deaths of parents and friends end relationships. People must shift emotional investments to others. Physical limitations may require a change in activities. 4 *Mental flexibility versus mental rigidity:* People use their past experiences as guides to solving new issues.	*Midlife transition (age 40—"give or take a decade"):* Midlife is stressful, as adolescence is stressful, because of the demands of entrance into a new stage of life. Much of the pain comes from having the maturity to face pain that was suppressed for years. Many men reassessed their past, reordered their attitudes toward sexuality, and seized one more chance to find new solutions to old needs. The best-adjusted men were the most generative and found these years (from 35 to 49) the happiest of their lives. *Tranquil fifties:* Males become more nurturant and expressive. Sexual differentiation lessens. The fifties are a generally mellower time of life.	*Midlife transition (age 40 to age 45):* Questioning one's life—values, desires, talents, goals; looking back over past choices and priorities; deciding where to go now; coming to terms with youthful dreams; developing a realistic view of self. *Entry life structure for middle adulthood (age 45 to age 50):* Reappraisal leads to a new life structure involving new choices. Some men retreat into a constricted—or well-organized, overly busy—middle age. *Age-50 transition* (age 50 to age 55):* Men who have not gone through their midlife crisis earlier may do so now. Others may modify the life structures they have formed in their mid-forties. *Culminating life structure for middle adulthood* (age 55 to 60):* Men complete middle adulthood; a time of fulfillment. *Late adult transition* (age 60 to age 65):* Middle age ends; preparation for late adulthood.	*Struggle for independent identity:* The woman typically seeks to affirm herself and her values through education, career, or a new relationship. She seeks appropriate work or training, clarification of values, or self-discovery. Often her new independence and assertiveness bring unpleasant consequences, like being passed over at work or being left by a husband. Common problems involve difficult relationships with others or overload, caused by other people's demands, economic strain, or job responsibilities. The early fifties emerge as the "prime of life." Benefits of this age may include good health, the empty nest, a feeling of control over one's life, a balance of "masculine" and "feminine" traits.

*Projected.
SOURCES: Erikson, 1950; Helson, 1992; Jung, 1953; Levinson, 1978, 1986; Mitchell & Helson, 1990; Peck, 1955; Vaillant, 1977.

Erik Erikson: Crisis 7—Generativity versus Stagnation

Erikson also saw the years around age 40 as a critical time, when people go through their seventh normative crisis, **generativity versus stagnation.** *Generativity* is the concern of mature adults for establishing and guiding the next generation. Looking ahead to the waning of their own lives, people feel a need to participate in the continuation of life. If this need is not met, people become *stagnant*—inactive or lifeless.

The impulse to foster development of the young is not limited to guiding one's own children. It can be expressed through activities like teaching and *mentorship*—a mutually fulfilling relationship that satisfies a younger protégé's need for guidance as well as an older person's need for generativity. Generativity can also take the form of productivity or creativity (as in the arts) or of self-generation, the further development of personal identity. (Generativity corresponds to Schaie's "responsible" and "executive" stages of cognitive development in midlife, discussed in Chapters 12 and 14, which involve practical problem solving on behalf of others.)

As in all of Erikson's stages, it is the *balance* of one trait over its opposite that is important. Even the most creative person goes through stagnant or fallow periods, gathering energy for the next project; but too much stagnation can result in self-indulgence or even in physical or psychological invalidism. The "virtue" of this period is *care:* "a widening commitment to *take care of* the persons, the products, and the ideas one has learned *to care for*" (Erikson, 1985, p. 67).

Erikson (1985) believes that people who have not been parents do not easily achieve generativity. He urges childless adults to acknowledge a sense of loss and to find other outlets for generative tendencies—as through helping children in developing countries, coaching a sports team, or leading a scout troop. However, many people who have cared for their own children for years may need to take care of themselves for a while before they can again focus on nurturing others. Furthermore, Erikson's view that childless people have trouble achieving generativity is considered narrow by many psychologists.

Robert Peck: Four Adjustments of Middle Age

Expanding on Erikson's concepts, Peck (1955) sees four psychological developments as critical to successful adjustment in middle age:

Coaching a Little League baseball team is one form of what Erikson calls *generativity.* Many middle-aged people fulfill this need to establish and guide the next generation by helping other people's children, in addition to or instead of their own. *(Bob Daemmrich/Stock, Boston)*

1 *Valuing wisdom versus valuing physical powers: Wisdom,* defined as the ability to make the best choices in life, seems to depend largely on life experience and on opportunities for a wide range of relationships and situations. Sometime between the late thirties and the late forties, most well-adjusted people appreciate that their wisdom more than makes up for their diminished physical strength, stamina, and youthful appearance.

2 *Socializing versus sexualizing in human relationships:* People redefine the men and women in their lives, valuing them as individuals, as friends, and as companions rather than primarily as sex objects. Thus they can appreciate the unique personalities of others and can reach a greater depth of understanding.

3 *Emotional flexibility versus emotional impoverishment:* The ability to shift emotional investment from one person to another and from one activity to another becomes crucial during middle age. Parents, spouses, and friends are more likely to die, and children have matured and become independent. Also, middle-aged people may have to change their activities because of physical limitations.

4 *Mental flexibility versus mental rigidity:* By midlife, many people have worked out a set of answers to life's important questions. But when they let these answers control them rather than continue to seek out new answers, they become set in their ways and closed to new ideas. Those who remain flexible use their experiences and the answers they have already found as provisional guides to the solution of new problems.

None of these developments need wait until middle age; some may already have occurred in early adulthood. If they do not take place by midlife, however, Peck doubts that the person will be able to make a successful emotional adjustment.

Men's Development in Middle Adulthood

George Vaillant: Introspection and Transition

The longitudinal research reported by Vaillant and known as the Grant Study (see Chapter 13) followed male college students into later adulthood and identified a midlife transition at about age 40. After the stage of career consolidation, which usually occurred during the thirties, many of the men abandoned the "compulsive, unreflective busywork of their occupational apprenticeships and once more [became] explorers of the world within" (Vaillant, 1977, p. 220). Neugarten (1977), a prominent advocate of the timing-of-events model, also observed this tendency toward introspection in middle age; she calls it *interiority.* Introspection, or interiority, echoes Jung's concept of turning inward as a necessity in middle age; but it seems to vary with personality. (This issue and the question of other personality changes in midlife are discussed in Box 15-1.)

The midlife transition may be stressful because of the demands made by a new stage of life, such as changing the parenting role to meet the needs of teenage children. Many men reassess their past, come to terms with long-suppressed feelings about their parents, and reorder their attitudes toward sexuality.

However, for the men in the Grant Study, the transition years rarely assumed crisis dimensions. These men were no more likely to get divorced, to be disenchanted with their jobs, or to become depressed at midlife than at any other time during the life span. By their fifties, the best-adjusted men in the group actually saw the years from 35 to 49 as the *happiest* in their lives.

Support for Erikson's theory appeared in the finding that the best-adjusted men were also the most generative, as measured by their responsibility for other people at work, their gifts to charity, and their children—whose academic achievements equaled those of their fathers. In midlife the men were four times more likely to cope with life events in such mature ways as using altruism and humor than in immature ways like drinking or becoming hypochondriacs (Vaillant, 1989).

The fifties were a generally mellower and more tranquil time of life than the forties. Vaillant noted some of the same traits seen by others: a lessening of sexual differentiation with advancing age—which Brim (1974) calls the "normal unisex of later life"—and a tendency for men to become more nurturant and expressive.

Daniel Levinson: Changing Life Structures

Levinson and his associates (1978, 1980, 1986) describe midlife as a time when life structures "always" change appreciably. Of the 40 men in Levinson's sample, 32 found the time between ages 40 and 45 a time of crisis, when they often felt upset and acted irrationally. He believes that such turmoil is inevitable as people question previously held values. However, reevaluation is healthy, helping people come to terms with youthful dreams and allowing them to emerge with a more realistic view of themselves.

Between ages 45 and 50, men carve out new life structures, possibly by taking a new job or a new wife (as did Levinson himself) or by changing patterns of work or relationships. Those who make no changes lead a boring, constricted life in middle age or are busy and well organized—but unexcited. Those who do change their life structures often find middle age the most fulfilling and creative time of life. Levinson and his colleagues (1978) did not follow their original sample into their fifties and sixties, although they still made projections about these years (see Table 15-1).

Women's Development in Middle Adulthood

The normative-crisis models of Erikson, Levinson, and Vaillant have all been male-oriented in theory, in research samples, or in both. More recently, a number of researchers have examined women's experience at midlife. While they have found some similarities to male-based models, they have also found substantial differences.

Mastery, Pleasure, and Women's Adjustment

What factors contribute to women's healthy adjustment in the middle years? A study of almost 300 women between ages 35 and 55 offers some answers (Barnett, 1985; G. Baruch, Barnett, & Rivers, 1983). The investigators first interviewed 60 women: employed women who had never married, employed married mothers, employed childless wives, employed divorced mothers, married homemakers with and without children. On the basis of what the women said about the pleasures, problems, and conflicts in their lives, the re-

BOX 15-1 TAKE A STAND

DOES PERSONALITY CHANGE IN MIDDLE AGE?

"I'm a completely different person now from the one I was 20 years ago," said the 47-year-old architect, as six friends, all in their forties and fifties, nodded vigorously in agreement. Many people feel themselves changing at midlife. But are these changes deep-seated, or are they just on the surface? Is there a basic core of personality that remains stable throughout life?

These are controversial questions. For years, most psychologists believed that by young adulthood, personality is set like concrete. But in the 1970s, the image shifted to a seemingly limitless capacity for change throughout life (Z. Rubin, 1981). Now there are two camps. One believes that personality will remain stable unless a specific event occurs to produce change (Costa & McCrae, 1994); the other believes that change will occur unless something interferes with development (Brim & Kagan, 1980). Here is evidence for both viewpoints.

EVIDENCE FOR STABILITY OF PERSONALITY

■ Longitudinal studies find that bubbly junior high schoolers grow up to be cheerful 40-year-olds, complaining adolescents turn into querulous adults, assertive 20-year-olds become outspoken 30-year-olds, and people who cope well with problems of youth are equally able to handle problems of later life (J. Block, 1981; Costa & McCrae, 1981; Eichorn, Clausen, Haan, Honzik, & Mussen, 1981).

■ As people grow older, they tend to become more introverted and introspective. But people who were extroverts in their youth tend to remain more outgoing than other people. Extroversion, openness to new experience, and neuroticism (a mild emotional disturbance arising from anxiety) all remain quite stable

throughout adulthood, according to the results of a nationwide cross-sectional study of more than 10,000 people 32 to 88 years old (Costa et al., 1986). Certain traits do seem to soften with maturity. For example, although impulsive children usually grow up to be restless, impatient adults, as adults they are less impulsive than they had been earlier (M. A. Stewart & Olds, 1973).

■ Long-term personality characteristics, like optimism, seem to affect quality of life at various ages. People who "manage their lives well at time one, enjoy the fruits of their skills at time two, and tend to appraise their lives favorably at all times" (Mitchell & Helson, 1990, p. 454).

EVIDENCE FOR PERSONALITY CHANGE

■ One common change in midlife is a tendency to take on characteristics associated with the other sex. Men often become more open about feelings, more interested in intimate relationships, and more nurturing; women tend to become more assertive, self-confident, and achievement-oriented (Cytrynbaum et al., 1980; Helson & Moane, 1987; Livson, 1976; Neugarten, 1968). These findings support Jung's notion of "balancing" and suggest that middle-aged people who fail to develop the previously "disowned" parts of their personalities are more susceptible to emotional problems.

■ From ages 43 to 52, women graduates of Mills College became more self-confident, independent, decisive, dominant, and self-affirming than they had been earlier in life (see Table 15-2). They became less self-critical and saw themselves as closer to their ideal selves. They became more

comfortable with themselves, partly because they were adhering to their own personal standards, as well as social ones. And they increased on four measures of coping, suggesting that they grew in the ability to analyze issues, to accept complexity and uncertainty in situations, and to be more flexible in their thinking (Helson & Wink, 1992).

■ Some social scientists, citing historical observations of similar changes, suggest that the hormonal changes of midlife blur sexual distinctions (Rossi, 1980). Others offer a cultural explanation: at the same time that women are freer—because their children have grown up and left home—to develop nonmaternal abilities and to seek achievements in a career, men begin to wonder whether work is the most important thing in life after all (Gutmann, 1975, 1985). Now that younger women are more achievement-oriented and more likely to combine working with mothering, and younger men are more active in child rearing, we may no longer see this switch in personality at midlife. The changes we have seen may have less to do with gender than with the questions middle-aged people ask themselves as they evaluate their lives: "Is this all there is to life? Shouldn't I try other options while I still have time?"

So does personality change or remain stable? Or do people change in some ways and remain the same in others? Through experience and accomplishments, most adults gain in self-esteem and a sense of control over their lives, but basic temperament tends to remain constant (Costa & McCrae, 1994; Brim & Kagan, 1980). Your opinion about these issues would depend on your concept of what personality is.

A woman's well-being flourishes in multiple roles, which may include a positive experience with husband and children and a challenging, satisfying job. This mother is shown enjoying one of the pleasures of family life, one that may require her to redefine her role to reflect her children's independent status. *(Miriam White/The Stock Market)*

searchers drew up a questionnaire and gave it to a random sample of 238 other women. On average, the subjects had 2 years' education beyond high school; their incomes ranged from $4500 to over $50,000.

Two main factors influenced the women's mental health: how much *mastery*, or control, they felt they had over their lives, and how much *pleasure* they got from life. Neither criterion was related to age: older women felt just as good about themselves as younger ones. There was no evidence of a midlife crisis. Nor did simple relationships show up between well-being and whether a woman was married, had children, or was pre- or postmenopausal. What did emerge as vitally important was the combination of a woman's work and her intimate relationships.

Paid work was the single best predictor of mastery. A positive experience with husband and children (including a good sex life) was the best predictor of pleasure. And the single best key to general well-being was a challenging job that paid well and gave opportunity to use skills and make decisions. The women who scored highest overall on both mastery and pleasure were employed married mothers; the lowest scorers were childless homemakers.

Women's well-being, then, seems to flourish in multiple roles, despite the stress that goes along with active involvement in several important areas of life. It is even more stressful, apparently, to be underinvolved—to have too little to do, to have a job that is not challenging enough, or to have too few personal and occupational demands. These findings support those of Helson and Moane (1987; see Chapter 13), that women who commit themselves to career, family, or both show more personality growth between early and middle adulthood than those who do not.

"Rewriting of the Life Story": The Struggle for an Independent Identity

Ravenna Helson (1992) asked 88 women in their fifties about "the most unstable, confusing, troubled, or discouraged time in your life since college—the one with the most impact on your values, self-concept, and the way you look at the world" (p. 336). These mostly white and middle-class women were graduates of Mills College in Oakland, California; a number had been part of a longitudinal study since their student days.

The early forties turned out to be a time of great turmoil. Common enough to be considered a "stage" in women's development was a struggle for independent identity, status, and power, and the desire to achieve control over their lives. Correlations appeared among the age of these critical times, whether the women had children, and their ego identity status (as defined by Marcia; see Chapter 11).

Typical Crisis Themes

A number of the women's crises could be categorized by themes, which were often age-related. Typical themes among women in their early to mid-twenties were those of *bad self* and *bad partner*. In the "bad self" theme, women felt lonely, isolated, unattractive, inferior, and often passive. "Bad partner" themes often revolved around husbands who were substance abusers, suicide attempters, or exploitative.

In the periods around ages 30 and 40, the most common theme was a struggle for *independent identity*, often involving graduate training, a career, or a love affair (heterosexual or lesbian). Moving into middle age, between ages 36 and 46, were themes involving *unpleasant consequences of independence and assertiveness,* like rebuffs at work or abandonment by husbands. Later midlife themes, between ages 47 to 53, often focused on *troubling relationships* with partners, parents, or children; or on *overload,* sometimes caused by the demands of other people, sometimes by economic strain or heavy responsibilities at work.

Ego-Identity Status

By and large, for these women the years around age 30 held just as much turmoil as did their early forties. Then, by the early fifties, they had become more confident, assertive, and independent, and less critical of themselves (see Table 15-2). This normative personality change was unrelated to typical midlife events like the empty nest, menopause, or caring for aging parents (Helson & Wink, 1992).

The women's ego-identity statuses (Marcia, 1966) were related to the age of onset of their most difficult time (Helson, 1992). Women who were at

TABLE 15-2

Selected Feelings about Life by Women in Their Early Fifties

	More True Now	Less True Now
Identity questioning and turmoil:		
Excitement, turmoil about my impulses and potential	21	56
Searching for a sense of who I am	28	47
Anxious that I won't live up to my potential	25	47
Coming near the end of one road and not finding another	27	45
Assurance of status:		
Feeling established	78	11
Influence in my community or field of interest	63	24
A new level of productivity	70	11
Feeling selective in what I do	91	2
A sense of being my own person	90	3
Cognitive breadth and complexity:		
Bringing both feeling and rationality into decisions	76	1
Realizing larger patterns of meaning and relationship	72	7
Appreciating my complexity	69	10
Discovering new parts of myself	72	11
Present rather than future orientation:		
Focus on reality—meeting the needs of the day and not being too emotional about them	76	6
More satisfied with what I have; less worried about what I won't get	76	11
Feeling the importance of time's passing	76	10
Adjustment and relational smoothness:		
Feeling secure and committed	71	12
Feeling my life is moving well	74	15
Feeling optimistic about the future	58	20
A new level of intimacy	53	30
Doing things for others and then feeling exploited	14	56
Feeling very much alone	26	45
Feelings of competition with other women	7	63
Feeling angry at men and masculinity	14	52
Awareness of aging and reduced vitality:		
Looking old	70	15
Being treated as an older person	64	14
Reducing the intensity of my achievement efforts	44	26
Liking an active social life	27	52
Being very interested in sex	19	64

Note: The women judged whether each item was more applicable to them now than in their early forties, less applicable now than then, or about the same.
SOURCE: Helson & Wink, 1992.

the more developed statuses of *achieved* identity or *in moratorium* tended to experience their critical times in the middle periods, from ages 36 to 46. Women in the less adequate statuses of *diffused* and *foreclosed* identity tended to report their critical times either disproportionately early or late. Motherhood tended to delay the critical times; women without children were more likely to talk about difficult times before age 36, whereas mothers tended to place them later.

In some ways, then, while no period of life has a monopoly on change, these privileged women did, like the privileged men of the Levinson and Vaillant studies, reorganize their perceptions to bring a new meaning to the stories of their lives. Often this meant changing the course of their lives.

"The Prime of Life"

Is middle age the prime of life? Despite the prejudices in our society toward older people, and especially toward older women, many older women give especially high ratings to the early fifties. Among 700 Mills College alumnae, aged 26 to 80, who were studied in 1983, women in their early fifties most often described their lives as "first-rate." And in 1989, women in a longitudinal sample from Mills, who were in their early fifties, also rated their quality of life as high (Mitchell & Helson, 1990).

What makes this age so good? Generally, the women in this college-educated, privileged group were young enough to be in good health and old enough to have launched all their children and to have achieved a comfortable financial status. Life at home was simpler; the energy that had gone to children was redirected to partners, work, community, or themselves. They had developed high levels of confidence, involvement, security, and breadth of personality. The women with the most positive outlooks were optimistic in general; had good relationships, a positive self-concept, a feeling of control over their lives, active interests; and were managing their lives sensibly, showing the importance of basic personality traits. Also, they were most likely to rate their health high and to be living with a partner, but with no one else in the home.

These women's lives confirmed the findings of other researchers in some respects, but contradicted them in others. They were, as Neugarten had found, more aware of time and of the complex consciousness of middle age. They were likely to be caring for others, showing the generativity that Erikson proposed as critical for this age. However, they did not show a reversal of gender roles through cultivating the previously avoided side of themselves, as posited by Jung and Levinson. Instead, the highest quality of life was associated with a balance of the "masculine" trait of autonomy and the "feminine" involvement in an intimate relationship. Nor did they show much of the spiritual interest that a number of researchers have identified as typical of midlife.

It seems, then, that under certain favorable social conditions, midlife can be as good as life can get!

EVALUATING THE NORMATIVE-CRISIS MODEL

Several questions can be asked about the normative-crisis model of adult development: How widely does it apply? Is the midlife crisis really typical? To what extent does adult development depend on age? Can this predominantly male model of development be considered healthy? Let's examine these issues.

Can the Findings of Normative-Crisis Research Be Generalized to Other Populations?

The subjects of these normative-crisis studies have been, for the most part, privileged white men or women born in the 1920s or 1930s. Vaillant's sample included no black people; in Levinson's small sample of 40 men, 30 were middle- or upper-class, and only 5 were black; and the Mills College women graduates were also largely white and middle-class.

Let's look at the cohort issue. Many of the men in Vaillant's and Levinson's studies were born or grew up during the economic depression of the 1930s. They benefited from an expanding economy after World War II and may have succeeded at work far beyond their early expectations—and then burned out early. Their development may, then, be unusual rather than typical. The Mills College graduates' experiences also have to be looked at in terms of their backgrounds and the cohort they belonged to—a group of educated women who lived through a time of great change brought about partly by the women's movement and by new patterns in the workplace. They were influenced by these factors, along with such other influences as the cultural demands on women (especially wives and mothers), the socialization they

BOX 15-2   *WINDOW ON THE WORLD*

A SOCIETY WITHOUT MIDDLE AGE?

The universality of the "midlife crisis" is questionable even in our culture. What, then, happens in nonwestern cultures that do not even have a clear concept of middle age? One such culture is that of the Gusii in Africa, a society of 1 million people in western Kenya, where people believe in witchcraft and men take several wives (R. Levine, 1980).

Among the Gusii, childbearing is not confined to young adulthood; people continue to reproduce as long as they are physiologically able. The Gusii do have a "life plan" with well-defined expectations for each stage, but this plan is very different from what is accepted as normal in the United States today.

The Gusii have no words for "adolescent," "young adult," or "middle-aged." A man goes through only one recognized stage of life—*omomura,* or "warrior"—between his circumcision, which takes place between ages 9 and 11, and the marriage of his first child, when he becomes an elder. Thus the *omomura* phase may last anywhere from 25 to 40 or more years. Women have an additional stage between being circumcised and becoming elders—*omosubaati,* or "married women"—em-

Many Gusii in western Kenya become ritual practitioners after their children are grown, seeking spiritual powers to compensate for their waning physical strength. For women like the diviner shown here, ritual practice may be a way to wield power in a male-dominated society. *(Levine/Anthro-Photo)*

phasizing the greater importance of marriage in a woman's life.

Transitions in Gusii society, then, depend on life events, not on age. Status is gained from circumcision, from marriage (for women), from having children, and from becoming a parent of a married child (and thus a prospective grandparent). However, the Gusii have a "social clock," a set of expectations for when these events should normally occur. Women or men who are "off

time"—who marry and have their first child late or (worse) not at all—are subject to ridicule or ostracism.

Although the Gusii have no clearly labeled midlife transition, some of them do reassess their lives around the time they are old enough to be grandparents (typically by age 40). "Middle-aged Gusii experience their lives and future performance as limited, and this can occasion a midlife crisis from which they emerge as ritual practitioners," or healers (R. Levine, 1980, p. 99). Their physical strength and stamina are waning, and they know that they will not be able to cultivate their land or herd their cattle indefinitely, so they seek spiritual powers. The quest has a generative purpose, too: elders are responsible for protecting their children and grandchildren ritually from death or illness, even when the children are grown.

A disproportionate number of older women become either ritual practitioners or witches, seeking power either to help people or to harm them. Their motive may be to compensate for their lack of personal and economic power in a male-dominated society.

had received from infancy on, and often discriminatory practices by employers.

Cohorts with different experiences may develop quite differently. For instance, if the pattern for future cohorts involves alternating periods of education, work, and leisure throughout life, a midlife career change may be seen as routine, not as a sign of crisis. And as gender roles and women's status in the workplace change, both men and women will be affected.

Similarly, these findings cannot be generalized to people of other races or other socioeconomic levels. Also, these theories have not been tested in

other cultures, some of which appear not to have a concept of middle age (see Box 15-2).

How Typical Is the "Midlife Crisis"?

Many psychologists, challenging the notion that crisis is a hallmark of midlife, emphasize that "crisis, transition and change occur all through life" (Schlossberg, 1987, p. 74). They also hold that the transition to middle age may be stressful, but such stress does not necessarily amount to a crisis (Brim, 1977; Chiriboga, 1989; Farrell & Rosenberg, 1981; Haan, 1990; Rossi, 1980).

In one study, a group of men in their thirties who had achieved success quite young were already struggling with the kinds of issues commonly associated with middle age. They were asking themselves questions like "Was it worth it?" "What next?" and "What shall I do with the rest of my life?" (Taguiri & Davis, 1982, in Baruch et al., 1983). And although Helson (1992) found a period of turmoil at about age 40, she is reluctant to call this a "crisis." One reason may be the fact that many women in her study experienced their greatest crises in their twenties or early thirties.

Research that questions the universality of the midlife crisis also bears out the timing-of-events view that crises arise in response to *events*, not *age*. Events that used to characterize a certain time of life are no longer so predictable; this unpredictability may bring on crises, catching people unprepared and unable to cope (Neugarten & Neugarten, 1987). Whether a transition turns into a crisis depends less on age than on the circumstances of a person's life and the person's resources for dealing with them; "One person may go from crisis to crisis while another . . . experience[s] relatively few strains" (Schlossberg, 1987, p. 74).

It seems, then, that although adults do go through a transition at midlife, they also experience transitions earlier and later; and the timing and acuteness of the midlife transition and the way people cope with it depends on their life circumstances and personalities rather than on their age.

Is Adult Development Age-Linked?

The heart of the normative-crisis approach is the idea that development follows a definite age-linked sequence. Although Helson found a number of age-related themes, she offered this caveat: "These unpleasant or frightening times are familiar, but how much they fix our view of life seems to depend upon factors such as our gender role, the adequacy of our resources to solve problems and to change, and no doubt upon factors of culture and cohort" (1992, p. 344).

Normative-crisis studies, then, have been too limited to support a definite age-linked sequence of development. For example, as we have seen, the developmental tasks in Levinson's scheme were derived from an intensive study of only 40 men from one cohort. Although he interviewed and tested all the subjects, he obtained little evidence from which to generalize, even about middle-aged men in the cohort sampled, let alone about other groups of men, or any women.

How Healthy Is the Male Model?

Jung, Erikson, Peck, Vaillant, and Levinson all suggest that how men resolve developmental tasks tells us about their psychological health. Levinson stresses the importance of the degree to which a man realizes or modifies his early dream, and sees the value of relationships with mentor and "special woman" more as a means toward a goal than for their own sake. Even the "healthiest" men in his study were unlikely to have close friendships. In this model, healthy development is a matter mainly of personal achievement and separation from early relationships. Not until middle age does a man even begin to concern himself with the need for attachment. Vaillant (1977), too, emphasizes work and deemphasizes relationships.

The men in these two studies seem to be emotionally constricted. If accurate, the model is not only inappropriate for women, whose lives typically involve a rich network of relationships, but also offers a dubious view of healthy male development (Bergman, 1991; Gilligan, 1982).

Proponents of the self-in-relation theory (described in Chapter 1) suggest that men, like women, have a primary desire for connection with other people, that their greatest source of happiness lies in mutually empowering relationships, and, conversely, that their unhappiness is most often due to isolation or poor relationships (Bergman, 1991; Miller, 1991). Men too, say these theorists, develop their individual identities through connection, beginning with their parents and continuing throughout life. When, as is typical, boys are taught to disconnect from primary attachments, they turn away not only from the individual bonds but from the very process of connection.

In midlife, men may sense "a loss of meaning, an emptiness, loneliness, failure, rage, sadness, leading to further isolation, stagnation and stasis, and depression" (Bergman, 1991, p. 10). Such men often try hard to develop connection with others. It is ironic that this increased interest in intimate relationships often comes at midlife, when children are about to leave home or have already done so and wives may have adapted to a lack of intimacy in marriage by investing their emotions more deeply in other relationships. This late awareness of the need for intimacy may help to explain why, as we'll see, men seem more prone to greet the "empty nest" with regret while women welcome it with relief (L. B. Rubin, 1979). It may also explain why men and women so often have trouble communicating with each other.

Still, normative-crisis studies of adult development have captured both the professional and the public imagination, largely because of the main, and most important, message of age-oriented research: adults continue to change, develop, and grow. Whether or not people grow in the specific ways suggested by the normative-crisis approach, it challenges the notion that nothing important happens to personality in midlife or later.

PERSONAL RELATIONSHIPS AND TIMING OF EVENTS IN MIDLIFE

The timing-of-events model suggests that adults' development hinges on the events in people's lives. If this is so, we need to look at some of the major changes likely to occur during the middle years—changes that often have to do with relationships. Just as the changes that occur within individuals affect their ties with others, changes in relationships affect individual personalities.

We'll examine the relationships middle-aged people have with people in their own generation—spouses or other sexual partners, siblings, and friends; with the older generation; and with the younger generation. Middle-aged people must often redefine their roles as parents to meet the changing needs of adolescent and young adult children and at the same time redefine what it means to be sons and daughters to their own parents, who may now need their help. We'll examine how people cope with being in the midlife "sandwich" between maturing children and aging parents.

MARRIAGE AND DIVORCE

Midlife marriage today is very different from what it used to be. When life expectancies were shorter, with many women dying in childbirth, couples who remained together for 25, 30, or 40 years were rare. The most common pattern was for marriages to be broken by death and for survivors to remarry. Households were usually filled with children. People had many children, early and late, and expected them to live at home until they married. It was unusual for a middle-aged husband and wife to be alone together.

Today, more marriages end in divorce, but couples who manage to stay together can often look forward to 20 or more years of married life after the last child has left home.

Marital Satisfaction in Midlife

What happens to the quality of a longtime marriage? Marital satisfaction seems to follow a U-shaped curve. From an early high point, it declines until late middle age and then rises again through the first part of late adulthood (S. A. Anderson, Russell, & Schumm, 1983; Gilford, 1984; Gruber-Baldini & Schaie, 1986). The least happy time seems to be the period when most couples are heavily involved in child rearing and careers. *Positive* aspects of marriage (like cooperation, discussion, and shared laughter) seem to follow the U-shaped pattern, while *negative* aspects (like sarcasm, anger, and disagreement over important issues) decline from young adulthood through age 69 (Gilford, 1984; Gilford & Bengtson, 1979). This may be because many conflict-ridden marriages end along the way.

One 30-year study of 175 couples confirmed the U-shaped curve, using a quasi-longitudinal method (Gruber-Baldini & Schaie, 1986). It followed 22 couples for the entire time, and the rest for various lengths of time. This study found that the longer a couple were married, the more they resembled each other in their outlook on life and way of thinking—even in math skills. But this tendency toward like-mindedness halted temporarily, with the dip in marital satisfaction, during the child-rearing years.

The first part of the middle years, when many couples have teenage children making their way toward independence, tends to be stressful. The years right after the children leave home, however, may bring as much contentment as the honeymoon (H. Feldman & Feldman, 1977). Husband and wife now have more privacy than they have had in years, freedom to be spontaneous, fewer money worries, and a new chance to get to know each other. This "second honeymoon" may coincide with a "honeymoon stage" of retirement, but it may not last; another drop in marital satisfaction seems to occur after age 69 (Gilford, 1984; see Chapter 17).

Typical personality changes of middle age can alter husbands' and wives' expectations and interactions. Their ability to adjust to each other's changing needs can affect their satisfaction with married life. For example, the husband of a woman who goes to work for the first time may have trouble accepting her new assertiveness and her involvement in an outside life that does not include him (Zube, 1982). On the other hand, many men at midlife become more receptive to closer connections with other people, including their wives

BOX 15-3 PRACTICALLY SPEAKING

ENHANCING MARRIAGE AT MIDLIFE

Some of the normative events of midlife are likely to be stressful for one or both partners in a marriage. Whenever one person is under stress, there is likely to be a ripple effect, affecting people close to the stressed person. The one likely to be most affected is a spouse. As one husband commented, "When my wife is happy, I'm not always happy. But when she's unhappy, I'm sure to be unhappy, too."

Spouses can help each other deal with stress by showing love and support and by helping one another understand what is happening and how to deal with it. One way to communicate about sources of anxiety is to do an exercise like the one below, suggested by the Cooperative Extension Service of the Pennsylvania State University, as part of its program "Strengthen Your Family."

In this exercise, each spouse looks separately at each of the changes given in the following list, estimates how much stress it has already caused or might cause in the future, and checks off his or her responses. Then the couple look together at each item and talk about their answers, asking such questions as "Why did we rate the item the same or differently?" "How can we help each other deal with the stress?" and "Where else could we turn for help?"

	Estimated Stress:		
	Much	Some	Little
Children leave home	☐	☐	☐
Hair turns gray or falls out	☐	☐	☐
Wife goes back to work or to school	☐	☐	☐
You're no longer in the "young crowd" at work	☐	☐	☐
Wrinkles multiply	☐	☐	☐
You start to put on weight	☐	☐	☐
A parent dies	☐	☐	☐
Menopause begins	☐	☐	☐
Your back aches	☐	☐	☐
A son or daughter marries	☐	☐	☐
You're passed over for promotion by a younger worker	☐	☐	☐
You develop arthritis	☐	☐	☐
A brother or sister has a heart attack	☐	☐	☐
Your sex drive changes	☐	☐	☐
You become a grandparent	☐	☐	☐
You're bored with your job	☐	☐	☐

SOURCE: B. W. Davis, n.d.

and children, which helps their marriages (Bergman, 1991).

Marriages are often affected by stressful events in midlife (as listed in Box 15-3), but communication between partners can often mitigate such stress. Many couples, in fact, report that hard times have brought them closer (Robinson & Blanton, 1993).

The research on marital satisfaction has been criticized for its methodology. Much of the earlier research dealt with only the husband's or wife's attitude, not with both. Also, almost all studies have been cross-sectional; they show differences among couples of different cohorts rather than ex-ploring changes in the *same* couples. In addition, samples have typically included only couples in intact marriages, omitting those who divorced (Blieszner, 1986).

What Makes Middle-Aged Couples Divorce or Stay Together?

How a marriage fares in midlife may depend largely on its quality up to then. A marriage that has been basically good all along may be better than ever. The passionate love of newlyweds—the initial intense attraction with its wildly emotional ups and downs—may fade as day-to-day life together dispels the sense of mystery. But a strong marriage, even one of many years, may well fit Sternberg's definition of *consummate love* (1985a), which embodies passion, intimacy, and commitment (see Table 13-5).

In a shaky marriage, though, the "empty nest" may be a personal and marital crisis. With the children gone, a couple may realize that they no longer have much in common and may ask themselves whether they want to spend the rest of their lives together.

The divorce rate has gone up for middle-aged couples as well as for younger ones. Current rates suggest that the first marriage of about 1 woman in 8 will end in divorce after she reaches age 40 (Uhlenberg, Cooney, & Boyd, 1990). Middle-aged couples separate for many of the same reasons as younger ones—greater expectations for marriage, growing willingness to end an unsatisfactory relationship, increased acceptance of divorce, and less stringent divorce laws.

Divorce can be especially traumatic for middle-aged and older people, who expect their lives to be relatively settled. However, this may change as midlife divorce becomes a more normative event (A. J. Norton & Moorman, 1987). Since divorce often seems preferable to living out a frustrating, conflict-filled relationship, many people, even at this stage of life, end unhappy marriages.

Divorce has become so common that social scientists are now studying why some marriages do *not* break up. Among 300 couples who had been happily married for at least 15 years, both men and women tended to credit such reasons as a positive attitude toward the spouse as a friend and as a person; commitment to marriage; belief in the sanctity of marriage; and agreement on aims and goals in life. Happily married couples spent much time together and shared many activities (Lauer & Lauer, 1985).

These conclusions were confirmed by an in-depth study of 15 couples who had been married more than 30 years (Robinson & Blanton, 1993). The factors that emerged most consistently in these enduring marriages were enjoyable relationships and commitment—to both the idea of marriage and the individual mate. Other key characteristics were intimacy balanced with autonomy, good communication, similar perceptions of the relationship, and religious orientation. These factors were interrelated, with intimacy showing up as central, affecting or being affected by the other characteristics.

This study yielded practical implications for im-

proving marriages, such as: the value of programs that help couples see difficult times as opportunities for growth and increased closeness; the need to balance connection and autonomy; the importance of developing communication skills and of exploring different perceptions of the relationship; and an understanding by religious institutions of the ways they can contribute to strong marriages.

RELATIONSHIPS WITH SIBLINGS

After Harilyn was widowed in her fifties, her brother, whom she had previously seen no more than once a month, made a point of seeing her every week. He helped her with home repairs and financial decisions, and he and his wife included her in their social activities.

Many middle-aged siblings stay in touch and stand ready to help each other. Relationships with siblings are the longest-lasting in most people's lives and become even more important as people grow older. Some 85 percent of middle-aged adults have at least one living brother or sister; the average person has two. Siblings usually get together at least several times a year—in many cases, once a month or more. It is unusual for them to lose touch completely (Cicirelli, 1980).

Although childhood rivalry may continue during adulthood, many siblings (especially sisters) become closer. The arrival of children often brings siblings closer together, as do more upsetting events like divorce, widowhood, or the death of a family member. Although marriage often means less contact with siblings, it rarely affects the emotional quality of the relationship (Connidis, 1992). More than two-thirds of people with siblings feel close or very close to their brothers and sisters and have good relationships with them; more than three-fourths say that they get along well or very well (Cicirelli, 1980). Closeness—both emotional and geographic—and a sense of responsibility for the welfare of siblings are the most important influences on how often brothers and sisters see each other (Lee, Mancini, & Maxwell, 1990).

Issues sometimes arise over the care of elderly parents and questions of inheritance, especially if the sibling relationship has not been good. One study of 140 sibling pairs who were caring for one or both parents found that many of the respondents felt that they were doing more for their parents and deriving more satisfaction from helping them than their siblings were. But the closer the siblings were, the more they agreed on how much

Friends are a valuable source of companionship, support, and enjoyment in middle age. Being at the same stage of life and having similar interests are now the predominant factors in the choice of friends. *(Randy Taylor/Sygma)*

each gave up in their personal lives, how much each gave to their parents, and how easy or hard it would be to have the sibling do more (Lerner, Somers, Reid, Chiriboga, & Tierney, 1991). And among 95 married daughters caring for parents with dementia, siblings were a strong source of support—but also the most important source of stress involving other people (Suitor & Pillemer, 1993).

FRIENDSHIPS

People sometimes devote less time and energy to friendship in midlife than in other stages of life. They tend to be heavily involved with family and busy with work, and they often want to spend their free time building up security for retirement. Middle-aged people tend to have fewer friends than either newlyweds or people about to retire, and their friendships seem less complex.

Yet friendships do persist throughout middle age and are a strong source of emotional support and well-being (Baruch et al., 1983; House, Lan-

dis, & Umberson, 1988). Many of the friends of midlife are old friends, though people do make some new ones, often through organizations. Age is less of a factor in making friends now than is similarity in life stage, such as age of children, length of marriage, or occupational status (Troll, 1975). Diane, for example, has become friendly with mothers of Anna's classmates, some of whom are several years younger than she is—and with professional colleagues who are several years older.

What midlife friendships lack in quantity, they often make up for in quality, as people turn to friends for emotional support and practical guidance: for example, to help them deal with maturing children and aging parents (Suitor & Pillemer, 1993). As we noted in Chapter 13, close ties with others help to foster mental and physical health.

RELATIONSHIPS WITH MATURING CHILDREN

Parenthood is a continuous process of letting go. From the moment of birth, children's normal course of development leads to more and more independence from parents. During the parents' middle age, most families are in a definitive phase of this process. If things have gone well over the years, the parents can now celebrate their success in raising their children to be competent, well-assured young adults, ready to face the challenges of independence. But even those parents with the best of intentions and optimal parenting skills often find this transition difficult.

Adolescent Children: Issues for Parents

It is ironic that the people at the two times of life most frequently linked with emotional crises—adolescence and midlife—often live in the same household. It is usually middle-aged adults who are the parents of adolescent children. While dealing with their own special concerns, the parents have to deal daily with young people who are undergoing great physical, emotional, and social changes. Sometimes parents' own long-buried adolescent fantasies resurface as they see their children turning into sexual beings. Furthermore, seeing their children at the brink of adulthood makes parents realize even more sharply how much of their own life is behind them. The contrast in life stages create resentment and jealousy on the part of the parent—and an overidentification with the child's fantasies (H. Meyers, 1989).

An important task for parents is acceptance of children as they are, not as what the parents had hoped and dreamed they would be. In coming to terms with this reality, parents must realize that they do not have total control over their children, that they cannot make children into carbon copies or improved models of themselves. Parents have to face the fact that the directions their children choose may be very different from the ones the parents want them to follow.

This acceptance is so hard for many parents, and the need to break away is so strong for many young people, that the adolescent years can be hard on the whole family. As one father of three said, only partly in jest, just after his youngest child had gone off to college, "They make the last couple of years at home so miserable that their going isn't a trauma—it's a relief!"

When Children Leave: The "Empty Nest"

For years, people have talked about the *"empty nest"* crisis, a supposedly difficult transition, especially for women, when the last child leaves home. But although some women who have a heavy investment in mothering do have problems at this time, they are far outnumbered by those who find it liberating not to have children at home anymore (Barnett, 1985; Mitchell & Helson, 1990). Parents like to see their children frequently, although most enjoy the freedom of not feeling responsible for their day-to-day lives (White & Edwards, 1990).

The empty nest may be harder on fathers, who often react to it with regret that they did not spend more time with their children when they were younger (L. B. Rubin, 1979). This stage also appears to be harder on parents whose children do not become independent when the parents expect them to (Harkins, 1978) and on women who have not prepared for it by reorganizing their lives through work or other involvements (Targ, 1979).

Many women, in fact, are freed by the empty nest from the "chronic emergency of parenthood" (Cooper & Gutmann, 1987, p. 347). In one group of 50 mothers—25 "pre-empty nest" and 25 "post-empty nest"—the "post-empty nest" women had an active mastery style. When asked to tell stories about ambiguous pictures, the "pre-empty nest" women tended to tell stories of emotionally conflicted leave-takings from home, of maternal warmth and nurturance, and of rescuing others. The "post-empty nest" women told stories of leaving home joyfully to realize a personal goal, of a mother as mentor more than nurturer, and of achievement done for the self (Cooper & Gutmann, 1987). This confirms the findings by Mitchell and Helson (1990) that for women, the decade of the fifties—after the children had left home—constituted the "prime of life."

When Children Stay or Return: The Not-So-Empty Nest

What happens if the nest does *not* empty when expected or is refilled by fledgling adults returning home to live? As the timing-of-events model would predict, this phenomenon sometimes leads to tension as parents are forced to adjust to the presence of full-grown offspring.

The past two decades saw more young adults returning to live in their parents' homes (P. C.

At the same time that middle-aged parents acknowledge their teenage children's need to become independent of them, most parents are happy when they can give help to their maturing adolescents—and when their children welcome that help. *(Erika Stone)*

Even after the years of active parenting are over, parents are still parents, who help their children in many ways. One common kind of help is baby-sitting, a "natural" for a grandfather and granddaughter who enjoy each other's company. *(Jennifer Moebus)*

Glick & Lin, 1986a). Jobs were harder to get, housing costs climbed, couples were postponing marriage, and divorce and unwed parenthood were on the rise (Clemens & Axelson, 1985; P. C. Glick & Lin, 1986a). Child needs rather than parent needs are more important in determining when adults live with their parents; never-married people, and to a lesser extent, divorced or separated ones, are most likely to come "home" (Ward, Logan, & Spitze, 1992).

The arrangement works best when it's temporary and when the children are under age 22 (Clemens & Axelson, 1985). Parents appreciate help with household chores and with caring for younger children, and enjoy sharing leisure activities. But serious conflicts may arise, especially when the young person is unemployed and financially dependent. Disagreements also arise over household responsibilities, dress and lifestyle—particularly sex, alcohol, drugs, and choice of friends. The young adult is likely to feel isolated from peers and to have trouble establishing intimacy, and the return to the parental home may impede maturation. If, for example, the young adult socializes only with the parents' friends, rather than with his or her own peers, and does not assume adult responsibilities, she or he may become trapped on a plateau that discourages healthy psychological growth.

Meanwhile, the parents may have to postpone renewing their own intimacy, exploring personal interests, and resolving marital issues. The most difficult situation for parents seems to be the return of divorced or separated children with their own children (Aquilino & Supple, 1991).

The situation works best when parent and child negotiate their roles and responsibilities, acknowledging the child's movement toward full adult status and the parents' rights to privacy and independence.

Lifelong Parenting

The difficulty many parents have in treating their offspring as adults is illustrated by a story that Elliott Roosevelt used to tell about his mother, Eleanor. At a state dinner where she was seated next to him, she leaned over and whispered into his ear. When a friend later asked Elliott, then in his forties, what she had said, he answered, "She told me to eat my peas."

Even after the years of active parenting are over and all the children have flown the nest, parents are still parents. The midlife role of parent to young adults raises new issues and calls for new attitudes and behaviors. (This is also a time when the new role of grandparent is assumed, since the typical age for becoming a grandparent is the early fifties. But the role of grandparent often becomes more important later in life; we discuss it in Chapter 17.)

Young newly married adults (especially daughters) are closely tied to their middle-aged parents, who often help them financially or with baby-sitting or helping them get their first homes in order. Parents and adult children often visit each other, and young couples spend a great deal of time talking about their parents.

Parents and adult children generally enjoy each other's company and get along well. Some keep harmony by avoiding touchy intergenerational issues—somewhat like establishing "demilitarized zones" (Hagestad, 1984). Most parents of children 16 or over express satisfaction with their role of parent—85 percent in one nationwide survey of more than 3000 people (Umberson, 1992). Although 80 percent of these parents are happy with how their children turned out, only 23 percent are never bothered or upset as parents. Parenting concerns continue into old age: elderly parents whose children have serious problems are more likely to be depressed themselves (Pillemer & Suitor, 1991).

Parents in the prime of life generally continue to give their children more than they get from them (Troll, 1989). Their continuing support probably reflects the relative strength of middle-aged adults and the continuing needs of young adults, who are in what some psychologists consider the most stressful years in the life span (Pearlin, 1980). The balance of mutual aid tends to shift as the parents grow older.

RELATIONSHIPS WITH AGING PARENTS

A 45-year-old woman says, "My mother is my best friend. I can tell her anything." A 50-year-old man visits his retired father every evening, bringing him news and asking his opinions about problems in the family business. A 40-year-old divorced mother sees her parents more often now than she did during her 15 years of marriage and needs their help more now than at any time since her teens. A 55-year-old man, who cannot have a 10-minute conversation with his mother without an argument, says, "I wish she would die so I could feel guilty and get it over with." A couple in their early sixties find that the time they had hoped to spend traveling and playing with their grandchildren is being spent instead caring for both their widowed mothers.

Relationships between middle-aged people and their parents vary enormously, often reflecting the history of the bond (Leigh, 1982; Morgan, 1984). These ties are not static; they evolve constantly over the years. Parents continue to be important. Among 350 adult daughters, those who have good relationships with their parents are more likely to report high well-being, less likely to suffer anxiety or depression than those with poor relationships (Barnett, Kibria, Baruch, & Pleck, 1991). In midlife, many people can look at their parents objectively for the first time, neither idealizing them nor blaming them for mistakes and inadequacies. With maturity, it becomes possible to see parents as individuals who exhibit both strengths and weaknesses.

Something else happens during these years. One day a son or daughter picks up a roll of photos from the camera shop, looks at the latest pictures of a mother or father—and sees an old person. The middle-aged child realizes that the parent is no longer a pillar of strength to lean on but is now starting to lean on the child. It is now time for the adult child to show "filial responsibility." Help for aging parents takes many forms: offering financial support; helping in decision making and performing daily tasks, like shopping and cooking; and, if the parents become ill, infirm, or confused, assuming responsibility for managing their lives.

Contact with Parents

The picture that emerges from a growing body of research on middle-aged children and their parents is one of a strong bond growing out of attachment earlier in life—and continuing as long as both generations live (Cicirelli, 1989; Rossi & Rossi, 1990). Parents and children see and speak to each other often and generally get along well, with relatively little strain. In one study, 91 percent of adult children felt close or very close to their mothers, and 87 percent to their fathers (Cicirelli, 1981). The two generations often live near each other and see each other frequently. One study found that 75 percent of parents of children 16 years old or older report seeing children who don't live with them at least once a week (Umberson, 1992).

Since both generations want to be independent, adults and elderly parents usually do not live together unless that arrangement becomes necessary because the parent is too poor or too ill to live alone and has no other good option. Most older people do not want to burden their families; fewer than 1 percent of those who live alone say that they would rather live with their children (Commonwealth Fund Commission on Elderly People Liv-

By middle age, many people can look at their parents objectively, neither idealizing them nor exaggerating their shortcomings. This middle-aged daughter putting drops in her mother's eyes realizes that her mother is no longer a tower of strength but instead is beginning to lean on *her*. Mothers and daughters usually remain closer than any other combination of family members. *(Parke/Gamma Liaison)*

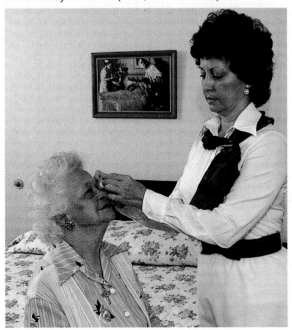

TABLE 15-3

Caregivers	
Category	Percent Who Provide Care
Gender	
Female	75
Male	25
Age	
Under 35	28
35–49	29
50–64	26
65 and older	15
Marital status	
Married	66
Not married	34
Children in household	
Yes	39
No	49
Current employment	
Full-time	42
Part-time	13
Retired	16
Not employed or homemaker	27

Note: A survey of 750 households found this profile of the people who provide unpaid care for an elderly relative or friend.
SOURCES: American Association of Retired Persons, 1989; "Juggling family," 1989, p. B8.

ing Alone, 1986). The younger family can find it inconvenient to absorb an extra person into a household, and the older person moving in with children has to make a major adjustment in day-to-day routines. Everyone's privacy—and relationships—may suffer.

Mothers and daughters are more likely to stay in close contact than any other combination of family members (Lee, Dwyer, & Coward, 1993; Troll, 1986). Large gender differences showed up in a study of African American adults and their parents. The children were more likely to visit their mothers than their fathers, and the mother-daughter relationship was especially strong (Spitze & Miner, 1992). Since adults are more likely to help the same-sex parent, this may partially explain the mother-daughter bond; older women are more likely to need help than older men (Lee et al., 1993). However, socialization patterns encouraging caregiving more in women than men is also a strong factor.

Mutual Help

Help flows back and forth between generations. "In general, parents give more services and money to their children throughout their life, and children give more emotional support, household help, and care during illness" (Troll, 1986, p. 23). Among working-class families, though, money is more likely to flow from child to parent (Troll et al., 1979). Parents usually do not expect to be "paid back" for what they have given their children, but instead are happy when they see their children turning out well and giving, in turn, to their own children. When in need, though, many parents do turn to their children for help.

Elderly parents tend to focus attention and aid on the child who needs them most. They may open their home to a child whose marriage has ended; and parents of disabled children often maintain their protective roles as long as they live. Elderly parents are more likely to give financial help and help with transportation to single adult children than married ones; they offer divorced children emotional support and help with child care and housework (Aldous, 1987). Unhappily married, divorced, and widowed adults often become closer to their parents, getting from them the support they are not getting from their spouses.

Caring for Parents

The generations get along best while parents are healthy and vigorous. When older people become infirm—especially if they suffer from mental deterioration or personality changes—the burden of caring for them may strain the relationship. Daughters, in particular, become distressed, because they are the ones who generally have this responsibility—most often for aging, ailing mothers (Troll, 1986). Today, the daughters are likely to be holding a full-time job, as well as having their own adolescent or young adult children (American Association of Retired Persons, 1989; see Table 15-3).

Even though mothers worry about losing their independence and being a burden on their children (Troll, 1986), adult children are the ones to whom many elderly women turn first when in need of care. In one study, more than half of the adult children surveyed felt some strain, and one-third reported substantial strain, in connection with helping their parents. The strain most often showed up as physical or emotional exhaustion and the feeling that a parent was impossible to satisfy (Cicirelli, 1980). African American daughters report less strain than white women do, but for both groups conflict between caregiving duties and the caregivers' personal and social life was a predictor of emotional strain (Mui, 1992).

This "sandwich generation"—torn between obligations to their parents and the need to help launch their own children—must allocate time, money, and energy to both generations. If they have full-time jobs, they may devote a large portion of nonworking hours to caring for parents, sometimes for years on end. Furthermore, the needs of aging parents seem to fall into the category of nonnormative, unanticipated demands. New parents expect to assume the full physical, financial, and emotional care of their babies, with the assumption that such care will gradually diminish as children grow up. Most people do not expect to have to care for their parents; they ignore the possibility of their parents' infirmity and rarely plan ahead for it. When it cannot be denied, they perceive it as interfering with other responsibilities and plans. Now that the fastest-growing group in our population is aged 85 and over, greater numbers of middle-aged people will find themselves in this position.

Feelings of strain are often highly subjective. Some, of course, are related to objective life circumstances; in one group of African American caregivers, women in poor health, with other conflicts in their lives, and the inability to take any time off from caregiving were most likely to feel strain (Mui, 1992). But often emotional issues dictate levels of strain—issues like conflicts with other family members, especially siblings—generally because the sibling did not give the expected amount of help (Strawbridge & Wallhagen, 1991). White caregivers, but not African Americans, also feel strain more when their relationship with their parents is not so good, and when they are having conflicts at work (Mui, 1992; Walker, Martin, & Jones, 1992). Middle-aged people often feel disappointment, anger, and guilt when they realize that they, rather than their parents, now have to be the strong ones. In addition, their anxiety over the anticipated end of their parents' lives is tinged with worry about their own mortality (Cicirelli, 1980; Troll, 1986).

Timing is another factor in these intergenerational strains. Parents who are looking forward to or are just experiencing the end of responsibility for their own children—and who now sense keenly that their own time on earth is limited—may feel that the need to care for their parents will deprive them of the chance to fulfill their own dreams. The sense of being "tied down," of not being able to take a vacation or make other plans, is, for some adult children, the hardest thing about caring for elderly parents (Robinson & Thurnher, 1981).

Still, children do care for their parents; they do not abandon them (Troll, 1986). Parents and children alike feel better when the care comes from feelings of attachment and not duty (Cantor, 1983; Robinson & Thurnher, 1981). Therefore, one psychologist who has studied intergenerational ties emphasizes that it is less effective to appeal to children's sense of obligation and more fruitful to encourage attachment behaviors like visiting and telephoning (Cicirelli, 1980). Children who are in touch with their parents can tell when help is needed, and they usually respond by giving it.

There are ways to reduce the strain of caregiving. The pressure of financial support for elderly parents has been greatly eased by such programs as social security, Supplemental Security Income, Medicare, and Medicaid. Other forms of support include work leaves for family members so they can give care when needed; free or low-cost programs where older people can go from morning till dinnertime; transportation and escort services; in-home services providing meals and housekeeping; and respite care, letting people whose elderly parents require daily attention get away for a few days.

Counseling and self-help groups can offer emotional support, pass on information about community resources, and help sons and daughters develop skills with their aging parents. One such program, which helped daughters recognize the limits of their ability to meet their mothers' needs and the value of encouraging their mothers' own self-reliance, lightened the daughters' burden somewhat and improved their relationships with their mothers; as a result the mothers became less lonely (Scharlach, 1987). When caregiving ends because of the parent's death, middle-aged adults must come to terms with their often ambivalent feelings (see Box 15-4).

As middle-aged adults enter the last stage of life, they often focus more on their legacy to their children and grandchildren. We'll see what these final years are like in Chapters 16 and 17.

520 PART SIX ■ MIDDLE ADULTHOOD

BOX 15-4   FOOD FOR THOUGHT

REACTING TO A PARENT'S DEATH

When Sally was 43 years old, her father, 76, died of a sudden heart attack. As the only surviving child, Sally took a much more active role in her mother's life until, 3½ years later, after many bouts of illness, her 79-year-old mother also died. For months after her mother's death, Sally felt depressed. Despite her recognition that losing one or both parents is a normative experience of midlife, she had not been prepared for her deep feelings of loss. In this she was fairly typical.

A parent's death is difficult for offspring of any age, no matter what the relationship in life has been. When the relationship has not been a good one, the death is sometimes even more disturbing as it arouses ambivalent feelings of loss mixed with relief, followed by guilt. But death may also help people deal with such developmental issues of middle age as coping with changes in the self, in social relationships, and in awareness of their own mortality (M. S. Moss & Moss, 1989).

With longer life expectancies, people are experiencing their parents' death at later ages, often in mid to late middle age (Hagestad, 1984). Let's look at the ways a parent's death can affect the bereaved adult's handling of midlife issues.* (We discuss the grieving process itself in Chapter 18.)

Personal changes: "Orphaned" middle-aged adults often experience a strengthening of the ego as they review a deceased parent's life and see it as relevant to their own. Their memories sometimes become selective, focusing on and identifying with the parent's good qualities. For the first time they may be able to accept and forgive the parent's failures, especially those toward themselves.

In addition, people are often prompted to review their own lives and to evaluate and revise their goals and current activities. There is a new awareness—especially after the death of both parents—of being the "older generation," no longer a child but a mature adult in the senior ranks. This awareness can be empowering to those who see themselves as wise "elders," or frightening to those without a sense of purpose in life.

Some people become more self-assertive and autonomous when their parents die; others, especially those whose identity had been intertwined with the parent, may worry about their own future or feel despair over their lack of self-fulfillment. Some experience a surge of creativity as they work through their loss by editing a parent's diary or memoirs, or writing their own.

Changes in other relationships: "Death ends a life but it does not end a relationship" (R. Anderson, 1980, p. 110). Even very old people often mention their parents as the most influential persons in their lives, and even a dead parent can be an ongoing presence in a son's or daughter's life (Troll & Smith, 1976). But death of a parent often brings changes in other relationships. If a child has been taking care of the parent, the parent's death may free the child to spend time and emotional energy on relationships that had been temporarily neglected, like those with a spouse or with children or grandchildren.

Recognizing the finality of death and the impossibility of saying anything more to the deceased parent, some people are motivated to resolve any conflicts in their ties to the living—now, while there is still time. Generally, there is little or no change in sibling relationships, but sometimes siblings who have been estranged realize that the parent who provided a link between them is no longer there, and they try to mend the rift themselves. People may also be moved to reconcile with an adult child.

Changes in attitudes toward time and death: A parent's death is inevitably a reminder of one's own mortality. It removes a "buffer" against death, leaving the child feeling older and unprotected. Many people, especially those whose parents died young, consider the parents' age at death significant for their own life span. Thus Arthur threw a large party for his fiftieth birthday, celebrating the fact that he had lived beyond his father's age. Other people are inspired to think about what they will do with their "bonus"—the extra years they have left to live.

The bond between parent and child, powerful in life, persists after death, becoming an "indelible legacy for later generations" (M. S. Moss & Moss, 1989, p. 110). This legacy can be unhappy if the parent's own life was unfulfilled. But adults who did not receive the kind of nurturing and guidance they would have liked from their own parents can often break the cycle and pass on more valuable gifts to their children.

source: M. S. and S. Z. Moss, 1989.

SUMMARY

MIDLIFE: THE NORMATIVE-CRISIS APPROACH

■ The "midlife crisis" is a stressful period during the early to middle forties that is triggered by a review and reevaluation of one's life. Research suggests that entering middle age does not necessarily result in a crisis; for many people this is just one of life's many transitions, and they adjust easily.

■ Some personality traits remain stable in adulthood, but growth and change do occur. Middle-aged people tend to become more introspective, and both sexes tend to take on characteristics associated with the other sex.

■ Carl Jung believed that people at midlife, freed from much of the obligation of child rearing, express personality characteristics that had previously been suppressed. Women become more assertive and men more emotionally expressive.

■ Erikson's seventh psychosocial crisis, occurring during middle age, is generativity versus stagnation. The generative person is concerned with establishing and guiding the next generation. A person who fails to develop generativity suffers from stagnation, self-indulgence, and perhaps physical and psychological invalidism.

■ Expanding on Erikson's concepts, Peck specified four psychological developments critical to successful adjustment during middle age: valuing wisdom versus valuing physical powers, socializing versus sexualizing, emotional flexibility versus emotional impoverishment, and mental flexibility versus mental rigidity.

■ The Grant Study of Harvard men (reported by Vaillant) and Levinson's study of 40 males suggest that the early forties are a potentially stressful time of transition. Some people experience a "crisis," although midlife does not necessarily involve this.

■ Normative-crisis research on middle-aged women suggests that women, too, go through midlife changes, but their subsequent lives are less settled than those of men. The early forties seem to be a particularly stressful time for women; the fifties appear to be a "prime time" of life.

■ Mastery and pleasure are important elements of well-being for middle-aged women. Both challenging, well-paid work and family commitments contribute to women's psychological health.

■ Because the Grant Study and Levinson's research focused mainly on privileged white men born in the 1920s or 1930s, their results may not be applicable to women, nonwhite people, and members of other cohorts and other cultures.

PERSONAL RELATIONSHIPS AND TIMING OF EVENTS IN MIDLIFE

■ The timing-of-events model suggests that development depends on the occurrence and timing of important events, which are often changes that take place in relationships.

■ Research on the quality of marriage in middle age suggests a dip in marital satisfaction during the years of child rearing, followed by an improved relationship after the children leave home.

■ The most important factors in marital longevity seem to be positive feelings about the spouse, a commitment to long-term marriage, and shared goals.

■ Bonds with siblings often become closer during middle age.

■ Middle-aged people tend to invest less time and energy in developing friendships than younger adults do, since their energies are devoted to family, work, and building up security for retirement.

■ Parents of adolescents need to come to terms with who their children are and with a loss of control over their children's lives.

■ The postparental years—when children have left—are often among the happiest. The "emptying of the nest" may be stressful, however, for fathers who have not been involved with child rearing, for parents whose children have not become independent when expected, and for mothers who have failed to prepare for the event.

■ Today, more young adults are living with their parents, often for economic reasons. Conflict between the two generations can put strains on the parents' marriage.

■ Middle-aged parents tend to remain involved with their young adult children and continue giving them more than they get from them.

■ Relationships between middle-aged adults and their parents are usually characterized by a strong bond of affection. Although older parents typically do not live with their adult children, they generally maintain frequent contact and offer and receive assistance.

■ Middle-aged people, especially daughters, may have to become caregivers to ailing, aging parents. This can be a source of considerable stress. Support programs can help relieve the strain of caregiving.

■ Reactions to parents' death are often profound and difficult. Death of a parent can precipitate changes in the self, in relationships with others, and in the personal meaning of time and of death.

KEY TERMS

midlife crisis (page 500)
generativity versus stagnation (503)
valuing wisdom versus valuing
  physical powers (503)

socializing versus sexualizing in
  human relationships (503)
emotional flexibility versus emotional impoverishment (503)

mental flexibility versus mental
  rigidity (503)
interiority (504)
"empty nest" (515)

SUGGESTED READINGS

Edinberg, M. A. (1987). *Talking with your aging parents.* Boston: Shambhala. The author, a clinical psychologist and director of the Center for the Study of Aging at the University of Bridgeport in Connecticut, suggests strategies for communicating with elderly parents about their special needs (for institutional care, extra help, and so on). The author also discusses how middle-aged children can cope with their own feelings of guilt regarding the burdens of family obligations.

Estés, C. P. (1992). *Women who run with the wolves: Myths and stories of the wild woman archetype.* New York: Ballantine. The author, a specialist in cross-cultural mythology who was trained as a Jungian analyst, draws on her Latino and Hungarian heritage, as well as the ancient and ethnic stories from other cultures. She analyzes and interprets these tales in terms of their relevance to women's psychology, especially regarding the importance of creativity in women's lives.

Gerson, K. (1993). *No man's land: Men's changing commitments to family and work.* New York: Basic Books. With the decline of the male breadwinner, deeply held beliefs about manhood and masculinity are being called into question. Here, in a series of life-history interviews, men discuss how their commitments are changing. Ideas are also offered for how we as individuals and a society can encourage progressive changes.

Heath, D. H. with Heath, H. E. (1991). *Fulfilling lives: Paths to maturity and success.* San Francisco: Jossey-Bass. Using vivid illustrations from the results of a longitudinal study, the author explores how adults find fulfillment in their lives.

Heilbrun, C. G. (1988). *Writing a woman's life.* New York: Norton. This provocative book by a feminist scholar and professor blends feminist theory with biographical information about a number of independent, achieving women to provide positive role models for a wide range of life experiences. The author maintains that traditional male-oriented ways of looking at women's lives have underestimated their possibilities.

Klagsbrun, F. (1985). *Married people: Staying together in the age of divorce.* New York: Bantam. A well-researched, sensitively written book that draws on published research, interviews with happily married couples, and the author's exploration of her own long-term marriage to examine such topics as the transition from passionate to companionate love, competition between spouses, the influence of family (including children) and friends on a couple's relationship, and sexuality.

Schreiber, L. A. (1990). *Midstream: The story of a mother's death and a daughter's renewal.* New York: Penguin. A lovingly observed memoir by a 40-year-old journalist of her mother's illness and death. The book chronicles this difficult experience with hope, humor, and anger.

PART SEVEN

LATE ADULTHOOD

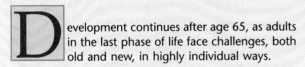

evelopment continues after age 65, as adults in the last phase of life face challenges, both old and new, in highly individual ways.

■ In **Chapter 16,** we look at some myths about aging, and at theories explaining the aging process. Most older people are in fairly good physical health, despite the changes that take place with age, and most are mentally sound as well. Some older persons do, of course, suffer physical or mental problems (or both), and we describe these problems, along with ways of preventing and treating them. We also examine the controversy over intellectual functioning in late life and conclude that although some abilities may diminish with age, there is a great deal of evidence that older people who

remain intellectually active retain their abilities and even increase their mental capacities in some ways.

■ In **Chapter 17,** we look at different patterns of aging, and we explore important relationships in late adulthood—with spouses, children, grandchildren, and siblings. We look at the ways people adjust to the loss of a spouse and at the role of sexuality in late life. We examine how older people live, either in the community or, for a small minority, in nursing homes. It becomes clearer than ever that although there are certain common patterns in the human experience, each person is an individual, and that people's individuality becomes more pronounced in the later years of life.

CHAPTER SIXTEEN

PHYSICAL AND INTELLECTUAL DEVELOPMENT IN LATE ADULTHOOD

Why not look at these new years of life in terms of continued or new roles in society, another stage in personal or even spiritual growth and development?

Betty Friedan,
The Fountain of Age, *1993*

■ **OLD AGE TODAY**

What Is Our Attitude toward Old Age?
Who Are the Elderly?
How Can We Make the Most of the Later
 Years?

PHYSICAL DEVELOPMENT

■ **LONGEVITY AND THE AGING PROCESS**

Life Expectancy
Why People Age: Two Theories

■ **PHYSICAL CHANGES OF OLD AGE**

Sensory and Psychomotor Functioning
The Brain in Late Adulthood
Other Physical Changes
Reserve Capacity

■ **HEALTH IN OLD AGE**

Health Care and Health Problems
Influences on Health and Fitness
Mental and Behavioral Disorders

INTELLECTUAL DEVELOPMENT

■ **ASPECTS OF INTELLECTUAL DEVELOPMENT**

Does Intelligence Decline in Late Adulthood?
How Does Memory Change in Late
 Adulthood?

■ **LIFELONG LEARNING: ADULT EDUCATION IN LATE LIFE**

■ **WORK AND RETIREMENT**

Why People Retire
How People Feel about Retirement
Making the Most of Retirement

■ **BOXES**

16-1 Window on the World: Aging in Asia
16-2 Practically Speaking: You and the Older
People in Your Life
16-3 Food for Thought: Wisdom in Late
Adulthood

ASK YOURSELF

- When does late adulthood begin, and what physical changes does it bring?
- What causes aging?
- What influences the health of older people?
- What are some reversible and irreversible mental and behavioral disorders?

- What factors affect intellectual functioning in late adulthood, and how can intellectual performance be improved?
- How can people make the most of retirement?

In Japan, the average person lives longer than anywhere else in the world, and old age is a mark of status. There—in contrast to most western countries, where it is considered rude to ask a person's age—travelers checking into hotels are often asked their age to ensure that they will receive the proper deference. At a man's sixtieth birthday celebration he wears a red vest symbolizing a rebirth into an advanced phase of life (Kimmel, 1988). Despite this respect for the old, however, a growing elderly population has brought challenges to Japan, as well as to other parts of Asia, as described in Box 16-1.

OLD AGE TODAY

In this chapter, we look at various aspects of late adulthood, including advances in longevity and how these result in greater numbers of older people in our society. We examine physical changes in old age and their implications for the health of elderly people. We also explore intellectual functioning in these years—how that affects and is affected by education, work, and other forms of mental stimulation. Finally, we discuss the issue of retirement. In Chapter 17, we emphasize the impact of such issues on social and emotional well-being.

WHAT IS OUR ATTITUDE TOWARD OLD AGE?

In our culture, aging is seen as negative. Many people even consider the word *old* taboo in polite society, and people of advanced years are now being called *senior citizens, golden-agers, elderly persons, older Americans,* or persons in the *harvest years* or *twilight years.* The newest—and perhaps most creative—euphemism is *chronologically gifted!*

Why do such terms seem desirable? For one thing, although everybody wants to live long, few want to be described as old. Then, those who use these terms want to counter *ageism:* prejudice or discrimination based on age, usually against older persons. Too often in our society, the word *old* connotes feebleness, incompetence, and narrow-mindedness. According to an analysis of 43 studies, older people are judged more negatively than younger ones on all characteristics studied, especially on competence and attractiveness (Kite & Johnson, 1988).

Interestingly, although television still presents stereotypes of older people, the stereotypes have changed from "comical, stubborn, eccentric, and foolish" to "powerful, affluent, healthy, active, admired, and sexy" (J. Bell, 1992, p. 305). Thus the great diversity of the elderly is still not acknowledged realistically. Furthermore, older women are still shown rarely—and when they are shown, they are likely to be subordinate to men. In real life, a growing number of women are investing the negative term *crone* with a new meaning emphasizing positive rebirth in old age (LeGuin, 1989).

WHO ARE THE ELDERLY?

Older people are an extremely diverse lot, with individual strengths and weaknesses. And late adulthood is a normal period of the life span, with its own special nature, developmental tasks, and opportunities for psychological growth.

"Young Old" and "Old Old"

According to social scientists who specialize in *gerontology,* the study of the aged and the aging process, many 70-year-olds today act and think as 50-year-olds did 10 or 20 years ago (Herz, in J. C. Horn & Meer, 1987). Today's elderly people can be described in two ways. The *young old,* the majority of older people, are those who—regardless of their actual age—are vital, vigorous, and active. The *old old* constitute the frail, infirm minority (Neugarten & Neugarten, 1987). Many problems of the "old old" are due not to aging itself, but to

BOX 16-1 WINDOW ON THE WORLD

AGING IN ASIA[1]

Asians often ask why American families put their parents into institutions and why a country as rich as the United States does not do more for its elderly people. But in recent years Asia has encountered some of the same problems as western nations in helping a growing population of older citizens.

Over the past 40 years or so, Asia has been the most successful region of the world in reducing fertility. Meanwhile, higher standards of living, better sanitary conditions, and immunization programs have extended the lives of older people. As a result, Asian nations now have a larger proportion of elderly citizens. It is projected that by 2025, the elderly in China, Hong Kong, Singapore, and Sri Lanka will constitute over 10 percent of the population; in Japan, the elderly will constitute over 20 percent.

At the same time, family structure has been changed by social trends: urbanization, migration, and an increase in women in the work force. Caring for the elderly at home has become less feasible, and governments and private agencies need to develop new policies.

It is hard to generalize about Asian countries, since they range from a highly developed, wealthy nation like Japan (which has the highest life expectancy in the world—at birth, 81.9 for women and 75.8 for men—U.S. Bureau of the Census, 1992c) to a very poor nation like Nepal (which has one of the world's lowest life expectancies—52.1 for women and 54.9 for men—Central Bureau of Statistics, 1992). Still, a common link among Asian nations has been a great respect for the aged, along with an expectation that when old people can no longer care for themselves, their families will care for them. But today, while both these patterns are still more preva-

Elderly Chinese people, like this woman, used to take for granted their place in their children's households. But today, although most elderly Asians still live with their children, they are less likely to want to do so than people were in the past, and their children are less prone to urge them to. China is one of several Asian countries that have passed laws obliging people to care for elderly relatives. *(Eastcott/Momatiuk/ Woodfin Camp & Associates)*

lent than in the west, they are eroding.

Although about three-quarters of elderly Asians live with their children, they are less likely to want to do so than older people were in the past, and their children are less prone to urge them to. Elderly Asians who are married, younger, live in rural areas, hold modern attitudes, and have highly educated children are more likely to have power in family decision making (Hong & Keith, 1992). However, in Japan older people living in three-generation households are more likely to commit suicide than elderly people living alone. And in Korea a survey found that only 7 percent of Koreans thought their children would care for them in their old age; 64 percent expected to care for themselves.

Some governments are trying to halt this erosion through legislation. China, Japan, and Singapore have all passed laws obliging people to care for elderly relatives, and Japan and Singapore provide tax relief to people who give their older relatives financial help. In Japan, also, lotteries for tenancy in public housing are set up so that

households with a member aged 60 or older have a 10 times greater chance of winning.

Institutionalization is seen as a last resort, to be used only for those elders who are destitute or without families. All the Asian countries have a lower percentage of people living in homes for the aged than the United States (where the rate is 5 percent): Japan, 1.5 percent; Singapore, 2.5 percent; Hong Kong, 1 percent; and China, 0.33 percent. Partly, this is simply because few such homes exist; social services administrators feel that more are needed.

A major controversy in Asia, as in the west, is whether housing priority, health care and other social services, and financial aid should be offered to people on the basis of age or of need. What will giving preference to the elderly mean for young families with small children? Will young families suffer? An aging population could place an unbearable burden on younger generations, with young workers being taxed heavily for pension funds. Or governments may have to cut back services for the young in order to fund services for the old.

Right now, in most Asian countries, either there is little in the way of social welfare for any age group or what there is favors the young. But the growth of senior citizens' clubs in Japan, Korea, Indonesia, the Philippines, Singapore, and Thailand will probably strengthen the political clout of the elderly, diverting more official funds their way. One result of the growing "gray power" has been the establishment of Respect for the Aged Day (September 15) in Japan and National Aging Day (April 13) in Thailand.

Most Asians can agree on goals—to help elderly people remain independent and productive as long as possible and, when they do need assistance, to help their families care for them. But reaching these goals is a difficult challenge.

[1]Unless otherwise noted, material in this box is from Martin, 1988.

lifestyle factors or diseases that may or may not accompany getting older.

It is becoming harder to draw the line between the end of middle adulthood and the beginning of late adulthood. If, as the saying goes, "you're as old as you feel," how would we classify Sally's father-in-law, who at the age of 84 was still working as an engineer and talking about putting money aside for his "twilight years"? Middle-aged and older people generally feel younger than the calendar would suggest (in contrast to teenagers, who feel older than they really are; or to young adults, who feel their own age—Montepare & Lachman, 1989).

The Graying of the Population

Not only is the older generation becoming "younger"; it is also becoming larger. By the year 2000, Americans aged 65 and over are expected to constitute 13 percent of the population, compared with almost 7 percent in 1940 (U.S. Bureau of the Census, 1992a). By 2030, the proportion will have risen to almost 22 percent (see Figure 16-1).

The ethnic diversity of the elderly is increasing: about 1 in 10 older persons is nonwhite, a proportion expected to double in the next 60 years (U.S. Bureau of the Census, 1992a). These aging members of minority groups are often reaping the bitter fruits of histories of poorly paid work and inadequate health care throughout life.

The "graying" of the population has several causes: the high birthrates of the late 1800s and the early to mid-1900s, the high immigration rates of the twentieth century, and a longer life expectancy due to medical advances. As the "baby boom" generation (people born in the late 1940s and the 1950s) ages, the proportion of older Americans will peak about a third of the way into the twenty-first century, after which it will drop again.

The Oldest Old

Since the number of healthy, vigorous people over age 65 is growing rapidly, we may soon begin to talk of old age as starting at 85. This age group, called the *oldest old,* is the fastest-growing segment of the United States population. In 1990, people 85 and over numbered 3 million, an increase of 232 percent between 1960 and 1990. (The total population increased by only 39 percent during these years.) By the middle of the twenty-first century, the oldest old could be nearly one-fourth of the elderly population (U.S. Bureau of the Census, 1992a).

Who are the oldest old? Where and how do they live? How is their health? What do they like to do? Some of the answers, based on 1980 and 1990 census data, are predictable; others unexpected.

Gender Differences

Because of men's lower life expectancy, there are only 38.6 men for every 100 women aged 85 and over in the United States today (U.S. Bureau of the Census, 1992a). Older women are three times more likely than men to be poor; the major reason for their impoverishment is the death of a husband. When wives die, their widowers tend to remarry quickly, an option rarely available to older women because there are fewer elderly men and the ones who are around tend to marry younger women.

Older women are also much more likely than

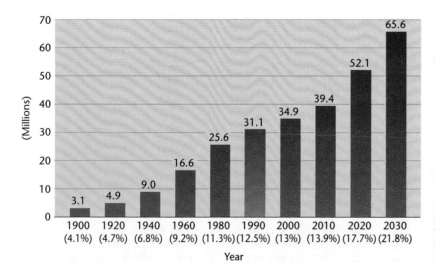

FIGURE 16-1
Population of the United States aged 65 and over, 1900–2030 (projected). Since the beginning of this century, the number of people aged 65 and over has continued to increase, both absolutely and relative to the rest of the population. This trend is expected to continue through the aging of the "baby boom" generation. (*Note:* Increments in years on the horizontal scale are uneven. Percentages at bottom of figure refer to percentage of the population aged 65 and over.) (*Source:* U.S. Bureau of the Census, 1992b.)

older men to live alone and to need help with such necessities of daily living as eating, dressing, bathing, preparing meals, managing money, and getting outside. The health problems of older women are likely to be long-term, chronic, disabling conditions, while men tend to develop fairly short-term fatal diseases. Because they often held fewer and lower-paid jobs, today's elderly women are less likely than men to have access to pension and Social Security benefits in their own names.

However, since women are now in the work force in much larger numbers than in previous years and tend to be younger than their husbands, many more will continue working after their husbands retire. This change should improve their financial situations and may also have as yet unknown implications for husband-wife relationships in later life.

Many of the currently old-old never went beyond eighth grade; future cohorts will have averaged more years of education than today's oldest old. This bodes well for the future, since better educated people tend to stay healthier longer and to be better off economically.

Health
A surprisingly large number of these oldest citizens need little medical care, but many do have health problems. At least one-fourth of those in selected studies were hospitalized in the previous year. Almost 10 percent are disabled and isolated—unable to use public transportation (Longino, 1987, 1988). Costs of health care for the oldest old are expected to soar; by 2040 Medicare costs may increase sixfold (Schneider & Guralnik, 1990). Successful cost containment will depend on the ability to prevent or cure disorders of old age that entail the greatest need for long-term care.

Life Circumstances
Most people over 85 live in their own homes, and 30 percent live alone. Fewer than one-fourth are in nursing homes, hospitals, or other institutions. Their average household income topped $20,000 in 1985; only 1 in 6 is poor. Future generations will be both better educated and more affluent (Longino, 1988).

Most of these people spend time with other people. More than half of an Iowa sample belong to professional, social, recreational, or religious groups and go to religious services at least once a week. More than 3 out of 4 see their children or other close relatives once a month (Longino, 1988).

Even at the last stage of life, then, it is misleading to generalize about people. What emerges is a picture not of "the elderly" but of individual human beings—some needy and frail, but most independent, healthy, and involved.

HOW CAN WE MAKE THE MOST OF THE LATER YEARS?

As the vigorous older population becomes more influential at the polls and in the marketplace, we are likely to see changes in government programs, housing, new products, and media attention. Research in both gerontology and *geriatrics,* the branch of medicine concerned with aging, has brought out the need for support services for the frail elderly, many of whom have outlived their savings and cannot pay for their own care.

But first we need to combat misconceptions about aging. These include the false beliefs that most old people are poorly coordinated, usually tired, and easily fall prey to infections; that they have many accidents and spend most of their time in bed; that they live in institutions; that they can neither remember nor learn; that they have no interest in sexual relationships; that they are isolated from others and depend on television or radio; that they do not use their time productively; and that they are grouchy, self-pitying, touchy, and cranky.

Such ageist myths hurt older people by emphasizing their problems rather than their strengths. A physician who does not bring up sexual issues with a 75-year-old heart patient denies the patient a source of fulfillment. An overprotective adult child encourages an aging parent to become dependent. A social worker who expects depression in old age in effect abandons an elderly client. Such attitudes affect how older people live and how they feel about themselves.

Even the positive stereotypes about old age, which picture it as a time of tranquility—a "golden age" of peace and relaxation when people harvest the fruits of their lifelong labors, or a carefree second childhood, spent idly on the golf course or at the card table, are not helpful, since they too ignore the diversity of older people and the opportunities of this time of life.

Learning about late adulthood can prepare you for what to expect when you get there and can suggest what you can do now to ensure that your stay there will be as pleasant as possible. Knowing what the aging process is like can also help you get along with, and enrich the lives of, the older people in your life (see Box 16-2).

BOX 16-2   PRACTICALLY SPEAKING

YOU AND THE OLDER PEOPLE IN YOUR LIFE

In the wealth of recent research on late adulthood, many findings can be applied to daily life. The following suggestions might make the lives of your parents, your grandparents, or other older people you care about happier and more comfortable.

▪ *Enrich yourself through the older person's experience:* Tape-record interviews in which you ask the older person about childhood memories, family members, experiences, and opinions about life. You will enhance your own knowledge and awareness, and the older person will be assured of the value of his or her wisdom and memories.

▪ *Encourage physical activity:* Take part in shared activities that you both enjoy, like walking, bicycling, dancing, or skating. Make such activities a regular weekly event. Find out what resources there are in the community. Good gifts are pool and "Y" memberships and exercise clothes, shoes, equipment, and accessories (like a walking stick).

▪ *Encourage mental activity:* Play

games that require thought, like word games, "twenty questions," and card games. Go to movies and plays together. Read a book together and discuss it. Find out what adult education courses are offered locally. Ask questions about subjects the older person knows about. Good gifts are games, books, and tickets.

▪ *Help with memory:* Present information in more than one way (write it down and give it orally, too). Be patient and reassuring about memory lapses, remembering that younger people forget things, too! Learn and teach some memory tricks. Good gifts are a pocket notebook and pen (for jotting down thoughts and things to do), a calendar (for writing appointments), and a note pad to keep near the phone.

▪ *For persons with hearing problems:* Speak somewhat more loudly than normal, but don't shout. Speak clearly and not too fast. Speak from a distance of 3 to 6 feet, in good light, so that your lip movements and gestures can be used as clues to your words. Don't chew,

eat, or cover your mouth while you're speaking. Turn off the radio and the television while you're talking. If the listener doesn't understand what you have said, rephrase your idea in short, simple sentences.

▪ *For persons with vision problems:* Install bright lighting at the top of staircases (most falls occur on the step at the top of the landing). Analyze lighting in work and reading areas to see that it is directed for greatest efficiency. Keep floor areas clutter-free, don't rearrange furniture, and get rid of "scatter rugs," which can easily be tripped over. Help get rid of unnecessary items in cupboards and bookshelves, and highlight often-used items with bright-colored markers. Good gifts include sunglasses (to be worn outside, so that less of an adjustment needs to be made upon coming indoors), a pocket or purse flashlight (for reading menus, concert programs, and the like), a magnifying glass to put in a pocket or hang on a chain, large-type reading matter, and a tape recorder and cassettes.

▪ PHYSICAL DEVELOPMENT

The onset of *senescence*—the period of the life span marked by changes in physical functioning associated with aging—varies greatly. One 80-year-old man can hear every word of a whispered conversation; another cannot hear the doorbell. One 70-year-old woman runs marathons; another cannot walk around the block.

The lengthening of life has focused attention on questions about aging. Why, for example, does senescence come earlier for some people than for others? In this section, we'll discuss life ex-

pectancy, and then we'll consider theories of why aging occurs. Then, we'll examine some physical changes often associated with aging and discuss what people can do to make the most of the abilities they have.

LONGEVITY AND THE AGING PROCESS

Eos, a mythological goddess, asked Zeus to allow Tithonus, the mortal she loved, to live forever. Zeus granted Tithonus immortality, and the lovers lived happily—for a while. Tithonus lived to a great age, until he became so infirm that he could not move. Yet he was denied the gift of death. To this day he lives on, where Eos finally put him away. Eos had made a grievous error; she had forgotten to ask Zeus to grant eternal youth along with eternal life.

In recognition of the tragedy of life extended so long that it is overburdened with infirmities, the motto of the Gerontological Society is: "To add life to years, not just years to life." The goal of research is not just to lengthen life but also to lengthen the vigorous and productive years.

LIFE EXPECTANCY

Trends in Life Expectancy

Today, most people can expect to grow old. A large elderly population is, however, something relatively recent. In 1900, babies born in the United States had an average *life expectancy* (the number of years a person is expected to live, based on statistical data) of about 47 years—in part because many died in infancy. By 1991, provisional statistics showed a life expectancy of 75.7 years—a 60 percent increase since 1900 (Wegman, 1992). In 1900, 1 in 5 white children and 1 in 3 children of other races died before age 5; and only 41 percent of newborns would survive to age 65, compared with 80 percent of 1990 newborns who are expected to live to this age (U.S. Bureau of the Census, 1992c). According to 1990 census data, an estimated 36,000 people are now over the age of 100 (U.S. Bureau of the Census, 1992a), and life expectancy is expected to continue rising.

These gains result from two major avenues of medical progress—the dramatic decline in infant and child mortality during the first half of this century, and the development of new treatments for many once-fatal illnesses.

Until recently, many gerontologists maintained that 110 years was about the upper limit of human longevity and that the average 80-year-old of today could expect to live only slightly longer than the 80-year-olds of the past. In this view, the aging human body is biologically programmed to fall apart, failing in response to one problem or another—a fall, the flu, or even hot weather.

But recent research on death rates of people in Sweden and Denmark, of rats, and of fruit flies seems to refute the idea of a preset life expectancy for every species (Barinaga, 1991a, 1991b). Preliminary results from a study of mortality in 1 million

Mediterranean fruit flies indicate that the probability of dying increases for the first third of the flies' life span and then seems to level off, so that at older ages life expectancy actually increases (Carey, Liedo, Orozco, & Vaupel, 1992; Curtsinger, Fukui, Townsend, & Vaupel, 1992).

Then, research on rats suggests a relationship between diet and life expectancy. Rats whose diets were changed to contain fewer calories have aged more slowly and lived longer (Masoro, 1988, 1992). Restricting calories in rats seems to change the use of glucose as a fuel in a way that offsets the long-term harmful effects of its use over many years. Findings like these, which cast doubt on the idea that other species have absolute life-span limits, may have implications for human beings.

There is evidence for the potential lengthening of the normal human life span. Death rates in Sweden have dropped dramatically in the last 50 years for people over 85. And computer studies of death patterns among Danish twins and among genetically identical strains of fruit flies suggest that most deaths result from accidents or disease rather than "old age" (Barinaga, 1991a, 1991b, 1992). Furthermore, better educated people tend to stay healthier longer, and future cohorts of the oldest old will have averaged more years of education than today's over-85s (U.S. Bureau of the Census, 1992a).

This does not mean, of course, that people will ever live forever, or even high into the hundreds. It does mean, though, that many deaths—even in the oldest old—are preventable and that life expectancy may well continue to rise, possibly to about 100 years of age.

Death Rates and Causes of Death

The dramatic increase in average life expectancy since the turn of the century reflects a sharp decline in *death rates* in the United States (the proportions of people of specific ages who die in a given year). Along with these declines have come changes in the leading causes of death. There have been fewer deaths from childbirth and infectious disease and more deaths from age-related conditions.

Heart disease remains by far the leading killer of people over 65, accounting for 40 percent of deaths. Other major causes of death in this age group are cancer (21 percent) and stroke (8 percent), followed by lung disease, pneumonia, influenza, diabetes, accidents, hardening of the arteries, kidney disease, and the bacterial infection, septicemia (USDHHS, 1991). Deaths from heart disease and stroke have declined over the past three decades, but cancer—especially lung cancer—has increased (USDHHS, 1991).

If cancer were eliminated as a cause of death, the average life span would be increased by less than 2 years, but if we could eliminate deaths due to heart disease, we would add 5 years to life expectancy at age 65, thus sharply increasing the proportion of the population 65 and older (USDHHS, 1991).

Race, Gender, and Life Expectancy

On average, white Americans live longer than nonwhite Americans, and women live longer than men (see Table 16-1). But nonwhite women live longer than white men.

Racial Differences

In the United States, life expectancy is about 4 years longer for white people than for black people. Only among black men is death more common *before* age 65 than afterward (U.S. Bureau of the Census, 1992c). Among those 85 and older, death rates are lowest for black women and highest for white men. Death rates show other racial and ethnic differences. For example, elderly black Americans have the highest rates of deaths from heart disease, followed by whites and Hispanics; Asians and Pacific Islanders have the lowest rates (USDHHS, 1991).

Gender Differences

The vulnerability of males continues throughout life, with major implications for older people. In 1900, there was only a 2-year difference in life expectancy between the sexes; but since World War II, longevity has increased twice as much for women as for men (Svanborg, 1985), so that the difference for babies born in 1991 was 7 years

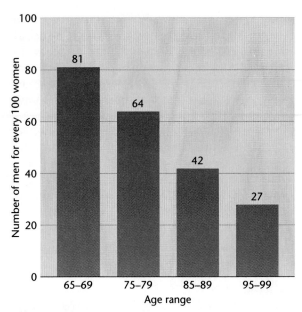

FIGURE 16-2
As the population ages, the proportion of women in the population increases. This has many ramifications, one of which is that elderly women are more likely than elderly men to be living alone and to need help from families and society. (*Source:* U.S. Bureau of the Census, 1992b.)

(Wegman, 1992). Elderly women now outnumber elderly men, 3 to 2 (see Figure 16-2).

What accounts for this greater longevity of women? Since the sex difference in life expectancy continues to increase in later life, and especially after age 65, some observers point to differences in lifestyles. For example, on the surface it might seem that women are sicker, since they report more illness, go to doctors more often, and stay in bed more often than men. But they may be more sensitive to changes in their bodies, leading them to report symptoms of illness earlier than men do, in time for them to be treated.

Another possible explanation is the greater level of social support enjoyed by older women. They are closer than men are to their siblings, they are more likely to have close friends they can confide in, and they derive more support from religious affiliation. Because social support has been linked to longer life (see Chapter 17), this may provide clues to women's longevity.

In any case, as one gerontologist stated, these older women "are the first great group of human beings in history to live such long lives in such large numbers. These are biological pioneers" (M. Lewis, 1983). Study of these women may yield valuable lessons in survival for both sexes.

TABLE 16-1

Life Expectancy at Birth in Years, by Sex and Race, 1991, in the United States			
	All Races	**White**	**Black**
Both sexes	75.7	76.4	72.2
Males	72.2	73	68.1
Females	79.1	79.7	76.2

SOURCE: Wegman, 1992 (provisional statistics).

Still, while some women consider old age the best time of life (Hurwich, 1982), others find these years a burden to bear rather than a bonus to enjoy. Older women are more likely than men to be widowed, to remain unmarried, and to have more years of poor health (U.S. Bureau of the Census, 1992c). Elderly women are more likely to suffer long-term disabling chronic diseases, whereas men are more apt to develop relatively short-term fatal ones (U.S. Bureau of the Census, 1992c).

For quality of life, men have the advantage. They tend to keep their health longer, have higher personal income, are more likely to be married, and have more years of active life and independence (S. Katz et al., 1983; Longino, 1987). Our male-dominated society might handle the problems of aging differently if more men were facing typical late-life problems.

WHY PEOPLE AGE: TWO THEORIES

Aging is a complex process influenced by heredity, nutrition, health, and environmental factors, and we do not know exactly why people's bodies function less efficiently as they grow old. None of the many theories of biological aging is universally accepted, but most of them take one of two basic approaches—"programmed" aging or aging as "wear and tear."

Programmed Aging

The *programmed-aging theory* maintains that in each species, the body ages according to a normal developmental pattern built into every organism; this program is subject to only minor modifications. Since each species has its own life expectancy and its own pattern of senescence, this pattern must be predetermined and inborn.

Leonard Hayflick (1974), who studied cells of many different animals, found a limit on the number of times normal cells will divide—about 50 times for human cells. This limit controls the life span, which he holds as about 110 years for humans. He suggests that people may have genes that become harmful later in life, causing deterioration. One area of deterioration may be the immune system, which seems to become "confused" in old age, so that it may attack the body itself.

Recent research transferred human chromosome 1 to hamsters and saw typical signs of aging, providing support for a cellular basis (Sugawara, Oshimura, Koi, Annab, & Barrett, 1990). Other re-

search reversed some effects of aging by administering human growth hormone to 21 men aged 61 to 81, suggesting that a decline with age in this hormone may cause fat to collect, muscles to wither, and organs to atrophy (Rudman et al., 1990).

Aging as Wear and Tear

The *wear-and-tear theory* holds that the body ages because of continuous use—that deterioration is the result of accumulated "insults." In this theory, the human body is comparable to a machine whose parts eventually wear out. For example, the cells of the heart and brain do not replace themselves, even early in life; when damaged, they die. The same thing seems to happen to other cells later in life: as they grow older, they are less able to repair or replace damaged components. Wear-and-tear theory suggests that internal and external stressors (including the accumulation of harmful materials, like chemical by-products of metabolism) aggravate the wearing-down process.

One line of research supporting "wear-and-tear" focuses on the harmful effects of *free radicals* (Stadtman, 1992; Wallace, 1992). These are specific forms of oxygen that are produced in the normal course of living, but which then become highly dangerous, altering—and damaging—such substances in the body as DNA, proteins, and fats. This effect on cellular functioning has been associated with the diseases of arthritis, muscular dystrophy, cataracts, and cancer (Stadtman, 1992). And there is some speculation that defective molecules in late life (possibly as the result of free-radical injury) may cause late-onset diabetes and Parkinson's and Alzheimer's diseases (Wallace, 1992). Thus, aging may result from such accumulations of irreversible destruction.

A recent study provides dramatic support for the free radical theory (Orr & Sohal, 1994). When fruit flies were given extra copies of the genes used to eliminate free radicals from cells, their life spans were extended by as much as one-third.

The difference between these two approaches is more than theoretical. If people are programmed to age, they can do little to retard the process; but if they age because of "insults" to the body, they may be able to live longer by eliminating stressors. The truth probably lies in a combination of the approaches: genetic programming may limit the absolute length of life, but wear and tear may affect how closely a person approaches the limit.

Along the same lines, some gerontologists distinguish between *primary aging,* a gradual, inevitable process of bodily deterioration that begins early in life and continues through the years; and *secondary aging,* the result of disease, abuse, and disuse—factors that are often avoidable and to some extent under people's control (Busse, 1987; J. C. Horn & Meer, 1987). Older people may not be able to stop their reflexes from slowing down or their hearing from becoming less acute; but by, for example, eating sensibly and keeping physically fit, many can and do stave off the secondary effects of aging.

PHYSICAL CHANGES OF OLD AGE

SENSORY AND PSYCHOMOTOR FUNCTIONING

After Sally's husband, Mark, retired from full-time work at age 62, he was able to devote more time to playing tennis. As a result, by the age of 72, he is playing longer, better, and more often than he ever has in his life. Yes, he feels arthritic twinges in his knee from time to time, but they do not stop him from any of his regular games—where he often plays with men 30 years his junior.

Mark's story is fairly typical of the middle- and upper-income "young old" in our society. There is a great deal of individual variation in the sensory and psychomotor abilities of older people, with many experiencing sharp declines and others finding their daily lives virtually unchanged. Among the "old old," impairments are likely to be more severe. Losses in vision or hearing have strong psychological consequences, as they deprive people of activities, social life, and independence.

Vision

Farsightedness (difficulty seeing things up close) usually stabilizes at about age 60, and with the help of glasses or contact lenses, most older people can see fairly well. After 65, however, serious visual problems that affect daily life are common. Many older adults have 20/70 vision or worse, have trouble perceiving depth or color, and experience problems doing a variety of activities dependent on vision. Some have trouble reading, doing close work, and shopping for and cooking food. Losses with age in visual contrast sensitivity

cause difficulty reading either very small or very large print (Akutsu, Legge, Ross, & Schuebel, 1991).

Driving is most seriously affected (especially at night), because older eyes cannot adapt as well to dim light, are more sensitive to glare, and create problems locating and reading signs. Most visual problems stem from deficits in five areas: near vision, light sensitivity, dynamic vision (reading moving signs), speed in processing what is seen, and visual search (locating a sign) (Kosnik, Winslow, Kline, Rasinski, & Sekuler, 1988; D. W. Kline et al., 1992). Besides curtailing daily activities, vision problems cause accidents in the home and outside it (Branch, Horowitz, & Carr, 1989).

Moderate vision problems can often be helped by corrective lenses, medical or surgical treatment, or changes in the environment (see Box 16-2). For example, more than half of people over 65 develop *cataracts,* cloudy or opaque areas in the lens of the eye that prevent light from passing through and thus cause blurred vision (USDHHS, 1993). But surgery to remove cataracts is usually very successful and is now the most common operation among Americans over 65. After surgery, patients may use special glasses or contact lenses or they may have plastic lenses implanted during the operation. In many cases, visual aids or other treatments may eliminate the need for surgery (USDHHS, 1993).

At worst, visual disorders can result in blindness. Half of the legally blind people in the United States are over 65, and retinal disorders are the leading cause of blindness among the elderly (National Institute on Aging, NIA, undated a). Glaucoma, another frequent cause of blindness, occurs when fluid pressure builds up, damaging the eye internally. Again, though, this disease can be treated and controlled. Although it seldom has early symptoms, it can be detected through routine vision checkups, and then treated with eye drops, medicine, laser treatments, or surgery.

Hearing

Although 7 out of 10 people between ages 65 and 74 and about half of those between 75 and 79 do *not* suffer from hearing loss, those who are hearing-impaired find that it interferes considerably with daily life (NIA, undated b). A difficulty in hearing high-frequency sounds makes it hard to hear what other people are saying, especially when there is competing noise from radio or television or there is a buzz of several people talking at once.

Hearing aids can compensate for hearing loss to some degree, but very few older people wear

The hearing aid in this man's ear makes it easier for him to understand his young granddaughter's high-pitched speech, but it may also magnify distracting background noise. More than 10 million older Americans have some degree of hearing loss, but only about 1 in 20 wears a hearing aid. Medical treatment, surgery, or special training can also help people with hearing problems. *(Barbara Kirk/The Stock Market)*

them. They can be hard to adjust to, since they magnify background noises as well as the sounds the wearer wants to hear. Furthermore, many people feel that wearing a hearing aid is like wearing a sign saying "I'm getting old."

Medical treatment, special training, and surgery are other ways to deal with hearing impairment. People should have their hearing checked if they find it hard to understand words; complain that other people are "mumbling"; cannot hear a dripping faucet or high notes in music; have a hissing or ringing noise in the ears; or do not enjoy parties, television, or concerts because they miss much of what goes on (NIA, n.d. b).

Taste and Smell

What you taste very often depends on what you can smell. When older people complain that their food does not taste good anymore, it may be because they have fewer taste buds in the tongue and also because the olfactory bulb—the organ in the brain that is responsible for the sense of smell—has withered.

Losses in the senses of smell and taste are considered a normal part of aging. One study of people between the ages of 19 and 95 found that women tended to retain these sensory abilities better than men, and that people taking medicine or being treated for medical problems experienced more loss (Ship & Weiffenbach, 1993). A study of elderly men found that they needed a greater intensity to taste sour, salty, and bitter flavors, but sweetness did not change (Spitzer, 1988). Many older people compensate for these losses by eating spicier and more highly seasoned food, but

some oversalt their food, possibly contributing to high blood pressure, and others eat less and become undernourished.

Strength, Coordination, and Reaction Time

Older people can do most of the same things that younger ones can, although they do these things more slowly (Birren, Woods, & Williams, 1980; Salthouse, 1985). But by and large, they have less strength than they once had and are limited in activities requiring endurance or the ability to carry heavy loads. However, they can benefit from strength training.

One program of high-resistance weight training led to significant gains in muscular strength, size, and functional mobility among 10 nursing home residents in their nineties (Fiatarone et al., 1990). This finding is important because people whose muscles have atrophied and who cannot get around well are more likely to suffer from falls and fractures and to need to depend upon other people for tasks in day-to-day living.

A general slowing down—which affects the quality of responses as well as response time—may result from environmental deprivation and depression, as well as from neurological changes (Butler & Lewis, 1982). But here, too, training can help. For 11 weeks, older people who had never before played videogames used "joy sticks" and "trigger buttons" to play such games as Breakout, Kaboom, and Ms. Pacman. At the end of the study, the videogame players had quicker reaction times than did a sedentary control group (Dustman, Emmerson, Steinhaus, Shearer, & Dustman, 1992).

This demonstrated ability to stimulate the cen-

Older people can do most of the things younger people can do, from reeling in a fish to reshingling a house. But older people take longer to do things because their reflex responses and information processing are slower. *(Cotton Coulson/Woodfin Camp & Associates)*

tral nervous system of elderly people can have many ramifications in preventing some of the problems caused by slowdowns in a number of areas. For example, it takes longer for older people to assess the environment, take in all the pertinent information, and make decisions. Slowed information processing makes older people ask others to repeat information that has been presented too quickly or not clearly enough; makes them do poorly on intelligence tests, especially timed tests; and can interfere with their ability to learn new information and to retrieve information from memory. And slowed reflex responses can result in accidental injuries or *incontinence*—loss of bladder or bowel control (Birren et al., 1980; Salthouse, 1985).

The combination of slower information processing, slower reaction time, and less efficient sensorimotor coordination can also make driving riskier. Drivers over age 65 have a high proportion of accidents, usually because of improper turns, failure to yield the right of way, and failure to obey traffic signs, rather than speeding (Sterns, Barrett, & Alexander, 1985).

Driving is important for older people: it can make the difference between active participation in society and enforced isolation. They can compensate for any loss of ability by driving more slowly and for shorter distances, choosing easier routes, and driving only in daylight (Sterns et al., 1985). In many communities, defensive driving courses and regular retesting of older drivers' vision, coordination, and reaction help to keep older drivers behind the wheel as long as possible. Meanwhile, highway engineers explore ways to make signs easier to read and intersections safer.

Most older people recognize the slowdown in their functioning and are sensibly cautious in their everyday activities. Society, too, needs to recognize this slowdown and the sensory changes that come with age and needs to redesign environments to help older adults manage their lives safely, comfortably, and productively.

THE BRAIN IN LATE ADULTHOOD

The brain of a healthy older person is very similar to that of a healthy younger person. Although the brain does change with age, the changes vary considerably from one person to another (D. A. Selkoe, 1991; D. J. Selkoe, 1992). In older people who do not have Alzheimer's disease or other brain disorders, the extent of anatomic brain change is modest and has little effect. The brains of healthy people in their eighties show almost as much activity as those of people in their twenties.

There is a great deal of controversy about the degree of brain change throughout adulthood. Some scientists have claimed that the older brain weighs less than does the brain of a younger person, because the overall number of nerve cells in it decreases. Others maintain that these claims were made on the basis of a flawed study and that, in fact, the number of brain cells does not decrease to any significant amount after early adulthood (Diamond, 1986; Diamond et al., 1985). If the nerve-cell-loss theory is correct, it could explain how various parts of the brain are affected, especially those areas important to learning, memory, planning, and other intellectual functions.

But not all brain changes are destructive. In fact, dendrites, the part of the neuron that communicates impulses to the cells, grow between middle age and early old age, possibly showing an effort to compensate for the loss of neurons. Although this growth stops in late old age, its presence earlier suggests that even in late adulthood, the brain is plastic and capable of some degree of regeneration (D. J. Selkoe, 1992).

OTHER PHYSICAL CHANGES

Aging also affects temperature and touch. The body adjusts more slowly to cold and becomes chilled more easily than that of a younger person. Exposure to outdoor cold and to poorly heated interiors may lower body temperature—a serious risk for the very old. Older people cannot cope as well with heat, either.

Even the skin at the tip of the fingers becomes less sensitive with age (J. C. Stevens, 1992). For most people, this lessening of spatial acuity of fingertip skin has little impact, but for those already disabled by blindness, it can interfere with the ability to read braille.

People sleep less in their later years; men especially tend to wake up during the night to urinate, and have trouble going back to sleep. Older people sleep more lightly, dream less, and have less deep sleep (Webb, 1987; Woodruff, 1985).

Many of the other changes associated with aging are obvious to even the most casual observer. Older skin tends to become paler and splotchier, taking on a parchment-like texture and losing elasticity. As some fat and muscle disappear, the skin may hang in folds and wrinkles. Varicose veins of the legs are more common. In both men and women, the hair on the head turns white and becomes thinner, and it sprouts in new places—on a woman's chin, out of a man's ears.

People may become shorter as the disks between their spinal vertebrae atrophy, and they may look even smaller because of stooped posture. In a minority of women, the chemical composition of the bones changes, causing a greater chance of fractures. This thinning of the bone may cause a "widow's hump" at the back of the neck (see Box 14-1).

The digestive system remains relatively efficient: the smooth muscles of the internal organs continue to operate well, and the liver and gallbladder hold up well. When obesity is present, however, it affects the circulatory system, the kidneys, and sugar metabolism; it contributes to degenerative disorders and tends to shorten life. All body systems and organs are more susceptible to disease, but the most serious change affects the heart. After age 55, its rhythm becomes slower and more irregular, deposits of fat accumulate around it and interfere with functioning, and blood pressure rises.

RESERVE CAPACITY

The human body has the equivalent of money in the bank for a rainy day. Normally, people do not use their organs and body systems to the limit; but extra capacity is available for extraordinary circumstances. This backup capacity, which lets body systems function in times of stress, is called *reserve capacity* (or *organ reserve*); it allows each organ to put forth 4 to 10 times as much effort as usual. Reserve capacity helps to preserve *homeostasis,* the maintenance of vital functions within their optimum range (Fries & Crapo, 1981).

With age, reserve levels drop. Although the decline is not usually noticeable in everyday life, older people cannot respond to the physical demands of stressful situations as quickly or efficiently as they used to. Someone who used to be able to shovel snow and then go skiing afterward may now exhaust the capacity of the heart just by shoveling. Young people can almost always survive pneumonia; older people often succumb to it. In the hectic traffic of modern roads, people need reserve capacity just to survive as pedestrians; but because older people cannot call upon fast reflexes, vigorous heart action, and rapidly responding muscles to get out of harm's way, they are more likely to be victims of traffic accidents. In general, then, as reserve capacity diminishes, people may become less able to care for themselves and more dependent on others.

HEALTH IN OLD AGE

Despite these physical changes, most elderly people are quite healthy. Three-fourths of noninstitutionalized people 65 to 74 years old, and two-thirds of those 75 and older rate their health as good, very good, or excellent (U.S. Bureau of the Census, 1992c). This is important, because people who rate their health as excellent are less likely to die in the near future than those who rate their health as poor (Wolinsky & Johnson, 1992b).

Affluent elderly people are likely to be healthier than poor ones; rural residents are most likely to have chronic conditions that limit their activity; and elderly white people tend to be healthier than elderly black people. The health status of elderly Hispanic Americans seems to fall between that of African Americans and whites (Markides, Coreil, & Rogers, 1989). These differences, reflecting disparities in lifestyle, preventive care, and access to and affordability of medical care, show the importance of nonbiological factors to health (Petchers & Milligan, 1988; U.S. Bureau of the Census, 1983).

HEALTH CARE AND HEALTH PROBLEMS

Most people over age 65 do not have to limit any major activities for health reasons. Not until age 85 and over do more than half the population report such limitations. And most older people do not need help with such everyday activities as eating, dressing, bathing, toileting, cooking, shopping, or housework. Limitations on what people can do increase with age, however, and they are more common among women, minority groups, and people with low incomes (U.S. Bureau of the Census, 1992c—see Fig. 16-3). The stereotype of the helpless, ill old person is not based on reality—even for the very old.

Medical Conditions

Most elderly people are in good health. However, chronic medical conditions become more frequent with age and may cause disability. Most older people have at least one chronic condition, but when the condition is not severe, it can usually be managed so that it does not interfere with daily life. The most common chronic conditions are arthritis, hypertension, hearing impairment, heart disease, orthopedic impairments, cataracts, and diabetes (AARP, 1992—see Fig. 16-4). Hip fractures are a particular danger for older people, especially older women; a woman over 65 has a 1-in-5 chance of breaking a hip (J. E. Brody, 1992b). But people over 65 have fewer colds, flu infections, and acute digestive problems than younger adults. The danger in old age is that a minor illness or injury—along with chronic conditions and loss of reserve capacity—may have serious repercussions.

Like younger workers, those over 65 miss an average of only 4 or 5 days each year due to illness (USDHHS, 1990). Even though activity is usually

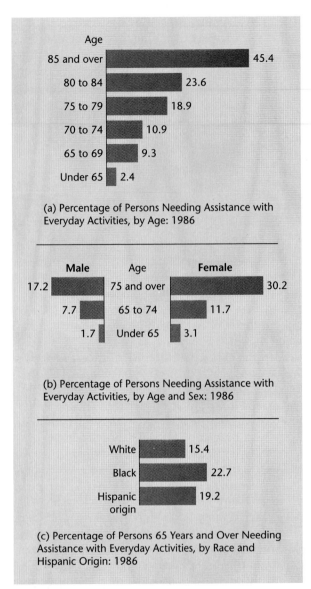

(a) Percentage of Persons Needing Assistance with Everyday Activities, by Age: 1986

(b) Percentage of Persons Needing Assistance with Everyday Activities, by Age and Sex: 1986

(c) Percentage of Persons 65 Years and Over Needing Assistance with Everyday Activities, by Race and Hispanic Origin: 1986

FIGURE 16-3
Most older people do not need help with everyday activities, but limitations on what people can do increase with age and are more common among women, minority groups, and people with low incomes. (*Source:* U.S. Bureau of the Census, 1992b.)

cut back longer for an acutely ill older person than it would be for someone younger, this amounts to a yearly average of only 31 days of curtailed activity (including 14 days sick in bed).

Overall, older people need more medical care than younger ones. They go to the doctor more often, are hospitalized more frequently, stay in the hospital longer, and spend more than 4 times as much money (an average of $5360 a year) on health care (U.S. Bureau of the Census, 1992c). Medicare (part of the social security system, available to

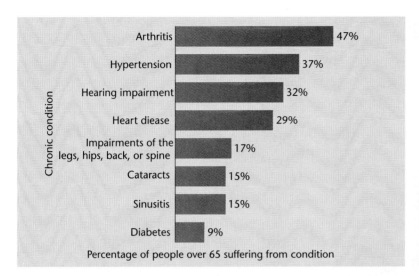

FIGURE 16-4
Although most older people are in good health, they are more subject to a number of chronic conditions. *Note:* These data refer only to the noninstitutionalized population. (*Source:* AARP, 1992.)

everyone over age 65), Medicaid (available only to low-income people), and other government programs cover about two-thirds of this cost. About one-fourth of the cost comes out of people's own pockets (or their families'); private insurance covers very little (AARP, 1992; Binstock, 1987).

Only a small percentage of elderly people live in nursing homes at any one time: 1.5 percent of those aged 65 to 74; 7 percent of those 75 to 84; and 22 percent of those over 85 (U.S. Bureau of the Census, 1992c). However, with the aging of the population, the need for such care is likely to increase. Some gerontologists estimate that by the time the "baby boomers" reach their eighties and nineties in about 2040, the proportion of those needing long-term care will have soared by about 2 to 3 times more than the 1986 figures (Kunkel & Applebaum, 1992). We'll discuss the issues relating to such care in Chapter 17.

Dental Health

Dental health is related to inborn tooth structure and to lifelong eating and dental habits. In one interview study, more than half of those 65 and over had not seen a dentist for 2 years or more (USDHHS, 1990). Extensive loss of teeth—a condition that is especially serious among the poor—may reflect inadequate (or no) dental care more than effects of aging.

Loss of teeth, along with tooth and gum problems, can have serious implications for nutrition. Since people with poor or missing teeth find many foods hard to chew, they tend to eat less and to shift to softer, sometimes less nutritious foods (Wayler, Kapur, Feldman, & Chauncey, 1982).

INFLUENCES ON HEALTH AND FITNESS

The American population as a whole has a higher standard of living, is eating better, and knows more about health. Furthermore, societal changes like better sanitation; immunization against once-fatal childhood diseases; and the widespread use of antibiotics to treat bronchitis, influenza, and pneumonia have contributed to better health.

But along with these positive changes have come negative ones—increases in cancer-causing agents in foods, in the workplace, and in the air we breathe; and a faster pace of life, which contributes to hypertension and heart disease. And living longer increases the likelihood of conditions and diseases that tend to occur late in life.

A person's chances of being reasonably healthy and fit in late life often depend on lifestyle—on the extent to which she or he has followed and continues to follow practices like those in Box 12-1.

Exercise and Diet

People who exercise tend to live longer (Rakowski & Mor, 1992). For years Diane's father walked from 2 to 4 miles a day in sunshine, rain, and snow. Other older walkers, who prefer climate-controlled conditions, log their miles in indoor malls. Indoors or out, exercise is just as valuable in late adulthood as it is earlier in the life span. A lifelong program of exercise may prevent many physical changes formerly associated with "normal aging," now thought to be caused by inactivity.

Regular exercise throughout adulthood appears

These enthusiastic square dancers are deriving the benefits of regular physical exercise in old age, along with having fun. They may well avoid some of the physical changes commonly—and apparently mistakenly—associated with "normal aging." Such changes are now thought to result from inactivity. *(Stacy Pick/Stock, Boston)*

to protect against hypertension, heart disease, and osteoporosis. It also seems to help maintain speed, stamina, and strength, and such basic functions as circulation and breathing. It reduces the chance of injuries by making joints and muscles stronger and more flexible, and it helps prevent or relieve lower-back pain and symptoms of arthritis. It may also improve mental alertness and cognitive performance, may help relieve anxiety and mild depression, and often improves morale (Clarkson-Smith & Hartley, 1989; Hill, Storandt, & Malley, 1993; Shay & Roth, 1992; Hawkins, Kramer, & Capaldi, 1992; Blumenthal et al., 1991).

For a number of reasons—diminished senses of taste and smell, dental problems, difficulty in shopping or preparing food, and inadequate incomes—many older people do not eat as well as they should. One study of 474 people between 65 and 98 years of age found that most did not get enough nutrients in their diet, and did not have enough energy. About 20 percent skipped lunch. The most commonly deficient nutrients were cal-

cium, zinc, and vitamins A and E (Ryan, Craig, & Finn, 1992).

MENTAL AND BEHAVIORAL DISORDERS

As the family and friends of an 80-year-old man watched him go downhill mentally, they assumed that he was becoming "senile." But his problem turned out to be the combined effects of several types of prescription drugs; when his medications were changed, his behavior returned to normal.

The confusion, forgetfulness, and personality changes sometimes associated with old age very often have physiological causes. The general term for such apparent intellectual deterioration is *dementia*. The word *senility*, frequently used to describe dementia in older people, is not a true medical diagnosis but a "wastebasket" term for a wide range of symptoms.

Contrary to another stereotype, dementia is not an inevitable part of aging. Most older people are in good mental health. Moderate memory loss is not necessarily a sign of dementia. (When younger people cannot remember something, they usually shrug it off; when older people forget, they may become alarmed, attributing simple forgetfulness to "senility.") Even if a person does suffer from dementia, treatment may be able to reverse it.

Reversible Mental Health Problems

Many older people mistakenly believe that they can do nothing about mental and behavioral problems because "you can't turn back the clock." Actually, some 100 such conditions—including about 15 percent of dementia cases—can be cured or alleviated. The most common are depression, delirium, intoxication caused by medications, and metabolic or infectious disorders. The next most common are malnutrition, anemia, alcoholism, low thyroid functioning, and head injury (NIA, 1980).

Unfortunately, many older people, especially those from minority groups and those who live in rural areas, do not get the help they need (Fellin & Powell, 1988; Roybal, 1988). Only a very small percentage of persons seen in psychiatric clinics are over age 60, and only a small percentage of people seen in community health centers are over 65 (Butler & Lewis, 1982).

Why is this? First, private treatment is expensive, not every community offers low-cost mental health services, and not enough programs reach out to find those in need. But this is not the entire story. Some mental health practitioners labor under the myth that the elderly cannot benefit from counseling or psychotherapy. And some older people are too proud to admit that they need help, are frightened of mental illness and feel that seeking help would mean they were "crazy," believe that they are "too old to change," or do not know that psychotherapy need not be long and costly.

Also, some people do not realize that their symptoms are treatable—especially when family members or insensitive clinicians dismiss disorders as irreversible "senility." Often the true cause of a problem becomes lost in a vicious circle. For example, people who slow down because they are depressed may fear that their brain is degenerating, and that belief depresses them even more, making them seem demented. But if they were treated for depression, they might begin acting "like themselves" again.

Depression

Many older people suffer from various more or less disabling aches and pains; have lost spouses, siblings, friends, and sometimes children; take mood-altering medicines; and feel that they have no control over their lives. Any one of these factors can make a person of any age depressed. An estimated 10 percent of elderly people living in the community show some signs of depression (Blazer, 1989).

Symptoms of depression are the same in old age as they are earlier in life—extreme sadness, lack of interest or enjoyment in life, loss of weight, insomnia, fatigue, feelings of worthlessness or inappropriate guilt, loss of memory, inability to concentrate, and thoughts of death or suicide (Blazer, 1989).

Support networks of family and friends can help older people ward off depression or find help for it. Help can also come from antidepressant drugs, from psychotherapy, or from various medical and community services.

Overmedication

Some apparent dementia turns out to be a side effect of drug intoxication. An older person may take as many as a dozen different medicines. Because physicians do not always ask what other medicines a patient is taking, they may prescribe drugs that interact harmfully. Also, because of age-related changes in the body's metabolism, a dosage that would be right for a 40-year-old may be an overdose for an 80-year-old.

Irreversible Mental Problems

Alzheimer's Disease

A respected poet cannot remember her own name, much less her poetry. A former industrial tycoon, swathed in a diaper, spends hours polishing his shoes. These are among the victims of *Alzheimer's disease,* a degenerative brain disorder that gradually robs people of intelligence, awareness, and even the ability to control their bodily functions—and finally kills them.

The great majority of elderly people do not suffer from this malady. Nevertheless, it is the most prevalent—and most feared—irreversible dementia. The extensive research and media attention given to the disease in recent years probably contribute to the dread so many middle-aged and older people harbor of succumbing to it. Although Alzheimer's disease occasionally strikes in middle age, most sufferers are over 65, with estimates of its prevalence varying from 2 to 10 percent of all people over 65 and from about 13 to 50 percent of people 85 and over (D. A. Evans et al., 1989; Folstein, Bassett, Anthony, Romanoski, & Nestadt, 1991; Skoog, Nilsson, Palmertz, Andreasson, & Svanborg, 1993).

Causes of Alzheimer's Disease   So far, the cause or causes of Alzheimer's disease are unknown. Early-

Some old people become depressed as a result of physical and emotional losses, and some apparent "brain disorders" are actually due to depression. But depression can often be relieved if older people seek help. *(Bill Gillette/Stock, Boston)*

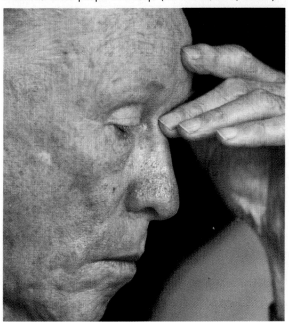

Most older people remain free from dementia. But some suffer from Alzheimer's disease, a brain disorder that affects all aspects of functioning. Three successive paintings of a windmill by the same artist show the progressive mental deterioration associated with this disorder. The artist did the first painting in his late sixties, at about the time that he began to show signs of the disease. In the second painting, done 7 years later, perspective is inaccurate, color sense is poor, and there is less attention to detail. When the artist made the third sketch, 2 years after the second, he could render only gross elements. *(NYT Pictures)*

appearing Alzheimer's disease has long been thought to be inherited; newer research has indicated that the late-onset type may also be inherited. Recently the presence of a particular gene was shown to be an important risk factor for Alzheimer's disease, predisposing people toward getting it both before and after age 65, and possi-

bly accounting for half of all patients with the disorder (Corder et al., 1993). Now, since there is no reliable treatment for preventing the disease, there would be no point to screening people for the presence of the gene. But should such treatment be developed, mass screening could identify people at risk, who could then receive preventive therapy.

Symptoms and Diagnosis   The first signs of Alzheimer's disease are often overlooked. They may include a tendency to garble telephone messages, some trouble using words, an inability to play a game of cards or tennis, or sudden episodes of extravagance. The most prominent early symptom is loss of memory, especially for recent events. More symptoms follow, such as confusion, irritability, restlessness, agitation, delirium, and impairment of judgment, concentration, orientation, and speech. As the disease progresses, symptoms become more pronounced and disabling. By the end, the victim cannot understand or use language, does not recognize family members, and cannot eat without help.

Diagnosing Alzheimer's disease is difficult. As of this writing, the only sure diagnosis depends on analysis of brain tissue, which can be done only by autopsy after death. The brain of a person with Alzheimer's disease shows tangles of nerve fibers, loss of cells, and other changes. These changes are far more pronounced in people suffering from Alzheimer's disease than in other elderly people, and they are more likely to occur in the hippocampus, the area of the brain associated with memory (Hyman, Van Hoesen, Damasio, & Barnes, 1984).

A recent clue is the discovery in autopsied brains of fragments of amyloid, a very tough protein that in normal amounts is essential for cell growth throughout the body. Some researchers believe that abnormal patches of this protein in the brain set up a chain reaction that kills brain cells. Since abnormal enzyme activity is part of the process, drugs that could deactivate some enzymes might block formation of amyloid (Sisodia, Koo, Beyreuther, Unterbeck, & Price, 1990; Whitson, Selkoe, & Cotman, 1989; Cai, Golde, & Younkin, 1993).

Doctors usually diagnose Alzheimer's disease in a living person by ruling out other conditions or by giving neurological or memory tests. One promising route to early diagnosis is the recent discovery that patients with Alzheimer's disease had a high level of a particular protein (glutamine synthetase) in their spinal fluid, compared with normal controls (Gunnersen & Haley, 1992).

Although Alzheimer's disease itself is still incurable, more accurate diagnosis would allow treatment of similar ailments that are sometimes misdiagnosed as Alzheimer's disease.

Treatment   Although no cure has been discovered for Alzheimer's disease, some drugs to improve memory and behavior show promise (Farlow et al., 1992; K. L. Davis et al., 1992; G. D. Cohen, 1987). Another line of research involves the grafting of fetal brain tissue (Gage, Bjorklund, Stenevi, Dunnett, & Kelly, 1984; M. B. Rosenberg et al., 1988).

Patients with Alzheimer's disease may also be helped by drugs that relieve agitation, lighten depression, or help them sleep. Proper nourishment and fluid intake, and exercise and physical therapy may help. Training can improve memory (McKitrick, Camp, & Black, 1992), and memory aids can help everyday functioning.

Probably the biggest help to both patient and family is the social and emotional support that can come through professional counseling and support groups (Blieszner & Shifflett, 1990). Family members suffer, too, from Alzheimer's disease, since the patient's inability to reciprocate expressions of affection and caring robs relationships of intimacy, while at the same time imposing a major burden of caregiving.

Other Irreversible Conditions

About 80 percent of cases of dementia among older people are caused either by Alzheimer's disease, a series of small strokes, or Parkinson's disease (D. J. Selkoe, 1992). When symptoms come on in several sudden steps, rather than gradually, stroke is the likeliest explanation. Small strokes can often be prevented by controlling hypertension through screening, a low-salt diet, and drugs (NIA, 1984). Brain implants of fetal tissue have improved the condition of some patients with Parkinson's disease (L. Thompson, 1992).

■ INTELLECTUAL DEVELOPMENT

Do older people continue to learn and grow intellectually, or does intelligence now falter and decline? We'll examine this controversial question, and then we'll look at memory in normal adults. Finally, we'll see how some older people keep their minds sharp and how they view work and retirement.

ASPECTS OF INTELLECTUAL DEVELOPMENT

DOES INTELLIGENCE DECLINE IN LATE ADULTHOOD?

When Sally's mother was 75, she was taken aback when a neighbor told her how "alert" she seemed. Sally's mother considered the comment patronizing and gratuitous—as well she might, in view of the fact that in most people, intellectual functioning does not decline in late adulthood.

Two Views of Intelligence

For years some psychologists have argued that "general intellectual decline in old age is largely a myth" (Baltes & Schaie, 1974, p. 35). Others have dismissed this view as rosy (J. L. Horn & Donaldson, 1976, 1977). To weigh these two points of view, we need to look at the results of intelligence tests that have been given to people of different ages, at the kinds of tests given, at the ways in which data have been collected, and at the kinds of intelligence being tested.

Fluid and Crystallized Intelligence: Which Is More Important?

The distinction between *fluid* and *crystallized* intelligence (see Chapter 14) is crucial to this controversy. Horn and his colleagues consider fluid abilities (those called on to solve new problems, tested by tasks outside a cultural context) to be at the heart of intelligence. They see the decline of these abilities in adulthood as the sign of a downhill slide.

Schaie and Baltes, on the other hand, maintain that while some abilities (mostly fluid) decline, other important abilities (mostly crystallized, the kind that depend on learning, life experience, and professional expertise) either hold their own or *increase* in later life. They stress the emergence of *new* abilities, like wisdom; cite studies suggesting that performance on fluid tests can be improved with training; and thus conclude that any assumption of an overall intellectual decline is unwarranted.

Fluid and Crystallized Intelligence: How Are They Tested?

Sequential Testing   Since longitudinal studies of intellectual functioning in later life did not show

TABLE 16-2

Tests of Primary Mental Abilities Given in Seattle Longitudinal Study of Adult Intelligence

Test	Ability Measured	Task	Type of Intelligence
Verbal meaning	Recognition and understanding of words	Find synonym by matching stimulus word with another word from multiple-choice list	Crystallized
Number	Applying numerical concepts	Check simple addition problems	Crystallized
Word fluency	Retrieving words from long-term memory	Think of as many words as possible beginning with a given letter, in a set time period	Part crystallized, part fluid
Spatial orientation	Rotating objects mentally in two-dimensional space	Select rotated examples of figure to match stimulus figure	Fluid
Inductive	Identifying regularities and inferring principles and rules	Complete a letter series	Fluid

SOURCE: Schaie, 1989.

the earlier and more marked declines that were reported in cross-sectional studies (see analysis of these two types of studies in Chapter 1), Schaie and his colleagues designed a new approach for studying changes in intellectual functioning. Their approach—*sequential testing* (see Chapter 1)—was designed to control both cohort differences and practice effects (Baltes, 1985; Schaie, 1979, 1983; Schaie & Herzog, 1983; Schaie & Strother, 1968).

Their now-classic sequential study began in 1956 with a battery of tests given to 500 randomly chosen volunteers (25 men and 25 women in each 5-year age interval from 20 to 70 years). Every 7 years, the original subjects were retested and new subjects were added. By 1984, more than 2000 people had been tested on timed tasks of primary mental abilities (described in Table 16-2). They also measured subjects on their degree of rigidity or flexibility and on the complexity of their lives, and they took health histories.

The major findings are that older people's intellectual functioning is variable, that it can improve as well as decline, and that it is influenced by the culture and the environment.

▪ *Variability among people:* About one-third of people over age 70 score higher than the average young adult, whereas some people's intellectual abilities begin to decline during their thirties, and for others, the decline begins in their sev-

enties. At age 81, less than half the subjects had declined consistently over the previous 7 years. A person's functioning is influenced by health, work, and education. Most fairly healthy adults do not experience any significant mental loss until at least about age 60 or later, and even then it appears that some of this loss may not be caused by aging but by other factors, and therefore might be preventable. If people live long enough, their intellectual functioning will begin to decline at some point; but very few people decline on all, or even most, abilities. Women seem to retain crystallized abilities longer, men do better on fluid abilities.

▪ *Multidirectionality of change:* Test scores of fluid intelligence begin to decline in young adulthood, but those of crystallized intelligence remain stable or even increase into the seventies. After this time, crystallized intelligence as measured on tests also declines, but the decline in test scores may be due to older people's slower response time, not to their capacity. It may also be due to the fact that tasks on tests were often developed for testing younger people, and these tasks may, therefore, be inappropriate for older test-takers. Older people may not be interested in solving problems involving mazes and puzzle boards!

▪ *Cultural and environmental influences:* Different cohorts show different patterns of intellectual functioning, as a result of different kinds of life experiences. For example, people who grew up more recently in the United States have more formal education, on the average; they have been exposed to more information through television; they have taken more tests and have taken them more recently; they are in better health; and they are likely to have jobs that depend on thinking rather than on physical labor. All these factors contribute to differences among cohorts. More recent cohorts scored higher on inductive reasoning and verbal meaning, whereas the other abilities showed varying patterns (see Figure 16-5).

■ *Influences on test performance:* Various physical and psychological factors may lower older people's test scores, leading to underestimation of their intelligence. They may have trouble hearing or seeing instructions, and poor coordination and agility may interfere with doing the tasks. People who do best on tests are physically fit, not fatigued, and have less disease, relatively low blood pressure, and fewer negative neurophysiological indicators (Furry & Baltes, 1973; Sands & Meredith, 1992; Schaie & Gribbin, 1975). High scorers also tend to have had a flexible personality style at midlife (Schaie, 1984) and to have an active lifestyle (Hultsch, Hammer, & Small, 1993).

The poorer showing of older people in cross-sectional studies may also be influenced by ***terminal drop,*** a decrease in intellectual performance shortly before death (Riegel & Riegel, 1972). Terminal drop affects abilities that are relatively unaffected by age, like vocabulary (N. White & Cunningham, 1988). This effect is also seen in people who die young; but it tends to bring down the average scores of an older sample, since more older people are likely to die in the near future.

In addition, just as for young people, attitudes toward a testing situation can affect the results. Older people may be anxious, especially if they are unfamiliar with the testing situation and have not taken tests for a long time. They may lack confidence in their ability to solve test problems, and the expectation that they will do poorly may become a self-fulfilling prophecy. Or they may lack motivation because doing as well as they can on intelligence tests does not mean much to them.

The time limits on most intelligence tests are particularly unfair to older people, since everything takes them longer than it once did. Older subjects do better when they are allowed as much time as they need (C. Herzog, 1989; J. L. Horn & Cattell, 1966; Schaie & Herzog, 1983). The emphasis on speed in western culture may result in incorrectly defining older people as less intelligent than younger ones.

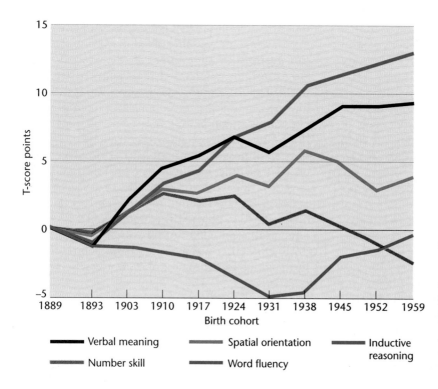

FIGURE 16-5
Cohort differences in scores on intelligence tests. In a group with mean birth years from 1889 to 1959, more recent cohorts scored higher on inductive reasoning and verbal meaning. Abilities with numbers, word fluency, and spatial orientation showed varying patterns. (*Source:* Schaie, 1989.)

Many older people, like this woman being taught by a high school student, are joining the computer age and learning new skills. Those who are motivated can put forth whatever effort is needed to maintain or expand their intellectual capacity. *(James Balog/Black Star)*

Furthermore, tests developed for children—to see whether they are acquiring the skills that define intellectual development earlier in life—appear to be inappropriate for older people. Older people do not seem to do as well on tests that they do not see as pertinent to real life. To learn about their intelligence, we need to measure the ability to deal with real-world challenges—tasks like balancing a checkbook, reading a railroad timetable, or making informed decisions about medical problems. We also need more research on the cognitive processes involved in intellectual functioning, and on how the elements of those processes may change with age.

Helping Older People Improve Their Intellectual Performance Everyone has had the experience of performing the same task better at one time than another. Your health and comfort, your level of fatigue or anxiety, your motivation, your study habits, and your skill in taking tests can all affect your test score. This variability, or modifiability, of a person's performance is called ***plasticity.***

Research has helped older people perform better on tests by identifying and doing something about factors that affect plasticity. Several studies have been based on the Adult Development and Enrichment Project (ADEPT), originated at Pennsylvania State University (Blieszner, Willis, & Baltes, 1981; Plemons, Willis, & Baltes, 1978; Willis, Blieszner, & Baltes, 1981).

In one study based on ADEPT (Blackburn, Papalia-Finlay, Foye, & Serlin, 1988), 69 healthy volunteers (average age about 70) were randomly assigned to three groups, each of which met for about 5 hours in small subgroups. The first group received formal training in figural relations (rules for determining the next figure in a series). The second group worked with the same training materials and problems but were *self-taught*—they had no formal instruction. A third, control, group received no training. Pretests and posttests contained some tasks like those in the training materials and other tasks that were quite different. Both experimental groups improved more than the control group, but the people in the second (self-taught) group maintained their gains better on a posttest after 1 month. Apparently the opportunity to work out their own solutions fostered more lasting learning than being taught a set of rules.

Findings like these show that training and practice can improve older people's performance even on tests of fluid intelligence. Much as aging athletes can often call upon physical reserves, older people who get training, practice, and social support seem to be able to draw upon mental reserves. Late adulthood need not be a time of intellectual decline if people are motivated and helped to put forth extra effort to keep up or improve their mental powers.

A New View: Mechanics and Pragmatics of Intelligence

Old age "adds as it takes away," said the poet William Carlos Williams in one of three books of verse written between his first stroke at the age of 68 and his death at age 79.

Paul Baltes and his colleagues (Baltes, 1993; Dixon and Baltes, 1986; Dixon, 1992) sketch a *dual-process model* of intellectual functioning in late adulthood. It includes aspects of intelligence that may continue to advance but are unlikely to show up on psychometric tests, as well as aspects that are subject to deterioration. This model identifies and seeks to measure two dimensions of intelligence:

1 *Mechanics of intelligence:* consist of content-free areas of information processing and problem solving. This is similar to fluid intelligence and is the area that most often declines with age.
2 *Pragmatics of intelligence:* include such potential growth areas as practical thinking, application of accumulated knowledge and skills, specialized expertise, professional productivity, and wisdom. This domain, which often develops in late adulthood, is similar to, although broader than, crystallized intelligence.

Older adults are likely to improve not in the basic cognitive "mechanics" they learned as children but rather in the "pragmatic" use of the information and know-how they have garnered from their education, work, and life experience.

Pragmatic intelligence can help people maintain or enhance their intellectual functioning through what Baltes (1993) calls *selective optimization with compensation.* That is, by doing what they are good at, older people can use their special abilities to compensate for their losses in other areas. This concept may help to explain how artists like Pablo Picasso and Georgia O'Keeffe, writers like George Bernard Shaw, and composers like Giuseppe Verdi were able to produce some of their finest works in their seventies and eighties.

An important part of pragmatic intelligence is wisdom (see Box 16-3 and Table 16-3).

HOW DOES MEMORY CHANGE IN LATE ADULTHOOD?

"I can't remember whether or not I put the sugar in that cake," Sally's mother said at age 73, when she was baking professionally. "I guess I really am getting old if I'm this forgetful." Yet until her death at age 79, Leah Wendkos remembered some 50 telephone numbers of a wide circle of friends, relatives, and customers; she never forgot an appointment; and she kept most of her recipes in her

head. Let's consider how this apparent contradiction might be understood.

The Three Memory Systems

Failing memory is often considered a sign of aging. The man who always kept his schedule in his head now has to write it in a calendar; the woman who takes several medicines now measures out each day's dosages and puts them where she is sure to see them.

Yet in memory too, older people's functioning varies greatly. There is no single capacity called *memory.* Memory involves three different storage systems—sensory memory, short-term (or working) memory, and long-term memory—each serving distinct purposes.

Sensory Memory
Your brain records whatever you see, hear, smell, taste, or touch—anything that comes in through the senses—and places the information in a temporary storage called *sensory memory,* where it stays very briefly. Images in sensory memory fade quickly unless they are transferred to short-term memory.

Iconic (visual) memory holds up well in late adulthood (Poon, 1985). Without this ability to register visual images (like an array of letters), you would be unable to read or to make sense of anything you saw.

Short-Term (or Working) Memory
When you look up a telephone number, it goes into your *short-term memory,* which holds information for about 20 seconds. Researchers assess short-term memory by asking a subject to repeat a sequence of numbers, either in the order in which they were presented (digit span forward) or in reverse order (digit span backward). Digit span forward ability holds up well with advancing age (Craik, 1977; Poon, 1985), but digit span backward performance is typically better in young adults than in elders (Lovelace, 1990).

Long-Term Memory
Long-term memory is long-term storage of information. Older people's long-term memory for newly learned information is different from their memory for material learned in the more distant past. Memory for newly learned material drops off significantly with advancing age: over a period of hours or days, younger adults can remember such newly learned material as word pairs and paragraphs better than older people do. But the

BOX 16-3 FOOD FOR THOUGHT

WISDOM IN LATE ADULTHOOD

What is wisdom? How can we recognize a wise response to life? Do people get wiser as they get older? To try to find answers to these questions, Jacqui Smith and Paul B. Baltes (1990) drew up criteria for wisdom, pulled together a panel of judges, and asked people of various ages to respond to practical problems of life planning.

These researchers defined *wisdom* in the context of fundamental matters of life as "expert knowledge in life planning, life management, and life review" (p. 495). Such knowledge would include insight into human development and good judgment, advice, and commentary about difficult life problems. A wise response would show knowledge about various conditions of life and recognition that no one solution is best for everyone, and would acknowledge that life is unpredictable.

Sixty well-educated German professionals—twenty aged 25 to 35, twenty aged 40 to 50, and twenty aged 60 to 81—were asked to come up with plans for resolving difficult life problems encountered by four fictitious characters (see Table 16-3). Their solutions were

then rated by the judges, all experienced human-services professionals.

Only 11 (5 percent) of the 240 responses (4 each from 60 subjects) were rated as "wise," which should not be surprising, since wisdom is extraordinary and rare. What may seem surprising is that wisdom was *not* shown more by the older subjects than by the younger ones. Instead, these 11 responses were distributed nearly evenly across the age groups: 3 young adults, 4 middle-aged adults, and 4 older adults.

The young and middle-aged subjects gave "wiser" responses to three of the problems—both normative and nonnormative problems of young people ("Elizabeth" and "Michael") and the normative problem of an older person ("Jack"). For the nonnormative problem of an older person ("Joyce"), no age group showed superiority. However, the oldest group gave its best answers to this last problem; all 4 of this group's "wise" responses were to this problem. Looking at the problems of young adults, older adults tended to be more dogmatic than younger and middle-aged adults and to show less

insight and knowledge about strategies and decision making.

The findings of this study suggest age-specific peaks in select areas. But both younger and older subjects showed more wisdom about life decisions that were nonnormative and unique to their own stage of life. Wisdom is not, then, confined to any one age group; it seems to emerge when people are faced with issues from current, everyday life. Although the older subjects did not produce all the top performances, they did contribute an equal share, showing that older adults can hold their own in "wisdom" (as defined here), especially in unexpected situations.

The researchers who conducted this study had drawn up their own definition of *wisdom*. How such a quality is defined affects research findings. Does their definition seem appropriate? How else could *wisdom* be defined? How else could its presence (or absence) be determined? And how can the wisdom of older people be applied to the problems of the elderly in contemporary society?

---

ability to recall long-ago events is not generally affected by advanced age (Poon, 1985; Craik, 1977).

Older adults are as proficient as younger ones in episodic memory (the ability to recall specific events or episodes), when they perceive the event to be recalled as distinctive. But younger people remember nondistinctive events better. Other types of memory that hold up well in late adulthood are procedural memory (remembering how to do something, like ride a bicycle) and memory for general knowledge (Camp, 1989; Cavanaugh, Kramer, Sinnott, Camp, & Markley, 1985; Kausler, 1990; Lachman & Lachman, 1980).

Why Does Memory Decline?

Investigators have offered several hypotheses to explain age differences in memory, particularly in long-term memory for recent events.

Biological Hypotheses

Some researchers point to neurological changes and other physiological changes connected with aging: the more a person deteriorates physically, the more loss of memory will take place. But so far, this biological approach appears to be more useful in explaining memory impairment in people with brain damage or other pathological conditions than in normal, healthy older adults (Poon,

BOX 16-3 (*Continued*)

WISDOM IN LATE ADULTHOOD

TABLE 16-3

Life-Planning Problems: A Fictitious Person Faces a Decision about Future Options

Young Target	Older Target
Type of life decision: Normative	
1 Elizabeth, 33 years old and a successful professional for 8 years, was recently offered a major promotion. Her new responsibilities would require an increased time commitment. She and her husband would also like to have children before it is too late. Elizabeth is considering the following options: she could plan to accept the promotion, or she could plan to start a family.	2 Up to now, Jack, 63 years old and married, has approached compulsory retirement at 65 with some anxiety. Recently, his company was taken over. The new management has decided to close the outer suburban branch in which Jack is employed. Jack is considering the following options: he can plan to take early retirement with full pay as compensation for 2 years, or he can plan to move to work in the company head office for 2 to 3 more years.
Type of life decision: Nonnormative	
3 Michael, a 28-year-old mechanic with two preschool-aged children, has just learned that the factory in which he is working will close in 3 months. At present, there is no possibility for further employment in this area. His wife has recently returned to her well-paid nursing career. Michael is considering the following options: he can plan to move to another city to seek employment, or he can plan to take full responsibility for child-care and household tasks.	4 Joyce, a 60-year-old widow, recently completed a degree in business management and opened her own business. She has been looking forward to this new challenge. She has just heard that her son has been left with two small children to care for. Joyce is considering the following options: She could plan to give up her business and live with her son, or she could plan to arrange for financial assistance for her son to cover child-care costs.

Note: The specific instruction following each problem is: "Formulate a plan that covers what __ should do and consider in the next 3 to 5 years. What extra pieces of information are needed?" Subjects were trained to think aloud.
SOURCE: J. Smith & Baltes, 1990, p. 497.

1985). However, recent studies suggest that degeneration in the frontal lobes of the brain is related to a decline in episodic memory in old age.

Processing Hypotheses

A second approach focuses on the three steps required to process information in memory: encoding, storage, and retrieval. Older people seem to be less efficient than younger ones at encoding information—preparing and "labeling" it for storage so that it will be easy to retrieve when needed. They are not as likely to think of ways to organize material to make it easier to remember (like putting names in alphabetical order). But when

given suggestions for organizing, older subjects remember as well as younger ones (Hultsch, 1971; Poon, 1985; Hess, Flannagan, & Tate, 1993).

Older people often have trouble retrieving information from memory. In one study, older people had some trouble *recalling* items they had learned, though they did just as well as younger people in *recognizing* the items (Hultsch & Dixon, 1990). If asked a question, they might not recall the right answer; but if presented with multiple-choice answers, they could recognize the correct response. Even though recognition memory seems to remain more stable with age than recall memory, it still takes older people a longer time to

Ruth Michael of Weslaco, Texas, graduated from college with honors at the age of 83, and now, as a volunteer, administers psychology tests to hospitalized patients. Many older people use the later years of life to obtain the education they couldn't afford or didn't have time for earlier in life. *(Dennis Wells)*

search their memories (T. R. Anders, Fozard, & Lillyquist, 1972).

Contextual Considerations

How do "contextual" factors account for individual differences in memory? Such factors might include motivation, intelligence, learning habits, and degree of familiarity with test items, as well as the type of task.

The designers of one study supported their hypothesis that memory would hold up better among people who are more intellectually able, flexible, and resourceful; who receive guidance in encoding and retrieval; or who are dealing with familiar material. The researchers compared three groups of 20 elderly volunteers (differing in verbal intelligence, daily activity levels, and socioeconomic status) with 20 undergraduate students. All subjects were tested individually on three verbal tasks, including recalling words from a list. The most intelligent, socially active, and affluent old people did best on all the tasks—about as well as the undergraduates. The least intelligent, least ac-

tive, and poorest old people did worst. The older people's performance was particularly good when the subjects were given cues to jog their memory than when they had to recall the words on their own (Craik, Byrd, & Swanson, 1987).

To speak of an across-the-board decline in memory, then, is seriously misleading. We need to ask: Which older people are we talking about? What tasks are they being asked to do? And how well prepared are they to do these tasks?

Memory Training

Aside from just giving people cues to help them organize or remember information, some investigators have offered more extensive memory training programs. These may emphasize *mnemonics* (techniques designed to help people remember, like visualizing a list of items or making associations between a face and a name), attention or relaxation training, or giving information about memory and aging. An analysis of 33 studies of people over 60 found that older people do benefit from memory training. The particular kind of mnemonic made little difference, and gains were largest for younger subjects, for those who received pretraining, and for those who were trained in groups and in short sessions (Verhaeghen, Marcoen, & Goossens, 1992). There is, then, considerable plasticity of memory performance for older people, but it does diminish with advancing age.

LIFELONG LEARNING: ADULT EDUCATION IN LATE LIFE

Research has found that the phrase "use it or lose it" applies as much to intellectual ability as to physical functioning. Continuing mental activity throughout life helps keep performance high, whether this activity involves reading, conversation, crossword puzzles, games like bridge or chess or other board games—or going back to school, as more and more mature adults are doing.

Qian Likun, a star student who walks to his classes on health care and ancient Chinese poetry, recently took part in a college-sponsored 2.3-mile foot race. This might not seem unusual, until you learn that Mr. Qian is 102 years old, one of thousands of students in China's network of "universities for the aged." More than 800 of these schools have been founded since the 1980s, showing China's commitment to its elderly population—and older people's willingness and ability to learn everything from basic reading and writing skills to esoteric subjects (Kristof, 1990).

In the United States, too, many older people use their new bounty of time to educate themselves. Since people who were well educated in their youth are more likely to seek more schooling later in life, and since education rates have been rising steadily (U.S. Bureau of the Census, 1983), the number of older people enrolled in educational programs will probably grow.

Many colleges offer tuition-free courses for older students. Low-cost Elderhostel programs offer 1- or 2-week minicourses in Shakespeare, geography, early American music, and a wide variety of other subjects. Some vocational programs give special attention to the needs of older women who have never worked for pay and who now must do so for either financial or emotional reasons.

Older people can learn new skills and information. They learn best when the materials and methods take into account the physiological, psychological, and intellectual changes that they may be going through. For example, they seem to do best when material is presented slowly and over a longer period of time with intervals in between, rather than in concentrated form. And students with visual or hearing problems benefit from clear, easily understandable audiovisual materials.

WORK AND RETIREMENT

At 79, Diane's father was still working fulltime at his law practice. When Sally's father, a furniture salesman, was 73, he lost his job because of the death of his employer; he received three offers of employment, took one, and worked until the day he died, at 76. More than 60 studies of job performance have yielded findings that show that older workers are more committed to their jobs than younger ones, that they exhibit less turnover and more job satisfaction (Rosen & Jerdee, 1988).

Perhaps because older people doing productive paid work represent only 3 percent of the work force (Schick, 1986), they are less visible than the stereotyped carefree retirees out playing golf. Over the past 40 years, moreover, the proportion of elderly people seeking work has fallen considerably. In 1990, only about 16 percent of men 65 and older were in the labor force, compared with almost 46 percent in 1950 (U.S. Department of Labor, 1980,

1987; U.S. Bureau of the Census, 1992c). Mainly, this is because more men now retire early and fewer are self-employed. Most of the research in work and retirement in late adulthood has focused on older men, but with the increased role of work in women's lives, women are now being studied more.

The proportion of older women (age 65 and over) who work has also decreased, but not as sharply—from about 10 percent in 1950 to about 9 percent in 1990. This probably reflects the fact that fewer women in this age group worked earlier in life and those who did tended to retire as early as possible because the kinds of work they could do were limited (AARP, 1986; Bird, 1987; U.S. Bureau of the Census, 1992b).

Retirement does not necessarily mean stopping paid work altogether. Many healthy retirees work part time, and part-timers account for a little more than half of older workers. Although there are probably some people over age 65 in almost every occupation, about 54 percent of older workers are white-collar and about 25 percent are self-employed (AARP, 1986; Bird, 1987; Schick, 1986; U.S. Bureau of the Census, 1992c).

WHY PEOPLE RETIRE

At one time almost all employers required their workers to retire at age 65. Then, laws were rewritten, first upping retirement age to 70, and then removing mandatory retirement age altogether, except for a few professions, such as airline pilots. Now, even though employers cannot force a worker to retire, many exert more or less subtle pressures on their older employees.

Most people leave their jobs at or before the retirement age their employers set. Economic status affects the age of retirement: workers who are still earning high wages are more likely to work longer, and lower-salary workers often retire as soon as they can afford to. Thanks to social security benefits (the principal source of income for the elderly) and private pension plans, many workers can retire and live relatively comfortably. (Issues related to income are discussed further in Chapter 17.)

Many private pension plans encourage early retirement by penalizing workers who are past their early sixties, and social security policies limit the income a recipient can earn. Changes in tax laws, pension plans, and company policies (like letting employees work part time at reduced pay) could

By using his leisure time to work as a volunteer in the field of health care, this retiree is helping not only the community but also himself. The self-esteem gained from using hard-won skills and from continuing to be a useful, contributing member of society is a valuable by-product of volunteer service. *(Joel Gordon)*

encourage more older workers to stay on the job (Ruhm, 1989).

HOW PEOPLE FEEL ABOUT RETIREMENT

A favorite adage of Sally's father—"It's better to be rich and healthy than poor and sick"—sums up how people feel about retirement. To no one's surprise, retirees who are not worried about money and who feel well are happier in retirement than those who miss their income and do not feel well enough to enjoy their leisure (Barfield & Morgan, 1974, 1978; Bossé, Aldwin, Levenson, & Workman-Daniels, 1991).

Use of time is also important. Many recent retirees relish the first long stretches of leisure time they have had since childhood. They enjoy spend-

ing it with family and friends and exploring new interests. After a while, though, they may begin to feel bored, restless, and useless. The most satisfied retirees tend to be physically fit people who are using their skills in part-time paid or volunteer work (Schick, 1986).

Retirement has little effect on physical health (Herzog, House, & Morgan, 1991), but it sometimes affects mental health (Bossé, Aldwin, Levenson, & Ekerdt, 1987). Among 1513 older men surveyed in the Boston Veterans Administration Normative Aging Study (a cross-sectional study), retirees were more likely than workers to report depression, obsessive-compulsive behavior, and physical symptoms that had no organic cause. Those who had retired early (before age 62) or late (after age 65) reported the most symptoms.

Of course, poor mental health might have been the reason some of these men retired. But it is also possible that the timing of retirement matters. Workers who are pressured to stop work before they want to may not have satisfying alternatives, or they may feel out of step with their peers. Workers who deferred retirement as long as possible because they enjoyed their work may now feel its loss keenly; those who continue working may do so because they want to feel valued and needed.

On the other hand, some people's morale and life satisfaction remain stable through both working and retirement years, and some retirees have higher morale than some workers (M. L. Cassidy, 1983; Palmore, Fillenbaum, & George, 1984). Once again, we see that we cannot describe any single effect of such a complex change in people's lives.

MAKING THE MOST OF RETIREMENT

Retirement is a major life transition. What can be done to help more people find it fulfilling? Two key elements are preparation before retirement and good use of time during retirement.

Planning Ahead

Ideally, planning for retirement should begin before middle age. It includes structuring life to make it enjoyable and productive, providing for financial needs, anticipating physical or emotional problems, and discussing how retirement will affect a spouse. Help can come from preretirement workshops, self-help books, and company-sponsored programs.

Using Leisure Time Well

Some retirees relish being able to sleep late, go fishing, or take in an afternoon movie. But many get more gratification from using the fruits of their experience in a more structured, "worklike" way, and programs have sprung up to tap this valuable resource. Retired business people share their experience with budding entrepreneurs, and retirees from many occupations tutor, counsel, and offer career advice to college students. Older persons serve as "foster" grandparents, and retired workers teach and supervise in such technical fields as drafting, automotive repairs, electronics, and computer technology.

Retirement could be made easier and more satisfying in the future by restructuring the course of life. Today, young adults usually plunge into education and careers, middle-aged people use most of their energy earning money, and older people have trouble filling their time. If people wove work, leisure, and study into their lives in a more balanced way at all ages, young adults would feel less pressure to establish themselves early, middle-aged people would feel less burdened, and older people would be more stimulated and would feel—and be—more useful. Such a change might make an important contribution to self-esteem and emotional well-being in old age, which we'll discuss in Chapter 17.

SUMMARY

OLD AGE TODAY

■ Negative stereotypes about old people reflect *ageism*—prejudice or discrimination based on age. Today, many old people are healthy, vigorous, and active. These people can be referred to as the *young old*, and the frail and infirm as the *old old*.

■ The number and proportion of old people in the United States population are greater today than ever before. This is due to high birthrates in the late eighteenth and early nineteenth centuries as well as high immigration rates.

■ People over 85 are the fastest-growing age group in America. They are largely widowed women.

■ Negative attitudes toward the elderly affect older people's feelings about themselves as well as society's treatment of them.

■ Senescence, the period in the life span marked by physical changes associated with aging, begins at different ages for different people.

LONGEVITY AND THE AGING PROCESS

■ Life expectancy has increased dramatically since 1900. American children born in 1991 have provisional life expectancy of 75.7 years. White people tend to live longer than black people, and women tend to live longer than men.

■ The death rate for older people has declined. Today, heart disease, cancer, and stroke are the three leading causes of death for people over age 65.

■ Most theories of why people age physically fall into two categories: aging as a programmed process and aging as a result of wear and tear to the body. Most likely, both of these factors influence aging.

■ Some gerontologists distinguish between primary aging, an inevitable process of bodily deterioration; and secondary aging, which results from the way people use their bodies and thus is largely preventable.

PHYSICAL CHANGES OF OLD AGE

■ There are vast individual differences in the timing and extent of the changes during late adulthood in sensory and perceptual abilities. Vision problems are especially common.

■ Older people experience a general slowing down of responses and of information processing. This slowdown requires them to make adjustments in many aspects of their lives. Training appears to be helpful.

■ Although the brain changes with age, the brain of a healthy older person is very similar to that of a healthy younger person.

■ A number of physical changes occur with advancing age, including some loss of skin coloring, texture, and elasticity; thinning and graying or whitening of hair; shrinkage of body size; and thinning of bones.

■ Most of the body systems generally continue to function fairly well, but the heart, in particular, becomes more susceptible to disease because of its decreased efficiency. The reserve capacity of the heart and other organs declines.

HEALTH IN OLD AGE

■ Most older people are reasonably healthy, especially if they follow a healthy lifestyle, incorporating exercise and sound nutrition. But incidence of illness and number of days of hospitalization are proportionally higher among older people than among younger people. Many older people are not hampered by chronic conditions, even though most have one or more.

- Loss of teeth and gum problems are common in late adulthood, especially when dental care has been inadequate. Very few people keep all their teeth until late in life.
- Most older people are in good mental health. Dementia, or intellectual deterioration, affects a minority of people of advanced age.
- Some forms of dementia, such as those caused by overmedication and depression, can be reversed with proper treatment; others, such as those brought on by Alzheimer's disease or by multiple strokes, are irreversible.

ASPECTS OF INTELLECTUAL DEVELOPMENT

- A major controversy concerns the maintenance or decline of intelligence in late adulthood. Test scores suggest that fluid intelligence, the ability to solve novel problems, appears to decline; but crystallized intelligence, which is based on learning and experience, tends to be maintained or even increases.
- Early cross-sectional research using psychometric tests of intelligence indicated decline, but this may reflect cohort differences more than aging; longitudinal studies indicate stability up to age 60 or so. Schaie's sequential studies suggest a more complex picture: intellectual functioning in late adulthood is marked by variability, multidirectionality, and susceptibility to cultural and environmental influences.
- Physical and psychological factors and test conditions can influence intellectual performance. Therefore, performance on intelligence tests may not be a precise measure of intellectual competence.
- Older people show considerable cognitive plasticity (modifiability) in intellectual performance. Their positive response to an intellectually supportive environment demonstrates that they can and do learn.
- Some aspects of intelligence seem to increase with age. Baltes proposes a dual-process model: the mechanics of intelligence often decline, but the pragmatics of intelligence (practical thinking, specialized

knowledge and skills, and wisdom) continue to grow. Successful aging, according to this theory, involves selective optimization with compensation (using special abilities to compensate for losses).

- While sensory memory, aspects of short-term memory, and remote long-term memory appear to be nearly as efficient in older adults as in younger people, long-term memory for recently learned information is often less efficient, probably because of problems with encoding (organization) and retrieval. The ability to recall distinctive events, procedural memory, and memory for general knowledge hold up well.
- Contextual factors may account for individual differences in recall. Like intelligence, memory functioning in older individuals varies greatly: more intelligent people may show little or no memory decline.
- Older people benefit from memory training.

LIFELONG LEARNING: ADULT EDUCATION IN LATE LIFE

- Continuing mental activity may be critical to keep older people mentally alert. Adult education programs can be designed to meet their needs.
- Learning and memory are interrelated. Older people can learn new skills and information, especially when it is presented slowly and over a longer period of time with intervals between exposures.

WORK AND RETIREMENT

- Some older people continue to work for pay, but the vast majority are retired. There is a trend toward retirement before age 65. However, many retired people find part-time paid or volunteer work.
- Retirement is a major transition of old age. It can be fulfilling, especially when the retiree has planned for it and uses leisure time well.

KEY TERMS

ageism (page 526)
gerontology (526)
senescence (530)
life expectancy (531)
programmed-aging theory (533)
wear-and-tear theory (533)
free radicals (533)
primary aging (534)

secondary aging (534)
reserve capacity (537)
dementia (540)
Alzheimer's disease (541)
terminal drop (545)
plasticity (546)
dual-process model (547)
mechanics of intelligence (547)

pragmatics of intelligence (547)
selective optimization with
    compensation (547)
sensory memory (547)
short-term memory (547)
long-term memory (547)

SUGGESTED READINGS

Cole, T. R. (1992).   *The journey of life: A cultural history of aging in America.* New York: Cambridge University Press. This engaging work, abundantly illustrated, traces the evolution of attitudes toward aging and the aged in America.

Dippel, R. L., & Hutton, J. T. (Eds.) (1991).   *Caring for the Alzheimer patient* (2d ed.). Buffalo, NY: Prometheus Books. This book is a compendium of articles by experts on Alzheimer's disease. It covers medical and physical aspects, environmental and behavioral problems, caregiver support, and ethical and legal issues.

Friedan, B. (1993).   *The fountain of age.* New York: Simon & Schuster. This pioneering feminist leader draws on the newest research on aging, along with her own and other people's personal experiences, to urge new ways of thought and action so that the years after 60 can be lived as a new life stage, full of opportunities for growth, development, and fulfillment.

Jarvik, L., & Small, G. (1990).   *Parentcare: A compassionate, commonsense guide for children and their aging parents.* New York: Bantam. This comprehensive volume by two psychiatrists who specialize in geriatrics takes a commonsense approach to problem solving. It covers mental and physical disabilities, common illnesses, legal questions, guilt, grief, commonly prescribed medications, and nutrition.

CHAPTER SEVENTEEN

PERSONALITY AND SOCIAL DEVELOPMENT IN LATE ADULTHOOD

There is still today
And tomorrow fresh with dreams:
Life never grows old

Rita Duskin, "Haiku,"
Sound and Light, 1987

■ **THEORY AND RESEARCH ON PERSONALITY DEVELOPMENT**

Erik Erikson: Crisis 8—Integrity versus Despair
Robert Peck: Three Adjustments of Late Adulthood
George Vaillant: Factors in Emotional Health
Research on Stability and Change in Personality
Approaches to "Successful Aging"
Personality and Patterns of Aging

■ **SOCIAL ISSUES RELATED TO AGING**

Income
Living Arrangements
Abuse of the Elderly

■ **PERSONAL RELATIONSHIPS IN LATE LIFE**

Marriage
Being Single Again: Divorce and Widowhood

Remarriage
Single Life: The "Never Marrieds"
Sexual Relationships
Relationships with Siblings
Friendships
Relationships with Adult Children
Childlessness
Grandparenthood and Great-Grandparenthood

■ **BOXES**

17-1 Food for Thought: Religion and Emotional Well-being in Late Life
17-2 Window on the World: Aging among African Americans, Hispanic Americans, and Other American Minority Groups
17-3 Practically Speaking: Visiting Someone in a Nursing Home
17-4 Window on the World: Extended Family Living in Latin America

- What important psychological tasks of late adulthood did Erikson and Peck identify?
- What personality and lifestyle patterns contribute to "successful aging"?
- How can society help older people deal with such issues as financial need and housing?
- How do relationships with family and friends provide emotional support to older people?

Dexter, 83, looks lovingly at his 81-year-old wife. "I always thought sunsets were more spectacular than sunrises, anyway," he says. "Now we're having some beautiful times in the evening of our lives." After each had been widowed and had lived alone, the two met at a senior citizens' dance. Now, after having been married for 2 years, Lizzie says, "This is the most well-rounded relationship I've ever had. Dexter and I are intellectual equals, and we have a lot of laughs together. Our story shows that it's never too late to find love and sex."

Love and sex are major social and personality issues throughout life. In late adulthood, they can go far to help people enjoy these years. The losses that Dexter and Lizzie suffered from widowhood are typical at this time of life—but so are the vigor and openness that let them begin a new relationship with each other.

Late adulthood is the developmental stage during which people clarify and find use for what they have learned over the years. People can continue to grow and adapt if they are flexible and realistic—if they learn how to conserve their strength, adjust to change and loss, and use these years productively. People now have a new awareness of time; and they want to use the time they have left to leave a legacy to their children or the world, pass on the fruits of their experience, and validate their lives as having been meaningful.

People who feel well, who can show their competence, and who feel in control of their lives are likely to have a strong enough sense of self to cope with losses like the death of loved ones, the relinquishing of work roles, and the diminution of bodily strength and sensory acuity. "Successful aging" *is* possible, and many people *do* experience the last stage of life positively.

In this chapter, we look at Erikson's and Peck's theories and at research on psychological development in late adulthood, and we examine some attempts to define *successful aging*. We discuss social issues and how older people's lives are af-

fected by how much money they have and where and how they live. Finally, we look at ties between older people and their families and friends, which greatly influence the quality of these last years.

THEORY AND RESEARCH ON PERSONALITY DEVELOPMENT

If I had my life to live over again, I'd try to make more mistakes the next time. I would relax. I would limber up. I would be sillier than I have been this trip. I know of very few things I would take seriously. I would be crazier. I would be less hygienic. I would take more chances. I would take more trips. I would climb more mountains, swim more rivers, and watch more sunsets. I would burn more gasoline. I would eat more ice cream and fewer beans. I would have more actual problems and fewer imaginary ones. (Stair, undated)

Nadine Stair—a participant in the Colorado Outward Bound School, which encourages adults of all ages to examine their lives and their values in the context of an outdoor experience—wrote these lines at the age of 85. In late adulthood, many people reexamine their lives, looking both backward and forward, and decide how to use the time left to them. Let's see what theory and research can tell us about this final phase of the search for self-knowledge.

ERIK ERIKSON: CRISIS 8—INTEGRITY VERSUS DESPAIR

In his final crisis, *integrity versus despair,* Erikson sees older people as confronting a need to accept their lives—how they have lived—in order to accept their approaching death. They struggle to achieve a sense of integrity, of the coherence and wholeness of life, rather than give way to despair over inability to relive their lives differently (Erikson, Erikson, & Kivnick, 1986).

People who succeed in this final, integrative

task—building on the outcomes of the seven previous crises—gain a sense of the order and meaning of their lives within the larger social order, past, present, and future. The "virtue" that develops during this stage is *wisdom,* an "informed and detached concern with life itself in the face of death itself" (Erikson, 1985, p. 61).

Wisdom, Erikson says, includes accepting the life one has lived, without major regrets over what could have been or what one should have done differently. It involves accepting one's parents as people who did the best they could and thus deserve love, even though they were not perfect. It implies accepting one's death as the inevitable end of a life lived as well as one knew how to live it. In sum, it means accepting imperfection in the self, in parents, and in life. (This definition of *wisdom* as acceptance of one's life and imminent death, and thus as an important psychological resource, differs from Smith and Baltes's cognitive definition of *wisdom,* described in Chapter 16.)

People who do not achieve acceptance are overwhelmed by despair, realizing that time is too short to seek other roads to integrity. While integrity must outweigh despair if this crisis is to be resolved successfully, Erikson believes that some despair is inevitable. People need to mourn—not only for their own misfortunes and lost chances but for the vulnerability and transience of the human condition.

Yet Erikson also believes that late life is a time to play, to recapture a childlike quality essential for creativity. The time for procreation is over, but creation can still take place. Even as the body's functions weaken and sexual energy may diminish, people can enjoy "an enriched bodily and mental experience" (1985, p. 64). Research bears out aspects of Erikson's position. For example, Carol Ryff and her associates (1982; Ryff & Baltes, 1976; Ryff & Heincke, 1983) found that both men and women were most concerned with integrity issues in later adulthood.

ROBERT PECK: THREE ADJUSTMENTS OF LATE ADULTHOOD

Peck (1955) expanded on Erikson's discussion of psychological development in late life, emphasizing three major necessary adjustments. These shifts allow older people to move beyond concerns with work, physical well-being, and mere existence to a broader understanding of the self and of life's purpose.

Older people achieve a sense of integrity, according to Erik Erikson, when they gain a sense of the order and meaning of their lives within the larger social order—past, present, and future. *(George Ancona/International Stock Photo)*

Peck's three adjustments are:

1 *Broader self-definition versus preoccupation with work roles:* The issue in this adjustment is the degree to which people define themselves by their work. Everyone has to ask: "Am I a worthwhile person only insofar as I can do a full-time job; or can I be worthwhile in other, different ways—as a performer of several other roles, and also because of the kind of person I am?" (Peck, 1955, in Neugarten, 1968, p. 90).

    Retirees especially need to redefine their worth as human beings. People need to explore themselves and find other interests to take the place of the work (whether centered in the marketplace or the home) that had given direction and structure to life. People are most likely to remain vital if they can be proud of personal attributes beyond their work. They need to recognize that their ego is richer and more diverse than the sum of their tasks at work.

2 *Transcendence of the body versus preoccupation with the body:* Physical decline creates the need

Older people, according to Robert Peck, need to find new interests and new sources of self-esteem to take the place of their former work roles and to make up for physical losses. An elderly person like the artist shown here, who can focus on relationships and absorbing activities, can often overcome physical discomforts. *(Nilo Lima/Photo Researchers)*

for a second adjustment: overcoming concerns with bodily condition and finding other sources of satisfaction. People who have emphasized physical well-being as the basis of a happy life may be plunged into despair by diminishing faculties or aches and pains. Those who focus on relationships and on activities that do not demand perfect health and youthful abilities adjust better.

An orientation away from preoccupation with the body should be developed by early adulthood, but it is in late life that this attitude is critically tested. Throughout life people need to cultivate mental and social powers that can grow with age, along with attributes like strength and muscular coordination that are likely to diminish over the years.

3 *Transcendence of the ego versus preoccupation with the ego:* Probably the hardest, and possibly the most crucial, adjustment for older people is to go beyond concern with themselves and their present lives and to accept the certainty of death.

How *can* people feel positive about their own death? They can recognize that they will achieve lasting significance through what they have done—the children they have raised, the contributions they have made to society, and the personal relationships they have forged. They transcend the ego by contributing to the well-being of others—and this, Peck says, sets human beings apart from animals.

GEORGE VAILLANT: FACTORS IN EMOTIONAL HEALTH

The Grant Study, a longitudinal study that began with college sophomores, was described in Chapters 13 and 15. The researchers in this study examined the physical and mental health of 173 of these men at age 65 (Vaillant & Vaillant, 1990). *Emotional health* at this age was defined as the "clear ability to play and to work and to love" (p. 31) and as having been happy over the previous decade.

It is surprising to see the very limited role that various factors played in emotional health. A happy marriage, a successful career, and a childhood free of such major problems as poverty or the death or divorce of parents were all unimportant in predicting good adjustment late in life. More influential was closeness to siblings at college age, suggesting a close family. Factors associated with poor adjustment at age 65 included major emotional problems in childhood and, before age 50, poor physical health, severe depression, alcoholism, and heavy use of tranquilizers.

Probably the most significant personality trait was the ability to handle life problems without blame, bitterness, or passivity—or, in the researchers' terms, to use "mature defense mechanisms" (see Chapter 13). The men who, over the years, had not collected injustices, complained, pretended nothing was wrong, or become bitter or prejudiced—and could thus respond appropriately to crises—were the best adjusted at age 65. The best adjusted 65-year-olds had been rated in college as well organized, steady, stable, and dependable; and throughout life they continued to show these traits, which were more important than being scholarly, analytic, or creative.

But some characteristics linked with good adjustment in young adulthood—like spontaneity and making friends easily—no longer mattered. Possibly the men who were eccentric and isolated early in life improved their social skills over the years, while the extroverted men did not develop other abilities that may, in the long run, be more valuable (Vaillant & Vaillant, 1990).

RESEARCH ON STABILITY AND CHANGE IN PERSONALITY

In our discussion of personality in middle age, we asked whether basic personality changes or remains stable. The answer seems to be that people change in some ways and remain the same in others. This also holds true for late adulthood. In the past, research on personality in late life seemed to point to a number of changes in the direction of more rigidity. However, for many years the only research on personality was cross-sectional. More recent studies, some longitudinal, some cross-sectional, and some sequential, lead to different conclusions.

A longitudinal study examined 192 Swedes aged 67 to 83 over 6-year periods in a dimension of personality and cognitive style called "field dependence-independence" (Hagberg, Samuelsson, Lindberg, & Dehlin, 1991). This characteristic is related to such traits as self-concept, identity, how outgoing or withdrawn a person is, and how much control people perceive that they have over their own lives. Typically, there is some stability in this personality characteristic. Significant change in this dimension (usually in the direction of greater dependence) was associated with death within 10 years. This might be because such a change in personality was brought on by such factors as illness, social losses, or other life crises. Or it might be related to depression or other psychiatric illnesses.

Another longitudinal study, of 74 Californians between ages 69 and 93, also found a combination of continuity and change over 14-year periods (Field & Millsap, 1991). Among five trait clusters studied, the most stable was *satisfaction*, a component that includes self-esteem, cheerfulness, satisfaction with one's self and one's circumstances, and a lack of worrisomeness and restlessness. The other highly stable dimension was *intellect*, which comprises cognitive functioning and open-mindedness. One dimension that increased was *agreeableness*, especially for the oldest old. Two that decreased were *extroversion* (including talkativeness, frankness, and excitability) and a dimension of *activity, energy, and health*. Changes like these show that development in late life is possible, and that people can change aspects of their personalities at any age.

The most extensive study in this area was a sequential examination that combined cross-sectional and longitudinal data involving more than 3000 older people. The researchers who conducted it concluded that personalities change very little over a 7-year period (Schaie & Willis, 1991). These authors maintain that most differences that show up in older people show change, not within individuals but across cohorts. They found two major cohort differences. The elderly of today are more flexible in personality, behavior, and attitude than were those of a previous generation, which should make them more adaptable to social change. On the other hand, the middle-aged and elderly of today show less social responsibility than did previous cohorts, demonstrating less concern for the needs of other people. If these generational changes continue, they may bode well for individual adjustment in old age, but carry serious consequences for our society as a whole.

The apparent contradictions in these three studies can be explained by focusing on the nature of the studies themselves. First of all, the *dimension studied* makes a difference. In their longitudinal study of older Californians, Field and Millsap found stability in some dimensions and change in others. Then, *nearness to death* makes a difference, as shown in the Swedish study of field dependence-independence. Although this research found considerable stability, it also found change, which was associated with death within 10 years. And finally, *cohort* makes a difference, as evidenced in the Schaie and Willis sequential studies, which found stability across age in individuals, along with significant change between cohorts. The different conclusions from these three studies emphasize the importance of interpreting data with a knowledge of how a given research project was conducted.

APPROACHES TO "SUCCESSFUL AGING"

Is a person who tranquilly watches the world go by from a rocking chair on the front porch making as healthy an adjustment to aging as one who is busy from morning till night? There is more than one way to age well, and the patterns that people follow vary with personality and life circumstances.

Let's look at two contrasting models of successful aging—disengagement theory and activity theory—and then at some personal definitions of successful aging. We'll then examine research findings about how people actually age.

Disengagement Theory

Samuel had been politically active as a younger man, and even after retirement from his job as a civil engineer he kept busy for a while—going to political meetings, writing for newsletters, and getting together for a weekly card game with old friends. But then he dropped out of one group after another; eventually, he even gave up his weekly poker game. This is the pattern of *disengagement* described by Cumming and Henry (1961).

Disengagement theory sees aging as a process of mutual withdrawal. Disengagement theory sees as normal, universal, and necessary for successful aging a pattern whereby older people voluntarily cut down their activities and commitments, while society encourages this by pressuring people to retire. More preoccupation with the self and less emotional investment in others are also considered normal. This decline in social interaction theoretically helps older people to keep their balance and benefits both the individual and society. Disengagement theory predicts that as people disengage, their morale remains high.

In many ways, disengagement theory runs counter to traditional American values of high activity; furthermore, the acceptance of disengagement as normal and desirable undercuts the premise beneath many social programs to help older adults. For these reasons, the presentation of this theory in 1961 led to the formulation of activity theory. (The history of these theories shows how scientific information can make an impact on public policy, and how, on the contrary, public reaction can influence scientists.)

Activity Theory

After Zora retired from her job as principal of an inner-city school, Zora turned her attention and energy to community projects. She started a local chapter of the Gray Panthers, an intergenerational activist group; she became an area coordinator for help to the homeless; and she volunteered to teach in a literacy program for young adults. After her husband died, she resumed a relationship with a man she had known 50 years before, going to church, movies, and other events together.

Zora's life exemplifies *activity theory*, which holds that the more active older people remain, the better they age. In this model, people who are aging successfully act like middle-aged people, keeping up as many activities as possible and finding substitutes for activities lost through retirement or death of a spouse or friends. In this view, a person's roles (worker, spouse, parent, and so on) are the major source of satisfaction in life; the greater the loss of roles through retirement, widowhood, distance from children, infirmity, or other causes, the less satisfied the person will be.

So far, research has not shown that either of these models is more accurate than the other. Some studies have found that activity in and of itself bears little relationship to satisfaction with life (Lemon, Bengson, & Peterson, 1972). Later studies suggested that the *kind* of activity matters: that older people heavily involved in *informal* activities (doing things with friends and family) were happier than those pursuing *formal* (structured group) activities or *solitary* activities (reading, watching television, and pursuing hobbies) (Longino & Kart, 1982). But a subsequent analysis indicated that how people feel about life is affected either not at all or only to the slightest degree by any kind of activity (M. A. Okun, Stick, Haring, & Witter, 1984). Furthermore, an analysis of the impact of activity on mortality over an 8-year period among 508 older Mexican Americans and Anglos found that level of activity was unrelated to time of death, once other factors like age, health, and gender were considered (D. J. Lee & Markides, 1990).

Nor has research on disengagement theory supported an overall relationship between disengagement and high morale; disengagement is *not* inevitable, universal, or consistently sought by elders (Palmore, 1981; Maddox, 1968; Reichard, Livson, & Peterson, 1962). Disengagement seems to be related less to age than to factors associated with aging, like poor health, widowhood, retirement, and poverty. It is influenced by the social environment. For example, when people work, they continue such work-related involvements as membership in trade unions, professional friend-

Author Betty Friedan, whose 1963 book, *The Feminine Mystique,* is credited with launching the women's movement in the United States, exemplifies successful aging as described by activity theory. At age 60, she went on the first Outward Bound survival expedition for people over 55. Now in her 70s, she teaches at universities in California and New York, and has just published her newest best-seller, *The Fountain of Age. (Marshall/Gamma-Liaison)*

ships, and reading in the field. When they lose or give up their jobs, they usually give up these activities. As we will see, other factors, like personality, help determine people's levels of activity—and their morale.

Disengagement may be more common in people close to death. Researchers measured and followed up engagement levels in older people, and found that those who had died in the interim had shown signs of disengagement 2 years before their death; the survivors had not. Thus disengagement may be a brief process, taking about 2 years rather than the 25 or 30 originally proposed (Lieberman & Coplan, 1970).

Personal Definitions of Aging Successfully

There are qualitative differences in the way people approach these last years of life. What are the components of successful aging?

In one study, researchers asked middle-aged adults (60 women and 9 men, average age 52) and older adults (61 women and 41 men, average age 73) to evaluate their present lives; to describe how they had changed or stayed the same; and to define "personal fulfillment," the "ideal person,"

"good" or "poor" adjustment for people their age, and "successful aging" (Ryff, 1989).

In both age groups, respondents defined "successful aging" mostly in terms of relationships with other people—unlike theorists who emphasize self-oriented factors like confidence, self-knowledge, and self-acceptance. Middle-aged and older people seem to consider self-related attributes less important than caring about and getting along with others.

Differences between the two age groups showed up when people were asked what they were unhappy about and what they would change if they could. Middle-aged people were most unhappy about family problems and would change themselves (as by exercising more) or accomplish more in schooling or careers. Older people, however, most commonly said that they were unhappy about nothing and would change nothing except health.

The fact that middle-aged people emphasized continuous growth and older people emphasized acceptance suggests that people age best if they can initiate change themselves but can accept the twists and turns of life—as long as they have good relationships with others.

PERSONALITY AND PATTERNS OF AGING

How do people cope with the losses and other stresses of late life? They may use a number of strategies (such as those listed in Table 17-1) and approaches tied in with religious beliefs and practices (as described in Box 17-1). But successful aging does not follow any single pattern. How older people adapt depends on their personalities and how they have adapted throughout life.

One classic study analyzed styles of aging by looking at subjects' personalities, activity level, and satisfaction with life (Neugarten, Havighurst, & Tobin, 1968). Researchers interviewed 159 men and women aged 50 to 90 and found four major personality types: *integrated, armor-defended, passive-dependent,* and *unintegrated.* They correlated these types with levels of activity in 11 social roles (such as parent, spouse, and club, church, or association member), rated the subjects by levels of life satisfaction, and identified patterns of aging.

Most of the subjects who expressed satisfaction with life were quite active, but some led less active lives. As people aged, they tended to be less active and to fill fewer social roles. The four

TABLE 17-1

Spontaneously Reported Emotion-regulating Coping Strategies Used by Older Adults during Stressful Experiences*

Rank Order	Frequency of Mention	
	Number	(%)
Religious	97	(17.4)
Kept busy	84	(15.1)
Accepted it	63	(11.3)
Support from family or friends	62	(11.1)
Help from professional	34	(6.1)
Positive attitude	31	(5.6)
Took one day at a time	29	(5.2)
Became involved in social activities	19	(3.4)
Planning and preparing beforehand	15	(2.7)
Optimized communication	13	(2.3)
Limited activities, didn't overcommit	11	(2.0)
Sought information	8	(1.4)
Exercised	8	(1.4)
Helped others more needy	7	(1.3)
Realized that time heals all wounds	7	(1.3)
Avoided situation	6	(1.1)
Experience of prior hardships	5	(.9)
Carried on for others' sake	5	(.9)
Ingested alcohol, tranquilizers	5	(.9)
Carried on as usual	4	(.7)
Took a vacation	3	(.5)
Realized others in same situation or worse	3	(.5)
Released emotion (cried or cursed)	3	(.5)
Lowered expectations or devalued	3	(.5)
Miscellaneous	31	(5.6)
Totals	556	(100.6†)

*100 older adults reported 556 coping behaviors for 289 stressful experiences.
†Due to rounding.
SOURCE: Koenig, George, & Siegler, 1988, p. 306.

major personality types, with associated patterns of aging, were as follows:

1 *Integrated:* Integrated people were functioning well, with a complex inner life, a competent ego, intact cognitive abilities, and a high level of satisfaction. They ranged from being very active and involved, with a wide variety of interests, to deriving satisfaction from one or two roles, to being self-contained and content.

2 *Armor-defended:* Armor-defended people were achievement-oriented, striving, and tightly controlled. Both those who stayed fairly active and those who limited their expenditures of energy, socializing, and experience showed moderate to high levels of satisfaction.

3 *Passive-dependent:* Passive-dependent people either sought comfort from others or were apathetic. Some, who depended on others, were moderately or very active and moderately or

BOX 17-1   *FOOD FOR THOUGHT*

RELIGION AND EMOTIONAL WELL-BEING IN LATE LIFE

Their health isn't what it was, they've lost old friends and beloved family members, they don't earn the money they once did, and their lives keep changing in countless stressful ways. Yet in general, older adults have fewer mental disorders and are more satisfied with life than younger ones. What accounts for this remarkable ability to cope?

In one study, interviewers asked 100 well-educated white men and women—aged 55 to 80, balanced for working-class and upper-middle-class status, and 90 percent Protestant—to describe the worst events in their lives and how they had dealt with them (Koenig, George, & Siegler, 1988). The respondents described 289 stressful events and 556 coping strategies.

Heading the list of the most frequent strategies (see Table 17-1) were behaviors associated with religion, cited by 58 percent of the women and 32 percent of the men. Almost three-fourths of these religious strategies consisted of placing trust and faith in God, praying, and getting help and strength from God. Other religious sources of help included friends from church, church activities, the minister, and the Bible.

The next most common strategy was taking one's mind off a problem by keeping busy—in work-related, social, recreational, and family activities; by reading or watching television; by working at hobbies; or by doing a variety of other things.

The third and fourth strategies involved acceptance—and other people. Many respondents were helped by the philosophy expressed in the "serenity prayer": "God grant me the serenity to accept things I cannot change, the courage to change those I can, and

the wisdom to know the difference." These people would think about a problem and do everything they could to resolve it—but then would accept the situation and get on with their lives. Support and encouragement from family and friends also helped; when asked, most people said that others had aided them through the bad times. Relatively few respondents had turned to a health worker; when they did, that person was four times more likely to be a personal physician than a mental health professional.

Other research has confirmed the supportive role of religion for the elderly, especially for women, African Americans, and the oldest of the old. Possible explanations include the social support offered by a religious community, the perception religion offers of a measure of control over life (as through prayer), and faith in God as a way of interpreting the stresses of life (believing, say, that one is part of a larger plan).

In a study of 836 older adults from two secular and three religiously oriented groups, morale was positively associated with three kinds of religious activity: organized (going to church or temple and taking part in the activities), informal (praying, reading the Bible), and spiritual (personal cognitive commitment to religious beliefs). The more religious people had higher morale and a better attitude toward aging, were more satisfied and less lonely. Women and people over 75 showed the strongest correlations between religion and well-being (Koenig, Kvale, & Ferrel, 1988).

The church has always been important to African Americans. At all ages, black women are more reli-

gious than black men. But religious involvement is high among men too, and the gender difference narrows or even reverses in the oldest groups (Levin & Taylor, 1993). Black elderly who feel supported by their church tend to report high levels of well-being, and the more religious older black people are, the more satisfaction they report with life (Walls & Zarit, 1991; Coke, 1992). For all ages and both sexes, the most common religious activity is personal prayer (Chatters & Taylor, 1989).

Since almost all the research on religion in the lives of older Americans has been cross-sectional, it is possible that turning toward religion in old age is a cohort effect rather than a result of aging. It is also likely, however, that as people think about the meaning of their lives and about death as the inevitable end, they may focus more on spiritual matters.

In any case, people can help the elderly better—either on a personal or a professional basis—if they know the most effective strategies for coping with life's challenges. Old people are often reluctant to seek or accept help unless it is offered in a way that is comfortable for them. Since the major source of poor morale in old age is poor health, physicians are usually the first line of help for the elderly. Doctors can help older patients by, for example, tactfully suggesting such supports as congregational work or speaking to a member of the clergy. Religious institutions can set up programs to reach and serve older persons. And friends and family can respect the value of an older person's religious beliefs and activities.

very satisfied. Others, who had been passive all their lives, did little and showed medium or low satisfaction.

4   *Unintegrated:* Unintegrated people were disorganized, with gross defects in psychological functioning, poor control over their emotions, and deteriorated thought processes. They managed to stay in the community, but with low activity and low satisfaction.

Clearly, people differ greatly in how they live the later years of life. Older people (like young ones) are influenced by health, work, money, and family status; furthermore, their personalities determine how they react to situations. They choose activities that make them feel good about themselves—that fit in with their abilities or their values—and they have different capacities to cope with life's stresses.

People tend to react to old age much as they have always reacted to life in general. People who cope well early in life, for example, also cope well later on (Neugarten, 1968, 1973; Neugarten et al., 1968). As Bernice Neugarten writes, "Aging is not a leveler of individual differences except, perhaps, at the very end of life. In adapting to both biological and social changes, the aging person continues to draw upon that which he has been, as well as that which he is" (1973, p. 329).

SOCIAL ISSUES RELATED TO AGING

The ability to cope with challenges may be sorely tested in late adulthood. On top of the physical problems that often accompany aging, the social circumstances of many older people are very trying, or even overwhelming. Two common issues are finances and living arrangements. A less common but growing problem is elder abuse.

INCOME

Government programs—social security and Medicare—have allowed today's elderly people, on the whole, to be at least as well off financially as younger people. In fact, the poverty rate is slightly less for people aged 65 and over than for children and young adults aged 18 to 24 (U.S. Bureau of the Census, 1992c).

Social security is the largest single source of income for older people in the United States. More than 90 percent receive social security benefits, which provide at least half the total income for 61 percent of beneficiaries. Pensions and earnings from work are also important sources of income (U.S. Bureau of the Census, 1992c). Older people who live in family households are better off financially than those who live alone or with nonrelatives.

Still, 3.7 million elderly people—more than one-fifth—are classified as poor or "near poor." Women (especially widows), minorities (see Box 17-2), single people, and people who worked at unskilled or service jobs are likeliest to be poor (U.S. Bureau of the Census, 1992c; Hurd, 1989). Married couples rarely become impoverished after retirement, especially if they have pension benefits. A husband's death, however, is a major risk factor for his widow: she is 4 times as likely as a married person to fall below the poverty line (Burkhauser, Holden, & Feaster, 1988).

Although fewer older people live in poverty today than in the past few decades, many people face poverty for the first time in old age. They can no longer work, and inflation has eroded their savings and pensions. Infirm or disabled people often outlive their savings at a time when their medical bills are soaring. Some get help from such public assistance programs as Supplemental Security Income, subsidized housing, Medicaid, and food stamps. Others either are not eligible or do not take part in these programs, often because they do not know what the programs offer or how to apply.

Medical progress helps people to live longer; now we need to make economic progress to let them live better. To help the poor elderly who are simply continuing a lifelong pattern of poverty, we need social policies to address poverty for all age groups. To help people who got by earlier in life but did not manage to save for their old age, we need insurance plans and programs to encourage saving. And to allay the risk of poverty resulting from the costs of long-term health care, we need a government-sponsored, self-supporting insurance program (Hurd, 1989).

LIVING ARRANGEMENTS

Almost 95 percent of older people live in the community (U.S. Department of Health and Human Services, USDHHS, 1990). About two-thirds of these live in families—most with spouses, the rest with children or other relatives. (These last tend to

BOX 17-2 WINDOW ON THE WORLD

AGING AMONG AFRICAN AMERICANS, HISPANIC AMERICANS, AND OTHER AMERICAN MINORITY GROUPS

Many problems of aging are especially troublesome for African Americans and Hispanic Americans, who make up about 10 percent of the elderly population. First of all, they tend to be poorer. Almost one-third of older African Americans and one-fourth of older Hispanics have incomes below the poverty line (American Association of Retired Persons, AARP, 1986). They also tend to be sicker: they are more likely to fall ill and less likely to get treatment. They tend to be less educated, to have histories of unemployment or under-employment, to live in poorer housing, and to have a shorter life expectancy than white people (see Chapter 14). Although their need for social and medical services is greater, they often live in areas in which services are least available.

A particular irony is that many minority-group workers do not get the social security and Medicare benefits they have earned. Often, after having contributed to these funds during their working years, they die too soon to collect benefits. This will become even more common after the year 2000, when social security benefits will not be available until age 67. Furthermore, since many jobs held by minority-group workers are not covered by social security, minority-group elderly people are more likely than others to be on Old Age Assistance.

Older people from various ethnic groups in the United States, and especially those who were born in other countries, often fail to take advantage of community and government services. They may not know what services are available; they may be too proud to accept help because they think of it as charity; or they may not want, or may not have enough money, to seek services beyond their own neighborhoods. Also, they may feel uncomfortable dealing with people who do not understand their ways of doing things—their food, their family traditions, or their housing patterns. Agencies that serve older people need to be sensitive to these concerns and should reach out to the needy elderly when they do not seek help themselves (Gelfand, 1982).

Some minority subcultures differ from the dominant culture in patterns of family life and standards of behavior. Among Hispanic families, for example, older people have traditionally received a great deal of respect. In these families (as in African American families), grandparents have played an important role in child rearing and have exerted considerable influence over family decisions.

In recent years, with assimilation, this pattern has been breaking down, so that the relations between the generations are becoming more like those in the population as a whole. Still, Hispanic people show a strong extended-family pattern, and the position of the elderly remains relatively high. Mexican Americans, for example, have "strong helping networks with their children." But those who rely heavily on their children tend to have low levels of psychological well-being, possibly because of their dependency (Markides & Krause, 1986; Lawrence, Bennett, & Markides, 1992).

African American families also have large kinship networks, with high levels of interaction and strong emotional bonds between the elderly and their extended families (R. J. Taylor & Chatters, 1991). The generations commonly help each other with money, child care, advice, and other supports. This aid usually adds to formal help from community and governmental agencies for the neediest family members (Gibson, 1986; Mindel, 1983). Older black women express more satisfaction with life than older black men, but for both sexes, the more family involvement there is, the greater life satisfaction people report (Coke, 1992).

Minority-group elderly people, then, are in most ways like the majority population. They do, however, have some special concerns, special needs, and special resources which policymakers and community service agencies need to keep in mind.

be in poor health; they may have moved in with other family members because they cannot care for themselves.) The other one-third live alone or with nonrelatives. The probability of living alone rises with age, and more women than men live alone (USDHHS, 1992—see Figure 17-1).

There are also ethnic differences in living arrangements. White women over 75 are more likely to live alone than black and Hispanic women of the same age, but white men under age 85 are less likely to live alone than their black and Hispanic counterparts (USDHHS, 1992—see Box 17-2 and Figure 17-2). And among elderly Americans of European ancestry, those whose roots are in

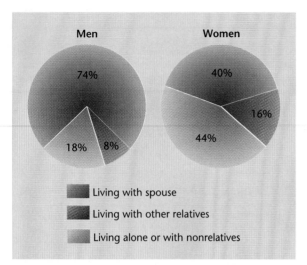

FIGURE 17-1
Living arrangements of noninstitutionalized people aged 65 and over, 1990. (*Source:* American Association of Retired People, AARP, 1991; based on data from U.S. Bureau of the Census.)

southern, central, or eastern Europe* are more likely to live with relatives than those whose forebears came from northwestern Europe.† These patterns hold, no matter how many generations have been in the United States (Clarke & Neidert, 1992). Social policymakers, then, need to take ethnicity into account. What is typical or ideal for one group may disrupt important social patterns in another.

The 9.2 million older people who live alone are at special risk. Almost 80 percent are women, 80 percent are widowed, and almost 50 percent have either no children or none living nearby. They are older and poorer on the average than elderly people who live with someone else. They are also more likely to be depressed and to worry about the future. Yet almost 90 percent value their independence and prefer to be on their own (U.S. Bureau of the Census, 1992c; Commonwealth Fund Commission on Elderly People Living Alone, 1986).

Living Independently

Fay's dream during the last years of her life, when she was in a nursing home, was to live in a room in a private home, so that she could regain her in-

*Southern European ancestry includes Italian, Greek, Spanish, and Portuguese. Central/eastern European ancestry includes Polish, Russian, Bulgarian, Czechoslovakian, Hungarian, Latvian, Romanian, Lithuanian, Serbo-Croation, Slovak, Yugoslavian, and Ukrainian.

†Northwestern European ancestry includes English, Irish, Scottish, Welsh, German, Austrian, Belgian, Dutch, French, Swiss, and Scandinavian.

dependence. But because she needed a high level of care and her daughter could neither care for her herself nor find an appropriate house, Fay remained in the nursing home until her death.

Most older people want to live in the community. Those who do report higher levels of well-being than those in institutions, even when their health is about the same (Chappell & Penning, 1979). But living arrangements can become a major problem as people age. A person may become too infirm to manage three flights of rickety steps. A neighborhood may deteriorate, and frail-looking older people may become the prey of young thugs. Mental or physical disability may keep a person who lives alone from being able to manage.

Some older people in these situations go to an institution, but in recent years creative social planning has enabled a growing number of older people to remain in the community. Many elderly people do not need or want to have their lives totally managed for them but have an impairment that makes it hard, if not impossible, to manage entirely on their own. Relatively minor forms of support—like meals, transportation, and home health aides—can often help them stay in their own homes. Older people usually want to stay in a familiar neighborhood, to be independent, to have privacy, to feel safe, and to have some social contacts (E. M. Brody, 1978; Lawton, 1981).

Most older people do not need much help, but those who do can usually get enough from one person so that they can remain in the community.

FIGURE 17-2
Percentage of persons 65 years and over living alone, by age, sex, race, and Hispanic origin, March 1990. (*Source:* USDHHS, 1992.)

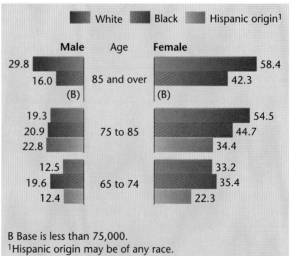

B Base is less than 75,000.
¹Hispanic origin may be of any race.

Married people get such help from the spouse; others most often get it from a child, most likely a daughter; and those who cannot call upon these people usually get help from a friend, rather than another relative (Chappell, 1991).

A variety of living arrangements, some traditional and some innovative, can help older people who fall between self-sufficiency and complete dependency (Steinbach, 1992; Hare & Haske, 1983–1984; Lawton, 1981). These include:

■ *Retirement and life-care communities:* Available only to well-off people, these often offer independent living units, with such services as cleaning, laundry, and meals. As residents age, they may use more extensive services, including health care in a nursing facility.

■ *Sharing a house:* Social agencies match people who need a place to live with people who have houses or apartments with extra rooms. Each person usually has a private room but shares living, eating, and cooking areas.

■ *Group homes:* A social agency that owns or rents a house brings together a small number of elderly residents and hires helpers to shop, cook, do heavy cleaning, drive the residents, and offer professional counseling. Residents care for their own personal needs and take some responsibility for day-to-day tasks.

■ *Accessory housing:* Independent units ("granny flats") are created so that an older person can live in a remodeled single-family home or in temporary quarters set up on the property of a single-family home. These units provide privacy for both parties, cut travel time and expense for the caregivers, and offer security and care for the elderly residents.

Many people in nursing homes do not need nursing care but have no better way to manage. With the high cost of such care and the reluctance of people to enter nursing homes, there are both humane and economic reasons to explore alternative living arrangements.

Living in Institutions

The vast majority of older people do not live in institutions. Most do not want to, and most of their families do not want them to. Older people often feel that placement in an institution is a sign of rejection; and children usually place their parents reluctantly, apologetically, and with great guilt. Sometimes, though, because of an older person's needs or a family's circumstances, such placement seems to be the only solution.

Residents of group retirement homes enjoy socializing. They also get help with shopping, cooking, and cleaning, while caring for their own personal needs and maintaining a sense of self-reliance. Such homes, usually run by social agencies, are among an array of alternatives for elderly people who do not need nursing care but are unable to be completely self-sufficient. *(Blair Seitz/Photo Researchers)*

Who Lives in Nursing Homes?

Although at any one time only about 5 percent of the over-65 population is living in an institution, the lifetime probability of spending time in a nursing home is much higher. A survey of close relatives of people who had died over age 25 found that 29 percent had spent some time in a nursing home and that the percentage rose sharply with age of death (Kemper & Murtaugh, 1991).

The single most important factor keeping people *out* of institutions is being married (Health Care Finance Administration, 1981). Most of the 1.8 million nursing home residents are widows, less than half can get around by themselves, more than half are mentally impaired, and one-third are incontinent (Wolinsky & Johnson, 1992a; U.S. Bureau of the Census, 1992c; AARP, 1986; Moss & Halamandaris, 1977; Ouslander, 1989). Another major factor that helps people to live in the community is taking part in such activities as seeing friends or relatives, going to church or temple or a senior center, or volunteering (Steinbach, 1992).

The elderly at highest risk of institutional living are those living alone, those who do not take part in social activities, those who perceive their health as poor, those whose daily activities are limited by poor health or disability, and those whose caregivers are overburdened (Steinbach, 1992; McFall & Miller, 1992).

As the population ages and women's life expectancy continues to increase faster than men's, the number of nursing home residents is expected

570 PART SEVEN ■ LATE ADULTHOOD

to swell. This will mean a need to build more homes and to finance them. The average cost of nursing home care today may well—especially if several years are involved—exhaust the funds of nearly all elderly people. Because of gaps in health insurance, both private and governmental, about half of all nursing home fees are paid privately. Health professionals, public officials, and private citizens need to come up with public policies for expanding, improving, and paying for such facilities (Kunkel & Applebaum, 1992).

What Makes a Good Nursing Home?

One essential element in good care is opportunity for residents to make decisions and exert some control over their daily lives (Langer & Rodin, 1976). Other essentials of a good nursing home are an experienced professional staff, specializing in care of the elderly; an adequate government insurance program; and a coordinated structure that can provide various levels of care as needed (Kayser-Jones, 1982). The ideal home should be lively, safe, hygienic, and attractive. It should offer stimulating activities and opportunities to socialize with people of both sexes and all ages. It should provide privacy so that (among other reasons) residents can be sexually active; and it should offer a full range of social, therapeutic, and rehabilitative services.

The best-quality care is provided by larger non-profit facilities with a high ratio of nurses to nursing aides (Pillemer & Moore, 1989). Residents are happier in such places, and so are their visitors. (For suggestions on visiting someone in a nursing home, see Box 17-3.)

Problems in Nursing Homes

In 1987, one-third of the nation's nursing homes did not meet minimum standards of legislation enacted that year, which could deny Medicare and Medicaid payments to nursing homes found substandard on three consecutive annual inspections.

A special horror is the abuse of elderly residents by staff members. In one telephone survey, 577 nurses and nurses' aides who worked in nursing homes told of many instances of abuse (Pillemer & Moore, 1989). More than one-third of the respondents (36 percent) had seen other staff members abusing patients physically—restraining them more than necessary; pushing, grabbing, shoving, pinching, slapping, hitting, or kicking them; or throwing things at them. Ten percent admitted having committed one or more of these acts themselves. Psychological abuse was even more com-

mon. Forty percent admitted committing it themselves, and 81 percent saw other staffers yell angrily at patients, insult them, swear at them, isolate them unnecessarily, threaten them, or refuse to give them food.

Furthermore, basic medical care is too often poor, with treatable conditions like depression and incontinence frequently misdiagnosed, drugs prescribed inappropriately, and patients kept oversedated and neglected. To improve care, more doctors need education in geriatrics, more mental health practitioners need to be involved, reimbursement policies need to offer incentives to health care workers for good long-term care, and systems should be set up to monitor prescription of medicines and other practices (Ouslander, 1989).

ABUSE OF THE ELDERLY

A shocking way for aging people to spend their final days is in the state of maltreatment known as *elder abuse*—neglect, or physical or psychological abuse, of dependent older persons. Although it can occur in institutions, it is most often suffered by frail elderly people living with their spouses or their children.

Such abuse can take the form of neglect, as in the withholding of food, shelter, clothing, medical care, money, or other assets. It can involve psychological torment: tongue-lashings, insults, swearing, or threats of violence or abandonment. It can also take the form of physical violence—beating, punching, burning, or using weapons against old people who cannot protect themselves.

Because of problems in defining elder abuse, as well as in reporting it, estimates of the number of cases per year vary from 600,000 to more than 1 million; it may, thus, involve 5 percent of the older population (Eastman, 1984). Elder abuse may be as underreported as child abuse and violence between younger spouses; a study in the Boston area suggests that only 1 case in 14 reaches public attention (Pillemer & Finkelhor, 1988).

The typical victim is an old person in poor health who lives with someone. Elderly people living alone—whether widowed, divorced, or never married—are at low risk. The abuser is more likely to be a spouse than a child, reflecting the fact that more older people live with spouses than with children; and the risk is greater when the caregiver is depressed (Pillemer & Finkelhor, 1988; Paveza et al., 1992). Although many older men are abused, abuse against women inflicts more injuries. Rates

BOX 17-3   PRACTICALLY SPEAKING

VISITING SOMEONE IN A NURSING HOME

Visiting someone in a nursing home can be a wrenching experience. It is painful for family members to witness the deterioration of once-keen mental faculties, to hear complaints that may have less to do with what the resident is actually complaining about than with the physical and emotional losses she or he has suffered, and to feel the depths of the older person's depression. One survey of family visitors found that many of them enjoyed fewer than half of their visits, mostly for these reasons (York & Calsyn, 1977).

Visitors cannot change most of these realities, but they can do something about another major problem—a lack of anything to do. Even if nursing home residents have suffered mental and sensory losses, they can engage in stimulating and comforting activities. A visitor can adapt the following suggestions to a particular resident's level of functioning (B. W. Davis, 1985).

■ *Call on the older person's strengths:* Ask him or her for advice in an area of expertise, like cooking, fishing, or crafts.
■ *Provide the opportunity to make decisions:* Ask the resident where she or he wants to go if you are going out for lunch or for a drive (going outdoors is usually a welcome treat for the homebound resident); ask what she or he wants to wear; ask advice on a gift to buy for a family member.
■ *Be a good listener:* When the older person wants to talk, pay attention even if you have heard the stories before. Be patient. Do not judge or argue. Listen to the feelings beneath the words. Hear complaints as a sympathetic listener without feeling that you need to do anything about them.
■ *Call on the older person's reserves of memories:* A person who forgets what happened 5 minutes ago may have vivid memories of the distant past.

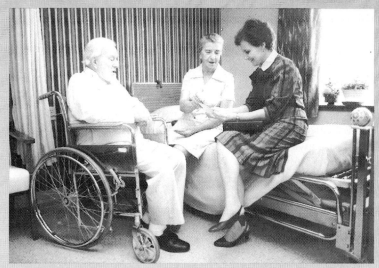

Most older people will never need to go to a nursing home. For those who do, visitors can enliven their visits with stimulating activities that call on the older person's strengths, interests, and memories. *(Blair Seitz/Photo Researchers)*

You might ask the resident to sing old songs with you; to tell you what his or her siblings were like; or to describe childhood celebrations, getting the first job, or meeting his or her spouse.
■ *Do a project together:* You could put together a scrapbook or a photo album, arrange flowers, make Christmas ornaments, do simple sewing or knitting, or do a jigsaw puzzle.
■ *Tape-record the older person:* You will be creating an oral history to pass down to future generations. At the same time, the older person will probably appreciate the opportunity to review his or her life and to think about some of its high points. Questions you might ask could cover decisions and turning points in the person's life, achievements she or he is proud of, wisdom that can be passed along, and events that she or he experienced or witnessed.
■ *Stimulate the senses:* Enhance the older person's experience of the world. Wear and talk about bright colors. Bring in beautifully illustrated books and calendars, and put up seasonal decorations. Play favorite

musical selections. Wear perfume or scented after-shave lotion and bring some for the resident. Bring favorite foods (that have been cleared with the nursing home staff). Most important—hug, hold hands, and touch the older person in comforting ways.
■ *Bring children to visit:* Older people are usually very happy to see young children, especially their grandchildren or great-grandchildren. Take along something to keep the children occupied.
■ *Offer practical help:* Give the resident a calendar to help him or her keep track of time, and mark the calendar with the dates of visits. Check to be sure the resident's eyeglasses are clean and a hearing aid is working and properly adjusted. Ask whether the older person has any special requests for you or the nursing staff.

Your visits are important to a person who lives in a nursing home, away from the familiar places and people of earlier life. You will enjoy them more yourself by following these guidelines.

of violence are high in families with an older person suffering from dementia; in these families punching, kicking, and other violent behavior is high in both directions (Paveza et al., 1992). Rates of abuse are no higher for minority elders, the poor, or people over age 75 (Pillemer & Finkelhor, 1988).

One way to help these victims is, when appropriate, to recognize elder abuse as a type of domestic violence. Outsiders will then be more likely to identify cases of abuse, and the elderly themselves will be aware that they do not have to put up with mistreatment.

Both victim and abuser need treatment (Hooyman, Rathbone-McCuan, & Klingbeil, 1982; Pillemer & Finkelhor, 1988). Abuse needs to be identified and reported, and the victims need to be protected in safe places, perhaps special apartments. Self-help groups may help victims acknowledge what is happening and find out how to stop it or get away from it. The abusers need treatment to recognize what they are doing and to reduce the stress of caregiving, especially when they are in poor health themselves. Some services offer caregivers education, emotional support, counseling, financial assistance, and substitute care to give them respite for a day, a weekend, or a week.

PERSONAL RELATIONSHIPS IN LATE LIFE

Most older people's lives are enriched by the presence of people who care about them and to whom they feel close.

The family is still the primary source of emotional support, and the late-life family has its own special characteristics (Brubaker, 1983; 1990). First of all, it is likely to be multigenerational. Most older people's families include at least three generations; many span four or five. The presence of so many people is enriching but also creates special pressures. Second, the late-life family has a long history, which also has its pluses and minuses. Long experience of coping with stresses can give older people confidence in dealing with whatever life sends their way. On the other hand, many elderly people are still resolving unfinished business of childhood or early adulthood. Third, a number of life events are especially typical of (though not confined to) older families: becoming a grandparent or great-grandparent, retiring from work, and losing a spouse to death.

Personal relationships, especially with family members, continue to be important into very old age (Johnson & Troll, 1992). Let's look at the relationships older people have with people of their own generation—spouses, siblings, and friends—and with their children and grandchildren. We'll also examine the lives of older adults who are divorced or widowed, have never married, and are childless.

MARRIAGE

"One wonderful thing about being married now," said Sylvia, 79, "is that Jake and I can have a "show and tell' session every morning when we tell each other about our aches and pains and know that the other one really cares how we feel. Then we can go through the day without boring anyone else with them!"

The long-term marriage, as we said earlier, is a relatively novel phenomenon; most marriages, like most people, used to have a shorter life span. Many men lost one or more wives in childbirth; and both wives and husbands often succumbed young to disease. Today, fiftieth anniversaries are more common, though many marriages are still severed earlier by death or divorce. Because women usually marry older men and usually live longer than men, many more men than women live with their spouses (see Figure 17-1).

Marital Happiness

Married couples who are still together in their sixties are more likely than middle-aged couples to report their marriage as satisfying. Many say that their marriage has gotten better over the years (Gilford, 1986). Since divorce has been easier to obtain for some years, spouses who are still together late in life have chosen to be together. The decision to divorce usually comes early in a marriage; partners who stay together despite difficulties are often able to work out their differences and eventually arrive at a mutually satisfying relationship.

Another possible reason older people report more satisfaction with marriage is that people of this age are more satisfied with life in general. Their satisfaction may stem from factors outside the marriage—work, the end of child rearing, or more money in the bank. Also, people may say that their marriage is happy as a conscious or unconscious justification for having stayed in it so long.

In a study of 17 marriages that had lasted from

50 to 69 years, nearly three-fourths were described—on the basis of interviews and observations over 50 years—as following one of two patterns: either basically happy over the years or happiest early and late with a dip in the middle (usually the child-rearing years). None of the marriages showed either a continuous increase or continuous decline in happiness (Weishaus & Field, 1988).

Strengths and Strains in Late-Life Marriage

Being in love is still important for successful marriage in late adulthood. Older spouses also value companionship and open expression of feelings, as well as respect and common interests. But problems may arise from differences in values, interests, and philosophies (Stinnett, Carter, & Montgomery, 1972).

A new freedom comes about as husband and wife shed the roles of breadwinner and child rearer, as they become more interested in each other's personality, and as they increasingly enjoy one another's company (Zube, 1982). Further, the ability of married people to handle the ups and downs of late adulthood with relative serenity may result from their mutual supportiveness. This reflects three important benefits of marriage: intimacy (sexual and emotional), interdependence (sharing of tasks and resources), and the partners' sense of belonging to each other (Atchley, 1985; Gilford, 1986).

The success of a marriage in late life may depend on the couple's ability to adjust to the personality changes of middle age, which often lead women and men in opposite directions (Zube, 1982). As the husband becomes less involved with work and more interested in intimacy, the wife may be more interested in personal growth and self-expression. In changing roles, couples may argue over household chores or the like.

Late-life marriages are often severely tested by one spouse's ill health. People who have to care for disabled mates may feel isolated, angry, and frustrated, especially when they are in poor health themselves (Gilford, 1986). Caring for a spouse with dementia is especially demanding, and often results in a sense of lost identity. Both personality and outside involvement affect how well caregivers can adjust to the demands on them. Those who are optimistic and well-adjusted to begin with and those who stay in touch with friends do best (Hooker, Monahan, Shifren, & Hutchinson, 1992; Skaff & Pearlin, 1992).

Some couples enjoy retirement because it offers

Many couples who are still together late in life, especially in the middle to late sixties, say that they are happier in marriage now than they were in their younger years. The most rewarding aspects of marriage include companionship and the ability to express feelings. Romance, fun, and sensuality have their place, too, as this couple in a hot tub demonstrate. *(Paul Fusco/Magnum)*

leisure time for traveling, spending time with children and grandchildren, and pursuing other interests together or separately. By and large, however, retirement does not make a marriage better (G. R. Lee & Shehan, 1989).

Problems most often arise in those situations when the husband retires and the wife is still working (G. R. Lee & Shehan, 1989). The wife may feel that her work load is unfair, since retirement-age husbands spend less than 8 hours a week, on average, on household chores, while their wives spend nearly 20 hours a week more and do more than three-fourths of the housework (Rexroat & Shehan, 1987). In one study, women who had not worked outside the home said that their husbands' retirement had both pros and cons. They missed their personal freedom, felt too many demands on their time, and had more "togetherness" than they wanted. Still, they felt needed in their new "job," and their morale was high (Keating & Cole, 1980).

Never before have so many couples stayed together long enough "to encounter the constellation of life-changing events" in late-life marriage. Some marriages "have built reserves of intimacy and belongingness on which to draw" (Gilford, 1986, p. 19). Others become overburdened.

BEING SINGLE AGAIN: DIVORCE AND WIDOWHOOD

Divorce in late life is rare; couples who take this step usually do it much earlier. Despite the increase in divorce over the past 20 years or so, very few people over age 65 are divorced and not remarried (see Figure 17-3). Given the high divorce rates for younger age groups in recent decades, however, the proportion is likely to rise in the future, and the gap between the sexes will probably widen (Uhlenberg, Cooney, & Boyd, 1990).

Divorced and separated people express much less satisfaction with family life than married people do. The men are less satisfied with friendships and activities not related to work, and the women's standard of living drops. For both sexes, mental illness and death rates are higher, perhaps because social support networks for older divorced people are inadequate (Uhlenberg & Myers, 1981). An increase in divorced older people will mean that they will be less able to help their children if *they* divorce (Uhlenberg et al., 1990).

Surviving the death of a spouse has other ramifications, which we'll discuss in Chapter 18, when we focus on issues of death and bereavement.

REMARRIAGE

After Norah's friend Alice died, Alice's widowed husband moved out of town. Some years later, back in town on a visit, he called on Norah, now widowed herself, and took her to lunch. She recalls:

FIGURE 17-3

Marital status of people aged 65 and over, 1990. (*Source:* American Association of Retired People, AARP, 1991; based on data from U.S. Bureau of the Census.)

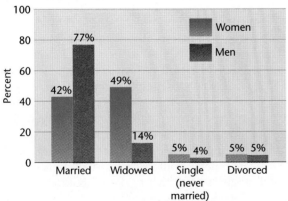

We began to write, and he called me up. Before I knew it, we decided to get married. I guess I didn't think I ever would [get married]. I didn't think I wanted to. [But] as he came, I kind of missed him when he didn't come, see? The more we saw of each other, the better we liked each other. It just worked into something. (Vinick, 1978, p. 361)

Norah's story is unusual—but her new husband's is not. Elderly widowers are more likely to remarry than widows, and men of any age are more likely than women to remarry after divorce. Men have more potential partners. Furthermore, they usually feel more need to remarry; women can handle their own household needs, are sometimes reluctant to give up survivors' pension rights, or do not want to end up caring for an infirm husband. As one woman put it, "I don't want to be a nurse or a purse."

In one study of 24 older couples who had remarried when both partners were over 60, most had been widowed and most had known each other during their first marriages or had been introduced by friends or relatives (Vinick, 1978). Why had they decided to marry again? Men tended to mention companionship and relief from loneliness, while women tended to mention their feelings toward their new husbands or the husbands' personal qualities. Almost all these people—who had been remarried for 2 to 6 years—were happy. These marriages were calmer than marriages earlier in life; the partners had a "live and let live" attitude.

Besides enhancing married couples' lives, remarriage can make society's burden lighter, since older married people are less likely than older people living alone to need help from community agencies or to enter institutions. It would be wise on pragmatic as well as humanitarian grounds to encourage remarriage by letting people keep their pensions and social security benefits and to encourage shared living like group housing.

SINGLE LIFE: THE "NEVER MARRIEDS"

Only about 5 percent of older men and women have never married (see Figure 17-3). When 22 never-married people, aged 60 to 94, were interviewed about their attitude toward getting old, they expressed less loneliness than the typical person of their age. They also seemed to be less affected by aging; they were more independent, had fewer social relationships, and were generally satisfied with life (Gubrium, 1975).

Never-married childless women in one study rated three kinds of relationships as important: bonds of blood (as a daughter, a sibling, and an aunt); parent-surrogate-type ties with younger people; and same-generation, same-sex friendships and companions (Rubinstein, Alexander, Goodman, & Luborsky, 1991). Few had key relationships with men. Older single women in another study appeared not to become lonely with the loss of friends and family, but they did feel lonely if they lost their health (Essex & Nam, 1987). Poor health undermines the sense of self-reliance and independence and may force people into dependent relationships with relatives they would rather not be with.

SEXUAL RELATIONSHIPS

Human beings are sexual beings from birth until death. Even though illness or frailty may sometimes prevent older people from acting on sexual feelings, the feelings persist. People can express sexuality in many ways other than genital contact—in touching, in closeness, in affection, in intimacy. An active sexual relationship, not defined by the performance standards of youth, can help to assure each partner of the other's love and affection and of each one's own continuing vitality.

The physical aspect of sex was not scientifically recognized as a normal element of the lives of older people until the 1960s, with the pioneering research of William H. Masters and Virginia E. Johnson and the findings of the Duke University Longitudinal Study. More recent reports also indicate a rich diversity of sexual experience well into late adulthood (Weg, 1985; Brecher & the Editors of Consumer Reports Books, 1984; B. D. Starr & Weiner, 1981).

After interviewing men and women over age 60, Masters and Johnson (1966, 1981) concluded that people who have active sexual lives during their younger years are likely to remain sexually active in later life. The most important factor in maintaining sexuality is consistent sexual activity over the years. A healthy man who has been sexually active can usually continue some form of active sexual expression into his seventies or eighties. Women are physiologically able to be sexually active as long as they live. The major barrier to a fulfilling sexual life for them is lack of a partner.

Sex is, of course, different in late adulthood from

Sexual relationships can be a vital part of life in late adulthood; they are by no means only a memory or an occasional foray into pleasures of the past. People who were sexually active when younger usually continue to be sexually active in late life, if partners are available. Sexuality can be expressed in closeness, touching, affection, and intimacy as well as in sexual intercourse. *(Bill Pierce, Time Magazine/Sygma)*

what it was earlier. Older people tend to feel less sexual tension, usually have less frequent sexual relations, and experience less physical intensity. The sexual flush and increased muscle tone that accompany arousal are still present, but to a lesser degree. With age, men take longer to develop an erection and to ejaculate, and have lower levels of the male sex hormone testosterone (Bremner, Vitiello, & Prinz, 1983). Women's breast engorgement, nipple erection, clitoral and labial engorgement, and other signs of sexual arousal are less intense than before. But older men and women can still reach orgasm, especially if they have been sexually active through the years.

Both men and women can enjoy their sexuality in late life. Sexual expression can be even more significant in the lives of older people if both young and old recognize it as normal and healthy. Older people need to accept their own sexuality without shame or embarrassment, and younger ones have to avoid ridiculing or patronizing older persons who show signs of healthy sexuality. Housing arrangements should give older men and women chances to socialize, with ample privacy. Medical and social workers should consider the sexual needs of the elderly: when possible, they should avoid prescribing drugs that interfere with sexual functioning; and when such a drug must be taken, the patient should be alerted about its effects. Professionals should discuss sexual activity matter-of-factly—for example, with a heart patient who may be embarrassed to ask about it.

RELATIONSHIPS WITH SIBLINGS

"When I die, don't you dare let my brother Pete come to my funeral," Sally's elderly mother told her daughter. "If he won't make up while I'm alive, I don't want him to do it after I'm dead." But another brother intervened as a peacemaker, and Leah and Pete reestablished the close ties they had had before a misunderstanding estranged them painfully for years. In their last years of life they were a source of great comfort to each other.

Sibling relationships are the longest-lasting ties in most people's lives. Since more than 75 percent of people aged 65 and older have at least one sibling, brothers and sisters play important roles in the support networks of older people (Scott & Roberto, 1981).

Research suggests that siblings have the same kinds of relationships in old age that they had in middle age: they see each other just as often and are just as involved (D. Field & Minkler, 1988). After establishing their own identities through career and family, they often make special efforts to renew ties after their children leave home. Earlier rivalry tends to be replaced by closeness and affection (Cicirelli, 1980; H. G. Ross, Dalton, & Milgram, 1980; Scott & Roberto, 1981).

Looking back, older people who feel close to their brothers or sisters express a sense of peace with life and with themselves, whereas those who are estranged from their siblings often feel upset, as if they have failed to live up to their family values. Siblings who have reestablished ties generally feel that they have accomplished something important (H. G. Ross et al., 1980). The closer people live to their siblings and the more siblings they have, the more likely they are to confide in them (Connidis & Davies, 1992).

Sisters are especially vital in maintaining family relationships; they challenge and stimulate each other and are emotionally supportive to their brothers. Older people who are close to their sisters feel better about life and worry less about aging than those without sisters, or without close ties to them (Cicirelli, 1977, 1989). And being close to a sister lifts the morale of older widows (O'Bryant, 1988). These effects may stem in part from wom-

en's nurturant behavior, which may be a cohort effect. As younger, less gender-typed men and women age, brothers may offer as much solace as sisters (Cicirelli, 1989). Even now, both brothers and sisters, as well as their children, are important sources of support for never-married women (Rubinstein et al., 1991).

Although older people feel closer to their children and grandchildren than to their siblings and are more likely to get help from children than from siblings, they usually turn to siblings before anyone else. For people who have only one or two children, or none, relationships with siblings in late life will probably be increasingly important as a source of emotional support and practical help (Rubinstein et al., 1991; Cicirelli, 1980; Scott & Roberto, 1981).

FRIENDSHIPS

Friendship is a unique relationship because people *choose* their friends. The element of choice may be especially important to older people, who may feel their control over their lives slipping away in many other areas (R. G. Adams, 1986). This helps to explain why most older people have close friends, and why those who have an active circle of friends are happier and healthier (Steinbach, 1992; Babchuk, 1978–1979; Lemon et al., 1972).

Well into old age, women continue to see their friends about as much as or more often than in the past, and feel the same way about them. Consistent with gender differences in friendship throughout life, older men see their friends less, see them more in group activities rather than on an intimate one-to-one basis, and consider friendship less important (D. Field & Minkler, 1988).

Although family members provide more reliable emotional support, older people enjoy time spent with their friends more than time spent with their families. In one study, 92 retired adults (52 women and 40 men) between ages 55 and 88 wore beepers for 1 week. At about 2-hour intervals, they were paged; then they filled out reports on what they were doing and with whom, and what they were thinking and feeling (Larson, Mannell, & Zuzanek, 1986). These people were generally more alert, excited, and emotionally aroused with friends than with family members, including their spouses. One reason may be that older people spend more active, enjoyable leisure time with friends but do household tasks or watch television with family. Older people feel a reciprocal sense of openness

Older people often enjoy the time they spend with friends more than the time they spend with family members. The openness and excitement of relationships with friends help older men and women rise above worries and problems. Intimate friendships give older people a sense of being valued and wanted and help them deal with the changes and crises of aging. *(Leonard Freed/Magnum)*

with their friends, and the lightheartedness and spontaneity of friendships help them rise above daily concerns.

Still, spending time with friends does not result in higher overall life satisfaction, while spending more time with a spouse does. It may be the very brevity and infrequency of the time spent with friends that give it its special flavor. Friends are a powerful source of *immediate* enjoyment, while the family provides a greater underlying sense of security and support.

Other studies have emphasized different aspects of friendship: common interests, social involvement, and mutual help (R. G. Adams, 1986). Intimacy may be the most important benefit of friendship, especially to older adults, who need to know that they are still valued and wanted despite physical and other losses (Essex & Nam, 1987). Friends and neighbors often take the place of family members who are far away.

Friends are a bulwark against the impact of stress on physical and mental health (Cutrona, Russell, & Rose, 1986). People who can confide their feelings and thoughts and can talk about their worries and pain with friends deal better with the changes and crises of aging (Genevay, 1986; Lowenthal & Haven, 1968). They also seem to extend their lives (Steinbach, 1992). In fact, one gerontologist has asked, "Could [men's] difficulty with self-disclosure and expression of feelings be factors in men's shorter life expectancy?" (Weg, 1987, p. 135). The importance of friends is highlighted by findings that most older people's morale depends more on how often they see their friends than on how often they see their children (Glenn & McLanahan, 1981).

RELATIONSHIPS WITH ADULT CHILDREN

For about 20 years, when Diane was living hundreds of miles away from her parents' New Jersey home, she kept in close touch with them by phone and mail. Since she moved to New York, only 20 minutes away, she was able to provide support during her father's illness and is now there to help her widowed mother.

Most older people see their children often—once or twice a week on an average—and feel even closer to them now. Most live near at least one child; they help their children in a number of ways, and when they need help themselves, their children are the first people they turn to and the ones likely to do the most (D. Field & Minkler, 1988). Older people in better health have more contacts with their families and report feeling closer to family members than do those in poorer health (Field, Minkler, Falk, & Leino, 1993).

How Parents Help Children

Many older people resume a more active parenting role when their adult children need help. Parents of divorced adults see their children more often after the divorce than they did before, and often take them into their homes. Parents are usually the primary caregivers for adult children who are mentally ill, moderately retarded, or otherwise disabled. And many parents of alcoholics and drug abusers support their children financially as well as emotionally (Greenberg & Becker, 1988).

In one study of 29 healthy white midwestern middle-class and working-class married couples, age 60 and over, their children's lives were a daily topic of conversation—especially when the children had problems. "Although they had left home years ago, these children remained psychologically present in their parents' thoughts and conversations" (Greenberg & Becker, 1988, p. 789). Parents helped by caring for grandchildren, inviting divorced daughters to live with them, paying for treatment for drug abuse, helping with household projects, giving advice (only when it was asked for, they said), and lending or giving money for a variety of purposes. In fact, more than half of the mothers and one-third of the fathers experienced significant stress because of their children's problems. The fathers' stress resulted more from their wives' reactions to the children's problems than from the problems themselves. For mothers, the most stressful relationships were those in which a daughter had broken off contact with the family; fathers' most stressful relationships were with sons who continued to depend on their parents for emotional or financial support.

Other research has shown that when an adult moves into the home of elderly parents, the parents report that the generations get along quite well (Suitor & Pillemer, 1987, 1988; see also the description of these studies in Chapter 15). Conflict was lowest in households with older adult children and households in which parent and child had the same or similar marital status. Such harmony may be explained in two ways. First, people who get along well are those most likely to choose to live together. But second, older parents may exaggerate harmony to make reality match their wishes. When parents and children do *not* get along, the parents' marriage is sometimes affected.

Thus, instead of thinking of older adults as freed from active parenting and its stresses, society needs to consider their continuing importance in their children's lives—and the need for programs to help them cope with their children's problems.

How Children Help Parents

People in our society do not fall as naturally into the cycle of care common in some other societies (see Box 17-4), in which older people expect to be cared for in their children's homes just as the parents once cared for the children. With such growing institutional supports as social security, Medicare, and Medicaid, many responsibilities have been shifted from the shoulders of adult children to various governmental agencies. And many mid-

dle-aged children who care for aging parents are torn between love and resentment, between duty toward their parents and obligations toward their spouses and children, and between wanting to do the right thing and not wanting to change their present style of life.

Still, adult children do help their aged parents in many ways—sometimes just by their existence. In one group of 150 "old-old" people in diverse socioeconomic circumstances, parents were more active with other relatives than were childless people. This suggests that children provide the link with other family members, especially, of course, grandchildren (Johnson & Troll, 1992).

Most adult children are conscious of their obligations to their parents, often expecting more of themselves than the parents do of them. In a study of 144 parent-child pairs (parents' ages ranged from 60 to 94; children, from 23 to 66), both generations considered the same three aspects of help to be most important (Hamon & Blieszner, 1990). These were helping parents to understand their resources, giving emotional support, and talking over matters of importance (see Table 17-2). Both generations thought it was important to be together on special occasions but gave little weight to living near or with each other, writing often, or adjusting work or family schedules to help parents. The children felt that they should give money to their parents, but the parents disapproved of this. In sum, elderly parents seem to care more about their children's feelings for them and how they show these feelings than about the concrete actions the children take.

In a study of 29 pairs of elderly widows and their caregiving daughters, researchers identified three kinds of relationships, characterized by either mutual enjoyment, ambivalence, or conflict (A. J. Walker & Allen, 1991). The daughters with the most rewarding ties to their mothers tended to have fewer children, not to be employed, and to have cared for their mothers for a shorter time than the daughters in the other two groups. Clearly, the rewards a daughter receives from helping her mother are colored by the other stresses in her life.

CHILDLESSNESS

Many parents say that one of the advantages of having children is being assured of care and companionship in their old age. But having children is not a guarantee of this; a far more important fac-

BOX 17-4 *WINDOW ON THE WORLD*

EXTENDED FAMILY LIVING IN LATIN AMERICA

In the colorful novels of Latin American authors like Isabel Allende, Gabriel Garcia Marquez, and Mario Llosa Vargas, households throb with the lively doings of grandparents, parents, and children, as well as uncles and aunts. Although these novelists infuse their stories with brilliant imaginative elements, this picture of three-generation life in one household is rooted in fact.

Most elderly Latin Americans live in extended-family households. In the six countries examined in the World Fertility Survey (Colombia, Costa Rica, the Dominican Republic, Mexico, Panama, and Peru), unmarried people were more likely than married people to live in such households. Overall, two-thirds of unmarried people lived in extended-family households, compared with about one-half of married people.

In this last respect, these countries are similar to the United States: two married couples rarely live together unless one couple is very old or very young. However, the differences are greater. In the United States, unmarried older people tend to live alone rather than with family; in Latin America, households commonly include family members outside the nuclear family unit.

Since gender is even more important in Latin America than North America in determining social roles, it is not surprising that women are more likely than men

Most elderly Latin Americans live in extended family households like this one among an Ecuadorian family of Otavalo Indians. Women and single elders are more likely to live in such households than are men and the married. *(Elliott Varner Smith/International Stock Photo)*

to live in extended-family households. This may reflect women's greater life expectancy, their closeness to their children, or their greater financial need. On the other hand, neither the age of an older person nor residence in a rural or urban setting affects the likelihood of living with relatives.

In the six countries surveyed, the proportion of extended families ranged from just over half (52 percent) in Mexico to almost two-thirds (64 percent) in the Dominican Republic. This may be due to

cultural differences between these countries—for example, whether the dominant cultural influence has been Caribbean (as in Costa Rica) or Andean (as in Peru). Both the larger overall difference between Latin America and North America and the smaller differences among these six countries show the importance of recognizing how culture helps to determine the way people lead their everyday lives.

SOURCE: deVos, 1990.

---

tor is the presence of a spouse. Married people are much less likely than single people to be institutionalized; the presence or absence of children does not seem to make much of a difference (Johnson & Catalano, 1981).

What is life like for the more than 5 million childless people who make up about 20 percent of the population over 65? Research has found little evidence of any important drawbacks associated with

nonparenthood in late life. Older people without children are no lonelier, no more negative about their lives, and no more afraid of death than those with children (Johnson & Catalano, 1981; Keith, 1983; Rempel, 1985). Widowed mothers, however, do have higher morale than childless widows (O'Bryant, 1988). And some older women do express regret over not having had children; the older they are, the more intense their regret

TABLE 17-2

Expectations for Behavior by Adult Children toward Their Parents

Item	Adult Children		Parents	
	%	Rank	%	Rank
Help understand resources	99.3	1	97.2	2
Give emotional support	97.2	2	95.7	3
Talk over matters of importance	96.5	3	98.6	1
Make room in home in emergency*	94.4	4	73.0	7
Sacrifice personal freedom*	93.7	5	81.0	6
Care when sick*	92.4	6	64.3	9
Be together on special occasions	86.0	7	86.7	5
Give financial help*	84.6	8	41.1	13
Give parents advice	84.0	9	88.7	4
Adjust family schedule to help*	80.6	10	57.4	10
Feel responsible for parent*	78.2	11	66.4	8
Adjust work schedule to help*	63.2	12	42.1	12
Parent should live with child*	60.8	13	36.7	15
Visit once a week	51.4	14	55.6	11
Live close to parent	32.2	15	25.7	16
Write once a week	30.8	16	39.4	14

Notes: (1) Ranking reflects percentage of respondents who "strongly agreed" or "agreed" with each item on the Hamon Filial Responsibility Scale. (2) Asterisk indicates significant differences in proportion of endorsement for children and parents.
SOURCE: Adapted from Hamon & Blieszner, 1990, p. P111.

seems to be (Alexander, Rubinstein, Goodman, & Luborsky, 1992).

GRANDPARENTHOOD AND GREAT-GRANDPARENTHOOD

Today's grandparents are likely to be designing rocking chairs rather than sitting in them, to be marketing cookies rather than baking them, and to be wearing jogging suits instead of aprons. This is partly because people usually become grandparents for the first time in middle age, at an average age of 50 for women and 52 for men (Troll, 1983). It is also because the role of grandparent is usually secondary to other roles in a person's life—despite a journalistic tendency to mention grandparenthood even when it is totally irrelevant, as in the case of a nurse who was identified as a "51-year-old grandmother" in a report of her conviction for poisoning her fiancé (Olds, 1987)!

Grandparenting *is* important to the 75 percent of people over 65 who have grandchildren, as well as to their children and to the grandchildren themselves. Since 75 percent of grandparents see their grandchildren at least once a week, one generation or the other is making the effort to visit (Troll,

1983). In general, satisfaction with grandchildren stays high into very old age, even though the generations see each other less often as children grow up (D. Field & Minkler, 1988).

A major study (consisting of interviews, group discussions, and case studies of a three-generational, nationally representative sample) found that "grandparents play a limited but important role in family dynamics" and that they have strong emotional ties to their grandchildren (Cherlin & Furstenberg, 1986, p. 26). Usually grandparents do not intervene directly in the children's upbringing. Instead, they enjoy the children's company through casual, frequent contact—even when the grandparents and the parents do not get along. When grandparents do *not* see their grandchildren often, it is usually because they live too far apart.

This norm of noninterference is likely to evaporate in times of trouble, when grandparents become a ready resource. Lillian E. Troll, who has done extensive studies of families in later life, sees grandparents as family "watchdogs" (1983). They stay on the fringes of their children's and grandchildren's lives, with varying degrees of involvement, but rarely play a strong role unless they *need* to. At times of crisis—after a divorce, for example, or during illness or money troubles—they step in and become more active. In good times, they watch to be sure that things are going well. African American grandparents, though, are more likely to act like parents even when there is no crisis (Cherlin & Furstenberg, 1986; see Box 17-2 on page 567).

Gender differences exist in grandparenting. Grandmothers tend to have closer, warmer relationships and to serve more often as surrogate parents than grandfathers do. The mother's parents are likely to be closer to the children than the father's parents and are more likely to become involved during a crisis (Cherlin & Furstenberg, 1986; Hagestad, 1978, 1982; Kahana & Kahana, 1970). Grandmothers tend to be more satisfied with grandparenting than grandfathers are (J. L. Thomas, 1986). Racial differences may influence the grandparent role, at least for men. One study found that grandfatherhood is more central to African Americans than to white men (Kivett, 1991).

Great-grandparents, too, find their role emotionally fulfilling. When 40 men and women, aged 71 to 90, were interviewed, 93 percent were enthusiastic about their status. Their comments— "Life is starting again in my family," "Seeing them grow keeps me young," "I never thought I'd live to see it," and the like—indicate a sense of personal and family renewal, appreciation of great-grandchildren as a source of diversion, and acknowledgment of the subjects' own longevity (Doka & Mertz, 1988, pp. 193–194). More than one-third of these people (mostly women) were close to their great-grandchildren; others were more remote and had more limited contacts. The ones who were close to the children were likely to live nearby and to be close to the children's parents and grandparents. They often helped out with loans, gifts, and baby-sitting. Most adapted to new situations and changed circumstances, and did as much as they could for their families.

This woman playing the piano while her disabled grandson sings along typifies today's active grandparent. The grandparent-grandchild relationship can bring a special element of fun, warmth, and caring, without the strains of child-rearing responsibilities. Grandparents are an important source of wisdom and a symbol of the continuity of family life. *(Will & Deni McIntyre/Photo Researchers)*

Both grandparents and great-grandparents are important to their families. They are sources of wisdom, companions in play, links to the past, and symbols of the continuity of family life. They are engaged in the ultimate generative function: expressing the human longing to transcend mortality by investing themselves in the lives of future generations.

SUMMARY

THEORY AND RESEARCH ON PERSONALITY DEVELOPMENT

■ Erik Erikson's final crisis is integrity versus despair, culminating in the virtue of wisdom. Old people need to accept their lives and their impending death; if they fail, they become overwhelmed with the realization that time is too short to begin another life and therefore will be unable to accept death.

■ Robert Peck specified three adjustments involved in successful aging: broader self-definition versus preoccupation with work roles, transcendence of the body versus preoccupation with the body, and transcendence of the ego versus preoccupation with the ego.

■ George Vaillant found that people who were able to handle life's problems without bitterness, blame, or passivity were best adjusted at age 65.

■ While some basic personality traits appear to remain stable in late adulthood, others shift.

■ Two models of successful aging are disengagement theory and activity theory. Disengagement theory characterizes successful aging by mutual withdrawal between society and the older person. Activity theory holds that the more active an old person remains, the more successfully she or he ages.

■ "Personal" definitions of successful aging emphasize relationships with others.

■ Research finds a variety of patterns of successful aging, associated with varying levels of activity.

SOCIAL ISSUES RELATED TO AGING

■ The financial situation for older people has improved, but still some 3.7 million of them live in poverty. Many become poor for the first time after retirement. Social security is the largest single source of income for elders in the United States.

■ Most older people live with members of their families. Of the almost 95 percent who are not institutionalized, about one-third live alone or with nonrelatives. The majority of the 9.2 million older people who live alone are widowed women.

■ Developing housing alternatives to institutionalization is a major challenge for society. Possibilities include retirement and life-care communities, sharing a house, group homes, and accessory housing.

■ Only 5 percent of people over 65 years old are institutionalized at any one time. Those most likely to be institutionalized are very old, frail women. Elder abuse is most often suffered by a frail older person living with a spouse or child.

PERSONAL RELATIONSHIPS IN LATE LIFE

■ Relationships are very important for older people, as they are for people of all ages. The family is still the primary source of emotional support.

■ As life expectancy increases, so does the potential longevity of marriage. Marriages that last into late adulthood (especially the early part of that period) tend to be relatively satisfying; but strains that arise from personality, health, and role changes may require adjustment by both partners.

■ Divorce is relatively uncommon among older people.

■ Remarriage in late adulthood tends to be a positive experience. Elderly widowers are more likely to remarry than elderly widows are.

■ People who reach late life without marrying seem to be more independent and less lonely than the typical person of their age.

■ Many older people are sexually active, though the degree of sexual tension and the frequency and intensity of sexual experience are generally lower than for younger adults.

■ Often relationships between siblings become closer in later life than they were in earlier adulthood. Sisters in particular make the effort to maintain these ties.

■ Friendships are important for immediate enjoyment, for intimacy, and for support in meeting the problems of aging.

■ Although elderly parents and their adult children do not typically live together, they frequently see or contact each other and offer each other assistance.

■ The presence or absence of children is not associated with important psychological or material rewards in old age.

■ Grandparents have close ties with their grandchildren and see them frequently unless they live too far away. Generally, grandparents today do not interfere with the way their grandchildren are raised but take a more active role in time of crisis. Great-grandparents also tend to find their roles emotionally fulfilling.

KEY TERMS

integrity versus despair (page 558)   activity theory (562)   elder abuse (570)
disengagement theory (562)

SUGGESTED READINGS

Biracree, T., & Biracree, N. (1991). *Over fifty: The resource book for the better half of your life.* New York: Harper. A comprehensive guide to finances, health care, recreation, education and travel opportunities, and housing for retired people, this book includes a directory of additional resources.

Elkind, D. (1990). *Grandparenting: Understanding today's children.* Glenview, IL: Scott, Foresman. David Elkind, a psychologist who has studied and written about stress in children, advises grandparents on dealing with typical problems that occur in each stage of a child's development. In addition, he offers suggestions on helping children and grandchildren cope with stress and on common problems faced by grandparents such as baby-sitting and relationships with teenagers.

Kidder, J. T. (1993). *Old friends.* New York: Houghton Mifflin. The prize-winning author offers a nonfiction portrait of two elderly men, thrust together as roommates in a nursing home. By musing over their lives together, the men, at first strangers, develop a deep and rewarding friendship. This study of old age reminds all of us of the possibility of continued renewal in the face of mortality.

Myerhof, B. (1984). *Number our days.* New York: Simon & Schuster. This study by an anthropologist of the process of aging focuses on a group of elderly people who attend a center for Jewish senior citizens. The book details their remarkable strength, vitality, and ability to meet life's challenges despite poverty and ill health.

Rose, X. (1990). *Widow's journey: A return to the loving self.* New York: Holt. This is a sensitive and moving account by a widowed psychotherapist of life after the death of a spouse; the ensuing feelings of guilt, anger, fear and isolation; and eventual readjustment.

PART EIGHT

THE END OF LIFE

Human beings are individuals; they undergo different life experiences and react to them in different ways. But one universal experience in the life cycle is its ending. The better people can understand and approach this inevitable event, the more fully they can live until it comes to them.

■ In **Chapter 18**, the final chapter in this book, we examine some important issues relating to the final stage of life: how people of different ages think and feel about death, how people face their own impending death, how they deal with the deaths of those they love, and what can be done to make their adjustment easier. We also look at the "right to die" and what it means with regard to "mercy killing" and suicide. We see that death is an integral element of the life span and that understanding the end of life helps us understand the whole of life.

CHAPTER EIGHTEEN

DEATH AND BEREAVEMENT

. . . The key to the question of death unlocks the door of life.

Elisabeth Kübler-Ross
Death: The Final Stage of Growth, *1975*

■ **THREE ASPECTS OF DEATH**

■ **FACING DEATH**

Attitudes toward Death and Dying across the
  Life Span
Confronting One's Own Death
Bereavement, Mourning, and Grief
Widowhood: Surviving A Spouse

■ **CONTROVERSIAL ISSUES OF DEATH
AND DYING**

Euthanasia and the Right to Die
Suicide

■ **FINDING A PURPOSE IN LIFE AND DEATH**

The Meaning of Death
Reviewing a Life

■ **BOXES**

18-1 Food for Thought: Postponing Death
18-2 Window on the World: Mourning
Customs among Traditional Jews
18-3 Take a Stand: Should Anencephalic
Babies Be Used as Organ Donors?
18-4 Practically Speaking: The Living Will
and Medical Durable Power of Attorney
18-5 Practically Speaking: Evoking Memories
for a "Life Review"

Death was once very much a part of daily life. People expected some of their children (or their sisters and brothers) to die in infancy or childhood. They saw relatives and friends succumb to an array of fatal illnesses at an early age. Before modern times, some 50 people out of every 1000 died in a typical year; and during periods of plague or natural disaster, the death rate might reach 40 percent—400 people out of every thousand. More than one-third of all babies died in infancy, and half of all children died before their tenth birthday (Lofland, 1986).

Since the turn of this century, advances in medicine and sanitation have brought a "mortality revolution" in modern developed countries (Lofland, 1986, p. 60). Death rates are typically below 9 percent; infant mortality has fallen to below 1 percent in the United States and even lower in much of Europe. Children are now more likely to reach adulthood, adults are more likely to reach old age, and older people are able to overcome illnesses that were once inevitably fatal. Death has become largely a phenomenon of late adulthood. People in the earlier phases of life rarely have to face death; thus when they reach the age when death becomes a more constant presence, they are likely to be ill-prepared for it (Lofland, 1986).

As death became something that happens mostly to the old and infirm, it moved to the periphery of younger people's consciousness. Care of the dying and the dead, once a familiar aspect of family life, is now usually done by professionals. People go to hospitals to die, and undertakers prepare their bodies for burial. When people speak of dying, they often use euphemisms like *passing away, passing on,* and *going to meet one's maker.* Although the AIDS scourge continues to take the lives of many young and middle-aged people, still many people in these age groups seldom meet death face to face, and many go through most of their lives without thinking much about their own death.

It is true that death is a constant presence in the media. The tendency of American popular culture to deny the personal reality of death seems to be coupled with a "pornographic" obsession with fantasies of violent death, as seen in horror movies and television shows. But real deaths—in battle, fires, and other disasters—are often little more than impersonal statistics on the evening news. Only a frightening event like an airplane crash, a suicide wave among teenagers, or an epidemic like the spread of AIDS brings death to the forefront of public awareness.

However, a healthier attitude toward death has emerged in recent years. Increasing numbers of people are seeking to understand death; to explore the emotional, moral, and practical issues surrounding it; and to try to make this certain outcome of every person's life as positive as possible. *Thanatology,* the study of death and dying, is arousing a great deal of interest as people recognize the importance of integrating death into life.

The terminal stage of life is a significant and valuable portion of the life course. If people live long enough, they are bound to have to deal with the death of people close to them. And, the awareness that they themselves will die one day can impart a special appreciation of life's pleasures and can make them think about the values they live by.

All deaths are different, just as all lives are different. The experience of dying is not the same for an accident victim, a patient with terminal cancer, a person who commits suicide, and someone who dies instantaneously of a heart attack. Nor is the experience of bereavement the same for their survivors. Yet all people are human; and just as there are commonalities in our lives, there are commonalities in death.

In this chapter we look at the biological, social, and psychological aspects of death (the state) and dying (the process). We see how people in different phases of life think about death. We explore efforts to ease the process of dying and the pain of bereavement through education about death, hospices for the terminally ill, and support organizations for the dying and their families. We examine different patterns of mourning across cultures, we look at the various forms grief can take, and we consider ways to help survivors handle bereavement. We also look at such controversial issues as the use of heroic measures to prolong life, euthanasia ("mercy killing"), and suicide, and especially at recent increases in suicide among adolescents. Finally, we look at how people can accept death by finding purpose in life.

THREE ASPECTS OF DEATH

There are at least three aspects of dying: the *biological*, the *social*, and the *psychological*, all of which have become increasingly controversial.

The legal definition of *biological* death varies from state to state, but in general, biological death is considered the cessation of bodily processes. A person may be pronounced dead when the heart stops beating for a significant period of time or when electrical activity in the brain stops. The criteria for death have become more complex with the development of medical apparatus that can prolong the basic signs of life indefinitely. People in a deep coma can be kept alive for years, even though they may have suffered irreversible brain damage and may never regain consciousness. Later in this chapter we will discuss the issue of whether or when such life supports as respirators and feeding tubes may be withheld or removed.

The *social* aspects of death revolve around funeral and mourning rituals and legal arrangements for the inheritance of power and wealth. A major problem in present-day American society is a lack of widely accepted conventions of behavior for people who know they are dying, for those around them, and for the survivors after the death of a loved one. Several conventions that do exist are rarely helpful either for dying people or for those close to them: isolating the dying in hospitals or nursing homes, refusing to discuss their condition with them, separating from them before death by

visiting less often, and thus leaving them to cope with death alone.

The *psychological* aspects of death involve the way people feel both about their own death as it draws near and about the death of those close to them. Most people today have a great deal of trouble coming to terms with the meaning of death. We need a more positive acceptance of the reality of death as a natural and expected phase of life.

FACING DEATH

ATTITUDES TOWARD DEATH AND DYING ACROSS THE LIFE SPAN

How do people of different ages think and feel about death? And how are they influenced by their cognitive, emotional, and experiential development?

Childhood

A first-grader, grieving for a classmate who had died after a violent beating, said, "I'll make a picture of Lisa and put it on her coffin and she'll sit up and become alive again" (Neuffer, 1987).

Most young children seem to think of death as

Sometime between ages 5 and 7, most children come to realize that death is permanent and that a dead animal, person, or flower will not come back to life. This girl, putting flowers on the grave of her pet kitten, has a natural, although sad, opportunity to develop a realistic understanding of death. *(J. Moore/The Image Works)*

a temporary state. Not until sometime between the ages of 5 and 7 do children usually understand that death is *irreversible*—that a dead person, animal, or flower cannot come to life again. At about the same age, children realize two other important concepts about death: first, that it is *universal* (all living things die); and second, that a dead person is *nonfunctional* (all life functions end at death). Before then, children may believe that certain groups of people (like teachers, parents, and children) do not die, that a person who is smart enough or lucky enough can avoid death, and that they themselves will be able to live forever. They may also believe that a dead person can still think and feel.

These observations about children's views of death emerge from a review of 40 studies that have been done since the 1930s, most of them based on interviews with children (Speece & Brent, 1984). All three concepts—irreversibility, universality, and the cessation of functions—usually develop at the time when, according to Piaget, children move from preoperational to concrete operational thinking. It seems likely that this cognitive leap allows a mature understanding of death. The importance of a child's cognitive development also comes through in children's common misunderstandings of euphemisms for death. When they are told that someone "expired" or that the family "lost" someone or that someone is "asleep" and will never awaken, they often become confused.

Children who are still thinking egocentrically usually cannot understand death, because it is beyond their personal experience. But preschool-age children who are terminally ill often *do* realize the imminence of their own death. One child, not quite 4 years old and suffering from a brain tumor, told hospital workers, "The Great Pumpkin is going to take me away, but I'm not ready." The following week, he woke up one morning and said, "The Great Pumpkin is coming to take me away—and now I'm ready to go with him." He died shortly thereafter (J. Finlay, personal communication, 1991).

Cultural experience, too, influences attitudes toward death. Children from poor families are more likely to associate death with violence, while middle-class children associate it with disease and old age (Bluebond-Langner, 1977).

Children sometimes express their grief in ways that are hard for adults to understand—through anger, acting out, or refusal to acknowledge a death, as if pretending that it has not happened will change reality. But children can be helped to understand death if they are introduced to the concept at an early age, in the context of their own ex-

perience, and are given opportunities to talk about the issues surrounding it. The death of a pet or of flowers may provide a natural opportunity. If another child dies, teachers and parents need to allay the surviving children's anxieties. (Later in this chapter we'll discuss some ways to help children with the concept of death.)

Adolescence

Adolescents tend to have highly romantic ideas about death: "adolescents make brave soldiers because they do not fear annihilation" so much as they are concerned about being "brave and glorious" (Pattison, 1977, p. 23). In their attempt to discover and express their identity, they are concerned with *how* they will live, not with how *long* they will live. This may partially explain the appeal of suicide to adolescents.

Furthermore, many adolescents are still thinking in egocentric ways and are in the grip of the *personal fable* (see Chapter 10). They believe that they can take almost any kind of risk without danger. They hitchhike, they drive recklessly, and they experiment with drugs—often with tragic results.

Terminally ill adolescents face death "in the contradictory and perplexing ways adolescents seem to face life" (Feifel, 1977, p. 177). The mysticism and intense interest in religion that are common in adolescence often become heightened. At the same time, mortally ill young people may deny their real condition and talk as if they are going to recover when, in fact, they know that they are not. Denial, and the accompanying repression of emotions, is a useful device that helps many sick young people deal with this crushing blow to their expectations for life. Terminally ill teenagers are far more likely to be angry than depressed. Their anger at the unfairness of their fate often erupts toward their parents, their doctors, their friends, or the world in general.

Adolescents mourning the death of a family member sometimes feel embarrassed talking to outsiders and may feel more comfortable grieving with their peers than with adults. Of course, there is no one way in which dying or grieving adolescents act; the way they handle the imminence of death reflects their individual personalities.

Young Adulthood

Most young adults—having finished their education, training, and courtship and having recently embarked on careers, marriage, or parenthood—

are eager to live the lives they have been preparing for. When they are suddenly taken ill or badly injured, young adults are likely to feel more intensely emotional about imminent death than people in any other period of life (Pattison, 1977). They feel extremely frustrated at the inability to fulfill their dreams. They have worked terribly hard—for nothing. Their frustration turns to rage, and that rage often makes young adults troublesome hospital patients.

They are difficult patients for another reason as well—the fact that the hospital workers responsible for their care are usually young adults themselves, and find it hard to deal with the thought of death for a person around their own age. Much of young adults' thought about death is evasive: people do not like to think about the possibility of their own death (Kastenbaum, 1977).

Middle Adulthood

When Saul Alinsky, a community organizer in Chicago, was asked what had made him decide to devote his life to organizing working-class people, he recalled a time when he had been gravely ill:

> I realized then that I was going to die. I had always known that in some abstract sense, of course, but for the first time I really *knew* it deep inside me. And I made up my mind that before I died I would do something that would really make a difference in the world (Alinsky, personal communication, 1966).

It is in middle age that most people really *know* deep inside themselves that they are indeed going to die. With the death of their parents, they are now the oldest generation. As they read the obituary pages—which they are likely to do more regularly at this age than they used to—they find more and more familiar names, and they may compare the ages with their own. Their bodies send them signals that they are not so young, agile, and hearty as they once were.

With this inner knowledge, middle-aged people perceive time in a new way. Previously, they thought of their lives in terms of the number of years they had lived since birth; but now they think of the number of years left to them until death, and of how to make the most of those years (Neugarten, 1967). The realization that death is certain is often an impetus for making a major life change. People take stock of their careers, their marriages, their relationships with their children, their friendships, their values, and how they spend their time.

These adolescents at a camp for cancer patients must face their own mortality, a subject to which many young people give little thought. Terminally ill adolescents handle the approach of death in varying ways that reflect their personalities. Some become angry, some turn to mysticism, and some deny the situation. *(Mary Ellen Mark)*

Late Adulthood

At 79, Sally's mother looked very small and frail in the middle of the hospital bed. "Don't feel sorry for me when I'm gone," she told her daughter. "I'm not afraid of death—I'm only afraid of living like this." Leah Wendkos—lonely since the death of her husband, both her sons, and her closest friends; sick and unable to pursue the activities she had enjoyed; and concerned about becoming a burden on her daughter—was ready to embrace death. It came only days after this conversation.

In general, older people are less anxious about death than middle-aged people (Bengtson, Cuellar, & Ragan, 1975). Through the years, as people lose friends and relatives, they gradually reorganize their thoughts and feelings to accept their own mortality. Also, physical problems and some of the other troubles of old age may diminish their pleasure in living. Those who feel that their lives have been meaningful are usually more able to accept the prospect of death than those who are still wondering about the point of having lived at all.

Some—like the 82-year-old woman who wrote the following lines within a few days before her second, and fatal, heart attack—have very complex feelings:

> I refuse to believe I am a piece of dust scuttering through uncaring space. I believe I count—that I have work to do—that there is need of me. I have a place. I want to live. The moment is Now—Now is my forever. I am still somebody—somebody on whom nothing is lost. With my last breath, I sing a psalm (Duskin, personal communication, February 1986).

Acknowledgment of death may be mixed with affirmation of the preciousness of the life that is slipping away.

CONFRONTING ONE'S OWN DEATH

How do people face the approach of their own death? By what processes do they accept the fact that their life will soon end? What kinds of psychological changes do they undergo when death is imminent? Professionals have closely observed persons close to death and have evolved theories to explain some of the psychological changes that occur as death approaches.

Changes Preceding Death

Psychological changes often begin to take place even before there are any physiological signs that a person is dying. In Chapter 16, we noted that a terminal drop in intellectual functioning often appears shortly before death, and in Chapter 17 we reported a study that showed a personality change at this time. Other changes, too, may show up during the terminal period.

Personality Changes

In one study, 80 people aged 65 to 91 were given batteries of psychological tests and followed over a 3-year period. Afterward, the researchers compared the scores of subjects who had died within a year after the last testing session with the scores of subjects who had lived an average of 3 years beyond that session (Lieberman & Coplan, 1970).

The subjects who had died within the year had lower scores on cognitive tests. They were also less introspective and more docile. Those who were dealing with some sort of crisis and were close to death were more afraid of and more preoccupied with death than people who were beset by similar crises but were not close to death. (Persons who were close to death but whose lives were relatively stable at the time showed neither special fear of death nor preoccupation with it.)

These observations suggest a mind-body relationship, in which physiological changes in the body are related to psychological changes, and vice versa. The changes are not simply effects of disease, since people who recovered from acute illnesses did not show the same pattern of personality decline as people who later died from the same kinds of illnesses. The people in this study talked freely about death. Many had worked out a personal meaning for death and had integrated it into their outlook on life.

Near-Death Experiences

Many people who have come close to death from drowning, cardiac arrest, or other causes have reported *near-death experiences.* These experiences often include a feeling of well-being, a new clarity of thinking, a sense of being out of one's body, and visions of bright lights. Three ways in which such experiences have been explained are as a prediction of a state of bliss after death (the *transcendental* theory); as a result of biological states that accompany the process of dying (the *physiological* theory); and as a response to the perceived threat of death (the *psychological* theory).

A recent study of such experiences, both in people who actually did come close to death and in others who only thought that they were close to death, found some support for all three theories (J. E. Owens, Cook, & Stevenson, 1990). Researchers studied the medical records and personal accounts of 28 hospital patients who would have died if doctors had not saved them, and of 30 who mistakenly thought they were in danger of dying. The two groups of patients had very similar sensations, a finding that lends support to the psychological theory. But those who had actually been near death reported near-death experiences more often—evidence for the physiological theory. And the researchers saw support for the transcendental theory in the fact that the dying patients reported clearer thinking, despite the likelihood that their brain functioning was in fact diminished.

So far, much of the work on near-death experiences has been anecdotal in nature and nonscientific, but, given the high level of interest the topic holds, there will undoubtedly be more rigorously scientific efforts to research it.

"Stages of Dying": Elisabeth Kübler-Ross

Elisabeth Kübler-Ross, a psychiatrist who works with dying people, is widely credited with having inspired the current interest in the psychology of death and dying. She found that most patients welcome an opportunity to speak openly about their condition, and that most are aware of being close to death even when they have not been told how sick they are.

After speaking with some 500 terminally ill patients, Kübler-Ross (1969, 1970) described five stages in coming to terms with death: (1) denial (refusal to accept the reality of what is happening); (2) anger; (3) bargaining for extra time (see Box 18-1 on page 594); (4) depression; and (5) ultimate acceptance. She also proposed a similar progression in the feelings of people facing imminent bereavement (Kübler-Ross, 1975).

Other professionals who work with dying patients point out that Kübler-Ross's "stages" are not true stages, as the term is used in other theories like Piaget's. Although the emotions that Kübler-Ross describes do commonly occur, not everyone goes through all five stages, and people may go through the stages in different sequences. A person may go back and forth between anger and depression, for example, or may feel both at once. Instead of the orderly progression in the theoretical model, dying people may show "a jumble of conflicting or alternating reactions running the gamut from denial to acceptance, with a tremendous variation affected by age, sex, race, ethnic group, social setting, and personality" (Butler & Lewis, 1982, p. 370). Unfortunately, some health professionals assume that these stages are inevitable and universal, and others feel that they have failed if they cannot bring a patient to "the ultimate goal, the big number 5—'acceptance' of death" (Leviton, 1977, p. 259).

Dying, like living, is an individual experience. For some people, denial or anger may be a healthier way to face death than calm acceptance. Thus Kübler-Ross's description—useful as it is in helping us understand the feelings of people who are facing the end of life—should not be held up as a model or a criterion for "the good death."

BEREAVEMENT, MOURNING, AND GRIEF

In the Asian nation of Nepal, Sally met Kami, a mountain-climbing guide whose good friend,

Elisabeth Kübler-Ross has been a pioneer in arousing popular and medical interest in death and dying. A psychiatrist who works with dying patients, she encourages them to talk about themselves and their feelings about impending death. On the basis of these discussions, she has theorized that there are five stages in coming to terms with death. *(Laurence Nelson/Black Star)*

Pemba, had died on an expedition. One of the climbers framed a photo he had taken of Pemba and sent it to his grieving parents. But since the Sherpas do not like to keep a picture of a dead person in the house, the family cut Pemba out of the photo. "This is the old way of thinking," said Kami, who keeps a photo of himself with Pemba, to remember their friendship. The different reactions of Pemba's family and his friend to the young man's death show how differently different cultures—and even different individuals within the same culture—handle grieving.

What do the terms *bereavement, mourning,* and *grief* mean? *Bereavement* is the objective *fact* of loss: the survivor's change in status, for example, from a wife to a widow or from a child to an orphan. *Mourning* refers to the *behavior* of the bereaved and the community after a death: the all-night Irish wake, at which friends and family keep a vigil and toast the memory of the dead person; the weeklong Jewish *shiva,* when the family remains at home to receive visitors (see Box 18-2 on pages 596–597); or flying a flag at half-mast after the death of a public figure. *Grief* is the *emotional response* of the bereaved, which can be expressed in many ways, from rage to a feeling of emptiness.

BOX 18-1   FOOD FOR THOUGHT

POSTPONING DEATH

Is there such a thing as a will to live? Can people postpone their own death so that they can celebrate a birthday, an anniversary, a grandchild's wedding, or some other meaningful event? Recent studies of patterns of death around important occasions suggest that some people can.

In a study of more than 2 million deaths from natural causes, researchers found that birthdays seem to affect men and women differently. Women were more likely to die in the week after their birthdays than at any other time of the year, while men were more likely to die just before their birthdays (Phillips, 1992). It is possible that birthdays may serve as an anticipated social event for women but a discouraging stock-taking for men.

Other studies examined death rates around two important holidays, each of which appeals strongly to one ethnic group and not to others, who can thus serve as control groups. On the Jewish holiday of Passover, more than 75 percent of American Jews attend a *seder* (a ceremonial dinner), usually conducted at home with close family members (D. P. Phillips & King, 1988). And during the Chinese Harvest Moon Festival, the senior woman of the house directs a ceremonial meal in her home (D. P. Phillips & Smith, 1990). This holiday emphasizes the symbolic importance of older women and is more important to them than to

young women or to men of any age. Passover usually falls near Easter (the last supper of Jesus and the disciples is said to have been a seder), and the Harvest Moon Festival occurs in autumn. But the timing of each changes from year to year by as much as 4 weeks.

In two California studies, death rates from natural causes were lower just before each holiday for the people to whom the holiday meant most, and higher just afterward. It seems as if some people who are close to death put forth every ounce of psychological and physical strength to stay alive for just one more celebration.

Jewish people showed a death rate lower than expected just before Passover and a higher death rate just after it. The effect was strongest when Passover fell on a weekend, when more people were expected to celebrate it; it was not affected by the specific date of the holiday (D. P. Phillips & King, 1988). The same pattern held true for elderly Chinese women, whose death rate was unusually low before the Harvest Moon Festival and unusually high afterward (D. P. Phillips & Smith, 1990). The pattern held for the three leading causes of death—heart disease, cancer, and stroke.

The "Passover effect" was especially strong among Jewish men, who have usually led the seder service. It was not found in African Americans, in Asians, or in Jewish

infants (none of whom celebrate Passover). The "Harvest Moon" effect did not appear among Jewish people or the general population, or among elderly Chinese men or younger Chinese women. It showed up only among women over age 75, the group to whom this holiday meant the most.

How might these effects work? It is not likely that stress or overeating causes high postholiday or postbirthday death rates, because these causes would not explain the very much lower death rates before the occasions. Perhaps psychosomatic processes let some people postpone death until they have reached an occasion important to them. In other words, they can will themselves to live just a little while longer. The opposite effect has also been found, in research that suggests that people who expect to die soon because of mythical, fatalistic beliefs do in fact die sooner than those who do not hold such beliefs (Phillips et al., 1993).

A variant of this effect has also shown up in two former presidents of the United States who died on the Fourth of July. Thomas Jefferson's last words were "Is it the Fourth?"

If health professionals and family members can develop strategies to emphasize the importance of certain occasions or to create new occasions, patients may be inspired to set goals for living to meet future events.

Traditional cultures help people deal with bereavement and grief through mourning rites that are universally understood and have accepted meanings. In our diversified culture, many mourners lack such reassuring structures. As old customs fall into disuse, the bereaved lose valuable supports for coping with their grief.

A Multicultural Perspective on Mourning

In our fast-paced, death-denying culture, the survivors of a person who has died are expected to express sadness at the time of death, but very soon thereafter to be brave, suppress their fears, remember the dead person but break their emotional bonds to them, and get on with the business of living. This approach, however, is not universal (Stroebe, Gergen, Gergen, & Stroebe, 1992).

In Japan, for example, religious rituals encourage survivors to maintain contact with the deceased. Mourners keep an altar in the home dedicated to the family ancestors; they talk to their dead loved ones and offer them food or cigars. On the other hand, among Native Americans, the Hopi aim to forget the dead person as quickly as possible. The Hopi believe that death brings pollution and that the spirits of the dead are to be feared; as a result, they—like the Sherpas of Nepal—do not keep photos or other reminders of the dead person. Muslims in Egypt express their grief by deeply emotional expressions of sorrow in the company of family and friends; Muslims in Bali are urged to laugh and be joyful and to suppress any expressions of sadness. Israeli parents of soldiers who died in wars often idealize them and remain preoccupied with them, sometimes to such a degree that their involvement with the dead sons interfere with their relationships to living children and other relatives.

Even in western society, patterns of grieving vary among different subgroups and across time. During the nineteenth century, for example, the evidence from 56 diaries shows that mourners did not try to break bonds with their loved ones, but instead tried to hold onto them. They prayed for them, talked about reunions in heaven, named children for them, used their wishes as guides to action, and tried to communicate with their spirits through seances and spirit mediums (Rosenblatt, 1983). And studies of present-day young widows and widowers suggest that many of them react similarly, usually continuing in their previous lifestyles and showing little interest in looking for a new partner.

The cultural context of grief, then, illustrates the point that there is no one "best" way to cope with death. What works in one culture or in one family may not in another. Therefore, in helping people handle grief, counselors need to take ethnic traditions and individual personalities into account.

Forms of Grief

Some people begin to mourn in anticipation, before a death actually occurs. After the death, grief may take one of several forms, or some combination.

Anticipatory Grief

The family and friends of a person who has been ill for a long time often prepare themselves for the loss through *anticipatory grief,* symptoms of grief experienced while the person is still alive. This sometimes helps survivors handle the actual death more easily when it does come (J. T. Brown & Stoudemire, 1983). In other cases, however, it seems to have little impact on adjustment after the death. One study of elderly widows found that those who had expected their husbands' death and "rehearsed" for widowhood, as by thinking and talking about the future, were no better or worse adjusted than women whose husbands died unexpectedly (C. D. Hill, Thompson, & Gallagher, 1988).

When anticipatory grief makes survivors disengage themselves from a dying person before death, it can create a devastating sense of isolation for the person who is dying.

"Grief Work": A Three-Phase Pattern

Grieving in the western world usually (but not always) follows a fairly predictable pattern. The bereaved person accepts the painful reality of the loss, gradually lets go of the bond with the dead person, readjusts to life without that person, and develops new interests and relationships. This process of "grief work" generally takes place in three phases—though, as with Kübler-Ross's stages, they may vary (J. T. Brown & Stoudemire, 1983; Schulz, 1978):

1 *Shock and disbelief:* The initial phase, which may take several weeks (especially after a sudden or unexpected death), is shock and disbelief. This may protect the bereaved from intense reactions. Survivors often feel lost, dazed, and confused. Shortness of breath, tightness in the chest or throat, nausea, and a feeling of emptiness in the abdomen are common. As awareness of the loss sinks in, the initial numbness gives way to overwhelming feelings of sadness, often expressed by frequent crying.

2 *Preoccupation with the memory of the person who has died:* The second phase, preoccupation with memories of the dead person, may last 6 months or longer. The survivor tries to come to terms with the death but cannot yet accept it. Frequent crying continues; and insomnia, fatigue, and loss of appetite are common. A widow may relive her husband's death and their entire relationship, going over all the details in her mind and in conversation, in an obsessive search for the meaning of his death. From time to time, she may be seized by a feeling that her

BOX 18-2   WINDOW ON THE WORLD

MOURNING CUSTOMS AMONG TRADITIONAL JEWS

Many ethnic groups follow special mourning customs, which provide a reassuring anchor amid the turbulence of loss. Such rituals allow death to occur with dignity and provide a wholesome, humane outlet for the feelings of those who are dying or bereft. For example, if you go to pay your respects to a Jewish family in which someone has just died, you can expect the following.

The funeral will probably take place within 1 or 2 days of the death; all who attend the funeral will be invited back to the home of the nearest relative, after the family and close friends return from the cemetery. Upon their return, those who went to the cemetery wash their hands or put them under a pitcher as someone else pours water over them. Then all present are invited to partake of food, much of which has been brought by visitors.

In an observant home, all the mirrors are covered or turned to the wall; the family members sit on hard wooden benches, wear torn strips of black ribbon pinned to their clothes, and wear slippers instead of shoes; and the men go unshaven. This continues during the period of *shiva,* the week following the death, when the family members are home and ready to receive visitors. Every evening during this week, a prayer service is held in the home.

Although most Jewish people no longer observe all the prescribed guidelines (A. Gordon, 1975; Heller, 1975), a look at what these practices are and how they speak to important psychological needs may be thought-provoking for Jews and non-Jews alike.

An Orthodox Jewish funeral is simple and realistic; it is meant to help the bereaved face their loss. The community provides emotional support and helps mourners begin the process of recovery by serving a meal at their home. Traditional cultures, like the Hasidic sect these mourners belong to, help people deal with death and grief through rituals that have culturally accepted meanings. *(Nathan Benn/Woodfin Camp & Associates)*

GUIDELINES FOR DYING

Jewish tradition views death as a natural part of life, to be faced directly and realistically.

■ Loved ones stay with a terminally ill patient as much as possible, offering comfort and support while encouraging him or her to prepare for the end. By never leaving the dying person alone, the survivors alleviate their own guilt. The deathbed vigil also keeps mourners from denying the reality of death.

■ Dying people are treated like living people, still able to handle their own affairs and take part in relationships until the moment of death.

■ The dying person puts material and spiritual affairs in order

by giving away possessions, blessing loved ones and giving them instruction or advice (the "ethical will"), and making a deathbed confession, repenting any wrongdoing. These communications represent a last contact with the familiar as the person is about to enter the unknown.

GUIDELINES FOR MOURNING

Judaism encourages mourners to express their grief and sorrow openly as a first step toward healing.

■ Mourners immediately make plans for the funeral and burial, acting on a wish to do all that they can for their loved one. By tearing their clothes (or wearing a symbolic strip of

(continued)

BOX 18-2   (Continued)

MOURNING CUSTOMS AMONG TRADITIONAL JEWS

black cloth) before the funeral, mourners symbolize severing the relationship with the person who has died.

■ The funeral is not ostentatious. It is realistic, to prevent mourners from denying the implications of death. The simple coffin (often a plain pine box) is kept closed. Children who were close to the deceased are likely to be there. The eulogy lets mourners reflect on their loss and pour out their grief in tears.

■ At the cemetery, mourners shovel dirt into the grave themselves. This final act of love and concern helps put the loved one to rest.

■ The year of mourning corresponds roughly to the stages of grief: "three days of deep grief, seven days of mourning, thirty days of gradual readjustment, and eleven months of remembrance and healing" (A. Gordon, 1975, p. 51). As they visit with each other and with friends throughout the week of *shiva*, mourners share memories of the deceased, talk about the death itself, and vent their emotions, while being reminded that life goes on. During the following year, the bereaved are gradually drawn back into the life of the community. At the end of the year, a ceremonial unveiling of the headstone signals the formal end of the mourning period. It is customary to name babies after family members who have died.

dead husband is present: she will hear his voice, sense his presence in the room, even see his face before her. She may have vivid dreams of him. These experiences diminish with time, though they may recur—perhaps for years— on such occasions as the anniversary of the marriage or of the death.

3 *Resolution:* The final phase, resolution, has arrived when the bereaved person resumes interest in everyday activities—when memories of the dead person bring fond feelings mingled with sadness, rather than sharp pain and longing. A widower may still miss his dead wife; but he knows that life must go on, and he becomes more active socially, getting out more, seeing people, resuming old interests, and perhaps discovering new ones. Many survivors feel a surge of strength and are proud to have recovered.

Other Patterns of Grieving

Recently, mental health professionals have found considerable differences in people's reactions to bereavement. The resolution of grief does not necessarily follow a straight line from shock to resolution. Mourning may continue for years, surfacing on anniversaries or other dates that are important to the bereaved person.

One team of psychologists reviewed studies of reactions to a major loss—not only the death of a loved one but also a loss of a different nature, paralysis induced by spinal injury. They found that

some common assumptions seem to be more myth than fact (Wortman & Silver, 1989).

Five common beliefs about loss are (1) everyone who suffers a severe loss will be distraught and probably depressed; (2) people who do not show such distress will have psychological problems later on; (3) a bereaved person has to "work through" a loss by focusing on it and trying to make sense of it; (4) the intense distress of mourning will come to an end within a fairly short period of time; and (5) people will eventually accept a loss, both intellectually and emotionally. These researchers say that none of these beliefs is valid.

First, they say, depression is not universal. From 3 weeks to 2 years after their loss, only from 15 to 35 percent of widows, widowers, and victims of spinal cord injury showed signs of depression.

Second, failure to show distress at the outset does not necessarily lead to problems later on. In fact, the subjects who were most upset immediately were likely to be most troubled up to 2 years later.

Third, not everyone needs to work through a loss or will benefit from working through it. Subjects who worked through their loss intensely at the beginning sometimes had more problems later.

Fourth, not everyone returns soon to normal functioning. Various follow-up studies have found that many normal children whose fathers died in wars still showed emotional and behavioral problems 3½ years later; that parents of children killed by drunk drivers were likely to be functioning poorly up to 7 years later; and that more than 40 percent of widows and widowers showed moderate to severe anxiety up to 4 years after the spouse's death, especially if it had been sudden.

Fifth, people cannot always resolve their grief and accept their loss. Parents and spouses of people who die in car accidents often have painful memories of the loved one even after many years have passed. And when people paralyzed by a spinal injury were interviewed 38 years after the injury, many still thought about and missed the things they could no longer do (Wortman & Silver, 1989).

This research found three main patterns of grieving. In the expected pattern, the mourner goes from high to low distress; in a second pattern, the mourner does not experience intense distress immediately or later; in a third pattern, the mourner remains distressed for a long time.

How Children Cope with Bereavement

Even today, when death in childhood or young adulthood is not as common as it used to be, at least in developed countries, 6 percent of American children under 10 have lost at least one parent. More have lost grandparents, many of whom played an important role in their lives; others mourn the deaths of siblings, other relatives, or friends (Committee on Psychosocial Aspects of Child and Family Health, 1992).

Children experience many of the same feelings of grief that adults do. But there are some special age-related aspects to their mourning, depending on their level of cognitive and emotional development. Furthermore, they often show their grief differently (see Table 18-1).

One reason for these differences is, as we pointed out earlier, children's limited cognitive development. A number of other factors can also make a death harder for children to accept. These include the loss in early childhood or early adolescence; a troubled relationship with the dead person before the death; a troubled surviving parent who depends too much on the child; the child's own previous behavioral or emotional problems; not enough family or community supports; and an unexpected death, especially one due to murder or suicide (AAP Committee on Psychosocial Aspects of Child and Family Health, 1992).

Parents or other caregivers can cushion the pain of loss in a number of ways. First, they need to help children understand that death is final, that they did not cause the death by their misbehavior or thoughts, and that the other person's death does not pose a fatal danger to them. They also need to reassure children that they will continue to be cared for by loving adults. In talking to children, adults should use the words *death* and *die*, since, as one hospice worker has said, "Kids are not uncomfortable with the word 'death.' We're uncomfortable with it. We should be using the language that children understand" (Ketcham, 1993). It is helpful to make as few changes in the children's environment, relationships, and daily activities as possible; to answer questions simply and honestly;

TABLE 18-1

Manifestations of Grief in Children

Under 3 years	3 to 5 years	School-age Children	Adolescents
Regression	Increased activity	Deterioration of school performance caused by loss of concentration, disinterest, lack of motivation, failure to complete assignments, and daydreaming in class	Depression
Sadness	Constipation		Somatic complaints
Fearfulness	Soiling		Delinquent behavior
Loss of appetite	Bed-wetting		Promiscuity
Failure to thrive	Anger and temper tantrums		Suicide attempts
Sleep disturbance	"Out-of-control" behavior		Dropping out of school
Social withdrawal	Nightmares	Resistance to attending school	
Developmental delay	Crying spells	Crying spells	
Irritability		Lying	
Excessive crying		Stealing	
Increased dependency		Nervousness	
Loss of speech		Abdominal pain	
		Headaches	
		Listlessness	
		Fatigue	

SOURCE: Adapted from Committee on Psychosocial Aspects of Child and Family Health, 1992.

and to share their own sadness and memories, encouraging children to talk about the dead person.

Helping People Deal with Dying and Bereavement

Implications of Research

Identifying the strengths—better coping styles, a particular religious or philosophical outlook, or other personal resources—that help some people mourn with less distress may help others to cope better with loss. Also, it may be unnecessary and even harmful to encourage or try to force mourners to "work through" a loss by experiencing anger, guilt, and depression. And recognition that grief may have a very long life may enable long-term mourners to get help without being considered "sick." By respecting different patterns of grief, professionals and laypeople alike can help people deal with loss without imposing the additional burden of making them feel that their reactions are abnormal.

With the growing realization that people can face death better if they understand it and get help to deal with it, several movements have arisen to help make dying and bereavement more humane. These include programs of grief therapy and death education, hospices to care for the terminally ill, and support groups and services for dying people and their families.

Grief Therapy

Most bereaved people are able, with the help of family and friends, to work through their grief and to resume normal lives. For some, however, *grief therapy*—a program to help the bereaved cope with their losses—is indicated.

Professional grief therapists focus on helping bereaved people express their sorrow and their feelings of loss, guilt, hostility, and anger. They encourage their clients to review their relationships with the deceased and to integrate the fact of the death into their lives so that they can be freed to develop new relationships and new ways of behaving toward surviving friends and relatives.

Organizations—such as Widow to Widow, Catholic Widow and Widowers Club, and Compassionate Friends (for parents of children who have died)—provide nonprofessional grief therapy, emphasizing the practical and emotional help that one person who has lost someone close can give to another.

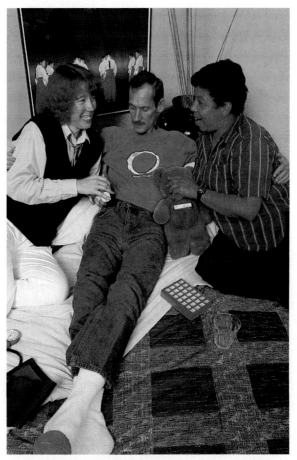

Hospice workers, like these helping a terminally ill AIDS patient, work together to ease patients' pain and treat their symptoms, to keep them as comfortable and alert as possible, to show both interest and kindness to them and their families, and to help the families deal with the patients' illness and death. *(James D. Wilson/Woodfin Camp & Associates)*

Hospices

"I had a fast-growing conviction," writes Norman Cousins in *Anatomy of an Illness* (1979), "that a hospital is no place for a person who is seriously ill" (p. 29). Many people are convinced that hospitals are even less appropriate for terminally ill patients. The typical hospital is set up to treat acute illness, with the goal of curing people and sending them home well; this goal is bound to be thwarted when a patient is terminally ill. Dying patients often receive needless tests and useless treatments, get less attention than patients with better chances of recovery, and are constrained by hospital rules that are not relevant for them.

The hospice movement began in response to a need for special facilities and special care for dying patients. *Hospice care*—warm, personal, patient- and family-centered care for the terminally ill—can be given in a hospital or another institution, at home, or through some combination of home and institution. Doctors, nurses, social workers, psychologists, aides, clergy, friends, and volunteers of various ages and backgrounds work together to ease patients' pain and treat their symptoms, to keep them as comfortable and alert as possible, to show both interest and kindness to them and their families, and to help the families deal with the patients' illness and death. Family members themselves are often an active part of hospice care.

In a study in which terminally ill cancer patients were randomly assigned either to standard hospital care or to hospice care, the main difference that emerged between the two groups was the frame of mind of the patients and their families. The hospice patients and the family members most involved with their day-to-day care were more satisfied than the hospital patients and their relatives. There were no differences between the two groups, however, in pain, symptoms, activities of daily living, emotional states, or expense. The difference, then, seems to reflect the greater time spent by the hospice teams in helping patients and their families cope with impending death (Kane, Wales, Bernstein, Leibowitz, & Kaplan, 1984).

Support Groups and Services

After Orville Kelly had been diagnosed as suffering from terminal cancer, he wrote:

> The death rate for any generation is 100 percent. We all die. However, I know what will probably kill me, while most people do not. We have no guarantee of how long we will live. But I believe it is truly the quality of life, not the quantity, that is most important. (O. Kelly, 1978, p. 63)

Spurred by his own initial difficulty in dealing with his diagnosis, Kelly founded Make Today Count, an organization where seriously ill patients and their families can talk about their feelings and the problems of living with terminal illness.

The Shanti Project, another support group, whose name derives from the Sanskrit word for "inner peace," was founded in the San Francisco Bay area by Charles Garfield, a psychologist concerned with offering compassionate care to the dying and their families. The project's hot line rings at all hours of the day and night, with requests from all over the country. One caller may ask for a volunteer to break the news to an elderly woman and her family that the woman is dying; a second

may ask for someone to counsel a man about to undergo chemotherapy, to let him know what to expect and to support him through the ordeal; a third may ask for someone to help the wife of a dying man cope with her own feelings so as to be as helpful as possible to her husband. Currently, the Shanti Project is devoting almost all its resources to help support terminally ill AIDS patients.

Death Education

"Why did my guinea pig die?" "When will it be alive again?" "How much should I tell terminally ill patients about their true situation?" These are just a few of the questions dealt with in *death education:* programs aimed at various age levels and groups to teach people about dying and grief and to help them deal with these issues in their personal and professional lives.

It is important for people to explore their own attitude toward death, to become familiar with the ways in which various cultures deal with death, and to be sensitive to its emotional ramifications, both for dying people and for survivors. Courses about death are offered to high school and college students; to social workers, doctors, nurses, and other professionals who work with dying people and survivors; and to the community. Teachers of young children can introduce discussions about death when they fit into the curriculum or into the children's experience. Learning about death helps people of all ages.

Goals of Death Education   What, specifically, can death education accomplish? Goals vary according to the students' ages and needs, but some are important for everyone. They include helping to allay death-related anxieties; helping people to develop their own individual belief systems, to see death as a natural end to life, and to prepare for their own death and the death of those close to them; teaching people humane ways to treat the dying; providing a realistic view of health care workers and their obligations to the dying and their families; offering an understanding of the dynamics of grief; helping suicidal people and those around them; helping consumers to decide on and purchase the kind of funeral services they want; and making dying as positive an experience as possible (Leviton, 1977).

Teaching Children about Death   Children are usually interested in talking about death with caring adults. They do best in a supportive atmosphere with an adult who is aware of children's varying cognitive levels and is sensitive to their individual feelings and experiences (Koocher, 1973).

Death education can help children on two levels—the relatively impersonal cognitive level and the more personal emotional level. On the cognitive level, teachers can raise the topic of death in social studies classes, by having students compare funeral practices and religious beliefs about death; and in science classes, where they can talk about the difference between what is "alive," what is "not alive," and what is "dead." On the emotional level, children's parents and teachers can respond to the death of a pet, of a person they know, or of a public figure, giving the children support for their feelings and helping them to express those feelings—by writing sympathy notes, for instance. Children's feelings can run deep. As one social worker says, "The death of a pet is not practice for something serious. It's the real thing" (Kutner, 1990, p. C8).

Teachers and parents need to walk a thin line to help children deal with a difficult topic like death without increasing their anxiety. Some excellent books are available to help children deal with death and other serious problems.

WIDOWHOOD: SURVIVING A SPOUSE

"As long as you have your husband, you're not old," said Julia, 75 and recently widowed. "But once he dies, old age sets in fast."

Widowhood is a burden that women are far likelier to carry than men, because not only do women tend to live longer than men, but their husbands tend to be older.

Adjusting to the Death of a Spouse

Aside from the pain of mourning, what does losing a spouse mean for the day-to-day life of the survivor? Roy, whose marriage of 56 years ended with his wife's sudden death, said, "One of the hardest things is feeling that I'm not *important* to one other person. My children love me, but they have their own families and their own lives to lead. I have good friends, but they're not the same either. Nobody can take Lil's place."

The widowed survivor of a long marriage faces a host of emotional and practical problems. A good marriage leaves a gaping emotional void: the loss of a lover, a confidant, a good friend, and a steady companion. Even in a bad marriage, the loss is felt.

For one thing, the survivor no longer has the role

By sharing his feelings about death with his granddaughter, this man can help allay the child's anxieties about it. Adults who discuss death with children need to be warm, supportive, and sensitive to the children's feelings. It is also important to remember that children vary in their cognitive readiness to understand death. *(Art Stein/Photo Researchers)*

of spouse. This may be especially hard for women who have structured their lives around caring for a husband and enjoying his company; but it also affects working people of both sexes who no longer have a partner to come home to, and retirees who have no one to talk to—or argue with. Social life also changes. Friends and family usually rally to the mourner's side immediately after the death, but then they go back to their own lives and the survivor has to carve out an entirely new life structure. Married friends, uncomfortable with the thought that this could happen to them too, may avoid the widowed person when they are most needed. Widowed people do see friends more often than married ones do, after a little time has passed (D. Field & Minkler, 1988).

Men and women adjust similarly to widowhood; both often feel like a "fifth wheel" with couples they have been friendly with for years (Brubaker, 1990). There are some differences, though. Men are more likely to see other women and to remarry; women—especially those in middle or late adulthood—usually make friends with other widows but have a hard time meeting and forming relationships with men (Brecher & the

Widowhood affects people differently, depending on personality and circumstances. It always takes time for the pain of loss to heal, but people who adjust best are those who have a sense of their own individual identity and a sturdy measure of self-sufficiency. The loneliness is still there, but the man who can, for example, keep house for himself and make social plans will be less disoriented by the loss of his wife. *(Gary M. Roberts/The Picture Cube)*

Editors of Consumer Reports Books, 1984; Lopata, 1977, 1979).

Widowed people of both sexes have higher rates of mental illness, especially depression, than married people (Balkwell, 1981). Physical health is most likely to be adversely affected when the loss occurs in the survivor's middle age; bereavement in young adulthood or old age usually does not affect the survivor's physical health nor alter prior patterns of medical care (Perkins & Harris, 1990; Wolinsky & Johnson, 1992a, 1992b). The women most likely to need counseling 6 months after their husbands' death are those who have few friends, do not feel close to their children, and have suffered a recent disability (Goldberg, Comstock, & Harlow, 1988).

A major problem for both sexes is economic hardship. When the husband has been the main breadwinner, his widow is deprived of his income. The widowed man, on his part, has to buy many of the services his wife provided. When both spouses have been employed, the loss of one income can be a major blow. Women who have prepared themselves financially—as by discussing pensions and insurance with their husbands—are better able to adjust after widowhood, partly, of course, because they understand their finances, but also because of the comforting feeling that their husbands loved them enough to help them plan for the future (O'Bryant & Morgan, 1989).

Like any life crisis, widowhood affects people differently, depending on personality and circumstances. It always takes time for the pain of loss to heal, but people can prepare better for widowhood (as for life in general) if they begin early to develop a strong sense of their own identity and a sturdy measure of self-sufficiency. A woman is less likely to be devastated by her husband's death if she is used to pursuing her own interests and knows how to manage the financial and practical details of her life. A man will cope better if he knows how to cook, do laundry, and make social plans.

Living as a Widow or Widower

The people who adjust best to widowhood are those who keep busy, develop new roles (as by taking on new paid or volunteer work), or become more deeply involved in activities. They see friends often (which helps more than frequent visits with their children), and they take part in community programs like support groups for widows (Balkwell, 1981; C. J. Barrett, 1978; Vachon, Lyall, Rogers, Freedmen-Letofky, & Freeman, 1980).

Most widows do not join organizations; they rely on their own informal support systems. The loneliest ones have few or no children, are in poor health, lost their husbands suddenly or unexpectedly or at a relatively early age, have been widowed for less than 6 years, or have few friends or social activities (Lopata, Heinemann, & Baum, 1982).

Many studies have found older people to be better adjusted to widowhood than younger people, but often the investigators have not considered the length of time a person has been widowed. One study, which did take this factor into account, found that being widowed early does *not* generally have a long-term effect on morale. Nor is it easier or harder to lose a husband or wife at an earlier or a later age—grief is grief, no matter when the loss occurs. However, older widows and widowers interviewed did tend to have somewhat higher morale than younger ones, no matter how long they had been widowed (Balkwell, 1985). The crucial factor may be availability of companions, especially widowed peers, or the fact that losing a spouse in old age is less of a shock than death in earlier years.

Quality of relationships may be more important than frequency of contact. Different relationships serve different purposes; a widow is more likely to seek out her children when she is worried or depressed but will turn to her brothers or sisters for financial help (T. B. Anderson, 1984).

CONTROVERSIAL ISSUES OF DEATH AND DYING

A pregnant woman learns that the fetus she is carrying has a defect so serious that the baby will not survive more than a few weeks after birth. She and her husband want to deliver the infant and to keep it alive long enough to donate their baby's organs to another child. This means declaring the infant "brain dead" if the organs are to be salvaged in a usable condition. What are the legal and moral ramifications? (See Box 18-3.)

A little girl has been so badly beaten by her stepfather that, according to a team of neurosurgeons, her brain has died. She is being maintained on a respirator, but there is no chance, they say, that she will ever walk, speak, or even think again. The girl's mother has requested that the respirator be disconnected, but the stepfather's attorney is attempting to prevent this, so that his client cannot be tried for murder. If hospital personnel do turn off the machines maintaining the child's breathing and heart action, who is responsible for her death—the stepfather or the hospital staff?

A 55-year-old woman is suffering from terminal cancer. With medical care she may live another year or two, but the likelihood is that she will become so weak that she will be confined to her bed most of the time, and that she will be in great pain. She asks her physician to give her a potent drug. He knows that an overdose will be fatal, and he strongly suspects that the woman plans to end her life at a time of her own choosing.

These are only a few examples of the hard choices that may face patients, families, and physicians today: choices involving the quality of life and the nature and circumstances of death. The field of medical ethics has expanded immensely in recent years, partly because of the complexity of issues that have always surrounded death and also in large part because of questions raised by recent technological advances. Many of these ethical and moral issues arise from such advances: antibiotics that enable older patients to survive one dread illness only to succumb to another; respirators that keep people alive and breathing when they are in a coma and show no brain activity or other physiological function; organ transplants that may achieve "miracles" at great risk.

The questions are endless. Should a doctor prescribe a medicine that will relieve pain but may shorten the patient's life? In a traumatic childbirth, if a doctor can save only one life, whose should it be—the mother's or the baby's? Is abortion a medical procedure, or is it murder? Do people have the right to take their own life? If so, under what circumstances? What is the legal liability of someone who helps a person commit suicide? Should a doctor tell a patient that an illness is terminal? If so, how? Should patients be told how long they are expected to live, so that they can put their affairs in order and prepare for death? Or will knowing the prognosis hasten death, becoming a self-fulfilling prophecy? Who decides that a life is not worth prolonging? Who decides when to stop treatment? What abuses are possible when such decisions must be made? How can abuses be prevented?

None of these questions has a simple answer. Each requires soul-searching by everyone involved. Since each situation is unique, each solution must be unique.

EUTHANASIA AND THE RIGHT TO DIE

A 79-year-old man visited his 62-year-old wife in a nursing home. Once a successful businesswoman, the wife, now suffering from advanced Alzheimer's disease, screamed constantly and was unable or unwilling to speak. The man pushed his wife's wheelchair into a stairwell, where he killed her with a pistol shot. The district attorney who prosecuted the husband called his action "classic first-degree murder." But the grand jury refused to indict, and he went free (Malcolm, 1984).

This husband seemed to be practicing *euthanasia,* or mercy killing. His act is an example of **active euthanasia,** action deliberately taken with the purpose of shortening a life in order to end suffering or to carry out the wishes of a terminally ill pa-

BOX 18-3   TAKE A STAND

SHOULD ANENCEPHALIC BABIES BE USED AS ORGAN DONORS?

In her eighth month of pregnancy, Laura Campo learned that she was carrying a fetus with anencephaly. Babies with this developmental disorder have no brain cortex—only the brain stem, which allows breathing and primitive reflexes. They have no chance for survival, and usually die within days or weeks of birth. The Campos decided to bear the child and to donate her organs to other babies; as soon as the baby girl was born, they requested that she be declared brain dead. Without such a declaration and immediate steps to preserve or transplant her organs, the organs might deteriorate to the point where they could not be used. But the Florida Supreme Court declared her not technically "brain dead," since the legal definition of death in Florida, as in most states, requires "irreversible cessation of all functions of the entire brain, including the brain stem." Ten days after birth the baby died when her lungs failed. None of her organs were usable.

This is another difficult ethical decision, in which people of good will have presented arguments both for and against taking steps toward organ donation. Which point of view would you take, after considering the following arguments on either side?

THE CASE FOR NOT USING THE BABY'S ORGANS

1 *Removing vital organs before death would allow the active killing of a human being:* Creating an exception to this rule would reduce the value of human life.

2 *This could set a dangerous precedent:* There might be a temptation to bend rules and expand the category of living organ sources to include infants who might otherwise have survived, and eventually to take adult organs from unconscious patients.

3 *Such practices could encourage having babies, or keeping them alive, for the purpose of "harvesting" their organs:* One such case has already been reported, in which a child was conceived for the prime purpose of using her as a bone marrow donor to save the life of her older sister.

THE CASE FOR USING THE BABY'S ORGANS

1 *A baby with anencephaly does not have a meaningful human life:* Such a baby cannot hear, see, smell, feel, taste, think, or grow, and will definitely die within weeks. Using the baby's organs to help other infants will give this baby's life meaning, by turning death into life. The heart, kidneys, lungs, and skin of one infant could conceivably save the lives of five or six other babies who have diseased, nonfunctioning organs.

2 *Special criteria for brain death can be set for anencephaly:* Strict standards can be spelled out so that this condition, and only this condition, will render an infant eligible to be an organ donor. This would prevent the possibility of "harvesting" the organs of children who might have a chance for life, even though they would be disabled.

3 *The need for healthy child-size organs is great:* About 5000 American children every year need pediatric organ transplants, but no more than 1300 get them. Of children younger than 2 years of age registered to receive transplants, an estimated 30 to 50 percent die before an organ becomes available.

4 *Anencephalic infants are ideal organ donors:* Adult organs are too big to transplant into children, and organs from children who die of disease are damaged, so the only source is sudden traumatic death, usually car accidents. Between 1000 and 2000 anencephalic babies are born every year in the United States; their organs are healthy and small enough to help other sick babies.

What do *you* think?

SOURCES: Committee on Bioethics, 1992; Kolata, 1992.

tient. *Passive euthanasia* is mercy killing which takes the form of withholding treatment that might extend life, such as medication, life-support systems, or feeding tubes.

Although active euthanasia is highly controversial, most people are not in favor of preserving life in all cases. In a *New York Times*-CBS Poll taken in 1990, 53 percent of the respondents said that doctors should be allowed to assist an ill person in taking his or her own life (Malcolm, 1990).

Active euthanasia may become more common, perhaps following the pattern in the Netherlands. A law passed there in 1993 sanctioned euthanasia, under strict conditions. The request must be made freely and over a period of time by the patient, un-pressured by others; the patient's suffering must be unbearable and without hope of recovery; another physician must agree on the advisability of euthanasia and on the method; and a complete report must be written. Active euthanasia remains technically illegal, but is permitted under these medical guidelines. A government study estimated that in 1990, voluntary euthanasia accounted for 2300 deaths and doctor-assisted suicides for 400 cases—a total of about 2 percent of all deaths in that year (Simons, 1993).

In the United States, the changing attitudes over the past 25 years or so can be attributed to technologies that can keep patients alive indefinitely after the brain has, for all practical purposes, stopped functioning. But there are thorny ethical questions for society and for patients and their families. There is a pressing need to define and monitor a problem that one doctor has called "so fundamental that it has moved beyond the boundaries of medicine" (Carton, 1990, p. 2221).

The President's Commission for the Study of Ethical Problems in Medicine and Biomedical and Behavioral Research proposed that mentally competent patients and families acting on behalf of incompetent patients be allowed to halt medical treatment that keeps them alive without any hope of curing or improving their condition. The commission recommended that ending a life intentionally be forbidden but that doctors should be allowed to give drugs that are likely to shorten life if the reason for administering the drugs is to relieve pain (Schmeck, 1983).

Since the United States Supreme Court ruled that a person whose wishes are clearly known has a constitutional right to have life-sustaining treatment discontinued (Greenhouse, 1990), more people have specified in writing the kinds of measures they want—or do not want—taken if they become mentally incompetent or terminally ill. It is important to put these requests in legally enforceable form, since a recent survey of 1400 doctors and nurses in five major hospitals around the United States found that nearly half the attending doctors and nurses and 70 percent of resident doctors reported overtreating terminally ill patients, while failing to give them enough pain medication (Solomon, 1993).

A person's wishes can be spelled out in a document called a living will (see Box 18-4 on page 609, which also discusses durable power of attorney). In addition, many people choose to leave instruc-tions about what kind of funeral they want and how their bodies are to be disposed of (for example, by burial, cremation, or donation to a research facility or medical school).

SUICIDE

Most people find life so precious that they cannot understand why anyone would voluntarily end it. Yet in 1989, more than 30,000 people in the United States committed suicide, making it the eighth leading cause of death in the nation (U.S. Department of Health and Human Services, USDHHS, 1992). Suicide is increasing among young people and males, and decreasing among females. White people are almost twice as likely to kill themselves as black people. Elderly white men over 75 have especially high rates of suicide. The increased use of guns instead of less certain methods like poison may indicate that more people who commit suicide are determined to succeed. In fact, injuries from firearms are directly responsible for most suicides in the United States today (USDHHS, 1992). (See Figure 18-1 for age-related trends in suicide; Figure 18-2 for suicide rates by age, race, and sex; and Table 18-2 for major risk factors for suicide.)

Statistics probably understate the number of suicides, since many go unreported and some "accidental" deaths may actually be self-inflicted. Also, the figures do not include suicide *attempts.* Although there are about 5000 documented suicides a year among young people aged 15 to 24, some mental health professionals estimate that each year as many as 500,000 children and teenagers try to kill themselves and fail (Brody, 1992a).

Patterns of Suicide

Suicide among Children

"It wasn't an accident. I figured if I died it wouldn't hurt as much as if I lived." These were the words of a dying 5-year-old child (Turkington, 1983).

It is painfully hard to believe that young children can be so unhappy that they take their lives. Yet one study strongly suggests that many "accidents" among preschoolers may actually be deliberate attempts at suicide (P. A. Rosenthal & Rosenthal, 1984). Sixteen children aged 2½ to 5 who were diagnosed as suicidal—they had seriously injured themselves or had tried to do so

TABLE 18-2

Risk Factors for Suicide

Characteristic	Highest Risk
Sex	Male
Race	White
Age	Highest *rates:* over age 65, especially over 75 (but rates for younger people are increasing) Highest *numbers:* ages 15 to 34
Marital status	Divorced and widowed
Family history	Other family members have attempted or carried out suicide
Personal history	Previous suicide attempts or psychiatric treatment, current or previous stressful life events
Health	Depression, schizophrenia, alcohol or drug abuse, physical illness, panic attacks
Personality	Dependency, helplessness, hopelessness, inability to accept help, difficulty in forming close personal relationships, poor problem-solving ability (especially under stress), extreme anxiety, difficulty concentrating, extreme irritability, antisocial behaviors
Occupational status	Unemployed people; medical doctors
Geographic location (U.S.)	The west (lowest rates in the northeast)
Season of year	Spring (March, April, May)
Other factors	Presence of a handgun in the home

SOURCES: Boyer & Guthrie, 1985; *Harvard Medical School Health Letter,* 1986; Kellermann et al., 1992; Meehan, 1990; *Morbidity and Mortality Weekly Report,* MMWR, 1985; U.S. Department of Health and Human Services, USDHHS, 1990, 1992; Weissman, Klerman, Markowitz, & Ouellette, 1989.

(13 of them more than once)—were compared with 16 children of the same ages who had serious behavioral problems but were not considered suicidal. The children diagnosed as suicidal were more aggressive, seemed more depressed, had more morbid ideas, ran away more, and were less likely to cry after being hurt than were the other children. Most of the suicidal children had parents who did not want them and who abused or neglected them; six had been separated from their parents by divorce, foster placement, adoption, or death; and all showed disturbed attachment behavior. Play therapy brought out the children's reasons for trying to kill themselves: to punish themselves, to escape or remedy their painful situations, or to be reunited with a loved, nurturing person (like a dead father).

The psychiatrists who conducted this study rec-

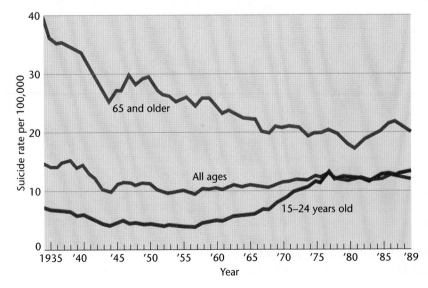

FIGURE 18-1
Suicide rates in the United States by age, showing changes from 1935 to 1989. (*Source:* National Center for Health Statistics, 1992.)

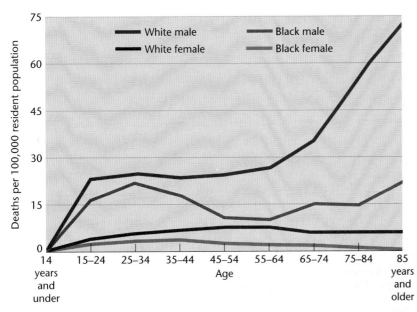

FIGURE 18-2

Suicide rates in the United States in 1989, by sex, race, and age. (*Source:* U.S. Department of Health and Human Services, USDHHS, 1992.)

ommend asking preschoolers about their accidents to try to uncover underlying psychological causes. Very young children may be particularly at risk because they generally believe (as did half of the children in this study) that death is reversible.

Suicide among Adolescents

A 16-year-old girl, constantly at odds with her parents because they disapprove of her boyfriend, breaks up with the boy. The next morning, her sister discovers her body next to an empty bottle of sleeping pills. An 18-year-old boy, despondent after a traffic accident that has resulted in the "totaling" of his car, the revocation of his driver's license, and a forthcoming trial, jumps off an icy bridge to his death.

These two teenagers are among a growing number of young people who see no way out of bad times in their life other than ending it. Suicide rates among teenagers—especially boys—have soared. Suicide is the second leading cause of death for 15- to 24-year-old white males and the third leading cause for this age group generally (USDHHS, 1992). The leading cause of death is accidents, some of which may actually be suicides (National Center for Health Statistics, in L. Eisenberg, 1986).

What makes life intolerable to so many young people? Some child-study professionals believe that suicide rates among teenagers have risen because today's adolescents are under much more stress than their counterparts in earlier days (Elkind, 1984). But many young people who attempt suicide do not want to die. They only want to change their lives, and their suicide attempts are desperate pleas for attention and help. Through impulsiveness or miscalculation, they often die before help can reach them.

Many young people who try to kill themselves have histories of emotional illness; common diagnoses are depression, drug and alcohol abuse, and unstable personality. They tend to be impulsive, to have poor control, and to have low tolerance for frustration and stress (Slap, Vorters, Chaudhuri, & Centor, 1989). They are also likely to think poorly of themselves, to live in a family torn by strife and one they experience as nonsupportive to them, to have inadequate relationships outside the family, and to feel hopeless (Swedo et al., 1991). Drugs and alcohol play a part in about half of all teenage suicide attempts (National Committee for Citizens in Education, NCCE, 1986).

Suicidal adolescents are often in conflict with their parents, unable to call on them for support when they feel lonely and unloved. Many come from troubled families, and a high proportion have been abused or neglected (Deykin, Alpert, & McNamarra, 1985). Although school problems are common, for either academic or behavior reasons, poor performance is not universal. Among a group of high-achieving high school juniors and seniors, 31 percent had considered suicide and 4 percent had tried it (*Who's Who among American High School Students*, in NCCE, 1986). Low achievers may feel that their lives are worthless; high achievers may feel under too much pressure to perform.

Several studies have assessed the impact of television. In one, the researchers compared the number of teenage suicides in California, Pennsylvania,

"Suicide High" is what people in Omaha, Nebraska, began calling Bryan High School after three students there committed suicide within five days. Suicide has become the second leading cause of death among adolescents (after accidents—some of which may be suicides). Guidance counselors like this one try to alleviate the anxiety of classmates of young suicide victims and to prevent more young people from taking their own lives. (Ted Kirk)

and the New York City area for two time periods—the 2 weeks *after* the broadcast of each of three fictional movies about suicide and the 2 weeks *before* the movies were shown. These researchers found no increase after the broadcasts and concluded that there is no reason to worry that fiction on television induces young people to kill themselves (D. P. Phillips & Paight, 1987). Another study, however, found that suicides do increase following extensive reporting of *real* suicides (D. P. Phillips & Carstensen, 1986). This may be related to a greater identification with real people than with fictional characters, or to the greater repetition in the reporting of a real case as compared with a single presentation of a fictional drama.

Given the alarming rise in suicide among young people, more research on this topic needs to be undertaken. Meanwhile, the family and friends of an adolescent who may be contemplating suicide can often help.

Suicide among Adults

Audience members at a Metropolitan Opera performance of Verdi's *Macbeth* were horrified when, during the intermission, an elderly man plunged to his death from an upper balcony. An 82-year-

old singing coach who had lived for his music and his friends, Bantcho Bantchevsky had been lively and gregarious until his health began to deteriorate a few months before. His depression grew until he took his life, dying in the theatrical manner in which he had lived (Okun, 1988).

Suicide among adults often occurs in conjunction with depression or with debilitating physical illness. About 15 percent of depressed people eventually kill themselves, accounting for some 30 to 70 percent of suicides in the United States (USDHHS, 1990). Although in absolute numbers most suicides occur among young white males (aged 15 to 34), the highest *rate* of suicide in the entire population is among white men over the age of 85. For white women, the rates are highest in middle age. Black men and women are most vulnerable as young adults (see Figure 18-2).

The suicide rates for adults may be even higher than they seem, since many deaths may not be recognized as self-inflicted. Some may look like traffic accidents, accidental overdoses of drugs, or forgetfulness—unintentional failure to take life-preserving medicine.

Why do older adults commit suicide? One explanation is despair over a progression of losses that they are helpless to stop: of work, of friends, of a spouse, of children, of memory, of health, and finally of self-esteem and hope. Some elderly people feel that the quality of life is too low to continue living. Older white men seem to find it especially hard to face the deprivations of old age, possibly because of overidentification with their work roles, leaving them without identity after they stop working.

Psychotherapy, medication, or increased social contacts can often help to lessen a person's feeling of isolation, lift depression, and restore an interest in life. At other times—especially when an older person has a disabling or painful illness—all efforts fail.

Preventing Suicide

In some quarters, ending one's life is seen as a rational decision, given certain circumstances, such as terminal illness; and suicide is considered a right to be defended. There is growing support for "right to die" legislation, which removes the criminal connotations from suicide and gives mature people the right to end their lives when they see fit.

Another view, however, is that while we can empathize with people who have committed suicide, we should try to thwart a suicide that has not yet

BOX 18-4 PRACTICALLY SPEAKING

THE LIVING WILL AND MEDICAL DURABLE POWER OF ATTORNEY

People who receive extraordinary measures to prolong life are often unconscious or mentally incompetent by the time these measures are put into effect. Such a condition can befall a person *of any age* who has been injured or become ill. By deciding ahead of time what kind of care you want and communicating these decisions to others, you can do much to ensure that you receive the extent of care that you want. This can be done through such documents as a *living will* and a *medical durable power of attorney.* If your state has legislation for either or both documents, you need to use the legally approved wording.

A *living will* should be addressed—and copies of it should be given—to your family doctor, your attorney, and close family members. It specifies that if the time comes when you can no longer take part in decisions for your own future, this statement will stand as an expression of your wishes and directions, while you are still of sound mind.

You may, for example, direct that if a situation should arise in which there is no reasonable expectation of recovery from extreme physical or mental disability, you be allowed to die and not be kept alive by medications, artificial

means, or "heroic measures." You may also, of course, use a living will to request such measures to keep you alive as long as possible. You may request pain-relieving medication even though it may shorten your life. You may spell out specific provisions with regard to—for example—cardiac resuscitation, mechanical respiration, antibiotics, tube feeding, and permission to offer your organs as transplants to other people.

Some "living will" legislation applies only to terminally ill patients—not to patients who are incapacitated by illness or injury but may live many years in severe pain, who are in a coma, or who are in some other greatly disabled state. Therefore, it is advisable to draw up a durable power of attorney, an instrument that appoints another person to make decisions in the event of your incompetence. A number of states have enacted statutes expressly for decisions about health care, known as a *medical durable power of attorney.* In these states, filling out a form is all that is required; you do not have to consult an attorney.

Depending on the statute, the agent you appoint (someone you trust and have confidence in) may give, withdraw, or withhold consent to specific medical or surgical

measures; hire and fire medical personnel; gain access to your medical records; go to court to carry out your wishes; spend or withhold funds for treatment; and interpret your living will.

REMEMBER

■ Both documents need to be signed and dated before two witnesses who are not blood relatives and to whom you are not leaving property.
■ For the medical durable power of attorney, you must have your signature notarized. If you choose more than one proxy for decision making on your behalf (a good idea in case your first choice is not available), give an order of priority (1, 2, 3, etc.).
■ Give a copy to your doctor to keep in your medical file, and be sure that she or he agrees to abide by your wishes.
■ Give copies to close relatives, friends, or both.
■ Keep a copy for yourself.
■ Tell the above people about your intentions now.
■ Look over your living will once a year. Redate it and initial the new date to make it clear that your wishes are unchanged.

been carried out. According to this viewpoint, suicide is not so much a wish for death as a desire to avoid unbearable pain, either physical or emotional, and we need to find ways to reduce that pain.

What Society Can Do
Society can take steps on many levels, starting at the most basic—promoting physical and mental health (Meehan, 1990). Schools can begin early to help children learn how to solve problems and cope with stress. Programs to enhance self-esteem should also be directed toward young children and continued through the school years.

Identifying children, young people, and adults who are at high risk is important, so that counseling and guidance can be offered. Often the first resource is a crisis center or telephone hot line, which can offer immediate support as well as referral to a mental health professional. Most communities and hospitals have suicide-prevention hot lines which people can call to talk with someone about their problems, and most college counseling departments provide suicide-prevention services. Intervention is especially urgent for people who have already talked about or attempted suicide, since studies show that 10 to 40 percent of people who commit suicide have attempted it at least once before (Meehan, 1990).

Steps can also be taken to reduce access to common methods of suicide. Gun control legislation would probably decrease such deaths. Suicide rates declined in England and Wales between 1960 and 1975, apparently as a result of the elimination of coal gas containing carbon monoxide, the use of which had been a popular method (J. H. Brown, 1979). In the United States and in Australia, the number of suicides from barbiturates declined in proportion to the number of prescriptions written. The number of suicides involving guns has risen in recent years; the ready availability of firearms in the home is associated with a higher risk of suicide (Kellermann et al., 1992). Many suicides are impulsive; if a convenient means is not at hand, the depressed person may not go any further or may at least defer action long enough to get help. Furthermore, a person who leans toward one method may be reluctant to use another (L. Eisenberg, 1980).

What Family and Friends Can Do

After a person has committed suicide, people close to him or her are usually overwhelmed not only with grief but also with guilt. They ask themselves, "Why didn't I know? Why didn't I do something?"

A person intent on suicide will sometimes carefully conceal his or her plans; but very often, warning signals appear long before the deed. Sometimes an attempt at suicide is a call for help, and people die because they are more successful than they intended to be.

Warning Signs of Suicide These include withdrawal from family or friends; talking about death, the hereafter, or suicide; giving away prized possessions; drug or alcohol abuse; and personality changes, such as unusual anger, boredom, or apathy. Signs of depression may include unusual neglect of appearance; difficulty concentrating on work or school; staying away from usual activities; complaints of physical problems when nothing is organically wrong; sleeping or eating much more or much less than usual; loss of self-esteem; or feelings of helplessness, hopelessness, extreme anxiety, or panic.

Actions That Might Avert Suicide People are sometimes afraid to talk to someone about suicidal thoughts; they worry that they will put ideas into the mind of someone who has not already thought of suicide. On the contrary, such talk will bring feelings into the open. It is often valuable to turn to others who are in a position to do something—the person's parents or spouse, other family members, a close friend, or a therapist or counselor. It is better to break a confidence than to let someone die. Sometimes it is possible to relieve real-life pressures that seem intolerable, whether that means calling a rejecting lover, lending money, or interceding with an employer. Probably the most important action involves showing the person that she or he has other options besides death, even though none of them may be ideal.

FINDING A PURPOSE IN LIFE AND DEATH

For most of us, death comes at a time and in a way not of our choosing. It is the inevitable end to the journey that began at the moment of conception. As death approaches, people tend to look back over what they have made of themselves—how they have changed and grown. They ask themselves about the purpose of life and death, and try to sum up what their lives have meant.

THE MEANING OF DEATH

The central character of Tolstoy's short story "The Death of Ivan Ilyich" is racked by an illness that he knows will be fatal. In despair, he asks himself over and over again what meaning there is to his agony. Even greater than his physical suffering is his mental torment as he lies dying and becomes more and more convinced that he has wasted his life, that his life has been without purpose, and therefore that his death is equally pointless.

What Tolstoy dramatized in literature, contemporary social scientists are finding in the real world. Viktor Frankl (1965), a psychoanalyst who survived a Nazi death camp during World War II, observed that people need to find meaning in death if they are to find meaning in life. It also seems to be true that the greater purpose people find in their lives, the less they fear death. A researcher who administered attitudinal scales to 39 women whose average age was 76 found that those who saw the most purpose in life did indeed have the least fear of death (Durlak, 1973).

"There is no need to be afraid of death," Kübler-Ross wrote (1975, p. 164). Awareness of death, she says, is the key to personal growth and to the development of human potential:

It is the denial of death that is partially responsible for [people's] living empty, purposeless lives; for when you live as if you'll live forever, it becomes too easy to postpone the things you know that you must do. In contrast, when you fully understand that each day you awaken could be the last you have, you take the time *that day* to grow, to become more of who you really are, to reach out to other human beings. . . . For only when we understand the real meaning of death to human existence will we have the courage to become what we are destined to be. (pp. 164, 165)

REVIEWING A LIFE

The elderly doctor who is the hero of Ingmar Bergman's classic film *Wild Strawberries* dreams and thinks about his past and his coming death. Realizing how cold and unaffectionate he has been, he becomes warmer and more open in his last days. This film underscores the fact that personality can change at any time in the life span, no matter how late.

The doctor in *Wild Strawberries* was able to make his life more purposeful through a *life review,* a process of reminiscence that enables a person to see the significance of his or her life. It can also foster "ego integrity," which Erikson holds as the final important task in life. Older people's natural tendency to talk about the people, events, and feelings of past years is an important part of the life review. Life-review therapy can help make the review more conscious, deliberate, and efficient (Butler, 1961; M. I. Lewis & Butler, 1974). Some of the techniques for evoking memories that are used in life-review therapy are presented in Box 18-5.

By going over their lives, people may see their experiences and actions in a new light. They may have a chance to complete such unfinished tasks as reconciliation with estranged family members or friends. The sense of completion after accomplishing these tasks can be a comfort as people round out the time that remains to them.

Some kinds of reminiscences that arise during the process of life review foster integrity more than others do. One team of researchers identified six kinds of reminiscences (Wong & Watt, 1991). They are:

■ *Integrative:* these help people to accept their pasts as worthwhile, resolve past conflicts, and reconcile the discrepancy between what they considered ideal and what really occurred.
■ *Instrumental:* these focus on coping strategies,

Participating in a class reunion—sharing memories with people who played a part in formative experiences—is one way to review a life. Life review can help people see important events in a new light and can motivate them to seek a sense of closure by rebuilding damaged relationships or completing unfinished tasks. *(William Strode/Woodfin Camp & Associates)*

which solved problems in the past and can be drawn upon for the present.
■ *Escapist:* these glorify the past (often helping to protect self-esteem) and deprecate the present.
■ *Obsessive:* these are colored by feelings of guilt, bitterness, or despair over disturbing events.
■ *Transmissive:* these pass on cultural heritage and personal wisdom.
■ *Narrative:* these are descriptive, furnishing routine biographical information or telling interesting but not personally meaningful anecdotes.

Wong and Watt analyzed the reminiscences of 171 people between ages 65 and 95, about half of whom were judged to be higher than average in mental and physical health and adjustment, and about half of whom were below average on these measures. Those who were "aging successfully" showed more integrative and instrumental reminiscences and fewer obsessive and escapist ones than did their "unsuccessful" counterparts. Possibly for reasons related to the nature of the study, clear differences did not show up for the other two kinds of reminiscences. The overall conclusion, however, is clear: not all reminiscences are beneficial.

Some elderly people, in reviewing their lives, feel that they have wasted them or have injured

BOX 18-5   PRACTICALLY SPEAKING

EVOKING MEMORIES FOR A "LIFE REVIEW"

The following methods (adapted from M. I. Lewis & Butler, 1974) for uncovering hidden memories are used in life-review therapy. These methods are often useful and enjoyable, and can also be used fruitfully as part of an ongoing project with younger family members or friends. They can build a bridge between generations, help older people experience a creative ordering of their lives, and give younger people insights that may help them in their own old age.

■ *Written or taped autobiographies:* The incidents, experiences, and people included in these autobiographies are significant. It is also important to be aware of what is *not* here. (One successful professional man put together an extensive record of his life, with practically no mention of his two middle-aged children. When the therapist delved into this omission, the man revealed that he was estranged from both children and was then able to use the therapy to examine his feelings about them.)

■ *Pilgrimages (in person or through correspondence):* When possible, older people can take trips back to the locations of their birth, childhood, youth, and young adulthood. They can take photos and make notes to put their thoughts in order. If they cannot do this in reality, they can often contact people who are still living in these places. Failing that, they can summon up their memories. (One woman, who was still angry with her parents for forbidding her to go into the attic and had for years fantasized about what they were hiding from her, discovered on revisiting her childhood home that there were no stairs to the attic and that the prohibition had been simply for her safety.)

■ *Reunions:* Getting together with high school and college classmates, family members, or members of a religious or civic organization lets people see themselves next to their peers and other important people in their lives.

■ *Genealogy:* Developing a family tree can give a person a sense of continuity in history. The search is interesting and absorbing in itself, as people put ads in newspapers; visit cemeteries; and pore over town records, family documents, and records of churches, synagogues, or other religious organizations.

■ *Scrapbooks, photo albums, old letters, and other memorabilia:* The items that people have kept usually have a special, pleasurable meaning in their lives. By talking about them, older people can often recall long-forgotten events, acquaintances, and emotional experiences.

■ *Books, audiocassettes, and videocassettes of historical events in the person's lifetime:* Accounts of recent history, tape recordings of famous people, and magazines summarizing, say, 50 years of movies can serve as lively triggers for discussion among older people.

■ *Summation of lifework:* By summing up what they regard as their contributions to the world, older people get the sense that they have participated meaningfully in it. Some older people's summations have grown into published books, poems, and music.

■ *Focus on ethnic identity:* By concentrating on special traditions they experienced and enjoyed as members of their ethnic groups, older persons can appreciate their heritage and pass it on.

others, and now have no chance to compensate for or improve on the past. More often, though, they can make a balanced assessment, recognizing both successes and failures and "bequeathing" their values to those who may be able to carry them on.

Within our limited life span, none of us can realize all our capabilities, gratify all our desires, engage all our interests, or experience all the richness that life has to offer. The tension between virtually infinite possibilities for growth and a finite time in which to do the growing defines human life from beginning to end. By choosing which possibilities to pursue and by following them as far as we can in the time we have, each of us contributes to the unfinished story of human development.

SUMMARY

■ Recently there has been an upsurge in interest in American society concerning the topic of death. Thanatology is the study of death and dying.

THREE ASPECTS OF DEATH

■ There are at least three aspects of dying: the biological (cessation of body processes), the social (mourning customs and legal implications of death), and the psychological (emotional reactions to death).

FACING DEATH

■ Sometime between the ages of 5 and 7, most children develop the understanding that death is irreversible and universal and that all life functions end at death.

■ Adolescents tend to have romantic conceptions of death and to be caught up in the personal fable, believing that they can take risks without danger.

■ Young adults who are about to die resent their inability to fulfill the dreams they have worked to achieve.

■ It is usually in middle age that people fully realize the inevitability of their own death and begin thinking about how to make the most of their remaining years.

■ In late adulthood, many people accept the prospect of death more tranquilly, especially if they feel that they have led meaningful lives.

■ People often undergo both intellectual and personality changes shortly before death.

■ Elisabeth Kübler-Ross, a pioneer in the study of death and dying, proposes that there are five stages in coming to terms with death: denial, anger, bargaining, depression, and acceptance. However, these stages do not necessarily represent the healthiest progression for all persons.

■ Bereavement is the objective change in status of a survivor following a death. Mourning is the behavior of the bereaved person after a death. Grief is the emotional response of the bereaved period. Patterns of mouring and grief vary across and within cultures.

■ Anticipatory grief involves symptoms of grief experienced by a survivor while a dying person is still alive.

■ The usual pattern of grieving begins with shock and disbelief. This is followed by preoccupation with the memory of the dead person. The final phase, resolution, occurs when the survivor resumes interest in everyday activities. Recently, mental health professionals have found considerable differences in people's reactions to bereavement. Although children ex-

perience many of the same grief reactions adult do there are age-related aspects, based on their cognitive and emotional development.

■ Some bereaved people need help through formal grief therapy or from support groups in order to cope with grief.

■ The hospice movement has developed to provide patient- and family-centered care for persons with terminal illnesses and their loved ones. Hospice care can be given in a hospital, in another institution, or at home.

■ Death education helps people to understand their attitudes toward death, to become familiar with the ways various cultural groups deal with death, and to be aware of the needs of dying persons and survivors.

■ Support groups and services can help people deal with death, dying, and bereavement.

CONTROVERSIAL ISSUES OF DEATH AND DYING

■ Widowhood is more likely to befall women than men. The survivor of a marriage is likely to face many emotional and practical problems. The best adjusted are those who keep busy, develop new roles, or become more deeply involved in activities.

■ Active euthanasia is deliberate action that is taken to shorten a life in order to end suffering. Passive euthanasia is the withholding of treatment that might extend the life of a terminally ill patient.

■ Most people do not favor using advanced medical technology to prolong the lives of the terminally ill against their wishes. People can make "living wills" stating their wishes about the kinds of measures they want or do not want taken in case of terminal illness.

■ The highest suicide rate is among elderly white men. Suicide is increasing among teenagers, especially boys, and is the third leading cause of death in adolescence. The leading cause of death among adolescents is accidents, but many presumed "accidents" (even among preschoolers) may actually be suicides or attempted suicides.

FINDING A PURPOSE IN LIFE AND DEATH

■ Evidence suggests that the more purpose and meaning people find in their lives, the less they fear death.

■ Life review is a process of reminiscence that helps people to prepare for death by assessing the significance of their lives and also gives them a last chance to make changes or to complete unfinished tasks.

KEY TERMS

thanatology (page 588)

near-death experiences (592)

bereavement (593)

mourning (593)

grief (593)

anticipatory grief (596)

grief therapy (599)

hospice care (599)

death education (600)

active euthanasia (603)

passive euthanasia (604)

living will (609)

medical durable power of attorney (609)

life review (611)

SUGGESTED READINGS

Bombeck, E. (1989). *I want to grow hair, I want to grow up, I want to go to Boise: Children surviving cancer.* New York: Harper & Row. An upbeat, optimistic, heartwarming, funny (yes, funny) book based on interviews with children who are living with cancer. The resilience of the human spirit—not only the children's but also those of the other people in their lives—comes through in quotation after quotation.

Callahan, D. (1993). *The troubled dream of life: Living with mortality.* New York: Simon & Schuster. An expert on medical ethics offers his personal experiences and insight into the controversies surrounding euthanasia, assisted suicide, and the medical technologies that can prolong life. For society to resolve these issues, he says that we must think about death itself, clarifying its meaning in our lives.

Colt, G. H. (1991). *The enigma of suicide.* New York: Summit Books. This book examines suicide from the historical perspective, seeks to understand the act and possible prevention, and discusses paths to healing for those left behind. There is a separate chapter on teenage suicides.

Kübler-Ross, E. (Ed.) (1975). *Death: The final stage of growth.* Englewood Cliffs, NJ: Prentice-Hall. This book, the most accessible of Kübler-Ross's works, treats death as a normal part of human development.

It offers a spectrum of views from clergy, doctors, nurses, sociologists, terminally ill patients, and survivors, and compares the ways our culture and other cultures treat death.

Moses, M., with Perry, P. (1990). *Closer to the light: Learning from children's near-death experiences.* New York: Random House. A sensitive account by a pediatrician of the near-death experiences of children, how the children and their families understand this experience, how it affects their lives, and the implications for seriously ill adults as well as children.

Nuland, S. B. (1994). *How we die: Reflections on life's final chapter.* New York: Knopf. This warm and compassionate work aims to clarify and demythologize the experience of death. By focusing on the details of various ways of dying, the author helps us to understand what death is really like, dispelling cultural myths and inaccurate beliefs.

Taylor, N. (1993). *A necessary end.* New York: Nan A. Talese. In this work, beautifully illustrated with woodcuts, the author tells the story of his parents' death and of his search for meaning in their life and his own. Sometimes annoyed at his parents for their quirks, the author ultimately shows compassion for them as well as for the reader, recognizing that most of us will face the death of our own parents.

accommodation   Piagetian term for a change in an existing cognitive structure to cope with new information. (36)

achieving stage   Second of Schaie's five cognitive stages, in which young adults use knowledge to gain competence and independence and do best on tasks relevant to life goals they have established for themselves. (420)

acquisitive stage   First of Schaie's five cognitive stages, characterized by the child's and adolescent's learning of information and skills largely for their own sake. (420)

acting-out behavior   Misbehavior (such as lying or stealing) spurred by emotional turmoil. (331)

active euthanasia   Deliberate action taken to shorten the life of a terminally ill person in order to end suffering or to carry out the wishes of the patient; also called *mercy killing*. Compare with *passive euthanasia*. (603)

activity theory   Theory of aging that holds that in order to age successfully a person must remain as active as possible. Compare with *disengagement theory*. (562)

adaptation   Piagetian term for effective interaction with the environment (problem solving) through the complementary processes of assimilation and accommodation. (36)

adaptive mechanisms   Vaillant's term to describe the four characteristic ways people adapt to life: mature, immature, psychotic, and neurotic. (438)

adolescence   Developmental transition between childhood and adulthood; generally considered to be-

gin around age 12 or 13 and end in the late teens or early twenties. (342)

adolescent growth spurt   Sharp increase in height and weight that precedes sexual maturity. (346)

adolescent rebellion   "Storm and stress" characteristic of some but not all adolescents, encompassing both conflict within the family and a general alienation from adult society and its values. (390)

affective disorder   Disorder of mood. (332)

ageism   Prejudice or discrimination against a person (most commonly an older person) based on age. (526)

aggressive behavior   Hostile assault, physical or verbal, intended to hurt the recipient or establish dominance. (250)

alcoholism   Condition characterized by physical and emotional dependence on alcohol. (67)

alleles   Pair of inherited genes (similar or different) that affect a particular trait. (51)

Alzheimer's disease   Irreversible dementia (degenerative brain disorder) characterized by deterioration in memory, awareness, and control of bodily functions, eventually leading to death. (541)

ambivalent attachment   Pattern of attachment in which an infant becomes anxious before the primary caregiver leaves, is extremely upset during his or her absence, and both seeks and resists contact upon his or her return; also called *resistant attachment*. (177)

amniocentesis   Prenatal medical procedure in which a sample of amniotic fluid is withdrawn and

analyzed to determine whether any of certain genetic defects are present. (61)

androgynous   Personality type integrating positive characteristics typically thought of as masculine with positive characteristics typically thought of as feminine. (247)

animism   Tendency to attribute life to objects that are not alive. (218)

anorexia nervosa   Eating disorder, seen mostly in young women, in which people starve themselves. (353)

anoxia   Lack of oxygen, which may cause brain damage. (93)

anticipatory grief   Grief that begins before an expected death and sometimes helps family and friends to prepare for bereavement. (596)

Apgar scale   Standard measurement of a newborn's condition; it assesses appearance, pulse, grimace, activity, and respiration. (96)

artificial insemination   Injection of sperm into a woman's cervix in order to enable her to conceive. (458)

assimilation   Piagetian term for the incorporation of new information into an existing cognitive structure. (36)

attachment   Active, affectionate reciprocal relationship specifically between two persons (usually infant and parent), in which interaction reinforces and strengthens the link. (176)

attention deficit hyperactivity disorder (ADHD)   Syndrome characterized by inattention, impulsivity, and considerable activity at inappropriate times and places. (298)

authoritarian parents   In Baumrind's terminology, parents whose child-rearing style emphasizes the values of control and obedience and who use forceful punishment to make children conform to a set standard of conduct. Compare with *authoritative parents* and *permissive parents.* (257)

authoritative parents   In Baumrind's terminology, parents whose child-rearing style blends respect for a child's individuality with an effort to instill social values in the child. Compare with *authoritarian parents* and *permissive parents.* (257)

autonomy versus shame and doubt   According to Erikson, the second critical pair of alternatives in psychosocial development (from about 18 months to 3 years), in which toddlers develop a balance of autonomous control (independence, self-determination) over shame and doubt. (164)

autosomes   The 22 pairs of nonsex chromosomes. (49)

avoidant attachment   Pattern of attachment in which an infant rarely cries when separated from the primary caregiver and avoids contact upon his or her return. (177)

basic trust versus basic mistrust   According to Erikson's theory, the first critical balancing of alternatives in psychosocial development (from birth to about 18 months), in which the infant develops a sense of whether or not the world can be trusted; the quality of interaction with the mother in feeding is a primary determinant of the outcome of this stage. (163)

battered child syndrome   Pattern of child abuse and neglect first identified in 1962. (185)

Bayley Scales of Infant Development   Standardized test for measuring the intellectual development of infants; the test consists of a mental scale and a motor scale, each of which yields a development quotient (DQ), computed by comparing what a particular baby can do at a certain age with the performance of a large number of previously observed babies at the same age. (134)

behaviorism   School of psychology that emphasizes the study of observable behaviors and events and the role of environment in causing behavior. (30)

behavior modification   Therapeutic approach using principles of learning theory to encourage desired behaviors or eliminate undesired ones; also called *behavior therapy.* (255)

behavior therapy   See behavior modification. (333)

bereavement   Loss due to death, which leads to a change in the survivor's status (for example, from wife to widow). (593)

bilingual education   A system of teaching children in two languages—their native language and English. (301)

bilingualism   Fluency in two languages. (301)

birth trauma   Birth-related brain injury caused by oxygen deprivation, mechanical injury, or infection or disease at birth. (96)

Brazelton Neonatal Behavioral Assessment Scale   Neurological and behavioral test to measure neonates' response to the environment; it assesses interactive behaviors, motor behaviors, physiological control, and response to stress. (98)

bulimia nervosa   Eating disorder in which a person regularly eats huge quantities of food and then purges the body by laxatives or induced vomiting; most common in young women. (354)

burnout   Syndrome of emotional exhaustion and a sense that one can no longer accomplish anything on the job, often experienced by people in the helping professions. (492)

case studies   Scientific studies, each covering a single case or life, based on notes taken by observers or on published biographical materials. (14)

causality   Piagetian term for the recognition that certain events cause other events. (138)

centration   In Piaget's theory, a limitation of preoperational thought that leads the child to focus on one aspect of a situation and neglect

others, often leading to illogical conclusions. (215)

cephalocaudal principle   Principle that development proceeds in a head-to-toe direction, i.e., that upper parts of the body develop before lower parts. (107)

cerebral cortex   Upper layer of the brain, responsible for thinking and problem solving. (95)

cesarean delivery   Delivery of a baby by surgical removal from the uterus. (83)

child abuse   Maltreatment of a child involving physical injury. (185)

childhood depression   Affective disorder characterized by a child's inability to form and maintain friendships, have fun, concentrate, and display normal emotional reactions. (332)

child-directed speech (CDS)   Form of speech used by some adults to talk to babies or toddlers; includes simplified speech and a high-pitched voice; also called *motherese.* (151)

chorionic villus sampling   Prenatal diagnostic procedure in which tissue from villi (hairlike projections of the membrane surrounding the embryo) is analyzed for birth defects. (61)

chromosomes   Segments of DNA that carry the genes, the transmitters of heredity; in the normal human being, there are 46 chromosomes. (50)

circular reactions   In Piaget's terminology, processes by which the infant learns to reproduce desired occurrences originally discovered by chance. Piaget described three types of circular reactions: primary, secondary, and tertiary. (135)

classical conditioning   Kind of learning in which a previously neutral stimulus (a neutral stimulus is one that does not elicit a particular response) acquires the power to elicit a response after the stimulus is repeatedly associated with another stimulus that ordinarily does elicit the response. (31, 130)

climacteric   Period of 2 to 5 years during which a woman's body undergoes physiological changes that bring on menopause. (475)

code-switching A process of changing one's speech to match the situation, as in people who are bilingual. (302)

cognitive development Changes in thought processes that result in a growing ability to acquire and use knowledge. (34, 135)

cognitive perspective View of humanity that is concerned with the development of thought processes. Views people as active and emphasizes qualitative rather than quantitative change. (34)

cognitive play Forms of play that reveal and enhance children's cognitive development. (263)

cohabitation Living together and maintaining a sexual relationship without being legally married. (453)

cohort People growing up in the same place at the same time. (9)

commitment Marcia's term for personal investment in an occupation or system of beliefs (one of two elements crucial in identity formation; see also *crisis*). (382)

componential element In Sternberg's triarchic theory, the analytic aspect of intelligence, which determines how efficiently people process information and solve problems. (421)

concrete operations Third stage of Piagetian cognitive development (approximately from age 5–7 to age 11), during which children develop logical but not abstract thinking. (279)

conservation In Piaget's terminology, awareness that two objects of equal size remain equal in the face of perceived alteration (for example, a change in shape) so long as nothing has been added to or taken away from either object. (215, 279)

contextual element In Sternberg's triarchic theory, the practical aspect of intelligence, which determines how effectively people deal with their environment. (421)

control group In an experiment, a group of people who are similar to the people in the experimental group but who do not receive the treatment whose effects are to be measured. The results obtained with the control group are compared with the results obtained with the experimental group. (19)

conventional morality Kohlberg's Level II of moral reasoning, in which the standards of authority figures are internalized. (282)

convergent thinking Thinking aimed at finding the one "right" answer to a problem; traditional thinking. Compare with *divergent thinking*. (300)

coregulation Transitional stage during middle childhood in which parent and child share power over the child's behavior, the parent exercising general supervision and the child regulating his or her own specific activities. (320)

correlation Statistical relationship between variables. (14)

crisis Marcia's term for a period of conscious decision making (one of two elements crucial in identity formation; see also *commitment*). (382)

critical period Specific time during development when a given event will have the greatest impact. (10)

cross-modal transference Information-processing skill by which young children can identify by sight an item they felt with their hands earlier but did not see; shows a fairly high level of abstraction. (143)

cross-sectional study Study design in which people of different ages are assessed on one occasion, providing comparative information about different age cohorts. Compare with *longitudinal study*. (21)

cross-sequential study Study design that combines cross-sectional and longitudinal techniques by assessing people in a cross-sectional sample more than once. (22)

crystallized intelligence Type of intelligence, proposed by Cattell and Horn, involving the ability to remember and use learned information; it is relatively dependent on education and cultural background. Compare with *fluid intelligence*. (485)

culture-fair test Describing an intelligence test that deals with experiences common to various cultures, in an attempt to avoid placing test-takers at an advantage or disadvantage due to their cultural background. Compare with *culture-free test*. (289)

culture-free test Describing an intelligence test that, if it were possible to design, would have no culturally linked content. Compare with *culture-fair test*. (289)

data Information that is obtained through research. (23)

death education Programs to educate people about dying and grief to help them deal with these issues in their personal and professional lives. (600)

decenter In Piagetian terminology, to consider all significant aspects of a situation simultaneously. Decentration is characteristic of operational thought. (215, 279)

defense mechanisms According to Freudian theory, ways in which people unconsciously combat anxiety by distorting reality. (25)

deferred imitation In Piaget's terminology, reproduction of an observed behavior after the passage of time by calling up a stored symbol of it. (140, 214)

dementia Apparent intellectual and personality deterioration sometimes associated with old age and caused by a variety of irreversible and reversible physiological conditions; sometimes called *senility*. (540)

Denver Developmental Screening Test Test given to children 1 month to 6 years old to determine whether or not they are developing normally; it assesses gross motor skills, fine motor skills, language development, and personal and social development. (117)

deoxyribonucleic acid (DNA) Genetic substance that controls the makeup and functions of body cells. (50)

dependent variable In an experiment, the factor that may or may not change as a result of manipulation of the independent variable. (19)

depression Emotional disturbance in which a person feels unhappy and often has trouble eating, sleeping, or concentrating. (69,170)

discipline The ways in which adults try to form a child's character, self-control, and moral behavior. (320)

disengagement theory Theory of aging that holds that successful aging is characterized by mutual withdrawal between the older person and society. Compare with *activity theory*. (562)

disorganized-disoriented attachment Pattern of attachment in which an infant, after being separated from the primary caregiver, greets him or her brightly upon return, but then turns away, or approaches without looking at the caregiver. (177)

divergent thinking Thinking that produces a variety of fresh, diverse possibilities; creative thinking. Compare with *convergent thinking*. (300)

dizygotic twins Twins conceived by the union of two different eggs with two different sperm cells within a brief period of time; also called *fraternal*, or *two-egg, twins*. (47)

dominant inheritance Pattern of inheritance, described by Mendel, in which only the dominant trait of two competing traits is expressed. (50)

Down syndrome Most common chromosomal disorder, usually caused by an extra twenty-first chromosome and characterized by mild or moderate mental retardation, and by such physical signs as a downward-sloping skin fold at the inner corners of the eyes. (58)

drug therapy Use of drugs to treat emotional problems, sometimes in children. (333)

dual-process model Model of intellectual functioning, proposed by Paul B. Baltes, which identifies and seeks to measure two dimensions of intelligence: the mechanics of intelligence and the pragmatics of intelligence. (547)

durable power of attorney A legal instrument that appoints an individual to make decisions in the event of another person's incapacitation. (609)

dyslexia Common learning disability involving inability to learn to read or difficulty in doing so. (296)

ecological approach Bronfenbrenner's system of understanding development, which identifies four levels of environmental influence: the microsystem, mesosystem, exosystem, and macrosystem. (9,367)

ego In Freudian theory, an aspect of personality that develops during infancy and operates on the reality principle, seeking acceptable means of gratification in dealing with the real world. (25)

egocentrism In Piaget's terminology, a characteristic of preoperational thought consisting of inability to consider another's viewpoint; a form of egocentrism is also characteristic of adolescents. (217)

elaboration A strategy for remembering items that involves linking them together in an imagined scene or story. (286)

elder abuse Neglect or physical or psychological abuse of dependent older persons. (570)

electronic fetal monitoring Monitoring of fetal heartbeat by machine in labor and delivery. (84)

embryonic stage Second stage of gestation (2 to 8–12 weeks), characterized by rapid growth and development of major body systems and organs. (70)

emotional flexibility versus emotional impoverishment One of four adjustments of middle age described by Peck. (503)

emotions Subjective feelings such as sadness, joy, and fear, which arise in response to situations and experiences and are expressed through some kind of altered behavior. (165)

empty nest Term for the transitional phase of parenting following the last child's leaving the parents' home. (515)

enuresis Bed-wetting. (208)

environmental influences Nongenetic influences on development that are attributable to experiences with the outside world. (8)

equilibration In Piagetian terminology, the tendency to strive for equilibrium (balance) among cognitive elements within the organism and between it and the outside world. (36)

ethological approach An approach to studying behavior that considers behavior to be biologically determined, is concerned with the evolutionary basis of behaviors, relies on naturalistic observation, and emphasizes critical, or sensitive, periods for behavior development; sometimes used to study the mother-infant bond. (174)

executive stage Fourth of Schaie's cognitive stages, in which the middle-aged person responsible for societal systems integrates complex relationships on several levels. (420)

experiential element In Sternberg's triarchic theory, the insightful, creative aspect of intelligence, which determines how effectively people approach both novel and familiar tasks. (421)

experiment Rigorously controlled, replicable (that is, repeatable) procedure in which the researcher manipulates variables to assess their effect on each other. (17)

experimental group In an experiment, the group receiving the treatment under study; any changes in these people are compared with changes in the control group. (19)

external aids A memory strategy that requires the use of something outside the person, such as a list. (286)

extinction Cessation of a response, or its return to the baseline level, when the response is no longer reinforced. (33)

family therapy Psychological treatment in which parents and child are seen together by a therapist. (333)

fertilization Union of sperm and ovum to produce a zygote. (46)

fetal alcohol syndrome (FAS) Mental, motor, and developmental abnormalities (including stunted growth, facial and bodily malformations, and disorders of the central nervous system) affecting the offspring of some women who drink heavily during pregnancy. (76)

fetal stage Final stage of gestation (8–12 weeks to birth), characterized by increased detail of body parts and greatly elongated body size. (72)

fine motor skills Abilities like buttoning and copying figures, which involve the small muscles. (209)

fluid intelligence Type of intelligence, proposed by Cattell and Horn, involving ability to perceive relations, form concepts, and reason abstractly. It is considered dependent on neurological development and relatively free from influences of education and culture and is thus tested by novel problems or tasks with common cultural elements. Compare with *crystallized intelligence.* (485)

fontanels Soft spots on head of young infant. (93)

foreclosure Identity status described by Marcia in which a person who has not spent time considering alternatives (that is, has not been in crisis) is committed to other people's plans for his or her life. (383)

formal operations According to Piaget, the final stage of cognitive development, reached by some adolescents, which is characterized by the ability to think abstractly. (360)

free radicals Specific forms of oxygen that are produced in the normal course of living, but then become dangerous and damage body substances such as DNA, proteins, and fats; support the "wear-and-tear" theory of aging. (533)

gamete Sex cell (sperm or ovum). (46)

gender Significance of being male or female. (241)

gender constancy Realization that one's sex will always stay the same. Also called *gender conservation.* (244)

gender differences Differences between males and females that may or may not be based on biological differences. (246)

gender identity Awareness, developed in early childhood, that one is male or female. (241)

gender roles Behaviors, interests, attitudes, and skills that a culture considers appropriate for males and females and expects them to fulfill. (241)

gender schema In Bem's theory, a mentally organized pattern of behavior that helps a child sort out information about what it means to be male or female. (244)

gender-schema theory Theory that children socialize themselves in their gender roles by developing the concept of what it means to be male or female. (244)

gender stereotypes Exaggerated generalizations about male or female role behavior. (246)

gender-typing Socialization process by which a child, at an early age, learns the appropriate gender role. (246)

gene Basic functional unit of heredity, which determines an inherited characteristic. (50)

generativity versus stagnation According to Erikson, the seventh critical alternative of psychosocial development, in which the mature adult develops a concern with establishing and guiding the next generation or else experiences stagnation (a sense of inactivity or lifelessness). (503)

genetic counseling Clinical service that advises couples of their probable risk of having children with particular hereditary defects. (59)

genetics Study of hereditary factors affecting development. (49)

genotype Underlying genetic composition that causes certain traits to be expressed; may vary without causing changes in phenotype, because of the presence of recessive genes. (51)

germinal stage First 2 weeks of prenatal development, characterized by rapid cell division and increasing complexity; the stage ends when the conceptus attaches itself to the wall of the uterus. (70)

gerontology The study of the aged and the process of aging. (526)

giftedness Exceptional potential in any of the following areas: general intellectual ability, specific academic aptitudes, leadership, talent in the arts, creativity, psychomotor ability. (299)

global self-worth In Harter's theory, children's favorable opinion of themselves. (310)

grief Emotional response of the bereaved to a death. (593)

grief therapy Program to help the bereaved cope with loss. (599)

gross motor skills Physical skills like jumping and running, which involve the large muscles. (209)

habituation Simple type of learning in which familiarity with a stimulus results in loss of interest and reduces or stops the response. (129)

heredity Inborn influences on development, carried on the genes inherited from the parents. (8, 49)

heterosexual Describing a person whose sexual orientation is toward the other sex. (386)

heterozygous Possessing two dissimilar alleles for a trait. (51)

holophrase Single word that conveys a complete thought; the typical speech form of children aged 12 to 18 months. (148)

homosexual Describing a person whose sexual orientation is toward the same sex. (386)

homozygous Possessing two similar alleles for a trait. (51)

horizontal décalage Piagetian term for a child's inability to transfer learning about one type of conservation to other types, because of which the child masters different types of conservation tasks for the first time at different ages (for example, learning substance conservation before either weight conservation or volume conservation). (280)

hospice care Warm, personal patient- and family-centered care for a person with a terminal illness. (599)

human development Scientific study of quantitative and qualitative ways in which people change and stay the same over time. (3)

humanistic perspective View of humanity that sees people as having the ability to foster their own positive, healthy development through the distinctively human capacities for choice, creativity, and self-realization. (37)

hypertension High blood pressure. (480)

hypothesis Possible explanation for a phenomenon, used to predict the outcome of an experiment. (23)

id In Freudian theory, the instinctual aspect of personality (present at birth) that operates on the pleasure principle, seeking immediate gratification. (25)

ideal self Person's concept of who he or she would like to be; compare with *real self*. (309)

identification Process by which a person acquires characteristics, beliefs, attitudes, values, and behaviors of another person or of a group; an important personality development of early childhood. (241)

identity achievement Identity status, described by Marcia, which is characterized by commitment to choices made following a crisis period, or period spent in thinking about alternatives. (383)

identity diffusion Identity status, described by Marcia, which is characterized by absence of commitment and may or may not follow a period of considering alternatives (crisis). (383)

identity versus identity confusion According to Eriksonian theory, the fifth critical alternative of psychosocial development, in which an adolescent must determine his or her own sense of self (identity), including the role she or he is to play in society. (380)

imaginary audience Observer who exists only in an adolescent's mind and is as concerned with the adolescent's thoughts and actions as is the adolescent himself or herself. (363)

imaginative play Play involving imaginary situations; also called

fantasy play, dramatic play, or *pretend play.* (265)

independent segregation Mendel's law that hereditary traits are transmitted separately. (51)

independent variable In an experiment, the variable over which the experimenter has control. Compare *dependent variable.* (19)

individual psychotherapy Psychological treatment in which a therapist sees a troubled person, sometimes a child, one-on-one. (333)

industry versus inferiority In Erikson's theory, the fourth critical alternative of psychosocial development, occurring during middle childhood, in which children must learn the productive skills their culture requires or else face feelings of inferiority. (310)

infantile autism Developmental disorder that begins with the first 2½ years of life and is characterized by lack of responsiveness to other people. (67)

infant mortality rate Proportion of babies born who die in the first year of life. (103)

infertility Inability to conceive after 12 or more months of trying. (456)

information-processing approach Study of intellectual development by analyzing the mental processes that underlie intelligent behavior; the manipulation of symbols and perceptions to acquire information and solve problems. (142)

initiative versus guilt According to Erikson, the third crisis of psychosocial development, occurring between the ages of 3 and 6, in which children must balance the urge to form and carry out goals with their moral judgments about what they want to do. Children develop initiative when they try out new things and are not overwhelmed by failure. (241)

integrity versus despair According to Erikson, the eighth and final critical alternative of psychosocial development, in which people in late adulthood either accept their lives as a whole and thus accept death or yield to despair that their lives cannot be relived. (558)

intelligence quotient (IQ) tests Tests used to assess *how much* a person has of certain abilities like comprehension and reasoning. (224)

intelligent behavior Behavior that is goal-oriented (conscious and deliberate) and adaptive (used to identify and solve problems). (132)

interiority In Neugarten's terminology, a concern with inner life (introversion or introspection), which generally increases as people grow older. (504)

interview Research technique in which people are asked to state their attitudes, opinions, or histories. (17)

intimacy versus isolation According to Erikson, the sixth critical alternative of psychosocial development, in which young adults either make commitments to others or face a possible sense of isolation and consequent self-absorption. (436)

invisible imitation Imitation with parts of one's body that one cannot see; e.g., the mouth. (139)

in vitro fertilization Fertilization of an ovum outside the mother's body. (459)

irreversibility In Piaget's theory, a limitation on preoperational thinking consisting of failure to understand that an operation can be reversed, restoring the original condition. (215)

karyotype Chart in which photomicrographs of a person's chromosomes are arranged according to size and structure to reveal any chromosomal abnormalities. (59)

laboratory observation Research method in which all subjects are placed in the same situation, the laboratory, where the surroundings are under the researcher's control. (16)

language acquisition device (LAD) In Noam Chomsky's nativist theory, an inborn mental structure that enables children to build linguistic rules by analyzing the language they hear. (151)

lanugo Fuzzy prenatal body hair, which drops off within a few days after birth. (93)

learning Long-lasting change in behavior that occurs as a result of experience. (128)

learning disabilities (LDs) Disorders that interfere with specific aspects of learning and school achievement. (296)

learning perspective theory Theory that behavior is learned from experience. The two major branches are traditional learning theory (behaviorism) and social-learning theory. (30,150)

life expectancy The number of years a person is expected to live, based on statistical data. (531)

life review Reminiscence about one's life in order to see its significance. (611)

life structure According to Levinson, the basic pattern of a person's life at a given time, consisting of internal and external aspects that shape and are shaped by the person's relationship with the environment. (439)

linguistic speech Speech designed to convey meaning. (148)

living will Document specifying the type of care wanted by the maker in the event of terminal illness. (609)

longitudinal study Study design in which data are collected about the same people over a period of time, to assess developmental changes that occur with age. Compare with *cross-sectional study*. (21)

long-term memory Store of permanent or long-lasting memories, which may be retrieved with varying degrees of ease depending on the efficiency of organization and storage. Long-term memory for newly learned information diminishes with aging, but long-term memory for memories acquired in the distant past does not generally diminish appreciably. Compare with *short-term memory*. (547)

low birthweight Weight of less than 5½ pounds at birth because of prematurity or being small for date. (100)

mainstreaming Integration of disabled and nondisabled children in the regular classroom. (298)

male climacteric Period of physiological, emotional, and psychological change involving a man's reproductive system and other body systems. (478)

masturbation Sexual self-stimulation. (385)

maternal blood test Prenatal diagnostic procedure to detect the presence of fetal abnormalities, used particularly when the fetus is at risk of defects in the central nervous system. (61)

maturation Unfolding of a biologically determined, age-related sequence of behavior patterns programmed by the genes, including the readiness to master new abilities. (63, 128)

mechanics of intelligence In the dual-process model of Baltes, the abilities to process information and solve problems, irrespective of content; the area of intellect in which there is often an age-related decline. Compare with *pragmatics of intelligence*. (547)

meconium Fetal waste matter, excreted during the first few days after birth. (94)

medical durable power of attorney Appointment of an agent to give, withdraw, or withhold consent to specific medical or surgical procedures when the patient is unable to do so. (609)

medicated delivery Childbirth in which the mother receives anesthesia. (82)

menarche First menstruation. (347)

menopause Cessation of menstruation and of ability to bear children, typically around age 50. (475)

mental flexibility versus mental rigidity One of four adjustments of middle age described by Peck. (503)

mental retardation Below-average intellectual functioning, a deficiency in adaptive behavior appropriate to current age, and the appearance of such characteristics before age 18. (296)

metacommunication Understanding of the processes involved in communication; metacommunication increases during middle childhood. (292)

metamemory Understanding of how memory works. (286)

midlife crisis Potentially stressful life period precipitated by the review and re-evaluation of one's past, typically occurring in the early to middle forties. (500)

mnemonic devices Strategies to aid memory. (285)

monozygotic twins Twins resulting from the division of a single zygote after fertilization; also called *identical*, or *one-egg, twins*. (47)

morality of constraint First of Piaget's two stages of moral development, characterized by rigid, simplistic judgments; also called *heteronomous morality*. (280)

morality of cooperation Second of Piaget's two stages of moral development, characterized by moral flexibility; also called *autonomous morality*. (281)

moratorium Identity status, described by Marcia, in which a person is currently considering alternatives (in crisis) and seems headed for commitment. (383)

mother-infant bond A mother's feeling of close, caring connection with her newborn. (175)

mourning Behavior of the bereaved and the community after a death. (593)

multifactorial inheritance Pattern of inheritance in which a single trait is affected by a combination of genetic and environmental factors. (52)

multiple alleles Genes that have three or more alternative forms. (52)

mutual-regulation model A process by which infant and caregiver communicate emotional states to each other and respond appropriately. (168)

nativism Theory that views human beings as having an inborn capacity for language acquisition. (150)

natural childbirth Method of childbirth, developed by Dr. Grantly Dick-Read, that seeks to prevent pain by eliminating the mother's fear of childbirth. (83)

naturalistic observation Method of research in which people's behavior is studied in natural settings without the observer's intervention or manipulation. (15)

near-death experiences Those experiences reported by people who have come close to death but have not died; these include a feeling of well-being, enhanced clarity of thinking, and visions of bright lights. (592)

negativism Behavior characteristic of toddlers, in which they express their desire for independence by resisting almost everything they are asked to do. (164)

neglect The withholding of adequate care from a child; usually refers to physical needs such as food, clothing, and supervision. (185)

neonatal period First 4 weeks of life, a time of transition from intrauterine dependency to independent existence. (92)

neonate Newborn baby. (92)

nonnormative life events In the timing-of-events model, life experiences which are unusual and thus not normally anticipated, or are ordinary but come at unexpected times, and which may have a major impact on development. (442)

nonorganic failure to thrive Emotional neglect resulting in a baby's failure to grow and gain weight at home despite adequate nutrition. (185)

normative-crisis model Theoretical model, typified by the work of Erikson, Levinson, and Vaillant, that describes social and emotional development in terms of a definite sequence of age-related changes. Compare with *timing-of-events model.* (436)

normative life events In the timing-of-events model, expected life experiences that occur at customary times. (442)

novelty preference The greater length of time babies spend looking at new stimuli rather than familiar ones. (143)

obesity Overweight marked by skinfold measurement in the 85th percentile. (352)

object permanence In Piaget's terminology, the understanding that

a person or object still exists when out of sight. (137)

operant (instrumental) conditioning Form of learning in which a response continues to be made because it has been reinforced or stops being made because it has been punished; also called *instrumental conditioning,* because the learner is instrumental in changing the environment to bring about either reinforcement or punishment. (32, 131)

operational thinking In Piaget's terminology, mental manipulation of symbols and signs to carry out logical operations. (279)

organization (1) Piagetian term for integration of knowledge into a system to make sense of the environment. (36) (2) Mnemonic device consisting of categorizing material to be remembered. (286)

osteoporosis Condition affecting 1 in 4 postmenopausal women, in which the bones become thinner and more susceptible to fractures. (475)

Otis-Lennon School Ability Test Group intelligence test for kindergarten to twelfth grade, covering classification, verbal and numerical concepts, general information, and ability to follow directions. (286)

ovulation Expulsion of ovum from ovary, which occurs about once every 28 days from puberty to menopause. (46)

ovum transfer Method of fertilization in which a woman who cannot produce normal ova use ova donated by fertile women. (459)

passive euthanasia Deliberate withholding of life-prolonging treatment from a terminally ill person in order to minimize suffering or to carry out the wishes of the patient. Compare with *active euthanasia.* (604)

permissive parents In Baumrind's terminology, parents whose childrearing style emphasizes the values of self-expression and self-regulation. Compare with *authoritarian parents* and *authoritative parents.* (257)

personal fable Conviction, typical in adolescence, that one is special,

unique, and not subject to the rules that govern the rest of the world. (363)

personality Person's unique and relatively consistent way of feeling, thinking, and behaving. (66,162)

phenotype Observable characteristic of a person. (51)

Piagetian approach Study of intellectual development by describing qualitative stages, or typical changes, in children's and adolescents' cognitive functioning; proposed by Jean Piaget. (135)

plasticity Variability or modifiability of a given person's performance. (546)

postconventional morality Kohlberg's Level III of moral reasoning, in which morality is fully internal. (282)

postformal thought Mature type of thought which contains subjectivity and reliance on intuition as well as the pure logic characteristic of formal operational thought. (422)

pragmatics of intelligence In the dual-process model of Baltes, the dimension of intelligence that tends to grow with age and includes practical thinking, application of accumulated knowledge and skills, specialized expertise, professional productivity, and wisdom. Compare with *mechanics of intelligence.* See *dual-process model.* (547)

preconventional morality Kohlberg's Level I of moral reasoning, in which control is external and rules are obeyed in order to gain rewards or avoid punishment. (282)

prejudice Negative attitude toward someone because of his or her membership in a particular group, such as a religious or racial group. (315)

prelinguistic speech Forerunner of linguistic speech; includes crying, cooing, babbling, and accidental and deliberate imitation of sounds without understanding their meaning. (146)

premenstrual syndrome (PMS) Disorder producing symptoms of physical discomfort and emotional tension before a menstrual period. (419)

preoperational stage In Piaget's theory, the second major period of intellectual development (approximately from age 2 to age 7), in which children can think about things not physically present by using mental representations but are limited by their inability to use logic. (214)

prepared childbirth Method of childbirth, developed by Dr. Ferdinand Lamaze, that uses instruction, breathing exercises, and social support to remove fear and pain. (83)

presbycusis Gradual loss of hearing that occurs during middle age, especially with regard to sounds at the upper frequencies. (473)

presbyopia Farsightedness associated with aging, resulting when the lens of the eye becomes less elastic. (473)

preterm babies Babies born before thirty-seventh week of gestation, dated from the mother's last menstrual period; also called *premature babies*. (100)

primary aging Gradual process of bodily deterioration that begins early in life and continues through the life span. Compare with *secondary aging*. (534)

primary sex characteristics Characteristics directly related to reproduction; specifically, the male and female sex organs. These enlarge and mature during adolescence. See *secondary sex characteristics*. (347)

private speech Talking aloud to oneself with no intent to communicate; common in early and middle childhood. (223)

programmed-aging theory Theory that bodies age in accordance with a normal development pattern built into every organism of a particular species; compare with *wear-and-tear theory of aging*. (533)

Project Head Start Compensatory preschool education program begun in the United States in 1965. (233)

prosocial behavior Behavior intended to help others without external reward. (254)

proximodistal principle Principle that development proceeds from within to without; i.e., that parts of the body near the center develop before the extremities. (108)

psychoanalytic perspective View of humanity concerned with the unconscious forces motivating human behavior. (24)

psychological maltreatment Action or failure to act that damages children's behavioral, cognitive, emotional, or physical functioning and may keep children from realizing their full potential as adults. (334)

psychometric approach Study of intellectual development by attempting to measure quantitatively the factors that appear to make up intelligence. (131)

psychosexual development In Freudian theory, an unvarying sequence of stages of personality development during infancy, childhood, and adolescence, in which gratification shifts from the mouth to the anus and then to the genitals. (25)

psychosocial development Theory of Erikson that societal and cultural influences play a major part in healthy personality development. According to this theory, development occurs in eight maturationally determined stages throughout the life span, each revolving around a particular crisis or turning point in which the person is faced with achieving a healthy balance between alternative positive and negative traits. (29)

puberty Process by which a person attains sexual maturity and is able to reproduce. (342)

punishment In operant conditioning, a stimulus that, when administered following a particular behavior, decreases the probability that the behavior will be repeated. (32)

qualitative change Change in kind, structure, or organization, such as the nature of a person's intelligence or the way the mind works. (3)

quantitative change Change in number or amount of something, such as height, weight, or vocabulary. (3)

random sample Type of sample that ensures representativeness because each member of the population has an equal chance to be selected. (19)

real self Person's concept of who he or she actually is. Compare with *ideal self*. (309)

recall Ability to reproduce material from memory without being presented with it again. Compare with *recognition*. (212)

recessive inheritance Expression of a recessive (nondominant) trait, which, according to Mendel, occurs only if the offspring receives the same recessive gene from both parents. (51)

recognition Ability to identify previously learned material when presented with it again; tested by asking a person to choose the correct answer from among several possibilities. Compare with *recall*. (212)

reflex behaviors Automatic responses to external stimulation. Reflexes—by their presence or disappearance—are early signs of an infant's neurological growth. (96)

rehearsal Mnemonic device consisting of conscious repetition. (285)

reinforcement In operant conditioning, a stimulus that, when administered following a particular behavior, increases the probability that the behavior will be repeated. (32)

reintegrative stage Fifth of Schaie's cognitive stages, in which older people focus energy on tasks that have meaning for them. (420)

relational theory Theory, proposed by Miller, that all personality growth occurs within emotional connections, not separate from them, beginning in infancy. (29)

reliability Consistency of a test in measuring performance. (224)

reliable Describing a test that is consistent in measuring performance. (224)

representational ability Capacity to mentally represent objects and experiences without needing a stimulus, largely through the use of symbols. (138)

reserve capacity Ability of body organs and systems to put forth 4 to 10 times as much effort as usual in times of stress or dysfunction; also called *organ reserve*. (537)

responsible stage Third of Schaie's five cognitive stages, in which middle-aged people are concerned with long-range goals and practical problems often related to their responsibility for others. (420)

sample In an experiment, the group of subjects chosen to represent the entire population under study. (19)

scaffolding The temporary support that parents and others give a child to do a task. (226)

schemes In Piaget's terminology, basic cognitive structures that an infant uses to interact with the environment; organized patterns of thought and behavior. (35, 136)

schizophrenia A group of mental disorders characterized by loss of contact with reality and such symptoms as delusions, hallucinations, and thought disturbances. (67)

school phobia Unrealistic fear of school, probably reflecting separation anxiety. (331)

scientific method System of established principles of scientific inquiry, including careful observation and recording of data, testing of alternative hypotheses, and widespread dissemination of findings and conclusions so that other scientists can learn from, analyze, repeat, and build on the results. (14)

secondary aging Aging processes that result from disease and bodily abuse and disuse, factors that may be subject to the person's own control. Compare with *primary aging*. (534)

secondary sex characteristics Physiological characteristics of the sexes which develop during adolescence (and do not involve the sex organs), including breast development in females, broadened shoulders in males, growth of body hair in both sexes, and adult skin and adult

voices of men and women. See *primary sex characteristics*. (347)

secular trend Trend that can be seen only by observing several generations. A secular trend toward earlier attainment of adult height and sexual maturity began a century ago and appears to have ended in the United States. (346)

secure attachment Attachment pattern in which an infant can separate readily from the primary caregiver and actively seeks out the caregiver upon return. (177)

selective optimization with compensation In the dual-process model of Baltes, the ability of older people to maintain or enhance their intellectual functioning through the use of special abilities to compensate for losses in other areas. (547)

self-awareness Realization, beginning in infancy, of separateness from other people and things, allowing reflection on one's own actions in relation to social standards. (166)

self-care children Children who regularly care for themselves at home without adult supervision. (323)

self-concept Sense of self, including self-understanding and self-control or self-regulation. (308)

self-definition External and psychological characteristics by which a person describes himself or herself. (308)

self-esteem Person's positive self-evaluation or self-image. (309)

self-fulfilling prophecy Expectation or prediction of behavior that tends to come true because it leads people to act as if it were already true. (294)

self-regulation Child's independent control of behavior to conform to understood social expectations. (164)

senescence Period of the life span marked by changes in physical functioning associated with aging; begins at different ages for different people. (530)

sensorimotor stage First of Piaget's stages of cognitive development, when infants (from birth to 2 years)

learn through their developing senses and motor activities. (135)

sensory memory Fleeting awareness of images or sensations, which disappears quickly unless transferred to short-term memory. (547)

separation anxiety Distress shown by an infant, usually beginning in the second half of the first year, when a familiar caregiver leaves; it is commonly a sign that attachment has occurred. (183)

separation anxiety disorder Condition involving excessive anxiety for at least 2 weeks, concerning separation from people to whom a child is attached. (331)

sex chromosomes Pair of chromosomes that determines sex: XX in the normal female, XY in the normal male. (49)

sex differences Physical differences between males and females. (245)

sex-linked inheritance Pattern of inheritance in which certain characteristics carried on the sex chromosomes (usually the X chromosome) are transmitted differently to males and females. (52)

sexual abuse Any kind of sexual contact between a child and an older person, or any sexual activity between adults to which one of the participants has not consented. (185)

sexually transmitted diseases (STDs) Diseases transmitted by sexual contact; also called *venereal diseases*. (357)

sexual orientation Sexual interest either in the other sex (heterosexual orientation) or in the same sex (homosexual orientation), usually first expressed during adolescence; also called *sexual preference*. (386)

shaping In operant conditioning, a method of bringing about a new response by reinforcing responses that are progressively more like it. (33)

short-term memory Working memory, the active repository of information currently being used; its capacity is limited but increases rapidly during middle childhood and is relatively unaffected by aging. Material in short-term memory disappears after about 20 seconds unless transferred to long-term memory. (547)

small-for-date babies Babies whose birthweight is less than that of 90 percent of babies of the same gestational age, as a result of slow fetal growth. (100)

socialization Process of learning the behaviors considered appropriate in one's culture. (174)

socializing versus sexualizing in human relationships One of four adjustments of middle age described by Peck. (503)

social-learning theory Theory, proposed chiefly by Bandura, that behaviors are learned by observing and imitating models and are maintained through reinforcement. (33)

social play Play in which children interact with other children, commonly regarded as a sign of social competence. (263)

social referencing Understanding an ambiguous situation by seeking out another person's perception of it. (169)

social speech Speech intended for a listener. (223)

spontaneous abortion Natural expulsion from the uterus of a conceptus that cannot survive outside the womb; also called *miscarriage*. (70)

standardized norms Standards for determining mental age of persons who take an intelligence test, obtained from scores of a large, representative sample of children who took the test while it was in preparation. (224)

Stanford-Binet Intelligence Scale Individual intelligence test used primarily with children to measure practical judgment, memory, and spatial orientation. (225)

states of arousal Periodic variations in an infant's daily cycles of wakefulness, sleep, and activity. (108)

status offender Juvenile charged with committing an act that would not be considered criminal if the offender were older (for example, being truant, running away from home, or engaging in sexual intercourse). (402)

Strange Situation Research technique used to assess the attachment between a mother and her infant. (177)

stranger anxiety Phenomenon that often occurs during the second half of a child's first year (in conjunction with separation anxiety), when the infant becomes wary of strange people and places; commonly a sign that attachment has occurred. (183)

stress The organism's physiological and psychological reaction to demands made on it. (480)

substantive complexity Degree to which a person's work requires thought and independent judgment. (493)

sudden infant death syndrome (SIDS) Sudden and unexpected death of an apparently healthy infant. (105)

superego According to Freudian theory, the aspect of personality representing values that parents and other agents of society communicate to a child. It develops around the age of 5 or 6 as a result of resolution of the Oedipus or Electra complex. (25)

surrogate motherhood Method of conception in which a woman who is not married to a man agrees to bear his baby and then give the child to the father and his wife. (459)

symbol In Piaget's terminology, an idiosyncratic mental representation of a sensory experience. (214)

symbolic function In Piaget's terminology, ability to learn by using mental representations (symbols or signs) to which a child has attached meaning; this ability, characteristic of preoperational thought, is shown in deferred imitation, symbolic play, and language. (214)

symbolic play In Piaget's terminology, play in which a child makes an object stand for something else. (214)

tacit knowledge Information that is not formally taught or openly expressed but is necessary to get ahead; includes self-management and management of tasks and of others. (422)

temperament Person's character-

istic style of approaching and reacting to people and situations. (66, 171)

teratogenic Capable of causing birth defects. (73)

terminal drop Sudden decrease in intellectual performance shortly before death. (545)

thanatology Study of death and dying. (588)

theory Set of related statements about data that helps scientists to explain, interpret, and predict behavior. (23)

timing-of-events model Theoretical model, advocated by Neugarten, that describes adult social and emotional development as a response to whether the occurrence and timing of important life events is expected or unexpected. Compare with *normative-crisis model*. (442)

transduction In Piaget's terminology, a preoperational child's tendency to mentally link particular experiences without the use of inductive or deductive logic, sometimes resulting in false conclusions. (217)

transitional objects Objects—commonly soft, cuddly ones—used repeatedly at bedtime to help a child make the transition from dependence to independence. (208)

triangular theory of love Sternberg's theory that love is composed of three elements: intimacy, passion, and commitment. (444)

ultrasound Prenatal medical procedure using high-frequency sound waves to detect the outline of a fetus, judge gestational age, detect multiple pregnancies, detect abnormalities or death of the fetus, and determine whether the pregnancy is progressing normally. (62)

valid Describing a test that measures what it is supposed to measure. (224)

valuing wisdom versus valuing physical powers One of four adjustments of middle age described by Peck. (503)

vernix caseosa Oily substance on a neonate's skin that protects against infection. (93)

visible imitation Imitation with parts of one's body that one can see, such as the hands and the feet. (139)

visual cliff Apparatus designed to give an illusion of depth and used to assess depth perception in infants. (114)

visual preference An infant's tendency to look longer at certain stimuli than at others, which depends on the ability to differentiate between sights. (115)

visual-recognition memory Ability to remember and recognize a visual stimulus. (142)

wear-and-tear theory Theory that bodies age because of continuous use and accumulated "insults." Compare with *programmed-aging theory*. (533)

Wechsler Intelligence Scale for Children (WISC-R) Individual intelligence test for schoolchildren that yields separate scores for verbal and performance subtests and a total score. (225,286)

Wechsler Preschool and Primary Scale of Intelligence (WPPSI-R) Individual intelligence test for children aged 4 to 6½ that includes verbal and performance subtests. (225)

zone of proximal development (ZPD) Vygotsky's term for the level at which children can *almost* perform a task on their own and, with appropriate teaching, *can* perform it. (225)

zygote One-celled organism resulting from the union of sperm and ovum. (46)

Abbey, A., Andrews, F. M., & Halman, J. (1992). Infertility and subjective well-being: The mediating roles of self-esteem, internal control, and interpersonal conflict. *Journal of Marriage and the Family, 54,* 408–417.

Abramovitch, R., Corter, C., & Lando, B. (1979). Sibling interaction in the home. *Child Development, 50,* 997–1003.

Abramovitch, R., Corter, C., Pepler, D., & Stanhope, L. (1986). Sibling and peer interactions: A final follow-up and comparison. *Child Development, 57,* 217–229.

Abramovitch, R., Pepler, D., & Corter, C. (1982). Patterns of sibling interaction among preschool-age children. In M. E. Lamb (Ed.), *Sibling relationships: Their nature and significance across the lifespan.* Hillsdale, NJ: Erlbaum.

Abrams, B., & Parker, J. D. (1990). Maternal weight gain in women with good pregnancy outcome. *Obstetrics and Gynecology, 76*(1), 1–7.

Abroms, K., & Bennett, J. (1981). Changing etiological perspectives in Down's syndrome: Implications for early intervention. *Journal of the Division for Early Childhood, 2,* 109–112.

Abt Associates. (1978). *Children at the center: Vol. 1. Summary findings and policy implications of the National Day Care Study.* Washington, DC: U.S. Department of Health, Education, and Welfare.

Acredolo, L., & Goodwyn, S. (1988). Symbolic gesturing in normal infants. *Child Development, 59,* 450–466.

Action for Children's Television (undated). *Treat TV with T. L. C.* One-page flyer. Newtonville, MA: Author

Adams, D. (1983). *The psychosocial development of professional black women's lives and the consequences of careers for their personal happiness.* Unpublished doctoral dissertation, Wright Institute, Berkeley, CA.

Adams, G., Adams-Taylor, S., & Pittman, K. (1989). Adolescent pregnancy and parenthood: A review of the problem, solutions, and resources. *Family Relations, 38,* 223–229.

Adams, L. A., & Rickert, V. I. (1989). Reducing bedtime tantrums: Comparison between positive routines and graduated extinction. *Pediatrics, 84,* 756–761.

Adams, R. G. (1986). Friendship and aging. *Generations, 10*(4), 40–43.

Ainsworth, M. D. S. (1967). *Infancy in Uganda; infant care and the growth of love.* Baltimore: Johns Hopkins Press.

Ainsworth, M. D. S. (1969). Object relations, dependency, and attachment: A theoretical review of the infant-mother relationship. *Child Development, 40,* 969–1025.

Ainsworth, M. D. S. (1979). Infant-mother attachment. *American Psychologist, 34*(10), 932–937.

Ainsworth, M. D. S., & Bell, S. (1977). Infant crying and maternal responsiveness: A rejoinder to Gerwitz and Boyd. *Child Development, 48,* 1208–1216.

Ainsworth, M. D. S., Blehar, M. C., Waters, E., & Wall, S. (1978). *Patterns of attachment: A psychological study of the strange situation.* Hillsdale, NJ: Erlbaum.

Akutsu, H., Legge, G. E., Ross, J. A., & Schuebel, K. J. (1991). Psychophysics of reading-X. Effects of age-related changes in vision. *Journal of Gerontology, 46*(6), P325–331.

Alan Guttmacher Institute. See under *Guttmacher.*

Aldous, J. J. (1987). Family life of the elderly and near-elderly. *Journal of Marriage and the Family, 49*(2), 227–234.

Alemi, B., Hamosh, M., Scanlon, J. W., Salzman-Mann, C., & Hamosh, P. (1981). Fat digestion in very low birthweight infants: Effects of addition of human milk to low-birth-weight formula. *Pediatrics, 68*(4), 484–489.

Alexander, B. B., Rubinstein, R. L., Goodman, M., & Luborsky, M. (1992). A path not taken: A cultural analysis of regrets and childlessness in the lives of older women. *Gerontologist, 32*(5), 618–626.

Allore, R., O'Hanlon, D., Price, R., Neilson, K., Willard, H. F., Cox, D. R., Marks, A., & Dun, R. J. (1988). Gene encoding the B subunit of S100 protein is on chromosome 21: Implications for Down syndrome. *Science, 239,* 1311–1313.

Almy, M., Chittenden, E., & Miller, P. (1966). *Young children's thinking: Some aspects of Piaget's theory.* New York: Teachers College Press.

Alsaker, F. D. (1992). Pubertal timing, overweight, and psychological adjustment. *Journal of Early Adolescence, 12*(4), 396–419.

Altemeir, W. A., O'Connor, S. M., Sherrod, K. B., & Vietze, P. M. (1985). Prospective study of antecedents for nonorganic failure to thrive. *Journal of Pediatrics, 106,* 360–365.

Alvarez, W. F. (1985). The meaning of maternal employment for mothers and their perceptions of their three-year-old children. *Child Development, 56,* 350–360.

Amabile, T. A., & Rovee-Collier, C. (1991). Contextual variation and memory retrieval at six months. *Child Development, 62,* 1155–1166.

Amato, P. R. (1987). Family processes in one-parent, stepparent, and intact families: The child's point of view. *Journal of Marriage and the Family, 49,* 327–337.

Amato, P. R., & Keith, B. (1991a). Parental divorce and adult well-being: A meta-analysis. *Journal of Marriage and the Family, 53,* 43–58.

Amato, P. R., & Keith, B. (1991b). Parental divorce and the well-being of children: A meta-analysis. *Psychological Bulletin, 110*(1), 26–46.

Amato, P. R., Kurdek, L. A., Demo, D. H., & Allen, K. R. (1993). Children's adjustment to divorce: Theories, hypotheses, and empirical support. *Journal of Marriage and the Family, 55*(1), 23–54.

American Academy of Pediatrics (AAP). (1973). The ten-state nutrition survey: A pediatric perspective. *Pediatrics, 51*(6), 1095–1099.

American Academy of Pediatrics (AAP). (1986a). *Day care facts and figures.* Elk Grove Village, IL: Author.

American Academy of Pediatrics (AAP). (1986b). *How to be your child's TV guide: Guidelines for constructive viewing.* Elk Grove Village, IL: Author.

American Academy of Pediatrics (AAP). (1986c). *Positive approaches to day care dilemmas: How to make it work.* Elk Grove Village, IL: Author.

American Academy of Pediatrics (AAP). (1989). Follow-up or weaning formulas. *Pediatrics, 83*(6), 1067.

American Academy of Pediatrics (AAP). (1992, January 15). *AAP proposes handgun ban, other measures to curb firearm deaths, injuries.* News release. Elk Grove Village, IL: Author.

American Academy of Pediatrics (AAP). (1992, Spring). Bedtime doesn't have to be a struggle. *Healthy Kids,* pp. 4–10.

American Academy of Pediatrics (AAP) Committee on Accident and Poison Prevention. (1990). Bicycle helmets. *Pediatrics, 85*(1), 229–230.

American Academy of Pediatrics (AAP) Committee on Adolescence. (1987). Alcohol use and abuse: A pediatric concern. *Pediatrics, 79*(3), 450–453.

American Academy of Pediatrics (AAP) Committee on Bioethics. (1992). Infants with anencephaly as organ sources: Ethical considerations. *Pediatrics, 89*(6), 1116-1119.

American Academy of Pediatrics (AAP) Committee on Bioethics. (1992, July). Ethical issues in surrogate motherhood. *AAP News,* pp. 14–15.

American Academy of Pediatrics (AAP) Committee on Children with Disabilities. (1992). Learning disabilities, dyslexia, and vision. *Pediatrics, 90*(1), 124–125.

American Academy of Pediatrics (AAP) Committee on Children with Disabilities and Committee on Drugs. (1987). Medication for children with an attention deficit disorder. *Pediatrics, 80*(5), 758–760.

American Academy of Pediatrics (AAP) Committee on Drugs. (1978). Effects of medication during labor and delivery on infant outcome. *Pediatrics, 62*(3), 402–403.

American Academy of Pediatrics (AAP) Committee on Drugs. (1982). Psychotropic drugs in pregnancy and lactation. *Pediatrics, 69*(2), 241–243.

American Academy of Pediatrics (AAP) Committee on Fetus and Newborn. (1986). Use and abuse of the Apgar scale. *Pediatrics, 78*(6), 1148–1149.

American Academy of Pediatrics (AAP) Committee on Genetics. (1992). Issues in newborn screening. *Pediatrics, 89*(2), 345–349.

American Academy of Pediatrics (AAP) Committee on Infectious Diseases. (1992). Universal hepatitis B immunization. *Pediatrics, 89*(4), 795–800.

American Academy of Pediatrics (AAP) Committee on Nutrition. (1981). Nutritional aspects of obesity in infancy and childhood. *Pediatrics, 68*(6), 880–883.

American Academy of Pediatrics (AAP) Committee on Nutrition. (1992a). Statement on cholesterol. *Pediatrics, 90*(3), 469–473.

American Academy of Pediatrics (AAP) Committee on Nutrition. (1992b). The use of whole cow's milk in infancy. *Pediatrics, 89*(6), 1105–1109.

American Academy of Pediatrics (AAP) Committee on Pediatric Aspects of Physical Fitness, Recreation, and Sports. (1981). Competitive athletics for children of elementary school age. *Pediatrics, 67*(6), 927-928.

American Academy of Pediatrics (AAP) Committee on Psychosocial Aspects of Child and Family Health (1992). The pediatrician and childhood bereavement. *Pediatrics, 89*(3), 516–518.

American Academy of Pediatrics (AAP) Committee on Sports Medicine and Committee on School Health. (1989). Organized athletics for preadolescent children. *Pediatrics, 84*(3), 583–584.

American Academy of Pediatrics (AAP) Committee on Sports Medicine and Fitness. (1992). Fitness, activity, and sports participation in the preschool child. *Pediatrics, 90*(6), 1002–1004.

American Academy of Pediatrics (AAP) Committee on Substance Abuse and Committee on Children with Disabilities. (1993). Fetal alcohol syndrome and fetal alcohol effects. *Pediatrics, 91*(5), 1004–1006.

American Academy of Pediatrics (AAP) Task Force on Blood Pressure Control in Children. (1987). Report of the second task force on blood pressure control in children. *Pediatrics, 79*(1), 1–25.

American Academy of Pediatrics (AAP) Task Force on Circumcision. (1989). Report on the task force on circumcision. *Pediatrics, 84*(4), 1155–1160.

American Academy of Pediatrics (AAP) Task Force on Infant Positioning and SIDS. (1992). Positioning and SIDS. *Pediatrics, 89*(6), 1120–1126.

American Academy of Pediatrics (AAP) Task Force on Pediatric AIDS. (1991). Education of children with human immunodeficiency virus infection. *Pediatrics, 88*(3), 645–648.

American Association of Retired Persons (AARP). (1986). *A profile of older Americans.* Brochure. Washington, DC: Author.

American Association of Retired Persons (AARP). (1989, March). *Working caregivers report.* Washington, DC: Author.

American Association of Retired Persons (AARP). (1991). *A profile of older Americans.* Brochure. Washington, DC: Author.

American Association of Retired Persons (AARP). (1992). *A profile of older Americans.* Brochure. Washington, DC: Author.

American Cancer Society. (1985). *1985 cancer facts and figures.* Pamphlet. Washington, DC: Author.

American Cancer Society. (1993). Cancer statistics, 1993. *Cancer Journal for Clinicians, 43*(1), 7–26.

American Council on Science and Health. (1985). *Premenstrual syndrome.* Pamphlet. Summit, NJ: Author.

American Heart Association. (1990). *The healthy American diet.* Dallas: Author.

American Heart Association. (1993). *Heart and stroke fact statistics.* Dallas: Author.

Anand, K. J. S., & Hickey, P. R. (1987). Pain and its effect in the human neonate and fetus. *New England Journal of Medicine, 317*(21), 1321–1329.

Anand, K. J. S., & Hickey, P. R. (1992). Halothane-morphine compared with high-dose sufentanil for anesthesia in post-operative analgesia in neonatal cardiac surgery. *New England Journal of Medicine, 326*(1), 1–9.

Anastasi, A. (1958). Heredity, environment, and the question "how?" *Psychological Review, 65*(4), 197–208.

Anastasi, A. (1988). *Psychological testing* (6th ed.). New York: Macmillan.

Anders, T., Caraskadon, M., & Dement, W. (1980). Sleep and sleepiness in children and adolescents. In I. Litt (Ed.), Adolescent medicine. *Pediatric Clinics of North America, 27*(1), 29–44.

Anders, T. R., Fozard, J. L., & Lillyquist, T. D. (1972). Effects of age upon retrieval from short-term memory. *Developmental Psychology, 6*(2), 214–217.

Anderson, R. (1980). I never sang for my father. In R. G. Lyell (Ed.), *Middle age, old age* (pp. 55–110). New York: Harcourt Brace Jovanovich.

Anderson, S. A., Russell, C. S., & Schumm, W. R. (1983). Perceived marital quality and family life-cycle categories: A further analysis. *Journal of Marriage and the Family, 45,* 127–139.

Anderson, T. B. (1984). Widowhood as a life transition: Its impact on kinship ties. *Journal of Marriage and the Family, 46,* 105–114.

Andersson, B. E. (1992). Effects of daycare on cognitive and socioemotional competence of thirteen-year-old Swedish children. *Child Development, 63,* 20–36.

Anson, O. (1989). Marital status and women's health revisited: The importance of a proximate adult. *Journal of Marriage and the Family, 51,* 185–194.

Anthony, E. J., & Koupernik, C. (Eds.). (1974). *The child in his family: Children at psychiatric risk,* Vol. 3. New York: Wiley.

Antonarakis, S. E., & Down Syndrome Collaborative Group. (1991). Parental origin of the extra chromosome in trisomy 21 as indicated by analysis of DNA polymorphisms. *New England Journal of Medicine, 324,* 872–876.

Apgar, V. (1953). A proposal for a new method of evaluation of the newborn infant. *Current Research in Anesthesia and Analgesia, 32,* 260–267.

Aquilino, W. S., & Supple, K. R. (1991). Parent-child relations and parent's satisfaction with living arrangements when adult children live at home. *Journal of Marriage and the Family, 53,* 13–27.

Arend, R., Gove, F., & Sroufe, L. A. (1979). Continuity of individual adaptation from infancy to kindergarten: A predictive study of ego-resiliency and curiosity in preschoolers. *Child Development, 50,* 950–959.

Ariès, P. (1962). *Centuries of childhood.* New York: Vintage.

Armstrong, B. G., McDonald, A. D., & Sloan, M. (1992). Cigarette, alcohol, and coffee consumption and spontaneous abortion. *American Journal of Public Health, 81,* 85.

Asendorpf, J. B., & Baudonniere, P-M. (1993). Self-awareness and other-awareness: Mirror self-recognition and synchronic imitation among unfamiliar peers. *Developmental Psychology, 29*(1), 88–95.

Ash, P., Vennart, J., & Carter, C. (1977, April 16). The incidence of hereditary disease in man. *The Lancet,* pp. 849–851.

Asher, J. (1987). Born to be shy? *Psychology Today, 21*(4), 54–64.

Asher, S., Renshaw, P., Geraci, K., & Dor, A. (1979, March). *Peer acceptance and social skill training: The selection of program content.* Paper presented at the meeting of the Society for Research in Child Development, San Francisco.

Aslin, R. N. (1987). Visual and auditory development in infancy. In J. D. Osofsky (Ed.), *Handbook of infant development* (2d ed.). New York: Wiley.

Associated Press. (1987, November 30). Infant survives on chips when family dies. *The New York Times,* p. A16.

Atchley, R. (1985). *Social forces and aging* (4th ed). Belmont, CA: Wadsworth.

Aylward, G. P., Pfeiffer, S. I., Wright, A., & Verhulst, S. J. (1989). Outcome studies of low birth weight infants published in the last decade: A metaanalysis. *Journal of Pediatrics, 115,* 515–520.

Azmitia, M., & Hesser, J. (1993). Why siblings are important agents of cognitive development: A comparison of siblings and peers. *Child Development, 64*(2), 430–444.

Babchuk, N. (1978–1979). Aging and primary relations. *International Journal of Aging and Human Development, 9*(2), 137–151.

Babson, S. G., & Clark, N. G. (1983). Relationship between infant death and maternal age. *Journal of Pediatrics, 103*(3), 391–393.

Bachman, J. G., & Schulenberg, J. (1993). How part-time work intensity relates to drug use, problem behavior, time use, and satisfaction among high school seniors: Are these consequences or merely correlates? *Developmental Psychology, 29*(2), 220–235.

Bachrach, C. A., London, K. A., & Maza, P. L. (1991). On the path to adoption: Adoption seeking in the United States, 1988. *Journal of Marriage and the Family, 53,* 705–718.

Backett, K. (1987). The negotiation of fatherhood. In C. Lewis and M. O'Brien (Eds.). *Reassessing fatherhood: New observations on fathers and the modern family.* London: Sage.

Baillargeon, R., & DeVos, J. (1991). Object permanence in young infants: Fur-

ther evidence. *Child Development, 62,* 1227–1246.

Baird, P. A., & Sadovnick, A. D. (1987). Life expectancy in Down syndrome. *Journal of Pediatrics, 110,* 849–854.

Baldwin, W., & Cain, V. S. (1980). The children of teenage parents. *Family Planning Perspectives, 12,* 34.

Balkwell, C. (1981). Transition to widowhood: A review of the literature. *Family Relations, 30,* 117–127.

Balkwell, C. (1985). Transition to widowhood: A review of the literature. *Family Relations, 34,* 577–581

Baltes, P. B. (1985). *The aging of intelligence: On the dynamics between growth and decline.* Unpublished manuscript.

Baltes, P. B. (1993). The aging mind: Potential and limits. *Gerontologist, 33,* 580–594.

Baltes, P. B., & Baltes, M. M. (1990). Psychological perspectives on successful aging: The model of selective optimization with compensation. In P. B. Baltes & M. M. Baltes (Eds.), *Successful aging: Perspectives from the behavioral sciences.* Cambridge, MA: Cambridge University Press.

Baltes, P. B., Reese, H. W., & Lipsitt, L. (1980). Life-span developmental psychology. *Annual Review of Psychology, 31,* 65–110.

Baltes, P. B., & Schaie, K. W. (1974). Aging and IQ: The myth of the twilight years. *Psychology Today, 7*(10), 35–38.

Bandura, A. (1960). *Relationship of family patterns to child behavior disorders* (Progress report, USPHS, Project. No. M-1734). Stanford, CA: Stanford University.

Bandura, A., & Huston, A. (1961). Identification as a process of incidental learning. *Journal of Abnormal and Social Psychology, 63*(12), 311–318.

Bandura, A., Ross, D., & Ross, S. A. (1961). Transmission of aggression through imitation of aggressive models. *Journal of Abnormal and Social Psychology, 63,* 575–582.

Bandura, A., Ross, D., & Ross, S. A. (1963). Imitation of film-mediated aggressive models. *Journal of Abnormal and Social Psychology, 66*(1), 3–11.

Barbanel, J. (1990, September 26). Chancellor has plan to distribute condoms to students in New York. *The New York Times,* pp. A1, B3.

Bardouille-Crema, A., Black, K. N., & Feldhusen, J. (1986). Performance on Piagetian tasks of black children of differing socioeconomic levels. *Developmental Psychology, 22*(6), 841–844.

Barfield, R. E., & Morgan, J. N. (1974). *Early retirement: The decision and the experience and a second look.* Ann Arbor, MI: Institute for Social Research.

Barfield, R. E., & Morgan, J. N. (1978). Trends in satisfaction with retirement. *Gerontologist, 18*(1), 19–23.

Barinaga, M. (1991a). A new buzz in the medfly debate. *Science, 253*(5026), 1351.

Barinaga, M. (1991b). How long is the human life-span? *Science, 254*(5034), 936–938.

Barinaga, M. (1992). Mortality: Overturning received wisdom. *Science, 258,* 398–399.

Barnes, A., Colton, T., Gunderson, J., Noller, K., Tilley, B., Strama, T., Townsend, D., Hatab, P., & O'Brien, P. (1980). Fertility and outcome of pregnancy in women exposed in utero to diethylstilbestrol. *New England Journal of Medicine, 302*(11), 609–613.

Barnes K. E. (1971). Preschool play norms: A replication. *Developmental Psychology, 5*(1), 99–103.

Barnett, R. (1985, March 2). *We've come a long way—but where are we and what are the rewards?* Presentation at conference, Women in Transition, New York University's School of Continuing Education, Center for Career and Life Planning, New York.

Barnett, R. C., Kibria, N., Baruch, G. K., & Pleck, J. H. (1991). Adult daughter-parent relationships and their association with daughters' subjective well-being and psychological distress. *Journal of Marriage and the Family, 53,* 29–42.

Barnett, R. C., Marshall, N. L., & Pleck, J. H. (1992). Men's multiple roles and their relationship to men's psychological distress. *Journal of Marriage and the Family, 54,* 358–367.

Barrett, C. J. (1978). Effectiveness of widows' groups in facilitating change. *Journal of Counseling and Clinical Psychology, 46*(1), 20–31.

Barrett, D. E., Radke-Yarrow, M., & Klein, R. E. (1982). Chronic malnutrition and child behavior: Effects of early caloric supplementation on social and emotional functioning at school age. *Developmental Psychology, 18,* 541–556.

Barrett-Connor, E., Chang, J. C., & Edelstern, S. L. (1994). Coffee-associated osteoporosis offset by daily milk consumption. *Journal of the American Medical Association, 271,* 280–283.

Baruch, G., Barnett, R., & Rivers, C. (1983). *Lifeprints.* New York: McGraw-Hill.

Baruch, G. K., & Barnett, R. C. (1986). Fathers' participation in family work and children's sex-role attitudes. *Child Development, 57,* 1210–1223.

Bass, J. L., Brennan, P., Mehta, K. A., & Kodzis, S. (1990). Pediatric problems in a suburban shelter for homeless families. *Pediatrics, 85,* 33–38.

Bass, M., Kravath, R. E., & Glass, L. (1986). Death-scene investigation in sudden infant death. *New England Journal of Medicine, 315,* 100–105.

Bassuk, E. L. (1991). Homeless families. *Scientific American, 265*(6), 66–74.

Bassuk, E. L., & Rosenberg, L. (1990). Psychosocial characteristics of homeless children and children with homes. *Pediatrics, 85*(30), 257–261.

Bassuk, E. L., & Rubin, L. (1987). Homeless children: A neglected population.

American Journal of Orthopsychiatry, 57(2), 279–286.

Bates, E., Bretherton, I., & Snyder, L. (1988). *From first words to grammar: Individual differences and dissociable mechanisms.* New York: Cambridge University Press.

Bates, E., O'Connell, B., & Shore, C. (1987). Language and communication in infancy. In J. D. Osofsky (Ed.), *Handbook of infant development* (2d ed.). New York: Wiley.

Battelle, P. (1981, February). The triplets who found each other. *Good Housekeeping,* pp. 74–83.

Bauer, D. (1976). An exploratory study of developmental changes in children's fears. *Journal of Child Psychology and Psychiatry, 17,* 69–74.

Baughman, E. E. (1971). *Black Americans.* New York: Academic Press.

Baumrind, D. (1971). Harmonious parents and their preschool children. *Developmental Psychology, 41*(1), 92–102.

Baumrind, D., & Black, A. E. (1967). Socialization practices associated with dimensions of competence in preschool boys and girls. *Child Development, 38*(2), 291–327.

Baydar, N., & Brooks-Gunn, J. (1991). Effects of maternal employment and child-care arrangements on preschoolers' cognitive and behavioral outcomes: Evidence from the children of the National Longitudinal Survey of Youth. *Developmental Psychology, 27*(6), 932–945.

Bayley, N. (1965). Comparisons of mental and motor test scores for age 1–15 months by sex, birth order, race, geographic location, and education of parents. *Child Development, 36,* 379–411.

Bayley, N. (1969). *Bayley scales of infant development.* New York: Psychological Corporation.

Bayley, N. (1993). *Bayley scales of infant development: II.* New York: Psychological Corporation.

Bayley, N., & Oden, M. (1955). The maintenance of intellectual ability in gifted adults. *Journal of Gerontology, 10,* 91–107.

Beautrais, A. L., Fergusson, D. M., & Shannon, F. T. (1982). Life events and childhod morbidity: A prospective study. *Pediatrics, 70*(6), 935–940.

Beckwith, L., & Cohen, S. E. (1989). Maternal responsiveness with preterm infants and later competency. In M. H. Bornstein (Ed.), Maternal responsiveness: Characteristics and consequences. *New Directions for Child Development,* No. 43. San Francisco: Jossey-Bass.

Behrman, R. E. (1985). Preventing low birth weight: A pediatric perspective. *Journal of Pediatrics, 107*(6), 842–854.

Behrman, R. E., & Vaughan, V. C. (Eds.). (1983). *Nelson textbook of pediatrics* (12th ed.). Philadelphia: Saunders.

Belbin, R. M. (1967). Middle age: What happens to ability? In R. Owen (Ed.), *Middle age.* London: BBC.

Bell, J. (1992). In search of a discourse on aging: The elderly on television. *Gerontologist, 32*(3), 305–311.

Bell, R. R. (1983). *Marriage and family interaction* (6th ed.). Homewood, IL: Dorsey.

Bell, S., & Ainsworth, M. D. S. (1972). Infant crying and maternal responsiveness. *Child Development, 43,* 1171–1190.

Bellinger, D., Leviton, A., Watermaux, C., Needleman, H., & Rabinowitz, M. (1987). Longitudinal analyses of prenatal and postnatal lead exposure and early cognitive development. *New England Journal of Medicine, 316*(17), 1037–1043.

Belloc, N. B., & Breslow, L. (1972). Relationship of physical health status and health practices. *Preventive Medicine, 1*(3), 409–421.

Belsky J. (1979). Mother-father-infant interaction: A naturalistic observational study. *Developmental Psychology, 15,* 601–607.

Belsky, J. (1980). A family analysis of parental influence on infant exploratory competence. In F. A. Pedersen (Ed.), *The father-infant relationship: Observational studies in a family setting.* New York: Praeger.

Belsky, J. (1984). Two waves of day care research: Developmental effects and conditions of quality. In R. Ainslie (Ed.), *The child and the day care setting.* New York: Praeger.

Belsky, J., Lang, M., & Huston, T. L. (1986). Sex typing and division of labor as determinants of marital change across the transition to parenthood. *Journal of Personality and Social Psychology, 50,* 517–522.

Belsky, J., & Rovine, M. J. (1988). Nonmaternal care in the first year of life and the security of infant-parent attachment. *Child Development, 59,* 157–167.

Belsky, J., & Rovine, M. J. (1990). Patterns of marital change across the transition to parenthood: Pregnancy to three years postpartum. *Journal of Marriage and the Family, 52,* 5–19.

Beltramini, A. U., & Hertzig, M. E. (1983). Sleep and bedtime behavior in preschool-aged children. *Pediatrics, 71*(2), 153–158.

Bem, S. L. (1974). The measurement of psychological androgyny. *Journal of Consulting and Clinical Psychology, 42,* 155–162.

Bem, S. L. (1976). Probing the promise of androgyny. In A. G. Kaplan & J. P. Bean (Eds.), *Beyond sex-role stereotypes: Readings toward a psychology of androgyny.* Boston: Little, Brown.

Bem, S. L. (1983). Gender schema theory and its implications for child development: Raising gender-aschematic children in a gender-schematic society. *Signs, 8,* 598–616.

Bem, S. L. (1985). Androgyny and gender schema theory: A conceptual and empirical integration. In T. B. Son-

dregger (Ed.), *Nebraska Symposium on Motivation, 1984. Psychology and gender.* Lincoln: University of Nebraska Press.

Benbow, C. P., & Stanley, J. C. (1983). Sex differences in mathematical ability: More facts. *Science, 222,* 1029–1031.

Benbow, C. P., & Stanley, J. C. (1990). Sex differences in mathematical ability: Fact or artifact? *Science, 210,* 1262–1264.

Bengston, V., Cuellar, J. A., & Ragan, P. (1975, October 29). Group contrasts in attitudes toward death: Variation by race, age, occupational status and sex. Paper presented at the annual meeting of the Gerontological Society, Louisville, KY.

Benn, R. K. (1986). Factors promoting secure attachment relationships between employed mothers and their sons. *Child Development, 57,* 1224–1231.

Benner, P. (1984). *From novice to expert: Excellence and practice in clinical nursing practice.* Reading, MA: Addison-Wesley.

Benson, J. B., & Uzgiris, I. C. (1985). Effect of self-inflicted locomotion on infant search activity. *Developmental Psychology, 21*(6), 923–931.

Berardo, D. H., Sheehan, C. L., & Leslie, G. R. (1987). A residue of tradition: Jobs, careers, and spouses' time in housework. *Journal of Marriage and the Family, 49,* 381–390.

Berger, R. M. (1982). *Gay and gray: The older homosexual male.* Urbana: University of Illinois Press.

Bergman, A. B., Larsen, R. M., & Mueller, B. A. (1986). Changing spectrum of serious child abuse. *Pediatrics, 77*(1), 113–116.

Bergman, S. J. (1991). *Men's psychological development: A relational perspective.* Work in Progress No. 48, The Stone Center, Wellesley College, Wellesley, MA.

Berk, L. E. (1986). Private speech: Learning out loud. *Psychology Today, 20*(5), 34–42.

Berk, L. E., & Garvin, R. A. (1984). Development of private speech among low-income Appalachian children. *Developmental Psychology, 20*(2), 271–286.

Berkowitz, G. S., Skovron, M. L., Lapinski, R. H., & Berkowitz, R. L. (1990). Delayed childbearing and the outcome of pregnancy. *New England Journal of Medicine, 322,* 659–664.

Berman, C. (1981). *Making it as a stepparent: New roles/new rules.* New York: Bantam.

Berman, P. W. (1987). Children caring for babies: Age and sex differences in response to infant signals and to the social context. In N. Eisenberg (Ed.), *Contemporary topics in developmental psychology.* New York: Wiley-Interscience.

Berman, P. W., & Goodman, V. (1984). Age and sex differences in children's responses to babies: Effects of adult caretaking requests and instructions. *Child Development, 55,* 1071–1077.

Berman, S. M., MacKay, H. T., Grimes, D. A., & Binkin, N. J. (1985). Deaths from spontaneous abortion in the

United States. *Journal of the American Medical Association, 253,* 3119–3123.

Bernard, J. L., & Bernard, M. L. (1984). The abusive male seeking treatment: Jekyll and Hyde. *Family Relations, 33,* 543–547.

Bernard-Bonnin, A.-C., Gilbert, S., Rousseau, E., Masson, P., & Maheux, B. (1991). Television and the 3- to 10-year-old child. *Pediatrics, 88*(1), 48–54.

Berndt, T. J. (1982). The features and effects of friendship in early adolescence. *Child Development, 53,* 1447–1460.

Berndt, T. J., & Perry, T. B. (1990). Distinctive features and effects of early adolescent friendships. In R. Montemayor, G. R. Adams, & T. P. Gullotta (Eds.), *From childhood to adolescence: A transitional period?* Newbury Park, CA: Sage.

Bernstein, G. A., & Garfinkel, B. D. (1988). Pedigrees, functioning, and psychopathology in families of school phobic children. *American Journal of Psychiatry, 145,* 70–74.

Berrueta-Clement, J. R., Schweinhart, L. J., Barnett, W. S., Epstein, A. S., & Weikart, D. P. (1985). *Changed lives: The effects of the Perry Preschool program on youths through age 19.* Ypsilanti, MI: High Scope.

Berscheid, E., & Campbell, B. (1981). The changing longevity of heterosexual close relationships.. In M. J. Lerner & S. C. Lerner (Eds.), *The justice motive in social behavior.* New York: Plenum.

Berscheid, E., Walster, E., & Bohrnstedt, G. (1973). The happy American body: A survey report. *Psychology Today, 7*(6), 119–131.

Bertenthal, B. I., & Campos, J. J. (1987). New directions in the study of early experience. *Child Development, 58,* 560–567.

Bertenthal, B. I., Campos, J. J., & Barrett, K. C. (1984). Self-produced locomotion: An organizer of emotional, cognitive, and social development in infancy. In R. N. Emde & R. J. Harmon (Eds.), *Continuities and discontinuities in development.* New York: Plenum.

Beumont, P. J. V., Russell, J. D., & Touyz, S. W. (1993). Treatment of anorexia nervosa. *The Lancet, 341,* 1635–1640.

Bianchi, S. M., & Spain, D. (1986). *American women in transition.* New York: Russell Sage Foundation.

Bielby, D., & Papalia, D. (1975). Moral development and perceptual role-taking egocentrism: Their development and interrelationship across the life span. *International Journal of Aging and Human Development, 6*(4), 293–308.

Bierman, K. L., & Furman, W. (1984). The effects of social skills training and peer involvement on the social adjustment of preadolescents. *Child Development, 55,* 151–162.

Biller, H. B. (1981). The father and sex role development. In M. E. Lamb (Ed.), *The role of the father in child development.* New York: Wiley.

Binstock, R. H. (1987). Health care: Organization, use and financing. In G. L. Maddox (Ed.), *The encyclopedia of aging* (p. 308). New York: Springer.

Birch, L. L., Johnson, S. L., Andresen, G., Peters, J. C., & Schulte, M. C. (1991). The variability of young children's energy intake. *New England Journal of Medicine, 324,* 232–235.

Bird, C. (1987, June–July). The shape of work to come. *Modern Maturity,* pp. 33–45.

Birns, B. (1976). The emergence and socialization of sex differences in the earliest years. *Merrill-Palmer Quarterly, 22,* 229–254.

Birren, J. E., Woods, A. M., & Williams, M. V. (1980). Behavioral slowing with age: Causes, organization, and consequences. In L. W. Poon (Ed.), *Aging in the 1980s.* Washington, DC: American Psychological Association.

Blackburn, J. A., Papalia-Finlay, D., Foye, B. F., & Serlin, R. C. (1988). Modifiability of figural relations performance among elderly adults. *Journal of Gerontology, 43*(3), P87–89.

Blair, S. N., Kohl, H. W., Paffenberger, R. S., Clark, D. G., Cooper, K. H., & Gibbons, L. W. (1989). Physical fitness and all-cause mortality: A prospective study of healthy men and women. *Journal of the American Medical Association, 262,* 2395–2401.

Blass, E. M., Ganchrow, J. R., & Steiner, J. E. (1984). Classical conditioning in newborn humans 2–24 hours of age. *Infant Behavior and Development, 7,* 223–235.

Blauvelt, H. (1955). Dynamics of the mother-newborn relationship in goats. In B. Schaffner (Ed.), *Group processes.* New York: Macy Foundation.

Blazer, D. (1989). Depression in the elderly. *New England Journal of Medicine, 320*(3), 164–166.

Blieszner, R. (1986). Trends in family gerontology research. *Family Relations, 35,* 555–562.

Blieszner, R., & Shifflett, P. A. (1990). The effects of Alzheimer's disease on close relationships between patients and caregivers. *Family Relations, 39,* 57–62.

Blieszner, R., Willis, S. L., & Baltes, P. B. (1981). Training research on induction ability: A short-term longitudinal study. *Journal of Applied Development Psychology, 2,* 247–265.

Block, J. (1981). Some enduring and consequential structures of personality. In A. I. Rabin et al. (Eds.), *Further explorations in personality.* New York: Wiley.

Bloom, B. S. (1985). *Developing talent in young people.* New York: Ballantine.

Bloom, D. E., & Pebley, A. R. (1982). Voluntary childlessness: A review of the evidence and its implications. *Population Research and Policy Review, 1,* 203–234.

Bluebond-Languer, M. (1977). Meanings of death to children. In H. Feifel (Ed.), *New meanings of death* (pp. 47–66). New York: McGraw-Hill.

Blum, R. (1987). Contemporary threats to adolescent health in the United States. *Journal of the American Medical Association, 257*(24), 3390–3395.

Blumenthal, J. A., Emery, C. F., Madden, D. J., Schniebolk, S., Walsh-Riddle, M., George, L. K., McKee, D. C., Higginbotham, M. B., Cobb, F. R., & Coleman, R. E. (1991). Long-term effects of exercise on psychological functioning in older men and women. *Journal of Gerontology, 46*(6), P352–361.

Blyth, D. A., & Foster-Clark, F. S. (1987). Gender differences in perceived intimacy with different members of adolescents' social networks. *Sex Roles, 17,* 689–718.

Blyth, D. A., et al. (1981). The effects of physical development on self-image and satisfaction with body-image for early adolescent males. In R. G. Simmons (Ed.), *Research on community and mental health,* Vol. 2. Greenwich, CT: JAI.

Blyth, D. A., Simmons, R. G., & Carlton-Ford, S. (1983). The adjustment of early adolescents to school transitions. *Journal of Early Adolescence, 3*(1–2), 105–120.

Bolger, N., DeLongis, A., Kessler, R. C., & Schilling, E. A. (1989). Effects of daily stress on negative mood. *Journal of Personality and Social Psychology, 57*(5), 808–818.

Bolles, E. B. (1982). *So much to say.* New York: St. Martin's.

Bornstein, M., Kessen, W., & Weiskopf, S. (1976). The categories of hue in infancy. *Science, 191,* 201–202.

Bornstein, M. H. (1985). How infant and mother jointly contribute to developing cognitive competence in the child. *Proceedings of the National Academy of Science, 82,* 7470–7473.

Bornstein, M. H., & Sigman, M. D. (1986). Continuity in mental development from infancy. *Child Development, 57,* 251–274.

Bornstein, M. H., & Tamis-LeMonda, C. S. (1989). Maternal responsiveness and cognitive development in children. In M. H. Bornstein (Ed.), Maternal responsiveness: Characteristics and consequences, *New Directions for Child Development.* No. 43. San Francisco: Jossey-Bass.

Bossé, R., Aldwin, C. M., Levenson, M. R., & Ekerdt, D. J. (1987). Mental health differences among retirees and workers: Findings from the Normative Aging Study. *Psychology and Aging, 2*(4), 383–389.

Bossé, R., Aldwin, C. M., Levenson, M. R., & Workman-Daniels, K. (1991). How stressful is retirement? Findings from the Normative Aging Study. *Journal of Gerontology, 46*(1), P9–14.

Boulton, M. G. (1983). *On being a mother: A study of women with pre-school children.* London: Tavistock.

Bouza, A. V. (1990). *The police mystique: An insider's look at cops, crime, and the criminal justice system.* New York: Plenum.

Bowes, W., Brackbill, Y., Conway, E., & Steinschneider, A. (1970). The effects of obstetrical medication on fetus and infant. *Monographs of the Society for Research in Child Development, 35,* 3–25.

Bowlby, J. (1951). Maternal care and mental health. *Bulletin of the World Health Organization, 3,* 355–534.

Bowlby, J. (1958). The nature of the child's tie to his mother. *International Journal of Psychoanalysis, 39,* 1–23.

Bowlby, J. (1960). Separation anxiety. *International Journal of Psychoanalysis, 41,* 89–113.

Bowman, J. A., Sanson-Fisher, R. W., & Webb, G. R. (1987). Intervention in preschools to increase the use of safety restraints by preschool children. *Pediatrics, 79,* 103–109.

Boyer, J. L., & Guthrie, L. (1985). Assessment and treatment of the suicidal patient. In E. E. Beckham & W. R. Leber, *Handbook of depression.* Homewood, IL: Dorsey.

Boysson-Bardies, B., Sagart, L., & Durand, C. (1984). Discernible differences in the babbling of infants according to target language. *Journal of Child Language, 11,* 1–15.

Brackbill, Y., & Broman, S. H. (1979). *Obstetrical medication and development in the first year of life.* Unpublished manuscript.

Bracken, M., Holford, T., White, C., & Kelsey, J. (1978). Role of oral contraception in congenital malformations of offspring. *International Journal of Epidemiology, 7*(4), 309–317.

Bradley, R., & Caldwell, B. (1982). The consistency of the home environment and its relation to child development. *International Journal of Behavioral Development, 5,* 445–465.

Bradley, R., Caldwell, B., & Rock, S. (1988). HOME environment and school performance: A ten-year follow-up and examination of three models of environmental action. *Child Development, 59,* 852–867.

Bradley, R. H. (1989). Home measurement of maternal responsiveness. In M. H. Bornstein (Ed.), Maternal responsiveness: Characteristics and consequences. *New Directions for Child Development.* No. 43. San Francisco: Jossey-Bass.

Bradley, R. H., et al. (1989). Home environment and cognitive development in the first 3 years of life: A collaborative study involving six sites and three ethnic groups in North America. *Developmental Psychology, 25*(2), 217–235.

Braine, M. (1976). Children's first word combinations. *Monographs of the Society for Research in Child Development, 41*(1, Serial No. 164).

Branch, L. G., Horowitz, A., & Carr, C. (1989). The implications for everyday life of incident of self-reported visual decline among people over age 65 living in the community. *Gerontologist, 29*(3), 359–365.

Brandes, J. M., Scher, A., Itzkovits, J., Thaler, I., Sarid, M., & Gershoni-Baruch, R. (1992). Growth and development of children conceived by in vitro fertilization. *Pediatrics, 90*(3), 424–429.

Brass, L. M., Isaacsohn, J. L., Merikangas, K. R., & Robinette, C. D. (1992). A study of twins and stroke. *Stroke, 23*(2), 221–223.

Braungart, J. M., Plomin, R., DeFries, J. C., & Fulker, D. W. (1992). Genetic influence on tester-rated infant temperament as assessed by Bayley's Infant Behavior Record: Nonadoptive and adoptive siblings and twins. *Developmental Psychology, 28*(1), 40–47.

Bray, D. W., & Howard, A. (1983). The AT&T longitudinal study of managers. In K. W. Schaie (Ed.), *Longitudinal studies of adult psychological development.* New York: Guilford.

Brazelton, T. B. (1973). *Neonatal behavioral assessment scale.* Philadelphia: Lippincott.

Brecher, E., & the Editors of Consumer Reports Books. (1984). *Love, sex, and aging: A Consumers Union report.* Boston: Little, Brown.

Bremner, W. J., Vitiello, M. V., & Prinz, P. N. (1983). Loss of circadian rhythmicity in blood testosterone levels with aging in normal men. *Journal of Clinical Endocrinology and Metabolism, 56,* 1278–1281.

Breslow, L., & Breslow, N. (1993). Health practices and disability: Some evidence from Alameda County. *Preventive Medicine, 22*(1), 86–95.

Bretherton, I. (1991). Intentional communication and the development of an understanding of mind. In D. Frye & C. Moore (Eds.), *Children's theories of mind: Mental states and social understanding.* Hillsdale, NJ: Erlbaum.

Brewster, A. B. (1982). Chronically ill hospitalized children's concepts of their illness. *Pediatrics, 69,* 355–362.

Briley, M. (1980, July-August). Burnout stress and the human energy crisis. *Dynamic Years,* pp. 36–39.

Brim, O. G. (1974). *Theories of the male mid-life crisis.* Address at the Annual Convention of the American Psychological Association, New Orleans.

Brim, O. G. (1977). Theories of the male mid-life crisis. In N. Schlossberg & A. Entine (Eds.), *Counseling adults.* Monterey, CA: Brooks/Cole.

Brim, O. G., & Kagan, K. (Eds.). (1980). *Constancy and change in human development.* New York: Wiley.

Brim, O. G., & Ryff, C. D. (1980). On the properties of life events. In P. B. Baltes & O. G. Brim (Eds.), *Life-span development and behavior,* Vol. 3. New York: Academic Press.

Brittain, C. (1963). Adolescent choices and parent-peer cross-pressures. *American Sociological Review, 28,* 385–391.

Brodbeck, A. J., & Irwin, O. C. (1946). The speech behavior of infants without families. *Child Development, 17,* 145–156.

Brody, E. B., & Brody, N. (1976). *Intelligence.* New York: Academic Press.

Brody, E. M. (1978). Community housing for the elderly. *Gerontologist, 18*(2), 121–128.

Brody, J. (1990, October 11). Sedentary living, not cholesterol, is the nation's leading culprit in fatal heart attacks. *The New York Times,* p. B12.

Brody, J. E. (1992a, June 16). Suicide myths cloud efforts to save children. *The New York Times,* p. C1.

Brody, J. E. (1992b, December 9). Hip fracture: A potential killer that can be avoided. *The New York Times,* p. C16.

Brody, L. R., Zelazo, P. R., & Chaika, H. (1984). Habituation-dishabituation to speech in the neonate. *Developmental Psychology, 20,* 114–119.

Bromley, D. B. (1974). *The psychology of human aging* (2d ed.). Middlesex, England: Penguin.

Bronfenbrenner, U. (1979). *The ecology of human development.* Cambridge, MA: Harvard University Press.

Bronfenbrenner, U., Alvarez, W. F., & Henderson, C. R. (1984). Working and watching: Maternal employment and parents' perceptions of their three-year-old children. *Child Development, 55,* 1362–1378.

Bronfenbrenner, U., Belsky, J., & Steinberg, L. (1977). *Daycare in context: An ecological perspective on research and public policy.* Review prepared for Office of the Assistant Secretary for Planning and Evaluation, U.S. Department of Health, Education, and Welfare.

Bronfenbrenner, U., & Crouter, A. (1982). Work and family through time and space. In S. B. Kamerman & C. D. Hayes (Eds.), *Families that work: Children in a changing world.* Washington, DC: National Academy.

Bronson, F. H., & Desjardins, C. (1969). Aggressive behavior and seminal vesicle function in mice: Differential sensitivity to androgen given neonatally. *Endocrinology, 85,* 871–975.

Bronstein, P. (1988). Father-child interaction: Implications for gender role socialization. In P. Bronstein & C. P. Cowan (Eds.), *Fatherhood today: Men's changing role in the family.* New York: Wiley.

Brooke, J. (1988, April 26). Technology aids vaccination effort. *The New York Times,* p. C3.

Brooks-Gunn, J. (1988). Pubertal processes and the early adolescent transition. In W. Damon (Ed.), *Child development today and tomorrow.* San Francisco: Jossey-Bass.

Brooks-Gunn, J., & Furstenberg, F. F. (1986). The children of adolescent mothers: Physical, academic, and psychological outcomes. *Developmental Review, 6,* 224–251.

Brooks-Gunn, J., & Reiter, E. O. (1990). The role of pubertal processes. In S. S. Feldman & G. R. Elliott (Eds.), *At the threshold: The developing adolescent.* Cambridge, MA: Harvard University Press.

Brophy, J. E., & Good, T. L. (1974). *Teacher-student relationships.* New York: Holt.

Brown, B. B., Clasen, D. R., & Eicher, S. A. (1986). Perceptions of peer pressure, peer conformity dispositions, and self-reported behavior among adolescents. *Developmental Psychology, 22,* 521–530.

Brown, B. B., Mounts, N., Lamborn, S. D., & Steinberg, L. (1993). Parenting practices and peer group affiliation in adolescence. *Child Development, 64,* 467–482.

Brown, J. D., Childers, K. W., & Waszak, C. S. (1988, June). *Television and adolescent sexuality.* Paper presented at the conference on "Television and Teens: Health Implications," Manhattan Beach, CA.

Brown, J. E. (1983). *Nutrition for your pregnancy.* Minneapolis: University of Minnesota Press.

Brown, J. H. (1979). Suicide in Britain: More attempts, fewer deaths, lessons for public policy. *Archives of General Psychiatry, 36,* 1119–1124.

Brown, J. L. (1987). Hunger in the U. S. *Scientific American, 256*(2), 37–41.

Brown, J. T., & Stoudemire, A. (1983). Normal and pathological grief. *Journal of the American Medical Association, 250,* 378–382.

Brown, L. M., & Gilligan, C. (1990, April). *The psychology of women and the development of girls.* Paper presented at the Laurel-Harvard Conference on the Psychology of Women and the Education of Girls, Cleveland.

Brown, P., & Elliott, H. (1965). Control of aggression in a nursery school class. *Journal of Experimental Child Psychology, 2,* 103–107.

Brown, R. (1973a). Development of the first language in the human species. *American Psychologist, 28*(2), 97–106.

Brown, R. (1973b). *A first language: The early stage.* Cambridge, MA: Harvard University Press.

Brown, R., Cazden, C. B., & Bellugi, U. (1969). The child's grammar from I to III. In J. P. Hill (Ed.), *Minnesota symposia on child psychology,* Vol. 2. Minneapolis: University of Minnesota Press.

Brown, S. S. (1985). Can low birth weight be prevented? *Family Planning Perspectives, 17*(3), 112–118.

Browne, A., & Finkelhor, D. (1986). Impact of child sexual abuse: A review of research. *Psychological Bulletin, 99*(1), 66–77.

Brozan, N. (1990, November 29). Less visible but heavier burdens as AIDS attacks people over 50. *The New York Times,* pp. A1, A16.

Brubaker, T. (1983). Introduction. In T. Brubaker (Ed.), *Family relationships in later life.* Beverly Hills, CA: Sage.

Brubaker, T. H. (1990). Families in later life: A burgeoning research area. *Journal of Marriage and the Family, 52,* 959–981.

Bryer, J. B., Nelson, B. A., Miller, J. J., & Krol, P.A. (1987). Childhood sexual and physical abuse as factors in adult psychiatric illness. *American Journal of Psychiatry, 144*(11), 1426–1430.

Buhrmester, D., & Furman, W. (1990). Perceptions of sibling relationships during middle childhood and adolescence. *Child Development, 61,* 138–139.

Buie, J. (1987, April 8). Pregnant teenagers: New view of old solution. *Education Week,* p. 32.

Bukowski, W. M., & Kramer, T. L. (1986). Judgments of the features of friendship among early adolescent boys and girls. *Journal of Early Adolescence, 6,* 331–338.

Bullen, B. A., Skrinar, G. S., Beitins, I., von Mering, G., Turnbull, B. A., & McArthur, J. W. (1985). Induction of menstrual disorders by strenuous exercise in untrained women. *New England Journal of Medicine, 312,* 1349–1353.

Bullock, K. D., Reed, R. J., & Grant, I. (1992). Reduced mortality risk in alcoholics who achieve long-term abstinence. *Journal of the American Medical Association, 267*(5), 668–672.

Bumpass, L., Sweet, J., & Martin, T. C. (1990). Changing patterns of remarriage. *Journal of Marriage and the Family, 52,* 747–756.

Bumpass, L. L., & Sweet, J. A. (1988). *Preliminary evidence on cohabitation.* NSFH Working Paper No. 2. Center for Demography and Ecology, University of Wisconsin-Madison.

Bumpers, D. (1984). Securing the blessings of liberty for posterity: Preventive health care for children. *American Psychologist, 39,* 896–900.

Burgess, A. W., Hartman, C. R., & McCormack, A. (1987). Abused to abuser: Antecedents of socially deviant behaviors. *American Journal of Psychiatry, 144*(11), 1431–1436.

Burkhauser, R. V., Holden, K. C., & Feaster, D. (1988). Incidence, timing, and events associated with poverty: A dynamic view of poverty in retirement. *Journal of Gerontology, 43*(2), S46–52.

Burns, A. (1992). Mother-headed families: An international perspective and the case of Australia. *Social Policy Report of the Society for Research in Child Development, VI*(1), Spring, 1992.

Burstin, H. R., Lipsitz, S. R., & Brennan, T. A. (1992). Socioeconomic status and risk for substandard medical care. *Journal of the American Medical Association, 268,* 2383–2387.

Bush, T. L., Cowan, L. D., Barrett-Connor, E., Criqui, M. H., Karon, J. M., Wallace, R. B., Tyroler, H. A., & Rifkind, B. M. (1983). Estrogen use and all-cause mortality: Preliminary results from the Lipid Research Clinics program follow-up study. *Journal of the American Medical Association, 249*(7), 903–906.

Busse, E. W. (1987). Primary and secondary aging. In G. L. Maddox (Ed.), *The encyclopedia of aging* (p. 534). New York: Springer.

Bussey, K. (1992). Children's lying and truthfulness: Implications for children's testimony. In S. J. Ceci, M. DeS. Leichtman, & M. E. Putnick (Eds.), *Cognitive and social factors in early deception.* Hillsdale, NJ: Erlbaum.

Bustillo, M., Buster, J. E., Cohen, S. W., Hamilton, F., Thorneycroft, I. H., Simon, J. A., Rodi, I. A., Boyers, S., Marshall, J. R., Louw, J. A., Seed, R., & Seed, R. (1984). Delivery of a healthy infant following nonsurgical ovum transfer. *Journal of the American Medical Association, 251*(7), 889.

Butler, R. (1961). Re-awakening interests. *Nursing Homes: Journal of American Nursing Home Association, 10,* 8–19.

Butler, R., & Lewis, M. (1982). *Aging and mental health* (3d ed.). St. Louis: Mosby.

Butterfield, E., & Siperstein, G. (1972). Influence of contingent auditory stimulation upon nonnutritional suckle. In J. Bosma (Ed.), *Oral sensation and perception: The mouth of the infant.* Springfield, IL: Thomas.

Cahan, S., & Cohen, M. (1989). Age versus schooling effects on intelligence development. *Child Development, 60,* 1239–1249.

Cai, X., Golde, T. E., & Younkin, S. C. (1993). Release of excess amyloid B protein from a mutant amyloid B protein precursor. *Science, 259,* 514–516.

Cain, V. S., & Hofferth, S. L. (1989). Parental choice of self-care for school-age children. *Journal of Marriage and the Family, 51,* 65–77.

Cain, W. S., Reid, F., & Stevens, J. C. (1990). Missing ingredients: Aging and the discrimination of flavor. *Journal of Nutrition for the Elderly, 9,* 3–15.

Cairns, R. B., Cairns, B. D., & Neckerman, H. J. (1989). Early school dropout: Configurations and determinants. *Child Development, 60,* 1437–1452.

Calkins, S. D., & Fox, N. A. (1992). The relations among infant temperament, security of attachment, and behavioral inhibition at twenty-four months. *Child Development, 63,* 1456–1472.

Calvert, S. L., & Huston, A. C. (1987). Television and children's gender schemata. In L. S. Liben & M. L. Signorella (Eds.), *Children's gender schemata.* San Francisco: Jossey-Bass.

Calvo, E. B., Galindo, A. C., & Aspres, N. B. (1992). Iron status in exclusively breast-fed infants. *Pediatrics, 90,* 375–379.

Camp, C. J. (1989). World-knowledge systems. In L. W. Poon, D. C. Rubin, & B. A. Wilson (Eds.), *Everyday cognition in adulthood and late life.* Cambridge, England: Cambridge University Press.

Campbell, A., Converse, P. E., & Rodgers, W. L. (1975). *The quality of American life: Perceptions, evaluations, and satisfactions.* New York: Russell Sage Foundation.

Campbell, F. L., Townes, B. D., & Beach, L. R. (1982). Motivational bases of childbearing decisions. In G. L. Fox (Ed.), *The childbearing decision: Fertility, attitudes, and behavior.* Beverly Hills, CA: Sage.

Campos, J., Bertenthal, B., & Benson, N. (1980, April). *Self-produced locomotion and the extraction of form invariance.* Paper presented at the meeting of the International Conference on Infant Studies, New Haven.

Campos, J. J., Langer, A., & Krowitz, A. (1970). Cardiac responses on the visual cliff in prelocomotor human infants. *Science, 170,* 196–197.

Cantor, M. H. (1983). Strain among caregivers: A study of experience in the United States. *Gerontologist, 23*(6), 597–604.

Caplan, N., Choy, M. H., & Whitmore, J. K. (1992, February). Indochinese refugee families and academic achievement. *Scientific American,* 36–42.

Capute, A. J., Shapiro, B. K., & Palmer, F. B. (1987). Marking the milestones of language development. *Contemporary Pediatrics, 4*(4), 24.

Cardenas, J.A. (1977). Response I. In N. Epstein (Ed.), *Language, ethnicity and the schools.* Washington, DC: Institute for Educational Leadership.

Carey, J. R., Liedo, P., Orozco, D., & Vaupel, J. W. (1992). Slowing of mortality rates at older ages in large medfly cohorts. *Science, 258,* 457–461.

Cargan, L. (1981). Singles: An examination of two stereotypes. *Family Relations, 30,* 377–385.

Carlo, G., Knight, G. P., Eisenberg, N., & Rotenberg, K. J. (1991). Cognitive processes and prosocial behaviors among children: The role of affective attributions and reconciliations. *Developmental Psychology, 27*(3), 456–461.

Carlson, B. E. (1984). The father's contribution to child care: Effects on children's perceptions of parental roles. *American Journal of Orthopsychiatry, 54*(1), 123–136.

Carlton-Ford, S., & Collins, W. A. (1988, August). *Family conflict: Dimensions, differential reporting, and developmental differences.* Paper presented at the annual meeting of the American Sociological Association, Chicago.

Carpenter, M. W., Sady, S. P., Hoegsberg, B., Sady, M. A., Haydon, B., Cullinane, E. M., Coustan, D. R., & Thompson, P. D. (1988). Fetal heart rate response to maternal exertion.

Journal of the American Medical Association, 259(20), 3006–3009.

Carrera, M. A. (1986, April 11). *Future directions in teen pregnancy prevention.* Talk presented to the annual meeting of the Society for the Scientific Study of Sex, Eastern Region.

Carroll, J. L., & Rest, J. R. (1982). Moral development. In B. Wolman (Ed.), *Handbook of developmental psychology.* Englewood Cliffs, NJ: Prentice-Hall.

Carter, D., & Welch, D. (1981). Parenting styles and children's behavior. *Family Relations, 30,* 191–195.

Carton, R. W. (1990). The road to euthanasia. *Journal of the American Medical Association, 263*(16), 2221.

Casey, P. H., Bradley, R., & Wortham, B. (1984). Social and nonsocial home environment of infants with nonorganic failure-to-thrive. *Pediatrics, 73*(3), 348–353.

Casey, R. J., & Berman, J. S. (1985). The outcome of psychotherapy with children. *Psychological Bulletin, 98*(2), 388–400.

Casper, R. C., & Offer, D. (1990). Weight and dieting concerns in adolescents, fashion or symptom? *Pediatrics, 86*(3), 384–390.

Cassell, C. (1984). *Swept away.* New York: Simon & Schuster.

Cassidy, J. (1986). The ability to negotiate the environment: An aspect of infant competence as related to quality of attachment. *Child Development, 57,* 331–337.

Cassidy, M. L. (1983). The effect of retirement on emotional well-being: A comparison of men and women. *Dissertation Abstracts International, 43*(9-A), 3118.

Cattell, R. B. (1965). *The scientific analysis of personality.* Baltimore: Penguin.

Cavanaugh, J. C., Kramer, D. A., Sinnott, J. D., Camp, C. J., & Markley, R. P. (1985). On missing links and such: Interfaces between cognitive research and everyday problem-solving. *Human Development, 28,* 146–168.

Ceci, S. J. (1991). How much does schooling influence general intelligence and its cognitive components? A reassessment of the evidence. *Developmental Psychology, 27*(5), 703–722.

Ceci, S. J., & Leichtman, M. DeS. (1992). "I know that you know that I know that you broke the toy": A brief report of recursive awareness among 3-year-olds. In S. J. Ceci, M. DeS. Leichtman, & M. E. Putnick (Eds.), *Cognitive and social factors in early deception.* Hillsdale, NJ: Erlbaum.

Celis, W. (1990). More states are laying school paddle to rest. *The New York Times,* pp. A1, B12.

Celis, W. (1991, November 27). Bilingual teaching: A new focus on both tongues. *The New York Times,* p. B6.

Centers for Disease Control. (1980). *Risk factor update.* Atlanta: U.S. Department of Health and Human Services.

Centers for Disease Control. (1983). *Child Development Surveillance Summaries,* Vol. 32. Atlanta: Author.

Centers for Disease Control. (1986). Statistical information. Atlanta: Author.

Centers for Disease Control. (1993). Rates of cesarean delivery—United States, 1991. *Morbidity and Mortality Weekly Report, 42,* 285–289.

Central Bureau of Statistics. (1992). *Statistical pocket book 1992.* Kathmandu, Nepal: Ratna Offset Press.

Chance, P., & Fischman, J. (1987). The magic of childhood. *Psychology Today, 21*(5), 48–58.

Chapman, A. H. (1974). *Management of emotional problems of children and adolescents* (2d ed.). Philadelpia: Lippincott.

Chappell, N. L. (1991). Living arrangements and sources of caregiving. *Journal of Gerontology, 46*(1), S1–8.

Chappell, N. L., & Penning, M. J. (1979). The trend away from institutionalization. *Research on Aging, 1*(1), 162–287.

Charness, M. E., Simon, R. P., & Greenberg, D. A. (1989). Ethanol and the nervous system. *New England Journal of Medicine, 321*(7), 442–454.

Chasnoff, I. J., Griffith, D. R., Freier, C., & Murray, J. (1992). Cocaine/polydrug use in pregnancy: Two-year follow-up. *Pediatrics, 89*(2), 284–289.

Chasnoff, I. J., Griffith, D. R., MacGregor, S., Dirkes, K., & Burns, K. A. (1989). Temporal patterns of cocaine use in pregnancy: Perinatal outcomes. *Journal of the American Medical Association, 261*(12), 1741–1744.

Chatters, L. M., & Taylor, R. J. (1989). Age differences in religious participation among black adults. *Journal of Gerontology, 44*(5), S183–189.

Chavez, G. F., Mulinare, J., & Cordero, J. F. (1989). Maternal cocaine use during early pregnancy as a risk factor for congenital urogenital anomalies. *Journal of the American Medical Association, 262*(6), 795–798.

Chen, C., & Stevenson, H. W. (1989). Homework: A cross-cultural examination. *Child Development, 60,* 551–561.

Cherlin, A., & Furstenberg, F. F. (1986). Grandparents and family crisis. *Generations, 10*(4), 26–28.

Chervenak, F. A., Isaacson, G., & Mahoney, M. J. (1986). Advances in the diagnosis of fetal defects. *New England Journal of Medicine, 315*(5), 305–307.

Chess, S. (1983). Mothers are always the problem—or are they? Old wine in new bottles. *Pediatrics, 71*(6), 974–976.

Chess, S., & Thomas, A. (1982). Infant bonding: Mystique and reality. *American Journal of Orthopsychiatry, 52*(2), 213–222.

Child Welfare League of America. (1986). *Born to run: The status of child abuse in America.* Washington, DC: Author.

Children's Defense Fund (1993). Birth to teens. *CDF Reports,* 0276-6531.

Chilman, C. W. (1980). *Adolescent sexuality in a changing American society: Social and psychological perspectives* (NIH Publication No. 80–1426). Bethesda, MD: National Institutes of Health.

Chira, S. (1988, July 27). In Japan, the land of the rod, an appeal to spare the child. *The New York Times*, pp. A1, A10.

Chiriboga, D. A. (1989). Mental health at the midpoint: Crisis, challenge, or relief. In S. Hunter & M. Sundel (Eds.), *Midlife myths*. Newbury Park, CA: Sage.

Chiriboga, D. A., & Thurnher, M. (1975). Concept of self. In M. F. Lowenthal, M. Thurnher, & D. A. Chiriboga & Associates (Eds.), *Four stages of life: A comparative study of women and men facing transitions*. San Francisco: Jossey-Bass.

Chisolm, J. S. (1983). *Navajo infancy: An ethological study of child development*. New York: Aldine.

Chissell, J. T. (1989, July 16). Paper delivered at symposium on race, racism, and health at National Medical Association's 94th annual convention, Orlando, Florida.

Chodorow, N. (1978). *The reproduction of mothering*. Berkeley: University of California Press.

Chomsky, C. S. (1969). *The acquisition of syntax in children from five to ten*. Cambridge, MA: Massachusetts Institute of Technology (MIT) Press.

Chomsky, N. (1957). *Syntactic structure*. The Hague: Mouton.

Chomsky, N. (1972). *Language and mind* (2d ed.). New York: Harcourt Brace Jovanovich.

Chumlea, W. C. (1982). Physical growth in adolescence. In B. B. Wolman (Ed.), *Handbook of developmental psychology*. Englewood Cliffs, NJ: Prentice-Hall.

Cicirelli, V. G. (1976a). Family structure and interaction: Sibling effects on socialization. In M. F. McMillan & S. Henao (Eds.), *Child psychiatry: Treatment and research*. New York: Brunner/Mazel.

Cicirelli, V. G. (1976b). Siblings teaching siblings. In V. L. Allen (Ed.), *Children as teachers: Theory and research on tutoring*. New York: Academic Press.

Cicirelli, V. G. (1977). Relationship of siblings to the elderly person's feelings and concerns. *Journal of Gerontology*, 12(3), 317–322.

Cicirelli, V. G. (1980, December). *Adult children's views on providing services for elderly parents*. Report to the Andrus Foundation.

Cicirelli, V. G. (1981, April). *Interpersonal relationships of siblings in the middle part of the life span*. Paper presented at the biennial meeting of the Society for Research in Child Development, Boston.

Cicirelli, V. G. (1989a). Feelings of attachment to siblings and well-being in later life. *Psychology and Aging*, 4(2), 211–216.

Cicirelli, V. G. (1989b). Helping relationships in later life: A reexamination. In J. A. Mancini (Ed.), *Aging parents and adult children*. Lexington, MA: D. C. Heath.

Clark, E. V. (1983). Meanings and concepts. In P. H. Mussen (Ed.), *Handbook of child psychology*. New York: Wiley.

Clark, R. A., & Gecas, V. (1977). *The employed father in America: A role competition analysis*. Paper presented at the annual meeting of the Pacific Sociological Association.

Clarke, C. J., & Neidert, L. J. (1992). Living arrangements of the elderly: An examination of differences according to ancestry and generation. *Gerontologist*, 32(6), 796–804.

Clarke-Stewart, A. (1977). *Child care in the family: A review of research and some propositions for policy*. New York: Academic Press.

Clarke-Stewart, A. (1992). Consequences of child care for children's development. In A. Booth (Ed.), *Child care in the 1990s: Trends and consequences*. Hillsdale, NJ: Erlbaum.

Clarke-Stewart, K. A. (1987). Predicting child development from day care forms and features: The Chicago study. In D. A. Phillips (Ed.), *Quality in child care: What does the research tell us? Research Monographs of the National Association for the Education of Young Children*. Washington, DC: National Association for the Education of Young Children.

Clarke-Stewart, K. A. (1989). Infant day care: Maligned or malignant. *American Psychologist*, 44(2), 266–273.

Clarkson-Smith, L., & Hartley, A. A. (1989). Relationship between physical exercise and cognitive abilities in older adults. *Psychology and Aging*, 4(2), 183–189.

Clausen, J. A. (1993). *American lives*. New York: Free Press.

Clemens, A. W., & Axelson, L. J. (1985). The not-so-empty nest: Return of the fledgling adult. *Family Relations*, 34, 259–264.

Cobrinick, P., Hood, R., & Chused, E. (1959). Effects of maternal narcotic addiction on the newborn infant. *Pediatrics*, 24, 288–290.

Cohen, G. D. (1981). *Depression and the elderly*. (DHHS Publication No. ADM 81–923). Washington, DC: U.S. Government Printing Office.

Cohen, G. D. (1987). Alzheimer's disease. In G. L. Maddox (Ed.), *The encyclopedia of aging* (pp. 27–30). New York: Springer.

Cohen, S., Lichtenstein, E., Prochaska, J. O., Rossi, J. S., Gutz, E. R., Carr, C. R., Orleans, C. T., Schoenbach, V. J., Biener, L., Abrams, D., DiClemente, C., Curry, S., Marlatt, G. A., Cummings, K. M., Emont, S. L., Grovino, G., & Ossip-Klein, D. (1989). Debunking myths about self-quitting: Evidence from 10 prospective studies of persons who attempt to quit smoking by themselves. *American Psychologist*, 44(11), 1355–1365.

Cohn, J. F., & Tronick, E. Z. (1983). Three-month-old infants' reaction to simulated maternal depression. *Child Development*, 54, 185–193.

Cohn, L. D. (1991). Sex differences in the course of personality development: A meta-analysis. *Psychological Bulletin*, 109, 252–266.

Coke, M. M. (1992). Correlates of life satisfaction among elderly African-Americans. *Journal of Gerontology*, 47(5), P316–320.

Colby, A., & Damon, W. (1993). Gaining insight into the lives of moral leaders. *Chronicle of Higher Education*, 39(20), 83–84.

Colby, A., Kohlberg, L., Gibbs, J., & Lieberman, M. (1983). A longitudinal study of moral development. *Monographs of the Society for Research in Child Development*, 48(1–2, Serial No. 200).

Cole, C., & Rodman, H. (1987). When school-age children care for themselves: Issues for family life educators and parents. *Family Relations*, 36, 92–96.

Cole, D. A. (1991). Changes in self-perceived competence as a function of peer and teacher evaluation. *Developmental Psychology*, 27(4), 682–688.

Cole, P. M., Barrett, K. C., & Zahn-Waxler, C. (1992). Emotion displays in two-year-olds during mishaps. *Child Development*, 63, 314–324.

Coleman, J. (1980). Friendship and the peer group in adolescence. In J. Adelson (Ed.), *Handbook of adolescent development*. New York: Wiley.

Coles, R., & Stokes, G. (1985). *Sex and the American teenager*. New York: Harper & Row.

Colligan, M. J., Smith, & Hurrell, J. J. (1977). Occupational incidence rates of mental health disorders. *Journal of Human Stress*, 3, 34–39.

Collin, M. F., Halsey, C. L., & Anderson, C. L. (1991). Emerging developmental sequelae in the "normal" extremely low birth weight infant. *Pediatrics*, 88, 115–120.

Collins, R. C., & Deloria, D. (1983). Head Start research: A new chapter. *Children Today*, 12(4), 15–19.

Collins, W. A. (Ed.). (1984). *Development during middle childhood: The years from six to twelve*. Washington, DC: National Academy.

Collins, W. A. (1990). Parent-child relationships in transition to adolescence: Continuity and change in interaction, affect, and cognition. In R. Montemayor, G. R. Adams, & T. P. Gullotta (Eds.), *From childhood to adolescence: A transitional period?* Newbury Park, CA: Sage.

Commonwealth Fund Commission on Elderly People Living Alone. (1986). *Problems facing elderly Americans living alone*. New York: Louis Harris & Associates.

Condon, W., & Sander, L. (1974). Synchrony demonstrated between movements of the neonate and adult speech. *Child Development, 45,* 456–462.

Condry, J. C., & Condry, S. (1974). *The development of sex differences: A study of the eye of the beholder.* Unpublished manuscript, Cornell University, Ithaca, NY.

Conger, J. J. (1988). Hostages to fortune: Youth, values, and the public interest. *American Psychologist, 43*(4), 291–300.

Conger, J. J., & Petersen, A. C. (1984). *Adolescence and youth.* New York: Harper & Row.

Congressional Caucus for Women's Issues. (1987). *The American woman, 1987–88.* Washington, DC: Author.

Connecticut Early Childhood Education Council (CECEC). (1983). *Report on full-day kindergarten.* Author.

Conners, C. K. (1988). Does diet affect behavior and learning in hyperactive children? *Harvard Medical School Mental Health Letter, 5*(5), 7–8.

Connidis, I. A. (1992). Life transitions and the adult sibling tie: A qualitative study. *Journal of Marriage and the Family, 54,* 972–982.

Connidis, I. A., & Davies, L. (1992). Confidants and companions: Choices in later life. *Journal of Gerontology, 47*(30), S115–122.

Coons, S., & Guilleminault, C. (1982). Development of sleep-wake patterns and non-rapid eye movement sleep stages during the first six months of life in normal infants. *Pediatrics, 69*(6), 793–798.

Cooper, K. L., & Gutmann, D. L. (1987). Gender identity and ego mastery style in middle-aged, pre- and post-empty nest women. *Gerontologist, 27*(3), 347–352.

Cooper, R. P., & Aslin, R. N. (1990). Preference for infant-directed speech in the first month after birth. *Child Development, 61,* 1584–1595.

Corbin, C. (1973). *A textbook of motor development.* Dubuque, IA: Brown.

Corder, E. H., Saunders, A. M., Strittmatter, W. J., Schmechel, D. E., Gaskell, P. C., Small, G. M., Roses, A. D., Haines, J. L., & Pericak-Vance, M. A. (1993). Gene dose of apolipoprotein E Type 4 allele and the risk of Alzheimer's disease in late onset families. *Science, 261,* 921–923.

Correa, P., Pickle, L. W., Fontham, E., Lin, Y., & Haenszel, W. (1983, September 10). Passive smoking and lung cancer. *The Lancet,* pp. 595–597.

Costa, P. J., & McCrae, R. R. (1994). Set like plaster? Evidence for the stability of adult personality. In T. F. Heatherton & J. L. Weinberger (Eds.), *Can personality change?*, Washington, DC: American Psychological Association.

Costa, P. T., & McCrae, R. R. (1981). Still stable after all these years: Personality as a key to some issues in adulthood and old age. In P. B. Baltes & O. G. Brim (Eds.), *Lifespan development and behavior,* Vol. 3. New York: Academic Press.

Costa, P. T., McCrae, R. R., Zonderman, A. B., Barbano, H. E., Lebowitz, B., & Larson, D. M. (1986). Cross-sectional studies of personality in a national sample: 2. Stability in neuroticism, extraversion, and openness. *Psychology and Aging, 1*(2), 144–149.

Costanzo, P. R., & Shaw, M. E. (1966). Conformity as a function of age level. *Child Development, 37,* 967–975.

Costello, A. J., Edelbrock, C., Burns, B. J., Dulcan, M. K., Brent, D., & Janiszewsku, S. (1988). Psychiatric disorders in pediatric primary care. *Archives of General Psychiatry, 45*(12), 1107–1116.

Coster, W. J., Gersten, M. S., Beeghly, M., & Cicchetti, D. (1989). Communicative functioning in maltreated toddlers. *Developmental Psychology, 25*(6), 1020–1029.

Council on Ethical and Judicial Affairs. (1990). Black-white disparities in health care. *Journal of the American Medical Association, 263,* 2344–2346.

Council on Scientific Affairs of the American Medical Association. (1989). Dyslexia. *Journal of the American Medical Association, 261*(15), 2236–2239.

Council on Scientific Affairs of the American Medical Association. (1991). Hispanic health in the United States. *Journal of the American Medical Association, 265*(2), 248–252.

Courchesne, E., Yeung-Courchesne, R., Press, G. A., Hesselink, J. R., & Jernigan, T. L. (1988). Hypolasia of cerebellar vermae lobules VI and VII in autism. *New England Journal of Medicine, 318,* 1349–1354.

Cousins, N. (1979). *Anatomy of an illness as perceived by the patient.* New York: Norton.

Cowan, M. W. (1979). The development of the brain. *Scientific American, 241,* 112–133.

Cox, J., Daniel, N., & Boston, B. O. (1985). *Educating able learners: Programs and promising practices.* Austin: University of Texas Press.

Cox, M. J., Owen, M. T., Henderson, V. K., & Margand, N. A. (1992). Prediction of infant-father and infant-mother attachment. *Developmental Psychology, 28*(3), 474–483.

Craft, M. J., Montgomery, L. A., & Peters, J. (1992, October 2). *Comparative study of responses in preschool children to the birth of an ill sibling.* Nursing seminar series presentation, University of Iowa College of Nursing, Iowa City.

Craik, F. I. M. (1977). Age differences in human memory. In J. E. Birren & K. W. Schaie (Eds.), *Handbook of the psychology of aging.* New York: Van Nostrand Reinhold.

Craik, F. I. M., Byrd, M., & Swanson, J. M. (1987). Patterns of memory loss in three elderly samples. *Psychology and Aging, 2*(1), 79–86.

Crain-Thoreson, C., & Dale, P. S. (1992). Do early talkers become early readers? Linguistic precocity, preschool language, and emergent literacy. *Developmental Psychology, 28*(3), 421–429.

Cratty, B. (1979). *Perceptual and motor development in infants and children* (2d ed.). Englewood Cliffs, NJ: Prentice-Hall.

Crisp, A. H., Queenan, M., & D'Souza, M. F. (1984, March 17). Myocardial infarction and the emotional climate. *The Lancet,* 616–618.

Crnic, K. A., & Greenberg, M. T. (1990). Minor parenting stresses with young children. *Child Development, 61,* 1628–1637.

Croake, J. W. (1973). The changing nature of children's fears. *Child Study Journal, 3*(2), 91–105.

Crockett, L. J., & Petersen, A. C. (1987). Pubertal status and psychosocial development: Findings from the Early Adolescent Study. In R. M. Lerner & T. T. Foch (Eds.), *Biological-psychosocial interactions in early adolescence: A lifespan perspective.* Hillsdale, NJ: Erlbaum.

Cross-National Collaborative Group. (1992). The changing rate of major depression: Cross-national comparisons. *Journal of the American Medical Association, 268*(21), 3098–3105.

Csikszentmihalyi, M., & Larson, R. (1984). *Being adolescent: Conflict and growth in the teenage years.* New York: Basic Books.

Cumming, E., & Henry, W. (1961). *Growing old.* New York: Basic Books.

Cummings, E. M., Iannotti, R. J., & Zahn-Waxler, C. (1989). Aggression between peers in early childhood: Individual continuity and developmental change. *Child Development, 60,* 887–895.

Cummins, J. (1986). Empowering minority students: A framework for intervention. *Harvard Educational Review, 56,* 18–36.

Cunningham, N., Anisfeld, E., Casper, V., & Nozyce, M. (1987, February 14). Infant carrying, breast feeding, and mother-infant relations. *The Lancet,* p. 379.

Curtiss, S. (1977). *Genie.* New York: Academic Press.

Curtsinger, J. W., Fukui, H. H., Townsend, D. R., & Vaupel, J. W. (1992). Demography of genotypes: Failure of the limited life-span paradigm in Drosophila melanogaster. *Science, 258,* 461–463.

Cushman, R., Down, J., MacMillan, N., & Waclawik, H. (1991). Helmet promotion in the emergency room following bicycle injury: A randomized trial. *Pediatrics, 88*(1), 43–47.

Cutrona, C., Russell, D., & Rose, J. (1986). Social support and adaptation to stress by the elderly. *Journal of Psychology and Aging, 1*(1), 47–54.

Cytrynbaum, S., Bluum, L., Patrick, R., Stein, J., Wadner, D., & Wilk, C. (1980). Midlife development: A personality and social systems perspective. In L. Poon (Ed.), *Aging in the 1980s*. Washington, DC: American Psychological Association.

Daley, S. (1991, January 9). Little girls lose their self-esteem on way to adolescence, study finds. *The New York Times*, p. B6.

D'Alton, M. E., & DeCherney, A. H. (1993). Prenatal diagnosis. *New England Journal of Medicine, 32*(2), 114–120.

Damon, W. (1984). Peer education: The untapped potential. *Journal of Applied Developmental Psychology, 5*, 331–343.

Dan, A. J., & Bernhard, L. A. (1989). Menopause and other health issues for midlife women. In S. Hunter & M. Sundel (Eds.), *Midlife myths*. Newbury Park, CA: Sage.

Daniels, D., & Plomin, R. (1985). Origins of individual differences in infant shyness. *Developmental Psychology, 21*(1), 118–121.

Danish, S. J. (1983). Musings about personal competence: The contributions of sport, health, and fitness. *American Journal of Community Psychology, 11*(3), 221–240.

Danish, S. J., & D'Augelli, A. R. (1980). Promoting competence and enhancing development through life development intervention. In L. A. Bond & J. C. Rosem (Eds.), *Competence and coping during adulthood*. Hanover, NH: University Press of New England.

Danish, S. J., Smyer, M. A., & Nowak, C. A. (1980). Development intervention: Enhancing life-event processes. In P. B. Baltes & O. G. Brim (Eds.), *Lifespan development and behavior*, Vol. 3. New York: Academic Press.

Darlington, R. B. (1991). The long-term effects of model preschool programs. In L. Okagaki & R. J. Sternberg (Eds.), *Directors of development: Influences on the development of children's thinking*. Hillsdale, NJ: Erlbaum.

Datan, N., Rodeheaver, D., & Hughes, F. (1987). Adult development and aging. *Annual Review of Psychology, 38*, 153–180.

Davidson, J., & Smith, R. (1990). Traumatic experiences in psychiatric outpatients. *Journal of Traumatic Stress, 3*(3), 459–475.

Davidson, J. E., & Sternberg, R. J. (1984). The role of insight in intellectual giftedness. *Gifted Child Quarterly, 28*(2), 58–64.

Davidson, R. J., & Fox, N. A. (1989). Frontal brain asymmetry predicts infants' response to maternal separation. *Journal of Abnormal Psychology, 948*(2), 58–64.

Davis, B. W. (1985). *Visits to remember: A handbook for visitors of nursing home residents*. University Park: Pennsylvania State University Cooperative Extension Service.

Davis, B. W. (undated). *Celebrate your marriage* (Marriage Strength Builder No. 4, Learn-at-Home Program). University Park: Pennsylvania State University Cooperative Extension Service.

Davis, K. E. (1985, February). Near and dear: Friendship and love compared. *Psychology Today, 19*, 22–30.

Davis, K. L., et al. (1992). A double-blind placebo-controlled multicenter study of tacrine for Alzheimer's disease. *New England Journal of Medicine, 327*, 1253–1259.

Dawson, G., Klinger, L. G., Panagiotides, H., Hill, D., & Spieker, S. (1992). Frontal lobe activity and affective behavior of infants of mothers with depressive symptoms. *Child Development, 63*, 725–737.

Dawson-Hughes, B., Dallal, G. E., Krall, E. A., Sadowski, L. Sahyoun, N., & Tannenbaum, S. (1990). A controlled trial of the effect of calcium supplementation on bone density in postmenopausal women. *New England Journal of Medicine, 323*, 878–883.

Deaux, K. (1985). Sex and gender. *Annual Review of Psychology, 36*, 49–81.

DeBuono, B. A., Zinner, S. H., Daamen, M., & McCormack, W. M. (1990). Sexual behavior of college women in 1975, 1980, and 1989. *New England Journal of Medicine, 322*, 821–825.

DeCasper, A., & Fifer, W. (1980). Newborns prefer their mothers' voices. *Science, 208*, 1174–1176.

Decker, M. D., Dewey, M. J., Hutcheson, R. H., & Schaffner, W. (1984). The use and efficacy of child restraint devices. *Journal of the American Medical Association, 252*(18), 2571–2575.

DeFrain, J., & Ernst, L. (1978). The psychological effects of sudden infant death syndrome on surviving family members. *Journal of Family Practice, 6*(5), 985–989.

DeFrain, J., Taylor, J., & Ernst, L. (1982). *Coping with sudden infant death*. Lexington, MA: Heath.

DeFries, J. C., Fulker, D. W., & LaBuda, M. C. (1987). Evidence for a genetic etiology in reading disability of twins. *Nature, 329*, 537–539.

Dekovic, M. & Janssens, J. M. A. M. (1992). Parents' child-rearing style and child's sociometric status. *Developmental Psychology, 28*(5), 925–932.

Demo, D. H. (1991). A sociological perspective on parent-adolescent disagreements. *New Directions for Child Development, 51*, 111–118.

Demo, D. H. (1992). Parent-child relations: Assessing recent changes. *Journal of Marriage and the Family, 54*, 104–117.

Denney, N. W. (1972). Free classification in preschool children. *Child Development, 43*, 1161–1170.

Denney, N. W., & Palmer, A. M. (1981). Adult age differences on traditional and practical problem-solving measures. *Journal of Gerontology, 36*(3), 323–328.

Denney, N. W., & Pearce, K. A. (1989). A developmental study of practical problem solving in adults. *Psychology and Aging, 4*(4), 438–442.

Dennis, W. (1960). Causes of retardation among institutional children: Iran. *Journal of Genetic Psychology, 96*, 47–59.

Denny, F. W., & Clyde, W. A. (1983). Acute respiratory tract infections: An overview. In W. A. Clyde & F. W. Denny (Eds.), Workshop on acute respiratory diseases among children of the world. *Pediatric Research, 17*, 1026–1029.

deRegt, R. H., Minkoff, H. L., Feldman, J., & Schwartz, R. H. (1986). Relation of private or clinic care to the cesarean birth rate. *New England Journal of Medicine, 315*, 619–624.

deVos, S. (1990). Extended family living among older people in six Latin American countries. *Journal of Gerontology, 45*(3), S87–94.

DeVries, M. W., & Sameroff, A. J. (1984). Culture and temperament: Influence on infant temperament in three East African societies. *American Journal of Orthopsychiatry, 54*(1), 83–96.

Deykin, E. Y., Alpert, J. J., & McNamarra, J. J. (1985). A pilot study of the effect of exposure to child abuse or neglect on adolescent suicidal behavior. *American Journal of Psychiatry, 142*(11), 1299–1303.

Diagnostic and statistical manual of mental disorders (3d ed., rev.) (DSM III-R). (1987). Washington, DC: American Psychiatric Association.

Diamond, M. (1986, August). *The changing brain: Age, sex and environment*. Address to the Commonwealth Club, San Francisco.

Diamond, M., et al. (1985). Plasticity in the 904 day old male rat cerebral cortex. *Experimental Neurology, 87*, 309–317.

Diaz, R. M. (1983). Thought and two languages: The impact of bilingualism on cognitive development. *Review of Research in Education, 10*, 23–54.

Dickson, W. P. (1979). Referential communication performance from age 4 to 8: Effects of referent type, context, and target position. *Developmental Psychology, 15*(4), 470–471.

Dien, D. S. F. (1982). A Chinese perspective on Kohlberg's theory of moral development. *Developmental Review, 2*, 331–341.

Dietz, W. H., & Gortmaker, S. L. (1985). Do we fatten our children at the television set? Obesity and television viewing in children and adolescents. *Pediatrics, 75*, 807–812.

Dimant, R. J., & Bearison, D. J. (1991). Development of formal reasoning during successive peer interactions. *Developmental Psychology, 27*(2), 277–284.

Dishion, T. J., Patterson, G. R., Stoolmiller, M., & Skinner, M. L. (1991). Family, school, and behavioral antecedents to early adolescent involvement with antisocial peers. *Developmental Psychology, 27*(1), 172–180.

Dixon, R. A. (1992). Contextual approaches to adult intellectual development. In R. Sternberg & C. A. Berg (Eds.), *Intellectual Development.* Cambridge, England: Cambridge University Press.

Dixon, R. A., & Baltes, P. B. (1986). Toward life-span research on the functions and pragmatics of intelligence. In R. J. Sternberg & R. K. Wagner (Eds.), *Practical intelligence: Nature and origins of competence in the everyday world.* New York: Cambridge University Press.

Doctors rule out transplant from organs of hanged boy. (1984, November 23). *The New York Times,* p. A26.

Dodge, K. A., Bates, J. E., & Pettit, G. S. (1990). Mechanisms in the cycle of violence. *Science, 250,* 1678–1683.

Dodge, K. A., Cole, J. D., Pettit, G. S., & Price, J. M. (1990). Peer status and aggression in boys' groups: Developmental and contextual analysis. *Child Development, 61,* 1289–1309.

Doering, C. H., Kraemer, H. C., Brodie, H. K. H., & Hamburg, D. A. (1975). A cycle of plasma testosterone in the human male. *Journal of Clinical Endocrinology and Metabolism, 40,* 492–500.

Doherty, W. J., & Jacobson, N. S. (1982). Marriage and the family. In B. Wolman (Ed.), *Handbook of developmental psychology.* Englewood Cliffs, NJ: Prentice-Hall.

Doka, K. J., & Mertz, M. E. (1988). The meaning and significance of great-grandparenthood. *Gerontologist, 28*(2), 192–197.

Doman, G. (1979). *How to teach your baby to read.* Philadelphia: The Better Baby Press.

Doman, G. (1984). *How to multiply your baby's intelligence.* Garden City, NY: Doubleday.

Donovan, P. (1993). *Testing positive: Sexually transmitted diseases and the public health response.* New York: Alan Guttmacher Institute.

Doppelt, J. E., & Wallace, W. L. (1955). Standardization of the Wechsler Adult Intelligence Scale for older persons. *Journal of Abnormal and Social Psychology, 51,* 312–330.

Dore, J. (1975). Holophrases, speech acts, and language universals. *Journal of Child Language, 2,* 21–40.

Dornbusch, S. M., Carlsmith, J. M., Bushwall, S. J., Ritter, P. L., Leiderman, H., Hastorf, A. H., & Gross, R. T. (1985). Single parents, extended households, and the control of adolescents. *Child Development, 56,* 326–341.

Dornbusch, S. M., Ritter, P. L., Leiderman, P. H., Roberts, D. F., & Fraleigh, M. J. (1987). The relation of parenting style to adolescent school performance. *Child Development, 58,* 1244–1257.

Dove, J. (undated). *Facts about anorexia nervosa.* Bethesda, MD: National Institutes of Health, Office of Research Reporting, National Institute of Child Health and Human Development.

Downey, D. B., & Powell, B. (1993). Do children in single-parent households fare better living with same-sex parents? *Journal of Marriage and the Family, 55*(1), 55–71.

Doyle, A. B., Doehring, P., Tessier, O., deLorimier, S., & Shapiro, S. (1992). Transitions in children's play: A sequential analysis of states preceding and following social pretense. *Developmental Psychology, 28*(1), 137–144.

Dreyer, P. H. (1982). Sexuality during adolescence. In B. B. Wolman (Ed.), *Handbook of developmental psychology.* Englewood Cliffs, NJ: Prentice-Hall.

Droege, R. (1982). *A psychosocial study of the formation of the middle adult life structure in women.* Unpublished doctoral dissertation, California School of Professional Psychology, Berkeley, CA.

Duncan, B., Ey, J., Holberg, C. J., Wright, A. L., Martinez, F. D., & Taussig, L. M. (1993). Exclusive breast-feeding for at least four months protects against otitis media. *Pediatrics, 91,* 867–872.

Dungy, C. I., Christensen-Szalanski, J., Losch, M., & Russell, D. (1992). Effect of discharge samples on duration of breast-feeding. *Pediatrics, 90*(2), 233–236.

Dunn, J. (1983). Sibling relationships in early childhood. *Child Development, 54,* 787–811.

Dunn, J. (1985). *Sisters and brothers.* Cambridge, MA: Harvard University Press.

Dunn, J. (1991). Young children's understanding of other people: Evidence from observations within the family. In D. Frye & C. Moore (Eds.), *Children's theories of mind: Mental states and social understanding.* Hillsdale, NJ: Erlbaum.

Dunn, J., Brown, J., & Beardsall, L. (1991). Family talk about feeling states and children's later understanding of others' emotions. *Developmental Psychology, 27*(3), 448–455.

Dunn, J., Brown, J., Slomkowski, C., Tesla, C., & Youngblade, L. (1991). Young children's understanding of other people's feelings and beliefs: Individual differences and antecedents. *Child Development, 62,* 1352–1366.

Dunn, J., & Kendrick, C. (1982). *Siblings: Love, envy and understanding.* Cambridge, MA: Harvard University Press.

Dunne, R. G., Asher, K. N., & Rivara, F. P. (1992). Behavior and parental expectations of child pedestrians. *Pediatrics, 89*(3), 486–490.

DuPont, R. L. (1983). Phobias in children. *Journal of Pediatrics, 102*(6), 999–1002.

Durlak, J. A. (1973). Relationship between attitudes toward life and death among elderly women. *Developmental Psychology, 8*(1), 146.

Dustman, R. E., Emmerson, R. Y., Steinhaus, L. A., Shearer, D. E., & Dustman, T. J. (1992). The effects of videogame playing on neuropsychological performance of elderly individuals. *Journal of Gerontology, 47*(3), P168–171.

Dwyer, T., Ponsonby, A. B., Newman, N. M., & Gibbons, L. E. (1991). Prospective cohort study of prone sleeping position and sudden infant death syndrome. *The Lancet, 337,* 1244–1247.

Dyslexia. (1989, September 23). *The Lancet,* pp. 719–720.

Easterbrooks, M. A. (1989). Quality of attachment to mother and to father: Effects of perinatal risk status. *Child Development, 60,* 825–830.

Easterbrooks, M. A., & Goldberg, W. A. (1984). Toddler development in the family: Impact of father involvement and parenting characteristics. *Child Development, 55,* 740–752.

Easterlin, R. A. (1980). *Birth and fortune.* New York: Basic Books.

Eastman, P. (1984). Elders under siege. *Psychology Today, 18*(1), 30.

Eccles, J. S., Midgley, C., Wigfield, A., Buchanan, C. M., Reuman, D., Flanagan, C., & MacIver, D. (1993). Development during adolescence: The impact of stage-environment on young adolescents' experiences in schools and in families. *American Psychologist, 48*(2), 90–101.

Eckenrode, J., Laird, M., & Doris, J. (1993). School performance and disciplinary problems among abused and neglected children. *Developmental Psychology, 29*(1), 53–62.

Eckerman, C. O., Davis, C. C., & Didow, S. M. (1989). Toddlers' emerging ways of achieving social coordination with a peer. *Child Development, 60,* 440–453.

Eckerman, C. O., & Stein, M. R. (1982). The toddler's emerging interactive skills. In K. H. Rubin & H. S. Ross (Eds.), *Peer relationships and social skills in childhood.* New York: Springer-Verlag.

Egbuono, L., & Starfield, B. (1982). Child health and social status. *Pediatrics, 69*(5), 550–557.

Egeland, B., & Farber, E. A. (1984). Infant-mother attachment: Factors related to its development and changes over time. *Child Development, 55,* 753–771.

Egeland, B., & Sroufe, L. A. (1981). Attachment and early maltreatment. *Child Development, 52,* 44–52.

Egertson, H. A. (1987, May 20). Recapturing kindergarten for 5-year-olds. *Education Week,* pp. 28, 19.

Ehrhardt, A. A., & Money, J. (1967). Progestin induced hermaphroditism: I.Q. and psychosocial identity. *Journal of Sexual Research, 3,* 83–100.

Eichorn, D. H., Clausen, J. A., Haan, N., Honzik, M. P., & Mussen, P. H. (1981). *Present and past in midlife.* New York: Academic Press.

Eiger, M. S., & Olds, S. W. (1987). *The complete book of breastfeeding* (rev. ed.). New York: Workman.

Eimas, P. (1985). The perception of speech in early infancy. *Scientific American, 252*(1), 46–52.

Eimas, P., Siqueland, E., Jusczyk, P., & Vigorito, J. (1971). Speech perception in infants. *Science, 171,* 303–306.

Einbender, A. J., & Friedrich, W. N. (1989). Psychological functioning and behavior of sexually abused girls. *Journal of Consulting and Clinical Psychology, 57*(1), 155–157.

Einstein, E. (1979, April). Stepfamily lives. *Human Behavior,* pp. 63–68.

Eisen, L. N., Field, T. M., Bandstra, E. S., Roberts, J. P., Morrow, C., Larson, S. K., & Steele, B. M. (1991). Perinatal cocaine effects on neonatal stress behavior and performance on the Brazelton scale. *Pediatrics, 88*(3), 477–480.

Eisen, M., & Zellman, G. L. (1987). Changes in incidence of sexual intercourse of unmarried teenagers following a community-based sex education program. *Journal of Sex Research, 23*(4), 527–544.

Eisenberg, A., Murkoff, H. E., & Hathaway, S. E. (1984, 1986). *What to expect when you're expecting* (2d ed.). New York: Workman.

Eisenberg, L. (1980). Adolescent suicide: On taking arms against a sea of troubles. *Pediatrics, 66,* 315–320.

Eisenberg, L. (1986). Does bad news about suicide beget bad news? *New England Journal of Medicine, 315,* 705–706.

Eisenberg, N., Fabes, R. A., Schaller, M., & Miller, P. A. (1989). Sympathy and personal distress: Development, gender differences, and interrelations of indexes. In N. Eisenberg (Ed.), *Empathy and related emotional responses. New Directions in Child Development, 44.* San Francisco: Jossey-Bass.

Eisenson, J., Auer, J. J., & Irwin, J. V. (1963). *The psychology of communication.* New York: Appleton-Century-Crofts.

Elkind, D. (1981). *The hurried child.* Reading, MA: Addison-Wesley.

Elkind, D. (1984). *All grown up and no place to go.* Reading, MA: Addison-Wesley.

Elkind, D. (1987a). *Miseducation.* New York: Knopf.

Elkind, D. (1987b). Superkids and super problems. *Psychology Today, 21*(5), 60–61.

Ellis, L., & Ames, M. A. (1987). Neurohormonal functioning and sexual orientation: A theory of homosexuality-heterosexuality. *Psychological Bulletin, 101*(2), 233–258.

Emde, R. N. (1992). Individual meaning and increasing complexity: Contributions of Sigmund Freud and Rene Spitz to developmental psychology. *Developmental Psychology, 28*(3), 347–359.

Emde, R. N., Plomin, R., Robinson, J., Corley, R., DeFries, J., Fulker, D. W., Reznick, J. S., Campos, J., Kagan, J., & Zahn-Waxler, C. (1992). Temperament, emotion, and cognition at 14 months: The MacArthur longitudinal twin study. *Child Development, 63,* 1437–1455.

Emery, R. E. (1989). Family violence. *American Psychologist, 44*(2), 321–328.

Emmerick, H. (1978). The influence of parents and peers on choices made by adolescents. *Journal of Youth and Adolescence, 7*(2), 175–180.

Epstein, J. L. (1984, May). Single parents get involved in children's learning [Summary]. *CSOS Report.* Baltimore, MD: Johns Hopkins University Center for Social Organization of Schools (CSOS).

Epstein, L. H., & Wing, R. R. (1987). Behavioral treatment of childhood obesity. *Psychological Bulletin, 101*(3), 331–342.

Erikson, E. H. (1950). *Childhood and society.* New York: Norton.

Erikson, E. H. (1964). *Insight and responsiblity.* New York: Norton.

Erikson, E. H. (1968). *Identity: Youth and crisis.* New York: Norton.

Erikson, E. H. (1973). The wider identity. In K. Erikson (Ed.), *In search of common ground: Conversations with Erik H. Erikson and Huey P. Newton.* New York: Norton.

Erikson, E. H. (1985). *The life cycle completed.* New York: Norton.

Erikson, E. H., Erikson, J. M., & Kivnick, H. Q. (1986). *Vital involvement in old age.* New York: Norton.

Eron, L. D. (1980). Prescription for reduction of aggression. *American Psychologist, 35*(3), 244–252.

Eron, L. D. (1982). Parent-child interaction, television violence, and aggression in children. *American Psychologist, 37*(2), 197–211.

Espenschade, A. (1960). Motor development. In W. R. Johnson (Ed.), *Science and medicine of exercise and sports.* New York: Harper & Row.

Essex, M. J., & Nam, S. (1987). Marital status and loneliness among older women: The differential importance of close family and friends. *Journal of Marriage and the Family, 49,* 93–106.

Estes, E. H. (1969). Health experience in the elderly. In E. Busse & E. Pfeiffer (Eds.), *Behavior and adaptation in late life.* Boston: Little, Brown.

European Collaborative Study (1992). Risk factors for mother-to-child transmission of HIV-1. *The Lancet, 339,* 1007–1012.

Evans, D. A., Funkenstein, H., Albert, M. A., Scherr, P. A., Cook, N. R., Chown, M. J., Hebert, L. E., Hennekens, C. H., & Taylor, J. O. (1989). Prevalence of Alzheimer's disease in a community population of older persons: Higher than previously reported. *Journal of the American Medical Association, 262*(18), 2551–2556.

Evans, G. (1976). The older the sperm . . . *Ms., 4*(7), 48–49.

Evans, R. I. (1967). *Dialogue with Erik Erikson.* New York: Harper & Row.

Eveleth, P. B., & Tanner, J. M. (1976). *Worldwide variation in human growth.* London: Cambridge University Press.

Ewigman, B. G., Crane, J. P., Frigoletto, F. D., Lefevre, M. L., Bain, R. P., McNellis, D., & the RADIUS Study Group. (1993). Effect of prenatal ultrasound screening on perinatal outcome. *New England Journal of Medicine, 329,* 821–827.

Fabes, R. A., & Eisenberg, N. (1992). Young children's coping with interpersonal anger. *Child Development, 63,* 116–128.

Fagan, J. F. (1982). Infant memory. In T. M. Field, A. Huston, H. Quay, L. Troll, & G. Finley (Eds.), *Review of human development.* New York: Wiley.

Fagan, J. F., & McGrath, S. K. (1981). Infant recognition memory and later intelligence. *Intelligence, 5,* 121–130.

Fagan, J. W., Morrongiello, B. A., Rovee-Collier, C., & Gekoski, M. J. (1984). Expectancies and memory retrieval in three-month-old infants. *Child Development, 55,* 936–943.

Falbo, T., & Polit, D. F. (1986). Quantitative review of the only child literature: Research evidence and theory development. *Psychological Bulletin, 100*(2), 176–189.

Falbo, T., & Poston, D. L. (1993). The academic, personality, and physical outcomes of only children in China. *Child Development, 64,* 18–35.

Fallot, M. E., Boyd, J. L., & Oski, F. A. (1980). Breast-feeding reduces incidence of hospital admissions for infection in infants. *Pediatrics, 65*(6), 1121–1124.

Fallows, J. (1986, November 24). Viva bilingualism. *The New Republic,* pp. 18–19.

Fantuzzo, J. W., Jurecic, L., Stoval, A., Hightower, A. D., Goiins, C., & Schachtel, D. (1988). Effects of adult and peer social initiations on the social behavior of withdrawn, maltreated preschool children. *Journal of Consulting and Clinical Psychology, 56*(1), 34–39.

Fantz, R. L. (1963). Pattern vision in newborn infants. *Science, 140,* 296–297.

Fantz, R. L. (1964). Visual experience in infants: Decreased attention to familiar patterns relative to novel ones. *Science, 146,* 668–670.

Fantz, R. L. (1965). Visual perception from birth as shown by pattern selectivity. In H. E. Whipple (Ed.), New issues in infant development. *Annals of the New York Academy of Science, 118,* 793–814.

Fantz, R. L., Fagen, J., & Miranda, S. B. (1975). Early visual selectivity. In L. Cohen & P. Salapatek (Eds.), *Infant perception: From sensation to cognition: Vol. 1. Basic visual processes* (pp. 249–341). New York: Academic Press.

Fantz, R. L., & Nevis, S. (1967). Pattern preferences and perceptual-cognitive development in early infancy. *Merrill-Palmer Quarterly, 13*, 77–108.

Farlow, M., Gracon, S. I., Hershey, L. A., Lewis, K. W., Sadowsky, C. H., Dolan-Ureno, J., for the Tacrine Study Group. (1992). A controlled trial of Tacrine in Alzheimer's disease. *Journal of the American Medical Association, 268*, 2523–2529.

Farnsworth, C. H. (1993, February 2). Anti-woman bias may bring asylum. *The New York Times*, p. A8.

Farrell, M. P., & Rosenberg, S. D. (1981). *Men at midlife.* Boston: Auburn.

Farrow, J. A., Rees, J. M., & Worthington-Roberts, B. S. (1987). Health, developmental, and nutritional status of adolescent alcohol and marijuana abusers. *Pediatrics, 79*(2), 218–223.

Feagans, L. (1983). A current view of learning disabilities. *Journal of Pediatrics, 102*(4), 487–493.

Feazell, C. S., Mayers, R. S., & Deschner, J. (1984). Services for men who batter: Implications for programs and policies. *Family Relations, 33*, 217–223.

Feifel, H. (1977). *New meanings of death.* New York: McGraw-Hill.

Fein, G. (1981). Pretend play in childhood: An integrative review. *Child Development. 52*, 1095–1118.

Feinberg, I. (1982). Schizophrenia: Caused by a fault in programmed synaptic elimination during adolescence. *Journal of Psychiatric Research, 17*, 319–334.

Feinman, S., & Lewis, M. (1983). Social referencing at ten months: A second-order effect on infants' responses. *Child Development, 54*, 878–887.

Feldman, H. (1981). A comparison of intentional parents and intentionally childless couples. *Journal of Marriage and the Family, 43*(3), 593–600.

Feldman, H., & Feldman, M. (1977). *Effect of parenthood at three points on marriage.* Unpublished manuscript.

Feldman, H., Goldin-Meadow, S., & Gleitman, L. (1979). Beyond Herodotus: The creation of language by linguistically deprived deaf children. In A. Lock (Ed.), *Action, gesture and symbol: The emergence of language.* New York: Academic Press.

Feldman, R. D. (1982). *Whatever happened to the quiz kids: Perils and profits of growing up gifted.* Chicago: Chicago Review Press.

Fellin, P. A., & Powell, T. J. (1988). Mental health services and older adult minorities: An assessment. *Gerontologist, 28*(4), 442–446.

Fergusson, D. M., Horwood, L. J., & Shannon, F. T. (1986). Factors related to the age of attainment of nocturnal bladder control: An 8-year longitudinal study. *Pediatrics, 78*, 884–890.

Fetterly, K., & Graubard, M. S. (1984, March 23). Racial and educational factors associated with breast-feeding—United States, 1969 and 1980. *Morbidity and Mortality Weekly Report (MMWR)*, pp. 153–154.

Fiatarone, M. A., Marks, E. C., Ryan, N. D., Meredith, C. N., Lipsitz, L. A., & Evans, W. J. (1990). High-intensity strength training in nonagenarians: Effects on skeletal muscles. *Journal of the American Medical Association, 263*, 3029–3034.

Field, D. (1977). The importance of the verbal content in the training of Piagetian conservation skills. *Child Development, 52*, 326–334.

Field, D. (1981). Can preschool children really learn to conserve? *Child Development, 52*, 326–334.

Field, D., & Millsap, R. E. (1991). Personality in advanced old age: Continuity or change? *Journal of Gerontology, 46*(6), P299–308.

Field, D., & Minkler, M. (1988). Continuity and change in social support between young-old and old-old or very-old age. *Journal of Gerontology, 43*(4), P100–106.

Field, D., Minkler, M., Falk, R. F., & Leino, E. V. (1993). The influence of health on family contacts and family functioning in advanced old age: A longitudinal study. *Journal of Gerontology, 48*(1), P18–28.

Field, T. (1991). Quality infant day-care and grade school behavior and performance. *Child Development, 62*, 863–870.

Field, T. M. (1978). Interaction behaviors of primary versus secondary caretaker fathers. *Developmental Psychology, 14*, 183–184.

Field, T. M. (1986). Interventions for premature infants. *Journal of Pediatrics, 109*(1), 183–190.

Field, T. M. (1987). Interaction and attachment in normal and atypical infants. *Journal of Consulting and Clinical Psychology, 55*(6), 853–859.

Field, T. M., & Roopnarine, J. L. (1982). Infant-peer interaction. In T. M. Field, A. Huston, H. C. Quay, L. Troll, & G. Finley (Eds.), *Review of human development.* New York: Wiley.

Field, T. M., Sandberg, D., Garcia, R., Vega-Lahr, N., Goldstein, S., & Guy, L. (1985). Pregnancy problems, postpartum depression, and early infant-mother interactions. *Developmental Psychology, 21*(6), 1152–1156.

Field, T. M., Widmayer, S., Greenberg, R., & Stoller, S. (1982). Effects of parent training on teenage mothers and their infants. *Pediatrics, 69*(6), 703–707.

Field, T. M., Woodson, R., Greenberg, R., & Cohen, D. (1982). Discrimination and imitation of facial expressions by neonates. *Science, 218*, 179–181.

Fielding, J. E., & Phenow, K. J. (1988). Health effects of involuntary smoking. *New England Journal of Medicine, 319*(22), 1452–1460.

Finegan, J. A. K., Quarrington, B. J., Hughes, H. E., Mervyn, J. M., Hood, J. E., Zacher, J. E., & Boyden, M. (1990). Child outcome following mid-trimester amniocentesis: Development, behaviour, and physical status at age 4 years. *British Journal of Obstetrics and Gynaecology, 97*, 32.

Fingerhut, L. A., & Kleinman, J. C. (1990). International and interstate comparisons of homicide among young males. *Journal of the American Medical Association, 263*(4), 3292–3295.

Fiore, M. C., Novotny, T. E., Pierce, J. P., et al. (1990). Methods used to quit smoking in the United States: Do cessation programs help? *Journal of the American Medical Association, 263*, 2760–2765.

Fitness Finders. (1984). *Feelin' good.* Spring Arbor, MI: Author.

Fivush, R., Hudson, J., & Nelson, K. (1983). Children's long term memory for a novel event: An exploratory study. *Merrill-Palmer Quarterly, 30*, 303–316.

Flanagan, C. A., & Eccles, J. S. (1993). Changes in parents' work status and adolescents' adjustment at school. *Child Development, 64*(1), 246–257.

Flavell, J. H., Beach, D., & Chinsky, J. (1966). Spontaneous verbal rehearsal in a memory task as a function of age. *Child Development, 37*, 283–299.

Flavell, J. H., Speer, J. R., Green, F. L., & August, D. L. (1981). The development of comprehension monitoring and knowledge about communication. *Monographs of the Society for Research in Child Development, 46*(5, Serial No. 192).

Fluoxetine-Bulimia Collaborative Study Group. (1992). Fluoxetine in the treatment of bulimia nervosa: A multicenter placebo-controlled, double-blind trial. *The Archives of General Psychiatry, 49*, 139–147.

Folstein, M. F., Bassett, S. S., Anthony, J. C., Romanoski, A. J., & Nestadt, G. R. (1991). Dementia: Case ascertainment in a community survey. *Journal of Gerontology, 46*(4), M132–138.

Fomon, S. J., Filer, L. J., Anderson, T. A., & Ziegler, E. E. (1979). Recommendations for feeding normal infants. *Pediatrics, 63*(1), 52–59.

Ford, J., Zelnik, M., & Kantner, J. (1979, November). *Differences in contraceptive use and socioeconomic groups of teenagers in the United States.* Paper presented at the meeting of the American Public Health Association, New York.

Forman, M. R., Graubard, B. I., Hoffman, H. J., Beren, R., Harley, E. E., & Bennett, P. (1984). The Pima infant feeding study: Breast feeding and gastroenteritis in the first year of life. *American Journal of Epidemiology, 119*(3), 335–349.

Fraga, C. G., Motchnik, P. A., Shigenaga, M. K., Helbock, H. J., Jacob, R. A., & Ames, B. N. (1991). Ascorbic acid protects against endogenous oxidative DNA damage in human sperm. *Proceedings of the National Academy of Sciences of the United States of America, 88,* 11003–11006.

Frank, S. J., Avery, C. B., & Laman, M. S. (1988). Young adults' perception of their relationships with their parents: Individual differences in connectedness, competence, and emotional autonomy. *Developmental Psychology, 24*(5), 729–737.

Frankenburg, W. K., Dodds, J., Archer, P., Shapiro, H., & Bresnick, B. (1992). The Denver II: A major revision and restandardization of the Denver Developmental Screening Test. *Pediatrics, 89,* 91–97.

Frankenburg, W. K., Dodds, J. B., Fandal, A. W., Kazuk, E., & Cohrs, M. (1975). *The Denver developmental screening test: Reference manual.* Denver: University of Colorado Medical Center.

Frankl, V. (1965). *The doctor and the soul.* New York: Knopf.

Freedman, D. G. (1979, January). Ethnic differences in babies. *Human Nature,* pp. 15–20.

Freud, A. (1946). *The ego and the mechanisms of defense.* New York: International Universities Press.

Freud, S. (1953). *A general introduction to psychoanalysis* (J. Riviere, Trans.). New York: Perma-books.

Frezza, M., DiPadova, C., Pozzato, G., Terpin, M., Baraona, E., & Lieber, C. S. (1990). High blood alcohol levels in women: The role of decreased gastric alcohol dehydrogenase activity and first-pass metabolism. *New England Journal of Medicine, 322,* 95–99.

Fried, P. A., Watkinson, B., & Willan, A. (1984). Marijuana use during pregnancy and decreased length of gestation. *American Journal of Obstetrics and Gynecology, 150,* 23–27.

Friedman, M., & Rosenman, R. H. (1974). *Type A behavior and your heart.* New York: Knopf.

Fries, J. F., & Crapo, L. M. (1981). *Vitality and aging.* San Francisco: Freeman.

Frisch, H. (1977). Sex stereotypes in adult-infancy play. *Child Development, 48,* 1671–1675.

Fromkin, V., Krashen, S., Curtiss, S., Rigler, D., & Rigler, M. (1974). The development of language in Genie: Acquisition beyond the "critical period." *Brain and Language, 15*(9), 28–34.

Fuchs, D., & Fuchs, L. S. (1986). Test procedure bias: A meta-analysis of examiner familiarity effects. *Review of Educational Research, 56,* 243–262.

Fuchs, F. (1980). Genetic amniocentesis. *Scientific American, 242*(6), 47–53.

Fuchs, L. S., & Fuchs, D. (1986). Effects of systematic formative evaluation of student achievement: A meta-analysis. *Exceptional Children, 53,* 199–205.

Furman, W. (1982). Children's friendships. In T. M. Field, A. Huston, H. C. Quay, L. Troll, & G. E. Finley (Eds.), *Review of human development.* New York: Wiley.

Furman, W., & Bierman, K. L. (1983). Developmental changes in young children's conceptions of friendship. *Child Development, 54,* 549–556.

Furman, W., & Buhrmester, D. (1985). Children's perceptions of the personal relationships in their social networks. *Developmental Psychology, 21*(6), 1016–1024.

Furry, C. A., & Baltes, P. B. (1973). The effect of age differences in ability-extraneous performance variables on the assessment of intelligence in children, adults, and the elderly. *Journal of Gerontology, 28*(1), 73–80.

Furst, K. (1983). *Origins and evolution of women's dreams in early adulthood.* Unpublished doctoral dissertation, California School of Professional Psychology, Berkeley, CA.

Furstenberg, F. F., Brooks-Gunn, J., & Morgan, S. P. (1987). Adolescent mothers and their children in later life. *Family Planning Perspectives, 19,* 142–152.

Furstenberg, F. F., Levine, J. A., & Brooks-Gunn, J. (1990). The children of teenage mothers: Patterns of early childbearing in two generations. *Family Planning Perspectives, 22*(2), 54–61.

Futterman, D., Hein, K., Reuben, N., Dell, R., Shaffer, N. (1993). Human immunodeficiency virus-infected adolescents: The first 50 patients in a New York City program. *Pediatrics, 91*(4), 730–735.

Gaensbauer, T., & Hiatt, S. (1984). *The psychobiology of affective development.* Hillsdale, NJ: Erlbaum.

Gaertner, S. L., Mann, J., Murrell, A., & Dovidio, J. F. (1989). Reducing intergroup bias: The benefits of recategorization. *Journal of Personality and Social Psychology, 57*(2), 239–249.

Gage, F. H., Bjorklund, A., Stenevi, U., Dunnett, S. B., & Kelly, P. A. T. (1984). Intrahippocampal septal grafts ameliorate learning impairments in aged rats. *Science, 22,* 533–536.

Galambos, N. L., Petersen, A. C., & Lenerz, K. (1988). Maternal employment and sex typing in early adolescence: Contemporaneous and longitudinal relations. In A. D. Gottfried and A. W. Gottfried (Eds.), *Maternal employ-*

ment and children's development: Longitudinal research. New York: Plenum.

Gamble, T. J., & Zigler, E. (1986). Effects of infant day care: Another look at the evidence. *American Journal of Orthopsychiatry, 56*(1), 26–42.

Gans, J. E. (1990). *America's adolescents: How healthy are they?* Chicago: American Medical Association.

Garbarino, J., Dubrow, N., Kostelny, K., & Pardo, C. (1992). *Children in danger: Coping with the consequences of community violence.* San Francisco: Jossey-Bass.

Garcia-Coll, C., Kagan, J., & Reznick, J. S. (1984). Behavioral inhibition in young children. *Child Development, 55,* 1005–1019.

Garcia-Coll, C. T., Halpern, L. F., Vohr, B. R., Seifer, R., & Oh, W. (1992). Stability and correlates of change of early temperament in preterm and full-term infants. *Infant Behavior and Development, 15,* 137–153.

Gardner, H. (1981, July). [Interview with Howard Gruber]. Breakaway minds. *Psychology Today,* pp. 64–71.

Gardner, H. (1983). *Frames of mind: The theory of multiple intelligences.* New York: Basic Books.

Gardner, H. (1989, December). Learning, Chinese-style. *Psychology Today,* pp. 54–56.

Garland, J. B. (1982, March). *Social referencing and self-produced locomotion.* Paper presented at the meeting of the International Conference on International Studies, Austin, TX.

Garmezy, N. (1983). Stressors of childhood. In N. Garmezy & M. Rutter (Eds.), *Stress, coping and development in children.* New York: McGraw-Hill.

Garn, S. M. (1980). Continuities and change in maturational timing. In O. G. Brim, Jr., & J. Kagan (Eds.), *Constancy and change in human development.* Cambridge, MA: Harvard University Press.

Garner, D. M. (1993). Pathogenesis of anorexia nervosa. *The Lancet, 341,* 1631–1635.

Garrison, W. T., & Earls, F. J. (1986). Epidemiological perspectives on maternal depression and the young child. In E. Z. Tronick & T. Field (Eds.), *Maternal depression and infant disturbances.* San Francisco: Jossey-Bass.

Gavotos, L. A. (1959). Relationships and age differences in growth measures and motor skills. *Child Development, 30,* 333–340.

Geber, M. (1962). Longitudinal study and psychomotor development among Baganda children. *Proceedings of the Fourteenth International Congress of Applied Psychology, 3,* 50–60.

Geber, M., & Dean, R. F. A. (1957, June 16). The state of development of newborn African children. *The Lancet,* pp. 1216–1219.

Gecas, V., & Seff, M. A. (1990). Families and adolescents: A review of the 1980s.

Journal of Marriage and the Family, 52, 941–958.

Gelfand, D. E. (1982). *Aging: The ethnic factor.* Boston: Little, Brown.

Gelles, R. J., & Maynard, P. E. (1987). A structural family systems approach to intervention in cases of family violence. *Family Relations, 36,* 270–275.

Gelman, R., Bullock, M., & Meck, E. (1980). Preschoolers' understanding of simple object transformations. *Child Development, 51,* 691–699.

Gelman, R., Spelke, A., & Meck, E. (1983). [Work on animism in childhood].

General Mills, Inc. (1977). *Raising children in a changing society.* Minneapolis, MN: Author.

General Mills, Inc. (1981). *General Mills American family report 1980–81: Families at work: Strengths and strains.* Minneapolis, MN: Author.

Genevay, B. (1986). Intimacy as we age. *Generations, 10*(4), 12–15.

Gesell, A. (1929). Maturation and infant behavior patterns. *Psychological Review, 36,* 307–319.

Getzels, J. W. (1964). Creative thinking, problem-solving, and instruction. In *Yearbook of the National Society for the Study of Education,* Part 1, pp. 240–267. Chicago: University of Chicago Press.

Getzels, J. W. (1984, March). *Problem-finding and creativity in higher education.* [The Fifth Rev. Charles F. Donovan, S. J., Lecture]. Boston College, School of Education, Boston.

Getzels, J. W., & Jackson, P. W. (1962). *Creativity and intelligence: Explorations with gifted students.* New York: Wiley.

Gibson, R. C. (1986). Older black Americans. *Generations, 10*(4), 35–39.

Gil, D. G. (1971). Violence against children. *Journal of Marriage and the Family, 33*(4), 637–648.

Gilford, R. (1984). Contrasts in marital satisfaction throughout old age: An exchange theory analysis. *Journal of Gerontology, 39,* 325–333.

Gilford, R. (1986). Marriages later in life. *Generations, 10*(4), 16–20.

Gilford, R., & Bengston, V. (1979). Measuring marital satisfaction in three generations: Positive and negative dimensions. *Journal of Marriage and the Family, 41,* 387–398.

Gilligan, C. (1982). *In a different voice: Psychological theory and women's development.* Cambridge, MA: Harvard University Press.

Gilligan, C. (1987). Adolescent development reconsidered. In E. E. Irwin (Ed.), *Adolescent social behavior and health.* San Francisco: Jossey-Bass.

Ginsburg, H., & Miller, S. M. (1982). Sex differences in children's risk-taking behavior. *Child Development, 53,* 426–428.

Ginsburg, H., & Opper, S. (1979). *Piaget's theory of intellectual development* (2d ed.). Englewood Cliffs, NJ: Prentice-Hall.

Glass, R. B. (1986). Infertility. In S. S. C. Yen & R. B. Jaffe (Eds.), *Reproductive endocrinology: Physiology, pathophysiology, and clinical management* (2d ed.). Philadelphia: Saunders.

Gleitman, L. R., Newport, E. L., & Gleitman, H. (1984). The current status of the motherese hypothesis. *Journal of Child Language, 11,* 43–79.

Glenn, N. D. (1987). Marriage on the rocks. *Psychology Today, 21*(10), 20–21.

Glenn, N. D. (1991). The recent trend in marital success in the United States. *Journal of Marriage and the Family, 53,* 261–270.

Glenn, N. D., & McLanahan, S. (1981). The effects of offspring on the psychological well-being of older adults. *Journal of Marriage and the Family, 43*(2), 409–421.

Glick, J. (1975). Cognitive development in cross-cultural perspective. In F. Horowitz (Ed.), *Review of child development research,* Vol. 4, pp. 595–654. Chicago: University of Chicago Press.

Glick, P. C. (1988). Fifty years of family demography: A record of social change. *Journal of Marriage and the Family, 50,* 861–873.

Glick, P. C. (1989). Remarried families, stepfamilies, and stepchildren: A brief demographic profile. *Family Relations, 38,* 24–27.

Glick, P. C., & Lin, S.-L. (1986a). More young adults are living with their parents: Who are they? *Journal of Marriage and the Family, 48,* 107–112.

Glick, P. C., & Lin, S.-L. (1986b). Recent changes in divorce and remarriage. *Journal of Marriage and the Family, 48*(4), 737–747.

Golbus, M., Loughman, W., Epstein, C., Hallbasch, G., Stephens, J., & Hall, B. (1979). Prenatal genetic diagnosis in 3000 amniocenteses. *New England Journal of Medicine, 300*(4), 157–163.

Gold, D., & Andres, D. (1978a). Developmental comparison between adolescent children with employed and nonemployed mothers. *Merrill-Palmer Quarterly, 24,* 243–254.

Gold, D., & Andres, D. (1978b). Relations between maternal employment and development of nursery school children. *Canadian Journal of Behavioral Science, 10,* 116–129.

Gold, D., Andres, D., & Glorieux, J. (1979). The development of Francophone nursery-school children with employed and non-employed mothers. *Canadian Journal of Behavioral Science, 11,* 169–173.

Gold, M., & Yanof, D. S. (1985). Mothers, daughters, and girlfriends. *Journal of Personality and Social Psychology, 49*(3), 654–659.

Goldberg, E. L., Comstock, G. W., & Harlow, S. D. (1988). Emotional problems in widowhood. *Journal of Gerontology, 43*(6), S206–208.

Golden, M., Birns, B., & Bridger, W. (1973). *Review and overview: Social class and cognitive development.* Paper presented at the meeting of the Society for Research in Child Development, Philadelphia.

Goldman, L., & Toteson, A. N. A. (1991). Uncertainty about postmenopausal estrogen. *New England Journal of Medicine, 325*(11), 800–802.

Goldschmid, M. L., & Bentler, P. M. (1968). The dimensions and measurement of conservation. *Child Development, 39,* 787–815.

Goldsmith, M. F. (1989). 'Silent epidemic' or 'social disease' makes STD experts raise their voices. *Journal of the American Medical Association, 261*(24), 3509–3510.

Goleman, D. (1990a, April 24). Anger over racism is seen as a cause of blacks' high blood pressure. *The New York Times,* p. C3.

Goleman, D. (1990b, May 10). Why girls are prone to depression. *The New York Times,* p. B15.

Gopnick, A., & Meltzoff, A. (1987). Relations between semantic and cognitive development in the one-word stage: The specificity hypothesis. *Child Development, 57,* 1040–1053.

Gorbach, S. L., Zimmerman, D. R., & Woods, M. (1984). *The doctors' anti-breast cancer diet.* New York: Simon & Schuster.

Gordon, A. (1975). The Jewish view of death: Guidelines for mourning. In E. Kübler-Ross (Ed.), *Death: The final stage of growth.* Englewood Cliffs, NJ: Prentice-Hall.

Gortmaker, S. L., Dietz, W. H., Sobol, A. M., & Wehler, C. A. (1987). Increasing pediatric obesity in the United States. *American Journal of the Diseases of Childhood, 141,* 535–540.

Goslin, D. A. (Ed.). (1969). *Handbook of socialization theory and research.* Skokie, IL: Rand-McNally.

Gottesman, I. I. (1993). Origins of schizophrenia: Past and prologue. In R. P. Plomin & G. E. McClearn (Eds.), *Nature, nurture, and psychology.* Washington, DC: American Psychological Association.

Gottman, J. M., & Katz, L. F (1989). Effects of marital discord on young children's peer interaction and health. *Developmental Psychology, 25*(3), 373–381.

Gottman, J. M., & Krokoff, L. J. (1989). Marital interaction and satisfaction: A longitudinal view. *Journal of Consulting and Clinical Psychology, 57*(1), 47–52.

Gould, J. B., Davey, B., & Stafford, R. S. (1989). Socioeconomic differences in rates of cesarean section. *New England Journal of Medicine, 321*(4), 233–239.

Graziano, A. M., & Mooney, K. C. (1982). Behavioral treatment of "nightfears" in children: Maintenance and improvement at 2½ to 3-year-old follow-up. *Journal of Counseling and Clinical Psychology, 50*(4), 598–599.

Greenberg, J., & Becker, M. (1988). Aging parents as family resources. *Gerontologist, 28*(6), 786–790.

Greenberger, E., & Steinberg, L. (1986). *When teenagers work.* New York: Basic Books.

Greenhouse, L. (1990, June 26). Justices find a right to die, but the majority sees need for clear proof of intent. *The New York Times,* pp. A1, A18, A19.

Grief, E. B., & Ulman, K. J. (1982). The psychological impact of menarche on early adolescent females: A review of the literature. *Child Development, 53,* 1413–1430.

Gross, R. T., & Duke, P. (1980). The effect of early versus late maturation on adolescent behavior. In I. Litt (Ed.), *Symposium on adolescent medicine. Pediatric Clinics of North America, 27*(1), 71–78.

Grotevant, H., & Durrett, M. (1980). Occupational knowledge and career development in adolescence. *Journal of Vocational Behavior, 17,* 171–182.

Gruber-Baldini, A., & Schaie, K. W. (1986, November 21). *Longitudinal-sequential studies of marital assortivity.* Paper presented at the annual meeting of the Gerontological Society of America, Chicago.

Gruen, G., Korte, J., & Baum, J. (1974). Group measure of locus of control. *Developmental Psychology, 10*(5), 683–686.

Gruson, L. (1992, April 22). Gains in deciphering genes set off effort to guard data against abuses. *The New York Times,* p. C12.

Gualtieri, T., & Hicks, R. E. (1985). An immunoreactive theory of selective male affliction. *Behavioral and Brain Sciences, 8,* 427–441.

Gubrium, F. F. (1975). Being single in old age. *International Journal of Aging and Human Development, 6*(1), 29–41.

Guidubaldi, J., & Perry, J. D. (1985). Divorce and mental health sequelae for children: A two year follow-up of a nationwide sample. *Journal of the American Academy of Child Psychiatry, 24*(5), 531–537.

Guilford, J. P. (1959). Three faces of intellect. *American Psychologist, 14,* 469–479.

Gunnar, M. R., Larson, M. C., Hertsgaard, L., Harris, M. L., & Brodersen, L. (1992). The stressfulness of separation among nine-month-old infants: Effects of social context variables and infant temperament. *Child Development, 63,* 290–303.

Gunnersen, D., & Haley, B. (1992). Detection of glutamine synthetase in the cerebrospinal fluid of Alzheimer diseased patients: A potential diagnostic biochemical marker. *Proceedings of the National Academy of Sciences of the*

United States of America, 89(24), 11949–11953.

Guskin, J. P. (1990, Spring). State of the college address. *The Antiochian, 60,* 10–13.

Gutmann, D. (1975). Parenting: A key to the comparative study of the life cycle. In N. Datan & L. H. Ginsberg (Eds.), *Life-span developmental psychology: Normative life crises.* New York: Academic Press.

Gutmann, D. (1977). The cross-cultural perspective: Notes toward a comparative psychology of aging. In J. Birren & K. W. Schaie (Eds.), *Handbook of the psychology of aging.* New York: Van Nostrand Reinhold.

Gutmann, D. (1985). The parental imperative revisited. In J. Meachem (Ed.), *Family and individual development.* Basel: Karger.

Alan Guttmacher Institute. (1981). *Teenage pregnancy: The problem that hasn't gone away.* New York: Viking.

Haan, N. (1990). Personality at midlife. In S. Hunter & M. Sundel (Eds.), *Midlife myths.* Newbury Park, CA: Sage.

Haan, N., & Day, D. (1974). A longitudinal study of change and sameness in personality development: Adolescence to later adulthood. *International Journal of Aging and Human Development, 5*(1), 11–39.

Haddow, J. E., Palomaki, G. E., Knight, G. J., Williams, J., Polkkiner, A., Canick, J. A., Saller, D. N., & Bowers, G. B. (1992). Prenatal screening for Down's syndrome with use of material serum markers. *New England Journal of Medicine, 327,* 588–593.

Hadeed, A. J., & Siegel, S. R. (1989). Maternal cocaine use during pregnancy: Effect on the newborn infant. *Pediatrics, 84*(2), 205–210.

Hadley, J. (1984, July–August). Facts about childhood hyperactivity. *Children Today,* pp. 8–13.

Hagberg, B., Samuelsson, G., Lindberg, B., & Dehlin, O. (1991). Stability and change of personality in old age and its relation to survival. *Journal of Gerontology, 46*(6), P285–291.

Hagestad, G. O. (1978). *Patterns of communication and influence between grandparents and grandchildren in a changing society.* Paper presented at the meeting of the World Conference of Sociology, Uppsala, Sweden.

Hagestad, G. O. (1982). *Issues in the study of intergenerational continuity.* Paper presented at the National Council on Family Relations Theory and Methods Workshop, Washington, DC.

Hagestad, G. O. (1984). *Family transitions in adulthood: Some recent changes and their consequences.* Paper presented at the annual meeting of the Gerontological Society of America, San Antonio, TX.

Haith, M. M. (1986). Sensory and perceptual processes in early infancy. *Journal of Pediatrics, 109*(1), 158–171.

Hakuta, K., & Garcia, E. E. (1989). Bilingualism and education. *American Psychologist, 44*(2), 374–379.

Hall, E. (1983). A conversation with Erik Erikson. *Psychology Today, 17*(6), 22–30.

Hall, E. G., & Lee, A. M. (1984). Sex differences in motor performance of young children: Fact or fiction? *Sex Roles, 10,* 217–230.

Hall, G. S. (1916). *Adolescence.* New York: Appleton. (Original work published 1904.)

Hall, G. S. (1922). *Senescence: The last half of life.* New York: Appleton.

Hamer, D. H., Hu, S., Magnuson, V. L., Hu, N., & Pattatucci, A. M. L. (1993). A linkage between DNA markers on the X chromosome and male sexual orientation. *Science, 261,* 321–327.

Hamilton, S., & Crouter, A. (1980). Work and growth: A review of research on the impact of work experience on adolescent development. *Journal of Youth and Adolescence, 9*(4), 323–338.

Hammond, C. B., Jelovsek, F. R., Lee, K. L., Creasman, W. T., & Parker, R. T. (1979). Effects of long-term estrogen replacement therapy. II: Neoplasia. *American Journal of Obstetrics and Gynecology, 133,* 537–547.

Hamon, R. R., & Blieszner, R. (1990). Filial responsibility expectations among adult child-older parent pairs. *Journal of Gerontology, 45*(3), P110–112.

Handyside, A. H., Lesko, J. G., Tarín, J. J., Winston, R. M. L., & Hughes, M. R. (1992). Birth of a normal girl after in vitro fertilization and preimplantation diagnostic testing for cystic fibrosis. *New England Journal of Medicine, 327*(13), 905–909.

Hanley, R. (1988a, February 4). Surrogate deals for mothers held illegal in Jersey. *The New York Times,* pp. A1, B6.

Hanley, R. (1988b, February 4). Legislators are hesitant on regulating surrogacy. *The New York Times,* p. B7.

Hanson, S. M. H. (1988). Divorced fathers with custody. In P. Bronstein & C. P. Cowan (Eds.), *Fatherhood today: Men's changing role in the family.* New York: Wiley.

Hardy-Brown, K., & Plomin, R. (1985). Infant communicative development: Evidence from adoptive and biological families for genetic and environmental influences on rate differences. *Developmental Psychology, 21*(2), 378–385.

Hardy-Brown, K., Plomin, R., & DeFries, J. C. (1981). Genetic and environmental influences on rate of communicative development in the first year of life. *Developmental Psychology, 17,* 704–717.

Hare, P. H., & Haske, M. (1983–1984, December–January). Innovative living arrangements: A source of long-term care. *Aging,* pp. 3–8.

Harkins, E. (1978). Effects of empty nest transition on self-report of psychological and physical well-being. *Journal of Marriage and the Family, 40*(3), 549–556.

Harlow, H. F., & Harlow, M. K. (1962). The effect of rearing conditions on behavior. *Bulletin of the Menninger Clinic, 26,* 213–224.

Harlow, H. F., & Zimmerman, R. R. (1959). Affectional responses in the infant monkey. *Science, 130,* 421–432.

Harris, L., & Associates. (1986). *American teens speak: Sex, myths, TV and birth control: The Planned Parenthood poll.* New York: Planned Parenthood Federation of America.

Harris, R., & Bologh, R. W. (1985). The dark side of love: Blue- and white-collar wife abuse. *Victimology.*

Harrison, A. O., Wilson, M. N., Pine, C. J., Chan, S. Q., & Buriel, R. (1990). Family ecologies of ethnic minority children. *Child Development, 61,* 347–362.

Harrison, M. (1982). *Self-help for premenstrual syndrome.* Cambridge, MA: Matrix.

Hart, C. H., DeWolf, M., Wozniak, P., & Burts, D. C. (1992). Maternal and paternal disciplinary styles: Relations with preschoolers' playground behavioral orientation and peer status. *Child Development, 63,* 879–892.

Hart, C. H., Ladd, G. W., & Burleson, B. R. (1990). Children's expectations of the outcome of social strategies: Relations with sociometric status and maternal disciplinary style. *Child Development, 61,* 127–137.

Hart, S. N., & Brassard, M. R. (1987). A major threat to children's mental health: Psychological maltreatment. *American Psychologist, 42*(2), 160–165.

Hartmann, E. (1981). The strangest sleep disorder. *Psychology Today, 15*(4), 14–18.

Hartshorne, H., & May, M. A. (1928–1930). *Studies in the nature of character,* Vols. 1–3. New York: Macmillan.

Hartup, W. W. (1984). The peer context in middle childhood. In W. A. Collins (Ed.), *Development during middle childhood: The years from six to twelve.* Washington, DC: National Academy.

Hartup, W. W. (1989). Social relationships and their developmental significance. *American Psychologist, 44*(2), 120–126.

Harvard Medical School Health Letter. (1986, February). Suicide, Part 1. *2*(8), 1–4.

Harvey, B. (1990, April 30). Talk before the American Academy of Pediatrics Spring Session, Seattle.

Haskett, M. E., & Kistner, J. A. (1991). Social interaction and peer perceptions of young physically abused children. *Child Development, 62,* 979–990.

Haskins, R. (1989). Beyond metaphor: The efficacy of early childhood education. *American Psychologist, 44*(2), 274–282.

Haswell, K., Hock, E., & Wenar, C. (1981). Oppositional behavior of pre-

school children: Theory and prevention. *Family Relations, 30,* 440–446.

Haugh, S., Hoffman, C., & Cowan, G. (1980). The eye of the very young beholder: Sex typing of infants by young children. *Child Development, 51,* 598–600.

Hawkins, H. L., Kramer, A. F., & Capaldi, D. (1992). Aging, exercise, and attention. *Psychology and Aging, 7*(4), 643–653.

Hawley, T. L., & Disney, E. R. (1992). Crack's children: The consequences of maternal cocaine abuse. *Social Policy Report of the Society for Research in Child Development, VI*(4), 1–23.

Hay, D. F., Pedersen, J., & Nash, A. (1982). Dyadic interaction in the first year of life. In K. H. Rubin & H. S. Ross (Eds.), *Peer relationships and social skills in children.* New York: Springer.

Hayden, A., & Haring, N. (1976). Early intervention for high risk infants and young children: Programs for Down's syndrome children. In T. D. Tjossem (Ed.), *Intervention strategies for high risk infants and young children* (pp. 573–607). Baltimore: University Park Press.

Hayflick, L. (1974). The strategy of senescence. *Gerontologist, 14*(1), 37–45.

Hazen, N. L., & Black, B. (1989). Preschool peer communication skills: The role of social status and interaction context. *Child Development, 60,* 867–876.

Health Care Finance Administration. (1981). *Long term care: Background and future directions.* Washington, DC: U.S. Department of Health and Human Services.

Healy, B. (1991). The Yentl syndrome. *New England Journal of Medicine, 325*(4), 274–276.

Heard Museum of Anthropology and Primitive Art. (1987). [Curatorial notes for exhibit on Apache sunrise ceremony]. Phoenix, AZ.

Heller, Z. I. (1975). The Jewish view of dying: Guidelines for dying. In E. Kübler-Ross (Ed.), *Death: The final stage of growth.* Englewood Cliffs, NJ: Prentice-Hall.

Helmreich, W. (1991). *Against all odds: Holocaust survivors and the successful lives they made in America.* New York: Simon and Schuster.

Helson, R. (1992). Women's difficult times and the rewriting of the life story. *Psychology of Women Quarterly, 16,* 331–347.

Helson, R., & Moane, G. (1987). Personality change in women from college to midlife. *Journal of Personality and Social Psychology, 53*(1), 176–186.

Helson, R., & Picano, J. (1990). Is the traditional role bad for women? *Journal of Personality and Social Psychology, 59*(2), 311–320.

Helson, R., & Wink, P. (1992). Personality change in women from the early 40s to the early 50s. *Psychology and Aging, 7*(1), 46–55.

Henderson, A. (1987). *The evidence continues to grow: Parent involvement improves student achievement.* Columbia, MD: National Committee for Citizens in Education.

Henig, R. M. (1989, December 24). High-tech fortunetelling. *The New York Times Magazine,* pp. 20–22.

Henker, B., & Whalen, C. K. (1989). Hyperactivity and attention deficits. *American Psychologist, 44*(2), 216–223.

Henker, F. O. (1981). Male climacteric. In J. G. Howells (Ed.), *Modern perspectives in the psychiatry of middle age.* New York: Brunner/Mazel.

Henly, W. L., & Fitch, B. R. (1966). Newborn narcotic withdrawal associated with regional enteritis in pregnancy. *New York Journal of Medicine, 66,* 2565–2567.

Henrich, J. B. (1992). The postmenopausal estrogen/breast cancer controversy. *Journal of the American Medical Association, 268*(14), 1900–1902.

Hermanson, B., Omenn, G. S., Kronmal, R. A., Gersh, B. J., & Participants in the Coronary Artery Surgery Study. (1988). Beneficial six-year outcome of smoking cessation in older men and women with coronary artery disease. *New England Journal of Medicine, 319*(21), 1365–1369.

Herold, E. S., & Goodwin, M. S. (1981). Premarital sexual guilt and contraceptive attitudes and behavior. *Family Relations, 30,* 247–253.

Herzog, A. R., House, J. S., & Morgan, J. N. (1991). Relation of work and retirement to health and well-being in older age. *Psychology and Aging, 6*(2), 202–211.

Herzog, C. (1989). Influences of cognitive slowing on age differences in intelligence. *Developmental Psychology, 25*(4), 636–651.

Herzog, D. B., Keller, M. B., & Lavori, P. W. (1988). Outcome in anorexia nervosa and bulimia. *Journal of Nervous and Mental Diseases, 176,* 131–143.

Hess, T. M., Flannagan, D. A., & Tate, C. S. (1993). Aging and memory for schematically organized verbal material. *Journal of Gerontology, 48*(1), P37–44.

Hetherington, E. M. (1965). A developmental study of the effects of sex of the dominant parent on sex role preference, identification and imitation in children. *Journal of Personality and Social Psychology, 2,* 188–194.

Hetherington, E. M. (1980). Children and divorce. In R. Henderson (Ed.), *Parent-child interaction: Theory, research and prospect.* New York: Academic Press.

Hetherington, E. M. (1987). Family relations six years after divorce. In K. Pasley & M. Ihinger-Tallman (Eds.), *Remarriage and stepparenting: Current research and theory.* New York: Guilford.

Hetherington, E. M., Cox, M., & Cox, R. (1975). *Beyond father absence: Conceptualizing effects of divorce.* Paper presented at the meeting of the Society for Research in Child Development, Denver.

Hetherington, E. M., Stanley-Hagan, M., & Anderson, E. (1989). Marital transitions: A child's perspective. *American Psychologist, 44*(2), 303–312.

Hewlett, B. S. (1987). Intimate fathers: Patterns of paternal holding among Aka pygmies. In M. E. Lamb (Ed.), *The father's role: Cross-cultural perspectives.* Hillsdale, NJ: Erlbaum.

Heyns, B., & Catsambis, S. (1986). Mother's employment and children's achievement: A critique. *Sociology of Education, 59,* 140–151. [See also Reply to Milne, Myers, & Ginsburg, 154–155].

Hier, D. B., & Crowley, W. F. (1982). Spatial ability in androgen-deficient men. *New England Journal of Medicine, 20,* 1202–1205.

Hill, C. D., Thompson, L. W., & Gallagher, D. (1988). The role of anticipatory bereavement in older women's adjustment to widowhood. *Gerontologist, 28*(6), 792–796.

Hill, C. R., & Stafford, F. P. (1980). Parental care of children: Time diary estimate of quantity, predictability, and variety. *Journal of Human Resources, 15,* 219–239.

Hill, J. P. (1987). Research on adolescents and their families: Past and prospect. In E. E. Irwin (Ed.), *Adolescent social behavior and health.* San Francisco: Jossey-Bass.

Hill, R. D., Storandt, M., & Malley, M. (1993). The impact of exercise training on psychological function in older adults. *Journal of Gerontology, 48*(1), 12–17.

Hinds, M. (1991, July 17). Nationwide revolution in education is giving handicapped a headstart. *The New York Times,* p. A19.

Hinds, M. deC. (1985, January 31). For older people, communal living has its rewards. *The New York Times,* pp. C1, C8.

Hirsch, J. (1972). Can we modify the number of adipose cells? *Postgraduate Medicine, 51*(5), 83–86.

Hirsh-Pasek, K. (1991). Pressure or challenge in preschool? How academic environments affect children. In L. Rescorla, M. C. Hyston, & K. Hirsh-Pasek (Eds.), *Academic instruction in early childhood: Challenge or pressure?* San Francisco: Jossey-Bass.

Hirsh-Pasek, K., Hyson, M. C., & Rescorla, L. (1989, August). *Academic environments in early childhood: Challenge and pressure.* Paper presented at the annual meeting of the American Psychological Association, New Orleans.

Hoff-Ginsberg, E. (1985). Relations between discourse properties of mothers' speech and their children's syntactic growth. *Journal of Child Language, 12,* 367–385.

Hoff-Ginsberg, E. (1986). Function and structure in maternal speech: Their relation to the child's development of syntax. *Developmental Psychology, 22*(2), 155–163.

Hoff-Ginsberg, E. (1991). Mother-child conversation in different social classes and communicative settings. *Child Development, 62,* 782–796.

Hoff-Ginsberg, E., & Shatz, M. (1982). Linguistic input and the child's acquisition of language. *Psychological Bulletin, 92*(1), 3–26.

Hofferth, S. L. (1979). Day care in the next decade: 1980–1990. *Journal of Marriage and the Family, 41*(3), 649–658.

Hoffman, E. L., & Bennett, F. C. (1990). Birth weight less than 800 grams: Changing outcomes and influences of gender and gestation number. *Pediatrics, 86*(1), 27–34.

Hoffman, L. (1979). Maternal employment. *American Psychologist, 34*(10), 859–865.

Hoffman, L. (1986). Work, family, and the child. In M. S. Pallak & R. O. Perloff (Eds.), *Psychology and work: Productivity, change, and employment.* Washington, DC: American Psychological Association.

Hoffman, L. W. (1984). Work, family, and the socialization of the child. In R. D. Parke (Ed.), *The family.* Chicago: University of Chicago Press.

Hoffman, L. W. (1989). Effects of maternal employment in the two-parent family: A review of recent research. *American Psychologist, 44*(2), 283–292.

Hoffman, M. (1970). Moral development. In P. H. Mussen (Ed.), *Carmichael's manual of child psychology.* New York: Wiley.

Hoffman, M. (1977). Sex differences in empathy and related behaviors. *Psychological Bulletin, 84,* 712–722.

Hoffman, M., & Hoffman, L. W. (Eds.). (1964). *Review of child development research.* New York: Russell Sage Foundation.

Holmes, T. H., & Rahe, R. H. (1976). The social readjustment rating scale. *Journal of Psychosomatic Research, 11,* 213.

Holt, R. R. (1982). Occupational stress. In L. Goldberger & S. Breznitz (Eds.), *Handbook of stress.* New York: Free Press.

Hong, S., & Keith, P. M. (1992). The status of the aged in Korea: Are the modern more advantaged? *The Gerontologist, 32*(2), 197–202.

Honzik, M. P., Macfarlane, J. W., & Allen, L. (1948). The stability of mental test performance between two and 18 years. *Journal of Experimental Education, 17,* 309–323.

Hooker, E. (1957). The adjustment of the male overt homosexual. *Journal of Projective Techniques, 21,* 18–31.

Hooker, K., Monahan, D., Shifren, K., & Hutchinson, C. (1992). Mental and physical health of spouse caregivers: The role of personality. *Psychology and Aging, 7*(3), 367–375.

Hooyman, N. R., Rathbone-McCuan, E., & Klingbeil, K. (1982). Serving the vulnerable elderly. *Urban and Social Change Review, 15*(2), 9–13.

Hopper, J. L., & Seeman, E. (1994). The bone density of female twins discordant for tobacco use. *New England Journal of Medicine, 330,* 387–392.

Horn, J. (1983). The Texas adoption project: Adopted children and their intellectual resemblance to biological and adoptive parents. *Child Development, 54,* 268–275.

Horn, J. C., & Meer, J. (1987). The vintage years. *Psychology Today, 21*(5), 76–90.

Horn, J. L. (1967). Intelligence—Why it grows, why it declines. *Transition, 5*(1), 23–31.

Horn, J. L. (1968). Organization of abilities and the development of intelligence. *Psychological Review, 75,* 242–259.

Horn, J. L. (1970). Organization of data on life-span development of human abilities. In L. R. Goulet & P. B. Baltes (Eds.), *Life-span developmental psychology: Theory and research.* New York: Academic Press.

Horn, J. L., & Cattell, R. B. (1966). Age differences in primary mental ability factors. *Journal of Gerontology, 21,* 210–220.

Horn, J. L., & Donaldson, G. (1976). On the myth of intellectual decline in adulthood. *American Psychologist, 31,* 701–719.

Horn, J. L., & Donaldson, G. (1977). Faith is not enough: A response to the Baltes-Schaie claim that intelligence does not wane. *American Psychologist, 32,* 369–373.

Horn, J. L., & Donaldson, G. (1980). Cognitive development II: Adulthood development of human abilities. In O. G. Brim & J. Kagan (Eds.), *Constancy and change in human development.* Cambridge, MA: Harvard University Press.

Horn, J. L., & Hofer, S. M. (1992). Major abilities and development in the adult period. In R. J. Sternberg & C. A. Berg (Eds.), *Intellectual development.* Cambridge, England: Cambridge University Press.

Horner, R. D., Matchar, D. B., Divine, G. W., & Feussner, J. R. (1991). Racial variations in ischemic, stroke-related physical and function impairments. *Stroke, 22*(12), 1491–1501.

Horowitz, F. D. (1992). John B. Watson's legacy: Learning and environment. *Developmental Psychology, 28*(3), 360–367.

Horowitz, F. D., & O'Brien, M. (1986). Gifted and talented children: State of knowledge and directions for research. *American Psychologist, 41*(10), 1147–1152.

Horwitz, S. M., Leaf, P. J., Leventhal, J. M., Forsyth, B., & Speechley, K. N. (1992). Identification and management of psychosocial and developmental problems in community-based primary pediatrics practices. *Pediatrics,* 89(3), 480–485.

House, S. J., Landis, K. R., & Umberson, D. (1988). Social relationships and health. *Science, 241,* 540–544.

Householder, J., Hatcher, R. Burns, W., & Chasnoff, I. (1982). Infants born to narcotic-addicted mothers. *Psychological Bulletin, 92,* 453–468.

Howard, M. (1983). Postponing sexual involvement: A new approach. *SIECUS Report, 11*(4), 5–6, 8.

Howes, C., & Matheson, C. C. (1992). Sequences in the development of competent play with peers: Social and social pretend play. *Developmental Psychology, 28*(5), 961–974.

Howie, P. W., et al. (1990). Protective effect of breastfeeding against infection. *British Journal of Medicine, 300,* 11.

Hu, Y., & Goldman, N. (1990). Mortality differentials by marital status: An international comparison. *Demography, 27*(2), 233–250.

Hudson, J. I., & Pope, H. G. (1990). Affective spectrum disorder: Does antidepressant response identify a family of disorders with a common pathophysiology? *American Journal of Psychiatry, 147*(5), 552–564.

Hughes, M. (1975). *Egocentrism in preschool children.* Unpublished doctoral dissertation, Edinburgh University, Edinburgh.

Hultsch, D. F. (1971). Organization and memory in adulthood. *Human Development, 14,* 16–29.

Hultsch, D. F., & Dixon, R. A. (1990). Learning and memory in aging. In J. E. Birren & K. W. Schaie (Eds.), *Handbook of the Psychology of Aging.* San Diego: Academic Press.

Hultsch, D. F., Hammer, M., & Small, B. J. (1993). Age differences in cognitive performance in later life: Relationships to self-reported health and activity life style. *Journal of Gerontology, 48*(1), P1–11.

Humphrey, L. L. (1986). Structural analysis of parent-child relationships in eating disorders. *Journal of Abnormal Psychology, 95*(4), 395–402.

Hunt, B., & Hunt, M. (1974). *Prime time.* New York: Stein & Day.

Hunt, C. E., & Brouillette, R. T. (1987). Sudden infant death syndrome: 1987 perspective. *Journal of Pediatrics, 110*(5), 669–678.

Hunt, M. M. (1974). *Sexual behavior in the 1970's.* New York: Dell.

Hurd, M. D. (1989). The economic status of the elderly. *Science, 244,* 659–664.

Hurwich, C. (1982). *Vital women in their seventies and eighties.* Unpublished thesis, Antioch University West, San Francisco.

Huston, A. C., Wright, J. C., Rice, M. L., Kerkman, D., & St. Petes, M. (1990). Development of television viewing patterns in early childhood: A longi-

tudinal investigation. *Developmental Psychology, 26*(3), 409–420.

Huttenlocher, J., Haight, W., Bryk, A., Seltzer, M., & Lyons, T. (1991). Early vocabulary growth: Relation to language input and gender. *Developmental Psychology, 27*(2), 236–248.

Hwang, C.-P., & Broberg, A. G. (1992). The historical and social context of child care in Sweden. In M. D. Lamb, K. J. Sternberg, C.-P. Hwang, & A. G. Broberg (Eds.), *Child care in context.* Hillsdale, NJ: Erlbaum.

Hyde, J., & Linn, M. C. (1988). Gender differences in verbal abilities: A meta-analysis. *Psychological Bulletin, 104*(1), 53–69.

Hyde, J. S. (1986). *Understanding human sexuality* (3d ed.). New York: McGraw-Hill.

Hyde, J. S., Fennema, E., & Lamon, S. J. (1990). Gender differences in mathematics performance: A meta-analysis. *Psychological Bulletin, 107*(2), 139–155.

Hyman, B. T., Van Hoesen, G. W., Damasio, A. R., & Barnes, C. L. (1984). Alzheimer's disease: Cell-specific pathology isolates hippocampal formation. *Science, 225,* 1168–1170.

Hynd, G. W., & Semrud-Clikeman, M. (1989). Dyslexia and brain morphology. *Psychological Bulletin, 106*(3), 447–482.

Infant Health and Development Program. (1990). Enhancing the outcomes of low-birth-weight, premature infants. *Journal of the American Medical Association, 263*(22), 3035–3042.

Infante-Rivard, C., Fernández, A., Gauthier, R., David, M., & Rivard, G.-E. (1993). Fetal loss associated with caffeine intake before and during pregnancy. *Journal of the American Medical Association, 270,* 2940–2943.

Ingram, D. D., Makuc, D., & Kleinman, J. C. (1986). National and state trends in use of prenatal care, 1970–1983. *American Journal of Public Health, 76*(4), 415–423.

Institute for Social Research. (1985). How children use time. In *Time, goods and well-being.* Ann Arbor: University of Michigan.

Interagency Committee on Learning Disabilities. (1987). *Learning disabilities: A report to the U. S. Congress.*

Isabella, R. A., Belsky, J., & von Eye, A. (1989). Origins of mother-infant attachment: An examination of interactional synchrony during the infant's first year. *Developmental Psychology, 25*(1), 12–21.

Izard, C. E. (1971). *The face of emotions.* New York: Appleton-Century-Crofts.

Izard, C. E. (1977). *Human emotions.* New York: Plenum.

Izard, C. E., Huebner, R. R., Resser, D., McGinness, G. C., & Dougherty, L. M. (1980). The young infant's ability to produce discrete emotional expres-

sions. *Developmental Psychology, 16*(2), 132–140.

Izard, C. E., & Malatesta, C. Z. (1987). Perspectives on emotional development I: Differential emotions theory of early emotional development. In J. D. Osofsky (Ed.), *Handbook of infant development* (2d ed.). New York: Wiley.

Jacklin, C. N. (1989). Female and male: Issues of gender. *American Psychologist, 44*(2), 127–133.

Jacobson, J. L., Jacobson, S. W., Fein, G. G., Schwartz, P. M., & Dowler, J. K. (1984). Prenatal exposure to an environmental toxin: A test of the multiple effects model. *Developmental Psychology, 20*(4), 523–532.

Jacobson, J. L., Jacobson, S. W., & Humphrey, H. E. B. (1990). Effects of in utero exposure to polychlorinated biphenyls and related contaminants on cognitive functioning in young children. *Journal of Pediatrics, 116,* 38–45.

Jacobson, J. L., Jacobson, S. W., Padgett, R. J., Brumitt, G. A., & Billings, R. L. (1992). Effects of prenatal exposure on cognitive processing and efficiency and sustained attention. *Developmental Psychology, 28*(2), 297–306.

Jacobson, J. L., & Wille, D. E. (1986). The influence of attachment pattern on developmental changes in peer interaction from the toddler to the preschool period. *Child Development, 57,* 338–347.

Jacobson, S. W., Fein, G. G., Jacobson, J. L., Schwartz, P. M., & Dowler, J. K. (1985). The effect of intrauterine PCB exposure on visual recognition memory. *Child Development, 56,* 853–860.

Jacobson, S. W., Jacobson, J. L., & Frye, K. F. (1991). Incidence and correlates of breast-feeding in socioeconomically disadvantaged women. *Pediatrics, 88,* 728–736.

Jacques, E. (1967). The mid-life crisis. In R. Owen (Ed.), *Middle age.* London: BBC.

Janos, P. M., & Robinson, N. M. (1985). Psychosocial development in intellectually gifted children. In F. D. Horowitz & M. O'Brien (Eds.), *The gifted and talented: Developmental perspectives* (pp. 251–295). Washington, DC: American Psychological Association.

Jarvik, L. F., Kallmann, F., & Klaber, N. M. (1957). Changing intellectual functions in senescent twins. *Acta Genetic Statistica Medica, 7,* 421–430.

Jaslow, C. K. (1982). *Teenage pregnancy* (ERIC/CAPS Fact Sheet). Ann Arbor, MI: Counseling and Personnel Services Clearinghouse.

Jason, J. M. (1989). Infectious disease-related deaths of low birth weight infants, United States, 1968 to 1982. *Pediatrics, 84*(2), 296–303.

Jay, M. S., DuRant, R. H., Shoffitt, T., Linder, C. W., & Litt, I. F. (1984). Effect of peer counselors on adolescent compliance in use of oral contraceptives. *Pediatrics, 73*(2), 126–131.

Jelliffe, D., & Jelliffe, E. (1974). *Fat babies: Prevalence, perils and prevention.* London: Incentive Press.

Jensen, A. R. (1969). How much can we boost IQ and scholastic achievement? *Harvard Educational Review, 39,* 1–123.

Jersild, A. T., & Holmes, F. (1935). Children's fears. *Child Development Monographs, 6*(Whole No. 20).

Jiao, S., Ji, G., & Jing, Q. (1986). Comparative study of behavioral qualities of only children and sibling children. *Child Development, 57,* 357–361.

Johnson, C. L., & Catalano, D. J. (1981). Childless elderly and their family supports. *Gerontologist, 21*(6), 610–618.

Johnson, C. L., & Troll, L. (1992). Family functioning in late late life. *Journal of Gerontology, 47*(2), S66–72.

Johnson, R. K., Smiciklas-Wright, H., Crouter, C., & Willits, F. K. (1992). Maternal employment and the quality of young children's diets: Empirical evidence based on the 1987–1988 nationwide food consumption inquiry. *Pediatrics, 90*(2), 245–249.

Johnston, L. D., Bachman, J. G., & O'Malley, P. M. (1982). *Student drug use, attitudes, and beliefs: National trends, 1975–1982.* Rockville, MD: National Institute on Drug Abuse.

Jones, D. C., Swift, D. J., & Johnson, M. A. (1988). Nondeliberate memory for a novel event among preschoolers. *Developmental Psychology, 24*(5), 641–645.

Jones, E. (1961). *The life and work of Sigmund Freud* (Edited and abridged by L. Trilling & S. Marcus). New York: Basic Books.

Jones, E. F., Forrest, J. D., Goldman, N., Henshaw, S. K., Lincoln, R., Rosoff, J. I., Westoff, C. F., Wulf, W., & Wulf, D. (1985). Teenage pregnancy in developed countries: Determinants and policy implications. *Family Planning Perspectives, 17,* 53–63.

Jones, M. C. (1957). The late careers of boys who were early- or late-maturing. *Child Development, 28,* 115–128.

Jones, H., & Conrad, H. (1933). The growth and decline of intelligence: A study of a homogeneous group between the ages of 10 and 60. *Genetic Psychology Monographs, 13,* 223–298.

Jones, M. C. (1958). The study of socialization patterns at the high school level. *Journal of Genetic Psychology, 93,* 87–111.

Jones, M. C., & Mussen, P. H. (1958). Self-conceptions, motivations, and interpersonal attitudes of early- and late-maturing girls. *Child Development, 29,* 491–501.

Jones, R. O., Nagashima, A. W., Hartnett-Goodman, M. M., & Goodlin, R. C. (1991). Rupture of low transverse cesarean scars during trial of labor. *Obstetrics and Gynecology, 77*(6), 815–817.

Jost, H., & Sontag, L. (1944). The genetic factor in autonomic nervous system function. *Psychosomatic Medicine, 6,* 308–310.

Juggling family, job, and aged dependent. (1989, January 26). *The New York Times,* p. B8.

Jung, C. G. (1953). The stages of life. In H. Read, M. Fordham, & G. Adler (Eds.), *Collected works,* Vol. 2. Princeton, NJ: Princeton University Press. (Original work published 1931.)

Jung, C. G. (1966). Two essays on analytic psychology. In *Collected works,* Vol. 7. Princeton, NJ: Princeton University Press.

Kagan, J. (1958). The concept of identification. *Psychological Review, 65*(5), 296–305.

Kagan, J. (1971). *Personality development.* New York: Harcourt Brace Jovanovich.

Kagan, J. (1982). Canalization of early psychological development. *Pediatrics, 70*(3), 474–483.

Kagan, J. (1989). *Unstable ideas: Temperament, cognition, and self.* Cambridge, MA: Harvard University Press.

Kagan, J., Reznick, J. S., Clarke, C., Snidman, N., & Garcia-Coll, C. (1984). Behavioral inhibition to the unfamiliar. *Child Development, 55,* 2212–2225.

Kahana, B., & Kahana, E. (1970). Grandparents from the perspective of the developing grandchild. *Developmental Psychology, 3*(1), 98–105.

Kalmuss, D., Davidson, A., & Cushman, L. (1992). Parental expectations, experiences, and adjustment to parenthood: A test of the violated expectations framework. *Journal of Marriage and the Family, 54,* 516–526.

Kalmuss, D. S., & Straus, M. A. (1982). Wife's marital dependency and wife abuse. *Journal of Marriage and the Family, 44,* 277–286.

Kamin, L. J. (1974). *The science and politics of IQ.* Potomac, MD: Erlbaum.

Kamo, Y. (1988). Determinants of the household division of labor: Resources, power, and ideology. *Journal of Family Issues, 9,* 177–200.

Kandel, D. B., Davies, M., Karus, D., & Yamaguchi, K. (1986). The consequences in young adulthood of adolescent drug involvement. *Archives of General Psychiatry, 43,* 746–754.

Kane, R. I., Wales, J., Bernstein, L., Leibowitz, A., & Kaplan, S. (1984, April 21). A randomized controlled trial of hospice care. *The Lancet,* pp. 890–894.

Kaplan, H., & Dove, H. (1987). Infant development among the Ache of East Paraguay. *Developmental Psychology, 23*(2), 190–198.

Kastenbaum, R. (1977). The kingdom where nobody dies. In S. Zarit (Ed.), *Readings in aging and death: Contemporary perspectives.* New York: Harper & Row.

Katz, L. (1987). Early education: What should young children be doing? In S. L. Kagan & E. F. Zigler (Eds.), *Early schooling: The national debate.* New Haven, CT: Yale University Press.

Katz, P. A. (1987). Variations in family constellation: Effects on gender schemata. In L. S. Liben & M. L. Signorella (Eds.), *Children's gender schemata.* San Francisco: Jossey-Bass.

Katz, S., Branch, L. G., Branson, M. H., Papsidero, J. A., Beck, J. C., & Greer, D. S. (1983). Active life expectancy. *New England Journal of Medicine, 309,* 1218–1224.

Kaufman, J., & Zigler, E. (1987). Do abused children become abusive parents? *American Journal of Orthopsychiatry, 57*(2), 186–192.

Kausler, D. H. (1990). Automaticity of encoding and episodic memory processes. In E. A. Lovelace (Ed.), *Aging and cognition: Mental processes, self awareness, and interventions.* North Holland: Elsevier.

Kawachi, I., Colditz, G. A., Stampfer, M. J., Willett, W. C., Manson, J. E., Rosner, B., Speizer, F. E., & Hennekens, C. H. (1993). Smoking cessation and decreased risk of stroke in women. *Journal of the American Medical Association, 269,* 232–236.

Kaye, W. H., Weltzin, T. E., Hsu, L. K. G., & Bulik, C. M. (1991). An open trial of fluoxetine in patients with anorexia nervosa. *The Journal of Clinical Psychiatry, 52,* 464–471.

Kayser-Jones, J. A. (1982). Institutional structures: Catalysts of or barriers to quality care for the institutionalized aged in Scotland and the U. S. *Social Science Medicine, 16,* 935–944.

Keating, N., & Cole, P. (1980). What do I do with him 24 hours a day? Changes in the housewife role after retirement. *Gerontologist, 20,* 84–89.

Keeney, T. J., Canizzo, S. R., & Flavell, J. H. (1967). Spontaneous and induced verbal rehearsal in a recall task. *Child Development, 38,* 953–966.

Keith, P. M. (1983). A comparison of the resources of parents and childless men and women in very old age. *Family Relations, 32,* 403–409.

Kellermann, A. L., Rivara, F. P., Somes, G., Reay, D. T., Francisco, J., Banton, J. G., Prodzinski, J., Flinger, C., & Hackman, B. B. (1992). Suicide in the home in relation to gun ownership. *New England Journal of Medicine, 327,* 467–472.

Kelley, J. L., Power, T. G., & Wimbush, D. D. (1992). Determinants of disciplinary practices in low-income black mothers. *Child Development, 63,* 573–582.

Kelly, J. B. (1982). Divorce: The adult perspective. In B. Wolman (Ed.), *Handbook of developmental psychology.* Englewood Cliffs, NJ: Prentice-Hall.

Kelly, J. B. (1987, August). *Longer-term adjustment in children of divorce: Converging findings and implications for practice.* Paper presented at the annual meeting of the American Psychological Association, New York.

Kelly, O. (1978). Living with a life-threatening illness. In M. C. Garfield (Ed.), *Psychosocial care of the dying patient* (pp. 59–66). New York: McGraw-Hill.

Kempe, C. H., et al. (1962). The battered child syndrome. *Journal of the American Medical Association, 181*(Part1), 17–24.

Kemper, P., & Murtaugh, C. M. (1991). Lifetime use of nursing home care. *New England Journal of Medicine, 324*(8), 595–600.

Kendall-Tackett, K. A., Williams, L. M., & Finkelhor, D. (1993). Impact of sexual abuse on children: A review and synthesis of recent empirical studies. *Psychological Bulletin, 113*(1), 164–180.

Kendler, K. S., Heath, A. C., Neale, M. C., Kessler, R. C., & Eaves, L. J. (1992). A population-based twin study of alcoholism in women. *Journal of the American Medical Association, 268*(14), 1877–1882.

Kennell, J., Klaus, M., McGrath, S., Robertson, S., & Hinckley, C. (1991). Continuous emotional support during labor in a US hospital. *Journal of the American Medical Association, 265,* 2197–2201.

Kerr, B. A. (1985). *Smart girls, gifted women.* Columbus, OH: Ohio Psychology.

Kessen, W., Haith, M., Salapatek, P. (1970). Infancy. In P. H. Mussen (Ed.), *Carmichael's manual of the child psychology,* Vol. 1 (3d ed.). New York: Wiley.

Kessler-Harris, A. (1987). The debate over equality for women in the workplace: Recognizing differences. In N. Gerstel & H. E. Gross (Eds.), *Families and work.* Philadelphia: Temple University Press.

Kestenbaum, R., Farber, E. A., & Sroufe, L. A. (1989). Individual differences in empathy among preschoolers: Relation to attachment history. In N. Eisenberg (Ed.), Empathy and related emotional responses. *New Directions in Child Development, 44.* San Francisco: Jossey-Bass.

Ketcham, D. (1990, September 30). About Long Island: The loneliness of divorce. *The New York Times,* pp. L.I. 1, 11.

Ketcham, D. (1993, March 14). About Long Island: When children have to deal with a loved one's death. *The New York Times,* p. L.I. 2

Kimmel, D. C. (1980). *Adulthood and aging* (2d ed.). New York: Wiley.

Kimmel, D. C. (1988). Ageism, psychology, and public policy. *American Psychologist, 43*(3), 175–178.

Kimura, D. (1989, November). Monthly fluctuation in sex hormones affect women's cognitive skills. *Psychology Today,* pp. 63–66.

King, D. (1993, March). Age-old questions [Letter to the editor]. *New Woman,* p. 14.

Kinsey, A. C., Pomeroy, W., & Martin, C. D. (1948). *Sexual behavior in the human male.* Philadelphia: Saunders.

Kinsey, A. C., Pomeroy, W., Martin, C. E., & Gebhard, P.H. (1953). *Sexual behavior in the human female.* Philadelphia: Saunders.

Kite, M. E., & Johnson, B. T. (1988). Attitudes toward older and younger adults: A meta-analysis. *Psychology and Aging, 3*(3), 232–244.

Kitson, G. C., & Morgan, L. A. (1990). The multiple consequences of divorce: A decade review. *Journal of Marriage and the Family, 52,* 913–924.

Kitson, G. C., & Roach, M. J. (1989). Independence and social and psychological adjustment in widowhood and divorce. In D. A. Lund (Ed.), *Older bereaved spouses: Research with practical implications.* New York: Hemisphere Press.

Kivett, V. R. (1991). Centrality of the grandfather role among older rural Black and white men. *Journal of Gerontology, 46*(5), S250–258.

Klaus, M. H., & Kennell, J. H. (1976). *Maternal-infant bonding.* St. Louis: Mosby.

Klaus, M. H., & Kennell, J. H. (1982). *Parent-infant bonding* (2d ed.). St. Louis: Mosby.

Klebanoff, M. A., Shiono, P. H., & Rhoads, G. G. (1990). Outcome of pregnancy in a national sample of resident physicians. *New England Journal of Medicine, 323,* 1040–1045.

Kleinberg, F. (1984). Sudden infant death syndrome. *Mayo Clinic Proceedings, 59,* 352–357.

Kleinman, J. C., Cooke, M., Machlin, S., & Kessel, S. S. (1983). *Variations in use of obstetric technology* (DHHS Publication No. PHS 84-1232). Washington, DC: U.S. Government Printing Office.

Kleinman, J. C., & Kiely, J. L. (1990). Postneonatal mortality in the United States: An international perspective. *Pediatrics, 86*(6, Pt. 2), 1091–1097.

Klerman, G. L. (1989). Treatment of alcoholism. *New England Journal of Medicine, 320*(6), 394–395.

Klerman, G. L., & Weissman, M. M. (1989). Increasing rates of depression. *Journal of the American Medical Association, 261,* 2229–2235.

Klesges, R. C., Shelton, M. L., & Klesges, L. M. (1993). Effects of television on metabolic rate: Potential implications for childhood obesity. *Pediatrics, 91*(2), 281–295.

Kline, D. W., Kline, T. J. B., Fozard, J. L., Kosnik, W., Schieber, F., & Sekuler, R. (1992). Vision, aging, and driving: The problems of older drivers. *Journal of Gerontology, 47*(1), P27–34.

Kline, M., Johnston, J. R., & Tschann, J. M. (1991). The long shadow of marital conflict: A model of children's postdivorce adjustment. *Journal of Marriage and the Family, 53,* 297–309.

Kline, M., Tshann, J. M., Johnston, J. R., & Wallerstein, J. S. (1989). Children's adjustment in joint and sole physical custody families. *Developmental Psychology, 25*(3), 430–438.

Knitzer, J. (1984). Mental health services to children and adolescents. *American Psychologist, 39,* 905–911.

Kochanska, G. (1992). Children's interpersonal influence with mothers and peers. *Developmental Psychology, 28*(3), 491–499.

Koenig, H. G., George, L. K., & Siegler, I. C. (1988). The use of religion and other emotion-regulating coping strategies among older adults. *Gerontologist, 28*(3), 303–310.

Koenig, H. G., Kvale, J. N., & Ferrel, C. (1988). Religion and well-being in later life. *Gerontologist, 28*(1), 18–28.

Koff, E., Rierdan, J., & Sheingold, K. (1982). Memories of menarche: Age, preparation, and prior knowledge as determinants of initial menstrual experience. *Journal of Youth and Adolescence, 11,* 1–9.

Kohlberg, L. (1966). A cognitive-developmental analysis of children's sex-role concepts and attitudes. In E. E. Maccoby (Ed.), *The development of sex differences.* Stanford, CA: Stanford University Press.

Kohlberg, L. (1968). The child as a moral philosopher. *Psychology Today, 2*(4), 25–30.

Kohlberg, L. (1969). Stage and sequence: The cognitive-developmental approach to socialization. In D. A. Goslin (Ed.), *Handbook of socialization theory and research.* Chicago: Rand McNally.

Kohlberg, L. (1973). Continuities in childhood and adult moral development revisited. In P. Baltes & K. W. Schaie (Eds.), *Life-span developmental psychology: Personality and socialization.* New York: Academic Press.

Kohlberg, L. (1981). *Essays on moral development.* San Francisco: Harper & Row.

Kohlberg, L., & Gilligan, C. (1971, Fall). The adolescent as a philosopher: The discovery of the self in a postconventional world. *Daedalus,* pp. 1051–1086.

Kohlberg, L., Yaeger, J., & Hjertholm, E. (1968). Private speech: Four studies and a review of theories. *Child Development, 39,* 691–736.

Kohn, M. L. (1980). Job complexity and adult personality. In N. J. Smelser & E. H. Erikson (Eds.), *Themes of work and love in adulthood.* Cambridge, MA: Harvard University Press.

Kolata, G. (1986). Obese children: A growing problem. *Science, 232,* 20–21.

Kolata, G. (1988, March 29). Fetuses treated through umbilical cords. *The New York Times,* p. C3.

Kolata, G. (1992, April 5). A malformed infant's brief life forces an issue of medical ethics. *The New York Times,* p. E2.

Kolb, B. (1989). Brain development, plasticity, and behavior. *American Psychologist, 44*(9), 1203–1212.

Koocher, G. (1973). Childhood, death, and cognitive development. *Developmental Psychology, 9,* 369–375.

Kopp, C. B. (1982). Antecedents of self-regulation. *Developmental Psychology, 18*(2), 199–214.

Kopp, C. B., & Kaler, S. R. (1989). Risk in infancy: Origins and implications. *American Psychologist, 44*(2), 224–230.

Kopp, C. B., & McCall, R. B. (1982). Predicting later mental performance for normal, at-risk, and handicapped infants. In P. B. Baltes & O. G. Brim (Eds.), *Life-span development and behavior,* Vol. 4. New York: Academic Press.

Korner, A. F., Zeanah, C. H., Linden, J., Berkowitz, R. I., Kraemer, H. C., & Agras, W. S. (1985). The relationship between neonatal and later activity and temperament. *Child Development, 56,* 38–42.

Kosnik, W., Winslow, L., Kline, D., Rasinski, K., & Sekuler, R. (1988). Visual changes in daily life throughout adulthood. *Journal of Gerontology, 43*(3), P63–70.

Kotelchuck, M. (1973, March). *The nature of the infant's tie to his father.* Paper presented at the meeting of the Society for Research in Child Development, Philadelphia.

Kraemer, H. C., Korner, A., Anders, T., Jacklin, C. N., & Dimiceli, S. (1985). Obstetric drugs and infant behavior: A reevaluation. *Journal of Pediatric Psychology, 10,* 345–353.

Kramer, J., Hill, K., & Cohen, L. (1975). Infants' development of object permanence: A refined methodology and new evidence for Piaget's hypothesized ordinality. *Child Development, 46,* 149–155.

Krauss, R., & Glucksberg, S. (1977). Social and nonsocial speech. *Scientific American, 263*(2), 100–105.

Kreutzer, M., & Charlesworth, W. R. (1973, March). *Infant recognition of emotions.* Paper presented at the meeting of the Society for Research in Child Development, Philadelphia.

Kreutzer, M., Leonard, C., & Flavell, J. (1975). An interview study of children's knowledge about memory. *Monographs of the Society for Research in Child Development, 40*(1, Serial No. 159).

Kristof, N. D. (1990, December 6). At 102, he's back in school, with many like him. *The New York Times,* p. A4.

Kristof, N. D. (1991, June 17). A mystery from China's census: Where have young girls gone? *The New York Times,* pp. A1, A8.

Kristof, N. D. (1993, April 25). China's crackdown on births: A stunning, and harsh, success. *The New York Times,* pp. A1, 12.

Kropp, J. P., & Haynes, O. M. (1987). Abusive and nonabusive mothers' ability to identify general and specific emotional signals of infants. *Child Development, 58,* 187–190.

Kruper, J. C., & Uzgiris, I. (1987). Fathers' and mothers' speech to young infants. *Journal of Psycholinguistic Research, 16*(6), 597–614.

Ku, L. C., Sonenstein, F. L., & Pleck, J. H. (1992). The association of AIDS education and sex education with sexual behavior and condom use among teenage men. *Family Planning Perspectives, 24,* 100–106.

Kübler-Ross, E. (1969). *On death and dying.* New York: Macmillan.

Kübler-Ross, E. (1970). *On death and dying* (paperback ed.). New York: Macmillan.

Kübler-Ross, E. (Ed.). (1975). *Death: The final stage of growth.* Englewood Cliffs, NJ: Prentice-Hall.

Kuhl, P. K., Williams, K. A., Lacerda, F., Stevens, K. N., & Lindblom, B. (1992). Linguistic experience alters phonetic perception in infants by 6 months of age. *Science, 255,* 606–608.

Kunkel, S. R., & Applebaum, R. A. (1992). Estimating the prevalence of long-term disability for an aging society. *Journal of Gerontology, 47*(5), S253–260.

Kupersmidt, J. B., & Coie, J. D. (1990). Preadolescent peer status, aggression, and school adjustment as predictors of externalizing problems in adolescence. *Child Development, 61,* 1350–1362.

Kupfersmid, J., & Wonderly, D. (1980). Moral maturity and behavior: Failure to find a link. *Journal of Youth and Adolescence, 9*(3), 249–261.

Kutner, L. (1990, August 2). Parent & child. *The New York Times,* p. C8.

Labbok, M. H., & Hendershot, G. E. (1987). Does breastfeeding protect against malocclusion? An analysis of the 1981 child health supplement to the National Health Interview Survey. *American Journal of Preventive Medicine, 3,* 4.

Labouvie-Vief, G. (1985). Intelligence and cognition. In J. E. Birren & K. W. Schaie (Eds.), *Handbook of the psychology of aging* (2d ed.). New York: Van Nostrand Reinhold.

Labouvie-Vief, G. (1986). Modes of knowledge and the organization of development. In M. L. Commons, L. Kohlberg, F. Richards, & J. Sinnott (Eds.), *Beyond formal operations 3: Models and methods in the study of adult and adolescent thought.* New York: Praeger.

Labouvie-Vief, G., Adams, C., Hakim-Larson, J., Hayden, M., & DeVoe, M. (1987). *Modes of text processing from preadolescence to mature adulthood.* Unpublished manuscript, Wayne State University, Detroit.

Labouvie-Vief, G., & Hakim-Larson, J. (1989). Developmental shifts in adult thought. In S. Hunter & M. Sondel (Eds.), *Midlife myths.* Newbury Park, CA: Sage.

Labouvie-Vief, G., Schell, D. A., & Weaver-dyck, S. E. (1982). *Recall deficit in the aged: A fable recalled.* Unpublished manuscript, Wayne State University, Detroit.

Lachman, J. L., & Lachman, R. (1980). Age and the acquisition of world knowledge. In L. W. Poon, J. L. Fozard, L. S. Cermak, D. Arenberg, & L. W. Thompson (Eds.), *New directions in memory and aging.* Hillsdale, NJ: Erlbaum.

Ladd, G. W., & Colter, B. S. (1988). Parents' management of preschooler's peer relations: Is it related to children's social competence? *Developmental Psychology, 24*(1), 109–117.

Lagercrantz, H., & Slotkin, T. A. (1986). The "stress" of being born. *Scientific American, 254*(4), 100–107.

Lamb, M. E. (1977). Father-infant and mother-infant interaction in the first year of life. *Child Development, 48,* 167–181.

Lamb, M. E. (1978). Influence of the child on marital quality and family interaction during the prenatal, perinatal, and infancy periods. In R. Lerner & G. Spanier (Eds.), *Child influences on marital and family interaction: A life-span perspective.* New York: Academic.

Lamb, M. E. (1981). The development of father-infant relationships. In M. E. Lamb (Ed.), *The role of the father in child development* (2d ed.). New York: Wiley.

Lamb, M. E. (1982a). The bonding phenomenon: Misinterpretations and their implications. *Journal of Pediatrics, 101*(4), 555–557.

Lamb, M. E. (1982b). Early contact and maternal-infant bonding: One decade later. *Pediatrics, 70*(5), 763–768.

Lamb, M. E. (1987a). Predictive implications of individual differences in attachment. *Journal of Consulting and Clinical Psychology, 55*(6), 817–824.

Lamb, M. E. (1987b). *The father's role: Cross-cultural perspectives.* Hillsdale, NJ: Erlbaum.

Lamb, M. E., Campos, J. J., Hwang, C. P., Leiderman, P. H., Sagi, A., & Svejda, M. (1983). Maternal-infant bonding: A joint rebuttal. *Pediatrics, 72*(4), 574–575.

Lamb, M. E., Frodi, A. M., Frodi, M., & Hwang, C. P. (1982). Characteristics of maternal and paternal behavior in traditional and non-traditional Swedish families. *International Journal of Behavior Development, 5,* 131–151.

Lamb, M. E., Frodi, M., Hwang, C. P., & Frodi, A. M. (1983). Effects of paternal involvement on infant preferences for mothers and fathers. *Child Development, 54,* 450–458.

Lamb, M. E., & Sternberg, K. J. (1992). Sociocultural perspectives on nonparental child care. In M. D. Lamb, K. J. Sternberg, C-P. Hwang, & A. G.

Broberg (Eds.), *Child care in context.* Hillsdale, NJ: Erlbaum.

Lamborn, S. D., Mounts, N. S., Steinberg, L., & Dornbusch, S. M. (1991). Patterns of competence and adjustment among adolescents from authoritative, authoritarian, indulgent, and neglectful families. *Child Development, 62,* 1049–1065.

Lampl, M., Veldhuis, J. D., & Johnson, M. (1992). Saltation and stasis: A model of human growth. *Science, 258*(5083), 801–803.

Landesman-Dwyer, S., & Emanuel, I. (1979). Smoking during pregnancy. *Teratology, 19,* 119–126.

Landy, F. J. (1992, February 19). *Research on the use of fitness tests for police and fire fighting jobs.* Presentation to the Second Annual Scientific Psychology forum of the APA, Washington, DC.

Lange, G., MacKinnon, C. E., & Nida, R. E. (1989). Knowledge, strategy, and motivational contributions to preschool children's object recall. *Developmental Psychology, 25*(5), 772–779.

Langer, E., & Rodin, J. (1976). The effects of choice and enhanced personal responsibility in an institutional setting. *Journal of Personality and Social Psychology, 34*(2), 191–198.

LaRossa, R. (1988). Fatherhood and social change. *Family Relations, 34,* 451–457.

LaRossa, R., & LaRossa, M. M. (1981). *Transition to parenthood: How infants change families.* Beverly Hills, CA: Sage.

Larson, R., & Lampman-Petraitis, C. (1989). Daily emotional states as reported by children and adolescents. *Child Development, 60,* 1250–1260.

Larson, R., Mannell, R., & Zuzanek, J. (1986). Daily well-being of older adults with friends and family. *Psychology and Aging, 1*(2), 117–126.

Larson, R., & Richards, M. H. (1991). Daily companionship in late childhood and early adolescence: Changing developmental contexts. *Child Development, 62,* 284–300.

Laudenslager, M. L., Ryan, S. M., Drugan, R. C., Hyson, R. L., & Maier, S. F. (1983). Coping and immunosuppression: Inescapable but not escapable shock suppresses lymphocyte proliferation. *Science, 221,* 568–570.

Lauer, J., & Lauer, R. (1985). Marriages made to last. *Psychology Today, 19*(6), 22–26.

Lawrence, R. H., Bennett, J. M., & Markides, K. S. (1992). Perceived intergenerational solidarity and psychological distress among older Mexican Americans. *Journal of Gerontology, 47*(2), S55–65.

Lawton, M. P. (1981). Alternate housing. *Journal of Gerontological Social Work, 3*(3), 61–79.

Lazarus, R. S. (1981). Little hassles can be hazardous to health. *Psychology Today, 15*(7), 58–62.

Lederberg, A. R., & Mobley, C. E. (1990). The effect of hearing impairment on the quality of attachment and mother-toddler interaction. *Child Development, 61,* 1596–1604.

Lederman, S. A. (1992). Estimating infant mortality from human immunodeficiency virus and other causes in breast-feeding and bottle-feeding populations. *Pediatrics, 89*(2), 290–296.

Lee, D. J., & Markides, K. S. (1990). Activity and mortality among aged people over an eight-year period. *Journal of Gerontology, 45*(1), S39–42.

Lee, G. R., Dwyer, J. W., & Coward, R. T. (1993). Gender differences in parent care: Demographic factors and some gender preferences. *Journal of Gerontology, 48*(1), S9–16.

Lee, G. R., & Shehan, C. L. (1989). Retirement and marital satisfaction. *Journal of Gerontology, 44*(6), S226–230.

Lee, I.-M., & Paffenbarger, R. S. (1992). Changes in body weight and longevity. *Journal of the American Medical Association, 268,* 2045–2049.

Lee, P. R., Franks, P., Thomas, G. S., & Paffenbarger, R. S. (1981). *Exercise and health: The evidence and its implications.* Cambridge, MA: Oelgeschlager, Gunn, & Hain.

Lee, T. R., Mancini, J. A., & Maxwell, J. W. (1990). Sibling relationships in adulthood: Current patterns and motivations. *Journal of Marriage and the Family, 52,* 431–440.

Lees, B., Molleson, T., Arnett, T. R., & Stevenson, J. C. (1993). Differences in proximal femur bone density over two centuries. *The Lancet, 341,* 673–675.

LeGuin, U. (1989). *Dancing at the edge of the world.* New York: Grove.

Lehman, D. R., & Nisbett, R. E. (1990). A longitudinal study of the effects of undergraduate training on reasoning. *Developmental Psychology, 26*(6), 952–960.

Lehmkuhle, S., Garzia, R. P., Turner, L., Hash, T., & Baro, J. A. (1993). A defective visual pathway in children with reading disability. *New England Journal of Medicine, 328*(14), 989–996.

Leigh, G. K. (1982). Kinship interaction over the family life span. *Journal of Marriage and the Family, 44*(1), 197–208.

Leland, C., et al. (1979). *Men and women learning together: Co-education in the 1980's.* Findings presented at conference, Men/Women/College, The Educational Implications of Sex Roles in Transition. December 1–2, 1978, at Brown University. Report published by Ford, Rockefeller, and Carnegie Foundations.

Lelwica, M., & Haviland, J. (1983). *Ten-week-old infants' reactions to mothers' emotional expressions.* Paper presented at the biennial meeting of the Society for Research in Child Development, Detroit.

Lemon, B., Bengtson, V., & Peterson, J. (1972). An exploration of the activity theory of aging: Activity types and life satisfaction among inmovers to a retirement community. *Journal of Gerontology, 27*(4), 511–523.

Lenneberg, E. H. (1967). *Biological functions of language.* New York: Wiley.

Lenneberg, E. H. (1969). On explaining language. *Science, 164*(3880), 635–643.

Lerner, J. V., & Galambos, N. L. (1985). Maternal role satisfaction, mother-child interaction, and child temperament: A process model. *Developmental Psychology, 21*(6), 1157–1164.

Lerner, M. J., Somers, D. G., Reid, D., Chiriboga, D., & Tierney, M. (1991). Adult children as caregivers: Egocentric biases in judgments of sibling contributions. *Gerontologist, 31*(6), 746–755.

Lester, B. M. (1979). A synergistic process approach to the study of prenatal malnutrition. *International Journal of Behavioral Development, 2,* 377–394.

Lester, B. M., Corwin, M. J., Sepkoski, C., Seifer, R., Peucker, M., McLaughlin, S., & Golub, H. L. (1991). Neurobehavioral syndromes in cocaine-exposed infants. *Child Development, 62,* 694–705.

Lester, B. M., & Dreher, M. (1989). Effects of marijuana use during pregnancy on newborn cry. *Child Development, 60,* 765–771.

Lester, R., & Van Theil, D. H. (1977). Gonadal function in chronic alcoholic men. *Advances in Experimental Medicine and Biology, 85A,* 339–414.

LeVay, S. (1991). A difference in hypothalamic structure between heterosexual and homosexual men. *Science, 253,* 1034–1037.

Leveno, K. J., Cunningham, F. G., Nelson, S., Roark, M., Williams, M. L., Guzick, D., Dowling, S., Rosenfeld, C. R., & Buckley, A. (1986). A prospective comparison of selective and universal electronic fetal monitoring in 34,995 pregnancies. *New England Journal of Medicine, 315,* 615–619.

Levin, J. S., & Taylor, R. J. (1993). Gender and age differences in religiosity among Black Americans. *Gerontologist, 33*(1), 16–23.

Levine, M. D. (1987). *Developmental variation and learning disorders.* Cambridge, MA: Educators Publishing.

Levine, R. (1980). Adulthood among the Gusii of Kenya. In N. J. Smelser & E. H. Erikson (Eds.), *Themes of work and love in adulthood* (pp. 77–104). Cambridge, MA: Harvard University Press.

Levinson, D. (1978). *The seasons of a man's life.* New York: Knopf.

Levinson, D. (1980). Toward a conception of the adult life course. In N. J. Smelser & E. H. Erikson (Eds.), *Themes of work and love in adulthood* (pp. 265–290). Cambridge, MA: Harvard University Press.

Levinson, D. (1986). A conception of adult development. *American Psychologist, 41*(1), 3–13.

Leviton, D. (1977). Death education. In H. Feifel (Ed.), *New meanings of death* (pp. 253–272). New York: McGraw-Hill.

Levy, D. M. (1966). *Maternal overprotection.* New York: Norton.

Levy, G. D., & Carter, D. B. (1989). Gender schema, gender constancy, and gender-role knowledge: The roles of cognitive factors in preschoolers' gender-role stereotype attributions. *Developmental Psychology, 25*(3), 444–449.

Levy-Shiff, R., Hoffman, M. A., Mogilner, S., Levinger, S., & Mogilner, M. B. (1990). Fathers' hospital visits to their preterm infants as a predictor of father-infant relationship and infant development. *Pediatrics, 86*(2), 289–293.

Lewin, T. (1988, March 22). Despite criticism, fetal monitors are likely to remain in wide use. *The New York Times,* p. 24.

Lewin, T. (1992, November 7). Doctors consider a specialty focusing on women's health. *The New York Times,* pp. A1,10.

Lewis, C., & Ventura, S. (1990, October). Birth and fertility rates by education: 1980 and 1985. *Vital and Health Statistics, 21*(49), 1–40. Hyattsville, MD: National Center for Health Statistics.

Lewis, D. O., Pincus, J. H., et al. (1988). Neuropsychiatric, psychoeducational and family characteristics of 14 juveniles condemned to death in the United States. *American Journal of Psychiatry, 145,* 584–589.

Lewis, G., David, A., Andreasson, S., and Allebeck, P. (1992). Schizophrenia and city life. *The Lancet, 340,* 137–140.

Lewis, M. (1983, March 23). *Older women and health.* Testimony at the hearings of the New York State Assembly Standing Committee on Aging, New York.

Lewis, M. (1987). Social development in infancy and early childhood. In J. D. Osofsky (Ed.), *Handbook of infant development* (2d ed.). New York: Wiley.

Lewis, M. (1992). Shame, the exposed self. *Zero to Three, XII*(4), 6–10.

Lewis, M., & Brooks, J. (1974). Self, other, and fear: Infants' reactions to people. In H. Lewis & L. Rosenblum (Eds.), *The origins of fear: The origins of behavior,* Vol. 2. New York: Wiley.

Lewis, M., Worobey, J., Ramsay, D. S., & McCormack, M. K. (1992). Prenatal exposure to heavy metals: Effect on childhood cognitive skills and health status. *Pediatrics, 89*(6), 1010–1015.

Lewis, M. I., & Butler, R. N. (1974). Life-review therapy: Putting memories to work in individual and group psychotherapy. *Geriatrics, 29,* 165–173.

Li, C. Q., Windsor, R. A., Perkins, L., Goldenberg, R. L., & Lowe, J. B. (1993). The impact on infant birth weight and gestational age of cotinine-validated smoking reduction during pregnancy. *Journal of the American Medical Association, 269,* 1519–1524.

Lickona, T. (1973, March). *An experimental test of Piaget's theory of moral development.* Paper presented at the meeting of the Society for Research in Child Development, Philadelphia.

Lickona, T. (Ed.). (1976). *Moral development and behavior.* New York: Holt.

Lieberman, M., & Coplan, A. (1970). Distance from death as a variable in the study of aging. *Developmental Psychology, 2*(1), 71–84.

Liebert, R. M. (1972). Television and social learning: Some relationships between viewing violence and behaving aggressively. In J. P. Murray, E. A. Rubinstein, & G. A. Comstock (Eds.), *Television and social behavior,* Vol. 2. Washington, DC: U.S. Government Printing Office.

Lieven, E. M. (1978). Conversations between mothers and young children. In N. Waterson & E. Snow (Eds.), *The development of communication: Social and pragmatic factors in language acquisition.* New York: Wiley.

Lightfoot-Klein, H. (1989). *Prisoners of ritual.* Binghamton, NY: Haworth.

Lindsey, R. (1984, January 15). A new generation finds it hard to leave the nest. *The New York Times,* p. A18.

Lindsey, R. (1988, February 1). Circumcision under criticism as unnecessary to newborn. *The New York Times,* pp. A1, A20.

Linney, J. A., & Seidman, E. (1989). The future of schooling. *American Psychologist, 44*(2), 336–340.

Lipid Research Clinics Program. (1984a). The lipid research clinic coronary primary prevention trial results: I. Reduction in incidence of coronary heart disease. *Journal of the American Medical Association, 251,* 351–364.

Lipid Research Clinics Program. (1984b). The lipid research clinic coronary primary prevention trial results: II. The relationship of reduction in incidence of coronary heart disease to cholesterol lowering. *Journal of the American Medical Association, 251,* 365–374.

Lipsitt, L. (1982). Infant learning. In T. M. Field, A. Huston, H. Quay, L. Troll, & G. Finley (Eds.), *Review of human development.* New York: Wiley.

Lipsitt, L. (1986). Learning in infancy: Cognitive development in babies. *Journal of Pediatrics, 109*(1), 172–182.

Little, R. E., Anderson, K. W., Ervin, C. H., Worthington-Roberts, B., & Clarren, S. K. (1989). Maternal alcohol use during breast-feeding and infant mental and motor development at one year. *New England Journal of Medicine, 321,* 425–430.

Livson, F. (1976). *Sex differences in personality development in the middle adult years: A longitudinal study.* Paper presented at the annual meeting of the Gerontological Society, Louisville, KY.

Livson, N., & Peskin, H. (1980). Perspectives on adolescence from longitudinal research. In J. Adelson (Ed.), *Handbook of adolescent psychology.* New York: Wiley.

Lo, Y.-M. D., Patel, P., Wainscoat, J. S., Sampietro, M., Gillmer, M. D. G., & Fleming, K. A. (1989, December 9). Prenatal sex determination by DNA amplification from maternal peripheral blood. *The Lancet,* pp. 1363–1365.

Localia, A. R., Lawthers, A. G., Bengston, J. M., Hebert, L. E., Weaver, S. L., Brennan, T. A., & Landis, R. (1993). Relationship between malpractice and Cesarean delivery. *Journal of the American Medical Association, 269,* 366–373.

Lock, A., Young, A., Service, V., & Chandler, P. (1990). Some observations on the origin of the pointing gesture. In V. Volterra & C. J. Erting (Eds.), *From gesture to language in hearing and deaf children.* New York: Springer.

Lock, M. (1991). Contested meanings of the menopause. *The Lancet, 337,* 1270–1272.

Loda, F. A. (1980). Day care. *Pediatrics in Review, 1*(9), 277–281.

Loeber, R., & Dishion, T. (1983). Early predictors of male delinquency: A review. *Psychological Bulletin, 94,* 68–99.

Loehlin, J., Lindzey, G., & Spuhler, J. (1975). *Race differences in intelligence.* San Francisco: Freeman.

Lofland, L. H. (1986). When others die. *Generations, 10*(4), 59–61.

London, K., Mosher, W., Pratt, W., & Williams, L. (1989). *Preliminary findings from the NSFG, Cycle IV.* Paper presented at the annual meeting of the Population Association of America, Baltimore, MD.

Long-term outlook for children with sex chromosome abnormalities. (1982, July 3). *The Lancet,* p. 27.

Longino, C. F. (1987). *The oldest Americans: State profiles for data-based planning.* Coral Gables, FL: University of Miami Department of Sociology.

Longino, C. F. (1988). Who are the oldest Americans? *Gerontologist, 28*(4), 515–523.

Longino, C. F., & Kart, C. S. (1982). Explicating activity theory: A formal replication. *Journal of Gerontology, 37*(6), 713–721.

Lonigan, C. J., Fischel, J. E., Whitehurst, G. J., Arnold, D. S., & Valdez-Menchaca, M. C. (1992). The role of otitis media in the development of expressive language disorder. *Developmental Psychology, 28*(3), 430–440.

Looft, W. R. (1971). *Toward a history of life-span developmental psychology.* Unpublished manuscript, University of Wisconsin, Madison.

Lopata, H. (1977, September–October). Widows and widowers. *Humanist,* pp. 25–28.

Lopata, H. (1979). *Women as widows.* New York: Elsevier.

Lopata, H., Heinemann, G. D., & Baum, J. (1982). Loneliness: Antecedents and coping strategies in the lives of widows. In L. A. Peplau & D. Perlman (Eds.), *Loneliness: A sourcebook of current theory, research, and therapy* (pp. 310–326). New York: Wiley.

Lorenz, K. (1957). Comparative study of behavior. In C. H. Schiller (Ed.), *Instinctive behavior*. New York: International Press.

Lott, I. T., Bocian, M., Pribram, H. W., & Leitner, M. (1984). Fetal hydrocephalus and ear anomalies associated with maternal use of isotretinoin. *Journal of Pediatrics, 105,* 597–600.

Louis Harris & Associates. *See* Harris, L., & Associates.

Lovelace, E. A. (1990). Basic concepts in cognition and aging. In E. A. Lovelace (Ed.), *Aging and cognition: Mental processes, self awareness, and interventions.* North-Holland, Amsterdam, Netherlands: Elsevier.

Lowenthal, M., & Chiriboga, D. (1972). Transition to the empty nest: Crisis, challenge, or relief? *Archives of General Psychiatry, 26,* 8–14.

Lowenthal, M., & Haven, C. (1968). Interaction and adaptation: Intimacy as a critical variable. In B. Neugarten (Ed.), *Middle age and aging.* Chicago: University of Chicago Press.

Lozoff, B., Wolf, A. W., & Davis, N. S. (1985). Sleep problems seen in pediatric practice. *Pediatrics, 75,* 477–483.

Lufkin, E. G., et al. (1992). Treatment of postmenopausal osteoporosis with transdermal estrogen. *Annals of Internal Medicine, 117,* 1–9.

Lutjen, P., Trounson, A., Leeton, J., Findlay, J., Wood, C., & Renou, P. (1984). The establishment and maintenance of pregnancy using in vitro fertilization and embryo donation in a patient with primary ovarian failure. *Nature, 307,* 174–175.

Lyons-Ruth, K., Alpern, L., & Repacholi, B. (1993). Disorganized infant attachment classification and maternal psychosocial problems as predictors of hostile-aggressive behavior in the preschool classroom. *Child Development, 64,* 572–585.

Lyons-Ruth, K., Connell, D. B., & Grunebaum, H. U. (1990). Infants at social risk: Services as mediators of infant development and security of attachment. *Child Development, 61,* 85–98.

Lystad, M. (1975). Violence at home: A review of literature. *American Journal of Orthopsychiatry, 45*(3), 328–345.

Lytton, H., & Romney, D. M. (1991). Parents' differential socialization of boys and girls: A meta-analysis. *Psychological Bulletin, 109*(2), 267–296.

Maccoby, E. (1980). *Social development.* New York: Harcourt Brace Jovanovich.

Maccoby, E. (1984). Middle childhood in the context of the family. In W. A. Collins (Ed.), *Development during middle childhood: The years from six to twelve.* Washington, DC: National Academy.

Maccoby, E., & Jacklin, C. (1974). *The psychology of sex differences.* Stanford, CA: Stanford University Press.

Maccoby, E. E. (1988). Gender as a social category. *Developmental Psychology, 24*(6), 755–765.

Maccoby, E. E. (1990). Gender and relationships: A developmental account. *American Psychologist, 45*(4), 513–520.

Macey, T. J., Harmon, R. J., & Easterbrooks, M. A. (1987). Impact of premature birth on the development of the infant in the family. *Journal of Consulting and Clinical Psychology, 55*(6), 846–852.

Macfarlane, A. (1975). Olfaction in the development of social preferences in the human neonate. In *Parent-infant interaction* (CIBA Foundation Symposium, 33). Amsterdam: Elsevier.

MacTurk, R. H., & Koester, L. S. (1991, April 19). *Social referencing in 12- and 18-month-old deaf and hearing infants.* Paper presented at the biennial meeting of Society for Research in Child Development, Seattle.

Maddox, G. (1968). Persistence of life style among the elderly. In B. Neugarten (Ed.), *Middle age and aging.* Chicago: University of Chicago Press.

Maddox, G. (Ed.). (1987). *The encyclopedia of aging.* New York: Springer.

Madison, P. (1969). *Personality development in college.* Reading, MA: Addison-Wesley.

Maeroff, G. I. (1984, October 29). Interest in learning foreign languages rises. *The New York Times,* p. A1.

Main, M. (1987). *Working models of attachment in adolescence and adulthood.* Symposium presented at the Society of Research in Child Development, Baltimore, MD.

Main, M., & Solomon, J. (1986). Discovery of an insecure, disorganized/disoriented attachment pattern: Procedures, findings, and implications for the classification of behavior. In M. Yogman & T. B. Brazelton (Eds.), *Affective development in infancy.* Norwood, NJ: Ablex.

Malcolm, A. H. (1984, September 23). Many see mercy in ending empty lives. *The New York Times,* pp. A1, 56.

Malcolm, A. H. (1990, June 9). Giving death a hand: Rending issue. *The New York Times,* p. A6.

Malloy, M. H., Rhoads, G. G., Schramm, W., & Land, G. (1989). Increasing Cesarean section rates in very low-birth weight infants: Effect on outcome. *Journal of the American Medical Association, 262,* 1475–1478.

Malmquist, C. P. (1983). Major depression in childhood: Why don't we know more? *American Journal of Orthopsychiatry, 53*(2), 262–268.

Mamay, P. D., & Simpson, P. L. (1981). Three female roles in television commercials. *Sex Roles, 7*(12), 1223–1232.

Mandler, J. M. (1990). A new perspective on cognitive development in infancy. *American Scientist, 78,* 236–243.

Mannuzza, S., Klein, R. G., Bonagura, N., Konig, P. H., & Shenker, R. (1988). Hyperactive boys almost grown up. II. Status of subjects without a mental disorder. *Archives of General Psychiatry, 45,* 13–18.

Manosevitz, M., Prentice, N. M., & Wilson, F. (1973). Individual and family correlates of imaginary companions in preschool children. *Developmental Psychology, 8*(1), 72–79.

Mansfield, R. S., & Busse, T. V. (1981). *The psychology of creativity and discovery: Scientists and their work.* Chicago: Nelson-Hall.

Maratsos, M. (1973). Nonegocentric communication abilities in preschool children. *Child Development, 44,* 697–700.

March of Dimes Birth Defects Foundation (1983, rev. 1987). *Genetic counseling.* White Plains, NY: Author.

Marcia, J. E. (1966). Development and validation of ego identity status. *Journal of Personality and Social Psychology, 3*(5), 551–558.

Marcia, J. E. (1979, June). *Identity status in late adolescence: Description and some clinical implications.* Address given at a symposium on identity development, Rijksuniversitat Groningen, Netherlands.

Marcia, J. E. (1980). Identity in adolescence. In J. Adelson (Ed.), *Handbook of adolescent psychology.* New York: Wiley.

Markides, K. S., Coreil, J., & Rogers, L. P. (1989). Aging and health among Southwestern Hispanics. In K. S. Markides (Ed.), *Aging and health: Perspectives on gender, race, ethnicity, and class.* Newbury Park, CA: Sage.

Markides, K. S., & Krause, N. (1986). Older Mexican Americans. *Generations, 10*(4), 31–34.

Markoff, J. (1992, October 12). Miscarriages tied to chip factories. *The New York Times,* pp. A1, D2.

Markus, H., & Nurius, P. S. (1984). Self-understanding and self-regulation in middle childhood. In W. A. Collins (Ed.), *Development during middle childhood: The years from six to twelve.* Washington, DC: National Academy.

Marquis, K. S., & Detweiler, R. A. (1985). Does adopted mean different? An attributional analysis. *Journal of Personality and Social Psychology, 48,* 1054–1066.

Martin, G. B., & Clark, R. D. (1982). Distress crying in neonates: Species and peer specificity. *Developmental Psychology, 18*(1), 3–9.

Martin, L. G. (1988). The aging of Asia. *Journal of Gerontology, 43*(4), S99–113.

Martin, T. C., & Bumpass, L. L. (1989). Recent trends in marital disruption. *Demography, 26*(1), 37–51.

Martinez, G. A., & Krieger, F. W. (1985). The 1984 milk-feeding patterns in the United States. *Pediatrics, 76*, 1004–1008.

Marzano, R. J., & Hutchins, C. L. (1987). *Thinking skills: A conceptual framework.* (ERIC Document Reproduction Service No. ED 266436)

Maslach, C., & Jackson, S. E. (1985). Burnout in health professions: A social psychological analysis. In G. Sanders & J. Suls (Eds.), *Social psychology of health and illness.* Hillsdale, NJ: Erlbaum.

Maslow, A. (1954). *Motivation and personality.* New York: Harper & Row.

Maslow, A. (1968). *Toward a psychology of being.* Princeton, NJ: Van Nostrand Reinhold.

Masoro, E. J. (1988). Minireview: Food restriction in rodents: An evaluation of its role in the study of aging. *Journal of Gerontology, 43*(3), S59–64.

Masoro, E. J. (1992). The role of animal models in meeting the gerontologic challenge of the 21st century. *Gerontologist, 32*(5), 627–633.

Massey, C. M., & Gelman, R. (1988). Preschoolers' ability to decide whether a photographed unfamiliar object can move itself. *Developmental Psychology, 24*(3), 307–317.

Masters, W. H., & Johnson, V. E. (1966). *Human sexual response.* Boston: Little, Brown.

Masters, W. H., & Johnson, V. E. (1981). Sex and the aging process. *Journal of the American Geriatrics Society, 29*, 385–390.

Matas, L., Arend, R., & Sroufe, L. A. (1978). Continuity of adaptation in the second year: The relationship between quality of attachment and later competence. *Child Development, 49*, 547–556.

Matheny, K. B., & Cupp, P. (1983). Control, desirability, and anticipation as moderating variables between life changes and illness. *Journal of Human Stress, 9*(2), 14–23.

Matlin, M. W. (1987). *The psychology of women.* New York: Holt, Rinehart, & Winston.

Matsukura, S., Taminato, T., Kitano, N., Seino, Y., Hamada, H., Uchihashi, M., Nakajima, H., & Hirata, Y. (1984). Effects of environmental tobacco smoke on urinary cotinine excretion in nonsmokers. *New England Journal of Medicine, 311*(13), 828–832.

Matthews, K. A. (1992). Myths and realities of menopause. *Psychosomatic Medicine, 54*, 1–9.

Matthews, K. A., & Rodin, J. (1989). Women's changing work roles: Impact on health, family, and public policy. *American Psychologist, 44*(1), 1389–1393.

Maxwell, L. (1987, January). *Eight pointers on teaching children to think* (Research in Brief, IS 87-104 RIB). Washington, DC: U.S. Department of Education, Office of Educational Research and Improvement.

Mayer, J. (1973). Fat babies grow into fat people. *Family Health, 5*(3), 24–26.

McAlister, A. L., Perry, C., & Maccoby, N. (1979). Adolescent smoking: Onset and prevention. *Pediatrics, 63*(4), 650–658.

McAnarney, E. R., & Hendee, W. R. (1989). Adolescent pregnancy and its consequences. *Journal of the American Medical Association, 262*(1), 74–77.

McCall, R. B., Appelbaum, M. I., & Hogarty, P. S. (1973). Developmental changes in mental performance. *Monographs of the Society for Research in Child Development, 38* (Serial No. 150).

McCall, R. B., & Carriger, M. S. (1993). A meta-analysis of infant habituation and recognition memory performance as predictors of later IQ. *Child Development, 64*, 57–79.

McCann, I. L., & Holmes, D. S. (1984). Influence of aerobic exercise on depression. *Journal of Personality and Social Psychology, 46*(5), 1142–1147.

McCartney, K. (1984). Effect of quality of day care environment on children's language development. *Developmental Psychology, 20*(2), 244–260.

McClelland, D., Constantian, C., Regalado, D., & Stone, C. (1978). Making it to maturity. *Psychology Today, 12*(1), 42–53, 114.

McCord, C., & Freeman, H. P. (1990). Excess mortality in Harlem. *New England Journal of Medicine, 322*, 173–177.

McDaniel, K. D. (1986). Pharmacological treatment of psychiatric and neurodevelopmental disorders in children and adolescents (Part 1, Part 2, Part 3). *Clinical Pediatrics, 25*(2, 3, 4), 65–71, 198–224.

McDonald, A. D., Armstrong, B. G., and Sloan, M. (1992a). Cigarette, alcohol, and coffee consumption and congenital defects. *American Journal of Public Health, 82*, 91.

McDonald, A. D., Armstrong, B. G., and Sloan, M. (1992b). Cigarette, alcohol, and coffee consumption and prematurity. *American Journal of Public Health, 82*, 87.

McFall, S., & Miller, B. H. (1992). Caregiver burden and nursing home admission of frail elderly patients. *Journal of Gerontology, 47*(2), S73–79.

McFarland, R. A., Tune, G. B., & Welford, A. (1964). On the driving of automobiles by older people. *Journal of Gerontology, 19*, 190–197.

McGauhey, P. J, Starfield, B., Alexander, C., & Ensminget, M. E. (1991). Social environment and vulnerability of low birth weight children: A social-epidemiological perspective. *Pediatrics, 88*, 943–953.

McGee, R., Partridge, F., Williams, S., & Silva, P. A. (1991). A twelve-year follow-up of preschool hyperactive children. *Journal of the American Academy of Child and Adolescent Psychiatry, 30*, 224–232.

McGinnis, J. M., Richmond, J. B., Brandt, E. N., Windom, R. E., & Mason, J. O. (1992). Health progress in the United States: Results of the 1990 objectives for the nation. *Journal of the American Medical Association, 268*(18), 2545–2552.

McGraw, M. B. (1940). Neural maturation as exemplified in the achievement of bladder control. *Journal of Pediatrics, 16*, 580–589.

McGue, M. (1993). From proteins to cognitions: The behavioral genetics of alcoholism. In R. P. Plomin & G. E. McClearn (Eds.), *Nature, nurture, and psychology.* Washington, DC: American Psychological Association.

McGue, M., Bacon, S., & Lykken, D. T. (1993). Personality stability and change in early adulthood: A behavioral genetic analysis. *Developmental Psychology, 21*(1), 96–109.

McGue, M., Bouchard, T. J., Iacono, W. G., & Lykken, D. T. (1993). Behavioral genetics of cognitive ability: A lifespan perspective. In R. P. Plomin & G. E. McClearn (Eds.), *Nature, nurture, and psychology.* Washington, DC: American Psychological Association.

McGuinness, D. (1986, February 5). Facing the "learning disabilities" crisis. *Education Week*, pp. 28, 22.

McKenry, P. C., Walters, L. H., & Johnson, C. (1979). Adolescent pregnancy: A review of the literature. *Family Coordinator, 23*(1), 17–28.

McKinley, D. (1964). *Social class and family life.* New York: Free Press.

McKinney, K. (1987, March). *A look at Japanese education today* (Research in Brief, IS 87-107 RIB). Washington, DC: U.S. Department of Education, Office of Educational Research and Improvement.

McKitrick, L. A., Camp, C. J,. & Black, F. W. (1992). Prospective memory intervention in Alzheimer's disease. *Journal of Gerontology, 47*(5), P337–343.

McLanahan, S., & Booth, K. (1989). Mother-only families: Problems, prospects, and politics. *Journal of Marriage and the Family, 51*, 557–580.

McLaughlin, B. (1985). *Second language acquisition in childhood: Vol. 2. School-age children* (2d ed.). Hillsdale, NJ: Erlbaum.

McLoyd, V. (1989). Socialization and development in a changing economy: The effects of paternal job and income loss on children. *American Psychologist, 44*(2), 293–302.

McLoyd, V. C. (1990). The impact of economic hardship on Black families and children: Psychological distress, parenting, and socioemotional development. *Child Development, 61*(2), 311–346.

McNally, J. W., & Mosher, W. D. (1991, May 14). AIDS-related knowledge and behavior among women 15–44 years of age: United States, 1988. *Advance Data, 200.*

Mead, M. (1928). *Coming of age in Samoa.* New York: Morrow.

Mead, M. (1935). *Sex and temperament in three primitive societies.* New York: Morrow.

Mednick, B. R., Baker, R. L., & Sutton-Smith, B. (1979). *Teenage pregnancy and perinatal mortality* (Contract No. 1-117–82807). Unpublished paper reporting on a study supported by the U.S. Department of Health, Education, and Welfare.

Medrich, E. A., Roizen, J. A., Rubin, V., & Buckley, S. (1982). *The serious business of growing up.* Berkeley: University of California Press.

Meehan, P. J. (1990). Prevention: The endpoint of suicidology. *Mayo Clinic Proceedings, 65,* 115–118.

Melnick, S., Cole, P., Anderson, B. A., & Herbst, A. (1987). Rates and risks of diethylstillbestrol-related clear-cell adenocarcinoma of the vagina and cervix. *New England Journal of Medicine, 316,* 514–516.

Meltzoff, A. & Gopnik, A. (1993). The role of imitation in understanding persons and developing a theory of mind. In S. Baron-Cohen, H. Tager-Flusberg, & D. J. Cohen (Eds.), *Understanding others minds: Perspectives from autism.* Oxford, England: Oxford University Press.

Meltzoff, A. N. (1985). Immediate and deferred imitation in fourteen- and twenty-four-month-old infants. *Child Development, 56,* 62–72.

Meltzoff, A. N. (1988a). Infant imitation after a 1-week delay: Long-term memory for novel acts and multiple stimuli. *Developmental Psychology, 24*(4), 470–476.

Meltzoff, A. N. (1988b). Infant imitation and memory: Nine-month-olds in immediate and deferred tests. *Child Development, 59,* 217, 225.

Meltzoff, A. N., & Borton, R. W. (1979). Intermodal matching by human neonates. *Nature, 282,* 403–404.

Meltzoff, A. N., & Moore, M. K. (1983). Newborn infants imitate adult facial gestures. *Child Development, 54,* 702–709.

Meltzoff, A. N., & Moore, M. K. (1989). Imitation in newborn infants: Exploring the range of gestures imitated and the underlying mechanisms. *Developmental Psychology, 25*(6), 954–962.

Meltzoff, A. N., & Moore, M. K. (1992). Early imitation within a functional framework: The importance of person identity, movement, and development. *Infant Behavior and Development, 15,* 479–505.

Menken, J., Trussell, J., & Larsen, U. (1986). Age and infertilty. *Science, 233,* 1389–1394.

Meredith, N. V. (1969). Body size of contemporary groups of eight-year-old children studied in different parts of the world. *Monographs of the Society for Research in Child Development, 34*(1).

Meyer, D. R., & Garasky, S. (1993). Custodial fathers: Myths, realities, and child support policy. *Journal of Marriage and the Family, 55*(1), 73–89.

Meyers, A. F., Sampson, A. E., Weitzman, M., Rogers, B. L., & Kayne, H. (1989). School breakfast program and school performance. *American Journal of Diseases of Children, 143,* 1234–1239.

Meyers, H. (1989). The impact of teenaged children on parents. In J. M. Oldham & R. S. Liebert (Eds.), *The middle years.* New Haven: Yale University Press.

Michaels, D., & Levine, C. (1992). Estimates of the number of motherless youth orphaned by AIDS in the United States. *Journal of the American Medical Association, 268*(24), 3456–3461.

Miles, C., & Miles, W. (1932). The correlation of intelligence scores and chronological age from early to late maturity. *American Journal of Psychology, 44,* 44–78.

Miller, B., & Gerard, D. (1979). Family influences on the development of creativity in children: An integrative review. *Family Coordinator, 28*(3), 295–312.

Miller, B. C., & Moore, K. A. (1990). Adolescent sexual behavior, pregnancy, and parenting: Research through the 1980s. *Journal of Marriage and the Family, 52,* 1025–1044.

Miller, B. C., & Myers-Walls, J. A. (1983). Parenthood: Stresses and coping strategies. In H. I. McCubbin & C. R. Figley (Eds.), *Stress and the family: Vol. 1. Coping with normative transitions.* New York: Brunner/Mazel.

Miller, C. A. (1987). Infant mortality in the U. S. *Scientific American, 253,* 31–37.

Miller, E., Cradock-Watson, J. E., & Pollock, T. M. (1982, October 9). Consequences of confirmed maternal rubella at successive stages of pregnancy. *The Lancet,* pp. 781–784.

Miller, J. B. (1991). The development of women's sense of self. In J. V. Jordan, A. G. Kaplan, J. B. Miller, I. P. Stiver, & J. L. Surrey (Eds.), *Women's growth in connection: Writings from the Stone Center.* New York: Guilford Press.

Miller, L. B., & Bizzel, R. P. (1983). Long-term effects of four preschool programs: Sixth, seventh, and eighth grades. *Child Development, 54,* 727–741.

Miller, P. M., Danaher, D. L., & Forbes, D. (1986). Sex-related strategies in coping with interpersonal conflict in children aged five and seven. *Developmental Psychology, 22*(4), 543–548.

Miller, V., Onotera, R. T., & Deinard, A. S. (1984). Denver developmental screening test: Cultural variations in southeast Asian children. *Journal of Pediatrics, 104*(3), 481–482.

Miller-Jones, D. (1989). Culture and testing. *American Psychologist, 44*(2), 360–366.

Mills, J. L., Graubard, B. I., Harley, E. E., Rhoads, G. G., & Berendes, H. W. (1984). Maternal alcohol consumption and birth weight: How much drinking is safe during pregnancy? *Journal of the American Medical Association, 252,* 1875–1879.

Mills, J. L., Holmes, L. B., Aarons, J. H., Simpson, J. L., Brown, Z. A., Jovanovic-Peterson, L. G., Conley, M. R., Graubard, B. I., Knopp, R. H., & Metzger, B. E. (1993). Moderate caffeine use and the risk of spontaneous abortion and intrauterine growth retardation. *Journal of the American Medical Association, 269,* 593–597.

Millstein, S. G. (1989). Adolescent health: Challenges for behavioral scientists. *American Psychologist, 44*(5), 837–842,

Millstein, S. G., Irwin, C. E., Adler, N. E., Cohn, L. D., Kegeles, S. M., & Dolcini, M. M. (1992). Health-risk behaviors and health concerns among young adolescents. *Pediatrics, 89,* 422–428.

Milne, A. M., Myers, D. E., Rosenthal, A. S., & Ginsburg, A. (1986). Single parents, working mothers, and the educational achievement of school children. *Sociology of Education, 59,* 125–139.

Milunsky, A. (1992). *Heredity and your family's health.* Baltimore, MD: Johns Hopkins.

Milunsky, A., Ulsiskas, M., et al. (1992). Maternal heat exposure and neural tube defects. *Journal of the American Medical Association, 268,* 882–885.

Mindel, C. H. (1983). The elderly in minority families. In T. H. Brubaker (Ed.), *Family relationships in later life.* Beverly Hills, CA: Sage.

Miranda, S., Hack, M., Fantz, R., Fanaroff, A., & Klaus, M. (1977). Neonatal pattern vision: Predictor of future mental performance? *Journal of Pediatrics, 91*(4), 642–647.

Mitchell, B. A., Wister, A. V., & Burch, T. K. (1989). The family environment and leaving the parental home. *Journal of Marriage and the Family, 51,* 605–613.

Mitchell, E. A., Ford, R. P. K., Stewart, A. W., Taylor, B. J., Bescroft, D. M. O., Thompson, J. M. P., Scragg, R., Hassall, I. B., Barry, D. M. J., Allen, E. M., & Roberts, A. P. (1993). Smoking and the sudden infant death syndrome. *Pediatrics, 91,* 893–896.

Mitchell, V., & Helson, R. (1990). Women's prime of life: Is it the 50s? *Psychology of Women Quarterly, 16,* 331–347.

Miyake, K., Chen, S., & Campos, J. (1985). Infants' temperament, mothers' mode of interaction and attachment in Japan: An interim report. In I. Bretherton & E. Waters (Eds.), Growing points of attachment theory and research. *Monographs of the Society for Research in Child Development, 50*(1–2, Serial No. 109), 276–297.

Moely, B. E., Hart, S. S., Leal, L., Santulli, K. A., Rao, N., Johnson, T., & Hamilton, L. B. (1992). The teacher's role in facilitating memory and study strategy development in the elementary school classroom. *Child Development, 63*, 653–672.

Moffitt, T. E., Caspi, A., Belsky, J., & Silva, P. A. (1992). Childhood experience and the onset of menarche: A test of a sociobiological model. *Child Development, 63*(1), 47–58.

Money, J., Ehrhardt, A., & Masica, D. N. (1968). Fetal feminization induced by androgen insensitivity in the testicular feminizing syndrome: Effect on marriage and maternalism. *Johns Hopkins Medical Journal, 123*, 105–114.

Montemayor, R. (1983). Parents and adolescents in conflict: All families some of the time and some families most of the time. *Journal of Early Adolescence, 3*, 83–103.

Montepare, J. M., & Lachman, M. E. (1989). "You're only as old as you feel": Self-perceptions of age, fears of aging, and life satisfaction from adolescence to old age. *Psychology and Aging, 4*(1), 73–78.

Moore, A. U. (1960). *Studies on the formation of the mother-neonate bond in sheep and goats.* Paper presented at the meeting of the American Psychological Association.

Moore, C., & Frye, D. (1991). The acquisition and utility of theories of mind. In D. Frye & C. Moore (Eds.), *Children's theories of mind: Mental states and social understanding.* Hillsdale, NJ: Erlbaum.

Moore, N., Evertson, C., & Brophy, J. (1974). Solitary play: Some functional reconsiderations. *Developmental Psychology, 10*(5), 830–834.

Morbidity and Mortality Weekly Report (MMWR). (1985, June 21). *Suicide—U.S., 1970–1980.*

Morbidity and Mortality Weekly Report (MMWR). (1987, August 14). *Update: Acquired immunodeficiency syndrome—United States.*

Morbidity and Mortality Weekly Report (MMWR). (1989). *Apparent per capita ethanol consumption—United States, 1977–1986.* 38(46), 800–803.

Morbidity and Mortality Weekly Report (MMWR). (1993, March 12). *Infant mortality—United States, 1990.* 42(9), 161–165.

Morgan, L. (1984). Changes in family interaction following widowhood. *Journal of Marriage and the Family, 46*(2), 323–331.

Morison, P., & Masten, A. S. (1991). Peer reputation in middle childhood as a predictor of adaptation in adolescence: A seven-year follow-up. *Child Development, 62*, 991–1007.

Morland, J. (1966). A comparison of race awareness in northern and southern children. *American Journal of Orthopsychiatry, 36*, 22–31.

Morris, R., & Kralochwill, T. (1983). *Treating children's fears and phobias: A behavioral approach.* Elmsford, NY: Pergamon.

Mosher, W. D., & McNally, J. W. (1991). Contraceptive use at first premarital intercourse: United States, 1965–1988. *Family Planning Perspectives, 23*(3), 108–116.

Mosher, W. D., & Pratt, W. F. (1990). Fecundity and infertility in the United States. Advance Data. *Vital and Health Statistics, 192.*

Moskowitz, B. A. (1978). The acquisition of language. *Scientific American, 239*(5), 92–108.

Moss, F., & Halamandaris, V. (1977). *Too old, too sick, too bad.* Germantown, MD: Aspen Systems.

Moss, M. S., & Moss, S. Z. (1989). The death of a parent. In R. A. Kalish (Ed.), *Midlife loss: Coping strategies.* Newbury Park, CA: Sage.

Mossberg, H.-O. (1989, August 26). 40-year follow-up of overweight children. *The Lancet*, pp. 491–493.

MRC Vitamin Study Research Group. (1991). Prevention of neural tube defects: Results of the Medical Research Council vitamin study. *The Lancet, 338*, 131–137.

Mui, A. C. (1992). Caregiver strain among black and white daughter caregivers: A role theory perspective. *Gerontologist, 32*(2), 203–212.

Murphy, C. M., & Bootzin, R. R. (1973). Active and passive participation in the contact desensitization of snake fear in children. *Behavior Therapy, 4*, 203–211.

Murphy, D. P. (1929). The outcome of 625 pregnancies in women subjected to pelvic radium roentgen irradiation. *American Journal of Obstetrics and Gynecology, 18*, 179–187.

Murray, A. D., Dolby, R. M., Nation, R. L., & Thomas, D. B. (1981). Effects of epidural anesthesia on newborns and their mothers. *Child Development, 52*, 71–82.

Murstein, B. I. (1980). Mate selection in the 1970s. *Journal of Marriage and the Family, 42*, 777–792.

Mussen, P. H., & Eisenberg-Berg, N. (1977). *Roots of caring, sharing, and helping: The development of prosocial behavior in children.* San Francisco: Freeman.

Mussen, P. H., & Jones, M. C. (1957). Self-conceptions, motivations, and interpersonal attitudes of late- and early-maturing boys. *Child Development, 28*, 243–256.

Mussen, P. H., & Rutherford, E. (1963). Parent-child relations and parental personality in relation to young children's sex role preferences. *Child Development, 34*, 589–607.

Must, A., Jacques, P. F., Dallal, G. E., Bajema, C. J., & Dietz, W. H. (1992). Long-term morbidity and mortality of overweight adolescents. *New England Journal of Medicine, 327*(19), 1350–1355.

Muuss, R. E. H. (1988). *Theories of adolescence* (5th ed.). New York: Random House.

Myers, J. K., Weissman, M. M., Tischler, G. L., Holzer, C. E., Leaf, P. J., Orvaschel, H., Burke, J. D., Kramer, M., & Stoltzman, R. (1984). Six-month prevalence of psychiatric disorders in three communities. *Archives of General Psychiatry, 41*(10), 959–967.

Myers, N., & Perlmutter, M. (1978). Memory in the years from 2 to 5. In P. Ornstein (Ed.), *Memory development in children.* Hillsdale, NJ: Erlbaum.

Myers-Walls, J. A. (1984). Balancing multiple role responsibilities during the transition to parenthood. *Family Relations, 33*, 267–271.

Naeye, R. L., & Peters, E. C. (1984). Mental development of children whose mothers smoked during pregnancy. *Obstetrics and Gynecology, 64*, 601.

Nathanson, C. A., & Lorenz, G. (1982). Women and health: The social dimensions of biomedical data. In J. Z. Giele (Ed.), *Women in the middle years.* New York: Wiley.

National Assessment of Educational Progress. (1982). *Reading comprehension of American youth: Do they understand what they read?* (Report No. 11-R-02). Denver: Education Commission of the States.

National Association of Children's Hospitals and Related Institutions (NACHRI) & American Academy of Pediatrics (AAP). (1990). *The fate of our children's health: Assessing progress in the 1980s, prospects for the 1990s.* Brochure.

National Center for Education Statistics (NCES). (1983). High school dropouts: Descriptive information from high school and beyond. *NCES Bulletin.* Washington, DC: U.S. Department of Education.

National Center for Education Statistics (NCES). (1984). *The condition of education* (Publication No. NCES-84-401). Washington, DC: U.S. Government Printing Office.

National Center for Education Statistics (NCES). (1985). *The relationship of parental involvement to high school grades* (Publication No. NCES-85-205b). Washington, DC: U.S. Department of Education.

National Center for Education Statistics (NCES). (1987). *Who drops out of high school? From high school and beyond.* Washington, DC: Office of Educational

Research and Improvement, U.S. Department of Education.

National Center for Education Statistics (NCES). (1989a). *National higher education statistics: Fall, 1989* (Publication No. NCES-90-379). Washington, DC: U.S. Department of Education.

National Center for Education Statistics (NCES). (1989b). *Pocket projections* (Publication No. NCES-89-649). Washington, DC: U.S. Department of Education.

National Center for Education Statistics (NCES). (1991, December). *National higher education statistics, Fall 91.* (Publication No. NCES 92-038). Washington, DC: Office of Educational Research and Improvement, U.S. Department of Education.

National Center for Health Statistics. (1986). *Maternal weight gain and the outcome of pregnancy, United States, 1980. Vital Statistics.* (DHHS Publication No. 86-1992). Washington, DC: U.S. Government Printing Office.

National Center for Health Statistics. (1987). Final mortality statistics, 1985, advanced report. *Monthly Vital Statistics Report, 36*(5, supplement).

National Center for Health Statistics. (1990). *Health United States 1989 and prevention profile* (DHHS Publication No. 90-1232). Washington, DC: U.S. Government Printing Office.

National Center for Health Statistics. (1992). Statistics on suicide rates in the United States, 1935–1989.

National Coalition on Television Violence. (undated). *Action alert: War toys/cartoons more violent.* Champaign, IL: Author.

National Commission for the Protection of Human Subjects of Biomedical and Behavioral Research. (1978). Report.

National Commission on Excellence in Education. (1983, April). *A nation at risk: The imperative for educational reform* (Stock No. 065-000-00177-2). Washington, DC: U.S. Government Printing Office.

National Commission on Youth. (1980). *The transition to adulthood: A bridge too long.* New York: Westview Press.

National Committee for Citizens in Education (NCCE). (1986, Winter Holiday). Don't be afraid to start a suicide prevention program in your school. *Network for Public Schools,* pp. 1,4.

National Institute of Child Health and Human Development. (1978). Smoking in children and adolescents. *Pediatric Annals, 7*(9), 130–131.

National Institute of Education (NIE). (1984). *Involvement in learning: Realizing the potential of American higher education.* Washington, DC: Author.

National Institute of Mental Health (NIMH). (1982). *Television and behavior: Ten years of scientific progress and implications for the eighties, Vol. 1: Summary report* (DHHS Publication No. ADM 82-1195). Washington, DC: U.S. Government Printing Office.

National Institute on Aging (NIA). (1980). *Senility: Myth or madness.* Washington, DC: U.S. Government Printing Office.

National Institute on Aging (NIA). (1984). *Be sensible about salt.* Washington, DC: U.S. Government Printing Office.

National Institute on Aging (NIA). (undated a). *Age Page: Aging and your eyes.* Bethesda, MD: U.S. Government Printing Office.

National Institute on Aging (NIA). (undated b). *Age Page: Hearing and the elderly.* Bethesda, MD: U.S. Government Printing Office.

National Institute on Alcohol Abuse and Alcoholism (NIAAA). (1981, October). *Fact sheet: Selected statistics on alcohol and alcoholism.* Rockville, MD: National Clearinghouse for Alcohol Information.

National Institute on Drug Abuse. (1993). *Monitoring the future survey.* Washington, DC: U.S. Government Printing Office.

National Institutes of Health (NIH). (1984). *Osteoporosis* (1984-421-132:4652). Consensus Development Conference Statement, 5(3). Bethesda, MD: U.S. Government Printing Office.

National Institutes of Health (NIH). (1985). *Health implications of obesity.* Consensus Development Conference Statement, 5(9). Washington, DC: U.S. Government Printing Office.

National Osteoporosis Foundation. (1992). Stand UP to osteoporosis: Your guide to staying healthy and independent through prevention and treatment. Brochure. Washington, DC: Author.

National Research Council (NRC). (1987). *Risking the future: Adolescent sexuality, pregnancy, and childbearing,* Vol. 2. Washington, DC: National Academy Press.

Needleman, H. L, & Gatsonis, C. A. (1990). Low-level lead exposure and the IQ of children: A meta-analysis of modern studies. *Journal of the American Medical Association, 263,* 673–678.

Neiswender, M, Birren, J., & Schaie, K. W. (1975). *Age and the experience of love in adulthood.* Paper presented at the annual meeting of the American Psychological Association, Chicago.

Nelson, K. (1973). Structure and strategy in learning to talk. *Monographs of the Society for Research in Child Development, 38*(1–2).

Nelson, K. (1981). Individual differences in language development: Implications for development and language. *Developmental Psychology, 17*(2), 170–187.

Nelson, K. (1989). Remembering: A functional developmental perspective. In P. R. Solomon, G. R. Goethels, C. M. Kelley, & B. R. Stephens (Eds.), *Memory: An interdisciplinary approach.* New York: Springer-Verlag.

Neuffer, E. (1987, November 14). School parents wrestle with Lisa's death. *The New York Times,* p. A29.

Neugarten, B. (1967). The awareness of middle age. In R. Owen (Ed.), *Middle age.* London: BBC.

Neugarten, B. (1968). Adult personality: Toward a psychology of the life cycle. In B. Neugarten (Ed.), *Middle age and aging.* Chicago: University of Chicago Press.

Neugarten, B. (1973). Personality change in late life: A developmental perspective. In C. Eisdorfer & M. P. Lawton (Eds.), *The psychology of adult development and aging.* Washington, DC: American Psychological Association.

Neugarten, B. (1977). Personality and aging. In J. Birren & K. W. Schaie (Eds.), *Handbook of the psychology of aging* (pp. 626–649). New York: Van Nostrand Reinhold.

Neugarten, B., & Hagestad, G. (1976). Age and the life course. In H. Binstock & E. Shanas (Eds.), *Handbook of aging and the social sciences.* New York: Van Nostrand Reinhold.

Neugarten, B., Havighurst, R., & Tobin, S. (1968). Personality and patterns of aging. In B. Neugarten (Ed.), *Middle age and aging.* Chicago: University of Chicago Press.

Neugarten, B., Moore, J. W., & Lowe, J. C. (1965). Age norms, age constraints, and adult socialization. *American Journal of Sociology, 70,* 710–717.

Neugarten, B., & Neugarten, D. A. (1987). The changing meanings of age. *Psychology Today, 21*(5), 29–33.

Neugarten, B., Wood, V., Kraines, R., & Loomis, B. (1963). Women's attitudes toward the menopause. *Vita Humana, 6,* 140–151.

Newacheck, P. W. (1989). Improving access to health services for adolescents from economically disadvantaged families. *Pediatrics, 84*(6), 1056–1063.

Newacheck, P. W., McManus, M. A., & Gephart, J. (1992). Health insurance coverage of adolescents: A current profile and assessment of trends. *Pediatrics, 90*(4), 589–596.

Newcomb, A. F., Bukowski, W. M., & Pattee, L. (1993). Children's peer relations: A meta-analytic review of popular, rejected, neglected, controversial, and average sociometric status. *Psychological Bulletin, 113*(1), 99–128.

Newhouse News Service. (1987, September 25). Sex still factor in student job goals. *Chicago Sun-Times,* p. 37.

Newman, P. R. (1982). The peer group. In B. Wolman (Ed.), *Handbook of developmental psychology.* Englewood Cliffs, NJ: Prentice-Hall.

Newport, E. I. (1992, June). *Critical periods and creolization: Effects of matura-*

tional states and input on the acquisition of language. Paper presented at the American Psychological Society meeting in San Diego.

Newport, E. L., & Singleton, J. L. (1992, June). Paper presented at the meeting of the American Psychological Association, San Diego.

Newson, J., Newson, E., & Mahalski, P. A. (1982). Persistent infant comfort habits and their sequelae at 11 and 16 years. *Journal of Child Psychology and Psychiatry, 23,* 421–436.

Nisan, M., & Kohlberg, L. (1982). Universality and variation in moral judgment: A longitudinal and cross-sectional study in Turkey. *Child Development, 53,* 865–876.

Noberini, M., & Neugarten, B. (1975). *A follow-up study of adaptation in middle-aged women.* Paper presented at the annual meeting of the Gerontological Society, Portland, OR.

Noll, R. B., Zucker, R. A., Fitzgerald, H. E., & Curtis, W. J. (1992). Cognitive and motoric functioning of sons of alcoholic fathers and controls: The early childhood years. *Developmental Psychology, 28*(4), 665–675.

Nordlicht, S. (1979). Effects of stress on the police officer and family. *New York State Journal of Medicine, 79,* 400–401.

Norton, A. J., & Moorman, J. E. (1987). Current trends in marriage and divorce among American women. *Journal of Marriage and the Family, 49*(1), 3–14.

Notelovitz, M., & Ware, M. (1983). *Stand tall: The informed woman's guide to preventing osteoporosis.* Gainesville, FL: Triad; © 1982.

Notzon, F. C. (1990). International differences in the use of obstetric interventions. *Journal of the American Medical Association, 263*(24), 3286–3291.

Notzon, F. C., Placek, P. J., & Taffel, S. M. (1987). Comparisons of national cesarean-section rates. *New England Journal of Medicine, 316,* 386–389.

Nugent, J. K. (1991). Cultural and psychological influences on the father's role in infant development. *Journal of Marriage and the Family, 53,* 475–485.

Nussbaum, M., Shenker, I. R., Baird, D., & Saravay, S. (1985). Follow-up investigation in patients with anorexia nervosa. *Journal of Pediatrics, 106,* 835–840.

Oakley, D., Sereika, S., & Bogue, E. (1991). Oral contraceptive pill use after an initial visit to a family planning clinic. *Family Planning Perspectives, 23*(4), 150–154.

Oberklaid, F., Sanson, A., Pedlow, R., & Prior, M. (1993). Predicting preschool behavior problems from temperament and other variables in infancy. *Pediatrics, 91*(1), 113–120.

Oberlander, T. F., Barr, R. G., Young, S. N., & Brian, J. A. (1992). Short-term effects of feed composition on sleeping and crying in newborns. *Pediatrics, 90*(5), 733–740.

O'Bryant, S. L. (1988). Sibling support and older widows' well-being. *Journal of Marriage and the Family, 50,* 173–183.

O'Bryant, S. L., & Morgan, L. A. (1989). Financial experience and well-being among mature widowed women. *Gerontologist, 29*(2), 245–251.

O'Connor, M. J., Cohen, S., & Parmelee, A. H. (1984). Infant auditory discrimination in preterm and full-term infants as a predictor of 5-year intelligence. *Developmental Psychology, 20,* 159–165.

O'Connor, M. J., Sigman, M., & Brill, N. (1987). Disorganization of attachment in relation to maternal alcohol consumption. *Journal of Consulting and Clinical Psychology, 55*(6), 831–836.

Offer, D. (1969). *The psychological world of the teenager: A study of normal adolescent boys.* New York: Basic Books.

Offer, D., & Offer, J. B. (1974). Normal adolescent males: The high school and college years. *Journal of the American College Health Association, 22,* 209–215.

Offer, D., Ostrov, E., & Howard, K. I. (1989). Adolescence: What is normal? *American Journal of Diseases of Children, 143,* 731–736.

Offer, D., Ostrov, E., & Marohn, R. C. (1972). *The psychological world of the juvenile delinquent.* New York: Basic Books.

Office of Technology Assessment (1988). Artificial insemination practice in the United States: Summary of a 1987 survey. Washington, DC: U.S. Government Printing Office.

Okun, M. A., Stick, W. A., Haring, M. J., & Witter, R. A. (1984). The social activity/subjective well-being relation: A quantitative synthesis. *Research on Aging, 6,* 45–65.

Okun, S. (1988, January 29). Opera coach died in his "house of worship." *The New York Times,* pp. B1, B3.

Olds, S. W. (1987, January). America's grandmother fixation. *Ms.,* p. 104.

Olds, S. W. (1989). *The working parents' survival guide.* Rocklin, CA: Prima.

O'Leary, K. D., Barling, J., Arias, I., Rosenbaum, A., Malone, J., & Tyree, A. (1989). Prevalence and stability of physical aggression between spouses: A longitudinal analysis. *Journal of Consulting and Clinical Psychology, 57*(2), 263–268.

Oliner, S. P., & Oliner, P. M. (1988). *The altruistic personality: Rescuers of Jews in Nazi Europe.* New York: Free Press.

Oller, D. K., & Eilers, R. (1988). The role of audition in infant babbling. *Child Development, 59,* 441–449.

Olsen-Fulero, L. (1982). Style and stability in mother conversational behavior: A study of individual differences. *Journal of Child Language, 9,* 543–564.

Orentlicher, D. (1990). Genetic screening by employers. *Journal of the American Medical Association, 263*(7), 1005–1008.

Organization for Economic Cooperation and Development (OECD). (1992). *OECD indicators: Education at a glance.* (Publication No. 96-92943-99). Paris: Author.

Orr, W. C., & Sohal, R. S. (1994). Extension of life-span by overexpression of superoxide dimutase and catalase in drosphila melanogaster. *Science, 263,* 1128–1130.

Ostrea, E. M., Brady, M., Gause, S., Raymundo, A. L., & Stevens, M. (1992). Drug screening of newborns by meconium analysis: A large-scale, prospective, epidemiologic study. *Pediatrics, 89*(1), 107–113.

Ostrea, E. M., & Chavez, C. J. (1979). Perinatal problems (excluding neonatal withdrawal) in maternal drug addiction: A study of 830 cases. *Journal of Pediatrics, 94*(2), 292–295.

Oswald, P. F., & Peltzman, P. (1974). The cry of the human infant. *Scientific American, 230*(3), 84–90.

Otis, A. S., & Lennon, R. T. (1967). *Otis-Lennon Mental Ability Test* (Primary Levels I and II). New York: Harcourt Brace.

Otten, M. W., Teutsch, S. M., Williamson, D. F., & Marks, J. S. (1990). The effect of known risk factors on the excess mortality of black adults in the United States. *Journal of the American Medical Association, 263*(6), 845–850.

Ouslander, J. G. (1989). Medical care in nursing homes. *Journal of the American Medical Association, 262*(18), 2582–2591.

Owens, J. E., Cook, E. W., & Stevenson, I. (1990). Features of "near-death experience" in relation to whether or not patients were near death. *The Lancet, 336,* 1175–1177.

Owens, J. F., Matthews, K. A., Wing, R., & Kuller, L. H. (1992). Can physical activity mitigate the effects of aging in middle-aged women? *Circulation, 85*(3), 1265–1270.

Owens, W. A. (1966). Age and mental abilities: A second adult follow-up. *Journal of Educational Psychology, 57*(6), 311–325.

Padilla, A. M., Lindholm, K. J., Chen, A., Duran, R., et al. (1991). The English-only movement: Myths, reality, and implications for psychology. *American Psychologist, 46*(2), 120–130.

Palmore, E. (1981). *Social patterns in normal aging: Findings from the Duke Longitudinal Study.* Durham, NC: Duke University Press.

Palmore, E. B., Fillenbaum, G. G., & George, L. K. (1984). Consequences of retirement. *Journal of Gerontology, 39,* 109–116.

Paloma, M. M. (1972). Role conflict and the married professional woman. In C. Safilious-Rothschild (Ed.), *Toward a sociology of women.* Lexington, MA: Xerox.

Papalia, D. (1972). The status of several conservation abilities across the life-span. *Human Development, 15,* 229–243.

Papousek, H. (1959). A method of studying conditioned food reflexes in young children up to age six months. *Pavlovian Journal of Higher Nervous Activity, 9,* 136–140.

Papousek, H. (1960a). Conditioned motor alimentary reflexes in infants: 1. Experimental conditioned sucking reflex. *Ceskoslovenska Pediatrie, 15,* 861–872.

Papousek, H. (1960b). Conditioned motor alimentary reflexes in infants: 2. A new experimental method of investigation. *Ceskoslovenska Pediatrie, 15,* 981–988.

Papousek, H. (1961). Conditioned head rotation reflexes in infants in the first months of life. *Acta Paediatrica, 50,* 565–576.

Pappas, G., Queen, S., Hadden, W., & Fisher, G. (1993). The increasing disparity in mortality between socioeconomic groups in the United States, 1960 and 1986. *New England Journal of Medicine, 329,* 103–109.

Paris, S. G., & Lindauer, B. K. (1976). The role of influence in children's comprehension and memory for sentences. *Cognitive Psychology, 8,* 217–227.

Parke, R. D. (1977). Some effects of punishment on children's behavior–revisited. In E. M. Hetherington & R. D. Parke (Eds.), *Contemporary readings in child psychology.* New York: McGraw-Hill.

Parke, R. D., Grossman, K., & Tinsley, B. R. (1981). Father-mother-infant interaction in the newborn period: A German-American comparison. In T. M. Field, A. M. Sostek, P. Viete, & P. H. Leideman (Eds.), *Culture and early interaction.* Hillsdale, NJ: Erlbaum.

Parke, R. D., & Tinsley, B. R. (1981). The father's role in infancy: Determinants of involvement in caregiving and play. In M. E. Lamb (Ed.), *The role of the father in child development* (2d ed.). New York: Wiley.

Parker, J. G., & Asher, S. R. (1987). Peer relations and later personal adjustment: Are low-accepted children at risk? *Psychological Bulletin, 102*(3), 357–389.

Parlee, M. B. (1983). Menstrual rhythms in sensory processes: A review of fluctuations in vision, olfaction, audition, taste, and touch. *Psychological Bulletin, 93*(3), 539–548.

Parmelee, A. H., Wenner, W. H., & Schulz, H. R. (1964). Infant sleep patterns: From birth to 16 weeks of age. *Journal of Pediatrics, 65,* 576.

Parmentier, M., Libert, F., Schurmans, S., Schiffmann, S., Lefort, A., Eggerickx, D., Mollereau, C., Gerard, C., Perret, J., et al. (1992). Expression of members of the putative olfactory receptor gene family in mammalian germ cells. *Nature, 355*(6359), 453–455.

Parten, M. (1932). Social play among preschool children. *Journal of Abnormal and Social Psychology, 27,* 243–269.

Passuth, P., Maines, D., & Neugarten, B. L. (1984, April). *Age norms and age constraints twenty years later.* Paper presented at Midwest Sociological Society meeting, Chicago.

Patterson, C. J., Kupersmidt, J. B., & Griesler, P. C. (1990). Children's perceptions of self and of relationships with others as a function of sociometric status. *Child Development, 61,* 1335–1349.

Patterson, G. R., Chamberlain, P., & Reid, J. B. (1982). A comparative evaluation of a parent-training program. *Behavior Therapy, 13*(5), 638–650.

Patterson, G. R., DeBaryshe, B. D., & Ramsey, E. (1989). A developmental perspective on antisocial behavior. *American Psychologist, 44*(2), 329–335.

Patterson, G. R., Reid, J. B., & Dishion, T. J. (in press). *Antisocial boys.* Eugene, OR: Castalia.

Patterson, G. R., & Stouthamer-Loeber, M. (1984). The correlation of family management practices and delinquency. *Child Development, 55,* 1299–1307.

Pattison, E. M. (1977). The experience of dying. In E. M. Pattison (Ed.), *The experience of dying.* Englewood Cliffs, NJ: Prentice-Hall.

Paveza, G. J., Cohen, D., Eisdorfer, C., Freels, S., Semla, T., Ashford, J. W., Gorelick, P., Hirschman, R., Luchins, D., & Levy, P. (1992). Severe family violence and Alzheimer's disease: Prevalence and risk factors. *Gerontologist, 32*(4), 493–497.

Pearlin, L. I. (1980). Life strains and psychological distress among adults. In N. J. Smelser & E. H. Erikson (Eds.), *Themes of work and love in adulthood.* Cambridge, MA: Harvard University Press.

Pease, D., & Gleason, J. B. (1985). Gaining meaning: Semantic development. In J. B. Gleason (Ed.), *The development of language.* Columbus, OH: Merrill.

Pebley, A. R. (1981). Changing attitudes toward the timing of first birth. *Family Planning Perspectives, 13*(4), 171–175.

Peck, R. C. (1955). Psychological developments in the second half of life. In J. E. Anderson (Ed.), *Psychological aspects of aging.* Washington, DC: American Psychological Association.

Pedersen, F. A., Cain, R., & Zaslow, M. (1982). Variation in infant experience associated with alternative family roles. In L. Laosa & I. Sigel (Eds.), *The family as a learning environment.* New York: Plenum.

Pedersen, F. A., Rubenstein, J. L., & Yarrow, L. J. (1979). Infant development in father-absent families. *Journal of Genetic Psychology, 135,* 51–61.

Pedersen, E., Faucher, T. A., & Eaton, W. W. (1978). A new perspective of the effects of first-grade teachers on children's subsequent adult status. *Harvard Educational Review, 48,* 1–31.

Peel, E. A. (1967). *The psychological basis of education* (2d ed.). Edinburgh: Oliver & Boyd.

Perkins, H. W., & Harris, L. B. (1990). Familial bereavement and health in adult life course perspective. *Journal of Marriage and the Family, 52,* 233–241.

Perlmutter, M., Behrend, S. D., Kuo, F., & Muller, A. (1989). Social influences on children's problem solving. *Developmental Psychology, 25*(5), 744–754.

Perris, E. E., Myers, N. A., & Clifton, R. K. (1990). Long-term memory for a single infancy experience. *Child Development, 61,* 1796–1807.

Perrucci, C. C., & Targ, D. B. (1988). Effects of a plant closing on marriage and family life. In P. Voydanoff & L. C. Majka (Eds.), *Families and economic distress: Coping strategies and social policy.* Newbury Park, CA: Sage.

Perry, W. G. (1970). *Forms of intellectual and ethical development in the college years.* New York: Holt.

Persson-Blennow, I., & McNeil, T. F. (1981). Temperament characteristics of children in relation to gender, birth order, and social class. *American Journal of Orthopsychiatry, 51,* 710–714.

Peskin, H. (1967). Pubertal onset and ego functioning. *Journal of Abnormal Psychology, 72,* 1–15.

Peskin, H. (1973). Influence of the developmental schedule of puberty on learning and ego functioning. *Journal of Youth and Adolescence, 2,* 273–290.

Petchers, M. K., & Milligan, S. E. (1988). Access to health care in a black urban elderly population. *Gerontologist, 28*(2), 213–217.

Petitto, L. A., & Marentette, P. F. (1991). Babbling in the manual mode: Evidence for the ontogeny of language. *Science, 251,* 1493–1495.

Petri, E. (1934). Untersuchungen zur Erbedingheir der Menarche. *Z Morph Anthr, 33,* 43–48.

Pettigrew, T. F. (1964). Negro American intelligence. In T. F. Pettigrew (Ed.), *Profile of the Negro American* (pp. 100–135). Princeton, NJ: Van Nostrand Reinhold.

Pettit, E. J., & Bloom, B. L. (1984). Whose decision was it? The effects of initiator status on adjustment to marital disruption. *Journal of Marriage and the Family, 46*(3), 587–595.

Phillips, D., McCartney, K., & Scarr, S. (1987). Child-care quality and children's social development. *Developmental Psychology, 23*(4), 537–543.

Phillips, D. P. (1992). The birthday: Lifeline or deadline? *Psychosomatic Medicine, 54*(5), 532–542.

Phillips, D. P., & Carstensen, L. L. (1986). Clustering of teenage suicides after television news stories about suicide. *New England Journal of Medicine, 315*(11), 685–689.

Phillips, D. P., & King, E. W. (1988, September 24). Death takes a holiday:

Mortality surrounding major social occasions. *The Lancet*, pp. 728–732.

Phillips, D. P., & Paight, B. A. (1987). The impact of televised movies about suicide. *New England Journal of Medicine, 317*(13), 809–811.

Phillips, D. P., Ruth, T. E., & Wagner, L. M. (1993). Psychology and survival. *The Lancet, 342*, 1142–1145.

Phillips, D. P., & Smith, D. G. (1990). Postponement of death until symbolically meaningful occasions. *Journal of the American Medical Association, 263*, 1947–1951.

Piaget, J. (1932). *The moral judgment of the child*. New York: Harcourt Brace.

Piaget, J. (1951). *Play, dreams, and imitation* (C. Gattegno & F. M. Hodgson, Trans.). New York: Norton.

Piaget, J. (1952). *The origins of intelligence in children*. New York: International Universities Press.

Piaget, J. (1962). Comments on Vygotsky's critical remarks concerning *The language and thought of the child*, and *Judgment and reasoning in the child*. In L. S. Vygotsky, *Thought and language*. Cambridge, MA: Massachusetts Institute of Technology (MIT) Press.

Piaget, J., & Inhelder, B. (1967). *The child's conception of space*. New York: Norton.

Pillemer, K., & Finkelhor, D. (1988). The prevalence of elder abuse: A random sample survey. *Gerontologist, 28*(1), 51–57.

Pillemer, K., & Moore, D. W. (1989). Abuse of patients in nursing homes: Findings from a survey of staff. *Gerontologist, 29*(3), 314–320.

Pillemer, K., & Suitor, J. J. (1991). "Will I ever escape my child's problems?": Effects of adult children's problems on elderly parents. *Journal of Marriage and the Family, 53*, 585–594.

Pincus, T., Callahan, L. F., & Burkhauser, R. V. (1987). Most chronic diseases are reported more frequently by individuals with fewer than 12 years of formal education in the age 18–64 United States population. *Journal of Chronic Diseases, 40*(9), 865–874.

Pines, M. (1983, November). Can a rock walk? *Psychology Today, 15*(9), 44–54.

Pipp, S., Easterbrooks, M. A., & Harmon, R. J. (1992). The relation between attachment and knowledge of self and mother in one- to three-year-old infants. *Child Development, 63*, 738–750.

Plemons, J., Willis, S., & Baltes, P. (1978). Modifiability of fluid intelligence in aging: A short-term longitudinal training approach. *Journal of Gerontology, 33*(2), 224–231.

Plomin, R. (1989). Environment and genes: Determinants of behavior. *American Psychologist, 44*(2), 105–111.

Plomin, R. (1990). The role of inheritance in behavior. *Science, 248*, 183–188.

Plomin, R., Pedersen, N. L., McClearn, G. E., Nesselroade, J. R., & Bergeman,

C. S. (1988). EAS temperaments during the last half of the life span: Twins reared apart and twins reared together. *Psychology and Aging, 3*, 43–50.

Plomin, R., & Rende, R. (1991). Human behavioral genetics. In M. R. Rosenzweig & L. W. Porter (Eds.), *Annual Review of Psychology*, Vol. 42. Palo Alto, CA: Annual Reviews, Inc.

Poland, R. L. (1990). The question of routine neonatal circumcision. *New England Journal of Medicine, 322*(18), 1312–1315.

Pollack, R. F. (1985, March 14). A wrong way to see the aged. *The New York Times*, p. A27.

Pollock, L. A (1983). *Forgotten children*. Cambridge, MA: Cambridge University Press.

Poon, L. W. (1985). Differences in human memory with aging: Nature, causes, and clinical implications. In J. E. Birren & K. W. Schaie (Eds.), *Handbook of the psychology of aging* (2d ed.). New York: Van Nostrand Reinhold.

Pope, A. W., Bierman, K. L., & Mumma, G. H. (1991). Aggression, hyperactivity, and inattention-immaturity: Behavior dimensions associated with peer rejection in elementary school boys. *Developmental Psychology, 27*(4), 663–671.

Posner, J. K., & Vandell, D. L. (undated). *Low-income children's after school care: Are there beneficial effects of after school programs?* Unpublished manuscript, University of Wisconsin-Madison.

Power, T. G., & Chapieski, M. L. (1986). Childrearing and impulse control in toddlers: A naturalistic investigation. *Developmental Psychology, 22*(2), 271–275.

Poznanski, E. O. (1982). The clinical phenomenology of childhood depression. *American Journal of Orthopsychiatry, 52*(2), 308–313.

Pratt, M. W., Kerig, P., Cowan, P. A., & Cowan, C. P. (1988). Mothers and fathers teaching 3-year-olds: Authoritative parenting and adult scaffolding of young children's learning. *Developmental Psychology, 24*(6), 832–839.

Pratt, W. B. (1990). *Premarital sexual behavior, multiple sexual partners, and marital experience*. Paper presented at the annual meeting of the Population Association of America, Toronto.

Prechtl, H. F. R., & Beintema, D. J. (1964). *The neurological examination of the full-term newborn infant: Clinics in developmental medicine* (No. 12). London: Heinemann.

Prevention Index '93: A report card on the nation's health. (1993). Emmaus, PA: Rodale.

Pugh, D. (1983, November 11). Bringing an end to mutilation. *New Statesman*, pp. 8–9.

Purnick, N. (1984, November 26). City tries to keep young mothers in school. *The New York Times*, p. B1.

Pynoos, R. S., Frederick, C., Nader, K., Arroyo, W., Steinberg, A., Eth, S., Nunez, F., & Fairbanks, L. (1987). Life threat and post-traumatic stress in school-age children. *Archives of General Psychiatry, 44*, 1057–1063.

Quinby, N. (1985, October). On testing and teaching intelligence: A conversation with Robert Steinberg. *Educational Leadership*, pp. 50–53.

Rabiner, D., & Coie, J. (1989). Effect of expectancy induction on rejected peers' acceptance by unfamiliar peers. *Developmental Psychology, 25*(3), 450–457.

Rachal, J. V., Guess, L. L., Hubbard, R. L., Maisto, S. A., Cavanaugh, E. R., Waddell, R., & Benrud, C. H. (1980). *Adolescent drinking behavior: Vol. 1. The extent and nature of adolescent alcohol and drug use*. Research Triangle Park, NC: Research Triangle Institute.

Radin, N. (1981). The role of the father in cognitive, academic, and intellectual development. In M. E. Lamb (Ed.), *The role of the father in child development*. New York: Wiley.

Radin, N. (1988). Primary caregiving fathers of long duration. In P. Bronstein & C. P. Cowan (Eds.), *Fatherhood today: Men's changing role in the family*. New York: Wiley.

Raffaelli, M., & Larson, R. W. (1987). *Sibling interactions in late childhood and early adolescence*. Paper presented at the biennial meeting of the Society for Research in Child Development, Baltimore.

Rafferty, Y., & Shinn, M. (1991). Impact of homelessness on children. *American Psychologist, 46*(11), 1170–1179.

Ragozin, A. S., Basham, R. B., Crnic, K. A., Greenberg, M. T., & Robinson, N. M. (1982). Effects of maternal age on parenting role. *Developmental Psychology, 18*(4), 627–634.

Rakowski, W., & Mor, V. (1992). The association of physical activity with mortality among older adults in The Longitudinal Study of Aging. *Journal of Gerontology, 47*(4), M122–129.

Raskin, P. A., & Israel, A. C. (1981). Sex-role imitation in children: Effects of sex of child, sex of model, and sex-role appropriateness of modelled behavior. *Sex Roles, 1*, 1067–1076.

Rassin, D. K., Richardson, J., Baranowski, T., Nader, P. R., Guenther, N., Bee, D. E., & Brown, J. P. (1984). Incidence of breast-feeding in a low socioeconomic group of mothers in the United States: Ethnic patterns. *Pediatrics, 73*, 132–137.

Raven, J. C. (1983). *Raven progressive matrices test*. San Antonio, TX: Psychological Corporation.

Ravitch, D. (1983). The education pendulum. *Psychology Today, 17*(10), 62–71.

Read, M. S., Habicht, J.-P., Lechtig, A., & Klein, R. E. (1973, May). *Maternal malnutrition, birth weight, and child de-*

velopment. Paper presented at the International Symposium on Nutrition, Growth, and Development, Valencia, Spain.

Redding, R. E., Harmon, R. J., & Morgan, G. A. (1990). Maternal depression and infants' mastery behaviors. *Infant Behavior and Development, 113,* 391–396.

Reese, H. W. (1977). Imagery and associative memory. In R. V. Kali & J. W. Hagen (Eds.), *Perspectives on the development of memory and cognition.* Hillsdale, NJ: Erlbaum.

Reichard, S., Livson, F., & Peterson, P. (1962). *Aging and personality: A study of 87 older men.* New York: Wiley.

Reid, I. R., Ames, R. W., Evans, M. G., Gamble, G. D., & Sharpe, S. J. (1993). Effect of calcium supplementation on bone loss in postmenopausal women. *New England Journal of Medicine, 328*(7), 460–464.

Reid, J. R., Patterson, G. R., & Loeber, R. (1982). The abused child: Victim, instigator, or innocent bystander? In D. J. Berstein (Ed.), *Response structure and organization.* Lincoln: University of Nebraska Press.

Reid, R. L., & Yen, S. S. C. (1981). Premenstrual syndrome. *American Journal of Obstetrics and Gynecology, 139*(1), 85–104.

Reissland, N. (1988). Neonatal imitation in the first hour of life: Observations in rural Nepal. *Developmental Psychology, 24,* 464–469.

Remafedi, G., Resnick, M., Blum, R., & Harris, L. (1992). Demography of sexual orientation in adolescents. *Pediatrics, 89*(4), 714–721.

Rempel, J. (1985). Childless elderly: What are they missing? *Journal of Marriage and the Family, 47*(2), 343–348.

Renzulli, J. S., & McGreevy, A. M. (1984). *A study of twins included and not included in gifted programs.* Storrs: University of Connecticut School of Education.

Rescorla, L. (1991). Early academics: Introduction to the debate. In L. Rescorla, M. C. Hyson, & K. Hirsh-Pasek (1991), Academic instruction in early childhood: Challenge or pressure? *New Directions in Child Development, 53,* 5–11.

Restak, R. (1984). *The brain.* New York: Bantam.

Rexroat, C., & Shehan, C. (1987). The family life cycle of spouses' time in housework. *Journal of Marriage and the Family, 49,* 737–750.

Reznick, J. S., & Goldfield, B. A. (1992). Rapid change in lexical development in comprehension and production. *Developmental Psychology, 28*(3), 406–413.

Reznick, J. S., Kagan, J., Snidman, N., Gersten, M., Baak, K., & Rosenberg, A. (1986). Inhibited and uninhibited children: A follow-up study. *Child Development, 57,* 660–680.

Rheingold, H. L. (1956). The modification of social responsiveness in insti-

tutionalized babies. *Monographs of the Society for Research in Child Development, 21*(Serial No. 63).

Rheingold, H. L. (1985). Development as the acquisition of familiarity. *Annual Review of Psychology, 36,* 1–17.

Rhoads, G. G., & Kagan, A. (1983, March 5). The relationship of coronary disease, stroke, and mortality to weight in youth and middle age. *The Lancet,* pp. 492–495.

Rhodes, S. R. (1983). Age-related differences in work attitudes and behaviors: A review and conceptual analysis. *Psychological Bulletin, 93*(2), 328–367.

Rice, M. L. (1989). Children's language acquisition. *American Psychologist, 44*(2), 149–156.

Richards, M. P. M. (1971). Social interaction in the first week of human life. *Psychiatria, Neurologia, Neurochirugia, 74,* 35–42.

Richardson, D. W., & Short, R. V. (1978). Time of onset of sperm production in boys. *Journal of Biosocial Science, 5,* 15–25.

Ridenour, M. V. (1982). Infant walkers: Development tool or inherent danger. *Perceptual & Motor Skills, 55,* 1201–1202.

Rieder, M. J., Schwartz, C., & Newman, J. (1986). Patterns of walker use and walker injury. *Pediatrics, 78*(3), 488–493.

Riegel, K. F., & Riegel, R. M. (1972). Development, drop, and death. *Developmental Psychology, 6,* 309–316.

Rierdan, J., Koff, E., & Flaherty, J. (1986). Conceptions and misconceptions of menstruation. *Women and Health, 10*(4), 33–45.

Rierdan, J., Koff, E., & Stubbs, M. L. (1988). Gender, depression, and body image in early adolescents. *Journal of Early Adolescence, 8*(2), 109–117.

Rierdan, J., Koff, E., & Stubbs, M. L. (1989). A longitudinal analysis of body image as a predictor of the onset and persistence of adolescent girls' depression. *Journal of Early Adolescence, 9*(4), 454–466.

Rieser, J., Yonas, A., & Wilkner, K. (1976). Radial localization of odors by human newborns. *Child Development, 47,* 856–859.

Rindfuss, R. R., Morgan, S. P., & Swicegood, G. (1988). *First births in America.* Berkeley: University of California Press.

Rindfuss, R. R., & St. John, C. (1983). Social determinants of age at first birth. *Journal of Marriage and the Family, 45,* 553–565.

Ritvo, E. R., Freeman, B. J., Mason-Brothers, A., Mo, A., & Ritvo, A. M. (1985). Concordance for the syndrome of autism in 40 pairs of afflicted twins. *American Journal of Psychiatry, 142,* 74–77.

Rivara, F. P., Bergman, A. B., & Drake, C. (1989). Parental attitudes and practices toward children as pedestrians. *Pediatrics, 84*(6), 1017–1021.

Roberts, E. J., Kline, D., & Gagnon, J. (1978). *Family life and sexual learning: A study of the role of parents in the sexual learning of children.* New York: Project on Human Sexual Development, Population Education.

Roberts, G. C., Block, J. H., & Block, J. (1984). Continuity and change in parents' child-rearing practices. *Child Development, 55,* 586–597.

Roberts, P., & Newton, P. M. (1987). Levinsonian studies of women's adult development. *Psychology and Aging, 2*(2), 154–163.

Robertson, L. F. (1984, November). Why we went back to half-days. *Principal,* pp. 22–24.

Robinson, B., & Thurnher, M. (1981). Taking care of aged parents: A family cycle transition. *Gerontologist, 19*(6), 586–593.

Robinson, I., Ziss, K., Ganza, B., Katz, S., & Robinson, E. (1991). Twenty years of the sexual revolution, 1965–1985: An update. *Journal of Marriage and the Family, 53,* 216–220.

Robinson, J. L., Kagan, J., Reznick, J. S., & Corley, R. (1992). The heritability of inhibited and uninhibited behavior: A twin study. *Developmental Psychology, 28*(6), 1030–1037.

Robinson, L. C., & Blanton, P. W. (1993). Marital strengths in enduring marriages. *Family Relations, 42,* 38–45.

Robison, L. L., Buckley, J. D., Daigle, A. E., Wells, R., Benjamin, D., Arthur, D. C., & Hammond, G. D. (1989). Maternal drug use and risk of childhood nonlymphoblastic leukemia among offspring. *Cancer, 63,* 1904–1911.

Robson, K. S. (1967). The role of eye-to-eye contact in maternal-infant attachment. *Journal of Child Psychology and Psychiatry, 8,* 13–25.

Roche, A. F. (1981). The adipocyte-number hypothesis. *Child Development, 52,* 31–43.

Rock, D. A., Ekstrom, R. B., Goertz, M. E., Hilton, T. L., & Pollack, J. (1985). *Factors associated with decline of test scores of high school seniors, 1972 to 1980.* Washington, DC: U.S. Department of Education, Center for Statistics.

Rodman, H., & Cole, C. (1987). Latchkey children: A review of policy and resources. *Family Relations, 36,* 101–105.

Rogers, M. F., White, C. R., Sanders, R., Schable, C., Ksell, T. E., Wasserman, R. L., Ballanti, J. A., Peters, S. M., & Wray, B. B. (1990). Lack of transmission of human immunodeficiency virus from infected children to their household contacts. *Pediatrics, 85*(2), 210–214.

Rogoff, B., & Morelli, G. (1989). Perspectives on children's development from cultural psychology. *American Psychologist, 44*(2), 343–348.

Romero-Gwynn, E., & Carias, L. (1989). Breast-feeding intentions and practice among Hispanic mothers in southern California. *Pediatrics, 84*(4), 626–631.

Roopnarine, J., & Field, T. (1984). Play interaction of friends and acquaintances in nursery school. In T. Field, J. Roopnarine, & M. Segal (Eds.), *Friendships in normal and handicapped children.* Norwood, NJ: Ablex.

Roopnarine, J., & Honig, A. S. (1985, September). The unpopular child. *Young Children,* pp. 59–64.

Rose, R. M., Gordon, T. P., & Bernstein, I. S. (1972). Plasma testosterone levels in the male rhesus: Influences of sexual and social stimuli. *Science, 178*(4061), 643–645.

Rose, S. A., Feldman, J. F., Wallace, I. F., & McCarton, C. (1991). Information processing at 1 year: Relation to birth status and developmental outcome during the first 5 years. *Developmental Psychology, 27*(5), 723–737.

Rosen, B., & Jerdee, T. (1988). Managing older workers' careers. *Research in Personnel and Human Resources Management, 6,* 37–74.

Rosen, J. G., & Gross, J. (1987). Prevalence of weight reducing and weight gaining in adolescent girls and boys. *Health Psychology, 6*(2), 131–147.

Rosen, L. A., Booth, S. R., Bender, M. E., McGrath, M. L., Sorrell, S., & Brabman, R. S. (1988). Effects of sugar (sucrose) on children's behavior. *Journal of Consulting and Clinical Psychology, 56*(4), 583–589.

Rosenberg, L., Palmer, J. R., & Shapiro, S. (1990). Decline in the risk of myocardial infarction among women who stop smoking. *New England Journal of Medicine, 322,* 213–217.

Rosenberg, M. B., Friedmann, T., Robertson, R. C., Tuszynski, M., Wolff, J. A., Breakefield, X. O., & Gage, F. H. (1988). Grafting genetically modified cells to the damaged brain: Restorative effects of NGF expression. *Science, 242,* 1575–1578.

Rosenberg, M. S. (1987). New directions for research on the psychological maltreatment of children. *American Psychologist, 42*(2), 166–171.

Rosenblatt, P. (1983). *Bitter, bitter tears: Nineteenth century diarists and twentieth century grief theories.* Minneapolis: University of Minnesota Press.

Rosenfeld, A., & Stark, E. (1987). The prime of our lives. *Psychology Today, 21*(5), 62–72.

Rosenthal, M. K. (1982). Vocal dialogues in the neonatal period. *Developmental Psychology, 18*(1), 17–21.

Rosenthal, P. A., & Rosenthal, S. (1984). Suicidal behavior by preschool children. *American Journal of Psychiatry, 141*(4), 520–525.

Rosenthal, R., & Jacobson, L. (1968). *Pygmalion in the classroom.* New York: Holt.

Rosenzweig, M. R. (1984). Experience, memory, and the brain. *American Psychologist, 39,* 365–376.

Rosenzweig, M. R., & Bennett, E. L. (Eds.). (1976). *Neural mechanisms of learning and memory.* Cambridge, MA: Massachusetts Institute of Technology (MIT) Press.

Rosetti-Ferreira, M. C. (1978). Malnutrition and mother-infant asynchrony: Slow mental development. *International Journal of Behavioral Development, 1,* 207–219.

Ross, C. E., Mirowsky, J., & Goldsteen, K. (1990). The impact of the family on health: A decade in review. *Journal of Marriage and the Family, 52,* 1059–1078.

Ross, G., Lipper, E. G., & Auld, P. A. M. (1991). Educational status and school-related abilities of very low birth weight premature children. *Pediatrics, 88,* 1125–1134.

Ross, H. G., Dalton, M. J., & Milgram, J. I. (1980, November). *Older adults' perceptions of closeness in sibling relationships.* Paper presented at the annual meeting of the Gerontological Society, San Diego, CA.

Rossi, A. S. (1980). Aging and parenthood in the middle years. In P. B. Baltes & O. G. Brim (Eds.), *Life-span development and behavior,* Vol. 3. New York: Academic Press.

Rossi, A. S., & Rossi, P. H. (1990). *Of human bonding: Parent-child relations across the life course.* New York: Aldine de Gruyter.

Rovee-Collier, C. (1987). Learning and memory in infancy. In J. D. Osofsky (Ed.), *Handbook of infant development* (2d ed.). New York: Wiley.

Rovee-Collier, C., & Fagan, J. (1976). Extended conditioning and 24-hour retention in infants. *Journal of Experimental Child Psychology, 21,* 1.

Rovee-Collier, C., & Fagan, J. (1981). The retrieval of memory in early infancy. In L. P. Lipsitt (Ed.), *Advances in infancy research,* Vol. 1. Norwood, NJ: Ablex.

Rovee-Collier, C., & Lipsitt, L. (1982). Learning, adaptation, and memory in the newborn. In P. Stratton (Ed.), *Psychobiology of the human newborn.* New York: Wiley.

Rovee-Collier, C., Schechter, A., Shyi, G., & Shields, P. (1992). Perceptual identification of contextual attributes and infant memory retrieval. *Developmental Psychology, 28*(2), 307–318.

Roybal, E. R. (1988). Mental health and aging. *American Psychologist, 43*(3), 184–189.

Ruberman, W., Weinblatt, E., Goldberg, J. D., & Chaudhary, B. S. (1984). Psychosocial influences on mortality after myocardial infarction. *New England Journal of Medicine, 311,* 552–559.

Rubin, A. (1977, September). Birth injuries. *Hospital Medicine,* pp. 114–130.

Rubin, D. H., Krasilnikoff, P. A., Leventhal, J. M., Weile, B., & Berget, A. (1986, August 23). Effect of passive smoking on birth-weight. *The Lancet,* pp. 415–417.

Rubin, D. H., Leventhal, J. M., Krasilnikoff, P. A., Kuo, H. S., Jekel, J. F., Weile, B., Levee, A., Kurzon, M., & Berget, A. (1990). Relationship between infant feeding and infectious illness: A prospective study of infants during the first year of life. *Pediatrics, 85,* 464–471.

Rubin, K. (1982). Nonsocial play in preschoolers: Necessary evil? *Child Development, 53,* 651–657.

Rubin, K., Maioni, T. L., & Hornung, M. (1976). Free play behaviors in middle-class and lower-class preschoolers: Parten and Piaget revisited. *Child Development, 47,* 414–419.

Rubin, K., Watson, K., & Jambor, T. (1978). Free-play behaviors in preschool and kindergarten children. *Child Development, 49,* 534–546.

Rubin, L. B. (1979). *Women of a certain age.* New York: Harper & Row.

Rubin, L. B. (1982). Sex and sexuality: Women at midlife. In M. Kirkpatricks (Ed.), *Women's sexual experiences: Exploration of the dark continent* (pp. 61–82). New York: Plenum.

Rubin, Z. (1981). Does personality really change after 20? *Psychology Today, 15*(3), 18–27.

Rubinstein, R. L. Alexander, B. B., Goodman, M., & Luborsky, M. (1991). Key relationships of never married, childless older women: A cultural analysis. *Journal of Gerontology, 46*(5), S270–277.

Ruble, D. N., & Brooks-Gunn, J. (1982). The experience of menarche. *Child Development, 53,* 1557–1566.

Rudman, D., Axel, G. F., Hoskote, S. N., Gergans, G. A., Lalitha, P. Y., Goldberg, A. F., Schlenker, R. A., Cohn, L., Rudman, I. W., & Mattson, D. E. (1990). Effects of human growth hormone in men over 60 years old. *New England Journal of Medicine, 323*(1), 1–6.

Ruhm, C. J. (1989). Why older Americans stop working. *Gerontologist, 29*(3), 294–299.

Rule, S. (1981, June 11). The battle to stem school dropouts. *The New York Times,* pp. A1, B10.

Russell, A., & Finnie, V. (1990). Preschool children's social status and maternal instructions to assist group entry. *Developmental Psychology, 26*(4), 603–611.

Rutter, M. (1971). Parent-child separation: Psychological effects on the children. *Journal of Child Psychology and Psychiatry, 12,* 233–260.

Rutter, M. (1979a). Maternal deprivation, 1972–1978: New findings, new concepts, new approaches. *Child Development, 50,* 283–305.

Rutter, M. (1979b). Separation experiences: A new look at an old topic. *Pediatrics, 95*(1), 147–154.

Rutter, M. (1983). Stress, coping, and development: Some issues and some questions. In N. Garmezy & M. Rutter (Eds.), *Stress, coping, and development in children.* New York: McGraw-Hill.

Rutter, M. (1984). Resilient children. *Psychology Today, 18*(3), 57–65.

Rutter, M. (1987). Continuities and discontinuities from infancy. In J. Osofsky (Ed.), *Handbook of infant development*. New York: Wiley.

Ryan, A. S., Craig, L. D., & Finn, S. C. (1992). Nutrient intakes and dietary patterns of older Americans: A national study. *Journal of Gerontology, 47*(5), M145–150.

Ryan, A. S., Rush, D., Krieger, F. W., & Lewandowski, G. E. (1991). Recent decline in breast-feeding in the United States, 1984 through 1989. *Pediatrics, 88*, 719–727.

Ryerson, A. J. (1961). Medical advice on child rearing, 1550–1900. *Harvard Educational Review, 31*, 302–323.

Ryff, C. D. (1982). Self-perceived personality change in adulthood and aging. *Journal of Personality and Social Psychology, 42*(1), 108–115.

Ryff, C. D. (1989). In the eye of the beholder: Views of psychological well-being among middle-aged and older adults. *Psychology and Aging, 4*(2), 195–210.

Ryff, C. D., & Baltes, P. B. (1976). Value transition and adult development in women: The instrumentality-terminality sequence hypothesis. *Developmental Psychology, 12*(6), 567–568.

Ryff, C. D., & Heincke, S. G. (1983). Subjective organization of personality in adulthood and aging. *Journal of Personality and Social Psychology, 44*(4), 807–816.

Rymer, R. (1993). *An abused child: Flight from silence*. New York: Harper Collins.

Sabatelli, R. M., Meth, R. L., & Gavazzi, S. M. (1988). Factors mediating the adjustment to involuntary childlessness. *Family Relations, 37*, 338–343.

Sacco, R. L., Hauser, W. A., & Mohr, J. P. (1991). Hospitalized stroke in blacks and Hispanics in northern Manhattan. *Stroke, 22*(12), 1491–1496.

Sachs, B. P., McCarthy, B. J., Rubin, G., Burton, A., Terry, J., & Tyler, C. W. (1983). Cesarean section. *Journal of the American Medical Association, 250*(16), 2157–2159.

Sacks, J. J., Smith, J. D., Kaplan, K. M., Lambert, D. A., Sattin, W., & Sikes, K. (1989). The epidemiology of injuries in Atlanta day-care centers. *Journal of the American Medical Association, 262*(12), 1641–1645.

Sadowitz, P. D., & Oski, F. A. (1983). Iron status and infant feeding practices in an urban ambulatory center. *Pediatrics, 72*(1), 33–36.

Sagi, A., & Hoffman, M. (1976). Empathic distress in newborns. *Developmental Psychology, 12*(2), 175–176.

Saigal, S., Szatmari, P., Rosenbaum, P., Campbell, D., & King, S. (1990). Intellectual and functional status at school entry of children who weighed 1000 grams or less at birth: A regional perspective of births in the 1980s. *Journal of Pediatrics, 116*, 409–416.

Salthouse, T. A. (1985). Speed of behavior and its implications for cognition. In J. E. Birren & K. W. Schaie (Eds.), *Handbook of the psychology of aging*. New York: Van Nostrand Reinhold.

Salzinger, S., Feldman, R. S., Hammer, M., & Rosario, M. (1993). Effects of physical abuse on children's social relations. *Child Development, 64*, 169–187.

Sandler, D. P., Everson, R. B., Wilcox, A. J., & Browder, J. P. (1985). Cancer risk in adulthood from early life exposure to parents' smoking. *American Journal of Public Health, 75*, 487–492.

Sands, L. P., & Meredith, W. (1992). Blood pressure and intellectual functioning in late midlife. *Journal of Gerontology, 47*(2), P81–84.

Santer, L. J., & Stocking, C. B. (1991). Safety practices and living conditions of low-income urban families. *Pediatrics, 88*(6), 111–118.

Santrock, J. W., Sitterle, K. A., & Warshak, R. A. (1988). Parent-child relationships in stepfather families. In P. Bronstein & C. P. Cowan (Eds.), *Fatherhood today: Men's changing role in the family*. New York: Wiley.

Sapienza, C. (1990, October). Parental imprinting of genes. *Scientific American*, pp. 52–60.

Saravis, S., Schachar, R., Zlotkin, S., Leiter, L. A., & Anderson, H. (1990). Aspartame: Effects on learning, behavior, and mood. *Pediatrics, 86*, 75–83.

Sauer, M. V., Paulson, R. J., & Lobo, R. A. (1990). A preliminary report on oocyte donation extending reproductive potential to women over 40. *New England Journal of Medicine, 323*, 1157–1160.

Scarborough, H. S. (1990). Very early language deficits in dyslexic children. *Child Development, 61*, 1728–1743.

Scarr, S., Phillips, D., & McCartney, K. (1989). Working mothers and their families. *American Psychologist, 44*(11), 1402–1409.

Scarr, S., & Weinberg, R. (1983). The Minnesota adoption study: Genetic differences and malleability. *Child Development, 54*, 260–267.

Schafer, R. (1980). *Narrative action in psychoanalysis*. Worcester, MA: Clark University Press.

Schaie, K. W. (1977–1978). Toward a stage theory of adult cognitive development. *Journal of Aging and Human Development, 8*(2), 129–138.

Schaie, K. W. (1979). The primary mental abilities in adulthood: An exploration in the development of psychometric intelligence. In P. B. Baltes & O. G. Brim (Eds.), *Life-span development and behavior*, Vol. 2. New York: Academic Press.

Schaie, K. W. (1983). The Seattle longitudinal study: A twenty-one-year investigation of psychometric intelligence. In K. W. Schaie (Ed.), *Longitudinal studies of adult personality development*. New York: Guilford.

Schaie, K. W. (1984). Midlife influences upon intellectual functioning in old age. *Journal of Behavioral Development, 7*, 463–478.

Schaie, K. W. (1989). The hazards of cognitive aging. *Gerontologist, 29*(4), 484–493.

Schaie, K. W., & Gribbin, K. (1975). Adult development and aging. *Annual Review of Psychology, 26*, 65–96.

Schaie, K. W., & Herzog, C. (1983). Fourteen-year cohort sequential analyses of adult intellectual development. *Developmental Psychology, 19*(4), 531–543.

Schaie, K. W., & Strother, C. (1968). A cross-sequential study of age changes in cognitive behavior. *Psychological Bulletin, 70*, 671–680.

Schaie, K. W., & Willis, S. L. (1991). Adult personality and psychomotor performance: Cross-sectional and longitudinal analysis. *Journal of Gerontology, 46*(6), P275–284.

Schanberg, S. M., & Field, T. M. (1987). Sensory deprivation illness and supplemental stimulation in the rat pup and preterm human neonate. *Child Development, 58*, 1431–1447.

Scharlach, A. E. (1987). Relieving feelings of strain among women with elderly mothers. *Psychology and Aging, 2*(1), 9–13.

Schechtman, V. L., Harper, R. M., Wilson, A. J., & Southall, D. P. (1992). Sleep state organization in normal infants and victims of the sudden infant death syndrome. *Pediatrics, 89*, 865–870.

Schick, F. L. (Ed.). (1986). *Statistical handbook on aging Americans*. Phoenix, AZ: Oryz.

Schindler, P. J., Moely, B. E., & Frank, A. L. (1987). Time in day care and social participation in young children. *Developmental Psychology, 23*(2), 255–261.

Schiro, A. (1988, August 25). Parents agree to detente in the clothes wars. *The New York Times*, pp. C1, C6.

Schlossberg, N. K. (1987). Taking the mystery out of change. *Psychology Today, 21*(5), 74–75.

Schmeck, H. M. (1976, June 10). Trend in growth of children lags. *The New York Times*, p. A13.

Schmeck, H. M. (1983, March 22). U.S. panel calls for patients' right to end life. *The New York Times*, pp. A1, C7.

Schmidt, W. E. (1988, April 6). Graying of America prompts new highway safety efforts. *The New York Times*, pp. A1, A17.

Schmitt, B. D., & Kempe, C. H. (1983). Abusing neglected children. In R. E. Berhman & V. C. Vaughn (Eds.), *Nelson textbook of pediatrics* (12th ed.). Philadelphia: Saunders.

Schmitt, M. H. (1970). Superiority of breastfeeding: Fact or fancy? *American Journal of Nursing*, 1488–1493.

Schnall, P. L., Pieper, C., Schwartz, J. E., Karasek, R. A., Schlussel, Y., Devereux, R. B., Ganau, A., Alderman, M., Warren, K., & Pickering, T. G. (1990). The relationship between 'job strain,' workplace diastolic blood pressure, and left ventricular mass index: Results of a case-control study. *Journal of the American Medical Association, 263,* 1929–1935.

Schneider, E. L., & Guralnik, J. M. (1990). The aging of America: Impact on health care costs. *Journal of the American Medical Association, 263*(17), 2335–2340.

Schoen, E. J. (1990). The status of circumcision of newborns. *New England Journal of Medicine, 322*(18), 1308–1312.

Schoen, R. (1992). First unions and the stability of first marriages. *Journal of Marriage and the Family, 54,* 281–284.

Schoendorf, K. C., Hogue, C. J. R., Kleinman, J. C., & Rowley, D. (1992). Mortality among infants of black as compared with white college-educated parents. *New England Journal of Medicine, 326,* 1522–1526.

Schoendorf, K. C., & Kiely, J. L. (1992). Relationship of sudden infant death syndrome to maternal smoking. *Pediatrics, 90*(6): 905–908.

Schor, E. L. (1987). Unintentional injuries: Patterns within families. *American Journal of the Diseases of Children, 141,* 1280.

Schuckit, M. A. (1985). Genetics and the risk for alcoholism. *Journal of the American Medical Association, 254*(18), 2614–2617.

Schuckit, M. A. (1987). Biological vulnerability to alcoholism. *Journal of Consulting and Clinical Psychology, 55*(3), 301–309.

Schulman, S. (1986). Facing the invisible handicap. *Psychology Today, 20*(2), 58–64.

Schultz, D. P., & Schultz, S. E. (1986). *Psychology and industry today* (4th ed.). New York: Macmillan.

Schulz, R. (1978). *The psychology of death, dying, and bereavement.* Reading, MA: Addison-Wesley.

Schutter, S., & Brinker, R. (1992). Conjuring a new category of disability from prenatal cocaine exposure: Are the infants unique biological or caretaking casualties? *Topics in Early Childhood Special Education, 11,* 84–111.

Schvaneveldt, J. D., Lindauer, S. L. K., & Young, M. H. (1990). Children's understanding of AIDS: A developmental viewpoint. *Family Relations, 39,* 330–335.

Schweinhart, L. U., Weikart, D. P., & Larner, M. B. (1986). A report on the High/Scope preschool curriculum comparison study. *Early Childhood Research Quarterly, 1,* 15–45.

Scott, G. B., Hutto, C., Makuch, R. W., Mastrucci, M. T., O'Connor, T., Mitchell, C. D., Trapido, E. J., & Parks, W. P. (1989). Survival in children with perinatal acquired immunodeficiency virus type 1 infection. *New England Journal of Medicine, 321,* 1791–1796.

Scott, J. P. (1958). *Animal behavior.* Chicago: University of Chicago Press.

Scott, J. P., & Roberto, K. A. (1981, October). *Sibling relationships in late life.* Paper presented at the annual meeting of the National Council on Family Relations, Milwaukee.

Scott, J. R. (1991). Mandatory trial of labor after cesarean delivery: An alternative viewpoint. *Obstetrics and Gynecology, 77*(6), 811–814.

Sears, P., & Barbee, A. (1978). Career and life satisfaction among Terman's gifted women. In *The gifted and the creative: A fifty-year perspective.* Baltimore: Johns Hopkins University Press.

Sears, R. R., Maccoby, E. E., & Levin, H. (1957). *Patterns of child rearing.* New York: Harper & Row.

Seccombe, K. (1991). Assessing the costs and benefits of children: Gender comparisons among childfree husbands and wives. *Journal of Marriage and the Family, 53,* 191–202.

Selkoe, D. A. (1991). The molecular pathology of Alzheimer's disease. *Neuron, 6*(4), 487–498.

Selkoe, D. J. (1992). Aging brain, aging mind. *Scientific American, 267,* 135–142.

Sells, L. W. (1980). The mathematics filter and the education of women and minorities. In L. H. Fox, L. Brody, & I. Tobin (Eds.), *Women and the mathematical mystique.* Baltimore: Johns Hopkins University Press.

Selman, R. L., & Selman, A. P. (1979). Children's ideas about friendship: A new theory. *Psychology Today, 13*(4), 71–80, 114.

Sen, A. (1993). The economics of life and death. *Scientific American, 268*(5) 40–47.

Sexton, M., & Hebel, R. (1984). A clinical trial of change in maternal smoking and its effect on birth weight. *Journal of the American Medical Association, 251*(7), 911–915.

Sgawara, O., Oshimura, M., Koi, M., Annab, L. A., & Barrett, J. C. (1990). Induction of cellular senescence in immortalized cells by human chromosome 1. *Science, 247,* 707–710.

Shangold, M. (1978, May 14). Female runners advised to follow common sense. *The New York Times,* Sec. 5, p. 2.

Shannon, D. C., & Kelly, D. H. (1982a). SIDS and near-SIDS (Part 1). *New England Journal of Medicine, 306*(16), 959–965.

Shannon, D. C., & Kelly, D. H. (1982b). SIDS and near-SIDS (Part 2). *New England Journal of Medicine, 306*(17), 1022–1028.

Shannon, L. W. (1982). *Assessing the relationship of adult criminal careers to juvenile careers.* Iowa City, IA: University of Iowa, Iowa Urban Community Research Center.

Shatz, M., & Gelman, R. (1973). The development of communication skills: Modifications in the speech of young children as a function of listener. *Monographs of the Society for Research in Child Development, 38*(5, Serial No. 152).

Shay, K. A., & Roth, D. L. (1992). Association between aerobic fitness and visuospatial performance in healthy older adults. *Psychology and Aging, 7*(1), 15–24.

Shaywitz, S. E., Shaywitz, B. A., Fletcher, J. M., & Escobar, M. D. (1990). Prevalence of reading disability in boys and girls. *Journal of the American Medical Association, 246*(8), 998–1002.

Sheps, S., & Evans, G. D. (1987). Epidemiology of school injuries: A 2-year experience in a muncipal health department. *Pediatrics, 79*(1), 69–75.

Sherman, L. W., & Berk, R. A. (1984, April). The Minneapolis domestic violence experiment. *Police Foundation Reports,* pp. 1–8.

Sherman, L. W., & Cohn, E. G. (1989). The impact of research on legal policy: The Minneapolis domestic violence experiment. *Law and Society Review,* pp. 118–144.

Shields, P. J., & Rovee-Collier, C. (1992). Long-term memory for context-specific category information at six months. *Child Development, 63,* 245–259.

Ship, J. A., & Weiffenbach, J. M. (1993). Age, gender, medical treatment, and medication effects on smell identification. *Journal of Gerontology, 48*(1), M26–32.

Shipp, E. R. (1988, February 4). Decision could hinder surrogacy across nation. *The New York Times,* p. B6.

Siegel, O. (1982). Personality development in adolescence. In B. B. Woman (Ed.), *Handbook of developmental psychology.* Englewood Cliffs, NJ: Prentice-Hall.

Siegler, R. S., & Richards, S. (1982). The development of intelligence. In R. Sternberg (Ed.), *Handbook of human intelligence.* London: Cambridge University Press.

Sigman, M., Neumann, C., Jansen, A. A. J., & Bwibo, N. (1989). Cognitive abilities of Kenyan children in relation to nutrition, family characteristics, and education. *Child Development, 60,* 1463–1474.

Sigman, M. D., Kasari, C., Kwon, J.-H., & Yirmiya, N. (1992). Responses to the negative emotions of others by autistic, mentally retarded, and normal children. *Child Development, 63,* 796–807.

Signorielli, N., Gross, L., & Morgan, M. (1982). Violence in television programs: Ten years later. In D. Pearl, L. Bouthilet, & J. Lazar (Eds.), *Television and behavior: Ten years of scientific progress and implications for the eighties: Technical reviews,* Vol. 2. Washington, DC: National Institute of Mental Health.

Silverman, S. (1989). Scope, specifics of maternal drug use, effects on fetus are beginning to emerge from studies. *Journal of the American Medical Association, 261*(12), 1688–1689.

Silverstein, B., Perdue, L., Peterson, B., et al. (1986). The role of the mass media in promoting a thin standard of bodily attractiveness for women. *Sex Roles, 14*(9/10), 519–532.

Silverstein, B., Peterson, B., & Perdue, L. (1986). Some correlates of the thin standard of bodily attractiveness for women. *International Journal of Eating Disorders, 5*(5).

Simmons, R. G., Blyth, D. A., & McKinney, K. L. (1983). The social and psychological effects of puberty on white females. In J. Brooks-Gunn & A. C. Petersen (Eds.), *Girls at puberty: Biological and psychological perspectives.* New York: Plenum.

Simmons, R. G., Blyth, D. A., Van Cleave, E. F., & Bush, D. M. (1979). Entry into early adolescence: The impact of school structure, puberty, and early dating on self-esteem. *American Sociological Review, 44*(6), 948–967.

Simmons, R. G., Burgeson, R., Carlton-Ford, S., & Blyth, D. A. (1987). The impact of cumulative change in early adolescence. *Child Development, 58,* 1220–1234.

Simner, M. L. (1971). Newborn's response to the cry of another infant. *Developmental Psychology, 5*(1), 135–150.

Simons, C. (1987, March). They get by with a lot of help from their *kyoiku* mamas. *Smithsonian,* pp. 44–52.

Simons, M. (1993, February 10). Dutch parliament approves law permitting euthanasia. *The New York Times,* p. A10.

Simpson, R., Kelly, S. F., Atinson, H. P., Turner, M., Greiser, K., & Zhao, D. (1991). Abstract. In *Circulation, 84*(4), 11–334, No. 1330.

Singer, D. G., & Singer, J. L. (1990). *The house of make-believe: Play and the developing imagination.* Cambridge, MA: Harvard University Press.

Singer, J. L., & Singer, D. G. (1981). *Television, imagination, and aggression: A study of preschoolers.* Hillsdale, NJ: Erlbaum.

Singh, S., Forrest, J. D., & Torres, A. (1989). *Prenatal care in the United States: A state and county inventory.* New York: Alan Guttmacher Institute.

Singleton, L., & Asher, S. (1979). Racial integration and children's peer preferences: An investigation of developmental and cohort differences. *Child Development, 50,* 936–941.

Sisodia, S. S., Koo, E. H., Beyreuther, K., Unterbeck, A., & Price, D. L. (1990). Evidence that B-amyloid protein in Alzheimer's disease is not derived by normal processing. *Science, 248,* 492–495.

Skaff, M. M., & Pearlin, L. I. (1992). Caregiving: Role engulfment and the loss of self. *Gerontologist, 32*(5), 656–664.

Skinner, B. F. (1938). *The behavior of organisms: An experimental approach.* New York: Appleton-Century.

Skinner, B. F. (1957). *Verbal behavior.* New York: Appleton-Century-Crofts.

Sklar, L. S., & Anisman, H. (1981). Stress and cancer. *Psychological Bulletin, 89*(3), 369–406.

Skoe, E. E., & Gooden, A. (1993). Ethics of care and real-life moral dilemma content in male and female early adolescents. *Journal of Early Adolescence, 13*(2), 154–167.

Skolnick, A. (1990). It's important, but don't bank on exercise alone to prevent osteoporosis. *Journal of the American Medical Association, 263*(13), 1751–1752.

Skoog, I., Nilsson, L., Palmertz, B., Andreasson, L., & Svanborg, A. (1993). A population-based study for dementia in 85-year-olds. *New England Journal of Medicine, 328,* 153–158.

Slap, G. B., Vorters, D. F., Chaudhuri, S., & Centor, R. M. (1989). Risk factors for attempted suicide during adolescence. *Pediatrics, 84,* 762–772.

Slevin, J. D. (1986, October). Geniuses are made, not born. *The World and I, 1*(10).

Slobin, D. (1973). Cognitive prerequisites for the acquisition of grammar. In C. Ferguson & D. Slobin (Eds.), *Studies of child language development.* New York: Holt, Rinehart, & Winston.

Slobin, D. (1983). Universal and particular in the acquisition of language. In E. Wanner & L. Gleitman (Eds.), *Language acquisition: The state of the art.* Cambridge, England: Cambridge University Press.

Slobin, D. I. (1971). Universals of grammatical development in children. In W. Levelt & G. B. Flores d'Arcais (Eds.), *Advances in psycholinguistic research.* Amsterdam: New Holland.

Smelser, N. J. (1980). Issues in the study of work and love in adulthood. In N. J. Smelser & E. H. Erikson (Eds.), *Themes of work and love in adulthood.* Cambridge, MA: Harvard University Press.

Smetana, J. G., Yau, J., Restrepo, A., & Braeges, J. L. (1991). Adolescent-parent conflict in married and divorced families. *Developmental Psychology, 27*(6), 1000–1010.

Smilansky, S. (1968). *The effects of sociodramatic play on disadvantaged preschool children.* New York: Wiley.

Smith, D. W., & Wilson, A. A. (1973). *The child with Down's syndrome (mongolism).* Philadelphia: Saunders.

Smith, J., & Baltes, P. B. (1990). Wisdom-related knowlege: Age/cohort differences in response to life-planning problems. *Developmental Psychology, 26*(3), 494–505.

Smith, T. E. (1981). Adolescent agreement with perceived maternal and paternal educational goals. *Journal of Marriage and the Family, 43,* 85–93.

Smith, T. W. (1991). Adult sexual behavior in 1989: Number of partners, frequency of intercourse and risk of AIDS. *Family Planning Perspectives, 23*(3), 102–107.

Snarey, J. R. (1985). Cross-cultural universality of social-moral development: A critical review of Kohlbergian research. *Psychological Bulletin, 97,* 202–232.

Snow, C. E. (1972). Mother's speech to children learning language. *Child Development, 43,* 549–565.

Snow, C. E. (1977). Mother's speech research: From input to interaction. In C. E. Snow & C. A. Ferguson (Eds.), *Talking to children: Language input and acquisition.* London: Cambridge University Press.

Snow, C. E., Arlman-Rupp, A., Hassing, Y., Jobse, J., Jootsen, J., & Verster, J. (1976). Mothers' speech in three social classes. *Journal of Psycholinguistic Research, 5,* 1–20.

Snow, M. E., Jacklin, C. N., & Maccoby, E. E. (1983). Sex-of-child differences in father-child interaction at one year of age. *Child Development, 54,* 227–232.

Soddy, K., & Kidson, M. (1967). *Men in middle life, cross-cultural studies in mental health.* Philadelphia: Lippincott.

Solomon, M. (1993). Report of survey of doctors and nurses about treatment of terminally ill patients. *American Journal of Public Health, 83*(1), 23–25.

Solomons, H. (1978). The malleability of infant motor development. *Clinical Pediatrics, 17*(11), 836–839.

Sonenstein, F. L., Pleck, J. H., & Ku, L. C. (1989). Sexual activity, condom use, and AIDS awareness among adolescent males. *Family Planning Perspectives, 21,* 152–158.

Sonenstein, F. L., Pleck, J. H., & Ku, L. C. (1991). Levels of sexual activity among adolescent males in the United States. *Family Planning Perspectives, 23*(4), 162–167.

Song, M., & Ginsburg, H. P. (1987). The development of informal and formal mathematical thinking in Korean and U.S. children. *Child Development, 58,* 1286–1296.

Sontag, S. (1972, September 23). The double standard of aging. *Saturday Review,* pp. 29–38.

Sorce, J. F., Emde, R. N., Campos, J., & Klinnert, M. D. (1985). Maternal emotional signaling: Its effect on the visual cliff behavior of 1-year-olds. *Developmental Psychology, 21*(1), 195–200.

Sorensen, R. C. (1973). *Adolescent sexuality in contemporary America.* Tarrytown, NY: World.

Sorensen, T., Nielsen, G., Andersen, P., & Teasdale, T. (1988). Genetic and environmental influence of premature death in adult adoptees. *New England Journal of Medicine, 318,* 727–732.

Speece, M. W., & Brent, S. B. (1984). Children's understanding of death: A review of three components of a death concept. *Child Development, 55,* 1671–1686.

Spencer, M. B., & Markstrom-Adams, C. (1990). Identity processes among racial and ethnic minority children. *Child Development, 61,* 290–310.

Spirduso, W. W., & MacRae, P. G. (1990). Motor performance and aging. In J. E. Birren & K. W. Schaie (Eds.), *Psychology of aging* (3d ed.). New York: Academic Press.

Spitz, M. R., & Johnson, C. C. (1985). Neuroblastoma and paternal occupation: A case-control analysis. *American Journal of Epidemiology, 121*(6), 924–929.

Spitz, R. A. (1945). Hospitalism: An inquiry in the genesis of psychiatric conditioning in early childhood. In D. Fenschel et al. (Eds.), *Psychoanalytic studies of the child,* Vol. 1 (pp. 53–74). New York: International Universities Press.

Spitz, R. A. (1946). Hospitalism: A follow-up report. In D. Fenschel et al. (Eds.), *Psychoanalytic studies of the child,* Vol. 1 (pp. 113–117). New York: International Universities Press.

Spitze, G., & Miner, S. (1992). Gender differences in adult child contact among elderly black parents. *Gerontologist, 32,* 213–218.

Spitzer, M. E. (1988). Taste acuity in institutionalized and noninstitutionalized elderly men. *Journal of Gerontology, 43*(3), P71–74.

Spock, B., & Rothenberg, M. B. (1985). *Baby and child care.* New York: Pocket Books.

Sroufe, L. A. (1977). Wariness of strangers and the study of infant development. *Child Development, 48,* 731–746.

Sroufe, L. A. (1979). Socioemotional development. In J. Osofsky (Ed.), *Handbook of infant development.* New York: Wiley.

Sroufe, L. A. (1983). Individual patterns of adaptation from infancy to preschool. In M. Perlmutter (Ed.), *Proceedings of the Minnesota symposium on child psychology.* Hillsdale, NJ: Erlbaum.

Sroufe, L. A., Fox, N. E., & Pancake, V. R. (1983). Attachment and dependency in a developmental perspective. *Child Development, 54,* 1615–1627.

Sroufe, L. A., & Waters, E. (1976). The ontogenesis of smiling and laughter: A perspective on the organization of development in infancy. *Psychological Review, 83,* 173–189.

Sroufe, L. A., & Wunsch, J. (1972). The development of laughter in the first year of life. *Child Development, 43,* 1326–1344.

Stacey, M., Dearden, R., Pill, R., & Robinson, D. (1970). *Hospitals, children and their families: The report of a pilot study.* London: Routledge.

Stadtman, E. R. (1992). Protein oxidation and aging. *Science, 257,* 1220–1224.

Stafford, R. S. (1990). Alternative strategies for controlling rising cesarean section rates. *Journal of the American Medical Association, 263,* 683–687.

Stair, N. (undated). [Course reading]. Denver: Colorado Outward Bound School.

Stampfer, M. J., Colditz, G. A., Willett, W. C., Manson, J. E., Rosner, B., Speizer, F. E., & Hennekens, C. H. (1991). Postmenopausal estrogen therapy and cardiovascular disease. *New England Journal of Medicine, 325,* 756–762.

Stanley, A. (1990, May 7). Prodigy, 12, fights skeptics, hoping to be a doctor at 17. *The New York Times,* pp. A1, B2.

Starfield, B. (1991). Childhood morbidity: Comparisons, clusters, and trends. *Pediatrics, 88*(3), 519–526.

Starfield, B., Katz, H., Gabriel, A., Livingston, G., Benson, P., Hankin, J., Horn, S., & Steinwachs, D. (1984). Morbidity in childhood—A longitudinal view. *New England Journal of Medicine, 310,* 824–829.

Starr, B. D., & Weiner, M. B. (1981). *The Starr-Weiner report on sex and sexuality in the mature years.* New York: Stein & Day.

Staub, S. (1973). *The effect of three types of relationships on young children's memory for pictorial stimulus pairs.* Unpublished doctoral dissertation, Harvard University Graduate School of Education, Cambridge, MA.

Stein, P. J. (1976, September 3). *Being single: Bucking the cultural imperative.* Paper presented at the annual meeting of the American Sociological Association.

Steinbach, U. (1992). Social networks, institutionalization, and mortality among elderly people in the United States. *Journal of Gerontology, 47*(4), S183–190.

Steinberg, L. (1981). Transformations in family relations at puberty. *Developmental Psychology, 17,* 833–840.

Steinberg, L. (1986). Latchkey children and susceptibility to peer pressure: An ecological analysis. *Developmental Psychology, 22*(4), 433–439.

Steinberg, L. (1987a). Impact of puberty on family relations: Effect of pubertal status and pubertal timing. *Developmental Psychology, 23*(3), 451–460.

Steinberg, L. (1987b). Single parents, stepparents, and the susceptibility of adolescents to antisocial peer pressure. *Child Development, 58,* 269, 275.

Steinberg, L. (1988). Reciprocal relation between parent-child distance and pubertal maturation. *Developmental Psychology, 24*(1), 122–128.

Steinberg, L. (1990). Autonomy, conflict, and harmony in the family relationship. In S. Feldman & G. Elliott (Eds.), *At the threshold: The developing adolescent.* Cambridge, MA: Harvard University Press.

Steinberg, L., & Darling, N. (1994). The broader context of social influence in adolescence. In R. Silbereisen & E. Todt (Eds.), *Adolescence in context.* New York: Springer.

Steinberg, L., Dornbusch, S. M., & Brown, B. B. (1992). Ethnic differences in adolescent achievement: An ecological perspective. *American Psychologist, 47*(6), 723–729.

Steinberg, L., Fegley, S., & Dornbusch, S. M. (1993). Negative impact of part-time work on adolescent adjustment: Evidence from a longitudinal study. *Developmental Psychology, 29*(2), 171–180.

Steinberg, L., Lamborn, S. D., Dornbusch, S. M., & Darling, N. (1992). Impact of parenting practices on adolescent achievement: Parenting, school involvement, and encouragement to succeed. *Child Development, 47*(6), 723–729.

Steinberg, L., & Silverberg, S. B. (1986). Influences on marital satisfaction during the middle stages of the family life cycle. *Journal of Marriage and the Family, 49,* 751–760.

Steiner, J. E. (1979). Human facial expressions in response to taste and smell stimulation. *Advances in Child Development and Behavior, 13,* 257.

Stenchever, M. A., Williamson, R. A., Leonard, J., Karp, L. E., Ley, B., Shy, K., & Smith, D. (1981). Possible relationship between in utero diethylstilbestrol exposure and male fertility. *American Journal of Obstetrics and Gynecology, 140*(2), 186–193.

Stern, M., & Hildebrandt, K. A. (1986). Prematuring stereotyping: Effects on mother-infant interaction. *Child Development, 57,* 308–315.

Sternberg, R. J. (1985a). *A triangular theory of love.* Paper presented at the annual meeting of the American Psychological Association, Los Angeles.

Sternberg, R. J. (1985b). *Beyond IQ: A triarchic theory of human intelligence.* New York: Cambridge University Press.

Sternberg, R. J. (1986). *Intelligence applied: Understanding and increasing your intellectual skills.* San Diego: Harcourt Brace.

Sternberg, R. J. (1987, September 23). The use and misuses of intelligence testing: Misunderstanding meaning, users over-rely on scores. *Education Week,* pp. 28, 22.

Sternberg, R. J., & Barnes, M. L. (1985). Real and ideal other in romantic relationships: Is four a crowd? *Journal of Personality and Social Psychology, 49*(6), 1586–1608.

Sternberg, R. J., & Grajek, S. (1984). The nature of love. *Journal of Personality and Social Psychology, 47*(2), 312–329.

Sterns, H. L., Barrett, G. V., & Alexander, R. A. (1985). Accidents and the aging individual. In J. E. Birren & K. W. Schaie (Eds.), *Handbook of the psychol-*

ogy of aging. New York: Van Nostrand Reinhold.

Stevens, J. C. (1992). Aging and spatial acuity of touch. *Journal of Gerontology, 47*(1), P35–40.

Stevens, J. C., Cain, W. S., Demarque, A., & Ruthruff, A. M. (1991). On the discrimination of missing ingredients: Aging and salt flavor. *Appetite, 16,* 129–140.

Stevens, J. H., & Bakeman, R. (1985). A factor analytic study of the HOME scale for infants. *Developmental Psychology, 21*(6), 1106–1203.

Stevenson, H. W., Chen, C., & Lee, S.-Y. (1993). Mathematics achievement of Chinese, Japanese, and American children: Ten years later. *Science, 258*(5081), 53–58.

Stevenson, H. W., Chen, C., & Uttal, D. H. (1990). Beliefs and achievement: A study of black, white, and Hispanic children. *Child Development, 61,* 508–523.

Stevenson, H. W., & Lee, S. (1990). Contexts of achievement. *Monographs of the Society for Research in Child Development 55*(1–2, Serial No. 221).

Stevenson, H. W., Stigler, J. W., Lee, S., Lucker, G. W., Kitamura, S., & Hsu, C. (1985). Cognitive performance and academic achievement of Japanese, Chinese, and American children. *Child Development, 56,* 718–734.

Stevenson, M., & Lamb, M. (1979). Effects of infant sociability and the caretaking environment on infant cognitive performance. *Child Development, 50,* 340–349.

Stewart, M. A., & Olds, S. W. (1973). *Raising a hyperactive child.* New York: Harper & Row.

Stewart, R. B. (1983). Sibling attachment relationships: Child-infant interactions in the strange situation. *Developmental Psychology, 19*(2), 192–199.

Stewart, W. (1977). *A psychosocial study of the formation of the early adult life structure in women.* Unpublished doctoral dissertation, Columbia University, New York.

Stigler, J. W., Lee, S., & Stevenson, H. W. (1987). Mathematical classrooms in Japan, Taiwan, and the United States. *Child Development, 58,* 1272–1285.

Stinnett, N., Carter, L., & Montgomery, J. (1972). Older persons' perceptions of their marriages. *Journal of Marriage and the Family, 34,* 665–670.

Stipek, D. J., Gralinski, H., & Kopp, C. B. (1990). Self-concept development in the toddler years. *Developmental Psychology, 26*(6), 972–977.

Stjernfeldt, M., Berglund, K., Lindsten, J., & Ludvigsson, J. (1986, June 14). Maternal smoking during pregnancy and risk of childhood cancer. *The Lancet,* pp. 1350–1352.

Stocker, C., Dunn, J., & Plomin, R. (1989). Sibling relationships: Links with child temperament, maternal behavior, and family structure. *Child Development, 60,* 715–727.

Strauss, M. A., & Sweet, S. (1992). Verbal/symbolic aggression in couples: Incidence rates and relationships to personal characteristics. *Journal of Marriage and the Family, 54,* 346–357.

Strauss, M., Lessen-Firestone, J., Starr, R., & Ostrea, E. (1975). Behavior of narcotics-addicted newborns. *Child Development, 46,* 887–893.

Strawbridge, W. J., & Wallhagen, M. I. (1991). Impact of family conflict on adult child caregivers. *Gerontologist, 31*(6), 770–777.

Streissguth, A. P., Aase, J. M., Clarren, S. K., Randels, S. P., LaDue, R. A., & Smith, D. F. (1991). Fetal alcohol syndrome in adolescents and adults. *Journal of the American Medical Association, 265,* 1961–1967.

Streissguth, A. P., Barr, H. M., Sampson, P. D., Darby, B. L., Martin, D. C. (1989). IQ at age 4 in relation to maternal alcohol use and smoking during pregnancy. *Developmental Psychology, 25*(1), 3–11.

Streissguth, A. P., Martin, D. C., Barr, H. M., Sandman, B. M., Kirchner, G. L., & Darby, B. L. (1984). Intrauterine alcohol and nicotine exposure: Attention and reaction time in 4-year-old children. *Developmental Psychology, 20*(4), 533–541.

Stroebe, M., Gergen, M. M., Gergen, K. J., & Stroebe, W. (1992). Broken hearts or broken bonds: Love and death in historical perspective. *American Psychologist, 47*(10), 1205–1212.

Strube, M. J., & Barbour, L. S. (1984). Factors related to the decision to leave an abusive relationship. *Journal of Marriage and the Family, 46,* 837–844.

Stuart, M. J., Gross, S. J., Elrad, H., & Graeber, J. E. (1982). Effects of acetylsalicylis-acid ingestion on maternal and neonatal hemostatis. *New England Journal of Medicine, 307,* 909–912.

Students' learning and graduation rates slip. (1990, May 3). *The New York Times,* p. B12.

Stunkard, A. J., Foch, T. T., & Hrubec, Z. (1986). A twin study of human obesity. *Journal of the American Medical Association, 256*(1), 51–54.

Stunkard, A., Harris, J. R., Pedersen, N. L., & McClearn, G. E. (1990). The body-mass index of twins who have been reared apart. *New England Journal of Medicine, 322*(21), 1483–1487.

Sue, S., & Okazaki, S. (1990). Asian-American educational achievements: A phenomenon in search of an explanation. *American Psychologist, 45*(8), 913–920.

Sugawara, O., Oshimura, M., Koi, M., Annab, L. A., & Barrett, J. C. (1990). Induction of cellular senescence in immortalized cells by human chromosome 1. *Science, 247,* 707–710.

Suitor, J. J., & Pillemer, K. (1987). The presence of adult children: A source of stress for elderly married couples? *Journal of Marriage and the Family, 49,* 717–725.

Suitor, J. J., & Pillemer, K. (1988). Explaining intergenerational conflict when adult children and elderly parents live together. *Journal of Marriage and the Family, 50,* 1037–1047.

Suitor, J. J., & Pillemer, K. (1993). Support and interpersonal stress in the social networks of married daughters caring for parents with dementia. *Journal of Gerontology, 41*(1), S1–S8.

Sullivan, H. S. (1953). *The interpersonal theory of psychiatry.* New York: Norton.

Sullivan, J. F. (1989, December 5). Prenatal care offered to all in New Jersey. *The New York Times,* pp. B1, B8.

Sullivan, M. W. (1982). Reactivation: Priming forgotten memories in infants. *Child Development, 53,* 516.

Suomi, S., & Harlow, H. (1972). Social rehabilitation of isolate-reared monkeys. *Developmental Psychology, 6*(3), 487–496.

Surbey, M. K. (1990). Family composition, stress, and human menarche. In T. E. Ziegler & F. B. Bercovitch (Eds.), *Socioendocrinology of primate reproduction.* New York: Wiley-Liss.

Svanborg, A. (1985). Biomedical and environmental influences on aging. In R. N. Butler and H. P. Gleason (Eds.), *Productive aging.* New York: Springer-Verlag.

Swain, I. U., Zelazo, P. R., & Clifton, R. K. (1993). Newborn infants' memory for speech sounds retained over 24 hours. *Developmental Psychology, 29*(2), 312–323.

Swedo, S., Rettew, D. C., Kuppenheimer, M., Lum, D., Dolan, S., & Goldberger, E. (1991). Can adolescent suicide attempters be distinguished from at-risk adolescents? *Pediatrics, 88*(3), 620–629.

Sweetland, J. D., & DeSimone, P. A. (1987). Age of entry, sex, and academic achievement in elementary school children. *Psychology in the Schools, 24,* 406–412.

Tabor, A., Philip, J., Masden, M., Bang, J., Obel, E. B., & Norgaard-Pedersen, B. (1986, June 7). Randomized controlled trial of genetic amniocentesis in 4606 low-risk women. *The Lancet,* pp. 1287–1293.

Tager, I. B., Weiss, S. T., Munoz, A., Rosner, B., & Speizer, F. E. (1983). Longitudinal study of the effects of maternal smoking on pulmonary function in children. *New England Journal of Medicine, 309,* 699–703.

Tamir, L. M. (1989). Modern myths about men at midlife: An assessment. In S. Hunter & M. Sundel (Eds.), *Midlife myths.* Newbury Park, CA: Sage.

Tan, S. L., Royston, P., Campbell, S., Jacobs, H. S., Betts, J., Mason, B., & Edwards, R. G. (1992). Cumulative conception and live birth after in-vitro fertilisation. *The Lancet, 339,* 1390–1094.

Tanfer, K., & Horn, M. C. (1985). Contraceptive use, pregnancy and fertility patterns among single American women in their 20's. *Family Planning Perspectives, 17*(1), 10–19.

Tanner, J. M. (1973). Growing up. *Scientific American, 229*(3), 35–43.

Tanner, J. M. (1978). *Fetus into man: Physical growth from conception to maturity.* Cambridge, MA: Harvard University Press.

Targ, D. B. (1979). Toward a reassessment of women's experience at middle-age. *Family Coordinator, 28*(3), 377–382.

Task Force on Pediatric AIDS of the American Psychological Association. (1989). Pediatric AIDS and human immunodeficiency virus infection. *American Psychologist, 44*(2), 258–264.

Tate, C. S., Warren, A. R., & Hess, T. M. (1992). Adults' liability for children's "lie-ability": Can adults coach children to lie successfully? In S. J. Ceci, M. DeS. Leichtman, & M. E. Putnick (Eds.), *Cognitive and social factors in early deception.* Hillsdale, NJ: Erlbaum.

Taylor, A. R., Asher, S. R., & Williams, G. A. (1987). The social adaptation of mainstreamed mildly retarded children. *Child Development, 58,* 1321–1334.

Taylor, M., Cartwright, B. S., & Carlson, S. M. (1993). A developmental investigation of children's imaginary companions. *Developmental Psychology, 28*(2), 276–285.

Taylor, R. J., & Chatters, L. M. (1991). Extended family networks of older Black adults. *Journal of Gerontology, 46*(4), S210–217.

Tellegren, A., Lykken, D. T., Bouchard, T. J., Wilcox, K. J., Segal, N. L., & Rich, S. (1988). Personality similarity in twins reared apart and together. *Journal of Personality and Social Psychology, 54*(6), 1031–1039.

Teller, D. Y., & Bornstein, M. H. (1987). Infant color vision and color perception. In P. Salapatek & L. B. Cohen (Eds.), *Handbook of infant perception: Vol. 1. From sensation to perception* (pp. 185–236). Orlando, FL: Academic Press.

Terman, L. M., & Oden, M. H. (1959). *Genetic studies of genius: Vol. 5. The gifted group at mid-life.* Stanford, CA: Stanford University Press.

Termine, N. T., & Izard, C. E. (1988). Infants' responses to their mothers' expressions of joy and sadness. *Developmental Psychology, 24*(2), 223–229.

Thacker, S. B., Addiss, D. G., Goodman, R. A., Holloway, B. R., & Spencer, H. C. (1992). Infectious diseases and injuries in child day care. Opportunities for healthier children. *Journal of the American Medical Association, 268,* 1720–1726.

Thomas, A., & Chess, S. (1977). *Temperament and development.* New York: Brunner/Mazel.

Thomas, A., & Chess, S. (1984). Genesis and evolution of behavioral disorders: From infancy to early adult life. *American Journal of Orthopsychiatry, 141*(1), 1–9.

Thomas, A., Chess, S., & Birch, H. G. (1968). *Temperament and behavior disorders in children.* New York: New York University Press.

Thomas, D. (1985). The dynamics of teacher opposition to integration. *Remedial Education, 20*(2), 53–58.

Thomas, J. L. (1986). Gender differences in satisfaction with grandparenting. *Psychology and Aging, 1*(3), 215–219.

Thomas, R. (1979). *Comparing theories of child development.* Belmont, CA: Wadsworth.

Thompson, L. (1992). Fetal transplants show promise. *Science, 257,* 868–870.

Thompson, L., & Walker, A. J. (1989). Gender in families: Women and men in marriage, work, and parenthood. *Journal of Marriage and the Family, 51,* 845–871.

Thompson, L. A., Fagan, J. F., & Fulker, D. W. (1991). Longitudinal prediction of specific cognitive abilities from infant novelty preference. *Child Development, 62,* 530–538.

Thompson, R. A., Lamb, M. E., & Estes, D. (1982). Stability of infant-mother attachment and its relationship to changing life circumstances in an unselected middle-class sample. *Child Development, 53,* 144–148.

Thompson, S. K. (1975). Gender labels and early sex-role development. *Child Development, 46,* 339–347.

Thomson, E., & Colella, U. (1992). Cohabitation and marital stability: Quality or commitment? *Journal of Marriage and the Family, 54,* 259–267.

Thornton, A. (1989). Changing attitudes toward family issues in the United States. *Journal of Marriage and the Family, 51,* 873–893.

Tiger, L., & Shepher, J. (1975). *Women in the kibbutz.* New York: Harcourt Brace.

Timiras, P. S. (1972). *Developmental physiology and aging.* New York: Macmillan.

Tisdale, S. (1988). The mother. *Hippocrates, 2*(3), 64–72.

Tobin, J. J., Wu, D. Y. H., & Davidson, D. H. (1989). *Preschools in three cultures: Japan, China, and the United States.* New Haven: Yale University Press.

Tobin-Richards, M. H., Boxer, A. M., Kavrell, S. A. Mc., & Petersen, A. C. (1984). Puberty and its psychological and social significance. In R. M. Lerner and N. L. Galambos (Eds.), *Experiencing adolescence: A sourcebook for parents, teachers, and teens.* New York: Garland.

Tobin-Richards, M. H., Boxer, A. M., & Petersen, A. C. (1983). The psychological significance of pubertal change: Sex differences in perceptions of self during early adolescence. In J. Brooks-Gunn & A. C. Petersen (Eds.), *Girls at puberty: Biological, social, and psychological perspectives.* New York: Plenum.

Tomasello, M., Mannle, S., & Kruger, A. C. (1986). Linguistic environment of 1- and 2-year-old twins. *Developmental Psychology, 22*(2), 169–176.

Toner, B. B., Garfinkel, P. E., & Garner, D. M. (1986). Long-term follow-up of anorexia nervosa. *Psychosomatic Medicine, 48*(7), 520–529.

Tonkova-Yompol'skaya, R. V. (1973). Development of speech intonation in infants during the first two years of life. In C. A. Fergusin & D. Slobin (Eds.), *Studies of child language development.* New York: Holt.

Treffers, P. E., Eskes, M., Kleiverda, G., & van Alten, D. (1990). Home births and minimal medical interventions. *Journal of the American Medical Association, 246*(17), 2203, 2207–2208.

Trichopoulos, D., Molio, F., Tomatis, L., Agapitos, E., Delsedime, L., Zavitsanos, X., Kalandidi, K., Riboli, E., & Saracci, R. (1992). Active and passive smoking and pathological indications of lung cancer risk in an autopsy study. *Journal of the American Medical Association, 268*(13), 1697–1701.

Trickett, P. K., & Susman, E. J. (1988). Parental perceptions of child-rearing practices in physically abusive and non-abusive families. *Developmental Psychology, 24*(2), 270–276.

Troll, L. E. (1975). *Early and middle adulthood.* Monterey, CA: Brooks/Cole.

Troll, L. E. (1980). Grandparenting. In L. W. Poon (Ed.), *Aging in the 1980s.* Washington, DC: American Psychological Association.

Troll, L. E. (1983). Grandparents: The family watchdogs. In T. H. Brubaker (Ed.), *Family relationships in later life.* Beverly Hills, CA: Sage.

Troll, L. E. (1985). *Early and middle adulthood* (2d ed.). Monterey, CA: Brooks/Cole.

Troll, L. E. (1986). Parents and children in later life. *Generations, 10*(4), 23–25.

Troll, L. E. (1989). Myths of midlife intergenerational relationships. In S. Hunter & M. Sundel (Eds.), *Midlife myths.* Newbury Park, CA: Sage.

Troll, L. E., Miller, S., & Atchley, R. (1979). *Families in later life.* Belmont, CA: Wadsworth.

Troll, L. E., & Smith, J. (1976). Attachment through the life span. *Human Development, 3,* 156–171.

Tronick, E. (1972). Stimulus control and the growth of the infant's visual field. *Perception and Psychophysics, 11,* 373–375.

Tronick, E. Z. (1980). On the primacy of social skills. In D. B. Sawin, L. O. Walker, & J. H. Penticuff (Eds.), *The exceptional infant: Psychosocial risk in infant environment transactions.* New York: Brunner/Mazel.

Tronick, E. Z. (1989). Emotions and emotional communication in infants. *American Psychologist, 44*(2), 112–119.

Tronick, E. Z., & Gianino, A. F. (1986). The transmission of maternal depression to the infant. In E. Z. Tronick & T. Field (Eds.), *Maternal depression and infant disturbance.* San Francisco: Jossey-Bass.

Trotter, R. J. (1983). Baby face. *Psychology Today, 17*(8), 14–20.

Trotter, R. J. (1986). Profile: Robert J. Sternberg: Three heads are better than one. *Psychology Today, 20*(8), 56–62.

Trotter, R. J. (1987). You've come a long way, baby. *Psychology Today, 21*(5), 34–45.

Tsai, M., & Wagner, N. (1979). Incest and molestation: Problems of childhood sexuality. *Resident and Staff Physician,* pp. 129–136.

Tschann, J., Johnston, J. R., & Wallerstein, J. S. (1989). Resources, stressors, and attachment as predictors of adult adjustment after divorce: A longitudinal study. *Journal of Marriage and the Family, 51,* 1033–1046.

Tuma, J. M. (1989). Mental health services for children: The state of the art. *American Psychologist, 44*(2), 188–199.

Turkington, C. (1983, May). Child suicide: An unspoken tragedy. *APA Monitor,* p. 15.

Tyler, P. (1994, January 11). Chinese start a vitamin program to eliminate a birth defect. *The New York Times,* p. C3.

Uhlenberg, P., Cooney, T., & Boyd, R. (1990). Divorce for women after midlife. *Journal of Gerontology, 45*(1), 53–61.

Uhlenberg, P., & Myers, M. A. P. (1981). Divorce and the elderly. *Gerontologist, 21*(3), 276–282.

Umberson, D. (1992). Relationships between adult children and their parents: Psychological consequences for both generations. *Journal of Marriage and the Family, 54,* 664–674.

UNICEF. (1992). *State of the world's children.* New York: Oxford University Press.

United Nations. (1990). *Declaration of the world summit for children.* New York: Author.

U.S. Bureau of the Census. (1983). *America in transition: An aging society* (Current Population Reports, Series P23-128). Washington, DC: U.S. Government Printing Office.

U.S. Bureau of the Census. (1988). *Households, families, marital status and living arrangements: March 1988* (Advance Report, Series P20-432). Washington, DC: U.S. Government Printing Office.

U.S. Bureau of the Census. (1989). *Marital status and living arrangements, March 1988.*

U.S. Bureau of the Census. (1990). *Who's minding the kids? Child care arrangements: 1986–1987.* (Current Population Reports, Series P70-20). Washington, DC: U.S. Government Printing Office.

U.S. Bureau of the Census. (1991). *Household and family characteristics, March 1991.* (Publication No. AP-20–458). Washington, DC: U.S. Government Printing Office.

U.S. Bureau of the Census. (1992a, July). Growth of America's oldest-old population. *Profiles of America's elderly, No. 2.*

U.S. Bureau of the Census. (1992b). *Marital status and living arrangements: March 1991.* (Current Population Reports, Series P20-461). Washington, DC: U.S. Government Printing Office.

U.S. Bureau of the Census. (1992c). *Sixty-five plus in America.* (Current Population Reports, Special Studies, Series P23-178). Washington, DC: U.S. Government Printing Office.

U.S. Bureau of the Census. (1993). Statistics on characteristics of single-parent households.

U.S. Bureau of Labor. (1989) Statistics comparing percent of women in various occupations in 1975 and 1985.

U.S. Consumer Product Safety Commission. (1991). *Statistics on shopping cart safety.*

U.S. Department of Education. (1986a). *Participation in adult education, May 1984* (Office of Educational Research and Improvement Bulletin CS 86-308B). Washington, DC: Center for Education Statistics.

U.S. Department of Education. (1986b). *What works: Research about reading and learning.* Washington, DC: Office of Educational Research and Improvement. (Available from What Works, Pueblo, CO 81009.)

U.S. Department of Education. (1987). *Transition from high school to postsecondary education: Analytical studies* (Office of Educational Research and Improvement Publication No. CS 87-309C). Washington, DC: U.S. Government Printing Office.

U.S. Department of Education. (1991). *Digest of education statistics.* (Publication No. NCES 91-697). Washington, DC: U.S. Government Printing Office.

U.S. Department of Education. (1992). *Dropout rates in the U.S., 1991* (Publication No. NCES 92-129). Washington, DC: U.S. Government Printing Office.

U.S. Department of Health, Education, and Welfare (USDHEW). (1976). *Health, United States, 1975* (DHEW Publication No. HRA 76-1232). Rockville, MD: National Center for Health Statistics.

U.S. Department of Health and Human Services (USDHHS). (1980). *The status of children, youth, and families, 1979* (DHHS Publication No. OHDS 80-30274). Washington, DC: U.S. Government Printing Office.

U.S. Department of Health and Human Services (USDHHS). (1981a). *The prevalence of dental caries in U.S. children, 1979–1980. Survey* (NIH Publication No. 82-2245). Washington, DC: U.S. Government Printing Office.

U.S. Department of Health and Human Services (USDHHS). (1981b). Statistics on incidence of depression.

U.S. Department of Health and Human Services (USDHHS). (1982). *Prevention 82* (DHHS [PHS] Publication No. 82-50157). Washington, DC: U.S. Government Printing Office.

U.S. Department of Health and Human Services (USDHHS). (1984). *Child sexual abuse prevention: Tips to parents.* Washington, DC: Office of Human Development Services, Administration for Children, Youth, and Families. National Center on Child Abuse and Neglect.

U.S. Department of Health and Human Services (USDHHS). (1985). *Health, United States, 1985* (DHHS Publication No. PHS 86-1232). Washington, DC: U.S. Government Printing Office.

U.S. Department of Health and Human Services (USDHHS). (1986). *Health, United States, 1986, and Prevention Profile* (DDH Publication No. PHS 87-1232). Washington, DC: U.S. Government Printing Office.

U.S. Department of Health and Human Services (USDHHS). (1987). *Smoking and health: A national status report* (HHS PHS/Child Development Publication No. 87-8396). Washington, DC: U.S. Government Printing Office.

U.S. Department of Health and Human Services (USDHHS). (1988, June 21). *HHS News.*

U.S. Department of Health and Human Services (USDHHS). (1990). *Health United States 1989* (DHHS Publication No. PHS 90-1232). Washington, DC: U.S. Government Printing Office.

U.S. Department of Health and Human Services (USDHHS). (1991). *Aging America: Trends and projections.* (DHHS Publication No. [FCoA] 91-28001). Washington, DC: U.S. Government Printing Office.

U.S. Department of Health and Human Services (USDHHS). (1992). *Health United States 1991, and Prevention Profile.* (DHHS Publication No. PHS 92-1232). Washington, DC: U.S. Government Printing Office.

U.S. Department of Health and Human Services (USDHHS). (1993). *A cataract patient's guide.* (Publication No. PHS A93-0544). Washington, DC: U.S. Government Printing Office.

U.S. Department of Justice. (1988). Press release on juvenile offenders.

U.S. Department of Justice, Federal Bureau of Investigation (FBI). (1987, July 25). Press release on crimes in 1986.

U.S. Department of Labor. (1980). *Handbook of labor statistics.* Washington, DC: U.S. Government Printing Office.

U.S. Department of Labor. (1987). *Handbook of labor statistics.* Washington, DC: U.S. Government Printing Office.

U.S. Department of Labor. (1992). Statistics on employed civilians detailed by occupation, sex, race, and Hispanic origin. *Handbook of Labor Statistics.* Washington, DC: U.S. Government Printing Office.

Uzgiris, I. C., & Hunt, J. (1975). *Assessment in infancy.* Urbana: University of Illinois Press.

Vachon, M., Lyall, W., Rogers, J., Freedmen-Letofky, K., & Freeman, S.

(1980). A controlled study of self-help intervention for widows. *American Journal of Psychiatry, 137*(11), 1380–1384.

Vaillant, G. E. (1977). *Adaptation to life.* Boston: Little, Brown.

Vaillant, G. E. (1989). The evolution of defense mechanisms during the middle years. In J. M. Oldham & R. S. Liebert (Eds.), *The middle years.* New Haven: Yale University Press.

Vaillant, G. E., & Vaillant, C. O. (1990). Natural history of male psychological health, XII: A 45-year study of predictors of successful aging. *American Journal of Psychiatry, 147*(1), 31–37.

Valdes-Dapena, M. (1980). Sudden infant death syndrome: A review of the medical literature, 1974–1979. *Pediatrics, 66*(4), 597–614.

Valenzuela, M. (1990). Attachment in chronically underweight young children. *Child Development, 61,* 1984–1996.

Vandell, D. L., & Corasaniti, M. A. (1988). The relation between third graders' after-school care and social, academic, and emotional functioning. *Child Development, 59,* 868–875.

Vandell, D. L., & Ramanan, J. (1991a). Children of the National Longitudinal Survey of Youth: Choices in after-school care and child development. *Developmental Psychology, 27*(4), 637–643.

Vandell, D. L., & Ramanan, J. (1991b). *Mother-child pretend play and children's later competence with peers.* Unpublished manuscript, University of Wisconsin-Madison.

vanIJzendoorn, M. H., Goldberg, S., Kroonenberg, P. M., & Frenkel, O. J. (1992). The relative effects of maternal and child problems on the quality of attachment: A meta-analysis of attachment in clinical samples. *Child Development, 63,* 840–858.

Van Noord-Zaadstra, B. M., Looman, C. W. N., Alsbach, H., Habbema, J. D. F., teVelde, E. R., & Karbaat, J. (1991). Delaying childbearing: Effect of age on fecundity and outcome of pregnancy. *British Medical Journal, 302,* 1361.

Vaughan, V., McKay, R. J., & Behrman, R. (1979). *Nelson textbook of pediatrics* (11th ed.). Philadelphia: Saunders.

Verhaeghen, P., Marcoen, A., & Goossens, L. (1992). Improving memory performance in the aged through mnemonic training: A meta-analytic study. *Psychology and Aging, 7*(2), 242–251.

Veroff, J., Douvan, E., & Kulka, R. (1981). *The inner American.* New York: Basic Books.

Vinick, B. (1978). Remarriage in old age. *Family Coordinator, 27*(4), 359–363.

Visher, E., & Visher, J. (1983). Stepparenting: Blending families. In H. I. McCubbin & C. R. Figley (Eds.), *Stress and the family: Vol. 1. Coping with normative transitions.* New York: Brunner/Mazel.

Visher, E. B., & Visher, J. S. (1989). Parenting coalitions after remarriage: Dynamics and therapeutic guidelines. *Family Relations, 38,* 65–70.

Voydanoff, P. (1983). Unemployment: Family strategies for adaptation. In C. R. Figley & H. I. McCubbin (Eds.), *Stress and the family: Vol. II. Coping with catastrophe.* New York: Brunner/Mazel.

Voydanoff, P. (1990). Economic distress and family relations: A review of the eighties. *Journal of Marriage and the Family, 52,* 1099–1115.

Vuori, L., Christiansen, N., Clement, J., Mora, J., Wagner, M., & Herrera, M. (1979). Nutritional supplementation and the outcome of pregnancy: 2. Visual habituation at 15 days. *Journal of Clinical Nutrition, 32,* 463–469.

Vygotsky, L. S. (1956). *Selected psychological investigations.* Moscow: Izdstel'sto Akademii Pedagogicheskikh Nauk SSSR.

Vygotsky, L. S. (1962). *Thought and language.* Cambridge, MA: Massachusetts Institute of Technology (MIT) Press.

Vygotsky, L. S. (1978). *Mind in society: The development of higher psychological processes.* Cambridge, MA: Harvard University Press.

Wachs, T. (1975). Relation of infants' performance on Piaget's scales between 12 and 24 months and their Stanford Binet performance at 31 months. *Child Development, 46,* 929–935.

Wagner, R. K., & Sternberg, R. J. (1986). Tacit knowlege and intelligence in the everyday world. In R. J. Sternberg & R. K. Wagner (Eds.), *Practical intelligence: Nature and origins of competence in the everyday world.* Cambridge, England: Cambridge University Press.

Walk, R. D., & Gibson, E. J. (1961). A comparative and analytical study of visual depth perception. *Psychology Monographs, 75*(15).

Walker, A. J., & Allen, K. R. (1991). Relationships between caregiving daughters and their elderly mothers. *Gerontologist, 31*(3), 389–396.

Walker, A. J., Martin, S. S. K., & Jones, L. L. (1992). The benefits and costs of caregiving and care receiving for daughters and mothers. *Journal of Gerontology, 47*(3), S130–139.

Walker, L. J. (1984). Sex differences in the development of moral reasoning: A critical review. *Child Development, 55,* 677–691.

Walker, L. J., & Taylor, J. H. (1991). Family interactions and the development of moral reasoning. *Child Development, 62,* 264–283.

Wallace, D. C. (1992). Mitochondrial genetics: A paradigm for aging and degenerative diseases? *Science, 256,* 628–632.

Wallach, M. A., & Kogan, N. (1965). *Modes of thinking in young children: A study of the creativity-intelligence distinction.* New York: Holt.

Wallerstein, J. S. (1983). Children of divorce: The psychological tasks of the child. *American Journal of Orthopsychiatry, 53*(2), 230–243.

Wallerstein, J. S. (1987). Children of divorce: Report of a ten-year follow-up of early latency-age children. *American Journal of Orthopsychiatry, 57*(2), 199–211.

Wallerstein, J. S., & Kelly, J. B. (1980). *Surviving the break-up: How children actually cope with divorce.* New York: Basic Books.

Walls, C. T., & Zarit, S. H. (1991). Informal support from Black churches and the well-being of elderly Blacks. *Gerontologist, 31*(4), 490–495.

Walster, E., & Walster, G. W. (1978). *A new look at love.* Cambridge, MA: Addison-Wesley.

Walter, H. J., Vaughan, R. D., & Cohall, A. T. (1991). Psychosocial influences on acquired immunodeficiency syndrome risk-behaviors among high school students. *Pediatrics, 88,* 846–852.

Ward, R., Logan, J., & Spitze, G. (1992). The influence of parent and child needs on coresidence in middle and later life. *Journal of Marriage and the Family, 54,* 209–221.

Warren, K. S. (1988, March 19). Protecting the world's children: An agenda for the 1990s. *The Lancet,* p. 659.

Wasik, B. H., Ramey, C. T., Bryant, D. M., & Sparling, J. J. (1990). A longitudinal study of two early intervention strategies: Project CARE. *Child Development, 61,* 1682–1696.

Waters, E., Wippman, J., & Sroufe, L. A. (1979). Attachment, positive affect, and competence in the peer group: Two studies in construct validation. *Child Development, 50*(3), 821–829.

Watson, J. B. (1958). *Behaviorism* (rev. ed.). New York: Norton.

Watson, J. B., & Rayner, R. (1920). Conditioned emotional reactions. *Journal of Experimental Psychology, 3,* 1–14.

Wayler, A. H., Kapur, K. K., Feldman, R. S., & Chauncey, H. H. (1982). Effects of age and dentition status on measures of food acceptability. *Journal of Gerontology, 37*(3), 294–299.

Weathers, W. T., Crane, M. M., Sauvain, K. J., & Blackhurst, D. W. (1993). Cocaine use in women from defined population: Prevalence at delivery and effects on growth in infants. *Pediatrics, 91,* 350–354.

Webb, W. B. (1987). Disorders of aging sleep. *Interdisciplinary Topics in Gerontology, 22,* 1–12.

Webb, W. B., & Bonnet, M. (1979). Sleep and dreams. In M. E. Meyer (Ed.), *Foundations of contemporary psychology.* New York: Oxford University Press.

Weg, R. B. (1985). Sexuality in aging. In M. S. J. Pathy (Ed.), *Principles and practice of geriatric medicine.* New York: Wiley & Sons.

Weg, R. B. (1987). Intimacy and the later years. In G. Lesnoff-Caravaglia (Ed.),

Handbook of applied gerontology. New York: Human Science Press.

Weg, R. B. (1989). Sensuality/sexuality of the middle years. In S. Hunter & M. Sundel (Eds.), *Midlife myths.* Newbury Park, CA: Sage.

Wegman, M. E. (1986). Annual summary of vital statistics–1985. *Pediatrics, 78*(6), 943–956.

Wegman, M. E. (1991). Annual summary of vital statistics–1990. *Pediatrics, 88*(6), 1081–1092.

Wegman, M. E. (1992). Annual summary of vital statistics–1991. *Pediatrics, 90*(6), 835–845.

Weinberg, R. A. (1989). Intelligence and IQ: Landmark issues and great debates. *American Psychologist, 44*(2), 98–104.

Weishaus, S., & Field, D. (1988). A half century of marriage: Continuity or change? *Journal of Marriage and the Family, 50,* 763–774.

Weiss, B. D. (1992). Trends in bicycle helmet use by children: 1985 to 1990. *Pediatrics, 89*(1), 78–80.

Weiss, G. (1990). Hyperactivity in childhood. *New England Journal of Medicine, 323*(20), 1413–1415.

Weiss, L., & Lowenthal, M. (1975). Lifecourse perspectives on friendship. In M. Lowenthal, M. Thurner, & D. Chiriboga (Eds.), *Four stages of life.* San Francisco: Jossey-Bass.

Weissman, M. M., Gammon, D., John, K., Merikangas, K. R., Warner, V., Prusoff, B. A., & Sholomskas, D. (1987). Children of depressed parents: Increased psychopathology and early onset of major depression. *Archives of General Psychiatry, 44,* 847–853.

Weissman, M. M., Klerman, G. L., Markowitz, J. S., & Ouellette, R. (1989). Suicidal ideation and suicide attempts in panic disorders and attacks. *New England Journal of Medicine, 321*(18), 1209–1214.

Weitzman, M., Gortmaker, S., & Sobol, A. (1992). Maternal smoking and behavior problems of children. *Pediatrics, 90*(3), 342–349.

Wellman, H., & Lempers, J. (1977). The naturalistic communicative abilities of two-year-olds. *Child Development, 48,* 1052–1057.

Wells, A. S. (1988, September 7). For those at risk of dropping out, an enduring program that works. *The New York Times,* p. B9.

Wentz, K. R., & Marcuse, E. K. (1991). Diptheria-Tetanus-Pertussis vaccine and serious neurological illness: An updated review of the epidemiologic evidence. *Pediatrics, 87*(3), 287–296.

Werler, M. M., Shapiro, S., & Mitchell, A. A. (1993). Periconceptional folic acid exposure and risk of occurrent neural tube defects. *Journal of the American Medical Association, 269*(10), 1257–1261.

Werner, E. E. (1985). Stress and protective factors in children's lives. In A. R. Nichol (Ed.), *Longitudinal studies in child psychology and psychiatry.* New York: Wiley.

Werner, E. E. (1989). Children of the garden island. *Scientific American, 260*(4), 106–111.

Werner, E. E., Bierman, L., French, F. E., Simonian, K., Connor, A., Smith, R., & Campbell, M. (1968). Reproductive and environmental casualties: A report on the 10-year follow-up of the children of the Kauai pregnancy study. *Pediatrics, 42*(1), 112–127.

Werner, J. S., & Siqueland, E. R. (1978). Visual recognition memory in the preterm infant. *Infant Behavior and Development, 1,* 79–94.

West Berlin Human Genetics Institute. (1987). Study on effects of nuclear radiation at Chernobyl on fetal development.

Whiffen, V. E., & Gotlib, I. H. (1989). Infants of postpartum depressed mothers: Temperament and cognitive status. *Journal of Abnormal Psychology, 98*(3), 274–279.

Whisnant, L., & Zegans, L. (1975). A study of attitudes toward menarche in white middle class adolescent girls. *American Journal of Psychiatry, 132*(8), 809–814.

White, B. L. (1971, October). *Fundamental early environmental influences on the development of competence.* Paper presented at the Third Western Symposium on Learning: Cognitive Learning, Western Washington State College, Bellingham, WA.

White, B. L., Kaban, B., & Attanucci, J. (1979). *The origins of human competence.* Lexington, MA: Heath.

White, K. R. (1982). The relation between socioeconomic status and academic achievement. *Psychological Bulletin, 91*(3), 461–481.

White, L., & Edwards, J. N. (1990). Emptying the nest and parental well-being: An analysis of national panel data. *American Sociological Review, 55,* 235–242.

White, L. K. (1990). Determinants of divorce: A review of research in the eighties. *Journal of Marriage and the Family, 52,* 904–912.

White, N., & Cunningham, W. R. (1988). Is terminal drop pervasive or specific? *Journal of Gerontology, 43*(6), p141–144.

Whitehurst, G. I., Fischel, J. E., Caulfield, M., DeBaryshe, B. D., & Valdez-Menchaca, M. C. (1989). Assessment and treatment of early expressive language delay. In P. R. Zelazo & R. G. Barr (Eds.), *Challenges to developmental paradigms: Implications for theory, assessment and treatment.* Hillsdale, NJ: Erlbaum.

Whitehurst, G. J., Falco, F. L., Lonigan, C. J., Fischel, J. E., DeBaryshe, B. D., Valdez-Menchaca, M. D., & Caulfield, M. (1988). Accelerating language development through picture book reading. *Developmental Psychology, 24*(4), 552–559.

Whitson, J. S., Selkoe, D. J., & Cotman, C. W. (1989). Amyloid B protein enhances survival of hippocampal neurons in vitro. *Science, 243,* 1488–1490.

Wideman, M. V., & Singer, J. F. (1984). The role of psychological mechanisms in preparation for childbirth. *American Psychologist, 34,* 1357–1371.

Widom, C. S. (1989). The cycle of violence. *Science, 244,* 160–166.

Wilcox, A. J., Weinberg, C. R., O'Connor, J. F., Baird, D. D., Schlatterer, J. P., Canfield, R. E., Armstrong, E. G., & Nisula, B. C. (1988). Incidence of early loss of pregnancy. *New England Journal of Medicine, 319*(4), 189–194.

Willett, W. C., Hunter, D. J., Stampfer, M. J., Colditz, G., Manson, J. E., Spiegelman, D., Rosner, B., Hennekens, C. H., & Spiezer, F. E. (1992). Dietary fat and fiber in relation to risk of breast cancer. *Journal of the American Medical Association, 268,* 2037–2044.

Willett, W. C., Stampfer, M. J., Colditz, G. A., Rosner, B. A., Speizer, F. E. (1990). Relation of meat, fat, and fiber intake to the risk of colon cancer in a prospective study among women. *New England Journal of Medicine, 323,* 1664–1672.

Williams, B. C. (1990). Immunization coverage among preschool children: The United States and selected European countries. [Supplement to] *Pediatrics, 86*(6), Part 2, 1052–1056.

Williams, B. C., & Miller, C. A. (1991). *Preventive health care for young children: Findings from a 10-country study and directions for United States policy.* Arlington, VA: National Center for Clinical Infant Programs.

Williams, B. C., & Miller, C. A. (1992). Preventive health care for young children: Findings from a 10-country study and directions for United States policy. *Pediatrics, 89*(5), Supplement.

Williams, E. R., & Caliendo, M. A. (1984). *Nutrition: Principles, issues, and applications.* New York: McGraw-Hill.

Williams, J., Best, D., & Boswell, D. (1975). The measurement of children's racial attitudes in the early school years. *Child Development, 46,* 494–500.

Williams, T. M. (1978). *Differential impact of TV on children: A natural experiment in communities with and without TV.* Paper presented at the meeting of the International Society for Research on Aggression, Washington, DC.

Williamson, D. F., Kahn, H. S., Remington, P. L., & Anda, R. F. (1990). The 10-year incidence of overweight and major weight gain in U.S. adults. *Archives of Internal Medicine, 150,* 665–672.

Willis, S. L., Blieszner, R., & Baltes, P. B. (1981). Intellectual training research in aging: Modification of performance on the fluid ability of figural relations.

Journal of Educational Psychology, 73, 41–50.

Wilson, G., McCreary, R., Kean, J., & Baxter, J. (1979). The development of preschool children of heroin-addicted mothers: A controlled study. *Pediatrics, 63*(1), 135–141.

Winick, M. (1981, January). Food and the fetus. *Natural History,* pp. 16–81.

Winick, M., Brasel, J., & Rosso, P. (1972). Nutrition and cell growth. In M. Winick (Ed.), *Nutrition and development.* New York: Wiley.

Wiswell, T. E., & Geschke, D. W. (1989). Risks from circumcision during the first month of life compared with those for uncircumcised boys. *Pediatrics, 83*(6), 1011–1015.

Wittrock, M. C. (1980). Learning and the brain. In M. C. Wittrock (Ed.), *The brain and psychology.* New York: Academic Press.

Wolf, M. (1968). *The house of Lim.* Englewood Cliffs, NJ: Prentice-Hall.

Wolfe, D. A. (1985). Child-abusive parents: An empirical review and analysis. *Psychological Bulletin, 97*(3), 462–482.

Wolfe, D. A., Edwards, B., Manion, I., & Koverola, C. (1988). Early intervention for parents at risk of child abuse and neglect: A preliminary investigation. *Journal of Consulting and Clinical Psychology, 56*(1), 40–47.

Wolff, P. H. (1963). Observations on the early development of smiling. In B. M. Foss (Ed.), *Determinants of infant behavior,* Vol. 2. London: Methuen.

Wolff, P. H. (1966). The causes, controls, and organizations of behavior in the newborn. *Psychological Issues, 5*(1, Whole No. 17), 1–105.

Wolff, P. H. (1969). The natural history of crying and other vocalizations in early infancy. In B. M. Foss (Ed.), *Determinants of infant behavior,* Vol. 4. London: Methuen.

Wolinsky, F. D., & Johnson, R. J. (1992a). Widowhood, health status, and the use of health services by older adults: A cross-sectional and prospective approach. *Journal of Gerontology, 47*(1), S8–16.

Wolinsky, F. D., & Johnson, R. J. (1992b). Perceived health status and mortality among older men and women. *Journal of Gerontology, 47*(6), S304–312.

Wong, N. D., Hei, T. K., Qaqundah, P. Y., Davidson, D. M., Bassin, S. L., & Gold, K. V. (1992). Television viewing and pediatric hypercholesterolemia. *Pediatrics, 90*(1), 75–79.

Wong, P. T. P., & Watt, L. M. (1991). What types of reminiscences are associated with successful aging? *Psychology and Aging, 6*(2), 272–279.

Wood, D. (1980). Teaching the young child: Some relationships between social interaction, language, and thought. In D. Olson (Ed.), *The social foundations of language and thought.* New York: Norton.

Wood, D., Bruner, J., & Ross, G. (1976). The role of tutoring in problem solving. *Journal of Child Psychiatry and Psychology, 17,* 89–100.

Wood, D. L, Hayward, R. A., Corey, C. R., Freeman, H. E., & Shapiro, M. F. (1990). Access to medical care for children and adolescents in the United States. *Pediatrics, 86*(5), 666–673.

Woodruff, D. S. (1985). Arousal, sleep and aging. In J. E. Birren & K. W. Schaie (Eds.), *Handbook of the psychology of aging.* New York: Van Nostrand Reinhold.

Working Group on HIV Testing of Pregnant Women and Newborns. (1990). HIV infection, pregnant women, and newborns: A policy proposal for information and testing. *Journal of the American Medical Association, 264,* 2416–2420.

Working Women Education Fund. (1981). *Health hazards for office workers.* Cleveland, OH: Author.

Wortman, C. B., & Silver, R. C. (1989). The myths of coping with loss. *Journal of Consulting and Clinical Psychology, 57*(3), 349–357.

Wright, A. L., Holberg, C. J., Martinez, F. D., Morgan, W. J., & Taussig, L. M. (1989, October 14). Breast-feeding and lower respiratory tract illness in the first year of life. *British Medical Journal, 299,* 946–949.

Wright, J. T., Waterson, E. J., Barrison, I. G., Toplis, P. J., Lewis, I. G., Gordon, M. G., MacRae, K. D., Morris, N. F., & Murray Lyon, I. M. (1983, March 26). Alcohol consumption, pregnancy, and low birthweight. *The Lancet,* pp. 663–665.

Wurtman, R. J., & Wurtman, J. J. (1989). Carbohydrates and depression. *Scientific American, 260*(1), 68–75.

Wynn, K. (1992). Evidence against empiricist accounts of the original of numerical knowledge. *Mind and Language, 7,* 315–332.

Yamazaki, J. N., & Schull, W. J. (1990). Perinatal loss and neurological abnormalities among children of the atomic bomb. *Journal of the American Medical Association, 264,* 605–609.

Yazigi, R. A., Odem, R. R., Polakoski, K. L. (1991). Demonstration of specific binding of cocaine to human spermatoza. *Journal of the American Medical Association, 266,* 1956–1959.

Yllo, K., & Straus, M. A. (1981). Interpersonal violence among married and cohabiting couples. *Family Relations, 30,* 339–347.

Yogman, M. J. (1984). Competence and performance of fathers and infants. In A. MacFarlane (Ed.), *Progress in child health.* London: Churchill Livingston.

Yogman, M. J., Cooley, J., & Kindlon, D. (1988). Fathers, infants, and toddlers: A developing relationship. In P. Bronstein & C. P. Cowan (Eds.), *Fatherhood*

today: Men's changing role in the family. New York: Wiley.

Yogman, M. J., Dixon, S., Tronick, E., Als, H., & Brazelton, T. B. (1977, March). *The goals and structure of face-to-face interaction between infants and their fathers.* Paper presented at the meeting of the Society for Research in Child Development, New Orleans.

York, J. L., & Calsyn, R. J. (1977). Family involvement in nursing homes. *Gerontologist, 17*(6), 500–505.

Young, K. T., & Zigler, E. (1986). Infant and toddler day care: Regulations and policy implications. *American Journal of Orthopsychiatry, 56*(1), 43–55.

Youngblade, L. M., & Belsky, J. (1992). Parent-child antecedents of 5-year-olds' close friendships: A longitudinal analysis. *Developmental Psychology, 28*(4), 700–713.

Youngstrom, N. (1992). Inner-city youth tell of life in "a war zone." *APA Monitor,* 36–37.

Zabin, L. S., Hirsch, M. B., Smith, E. A., & Hardy, J. B. (1984). Adolescent sexual attitudes and behavior: Are they consistent? *Family Planning Perspectives, 15,* 16, 185.

Zabin, L. S., Kantner, J. F., & Zelnik, M. (1979). The risk of adolescent pregnancy in the first months of intercourse. *Family Planning Perspectives, 11*(4), 215–222.

Zahn-Waxler, C., Radke-Yarrow, M., Wagner, E., & Chapman, M. (1992). Development of concern for others. *Developmental Psychology, 28*(1), 126–136.

Zakariya, S. B. (1982, September). Another look at the children of divorce: Summary report of the study of school needs of one-parent children. *Principal,* pp. 34–37.

Zametkin, A. J., Nordahl, T. E., Gross, M., et al. (1990). Cerebral glucose metabolism in adults with hyperactivity of childhood onset. *New England Journal of Medicine, 323,* 1361–1366.

Zarbatany, L., Hartmann, D. P., & Rankin, D. B. (1990). The psychological functions of preadolescent peer activities. *Child Development, 61,* 1067–1080.

Zelazo, P. R., Kotelchuck, M., Barber, L., & David, J. (1977, March). *Fathers and sons: An experimental facilitation of attachment behaviors.* Paper presented at the meeting of the Society for Research in Child Development, New Orleans.

Zelnik, M., Kantner, J. F., & Ford, K. (1981). *Sex and pregnancy in adolescence.* Beverly Hills, CA: Sage.

Zelnik, M., & Shah, F. K. (1983). First intercourse among young Americans. *Family Planning Perspectives, 15*(2), 64–72.

Zeskind, P. S., & Iacino, R. (1984). Effects of maternal visitation to preterm infants in the neonatal intensive care unit. *Child Development, 55,* 1887–1893.

Zeskind, P. S., & Ramey, C. T. (1981). Preventing intellectual and interactional sequelae of fetal malnutrition: A longitudinal, transactional, and synergistic approach to development. *Child Development, 52,* 213–218.

Zigler, E. F. (1987). Formal schooling for four-year-olds? *North American Psychologist, 42*(3), 254–260.

Zimiles, H., & Lee, V. E. (1991). Adolescent family structure and educational progress. *Developmental Psychology, 27*(2), 314–320.

Zimmerman, D. (1993). Genital mutilation of women now is a challenge in the U.S. *Probe: David Zimmerman's newsletter on science, media, public policy, and health, 2*(4), 1, 4–5.

Zimmerman, I. L., & Bernstein, M. (1983). Parental work patterns in alternate families: Influence on child development. *American Journal of Orthopsychiatry, 53*(3), 418–425.

Zube, M. (1982). Changing behavior and outlook of aging men and women: Implications for marriage in the middle and later years. *Family Relations, 31*(1), 147–156.

Zuckerman, B., Frank, D., Hingson, R., Amaro, H., Levenson, S. M., Kayne, H., Parker, S., Vinci, R., Aboagye, K., Fried, L., Cabral, H., Timperi, R., & Bauchner, H. (1989). Effects of maternal marijuana and cocaine use on fetal growth. *New England Journal of Medicine, 320*(12), 762–768.

Zuckerman, B. S., & Beardslee, W. R. (1987). Maternal depression: A concern for pediatricians. *Pediatrics, 79*(1), 110–117.

Zuckerman, D. M., & Zuckerman, B. S. (1985). Television's impact on children. *Pediatrics, 75*(2), 233–240.

Zylke, J. W. (1989). Sudden infant death syndrome: Resurgent research offers hope. *Journal of the American Medical Association, 262*(12), 1565–1566.

PERMISSIONS ACKNOWLEDGMENTS

Table 9-1 Juster, F. T. (1985). How Children Use Time. *Time, Goods and Well-Being.* Reprinted by permission of the Institute for Social Research, University of Michigan.

Table 9-2 Zarbatany, L., Hartmann, D. P., & Rankin, D. B. (1990). The psychological functions of preadolescent peer activities. *Child Development, 61,* 1067–1080. © The Society for Research in Child Devlopment, Inc.

Table 9-3 Selman, R. L., & Selman, A. P. (1979). Children's ideas about friendship: A new theory. *Psychology Today, 13*(4), 71–80, 114. Reprinted with permission from *Psychology Today* Magazine. Copyright © 1979 (Sussex Publishers, Inc.).

CHAPTER 10

Figure 10-1 Gans, J. E. (1990). *America's Adolescents: How Healthy Are They?* American Medical Association, 1990.

Figure 10-2 Gortmaker, S. L., Dietz, W. H., Sobol, A. M., & Wehler, C. A. (1987). Increasing pediatric obesity in the United States. *American Journal of the Diseases of Childhood, 141,* 535–540. Reprinted by permission of the American Medical Association.

Table 10-6 Skoe, E. E., & Gooden, A. (1993). Ethics of care and real-life moral dilemma content in male and female early adolescents. *Journal of Early Adolescence, 13*(2), 154–167. Reprinted by permission of Sage Publications.

CHAPTER 11

Opening Quote Merriam, E. (1964). "Conversation with Myself" from *A Sky Full of Poems* by Eve Merriam. Copyright © 1964, 1970, 1973, 1986 by Eve Merriam. Copyright renewed © 1992 Eve Merriam. Reprinted by permission of Marian Reiner.

Figures 11-1 and 11-2 Csikszentmihalyi, M., & Larsen, R. (1984). From *Being Adolescent: Conflict and Growth in the Teenage Years* by Mihaly Csikszentmihalyi and Reed Larson. Copyright © 1984 by Basic Books, Inc. Reprinted by permission of BasicBooks, a division of HarperCollins Publishers, Inc.

Table 11-1 Marcia, J. E. (1980). Identity in adolescence. In Adelson, J. (ed.), *Handbook of Adolescent Psychology.* Copyright © 1980. Reprinted by permission of John Wiley & Sons, Inc.

Table 11-2 Marcia, J. E. (1966). Development and validation of ego identity status. *Journal of Personality and Social Psychology, 3*(5), 551–558. Copyright 1966 by the American Psychological Association. Adapted by permission.

CHAPTER 12

Figure 12-2 The New York Times, (1990). "Young Men at Risk," *The New York Times,* June 27, 1990. Copyright © 1990 by The New York Times Company. Reprinted by permission.

Table 12-1 Belloc, N. B., & Breslow, L. (1972). Relationship of physical health status and health practices. *Preventive Medicine, 1*(3), 409–421. Reprinted by permission of Academic Press.

Table 12-2 Holmes, T. N., & Rahe, R. H. (1976). The social readjustment rating scale. *Journal of Psychosomatic Research, 11*(213). Reprinted with permission of Elsevier Science Ltd. Pergamon Imprint, Oxford, England.

Table 12-3 Gilligan, C. (1982). Reprinted by permission of the publishers from *In A Different Voice* by Carol Gilligan, Cambridge Mass.: Harvard University Press, copyright © 1982 by Carol Gilligan.

CHAPTER 13

Box 13-3 Olds, S. W. (1989). From *The Working Parents Survival Guide.* Copyright © 1989 by S. W. Olds, from the book *The Working Parents Survival Guide,* published by Prima Publishing, Roseville, CA.

Figure 13-1 Burns, A. (1992). Mother-headed families: An international perspective and the case of Australia. *Social Policy Report of the Society for Research in Child Development, VI*(1), Spring, 1992. Reprinted by permission of The Society for Research in Child Development, Inc.

Table 13-2 Passuth, P., Maines, D., & Neugarten, B. L. (1984). Age Norms paper. Reprinted by permission of the authors.

Table 13-4 White, L. K. (1990). Determinants of divorce: A review of research in the eighties. *Journal of Marriage and the Family, 52,* 904–912. Schoen, R. (1992). First unions and the stability of first marriages. *Journal of Marriage and the Family, 54,* 291–284. Copyright 1990, 1992 by the National Council on Family Relations, 3989 Central Ave., NE, Suite 550, Minneapolis, MN 55421. Reprinted by permission.

Table 13-5 Bumpass, L. L., Sweet, J., & Martin, T. C. (1990). Changing patterns of remarriage. *Journal of Mariage and the Family, 52,* 747–756. Copyright 1990 by the National Council on Family Relations, 3989 Central Ave., NE, Suite 550, Minneapolis, MN 55421. Reprinted by permission.

CHAPTER 14

Box 14-1 Figure Notelovitz, M., & Ware, M. (1982). *Stand Tall: The Informed Woman's Guide to Preventing Osteoporosis.* Illustration © 1982 by Triad Publishing Company.

Figure 14-1 McCord, C., & Freeman, H. (1990). Excess mortality in Harlem. *The New England Journal of Medicine, 322,* 173–177. Reprinted by permission.

Figure 14-2 Raven, J. C. (1983). Raven progressive matrices test. A5 from the Raven *Standard Progressive Matrices.* Reproduced by permission of J. C. Raven Ltd.

Table 14-1 9 to 5, Working Women Education Fund, (1981). *Warning! Health Hazards for Office Workers,* 9. Reprinted by permission of 9 to 5, Working Women Education Fund.

Table 14-3 Horn, J. L., and Donaldson, G. (1980). Cognitive development: Adulthood development of human abilities. Reprinted by permission of the publishers from *Constancy and Change in Human Development* edited by Orville G. Brim and Jerome Kagan, Cambridge, Mass.: Harvard University Press, Copyright © 1980 by the President and Fellows of Harvard College.

CHAPTER 15

Opening Quote Huges, L. "Dream Deferred" from *The Panther and the Lash* by Langston Hughes. Copyright 1951 by Langston Huges. Reprinted by permission of Alfred A. Knopf, Inc.

Box 15-3 Davis, B. W. (undated). *Celebrate Your Marriage* (Marriage Strength Builder No. 4, Learn-at-Home Program). Reprinted by permission of Pennsylvania State University Cooperative Extension Service.

Table 15-2 Helson, R., & Wink, P. (1992). Personality change in women from the early 40s to the early 50s. *Psychology and Aging,* 7(1), 46–55. Copyright 1992 by the American Psychological Association. Reprinted by permission.

Table 15-3 American Association of Retired Persons (1989). *National Survey of Caregivers.* Copyright 1989, American Association of Retired Persons. Reprinted by permission.

CHAPTER 16

Figure 16-4 American Association of Retired Persons (1992). *A Profile of Older Americans: 1992.* Reprinted with the permission of the American Association of Retired Persons.

Figure 16-5 Schaie, K. W. (1989). The hazards of cognitive aging. *The Gerontologist,* 29(4), 484–493. Copyright by The Gerontological Society of America. Used with permission.

Table 16-1 Wegman, M. E. (1992). Annual summary of vital statistics—1991. *Pediatrics,* 90(6), 835–845. Reproduced by permission of *Pediatrics.* Copyright © 1992.

Table 16-2 Schaie, K. W. (1989). The hazards of cognitive aging. *The Gerontologist,* 29(4), 484–493, Copyright by The Gerontological Society of America. Used with permission.

Table 16-3 Smith, J., & Baltes, P. B. (1990). Wisdom-related knowledge: Age/cohort differences in response to life-planning problems. *Developmental Psychology,* 26(3), 494–505. Copyright 1990 by the American Psychological Association. Reprinted by permission.

CHAPTER 17

Opening Quote Haiku. From *Sound and Light.* Copyright 1987 Ruth Duskin Feldman and Bunny L. Shuch.

Box 17-4 DeVos, S. (1990). Extended family living among older people in six Latin American countries. *Journal of Gerontology: Social Sciences,* 45(3), 587–594. Copyright by The Gerontological Society of America. Used with permission.

Table 17-1 Koenig, H. G., George, L. K., & Seigler, I. C. (1988). The use of religion and other emotion-regulating coping strategies among older adults. *The Gerontologist,* 28(3), 303–310. Copyright by The Gerontological Society of America. Used with permission.

INDEXES

NAME INDEX

Abbey, A., 456
Abramovitch, R., 188, 259, 261, 262
Abrams, B., 73
Abroms, K., 58
Abt Associates, 191
Acredolo, L., 17, 148
Action for Children's Television, 248, 253
Adams, D., 441
Adams, G., 399, 400
Adams, L. A., 209
Adams, R. G., 486, 576, 578
Ainsworth, Mary D. S., 167, 176–178, 179
Akutsu, H., 534
Alan Guttmacher Institute (*see under* Guttmacher)
Aldous, J. J., 518
Alemi, B., 112
Alexander, B. B., 580
Alinsky, Saul, 591
Allende, Isabel, 579
Allore, R., 59
Almy, M., 280
Alsaker, F. D., 348, 349, 352
Altemeir, W. A., 185
Alvarez, W. F., 227
Amabile, 132
Amato, P. R., 325, 327, 328
Ambati, Balamurati Krishna, 299
American Academy of Pediatrics (AAP), 106, 111, 113, 191, 204, 209, 253, 335
  Committee on Accident and Poison Prevention, 278
  Committee on Adolescence, 356
  Committee on Bioethics, 459
  Committee on Children with Disabilities, 76, 296, 298
  Committee on Drugs, 76, 82, 298
  Committee on Fetus and Newborn, 98
  Committee on Genetics, 98

American Academy of Pediatrics (AAP) (*Cont.*):
  Committee on Infectious Diseases, 106*n*.
  Committee on Nutrition, 113, 114, 201
  Committee on School Health, 277, 278
  Committee on Sports Medicine and Fitness, 210, 277, 278
  Committee on Substance Abuse, 76
  Task Force on Blood Pressure Control in Children, 277
  Task Force on Circumcision, 118
  Task Force on Infant Positioning and SIDS, 105
  Task Force on Pediatric AIDS, 202
American Association of Retired Persons (AARP), 518, 538, 539, 551, 567, 568, 569, 574
American Cancer Society, 202, 356
American Council on Science and Health, 419
American Heart Association, 414, 415, 480
Anand, K. J. S., 116, 117
Anastasi, A., 63, 134, 224, 289, 300
Anders, T. R., 208, 550
Anderson, B. E., 193
Anderson, R., 520
Anderson, S. A., 511
Anderson, T. B., 603
Anson, O., 448, 465
Anthony, E. J., 268, 334
Antonarakis, S. E., 59, 81
Apgar, Virginia, 96, 98
Apter, T., 406
Aquilino, W. S., 516
Arend, R., 180
Ariès, Philippe, 11–12
Arjyal, B. P., 455
Armstrong, B. G., 76

Asendorpf, J. B., 189
Ash, P., 72
Asher, J., 68
Asher, S., 261
Aslin, R. N., 113
Associated Press, 154
Atchley, R., 573
Axline, V. M., 268
Aylward, G. P., 102
Azmitia, M., 330
Babchuk, N., 576
Babson, S. G., 105
Bachman, J. G., 374
Bachrach, C. A., 458
Backett, K., 461
Baillargeon, R., 139
Baird, P. A., 58
Baldwin, W., 399
Balkwell, C., 602
Baltes, P. B., 8, 543, 544, 547
Bandura, Albert, 24, 33, 242, 251, 252
Banner, L. W., 496
Barbanel, J., 401
Bardouille-Crema, A., 280
Barfield, R. E., 552
Baringa, M., 531
Barnes, A., 76
Barnes, K. E., 264
Barnett, R. C., 463, 504, 515, 517
Baron, N. S., 159
Barrett, C. J., 602
Barrett, D. E., 274
Barrett-Connor, E., 476
Bartholet, E., 467
Baruch, G., 321, 441, 493, 504, 510, 514
Bass, J. L., 206
Bass, M., 105
Bassuk, E. J., 205, 206, 207
Bassuk, E. L., 206
Bates, E., 145, 146, 147, 149
Battelle, P., 65
Bauer, D., 249
Baughman, E. E., 288

Baumrind, Diana, 257–258
Baydar, N., 192
Bayley, N., 115, 134, 288, 485
Beardsley, L., 237
Beautrais, A. L., 204
Beckman, P. J., 237
Beckwith, L., 144
Behrman, R. E., 86, 93, 100, 110, 274, 276, 346
Belbin, R. M., 473, 474
Belenky, M. F., 433
Bell, J., 526
Bell, R. R., 491
Bell, S., 167
Bellinger, D., 79
Belloc, N. B., 412
Belsky, J., 16, 174, 185, 190, 191, 192, 460
Beltramini, A. U., 208
Bem, Sandra L., 241, 242, 244, 247
Benbow, C. P., 375
Bengston, V., 591
Benn, R. K., 193, 194
Benner, P., 423
Benson, J. B., 120
Berardo, D. H., 429
Berger, G. S., 467
Berger, L., 305
Berger, R. M., 478–479
Bergman, A. B., 185
Bergman, S. J., 510, 512
Berk, L. E., 223, 224
Berkowitz, G. S., 79, 456
Berman, P. W., 246
Berman, S. M., 70
Bernard, J. L., 449
Bernard-Bonnin, A. C., 252, 253
Berndt, T. J., 396, 397
Bernstein, G. A., 332
Bernstein, Leonard, 494
Berrueta-Clement, J. R., 234
Berscheid, E., 350, 450
Bertenthal, B. I., 120
Bertenthal, B. L., 114, 120, 129

Beumont, P. J. V., 354
Bianchi, S. M., 447
Bielby, D., 423
Bierman, K. L., 318
Biller, H. B., 248
Binet, Alfred, 35, 133
Binstock, R. H., 539
Biracree, T., 583
Birch, L. L., 201
Bird, C., 496, 551
Birns, B., 173, 174
Birren, J. E., 474, 535, 536
Blackburn, J. A., 546
Blair, S. N., 415, 416
Blass, E. M., 130
Blauvelt, H., 175
Blazer, D., 541
Blieszner, R., 512, 543, 546
Block, J., 467, 505
Bloom, B. S., 300, 301
Bloom, D. E., 464
Bluebond-Langner, M., 590
Blum, R., 351
Blumenthal, J. A., 540
Blyth, D. A., 348, 367, 384, 397
Bolger, N., 492
Bolles, E. B., 223, 467
Bombeck, E., 614
Bornstein, M. H., 114, 133, 142, 143, 144, 225
Bossé, R., 552
Boulton, M. G., 461
Bouza, A. V., 449
Bowes, W., 130
Bowlby, John, 177, 179, 184
Bowman, J. A., 203
Boyer, J. L., 606
Boysson-Bardies, B., 146
Brackbill, Y., 82
Bracken, M., 75
Bradley, R. H., 155, 156
Braine, M., 149
Branch, L. G., 534
Brandes, J. M., 459
Brass, L. M., 65
Braungart, J. M., 172
Bray, D. W., 490
Brazelton, T. B., 98, 196, 268
Brecher, E., 474, 575, 601–602
Bremner, W. J., 575
Breslow, L., 413
Bretherton, I., 219
Brewster, A. B., 275
Briley, M., 492
Brim, O. G., 443, 504, 505, 509
Brittain, C., 398
Brodbeck, A. J., 150
Brody, E. B., 288
Brody, E. M., 568
Brody, J. E., 474, 538
Brody, L. R., 115
Bromley, D. B., 410
Bronfenbrenner, Urie, 9, 185, 191, 227, 319, 322, 367
Bronson, F. H., 247
Bronstein, P., 182, 248
Brooke, J., 107
Brooks-Gunn, J., 346, 390, 399
Brophy, J. E., 295
Brown, B. B., 393, 398

Brown, J. D., 353, 389
Brown, J. E., 75
Brown, J. H., 610
Brown, J. L., 74, 204, 205
Brown, J. T., 596, 597
Brown, L. M., 383, 384, 406
Brown, Louise, 459
Brown, P., 251
Brown, R., 149, 150, 159
Brown, S. S., 86, 100, 101, 102, 399
Browne, A., 185, 186
Brozan, N., 480
Brubaker, T. H., 572, 601
Bryer, J. B., 186
Buhrmester, D., 394, 394n.
Buie, J., 402
Bukowski, W. M., 397
Bullen, B. A., 348
Bullock, K. D., 417
Bumpass, L. L., 451, 453
Burgess, A. W., 186
Burkhauser, R. V., 566
Burns, A., 327, 328, 447, 449, 450
Burstin, H. R., 418
Bush, T. L., 477
Busse, E. W., 534
Bussey, K., 219
Bustillo, M., 459
Butler, R., 535, 540, 593, 611
Butterfield, E., 131
Byrne, K., 377

Cahan, S., 287, 288
Cain, V. S., 323
Cain, W. S., 473
Cairns, R. B., 372
Calkins, S. D., 179, 180
Callahan, D., 614
Calvert, K., 41
Calvert, S. L., 248
Calvo, E. B., 113
Camp, C. J., 548
Campbell, A., 446
Campbell, F. L., 455, 464
Campbell, Stuart, 13
Campo, Laura, 604
Campos, J. J., 114, 120
Cantor, M. H., 519
Caplan, N., 290, 291
Capute, A. J., 145
Cardenas, J. A., 302
Carey, J. R., 531
Cargan, L., 452, 453
Carlo, G., 254
Carlson, B. E., 321
Carlton-Ford, S., 391
Carpenter, M. W., 80
Carrera, M. A., 400
Carroll, J. L., 284
Carter, D., 258
Carton, R. W., 605
Casey, P. H., 185
Casey, R. J., 333
Casper, R. C., 353
Cassell, C., 400
Cassidy, J., 177
Cassidy, M. L., 552
Catherine of Aragon, 48
Cattell, R. B., 485
Cavanaugh, J. C., 548

Ceci, S. J., 219, 287, 289
Celis, W., 186, 301
Centers for Disease Control (CDC), 83, 107, 359, 360, 412
Central Bureau of Statistics, 527
Chance, P., 286, 301
Chapman, A. H., 331
Chappell, N. L., 568, 569
Charness, M. E., 76
Chasnoff, I. J., 77
Chatters, L. M., 565
Chavez, G. F., 77
Chess, Stella, 175
Child Welfare League of America, 185
Children's Defense Fund (CDF), 399
Chilman, C. W., 387
Chira, S., 291
Chiriboga, D. A., 509
Chisolm, J. S., 99, 183
Chissell, J. T., 483, 484
Chodorow, N., 441
Chomsky, C. S., 292, 293
Chomsky, Naom, 150, 151
Chudacoff, H. P., 41
Chumlea, W. C., 345, 346
Cicirelli, V. G., 330, 513, 517, 519, 576
Clark, E. V., 149
Clark, R. A., 322
Clarke, C. J., 568
Clarke-Stewart, K. Alison, 178, 180, 184, 190, 191, 192, 194, 226
Clarkson-Smith, L., 540
Clausen, John A., 13, 41
Clemens, A. W., 516
Cobrinick, P., 77
Cohen, G. D., 543
Cohen, S., 417
Cohn, J. F., 169
Cohn, L. D., 383
Coke, M. M., 567
Colby, Anne, 282, 487–488, 496
Cole, C., 323
Cole, P. M., 170
Cole, T. R., 555
Coleman, J., 395
Coles, R., 305, 338, 386, 389
Colligan, M. J., 492
Collin, M. F., 102
Collins, R. C., 233
Collins, W. A., 312, 391
Colt, G. H., 614
Comer, J. P., 338
Committee on Bioethics, 604
Committee on Psychosocial Aspects of Child and Family Health, 598
Commonwealth Fund Commission on Elderly People Living Alone, 517–518, 568
Condon, W., 151
Condry, J. C., 173
Conger, J. J., 342, 389, 400, 401
Congressional Caucus for Women's Issues, 427
Connecticut Early Childhood Edu-

cation Council (CECEC), 234
Conners, C. K., 298
Connidis, I. A., 513, 576
Coons, S., 109
Cooper, K. H., 496
Cooper, K. L., 515
Cooper, R. P., 152
Corbin, C., 210
Corder, E. H., 542
Correa, P., 416
Costa, P. J., 505
Costa, P. T., 505
Costanzo, P. R., 314
Costello, A. J., 330, 331
Coster, W. J., 186
Council on Ethical and Judicial Affairs, 483
Council on Scientific Affairs of the American Medical Association, 86, 296, 412, 480
Courchesne, E., 69
Cousins, Norman, 599
Cowan, C. P., 467
Cowan, M. W., 94
Cox, J., 301
Cox, M. J., 181
Craft, M. J., 204
Craik, F. I. M., 547, 548, 550
Crain-Thoreson, C., 149, 154
Cratty, B., 279
Crisp, A. H., 481
Crnic, K. A., 461
Croake, J. W., 249
Crockett, L. J., 349
Cross-National Collaborative Group, 69
Csikszentmihalyi, M., 390, 395, 396
Cumming, E., 562
Cummings, E. M., 250
Cummins, J., 302
Cunningham, N., 178
Curtiss, S., 14
Curtsinger, J. W., 531
Cushman, R., 278
Cutrona, C., 577
Cytrynbaum, S., 505

Daley, S., 384
D'Alton, M. E., 61, 62
Damon, William, 392, 487–488
Daniels, D., 68
Danish, S. J., 412, 442, 443
Darlington, R. B., 234
Darwin, Charles, 494
Datan, N., 489
Davidson, J., 335
Davidson, J. E., 300
Davidson, R. J., 183
Davis, B. W., 512, 571
Davis, K. E., 465
Davis, K. L., 543
Dawson, G., 170
Dawson-Hughes, B., 476
de la Tour, Georges, 11
Deaux, K., 249
DeBuono, B. A., 454
DeCasper, A., 115, 151
Decker, M. D., 203
DeFrain, J., 89, 105, 125
DeFries, J. C., 296, 297

Dekovic, M., 317
deMille, Agnes, 494
Demo, D. H., 312, 318, 319, 321, 328, 390
Denney, N. W., 220, 488
Dennis, W., 63, 122
Denny, F. W., 202
deRegt, R. H., 84
deVos, S., 579
DeVries, M. W., 173
Deykin, E. Y., 607
Diagnostic and Statistical Manual of Mental Disorders (DSM III-R), 69, 208, 209, 296, 298, 332, 353, 354, 386
Diamond, M., 536
Diaz, R. M., 302
Dick-Read, Grantly, 83
Dickson, W. P., 223
Dien, D. S. F., 424
Dietz, W. H., 274
Dimant, R. J., 362
Dippel, R. L., 555
Dishion, T. J., 404
Dixon, R. A., 547
Dodge, K. A., 186, 317
Doering, C. H., 478
Doherty, W. J., 448
Doka, K. J., 581
Doman, G., 231
Donovan, P., 357
Doppelt, J. E., 485
Dore, J., 146
Dornbusch, S. M., 370, 394
Dorris, M., 89
Dove, J., 353
Downey, D. B., 325
Doyle, A. B., 266
Dreyer, P. H., 386, 387
Droege, R., 441
Duncan, B., 112
Dungy, C. I., 112
Dunn, J., 188, 189, 219, 220
Dunne, R. G., 278
DuPont, R. L., 249
Durlak, J. A., 610
Duskin, Rita, 557
Dustman, R. E., 535
Dwyer, T., 105

Easterbrooks, M. A., 179, 181, 182
Easterlin, R. A., 404
Eastman, P., 570
Eccles, J. S., 367
Eckenrode, J., 186
Eckerman, C. O., 189
Edelman, M. W., 406
Edinberg, M. A., 522
Edison, Thomas, 296
Egbuono, L., 205
Egeland, B., 177, 178, 179, 186
Ehrhardt, A. A., 247
Eichorn, D. H., 505
Eiger, M. S., 111, 112, 125
Eimas, P., 115, 146, 151
Einbender, A. J., 186
Einstein, Albert, 153, 421
Einstein, E., 463
Eisen, L. N., 77, 130
Eisen, M., 400
Eisenberg, A., 74, 89

Eisenberg, L., 607, 610
Eisenberg, N., 246
Eisenson, J., 146
Elkind, David, 12, 334, 338, 362, 363, 377, 583, 607
Ellis, L., 386
Emde, R. N., 30, 172
Emery, R. E., 186
Emmerick, H., 398
Epstein, J. L., 328
Epstein, L. H., 274
Erikson, Erik H., 24, 27, 28–29, 41, 162–164, 240–241, 310, 311, 380–382, 407, 436–438, 441, 455, 486, 500, 502, 503, 504, 510, 558–559, 611
Eron, L. D., 252
Espenschade, A., 278
Essex, M. J., 575, 577
Estés, C. P., 522
European Collaborative Study, 79
Evans, D. A., 6, 541
Evans, G., 81
Evans, R. I., 29
Eveleth, P. B., 346
Ewigman, B. G., 62
Eyer, D. D., 196

Faber, A., 268
Fabes, R. A., 261, 262
Fagan, J. F., 129, 143
Fagan, J. W., 131
Falbo, T., 259, 260
Fallot, M. E., 112
Fallows, J., 302
Fantuzzo, J. W., 187
Fantz, R. L., 115, 129
Farlow, M., 543
Farnsworth, C. H., 344
Farrell, M. P., 509
Farrow, J. A., 356
Feagans, L., 297
Feazell, C. S., 449
Feifel, H., 590
Fein, G., 266
Feinberg, I., 94
Feinman, S., 183
Feldman, H., 151, 464, 511
Feldman, R. D., 375
Fellin, P. A., 540
Fergusson, D. M., 208
Fetterly, K., 112
Fiatarone, M. A., 535
Field, D., 221, 561, 576, 577, 580, 601
Field, Tiffany M., 16, 103, 140, 170, 180, 182, 189, 191, 192, 402
Fielding, J. E., 416
Finegan, J. A., 61
Fingerhut, L. A., 412
Finlay, J., 590
Fiore, M. C., 416–417
Fitness Finders, 277
Fitzgerald, Ella, 494
Fivush, R., 213
Flanagan, C. A., 367
Flavell, J. H., 285, 293
Fluoxitine-Bulimia   Collaborative Study Group, 354
Folstein, M. F., 541
Fomon, S. J., 113

Ford, J., 400
Forman, M. R., 112
Fraga, C. G., 80
Fraiberg, Selma, 91
Frank, Anne, 341
Frank, S. J., 440
Frankenburg, W. K., 117, 119
Frankl, Viktor, 610
Freedman, D. G., 99
Freedman, S. G., 377
Freud, Anna, 25, 28, 390
Freud, Sigmund, 24, 25–28, 30, 242, 383, 390, 424, 455
Frezza, M., 417
Fried, P. A., 76
Friedan, Betty, 525, 555, 563
Friedman, M., 482
Friedman, R., 89
Fries, J. F., 537
Frisch, H., 174
Fromkin, V., 14
Fuchs, D., 289
Fuchs, F., 61
Fuchs, L. S., 289
Furman, W., 261, 312, 316, 318
Furry, C. A., 545
Furst, K., 441
Furstenberg, F. F., 399

Gaensbauer, T., 166
Gaertner, S. L., 315
Gage, F. H., 543
Galambos, N. L., 393
Galland, Eddy, 65
Gamble, T. J., 192
Gans, J. E., 351
Garbarino, J., 335
Gárcia Marquez, Gabríel, 435, 579
Garcia-Coll, C. T., 68, 172
Gardner, Howard, 144, 287, 300, 305, 494
Garfield, Charles, 600
Garland, J. B., 121
Garmezy, N., 334
Garn, S. M., 349
Garner, D. M., 353, 354
Garrison, W. T., 170
Gavotos, L. A., 278
Geber, M., 288
Gecas, V., 395
Gelfand, D. E., 567
Gelles, R. J., 321, 449
Gelman, R., 218
General Mills, Inc., 322, 392
Genevay, B., 577
Gerson, K., 522
Gesell, A., 122, 123
Getzels, J. W., 300
Gibson, R. C., 567
Gil, D. G., 186
Gilford, R., 511, 572, 573
Gilligan, Carol, 282–284, 362, 365, 366, 383, 384, 424–425, 433, 438, 441, 510
Ginsburg, H., 159, 277, 360, 361*n*.
Ginzburg, Natalia, 271
Glass, R. B., 456
Gleitman, L. R., 153
Glenn, N. D., 446, 450, 577
Glick, J., 10

Glick, P. C., 174, 324, 452, 463, 515–516
Golbus, M., 61
Gold, D., 227, 393
Gold, M., 397
Goldberg, E. L., 602
Golden, M., 288
Goldman, L., 480
Goldschmid, M. L., 280
Goldsmith, M. F., 357, 359
Goleman, D., 350, 484
Gopnick, A., 220, 221
Gorbach, S. L., 415
Gordon, A., 595, 596
Gortmaker, S. L., 274, 352
Goslin, D. A., 284
Gottesman, I. I., 67
Gottman, J. M., 262, 448
Gould, J. B., 84
Graf, Steffi, 34
Graziano, A. M., 209
Greenberg, J., 577, 578
Greenberg, S. P., 246
Greenberger, E., 374, 377
Greenhouse, L., 605
Greenwood, S., 496
Greer, J., 467
Grief, E. B., 349
Griswold, R. L., 433
Gross, R. T., 348
Grotevant, H., 373
Gruber, Howard, 494
Gruber-Baldini, A., 511
Gruen, G., 299
Gruson, L., 64
Gualtieri, T., 49
Gubrium, F. F., 575
Guidubaldi, J., 324
Guilford, J. P., 300
Gunnar, M. R., 184
Gunnersen, D., 543
Gutmann, D., 488, 505
Guttmacher, Alan, Institute, 399, 401

Haan, N., 509
Haddow, J. E., 61
Hadeed, A. J., 77
Hadley, J., 298
Hagberg, B., 561
Hagestad, G. O., 516, 520, 581
Haith, M. M., 114, 116
Hakuka, K., 301
Hall, E. G., 278, 438
Hall, G. Stanley, 12, 390
Hamer, D. H., 386
Hamilton, S., 374
Hammond, C. B., 477
Hamon, R. R., 578, 580
Handyside, A. H., 62
Hanley, R., 459
Hanson, S. M. H., 327
Hardy, J. B, 467
Hardy, J. B., 406
Hardy-Brown, K., 151
Hare, P. H., 569
Harkins, E., 515
Harlow, Harry, 176
Harlow, Margaret, 176
Harris, Louis, & Associates, 387, 389, 399, 400, 401

Harris, R., 449
Harrison, A. O., 319
Harrison, M., 419
Hart, C. H., 254, 255, 317
Hart, D. A., 467
Hart, S. N., 334
Harter, Susan, 310, 311
Hartford, John, 161
Hartmann, E., 208
Hartshorne, H., 284
Hartup, W. W., 314, 315, 316, 317
Harvard Medical School Health Letter, 606
Harvey, B., 107
Haskett, M. E., 186
Haskins, R., 234
Haswell, K., 165
Haugh, S., 247
Hawkins, H. L., 540
Hawley, T. L., 77
Hay, D. F., 189
Hayden, A., 59
Hayflick, Leonard, 533
Hayghe, H., 431
Hazen, N. L., 223
Health Care Finance Administration, 569
Healy, B., 418, 419
Healy, J. M., 305
Heard Museum of Anthropology and Primitive Art, 343
Heath, D. H., 522
Heilbrun, C. G., 522
Heller, Z. I., 595
Helmreich, W., 334, 338
Helson, Ravenna, 442, 502, 505, 506, 507, 510
Henderson, A., 295
Henig, R. M., 64
Henker, B., 298
Henker, F. O., 478
Henly, W. L., 77
Henrich, J. B., 477
Henry III, King of England, 48
Heraclitus, 1
Hermanson, B., 417
Herold, E. S., 400
Herzog, A. R., 552
Herzog, C., 545
Herzog, D. B., 353
Hess, T. M., 549
Hetherington, E. M., 243, 324, 325, 328, 329
Hewlett, B. S., 182
Heyns, B., 322
Hier, D. B., 248
Hill, C. D., 597
Hill, C. R., 318
Hill, J. P., 390, 391, 398
Hill, R. D., 540
Hinds, M., 228
Hirsch, J., 114
Hirsh-Pasek, K., 230, 231
Hoff-Ginsburg, E., 151, 152–153
Hofferth, S. L., 189
Hoffman, E. L., 102
Hoffman, Lois Wladis, 180, 192, 194, 227, 321, 321n., 322, 393
Hoffman, M., 246, 281
Holmes, T. H., 481

Holt, R. R., 492
Hong, S., 527
Hooker, E., 386
Hooker, K., 573
Hooyman, N. R., 572
Hopper, J. L., 476
Hopson, D., 268
Horn, J., 66
Horn, J. C., 526, 534
Horn, J. L., 485, 486, 543, 545
Horner, R. D., 484
Horowitz, F. D., 34, 299, 300, 301
Horwitz, S. M., 275
House, S. J., 465, 514
Householder, J., 77
Howard, M., 401
Howes, C., 266
Howie, P. W., 112
Hu, Y., 448
Hudson, J. I., 354
Hughes, Langston, 499
Hughes, M., 219
Hultsch, D. F., 545, 549
Humphrey, L. L., 354
Hunt, B., 472, 474, 480
Hunt, C. E., 105
Hunt, M. M., 454
Hurd, M. D., 566
Hurwich, C., 533
Huston, A. C., 253
Huttenlocher, J., 153
Hwang, C.-P., 193
Hyde, J. S., 246, 375, 387, 406
Hyman, B. T., 542
Hynd, G. W., 297

Infant Health and Development Program, 103
Infante-Rivard, Fernández, 78
Ingersoll, B. D., 237
Ingram, D. D., 86
Inhelder, Barbel, 35, 220
Institute for Social Research, 312
Interagency Committee on Learning Disabilities, 296–297
Isabella, R. A., 178
Izard, C. E., 165, 166, 167, 171

Jacklin, C. N., 49
Jacobson, J. L., 79, 180
Jacobson, S. W., 79, 112
Jacques, E., 500
James, William, 113
Janos, P. M., 300
Jarvik, L. F., 65, 555
Jaslow, C. K., 401
Jason, J. M., 102
Jay, M. S., 401
Jeliffe, D., 114
Jensen, A. R., 288
Jersild, A. T., 249
Jiao, S., 260
Johnson, C. L., 572, 578, 579
Johnson, R. K., 201
Johnson, Virginia E., 575
Johnston, L. D., 357
Jones, D. C., 213
Jones, E., 25
Jones, E. F., 401
Jones, H., 485

Jones, M. C., 348, 349
Jones, R. O., 84
Jost, H., 65
Jung, C. G., 500, 501, 502, 508, 510

Kagan, Jerome, 4, 41, 68, 242, 243, 248
Kahana, B., 581
Kalmuss, D. S., 449, 460
Kamin, L. J., 288
Kamo, Y., 429
Kandel, D. B., 355
Kane, R. I., 600
Kaplan, A., 491, 492
Kaplan, H., 99, 100
Kastenbaum, R., 591
Katz, D., 41
Katz, L., 231
Katz, P. A., 248
Katz, S., 533
Kaufman, J., 186
Kausler, D. H., 548
Kawachi, I., 480
Kaye, W. H., 354
Kayser-Jones, J. A., 570
Keating, N., 573
Keeney, T. J., 286
Keith, P. M., 579
Keller, Helen, 296
Kellermann, A. L., 606, 610
Kelley, J. L., 258
Kelly, J. B., 324, 325, 329, 451
Kelly, Orville, 600
Kempe, C. H., 185
Kemper, P., 569
Kendall-Tackett, 186
Kendler, K. S., 67
Kennedy, P., 305
Kennell, J., 85
Kerr, B. A., 427
Kessen, W., 135
Kessler-Harris, A., 431
Kestenbaum, R., 254
Ketcham, D., 449, 598
Kidder, J. T., 583
Kidder, T., 305
Kimmel, D. C., 526
Kimura, D., 419
Kinsey, A. C., 454
Kite, M. E., 526
Kitson, G. C., 451
Kivett, V. R., 581
Klagsbrun, F., 522
Klaus, M. H., 175
Klebanoff, M. A., 80
Kleinberg, F., 105
Kleinman, J. C., 79, 105
Klerman, G. L., 69
Klesges, R. C., 277
Kline, D. W., 534
Kline, M., 325, 328
Knitzer, J., 332
Kochanska, G., 262
Koenig, H. G., 564, 565
Koff, E., 350
Kohlberg, Lawrence, 36, 224, 242, 244–245, 280, 282–284, 362, 364–365, 423–425, 487
Kohn, M. L., 493, 494
Kolata, G., 62, 274, 604
Kolb, B., 94, 95

Konner, M., 196
Koocher, G., 601
Kopp, C., 125
Kopp, C. B., 133, 134, 166, 224
Korner, A. F., 110
Kosnik, W., 534
Kotelchuck, M., 181
Kraemer, H. C., 82
Kramer, J., 138
Krauss, R., 223
Kreutzer, M., 168, 286
Kristof, N. D., 249, 551
Kropp, J. P., 185
Kruper, J. C., 16
Ku, L. C., 357
Kübler-Ross, Elisabeth, 587, 593, 597, 614
Kuhl, P. K., 146
Kunkel, S. R., 539, 570
Kuntzleman, C. T., 276
Kupersmidt, J. B., 317
Kupfersmid, J., 284
Kutner, L., 601

Labbok, M. H., 112
Labouvie-Vief, G., 422, 423, 486
Lachman, J. L., 548
Ladd, G. W., 262
Lagercrantz, H., 81, 83
Lamaze, Fernand, 83
Lamb, M. E., 175, 180, 181, 182, 188, 193, 429
Lamborn, S. D., 392
Lampl, M., 110
Landesman-Dwyer, S., 76, 77
Landy, F. J., 490
Lange, G., 212, 213
Langer, E., 570
Lansky, V., 338
LaRossa, R., 461
Larson, R., 390, 395, 576
Laudenslager, M. L., 481
Lauer, J., 513
Lawrence, R. H., 567
Lawton, M. P., 568, 569
Lazarus, R. S., 481
Leach, P., 125, 237
Lederberg, A. R., 179
Lederman, S. A., 79
Lee, D. J., 562
Lee, G. R., 518, 573
Lee, I. M., 414
Lee, P. R., 415
Lee, T. R., 513
Lees, B., 476
LeGuin, U., 526
Lehman, D. R., 362, 426
Lehmkuhle, S., 296
Leigh, G. K., 517
Leland, C., 427
Lelwica, M., 169
Lemon, B., 562, 576
Lenneberg, E. H., 11, 145, 146
Lerner, J. V., 173
Lerner, M. J., 514
Lester, B. M., 76, 77, 274
Lester, R., 80
LeVay, S., 386
Leveno, K. J., 85
Levin, J. S., 565

Levine, M. D., 297
Levine, R., 509
Levinson, Daniel, 437, 438, 439, 441, 501, 502, 504, 508, 510
Leviton, D., 593, 600
Levy, D. M., 247
Levy, G. D., 245
Levy-Schiff, R., 102
Lewin, T., 85, 418
Lewis, C., 455
Lewis, D. O., 402
Lewis, G., 67
Lewis, M., 80, 166, 532
Lewis, M. I., 611, 612
Li, C. Q., 76
Lickona, T., 252, 284
Lieberman, M., 563, 592
Liebert, R. M., 252
Lieven, E. M., 149
Lightfoot-Klein, H., 344
Lindbergh, Anne Morrow, 471
Linney, J. A., 368
Lipid Research Clinics Program, 414
Lipsitt, L., 94, 121, 130, 131
Little, R. E., 76
Livson, N., 348, 349
Lo, Y-M. D., 62
Localia, A. R., 84
Lock, A., 148
Lock, M., 478
Loda, F. A., 204
Loeber, R., 402
Loehlin, J., 288
Lofland, L. H., 588
London, K., 388
Longino, C. F., 529, 533
Lonigan, C. J., 153
Looft, W. R., 364
Lopata, H., 602
Lorenz, Konrad, 174, 175
Lott, I. T., 75
Lovelace, E. A., 547
Lowenthal, M., 577
Lozoff, B., 208
Lufkin, E. G., 476
Lutjen, P., 459
Lyons-Ruth, K., 170, 180
Lystad, M., 449
Lytton, H., 243, 248

McAlister, A. L., 356, 357
McArney, E. R., 399
McCall, R. B., 133, 142, 143
McCann, I. L., 415
McCartney, K., 153, 192
McClelland, D., 113, 258, 259
Maccoby, Eleanor E., 124, 243, 246, 267, 309, 319, 320
McCord, C., 482, 483
McDaniel, K. D., 209, 298
McDonald, A. D., 76
Macey, T. J., 179
McFall, S., 569
McFarland, R. A., 474
Macfarlane, A., 116
McGauhey, P. J., 102
McGee, R., 298
McGinnis, J. M., 351
McGraw, M. B., 122, 123–124
McGue, M., 66, 67

McGuinness, D., 297
McKenry, P. C., 399
McKinley, D., 186, 322
McKinney, K., 290
McKitrick, L. A., 543
McLanahan, S., 327, 328
McLaughlin, B., 302
McLoyd, V. C., 322
McNally, J. W., 453
MacTurk, R. H., 169
Madison, P., 426
Maeroff, G. I., 368
Main, M., 177, 488
Malcolm, A. H., 603, 604
Malloy, M. H., 83
Malmquist, C. P., 332
Malthus, Thomas, 494
Mamay, P. D., 248
Mandler, J. M., 139
Manginello, F. P., 125
Mannuzza, S., 298
Manosevitz, M., 266
Mansfield, R. S., 300, 301
Maratsos, M., 223
March of Dimes Birth Defects Foundation, 52
Marcia, James E., 382, 384, 385
Markides, K. S., 538, 567
Markoff, J., 80
Marks, J., 496
Markus, H., 309
Marquis, K. S., 458
Marston, S., 338
Martin, G. B., 189
Martin, L. G., 527
Martin, T. C., 449
Martinez, G. A., 112
Marzano, R. J., 294
Maslach, C., 492
Maslow, Abraham, 37–38
Masoro, E. J., 531
Massey, C. M., 218
Masters, William H., 475, 575
Matas, L., 179
Matheny, K. B., 481
Matlin, M. W., 246, 375
Matsukura, S., 416
Matthews, K. A., 431, 475, 477
Maxwell, L., 294
Mayer, J., 114
Mead, Margaret, 99, 390
Mednick, B. R., 399
Medrich, E. A., 312
Meehan, P. J., 606, 609–610
Melnick, S., 76
Melpomene Institute for Women's Health Research, 433
Meltzoff, A. N., 139, 140
Mendel, Gregor, 50–51, 52
Menken, J., 456
Meredith, N. V., 273
Merriam, Eve, 379
Meyer, D. R., 327
Meyers, A. F., 274
Meyers, H., 515
Michaels, D., 202
Miles, C., 485
Miller, B. C., 300, 388, 400, 461
Miller, C. A., 86
Miller, E., 78

Miller, Jean Baker, 24, 27–28, 29–30, 41, 441, 510
Miller, L. B., 230, 234
Miller, P. M., 246
Miller, V., 99
Miller-Jones, D., 288, 289
Mills, J. L., 76, 78
Millstein, S. G., 351
Milne, A. M., 328, 393
Milunsky, A., 58, 61, 79
Mindel, C. H., 567
Miranda, S., 115
Mitchell, B. A., 440
Mitchell, E. A., 105
Mitchell, V., 502, 505, 508, 515
Miyake, K., 180
Moely, B. E., 285
Moffitt, T. E., 349
Money, J., 247
Montaigne, 239
Montemayor, R., 391
Montepare, J. M., 528
Montessori, Maria, 228, 233
Moore, A. U., 175
Moore, C., 219
Moore, N., 264
Morbidity and Mortality Weekly Report (MMWR), 100, 101, 359, 417, 606
Morgan, L., 517
Morison, P., 317
Morland, J., 315
Morris, R., 250
Morrison, Toni, 494
Moses, M., 614
Mosher, W. D., 400, 456
Moskowitz, B. A., 153
Moss, F., 569
Moss, M. S., 520
Mossberg, H.-O., 114
Mozart, Wolfgang Amadeus, 301
MRC Vitamin Study Research Group, 74
Mui, A. C., 519
Murphy, C. M., 250
Murphy, D. P., 79
Murray, A. D., 82
Murstein, B. I., 444
Mussen, P. H., 243, 255, 348
Must, A., 352
Muuss, R. E. H., 284
Myerhof, B., 583
Myers, J. K., 69
Myers, N., 212
Myers-Walls, J. A., 461

Naeye, R. L., 77
Nash, Ogden, 307
Nathanson, C. A., 418, 419
National Assessment of Educational Progress, 312
National Association for the Education of Young Children, 229–230
National Association of Children's Hospitals and Related Institutions (NACHRI), 106, 204
National Center for Education Statistics (NCES), 368, 369, 370, 371, 372, 374, 426, 427, 428

National Center for Health Statistics, 75, 205, 455, 456, 606, 607
National Coalition on Television Violence, 253
National Commission for the Protection of Human Subjects of Biomedical and Behavioral Research, 22
National Commission on Excellence in Education, 299, 368
National Commission on Youth, 374
National Committee for Citizens in Education (NCCE), 607
National Institute of Aging (NIA), 534, 535, 540, 543
National Institute of Child Health and Human Development, 103, 356
National Institute of Education (NIE), 428
National Institute of Mental Health (NIMH), 252, 255
National Institute on Alcohol Abuse and Alcoholism (NIAAA), 417
National Institute on Drug Abuse (NIDA), 354, 355, 356
National Institutes of Health (NIH), 414, 418, 476
National Osteoporosis Foundation, 476
National Research Council (NRC), 399
Needleman, H. L., 79
Neiswender, M., 445
Nelson, K., 148, 149, 151, 152, 153, 213
Neuffer, E., 589
Neugarten, Bernice, 12, 442, 443, 472, 477, 501, 504, 505, 508, 510, 526, 559, 563, 566, 591
Newacheck, P. W., 351
Newcomb, A. F., 317
Newhouse News Service, 427
Newman, P. R., 395, 398
Newport, E. I., 151
Newson, J., 208
Nilsson, L., 89
Nin, Anaïs, 409
Nisan, M., 282
Noll, R. B., 227
Nordlicht, S., 322
Norton, A. J., 452, 513
Notelovitz, M., 415, 476
Notzon, F. C., 83, 84
Nugent, J. K., 181
Nuland, S. B., 614
Nussbaum, M., 354

Oakley, D., 399
Oberklaid, F., 173
Oberlander, T. F., 110
O'Bryant, S. L., 576, 579, 602
O'Connor, M. J., 115, 143, 177
Oehlenschlager, Adam G., 199
Offer, Daniel, 390, 391, 402, 404
Office of Technology Assessment, 459
O'Keeffe, Georgia, 547
Okun, M. A., 562
Okun, S., 608
Olds, S. W., 191, 323, 457, 580

O'Leary, K. D., 449
Oliner, S. P., 255
Oller, D. K., 146
Olsen-Fulero, L., 149
Orentlicher, D., 64
Orr, W. C., 533
Ostrea, E. M., 75, 77
Oswald, P. F., 167
Otten, M. W., 483
Ouslander, J. G., 569, 570
Owens, J. E., 592
Owens, J. F., 480
Owens, W. A., 485

Padilla, A. M., 301, 302
Palmore, E. B., 552, 562
Paloma, M. M., 461
Papousek, H., 131
Pappas, G., 418
Paris, S. G., 286
Parke, R. D., 181, 182, 256
Parker, J. G., 317
Parlee, M. B., 419
Parmelee, A. H., 108
Parmentier, M., 46
Parten, Mildred B., 263, 264
Passuth, P., 444
Pasteur, Louis, 494
Patterson, C. J., 317
Patterson, G. R., 186, 251, 253, 403
Pattison, E. M., 590, 591
Patton, George, 296
Paveza, G. J., 570, 572
Pavlov, Ivan, 24, 31
Pearlin, L. I., 517
Pease, D., 221
Pebley, A. R., 455
Peck, Robert C., 501, 502, 503–504,
    510, 559, 559–560
Pedersen, F. A., 182
Pederson, E., 294
Peel, E. A., 360
Perkins, H. W., 602
Perlmutter, M., 313
Perris, E. E., 132
Perrucci, 493
Perry, William G., 423, 426
Persson-Blennow, I., 172
Peskin, H., 348
Petchers, M. K., 538
Petitto, L. A., 146, 147
Petri, E., 65
Pettigrew, T. F., 288
Pettit, E. J., 451
Phillips, D., 192
Phillips, D. P., 594, 608
Piaget, Jean, 27–28, 34–37, 132,
    135–140, 142, 159, 166, 213–224,
    265, 272, 279, 280, 281, 360, 361,
    362, 365, 422, 423, 590
Picasso, Pablo, 547
Pillemer, K., 516, 570, 572
Pincus, T., 418
Pines, M., 218
Pinker, S., 159
Pipp, S., 180
Pippig, Uta, 411
Pittman, F., 433
Plemons, J., 546
Plomin, R., 65, 66–70

Poland, R. L., 118
Pollock, Linda A., 12
Poon, L. W., 547, 548–549
Pope, A. W., 317
Posner, J. K., 323
Poznanski, E. O., 332
Pratt, M. W., 226, 257
Pratt, W. B., 388
Prechtl, H. F. R., 109
Prevention Index '93: A Report
    Card on the Nation's Health,
    415, 416, 417, 480, 481
Pugh, D., 344
Purnick, N., 402
Pynoos, R. S., 334

Quinby, N., 289

Rabiner, D., 317, 318
Rachal, J. V., 356
Radford, J., 305
Radin, N., 182, 226, 227
Raffaelli, M., 394
Rafferty, Y., 206, 207
Ragozin, A. S., 456
Rakowski, W., 539
Raskin, P. A., 243
Rassin, D. K., 112
Raven, J. C., 485
Ravitch, D., 293
Read, M. S., 74
Redding, R. E., 170
Reese, H. W., 286
Reichard, S., 562
Reid, J. R., 185
Reid, R. L., 419
Reissland, N., 140
Remafedi, G., 386, 387
Rempel, J., 579
Renzulli, J. S., 300
Rescorla, L., 293
Restak, R., 95
Reuben, C., 89
Rexroat, C., 573
Reznick, J. S., 68, 145, 149
Rheingold, H. L., 143, 184
Rhoads, G. G., 414
Rhodes, S. R., 428, 430
Rice, M. L., 149, 153
Richards, M. P. M., 179
Richardson, D. W., 347
Ridenour, M. V., 122
Rieder, M. J., 122
Riegel, K. F., 545
Rierdan, J., 350
Rieser, J., 116
Rindfuss, R. R., 455
Ritvo, E. R., 69
Rivara, F. P., 278
Roberts, E. J., 385
Roberts, G. C., 320
Roberts, P., 441
Robertson, L. F., 234
Robinson, B., 519
Robinson, I., 387
Robinson, J. L., 67, 68
Robinson, L. C., 512, 513
Robison, L. L., 76
Robson, K. S., 179
Roche, A. F., 114

Rock, D. A., 368
Rockefeller, Nelson, 296
Rogers, M. F., 202
Rogoff, B., 10
Romero-Gwynn, E., 112
Roopnarine, J., 261, 262, 263
Roosevelt, Eleanor, 516
Roosevelt, Elliot, 516
Rose, R. M., 247
Rose, S. A., 143
Rose, X., 583
Rosen, B., 551
Rosen, J. G., 353
Rosen, L. A., 273
Rosenberg, L., 417
Rosenberg, M. B., 543
Rosenberg, M. S., 334
Rosenblatt, P., 596
Rosenfeld, A., 444
Rosenthal, M. K., 151
Rosenthal, P. A., 605
Rosenthal, R., 295
Rosenzweig, M. R., 95
Rosetti-Ferreira, M. C., 274
Ross, C. E., 446, 448
Ross, G., 102
Ross, H. G., 576
Rossi, A. S., 505, 509, 517
Rovee-Collier, C., 130, 131, 132
Roybal, E. R., 540
Ruberman, W., 482
Rubin, A., 96
Rubin, D. H., 80, 112
Rubin, K., 264, 265
Rubin, L. B., 475, 510, 515
Rubin, Z., 505
Rubinstein, R. L., 575, 576
Ruble, D. N., 349, 350
Rudman, D., 533
Ruhm, C. J., 552
Rule, S., 372
Russell, A., 262
Rutter, M., 175, 184, 185, 328, 334, 335
Ryan, A. S., 111, 540
Ryerson, A. J., 12
Ryff, Carol D., 559, 563
Rymer, R., 14, 41

Sabatelli, R. M., 456
Sacco, R. L., 484
Sachs, B. P., 83
Sacks, J. J., 204
Sadowitz, P. D., 113
Sagi, A., 189
Saigal, S., 102
Salthouse, T. A., 535, 536
Salzinger, S., 186
Sandler, D. P., 80
Sands, L. P., 545
Santer, L. J., 204
Santrock, J. W., 329
Sapienza, C., 52
Saravis, S., 273
Sauer, M. V., 459
Scarborough, H. S., 153, 154
Scarr, S., 66, 192
Schafer, R., 488
Schaie, K. Warner, 12, 420–421, 485,
    486, 544, 545, 561
Schanberg, S. M., 103

Scharlach, A. E., 519
Schechtman, V. L., 105
Schick, F. L., 551, 552
Schindler, P. J., 266
Schiro, A., 320
Schlossberg, N. K., 509, 510
Schmeck, H. M., 346, 605
Schmitt, B. D., 185
Schmitt, M. H., 113
Schnall, P. L., 492
Schneider, E. L., 529
Schnur, S., 467
Schoen, E. J., 118
Schoen, R., 448, 453
Schoendorf, K. C., 102, 104, 105
Schor, E. L., 277
Schorr, L., 237
Schreiber, L. A., 522
Schuckit, M. A., 67
Schulman, S., 296, 297
Schultz, D. P., 491
Schulz, R., 597
Schutter, S., 77
Schvaneveldt, J. D., 275
Schweinhart, L. U., 234
Scott, G. B., 79
Scott, J. P., 175, 576
Sears, P., 21
Sears, R. R., 258
Seccombe, K., 461
Seles, Monica, 34
Selkoe, D. A., 536
Selkoe, D. J., 536, 537, 543
Sells, L. W., 427
Selman, Robert L., 316
Sen, A., 483
Sexton, Anne, 45
Sexton, M., 76
Shafran, Robert, 65
Shakespeare, William, 49
Shangold, M., 348
Shannon, D. C., 105
Shannon, L. W., 404
Shapiro, J. L., 196
Shapiro, J. P., 41
Shatz, M., 223
Shaw, George Bernard, 547
Shay, K. A., 540
Shaywitz, S. E., 296
Shekerjian, D., 305
Sheps, S., 277, 278
Sherman, L. W., 186, 449
Shields, P. J., 132
Ship, J. A., 535
Shipp, E. R., 459
Siegel, O., 348
Siegler, R. S., 138, 285
Sigman, M. D., 169, 274
Signorielli, N., 252
Silverman, S., 75
Silverstein, B., 353
Simmons, R. G., 349, 367
Simner, M. L., 189
Simon, S. B., 338
Simon, Theodore, 133
Simons, C., 291
Simons, M., 605
Simpson, R., 484
Singer, D. G., 266
Singer, J. L., 266

Singh, S., 86
Singleton, L., 315
Sisodia, 542
Skaff, M. M., 573
Skinner, B. F., 24, 32, 150
Sklar, L. S., 481
Skoe, E. E., 366
Skolnick, A., 476
Skoog, I., 541
Slap, G. B., 607
Slevin, J. D., 231
Slobin, D. I., 149, 150
Smelser, N. J., 493
Smetana, J. G., 391
Smilansky, S., 265
Smith, D. W., 59
Smith, Jacqui, 548, 549
Smith, T. E., 374
Smith, T. W., 453, 454, 455
Snarey, J. R., 282
Snow, C. E., 152, 153
Snow, M. E., 182
Soddy, K., 474
Solomon, M., 605
Solomons, H., 99
Sonenstein, F. L., 387, 388
Song, M., 290, 291
Sontag, S., 478
Sorce, J. F., 169
Sorensen, R. C., 389, 390
Sorensen, T., 66
Speece, M. W., 590
Spencer, M. B., 385
Spirduso, W. W., 473, 474
Spitz, M. R., 80
Spitz, R. A., 183, 184
Spitze, G., 518
Spitzer, M. E., 535
Spock, B., 188
Sroufe, L. A., 163, 168, 180, 183, 254
Stacey, M., 185
Stadtman, E. R., 533
Stafford, R. S., 84
Stair, Nadine, 558
Stampfer, M. J., 480
Stanley, A., 299
Starfield, B., 202, 205, 274, 275
Starr, B. D., 474, 575
Staub, S., 212
Stein, P. J., 452
Steinbach, U., 569, 576, 577
Steinberg, L., 349, 370, 374, 390, 392,
    393, 394, 406
Steinberg, W., 496
Steiner, J. E., 116
Stenchever, M. A., 76
Stern, D. N., 196
Stern, M., 102
Sternberg, Robert J., 287–289, 300,
    421–422, 433, 444, 445, 513
Sterns, H. L., 536
Stevens, J. C., 473, 537
Stevens, J. H., 156
Stevenson, H. W., 290–291, 295
Stevenson, M., 189
Stewart, M. A., 298, 505
Stewart, R. B., 188
Stewart, W., 441
Stigler, J. W., 291
Stinnett, N., 573

Stipek, D. J., 166
Stiver, I., 492
Stjernfeldt, M., 77
Stocker, C., 395
Stoppard, M., 89
Straus, M., 78, 449
Strawbridge, W. J., 519
Streissguth, A. P., 76, 77
Stroebe, M., 596
Strube, M. J., 449
Stuart, M. J., 75–76
Stunkard, A. J., 65, 111, 274
Sue, S., 291
Sugawara, O., 533
Suitor, J. J., 514, 578
Sullivan, H. S., 316
Sullivan, J. F., 86
Sullivan, M. W., 131
Suomi, S., 176
Surbey, M. K., 349
Svanborg, A., 532
Swain, I. U., 131
Swedo, S., 607
Sweetland, J. D., 234

Tabor, A., 61
Tager, I. B., 416
Tamir, L. M., 490
Tan, S. L., 459
Tanfer, K., 400, 453
Tannen, D., 467
Tanner, J. M., 273, 348, 410
Targ, D. B., 515
Tate, C. S., 219
Taylor, A. R., 299
Taylor, M., 266
Taylor, N., 614
Taylor, R. J., 567
Taylor, S. E., 433
Tennyson, Alfred, Lord, 127
Terman, Lewis M., 12, 21, 300
Termine, N. T., 169
Thacker, S. B., 204
Thomas, A., 66, 171, 172, 189
Thomas, D., 299
Thomas, J. L., 581
Thomas, R., 37
Thompson, L. A., 142, 143, 429, 446,
    461, 543
Thompson, R. A., 179
Thompson, S. K., 244
Thomson, E., 453
Thornton, A., 443, 453, 455, 464
Tiger, L., 245
Timiras, P. S., 94, 473
Tisdale, S., 53–55
Tobin, J. J., 232, 233, 237
Tobin-Richards, M. H., 345, 350
Tomasello, M., 152
Toner, B. B., 353
Tonkova-Yampol'skaya, R. V., 146
Treffers, P. E., 87
Treiber, P. M., 237
Trichopoulos, D., 416
Trickett, P. K., 185
Troll, Lillian E., 410, 472, 473, 514,
    516, 518–520, 580
Tronick, E. Z., 113, 168, 169
Trotter, R. J., 171, 174, 421
Tsai, M., 185

Tschann, J., 451
Tuma, J. M., 333
Turecki, S., 268
Turkington, C., 605

Uhlenberg, P., 513, 574
Umberson, D., 516, 517
UNICEF, 101
United Nations, 107
U.S. Bureau of the Census, 189, 190,
    326, 327, 369, 446, 449, 452, 527,
    528, 531, 532, 533, 537, 538, 539,
    551, 566, 568, 569
U.S. Bureau of Labor, 431
U.S. Consumer Product Safety
    Commission, 204
U.S. Department of Education, 295,
    369, 371, 428, 489
U.S. Department of Health, Educa-
    tion, and Welfare (USDHEW), 276
U.S. Department of Health and
    Human Services (USDHHS), 49,
    69, 85, 86, 101, 104, 105, 106, 187,
    276, 331, 411, 416, 417, 419, 479,
    480, 482, 532, 534, 538, 539, 566,
    567, 568, 605, 606, 607, 608
U.S. Department of Justice, 403
U.S. Department of Labor, 430, 551
Upjohn Company, 358
Uzgiris, I. C., 138

Vachon, M., 602
Vaillant, George E., 1, 437–439, 441,
    501, 502, 504, 508, 510, 560–561, 561
Valdes-Dapena, M., 105
Valenzuela, M., 179
Van Noord-Zaadstra, B. M., 456
Vandell, D. L., 266, 323
vanIJzendoorn, M. H., 179
Vargas, Mario Llosa, 579
Vaughan, V., 48
Verdi, Giuseppe, 547
Verhaeghen, P., 550
Veroff, J., 322
Vinci, Leonardo da, 494
Vinick, B., 574
Visher, E. B., 329, 463
Voydanoff, P., 493
Vuori, L., 74
Vygotsky, Lev Semenovich, 224,
    225

Wachs, T., 138
Wagner, R. K., 422
Walk, R. D., 114
Walker, A., 377
Walker, A. J., 519, 578
Walker, L. J., 365, 424
Wallace, D. C., 533
Wallach, M. A., 300
Wallerstein, J. S., 324, 325, 327, 330
Walls, C. T., 565
Walster, E., 446
Walter, H. J., 357
Ward, R., 516
Wasik, B. H., 134
Waters, E., 180
Watson, John B., 24, 32, 130
Wayler, A. H., 539

Weathers, W. T., 78
Webb, W. B., 207, 537
Webber, J., 237
Weg, R. B., 475, 478, 575, 577
Wegman, M. E., 52, 101, 102, 103,
    103n., 104, 324, 531, 532
Weihenmayer, Erik, 430
Weinberg, R. A., 66
Weishaus, S., 573
Weiss, B. D., 278
Weiss, G., 298
Weiss, L., 397, 465
Weissman, M. M., 332, 606
Weitzman, M., 77
Wellman, H., 223
Wells, A. S., 372
Wendkos, Leah, 547, 591
Wentz, K. R., 106
Werler, M. M., 74
Werner, E. E., 96
Werner, J. S., 129
West Berlin Human Genetics Insti-
    tute, 80
Whiffen, V. E., 170
Whisnant, L., 350
White, B. L., 155, 156, 159
White, K. R., 370, 371
White, L., 515
White, L. K., 448
White, N., 545
Whitehurst, G. J., 17, 153, 154
Whitson, J. S., 542
Wideman, M. V., 83
Widom, C. S., 186
Wilcox, A. J., 70
Wilde, J. A., 159
Willett, W. C., 415
Williams, B. C., 98, 107, 203, 205
Williams, E. R., 201, 203, 273, 352
Williams, J., 315
Williams, T. M., 253
Williams, William Carlos, 546–547
Williamson, D. F., 414, 483
Willis, S. L., 546
Wilson, G., 77
Wilson, M. H., 237
Winfrey, Oprah, 5
Winick, M., 74, 75
Wiswell, T. E., 118
Wittrock, M. C., 95
Wolf, M., 424
Wolfe, D. A., 185, 186
Wolff, P. H., 109, 167, 168
Wolinsky, F. D., 537, 569, 602
Wong, N. D., 277
Wong, P. T. P., 611
Wood, D., 226
Wood, D. L., 205
Woodruff, D. S., 537
Working Group on HIV Testing of
    Pregnant Women and New-
    borns, 79
Working Women Education Fund,
    491
World Health Organization, 205
Worth, C., 125
Wortman, C. B., 597, 598
Wright, A. L., 112
Wright, Frank Lloyd, 494
Wright, J. T., 77

Wurtman, R. J., 419
Wynn, Karen, 140, 141

Yamazaki, J. N., 80
Yazigi, R. A., 80
Yllo, K., 449
Yogman, M. J., 181, 182

York, J. L., 571
Young, K. T., 192
Youngblade, L. M., 180, 182
Youngstrom, N., 335

Zabin, L. S., 388, 400
Zahn-Waxler, C., 254

Zakaria, S. B., 328
Zametkin, A. J., 298
Zarbatany, L., 313, 314
Zelazo, P. R., 181
Zelnik, M., 387
Zeskind, P. S., 74, 102
Zigler, E. F., 234, 235

Zimiles, H., 372
Zimmerman, D., 344
Zimmerman, I. L., 227
Zube, M., 511, 573
Zuckerman, B. S., 77, 170
Zuckerman, D. M., 248, 255
Zylke, J. W., 105

SUBJECT INDEX

Abortions, spontaneous, 70–73, 74, 76, 79, 625
Absenteeism, job, 430
Abuse:
    of children, 185–187, 616
    of elderly, 570–572, 618
    sexual, 185, 624
    of spouses, 449
Acceptance stage of dying, 593
Accidental injuries, 203–204, 277–278, 411, 413, 417
Accommodation, Piagetian, 36, 615
Ache culture (Paraguay), motor development in infants in, 99–100
Achieving stage, 420, 421, 615
Achondroplasia (dwarfism), 52
Acquired immune deficiency syndrome (AIDS) (see AIDS)
Acquisitive stage, 420, 421, 615
Acting-out behavior, 331, 615
Active euthanasia, 603–605, 615
Active sleep in infants, 109
Activity theory of aging, 562–563, 615
Acute lymphoblastic leukemia, 76
Adaptation, Piagetian, 36, 615
Adaptive mechanisms, 319, 438, 615
Addicted mothers, children of, 77–78
Adjustment, and temperament, 172–173
Adolescence, 342–406
    career development in, 372–375
    characteristics of, 7
    cognitive development in, 360–362
    cohort studies of, 404–405
    death in, 590
        by suicide, 607–608
        views of, 590
    defined, 342, 615
    egocentrism in, 362–364
    end of, 342, 343
    everyday life in, 395–398
    health concerns in, 351–360
    history of study of, 12
    maturation in, 344–350
    and middle-aged parents, 514–515
    moral development in, 364–366
    personality development in (see Personality and social development, in adolescence)
    pregnancy in, 398–402
    versus rites of passage, 342, 343
    secondary school during, 367–372
    as stage of parenting, 462

Adolescent growth spurt, 346–347, 615
Adolescent (Oakland) Growth Study, 12, 13
Adolescent rebellion, 390–391, 403, 615
Adoption, 458
Adoption studies, 65–68
Adult Development and Enrichment Project (ADEPT), studies based on, 546
Adult education:
    in late adulthood, 550–551
    in middle adulthood, 489
Adulthood:
    coming of, 342, 343
    history of study of, 12
    suicide in, 608
    (See also Late adulthood; Middle adulthood; Young adulthood)
Affective disorders, 332, 615
African Americans (see Racial differences)
Age:
    of children:
        and reactions to divorce, 322–327
        and spacing of sibling, 187–188
    declining consciousness of, 443
    effects on work, 428–430
    of parenthood:
        factors in young adulthood, 455–456, 457
        and risk of birth defects, 58–59, 61, 79, 81
Age-30 transition, 437, 442
Age-50 transition, 502
Age-graded influences, normative, 8
Ageism, 526, 529, 615
Aggressive behavior, 250–254
    in adolescence, 346, 372
    characteristics of, 250–251
    defined, 615
    and gender differences, 246
    hostile, 250
    instrumental, 250
    reducing, 253–254
    triggers of, 251–252
Aging:
    double standard of, 478–479
    history of study of, 12
    social issues related to, 566–572
    successful patterns of, 562–566
    theories of process of, 533–534
    (See also Late adulthood)
AIDS (acquired immune deficiency syndrome), 453–454
    in children, 202–203, 275

AIDS (acquired immune deficiency syndrome), (Cont.):
    effect on fetus, 78–79
    in middle adulthood, 480
    as sexually transmitted disease, 357, 359
Alcohol use and abuse:
    in adolescence, 355–356
    and adult health, 412, 413, 417
    hereditary factors in, 67
    during pregnancy, 74, 76, 618–619
    (See also Alcoholism)
Alcoholism, 226–227, 615 (See also Alcohol use and abuse)
Alleles, 51, 615
Alpha¹, antitrypsin deficiency, 53
Alpha fetaprotein (AFP), testing for, 61
Alpha thalassemia, 53, 62
Altruism, 254–255
Alzheimer's disease, 6, 541–543, 615
Ambivalent (resistant) attachment, 177–180, 615
Amniocentesis, 61, 615
Amniotic sac, 70
Anal stage, 26, 27
Androgens, 247–248, 345
Androgynous personality, 247, 615
Anencephaly, 54–55, 61, 604
Anesthetics:
    during childbirth, 82
    for newborns, 116, 117
Anger stage of dying, 593
Animal studies:
    of brain development, 95
    of mother-infant bonding, 174–176, 177
    purpose in studies of human development, 4
    of sex differences, 247
    and social-learning theory, 33
Animism:
    defined, 615
    of young children, 218
Anorexia nervosa, 352–354, 615
Anoxia, 93, 96, 615
Anticipatory grief, 596–597, 615
Anxiety:
    about strangers and separation, 183, 625
    in middle childhood, 331–332
Anxious (insecure) attachment, day care and, 193–194
Apache Indians, puberty rites of, 343
Apgar scale, 96–98, 615
Appalachian children, speech in, 224

Apparent hypocrisy, 364
Arapesh culture (New Guinea):
    middle childhood in, 310
    motor development of infants in, 99
Argumentativeness, 363
Armor-defended personality, 564
Artificial insemination, 458–459, 615
Asian cultures:
    aging in, 527
    children in:
        education performance of, 290–291
        learning style of, 144
        motor skills of, 99–100
        prelinguistic speech of, 146
        in preschools, 232
    (See also names of specific cultures)
Aspirin use during pregnancy, effects of, 75–76
Assessment:
    of creative thinking, 299–300
    of development, 134–135
        Bayley Scales of Infant Development, 134–135, 616
        Denver Developmental Screening Test, 99, 117, 617
        Infant Psychological Development Scales, 138
    of intelligence
        for disabled children, 134
        Stanford-Binet Intelligence Scale, 138, 224, 225, 280, 625
        Wechsler scales, 143–144, 224, 225, 286–287, 626
        (See also Psychometric approach)
    of neonates, 96–100, 616
    of practical problem solving, 488
    prenatal, 61–62
Assignment, random, in experiments, 19
Assimilation, Piagetian, 36, 615
Associative play, 264
Attachment, 176–180
    changes in, 179
    defined, 176, 615
    effects on early childhood, 179–180, 261–263
    and employment of mother, 192–195
    establishment of, 178–179
    and stranger and separation anxiety, 183, 625
Attention deficit hyperactivity disorder (ADHD), 52, 297–298, 615
Attention in infancy, 143
Authoritarian parents, 258

Authoritarian parents, *(Cont.)*:
  of adolescents, 369, 370
  defined, 257, 616
Authoritative parents, 262
  of adolescents, 369, 370, 393, 394
  and child development, 257, 258
  defined, 257, 616
  and popularity, 317
  and self-esteem, 317, 324–325
Autism, infantile, 67–69, 169, 219, 620
Autobiographies in life review, 612
Automobile accidents, 203, 278, 411, 413, 417
Autonomous morality, 281 (*See also* Morality, of cooperation)
Autonomy:
  defined, 164
  versus shame and doubt stage, 27, 163–164, 616
Autosomes, defined, 49, 616
Aversive events in operant conditioning, 32–33
Avoidant attachment, 177–180, 616

Babbling, 146, 147, 154
Babies (*see* Infancy and toddlerhood)
Babinski reflex, 97
Babkin reflex, 130–131
Baby biographies, 14
Baby booms, 528, 539
"Baby M" case, 459
Bargaining stage of dying, 593
Basic trust versus basic mistrust stage:
  characteristics of, 162–163
  defined, 27, 616
Battered child syndrome, 185, 616
Bayley Scales of Infant Development, 134–135, 616
"Becoming One's Own Man" (BOOM), 437
Bed-wetting, 208–209, 618
Behavior modification (behavior therapy), 33, 255, 333, 616
Behavior therapy (*see* Behavior modification)
Behavioral and mental disorders:
  hereditary factors in, 67–69
  in late adulthood, 540–543
  in middle childhood, 330–333
Behavioral assessment scale, Brazelton, 98–100, 616
Behaviorism, 30–33, 34, 150–151, 616
Bereavement, 593, 598–601, 616
Berkeley Longitudinal Studies, 12, 13
Beta thalassemia (Cooley's anemia), 53
Bilingual education, 501–502, 616
Bilingualism, 301–302, 616
Biological changes (*see* Physical development)
Biological death, defined, 589
Biological influences:
  on memory impairment, 548–550
  (*See also* Heredity)

Bipedal walking, 121
Birth, 81–87
  alternative settings for, 85–87
  contractions of, 81
  effects of trauma, 96
  methods of, 82–85
    cesarean section, 83–84, 616
    medicated delivery, 82, 621
    natural, 83, 621
    prepared, 83, 623
  stages of, 81
  stress at, 83–84, 96
  weight at (*see* Low birthweight)
  (*See also* Pregnancy; Prenatal development)
Birth control:
  education about, 401
  failure to use, 399–400, 401
Birth defects:
  as cause of infant mortality, 104
  environmental causes of:
    maternal (*see* Mothers, pregnant)
    paternal, 80–81
  hereditary, 52–60
  and organ donation, 604
  prenatal diagnosis of, 61–62
Birth trauma:
  defined, 616
  effects of, 96
Black people (*see* Racial differences)
Blastocyst, 70
Blended families, 329, 461–464
Blindness in late adulthood, 534
Blood tests, maternal, 61–62, 621
Blood type, incompatibility of between mother and fetus, 61, 79
Body image, adolescent, 348–350
Body transcendence versus body preoccupation, 559–560
Bonds, infant:
  with fathers, 180–181
  with mothers, 112, 174–176, 177, 621
Bones:
  in late adulthood, 352, 535, 537
  thinning of (osteoporosis), 352, 475, 476, 535, 537, 622
  (*See also* Growth, physical)
BOOM ("Becoming One's Own Man"), 437
Bottle-feeding, 112, 113
Brain:
  in Alzheimer's disease, 541–543
  development of, 94–96
  and fetal malnutrition, 74
  in late adulthood, 536–537
  reflex behavior controlled by, 94–96
Brazelton Neonatal Behavioral Assessment Scale, 98–100, 616
Breastfeeding, 74, 76, 78–79, 111–112
Breasts, budding of, 347
Breeding, selective, 63
Brothers and sisters (*see* Sibling relations)
Bulimia nervosa, 354, 616
Burnout, 492, 616

Caffeine intake during pregnancy, 78
Calcium for osteoporosis prevention, 476
Cancer, 415, 416
  in children, 202
  death from, 482, 532
  and diet, 415
  and estrogen, 475–477, 480
  and maternal drug use, 76, 77
Care, virtue of, 503
Career changes, midlife, 490–491
Career consolidation, 438–439
Career development:
  in adolescence, 372–375
  in young adulthood, 441–442
Careers (*see* Career development; Employment; Work)
Carriers of genetic defects, 56, 57
Case studies, 14–16, 616
Cataracts, 534
Catecholamine production at birth, 83–84
Causality:
  defined, 616
  and experimental methods, 17–19, 22
  and nonexperimental research methods, 14, 16
  preoperational understanding of, 218
  sensorimotor awareness of, 138
Cell division, 50, 70
Centration:
  defined, 215, 616
  egocentrism as, 217
Cephalocaudal principle, 107, 616
Cerebral cortex, 95, 616
Cesarean section, 83–84, 616
Child abuse and neglect, 185–187, 616, 622
Child-directed speech (motherese), 2–3, 151–153, 181, 616
Childbirth (*see* Birth)
Childhood depression, 332, 616
Childlessness, 464, 578–580
Children:
  and bereavement, 598–599
  and death
    in early childhood, 202, 203–204
    education about, 600–601, 617
    by suicide, 605–607
    views of, 589–590
  grown, parents of, 462, 513, 515, 577–578
  having (*see* Parents, becoming)
  social learning by, 33–34
  and studies of childhood, 11–12
  of teenage parents, 399
  understanding of illness by, 275
  (*See also* Early childhood; Infancy and toddlerhood; Middle childhood)
Chinese children:
  as only children, 260
  testing cognition of, 290–291
Chlamydia, 358
Cholesterol, and heart disease, 113, 414

Chorionic villus sampling (CVS), 61, 616
Chromosomes:
  abnormal, 57–59, 72
  defined, 50, 616
  determination of, 60, 61
  and sex determination, 48–49
  and sex-linked traits, 52, 57
Chronic conditions in late adulthood, 538–539
Cigarette smoking (*see* Smoking)
Circular reactions, 135–136, 616
Circulatory system of neonates, 93
Circumcision, 116, 117, 118
  female, 344
Classical conditioning, 31–32, 130–131, 616
Classification, by young children, 220–221
Cleft palate, 52
Climacteric, 475–477, 616–617
  male, 477–478, 621
Cocaine:
  maternal use during pregnancy, 77–78
  paternal use of, 80–81
Code-switching, 302, 617
Cognitive development:
  of Asian versus American children, 290–291
  defined, 34, 135, 617
  father's role in, 182
  gender differences in, 374–375
  and infant day care, 190–192
  informational-processing approach to, 143–144
  of middle adulthood, 486–489
Cognitive-developmental theory, 242, 244–245 (*See also* Piagetian approach)
Cognitive factors:
  in separation anxiety, 183
  in social-learning theory, 33–34
Cognitive perspective, 34–37, 617
  characteristics of, 24
  stages, theories of:
    Piagetian (*see* Piagetian approach)
    Schaie's, 420–421
Cognitive play, 263, 265, 617
Cognitive-social theory, 242, 244
Cohabitation, 453, 617
Cohort, defined, 9, 617
Cohort effects, in cross-sectional studies, 22
College, 426–428, 489
Coming-of-age, 342, 343, 344
Command generation, 488–489
Commitment:
  and crisis, 382–383
  defined, 617
  in love, 444–445
Communication:
  adolescent-parent, about sex, 389
  awareness of processes of (metacommunication), 292–293, 621
  by gestures, 17, 147–148
  with oneself, private speech as, 223–224, 623

Communication: (*Cont.*):
  with others using social speech, 223
  (*See also* Language development)
Compensation rule for conservation, 221–222, 280
Compensatory preschool programs, 233–234, 623
Competence:
  development of, 154–157
  and nonsocial play, 263–264
  and parenting styles, 257–258
  virtue of, 310, 311
Competent-connected relationship with parents, 440
Componential element of intelligence, 421, 617
Conception:
  difficulty with, 456–458
  new means of, 458–459
  process of, 46–47, 48–49
Concordance in twins, studies of, 65, 69
Concrete operations stage, 216
  and ability to classify, 220–221
  in adolescence, 361
  defined, 27, 617
  in middle childhood, 279–280
Conditioned stimuli and responses (CS and CR), 31
Conditioning:
  behavior modification (behavior therapy), 33, 255, 333, 616
  classical, 31–32, 130–131, 616
  operant (instrumental), 32–33, 131, 622
Conflicted relationship with parents, 440
Conformity in middle childhood, 314
Consanguinity studies, 65
Consent, informed, 22
Conservation, principle of, 617
  defined, 279, 617
  development in children, 215, 216, 221
  gender conservation (constancy), 619
  gender constancy (conservation), 244
  of weight, 279–280
Constraint, morality of, 280–281, 621
Constructive play, 265
Consummate love, 513
Contextual (practical) element of intelligence, 383, 421–422, 617
Contextual factors in recall, 550
Contraceptives:
  education about, 401
  failure to use, 399–400, 401
Contractions, birth, 81
Control:
  and coregulation, 320, 617
  internal, development of, 164, 165
  mastery, women's, and well-being, 504–506
  of stressors, 481
Control groups, 17, 19, 617

Conventional morality, 282, 283, 364–365, 424, 617
Convergent thinking, 300, 617
Cooing in infancy, 146
Cooley's anemia, 53
Cooperation, morality of, 281, 621
Cooperative play, 264
Coordination:
  in early childhood, 209–210
  in late adulthood, 535–536
  in middle adulthood, 473–474
Coregulation in middle childhood, 320, 617
Correlational studies, 14, 617
Cortex, cerebral, 95, 616
Cows' milk for infants, 113
Crack use during pregnancy, 77–78
Cramps, menstrual, 419
Crawling, by infants, 120–121, 122, 129
Creativity:
  and giftedness in children, 299–301
  in middle adulthood, 494
Crime, and juvenile delinquency, 22, 402–404
Crises:
  and commitment, 382–383
  defined, 617
  Eriksonian (*see* Psychosocial theory, Erikson's)
  identity, 28–29
  midlife, 479, 500–501, 509–510, 621
  universality of, 509
  (*See also* Normative-crisis model)
Critical (componential) element of intelligence, 421, 617
Critical periods:
  defined, 10–11, 617
  for mother-infant bonding, 175
Cross-cultural studies:
  of aging, 527, 567
  of child abuse, 186
  of child care and maternity leave, 193
  of coming-of-age, 342, 343, 344
  of death and mourning, 595–596
  of developmental behavior, 99–100
  of extended families, 579
  of gender differences, 248–249
  of growth in middle childhood, 273
  of immunization, 105–107
  importance of, 4
  of intelligence, 288–289
  of language acquisition, 146
  of learning style, 144
  of low birthweight, 101–102
  of marriage and divorce, 447
  of maternal care, 85–87
  of middle adulthood, 509
  of moral development, 424
  of only children in China, 260
  of parent-infant bonding, 181–182
  of preschools, 232
  purpose of, 10
  of temperament, 172–173

Cross-modal transference, 143, 617
Cross-sectional studies, 21–22, 484–485, 617
Cross-sequential studies, 22, 617
Crying in infancy:
  as communication, 146
  as emotion, 167
  and maternal cocaine use, 77
  as state, 109–110
Crystallized intelligence, 485–486, 543–546, 617
Culminating life structures:
  for early adulthood, 437, 441
  for middle adulthood, 502
Cultural bias, 288, 289
Cultural events, 443
Cultural-relativism schema, 245
Culture (*see* Cross-cultural studies)
Culture-fair tests, 289, 290–291, 617
Culture-free tests, 289, 290–291, 617
Cystic fibrosis, 52, 53, 62

Darwinian (grasping) reflex, 97
Data:
  defined, 617
  methods of collection, 21–22, 543–546
  theories from, 23
Day care, 227–234
  and illness, 204
  infant, 189–195
  influence on development, 228–231
  influence on play, 266–267
  and injuries, 204
  selecting, 191
Deaf children, language acquisition in, 147
Death, 588–613
  in adolescence, 607–608
  aspects of, 589
  attitudes toward, across life span, 589–592
  controversies about
    euthanasia and right to die, 603–605, 609
    suicide, 605–610
  in early childhood, 202, 203–204
  education about, 600–601, 617
  in infancy, 103–105
    and low birthweight, 102
    sudden infant death syndrome (SIDS), 104–105, 625
  in late adulthood, 531–532
    acceptance of, 559–560
    by suicide, 608
  life review in preparation for, 611–612
  meaning of, 610–611
  in middle adulthood, 482–484
  and near-death experiences, 592
  of parents, effect on children, 520
  postponing, 594
  psychological changes preceding, 592
  of spouse, 574
  stages in coming to terms with, 593
  survivors' dealing with, 593–603

Death, (*Cont.*):
  terminal illness preceding:
    attitudes during, 590, 593
    help during, 599–600
    prolonging life in, 603–605, 609
  in young adulthood, 411–412
Death education, 600–601, 617
Décalage, horizontal, 280, 619
Decentering, 279, 617
  absence of in preoperational stage, 215
Deception, avoiding in research, 22–23
Deduction, 217
Defense mechanisms, 26
  defined, 25, 617
  mature, 560–561
Deferred imitation, 140, 214, 617
Delinquency, juvenile, 22, 402–404
Delivery of baby, 82–85 (*See also* Birth, methods of)
Dementia, 540, 541–543, 573, 617
Denial stage of dying, 593
Dental health (*see* Teeth)
Denver Developmental Screening Test, 99, 117, 617
Deoxyribonucleic acid (DNA), 50, 617
Dependent relationship with parents, 440
Dependent variables, 19, 617
Depression:
  in adolescence, 346, 350
  in childhood, 332, 616
  defined, 170, 618
  effect of mothers' on infants, 170
  genetic basis for, 69
  in late adulthood, 541
  postpartum, 170
  as stage of dying, 593, 597
  and widowhood, 602
Depth perception in infants, 114, 129, 169, 626
DES (diethylstilbestrol), effects of, 75, 76
Despair stage of separation anxiety, 184
Detachment stage of separation anxiety, 184
Development:
  critical periods for, 10–11, 175, 617
  cultural differences in (*see* Cross-cultural studies)
  defined, 3–4
  ecological approach to, 9–10, 319, 367, 370, 618
  individual differences in, 6–8, 171–174
  influences on:
    contexts of, 10
    kinds of, 8–11
    from oneself, 4–5, 8, 33–34, 35
    timing of, 10–11
  kinds of, 6
    cognitive (*see* Cognitive development)
    intellectual (*see* Intellectual development)

Development (*Cont.*):
  moral (*see* Moral development, theories of)
  of personality (*see* Personality and social development)
  physical (*see* Physical development)
  and life span (*see* Adolescence; Death; Early childhood; Infancy and toddlerhood; Late adulthood; Middle adulthood; Prenatal development; Young adulthood)
  psychosexual, 25–28
  rates of, 6
  results of, 6
  study of:
    approach to, 4–5
    history of, 5–6, 11–12, 46
    practical implications of, 6
    (*See also* Research)
  theoretical perspectives on (*see* Theoretical perspectives on development)
  universals in, 10
Developmental tests, 134–135
  Bayley Scales of Infant Development, 134–135, 616
  Denver Developmental Screening Test, 99, 117, 617
  Infant Psychological Development Scales, 138
Diet (*see* Nutrition)
Diethylstilbestrol (DES), effects of, 75, 76
"Difficult" children, 171, 172
Disabled children:
  education for, 296–299
  intelligence testing of, 134
Disadvantaged adolescents, unprotected sex among, 400
Disadvantaged children, compensatory preschool for, 233–234
Disadvantaged infants, birthweight and mortality of, 100
Discipline:
  defined, 320, 618
  in early childhood, 251, 255–259
  in middle childhood, 319–320
Discrimination in infants, 129
Diseases and disorders:
  in adolescence, 351–360
  in early childhood, 201–203
  hereditary, 52–60
    Alzheimer's disease as, 541–543
    and environmental factors in, 67–69
    genetic counseling about, 59–60
  immunization for, 105–107, 274
  in infancy, 111, 112
  in late adulthood, 529, 534–536, 538–539, 540–543
  in middle adulthood, 479–482
  in middle childhood, 274–277
    emotional, 330–333
    understanding of illness, 275
  neonatal screening for, 98–100
  during pregnancy, 11, 78–79

Diseases and disorders (*Cont.*):
  risk factors for, 412–420
  sexually transmitted (STDs), 78–79, 357–360, 388, 389, 624
  terminal:
    attitudes during, 590, 593
    help during, 599–600
    prolonging life in, 603–605, 609
  in young adulthood, 411
Disengagement theory of aging, 562, 618
Disorganized-disoriented attachment, 177–180, 618
Divergent thinking, 300, 618
Divorce:
  children of, 322–327
  in late adulthood, 574
  in middle adulthood, 512–513
  in young adulthood, 447, 449–452
Dizygotic (fraternal) twins, 47, 618
DNA (deoxyribonucleic acid), 50, 617
Domestic violence, 449
Dominant inheritance, 50, 52, 56, 618
Donor eggs, 459
Double standard:
  of aging, 478–479
  of sexuality, 387
Down syndrome, 53, 58–59, 60, 61, 81, 96, 130, 296, 618
  (*See also* Mental retardation)
Dramatic (imaginative) play, 137, 265–266, 620
Dream, Levinsonian:
  female, 441
  male, 441
Drinking (*see* Alcohol use and abuse)
Driving:
  in late adulthood, 535, 537
  in middle adulthood, 474
Dropouts:
  college, 428
  secondary school, 371–372
  teenaged mothers as, 399
Drug intoxication in late adulthood, 541
Drug therapy, 333, 618
Drug use:
  in adolescence, 354–357
  effects of obstetric medication, 82
  effects on fetus, 11, 75–78, 80–81
  as health risk, 412, 413
  and infants, 116, 117
Drugs, fertility, 48
Dual-earner couples, 429
Dual-process model of intelligence, 547, 618
Duchenne's muscular dystrophy, 54, 61
Durable power of attorney, 605, 609, 618, 621
Dwarfism, 52, 81
Dying (*see* Death)
Dyslexia, 296–297, 618
Dysmenorrhea, 419

Early adult transition, 437
Early adulthood (*see* Young adulthood)

Early childhood, 200–268
  attachment effects in, 179–180, 261–263
  characteristics of, 7
  health in, 201–207
  intellectual development in (*see* Intellectual development, in early childhood)
  motor skills in, 209–210
  personality and social development in (*see* Personality and social development, in early childhood)
  physical changes in, 200–201
  sleep patterns and problems in, 207–209
  as stage of parenting, 462
"Easy" children, 171, 172
Eating disorders, 352–354
  anorexia nervosa, 352–354, 615
  bulimia nervosa, 354, 616
  (*See also* Obesity)
Eating habits (*see* Nutrition)
Ecological approach, 9–10, 319, 367, 370, 618
Ectoderm, 70
Education:
  about death, 600–601, 617
  and age of becoming a parent, 455
  (*See also* Schooling)
Education for All Handicapped Children Act (1975), 202, 298–299
Ego:
  defined, 25, 618
  development of:
    in Erikson's theory, 28–29
    in Freud's theory, 25
Ego differentiation versus work role preoccupation, 559
Ego-identity status, 507–509
Ego transcendence versus ego preoccupation, 560
Egocentrism:
  in adolescence, 362–364
  defined, 217, 618
  of only children, 260
  in young children, 217, 218–221, 223
Elaboration as mnemonic strategy, 286, 618
Elder abuse, 570–572, 618
Elderly people (*see* Late adulthood)
Electronic fetal monitoring, 84–85, 618
Embryo:
  development of, 71–72
  hazards to, 70–73
Embryonic disk, 70
Embryonic stage, 70–73, 618
Emotional disturbances:
  hereditary factors in, 67–69
  in late adulthood, 540–543
  in middle childhood, 330–333
Emotional flexibility versus emotional impoverishment, Peck's criterion of, 502, 503, 618
Emotional health, 560–561
Emotional neglect, 185–187, 622
Emotions:
  in adolescence, 348–350

Emotions (*Cont.*):
  defined, 165, 618
  development of, 166–167
  expression of, 167–168
  individual differences in, 171–174
  of infants, study of, 165–166
  between infants and adults, 168–170
  means of showing, 168–170
  "reading" of others', 169
  and religion, 565
Empathy in early childhood, 246, 251, 254
Employment:
  and dropouts, 372
  of mothers (*see* Working mothers)
  of parents of adolescents, 392–393
  (*See also* Work)
Empty nest, 513, 515, 618
Encoding and retrieval of information, 285, 549–550
Endoderm, 70
Engrossment, paternal, 181–182
Enriched environment and brain development, 96
Entering the Adult World (novice phase), 437
Entry life structures:
  for early adulthood, 437
  for middle adulthood, 502
Enuresis, 208–209, 618
Environment:
  and heredity, 60–70
    characteristics influenced by, 66
    and cultural differences in motor development, 99–100
    disorders influenced by, 67–69
    history of study of, 12
    in IQ performance, 288–289
    and language acquisition, 17
    nature-nurture controversy, 60–63
    studying relative effects of, 65–67
    (*See also* Heredity)
  prenatal:
    maternal, 73–80
    paternal influences in, 80–81
    (*See also* Mothers, pregnant)
Environmental influences:
  on brain development, 96
  on children from ethnic minorities, 319
  on competence, 154–157
  defined, 8, 618
  on effects of birth trauma, 96
  on emotional differences, 170
  in exosystem, 9–10
  on human development, 69–70, 79–81
  on intellectual functioning in maturity, 545
  on language acquisition, 151–153
  in macrosystem, 10
  in mesosystem, 9
  in microsystem, 9
  on motor development, 99–100, 121–122

Environmental influences (*Cont.*):
  on timing of puberty, 349
  weighing, in intellectual testing, 288–289
  (*See also* Cross-cultural studies)
Environmental manipulation, 63
Episodic memory, 548
Equilibration, Piagetian, 36, 618
Eriksonian theories (*see* Psychosocial theory, Erikson's)
Estrogen, 93, 345, 475–477, 480
Ethical issues:
  about death, 603–610
  about new means of conception, 459
  in genetic testing, 64
  in research, 22–23, 130
Ethical standards in research, 23
Ethological approach, 174–175, 618
Euthanasia, 603–605, 609
Examinations (*see* Assessment; Psychometric approach)
Executive stage, 420, 421, 618
Exercise, 412, 413, 415–416
  for bone growth, 476
  in late adulthood, 530, 539–540
  and menstruation, 348
  during pregnancy, 74, 80
  (*See also* Fitness, physical)
Exosystem, 9–10
Experience:
  and memory, 213
  and moral development, 423–424
Experiential element of intelligence, 421, 618
Experimental groups, 17, 19, 618
Experiments, 15, 17–21, 618
Expressions, emotional, of infants, 167–168
Extended-family homes, 579
External aids for memory, 286, 618
Extinction of response, 33, 618
Extramarital sex, 454–455
Eye-hand coordination, 210
Eyesight (*see* Vision)

Faces, infants' viewing of, 115, 121
Facial expressions, of infants, 166
Families:
  dual-earner, 429
  effects of disturbances in relationships, 183–187
  extended, 579
  late-life, characteristics of, 572–573
  in middle childhood, 290–291, 312–313, 317, 318–330, 336
  of minority-group elderly, 567
  and personality development in infancy, 174–187
  presence or absence of siblings, 187–189
  stepfamilies (blended or reconstituted families), 329, 461–464
  stranger and separation anxiety, 183
  (*See also* Fathers; Mothers; Parents; Sibling relations)
Family (consanguinity) studies, 65

Family (consanguinity) studies, (*Cont.*):
  (*See also* Adoption studies; Twin studies)
Family therapy, 333, 618
Fantasy period of career planning, 373
Fantasy (imaginative) play, 137, 265–266, 620
Fathers:
  and adolescent development, 349
  child-rearing, participation in, 321, 322, 460, 461, 463
  environmentally caused defects transmitted by, 80–81
  and gender development of children, 248
  of infants, 180–182
  and intelligence of children, 226–227
  relationships with children following divorce, 325, 327
  and school performance of adolescents, 369, 370
  teenage, 400, 402
  working, 322, 463
Fatness (*see* Obesity)
Fears:
  bedtime, 207–208
  conditioning of, 130–131
  in early childhood, 249–250
  school phobia, 331–332, 624
  of visual cliff, 129
Feeding:
  in Erikson's theory, 163
  of infants:
    bottle-feeding, 112, 113
    breastfeeding, 74, 76, 78–79, 111–112
    formula for, 112, 113
  (*See also* Nutrition)
Female circumcision, 344
Female genital mutilation (FGM), 344
Fertility drugs, 48
Fertilization, 70
  defined, 46, 618
  difficulty with, 456–458
  process of, 46–47, 48–49
  in vitro, 62, 459, 620
Fetal alcohol syndrome (FAS), 74, 76, 618–619
Fetal development (*see* Prenatal development)
Fetal stage, 72–73, 619
Fetal versus postnatal life, 94
Fidelity, virtue of, 381
Field dependence-independence, 561
Field experiments, 20
Financial situation:
  and health, 204–207
  in late adulthood, 566
  (*See also* Socioeconomic factors)
Fine motor skills, 209, 210, 619
First sentences, 149, 154
First words, 148–149, 154
Firstborn children and siblings, 187–188
Fitness, physical:
  in late adulthood, 530, 539–540

Fitness, physical (*Cont.*):
  in middle childhood, 274–277
  schoolchildren's, improving, 276–277
  in young adulthood, 412, 413, 415–416
  (*See also* Exercise)
Fixation, defined, 25
Fluid intelligence, 485–486, 543–546, 619
Fontanels, 93
Food intake (*see* Nutrition)
Foreclosure, identity status of, 383, 619
Formal operations stage:
  characteristics of, 360, 361–362
  defined, 27, 619
Formula, infant, 112, 113
Fragile X syndrome, 54
Fraternal (dizygotic) twins, 47, 618
Free radicals, 533, 619
Freudian theories (*see* Psychosexual theory, Freud's)
Friendship:
  adolescent, 395–397, 398
  among adults:
    in late adulthood, 576–577
    in middle adulthood, 514
    in young adulthood, 461, 464–465
  among children:
    in early childhood, 261–263
    in middle childhood, 315–316
Frustration and aggressive behavior, 251–252
Functional invariants, in Piaget's theory, 35–36
Functional play, 265
Functional relationships, understanding of in early childhood, 214–215

Games, 265, 311–313
Gametes (ovum and sperm), 46–47, 48–49, 456, 459, 619
Gastrointestinal system of neonates, 94
Gender, defined, 241, 619
Gender conservation (constancy), 244, 619
Gender differences:
  in adult's behavior toward children, 173–174, 181–182
  in aggressive behavior, 251–252
  attitudes toward, 246–247
  in child's adjustment to divorce, 325–327
  in college, 427
  defined, 246, 619
  in early childhood, 245–249
  in effects of maternal employment, 192–193, 321–322
  in grandparenting, 581
  in health, 418–420
  in identity formation, 383–384
  in intelligence, parental influence on, 226–227
  in juvenile delinquency, 402
  in Levinsonian development, 441–442, 504–508

Gender differences (*Cont.*):
  in life expectancy, 528–529, 532–533
  in midlife changes, 475–478, 504–508
  in midlife death, 482
  in moral development, 366, 424–425
  physical (*see* Sex differences)
  in relationship with parents, 440
  in remarriage, late-life, 574
  in sibling relationships, 329–330
  and similarities, 245–246
  in social world of middle childhood, 315
  sources of, 30, 247–249
  and vocational planning, 374–375
  in widowhood adjustment, 574
  work-related, 430–431, 441–442, 491*n*.
Gender identity, 241–245
  in cognitive-developmental theory, 244
  cognitive-social theory of, 244
  defined, 241, 619
  in social-learning theory, 243
Gender roles and gender-typing, 182, 241, 246, 248, 619 (*See also* Gender stereotypes)
Gender schema, 242, 244, 619
Gender-schema theory, 242, 244, 245, 619
Gender stereotypes:
  combating, 248
  defined, 246–247, 619
  fathers' reinforcement of, 248
  in media, 248
Gender-typing (*see* Gender roles and gender-typing; Gender stereotypes)
Gene therapy, 60
Genealogy in life review, 612
Generativity versus stagnation stage:
  characteristics of, 502, 503
  defined, 28, 619
Genes:
  defined, 50, 619
  dominant and recessive, 50–51, 52–57
Genetic counseling, 59–60, 619
Genetic imprinting, 52
Genetic testing, 64
Genetics, 49, 619 (*See also* Heredity)
"Genie" study, 14–15
Genital stage, 26, 28
Genital warts, 359
Genitality, Erikson's concept of, 436
Genotypes, 51, 619
Geriatrics, defined, 529
Germinal stage of prenatal development, 70, 619
Gerontology, defined, 526, 619
Gestation, 70 (*See also* Prenatal development)
Gestures, in language development, 17, 147–148
Giftedness, 12, 21, 299–301, 619

Glaucoma, 52
Global self-worth, 310–311, 619
Gonorrhea, 359
Grammar, command of:
  in early childhood, 222
  in middle childhood, 289–292, 293
Grandparenthood, 580–581
Grant Study of Adult Development, 438, 442, 504, 560–561
Grasping reflex, 97
Grief, 596–598, 619
  anticipatory, 596–597, 615
  defined, 593
  patterns of, 597–598
Grief therapy, 599, 619
Gross motor skills, 209, 210, 619
Group living arrangements for older people, 569
Growth, physical:
  adolescent growth spurt, 346–347, 615
  in early childhood, 200–201
  of infants and toddlers, 110–111
  insufficient, poverty and, 205
  in middle childhood, 272–274
  (See also Height; Physical development; Weight)
Gusii culture (Kenya), 509

Habituation:
  defined, 619
  in infancy, 129–130, 143, 144
Hair growth, adolescent, 347
Hand control in infants, 119
Handicapped children (see Disabled children)
Happiness, in marriage, 446, 513, 572–573
Harris poll of teenagers about sex, 388
Harvard Preschool Project, 154–155, 156
Head, of infants:
  control of, 119
  in neonates, 93
Head Start (see Project Head Start)
Health:
  in adolescence, 351–360
  changes related to, 473–474, 534–536
  defined, 412
  emotional, 560–561
  improving, 413
  influences on, 204–207, 411–420, 539–540
  in late adulthood, 537–543
  and marriage, 420, 446–448
  in middle adulthood, 479–482
  in middle childhood, 274–277
  problems (see Diseases and disorders)
  and retirement, 552
  in young adulthood, 411–420
Hearing:
  deafness, and language acquisition, 147
  in infancy, 115–116, 179
  in late adulthood, problems with, 530, 534–535

Hearing (Cont.):
  in middle adulthood, 473
Heart disease, risk factors for, 531–532
  cholesterol, 113, 414
  menopause, 480
  in middle childhood, 274, 276
  and stress, 481–482
  in young adulthood, 411, 414, 417
Height:
  in adolescence, 346–347
  in early childhood, 200–201
  hereditary influences on, 63, 65
  of infants and toddlers, 110–111
  in middle childhood, 273
  in young adulthood, 410
Heinz's dilemma, 282, 283–284, 423, 424, 487
Hemophilia, 54, 57, 61
Hepatitis B, 359
Heredity, 49–70
  and bed-wetting, 208–209
  defects transmitted by, 52–60
    Alzheimer's disease as, 541–543
    genetic counseling about, 59–60
    prenatal assessment of, 61–62
  defined, 8, 619
  dominant and recessive, 50–51, 52–57
  mechanisms of, 49–50
  and obesity, 274
  patterns of transmission in, 50–52
  sex-linked, 52, 57, 58–59, 624
  (See also Environment, and heredity)
Herpes simplex, 359
Heteronomous morality, 280–281
  (See also Morality, of constraint)
Heterosexual:
  defined, 386, 619
  teenagers, 387–389
Heterozygous versus homozygous organisms, 50, 51, 619
Hierarchy of needs, Maslow's, 37–38
High blood pressure (hypertension), 480, 620
Hispanic families, 567
Holophrase, defined, 148, 619
Home learning activities, 295
Home Observation for Measurement of the Environment (HOME), 155–156
Homelessness, and illness, 206–207
Homosexual, defined, 386, 619
Homosexuality, 386–387
Homozygous versus heterozygous organisms, 50, 51, 619
Hope, virtue of, 163
Horizontal décalage, 280, 619
Hormones:
  at birth, production of, 83–84
  and gender differences, 247–248, 418–419
  and menopause, 475–477
  sex (see Sex hormones)
  and sexual orientation, 386

Hospice care, 599–600, 619
Hospitalized children, 184–185
Hospitals, childbirth in, 85, 87
Housing arrangements for older people, 566–570
Human development:
  defined, 3, 619
  (See also Development)
Human Genome Project, 64
Humanistic perspective, 24, 37–38, 620
Hunger, and poverty, 205
Huntington's disease, 52
Hurried child, 334
Hyaline membrane disease, 102
Hyperactivity, 52, 297–298, 615
Hypertension, 480, 620
Hypocrisy, apparent, in adolescence, 364
Hypotheses:
  defined, 23, 620
  testing of, in formal operations stage, 361

Iconic (visual) memory, 547, 550
Id, 25, 620
Ideal self, 309, 620
Identical (monozygotic) twins, 47–48, 208–209, 621 (See also Twin studies)
Identification, 240, 241, 243, 620
Identified relationship with parents, 440
Identity:
  in Erikson's psychosocial theory, 28–29
  gender, 241–245, 619
  gender differences in paths to, 441–442
  sexual, achievement of, 385–389
  understanding of, in early childhood, 214–215
Identity achievement, 383, 620
Identity crisis, 28–29
Identity diffusion, 383, 620
Identity formation, in adolescence, 380–389
Identity rule for conservation, 221–222, 280
Identity statuses, 382–383
  gender differences in, 383–384
Identity versus identity confusion stage:
  characteristics of, 380–381
  defined, 27, 620
Illnesses (see Diseases and disorders)
Imaginary audience, 363, 620
Imaginative play, 137, 265–266, 620
Imitation:
  deferred, 140, 214, 617
  invisible, 140, 620
  in language development, 146, 147, 150
  of models, 33–34, 243, 251–252
  visible, 139–140, 626
Immunizations, 105–107, 274
Imprinting, 175
In vitro fertilization, 62, 459, 620
Inbreeding, 57

Income:
  and health, 204–207
  in late adulthood, 566
  (See also Socioeconomic factors)
Incomplete dominance, 52
Incontinence, 536
Incubators (isolettes), 102
Indecisiveness, 363–364
Independent identity, 506–507
Independent segregation, law of, 50–51, 620
Independent variables, 19, 620
Individual differences in development, 6–8
  of personality, 171–174
  of sociability, 189
Individual-differences scheme, 245–246
Individual events, 443
Individual psychotherapy, 333, 620
Individuated relationship, with parents, 440
Induction, 217
Industry versus inferiority stage:
  characteristics of, 310
  defined, 27, 620
Infancy and toddlerhood, 92–196
  characteristics of, 7
  cognitive structures in, 35–36
  cultural differences in, 99–100
  death in, 86, 103–105, 620
    sudden infant death syndrome (SIDS), 104–105, 625
  effects of childbirth medication during, 82
  effects of malnutrition in, 273–274
  family relationships in:
    effects of disturbances in, 183–187
    father-child, 180–182
    mother-child, 174–180, 182
    presence or absence of siblings, 187–189
    and stranger and separation anxiety, 183
  intellectual development in (see Intellectual development, in infancy and toddlerhood)
  methods of studying:
    case studies, 14–16
    laboratory observation, 16
    time sampling, 16
  personality and social development in (see Personality and social development, in infancy and toddlerhood)
  physical development in, 92–125
    growth, 110–111
    motor, 99–100, 117–124
    and nourishment, 111–113, 114
    principles of, 107–108
    of sensory capacities, 113–117, 129–130
    sex differences in, 124
    (See also Neonates)
  Piagetian schemes of, 35
  research findings about, practicing, 194
  as stage of parenting, 462

Infancy and toddlerhood (*Cont.*):
  state patterns in, 108–110
  as transition for parents, 459–461
Infant mortality, 86, 103–105, 620
  sudden infant death syndrome (SIDS), 104–105, 625
Infant mortality rate, 620
Infant Psychological Development Scales (IPDS), 138
Infantile autism, 67–69, 169, 219, 620
Infertility, 456–458, 620
Information-processing approach:
  characteristics of, 37, 133, 142–144
  defined, 620
  memory:
    in early childhood, 212–213
    in late adulthood, 549–550
    in middle childhood, 284–286
    slowness in late adulthood, 535–536
Informed consent, right of, 22
Inheritance (*see* Heredity)
Initiative versus guilt stage:
  characteristics of, 240–241
  defined, 27, 620
Injuries:
  accidental, 203–204, 277–278
  effects of at birth, 96
  in middle childhood, 277–278
Inner-to-outer infant development, 108
Insightful (experiential) element of intelligence, 421, 618
Institutionalization:
  of children, 63, 122, 183–184
  in late adulthood, 539, 569–570, 571
Instrumental (operant) conditioning, 32–33, 131, 622
  behavior modification (behavior therapy), 33, 255, 333, 616
Instrumental values, 561
Integrated personality, 564
Integrative thinking, 486–488
Integrity versus despair stage:
  characteristics of, 558–559
  defined, 28, 620
Intellectual development, 6
  in adolescence, 360–366
    secondary school, 367–372
    vocational planning, 372–375
  areas of (*see* Cognitive development; Intelligence; Language development; Memory; Moral development, theories of)
  in early childhood, 210–227
    cognitive, 213–221
    intelligence, 224–227
    language, 221–224, 228–231
    memory, 212–213
    wider environment for, 228–235
  in infancy and toddlerhood, 132–144
    competence, 154–157
    information-processing approach to, 133, 142–144
    language, 144–154

Intellectual development, (*Cont.*):
  learning (*see* Learning, in infancy and toddlerhood)
    Piagetian approach to, 133, 135–142
    psychometric approach to, 133–135, 138
  in late adulthood, 543–550, 551–552
  in middle adulthood, 484–489, 490–491
  in middle childhood, 278–302
    cognitive, 279–280
    education (*see* Middle childhood, school experience in)
    intelligence, 286–289
    language, 289–293
    memory, 284–286
    moral, 280–284
    understanding of illness, 275
  in young adulthood, 420–423
    career development, 428–431, 441–442
    college experience, 426–428
    moral, 423–425
Intellectual retardation, nature and nurture in, 60
Intelligence:
  crystallized, 485–486, 543–546, 617
  in early childhood, 224–227
  fluid, 485–486, 543–546, 619
  hereditary influences on, 66
  increasing, 289, 294
  in infants and toddlers, 133
  and information processing in infancy, 142–144
  in late adulthood, 543–550
  mechanics of, 547, 621
  in middle adulthood, 484–489
  in middle childhood, 286–289
  multiple kinds of, 300
  pragmatics of, 547, 622
  in young adulthood, 421–422
Intelligence quotient (IQ), 133–134
  and birthweight, 102
  in early childhood, 224, 225
  hereditary influences on, 66
  and infant sensory capacities, 115–116
  in middle adulthood, 484–486
  in middle childhood, 286–289, 299–300
Intelligence quotient (IQ) tests:
  and African-American children (*see* Racial differences)
  analysis, 288–289
  defined, 133, 620
  for disabled children, 134
  and early day care, 191–192
  to identify gifted students, 300
  (*See also* Assessment; Psychometric approach)
Intelligent behavior, defined, 132–133, 620
Interiority, 504, 620
Intermittent reinforcement, 33
Interview method, 15, 17, 620
Intimacy:
  adolescent, 397

Intimacy (*Cont.*):
  and identity, 381, 384
  versus isolation stage:
    characteristics of, 436–438
    defined, 28, 620
  in love, 444
  in marriage, 446
Intimate relationships:
  cohabitation, 453, 617
  love, 443–446
  parenthood and nonparenthood in, 455–464
  (*See also* Friendship; Marriage; Sexuality)
Invisible imitation, 140, 620
IQ (*see* Intelligence quotient)
Iranian orphanages, environmental deprivation in, 63, 122
Irreversibility of thought, 215–217, 620
Isolettes, use of, 102

Japanese:
  cancer in, and diet, 415
  children, educational performance of, 290–291
  older, 527
  and women's experience of menopause, 478
Jaundice, physiologic, 94, 622
Jews, dying and mourning by, 595–596
Job satisfaction, and age, 428–430
Jobs (*see* Employment; Work)
Jungian theory, 501, 502
Juvenile delinquency, 22, 402–404

Karyotype, defined, 59, 620
Kindergarten, 234–235
Kpelle culture (central Liberia), 10

Labor (birth):
  contractions of, 81
  stages of, 81
Laboratory experiments, 19–20
Laboratory observation, 15, 16, 620
Lamaze method of prepared childbirth, 83
Language acquisition device (LAD), 151, 620
Language development:
  and bilingual education, 301–302, 616
  critical period for, 11
  delayed, 2–3, 6, 153–154
  in early childhood, 16, 17–19, 221–224, 228–231
  in infancy and toddlerhood, 144–154
  influences on, 151–153, 155
  learning theory of, 150–151
  linguistic speech, 148–150, 621
  in middle childhood, 289–293
  milestones of, 145
  nativist view of, 150, 151, 621
  nature and nurture in, 63
  prelinguistic speech, 146–148, 154, 622–623
  stages of, 11, 146–150
  study of, 5
  (*See also* Communication)

Lanugo, defined, 93, 620
Latchkey (self-care) adolescents, 393
Latchkey (self-care) children, 323, 624
Late adult transition, 502
Late adulthood, 526–582
  aging patterns in, 562–566
  aging process in, theories of, 533–534
  characteristics of, 8
  cultural differences in, 527, 567
  death in, 531–532
    acceptance of, 559–560, 591–592
    suicide, 608
  health in, 537–543
  help with everyday life in, 530
  history of study of, 12
  intellectual development in, 543–550, 551–552
  latest stage of, 528–529
  life expectancy in, 528–529, 621
  misconceptions about, 529
  morality in, 487–488
  personal relationships in, 517–519, 572–581
  personality development in, theory and research on, 558–566
  physical changes in, 534–536
  social issues in, 566–572
Latency period, 26–28
Laughing, by infants, 168
Learning:
  defined, 128, 620–621
  in infancy and toddlerhood, 128–132
    classical conditioning, 130–131
    complex, 131
    habituation, 129–130, 143, 144, 619
    and maturation, 128–129, 621
    and memory, 131–132, 142–143
    operant conditioning, 32–33, 131, 622
  lifelong, 489, 550–551
  (*See also* Conditioning; Schooling)
Learning disabilities (LDs), 296–297, 621
Learning perspective, 24
  behaviorism, 30–33, 34, 150–151, 616
  characteristics of, 30–34
  defined, 30, 621
  evaluation of, 34, 243
  social-learning theory, 33–34, 150–151, 242–243, 625
Learning theory, 621
  evaluation of, 34, 243
  of language acquisition, 150–151
  social-learning theory, 33–34, 150–151, 242–243, 625
  traditional (behaviorism), 30–33, 34, 150–151, 616
Leisure time:
  after retirement, use of, 553
  in middle childhood, 311–313
Life eras, Levinson's, 439–442
  early adulthood, 437, 439–442
  middle adulthood, 502, 504

Life events:
normative and nonnormative, 8–9, 442–443, 549, 622
responding to, 443
stress from, 481
timing of, 442–443, 500–501, 509
(*See also names of individual events*)
Life expectancy, 531–533, 621
Life histories, comparing, 65
Life-planning problems, 549
Life review, 611–612, 621
Life span:
description of periods of, 6, 7–8
human potential throughout, 4
studies of, 12–14
(*See also* Adolescence; Death; Early childhood; Infancy and toddlerhood; Late adulthood; Prenatal development; Young adulthood)
Life structures, Levinson's, 439–442, 621
culminating:
for early adulthood, 437, 441
for middle adulthood, 502
entry:
for early adulthood, 437
for middle adulthood, 502
Linguistic development (*see* Language development)
Linguistic speech, 148–150, 621
"Little Albert" study, 32, 130–131
Living arrangements in late adulthood, 566–570
independence, 568–569
institutionalization, 539, 569–570, 571
Living wills, 605, 609, 621
Locomotion in infants and toddlers, 119–121
Long-term memory, 547–548, 621
Longitudinal studies, 12, 13, 21–22, 485, 543–546, 621
Love:
characteristics of, 443–446
consummate, 513
as Eriksonian virtue, 438
parental, effects of, 258–259
passionate, 444, 512–513
patterns of, 445
Low birthweight, 100–103
and birth trauma, 96
consequences of, 102
defined, 621
and infant mortality, 102, 105
and learning disabilities, 297
and maternal nutrition, 74
risk factors for, 100–101
treatment of, 102–103
Lying, 331

Macrosystem, 10
Mainstreaming, 298–299, 621
Make Today Count, 600
Male climacteric, 477–478, 621
Malnutrition:
adolescent mineral deficiencies, 352
and fetal development, 73–75

Malnutrition (*Cont.*):
in middle childhood, 273–274
and poverty, 205
(*See also* Nutrition)
Management:
of others, 422
of self, 422
of tasks, 422
Marijuana use:
in adolescence, 356
during pregnancy, 76
Marriage, 446–449
age at, 447, 448
alternatives to, 452–453, 574
benefits of, 446
and double standard of aging, 478–479
dual careers in, 429
and friendships, 461, 464–465
and happiness, 446, 513, 572–573
and health, 420, 446–448
lasting, reasons for, 512–513
in late adulthood, 572–573, 574
in middle adulthood, 511–513
parenthood's effect on, 459–461
remarriage, 451–452, 574
sexual activity in, 454
success in, 448–449
termination of:
by death, 574, 601–603
by divorce, 447, 449–452, 512–513, 574
violence in, 449
Massage, infant, 103
Mastery and pleasure, well-being from, 504–506
Mastery motivation, 212–213
Masturbation, 385–386, 621
Maternal blood tests, 61–62, 621
Maternal instinct, 82, 178–179
Maternity centers, 85
Mathematical performance, gender differences in, 375
Maturation, 344–350
cognitive, 361–362
defined, 63, 621
and learning, 128–129, 621
secular trends in, 342, 346, 624
Mature defense mechanisms, 560–561
Mature thinking, 489
Mechanics of intelligence, 547, 621
Meconium, defined, 94, 621
Media:
death in, 588
and gender stereotypes, 248
sexual activity influenced by, 388, 400
(*See also* Television)
Medical assessment of neonates, 96–100
Medical care:
need for, in late adulthood, 538–539
during pregnancy, 74, 75–76, 100–101
Medical durable power of attorney, 605, 609, 621
Medical risks for delivering underweight infants, 100–101

Medical x-rays during pregnancy, 11, 79
Medicated delivery, 82, 621
Medication, excessive, in late adulthood, 541
Meiosis versus mitosis, 50
Memory:
development of, 6
in early childhood, 212–213
evoking, for life review, 612
in infancy, 131–132, 142–143
influences on, 212–213
in late adulthood, 530, 547–550
long-term, 547–548, 621
loss of, with Alzheimer's disease, 541–543
in middle childhood, 284–286
mnemonic strategies for, 285–286, 550, 618, 621
sensory, 547, 624
short-term, 547, 625
Memory training, 550
Menarche, 347–348, 621
reaction to, 349–350
Menopause, 418–419, 475–477, 478, 621
Menstrual cycle:
beginning of (menarche), 347–350, 621
effects of, 419
premenstrual syndrome (PMS), 419, 623
reaction to, 349–350
(*See also* Fertilization)
Mental combinations, of toddlers, 136–138
Mental disturbances:
hereditary factors in, 67–69
in late adulthood, 540–543
in middle childhood, 330–333
Mental flexibility versus mental rigidity, Peck's criterion of, 502, 503, 621
Mental retardation, 296, 621
levels of, 297
nature and nurture in, 60
(*See also* Down syndrome)
Mentoring, 301, 441, 503
Mercy killing (euthanasia), 603–605, 609
Mesoderm, 70
Mesosystem, 9
Metacommunication, 292–293, 621
Metamemory, defined, 286, 621
Microsystem, 9
Middle adulthood, 472–521
characteristics of, 7
death in, 482–484, 591
defined, 472
friendship in, 514
in Gusii culture, 509
intellectual development in, 484–489, 490–491
marriage and divorce in, 511–513
midlife crisis in, 479, 500–501, 509–510, 621
morality in, 487–488
normative-crisis theory of, 501–511
parenthood during, 514–517

Middle adulthood, (*Cont.*):
personality change in, 505
physical aspects of, 473–484
relationship with aging parents, 517–520
sexuality in, 513
sibling relationships in, 513–514
Middle childhood, 272–337
characteristics of, 7
divorce of parents during, 322–327
emotional disturbances in, 330–333
everyday life in, 311–313
family relationships in, 290–291, 312–313, 317, 318–330, 336
growth and fitness in, 273
health in, 274–277
intellectual development in (*see* Intellectual development, in middle childhood)
motor development in, 277
peer group in, 313–318
school experience in, 293–302
for disabled children, 296–299
for gifted, talented, and creative children, 300–301
in Japan, 290–291
parents' involvement in, 295–296, 319, 328, 329
in single-parent families, 328
teaching approaches, 293–295
self-care during, 323, 624
self-concept in, 308–311
as stage of parenting, 462
stresses in, 334–336
coping with, 334–336
divorce, 322–327
in single-parent families, 327–330
Midlife crisis, 479, 500–501, 509–510, 621
Midlife transition, 437, 500, 502, 504–508, 509–510
Milk for infants, 111–113
Minerals in diet:
calcium for osteoporosis prevention, 476
deficiencies during adolescence, 352
Minority groups (*see* Racial differences)
Miscarriages (spontaneous abortions), 70–73, 74, 76, 79, 625
Mitosis versus meiosis, 50
Mnemonic strategies, 285–286, 550, 618, 621
Models, imitation of, 33–34, 243 and aggressive behavior, 251–252
Monozygotic (identical) twins, 47–48, 208–209, 621 (*See also* Twin studies)
Montessori method, 233
Moral development, theories of, 243, 280–284
in adulthood, 423–425
Kohlberg's, 282–284, 364–366, 423–424, 425
Piaget's, 280–282
psychoanalytic, 242

Morality:
  of constraint, 280–281, 621
  conventional, 282, 283, 364–365, 424, 617
  of cooperation, 281, 621
  earliest awareness of, 166–167
  in middle and late adulthood, 487–488
  postconventional, 282, 284, 365, 424, 622
  preconventional, 282, 283, 364, 622
Moratorium, adolescent:
  as identity status, 383, 621
  in psychosocial theory, 381
Moro (startle) reflex, 96, 97, 99
Mortality (see Death; Infant mortality)
Mother-infant bond, 112, 174–176, 177, 621
Motherese, 2–3, 151–153, 181, 616
Mothers:
  abusive and neglectful, 185–187
  adolescents' conflicts with, 390, 393
  age of, 58–59, 61, 79, 81, 455–456, 457
  and competence of children, 155–156
  and firstborn children, 188
  as friends of adolescent daughters, 398
  and infant language development, 151–153, 155
  of infants, 174–180, 455–456, 457
    attachment to, 176–180
    bonding in, 112, 174–176, 177, 621
    depressed, 170
    in Erikson's theory, 163
    working, 182, 189–195
  and intelligence of children, 133, 143–144, 227
  pregnant, 73–80
    blood tests for, 61–62, 621
    blood type incompatibility with fetus, 61, 79
    drug use by, 75–78
    exposure to x-rays, 11, 79
    external environmental hazards to, 79–80
    guidelines for risk reduction, 74
    illness of, 78–79
    nutrition of, 73–75
    risk factors for underweight infants, 101
    teenage, 398–402
  remarriage of, 325
  sensory discrimination of by newborns, 114
  surrogate, 459, 625
  working, 182, 189–195, 227, 320–322, 392–393, 429
  (See also Birth)
Motivation, for memory, 212–213
Motor development:
  accelerating, 122–124
  adult psychomotor functioning, 410–411

Motor development (Cont.):
  cultural differences in, 99
  in early childhood, 209–210
  environmental influences on, 99–100, 121–122
  in infancy and toddlerhood, 99–100, 117–124
  in middle childhood, 277
  milestones of, 117–121, 279
  psychomotor functioning, adult, 473–474, 535–536
Mountain task, Piaget's, 217
Mourning, 593, 594–596, 621
Multifactorial inheritance, defined, 52, 621
Multiple alleles, defined, 52, 621
Multiple births, 47–48 (See also Twin studies)
Murder, 412
Muscle coordination in early childhood, 209–210
Mutual-regulation model, 168–169, 621
Mutuality of devotion, virtue of, 438

"Naming explosion," 220–221
Narcotics-addicted mothers, effects of, 77–78
Nativism as view of language acquisition, 150, 151, 621
Natural childbirth, 83, 621
Natural experiments, 20
Natural selection, 99
Naturalistic observation, 15, 16, 622
Nature-nurture controversy, 60–63
Navajo Indians, motor development in infants, 99
Near-death experiences, 592, 622
Needs, Maslow's hierarchy of, 37–38
Negative reinforcement, 32
Negativism in toddlers, 162, 164, 165, 622
Neglect and abuse of children, 185–187, 622
Neonatal period, defined, 92, 622
Neonates, 92–107, 622
  body systems of, 93–94
  bonding with, 174–176, 180–181
  and brain development, 94–96
  conditioning of, 131
  effects of birth trauma on, 96
  low birthweight of, 102–103, 105
  medical and behavioral screening tests for, 96–100
  physical characteristics of, 92–93
  reflex behavior in, 96, 97, 116
    control over, 135, 136, 137
    smiling, 167–168
  responses to language, 151
  sensory capacities of, 113–117, 129–130
  states of, 108–110
Neural-tube defects, 54–55, 61, 74, 79
Neutral stimuli, 31, 130
Never-married people, 452–453, 574–575
New York Longitudinal Study (NYLS), 66–67, 171–173

Newborns (see Neonates)
Nicotine use (see Smoking)
Nightmares and night terrors, 208
Nocturnal emissions, 347
Nonexperimental research methods, 14–17
Nonnormative life events, 9, 442, 549, 622
Nonorganic failure to thrive, 185, 622
Nonparenthood (childlessness), 464, 578–580
Nonsocial play, 263–264
Normative-crisis model, 436–442, 501–511, 622
  analysis of, 442, 508–511
  Erikson's theory, 436–438, 502
  Levinson's theory, 439–442, 502, 504, 505, 510
  Peck's theory, 502, 559–560
  Vaillant's theory, 437, 438–439, 502, 504, 560–561
Normative life events and influences, 8–9, 442–443, 549, 622
Norms, standardized, 287, 625
Nourishment (see Nutrition)
Novelty preference, in infants, 143, 622
Novice phase of early adulthood, 437, 441
Number concepts, 140–142
Nursing home residents, 539, 569–570, 571
Nutrition:
  in adolescence, 352
  and adult health, 412, 413–415
  in early childhood, 201, 203
  in infancy, 111–113, 114, 273–274
  in late adulthood, 539–540
  in middle childhood, 273–274
  for osteoporosis prevention, 476
  and poverty, 205
  for pregnant women, 73–75

Oak School experiment, 295
Obesity:
  in adolescence, 352
  as adult health hazard, 414
  defined, 352, 622
  genetic factors in, 65
  and infancy, 114
  in middle childhood, 274
Object permanence:
  absence of, 135
  defined, 137, 622
  development of, 137–138, 139
  and first words, 149
Observation:
  laboratory, 15, 16, 620
  naturalistic, 15, 16, 622
Observer bias, 16
Obstetrics (see Birth)
Occupations (see Career development; Employment; Work)
Old age (see Late adulthood)
Old-old versus young-old, 526–528
Oldest old, 528–529
One-egg (monozygotic, identical) twins, 47–48, 208–209, 621 (See also Twin studies)

One-parent families:
  and adolescent development, 393–394
  and early childhood development, 227, 248
  in middle childhood, 327–330
  teenage, 398–402
Onlooker behavior, 264
Only children, 187, 259, 260
Operant (instrumental) conditioning, 32–33, 131, 622
  behavior modification (behavior therapy), 33, 255, 333, 616
Operational thinking, 279, 622
Opiate use during pregnancy, effects of, 77
Oral stage, 26, 27
Organ donation, 604
Organ reserve (see Reserve capacity)
Organization:
  defined, 622
  as mnemonic strategy, 286
  Piagetian, 36
Organized supplementary (cooperative) play, 264
Orphanages, children in, 183–184
  Iranian, 63, 122
Osteoporosis, 352, 475, 476, 535, 537, 622
Otis-Lennon School Ability Test, 287, 622
Ova:
  in multiple births, 47–48
  and sperm, 46–47, 48–49, 456, 459
Overmedication, dementia from, 541
Overweight (see Obesity)
Ovulation, 46, 419, 622
Ovum transfer, 459, 622

Pain, infants' sense of, 116–117, 118
Pain medication in childbirth, effects of, 82
Parallel play, 264
Parental deprivation, 183–184
Parenthood, 455–464
  lifelong, 516–517
Parenting styles:
  and adjustment to divorce, 324–325
  for adolescents, 369–370, 392
  of juvenile delinquents, 402–403
  and self-esteem, 317, 324–325
  types of, 257–258
Parents:
  abusive and neglectful, 185–187
  becoming:
    age of, 58–59, 61, 79, 81, 455–456, 457
    alternative methods for, 458–459
    choosing against, 464
    reasons for, 455
    timing of, 455–456, 457
    as transition, 459–461
  and career planning of adolescents, 373–374
  communication with adolescents about sex, 389

Parents (*Cont.*):
and competence of children, 140
conflict with adolescents, 390–392
of creative children, 300–301
death of, 520
of delinquents, 402–403
developing as, 462
effect of employment on adolescents, 392–393
elderly, 517–520, 577–578
of grown children, 462, 513, 515, 577–578
of infants and toddlers, 174–182, 459–461
in Erikson's theory, 163
SIDS victims, 105, 625
and state patterns, 109–110
as influence on play, 266–267
and intelligence of children, 133, 225–227
mature relationships with, 440
middle-aged, 514–517
peer pressure versus influence of, 397–398
psychological maltreatment by, 334
of school-age children, 312–313, 317, 318–330, 462
effect of divorce on, 322–327
employed mothers, 320–322
single, 327–330
school involvement of, 295–296, 319, 328, 329, 367–368, 369
and school performance of adolescents, 367–368, 369–371
and self-esteem, 317, 324–325
stepparents, 461–464
and temperament of children, 172–173
and young children's personality, 255–259
dealing with aggressive behavior, 251, 253–254
imitation, social-learning theory of, 243
issue of gender, 248
popularity, 261–263
prosocial children, 254–255, 623
(*See also* Fathers; Mothers)
Part-time jobs, 374
Passionate love, 444, 512–513
Passive-dependent personality, 564–566
Passive euthanasia, defined, 604–605, 622
Passive smoking, 416
Pedigree method, 63
Peer group:
in adolescence, 395–398, 403–404
in middle childhood, 313–318
Peer-group pressure versus parental influence, 397–398
Pendulum problem, Piaget's, 360–361
Permissive parents, 257, 258, 369–370, 622
Personal fables, 363, 590, 622
Personality:
balancing, 501, 503

Personality (*Cont.*):
defined, 66, 162, 622
hereditary aspects of, 66–67, 68
in middle adulthood, stress and, 481–482
psychoanalytical theories of (*see* Psychosexual theory, Freud's; Psychosocial theory, Erikson's)
(*See also* Personality and social development)
Personality and social development, 6
in adolescence, 380–406
identity formation, 380–389
problems, 398–404
relations with parents, 390–394
relations with peers, 395–398
sexuality, 385–389
theoretical perspectives on, 380–381
in early childhood, 240–268
aggressive behavior, 246, 250–254
effects of child-rearing practices, 255–259
fearfulness, 249–250
friendship, 261–263
gender effects on, 245–249
and play, 263–267
prosocial behavior, 254–255
sibling relations, 187–189, 259–261
theoretical views of, 240–245
in infancy and toddlerhood, 162–195
differences in, 171–174
emotions, 165–170
highlights of, 163
impact of early day care on, 192–195
self-control and self-regulation, 163–164, 165
sociability, 189
theories of, 162–164
in late adulthood, 558–582
patterns of successful aging, 562–566
personal relationships, 517–520, 572–581
social issues of aging, 566–572
theoretical perspectives on, 558–561
in middle adulthood, 481–482, 487–488, 500–521
in Gusii culture, 509
midlife crisis, 479, 500–501, 509–510, 621
normative-crisis theory of, 501–511
personal relationships, 511–520
question of change, 505
in middle childhood, 308–336
and divorce of parents, 322–327
emotional disturbances, 330–333
everyday life, 311–313
family relationships, 312–313, 317, 318–330, 336

Personality and social development (*Cont.*):
and nutrition, 273–274
peer group, 313–318
self-care, 323, 624
self-concept, 308–311
stress and resilience, 327–330, 334–336
in young adulthood, 436–466
in college, 426–428
intimate relationships, 443–465
models of, 436–443
(*See also* Personality)
Personality change, question of:
in late adulthood, 561
in middle adulthood, 505
Personality decline before death, 592
Phallic stage, 26, 27
Phenotypes, 51, 622
Phenylketonuria (PKU), screening for, 98
Phobias, school, 331–332, 624
Physical characteristics:
hereditary influences on, 65–66
of neonates, 92–93
Physical development, 6
in adolescence, 344–350
in early childhood, 200–201
in infancy and toddlerhood, 92–125 (*See also* Neonates)
growth, 110–111
motor, 99–100, 117–124
and nourishment, 111–113, 114
principles of, 107–108
of sensory capacities, 113–117, 129–130
sex differences in, 124
in late adulthood, 530–543
in middle adulthood, 473–484
in middle childhood, 272–278
prenatal (*see* Prenatal development)
in young adulthood, 410–411
Physical fitness:
and health in young adulthood, 412, 413, 415–416
in late adulthood, 539–540
in middle childhood, 276–277
schoolchildren's, improving, 276–277
Physiologic jaundice, 94, 622
Physiological changes in adolescence, 344–350
Physiological theory of death, 592
Physiological traits, hereditary influences on, 65–66
Physiology, in middle adulthood, 474
Piagetian approach:
analyses of, 138–142, 217–221
characteristics of, 34–36, 135–142
cognitive structures in, 35–36
defined, 622
evaluation of, 36–37
to language, 223–224
to moral development, 280–282
to play, 265
principles of development in, 35

Piagetian approach (*Cont.*):
stages of:
concrete operations stage, 27, 216, 220–221, 279–280, 361, 617
formal operations stage, 27, 360, 361–362, 619
preoperational stage, 27, 213–221, 280, 360–361, 623
sensorimotor stage, 27, 135–142, 624
summary of, 27–28
Pilgrimages in life review, 612
PKU (phenylketonuria), screening for, 98
Placenta, 70
Placing reflex, 97
Plasticity of performance, 546, 622
Play, 263–267
cognitive, 263, 265–266, 617
imaginative, 137, 265–266, 620
importance in early childhood, 263
in middle childhood, 311–313
nonsocial, 263–264
social, 263–264, 625
symbolic, 214, 625
Playmates:
factors in choice of, 261–262
help with finding, 263
Pleasure and mastery, well-being from, 504–506
Pleasure principle, 25
Polycystic kidney disease, 55
Popularity:
in early childhood, 261–263
in middle childhood, 316–318
Population, aging of, 528
Positive reinforcement, defined, 32
Postconventional morality, 282, 284, 365, 424, 622
Postformal thought, 422–423, 622
Postpartum depression, 170
Poverty:
in adolescence, 351
compensating for, with early education, 233–234
and hunger, 205
in late adulthood, 566
and teachers' expectations, 295
Practical (contextual) element of intelligence, 383, 421–422, 617
Practical problem solving in middle adulthood, 488–489
Pragmatics of intelligence, 547, 622
Precision grip, 119
Preconventional morality, 282, 283, 364, 622
Pregnancy, 46–81
spontaneous abortion of, 70–73, 74, 76, 79
teenage, 398–402
(*See also* Birth; Prenatal development)
Preimplantation genetic diagnosis, 62
Prejudice:
defined, 622
racial, in childhood, 315
Prelinguistic speech, 146–148, 154, 622–623

Premature (preterm) babies, 74, 100, 143, 623
Premenstrual syndrome (PMS), 419, 623
Prenatal care, 74, 75–76, 100–101
Prenatal development, 70–81
  assessment during, 61–62
  of brain, 94–96, 604
  characteristics of, 7
  critical periods of, 10–11
  environmental influences on, 73–81
    maternal (*see* Mothers, pregnant)
    paternal, 80–81
  month-by-month, 71–72
  and organ donation, 604
  stages of, 70–73
Prenatal studies, 63
Prenatal versus postnatal life, 94
Preoccupation phase of grief, 597
Preoperational stage:
  achievements of, 214–215
  assessing theory of, 217–221
  characteristics of, 213–221, 280, 360–361
  defined, 27, 623
  limitations of, 215–217
  symbolic function in, 214
Prepared childbirth, 83, 623
Presbyopia and presbycusis, 473, 623
Preschool, 227–234
Preschool years (*see* Early childhood)
Pretend (imaginative) play, 137, 265–266, 620
Preterm babies, 100, 143, 623
Primary aging, 534, 623
Primary circular reactions, 136, 137
Primary sex characteristics, 344, 347, 623
Privacy, right of, 23
Private speech, 223–224, 623
Problem solving in middle adulthood, 488–489
Procedural memory, 548
Processing of information (*see* Information-processing approach)
Programmed-aging theory, 533, 623
Project Head Start, 233–234, 623
Projection, 26
Prosocial behavior, 254–255, 623
Protest stage of separation anxiety, 184
Proximodistal principle, 108, 623
Pseudoautonomous relationship with parents, 440
Psychoanalytic perspective:
  characteristics of, 24, 25–28
  defined, 623
  evaluation of, 30, 242
  (*See also* Psychosexual theory, Freud's; Psychosocial theory, Erikson's)
Psychological aspects of death, defined, 589
Psychological changes preceding death, 592

Psychological effects:
  of adolescent physical changes, 348–350
  of infertility, 456
Psychological maltreatment, 334, 623
Psychological theory of death, 592
Psychological therapies, 333
Psychometric approach:
  analysis of, 288–289
  characteristics of, 133–135
  defined, 623
  in early childhood, 224–225
  to increasing intelligence, 134, 289
  information-processing approach and, 142–144
  in late adulthood, 543–546
  in middle adulthood, 484–486
  in middle childhood, 286–289, 300
  Piagetian approach combined with, 138
  in young adulthood, 422
  (*See also* Assessment)
Psychomotor functioning:
  in late adulthood, 535–536
  in middle adulthood, 473–474
  in young adulthood, 410–411
Psychosexual theory, Freud's:
  defense mechanisms in, 25, 26
  defined, 623
  stages of:
    anal stage, 26, 27
    genital stage, 27, 28
    latency period, 26–28
    oral stage, 26, 27
    phallic stage, 26, 27
  summary of, 27
Psychosocial moratorium, 381, 383, 621
Psychosocial theory, Erikson's:
  background of, 28–29
  characteristics of, 162–164
  defined, 623
  stages of:
    autonomy versus shame and doubt stage, 27, 163–164, 616
    basic trust versus basic mistrust stage, 27, 162–163, 616
    generativity versus stagnation stage, 28, 502, 503, 619
    identity versus identity confusion stage, 27, 380–381, 620
    industry versus inferiority stage, 27, 310, 620
    initiative versus guilt stage, 27, 240–241, 620
    integrity versus despair stage, 28, 558–559, 620
    intimacy versus isolation stage, 28, 436–438, 620
  summary of, 27–28
Psychotherapy, individual, 333, 620
Puberty, 342, 623
Puberty rites, 342, 343, 344
Pubescence and puberty, 342*n.*, 344–350, 623
Punishment, 255–256
  and aggressive behavior, 251, 254
  defined, 32–33, 623

Punishment (*Cont.*):
  versus discipline, 320
  effective, 256
  versus negative reinforcement, 32–33
  versus rewards, 256
Purpose, virtue of, 241

Qualitative changes, 3–4, 623
  learning theorists' emphasis on, 34
Quantitative versus qualitative changes, 3, 623

Racial differences:
  in aging, 567
  in deaths:
    infant, 104
    in middle adulthood, 482–484
    in young adulthood, 411–412
  in depression, 69
  in dropout rates, 371
  in genetic disorders, 58, 61–62
  in health, 482–484
  in identity formation, 385
  in IQ performance, 288–289
  in life expectancy, 532
  and prejudice in childhood, 315
  in prenatal care, 85–87
Radiation exposure during pregnancy, 80
Random sampling, 19, 623
Reaction formation, 26
Reaction time:
  in late adulthood, 535–536
  in middle adulthood, 473–474
Reading to children, 152, 154
Real self, 309, 623
Realistic period of career planning, defined, 373
Reality principle, 25
Reasoning, kinds of:
  deduction, induction, and transduction, 217
  formal (hypothetical-deductive), 360, 361–362
  moral, Kohlberg's theory of, 282–284, 364–366, 424
Rebellion, adolescent, 390–391, 403, 615
Recall and recognition, 212, 549–550, 623
Recessive inheritance, 51, 52–57, 623
Recognition and recall, 212, 549–550, 623
Reconstituted families, 329, 461–464
Reflex behaviors:
  control over, 135, 136, 137
  cultural differences in, 99
  defined, 623
  development of, 96, 97
  in infants, 116
  smiling as, 167–168
Regression, 26
Rehearsal as mnemonic strategy, 285–286, 623
Reinforcement:
  of aggressive behavior, 251

Reinforcement (*Cont.*):
  defined, 32, 623
  and language acquisition, theory of, 150–151
  in operant conditioning, 32, 131
  and punishment, 255–256
  in social-learning theory, 243
Reintegrative stage, 420, 421, 623
Relational theory, 27–28, 29–30, 623
Reliability of tests, 287–288, 623–624
Reliable, defined, 224, 624
Religion, and emotional well-being, 565
Remarriage, 451–452, 574
Representational ability, 138, 214, 624
Repression, 26
Reproduction:
  decline in capacity for, 475
  difficulty with, 456–458
  new means of, 458–459
  process of, 46–47, 48–49
Research, 12–23
  basic versus applied, 5
  case studies, 14–16, 616
  correlational studies, 14, 617
  data collection in, 21–22, 543–546
  ethical issues in, 22–23, 130
  ethical standards in, 23
  experimental methods of, 15, 17–21
  family, new trends in, 174
  on heredity versus environment, methods of, 65–66
  on identity, 381–385
  on infants, practicing findings of, 194
  interview method, 15, 17, 620
  laboratory observation, 15, 16, 620
  naturalistic observation, 15, 16, 622
  nonexperimental methods of, 14–17
  on personality changes, 561
  scientific method in, 14
  and theories, 23–24
Reserve capacity:
  defined, 537, 624
  loss of, 537
Resilient children, 334–336
Resistant (ambivalent) attachment, 177–180, 615
Resolution phase of grief, 597
Respiratory distress syndrome, 102
Respiratory factors in SIDS, 105
Respiratory system of neonates, 93
Respondent (classical) conditioning, 31–32, 130–131, 616
Responses:
  conditioned (CR), 31
  unconditioned (UCR), 31
Responsible stage, 420, 421, 624
Retirement, 528, 550–553, 573
Retrieval of information, 285, 549–550
Reunions in life review, 612
Reversibility rule for conservation, 221–222, 280
Rewards, use of, 256

Rh factor, 61, 79
Right to die, 603–605, 609
Rights of research subjects, 22–23
Rites of passage, 342, 343, 344
Role confusion, 381
Roles, gender, and gender-typing, 246, 248, 619
Rooting reflex, 97, 116
Rubella (German measles), 78

Safety, in middle childhood, 277–278
Samples, experimental, 19, 624
Scaffolding, 226, 257–258, 624
Schemata:
    in gender-schema theory, 244, 245
    of infants, 35–36, 136, 137, 624
Schizophrenia, 52, 67, 624
School phobia, 331–332, 624
Schoolchildren (*see* Middle childhood)
Schooling:
    achievement in:
        home influences on, in adolescence, 367–368, 369–372
        and maternal employment, 321–322
        and single-parent families, 328
    college, 426–428, 489
    for disabled children, 296–299
    educational trends in, 293–294
    8-4 pattern, 367
    for gifted, talented, and creative children, 300–301
    and health, 418
    in Japan, 290–291
    kindergarten, 234–235
    in late adulthood, 550–551
    in middle adulthood, 489
    in middle childhood, 293–302
    parents' involvement in, 295–296, 319, 328, 329, 367–368, 369
    preschool, 227–234
    secondary school, 367–372
    6-3-3 pattern, 367
    teachers, 293–295
        mainstreaming attitudes of, 299
        parental involvement by, 295–296
Scientific method, 14, 624
Screening (*see* Assessment; Psychometric approach)
Seat belts and restraints, use of, 203, 413
"Second honeymoon," 511
Secondary aging, 534, 624
Secondary circular reactions, 136, 137
Secondary school, 367–372
Secondary sex characteristics, 345, 347, 624
Secular trends, 342, 346, 624
Secure attachment, 177–180, 182, 183, 262–263, 624
Selective optimization with compensation, 547, 624
Self:
    ideal, 309, 620

Self (*Cont.*):
    real, 309, 623
Self-actualization, 37–38
Self-awareness:
    defined, 624
    development of, 166–167, 308
Self-care adolescents, 393
Self-care children, 323, 624
Self-centeredness in adolescence, 363
Self-concept:
    defined, 308, 624
    development of, 309–311
    in middle childhood, 308–311
    theoretical perspectives on, 310–311
Self-consciousness in adolescence, 363
Self-control:
    defined, 164
    development of, 163–164, 165
Self-definition, 308–309, 624
Self-esteem:
    and appearance, 350
    defined, 309, 624
    development of, 309–311
    female, research on, 384
    and parenting style, 317, 324–325
    right of, 23
Self-fulfilling prophecy, principle of, 294–295, 624
Self-recognition, 166, 308
Self-regulation:
    defined, 164, 624
    and self-control, development of, 163–164, 165
    and social regulation, coordination of, 309
Self-worth, global, 310–311, 619
Senescence, defined, 530, 624
Senility, defined, 540
Senses:
    infants' capacities, 113–117, 129–130
    in late adulthood, problems with, 530, 535, 537
    and menstrual cycle, 419
    in middle adulthood, 473
    in young adulthood, 411
Sensorimotor (functional) play, defined, 265
Sensorimotor stage:
    assessing theory of, 138–142
    cognitive concepts of, 137–138
    defined, 27, 135, 624
    research based on, 138–142
    substages of, 136–138
Sensory functioning (*see* Senses)
Sensory memory, 547, 624
Sentences:
    early childhood, 222
    first, 149, 154
Separation, infant-parent, 183–184
Separation anxiety, 183, 624
    defined, 6
    during hospitalization, 184–185
Separation anxiety disorder, 331, 332, 624
Sequential studies, 22
Sequential testing, 543–546
"Settling Down," 437

Sex cells (ovum and sperm), 46–47, 48–49, 456, 459
Sex characteristics:
    primary, 344, 347, 623
    secondary, 345, 347, 624
Sex chromosomes, 48–49, 624
    abnormality, 55, 58–59
    and sex-linked traits, 52, 57, 58–59
Sex determination, 48–49
Sex differences, 48–49, 624
    in adolescent growth, 344–346, 348–350
    in early childhood growth, 200–201
    versus gender differences, 245–246
    in health, 418–420
    hormonal, 247–248, 418–419
    in infancy, 124
    in motor abilities, 277
Sex hormones:
    androgens, 247–248, 345
    estrogen, 93, 345, 475–477, 480
    and menopause, 475–477
    at puberty, 345–346
    and sexual orientation, 386
    testosterone, 247, 345
Sex-linked inheritance, 52, 624
    defects transmitted by, 57, 58–59
Sexual abuse:
    of children, 185–187
    defined, 185, 624
Sexual evolution, 387–389
Sexual maturation, 344–350
Sexual orientation (sexual preference), 386, 624
Sexual theory, Freud's (*see* Psychosexual theory, Freud's)
Sexuality:
    adolescent, 357–360, 385–389
    Freud's emphasis on, 26–28
    and pregnancy, 398–402
    in late adulthood, 575–576
    in middle adulthood, 474–478, 513
    in young adulthood, 453–455
        healthful practices, 412
        in intimacy versus isolation stage, 436–438
Sexually transmitted diseases (STDs), 78–79, 357–360, 388, 389, 624
Shanti Project, 600
Shaping in operant conditioning, 33, 624
Shock and disbelief phase of grief, 597
Short-term memory, 547, 625
Shyness, 68
Sibling relations, 187–189, 259–261
    absence of, 187
    in adolescence, 394–395
    and individual environments, 69–70
    in late adulthood, 576
    in middle adulthood, 513–514
    in middle childhood, 329–330
    and sudden infant death syndrome (SIDS), 105
Sibling rivalry, 187–188, 259, 261

Sickle-cell anemia, 52, 55, 61, 62
SIDS (sudden infant death syndrome), 104–105, 625
Sight (*see* Vision)
Sight, infant, 113–114
Simple-to-complex development, 108
Single-parent homes:
    and adolescent development, 393–394
    and early childhood development, 227, 248
    in middle childhood, 327–330
    teenage, 398–402
Single people, 452–453, 574–575
Sioux Indians, socialization of, 29
Sisters and brothers (*see* Sibling relations)
Sitting in infancy, 119
Skin changes:
    in adolescence, 347
    in late adulthood, 537
Sleep disturbances, 208
Sleep patterns:
    in early childhood, 207–209
    in infancy, 105, 108–110
    in late adulthood, 537
Sleepwalking and sleeptalking, 208
Slow-to-warm-up child, defined, 172
Slowdown in late adulthood, 535–536, 545–546
Small-for-date babies, 100, 625
Smell, sense of:
    in late adulthood, 535
    in newborns, 116
Smiling, by infants, 167–168
Smoking:
    in adolescence, 356–357
    avoiding during pregnancy, 74
    effects on fetus, 76–77, 80, 100, 105
    as health risk, 412, 413, 416–417
    and osteoporosis, 476
Sociability, development of, 189
Social aspects of death, defined, 589
Social development (*see* Personality and social development)
Social interactions, and memory, 213
Social issues in late adulthood, 566–572
Social-learning theory, 33–34, 150–151, 242–243, 625
Social play, 263–264, 625
Social referencing, 121, 169, 183, 219, 625
Social regulation and self-regulation, 309
Social speech, 223, 625
Social theories:
    cognitive-social, 244
    psychosocial (*see* Psychosocial theory, Erikson's)
Socialization, 174, 248, 625
Socializing versus sexualizing, Peck's criterion of, 502, 503, 625
Sociodramatic play, 265–266

Socioeconomic factors:
  in birthweight, 100
  and cesarean delivery, 84
  compensating for with preschool
    programs, 233–234
  in depression, 170
  in health, 417–418, 482–484
  in IQ performance, 288–289
  in maternal employment's ef-
    fects on sons, 322
  in school performance, 370–371
  for single-parent families, 328
Solid foods for infants, 113
Solitary independent play, 264
Sound discrimination in infants,
  115–116
Speech:
  development of (see Language
    development)
  linguistic, 148–150, 621
  prelinguistic, 146–148, 154, 622–
    623
  private, 223–224, 623
  social, 223, 625
Speech therapy, 2–3
Sperm:
  abnormalities of, 80–81
  and ova, 46–47, 48–49, 456, 459
Spina bifida, 52, 54–55, 61
Spontaneous abortions, 70–73, 74,
  76, 79, 625
Spouse abuse, 449
Stages of childbirth, 81
Stages of development:
  of adult cognition, 420–421
  in cognitive perspective (see
    Piagetian approach)
  of friendship, 316
  in learning perspective, 34
  linguistic, 148–150
  moral:
    Gilligan's, 424–425
    Kohlberg's, 283–284, 364–366,
      423–424, 425
    Piaget's, 281
  in normative-crisis models, 436–
    442, 501–504
  as parents, 462
  prenatal, 70–73
  psychoanalytic theories of (see
    Psychosexual theory, Freud's;
    Psychosocial theory, Erikson's)
  of self-regulation, 163–164, 165
  in timing-of-events, 442–443
Stages of dying, Kübler-Ross's, 593
Standardized norms, 224, 287, 625
Standing in infancy, 121
Stanford-Binet Intelligence Scale,
  138, 224, 225, 288, 625
Startle (Moro) reflex, 96, 97, 99
States of arousal, 108–110, 625
Status offenders, 402, 625
Stealing, 331
Stepfamilies, 329, 461–464
Stepparenthood, 461–464
Stereotypes:
  ageist, 529
  gender, 246–247, 619
    combating, 248

Stereotypes (Cont.):
  fathers' reinforcement of, 248
  in media, 248
Stimuli:
  conditioned (CS), 31
  neutral, 31
  unconditioned (UCS), 31
Storage of information, 285, 549–
  550
Strange Situation, Ainsworth's,
  177, 180, 625
Stranger anxiety, 183, 625
Strength and coordination:
  in late adulthood, 535–536
  in middle adulthood, 473–474
Stress and stressors, 625
  in adolescence, 367–368
  at birth:
    effects of trauma, 96
    and hormone production, 83–84
  in childhood:
    coping with, 334–336
    divorce, 322–327
    and health, 204
    in single-parent families, 327–
      330
    sources of, 334–336
  defined, 480
  of dual-earner couples, 429
  of elderly parents, 519
  in late adulthood, coping strate-
    gies for, 564, 565
  from life events, 481
  in middle adulthood, 480–482,
    511–512
  and puberty, 349
  work-related, 491–492, 493
Sublimation, 26
Substance conservation, 280
Substantive complexity of work,
  493–495, 625
Sucking, by infants:
  in habituation studies, 129
  in operant conditioning, 131
Sudden infant death syndrome
  (SIDS), 104–105, 625
Suicide, 605–610
  among adolescents, 607–608
  among adults, 608
  among children, 605–607
  preventing, 608–610
Superego, 25, 625
"Superwoman syndrome," avoid-
  ing during pregnancy, 74
Support groups, during terminal
  illness, 600
Surrogate motherhood, 459, 625
Swimming reflex, 97
Symbolic function, 214, 625
Symbolic gesturing:
  and language acquisition, 147–
    148
  of toddlers, 17
Symbolic play, 214, 625
Symbolic thought, 136, 137, 140–
  142
Symbols, 214, 625
Syntax:
  early, 149

Syntax (Cont.):
  mastery of, 289–292, 293
Syphilis, 359

Tacit knowledge, 422, 625
Talented and gifted children, 300–
  301
Talking (see Communication; Language development)
Taste, sense of:
  in late adulthood, 535
  in middle adulthood, 473
  in newborns, 116
Tay-Sachs disease, 52, 55, 61
Teachers:
  expectations of, 294–295
  mainstreaming, attitudes to-
    ward, 299
  parental involvement by, 295–
    296
  (See also Schooling)
Teenage years (see Adolescence)
Teeth:
  in adolescence, 351
  in early childhood, 201
  in infancy, 110–111
  in late adulthood, 539
  in middle childhood, 276
Television:
  and adolescent sexuality, 388,
    400
  and gender stereotypes, 248
  guidelines for children's viewing
    of, 253
  in middle childhood, 312
  and obesity, 274, 276
  violence on, 252–253
Temperament:
  and adjustment, 172–173
  components of, 171
  defined, 171, 625
  differences in, 171–174
  influences on, 66–67, 68, 172–173
  and parents, 172–173
  patterns of, 171–172
Temperature regulation, in neonates, 94
Tentative period of career planning, defined, 373
Teratogenic factors, defined, 73,
  625
Terminal drop, 545, 625
Terminal illness:
  attitudes during, 590, 593
  help during, 599–600
  prolonging life in, 603–605, 609
"Terrible twos," 162, 164
Tertiary circular reactions, 136,
  137
Test-tube babies, 459
Testosterone, 247, 345
Tests (see Assessment; Psychometric approach)
Thanatology, defined, 588, 625
Theoretical perspectives on devel-
  opment, 24
  aging:
    process of, 533–534
    successful, 562–566

Theoretical perspectives on development (Cont.):
  cognitive, of personality, 24,
    34–37, 623
    in adolescence, 380–381
    in early childhood, 242–243
    in late adulthood, 558–561
      (See also Normative-crisis
      model)
    and timing-of-events model,
      442–443, 500–501, 510, 625
    (See also Piagetian approach)
  humanistic, 24, 37–38, 620
  intellectual (see Intellectual de-
    velopment)
  learning, of personality, 24 (See
    also Learning perspective)
  moral (see Moral development,
    theories of)
  psychoanalytic, 24 (see Psycho-
    analytic perspective)
  of self-concept, 310–311
Theories, 23–24, 625
Therapies:
  for childhood emotional distur-
    bances, 333
  drug, 333
  family, 333, 618
  grief, 599, 619
  psychological, 333
  psychotherapy, 333, 620
Thought:
  cognitive-stage approach to
    Piaget's (see Piagetian ap-
    proach)
    Schaie's, 420–421
  convergent, 300, 617
  divergent, 300, 618
  integrative, 486–488
  mature, 489
  objective, 422
  postformal, 622
  subjective, 422
  symbolic, 136, 137, 140–142
  teaching of, 294
Time sampling, 16
Timing-of-events model, 442–443,
  500–501, 510, 625
Tobacco use (see Smoking)
Toddlerhood (see Infancy and toddlerhood)
Toilet training:
  early, attempts at, 123–124
  and self-control, 164
Tonic neck reflex, 97
Top-to-bottom infant development,
  107
Torrance Tests of Creative Thinking, 300
Touch, infants' sense of, 116–117
Traditional learning theory (behav-
  iorism), 30–33, 34, 616
Transcendental theory of death, 592
Transduction, 217, 625
Transformations versus states, fail-
  ure to focus on, 217
Transitional objects, 208, 625
Transitions:
  empty nest, 513, 515, 618

Transitions (*Cont.*):
  Levinsonian, 437, 439–442, 502, 504–508
  midlife, 437, 500, 502, 504–508, 509–510
    parenthood, 459–461
    for women, 441–442, 504–508
Trauma:
  influence of, 26
  recovery from, 4
  (*See also* Birth trauma)
Treatment, experimental, 19
Triangular theory of love, 444, 625
Triarchic theory of intelligence, Sternberg's, 421–422
Trichomoniasis, 358
Trophoblast, 70
Twin births, 47–48
Twin studies, 65
  of disorders, 67, 69
  of intelligence, 66
  of motherese, 152
  of physical and physiological traits, 65–66
  of speeded-up motor development, 122, 123–124
  of toilet training, early, 123–124
Two-earner couples, 429
Two-egg (dizygotic, fraternal) twins, 47, 618
Type A behavior pattern, 482
Type B behavior pattern, 482

Ultrasound, 62, 625
Umbilical cord, 62, 70
Umbilical cord assessment, 62
Unconditioned stimuli and responses (UCS and UCR), 31
Unemployment, 492–493
Unintegrated personality, 566
Unmarried people, 452–453, 574–575
  sexuality among, 453–454
  teenage parents, 398–402
Unoccupied behavior, 264
Unpopular schoolchildren, 317–318

Vaccinations, 105–107, 274
Valid, defined, 224
Validity of tests, 288, 625
Values, and working mothers, 321
Valuing wisdom versus valuing physical powers, Peck's criterion of, 502, 503, 626
Variables:
  correlation of, 14

Variables(*Cont.*):
  defined, 14
  dependent, 19, 617
  independent, 19, 620
Venereal diseases (sexually transmitted diseases, STDs), 78–79, 357–360, 388, 389, 624
Verbal performance, gender differences in, 375
Vernix caseosa, defined, 93, 626
Violence:
  children's reactions to, 335
  between spouses, 449
  televised, 252–253
Virtues, Erikson's:
  care, 503
  competence, 310, 311
  fidelity, 381
  hope, 163
  love (mutuality of devotion), 438
  purpose, 241
  will, 164
  wisdom, 559
Visible imitation, 139–140, 626
Vision:
  in infancy, 113–114, 115, 129
  in late adulthood, problems with, 530, 534
  in middle adulthood, 473
  in middle childhood, 275–276
Visual cliff, 114, 129, 169, 626
Visual preferences, of infants, 115, 626
Visual-recognition memory, 142–143, 547, 550, 626
Vocabulary, growth of, 148–149
Vocational planning in adolescence, 372–375
Vocations (*see* Career development; Employment; Work)
Volume conservation, 280

Wakefulness in infancy, 108–110
Walkers, infant, 122
Walking:
  infants' mastery of, 121, 122
  in sleep, 208
Walking reflex, 97
Warts, genital, 359
Wear-and-tear theory of aging, 533, 626
Wechsler Intelligence Scale for Children (WISC-R), 286–287, 626
Wechsler Preschool and Primary Scale of Intelligence (WPPS), 143–144

Wechsler Preschool and Primary Scale of Intelligence (WPPSI-R), 225, 626
Weight:
  of adolescents, and eating disorders, 352–354
  and adults' health, 414
  conservation of, 279–280
  in early childhood, 200–201
  gain during pregnancy, 74, 75
  hereditary influences on, 63, 65
  of infants and toddlers, 93, 110–111 (*See also* Low birthweight)
  (*See also* Obesity)
Weight conservation, 280
Wet dreams, 347
Widowhood, 574, 601–603
Wife battering, 449
Will, virtue of, 164
Will to live, 594
Wisdom:
  as Eriksonian virtue, 559
  in late adulthood, 548–549
"Witch's milk," 93
Women:
  abused wives, 449
  osteoporosis prevention for, 476
  (*See also* Gender differences; Mothers)
Words:
  early childhood, 222
  first, 148–149, 154
Work:
  adolescents' planning for, 372–375
  age-related effects on, 428–430
  changing, in midlife, 490–491
  continuing education related to, 489
  creativity in, 494
  definition of self by, overcoming, 559
  developing a career, 372–375, 428–431, 441–442
  of dropouts, 372
  by dual-earner couples, 429
  gender and, 430–431, 441–442, 490–491, 491*n*.
  and health, 419–420
  in late adulthood, 551–552
  loss of, 492–493
  part-time, 374
  patterns in middle adulthood, 489–495
  retirement from, 528, 550–553
  stress related to, 491–492, 493

Work(*Cont.*):
  substantive complexity of, and intellectual flexibility, 493–495
  in young adulthood, 428–431, 441–442
  (*See also* Career development; Employment)
Workaholics, 490
Working mothers, 227, 320–322, 429
  of adolescents, 392–393
  child care arrangements of, 227–234
  of infants, 182, 189–195
  of young children, 227, 320–322

X chromosomes:
  abnormal number of, 58
  defined, 49
  sex-linked traits on, 52, 57, 58
X-ray exposure during pregnancy, 11, 79

Y chromosomes:
  abnormalities of, 58
  defined, 49
Young adulthood, 410–466
  characteristics of, 7
  death in, 411–412, 590–591
  intellectual development in, 420–423
    career development, 428–431, 441–442
    college experience, 426–428
    moral, 423–425
  Levinsonian era of, 437, 439–442
  and parents, 462, 515–517
  personality development in college, 426–428
    intimate relationships, 443–465
    models of, 436–443
  physical development in, 410–411
  for women, 441–442
Young-old versus old-old, 526–528
Yucatecan babies, motor development in, 99

Zone of proximal development (ZPD), 225, 226, 626
Zygotes, defined, 46, 626